The Discovery Bible

New American Standard New Testament

Reference Edition

H.E.L.P.S.
The Study System
of The Discovery Bible

Gary Hill

with consulting editor
Gleason L. Archer

MOODY PRESS
CHICAGO

Library of Congress Cataloging in Publication Data

Bible. N.T. English. New American Standard.
The discovery Bible. New Testament 1987.

  I. Hill, Gary, 1950- . II. Title.
BS2095.N35 1987   225.5′2   85-21475
ISBN 0-8024-4159-9

Printed in the United States of America

1 2 3 4 5 6 7 8 9 10 11 12 / 90 89 88 87

CONTENTS

The Discovery Bible

HELPS

HILL EMPHATIC LANGUAGE POINTER SYSTEM

PREFACE TO *THE DISCOVERY BIBLE*

The Discovery Bible represents a new dimension in biblical comprehension through a coding system to convey to the modern English reader at least three very important elements in the Greek language of the New Testament.

The scholar of Ancient Greek who has read the Bible through repeatedly in the original languages can appreciate the connotations and overtones of key words and phrases as they recur in the various books of the Bible. These scholars can build clusters of associations derived from the various other passages in which the words or phrases under study occur. These scholars enjoy and appreciate the same fine distinctions and nuances as those understood by the original ancient readers of Scripture.

What the scholar enjoys in the original Greek may now be experienced by the English reader who knows no Greek. He may find which English word or words in each sentence convey *emphasis* by virtue of the Greek word order. Second, he may become aware of the *mode of action* expressed by the present or aorist tenses (such as the subjunctive, the imperative, or the infinitive), whether the action is thought of as single and complete, or whether it is repetitive or incomplete. Third, he may be alerted to the *Greek synonym* underlying the English translation word (such as *love* or *redeem*, each of which may represent two or three different Greek synonyms with somewhat different connotations).

The introductory material will explain how the above-mentioned distinctions are conveyed in this edition of the *New American Standard Bible.* The purpose for choosing this modern translation is that, like the King James Version, it translates into English every translatable word in the original text. In the interest of more contemporary style, other recent versions tend to omit certain connectives or sentence adverbs that are important and may be coded under the system followed by *The Discovery Bible.*

Several years ago Gary Hill approached me, as a scholar of Ancient Greek, to assist him in his personal Bible study. Because they enriched his own understanding of Scripture, Gary soon came to realize the tremendous advantages to be received from these matters of *emphasis, mode of action,* and *synonym distinction.* He therefore resolved to produce a new edition of the Bible embodying these helpful features for the benefit of the entire church of Christ. This then is the rationale behind this new production, which in our view and in the view of many other Bible scholars represents an exciting new dimension to the art of Bible comprehension.

GLEASON L. ARCHER

H.E.L.P.S. Acknowledgments

The H.E.L.P.S. Study System of *The Discovery Bible* project is especially indebted to the meticulous oversight provided by Gleason L. Archer, who has compared the entire text of *The Discovery Bible New Testament* with each corresponding phrase of the Greek New Testament eight times. Dr. Archer's considerable abilities in the biblical languages have been of incalculable worth in forging the grammatical principles upon which this work is based. Other participants on the project included Jerry and Craig Rucin (assisting with synonym and verb tense placement), Shirley Hill, William and Pamela Dempsey, and Donald Lesher (manuscript preparation), without all of whom this project would have not have been possible.

Special appreciation is deserving to Mr. Lee Mitchell, M.B.A. Harvard University, who volunteered his background in marketing research, which helped to spawn the creative use of color and symbols.

GARY HILL

INTRODUCTION TO H.E.L.P.S.

Why is this called The "Discovery" Bible?

Through the highlighted words, symbols, and numbers every Bible reader can make life-changing discoveries by seeing the distinctions of the inspired original Greek text (upon which all New Testament translations are based) without having to learn one word of Greek!

The easy-to-follow discovery color shows each English reader at a glance the places where the sacred originals convey a special insight (discovery) that is often beyond the reach of ordinary translation. It is the aim of *The Discovery Bible* New Testament to:

- identify in the discovery color which words are emphatic (given stress) in the original text
- identify through symbols (^{x}, $\sim^{!}$, etc.) the colorful and vivid action conveyed by the different Greek verb tenses in the original text
- identify by superlinear numbers (5a,5b; 6a,6b; etc.) those words in the original text that are too closely related in meaning to be distinguished in English translation (i.e., Greek synonyms), yet may make a profound difference in understanding a given verse or passage

By paying careful attention to the words, symbols, and numbers in the discovery color, you will be able to gain in-depth insights into the Word of God. Experience the fresh excitement of your own personal discoveries from the Holy Scriptures—discoveries resting on the authority of the inspired original text.

Seeing the perfections of the Word of God through your own eyes will help to stimulate new interest in reading the Bible and in spending more time dwelling on divine truth.

To better understand the meaning of the Scriptures is to better know the life-changing power of its Author. For each Bible reader to personally discover this fuller knowledge of God and His will is the goal of *The Discovery Bible*.

abide [x] means this is a fact; a complete and specific action. It reads "If you (in fact) abide in Me..."

words [43b] This number refers the reader to a glossary of Greek words closely related in meaning, but often not distinguished in ordinary translation. Here, not the ordinary term for 'word,' but rather the specific spoken word of Christ.

bear [~] shows repeated or continuous action. It reads "...that you (continuously) bear much fruit..."

7 "If you abide[x] in Me, and My words[43b] abide[x] in you, ask[xi] whatever you wish, and it shall be done for you.

8 "By this is My Father glorified, that you bear[~] *much* fruit, and *so* prove to be *My* disciples.

9 "Just as the *Father* has loved[31a] Me, *I* have also loved *you;* abide[xi] in My love.

10 "If you keep[x] My commandments, you will abide in My love; just as *I* have kept[+] My Father's commandments, and abide in *His* love.

I By emphasizing Himself, Jesus is showing that obedience is necessary even for the Son of God to remain in the Father's love.

kept [+] means an action has already taken place and the results continue. It reads "...I have kept (in the past and still do now)..."

much fruit Jesus emphasizes these words to powerfully bring out the great abundance of results which accompany a new life in Him.

What do the highlighted words mean?

It is important for the Bible student to discover which words or phrases in each sentence or clause were given central importance or stress in the original languages of Scripture. The New Testament abounds in the use of word emphasis and stress. Greek, as an inflected language, has a special ability to stress or emphasize an important word by changing that word's *position* in the sentence. The Greek language is able to give special importance (emphasis) to a particular word by placing it out of the usual order in a position of prominence, or it may use the word in an intensive or distinctive form.

The words highlighted in the discovery color are those words that are stressed (emphatic) in the inspired original Greek text. Words that appear in the discovery color in ordinary type mean minor emphasis; those in *slanted* type mean *major emphasis*.[1] In this way, highlighted words can become "windows of discovery" for the reader.

1. The two levels of emphasis (*major* and minor) are determined by the forcefulness and unusualness of the word order in the underlying Greek text, as well as by the context. Sometimes they occur side by side—see Matthew 6:4 ("*your* alms") where "*your*" is even more strongly stressed in the Greek text than "alms."

Discovery color highlighting is the result of years of research regarding emphasis, word order, and mode of action in the Greek New Testament. It is important for the reader to understand that no claim for inerrancy is made for the special markings in the discovery color. Only the authoritative original text itself can be regarded as infallible and inerrant.

"What should I do when I see a highlighted word?"

Words are emphasized in the Greek originals for basically the same reason they are emphasized in any language—they have received added distinctiveness so that their special importance may not be overlooked or misunderstood.

Words are generally emphasized because of one of the three following reasons:

(1) to bring a sharpened *focus;* (2) to show *contrast;* or (3) to convey *intensity.*

If the meaning of a highlighted word seems unclear, its meaning will become clearer by considering one of these three reasons for emphasizing text.

1. *Focus.* Many "obvious" truths and insights often become plain only after we ponder and think about them. The Scripture writers emphasized *key facts* so that their full importance would not be diluted or overlooked. Highlighted words become keys to unlocking a rich and satisfying understanding of a passage of Scripture. Personal Bible reading can glow with fresh interest and new meaning as its emphasis and distinctive meanings are understood more clearly.

2. *Contrast.* Basic to the process of learning is taking note of how the object of attention is like or unlike what we already know. That is, we best understand what something *is* by how different or opposite it is to something *else.* For this reason, important truths in Scripture are often taught by showing how one member of a pair is dissimilar to the other member (e.g., *spirituality* and *carnality* are contrasted with each other in Romans 8). Contrasting words that are emphasized really say two things: what they *are,* and what they *are not;* that is, what is not explicitly stated, yet clearly implied. ("This is *mine!*" also means, "It's not *yours!*") For example, when Paul was about to be punished without trial in Jerusalem, he asked, "Is it lawful for you to scourge a man who is a *Roman?*" (i.e., as a legally protected full citizen to be spared such treatment because he was *a Jew who had the status of Roman citizenship).* Contrast (stated or unstated) is probably the most common kind of emphasis in the Scripture. A proper appreciation of contrast can illuminate many difficult passages.

3. *Intensification.* In English we often emphasize a word by intensifying it with another word, such as "I *really* want to go" or "It tasted *so good.*" The same is often done in Scripture—only without adding any additional words,

such as "very" or "really." When Paul emphatically says he hopes to send Timothy "soon," he really means *"very* soon."

Only when the reader grasps "how much" (or "to what extent") something is true, will he adequately appreciate what the Scripture writer really means to say. Taking into consideration the special level of intensity or the abnormal degree (magnitude) at which the statement is made furnishes a valuable key to a more adequate understanding of many passages of Scripture.

Why is emphasis important?

Whether or not we are conscious of it, all of us use emphasis on a continual basis. Even when we listen to a young child speak, we find it easy to detect which words are receiving special stress and importance by how loudly or softly something is spoken. When the speaker wishes the listener to give extra attention to a particular point, he will very often raise the pitch of his voice or vary the speed of the words he wants to be made emphatic. Indeed, the richer and more effective use of emphasis employed, the more interesting a speaker sounds to his listener. Monotone speaking makes even lively subjects sound boring. Without emphasis, communication can become an almost "lifeless lump of language."

Modern-day speakers illustrate the advantage of using emphasis effectively. What a difference there is between reading a verbatim message and actually hearing it preached before a crowd. The rise and fall of the voice, the changes from loud tone to soft, the various pauses, gestures of the hand, changes in facial expression, and so on, all combine to make a greater impact on the listener. Emphasis serves to let the emotion behind what is spoken come out more clearly and thus leaves a lasting *impression* as well as intelligible *expression*. Therefore, emphasis holds the attention of the listener and brings him into a personal involvement with subject matter. This personal involvement and focused attention on the part of the listener is probably the most important key to the art of communication. For this reason, the writings of the New Testament abound in the use of emphasis. However, instead of achieving emphasis by changing the intonation of the voice, the New Testament Greek original brings out emphasis *by the order in which the words are written.* As English speakers, we find this device hard to duplicate in our own tongue, because English, unlike Greek, is one of those languages that essentially lacks the ability to change the order of words without confusing the meaning intended by the speaker. Thus, to reverse the order of the *words* "The dog bit the man" to "The man bit the dog" is to reverse the *meaning.* This is because once the order of the words is changed, there is no longer any way of determining who is *doing* the action (the subject, "the dog") and who is *receiving* the action (the direct object, "man"). In Greek, however, special inflectional endings make these relationships perfectly clear regardless of the order of the words. Since subjects are in what is called the nominative case, and direct objects are in the accusative case, with distinc-

tive endings for each of these cases, variation in word order does not lead to confusion in the meaning of the speaker.

In approaching the New Testament (which was written in the Greek of the first century A.D.), the English reader must be aware that the order of the Greek words themselves is exactly right to communicate what the author wanted to stress.

The Discovery Bible does not attempt to introduce a novel or new-found way of reading the Scriptures, but rather brings before the English reader that which was commonly understood and appreciated by native Greek speakers since Bible times. The amazing abilities of the Greek language to express thought with beautiful accuracy doubtless furnished one of the reasons God selected it to record the written revelation of His Son (see Gal. 4:4).

The discovery color, then, enables the average English reader to detect, as he reads the *New American Standard Bible* translation, all those words that originally were given stress and special importance in the originals. To pay attention to the details and precisions built into the original text of Holy Scripture is to better appreciate and honor its divine Author. Knowing what is being given special stress is invaluable to readers in any language. Some of the advantages of using emphasis are:

1. *To bring out the emotion and energy behind the words that are said*

"I *heard* you" can show resentment and impatience at the prospect of being told something again. "I'll *take* it!" shows that the customer is not impassive or reluctant but has an enthusiastic attitude in making his purchase.

Emphasis can bring "words to life" in much the same way dynamics ("louds" and "softs") do to a musical score. Even the most beautiful songs ever written would sound dull and uninteresting if certain notes were not stressed more than others. A bland score of plain notes can be transformed into a musical masterpiece by the touch of a gifted pianist who emphasizes the right notes at the right times. So it is with language. Clear and forceful meaning depends on knowing and appreciating what words are being stressed. The highlighted words will help bring the dynamics and emotion of the original text, as composed under the influence of the Holy Spirit, to the English reader.

2. *To enable warnings and persuasions to really "hit home"*

A word may be emphasized so that the full extent or degree to which something is true will not be underestimated or go unheeded. The Scripture writers often made extensive use of emphasis when persuasion or warning was involved to ensure that their words would be fully convincing and carried out.

3. *To make Bible memorization easier*

Many people find that they remember more when they listen to a Bible message than when they read one. This is because we tend to remember what is emphasized. A speaker has the added advantage of being able to stress certain words with his voice. So, too, as the reader sees and feels what

was stressed in the original text through the highlighted words, he will find his comprehension and recall significantly increasing.

4. *To convey subtleties that are not easily communicated*

Emphasized words often convey something without directly stating it. Observe how different the meaning of the following four-word sentence is when emphasis is applied:

"I think Paul can" (a simple statement of fact—no emphasis)

"*I* think Paul can" (i.e., "Maybe you don't think so, but I do!")

"I *think* Paul can" (i.e., "I guess he can, but I am not positive")

"I think *Paul* can" (i.e., "Maybe others can't, but Paul, on the other hand, can")

"I think Paul *can*" (i.e., "I have no doubt about Paul's ability!")

It is clear from the above illustration that knowing what is being emphasized can make a great deal of difference in meaning. This example illustrates how emphasis can leave a stronger and more lasting impression by showing what is clearly implied but not explicitly stated.

EXPLANATION OF HIGHLIGHTED VERB SYMBOLS

A new world of Bible discovery lies in the colorful and vivid verb tenses of the Greek New Testament. That is, a kind of "motion picture show" occurs before the reader's eye when an action is described. This picturesque action is conveyed in *The Discovery Bible* through the use of eight different symbols. Each of the symbols (shown on the chart below) corresponds to specific verb tenses in the original Greek text. These symbols always appear at the upper right corner of the word they refer to. Therefore, a symbol always refers to a word on its left.

Because temporal distinction is so effectively conveyed in English translations, those verb forms selected to be shown by a specific symbol were principally confined to the non-indicative moods. Functionally defective verbs, pretero-presents, specialized uses, and so forth, did not permit us to indicate every occurrence of a given verb form.

~ present infinitive, subjunctive, and optative

ˣ aorist infinitive, subjunctive, and optative

~! present imperative

ˣ! aorist imperative

⊙ present imperative negated

⊘ aorist imperative (subjunctive) negated

→ perfect participle and indicative

ˣˣˣ imperfect indicative

Present Tense— ~ The present tense in Greek—signified by the symbol ~ —conveys continuous or habitual action. Examples of the uses of the present tense in Scripture include the following.

(1) Continuous or uninterrupted action—John 15:4, "As the branch cannot bear fruit of itself, unless it [continuously] abides~ in the vine, so neither can you unless you [continuously] abide~ in Me."

(2) Action that happens over and over again—Matthew 10:1, "He gave them authority over unclean spirits, to [repeatedly] cast~ them out, and to [over and over again] heal~ every kind of disease."

(3) Customary or habitual action—Matthew 7:12, "Therefore however you [customarily] want~ people to [customarily] treat~ you."

By supplying one of the following words or phrases that best suits the context, the Bible reader can significantly enhance his understanding of the

passages where the symbol ~ appears: *continuously, repeatedly, over and over again, uninterruptedly, constantly, keep on, customarily, habitually.*

Aorist Tense—ˣ The symbol ˣ represents the Greek aorist tense, which conveys "point action." This means the action is viewed as complete whole or one-time action. Such action (depending on the context) may indicate one of the following things.

(1) "Effective" or "successful" action—1 Timothy 1:3, "In order that you may [effectively] instructˣ certain men"; or again in 2 Timothy 2:4, "So that he may [successfully] pleaseˣ the one who enlisted him."
(2) "Single" (one time) action—Matthew 5:28, "Everyone who looks on a woman to lustˣ [i.e., even once] for her has committed."
(3) Action wrapped up as a "single package"—Luke 17:4, "And if he sinsˣ against you seven times a day, and returnsˣ to you seven times." Here "sinsˣ" and "returnsˣ" include all the possible occasions of these acts in one single idea.
(4) Action viewed as an anticipated fact or reality—John 15:7, "If you [really do] abideˣ in Me, and My words [really do] abideˣ in you."

The aorist tense then exhibits a certain range of meaning that can be brought out through the use of "helping" words. As the reader encounters the symbol ˣ he may supply from the following list the word or phrase that best suits that particular context: *effectively, successfully, completely, even once, ever, as a whole, indeed, in fact, actually, really do.*

The Greek New Testament possesses a marvelous ability to convey precisely how an order or command is to be understood. Because spiritual blessing and prosperity depend primarily on obeying God's commands, the importance of correctly understanding commands in Scripture can hardly be overstated. The two different ways *positive* commands are conveyed in the original text are discussed as follows.

Present Imperative—~! Orders or commands that are expected to have continuous or repeated application are given in the present tense. Therefore, the present imperative essentially means, "Follow this command as often as the situation or need arises." With that in mind, the words of 2 Corinthians 13:5 take on new meaning, "Test~! yourselves to see if you are in the faith; examine~! yourselves!" The present imperatives in this verse emphatically show that the danger of spiritual pride and the need of self-examination remain a constant consideration throughout the believer's life. The four present imperatives in 1 Corinthians 16:13, "Be~! on the alert, stand~! firm in the faith, act~! like men, be~! strong," each bring out the call to a *long-term commitment* conveyed by this tense.

Aorist Imperative—ˣ! In the aorist imperative we move away from the call to a long-term commitment of the present imperative to the call for a specific and definite decision. Thus our Lord's words in John 15:4, "Abideˣ! in Me," are not primarily dealing with a future kind of life-style, but rather

with a call for a definite preference regarding fellowship with Himself. The call to a decisive and dramatic choice is again clearly seen in the apostle Paul's exhortation "Be reconciled[x] to God!"

Summary and contrast of the present ([~]*) and aorist (*[x]*) imperatives.* An aorist imperative compels you to a choice; a present imperative commits you to a process.

An aorist imperative usually relates to a particular and specific situation; a present imperative usually relates to a more general and recurring situation.

An aorist imperative calls for a decisive choice to effectively accomplish an action, which in many cases is urgent and immediate; the present imperative calls for a long-term way of doing something.

The aorist imperative focuses on decision; the present imperative on the broader consideration of general policy and life-style.

Hence the order "Turn off the TV!" would be in the aorist tense, whereas a schoolteacher's order "Read books!" would be in the present tense.

Negative imperatives. As with positive commands ("Do this!"), the Greek language also has two ways of negative commands ("Don't do this!"). The distinctive shade of meaning that each conveys is often difficult to recapture in translation. The reader can gain significant insights by taking note of the symbols ([0], [o]), which show these two different kinds of negative commands (imperatives).

Negative Present Imperative—[0] In the majority of cases, the negative present imperative has the meaning *"Stop doing this!"* For example, in John 20:17 what Jesus said to Mary Magdalene was not so much, "Do not touch Me at all!" but rather, *"Stop touching Me!"* A. T. Robertson holds that as a general rule the negative present imperative is used to stop an action that is already going on, whereas the negative aorist imperative ([o]) is used to forbid an action that has not yet been done.[1] Thus the meaning of the apostle Paul's words "Do not be troubled[0]" is really, "Do not be troubled [*any longer*]!" (see Acts 20:10). We can see this illustrated again in Jesus' words to Thomas "Be not unbelieving[0]", which really have the force, *"Stop being unbelieving!"* (see John 20:27). Another meaning of the negative present imperative is "Go on refusing to do this each time the situation arises!" as in Romans 12:14 ("curse[0] not").

In summary, when the reader sees the symbol [0], he may supply from the following phrases the one that best suits the context: *Stop doing this! Do not let this continue any longer! Go on refusing to do this!*

Negative Aorist Imperative (Subjunctive)—[o] The negative aorist imperative has a different focus than the negative present imperative ([0]). Whereas

---

1. A. T. Robertson, *A Grammar of the Greek New Testament in the Light of Historical Research* (New York, 1931), p. 852.

the negative present imperative lays stress on forbidding that an action *continue*, the negative aorist imperative lays the stress on the action's *never happening at all*. This can be seen in Paul's words to Timothy in 2 Timothy 1:8, "Therefore do not be ashamed⁰ [i.e., never at any time] of the testimony of our Lord." The symbol ⁰ in this verse would have implied (in an accusing way) that Timothy had already been ashamed, whereas the symbol ⁰ used here conveys a total and absolute prohibition.

This kind of prohibition can be seen again in the words of Hebrews 12:25, "See to it that you do not refuse⁰ [i.e., at any time] Him who is speaking."

In summary, when the reader sees the symbol ⁰ , he is to consider one of the following phrases that best suits the context: *Never begin to do this! Do not do this at all! Don't even start this!* Whereas the symbol ⁰ envisions that the situation is likely to come up again and again (or is already going on), the symbol ⁰ conveys a somewhat more urgent, peremptory, or authoritative prohibition.

Perfect Tense—⁺ In the Greek New Testament, the perfect tense conveys a completed action that has lingering effects or that leaves an *ongoing result* or *condition*. Well-known grammarians H. W. Smyth and E. Burton describe an event in the perfect tense as "a completed action, the effects of which still continue in the present"[2] and a past action that "affirms an existing result."[3]

Very often the thought "and now still is" aptly recaptures the meaning of the perfect tense when supplied in translation. The following examples from the epistle to the Hebrews illustrate this point.

Hebrews 1:4, "He has inherited⁺ [and now still has] a more excellent name than they."

Hebrews 2:9, "Jesus, because of the suffering of death crowned⁺ [and now still is] with glory and honor."

Hebrews 12:2, "Jesus, . . . who for the joy set before Him endured the cross, . . . and has sat down⁺ [and now still is seated] at the right hand of the throne of God."

Perhaps the sense most often conveyed by the perfect tense, however, is the continuance of the *effect* of the action (not the action *itself*), which must be determined from each individual context. For example, in the cry of Jesus from the cross, "It is finished!⁺" (John 19:30), the perfect tense brings out that the results and effects of His sacrificial death are anything but over and finished. Another instance where a particular action is finished but the effects have a profoundly important ongoing significance is in Galatians 2:20, "I have been crucified⁺ with Christ."

The uses of the perfect tense throughout the New Testament, therefore, are often of great importance. Moreover, the meaning and significance of each occurrence must be determined by the context.

2. H. W. Smyth, *Greek Grammar* (Cambridge, Mass.: Harvard U., 1956), p. 434.
3. E. D. Burton, *Moods and Tenses in New Testament Greek* (Grand Rapids: Kregel, 1976).

Imperfect Tense—ˣˣˣ The imperfect tense is used primarily[4] in the Greek New Testament to convey repeated action in past time. In other words, an action that occurred more than once. An illustration of this is found in Mark 5:18 when the man who had been demon-possessed "was entreatingˣˣˣ" Jesus to permit him to accompany Him. The imperfect here shows that the man did not merely ask Jesus once, but rather had pleaded over and over with Him. Another graphic use of this tense is with the description of Jesus feeding the five thousand in Mark 6:41, "He blessed the food and broke the loaves and He kept givingˣˣˣ [repeatedly, over and over again] them to the disciples to set before them."

The imperfect tense is also used to convey habitual or customary action. It is thus used to describe Jesus' daily habit of teaching in the Temple in Matthew 26:55, "Have you come out . . . to arrest Me as against a robber? Every day I used to sitˣˣˣ in the temple teaching." Another illustration of this is found in 1 Peter 3:5, "For in this way in former times the holy women also, . . . used to [customarily] adornˣˣˣ themselves."

The symbol ˣˣˣ can also convey an action in *dramatic process* (Luke 4:39-41), as well as the multiple actions of a group, rather than just an individual (Luke 4:36, 42).

The symbol ˣˣˣ therefore signals that often "multiplied action" of some kind has taken place. Because this colorful action is often difficult to convey in translation, the reader is encouraged to consider the following words and phrases in each particular context to see which one best applies: *repeatedly, over and over again, kept on, customarily, habitually, began to, tried to.*

4. Other functions of the imperfect tense, such as the inceptive imperfect ("he began to write") and the conative imperfect ("he tried to write") in many cases were not marked in *The Discovery Bible*.

EXPLANATION OF COLOR-HIGHLIGHTED WORDS AND MARKS

Meaning of *Major* and Minor Emphasis

Every word that is emphatic by position or by intensified form is highlighted by the russet color. Minor emphasis is indicated by normal vertical type, major emphasis by *slanted* type. (This should not be confused with the *italicized words* in the NASB text that are used to indicate words not found in the original Hebrew, Aramaic, or Greek.) The distinction between major and minor emphasis was based on the combination of the unusualness of the word order and context. Major emphasis ordinarily involves some factor of antithesis or contrast in the immediate context; minor emphasis is applied to what is secondarily stressed in its word order or in its special form. Occasionally major and minor emphases are involved in two successive words. For example, in Hebrews 3:3 "worthy of *more* glory," the prime position of "*more*" *(pleionos)* reveals an even greater stress than the position of "glory" *(doxēs)*. These gradations or levels of stress in successive words should be carefully observed in order to appreciate the emphasis intended by the author (see also Matt. 14:33 and 16:26, where the expressions "*God's* Son" and "*whole* world" further illustrate this point).

The Discovery Bible does not attempt to show which words are emphatic *merely by their context*; rather, only those words that are emphasized by their position or distinctive form in the original Greek text have been highlighted. Hence, some emphatic passages (such as Matthew 27:51-53) have no highlighted words even though they are highly dramatic.

The meaning of the superior +—*"obligatory in position but emphatic in sense"*

The symbol + at the *left-hand* corner of a highlighted word indicates that the emphasis of that word was determined on the basis of context as well as its position in the underlying Greek text; that is, grammatical and contextual factors suggest that a word (or phrase) is being stressed, yet the Greek word order is either: (1) not *exclusively* used for emphasis (i.e., shared at times with non-emphatic occurrences[1]) or (2) in a "fixed" or immovable position.[2]

---

1. This is the case with certain words coming before the copula verb "to be," as in John 15:1, or before participles, as in 2 Peter 2:1.
2. This is particularly the case in elliptical constructions where the first member of a pair is emphasized by word order but the second is indeterminable because a word has been omitted in the Greek text as in 1 Corinthians 15:44 and 1 Thessalonians 2:4; see also Matthew 5:3, 12:31, where an emphatic idea occurs in a grammatical construction that *cannot* be stressed in Greek by word order.

Explanation of Color-Highlighted Words and Marks

When the mark † relates to several words as a single unit (i.e., a phrase), it appears on the last word of that phrase, as in Romans 1:16, "*power of †God.*"

The meaning of the superior mark ·—"*inherently emphatic whatever its position*"

This superior dot occurs on the upper left-hand corner of those words that are strengthened beyond their normal form. These words come in four types:[3] (1) emphatic personal pronouns, such as *emou, emoi, eme*—in contrast to the enclitic *mou, moi, me* (the first person pronoun singular); (2) emphatic possessive pronominal adjectives, such as *sos* (instead of enclitic *sou*) for "yours," or *emos* instead of *mou* for "my," as in Luke 22:19: "Do this in remembrance of *Me (emēn)*" rather than "my *(mou)* remembrance"; (3) strengthened adverbs with final *i*, such as *ouchi* (for *ouk*) and *nuni* for *nun* "now" (for example John 13:10, "but •not [*ouchi*] all of you"). (4) phrases in which near-synonyms are combined to lend greater force, as in Mark 9:2, where *kat' idian monous* can be rendered "by themselves"—literally "apart alone." Another instance of such intensification is the conscious imitation of the Hebrew infinitive absolute through the use of cognates (cf. Acts 7:34).

A fair number of independent personal pronouns used in the nominative case with verbs that already contain that pronoun in their inflected form are really emphatic. Such pronouns occur so frequently that they have not been marked by the superlinear dot. The same is true of many of the words highlighted by a preceding *kai* ("even, also") and the intensive personal pronoun *autos* ("himself").

---

3. These have not been highlighted in every case because these forms are not always emphatic in the Greek New Testament.

FOREWORD TO THE
NEW AMERICAN STANDARD BIBLE

SCRIPTURAL PROMISE

"The grass withers, the flower fades,
but the word of our God stands forever."
Isaiah 40:8

The New American Standard Bible has been produced with the conviction
that the words of Scripture as originally penned in the Hebrew, Aramaic, and
Greek were inspired by God. Since they are the eternal Word of God, the Holy
Scriptures speak with fresh power to each generation, to give wisdom that
leads to salvation, that men may serve Christ to the glory of God.

The Fourfold Aim
of
The Lockman Foundation

1. These publications shall be true to the original Hebrew, Aramaic, and
   Greek.

2. They shall be grammatically correct.

3. They shall be understandable to the masses.

4. They shall give the Lord Jesus Christ His proper place, the place which
   the Word gives Him; therefore, no work will ever be personalized.

PREFACE TO THE
NEW AMERICAN STANDARD BIBLE

In the history of English Bible translations, the King James Version is the most prestigious. This time-honored version of 1611, itself a revision of the Bishops' Bible of 1568, became the basis for the English Revised Version appearing in 1881 (New Testament) and 1885 (Old Testament). The American counterpart of this last work was published in 1901 as the American Standard Version. Recognizing the values of the American Standard Version, the Lockman Foundation felt an urgency to update it by incorporating recent discoveries of Hebrew and Greek textual sources and by rendering it into more current English. Therefore, in 1959 a new translation project was launched, based on the ASV. The result is the New American Standard Bible.

The American Standard Version (1901) has been highly regarded for its scholarship and accuracy. A product of both British and American scholarship, it has frequently been used as a standard for other translations. It is still recognized as a valuable tool for study of the Scriptures. The New American Standard Bible has sought to preserve these and other lasting values of the ASV.

Furthermore, in the preparation of this work numerous other translations have been consulted along with the linguistic tools and literature of biblical scholarship. Decisions about English renderings were made by consensus of a team composed of educators and pastors. Subsequently, review and evaluation by other Hebrew and Greek scholars outside the Editorial Board were sought and carefully considered.

The Editorial Board has continued to function since publication of the complete Bible in 1971. Minor revisions and refinements, recommended over the last several years, are presented in this edition.

NEW AMERICAN STANDARD BIBLE PRINCIPLES OF TRANSLATION

Modern English Usage: The attempt has been made to render the grammar and terminology in contemporary English. When it was felt that the word-for-word literalness was unacceptable to the modern reader, a change was made in the direction of a more current English idiom. In the instances where this has been done, the more literal rendering has been indicated in the notes.

Alternative Readings: In addition to the more literal renderings, notations have been made to include alternate translations, readings of variant manuscripts and explanatory equivalents of the text. Only such notations have been used as have been felt justified in assisting the reader's comprehension of the terms used by the original author.

Greek Text: Consideration was given to the latest available manuscripts with a view to determining the best Greek text. In most instances the 23rd edition of Eberhard Nestle's **Novum Testamentum Graece** was followed.

Greek Tenses: A careful distinction has been made in the treatment of the Greek aorist tense (usually translated as the English past, "He did") and the Greek imperfect tense (rendered either as English past progressive, "He was doing"; or, if inceptive, as "He *began* to do" or "He started to do"; or else if customary past, as "He used to do"). "Began" is italicized if it renders an imperfect tense, in order to distinguish it from the Greek verb for "begin."

On the other hand, not all aorists have been rendered as English pasts ("He did"), for some of them are clearly to be rendered as English perfects ("He has done"), or even as past perfects ("He had done"), judging from the context in which they occur. Such aorists have been rendered as perfects or past perfects in this translation.

As for the distinction between aorist and present imperatives, the translators have usually rendered these imperatives in the customary manner, rather than attempting any such fine distinction as "Begin to do!" (for the aorist imperative), or, "Continually do!" (for the present imperative).

As for sequence of tenses, the translators took care to follow English rules rather than Greek in translating Greek presents, imperfects and aorists. Thus, where English says, "We knew that he was doing," Greek puts it, "We knew that he does"; similarly, "We knew that he had done" is the Greek, "We knew that he did." Likewise, the English, "When he had come, they met him," is represented in Greek by: "When he came, they met him." In all cases a consistent transfer has been made from the Greek tense in the subordinate clause to the appropriate tense in English.

In the rendering of negative questions introduced by the particle **mē** (which always expects the answer "No") the wording has been altered from a mere, "Will he not do this?" to a more accurate, "He will not do this, will he?"

Editorial Board, THE LOCKMAN FOUNDATION

NEW AMERICAN STANDARD BIBLE
EXPLANATION OF
GENERAL FORMAT

Cross References are placed in a column adjoining the text on the page and listed under verse numbers to which they refer. Cross References in italics are parallel passages.

Footnotes are used only where the text especially requires them for clarification. Marginal notes have been deleted from this edition.

Paragraphs are designated by bold face numbers or letters.

Quotation Marks are used in the text in accordance with modern English usage.

"Thou," "Thee" and "Thy" are not used in this translation except in the language of prayer when addressing Deity.

Personal Pronouns are capitalized when pertaining to Deity.

Italics are used in the text to indicate words which are not found in the original Hebrew, Aramaic, or Greek but implied by it. Italics are used in the footnotes to signify alternate readings for the text.

Small Caps in the New Testament are used in the text to indicate Old Testament quotations or obvious allusions to Old Testament texts. Variations of Old Testament wording are found in New Testament citations depending on whether the New Testament writer translated from a Hebrew text, used existing Greek or Aramaic translations, or paraphrased the material. It should be noted that modern rules for the indication of direct quotation were not used in biblical times thus allowing freedom for omissions or insertions without specific indication of these.

Asterisks are used to mark verbs that are historical presents in the Greek which have been translated with an English past tense in order to conform to modern usage. The translators recognized that in some contexts the present tense seems more unexpected and unjustified to the English reader than a past tense would have been. But Greek authors frequently used the present tense for the sake of heightened vividness, thereby transporting their readers in imagination to the actual scene at the time of occurrence. However, the translators felt that it would be wise to change these historical presents to English past tenses.

NEW AMERICAN STANDARD BIBLE
ABBREVIATIONS AND
SPECIAL MARKINGS:

   Gr. = Greek translation of O.T. (Septuagint or LXX) or Greek text of N.T.

   Lit. = A literal translation

   Or = An alternate translation justified by the Hebrew, Aramaic, or Greek

   [ ] = In text, brackets indicate words probably not in the original writings

   [ ] = In margin, brackets indicate references to a name, place or thing similar to, but not identical with that in the text

   cf. = compare

   f., ff. = following verse or verses

   ms., mss. = manuscript, manuscripts

   v., vv. = verse, verses

THE NAMES AND ORDER OF
THE BOOKS OF
THE NEW TESTAMENT

New American Standard Bible

NEW TESTAMENT

The Gospel According to
Matthew

Genealogy of Jesus Christ

1 The book of the genealogy of Jesus Christ, the son of David, the son of Abraham.

2 To Abraham was born Isaac; and to Isaac, Jacob; and to Jacob, ªJudah and his brothers;

3 and to Judah were born Perez and Zerah by Tamar; and to Perez was born Hezron; and to Hezron, Ram;

4 and to Ram was born Amminadab; and to Amminadab, Nahshon; and to Nahshon, Salmon;

5 and to Salmon was born Boaz by Rahab; and to Boaz was born Obed by Ruth; and to Obed, Jesse;

6 and to Jesse was born David the king.

And to David was born Solomon by her *who had been the wife* of Uriah;

7 and to Solomon was born Rehoboam; and to Rehoboam, Abijah; and to Abijah, Asa;

8 and to Asa was born Jehoshaphat; and to Jehoshaphat, Joram; and to Joram, Uzziah;

9 and to Uzziah was born Jotham; and to Jotham, Ahaz; and to Ahaz, Hezekiah;

10 and to Hezekiah was born Manasseh; and to Manasseh, Amon; and to Amon, Josiah;

11 and to Josiah were born Jeconiah and his brothers, at the time of the deportation to Babylon.

12 And after the deportation to Babylon, to Jeconiah was born Shealtiel; and to Shealtiel, Zerubbabel;

13 and to Zerubbabel was born Abiud; and to Abiud, Eliakim; and to Eliakim, Azor;

14 and to Azor was born Zadok; and to Zadok, Achim; and to Achim, Eliud;

15 and to Eliud was born Eleazar; and to Eleazar, Matthan; and to Matthan, Jacob;

16 and to Jacob was born Joseph the husband of Mary, by whom was born †*Jesus,* who is called Christ.

17 Therefore all the generations from Abraham to David are fourteen generations; and from David to the deportation to

ªGr., *Judas.* Names of Old Testament characters will be given in their Old Testament form.

1:1
2 Sam. 7:12-16;
Ps. 89:3f.;
132:11; Is. 9:6f.;
11:1; Matt. 9:27;
Luke 1:32,69;
John 7:42; Acts
13:23; Rom. 1:3;
Rev. 22:16;
Matt. 1:1-6: *Luke
3:32-34;* Gen.
22:18; Gal. 3:16
1:3
Ruth 4:18-22;
1 Chr. 2:1-15;
Matt. 1:3-6

1:6
2 Sam. 11:27;
12:24

1:7
1 Chr. 3:10ff.

1:11
2 Kin. 24:14f.;
Jer. 27:20; Matt.
1:17
1:12
2 Kin. 24:14f.;
Jer. 27:20; Matt.
1:17

1:16
Matt. 27:17,22;
Luke 2:11; John
4:25
1:17
2 Kin. 24:14f.;
Jer. 27:20; Matt.
1:11,12

Babylon fourteen generations; and from the deportation to Babylon to *the time of* Christ fourteen generations.

Conception and Birth of Jesus

1:18
Matt. 12:46; Luke
1:27;
Luke 1:35

18 Now the birth of *Jesus Christ* was as follows. When His mother Mary had been betrothed to Joseph, before they came[x] together she was found to be with child by the Holy Spirit.

1:19
Deut. 22:20-24;
24:1-4; John 8:4,
5

19 And Joseph her husband, being a righteous man, and not wanting to disgrace[x] her, desired [b]to put[x] her away secretly.

1:20
Luke 2:4

20 But when he had considered this, behold, an angel of the Lord appeared to him in a dream, saying, "Joseph, son of David, do not be afraid[o] to take[x] Mary as your wife; for that which has been [c]conceived in her is of the Holy *Spirit.*

1:21
Luke 1:31; 2:21;
Luke 2:11; John
1:29; Acts 4:12;
5:31; 13:23,38,
39; Col. 1:20-23
1:22
Luke 24:44; Rom.
1:2-4
1:23
Is. 7:14;
Is. 9:6,7;
Is. 8:10

21 "And she will bear a Son; and you shall call His name Jesus, for it is *He* who will save His people from their sins."

22 Now all this took⁺ place that what was spoken by the Lord through the prophet might be *fulfilled,*[x] saying,

23 "Behold, the virgin shall be with child, and shall bear a Son, and they shall call His name Immanuel," which translated means, "⁺God with us."

24 And Joseph arose from his sleep, and did as the angel of the Lord commanded him, and took *her* as his wife,

1:25
Luke 2:7;
Matt. 1:21; Luke
2:21

25 and [d]kept[xx] her virgin until she gave birth to a Son; and he called His name Jesus.

Visit of the Wise Men

2:1
Mic. 5:2; Luke
2:4-7;
Luke 1:5

2 Now after Jesus was born in Bethlehem of Judea in the days of Herod the king, behold, [e]magi from the east arrived in Jerusalem, saying,

2:2
Jer. 23:5; 30:9;
Zech. 9:9; Matt.
27:11; Luke
19:38; 23:38;
John 1:49;
Num. 24:17

2 "Where is He who has been born King of the Jews? For we saw *His* star in the east, and have come to worship[x] Him."

3 And when Herod the king heard it, he was troubled, and all Jerusalem with him.

4 And gathering together all the chief priests and scribes of the people, he *began* to inquire of them where the Christ was to be born.

2:5
John 7:42

5 And they said to him, "In Bethlehem of Judea, for so it has been written⁺ by the prophet,

2:6
Mic. 5:2; John
7:42;
John 21:16

6 'And you, Bethlehem, land of Judah,
    Are by no means least among the leaders of
        Judah;
    For *out of you* shall come forth a Ruler,

[b]Or, *to divorce her* [c]Lit., *begotten* [d]Lit., *was not knowing her* [e]Pronounced may-ji, a caste of wise men specializing in astrology, medicine and natural science

WHO WILL SHEPHERD MY PEOPLE ISRAEL.' "

7   Then Herod secretly called the magi, and ascertained from them the time the star appeared.

8   And he sent them to Bethlehem, and said, "Go and make careful search[xl] for the Child; and when you have found[x] *Him*, report[xl] to me, that *I too* may come and worship[x] Him."

9   And having heard the king, they went their way; and lo, the star, which they had seen in the east, went[m] on before them, until it came and stood over where the Child was.

10   And when they saw the star, they rejoiced *exceedingly*[4] with *great* joy.

11   And they came into the house and saw the Child with Mary His mother; and they fell down and worshiped[44b] Him; and opening their treasures they presented to Him gifts of gold and frankincense and myrrh.

12   And having been warned *by God* in a dream not to return[x] to Herod, they departed for their own country by *another way.*

The Flight to Egypt

13   Now when they had departed, behold, an angel of the Lord *appeared to Joseph in a dream, saying, "Arise and take[xl] the Child and His mother, and flee to Egypt, and remain there until I tell[x] you; for Herod is going to search for the Child to destroy[x] Him."

14   And he arose and took the Child and His mother by night, and departed for Egypt;

15   and was there until the death of Herod, that what was spoken by the Lord through the prophet might be fulfilled,[x] saying, "OUT OF EGYPT DID I CALL MY SON."

Herod Slaughters Babies

16   Then when Herod saw that he had been tricked by the magi, he became very enraged, and sent and slew all the male children who were in Bethlehem and in all its environs, from two years old and under, according to the time which he had ascertained from the magi.

17   Then that which was spoken through Jeremiah the prophet was fulfilled, saying,

18   "A VOICE WAS HEARD IN RAMAH,
WEEPING AND *GREAT* MOURNING,
RACHEL WEEPING FOR HER CHILDREN;
AND SHE REFUSED[m] TO BE COMFORTED,[x]
BECAUSE THEY WERE NO MORE."

2:19
Matt. 1:20; 2:12,
13,22

2:22
Matt. 2:12,13,19
2:23
Luke 1:26; 2:39;
John 1:45,46;
Mark 1:24; John
18:5,7; 19:19
3:1
Matt. 3:1-12;
Mark 1:3-8; Luke
3:2-17; John
1:6-8,19-28;
Matt. 11:11-14;
16:14;
Josh. 15:61;
Judg. 1:16
3:2
Matt. 4:17;
Dan. 2:44; Matt.
4:17,23; 6:10;
10:7; Mark 1:15;
Luke 10:9f.;
11:20; 21:31
3:3
Luke 1:17,76;
Is. 40:3;
John 1:23
3:4
2 Kin. 1:8; Zech.
13:4; Matt. 11:8;
Mark 1:6;
Lev. 11:22
3:5
Mark 1:5;
Luke 3:3
3:6
Matt. 3:11,13-16;
Mark 1:5; John
1:25,26; 3:23;
Acts 1:5; 2:38-41;
10:37
3:7
Matt. 16:1ff.;
23:13,15;
Matt. 22:23; Acts
4:1; 5:17; 23:6ff.;
Matt. 12:34;
23:33;
1 Thess. 1:10
3:8
Luke 3:8; Eph.
5:8,9;
Acts 26:20
3:9
Luke 3:8; 16:24;
John 8:33,39,53;
Acts 13:26; Rom.
4:1; 9:7,8; Gal.
3:29
3:10
Luke 3:9;
Ps. 92:12-14;
Matt. 7:19; John
15:2
3:11
Mark 1:4,8; Luke
3:16; John 1:26f.;
Acts 1:5; 8:36,
38; 11:16;
John 1:33; Acts
2:3,4; Titus 3:5
3:12
Is. 30:24; 41:16;
Jer. 15:7; 51:2;
Luke 3:17;
Matt. 13:30;
Ps. 1:4;
Is. 66:24; Jer.
7:20; Matt.
13:41,42; Mark
9:43,48

19 But when Herod was dead, behold, an angel of the Lord *appeared in a dream to Joseph in Egypt, saying,

20 "Arise and take the^{xi} Child and His mother, and go into the land of Israel; for those who sought the Child's life are dead."

21 And he arose and took the Child and His mother, and came into the land of Israel.

22 But when he heard that Archelaus was reigning over Judea in place of his father Herod, he was afraid to go^x there. And being warned *by God* in a dream, he departed for the regions of Galilee,

23 and came and resided in a city called Nazareth, that what was spoken through the prophets might be fulfilled,^x "He shall be called a *Nazarene*."

John the Baptist Preaches

3 Now in those days John the Baptist *came, preaching in the wilderness of Judea, saying,

2 "Repent, for the kingdom of heaven is at hand."⁺

3 For this is the one referred to by Isaiah the prophet, saying,

"THE VOICE OF ONE CRYING IN THE WILDERNESS,
'MAKE^{xi} READY THE WAY OF THE LORD,
MAKE⁓ HIS PATHS STRAIGHT!' "

4 Now John himself had^{xxi} a garment of camel's hair, and a leather belt about his waist; and his food was locusts and wild honey.

5 Then Jerusalem was going^{xxi} out to him, and all Judea, and all the district around the Jordan;

6 and they were being baptized^{xxi} by him in the Jordan River, as they confessed[1] their sins.

7 But when he saw many of the Pharisees and Sadducees coming for baptism, he said to them, "You brood of vipers, who warned you to flee^x from the wrath^{7b} to come?

8 "Therefore bring^{xi} forth fruit in keeping with repentance;

9 and do not suppose[⊕] that you can say⁓ to yourselves, 'We have *Abraham* for our father'; for I say to you, that God is able from *these stones* to raise^x up children to Abraham.

10 "And the axe is already laid at the root of the trees; every tree therefore that does not bear good^{25b} fruit is cut down and thrown into the *fire*.

11 "As for me, *I* baptize you ᶠwith water for repentance, but He who is coming after me is mightier than I, and I am not fit to remove^x His sandals; *He* will baptize you with the Holy Spirit and fire.

12 "And His winnowing fork is in His hand, and He will

ᶠThe Gr. here can be translated *in, with* or *by*

thoroughly[1] clear His threshing floor; and He will gather His wheat into the barn, but He will burn up the chaff with *unquenchable* fire."

The Baptism of Jesus

13 Then Jesus *arrived from Galilee at the Jordan *coming* to John, to be baptized[x] by him.

14 But John tried to prevent[m1] Him, saying, "*I* have need to be baptized[x] by *You*, and do *You* come to •me?"

15 But Jesus answering said to him, "Permit[x16a] *it* at this time; for in this way it is †fitting for us to fulfill[x] all righteousness." Then he *permitted Him.

16 And after being baptized, Jesus went up immediately from the water; and behold, the heavens were opened, and he saw the Spirit of God descending as a dove, *and* coming upon Him,

17 and behold, a voice out of the heavens, saying, "This is gMy *beloved* Son, in whom I am well-pleased."

Temptation of Jesus

4 Then Jesus was led up by the Spirit into the wilderness to be tempted[x] by the devil.

2 And after He had fasted forty days and forty nights, He hthen became hungry.

3 And the tempter came and said to Him, "If You are the *Son* of God, command[x1] that these stones become *bread.*"

4 But He answered and said, "It is written,✝ 'MAN SHALL NOT LIVE ON *BREAD ALONE,* BUT ON EVERY WORD[43b] THAT PROCEEDS OUT OF THE MOUTH OF GOD.'"

5 Then the devil *took Him into the holy[28a] city; and he had Him stand on the pinnacle of the temple,

6 and *said to Him, "If You are the *Son* of God throw[x1] Yourself down; for it is written,✝

'HE WILL GIVE *HIS ANGELS* CHARGE CONCERNING YOU';
and
'ON *their* HANDS THEY WILL BEAR YOU UP,
LEST YOU STRIKE[x] YOUR FOOT AGAINST A STONE.'"

7 Jesus said[m] to him, "On the other hand, it is written,✝ 'YOU SHALL NOT iPUT THE LORD YOUR GOD TO THE TEST.'"[1]

8 Again, the devil *took Him to a *very high* mountain, and *showed Him all the kingdoms of the world, and their glory;

9 and he said to Him, "*All* these things will I give You, if You fall down and worship[x44b] me."

10 Then Jesus *said to him, "Begone, Satan! For it is written,✝

gLit., *My Son, the Beloved* hLit., *later, afterward* iOr, *tempt . . . God*

3:13
Matt. 3:13-17;
Mark 1:9-11;
Luke 3:21,22;
John 1:31-34;
Matt. 2:22

3:15
Ps. 40:7,8; John
4:34; 8:29

3:16
Mark 1:10; Luke
3:22; John 1:32;
Acts 7:56

3:17
Ps. 2:7; Is. 42:1;
Matt. 12:18; 17:5;
Mark 9:7; Luke
9:35; John 12:28

4:1
Matt. 4:1-11;
Mark 1:12,13;
Luke 4:1-13;
Heb. 4:15; James
1:14
4:2
Ex. 34:28; 1 Kin.
19:8
4:3
1 Thess. 3:5;
Matt. 14:33;
26:63; Mark 3:11;
5:7; Luke 1:35;
4:41; John 1:34,
49; Acts 9:20
4:4
Deut. 8:3
4:5
Neh. 11:1,18;
Dan. 9:24; Matt.
27:53
4:6
Ps. 91:11,12

4:7
Deut. 6:16

4:8
Matt. 16:26; 1
John 2:15-17

4:9
1 Cor. 10:20f.

4:10
Deut. 6:13; 10:20

'YOU SHALL WORSHIP THE LORD YOUR GOD, AND SERVE[38c] HIM ONLY.' "

4:11
Matt. 26:53; Luke
22:43; Heb. 1:14

11   Then the devil *left Him; and behold, angels came and *began* to minister[38a] to Him.

Jesus Begins His Ministry

4:12
Matt. 14:3; Mark
1:14; Luke 3:20;
John 3:24;
Mark 1:14; Luke
4:14; John 1:43;
2:11
4:13
Matt. 11:23; Mark
1:21; 2:1; Luke
4:23,31; John
2:12; 4:46f.
4:15
Is. 9:1

12   Now when He heard that John had been taken into custody, He withdrew into Galilee;

13   and leaving Nazareth, He came and settled in Capernaum, which is by the sea, in the region of Zebulun and Naphtali.

14   *This was* to fulfill[x] what was spoken through Isaiah the prophet, saying,

15   "THE LAND OF ZEBULUN AND THE LAND OF NAPHTALI,
         BY THE WAY OF THE SEA, BEYOND THE JORDAN,
            GALILEE OF THE [j]GENTILES—

4:16
Is. 9:2; 60:1-3;
Luke 2:32

16   "THE PEOPLE WHO WERE SITTING IN DARKNESS SAW A
            GREAT[26a] LIGHT,
         AND TO THOSE WHO WERE SITTING IN THE LAND AND
            SHADOW OF DEATH,
         UPON THEM A LIGHT DAWNED."

4:17
Mark 1:14,15;
Matt. 3:2
4:18
Matt. 4:18-22;
Mark 1:16-20;
Luke 5:2-11; John
1:40-42;
Matt. 15:29; Mark
7:31; Luke 5:1;
John 6:1;
Matt. 10:2; 16:18;
John 1:40-42
4:21
Matt. 10:2; 20:20
4:23
Mark 1:39; Luke
4:14,44;
Matt. 9:35; 13:54;
Mark 1:21; 6:2;
10:1; Luke 4:15;
6:6; 13:10; John
6:59; 18:20;
Matt. 3:2; 9:35;
24:14; Mark 1:14;
Luke 4:43; 8:1;
16:16; Acts
20:25; 28:31;
Matt. 8:16; 9:35;
14:14; 15:30;
19:2; 21:14;
Mark 1:34; 3:10;
Luke 4:40; 7:21;
Acts 10:38
4:24
Mark 7:26; Luke
2:2; Acts 15:23;
18:18; 20:3;
21:3; Gal. 1:21;
Matt. 8:16,28,33;
9:32; 12:22;
15:22; Mark
1:32; 5:15,16,18;
Luke 8:36; John
10:21;
Matt. 17:15;
Matt. 8:6; 9:2,6;
Mark 2:3,5,9;
Luke 5:24

17   From that time Jesus began to preach~ and say,~ "Repent, for the kingdom of heaven is at hand."+

The First Disciples

18   And walking by the Sea of Galilee, He saw two brothers, Simon who was called Peter, and Andrew his brother, casting a net into the sea; for they were fishermen.

19   And He *said to them, "Follow Me, and I will make you fishers of men."

20   And they immediately left the nets, and followed Him.

21   And going on from there He saw two other brothers, James the *son* of Zebedee, and John his brother, in the boat with Zebedee their father, mending their nets; and He called them.

22   And they immediately left the boat and their father, and followed Him.

Ministry in Galilee

23   And *Jesus* was going[m] about in all Galilee, teaching in their synagogues, and proclaiming the gospel of the kingdom, and healing[15a] every kind of disease and every kind of sickness among the people.

24   And the news about Him went out into all Syria; and they brought to Him all who were ill, taken with various diseases and

[j]Or, *nations*

pains, demoniacs, epileptics, paralytics; and He healed them.

25   And great multitudes followed Him from Galilee and Decapolis and Jerusalem and Judea and *from* beyond the Jordan.

4:25
Mark 3:7,8; Luke
6:17;
Mark 5:20; 7:31;
Matt. 4:15

The Sermon on the Mount
The Beatitudes

5 And when He saw the multitudes, He went up on the mountain; and after He sat down, His disciples came to Him.

5:1
Matt. ch. 5-7;
Luke 6:20-49;
Mark 3:13; Luke
6:17; 9:28; John
6:3,15

2   And opening His mouth He *began* to teach them, saying,

5:2
Matt. 13:35; Acts
8:35; 10:34;
18:14

3 "†Blessed are the poor in spirit, for *theirs* is the kingdom of heaven.

5:3
Matt. 5:3-12;
Luke 6:20-23;
Matt. 5:10; 19:14;
25:34; Mark
10:14; Luke 6:20;
22:29f.

4 "†Blessed are those who mourn, for *they* shall be comforted.

5 "†Blessed are the ᵏgentle,²³ᵇ for *they* shall inherit the earth.

6 "†Blessed are those who hunger and thirst for righteousness, for *they* shall be satisfied.

5:4
Is. 61:2; John
16:20; Rev. 7:17
5:5
Ps. 37:11
5:6
Is. 55:1,2; John
4:14; 6:48ff.; 7:37

7 "†Blessed are the merciful, for *they* shall receive mercy.

8 "†Blessed are the pure¹³ᶜ in heart, for *they* shall see *God*.

9 "†Blessed are the peacemakers, for *they* shall be called *sons of God*.

5:7
Prov. 11:17; Matt.
6:14,15; 18:33-35
5:8
Ps. 24:4;
Heb. 12:14;
1 John 3:2; Rev.
22:4
5:9
Matt. 5:45; Luke
6:35; Rom. 8:14

10 "†Blessed are those who have been persecuted⁺ for the sake of righteousness, for *theirs* is the kingdom of heaven.

5:10
1 Pet. 3:14;
Matt. 5:3; 19:14;
25:34; Mark
10:14; Luke 6:20;
22:29f.

11 "†Blessed are you when *men* castˣ insults at you, and persecuteˣ you, and sayˣ all kinds of evil¹⁰ᵇ against you falsely, on account of Me.

5:11
1 Pet. 4:14

12 "Rejoice,ᕁ' and be glad,ᕁ' for your reward in heaven is great,²⁶ᵇ for so they persecuted the prophets who were before you.

5:12
2 Chr. 36:16;
Matt. 23:37; Acts
7:52; 1 Thess.
2:15; Heb.
11:33ff.; James
5:10

Disciples and the World

13 "†You are the salt of the earth; but if the salt has becomeˣ tasteless, how will it be made salty *again*? It is good for nothing anymore, except to be thrown out and trampled˜ under foot by men.

5:13
Mark 9:50; Luke
14:34f.

14 "†You are the light of the world. A city set on a *hill* cannot be hidden.ˣ

5:14
Prov. 4:18; John
8:12; 9:5; 12:36

15 "Nor do *men* light a lamp, and put it under the peck-measure, but on the lampstand; and it gives light to all who are in the house.

5:15
Mark 4:21; Luke
8:16; 11:33; Phil.
2:15

16 "Let your light shineˣ' before men in such a way that they may seeˣ your good²⁵ᵇ works, and glorifyˣ your Father who is in heaven.

5:16
1 Pet. 2:12;
Matt. 9:8

17 "Do not think⊙ that I came to abolishˣ the Law or the Prophets; I did not come to abolish,ˣ but to fulfill.ˣ

5:17
Matt. 7:12

ᵏOr, *humble, meek*

5:18 Matt. 24:35; Luke 16:17

18 "For •truly I say to you, until heaven and earth pass[x] away,
•*not* the smallest letter or stroke shall pass[x] away from the Law,
until all is accomplished.

5:19 Matt. 11:11

19 "Whoever then annuls[x] one of the *least* of these commandments, and so teaches[x] others, shall be called *least* in the kingdom of heaven; but whoever keeps[x] and teaches[x] *them*, he shall
be called *great*[26a] in the kingdom of heaven.

5:20 Luke 18:11,12

20 "For I say to you, that unless your righteousness *surpasses*[x]
that of the scribes and Pharisees, you shall •*not* enter[x] the kingdom of heaven.

Personal Relationships

5:21 Matt. 5:27,33,38, 43; Ex. 20:13; Deut. 5:17; Deut. 16:18; 2 Chr. 19:5f.
5:22 Deut. 16:18; 2 Chr. 19:5f.; Matt. 10:17; 26:59; Mark 13:9; 14:55; 15:1; Luke 22:66; John 11:47; Acts 4:15; 5:21; 6:12; 22:30; 23:1; 24:20; Matt. 5:29f.; 10:28; 18:9; 23:15,33; Mark 9:43ff.; Luke 12:5; James 3:6
5:23 Matt. 5:24
5:24 Rom. 12:17,18

21 "You have heard that the ancients were told, 'YOU SHALL
NOT COMMIT MURDER' and 'Whoever commits[x] murder shall be
[l]liable to the court.'
22 "But *I* say to you that everyone who is angry with his
brother[m] shall be guilty before the court; and whoever shall say[x]
to his brother, '[n]Raca,' shall be guilty before [o]the supreme court;
and whoever shall say,[x] 'You fool,'[20c] shall be guilty *enough to go*
into the [p]fiery hell.[27b]
23 "If therefore you are presenting[~] your offering at the altar,
and there remember[x] that your brother has something against
you,
24 leave[x!] your offering there before the altar, and go your
way; *first* be reconciled[x!1] to your brother, and then come and
present[~!] your offering.

5:25 Prov. 25:8f.; Luke 12:58

25 "Make friends quickly with your opponent at law while you
are with him on the way, in order that your opponent may not
deliver[x] you to the judge, and the judge to the officer, and you be
thrown into prison.

5:26 Luke 12:59

26 "•Truly I say to you, you shall •*not* come[x] out of there, until
you have paid[x] up the last [q]cent.

5:27 Matt. 5:21,33,38, 43; Ex. 20:14; Deut. 5:18
5:28 2 Sam. 11:2-5; Job 31:1; Matt. 15:19; James 1:14,15
5:29 Matt. 18:9; Mark 9:47; Matt. 5:22

27 "You have heard that it was said, 'YOU SHALL NOT COMMIT
ADULTERY';
28 but *I* say to you, that everyone who looks on a woman to
lust[x] for her has committed adultery with her already in his heart.
29 "And if your right eye makes you stumble, tear[x!] it out, and
throw[x!] it from you; for it is better for you that *one* of the parts of
your body perish,[x] than for your whole body to be thrown[x] into
hell.[27b]

5:30 Matt. 18:8; Mark 9:43; Matt. 5:22

30 "And if your right hand makes you stumble, cut[x!] it off, and
throw[x!] it from you; for it is better for you that *one* of the parts of

[l]Or, *guilty before* [m]Some mss. insert here: *without cause* [n]Aramaic for *empty-head* or, *good for nothing* [o]Lit., *the Sanhedrin* [p]Lit., *Gehenna of fire* [q]Lit., *quadrans* (equaling two lepta or mites), i.e., 1/64 of a denarius

your body perish,[x] than for your whole body to go[x] into *hell.* [27b]

31 "And it was said, 'WHOEVER SENDS[x] HIS WIFE AWAY, LET HIM GIVE[xl] HER A CERTIFICATE OF DIVORCE';

32 but *I* say to you that everyone who divorces his wife, except for *the* cause of unchastity, makes her commit[x] adultery; and whoever marries a divorced[+] woman commits[x] adultery.

33 "Again, you have heard that the ancients were told, 'YOU SHALL NOT MAKE FALSE VOWS, BUT SHALL FULFILL YOUR VOWS TO THE LORD.'

34 "But *I* say to you, make[x] no oath at all, either by heaven, for it is the throne of God,

35 or by the earth, for it is the footstool of His feet, or by Jerusalem, for it is THE CITY OF THE GREAT KING.

36 "Nor shall you make[x] an oath by your head, for you cannot make[x] [+]*one* hair white or black.

37 "But let your statement be, 'Yes, yes' *or* 'No, no'; and anything beyond these is of [+]evil. [10b]

38 "You have heard that it was said, 'AN EYE FOR AN EYE, AND A TOOTH FOR A TOOTH.'

39 "But *I* say to you, do not resist[x] him who is evil;[10b] but whoever slaps you on your right cheek, turn[xl] to him the other also.

40 "And if anyone wants to sue[x] you, and take[x] your [r]shirt, let him have[xl] your [s]coat also.

41 "And whoever shall force you to go one mile, go with him two.

42 "Give[xl] to him who asks of you, and do not turn[⊙] away from him who wants to borrow[x] from you.

43 "You have heard that it was said, 'YOU SHALL LOVE[31a] YOUR NEIGHBOR, and hate your enemy.'

44 "But *I* say to you, love[~31a] your enemies, and pray[~l] for those who persecute you

45 in order that you may be sons of your Father who is in heaven; for He causes His sun to rise on *the* evil and *the* good, and sends rain on *the* righteous and *the* unrighteous.

46 "For if you love[x] those who love you, what reward have you? Do not even the tax-gatherers do the *same?*

47 "And if you greet[x] your brothers only, what do you do more *than others?* Do not even the Gentiles do the *same?*

48 "Therefore *you* are to be perfect, as your heavenly Father is perfect.

[r]Or, *tunic;* i.e., garment worn next to the body   [s]Or, *cloak;* i.e., outer garment

5:31
Deut. 24:1,3; Jer. 3:1; Matt. 19:7; Mark 10:4
5:32
Matt. 19:9; Mark 10:11f.; Luke 16:18; 1 Cor. 7:11f.
5:33
Matt. 5:21,27,38, 43; 23:16ff.; Lev. 19:12; Num. 30:2; Deut. 23:21, 23
5:34
James 5:12; Is. 66:1; Matt. 23:22
5:35
Is. 66:1; Acts 7:49; Ps. 48:2
5:37
Matt. 6:13; 13:19, 38; John 17:15; 2 Thess. 3:3; 1 John 2:13f.; 3:12; 5:18f.
5:38
Matt. 5:21,27,33, 43; Ex. 21:24; Lev. 24:20; Deut. 19:21
5:39
Matt. 5:39-42: *Luke 6:29,30;*1 Cor. 6:7
5:42
Deut. 15:7-11; Luke 6:34f.; 1 Tim. 6:18
5:43
Matt. 5:21,27,33, 38; Lev. 19:18; Deut. 23:3-6
5:44
Luke 6:27f.; 23:34; Acts 7:60; Rom. 12:20
5:45
Matt. 5:9; Luke 6:35; Acts 14:17
5:46
Luke 6:32
5:48
Lev. 19:2; Deut. 18:13; 2 Cor. 7:1; Phil. 3:12-15

Concerning Alms and Prayer

6:1
Matt. 6:5,16; 23:5

6 "Beware~¹ of practicing~ your righteousness before men to be noticed˟ by them; otherwise you have *no reward* with your Father who is in heaven.

6:2
Matt. 6:5,16;
23:5;
Matt. 6:5,16; Luke
6:24

2 "When therefore you give~ alms, do not sound⁹ a trumpet before you, as the hypocrites do in the synagogues and in the streets, that they may be honored˟ by men. •Truly I say to you, they have their reward in full.

3 "But when *you* give alms, do not let your left hand know⁹ what your right hand is doing

6:4
Jer. 17:10; Matt.
6:6,18; Heb. 4:13

4 that *your* alms may be in secret; and your Father who sees in secret will repay you.

6:5
Mark 11:25; Luke
18:11,13;
Matt. 6:1,16;
Matt. 6:2,16; Luke
6:24

5 "And when you pray,~ you are not to be as the hypocrites; for they love³¹ᵇ to stand and pray~ in the synagogues and on the street corners, in order to be seen˟ by men. •Truly I say to you, they have their reward in full.

6:6
Is. 26:20; Matt.
26:36-39; Acts
9:40;
Matt. 6:4,18

6 "But *you,* when you pray,~ go˟¹ into your inner room, and when you have shut your door, pray˟¹ to your Father who is in secret, and your Father who sees in secret will repay you.

6:7
1 Kin. 18:26f.

7 "And when you are praying, do not use⁹ meaningless repetition, as the Gentiles do, for they suppose that they will be heard for their *many words.*

6:8
Ps. 38:9;
69:17-19; Matt.
6:32; Luke 12:30

8 "Therefore do not be like⁹ them; for your Father knows what you need, before you ask˟⁹ᵃ Him.

6:9
Matt. 6:9-13:
Luke 11:2-4

9 "Pray,~¹ then, in this way:

'Our Father who art in heaven,
Hallowed˟¹ be Thy name.

6:10
Matt. 3:2; 4:17;
Matt. 26:42; Luke
22:42; Acts 21:14
6:11
Prov. 30:8; Is.
33:16; Luke 11:3
6:12
Ex. 34:7; Ps.
32:1; 130:4; Matt.
9:2; 26:28; Eph.
1:7; 1 John 1:7-9
6:13
John 17:15;
1 Cor. 10:13;
2 Thess. 3:3;
2 Tim. 4:18; 2
Pet. 2:9; 1 John
5:18;
Matt. 5:37
6:14
Matt. 7:2; Mark
11:25f.; Eph.
4:32; Col. 3:13
6:15
Matt. 18:35

10   'Thy kingdom come.˟¹
Thy will be done,˟¹
On earth as it is in heaven.

11   'Give˟¹ us this day our *daily bread.*

12   'And forgive˟¹²¹ᵃ us our debts, as *we also* have
forgiven our debtors.

13   'And do not lead⁹ us into temptation, but deliver˟¹¹⁸ᵇ
us from evil.¹⁰ᵇ [For Thine is the kingdom, and the
power, and the glory, forever. Amen.]'

14 "For if you forgive˟²¹ᵃ men for their transgressions,⁴⁰ᵇ your heavenly Father will also forgive you.

15 "But if you do not forgive˟ men, then your Father will not forgive your transgressions.

Concerning Fasting
True Treasure
Mammon

16 "And whenever you fast,~ do not put⊙ on a gloomy face as the hypocrites *do*, for they neglect their appearance in order to be seenˣ fasting by men. •Truly I say to you, they have their reward in full.

17 "But *you*, when you fast, anointˣ' *your* head, and washˣ' *your face*

18 so that you may not be seenˣ fasting by men, but by your Father who is in secret; and your Father who sees in secret will repay you.

19 "Do not lay⊙ up for yourselves treasures upon earth, where moth and rust destroy, and where thieves break in and steal.

20 "But lay~' up for yourselves treasures in heaven, where neither moth nor rust destroys, and where thieves do not break in or steal;

21 for where your treasure is, there will your *heart* be *also*.

22 "The lamp of the body is the eye; if therefore your eye is clear, your whole body will be full of light.

23 "But if your eye is bad,¹⁰ᵇ your whole body will be full of darkness. If therefore the light that is in you is darkness, how *great* is the darkness!

24 "No one can serve~³⁸ᵇ *two* masters; for either he will hate the one and love the other, or he will hold to one and despise the other. You cannot serve~ *God* and ʲmammon.

The Cure for Anxiety

25 "For this reason I say to you, do not be anxious⊙ for your life, *as to* what you shall eat,ˣ or what you shall drink;ˣ nor for your body, *as to* what you shall putˣ on. Is not life more than food, and the body than clothing?

26 "Lookˣ' at the birds of the air, that they do not sow, neither do they reap, nor gather into barns, and *yet* your heavenly Father feeds them. Are *you* not worth much more than they?

27 "And which of you by being anxious can addˣ a *single* cubit to his life's span?

28 "And why are you anxious about clothing? Observeˣ' how the lilies of the field grow; they do not toil nor do they spin,

29 yet I say to you that even Solomon in all his glory did not clothe himself like one of these.

30 "But if God so arrays the *grass of the field*, which is *alive*

ʲOr, *riches*

6:16
Is. 58:5;
Matt. 6:2

6:17
Ruth 3:3; 2 Sam.
12:20

6:18
Matt. 6:4,6

6:19
Prov. 23:4; Matt.
19:21; Luke
12:21,33; 18:22;
1 Tim. 6:9,10;
Heb. 13:5; James
5:2
6:20
Matt. 19:21; Luke
12:33; 1 Tim.
6:19
6:21
Luke 12:34
6:22
Matt. 6:22,23;
Luke 11:34,35
6:23
Matt. 20:15; Mark
7:22

6:24
1 Kin. 18:21;
Luke 16:13; Gal.
1:10; James 4:4;
Luke 16:9,11,13

6:25
Matt. 6:25-33;
Luke 12:22-31;
Matt. 6:27,28,31,
34; Luke 10:41;
12:11,22; Phil.
4:6; 1 Pet. 5:7
6:26
Job 35:11; 38:41;
Ps. 104:27,28;
Matt. 10:29ff.;
Luke 12:24
6:27
Matt. 6:25,28,31,
34; Luke 10:41;
12:11,22; Phil.
4:6; 1 Pet. 5:7;
Ps. 39:5
6:28
Matt. 6:25,27,31,
34; Luke 10:41;
12:11,22; Phil.
4:6; 1 Pet. 5:7
6:29
1 Kin. 10:4-7;
2 Chr. 9:4-6,
20-22
6:30
James 1:10,11; 1
Pet. 1:24;
Matt. 8:26;
14:31; 16:8

today and tomorrow is thrown into the furnace, *will He* not much more *do so for* you, O men of little faith?

6:31
Matt. 6:25,27,28, 34; Luke 10:41; 12:11,22; Phil. 4:6; 1 Pet. 5:7
6:32
Matt. 6:8; Phil. 4:19
6:33
Matt. 19:28; Mark 10:29f.; Luke 18:29f.; 1 Tim. 4:8
6:34
Matt. 6:25,27,28, 31; Luke 10:41; 12:11,22; Phil. 4:6; 1 Pet. 5:7

31 "Do not be anxious° then, saying, 'What shall we eat?'ˣ or 'What shall we drink?'ˣ or 'With what shall we clotheˣ ourselves?'

32 "For all *these things* the Gentiles eagerly[1] seek; for your heavenly Father knows that you need all these things.

33 "But seek~ˡ first His kingdom and His righteousness; and all these things shall be added to you.

34 "Therefore do not be anxious° for tomorrow; for tomorrow will care for itself. *Each* day has enough trouble of its own.

Concerning Judging Others

7:1
Matt. 7:1-5: *Luke 6:37f.,41f.*; Rom. 14:10,13
7:2
Mark 4:24; Luke 6:38
7:3
Rom. 2:1

7:4
Luke 6:42

7 "Do not judge° lest you be judged.ˣ

2 "For in the way you judge, you will be judged; and by your standard of measure, it will be measured to you.

3 "And why do you look at the speck that is in your brother's eye, but do not notice the *log* that is in your *own* eye?

4 "Or how can you say to your brother, 'Letˣˡ me takeˣ the speck out of your eye,' and behold, the log is in your own eye?

5 "You hypocrite, first takeˣˡ the *log* out of your own eye, and then you will see clearly[1] to takeˣ the speck out of your brother's eye.

7:6
Matt. 15:26

6 "Do not give° what is holy[28a] to dogs, and do not throw° your pearls before swine, lest they trample them under their feet, and turn and tearˣ you to pieces.

Encouragement to Pray

7:7
Matt. 7:7-11: *Luke 11:9-13*; Matt. 18:19; 21:22; Mark 11:24; John 14:13; 15:7,16; 16:23f.; James 1:5f.; 1 John 3:22; 5:14f.

7 "Ask, ~ˡ⁹ᵃ and it shall be given to you; seek, ~ˡ and you shall find; knock, ~ˡ and it shall be opened to you.

8 "For everyone who asks receives,[5b] and he who seeks finds, and to him who knocks it shall be opened.

9 "Or what man is there among you, when his son shall ask him for a loaf, will give him a *stone*?

10 "Or if he shall ask for a *fish,* he will not give him a *snake*, will he?

7:11
Ps. 84:11; Is. 63:7; Rom. 8:32; James 1:17

11 "If *you* then, being †*evil,* [10b] know how to give~ good[25a] gifts to your children, how much more shall your Father who is in heaven give what is good[25a] to those who ask Him!

7:12
Luke 6:31; Matt. 22:40; Rom. 13:8ff.; Gal. 5:14

12 "Therefore, however you want people to treat~ you, so treat~ˡ them, for this is the Law and the Prophets.

Ways Contrasted
Fruits Contrasted

7:13
Luke 13:24

13 "Enterˣˡ by the narrow gate; for the gate is *wide,* and the

way is *broad* that leads to destruction, and many are those who enter by it.

14 "For the gate is *small,* and the way is *narrow* + that leads to life,[30b] and few are those who find it.

15 "Beware[m] of the false prophets, who come to you in sheep's clothing, but inwardly are ravenous wolves.

16 "You will know[29b] them by their *fruits.* Grapes are not gathered from thorn *bushes,* nor figs from thistles, are they?

17 "Even so, every good[25a] tree bears *good*[25b] fruit; but the bad[10c] tree bears *bad*[10b] fruit.

18 "A good[25a] tree *cannot* produce~ *bad*[10b] fruit, nor can a bad[10c] tree produce~ *good*[25b] fruit.

19 "Every tree that does not bear *good*[25b] fruit is cut down and thrown into the *fire.*

20 "So[2] then, you will know[29b] them by their *fruits.*

21 "Not everyone who says to Me, 'Lord, Lord,' will enter the kingdom of heaven; but he who does the will of My Father who is in heaven.

22 "Many will say to Me on that day, 'Lord, Lord, did we not prophesy in *Your* name, and in *Your* name cast out *demons,* and in *Your* name perform *many* miracles?'

23 "And then I will declare to them, 'I +*never* knew[29a] you; DEPART FROM ME, YOU WHO PRACTICE LAWLESSNESS.'

The Two Foundations

24 "Therefore everyone who hears these words of Mine, and acts upon them, may be compared to a wise[35b] man, who built *his* house upon the rock.

25 "And the rain descended, and the floods came, and the winds blew, and burst against that house; and *yet* it did not fall, for it had been founded upon the rock.

26 "And everyone who hears these words of Mine, and does not act upon them, will be like a foolish[20c] man, who built *his* house upon the sand.

27 "And the rain descended, and the floods came, and the winds blew, and burst against that house; and it fell, and *great* was its fall."

28 The result was that when Jesus had finished these words, the multitudes were amazed[m1] at His teaching;

29 for He was teaching~ them as *one* having +authority, and not as their scribes.

7:15
Matt. 24:11,24;
Mark 13:22; Luke
6:26; Acts 13:6; 2
Pet. 2:1; 1 John
4:1; Rev. 16:13;
19:20; 20:10;
Ezek. 22:27; John
10:12; Acts 20:29
7:16
Matt. 7:20; 12:33;
Luke 6:44; James
3:12
7:17
Matt. 12:33,35

7:19
Matt. 3:10; Luke
3:9; 13:7; John
15:2,6
7:20
Matt. 7:16; 12:33;
Luke 6:44; James
3:12
7:21
Luke 6:46

7:22
Matt. 25:11f.;
Luke 13:25ff.;
Matt. 10:15

7:23
Ps. 6:8; Matt.
25:41; Luke 13:27

7:24
Matt. 7:24-27;
Luke 6:47-49;
Matt. 16:18;
James 1:22-25

7:28
Matt. 11:1; 13:53;
19:1; 26:1;
Matt. 13:54;
22:33; Mark 1:22;
6:2; 11:18; Luke
4:32; John 7:46

Jesus Cleanses a Leper
The Centurion's Faith

8 And when He had come down from the mountain, great multitudes followed Him.

8:2
Matt. 8:2-4; *Mark
1:40-44; Luke
5:12-14;*
Matt. 9:18; 15:25;
18:26; 20:20;
John 9:38; Acts
10:25
8:3
Matt. 11:5; Luke
4:27

2   And behold, a leper came to Him, and bowed™ down to Him, saying, "Lord, if You are willing,~ You can make× me clean."

3   And He stretched out His hand and touched him, saying, "I am willing; be cleansed."×¹ And immediately his leprosy was cleansed.

8:4
Matt. 9:30; 12:16;
17:9; Mark 1:44;
3:12; 5:43; 7:36;
8:30; 9:9; Luke
4:41; 8:56; 9:21;
Mark 1:44; Luke
5:14; 17:14;
Lev. 13:49; 14:2ff.
8:5
Matt. 8:5-13;
Luke 7:1-10
8:6
Matt. 4:24

4   And Jesus *said to him, "See~¹ that you tell× no one; but go, show×¹ *yourself* to the priest, and present×¹ the offering that Moses commanded, for a testimony to them."

5   And when He had entered Capernaum, a centurion came to Him, entreating Him,

6   and saying, "Lord, my servant is lying⁺ paralyzed at home, suffering great pain."

7   And He *said to him, "*I* will come and heal¹⁵ᵃ him."

8   But the centurion answered and said, "Lord, I am not worthy for You to come× under *my* roof, but just say×¹ the word,⁴³ᵃ and my servant will be healed.¹⁵ᵇ

8:9
Mark 1:27; Luke
9:1

9   "For *I, too*, am a man under authority, with soldiers *under me*; and I say to this one, 'Go!'×¹ and he goes, and to another, 'Come!' and he comes, and to my slave, 'Do×¹ this!' and he does *it*."

10   Now when Jesus heard *this*, He marveled, and said to those who were following, "●Truly I say to you, I have not found such great faith with anyone in *Israel*.

8:11
Is. 49:12; 59:19;
Mal. 1:11; Luke
13:29

11   "And I say to you, that many shall come from east and west, and ᵘrecline *at the table* with Abraham, and Isaac, and Jacob, in the kingdom of heaven;

8:12
Matt. 13:38;
Matt. 22:13;
25:30;
Matt. 13:42,50;
22:13; 24:51;
25:30; Luke 13:28
8:13
Matt. 9:22,29

12   but the sons of the kingdom shall be cast out into the outer darkness; in that place there shall be weeping and gnashing of teeth."

13   And Jesus said to the centurion, "Go your way; let it be done×¹ to you as you have *believed*." And the servant was healed¹⁵ᵇ *that very* hour.

Peter's Mother-in-law Healed
Many Healed

8:14
Matt. 8:14-16;
*Mark 1:29-34;
Luke 4:38-41*

14   And when Jesus had come to Peter's home, He saw his mother-in-law lying⁺ sick in bed with a fever.

ᵘOr, *dine*

15   And He touched her hand, and the fever left her; and she arose, and waited^m on Him.

16   And when evening had come, they brought to Him many who were demon-possessed; and He cast out the spirits with a word,^{43a} and healed^{15a} *all who were ill*

8:16
Matt. 4:24;
Matt. 4:23; 8:33

17   in order that what was spoken through Isaiah the prophet might be *fulfilled,*^x saying, *"HE HIMSELF* TOOK OUR *INFIRMITIES,* AND CARRIED AWAY OUR *DISEASES."*

8:17
Is. 53:4

Discipleship Tested

18   Now when Jesus saw a crowd around Him, He gave^x orders to depart to the other side.

8:18
Mark 4:35; Luke 8:22

19   And a certain scribe came and said to Him, "Teacher, I will follow You wherever You go."

8:19
Matt. 8:19-22;
Luke 9:57-60

20   And Jesus *said to him, "The foxes have holes, and the birds of the air *have* ┼nests; but the Son of Man has nowhere to lay~ His head."

8:20
Dan. 7:13; Matt. 9:6; 12:8,32,40;
13:41; 16:13,27f.;
17:9; 19:28;
26:64; Mark 8:38;
Luke 12:8; 18:8;
21:36; John 1:51;
3:13f.; 6:27;
12:34; Acts 7:56

21   And another of the disciples said to Him, "Lord, permit^{x16c} me first to go^x and bury^x my father."

22   But Jesus *said to him, "Follow~ Me; and allow^{x16a} the dead to bury^x their own dead."

8:22
Matt. 9:9; Mark 2:14; Luke 9:59,
60; John 1:43;
21:19

23   And when He got into the boat, His disciples followed Him.

8:23
Matt. 8:23-27;
Mark 4:36-41;
Luke 8:22-25

24   And behold, there arose a great storm in the sea, so that the boat was covered~ with the waves; but He Himself was asleep.

25   And they came to *Him,* and awoke Him, saying, "Save^{x1} *us,* Lord; we are perishing!"

8:25
Matt. 8:2; 9:18

26   And He *said to them, "Why are you timid, you men of little faith?" Then He arose, and rebuked the winds and the sea; and it became perfectly calm.

8:26
Matt. 6:30; 14:31;
16:8; 17:20

27   And the men marveled, saying, "What kind of a man is this, that even the winds and the sea obey *Him?"*

Jesus Casts Out Demons

28   And when He had come to the other side into the country of the Gadarenes, two men who were demon-possessed met Him as they were coming out of the tombs; *they were* so exceedingly violent that no one could~ pass^x by that road.

8:28
Matt. 8:28-34;
Mark 5:1-17;
Luke 8:26-37;
Matt. 4:24

29   And behold, they cried out, saying, "What do we have to do with You, Son of God? Have You come here to torment^x us before the time?"

8:29
Judg. 11:12;
2 Sam. 16:10;
19:22; 1 Kin.
17:18; 2 Kin.
3:13; 2 Chr.
35:21; Mark 1:24;
5:7; Luke 4:34;
8:28; John 2:4

30   Now there was at a distance from them a herd of many swine feeding. ~

31   And the demons *began* to entreat^m Him, saying, "If You are *going to* cast us out, send^xl us into the herd of swine."

32   And He said to them, "Begone!" And they came out, and went into the swine, and behold, the whole herd rushed down the steep bank into the sea and perished in the waters.

33   And the herdsmen ran away, and went to the city, and reported everything, including the *incident* of the demoniacs.

34   And behold, the whole city came out to meet Jesus; and when they saw Him, they entreated *Him* to depart^x from their region.

A Paralytic Cured

9   And getting into a boat, He crossed over, and came to His own city.

2   And behold, they were bringing to Him a paralytic, lying* on a bed; and Jesus seeing their faith said to the paralytic, "Take courage, My son, your *sins* are forgiven."

3   And behold, some of the scribes said to themselves, "This *fellow* blasphemes."

4   And Jesus knowing their thoughts said, "Why are you thinking evil^10b in your hearts?

5   "For which is easier, to say,^x 'Your *sins* are forgiven,' or to say,^x 'Rise, and walk'?

6   "But in order that you may know^29e that the Son of Man has *authority* on earth to forgive^~21a sins"—then He *said to the paralytic—"Rise, take^xl up your bed, and go home."

7   And he rose, and went home.

8   But when the multitudes saw *this*, they were filled with awe, and glorified God, who had given *such* authority to men.

Matthew Called

9   And as Jesus passed on from there, He saw a man, called Matthew, sitting in the tax office; and He *said to him, "Follow^~! Me!" And he rose, and followed Him.

10   And it happened that as He was reclining *at the table* in the house, behold many tax-gatherers and sinners came and were dining with Jesus and His disciples.

11   And when the Pharisees saw *this*, they said^m to His disciples, "Why is your Teacher eating with the *tax-gatherers* and *sinners*?"

12   But when He heard this, He said, "*It is* not those who are healthy who need a physician, but those who are sick.

13   "But go and learn^xl what *this* means, 'I DESIRE COMPASSION,

---

8:33
Matt. 4:24

8:34
Amos 7:12; Acts 16:39

9:1
Matt. 4:13; Mark 5:21

9:2
Matt. 9:2-8; *Mark 2:3-12; Luke 5:18-26*; Matt. 4:24; 9:6; Matt. 9:22; 14:27; Mark 6:50; 10:49; John 16:33; Acts 23:11; Mark 2:5,9; Luke 5:20,23; 7:48
9:3
Mark 3:28,29
9:4
Matt. 12:25; Luke 6:8; 9:47
9:5
Matt. 9:2,6; Mark 2:5,9; Luke 5:20, 23; 7:48
9:6
Matt. 8:20; John 5:27; Matt. 4:24; 9:2

9:8
Matt. 5:16; 15:31; Mark 2:12; Luke 2:20; 5:25,26; 7:16; 13:13; 17:15; 23:47; John 15:8; Acts 4:21; 11:18; 21:20; 2 Cor. 9:13; Gal. 1:24
9:9
Matt. 9:9-17; *Mark 2:14-22; Luke 5:27-38*; Matt. 10:3; Mark 2:14; 3:18; Luke 6:15; Acts 1:13; Matt. 8:22

9:11
Matt. 11:19; Mark 2:16; Luke 5:30; 15:2
9:12
Mark 2:17; Luke 5:31
9:13
Matt. 12:7; Hos. 6:6; Mark 2:17; Luke 5:32; 1 Tim. 1:15

ᵛAND NOT SACRIFICE,' for I did not come to callˣ the righteous, but sinners."

14 Then the disciples of John *came to Him, saying, "Why do we and the Pharisees fast, but Your disciples do not fast?"

15 And Jesus said to them, "The attendants of the bridegroom cannot mourn˜ as long as the bridegroom is *with them,* can they? But the days will come when the bridegroom is takenˣ away from them, and then they will fast.

16 "But no one puts a patch of unshrunk cloth on an ᵗold garment; for the patch pulls away from the garment, and a worse tear results.

17 "Nor do *men* put ᵗnew wine into ᵗold wineskins; otherwise the wineskins burst, and the wine pours out, and the wineskins are ruined; but they put ᵗnew wine into ᵗfresh wineskins, and both are preserved."

Miracles of Healing

18 While He was saying these things to them, behold, there came a *synagogue* official, and bowedᵐ down before Him, saying, "My daughter has just died; but come and layˣ Your hand on her, and she will live."

19 And Jesus rose and *began* to follow him, and *so did* His disciples.

20 And behold, a woman who had been suffering from a hemorrhage for *twelve* years, came up behind Him and touched the fringe of His cloak;

21 for she was sayingᵐ to herself, "If I only touchˣ His garment, I shall get well."

22 But Jesus turning and seeing her said, "Daughter, take courage; your faith has made* you well." And at *once* the woman was made well.

23 And when Jesus came into the official's house, and saw the flute-players, and the crowd in noisy disorder,

24 He *began* to say, "Depart; for the girl has *not died,* but is asleep." And they *began* laughing¹ at Him.

25 But when the crowd had been put out, He entered and took her by the hand; and the girl arose.

26 And this news went out into all that land.

27 And as Jesus passed on from there, two blind men followed Him, crying out, and saying, "Have mercyˣ on us, Son of David!"

28 And after He had come into the house, the blind men came

ᵛI.e., more than

9:14
Luke 18:12

9:18
Matt. 9:18-26;
Mark 5:22-43;
Luke 8:41-56;
Matt. 8:2

9:20
Num. 15:38;
Deut. 22:12; Matt.
14:36; 23:5

9:21
Matt. 14:36; Mark
3:10; Luke 6:19

9:22
Matt. 9:2;
Matt. 9:29; 15:28;
Mark 5:34; 10:52;
Luke 7:50; 8:48;
17:19; 18:42
9:23
2 Chr. 35:25; Jer.
9:17; 16:6; Ezek.
24:17
9:24
John 11:13; Acts
20:10

9:25
Acts 9:40;
Mark 9:27
9:26
Matt. 4:24; 9:31;
14:1; Mark 1:28,
45; Luke 4:14,37;
5:15; 7:17
9:27
Matt. 1:1; 12:23;
15:22; 20:30,31;
21:9,15; 22:42;
Mark 10:47,48;
12:35; Luke
18:38,39; 20:41f.

up to Him, and Jesus *said to them, "Do you believe that I am able to do[x] this?" They *said to Him, "Yes, Lord."

9:29
Matt. 8:13; 9:22

29   Then He touched their eyes, saying, "Be it done[xi] to you *according to your faith.*"

9:30
Matt. 8:4

30   And their eyes were opened. And Jesus sternly warned them, saying, "See *here,* let no one know[ml] *about this!*"

9:31
Matt. 4:24; 9:26;
14:1; Mark 1:28,
45; Luke 4:14,37;
5:15; 7:17
9:32
Matt. 12:22,24;
Matt. 4:24

31   But they went out, and spread the news about Him in all that land.

32   And as they were going out, behold, a dumb man, demon-possessed, was brought to Him.

9:33
Mark 2:12

33   And after the demon was cast out, the dumb man spoke; and the multitudes marveled, saying, "Nothing like *this* was ever seen in Israel."

9:34
Matt. 12:24; Mark
3:22; Luke 11:15;
John 7:20f.

34   But the Pharisees were saying,[xx] "He casts out the demons *by the ruler of the demons.*"

9:35
Matt. 4:23; Mark
1:14

35   And Jesus was going[m] about all the cities and the villages, teaching in their synagogues, and proclaiming the gospel of the kingdom, and healing every kind of disease and every kind of sickness.

9:36
Matt. 14:14;
15:32; Mark 6:34;
8:2;
Num. 27:17;
Ezek. 34:5; Zech.
10:2; Mark 6:34
9:37
Luke 10:2

36   And seeing the multitudes, He felt compassion for them, because they were distressed[+] and downcast[+] like sheep without a shepherd.

37   Then He *said to His disciples, "The harvest is plentiful, but the workers are few.

38   "Therefore beseech[xi] the Lord of the harvest to send[x] out workers into His harvest."

10:1
Mark 3:13-15;
6:7;
Matt. 9:35; Luke
9:1
10:2
Matt. 10:2-4;
Mark 3:16-19;
Luke 6:14-16;
Acts 1:13;
Matt. 4:18;
Matt. 4:21
10:3
John 1:43ff.;
John 11:16; 14:5;
20:24ff.; 21:2;
Matt. 9:9;
Mark 15:40;
Mark 3:18; Luke
6:16; Acts 1:13
10:4
Matt. 26:14; Luke
22:3; John 6:71;
13:2,26
10:5
Mark 6:7; Luke
9:2;
2 Kin. 17:24ff.;
Luke 9:52; 10:33;
17:16; John 4:9,
39f.; 8:48; Acts
8:25
10:6
Matt. 15:24

The Twelve Disciples
Instructions for Service

10   And having summoned His twelve disciples, He gave them authority over unclean spirits, to cast[~] them out, and to heal[~] every kind of disease and every kind of sickness.

2   Now the names of the twelve apostles are these: The first, Simon, who is called Peter, and Andrew his brother; and James the *son* of Zebedee, and John his brother;

3   Philip and Bartholomew; Thomas and Matthew the taxgatherer; James the *son* of Alphaeus, and Thaddaeus;

4   Simon the Zealot, and Judas Iscariot, the one who betrayed Him.

5   *These twelve* Jesus sent out after instructing them, saying, "Do not go[o] in *the* way of *the Gentiles,* and do not enter[o] *any* city of the *Samaritans;*

6   but rather go[ml] to the *lost* [+] sheep of the house of Israel.

7 "And as you go, preach,~ saying, 'The kingdom of heaven is *at hand.'*

8 "Heal~ *the sick,* raise~ *the dead,* cleanse~ *the lepers,* cast~ out *demons;* freely you received,[5b] freely give.[xi]

9 "Do not acquire[⊙] gold, or silver, or copper for your money belts,

10 or a bag for *your* journey, or even two tunics, or sandals, or a staff; for the worker is *worthy* of his support.

11 "And into whatever city or village you enter,[x] inquire[xi] who is worthy in it; and abide[xi] there until you go[x] away.

12 "And as you enter the house, give[xi] it your greeting.

13 "And if the house is worthy, let your *greeting of* peace come[xi] upon it; but if it is not worthy, let your *greeting of* peace *return*[xi] to you.

14 "And whoever does not receive[x] you, nor heed[x] your words, as you go out of that house or that city, shake[xi] off the dust of your feet.

15 "•Truly I say to you, it will be *more* †*tolerable* for *the* land of Sodom and Gomorrah in the day of judgment, than for that city.

A Hard Road before Them

16 "Behold, *I* send you out as sheep in the midst of wolves; therefore be~ shrewd[35b] as serpents, and innocent as doves.

17 "But beware~ of men; for they will deliver you up to *the* courts, and scourge you in their synagogues;

18 and you shall even be brought before governors and kings for My sake, as a testimony to them and to the Gentiles.

19 "But when they deliver[x] you up, do not become anxious[⊙] about how or what you will speak;[x] for it shall be given you in that hour what you are to speak.[x]

20 "For it is not *you* who speak, but *it is* the Spirit of your Father who speaks in you.

21 "And brother will deliver up brother to death, and a father *his* child; and children will rise up against parents, and cause them to be put to death.

22 "And you will be hated~ by all on account of My name, but it is the one who has endured to the end who will be saved.

23 "But whenever they persecute~ you in this city, flee to the next; for •truly I say to you, you shall •*not* finish[x] *going through* the cities of Israel, until the Son of Man comes.

The Meaning of Discipleship

24 "A disciple is not above his teacher, nor a slave above his master.

10:7
Matt. 3:2

10:9
Matt. 10:9-15;
Mark 6:8-11;
Luke 9:3-5;
10:4-12; Luke
22:35
10:10
1 Cor. 9:14;
1 Tim. 5:18

10:12
1 Sam. 25:6; Ps.
122:7,8

10:14
Acts 13:51

10:15
Matt. 11:22,24;
2 Pet. 2:6; Jude
7; Matt. 7:22;
11:22,24; 12:36;
Acts 17:31;
1 Thess. 5:4; Heb.
10:25; 2 Pet. 2:9;
3:7; 1 John 4:17;
Jude 6
10:16
Luke 10:3;
Gen. 3:1; Matt.
24:25; Rom.
16:19;
Hos. 7:11
10:17
Matt. 5:22;
Matt. 23:34; Mark
13:9; Luke 12:11;
Acts 5:40; 22:19;
26:11
10:19
Matt. 10:19-22:
Mark 13:11-13;
Luke 21:12-17;
Matt. 6:25; Luke
12:11,12
10:20
Luke 12:12; Acts
4:8; 13:9; 2 Cor.
13:3
10:21
Matt. 10:35,36;
Mark 13:12;
Mic. 7:6
10:22
Matt. 24:9; Luke
21:17; John
15:18ff.;
Matt. 24:13; Mark
13:13
10:23
Matt. 23:34;
Matt. 16:27f.

10:24
Luke 6:40; John
13:16; 15:20

10:25
Matt. 9:34;
2 Kin. 1:2; Matt.
12:24,27; Mark
3:22; Luke 11:15,
18,19

25 "It is enough for the disciple that he become^x as his teacher, and the slave as his master. If they have called the *head* of the house Beelzebul, how much more the members of his household!

10:26
Matt. 10:26-33;
Luke 12:2-9;
Mark 4:22; Luke
8:17; 12:2; 1 Cor.
4:5

26 "Therefore do not fear[⊙] them, for there is nothing covered⁺ that will not be revealed, and hidden that will not be known.

10:27
Luke 12:3;
Matt. 24:17; Acts
5:20

27 "What I tell you in the darkness, speak^{xl} in the light; and what you hear *whispered* in *your* ear, proclaim^{xl} upon the housetops.

10:28
Heb. 10:31;
Matt. 5:22; Luke
12:5

28 "And do not fear[⊙] those who kill the body, but are unable to kill^x the *soul;* but rather fear^{~l} Him who is able to destroy^x *both soul and body* in hell.^{27b}

10:29
Luke 12:6

29 "Are not *two* sparrows sold for *a* ^w*cent?* And *yet* not one of them will fall to the ground apart from your Father.

10:30
1 Sam. 14:45;
2 Sam. 14:11;
1 Kin. 1:52; Luke
21:18; Acts 27:34

30 "But the very hairs of *your* head are *all* numbered.⁺

10:31
Matt. 12:12

31 "Therefore do not fear;[⊙] *you* are of more value than *many sparrows.*

10:32
Luke 12:8; Rev.
3:5

32 "Everyone therefore who shall confess Me before men, *I* will *also* confess him before My Father who is in heaven.

10:33
Mark 8:38; Luke
9:26; 2 Tim. 2:12

33 "But whoever shall deny^x Me before men, *I* will *also* deny him before My Father who is in heaven.

10:34
Matt. 10:34,35;
Luke 12:51-53

34 "Do not think[⊙] that I came to bring^x peace on the earth; I did not come to bring^x peace, but a sword.

10:35
Mic. 7:6; Matt.
10:21; Luke 12:53

35 "For I came to SET^x A MAN AGAINST HIS FATHER, AND A DAUGHTER AGAINST HER MOTHER, AND A DAUGHTER-IN-LAW AGAINST HER MOTHER-IN-LAW;

10:36
Mic. 7:6; Matt.
10:21

36 and A MAN'S ENEMIES WILL BE THE MEMBERS OF HIS HOUSE-HOLD.

10:37
Deut. 33:9; Luke
14:26

37 "He who loves^{31b} father or mother more than Me is not worthy of Me; and he who loves^{31b} son or daughter more than Me is not worthy of Me.

10:38
Matt. 16:24; Mark
8:34; Luke 9:23;
14:27

38 "And he who does not take^{5b} his cross and follow after Me is not worthy of Me.

10:39
Matt. 16:25; Mark
8:35; Luke 9:24;
17:33; John 12:25

39 "He who has found his life shall lose it, and he who has lost his life for My sake shall find it.

10:40
Matt. 18:5; Luke
10:16; John
13:20; Gal. 4:14;
Mark 9:37; Luke
9:48; John 12:44

40 "He who receives you receives^{5a} *Me,* and he who receives *Me* receives Him who sent Me.

10:41
Matt. 25:44,45

41 "He who receives a prophet in *the* name of a prophet shall receive a *prophet's reward;* and he who receives a righteous man in the name of a righteous man shall receive a *righteous man's reward.*

10:42
Matt. 25:40; Mark
9:41

42 "And whoever in the name of a disciple gives^x to one of

^wGr., *assarion,* the smallest copper coin

these little ones even a cup of cold water to drink, •truly I say to you he shall •*not* lose[x] his reward."

John's Questions

11 And it came about that when Jesus had finished giving instructions to His twelve disciples, He departed from there to teach[~] and preach[~] in their cities.

2 Now when John in prison heard of the works of Christ, he sent *word* by his disciples,

3 and said to Him, "Are *You* the Expected One, or shall we look for someone *else?*"

4 And Jesus answered and said to them, "Go and report[xl] to John what you hear and see:

5 *the* BLIND RECEIVE SIGHT and *the* lame walk, *the* lepers are cleansed and *the* deaf hear, and *the* dead are raised up, and *the* POOR HAVE THE GOSPEL PREACHED TO THEM.

6 "And *blessed* is he who keeps from stumbling[x] over Me."

Jesus' Tribute to John

7 And as these were going *away,* Jesus began to speak[~] to the multitudes about John, "What did you go out into the wilderness to look[x] at? A reed shaken by the wind?

8 "But what did you go out to see?[x] A man dressed[•] in soft *clothing?* Behold, those who wear soft *clothing* are in kings' palaces.

9 "But why did you go out? To see[x] a *prophet?* Yes, I say to you, and one who is more than a prophet.

10 "This is the one about whom it is written,[•]

'BEHOLD, †I SEND MY MESSENGER BEFORE YOUR FACE,
WHO WILL PREPARE YOUR WAY BEFORE YOU.'

11 "•Truly, I say to you, among those born of women there has not arisen[•] *anyone* greater than John the Baptist; yet he who is least in the kingdom of heaven is greater than †he.

12 "And from the days of John the Baptist until now the kingdom of heaven suffers violence, and violent men take it by force.

13 "For all the prophets and the Law prophesied until John.

14 "And if you care to accept[x] *it, he himself* is Elijah, who was to come.

15 "He who has ears to hear, let him hear. [M]

16 "But to what shall I compare[x] this generation? It is like children sitting in the market places, who call out to the other *children,*

17 and say, 'We played the flute for you, and you did not dance; we sang a dirge, and you did not mourn.'

11:1
Matt. 7:28;
Matt. 9:35; Luke 23:5

11:2
Matt. 11:2-19;
Luke 7:18-35;
Matt. 4:12;
Matt. 14:3; Mark 6:17; Luke 9:7ff.
11:3
Ps. 118:26; Matt. 11:10; John 6:14; 11:27; Heb. 10:37

11:5
Is. 35:5f.; Matt. 8:3; 12:13;
Is. 61:1; Luke 4:18

11:6
Matt. 5:29; 13:57; 24:10; 26:31;
Mark 6:3; John 6:61; 16:1

11:7
Matt. 3:1

11:9
Matt. 14:5; 21:26;
Luke 1:76; 20:6

11:10
Mal. 3:1; Mark 1:2

11:12
Luke 16:16

11:14
Mal. 4:5; Matt. 17:10-13; Mark 9:11-13; Luke 1:17; John 1:21
11:15
Matt. 13:9,43;
Mark 4:9,23; Luke 8:8; 14:35; Rev. 2:7,11,17,29; 3:6, 13,22; 13:9

11:18
Matt. 3:4;
Luke 1:15;
Matt. 9:34; John
7:20; 8:48f.,52;
10:20
11:19
Matt. 9:11; Luke
5:29-32; 15:2

18 "For John came neither eating nor drinking, and they say, 'He has a *demon!*'

19 "The Son of Man came eating and drinking, and they say, 'Behold, a gluttonous man and a drunkard, a friend of *tax-gatherers* and sinners!' Yet wisdom is vindicated by her deeds."

The Unrepenting Cities

11:20
Luke 10:13-15

20 Then He began to reproach~ the cities in which most³ of His miracles were done, because they did not repent.

11:21
Matt. 11:21-23;
Luke 10:13-15;
Mark 6:45; 8:22;
Luke 9:10; John
1:44; 12:21;
Matt. 11:22;
15:21; Mark 3:8;
7:24,31; Luke
4:26; 6:17; Acts
12:20; 27:3;
Rev. 11:3
11:22
Matt. 10:15;
11:24; 12:36;
Rev. 20:11,12
11:23
Matt. 4:13;
Is. 14:13,15;
Ezek. 26:20;
31:14; 32:18,24;
Matt. 16:18; Luke
10:15; 16:23;
Acts 2:27,31;
Rev. 1:18; 6:8;
20:13f.;
Matt. 10:15
11:24
Matt. 10:15;
11:22

21 "Woe to you, Chorazin! Woe to you, Bethsaida! For if the miracles had occurred in *Tyre* and *Sidon* which occurred in you, they would have repented *long ago* in sackcloth and ashes.

22 "Nevertheless I say to you, it shall be more tolerable for *Tyre* and *Sidon* in *the* day of judgment, than for you.

23 "And you, Capernaum, will not be exalted to *heaven,* will you? You shall descend to *Hades;* for if the miracles had occurred in *Sodom* which occurred in you, it would have remained to this day.

24 "Nevertheless I say to you that it shall be more tolerable for the land of *Sodom* in *the* day of judgment, than for you."

Come to Me

11:25
Matt. 11:25-27;
Luke 10:21,22;
Luke 22:42;
23:34; John
11:41; 12:27,28;
Ps. 8:2; 1 Cor.
1:26ff.
11:26
Luke 22:42;
23:34; John
11:41; 12:27,28
11:27
Matt. 28:18; John
3:35; 13:3; 17:2;
John 7:29; 10:15;
17:25
11:28
Jer. 31:25; John
7:37
11:29
John 13:15; Eph.
4:20; Phil. 2:5;
1 Pet. 2:21;
1 John 2:6;
Jer. 6:16
11:30
1 John 5:3

25 At that time Jesus answered and said, "I praise Thee, O Father, Lord of heaven and earth, that Thou didst hide these things from *the* wise and intelligent and didst reveal them to babes.

26 "Yes, Father, for thus it was well-pleasing in Thy sight.

27 "All things have been handed over to Me by My Father; and no one knows²⁹ᵇ the Son, except the Father; nor does anyone know²⁹ᵇ the Father, except the Son, and anyone to whom the *Son* wills~ to reveal× *Him.*

28 "Come to Me, all who are weary and heavy-laden,· and *I* will give you rest.

29 "Take×ⁱ My yoke upon you, and learn×ⁱ from Me, for I am gentle and humble in heart; and YOU SHALL FIND REST FOR YOUR SOULS.

30 "For My yoke is easy, and My load¹²ᵇ is light."

Sabbath Questions

12:1
Matt. 12:1-8;
Mark 2:23-28;
Luke 6:1-5;
Deut. 23:25
12:2
Matt. 12:10; Luke
13:14; 14:3; John
5:10; 7:23; 9:16

12 At that time Jesus went on the Sabbath through the grainfields, and His disciples became hungry and began to pick~ the heads *of grain* and eat. ~

2 But when the Pharisees saw it, they said to Him, "Behold, Your disciples do what is not lawful to do~ on a Sabbath."

3   But He said to them, "Have you not read what *David* did, when he became hungry, he and his companions;

4   how he entered the house of God, and they ate the *conse-crated bread,* which was not lawful for him to eat,[x] nor for those with him, but for the priests alone?

12:4
1 Sam. 21:6

5   "Or have you not read in the Law, that on the *Sabbath* the priests in the temple break the Sabbath, and are *innocent?*

6   "But I say to you, that something *greater* than the temple is here.

12:6
2 Chr. 6:18; Is. 66:1,2; Matt. 12:41,42
12:7
Hos. 6:6; Matt. 9:13

7   "But if you had known what this means, 'I DESIRE COMPAS-SION, AND NOT A SACRIFICE,' you would not have condemned[14b] the innocent.

Lord of the Sabbath

8   "For the Son of Man is *Lord* of the Sabbath."

12:8
Matt. 8:20; 12:32, 40
12:9
Matt. 12:9-14; Mark 3:1-6; Luke 6:6-11
12:10
Matt. 12:2; Luke 13:14; 14:3; John 5:10; 7:23; 9:16
12:11
Luke 14:5

9   And departing from there, He went into their synagogue.

10   And behold, *there was* a man with a withered hand. And they questioned Him, saying, "Is it lawful to heal[x] on the *Sab-bath?"*—in order that they might accuse[x] Him.

11   And He said to them, "What man shall there be among you, who shall have one sheep, and if it falls[x] into a pit on the *Sabbath,* will he not take hold of it, and lift it out?

12   "Of how much more value then is a man than a sheep! So then, it is lawful to do[~] good on the Sabbath."

12:12
Matt. 10:31; Luke 14:1-6

13   Then He *said to the man, "Stretch[xi] out your hand!" And he stretched it out, and it was restored to normal, like the other.

12:13
Matt. 8:3; Acts 28:8

14   But the Pharisees went out, and counseled together against Him, *as to* how they might destroy[x] Him.

12:14
Matt. 26:4; Mark 14:1; Luke 22:2; John 7:30,44; 8:59; 10:31,39; 11:53
12:15
Matt. 4:23

15   But Jesus, aware of *this,* withdrew from there. And *many* followed Him, and He healed them all,

16   and warned them not to make[x] Him known,

12:16
Matt. 8:4; 9:30; 17:9

17   in order that what was spoken through Isaiah the prophet, might be fulfilled,[x] saying,

18   "BEHOLD, MY SERVANT WHOM I HAVE CHOSEN;
    MY BELOVED IN WHOM MY SOUL IS WELL-PLEASED;
    I WILL PUT MY SPIRIT UPON HIM,
    AND HE SHALL PROCLAIM JUSTICE TO THE GENTILES.

12:18
Is. 42:1;
Matt. 3:17; 17:5; Luke 4:18; John 3:34

19   "HE WILL NOT QUARREL, NOR CRY OUT;
    NOR WILL ANYONE HEAR HIS VOICE IN THE STREETS.

12:19
Is. 42:2

20   "A BATTERED[*] REED HE WILL NOT BREAK OFF,
    AND A SMOLDERING WICK HE WILL NOT PUT[x] OUT,
    UNTIL HE LEADS JUSTICE TO *VICTORY.*

12:20
Is. 42:3

21   "AND IN HIS NAME THE GENTILES WILL HOPE."

12:21
Rom. 15:12

The Pharisees Rebuked

22 Then there was brought to Him a demon-possessed man *who was* blind and dumb, and He healed him, so that the dumb man spoke~ and saw.~

23 And all the multitudes were amazed,ᵐ and *began* to say, "This *man* cannot be the Son of David, can he?"

24 But when the Pharisees heard it, they said, "This man casts out demons only by Beelzebul the ruler of the demons."

25 And knowing their thoughts He said to them, "Any kingdom divided against itself is laid waste; and any city or house divided against itself shall not stand.

26 "And if Satan casts out *Satan,* he is divided *against himself;* how then shall his kingdom stand?

27 "And if I by *Beelzebul* cast out demons, by whom do your sons cast them out? Consequently *they* shall be your *judges.*

28 "But if I cast out demons by the *Spirit of God,* then the kingdom of God has come upon you.

29 "Or how can anyone enterˣ the strong man's house and carryˣ off his property, unless he first bindsˣ the strong *man?* And †then he will plunder his house.

The Unpardonable Sin

30 "He who is not with Me is *against Me;* and he who does not gather with Me scatters.

31 "Therefore I say to you, any sin and blasphemy shall be forgiven men, but blasphemy against the †*Spirit* shall not be forgiven.

32 "And whoever shall speakˣ a word against the Son of Man, it shall be forgiven him; but whoever shall speakˣ against the Holy Spirit, it shall not be forgiven him, either in this age, or in the *age* to come.

Words Reveal Character

33 "Either makeˣˡ the tree good,²⁵ᵇ and its fruit good; or makeˣˡ the tree bad,¹⁰ᶜ and its fruit bad; for the tree is known²⁹ᵃ by its *fruit.*

34 "You brood of vipers, how can you, being evil,¹⁰ᵇ speak~ what is *good?*²⁵ᵃ For the mouth speaks out of that which fills the heart.

35 "The good man out of *his* good treasure brings forth what is good; and the evil man out of *his* evil treasure brings forth what is evil.

36 "And I say to you, that every careless word⁴³ᵇ that men shall

12:22
Matt. 12:22,24;
Luke 11:14,15;
Matt. 9:32,34;
Matt. 4:24; 2
Thess. 2:9
12:23
Matt. 9:27

12:24
Matt. 9:34

12:25
Matt. 12:25-29;
Mark 3:23-27;
Luke 11:17-22;
Matt. 9:4

12:26
Matt. 4:10; 13:19

12:27
Matt. 9:34;
Acts 19:13

12:28
1 John 3:8

12:30
Mark 9:40; Luke
9:50; 11:23

12:31
Matt. 12:31,32;
Mark 3:28-30;
Luke 12:10

12:32
Luke 12:10;
Matt. 13:22,39;
Mark 10:30; Luke
16:8; 18:30;
20:34,35; Eph.
1:21; 1 Tim. 6:17;
2 Tim. 4:10; Titus
2:12; Heb. 6:5

12:33
Matt. 7:16-18;
Luke 6:43,44;
John 15:4-7

12:34
Matt. 3:7; 23:33;
Luke 3:7;
1 Sam. 24:13; Is.
32:6; Matt. 12:34,
35; 15:18; Luke
6:45; Eph. 4:29;
James 3:2-12
12:35
Prov. 10:20,21;
25:11,12; Matt.
13:52; Col. 4:6
12:36
Matt. 10:15

speak, they shall render *account* for it in the day of judgment.

37 "For by your *words*[43a] you shall be justified, and by your *words* you shall be condemned."[14b]

The Desire for Signs

38 Then some of the scribes and Pharisees answered Him, saying, "Teacher, we want to see[x] a *sign* from You."

39 But He answered and said to them, "An evil and adulterous generation craves[1] for a *sign;* and *yet* no sign shall be given to it but the sign of Jonah the prophet;

40 for just as JONAH WAS THREE DAYS AND THREE NIGHTS IN THE BELLY OF THE SEA MONSTER, so shall the Son of Man be three days and three nights in the heart of the earth.

41 "The men of Nineveh shall stand up with this generation at the judgment, and shall condemn[14c] it because they repented at the preaching of Jonah; and behold, something greater[26b] than Jonah is here.

42 "*The* Queen of *the* South shall rise up with this generation at the judgment and shall condemn it, because she came from the ends of the earth to hear[x] the wisdom of Solomon; and behold, something greater[26b] than Solomon is here.

43 "Now when the unclean spirit goes[x] out of a man, it passes through waterless places, seeking rest, and does not find *it*.

44 "Then it says, 'I will *return* to my house from which I came'; and when it comes, it finds it unoccupied, swept,* and put* in order.

45 "Then it goes, and takes along with it *seven* other spirits more wicked than itself, and they go in and live there; and the *last state* of *that* man becomes worse than the first. That is the way it will also be with this *evil* generation."

Changed Relationships

46 While He was still speaking to the multitudes, behold, His mother and brothers were standing outside, seeking to speak[x] to Him.

47 And someone said to Him, "Behold, Your mother and Your brothers are standing outside seeking to speak[x] to You."

48 But He answered the one who was telling Him and said, "Who is My mother and who are My brothers?"

49 And stretching out His hand toward His disciples, He said, "Behold, My mother and My brothers!

50 "For whoever does[x] the will of My Father who is in heaven, *he* is My brother and sister and mother."

12:38
Matt. 16:1; Mark 8:11,12; Luke 11:16; John 2:18; 6:30; 1 Cor. 1:22
12:39
Matt. 12:39-42; *Luke 11:29-32;* Matt. 16:4

12:40
Jon. 1:17; Matt. 8:20; Matt. 16:21

12:41
Jon. 1:2; Jon. 3:5; Matt. 12:6,42

12:42
1 Kin. 10:1; 2 Chr. 9:1; Matt. 12:6,41

12:43
Matt. 12:43-45; *Luke 11:24-26*

12:45
Mark 5:9; Luke 11:26; Heb. 6:4-8; 2 Pet. 2:20

12:46
Matt. 12:46-50; *Mark 3:31-35; Luke 8:19-21;* Matt. 1:18; 2:11ff.; 13:55; Luke 1:43; 2:33f., 48,51; John 2:1,5, 12; 19:25f.; Acts 1:14;
Matt. 13:55; Mark 6:3; John 2:12; 7:3,5,10; Acts 1:14; 1 Cor. 9:5; Gal. 1:19

Jesus Teaches in Parables

13:1
Matt. 9:28; 13:36;
Matt. 13:1-15;
Mark 4:1-12;
Luke 8:4-10;
Mark 2:13
13:2
Luke 5:3

13 On that day Jesus went out of the house, and was sitting by the sea.

2 And great multitudes gathered to Him, so that He got into a boat and sat down, and the whole multitude was standing on the beach.

13:3
Matt. 13:10ff.;
Mark 4:2ff.

3 And He spoke many things to them in parables, saying, "Behold, the sower went out to sow;~

4 and as he sowed,~ some *seeds* fell beside the road, and the birds came and ate them up.

5 "And others fell upon the rocky places, where they did not have^m much soil; and immediately they sprang up, because they had no depth of soil.

6 "But when the *sun* had risen, they were scorched; and because they had no root, they withered away.

7 "And others fell among the thorns, and the thorns came up and choked them out.

13:8
Gen. 26:12; Matt.
13:23

8 "And others fell on the *good* soil, and *yielded^m a crop, some a hundredfold, some sixty, and some thirty.

13:9
Matt. 11:15; Rev.
2:7,11,17,29; 3:6,
13,22

9 "He who has ears, let him hear."~!

An Explanation

10 And the disciples came and said to Him, "Why do You speak to them in *parables?*"

13:11
Matt. 19:11;
20:23; John 6:65;
1 Cor. 2:10; Col.
1:27; 1 John 2:20,
27
13:12
Matt. 25:29; Mark
4:25; Luke 8:18;
19:26

11 And He answered and said to them, "To *you* it has been granted+ to know^x29a the mysteries of the kingdom of heaven, but to *them* it has not been granted.+

12 "For whoever has, to him shall *more* be given, and he shall have an abundance; but whoever does not have, even what he has shall be taken away from him.

13:13
Deut. 29:4; Is.
42:19,20; Jer.
5:21; Ezek. 12:2

13 "Therefore I speak to them in *parables;* because while seeing they do not see, and while hearing they do not hear, nor do they understand.^29f

13:14
Is. 6:9; Mark 4:12;
Luke 8:10; John
12:40; Acts
28:26,27; Rom.
10:16; 11:8

14 "And in their case the prophecy of Isaiah is being fulfilled, which says,

'YOU WILL KEEP^4 ON HEARING, BUT WILL *NOT
UNDERSTAND;^x
AND YOU WILL KEEP^4 ON SEEING, BUT WILL *NOT
PERCEIVE;^x

13:15
Is. 6:10; Ps.
119:70; Zech.
7:11; Luke 19:42;
John 8:43,44;
2 Tim. 4:4; Heb.
5:11

15 FOR THE HEART OF THIS PEOPLE HAS BECOME DULL,
AND WITH THEIR EARS THEY SCARCELY HEAR,
AND THEY HAVE CLOSED THEIR EYES
LEST THEY SHOULD SEE^x WITH THEIR EYES,

AND HEAR[x] WITH THEIR EARS,
AND UNDERSTAND[x] WITH THEIR HEART AND RETURN,[x]
AND I SHOULD HEAL THEM.'

16 "But blessed are *your* eyes, because they see; and your ears, because they hear.

17 "For •truly I say to you, that many prophets and righteous men desired to see[x] what you see, and did not see *it*; and to hear[x] what you hear, and did not hear *it*.

The Sower Explained

18 "Hear[xt] then the parable of the sower.

19 "When anyone hears the word of the kingdom, and does not understand[29f] it, the *evil one* comes and snatches away what has been sown• in his heart. This is the one on whom seed was sown beside the road.

20 "And the one on whom seed was sown on the rocky places, this is the man who hears the word, and immediately receives it with joy;

21 yet he has no *firm* root in himself, but is *only temporary*, and when affliction or persecution arises because of the word, immediately he falls away.

22 "And the one on whom seed was sown among the thorns, this is the man who hears the word, and the worry of the world, and the deceitfulness of riches choke the word, and it becomes *unfruitful.*

23 "And the one on whom seed was sown on the good soil, this is the man who hears the word[43a] and understands[29f] it; who indeed bears fruit, and brings forth, some a hundredfold, some sixty, and some thirty."

Tares among Wheat

24 He presented another parable to them, saying, "The kingdom of heaven may be compared to a man who sowed good seed in his field.

25 "But while men were sleeping,~ his enemy came and sowed [x]tares also among the wheat, and went away.

26 "But when the wheat sprang up and bore grain, then the *tares* became evident *also.*

27 "And the slaves of the landowner came and said to him, 'Sir, did you not sow *good seed* in •your field? How then does it have tares?'

28 "And he said to them, 'An enemy has done this!' And the

[x]Or, *darnel*, a weed resembling wheat

13:16
Matt. 13:16,17;
Luke 10:23,24;
Matt. 16:17; John 20:29
13:17
John 8:56; Heb. 11:13; 1 Pet. 1:10-12

13:18
Matt. 13:18-23;
Mark 4:13-20;
Luke 8:11-15
13:19
Matt. 4:23;
Matt. 5:37

13:21
Matt. 11:6

13:22
Matt. 12:32;
13:39; Mark 4:19;
Rom. 12:2; 1 Cor. 1:20; 2:6,8; 3:18;
2 Cor. 4:4; Gal. 1:4; Eph. 2:2;
Matt. 19:23;
1 Tim. 6:9,10,17
13:23
Matt. 13:8

13:24
Matt. 13:31,33, 45,47; 18:23;
20:1; 22:2; 25:1;
Mark 4:26-30;
Luke 13:18,20

slaves *said to him, 'Do you want us, then, to go and gather[x] them up?'

29 "But he *said, 'No; lest while you are gathering up the tares, you may root[x] up the wheat with them.

13:30
Matt. 3:12

30 'Allow[xi] both to grow~ together until the harvest; and in the time of the harvest I will say to the reapers, "First gather[xi] up the tares and bind[xi] them in bundles to burn[x] them up; but gather[xi] the wheat into my barn." ' "

The Mustard Seed

13:31
Matt. 13:31,32;
Mark 4:30-32;
Luke 13:18,19;
Matt. 13:24;
Matt. 17:20; Luke
17:6
13:32
Ezek. 17:23; Ps.
104:12; Ezek.
31:6; Dan. 4:12

31 He presented another parable to them, saying, "The kingdom of heaven is like a mustard seed, which a man took and sowed in his field;

32 and this is †smaller than all *other* seeds; but when it is full grown,[x] it is †*larger* than the garden plants, and becomes a tree, so that THE BIRDS OF THE AIR come and NEST~ IN ITS BRANCHES."

The Leaven

13:33
Matt. 13:33: Luke
13:21; Matt.
13:24;
Gen. 18:6; Judg.
6:19; 1 Sam. 1:24
13:34
Mark 4:34; John
10:6; 16:25

33 He spoke another parable to them, "The kingdom of heaven is like leaven, which a woman took, and hid in three pecks of meal, until it was all leavened."

34 All these things Jesus spoke[m] to the multitudes in parables, and He did not speak to them *without a parable,*

13:35
Ps. 78:2

35 so that what was spoken through the prophet might be *fulfilled,*[x] saying,

"I WILL OPEN MY MOUTH IN *PARABLES;*

I WILL UTTER THINGS HIDDEN⁺ SINCE THE FOUNDATION

OF THE WORLD."

The Tares Explained

13:36
Matt. 13:1;
Matt. 15:15
13:37
Matt. 8:20
13:38
Matt. 8:12;
John 8:44; Acts
13:10; 1 John
3:10;
Matt. 5:37
13:39
Matt. 12:32;
13:22,40,49;
24:3; 28:20; 1
Cor. 10:11; Heb.
9:26
13:40
Matt. 12:32;
13:22,39,49;
24:3; 28:20; 1
Cor. 10:11; Heb.
9:26
13:41
Matt. 8:20;
Matt. 24:31;
Zeph. 1:3

36 Then He left the multitudes, and went into the house. And His disciples came to Him, saying, "Explain[xi] to us the parable of the tares of the field."

37 And He answered and said, "The one who sows the good[25b] seed is the Son of Man,

38 and the field is the world; and *as for* the good seed, these are the sons of the kingdom; and the tares are the sons of the evil *one;*

39 and the enemy who sowed them is the devil, and the harvest is the end[1] of the age; and the reapers are angels.

40 "Therefore just as the tares are gathered up and burned with *fire,* so shall it be at the end[1] of the age.

41 "The Son of Man will send forth His angels, and they will

gather out of His kingdom all stumbling blocks, and those who commit lawlessness,

42   and will cast them into the furnace of fire; in that place there shall be weeping and gnashing of teeth.

13:42
Matt. 13:50;
Matt. 8:12

43 "Then THE RIGHTEOUS WILL SHINE FORTH AS THE SUN in the kingdom of their Father. He who has ears, let him hear. ∾ⁱ

13:43
Dan. 12:3;
Matt. 11:15

Hidden Treasure

44 "The kingdom of heaven is like a treasure hidden⁺ in the field, which a man found and hid; and from joy over it he goes and sells all that he has, and buys *that* field.

13:44
Matt. 13:24;
Matt. 13:46

A Costly Pearl

45 "Again, the kingdom of heaven is like a merchant seeking fine pearls,

13:45
Matt. 13:24

46   and upon finding one pearl of great value, he went and sold all that he had, and bought it.

A Dragnet

47 "Again, the kingdom of heaven is like a dragnet cast into the sea, and gathering *fish* of every kind;

13:47
Matt. 13:44

48   and when it was filled, they drew it up on the beach; and they sat down, and gathered the good *fish* into containers, but the bad they threw away.

49 "So it will be at the end¹ of the age; the angels shall come forth, and take out the wicked from among the righteous,

13:49
Matt. 13:39,40

50   and will cast them into the furnace of fire; there shall be weeping and gnashing of teeth.

13:50
Matt. 13:42;
Matt. 8:12

51 "Have you understood²⁹ᶠ all these things?" They *said to Him, "Yes."

52   And He said to them, "Therefore every scribe who has become a disciple of the kingdom of heaven is like a head of a household, who brings forth out of his treasure things new³⁴ᵃ and old."

Jesus Revisits Nazareth

53 And it came about that when Jesus had finished these parables, He departed from there.

13:53
Matt. 7:28

54   And coming to His home town He *began* teaching them in their synagogue, so that they became astonished, ∾ and said, ∾ "Where *did* this man *get* this wisdom, and *these* miraculous powers?

13:54
Matt. 13:54-58;
Mark 6:1-6;
Matt. 4:23;
Matt. 7:28

55 "Is not this the ⁺*carpenter's* son? Is not His mother called Mary, and His brothers, James and Joseph and Simon and Judas?

13:55
Matt. 12:46

13:56
Mark 6:3

56 "And His sisters, are they not *all with us?* Where then *did* this man *get* all these things?"

13:57
Matt. 11:6;
Mark 6:4; Luke
4:24; John 4:44

57 And they took^{xx} offense at Him. But Jesus said to them, "A prophet is not without honor except in his home town, and in his *own* household."

58 And He did not do many miracles there because of their unbelief.

John the Baptist Beheaded

14:1
Matt. 14:1-12;
Mark 6:14-29;
Matt. 14:1,2: *Luke*
9:7-9;
Mark 8:15; Luke
3:1,19; 8:3;
13:31; 23:7f.,11f.,
15; Acts 4:27;
12:1
14:2
Matt. 16:14; Mark
6:14; Luke 9:7
14:3
Matt. 14:1-12:
Mark 6:14-29;
Mark 8:15; Luke
3:1,19; 8:3;
13:31; 23:7f.,11f.,
15; Acts 4:27;
12:1;
Matt. 4:12; 11:2;
Matt. 14:6; Mark
6:17,19,22; Luke
3:19f.
14:4
Lev. 18:16; 20:21
14:5
Matt. 11:9
14:6
Matt. 14:3; Mark
6:17,19,22; Luke
3:19;
Matt. 14:1-12:
Mark 6:14-29;
Mark 8:15; Luke
3:1,19; 8:3;
13:31; 23:7f.,11f.,
15; Acts 4:27;
12:1

14 At that time Herod the tetrarch heard the news about Jesus,

2 and said to his servants, "This is John the Baptist; *he* has risen from the dead; and that is why miraculous powers are at work in him."

3 For when Herod had John arrested, he bound him, and put him in prison on account of Herodias, the wife of his brother Philip.

4 For John had been saying^{xx} to him, "It is not lawful for you to have her."

5 And although he wanted to put^x him to death, he feared the multitude, because they regarded^{xx} him as a *prophet.*

6 But when Herod's birthday came, the daughter of Herodias danced before *them* and pleased Herod.

7 Thereupon he promised^x with an *oath* to give^x her whatever she asked.

8 And having been prompted by her mother, she *said, "Give^{xi} me here on a platter the head of John the Baptist."

9 And although he was grieved, the king commanded *it* to be given^x because of his oaths, and because of his dinner guests.

10 And he sent and had John beheaded in the prison.

11 And his head was brought on a platter and given to the girl; and she brought *it* to her mother.

12 And his disciples came and took away the body and buried it; and they went and reported to Jesus.

Five Thousand Fed

14:13
Matt. 14:13-21;
Mark 6:32-44;
Luke 9:10-17;
John 6:1-13;
Matt. 15:32-38
14:14
Matt. 9:36;
Matt. 4:23

13 Now when Jesus heard *it,* He withdrew from there in a boat, to a lonely place by Himself; and when the multitudes heard *of this,* they followed Him on foot from the cities.

14 And when He went ashore, He saw a great multitude, and felt compassion for them, and healed their sick.

15 And when it was evening, the disciples came to Him, saying, "The place is *desolate,* and the time is already past; so

send[xi] the multitudes away, that they may go into the villages and buy[x] food for themselves."

16   But Jesus said to them, "They do not need to go[x] away; *you* give[xi] them *something* to eat!"[x]

17   And they *said to Him, "We have here only *five* loaves and *two* fish."

14:17
Matt. 16:9

18   And He said, "Bring them here to Me."

19   And ordering the multitudes to recline[x] on the grass, He took the five loaves and the two fish, and looking up toward heaven, He blessed *the food,* and breaking the loaves He gave them to the disciples, and the disciples *gave* to the multitudes,

14:19
1 Sam. 9:13;
Matt. 15:36;
26:26; Mark 6:41;
8:7; 14:22; Luke
24:30; Acts
27:35; Rom. 14:6

20   and they *all* ate, and were satisfied. And they picked up what was left over of the broken pieces, *twelve* full baskets.

14:20
Matt. 16:9; Mark
6:43; 8:19; Luke
9:17; John 6:13

21   And there were about five thousand men who ate, aside from women and children.

Jesus Walks on the Water

22   And immediately He made the disciples get[x] into the boat, and go[~] ahead of Him to the other side, while He sent[x] the multitudes away.

14:22
Matt. 14:22-33;
Mark 6:45-51;
John 6:15-21

23   And after He had sent the multitudes away, He went up to the mountain by Himself to pray;[x] and when it was evening, He was there *alone.*

14:23
Mark 6:46; Luke
6:12; 9:28; John
6:15

24   But the boat was already *many* [y] stadia away from the land, battered by the waves; for the wind was contrary.

25   And in the [z]fourth watch of the night He came to them, walking on the sea.

14:25
Matt. 24:43; Mark
13:35

26   And when the disciples saw Him walking on the *sea,* they were frightened, saying, "It is a [†]*ghost!*" And they cried out for fear.

14:26
Luke 24:37

27   But immediately Jesus spoke to them, saying, "Take courage,[~] it is I; do not be afraid."[⊖]

14:27
Matt. 9:2;
Matt. 17:7; 28:5,
10; Mark 6:50;
Luke 1:13,30;
2:10; 5:10; 12:32;
John 6:20; Rev.
1:17

28   And Peter answered Him and said, "Lord, if it is *You,* command[xi] me to come to You on the water."

29   And He said, "Come!"[x] And Peter got out of the boat, and walked on the water and came toward Jesus.

30   But seeing the wind, he became afraid, and beginning to sink,[~] he cried out, saying, "Lord, save[xi] me!"

31   And immediately Jesus stretched out His hand and took hold of him, and *said to him, "O you of little faith, why did you doubt?"

14:31
Matt. 6:30; 8:26;
16:8

32   And when they got into the boat, the wind stopped.

[y]A stadion was about 600 feet   [z]I.e., 3-6 a.m.

14:33
Matt. 4:3
33 And those who were in the boat worshiped Him, saying, "You are certainly *God's* Son!"

14:34
Matt. 14:34-36;
Mark 6:53-56;
John 6:24,25;
Mark 6:53; Luke
5:1
34 And when they had crossed over, they came to land at Gennesaret.

35 And when the men of that place recognized Him, they sent into all that surrounding district and brought to Him all who were sick;

14:36
Matt. 9:20;
Matt. 9:21; Mark
3:10; 6:56; 8:22;
Luke 6:19
36 and they *began* to entreat™ Him that they might just touch˟ the fringe of His cloak; and as many as touched *it* were cured.

Tradition and Commandment

15:1
Matt. 15:1-20;
Mark 7:1-23;
Mark 3:22; 7:1;
John 1:19; Acts
25:7
15:2
Luke 11:38
15 Then some Pharisees and scribes *came to Jesus from Jerusalem, saying,

2 "Why do Your disciples transgress the tradition of the elders? For they do not wash their hands when they eat~ bread."

3 And He answered and said to them, "And why do *you yourselves* transgress the commandment of God for the sake of your tradition?

15:4
Ex. 20:12; Deut.
5:16;
Ex. 21:17; Lev.
20:9
4 "For God said, 'HONOR~ YOUR FATHER AND MOTHER,' and, 'HE WHO SPEAKS EVIL OF FATHER OR MOTHER, LET HIM BE PUT~ TO DEATH.'

5 "But *you* say, 'Whoever shall say˟ to *his* father or mother, "Anything of mine you might have been helped˟ by has been given *to God*,"

6 he is •*not* to honor his father ᵃor his motherᵇ.' And *thus* you invalidated the word of God for the sake of your tradition.

7 "You hypocrites, rightly did Isaiah prophesy of you, saying,

15:8
Is. 29:13
8   'THIS PEOPLE HONORS ME WITH THEIR LIPS,
        BUT THEIR HEART IS FAR AWAY FROM ME.

15:9
Col. 2:22
9   'BUT IN VAIN DO THEY WORSHIP⁴⁴ᶜ ME,
        TEACHING AS DOCTRINES THE PRECEPTS OF MEN.' "

10 And after He called the multitude to Him, He said to them, "Hear,~ and understand.~¹²⁹ᶠ

15:11
Matt. 15:18; Acts
10:14,15; 1 Tim.
4:3
11 "Not what enters into the mouth defiles the man, but what proceeds out of the mouth, this defiles the man."

12 Then the disciples *came and *said to Him, "Do You know that the Pharisees were offended when they heard this statement?"

15:13
Is. 60:21; 61:3;
John 15:2; 1 Cor.
3:9
15:14
Matt. 23:16,24;
Luke 6:39
13 But He answered and said, "Every plant which *My heavenly Father* did not plant shall be rooted up.

14 "Let˟ᴵ them alone; they are *blind* guides ᶜof the blind. And if

ᵃMany mss. do not contain *or his mother*   ᵇi.e., by supporting them with it   ᶜSome mss. do not contain *of the blind*

a *blind man* guides~ a *blind man,* both will fall into a *pit."*

The Heart of Man

15 And Peter answered and said to Him, "Explain[x1] the parable to us."

15:15
Matt. 13:36

16 And He said, "Are *you* still lacking in understanding *also?*

17 "Do you not understand that everything that goes into the
mouth passes into the stomach, and is eliminated?

18 "But the things that proceed out of the mouth come from
the *heart,* and those defile[17a] the man.

15:18
Matt. 12:34; Mark
7:20

19 "For out of the *heart* come evil[10b] thoughts, murders, adulteries, fornications, thefts, false witness, slanders.

15:19
Gal. 5:19ff.

20 "These are the things which defile[17a] the man; but to eat[x]
with unwashed hands does not defile the man."

The Syrophoenician Woman

21 And Jesus went away from there, and withdrew into the
district of Tyre and Sidon.

15:21
Matt. 15:21-28;
Mark 7:24-30;
Matt. 11:21
15:22
Matt. 9:27;
Matt. 4:24

22 And behold, a Canaanite woman came out from that region, and *began* to cry[m] out, saying, "Have mercy[x1] on me, O
Lord, Son of David; my daughter is cruelly demon-possessed."

23 But He did not answer her a word. And His disciples came
to *Him* and kept asking[m] Him, saying, "Send[x1] her away, for she
is shouting out after us."

24 But He answered and said, "I was sent only to the lost*
sheep of the house of Israel."

15:24
Matt. 10:6

25 But she came and *began* to bow[m] down before Him, saying,
"Lord, help~[1] me!"

15:25
Matt. 8:2

26 And He answered and said, "It is not good to take[x] the
children's bread and throw[x] it to the dogs."

27 But she said, "Yes, Lord; but even the dogs feed on the
crumbs which fall from their masters' table."

28 Then Jesus answered and said to her, "O woman, your
faith is *great;*[26a] be it done[x1] for you as you wish." And her
daughter was healed[15b] at *once.*

15:28
Matt. 9:22

Healing Multitudes

29 And departing from there, Jesus went along by the Sea of
Galilee, and having gone up to the mountain, He was sitting
there.

15:29
Matt. 15:29-31;
Mark 7:31-37;
Matt. 4:18

30 And great multitudes came to Him, bringing with them
those who were lame, crippled, blind, dumb, and many others,
and they laid them down at His feet; and He healed them,

15:30
Matt. 4:23

31 so that the multitude marveled[x] as they saw the dumb

15:31
Matt. 9:8

speaking, the crippled restored, and the lame walking, and the blind seeing; and they glorified the God of Israel.

Four Thousand Fed

15:32
Matt. 15:32-39;
Mark 8:1-10;
Matt. 14:13-21;
Matt. 9:36

32 And Jesus called His disciples to Him, and said, "I feel compassion for the multitude, because they have remained with Me now three days and have nothing to eat;ˣ and I do not wish to sendˣ them away *hungry,* lest they faintˣ on the way."

33 And the disciples *said to Him, "Where would we get *so many* loaves in a desolate place to satisfyˣ *such a great* multitude?"

34 And Jesus *said to them, "How many loaves do you have?" And they said, "Seven, and a few small fish."

35 And He directed the multitude to sitˣ down on the ground;

15:36
Matt. 14:19;
26:27; Luke
22:17,19; John
6:11,23; Acts
27:35; Rom. 14:6
15:37
Matt. 16:10; Mark
8:8,20; Acts 9:25

36 and He took the seven loaves and the fish; and giving thanks, He broke them and started givingˣˣ them to the disciples, and the disciples *in turn,* to the multitudes.

37 And they *all* ate, and were satisfied, and they picked up what was left over of the broken pieces, *seven* large baskets full.

38 And those who ate were *four thousand* men, besides women and children.

15:39
Mark 3:9;
Mark 8:10

39 And sending away the multitudes, He got into the boat, and came to the region of Magadan.

Pharisees Test Jesus

16:1
Matt. 16:1-12;
Mark 8:11-21;
Matt. 3:7; 16:6,
11,12;
Matt. 12:38; Luke
11:16
16:2
Luke 12:54f.
16:3
Luke 12:56

16 And the Pharisees and Sadducees came up, and testing Him asked⁹ᶜ Him to showˣ them a sign from heaven.

2 But He answered and said to them, "When it is evening, you say, '*It will be* fair weather, for the sky is red.'

3 "And in the morning, '*There will be* a storm today, for the sky is red and threatening.' Do you know how to discern~ the *appearance of the sky,* but cannot *discern* the *signs of the times?*

16:4
Matt. 12:39; Luke
11:29

4 "An evil and adulterous generation seeksⁱ after a sign; and a *sign* will not be given it, except the sign of Jonah." And He left them, and went away.

5 And the disciples came to the other side and had forgotten to takeˣ bread.

16:6
Mark 8:15; Luke
12:1;
Matt. 3:7

6 And Jesus said to them, "Watch~ᵗ out and beware~ᵗ of the leaven of the Pharisees and Sadducees."

7 And they began to discuss among themselves, saying, "*It is* because we took *no bread.*"

16:8
Matt. 6:30; 8:26;
14:31

8 But Jesus, aware of this, said, "You men of little faith, why do you discuss among yourselves that you have *no bread?*

9 "Do you not yet understand²⁹ᵈ or remember the five loaves of the five thousand, and how many baskets you took up?

16:9
Matt. 14:17-21

10 "Or the seven loaves of the four thousand, and how many large baskets you took up?

16:10
Matt. 15:34-38

11 "How is it that you do not understand²⁹ᵈ that I did not speak to you concerning *bread?* But beware⁓ᵗ of the leaven of the Pharisees and Sadducees."

16:11
Matt. 16:6; Mark 8:15; Luke 12:1; Matt. 3:7; 16:6,12

12 Then they understood²⁹ᶠ that He did not say to beware⁓ of the leaven of bread, but of the teaching of the Pharisees and Sadducees.

16:12
Matt. 3:7; 5:20

Peter's Confession of Christ

13 Now when Jesus came into the district of Caesarea Philippi, He *began* asking His disciples, saying, "Who do people say that the Son of Man is?"

16:13
Matt. 16:13-16:
Mark 8:27-29;
Luke 9:18-20;
Mark 8:27;
Matt. 8:20; 16:27, 28

14 And they said, "Some *say* John the Baptist; and others, Elijah; but still others, Jeremiah, or one of the prophets."

16:14
Matt. 14:2;
Matt. 17:10; Mark 6:15; Luke 9:8; John 1:21

15 He *said to them, "But who do *you* say that I am?"

16 And Simon Peter answered and said, *"Thou* art the Christ, the Son of the living God."

16:16
Matt. 1:16; 16:20; John 11:27;
Matt. 4:3;
Ps. 42:2; Matt. 26:63; Acts

17 And Jesus answered and said to him, "†*Blessed* are you, Simon Barjona, because flesh and blood did not reveal *this* to you, but My Father who is in heaven.

14:15; Rom. 9:26;
2 Cor. 3:3; 6:16;
1 Tim. 3:15; 4:10;
1 Thess. 1:9;
Heb. 3:12; 9:14;
10:31; 12:22;
Rev. 7:2
16:17
John 1:42;
21:15-17;
1 Cor. 15:50; Gal.
1:16; Eph. 6:12;
Heb. 2:14
16:18
Matt. 4:18;
Matt. 11:23
16:19
Is. 22:22; Rev.
1:18; 3:7;
Matt. 18:18; John 20:23
16:20
Matt. 8:4; Mark
8:30; Luke 9:21;
Matt. 1:16; 16:16;
John 11:27

18 "And I also say to you that you are Peter, and upon this †rock I will build My *church;* and the gates of Hades shall not overpower it.

19 "I will give you the keys of the kingdom of heaven; and whatever you shall bind˟ on earth shall be bound⁺ in heaven, and whatever you shall loose˟ on earth shall be loosed⁺ in heaven."

20 Then He warned the disciples that they should tell˟ no one that He was the Christ.

Jesus Foretells His Death

21 From that time Jesus Christ began to show⁓ His disciples that He must go˟ to Jerusalem, and suffer˟ *many things* from the elders and chief priests and scribes, and be killed,˟ and be raised˟ up on the third day.

16:21
Matt. 16:21-28:
Mark 8:31-9:1;
Luke 9:22-27;
Matt. 12:40; 17:9,
12,22f.; 20:18f.;
27:63; Mark 9:12,
31; Luke 17:25;
18:32; 24:7; John
2:19

22 And Peter took Him aside and began to rebuke⁓ Him, saying, "God forbid *it,* Lord! This shall •*never* happen to You."

23 But He turned and said to Peter, "Get behind Me, Satan! You are a *stumbling block* to Me; for you are not setting your mind on God's interests, but man's."

16:23
Matt. 4:10

Discipleship Is Costly

16:24
Matt. 10:38; Luke
14:27

24   Then Jesus said to His disciples, "If anyone wishes to come after *Me,* let him deny[xl1] himself, and take[xl] up his cross, and follow[~l] Me.

16:25
Matt. 10:39

25   "For whoever wishes~ to *save* [x] his life shall lose it; but whoever loses[x] his life for My sake shall find it.

26   "For what will a man be profited, if he gains[x] the *whole* world, and forfeits[x] his *soul?* Or what will a man give in exchange for his soul?

16:27
Matt. 8:20;
Matt. 10:23; 24:3,
27,37,39; 26:64;
Mark 8:38; 13:26;
Luke 21:27; John
21:22; Acts 1:11;
1 Cor. 15:23; 1
Thess. 1:10; 4:16;
2 Thess. 1:7,10;
2:1,8; James
5:7f.; 2 Pet. 1:16;
3:4,12; 1 John
2:28; Rev. 1:7;
Ps. 62:12; Prov.
24:12; Rom. 2:6;
14:12; 1 Cor.
3:13; 2 Cor. 5:10;
Eph. 6:8; Col.
3:25; Rev. 2:23;
20:12; 22:12

27   "For the Son of Man is going to come in the glory of His Father with His angels; and WILL THEN RECOMPENSE EVERY MAN ACCORDING TO HIS DEEDS.

28   "•Truly I say to you, there are some of those who are standing here who shall•*not* taste[x] death until they see[x] the Son of Man coming in His kingdom."

The Transfiguration

16:28
Matt. 8:20;
Matt. 10:23; 24:3,
27,37,39; 26:64;
Mark 8:38; 13:26;
Luke 21:27; John
21:22; Acts 1:11;
1 Cor. 15:23; 1
Thess. 1:10; 4:16;
2 Thess. 1:7,10;
2:1,8; James
5:7f.; 2 Pet. 1:16;
3:4,12; 1 John
2:28; Rev. 1:7

17:1
Matt. 17:1-8:
Mark 9:2-8; Luke
9:28-36;
Matt. 26:37; Mark
5:37; 13:3

17   And six days later Jesus *took with Him Peter and James and John his brother, and *brought them up to a high mountain by themselves.

2   And He was transfigured before them; and His face *shone* like the sun, and His garments became as white as light.

3   And behold, *Moses* and *Elijah* appeared to them, talking with Him.

17:4
Mark 9:5; Luke
9:33

4   And Peter answered and said to Jesus, "Lord, it is good for us to be here; if You wish, I will make three tabernacles here, one for You, and one for Moses, and one for Elijah."

17:5
Mark 1:11; Luke
3:22; 2 Pet.
1:17f.;
Is. 42:1; Matt.
3:17; 12:18

5   While he was still speaking, behold, a bright cloud overshadowed them; and behold, a voice out of the cloud, saying, "This is My *beloved* Son, with whom I am well-pleased; listen[~] to Him!"

6   And when the disciples heard *this,* they fell on their faces and were much afraid.

17:7
Matt. 14:27

7   And Jesus came to *them* and touched them and said, "Arise,[x] and do not be afraid."[o]

8   And lifting up their eyes, they saw no one, except Jesus Himself alone.

17:9
Matt. 17:9-13:
Mark 9:9-13;
Matt. 8:4;
Matt. 8:20; 17:12,
22;
Matt. 16:21

9   And as they were coming down from the mountain, Jesus commanded them, saying, "Tell[x] the vision to no one until the Son of Man has risen[x] from the dead."

17:10
Mal. 4:5; Matt.
11:14; 16:14

10   And His disciples asked Him, saying, "Why then do the scribes say that *Elijah* must come first?"

11 And He answered and said, "Elijah is coming and will restore all things;

12 but I say to you, that Elijah already came, and they did not recognize[1] him, but did to him whatever they wished. So also the Son of Man is going to suffer at their hands."

17:12
Matt. 8:20; 17:9, 22

13 Then the disciples understood that He had spoken to them about *John the Baptist*.

The Demoniac

14 And when they came to the multitude, a man came up to Him, falling on his knees before Him, and saying,

17:14
Matt. 17:14-19:
Mark 9:14-28;
Matt. 17:14-18:
Luke 9:37-42

15 "Lord, have mercy[xl] on my son, for he is a lunatic, and is very ill; for he often falls into the fire, and often into the water.

17:15
Matt. 4:24

16 "And I brought him to Your disciples, and they could not cure[x] him."

17 And Jesus answered and said, "O unbelieving and per- verted+ generation, how long shall I be with you? How long shall I put up with you? Bring him here to Me."

18 And Jesus rebuked him, and the demon came out of him, and the boy was cured at *once*.

19 Then the disciples came to Jesus privately and said, "Why could *we* not cast[x] it out?"

20 And He *said to them, "Because of the littleness of your faith; for •truly I say to you, if you have~ faith as a mustard seed, you shall say to this mountain, 'Move[xl] from here to there,' and it shall move; and +*nothing* shall be impossible to you.

17:20
Matt. 21:21f.;
Mark 11:23f.;
Luke 17:6;
Matt. 13:31; Luke 17:6;
Matt. 17:9; 1 Cor. 13:2;
Mark 9:23; John 11:40

21 ["dBut this kind does not go out except by prayer and fasting."]

17:21
Mark 9:29

22 And while they were gathering together in Galilee, Jesus said to them, "The Son of Man is going to be delivered into the hands of men;

17:22
Matt. 17:22,23:
Mark 9:30-32;
Luke 9:44,45

23 and they will kill Him, and He will be raised on the third day." And they were deeply grieved.

17:23
Matt. 16:21; 17:9

The Tribute Money

24 And when they had come to Capernaum, those who col- lected the etwo-drachma *tax* came to Peter, and said, "Does your teacher not pay the etwo-drachma *tax*?"

17:24
Ex. 30:13; 38:26

25 He *said, "Yes." And when he came into the house, Jesus spoke to him first, saying, "What do you think, Simon? From whom do the kings of the earth collect customs or poll-tax, from their sons or from strangers?"

17:25
Rom. 13:7;
Matt. 22:17,19

dMany mss. do not contain this verse   eEquivalent to two denarii or two days' wages paid as a temple tax

26 And upon his saying, "From strangers," Jesus said to him, "Consequently[2] the *sons* are exempt.

17:27
Matt. 5:29,30;
18:6,8,9; Mark
9:42,43,45,47;
Luke 17:2; John
6:61; 1 Cor. 8:13

27 "But, lest we give them offense,[x] go to the sea, and throw[xl] in a hook, and take[xl] the *first fish* that comes up; and when you open its mouth, you will find a ʲstater. Take that and give[x] it to them for you and Me."

Rank in the Kingdom

18:1
Matt. 18:1-5;
Mark 9:33-37;
Luke 9:46-48;
Luke 22:24

18 At that time the disciples came to Jesus, saying, "Who then is greatest[26a] in the kingdom of heaven?"

2 And He called a child to Himself and set him before them,

18:3
Matt. 19:14; Mark
10:15; Luke
18:17; 1 Cor.
14:20; 1 Pet. 2:2

3 and said, "•Truly I say to you, unless you are converted[x] and become like children, you shall •*not* enter[x] the kingdom of heaven.

4 "Whoever then humbles himself as this child, he is the greatest in the kingdom of heaven.

5 "And whoever receives[x] one such child in My name receives *Me;*

18:6
Mark 9:42; Luke
17:2; 1 Cor. 8:12;
Matt. 17:27

6 but whoever causes[x] one of these little ones who believe in Me to stumble, it is better for him that a heavy millstone be hung[x] around his neck, and that he be drowned[x] in the depth of the sea.

Stumbling Blocks

18:7
Luke 17:1; 1 Cor.
11:19; 1 Tim. 4:1

7 "Woe to the world because of *its* stumbling blocks! For it is inevitable that stumbling blocks come; but woe to that man through whom the stumbling block comes!

18:8
Matt. 5:30; Mark
9:43

8 "And if your hand or your foot causes you to stumble, cut[xl] it off and throw[xl] it from you; it is better for you to enter[x] life crippled or lame, than having *two* hands or *two* feet, to be cast[x] into the ʲeternal fire.

18:9
Matt. 5:29; Mark
9:47;
Matt. 5:22

9 "And if your eye causes you to stumble, pluck[xl] it out, and throw[xl] it from you. It is better for you to enter[x] life with *one* eye, than having *two* eyes, to be cast[x] into the fiery hell.[27b]

18:10
Luke 1:19; Acts
12:15; Rev. 8:2

10 "See[ᵐ] that you do not despise[x] one of these little ones, for I say to you, that their angels in heaven *continually* behold the face of My Father who is in heaven.

18:11
Luke 19:10

11 ["⁹For the Son of Man has come to save that which was lost.]

Ninety-nine Plus One

18:12
Matt. 18:12-14;
Luke 15:4-7

12 "What do you think? If any man has a *hundred* sheep, and *one* of them has gone[x] astray, does he not leave the ninety-nine on the mountains and go and search for the one that is straying?

ʲOr, *shekel*, worth four drachmas   9Most ancient mss. do not contain this verse

13 "And if it turns out that he finds˟ it, •truly I say to you, he rejoices over it more than over the ninety-nine which have not gone⁺ astray.

14 "Thus it is not *the* will of your Father who is in heaven that one of these little ones perish.˟

Discipline and Prayer

15 "And if your brother ʰsins,˟ go and reprove˟ˡ him in ⁺private; if he listens˟ to you, you have won your brother.

16 "But if he does not listen˟ *to you,* take˟ˡ one or two more with you, so that BY THE MOUTH OF *TWO OR THREE WITNESSES* EVERY FACT MAY BE CONFIRMED.˟

17 "And if he refuses˟ to listen to them, tell˟ˡ it to the church; and if he refuses˟ to listen *even to the church,* let him be to you as a Gentile and a tax-gatherer.

18 "•Truly I say to you, whatever you shall bind˟ on earth shall be bound⁺ in heaven; and whatever you loose˟ on earth shall be loosed⁺ in heaven.

19 "Again I say to you, that if two of you *agree*˟ on earth about anything that they may ask,˟ it shall be done for them by My Father who is in heaven.

20 "For where two or three have gathered⁺ together in •*My* name, ⁺there I am in their midst."

Forgiveness

21 Then Peter came and said to Him, "Lord, how often shall my brother sin against me and I forgive²¹ᵃ him? Up to seven times?"

22 Jesus *said to him, "I do not say to you, up to seven times, but up to seventy times seven.

23 "For this reason the kingdom of heaven may be compared to a certain king who wished to settle˟ accounts with his slaves.

24 "And when he had begun to settle~ *them,* there was brought to him one who owed him ⁱ*ten thousand* talents.

25 "But since he did not have *the means* to repay,˟ his lord commanded him to be sold,˟ along with his wife and children and all that he had, and repayment to be made.˟

26 "The slave therefore falling down, prostratedᵐ himself before him, saying, 'Have patience˟ˡ with me, and I will repay you *everything.'*

27 "And the lord of that slave felt compassion and released him and forgave him the debt.

18:15
Lev. 19:17; Luke 17:3; Gal. 6:1; 2 Thess. 3:15;
James 5:19

18:16
Deut. 19:15; John 8:17; 2 Cor. 13:1; 1 Tim. 5:19; Heb. 10:28

18:17
1 Cor. 6:1ff.;
2 Thess. 3:6,14f.

18:18
Matt. 16:19; John 20:23

18:19
Matt. 7:7

18:20
Matt. 28:20

18:21
Matt. 18:15;
Luke 17:4

18:22
Gen. 4:24

18:23
Matt. 13:24;
Matt. 25:19

18:25
Luke 7:42;
Ex. 21:2; Lev. 25:39; 2 Kin. 4:1;
Neh. 5:5

18:26
Matt. 8:2

18:27
Luke 7:42

ʰMany mss. add here: *against you* ⁱAbout $10,000,000 in silver content but worth much more in buying power

28 "But that slave went out and found one of his fellow slaves who owed him a *hundred* ʲdenarii; and he seized him and *began* to choke *him*, saying, 'Pay^{xl} back what you owe.'

29 "So his fellow slave fell down and *began* to entreat him, saying, 'Have patience^{xl} with me and I will repay you.'

30 "He was unwilling^m however, but went and threw him in prison until he should pay^x back what was owed.

31 "So when his fellow slaves saw what had happened, they were deeply grieved and came and reported to their lord all that had happened.

32 "Then summoning him, his lord *said to him, 'You *wicked* slave, I forgave you *all that debt* because you entreated me.

18:33
Matt. 6:12; Eph. 4:32

33 'Should you not also have had mercy^x on your fellow slave, *even as I* had mercy on you?'

34 "And his lord, moved with anger, handed him over to the torturers until he should repay^x all that was owed him.

18:35
Matt. 6:14

35 "So shall My heavenly Father also do to you, if each of you does not forgive^{x21a} his brother from your heart."

Concerning Divorce

19:1
Matt. 7:28;
Matt. 19:1-9;
Mark 10:1-12

19 And it came about that when Jesus had finished these words, He departed from Galilee, and came into the region of Judea beyond the Jordan;

19:2
Matt. 4:23

2 and great multitudes followed Him, and He healed them there.

19:3
Matt. 5:31

3 And *some* Pharisees came to Him, testing Him, and saying, "Is it lawful *for a man* to divorce^x his wife for any cause at all?"

19:4
Gen. 1:27; 5:2

4 And He answered and said, "Have you not read, that He who created *them* from the beginning MADE THEM *MALE* AND *FEMALE*,

19:5
Gen. 2:24; Eph. 5:31;
1 Cor. 6:16

5 and said, 'FOR THIS CAUSE A MAN SHALL LEAVE HIS FATHER AND MOTHER, AND SHALL CLEAVE TO HIS WIFE; AND THE TWO SHALL BECOME ONE FLESH'?

6 "Consequently they are no longer two, but one flesh. What therefore God has joined together, let no *man* separate."^θ

19:7
Deut. 24:1-4;
Matt. 5:31

7 They *said to Him, "Why then did Moses command to GIVE^x HER A CERTIFICATE OF DIVORCE AND SEND^x *her* AWAY?"

8 He *said to them, "Because of your hardness of heart, Moses permitted^{6c} you to divorce^x your wives; but from the †beginning it has not been this way.

19:9
Matt. 5:32

9 "And I say to you, whoever divorces^x his wife, except for immorality, and marries^x another woman commits adultery."

ʲThe denarius was equivalent to one day's wage

10   The disciples *said to Him, "If the relationship of the man with his wife is *like* †*this,* it is better not to marry."ˣ

11   But He said to them, "Not all men *can* accept †this statement, but *only* those to whom it has been given.†

19:11
1 Cor. 7:7ff.;
Matt. 13:11

12   "For there are eunuchs who were born that way from their mother's womb; and there are eunuchs who were made eunuchs by men; and there are *also* eunuchs who made themselves eunuchs for the sake of the kingdom of heaven. He who is able to accept~ *this,* let him accept~ᴵ *it.*"

Jesus Blesses Little Children

13   Then *some* children were brought to Him so that He might layˣ His hands on them and pray;ˣ and the disciples rebuked them.

19:13
Matt. 19:13-15;
Mark 10:13-16;
Luke 18:15-17

14   But Jesus said, "Letˣᴵ the children alone, and do not hinderᶿ them from coming to Me; for the kingdom of heaven belongs to such as these."

19:14
Matt. 18:3; Mark
10:15; Luke
18:17; 1 Cor.
14:20; 1 Pet. 2:2;
Matt. 5:3

15   And after laying His hands on them, He departed from there.

The Rich Young Ruler

16   And behold, one came to Him and said, "Teacher, what good[25a] thing shall I doˣ[19a] that I may obtainˣ eternal life?"

19:16
Matt. 19:16-29;
Mark 10:17-30;
Luke 18:18-30;
Luke 10:25-28;
Matt. 25:46

17   And He said to him, "Why are you asking[9c] Me about what is good?[25a] There is *only* One who is good; but if you wish to enterˣ into *life,* keepˣᴵ the commandments."

19:17
Lev. 18:5; Neh.
9:29; Ezek. 20:21

18   He *said to Him, "Which ones?" And Jesus said, "You shall not commit murder; You shall not commit adultery; You shall not steal; You shall not bear false witness;

19:18
Ex. 20:13-16;
Deut. 5:17-20

19   Honor~ᴵ your father and mother; and You shall love[31a] your neighbor as yourself."

19:19
Ex. 20:12; Deut.
5:16;
Lev. 19:18

20   The young man *said to Him, "All *these things* I have kept; what am I still lacking?"

21   Jesus said to him, "If you wish to be †*complete,* go *and* sellˣᴵ your *possessions* and giveˣᴵ to *the* poor, and you shall have treasure in heaven; and come, follow~ᴵ Me."

19:21
Luke 12:33; 16:9;
Acts 2:45; 4:34f.;
Matt. 6:20

22   But when the young man heard this statement, he went away grieved; for he was one who owned *much* property.

23   And Jesus said to His disciples, "•Truly I say to you, it is hard for a rich man to enter the kingdom of heaven.

19:23
Matt. 13:22; Mark
10:23f.; Luke
18:24

24   "And again I say to you, it is †easier for a camel to goˣ through the *eye of a needle,* than for a rich man to enterˣ the kingdom of God."

19:24
Mark 10:25; Luke
18:25

25   And when the disciples heard *this*, they were very aston-ished^{m1} and said, "Then who can be saved?"^x

26   And looking upon *them* Jesus said to them, "With *men* this is impossible, but with †God all things are possible."

The Disciples' Reward

27   Then Peter answered and said to Him, "Behold, *we* have left everything and followed You; what then will there be for us?"

28   And Jesus said to them, "•Truly I say to you, that you who have followed Me, in the regeneration when the Son of Man will sit^x on His glorious throne, *you also* shall sit upon *twelve* thrones, judging the twelve tribes of Israel.

29   "And everyone who has left houses or brothers or sisters or father or mother^k or children or farms for •My name's sake, shall receive *many times as much,* and shall inherit *eternal life.*

30   "But many *who are first* will be last; and *the* †last, first.

Laborers in the Vineyard

20   "For the kingdom of heaven is like a landowner who went out early in the morning to hire^x laborers for his vineyard.

2   "And when he had agreed with the laborers for a ¹ denarius for the day, he sent them into his vineyard.

3   "And he went out about the ^mthird hour and saw others standing idle in the market place;

4   and to those he said, '*You too* go into the vineyard, and whatever is right I will give you.' And *so* they went.

5   "Again he went out about the ⁿsixth and the ninth hour, and did the same thing.

6   "And about the °eleventh *hour* he went out, and found others standing; and he *said to them, 'Why have you been standing here idle all day long?'

7   "They *said to him, 'Because no one hired us.' He *said to them, '*You too* go into the vineyard.'

8   "And when evening had come, the owner of the vineyard *said to his foreman, 'Call^x the laborers and pay^{xl} them their wages, beginning with the last *group* to the first.'

9   "And when those *hired* about the eleventh hour came, each one received a ¹denarius.

10   "And when those *hired* first came, they thought that they would receive †more; and *they also* received each one a ¹ denari-us.

kMany mss. add here, *or wife* ¹The denarius was equivalent to one day's wage ml.e., 9 a.m. nl.e., Noon and 3 p.m. ol.e., 5 p.m.

11 "And when they received it, they grumbled™ at the landowner,

12 saying, 'These last men have worked *only one* hour, and
you have made them *equal* to us who have borne the burden and
the scorching heat of the day.'

13 "But he answered and said to one of them, 'Friend, I am
doing you no wrong; did you not agree with me for a ᴾdenarius?

14 'Takeˣ what is yours and go your way, but I wish to giveˣ to
this *last man* the same as to you.

15 'Is it not lawful for me to doˣ what I wish with what is my
own? Or is your eye ⁺*envious* because I am ⁺*generous?*'²⁵ᵃ

16 "Thus the *last* shall be first, and the ⁺*first* last."

Death, Resurrection Foretold

17 And as Jesus was about to go up to Jerusalem, He took the
twelve *disciples* aside by themselves, and on the way He said to
them,

18 "Behold, we are going up to Jerusalem; and the Son of Man
will be delivered to the chief priests and scribes, and they will
condemn¹⁴ᶜ Him to death,

19 and will deliver Him to the Gentiles to mockˣ and scourgeˣ
and crucifyˣ *Him,* and on the third day He will be raised up."

Preferment Asked

20 Then the mother of the sons of Zebedee came to Him with
her sons, bowing down, and making a request of Him.

21 And He said to her, "What do you wish?" She *said to
Him, "Commandˣ that in Your kingdom these two sons of mine
may sit,ˣ one on Your right and one on Your left."

22 But Jesus answered and said, "You do not know what you
are asking for. Are you able to drinkˣ the cup that *I* am about to
drink?" They *said to Him, "We are able."

23 He *said to them, "My cup you shall drink; but to sitˣ on
My right and on *My* left, *this* is not Mine to give,ˣ but it is for
those for whom it has been prepared⁺ by My Father."

24 And hearing *this,* the ten became indignant with the two
brothers.

25 But Jesus called them to Himself, and said, "You know
that the rulers of the Gentiles lord it over them, and *their* great
men exercise authority over them.

26 "It is not so among you, but whoever wishes~ to become
⁺great²⁶ᵃ among you shall be your *servant,* ³⁸ᵃ

ᴾThe denarius was equivalent to one day's wage

20:12
Jon. 4:8; Luke
12:55; James
1:11

20:13
Matt. 22:12;
26:50

20:15
Deut. 15:9; Matt.
6:23; Mark 7:22

20:16
Matt. 19:30; Mark
10:31; Luke 13:30

20:17
Matt. 20:17-19;
*Mark 10:32-34;
Luke 18:31-33*

20:18
Matt. 16:21

20:19
Matt. 27:2; Acts
2:23; 3:13; 4:27;
21:11;
Matt. 16:21;
17:23; Luke
18:32f.

20:20
Matt. 20:20-28;
Mark 10:35-45;
Matt. 4:21; 10:2;
Matt. 8:2
20:21
Matt. 19:28

20:22
Is. 51:17,22; Jer.
49:12; Matt.
26:39,42; Luke
22:42; John 18:11

20:23
Acts 12:2; Rev.
1:9;
Matt. 13:11;
Matt. 25:34

20:25
Matt. 20:25-28;
Luke 22:25-27

20:26
Matt. 23:11; Mark
9:35; 10:43; Luke
22:26

27 and whoever wishes~ to be first among you shall be your *slave;*[38b]

20:28
Matt. 8:20;
Matt. 26:28; John
13:13ff.; 2 Cor.
8:9; Phil. 2:7; 1
Tim. 2:6; Titus
2:14; Heb. 9:28;
Rev. 1:5

28 just as the Son of Man did not come to be served,[x38a] but to serve,[x] and to give[x] His life a ransom for many."

Sight for the Blind

20:29
Matt. 20:29-34;
Mark 10:46-52;
Luke 18:35-43;
Matt. 9:27-31
20:30
Matt. 20:31;
Matt. 9:27

29 And as they were going out from Jericho, a great multitude followed Him.

30 And behold, two blind men sitting by the road, hearing that Jesus was passing by, cried out, saying, "Lord, have mercy[xi] on us, Son of David!"

20:31
Matt. 9:27

31 And the multitude sternly told[x] them to be quiet; but they cried out all the more, saying, "Lord, have mercy[xi] on us, Son of David!"

32 And Jesus stopped and called them, and said, "What do you want Me to do[x] for you?"

33 They *said to Him, "Lord, *we want* our eyes to be opened."[x]

34 And moved with compassion, Jesus touched their eyes; and immediately they regained their sight and followed Him.

The Triumphal Entry

21:1
Matt. 21:1-9;
Mark 11:1-10;
Luke 19:29-38;
Matt. 24:3; 26:30;
Mark 11:1; 13:3;
14:26; Luke
19:29,37; 21:37;
22:39; John 8:1;
Acts 1:12

21 And when they had approached Jerusalem and had come to Bethphage, to the Mount of Olives, then Jesus sent two disciples,

2 saying to them, "Go⌢ into the village opposite you, and immediately you will find a donkey tied⁺ *there* and a colt with her; untie *them,* and bring[xi] *them* to Me.

3 "And if anyone says[x] something to you, you shall say, 'The Lord has need of them,' and immediately he will send them."

21:4
Matt. 21:4-9;
Mark 11:7-10;
Luke 19:35-38;
John 12:12-15
21:5
Is. 62:11; Zech.
9:9

4 Now this took place that what was spoken through the prophet might be *fulfilled,*[x] saying,

5 "SAY[xi] TO THE DAUGHTER OF ZION,
'BEHOLD YOUR KING IS COMING TO YOU,
GENTLE, AND MOUNTED⁺ ON A DONKEY,
EVEN ON A COLT, THE FOAL OF A BEAST OF BURDEN.' "

6 And the disciples went and did just as Jesus had directed them,

7 and brought the donkey and the colt, and laid on them their garments, on which He sat.

21:8
2 Kin. 9:13

8 And most[3] of the multitude spread *their* garments in the road, and others were cutting[m] branches from the trees, and spreading[m] them in the road.

9　And the multitudes going before Him, and those who followed after were crying^m out, saying,

> "Hosanna to the Son of David;
> BLESSED⁺ IS HE WHO COMES IN THE NAME OF THE
> LORD;
> Hosanna in the highest!"

10　And when He had entered Jerusalem, all the city was stirred, saying, "Who is this?"

11　And the multitudes were saying,^m "This is the prophet Jesus, from Nazareth in Galilee."

Cleansing the Temple

12　And Jesus entered the temple and cast out all those who were buying and selling in the temple, and overturned the *tables of the moneychangers* and the ⁺*seats* of those who were selling doves.

13　And He *said to them, "It is written, ⁺ 'MY HOUSE SHALL BE CALLED A *HOUSE OF PRAYER'*; but *you* are making it a ROBBERS' DEN."

14　And *the* blind and *the* lame came to Him in the temple, and He healed them.

15　But when the chief priests and the scribes saw the wonderful things that He had done, and the children who were crying out in the temple and saying, "Hosanna to the Son of David," they became indignant,

16　and said to Him, "Do You hear what these are saying?" And Jesus *said to them, "Yes; have you never read, 'OUT OF THE *MOUTH OF INFANTS AND NURSING BABES* THOU HAST PREPARED PRAISE FOR THYSELF'?"

17　And He left them and went out of the city to Bethany, and lodged there.

The Barren Fig Tree

18　Now in the morning, when He returned to the city, He became hungry.

19　And seeing a lone fig tree by the road, He came to it, and found ⁺nothing on it except leaves only; and He *said to it, "No longer shall there ever be *any* fruit from *you*." And at *once* the fig tree withered.

20　And seeing *this*, the disciples marveled, saying, "How did the fig tree wither at once?"

21　And Jesus answered and said to them, "•Truly I say to you, if you have~ faith, and do not doubt,ˣ you shall not only do what

21:9
Matt. 9:27;
Ps. 118:26;
Luke 2:14

21:11
Matt. 21:26; Mark
6:15; Luke 7:16,
39; 13:33; 24:19;
John 1:21,25;
4:19; 6:14; 7:40;
9:17; Acts 3:22f.;
7:37;
Matt. 2:23
21:12
Matt. 21:12-16;
Mark 11:15-18;
Luke 19:45-47;
Matt. 21:12,13;
John 2:13-16;
Ex. 30:13;
Lev. 1:14; 5:7;
12:8
21:13
Is. 56:7;
Jer. 7:11

21:14
Matt. 4:23

21:15
Matt. 9:27

21:16
Ps. 8:2; Matt.
11:25

21:17
Matt. 26:6; Mark
11:1,11,12; 14:3;
Luke 19:29;
24:50; John 11:1,
18; 12:1

21:18
Matt. 21:18-22;
Mark 11:12-14,
20-24
21:19
Luke 13:6-9

21:21
Matt. 17:20; Mark
11:23; Luke 17:6;
James 1:6

was done to the fig tree, but even if you say[x] to *this mountain,* 'Be taken[xi] up and cast[xi] into the sea,' it shall happen.

21:22
Matt. 7:7

22 "And all things you ask[x9a] in prayer, believing, you shall receive."[5b]

Authority Challenged

21:23
Matt. 21:23-27;
Mark 11:27-33;
Luke 20:1-8;
Matt. 26:55

23 And when He had come into the temple, the chief priests and the elders of the people came to Him as He was teaching, and said, "By what authority are You doing these things, and who gave *You* this authority?"

24 And Jesus answered and said to them, "*I* will ask you one thing *too,* which if you tell[x] Me, *I* will *also* tell *you* by what authority I do these things.

25 "The baptism of John was from *what source,* from heaven or from men?" And they *began* reasoning[m] among themselves, saying,[x] "If we say, 'From heaven,' He will say to us, 'Then why did you not believe him?'

21:26
Matt. 11:9; Mark
6:20

26 "But if we say,[x] 'From men,' we fear the multitude; for they all hold John to be a *prophet.*"

27 And answering Jesus, they said, "We do not know." He *also* said[m] to them, "Neither will *I* tell you by what authority I do these things.

Parable of Two Sons

21:28
Matt. 20:1; 21:33

28 "But what do you think? A man had two sons, and he came to the first and said, 'Son, go work[m] today in the vineyard.'

29 "And he answered and said, 'I will, sir'; and he did not go.

30 "And he came to the second and said the same thing. But he answered and said, 'I will not'; *yet* he afterward regretted *it* and went.

21:31
Luke 7:29,37-50

31 "Which of the two did the will of his father?" They *said, "The latter." Jesus *said to them, "•Truly I say to you that the tax-gatherers and harlots will get into the kingdom of God before you.

21:32
Luke 3:12; 7:29f.

32 "For John came to you in the way of righteousness and you did not believe him; but the tax-gatherers and harlots did believe him; and *you,* seeing this, did not even feel remorse afterward so as to believe[x] him.

Parable of the Landowner

21:33
Matt. 21:33-46;
Mark 12:1-12;
Luke 20:9-19;
Is. 5:1,2;
Matt. 20:1; 21:28;
Matt. 25:14

33 "Listen[xi] to another parable. There was a landowner who PLANTED A VINEYARD AND PUT A WALL AROUND IT AND DUG A WINE PRESS IN IT, AND BUILT A TOWER, and rented it out to vine-growers, and went on a journey.

34 "And when the harvest time approached, he sent his slaves to the vine-growers to receive^x his produce.

21:34
Matt. 22:3

35 "And the vine-growers took his slaves and beat one, and killed another, and stoned a third.

36 "Again he sent another group of slaves larger than the first; and they did the same thing to them.

21:36
Matt. 22:4

37 "But afterward he sent his son to them, saying, 'They will respect my son.'

38 "But when the vine-growers saw the son, they said among themselves, 'This is the heir; come, let us kill^x him, and seize^x his inheritance.'

39 "And they took him, and threw him out of the vineyard, and killed him.

40 "Therefore when the owner of the vineyard comes, what will he do to those vine-growers?"

41 They *said to Him, "He will bring those *wretches* to a wretched^4 end, and will rent out the vineyard to other vine-growers, who will pay him the proceeds at the *proper* seasons."

21:41
Matt. 8:11f.; Acts
13:46; 18:6;
28:28

42 Jesus *said to them, "Did you never read in the Scriptures,

21:42
Ps. 118:22f.; Acts
4:11; Rom. 9:33;
1 Pet. 2:7

'THE STONE WHICH THE BUILDERS †REJECTED,
THIS BECAME THE CHIEF CORNER *stone*;
THIS CAME ABOUT *FROM THE LORD*,
AND IT IS MARVELOUS IN OUR EYES'?

43 "Therefore I say to you, the kingdom of God will be taken away from you, and be given to a nation producing the fruit of it.

44 "And he who falls on †*this* stone will be broken to pieces;^{1} but on whomever it falls,^{x} it will scatter him like dust."

21:44
Is. 8:14,15

45 And when the chief priests and the Pharisees heard His parables, they understood that He was speaking about *them*.

46 And when they sought to seize^x Him, they feared the multitudes, because they held^m Him to be a *prophet*.

21:46
Matt. 21:26;
Matt. 21:11

Parable of the Marriage Feast

22 And Jesus answered and spoke to them again in parables, saying,

2 "The kingdom of heaven may be compared to a king, who gave a wedding feast for his son.

22:2
Matt. 13:24;
22:2-14; Luke
14:16-24;
Luke 12:36; John
2:2

3 "And he sent out his slaves to call^x those who had been invited$^+$ to the wedding feast, and they were unwilling^m to come.

22:3
Matt. 21:34
22:4
Matt. 21:36

4 "Again he sent out other slaves saying, 'Tell^x those who have been invited,$^+$ "Behold, I have prepared$^+$ my dinner; my oxen and my fattened livestock are *all* butchered$^+$ and everything is ready; come to the wedding feast." '

5 "But they paid no attention and went their way, one to his own farm, another to his business,

6 and the rest seized his slaves and mistreated them and killed them.

7 "But the king was enraged and sent his armies, and destroyed those murderers, and set their city on *fire.*

8 "Then he *said to his slaves, 'The wedding is *ready,* but those who were invited⁺ were not worthy.

22:9
Ezek. 21:21;
Obad. 14

9 'Go ᴹ therefore to the main highways, and as many as you findˣ *there,* inviteˣᴵ to the wedding feast.'

10 "And those slaves went out into the streets, and gathered together all they found, both evil¹⁰ᵇ and good;²⁵ᵃ and the wedding hall was filled with dinner guests.

22:11
2 Kin. 10:22;
Zech. 3:3,4

11 "But when the king came in to lookˣ over the dinner guests, he saw there a man *not* dressed⁺ in wedding clothes,

22:12
Matt. 20:13;
26:50

12 and he *said to him, 'Friend, how did you come in here without wedding clothes?' And he was speechless.

22:13
Matt. 8:12; 25:30;
Luke 13:28

13 "Then the king said to the servants, 'Bind him hand and foot, and castˣᴵ him into the outer darkness; in that place there shall be weeping and gnashing of teeth.'

22:14
Matt. 24:22;
2 Pet. 1:10; Rev.
17:14

14 "For many are called, but few *are* chosen."

Tribute to Caesar

22:15
Matt. 22:15-22;
Mark 12:13-17;
Luke 20:20-26

15 Then the Pharisees went and counseled together how they might trapˣ Him in what He said.

22:16
Mark 3:6; 8:15;
12:13

16 And they *sent their disciples to Him, along with the Herodians, saying, "Teacher, we know that You are ⁺truthful and teach the way of God in *truth,* and defer to no one; for You are not partial to any.

22:17
Matt. 17:25;
Luke 2:1; 3:1

17 "Tellˣᴵ us therefore, what do You think? Is it lawful to giveˣ a poll-tax to Caesar, or not?"

18 But Jesus perceived²⁹ᵃ their malice, and said, "Why are you testing Me, you hypocrites?

22:19
Matt. 17:25

19 "Showˣᴵ Me the coin *used* for the poll-tax." And they brought Him a denarius.

20 And He *said to them, "Whose likeness and inscription is this?"

22:21
Mark 12:17; Luke
20:25; Rom. 13:7

21 They *said to Him, "Caesar's." Then He *said to them, "Then renderˣᴵ to Caesar the things that are Caesar's; and to God the things that are God's."

22:22
Mark 12:12

22 And hearing *this,* they marveled, and leaving Him, they went away.

Jesus Answers the Sadducees

23   On that day *some* Sadducees (who say there is no *resurrection*) came to Him and questioned Him,

24   saying, "Teacher, Moses said, 'IF A MAN DIES,ˣ HAVING NO CHILDREN, HIS BROTHER AS NEXT OF KIN SHALL MARRY HIS WIFE, AND RAISE UP AN OFFSPRING TO HIS BROTHER.'

25   "Now there were *seven* brothers with us; and the first married and died, and having no offspring left his wife to his brother;

26   so also the second, and the third, down to the seventh.

27   "And last of all, the woman died.

28   "In the resurrection therefore whose wife of the seven shall she be? For they all had her."

29   But Jesus answered and said to them, "You are mistaken, not understanding[29e] the Scriptures, or the power[32a] of God.

30   "For in the resurrection they neither marry, nor are given in marriage, but are *like angels in heaven.*

31   "But regarding the resurrection of the dead, have you not read that which was spoken to you by God, saying,

32   '†*I* AM THE GOD OF ABRAHAM, AND THE GOD OF ISAAC, AND THE GOD OF JACOB'? He is not the God of the dead but of the living."

33   And when the multitudes heard *this,* they were astonished[ᵐ1] at His teaching.

34   But when the Pharisees heard that He had put the Sadducees to silence, they gathered themselves together.

35   And one of them, [q]a lawyer, asked Him *a question,* testing Him,

36   "Teacher, which is the great[26a] commandment in the Law?"

37   And He said to him, " 'YOU SHALL LOVE[31a] THE LORD YOUR GOD WITH ALL YOUR HEART, AND WITH ALL YOUR SOUL, AND WITH ALL YOUR MIND.'[33a]

38   "This is the great and foremost commandment.

39   "The second is like it, 'YOU SHALL LOVE[31a] YOUR NEIGHBOR AS YOURSELF.'

40   "On *these two commandments* depend the whole Law and the Prophets."

41   Now while the Pharisees were gathered⁺ together, Jesus asked them a question,

42   saying, "What do you think about the Christ, whose son is He?" They *said to Him, *"The son* of David."

[q]I.e., an expert in the Mosaic law

22:23
Matt. 22:23-33;
Mark 12:18-27;
Luke 20:27-40;
Matt. 3:7;
Acts 23:8
22:24
Deut. 25:5

22:29
John 20:9

22:30
Matt. 24:38; Luke
17:27

22:32
Ex. 3:6

22:33
Matt. 7:28

22:34
Matt. 22:34-40;
Mark 12:28-31;
Luke 10:25-37;
Matt. 3:7
22:35
Luke 7:30; 10:25;
11:45,46,52;
14:3; Titus 3:13

22:37
Deut. 6:5

22:39
Lev. 19:18; Matt.
19:19; Gal. 5:14

22:40
Matt. 7:12

22:41
Matt. 22:41-46;
Mark 12:35-37;
Luke 20:41-44
22:42
Matt. 9:27

22:43
2 Sam. 23:2; Rev.
1:10; 4:2

43 He *said to them, "Then how does David in the Spirit call Him 'Lord,' saying,

22:44
Ps. 110:1; Matt.
26:64; Mark
16:19; Acts
2:34f.; 1 Cor.
15:25; Heb. 1:13;
10:13

44 'THE LORD SAID TO MY LORD,
  "SIT AT MY RIGHT HAND,
    UNTIL I PUT[x] THINE ENEMIES BENEATH THY FEET" '?

45 "If David then calls Him 'Lord,' how is He *his son?"

22:46
Mark 12:34; Luke
14:6; 20:40

46 And no one was able[m] to answer[x] Him a word, nor did anyone dare from that day on to ask[x9c] Him another question.

Pharisaism Exposed

23:1
Matt. 23:1-7;
Mark 12:38,39;
Luke 20:45,46
23:2
Deut. 33:3f.; Ezra
7:6,25; Neh. 8:4

23 Then Jesus spoke to the multitudes and to His disciples,
2 saying, "The scribes and the Pharisees have seated themselves in the chair of *Moses;*

3 therefore all that they tell[x] you, do[xl] and observe,[~] but do not do[⊖] *according to their deeds;* for they say *things,* and do not do *them.*

23:4
Luke 11:46; Acts
15:10

4 "And they tie up *heavy* loads, and lay them on men's shoulders; but *they themselves* are unwilling to move[x] them with *so much as* a *finger.*

23:5
Matt. 6:1,5,16;
Ex. 13:9; Deut.
6:8; 11:18;
Matt. 9:20

5 "But they do *all their deeds* to be noticed[x] by men; for they broaden their [r]phylacteries, and lengthen the tassels *of their garments.*

23:6
Luke 11:43; 14:7;
20:46

6 "And they love[31b] the place of honor at banquets, and the chief seats in the synagogues,

23:7
Matt. 23:8; 26:25,
49; Mark 9:5;
10:51; 11:21;
John 1:38,49; 3:2,
26; 4:31; 6:25;
9:2; 11:8; 20:16
23:8
James 3:1;
Matt. 23:7; 26:25,
49; Mark 9:5;
10:51; 11:21;
14:45; John 1:38,
49; 3:2,26; 4:31;
6:25; 9:2; 11:8;
20:16
23:9
Matt. 6:9; 7:11
23:11
Matt. 20:26
23:12
Luke 14:11; 18:14

7 and respectful greetings in the market places, and being called[~] by men, Rabbi.

8 "But do not be called[⊖] Rabbi; for One is *your* Teacher, and you are all *brothers.*

9 "And do not call[⊖] *anyone* on earth your *father;* for One is *your* Father, He who is in heaven.

10 "And do not be called[⊖] leaders; for One is your Leader, *that is, Christ.*

11 "But the greatest[26a] among you shall be your *servant.* [38a]

12 "And whoever exalts himself shall be humbled; and whoever humbles himself shall be exalted.

Seven Woes

23:13
Matt. 23:15,16,
23,25,27,29;
Luke 11:52

13 "But woe to you, scribes and Pharisees, hypocrites, because you shut off the kingdom of heaven from men; for *you* do not enter in *yourselves,* nor do you allow those who are entering to go[x] in.

23:14
Mark 12:40; Luke
20:47

14 ["[s]Woe to you, scribes and Pharisees, hypocrites, because

[r]i.e., small boxes containing Scripture texts worn for religious purposes   [s]This verse not found in the earliest mss.

you devour[1] widows' houses, even while for a pretense you make long prayers; therefore you shall receive greater condemnation.]

15 "Woe to you, scribes and Pharisees, hypocrites, because you travel about on sea and land to make[x] one proselyte; and when he becomes one, you make him twice as much a son of hell as yourselves.

16 "Woe to you, blind guides, who say, 'Whoever swears[x] by the temple, that is nothing; but whoever swears[x] by the gold of the temple, he is obligated.'

17 "You fools and blind men; which is more important, the gold, or the temple that sanctified the gold?

18 "And, 'Whoever swears[x] by the altar, *that* is nothing, but whoever swears[x] by the offering upon it, he is obligated.'

19 "You blind men, which is more important, the offering or the altar that sanctifies the offering?

20 "Therefore he who swears, swears *both* by the altar and by everything on it.

21 "And he who swears by the temple, swears *both* by the temple and by Him who dwells within it.

22 "And he who swears by heaven, swears *both* by the throne of God and by Him who sits upon it.

23 "Woe to you, scribes and Pharisees, hypocrites! For you tithe mint and dill and cummin, and have neglected the weightier provisions of the law: justice and mercy and faithfulness; but *these* are the things you should[m] have done[x] without neglecting[~] the others.

24 "You blind guides, who strain out a gnat and swallow a [†]*camel!*

25 "Woe to you, scribes and Pharisees, hypocrites! For you clean the outside of the cup and of the dish, but inside they are full of robbery and self-indulgence.

26 "You blind Pharisee, first clean[xi] the inside of the cup and of the dish, so that the outside of it may become clean also.

27 "Woe to you, scribes and Pharisees, hypocrites! For you are like whitewashed[•] tombs which on the [†]outside appear beautiful, but [†]inside they are full of dead men's bones and all uncleanness.

28 "Even so *you too* outwardly appear righteous to men, but inwardly you are full of hypocrisy and lawlessness.

29 "Woe to you, scribes and Pharisees, hypocrites! For you build the tombs of the prophets and adorn the monuments of the righteous,

30 and say, 'If we had been *living* in the days of our fathers,

23:15 Acts 2:10; 6:5; 13:43; Matt. 5:22

23:16 Matt. 15:14; 23:24; Matt. 5:33-35

23:17 Ex. 30:29

23:19 Ex. 29:37

23:21 1 Kin. 8:13; Ps. 26:8; 132:14

23:22 Is. 66:1; Matt. 5:34

23:23 Matt. 23:13; Luke 11:42

23:24 Matt. 23:16

23:25 Mark 7:4; Luke 11:39f.

23:26 Mark 7:4; Luke 11:39f.

23:27 Luke 11:44; Acts 23:3

23:29 Luke 11:47f.

we would not have been partners with them in *shedding* the blood of the prophets.'

23:31
Matt. 23:34,37;
Acts 7:51f.

31 "Consequently you bear witness against yourselves, that you are *sons* of those who murdered the prophets.

32 "Fill^xi up then the measure *of the guilt* of your fathers.

23:33
Matt. 3:7; Luke
3:7;
Matt. 5:22

33 "You serpents, you brood of vipers, how shall you escape^x the sentence of hell?^27b

23:34
Matt. 23:34-36;
Luke 11:49-51;
2 Chr. 36:15,16;
Matt. 10:17;
Matt. 10:23

34 "Therefore, behold, *I* am sending you prophets and wise men and scribes; some of them you will kill and crucify, and some of them you will scourge in your synagogues, and persecute from city to city,

23:35
Gen. 4:8ff.; Heb.
11:4;
Zech. 1:1;
2 Chr. 24:21

35 that upon *you* may fall *the guilt of* all the righteous blood shed on earth, from the blood of righteous Abel to the blood of Zechariah, the son of Berechiah, whom you murdered between the temple and the altar.

23:36
Matt. 10:23;
24:34

36 "•Truly I say to you, *all* these things shall come upon †*this* generation.

Lament over Jerusalem

23:37
Matt. 23:37-39;
Luke 13:34,35;
Matt. 5:12;
Ruth 2:12

37 "O Jerusalem, Jerusalem, who kills the prophets and stones those who are sent• to her! How often I wanted to gather^x your children together, the way a hen gathers her chicks under her wings, and you were unwilling.

23:38
1 Kin. 9:7f.; Jer.
22:5
23:39
Ps. 118:26; Matt.
21:9

38 "Behold, your house is being left to you desolate!

39 "For I say to you, from now on you shall •not see^x Me until you say,^x '†Blessed• is He who comes in the name of the Lord!' "

Signs of Christ's Return

24:1
Matt. 24:1-51;
Mark 13; Luke
21:5-36;
Matt. 21:23

24 And Jesus came out from the temple and was going away when His disciples came up to point^x out the temple buildings to Him.

24:2
Luke 19:44

2 And He answered and said to them, "Do you not see all these things? •Truly I say to you, •not one stone here shall be left^x upon another, which will not be torn down."

24:3
Matt. 21:1;
Matt. 16:27f.;
24:27,37,39

3 And as He was sitting on the Mount of Olives, the disciples came to Him privately, saying, "Tell^xi us, when will these things be, and what *will be* the sign of •Your coming, and of the end^1 of the age?"

24:4
Jer. 29:8

4 And Jesus answered and said to them, "See ᵙ to it that no one misleads^x you.

24:5
Matt. 24:11,24;
Acts 5:36f.;
1 John 2:18; 4:3
24:6
Rev. 6:4

5 "For many will come in My name, saying, '*I* am the Christ,' and will mislead *many*.

6 "And you will be hearing~ of wars and rumors of wars;

see⁓ᴵ that you are not frightened,° for *those things* must take place, but *that* is not †yet the end.

7 "For nation will rise against nation, and kingdom against kingdom, and in various places there will be famines and earth-quakes.

8 "But all these things are *merely* the beginning of birth pangs.

9 "Then they will deliver you to tribulation, and will kill you, and you will be hated⁓ by all nations on account of My name.

10 "And at that time *many* will fall away and will deliver up one another and hate one †another.

11 "And many false prophets will arise, and will mislead many.

12 "And because lawlessness is increased,ˣ most people's love will grow cold.

13 "But the one who endures to the end, he shall be saved.

14 "And this gospel of the kingdom shall be preached in the whole world for a witness to all the nations, and then the *end* shall come.

Perilous Times

15 "Therefore when you seeˣ the ABOMINATION OF DESOLATION which was spoken of through Daniel the prophet, standing⁺ in the holy place (let the reader understand⁓ᴵ²⁹ᵈ),

16 then let those who are in Judea flee to the mountains;

17 let him who is on the housetop not go° down to getˣ the things out that are in his house;

18 and let him who is in the field not turn° back to getˣ his cloak.

19 "But woe to those who are with child and to those who nurse babes in those days!

20 "But pray⁓ᴵ that your flight may not be in the winter, or on a Sabbath;

21 for then there will be a *great*²⁶ᵃ *tribulation,* such as has not occurred since the beginning of the world until now, nor •*ever shall.*

22 "And unless those days had been cut short, *no life* would have been saved; but for the sake of the *elect* those days shall be cut short.

23 "Then if anyone saysˣ to you, 'Behold, here is the Christ,' or 'There *He is,*' do not believe° him.

24 "For false Christs and false prophets will arise and will show great²⁶ᵃ signs and wonders, so as to mislead,ˣ if possible, even the elect.

25 "Behold, I have told⁺ you in advance.

24:7
2 Chr. 15:6; Is. 19:2; Rev. 6:8,12; Acts 11:28; Rev. 6:5,6

24:8
Matt. 24:8-20; Luke 21:12-24
24:9
Matt. 10:17; John 16:2;
Matt. 10:22; John 15:18ff.
24:10
Matt. 11:6
24:11
Matt. 7:15; 24:24

24:13
Matt. 10:22
24:14
Matt. 4:23; Rom. 10:18; Col. 1:6,23; Luke 2:1; 4:5; Acts 11:28; 17:6, 31; 19:27; Rom. 10:18; Heb. 1:6; 2:5; Rev. 3:10; 16:14
24:15
Dan. 9:27; 11:31; 12:11; Mark 13:14; Luke 21:20; John 11:48; Acts 6:13f.; 21:28; Mark 13:14; Rev. 1:3
24:17
1 Sam. 9:25; 2 Sam. 11:2; Matt. 10:27; Luke 5:19; 12:3; 17:31; Acts 10:9

24:19
Luke 23:29

24:21
Dan. 12:1; Joel 2:2; Matt. 24:29

24:22
Matt. 22:14; 24:24,31; Luke 18:7

24:23
Luke 17:23f.

24:24
Matt. 7:15; 24:11; John 4:48; 2 Thess. 2:9; Matt. 22:14; 24:22,31; Luke 18:7

26 "If therefore they say˟ to you, 'Behold, He is in the wilderness,' do not go⊖ forth, *or*, 'Behold, He is in the inner rooms,' do not believe⊖ *them.*

24:27
Luke 17:24;
Matt. 24:3,37,39;
Matt. 8:20
24:28
Job 39:30; Ezek.
39:17; Hab. 1:8;
Luke 17:37

27 "For just as the lightning comes from the east, and flashes even to the west, so shall the coming of the Son of Man be.

28 "Wherever the corpse is, there the vultures will gather.

The Glorious Return

24:29
Matt. 24:21;
Is. 13:10; 24:23;
Ezek. 32:7; Joel
2:10,31; 3:15f.;
Amos 5:20; 8:9;
Zeph. 1:15; Matt.
24:29-35; Acts
2:20; Rev.
6:12-17; 8:12;
Is. 34:4; Rev.
6:13
24:30
Matt. 24:3; Rev.
1:7;
Dan. 7:13; Matt.
16:27; 24:3,37,39
24:31
Matt. 13:41;
Ex. 19:16; Deut.
30:4; Is. 27:13;
Zech. 9:14; 1 Cor.
15:52; 1 Thess.
4:16; Heb. 12:19;
Rev. 8:2; 11:15;
Matt. 24:22;
Dan. 7:2; Zech.
2:6; Rev. 7:1

29 "But immediately after the tribulation of those days THE SUN WILL BE DARKENED, AND THE MOON WILL NOT GIVE ITS LIGHT, AND THE STARS WILL FALL from the sky, and the powers of the heavens will be shaken,

30 and then the sign of the Son of Man will appear in the sky, and then all the tribes of the earth will ✝mourn, and they will see the SON OF MAN COMING ON THE CLOUDS OF THE SKY with power and *great*[26b] glory.

31 "And He will send forth His angels with A GREAT TRUMPET and THEY WILL GATHER TOGETHER His elect from the four winds, from one end of the sky to the other.

Parable of the Fig Tree

32 "Now learn˟ᴵ the parable from the fig tree: when its branch has already become tender, and puts˜ forth its leaves, you know[29a] that summer is *near;*

24:33
James 5:9; Rev.
3:20

33 even so you too, when you see˟ all these things, recognize˜ᴵ that He is near, *right* at the door.

24:34
Matt. 10:23;
16:28; 23:36

34 "•Truly I say to you, this generation will •*not* pass˟ away until all these things take place.

24:35
Matt. 5:18; Mark
13:31; Luke 21:33

35 "Heaven and earth will pass away, but My words[43a] shall •*not* pass˟ away.

24:36
Mark 13:32; Acts
1:7

36 "But of *that* day and hour no one knows, not even the angels of heaven, nor the Son, but the Father alone.

24:37
Matt. 16:27; 24:3,
30,39;
Gen. 6:5; 7:6-23;
Luke 17:26f.
24:38
Matt. 22:30;
Gen. 7:7

37 "For the coming of the Son of Man will be just like the days of Noah.

38 "For as in those days which were before the flood they were eating and drinking, they were marrying and giving in marriage, until the day that Noah entered the ark,

24:39
Matt. 16:27; 24:3,
30,37

39 and they did not understand until the flood came and took them all away; so shall the coming of the Son of Man be.

40 "Then there shall be two men in the field; one will be taken, and one will be left.

24:41
Luke 17:35;
Ex. 11:5; Deut.
24:6; Is. 47:2

41 "Two women *will be* grinding at the mill; one will be taken, and one will be left.

Be Ready for His Coming

42 "Therefore be on the alert, ⁀ˡ for you do not know which day your Lord is coming.

43 "But be sure⁀ˡ of this, that if the head of the house had known at what time of the night the thief was coming, he would have been on the alert and would not have allowed his house to be brokenˣ into.

44 "For this reason *you* be ready⁀ˡ *too;* for the Son of Man is coming at an hour when you do not think *He will.*

45 "Who then is the faithful and sensible³⁵ᵇ slave³⁸ᵇ whom his master put in charge of his household to giveˣ them their food at the proper time?

46 "†Blessed is *that* slave³⁸ᵇ whom his master finds so doing when he comes.

47 "•Truly I say to you, that he will put him in charge of *all his possessions.*

48 "But if that evil¹⁰ᵃ slave saysˣ in his heart, 'My master is not coming for a *long time,'*

49 and shall beginˣ to beat~ his fellow slaves and eat~ and drink~ with drunkards;

50 the master of that slave will come on a day when he does not expect *him* and at an hour which he does not know,

51 and shall cut him in pieces and assign him a place with the *hypocrites;* weeping shall be there and the gnashing of teeth.

Parable of Ten Virgins

25 "Then the kingdom of heaven will be comparable to ten virgins, who took their lamps, and went out to meet the bridegroom.

2 "And five of them were foolish,²⁰ᶜ and five were prudent.³⁵ᵇ

3 "For when the foolish took their lamps, they took no *oil* with them,

4 but the prudent took oil in flasks along with their lamps.

5 "Now while the bridegroom was delaying, they all got drowsy and *began* to sleep.

6 "But at midnight there was a shout, 'Behold, the bridegroom! Come out to meet *him.'*

7 "Then all those virgins rose, and trimmed their lamps.

8 "And the foolish said to the prudent, 'Giveˣˡ us some of your oil, for our lamps are going out.'

9 "But the prudent answered, saying, 'No, there will •*not* beˣ enough for us and you *too;* go instead to the dealers and buyˣˡ *some* for yourselves.'

24:42
Matt. 24:43,44; 25:10,13; Luke 12:39f.; 21:36

24:43
Matt. 24:42,44; 25:10,13; Luke 12:39f.; 21:36; Matt. 14:25; Mark 6:48; 13:35; Luke 12:38

24:44
Matt. 24:42,43; 25:10,13; Luke 12:39f.; 21:36; Matt. 24:27

24:45
Matt. 24:45-51; *Luke 12:42-46;* Matt. 25:21,23; Luke 16:10; Matt. 7:24; 10:16; 25:2ff.; Matt. 25:21,23

24:47
Matt. 25:21,23

24:51
Matt. 8:12

25:1
Matt. 13:24; John 18:3; Acts 20:8; Rev. 4:5; 8:10

25:2
Matt. 7:24; 10:16; 25:2ff.

25:4
Matt. 7:24; 10:16; 25:2ff.

25:9
Matt. 7:24; 10:16; 25:2ff.

25:10
Matt. 24:42ff.;
Luke 12:35f.;
Matt. 7:21ff.; Luke
13:25
10 "And while they were going away to make[x] the purchase, the bridegroom *came,* and those who were ready went in with him to the wedding feast; and the door was shut.

25:11
Matt. 7:21ff.; Luke
13:25
11 "And later the other virgins also came, saying, 'Lord, lord, open[xi] up for us.'

12 "But he answered and said, '•Truly I say to you, I do not know you.'

25:13
Matt. 24:42ff.
13 "Be on the alert[m] then, for you do not know the day nor the hour.

Parable of the Talents

25:14
Matt. 25:14-30;
Luke 19:12-27;
Matt. 21:33
14 "For *it is* just like a man *about* to go on a journey, who called his own slaves, and entrusted his possessions to them.

25:15
Matt. 18:24; Luke
19:13;
Matt. 21:33
15 "And to one he gave *five* talents, to another, +*two,* and to another, +*one,* each according to his own ability; and he went on his journey.

25:16
Matt. 18:24; Luke
19:13
16 "Immediately the one who had received the five talents went and traded with them, and gained five more talents.

17 "In the same manner the one who *had received* the two *talents* gained two more.

18 "But he who received the one *talent* went away and dug in the ground, and hid his master's money.

25:19
Matt. 18:23
19 "Now after a long time the master of those slaves *came and *settled accounts with them.

25:20
Matt. 18:24; Luke
19:13
20 "And the one who had received the five talents came up and brought *five* more talents, saying, 'Master, you entrusted five talents to me; see, I have gained *five more talents.'*

25:21
Matt. 24:45,47;
25:23;
Luke 12:44;
22:29; Rev. 3:21;
21:7
21 "His master said to him, 'Well done, good[25a] and faithful slave;[38b] you were faithful with a *few things,* I will put you in charge of *many things,* enter[xi] into the joy of your master.'

25:22
Matt. 18:24; Luke
19:13
22 "The one also who *had received* the two talents came up and said, 'Master, you entrusted to me two talents; see, I have gained *two more talents.'*

25:23
Matt. 24:45,47;
25:21
23 "His master said to him, 'Well done, good[25a] and faithful slave;[38b] you were faithful with a *few things,* I will put you in charge of *many things;* enter[xi] into the joy of your master.'

25:24
Matt. 18:24; Luke
19:13
24 "And the one also who had received• the one talent came up and said, 'Master, I knew you to be a *hard* man, reaping where you did not sow, and gathering where you scattered no *seed.*

25 'And I was afraid, and went away and hid your talent in the ground; see, you have what is yours.'

26 "But his master answered and said to him, 'You wicked,

lazy slave, you knew that I reap where I did not sow, and gather where I scattered no *seed*.

27 'Then you ought^m to have put^x my money in the bank, and on my arrival *I* would have received my *money* back with interest.

28 'Therefore take^{xi} away the talent from him, and give^{xi} it to the one who has the ten talents.'

29 "For to everyone who has shall *more* be given, and he shall have an abundance; but from the one who does not have, even what he does have shall be taken away.

25:29
Matt. 13:12; Mark 4:25; Luke 8:18; John 15:2

30 "And cast^{xi} out the *worthless slave* into the outer darkness; in that place there shall be weeping and gnashing of teeth.

25:30
Matt. 8:12; 22:13; Luke 13:28

The Judgment

31 "But when the Son of Man comes in His glory, and all the angels with Him, then He will sit on His glorious throne.

25:31
Matt. 16:27f.; 1 Thess. 4:16; 2 Thess. 1:7; Heb. 9:28; Jude 14; Rev. 1:7; Matt. 19:28

32 "And all the nations will be gathered before Him; and He will separate them from one another, as the shepherd separates the sheep from the goats;

25:32
Matt. 13:49; 2 Cor. 5:10; Ezek. 34:17,20

33   and He will put the sheep on His right, and the goats on the left.

25:33
1 Kin. 2:19; Ps. 45:9; Eccl. 10:2

34 "Then the King will say to those on His right, 'Come, you who are blessed⁺ of My Father, inherit^{xi} the kingdom prepared⁺ for you from the foundation of the world.

25:34
Matt. 5:3; 19:29; Luke 12:32; 1 Cor. 6:9; 15:50; Gal. 5:21; James 2:5; Matt. 13:35; Luke 11:50; John 17:24; Eph. 1:4; Heb. 4:3; 9:26; 1 Pet. 1:20; Rev. 13:8; 17:8

35 'For I was †hungry, and you gave Me *something* to eat;^x I was thirsty, and you gave Me drink; I was a stranger, and you invited Me in;

25:35
Is. 58:7; Ezek. 18:7,16; James 2:15,16; Job 31:32; Heb. 13:2

36 †naked, and you clothed Me; I was †sick, and you visited Me; I was in prison, and you came to Me.'

25:36
Is. 58:7; Ezek. 18:7,16; James 2:15,16; James 1:27; 2 Tim. 1:16f.

37 "Then the righteous will answer Him, saying, 'Lord, when did we see *You* hungry, and feed You, or thirsty, and give You drink?

38 'And when did we see *You* a stranger, and invite You in, or naked, and clothe You?

39 'And when did we see *You* sick, or in prison, and come to You?'

40 "And the King will answer and say to them, '•Truly I say to you, to the extent that you did it to one of these brothers of Mine, *even* the *least of them*, you did it to Me.'

25:40
Matt. 25:34; Luke 19:38; Rev. 17:14; 19:16; Prov. 19:17; Matt. 10:42; Heb. 6:10

41 "Then He will also say to those on His left, 'Depart from Me, accursed⁺ ones, into the †eternal fire which has been prepared⁺ for the devil and his angels;

25:41
Matt. 7:23; Mark 9:48; Luke 16:24; Jude 7; Matt. 4:10; Rev. 12:9

42   for I was hungry, and you gave Me *nothing* to eat;^x I was thirsty, and you gave Me nothing to drink;

43   I was a stranger, and you did not invite Me in; naked, and

you did not clothe Me; sick, and in prison, and you did not visit Me.'

44 "Then *they themselves also* will answer, saying, 'Lord, when did we see *You* hungry, or thirsty, or a stranger, or naked, or sick, or in prison, and did not take care of You?'

45 "Then He will answer them, saying, '•Truly I say to you, to the extent that you did not do it to one of the *least* of these, you did not do it to *Me.*'

46 "And these will go away into eternal punishment, but the righteous into eternal life."

The Plot to Kill Jesus

26 And it came about that when Jesus had finished all these words, He said to His disciples,

2 "You know that after two days the Passover is coming, and the Son of Man is *to be* delivered up for crucifixion."ˣ

3 Then the chief priests and the elders of the people were gathered together in the court of the high priest, named Caiaphas;

4 and they plotted together to seizeˣ Jesus by *stealth,* and killˣ *Him.*

5 But they were saying,ᵐ "Not during the festival, lest a riot occur among the people."

The Precious Ointment

6 Now when Jesus was in Bethany, at the home of Simon the leper,

7 a woman came to Him with an alabaster vial of *very costly* perfume, and she poured it upon His head as He reclined *at the table.*

8 But the disciples were indignant when they saw *this,* and said, "Why this waste?

9 "For this *perfume* might haveᵐ been soldˣ for a high price and *the money* givenˣ to the poor."

10 But Jesus, aware of this, said to them, "Why do you bother the woman? For she has done a *good*²⁵ᵇ deed to Me.

11 "For the poor you have with you always; but you do not always have *Me.*

12 "For when she poured this perfume upon My body, she did it to prepare Me for *burial.*ˣ

13 "•Truly I say to you, wherever this gospel is preachedˣ in the whole world, what *this woman* has done shall also be spoken of in memory of her."

25:46
Dan. 12:2; John
5:29; Acts 24:15;
Matt. 19:29; John
3:15f.,36; 5:24;
6:27,40,47,54;
17:2f.; Acts
13:46,48; Rom.
2:7; 5:21; 6:23;
Gal. 6:8; 1 John
5:11
26:1
Matt. 7:28
26:2
Matt. 26:2-5;
Mark 14:1,2; Luke
22:1,2;
John 11:55; 13:1;
Matt. 10:4
26:3
John 11:47;
Matt. 26:58,69;
27:27; Mark
14:54,66; 15:16;
Luke 22:55; John
18:15;
Matt. 26:57; Luke
3:2; John 11:49;
18:13,14,24,28;
Acts 4:6
26:4
Matt. 12:14
26:5
Matt. 27:24
26:6
Matt. 26:6-13;
Mark 14:3-9;
Luke 7:37-39;
John 12:1-8;
Matt. 21:17
26:7
Luke 7:37f.
26:11
Deut. 15:11; Mark
14:7; John 12:8
26:12
John 19:40
26:13
Mark 14:9

Judas' Bargain

14 Then one of the twelve, named Judas Iscariot, went to the chief priests,

15 and said, "What are you willing to give[x] me to deliver Him up to you?" And they weighed out to him thirty pieces of silver.

16 And from then on he *began* looking for a good opportunity to betray[x] Him.

17 Now on the first *day* of Unleavened Bread the disciples came to Jesus, saying, "Where do You want us to prepare[x] for You to eat[x] the Passover?"

18 And He said, "Go into the city to a certain man, and say[xi] to him, 'The Teacher says, "My time is at [†]hand; I *am to* keep the Passover at *your house* with My disciples." ' "

19 And the disciples did as Jesus had directed them; and they prepared the Passover.

The Last Passover

20 Now when evening had come, He was reclining *at the table* with the twelve disciples.

21 And as they were eating, He said, "•Truly I say to you that one of you will betray Me."

22 And being deeply grieved, they each one began to say[~] to Him, "Surely not *I*, Lord?"

23 And He answered and said, "He who dipped his hand with Me in the bowl is the one who will betray Me.

24 "The Son of Man *is to* go, just as it is written[+] of Him; but woe to *that* man by whom the Son of Man is betrayed! It would have been good for *that* man if he had *not been born.*"

25 And Judas, who was betraying Him, answered and said, "Surely it is not [†]*I*, Rabbi?" He *said to him, "*You* have said *it* yourself.*"

The Lord's Supper Instituted

26 And while they were eating, Jesus took *some* bread, and after a blessing, He broke *it* and gave *it* to the disciples, and said, "Take,[xi] eat;[xi] this is My body."

27 And when He had taken a cup and given thanks, He gave *it* to them, saying, "Drink[xi] from it, all of you;

28 for this is My blood of the covenant, which is poured out for many for forgiveness of sins.

29 "But I say to you, I will •not drink[x] of this fruit of the vine from now on until that day when I drink it new[34a] with you in My Father's kingdom."

26:14
Matt. 26:14-16;
Mark 14:10,11;
Luke 22:3-6;
Matt. 10:4; 26:25,
47; 27:3; John
6:71; 12:4; 13:26;
Acts 1:16
26:15
Matt. 10:4;
Ex. 21:32; Zech.
11:12
26:17
Matt. 26:17-19;
Mark 14:12-16;
Luke 22:7-13;
Ex. 12:18-20
26:18
Mark 14:13; Luke
22:10;
John 7:6,8
26:20
Matt. 26:20-24;
Mark 14:17-21
26:21
Luke 22:21-23;
John 13:21f.
26:23
Ps. 41:9; John
13:18,26
26:24
Matt. 26:31,54,
56; Mark 9:12;
Luke 24:25-27,
46; Acts 17:2f.;
26:22f.; 1 Cor.
15:3; 1 Pet.
1:10f.;
Matt. 18:7; Mark
14:21
26:25
Matt. 26:14;
Matt. 23:7; 26:49;
Matt. 26:64;
27:11; Luke 22:70
26:26
Matt. 26:26-29;
Mark 14:22-25;
Luke 22:17-20;
1 Cor. 11:23-25;
1 Cor. 10:16;
Matt. 14:19
26:28
Ex. 24:8; Heb.
9:20;
Matt. 20:28

26:30
Matt. 26:30-35;
Mark 14:26-31;
Luke 22:31-34;
Matt. 21:1
26:31
Matt. 11:6;
Zech. 13:7;
John 16:32

26:32
Matt. 28:7,10,16;
Mark 16:7

26:34
Matt. 26:75; John
13:38;
Mark 14:30
26:35
John 13:37

30 And after singing a hymn, they went out to the Mount of Olives.

31 Then Jesus *said to them, "*You* will all fall away because of Me this night, for it is written,⁺ 'I WILL STRIKE DOWN THE SHEP-HERD, AND THE SHEEP OF THE FLOCK SHALL BE SCATTERED.'

32 "But after I have been raised,ˣ I will go before you to Galilee."

33 But Peter answered and said to Him, "*Even* though all may fall away because of You, *I* will †never fall away."

34 Jesus said to him, "•Truly I say to you that this *very* night, before a cock crows,ˣ you shall deny Me three times."

35 Peter *said to Him, "Even if I have~ to *die*ˣ with You, I will •*not* deny You." All the disciples said the same thing too.

The Garden of Gethsemane

26:36
Matt. 26:36-46;
Mark 14:32-42;
Luke 22:40-46;
Mark 14:32; Luke
22:39; John 18:1
26:37
Matt. 4:21; 17:1;
Mark 5:37

26:38
John 12:27;
Matt. 26:40,41

26:39
Matt. 20:22;
Matt. 26:42; Mark
14:36; Luke
22:42; John 6:38

26:40
Matt. 26:38

26:41
Matt. 26:38;
Mark 14:38

26:42
Matt. 20:22;
Matt. 26:39; Mark
14:36; Luke
22:42; John 6:38

26:45
Mark 14:41; John
12:27; 13:1

36 Then Jesus *came with them to a place called Gethsemane, and *said to His disciples, "Sitˣˡ here while I go over there and pray."ˣ

37 And He took with Him Peter and the two sons of Zebedee, and began to be grieved~ and distressed. ~

38 Then He *said to them, "My soul is *deeply*¹ grieved, to the point of death; remainˣˡ here and keep watch⌣ with Me."

39 And He went a little beyond *them,* and fell on His face and prayed, saying, "My Father, if it is possible, let this cup passˣˡ from Me; yet not as *I* will, but as †*Thou* wilt."

40 And He *came to the disciples and *found them sleeping, and *said to Peter, "So, you *men* could not keep watchˣ with Me for *one* hour?

41 "Keep watching⌣ and praying,⌣ that you may not enterˣ into temptation; the spirit is willing, but the flesh is weak."

42 He went away again a second time and prayed, saying, "My Father, if this cannot passˣ away unless I drinkˣ it, Thy will be done."ˣˡ

43 And again He came and found them sleeping, for *their* eyes were heavy.⁺

44 And He left them again, and went away and prayed a third time, saying the same thing once more.

45 Then He *came to the disciples, and *said to them, "Are you still sleeping⌣ and taking⌣ your rest? Behold, the hour is at hand⁺ and the Son of Man is being betrayed into the hands of sinners.

46 "Arise, let us be going;~ behold, the one who betrays Me is at hand!"⁺

Jesus' Betrayal and Arrest

47   And while He was still speaking, behold, Judas, one of the twelve, came up, accompanied by a great multitude with swords and clubs, from the chief priests and elders of the people.

48   Now he who was betraying Him gave them a sign, saying, "Whomever I shall kiss,ˣ *He* is the one; seizeˣⁱ Him."

49   And immediately he went to Jesus and said, "Hail, Rabbi!" and kissedⁱ Him.

50   And Jesus said to him, "Friend, *do* what you have come for." Then they came and laid hands on Jesus and seized Him.

51   And behold, one of those who were with Jesus reached and drew out his sword, and struck the slave of the high priest, and cut off his ear.

52   Then Jesus *said to him, "Putˣⁱ your sword back into its place; for all those who take up the sword shall perish *by the sword*.

53   "Or do you think that I cannot appealˣ to My Father, and He will at once put at My disposal more than *twelve* ⁱlegions of angels?

54   "How then shall the Scriptures be fulfilled,ˣ that it must happen this way?"

55   At that time Jesus said to the multitudes, "Have you come out with swords and clubs to arrestˣ Me as against a *robber?* Every day I used to sitᵐ in the temple teaching and you did not seize Me.

56   "But all this has taken place that the Scriptures of the prophets may be fulfilled."ˣ Then *all* the disciples left Him and fled.

Jesus before Caiaphas

57   And those who had seized Jesus led Him away to Caiaphas, the high priest, where the scribes and the elders were gathered together.

58   But Peter also was followingᵐ Him at a distance as far as the courtyard of the high priest, and entered in, and sat down with the officers to seeˣ the outcome.

59   Now the chief priests and the *whole* Council kept trying to obtainᵐ false testimony against Jesus, in order that they might putˣ Him to death;

60   and they did not find *any*, even though many false witnesses came forward. But later on two came forward,

61   and said, "This man stated,ᵐ 'I am able to destroyˣ the temple of God and to rebuildˣ it in *three days*.'"

ⁱA legion equaled 6,000 troops

26:47
Matt. 26:47-56;
Mark 14:43-50;
Luke 22:47-53;
John 18:3-11;
Matt. 26:14

26:49
Matt. 23:7; 26:25

26:50
Matt. 20:13;
22:12

26:51
Mark 14:47; Luke
22:50; John
18:10;
Luke 22:38

26:52
Gen. 9:6; Rev.
13:10

26:53
Mark 5:9,15; Luke
8:30;
Matt. 4:11

26:54
Matt. 26:24

26:55
Mark 12:35;
14:49; Luke 4:20;
19:47; 20:1;
21:37; John 7:14,
28; 8:2,20; 18:20

26:56
Matt. 26:24

26:57
Matt. 26:57-68;
Mark 14:53-65;
John 18:12f.,
19-24;
Matt. 26:3
26:58
John 18:15;
Matt. 26:3;
Matt. 5:25; John
7:32,45f.; 19:6;
Acts 5:22,26
26:59
Matt. 5:22

26:60
Deut. 19:15

26:61
Matt. 27:40; Mark
14:58; 15:29;
John 2:19; Acts
6:14

62   And the high priest stood up and said to Him, "Do You make no answer? What is it that these men are testifying against You?"

26:63
Matt. 27:12,14;
John 19:9;
Matt. 26:63-66;
Luke 22:67-71;
Lev. 5:1;
Matt. 16:16;
Matt. 4:3
26:64
Matt. 26:25;
Ps. 110:1; Mark 14:62;
Dan. 7:13; Matt. 16:27f.
26:65
Num. 14:6; Mark 14:63; Acts 14:14

63   But Jesus kept silent.ᵐ And the high priest said to Him, "I adjure You by the living God, that You tellˣ us whether *You* are the Christ, the Son of God."

64   Jesus *said to him, "*You* have said it *yourself*; nevertheless I tell you, hereafter you shall see THE SON OF MAN SITTING AT THE RIGHT HAND OF POWER,³²ᵃ and COMING ON THE CLOUDS OF HEAVEN."

65   Then the high priest tore his robes, saying, "He has blasphemed! What further need do we have of witnesses? Behold, you have now heard the blasphemy;

26:66
Lev. 24:16; John 19:7

66   what do you think?" They answered and said, "He is *deserving of* ⁺*death!*"

26:67
Is. 50:6; Matt. 26:67,68; Luke 22:63-65; John 18:22;
Matt. 27:30; Mark 10:34
26:68
Mark 14:65; Luke 22:64

67   Then they spat in His face and beat Him with their fists; and others slapped Him,

68   and said, "Prophesyˣᵗ to us, You Christ; who is the one who hit You?"

Peter's Denials

26:69
Matt. 26:69-75;
Mark 14:66-72;
Luke 22:55-62;
John 18:16-18, 25-27;
Matt. 26:3

69   Now Peter was sitting outside in the courtyard, and a certain servant-girl came to him and said, "*You too* were with Jesus the Galilean."

70   But he denied *it* before them all, saying, "I do not know what you are talking about."

71   And when he had gone out to the gateway, another *servant-girl* saw him and *said to those who were there, "This man was with Jesus of Nazareth."

72   And again he denied *it* with an oath, "I do not know the man."

26:73
Mark 14:70; Luke 22:59; John 18:26

73   And a little later the bystanders came up and said to Peter, "Surely *you too* are *one* of them; for the way you talk *gives you away*."

74   Then he began to curse˜ and swear,˜ "I do not know the man!" And immediately a cock crowed.

26:75
Matt. 26:34

75   And Peter remembered the word which Jesus had said, ⁺ "Before a cock crows,ˣ you will deny Me three times." And he went out and wept *bitterly*.

Judas' Remorse

27:1
Mark 15:1; Luke 22:66; John 18:28

27   Now when morning had come, all the chief priests and the elders of the people took counsel against Jesus to putˣ Him to death;

2   and they bound Him, and led Him away, and delivered Him up to Pilate the governor.

3   Then when Judas, who had betrayed Him, saw that He had been condemned,[14c] he felt remorse and returned the thirty pieces of silver to the chief priests and elders,

4   saying, "I have sinned by betraying *innocent* blood." But they said, "What is that to ⁺us? See *to that yourself!*"

5   And he threw the pieces of silver into the sanctuary and departed; and he went away and hanged himself.

6   And the chief priests took the pieces of silver and said, "It is not lawful to put[x] them into the temple treasury, since it is the price of blood."

7   And they counseled together and with the money bought the Potter's Field as a burial place for strangers.

8   For this reason that field has been called the Field of Blood to this day.

9   Then that which was spoken through Jeremiah the prophet was fulfilled, saying, "AND THEY TOOK THE THIRTY PIECES OF SILVER, THE PRICE[4] OF THE ONE WHOSE PRICE HAD BEEN SET⁺ by the sons of Israel;

10   AND THEY GAVE THEM FOR THE POTTER'S FIELD, AS THE LORD DIRECTED ME."

Jesus before Pilate

11   Now Jesus stood before the governor, and the governor questioned Him, saying, "Are *You* the King of the Jews?" And Jesus said to him, "*It is as* you say."

12   And while He was being accused~ by the chief priests and elders, He made no answer.

13   Then Pilate *said to Him, "Do You not hear how many things they testify against You?"

14   And He did not answer him with regard to even a *single* charge, so that the governor was *quite* amazed. ~

15   Now at *the* feast the governor was accustomed to release~ for the multitude *any* one prisoner whom they wanted.ᵐ

16   And they were holdingᵐ at that time a notorious prisoner, called Barabbas.

17   When therefore they were gathered⁺ together, Pilate said to them, "Whom do you want me to release[x] for you? Barabbas, or Jesus who is called Christ?"

18   For he knew that because of *envy* they had delivered Him up.

19   And while he was sitting on the judgment seat, his wife sent to him, saying, "Have nothing to do with that righteous

27:2
Matt. 20:19;
Luke 3:1; 13:1;
23:12; Acts 3:13;
4:27; 1 Tim. 6:13
27:3
Matt. 26:14;
Matt. 26:15

27:4
Matt. 27:24

27:5
Matt. 26:61; Luke
1:9,21;
Acts 1:18

27:8
Acts 1:19

27:9
Zech. 11:12

27:10
Zech. 11:13

27:11
Matt. 27:11-14;
Mark 15:2-5;
Luke 23:2,3; John
18:29-38;
Matt. 2:2;
Matt. 26:25
27:12
Matt. 26:63; John
19:9

27:14
Matt. 27:12; Mark
15:5; Luke 23:9;
John 19:9
27:15
Matt. 27:15-26;
Mark 15:6-15;
Luke 23:[17]-25;
John 18:39-19:16

27:17
Matt. 1:16; 27:22

27:19
John 19:13; Acts
12:21; 18:12,16f.;
25:6,10,17;
Matt. 27:24;
Gen. 20:6; 31:11;
Num. 12:6; Job
33:15; Matt.
1:20; 2:12f.,19,
22

Man; for last night I suffered *greatly* in a dream because of Him."

27:20
Acts 3:14

20   But the chief priests and the elders persuaded the multitudes to ask[x] for Barabbas, and to put[x] *Jesus* to death.

21   But the governor answered and said to them, "Which of the two do you want me to release[x] for you?" And they said, "Barabbas."

27:22
Matt. 1:16

22   Pilate *said to them, "Then what shall I do[x] with Jesus who is called Christ?" They all *said, "Let Him be crucified!"[xl]

23   And he said,[m] "Why, what evil[10a] has He done?" But they kept shouting[m] all the more, saying, "Let Him be crucified!"[xl]

27:24
Matt. 26:5;
Deut. 21:6-8;
Matt. 27:19;
Matt. 27:4

24   And when Pilate saw that he was accomplishing nothing, but rather that a riot was starting, he took water and washed his hands in front of the multitude, saying, "I am †innocent of this Man's blood; see *to that yourselves.*"

27:25
Josh. 2:19; Acts
5:28

25   And all the people answered and said, "His blood *be* on us and on our children!"

27:26
Mark 15:15; Luke
23:16; John 19:1

26   Then he released Barabbas for them; but after having Jesus scourged, he delivered Him to be crucified.[x]

Jesus Is Mocked

27:27
Matt. 27:27-31;
Mark 15:16-20;
Matt. 26:3; John
18:28,33; 19:9;
Acts 10:1
27:28
Mark 15:17; John
19:2
27:29
Mark 15:17; John
19:2;
Mark 15:18; John
19:3
27:30
Matt. 26:67; Mark
10:34; 14:65;
15:19
27:31
Mark 15:20
27:32
Matt. 27:32: *Mark
15:21; Luke
23:26;* John
19:17;
Acts 2:10; 6:9;
11:20; 13:1

27   Then the soldiers of the governor took Jesus into the Praetorium and gathered the whole *Roman* cohort around Him.

28   And they stripped Him, and put a *scarlet* robe on Him.

29   And after weaving a crown of thorns, they put it on His head, and a reed in His right hand; and they kneeled down before Him and mocked Him, saying, "Hail, King of the Jews!"

30   And they spat on Him, and took the reed and *began* to beat[m] Him on the head.

31   And after they had mocked Him, they took His robe off and put His garments on Him, and led Him away to crucify[x] *Him*.

32   And as they were coming out, they found a man of Cyrene named Simon, whom they pressed into service to bear[x] His cross.

The Crucifixion

27:33
Matt. 27:34-44;
*Mark 15:22-32;
Luke 23:33-43;
John 19:17-24;*
Luke 23:33; John
19:17
27:34
Ps. 69:21;
Mark 15:23
27:35
Ps. 22:18
27:36
Matt. 27:54

33   And when they had come to a place called Golgotha, which means Place of a Skull,

34   they gave Him wine to drink[x] mingled† with gall; and after tasting *it*, He was unwilling to drink.[x]

35   And when they had crucified Him, they divided up His garments among themselves, casting lots;

36   and sitting down, they *began* to keep watch[m] over Him there.

27:37
Mark 15:26; Luke
23:38; John 19:19

37   And they put up above His head the charge against Him which read,† "THIS IS JESUS THE KING OF THE JEWS."

38   At that time two robbers *were crucified with Him, one on the right and one on the left.

39   And those passing by were hurling [m] abuse at Him, wagging their heads,

40   and saying, "You who *are going to* destroy the temple and rebuild it in *three*days, save[xl] Yourself! If You are the *Son* of God, come[xl] down from the cross."

41   In the same way the chief priests also, along with the scribes and elders, were mocking *Him,* and saying,[m]

42   "He saved *others;* He cannot save[x] *Himself.* He is the King of Israel; let Him now come[xl] down from the cross, and we shall believe in Him.

43   "HE TRUSTS [*] IN GOD; LET HIM DELIVER[xl] [18b] *Him* now, IF HE TAKES PLEASURE IN HIM; for He said, 'I am the Son of *God.'*"

44   And the robbers also who had been crucified with Him were casting[m] the same insult at Him.

45   Now from the [u]sixth hour darkness fell upon all the land until the [v] *ninth*hour.

46   And about the ninth hour Jesus cried out with a loud voice, saying, "ELI, ELI, LAMA SABACHTHANI?" that is, "MY GOD, MY GOD, WHY HAST THOU FORSAKEN ME?"

47   And some of those who were standing there, when they heard it, *began* saying,[m] "This man is calling for *Elijah.*"

48   And immediately one of them ran, and taking a sponge, he filled it with sour wine, and put it on a reed, and gave[m] Him a drink.

49   But the rest *of them* said,[m] "Let us see[x] whether Elijah will come to save Him."[w]

50   And Jesus cried out again with a loud voice, and yielded up *His* spirit.

51   And behold, the veil of the temple was torn in two from top to bottom, and the earth shook; and the rocks were split,

52   and the tombs were opened; and many bodies of the saints who had fallen[*] asleep were raised;

53   and coming out of the tombs after His resurrection they entered the holy city and appeared to many.

54   Now the centurion, and those who were with him keeping guard over Jesus, when they saw the earthquake and the things that were happening, became very frightened and said, "Truly this was the Son of *God!*"

55   And many women were there looking on from a distance, who had followed Jesus from Galilee, ministering to Him,

[u]i.e., noon   [v]i.e., 3 p.m.   [w]Some early mss. add: *And another took a spear and pierced His side, and there came out water and blood.* (cf. John 19:34)

27:39
Job 16:4; Ps. 22:7; 109:25; Lam. 2:15; Mark 15:29
27:40
Matt. 26:61; John 2:19; Matt. 27:42

27:42
Mark 15:31; Luke 23:35; Matt. 27:37; Luke 23:37; John 1:49; 12:13
27:43
Ps. 22:8

27:44
Luke 23:39-43

27:45
Matt. 27:45-56: *Mark 15:33-41;* Luke 23:44-49
27:46
Ps. 22:1

27:48
Ps. 69:21; Mark 15:36; Luke 23:36; John 19:29

27:50
Mark 15:37; Luke 23:46; John 19:30

27:51
Matt. 27:51-56: *Mark 15:38-41;* Luke 23:47-49; Ex. 26:31ff.; Mark 15:38; Luke 23:45; Heb. 9:3; Matt. 27:54
27:52
Acts 7:60
27:53
Matt. 4:5
27:54
Mark 15:39; Luke 23:47; Matt. 27:36; Matt. 27:51; Matt. 4:3; 27:43

27:55
Mark 15:40f.; Luke 23:49; John 19:25; Mark 15:41; Luke 8:2,3

27:56
Matt. 28:1; Mark
15:40,47; 16:9;
Luke 8:2; John
19:25; 20:1,18;
Matt. 20:20

56 among whom was Mary Magdalene, *along with* Mary the mother of James and Joseph, and the mother of the sons of Zebedee.

Jesus Is Buried

27:57
Matt. 27:57-61;
Mark 15:42-47;
Luke 23:50-56;
John 19:38-42

57 And when it was evening, there came a rich man from Arimathea, named Joseph, who himself had also become a disciple of Jesus.

58 This man went to Pilate and asked for the body of Jesus. Then Pilate ordered *it* to be given[x] over *to him.*

59 And Joseph took the body and wrapped it in a clean linen cloth,

27:60
Matt. 27:66; 28:2;
Mark 16:4

60 and laid it in his own new tomb, which he had hewn out in the rock; and he rolled a large stone against the entrance of the tomb and went away.

27:61
Matt. 27:56; 28:1

61 And Mary Magdalene was there, and the other Mary, sitting opposite the grave.

27:62
Mark 15:42; Luke
23:54; John
19:14,31,42

62 Now on the next day, which is *the one* after the preparation, the chief priests and the Pharisees gathered together with Pilate,

27:63
Matt. 16:21;
17:23; 20:19;
Mark 8:31; 9:31;
10:34; Luke 9:22;
18:31-33

63 and said, "Sir, we remember that when He was still alive that deceiver said, '*After three days* I *am* to rise again.'

64 "Therefore, give[xi] orders for the grave to be made[x] secure until the third day, lest the disciples come and steal[x] Him away and say[x] to the people, 'He has risen from the dead,' and the last deception will be worse than the first."

27:65
Matt. 27:66;
28:11

65 Pilate said to them, "You have a guard; go, make[xi] it *as* secure as you know how."

27:66
Matt. 27:65;
28:11;
Dan. 6:17;
Matt. 27:60; 28:2;
Mark 16:4

66 And they went and made the grave secure, and along with the guard they set a seal on the stone.

Jesus Is Risen!

28:1
Matt. 28:1-8;
Mark 16:1-8;
Luke 24:1-10;
John 20:1-8;
Matt. 27:56,61

28 Now after the Sabbath, as it began to dawn toward the first *day* of the week, Mary Magdalene and the other Mary came to look[x] at the grave.

28:2
Luke 24:4; John
20:12;
Matt. 27:66; Mark
16:4

2 And behold, a *severe* earthquake had occurred, for an angel of the Lord descended from heaven and came and rolled away the stone and sat upon it.

28:3
Dan. 7:9; 10:6;
Mark 9:3; John
20:12; Acts 1:10

3 And his appearance was like lightning, and his garment as white as snow;

4 and the guards *shook for fear* of him, and became like dead men.

28:5
Matt. 14:27;
28:10; Rev. 1:17

5 And the angel answered and said to the women, "Do not

be afraid;° for I know that you are looking for Jesus who has been crucified. ⁺

6 "He is not here, for He has risen, just as He said. Come, see*ˡ the place where He was lying.

7 "And go quickly and tell*ˡ His disciples that He has risen from the dead; and behold, He is going before you into Galilee, *there* you will see Him; behold, I have told you."

8 And they departed quickly from the tomb with fear and great joy and ran to report* it to His disciples.

9 And behold, Jesus met them and greeted them. And they came up and took hold of His feet and worshiped Him.

10 Then Jesus *said to them, "Do not be afraid;° go and take*ˡ word to My brethren to leave* for Galilee, and *there* they shall see Me."

11 Now while they were on their way, behold, some of the guard came into the city and reported to the chief priests all that had happened.

12 And when they had assembled with the elders and counseled together, they gave a *large sum of money* to the soldiers,

13 and said, "You are to say,*ˡ 'His disciples came by night and stole Him away while we were *asleep.'*

14 "And if *this* should come* to the governor's ears, *we* will win him over and keep you out of trouble."

15 And they took the money and did as they had been instructed; and this story was widely spread among the Jews, *and is* to this day.

The Great Commission

16 But the eleven disciples proceeded to Galilee, to the mountain which Jesus had designated.

17 And when they saw Him, they worshiped *Him*; but some were doubtful.

18 And Jesus came up and spoke to them, saying, "*All authority* has been given to Me in heaven and on earth.

19 "Go therefore and make disciples*ˡ of all the nations, baptizing them in the name of the Father and the Son and the Holy Spirit,

20 teaching them to observe～ all that I commanded you; and lo, *I* am *with you* always, even to the end¹ of the age."

28:6
Matt. 12:40;
16:21; 27:63

28:7
Matt. 26:32;
28:10,16; Mark
16:7

28:10
Matt. 14:27; 28:5;
John 20:17; Rom.
8:29; Heb. 2:11f.,
17;
Matt. 26:32; 28:7,
16
28:11
Matt. 27:65,66

28:14
Matt. 27:2

28:15
Matt. 9:31; Mark
1:45;
Matt. 27:8
28:16
Matt. 26:32; 28:7,
10; Mark 15:41;
16:7
28:17
Mark 16:11
28:18
Dan. 7:13f.; Matt.
11:27; 26:64;
Rom. 14:9; Eph.
1:20-22; Phil.
2:9f.; Col. 2:10; 1
Pet. 3:22
28:19
Mark 16:15f.;
Matt. 13:52; Acts
1:8; 14:21;
Matt. 25:32; Luke
24:47;
Acts 2:38; 8:16;
Rom. 6:3; 1 Cor.
1:13,15ff.; Gal.
3:27
28:20
Matt. 18:20; Acts
18:10;
Matt. 13:39

The Gospel According to
Mark

Preaching of John the Baptist

1:1
Matt. 4:3
1:2
Mark 1:2-8: Matt.
3:1-11; Luke
3:2-16;
Mal. 3:1; Matt.
11:10; Luke 7:27
1:3
Is. 40:3; Matt. 3:3;
Luke 3:4; John
1:23

1 The beginning of the gospel of Jesus Christ, ^athe Son of God. 2 As it is written* in Isaiah the prophet,

"BEHOLD, I SEND MY MESSENGER BEFORE YOUR FACE,
WHO WILL PREPARE YOUR WAY;
3 THE VOICE OF ONE CRYING IN THE WILDERNESS,
'MAKE ^{xi} READY THE WAY OF THE LORD,
MAKE ^m HIS PATHS STRAIGHT.' "

1:4
Acts 13:24;
Luke 1:77

4 John the Baptist appeared in the wilderness ^bpreaching a baptism of repentance for the forgiveness of sins.

5 And all the country of Judea was going^m out to him, and all the people of Jerusalem; and they were being baptized^m by him in the Jordan River, confessing¹ their sins.

1:6
2 Kin. 1:8

6 And John was clothed* with camel's hair and *wore* a leather belt around his waist, and his diet was locusts and wild honey.

7 And he was preaching,^m and saying, "After me One is coming who is mightier than I, and I am not fit to stoop down and untie^x the thong of His sandals.

8 "*I* baptized you ^cwith water; but *He* will baptize you ^cwith the Holy Spirit."

The Baptism of Jesus

1:9
Mark 1:9-11:
Matt. 3:13-17;
Luke 3:21,22;
Matt. 2:23; Luke
2:51

9 And it came about in those days that Jesus came from Nazareth in Galilee, and was baptized by John in the Jordan.

10 And immediately coming up out of the water, He saw the heavens opening, and the Spirit like a dove descending upon Him;

1:11
Ps. 2:7; Is. 42:1;
Matt. 3:17; 12:18;
Mark 9:7; Luke
3:22
1:12
Mark 1:12,13:
Matt. 4:1-11;
Luke 4:1-13
1:13
Matt. 4:10

11 and a voice came out of the heavens: " *Thou* art My *beloved* Son, in *Thee* I am well-pleased."

12 And immediately the Spirit *impelled Him *to go* out into the wilderness.

13 And He was in the wilderness forty days being tempted by Satan; and He was with the wild beasts, and the angels were ministering ^m to Him.

^aMany mss. do not contain *the Son of God* ^bOr, *proclaiming* ^cThe Gr. here can be translated *in, with* or *by*

Jesus Preaches in Galilee

14   And after John had been taken[x] into custody, Jesus came into Galilee, preaching the gospel of God,

15   and saying, "The time is *fulfilled,*[+] and the kingdom of God is at hand;[+] repent and believe [~] in the gospel."

16   And as He was going along by the Sea of Galilee, He saw Simon and Andrew, the brother of Simon, casting a net in the sea; for they were fishermen.

17   And Jesus said to them, "Follow Me, and I will make you become fishers of men."

18   And they immediately left the nets and followed Him.

19   And going on a little farther, He saw James the *son* of Zebedee, and John his brother, who were also in the boat mending the nets.

20   And immediately He called them; and they left their father Zebedee in the boat with the hired servants, and went away to follow Him.

21   And they *went into Capernaum; and immediately on the Sabbath He entered the synagogue and *began* to teach.

22   And they were amazed[m1] at His teaching; for He was teaching[~] them as *one* having [†]authority, and not as the scribes.

23   And just then there was in their synagogue a man with an unclean spirit; and he cried out,

24   saying, "What do we have to do with You, Jesus [d]of Nazareth? Have You come to destroy[x] us? I know[29e] who You are—the Holy[28a] One of God!"

25   And Jesus rebuked him, saying, "Be quiet, [xl] and come[xl] out of him!"

26   And throwing him into convulsions, the unclean spirit cried out with a loud voice, and came out of him.

27   And they were all amazed, so that they debated[~] among themselves, saying, "What is this? A *new*[34a] teaching with authority! He commands even the *unclean spirits,* and they obey Him."

28   And *immediately* the news about Him went out everywhere into all the surrounding district of Galilee.

Multitudes Healed

29   And immediately after they had come out of the synagogue, they came into the house of Simon and Andrew, with James and John.

[d]Lit., *the Nazarene*

1:14
Matt. 4:12;
Matt. 4:23

1:15
Gal. 4:4; Eph.
1:10; 1 Tim. 2:6;
Titus 1:3;
Matt. 3:2; Acts
20:21
1:16
Mark 1:16-20:
Matt. 4:18-22;
Luke 5:2-11; John
1:40-42

1:21
Mark 1:21-28:
Luke 4:31-37;
Matt. 4:23; Mark
1:39; 10:1
1:22
Matt. 7:28

1:24
Matt. 8:29;
Matt. 2:23; Mark
10:47; 14:67;
16:6; Luke 4:34;
24:19; Acts 24:5;
Luke 1:35; 4:34;
John 6:69; Acts
3:14

1:27
Mark 10:24,32;
16:5,6

1:29
Mark 1:29-31:
Matt. 8:14,15;
Luke 4:38,39;
Mark 1:21,23

30   Now Simon's mother-in-law was lying sick with a fever; and immediately they *spoke to Him about her.

31   And He came to her and raised her up, taking her by the hand, and the fever left her, and she ᵉwaitedᵐ on them.

32   And when evening had come, after the sun had set, they *began* bringingᵐ to Him all who were ill and those who were demon-possessed.

33   And the whole city had gathered⁺ at the door.

34   And He healed many who were ill with various diseases, and cast out *many* demons; and He was not permittingᵐ the demons to speak,~ because they ᶠknew who He was.

35   And in the early morning, while it was still dark, He arose and went out and departed to a lonely place, and was prayingᵐ there.

36   And Simon and his companions hunted¹ for Him;

37   and they found Him, and *said to Him, "Everyone is looking for You."

38   And He *said to them, "Let us go~ somewhere else to the towns nearby, in order that I may preachˣ there also; for that is what I came out for."

39   And He went into their synagogues throughout all Galilee, preaching and casting out the demons.

40   And a leper *came to Him, beseeching Him and falling on his knees before Him, and saying to Him, "If You are willing,~ You can make me clean."ˣ

41   And moved with compassion, He stretched out His hand, and touched him, and *said to him, "I am willing; be cleansed."ˣˡ

42   And immediately the leprosy left him and he was cleansed.

43   And He sternly warned him and immediately sent him away,

44   and He *said to him, "See~ᴵ that you sayˣ nothing to anyone; but go, showˣˡ *yourself* to the priest and offerˣˡ for your cleansing what Moses commanded, for a testimony to them."

45   But he went out and began to proclaim~ it freely and to spread~ the news about, to such an extent that Jesus could~ no longer publicly enterˣ a city, but ᵍstayed out in unpopulated areas; and they were comingᵐ to Him from everywhere.

The Paralytic Healed

2   And when He had come back to Capernaum several days afterward, it was heard that He was at home.

2   And *many* were gathered together, so that there was no

Margin cross-references:

1:32
Mark 1:32-34;
Matt. 8:16,17;
Luke 4:40,41;
Matt. 8:16; Luke
4:40;
Matt. 4:24
1:33
Mark 1:21
1:34
Matt. 4:23

1:35
Mark 1:35-38;
Luke 4:42,43;
Matt. 14:23; Luke
5:16

1:39
Matt. 4:23; 9:35;
Mark 1:23; 3:1

1:40
Mark 1:40-44;
Matt. 8:2-4; Luke
5:12-14;
Matt. 8:2; Mark
10:17; Luke 5:12

1:44
Matt. 8:4;
Lev. 14:1-32

1:45
Matt. 28:15; Luke
5:15;
Mark 2:2,13; 3:7;
Luke 5:17; John
6:2

2:2
Mark 1:45; 2:13

longer room, even near the door; and He was speaking[m] the word to them.

3　And they *came, bringing to Him a paralytic, carried by four men.

4　And being unable to get[x] to Him because of the crowd, they removed the roof above Him; and when they had dug an opening, they let down the pallet on which the paralytic was lying.[m]

5　And Jesus seeing their faith *said to the paralytic, "My [h]son, your *sins* are forgiven."

6　But there were some of the scribes sitting~ there and reasoning~ in their hearts,

7　"Why does this man speak that way? He is blaspheming; who can forgive~ sins but God alone?"

8　And immediately Jesus, aware[1] in His spirit that they were reasoning that way within themselves, *said to them, "Why are you reasoning about these things in your hearts?

9　"Which is easier, to say[x] to the paralytic, 'Your *sins* are forgiven'; or to say,[x] 'Arise, and take[xi] up your pallet and walk'?

10　"But in order that you may know[29e] that the Son of Man has authority on earth to forgive~[21a] sins"—He *said to the paralytic—

11　"I say to you, rise, take[xi] up your pallet and go home."

12　And he rose and immediately took up the pallet and went out in the sight of all; so that they were all amazed~ and were glorifying~ God, saying, "We have never seen anything like this."

13　And He went out again by the seashore; and all the multitude were coming[m] to Him, and He was teaching[m] them.

Levi (Matthew) Called

14　And as He passed by, He saw Levi the *son* of Alphaeus sitting in the tax office, and He *said to him, "Follow[~l] Me!" And he rose and followed Him.

15　And it came about that He was reclining~ *at the table* in his house, and many tax-gatherers and sinners were dining[m] with Jesus and His disciples; for there were many of them, and they were following[m] Him.

16　And when the scribes of the Pharisees saw that He was eating with the sinners and tax-gatherers, they *began* saying to His disciples, "Why is He eating and drinking with *tax-gatherers* and *sinners?*"

17　And hearing this, Jesus *said to them, "*It is* not those who

[h]Lit., *child*

2:3
Mark 2:3-12:
Matt. 9:2-8; Luke 5:18-26;
Matt. 4:24
2:4
Luke 5:19;
Matt. 4:24

2:5
Matt. 9:2

2:7
Is. 43:25

2:9
Matt. 4:24

2:12
Matt. 9:8;
Matt. 9:33

2:13
Mark 1:45

2:14
Mark 2:14-17:
Matt. 9:9-13;
Luke 5:27-32;
Matt. 9:9;
Matt. 8:22

2:16
Luke 5:30; Acts 23:9;
Matt. 9:11

2:17
Matt. 9:12,13;
Luke 5:31,32

are healthy who need a physician, but those who are sick; I did not come to call[x] the righteous, but sinners."

2:18
Mark 2:18-22;
Matt. 9:14-17;
Luke 5:33-38

18   And John's disciples and the Pharisees were fasting;[~] and they *came and *said to Him, "Why do John's disciples and the disciples of the Pharisees fast, but •Your disciples do not fast?"

19   And Jesus said to them, "While the bridegroom is with them, the attendants of the bridegroom do not fast,[~] do they? So long as they have the bridegroom with them, they cannot fast.[~]

2:20
Matt. 9:15; Luke
17:22

20   "But the days will come when the bridegroom is taken[x] away from them, and then they will fast in that day.

21   "No one sews a patch of unshrunk cloth on an [+]old garment; otherwise the patch pulls away from it, the new from the old, and a worse tear results.

22   "And no one puts [+]new wine into [+]old wineskins; otherwise the wine will burst the skins, and the wine is lost, and the skins as well; but one puts [+]new wine into [+]fresh wineskins."

Question of the Sabbath

2:23
Mark 2:23-28:
Matt. 12:1-8;
Luke 6:1-5;
Deut. 23:25

23   And it came about that He was passing[~] through the grainfields on the Sabbath, and His disciples began to make[~] their way along while picking the heads of grain.

2:24
Matt. 12:2

24   And the Pharisees were saying[m] to Him, "See here, why are they doing what is not lawful on the Sabbath?"

25   And He *said to them, "Have you never read what David did when he was in need and became hungry, he and his companions:

2:26
1 Sam. 21:1;
2 Sam. 8:17;
1 Chr. 24:6;
Lev. 24:9

26   how he entered the house of God in the time of Abiathar the high priest, and ate the consecrated bread, which is not lawful for anyone to eat[x] except the priests, and he gave it also to those who were with him?"

2:27
Ex. 23:12; Deut.
5:14;
Col. 2:16

27   And He was saying[m] to them, "The Sabbath was made for man, and not man for the Sabbath.

28   "Consequently, the Son of Man is Lord even of the Sabbath."

Jesus Heals on the Sabbath

3:1
Mark 3:1-6: Matt.
12:9-14; Luke
6:6-11;
Mark 1:21,39
3:2
Luke 6:7; 14:1;
20:20;
Matt. 12:10; Luke
6:7; 11:54

3   And He entered again into a synagogue; and a man was there with a withered[•] hand.

2   And they were watching[m1] Him to see if He would heal him on the Sabbath, in order that they might accuse[x] Him.

3   And He *said to the man with the withered hand, "Rise and come forward!"

4   And He *said to them, "Is it lawful on the Sabbath to do

good[x] or to do harm,[x] to save[x] a life or to kill?"[x] But they kept silent.[m]

5 And after looking around at them with anger, grieved[l] at their hardness of heart, He *said to the man, "Stretch[x] out your hand." And he stretched it out, and his hand was restored.

6 And the Pharisees went out and immediately *began* taking[m] counsel with the Herodians against Him, *as to* how they might destroy[x] Him.

7 And Jesus withdrew to the sea with His disciples; and a great multitude from Galilee followed; and *also* from Judea,

8 and from Jerusalem, and from Idumea, and beyond the Jordan, and the vicinity of Tyre and Sidon, a *great* multitude heard of all that He was doing[m] and came to Him.

9 And He told His disciples that a boat should stand[~] ready for Him because of the multitude, in order that they might not crowd[~] Him;

10 for He had healed *many,* with the result that all those who had[m] afflictions pressed[~] about Him in order to touch[x] Him.

11 And whenever the unclean spirits beheld[m] Him, they would fall[m] down before Him and cry[m] out, saying, "*You* are the Son of God!"

12 And He earnestly warned[m] them not to make[x] Him known.

The Twelve Are Chosen

13 And He *went up to the mountain and *summoned those whom *He Himself* wanted,[m] and they came to Him.

14 And He appointed twelve[i], that they might be with Him, and that He might send[~] them out to preach,[~]

15 and to have authority to cast[~] out the demons.

16 And He appointed the twelve: Simon (to whom He gave the name Peter),

17 and James, the *son* of Zebedee, and John the brother of James (to them He gave the name Boanerges, which means, "Sons of Thunder");

18 and Andrew, and Philip, and Bartholomew, and Matthew, and Thomas, and James the *son* of Alphaeus, and Thaddaeus, and Simon the Zealot;

19 and Judas Iscariot, who also betrayed Him.

20 And He *came [j]home, and the multitude *gathered again, to such an extent that they could[~] not even eat[x] a meal.

21 And when His own [k]people heard *of this,* they went out to

---

iSome early mss. add: *whom He named apostles*   jLit., *into a house*   kOr, *kinsmen*

3:5
Luke 6:10

3:6
Matt. 22:16; Mark 12:13

3:7
Mark 3:7-12:
Matt. 12:15,16;
Luke 6:17-19;
Matt. 4:25; Luke 6:17
3:8
Josh. 15:1,21;
Ezek. 35:15;
36:5;
Matt. 11:21
3:9
Mark 4:1; Luke 5:1-3

3:10
Matt. 4:23;
Mark 5:29,34;
Luke 7:21;
Matt. 9:21; 14:36;
Mark 6:56; 8:22
3:11
Matt. 4:3

3:12
Matt. 8:4

3:13
Matt. 5:1; Luke 6:12;
Matt. 10:1; Mark 6:7; Luke 9:1

3:16
Mark 3:16-19:
Matt. 10:2-4;
Luke 6:14-16;
Acts 1:13

3:20
Mark 2:1; 7:17;
9:28;
Mark 1:45; 3:7;
Mark 6:31
3:21
Mark 3:31f.;
John 10:20; Acts 26:24

take^x custody of Him; for they were saying,^m "He has lost His senses."

3:22
Matt. 15:1;
Matt. 10:25;
11:18;
Matt. 9:34

22   And the scribes who came down from Jerusalem were saying,^m "He is possessed by *Beelzebul*," and "He casts out the demons *by the ruler of the demons."*

3:23
Mark 3:23-27:
Matt. 12:25-29;
Luke 11:17-22;
Matt. 13:3ff.;
Mark 4:2ff.;
Matt. 4:10

23   And He called them to Himself and began speaking to them in parables, "How can Satan cast[~] out *Satan?*

24   "And if a kingdom is divided^x *against* itself, that kingdom cannot stand.^x

25   "And if a house is divided^x *against* itself, that house will not be able to stand.^x

3:26
Matt. 4:10

26   "And if Satan has risen up against himself and is divided, he cannot stand,^x but he is finished!

3:27
Is. 49:24,25

27   "But no one can enter the strong man's house and plunder^x his property unless he first *binds*^x the strong man, and [†]then he will plunder his house.

3:28
Matt. 12:31,32;
Mark 3:28-30;
Luke 12:10
3:29
Luke 12:10

28   "•Truly I say to you, *all* sins shall be forgiven the sons of men, and whatever blasphemies they utter;^x

29   but whoever blasphemes^x against the Holy Spirit never has forgiveness, but is guilty of an *eternal* sin"—

30   because they were saying,^m "He has an *unclean spirit."*

3:31
Mark 3:31-35:
Matt. 12:46-50;
Luke 8:19-21

31   And His mother and His brothers *arrived, and standing outside they sent *word* to Him, and called Him.

32   And a multitude was sitting around Him, and they *said to Him, "Behold, Your mother and Your brothers^l are outside looking for You."

33   And answering them, He *said, "Who are My mother and My brothers?"

3:34
Matt. 12:49

34   And looking about on those who were sitting around Him, He *said, "Behold, My mother and My brothers!

3:35
Eph. 6:6; Heb.
10:36; 1 Pet. 4:2;
1 John 2:17

35   "For whoever does^x the will of God, *he* is My brother and sister and mother."

Parable of the Sower and Soils

4:1
Mark 4:1-12:
Matt. 13:1-15;
Luke 8:4-10;
Mark 2:13; 3:7;
Luke 5:1-3

4   And He began to teach[~] again by the sea. And such a *very*³ *great multitude* gathered to Him that He got into a boat in the sea and sat down; and the whole multitude was by the sea on the land.

4:2
Matt. 13:3ff.;
Mark 3:23; 4:2ff.

2   And He was teaching^m them many things in parables, and was saying^m to them in His teaching,

3   "Listen^{~!} *to this!* Behold, the sower went out to sow;^x

4   and it came about that as he was sowing, [~] some *seed* fell beside the road, and the birds came and ate it up.

^lLater mss. add: *and Your sisters*

5 "And other *seed* fell on the rocky *ground* where it did not have much soil; and immediately it sprang up because it had no depth of soil.

6 "And after the *sun* had risen, it was scorched; and because it had no root, it withered away.

7 "And other *seed* fell among the thorns, and the thorns came up and choked it, and it yielded no crop.

8 "And other *seeds* fell into the *good* soil and as they grew up and increased, they yielded^m a crop and produced^m thirty, sixty, and a hundredfold."

9 And He was saying,^m "He who has ears to hear,~ let him hear."~!

4:9
Matt. 11:15; Mark 4:23; Rev. 2:7,11, 17,29

10 And as soon as He was alone, His followers, along with the twelve, *began* asking^m Him *about* the parables.

11 And He was saying^m to them, "To *you* has been given+ the mystery of the kingdom of God; but *those* who are outside get everything in *parables,*

4:11
1 Cor. 5:12f.; Col. 4:5; 1 Thess. 4:12; 1 Tim. 3:7; Mark 3:23; 4:2

12 in order that WHILE SEEING, THEY MAY SEE~ AND NOT PERCEIVE;^x AND WHILE HEARING, THEY MAY HEAR~ AND NOT UNDERSTAND~^{29f} LEST THEY RETURN^x AND BE FORGIVEN."^x

4:12
Is. 6:9f.; 43:8; Jer. 5:21; Ezek. 12:2; Matt. 13:14; Luke 8:10; John 12:40; Rom. 11:8

Explanation

13 And He *said to them, "Do you not understand^{29e} this parable? And how will you understand^{29a} *all the parables?*

14 "The sower sows the *word.* ^{43a}

4:13
Mark 4:13-20;
Matt. 13:18-23;
Luke 8:11-15

15 "And these are the ones who are beside the road where the word is sown; and when they hear,^x immediately *Satan* comes and takes away the word which has been sown+ in them.

4:15
Matt. 4:10f.; 1 Pet. 5:8; Rev. 20:2,3,7-10

16 "And in a similar way these are the ones on whom seed was sown on the rocky *places,* who, when they hear^x the word, immediately receive it with joy;

17 and they have no *firm* root in themselves, but are *only temporary;* then, when affliction or persecution arises because of the word, immediately they fall away.

18 "And others are the ones on whom seed was sown among the thorns; these are the ones who have heard the word,

19 and the worries of the ^mworld, and the deceitfulness of riches, and the desires for other things enter in and choke the word, and it becomes *unfruitful.*

4:19
Matt. 13:22; Rom. 12:2; Eph. 2:2; 6:12; Prov. 23:4; 1 Tim. 6:9,10,17

20 "And those are the ones on whom seed was sown on the *good* soil; and they hear the word and accept it, and bear fruit, thirty, sixty, and a hundredfold."

4:20
John 15:2ff.;
Rom. 7:4

21 And He was saying to them, "A lamp is not brought to be

4:21
Matt. 5:15; Luke 8:16; 11:33

^mOr, *age*

put[x] *under a peck-measure,* is it, or *under a* †*bed?* Is it not *brought* to be put[x] on the *lampstand?*

4:22
Matt. 10:26; Luke
8:17; 12:2

22 "For nothing is hidden, except to be revealed;[x] nor has *anything* been secret, but that it should come to light.

4:23
Matt. 11:15; 13:9,
43; Mark 4:9;
Luke 8:8; 14:35;
Rev. 3:6,13,22;
13:9

23 "If any man has ears to hear,~ let him hear."~!

4:24
Matt. 7:2; Luke
6:38

24 And He was saying to them, "Take care~! what you listen to. By your standard of measure it shall be measured to you; and more shall be given you besides.

4:25
Matt. 13:12;
25:29; Luke 8:18;
19:26

25 "For whoever has, to him shall *more* be given; and whoever does not have, even what he has shall be taken away from him."

Parable of the Seed

26 And He was saying, "The kingdom of God is like a man who casts[x] seed upon the soil;

27 and goes~ to bed at night and gets~ up by day, and the seed sprouts~ up and grows~—how, he himself does not know.

28 "The soil produces crops *by itself;* first the blade, then the head, then the mature grain in the head.

4:29
Joel 3:13

29 "But when the crop permits,[x] he immediately puts in the sickle, because the harvest has come."⁺

Parable of the Mustard Seed

4:30
Mark 4:30-32;
Matt. 13:31,32;
Luke 13:18,19;
Matt. 13:24

30 And He said, "How shall we ⁿpicture[x] the kingdom of God, or by what parable shall we present[x] it?

31 "*It is* like a mustard seed, which, when sown[x] upon the soil, though it is smaller than all the seeds that are upon the soil,

4:32
Ezek. 17:23; Ps.
104:12; Ezek.
31:6; Dan. 4:12

32 yet when it is sown,[x] grows up and becomes larger than all the garden plants and forms large branches; so that THE BIRDS OF THE °AIR can NEST~ UNDER ITS SHADE."

33 And with *many* such parables He was speaking[m] the word to them as they were able[m] to hear~ it;

4:34
Matt. 13:34; John
10:6; 16:25;
Luke 24:27

34 and He did not speak[m] to them *without a parable;* but He was explaining[m] everything *privately* to His own disciples.

Jesus Stills the Sea

4:35
Mark 4:35-41;
Matt. 8:18,23-27;
Luke 8:22,25

35 And on that day, when evening had come, He *said to them, "Let us go[x] over to the other side."

4:36
Mark 3:9; 4:1;
5:2,21

36 And leaving the multitude, they *took Him along with them, just as He was, in the boat; and other boats were with Him.

37 And there *arose a fierce gale of wind, and the waves were breaking[m] over the boat so much that the boat was already filling~ up.

38 And He Himself was in the stern, asleep~ on the cushion;

ⁿLit., *compare* °Or, *sky*

and they *awoke Him and *said to Him, "Teacher, do You not care that we are perishing?"

39   And being aroused, He rebuked the wind and said to the sea, "Hush, be still." And the wind died down and it became perfectly calm.

4:39
Ps. 65:7; 89:9;
107:29; Matt.
8:26; Luke 8:24

40   And He said to them, "Why are you so timid? How is it that you have no faith?"

4:40
Matt. 14:31; Luke
8:25

41   And they became very much •afraid⁴ and said™ to one another, "Who then is this, that even the wind and the sea obey Him?"

The Gerasene Demoniac

5   And they came to the other side of the sea, into the country of the Gerasenes.

5:1
Mark 5:1-17;
Matt. 8:28-34;
Luke 8:26-37
5:2
Mark 3:9; 4:1,36;
5:21;
Mark 1:23

2   And when He had come out of the boat, immediately a man from the tombs with an unclean spirit met Him,

3   and he had™ his dwelling among the tombs. And *no* ⁺*one* was able™ to bind˟ him anymore, even with a *chain;*

4   because he had often been bound⁺ with shackles and chains, and the chains had been torn⁺ apart by him, and the shackles broken⁺ in ⁺pieces, and no one was strong™ enough to subdue˟ him.

5   And constantly night and day, among the tombs and in the mountains, he was crying~ out and gashing~ himself with stones.

6   And seeing Jesus from a distance, he ran up and bowed down before Him;

7   and crying out with a loud voice, he *said, "What do I have to do with You, Jesus, Son of the Most High God? I implore You by God, do not torment⁹ me!"

5:7
Matt. 8:29;
Matt. 4:3;
Luke 8:28; Acts
16:17; Heb. 7:1

8   For He had been saying™ to him, "Come˟ⁱ out of the man, you unclean spirit!"

9   And He was asking™ him, "What is your name?" And he *said to Him, "My name is Legion; for we are ⁺*many.*"

5:9
Matt. 26:53; Mark
5:15; Luke 8:30

10   And he *began* to entreat™ Him earnestly not to send˟ them out of the country.

11   Now there was a big herd of swine feeding~ there on the mountain.

12   And *the demons* entreated Him, saying, "Send˟ⁱ us into the swine so that we may enter˟ *them.*"

13   And He gave them permission. And coming out, the unclean spirits entered the swine; and the herd rushed down the steep bank into the sea, about two thousand *of them;* and they were drowned™ in the sea.

14   And their herdsmen ran away and reported it in the city and *out* in the country. And *the people* came to see^x what it was that had happened.⁺

5:15
Matt. 4:24; Mark
5:16,18;
Luke 8:27;
Luke 8:35;
Mark 5:9

15   And they *came to Jesus and *observed the man who had been demon-possessed sitting down, clothed⁺ and in his right mind, the very man who had had⁺ the "legion"; and they became frightened.

5:16
Matt. 4:24; Mark
5:15

16   And those who had seen it described to them how it had happened to the demon-possessed man, and *all* about the swine.

5:17
Matt. 8:34; Acts
16:39

17   And they began to entreat~ Him to depart^x from their region.

5:18
Mark 5:18-20:
Luke 8:38,39;
Matt. 4:24; Mark
5:15,16

18   And as He was getting into the boat, the man who had been demon-possessed was entreating^m Him that he might *accompany* Him.

5:19
Luke 8:39

19   And He did not let him, but He *said to him, "Go home to your people and report^x to them ᴾwhat great things the Lord has done⁺ for you, and *how* He had mercy on you."

5:20
Ps. 66:16;
Matt. 4:25; Mark
7:31

20   And he went away and began to proclaim~ in Decapolis what great things *Jesus* had done for him; and everyone marveled.^m

Miracles and Healing

5:21
Matt. 9:1; Luke
8:40;
Mark 4:36;
Mark 4:1

21   And when Jesus had crossed over again in the boat to the other side, a great multitude gathered about Him; and He stayed by the seashore.

5:22
Mark 5:22-43:
Matt. 9:18-26;
Luke 8:41-56;
Matt. 9:18; Mark
5:35,36,38; Luke
8:49; 13:14; Acts
13:15; 18:8,17
5:23
Mark 6:5; 7:32;
8:23; 16:18; Luke
4:40; 13:13; Acts
6:6; 9:17; 28:8

22   And one of the synagogue officials named Jairus *came up, and upon seeing Him, *fell at His feet,

23   and *entreated Him earnestly, saying, "My little daughter is at the point of death; *please* come and lay^x Your hands on her, that she may get^x well and live."^x

24   And He went off with him; and a great multitude was following^m Him and pressing^m in on Him.

25   And a woman who had had a hemorrhage for *twelve* years,

26   and had endured *much* at the hands of many physicians, and had spent all that she had and was not helped at all, but rather had grown *worse,*

27   after hearing about Jesus, came up in the crowd behind *Him,* and touched His cloak.

28   For she thought,^m "If I just touch^x His garments, I shall get well."

5:29
Mark 3:10; 5:34

29   And immediately the flow of her blood was dried up; and she felt in her body that she was healed^{+15b} of her affliction.

ᴾOr, *everything that*

30 And immediately Jesus, perceiving[29b] in Himself that the power[32a] *proceeding* from Him had gone forth, turned around in the crowd and said,[m] "Who touched *My* garments?"

31 And His disciples said[m] to Him, "You see the multitude pressing in on You, and You say, 'Who touched [†]Me?'"

32 And He looked[m] around to see[x] the woman who had done this.

33 But the woman fearing and trembling, aware of what had happened[+] to her, came and fell down before Him, and told Him the whole truth.

34 And He said to her, "Daughter, your faith has made[+] you well; go in peace, and be healed of your affliction."

35 While He was still speaking, they *came from the *house of* the synagogue official, saying, "Your daughter has died; why trouble the Teacher anymore?"

36 But Jesus, overhearing what was being spoken, *said to the synagogue official, "Do not be afraid[⊙] *any longer*, only believe."[~¹]

37 And He allowed no one to follow[x] with Him, except Peter and James and John the brother of James.

38 And they *came to the house of the synagogue official; and He *beheld a commotion, and *people* loudly weeping and wailing.

39 And entering in, He *said to them, "Why make a commotion and weep? The child has not died, but is asleep."

40 And they *began* laughing[m¹] at Him. But putting them all out, He *took along the child's father and mother and His own companions, and *entered *the room* where the child was.

41 And taking the child by the hand, He *said to her, "Talitha kum!" (which translated means, "Little girl, I say to you, arise!").

42 And immediately the girl rose and *began* to walk;[m] for she was twelve years old. And immediately they were *completely*[1] •astounded.

43 And He gave them strict orders that no one should know[x] about this; and He said that *something* should be given[x] her to eat.[x]

Teaching at Nazareth

6 And He went out from there, and He *came into His home town; and His disciples *followed Him.

2 And when the Sabbath had come, He began to teach[~] in the synagogue; and the many listeners were astonished,[m¹] saying, "Where did this man *get* these things, and what is *this* wisdom given to Him, and such miracles as these performed by His hands?

5:30
Luke 5:17

5:34
Matt. 9:22;
Luke 7:50; 8:48;
Acts 16:36;
James 2:16;
Mark 3:10; 5:29
5:35
Mark 5:22

5:36
Mark 5:22;
Luke 8:50

5:37
Matt. 17:1; 26:37

5:38
Mark 5:22

5:41
Luke 7:14; Acts
9:40

5:43
Matt. 8:4

6:1
Mark 6:1-6; *Matt.
13:54-58*;
Matt. 13:54,57;
Luke 4:16,23
6:2
Matt. 4:23; Mark
10:1;
Matt. 7:28

6:3
Matt. 13:55;
Matt. 12:46;
Matt. 13:56;
Matt. 11:6

3 "Is not this the carpenter, the son of Mary, and brother of James, and Joses, and Judas, and Simon? Are not His sisters here with us?" And they took^m offense at Him.

6:4
Matt. 13:57; John
4:44;
Mark 6:1

4 And Jesus said to them, "A prophet is not without honor except in his home town and among his *own* relatives and in his *own* household."

6:5
Mark 5:23

5 And He could^m do^{x19a} no miracle there except that He laid His hands upon a few sick people and healed them.

6:6
Matt. 9:35; Mark
1:39; 10:1; Luke
13:22

6 And He wondered^m at their unbelief.

And He was going^m around the villages teaching.

The Twelve Sent Out

6:7
Mark 6:7-11;
Matt. 10:1,9-14;
Luke 9:1,3-5;
Luke 10:4-11;
Matt. 10:1,5;
Mark 3:13; Luke
9:1;
Luke 10:1
6:8
Matt. 10:10

7 And He *summoned the twelve and began to send~ them out in pairs; and He was giving^m them authority over the unclean spirits;

8 and He instructed them that they should take~ nothing for *their* journey, except a mere staff; no bread, no bag, no money in their belt;

9 but *to* wear* sandals; and *He added,* "Do not put° on two ^qtunics."

10 And He said to them, "Wherever you enter^x a house, stay^{x1} there until you leave^x town.

6:11
Matt. 10:14; Acts
13:51

11 "And any place that does not receive^x you or listen^x to you, as you go out from there, shake^{x1} off the dust from the soles of your feet for a testimony against them."

6:12
Matt. 11:1; Luke
9:6
6:13
James 5:14

12 And they went out and preached that *men* should repent.~

13 And they were casting^m out *many* demons and were anointing^m with oil many sick people and healing^{m15a} them.

John's Fate Recalled

6:14
Mark 6:14-29;
Matt. 14:1-12;
Mark 6:14-16;
Luke 9:7-9;
Matt. 14:2; Luke
9:19

14 And King Herod heard *of it,* for His name had become *well known;* and *people* were saying,^m "John the Baptist has risen* from the dead, and that is why these *miraculous powers* are at work in Him."

6:15
Matt. 16:14; Mark
8:28;
Matt. 21:11

15 But others were saying,^m "He is *Elijah.*" And others were saying,^m *"He is* a prophet, like one of the prophets *of old.*"

16 But when Herod heard *of it,* he kept saying,^m *"John,* whom *I* beheaded, has risen!"

6:17
Matt. 14:3; Luke
3:19

17 For Herod himself had sent and had John arrested and bound in prison on account of Herodias, the wife of his brother Philip, because he had married her.

6:18
Matt. 14:4

18 For John had been saying^m to Herod, "It is not lawful for you to have your brother's wife."

^qOr, *inner garments*

19 And Herodias had^ᴹ a grudge against him and wanted^ᴹ to put^x him to death and could^ᴹ not *do so;*

6:19
Matt. 14:3

20 for Herod was afraid^ᴹ of John, knowing that he was a righteous and holy[28a] man, and kept^ᴹ him safe.[1] And when he heard him, he was very perplexed;^ᴹ but he used to enjoy listening^ᴹ to him.

6:20
Matt. 21:26

21 And a strategic day came when Herod on his birthday gave a banquet for his lords and military commanders and the leading men of Galilee;

6:21
Esth. 1:3; 2:18;
Luke 3:1

22 and when the daughter of Herodias herself came in and danced, she pleased Herod and his dinner guests; and the king said to the girl, "Ask^{xi} me for whatever you want~ and I will give it to you."

6:22
Matt. 14:3

23 And he swore to her, "Whatever you ask^x of me, I will give it to you; up to half of my kingdom."

6:23
Esth. 5:3,6; 7:2

24 And she went out and said to her mother, "What shall I ask^x for?" And she said, "The head of John the Baptist."

25 And *immediately* she came in haste before the king and asked, saying, "I want you to give^x me right away the head of John the Baptist on a platter."

26 And although the king was very[1] sorry, *yet* because of his oaths and because of his dinner guests, he was unwilling to refuse^x her.

27 And immediately the king sent an executioner and commanded *him* to bring^x *back* his head. And he went and had him beheaded in the prison,

28 and brought his head on a platter, and gave it to the girl; and the girl gave it to her mother.

29 And when his disciples heard *about this,* they came and took away his body and laid it in a tomb.

30 And the apostles *gathered together with Jesus; and they reported to Him all that they had done and taught.

6:30
Luke 9:10;
Matt. 10:2; Mark
3:14; Luke 6:13;
9:10; 17:5; 22:14;
24:10; Acts 1:2,
26

31 And He *said to them, "Come away by yourselves to a lonely place and rest^{xi} a while." (For there were many *people* coming and going, and they did not even have^ᴹ time to eat.)^x

6:31
Mark 3:20

32 And they went away in the boat to a lonely place by themselves.

6:32
Mark 6:32-44;
Matt. 14:13-21;
Luke 9:10-17;
John 6:5-13;
Mark 8:2-9;
Mark 3:9; 4:36;
6:45

Five Thousand Fed

33 And *the people* saw them going, and *many* recognized *them,* and they ran there together on foot from all the cities, and got there ahead of them.

6:34
Matt. 9:36;
Num. 27:17;
1 Kin. 22:17;
2 Chr. 18:16;
Zech. 10:2

34 And when He went ashore, He saw a great multitude, and He felt compassion for them because they were like sheep

without a shepherd; and He began to teach~ them many things.

35　And when it was already *quite late,* His disciples came up to Him and *began* saying,ᵐ "The place is *desolate* and it is already *quite late;*

36　sendˣⁱ them away so that they may go into the surrounding countryside and villages and buyˣ themselves something to eat."ˣ

6:37
John 6:7;
Matt. 18:28; Luke 7:41

37　But He answered and said to them, "*You* giveˣⁱ them *something* to eat!"ˣ And they *said to Him, "Shall we go and spendˣ *two hundred* ʳ*denarii* on bread and give them *something* to eat?"ˣ

38　And He *said to them, "How many loaves do you have? Go look!"ˣⁱ And when they found out, they *said, "ᵗ*Five* and *two* fish."

39　And He commanded them all to reclineˣ by groups on the green grass.

40　And they reclined in companies of hundreds and of fifties.

6:41
Matt. 14:19

41　And He took the five loaves and the two fish, and looking up toward heaven, He blessed *the food* and broke the loaves and He kept givingᵐ *them* to the disciples to set~ before them; and He divided up the *two fish* among them all.

42　And they *all* ate and were satisfied.

6:43
Matt. 14:20

43　And they picked up *twelve* full baskets of the broken pieces, and also of the fish.

6:44
Matt. 14:21

44　And there were *five thousand* men who ate the loaves.

Jesus Walks on the Water

6:45
Mark 6:45-51;
Matt. 14:22-32;
John 6:15-21;
Mark 6:32;
Matt. 11:21; Mark 8:22
6:46
Acts 18:18,21; 2 Cor. 2:13;
Matt. 14:23

45　And immediately He made His disciples getˣ into the boat and go~ ahead of *Him* to the other side to Bethsaida, while He Himself was sending the multitude away.

46　And after bidding them farewell, He departed to the mountain to pray.ˣ

47　And when it was evening, the boat was in the midst of the sea, and He *was* alone on the land.

6:48
Matt. 24:43; Mark 13:35

48　And seeing them straining~ at the oars, for the wind was against them, at about the fourth watch of the night, He *came to them, walking on the sea; and He intendedᵐ to passˣ by them.

49　But when they saw Him walking on the *sea,* they supposed that it was a ᵗ*ghost,* and cried out;

6:50
Matt. 9:2;
Matt. 14:27

50　for they all saw Him and were frightened. But immediately He spoke with them and *said to them, "Take courage; it is *I,* do not be afraid."ᴼ

6:51
Mark 6:32

51　And He got into the boat with them, and the wind stopped; and they were *greatly* astonished,ᵐ

ʳThe denarius was equivalent to one day's wage

52   for they had not gained any insight from the *incident of* the loaves, but their heart was †hardened.*

Healing at Gennesaret

53   And when they had crossed over they came to land at Gennesaret, and moored to the shore.

54   And when they had come out of the boat, immediately *the people* recognized Him,

55   and ran about that whole country and began to carry~ about on their pallets those who were sick, to the place they heard™ He was.

56   And wherever He entered™ villages, or cities, or country-side, they were laying™ the sick in the market places, and entreat-ing™ Him that they might just touch˟ the *fringe of His cloak;* and as many as touched it were being cured.™

Followers of Tradition

7   And the Pharisees and some of the scribes gathered together around Him when they had come from Jerusalem,

2   and had seen that some of His disciples were eating their bread with *impure hands,* that is, unwashed.

3   (For the Pharisees and all the Jews do not eat unless they carefully wash˟ their hands, *thus* observing the traditions of the elders;

4   and *when they come* from the market place, they do not eat unless they cleanse˟ themselves; and there are *many* other things which they have received in order to observe,~ such as the washing of cups and pitchers and copper pots.)

5   And the Pharisees and the scribes *asked Him, "Why do Your disciples not walk according to the tradition of the elders, but eat their bread with *impure hands?"*

6   And He said to them, "Rightly did Isaiah prophesy of you hypocrites, as it is written,*

'THIS PEOPLE HONORS ME WITH THEIR LIPS,
BUT THEIR HEART IS FAR AWAY FROM ME.

7   'BUT IN VAIN DO THEY WORSHIP ⁴⁴ᶜ ME,
TEACHING AS DOCTRINES THE PRECEPTS OF MEN.'

8   "Neglecting the commandment of God, you hold to the tradition of men."

9   He was also saying™ to them, "You nicely set aside the commandment of God in order to keep˟ *your tradition.*

10   "For Moses said, 'HONOR~ᴵ YOUR FATHER AND YOUR MOTH-ER'; and, 'HE WHO SPEAKS EVIL OF FATHER OR MOTHER, LET HIM BE PUT~ᴵ TO *DEATH*';

6:52
Mark 8:17ff.;
Rom. 11:7

6:53
Mark 6:53-56;
Matt. 14:34-36;
John 6:24,25

6:56
Mark 3:10;
Matt. 9:20

7:1
Mark 7:1-23;
Matt. 15:1-20;
Matt. 15:1
7:2
Matt. 15:2; Mark
7:5; Luke 11:38;
Acts 10:14,28;
11:8; Rom. 14:14;
Heb. 10:29; Rev.
21:27
7:3
Mark 7:5,8,9,13;
Gal. 1:14
7:4
Matt. 23:25

7:5
Mark 7:3,8,9,13;
Gal. 1:14;
Mark 7:2

7:6
Is. 29:13

7:7
Is. 29:13

7:8
Mark 7:3,5,9,13;
Gal. 1:14

7:9
Mark 7:3,5,8,13;
Gal. 1:14

7:10
Ex. 20:12; Deut.
5:16;
Ex. 21:17; Lev.
20:9

7:11
Lev. 1:2; Matt.
27:6
11   but *you* say, 'If a man says[x] to *his* father or *his* mother, anything of mine you might have been helped[x] by is Corban (that is to say, [s]given *to God*),'

12   you no longer permit him to do[x] anything for *his* father or *his* mother;

7:13
Mark 7:3,5,8,9;
Gal. 1:14
13   *thus* invalidating the word of God by your tradition which you have handed down; and you do *many* things such as that.''

The Heart of Man

14   And after He called the multitude to Him again, He *began* saying to them, ''Listen[xl] to Me, all of you, and understand:[xl29f]

15   there is nothing outside the man which going into him can defile[x17a] him; but the things which proceed out of the man are what defile the man.

16   [''[t]If any man has ears to hear, let him hear.'']

7:17
Mark 2:1; 3:20;
9:28;
Matt. 15:15
17   And when leaving the multitude, He had entered the house, His disciples questioned[m] Him about the parable.

18   And He *said to them, ''Are *you* so lacking in understanding *also?* Do you not understand[29d] that whatever goes into the man from outside cannot defile[x17a] him;

7:19
Rom. 14:1-12;
Col. 2:16;
Luke 11:41; Acts
10:15; 11:9
7:20
Matt. 15:18; Mark
7:23
19   because it does not go into his heart, but into his stomach, and is eliminated?'' (*Thus He* declared all foods clean.)

20   And He was saying, ''That which proceeds out of the man, that is what defiles the man.

21   ''For from within, out of the heart of men, proceed the evil[10a] thoughts, fornications, thefts, murders, adulteries,

7:22
Matt. 6:23; 20:15
22   deeds of coveting *and* wickedness, *as well as* deceit, sensuality, envy, slander, pride *and* foolishness.

23   ''All these evil[10b] things proceed from within and defile[17a] the man.''

The Syrophoenician Woman

7:24
Mark 7:24-30;
Matt. 15:21-28;
Matt. 11:21; Mark
7:31
24   And from there He arose and went away to the region of Tyre[u]. And when He had entered a house, He wanted[m] no one to know[x] *of it;* yet He could not escape[x] notice.

25   But after hearing of Him, a woman whose little daughter had[m] an unclean spirit, immediately came and fell at His feet.

26   Now the woman was a [v]Gentile, of the Syrophoenician race. And she kept asking[m] Him to cast[x] the demon out of her daughter.

27   And He was saying[m] to her, ''Let[xl] the *children* be satisfied[x]

[s]Or, *a gift, an offering*   [t]Many mss. do not contain this verse   [u]Some early mss. add: *and Sidon*
[v]Lit., *Greek*

first, for it is not good to take* the children's bread and throw* it to the *dogs.*"

28 But she answered and *said to Him, "Yes, Lord, *but* even the dogs under the table feed on the children's crumbs."

29 And He said to her, "Because of this answer go your way; the demon has gone⁺ out of your daughter."

30 And going back to her home, she found the child lying⁺ on the bed, the demon having departed.⁺

31 And again He went out from the region of Tyre, and came through Sidon to the Sea of Galilee, within the region of Decapolis.

32 And they *brought to Him one who was deaf and spoke with difficulty, and they *entreated Him to lay* His hand upon him.

33 And He took him aside from the multitude by himself, and put His fingers into his ears, and after spitting, He touched his tongue *with the saliva;*

34 and looking up to heaven with a deep sigh, He *said to him, "Ephphatha!" that is, "Be opened!"*ˣˡ*

35 And his ears were *opened,* and the impediment of his tongue was removed, and he *began* speakingᵐ *plainly.*

36 And He gave them orders not to tell~ anyone; but the more He orderedᵐ them, the more³ •widely they continued to proclaimᵐ it.

37 And they were utterly¹ astonished,ᵐ saying, "He has done⁺ all things well; He makes even the deaf to hear,~ and the dumb to speak."~

Four Thousand Fed

8 In those days again, when there was a great multitude and they had nothing to eat,* He called His disciples and *said to them,

2 "I feel compassion for the multitude because they have remained with Me now three days, and have nothing to eat;*

3 and if I send* them away hungry to their home, they will faint on the way; and some of them have come from a distance."

4 And His disciples answered Him, "Where will anyone be able to *find enough to* satisfy* these men with bread *here* in a desolate place?"

5 And He was asking them, "How many loaves do you have?" And they said, "Seven."

6 And He *directed the multitude to sit* down on the ground; and taking the seven loaves, He gave thanks and broke

7:31
Mark 7:31-37;
Matt. 15:29-31;
Matt. 11:21; Mark 7:24;
Matt. 4:18;
Matt. 4:25; Mark 5:20
7:32
Mark 5:23

7:33
Mark 8:23

7:34
Mark 8:12

7:36
Matt. 8:4;
Mark 1:45

8:1
Mark 8:1-9; *Matt. 15:32-39;* Mark 6:34-44

8:2
Matt. 9:36; Mark 6:34

them, and started giving^m them to His disciples to serve~ to them, and they served them to the multitude.

8:7
Matt. 14:19

7   They also had a *few* small fish; and after He had blessed them, He ordered these to be served~ as well.

8:8
Matt. 15:37; Mark 8:20

8   And they ate and were satisfied; and they picked up *seven* large baskets full of what was left over of the broken pieces.

9   And about four thousand were *there;* and He sent them away.

8:10
Matt. 15:39

10   And immediately He entered the boat with His disciples, and came to the district of Dalmanutha.

8:11
Mark 8:11-21;
Matt. 16:1-12;
Matt. 12:38

11   And the Pharisees came out and began to argue~ with Him, seeking from Him a sign from heaven, to test Him.

8:12
Mark 7:34;
Matt. 12:39

12   And sighing deeply in His spirit, He *said, "Why does this generation seek[1] for a sign? •Truly I say to you, no sign shall be given to this generation."

13   And leaving them, He again embarked and went away to the other side.

14   And they had forgotten to take^x bread; and did not have more than one loaf in the boat with them.

8:15
Matt. 16:6; Luke 12:1;
Matt. 14:1; 22:16

15   And He was giving^m orders to them, saying, "Watch^m out! Beware^m of the leaven of the Pharisees and the leaven of Herod."

16   And they *began* to discuss^m with one another *the fact* that they had *no bread.*

8:17
Mark 6:52

17   And Jesus, aware of this, *said to them, "Why do you discuss *the fact* that you have no bread? Do you not yet see^{29d} or understand?^{29f} Do you have a *hardened•* heart?

8:18
Jer. 5:21; Ezek. 12:2; Mark 4:12

18   "HAVING EYES, DO YOU NOT SEE? AND HAVING EARS, DO YOU NOT HEAR? And do you not remember,

8:19
Mark 6:41-44;
Matt. 14:20

19   when I broke the *five loaves* for the five thousand, how many baskets full of broken pieces you picked up?" They *said to Him, "†*Twelve.*"

8:20
Mark 8:6-9;
Mark 8:8

20   "And when *I broke* the †*seven* for the four thousand, how many large baskets full of broken pieces did you pick up?" And they *said to Him, "†*Seven.*"

8:21
Mark 6:52

21   And He was saying to them, "Do you not yet understand?"

8:22
Matt. 11:21; Mark 6:45;
Mark 3:10

22   And they *came to Bethsaida. And they *brought a blind man to Him, and *entreated Him to touch^x him.

8:23
Mark 7:33;
Mark 5:23

23   And taking the blind man by the hand, He brought him out of the village; and after spitting on his eyes, and laying His hands upon him, He asked^m him, "Do you see anything?"

24   And he looked up and said,^m "I see men, for I am seeing *them* like trees, walking about."

25   Then again He laid His hands upon his eyes; and he looked intently and was restored, and *began* to see^m everything *clearly.*

26   And He sent him to his home, saying, "Do not even enter[◎] the village."

8:26
Mark 8:23

Peter's Confession of Christ

27   And Jesus went out, along with His disciples, to the villages of Caesarea Philippi; and on the way He questioned^m His disciples, saying to them, "Who do people say that I am?"

8:27
Mark 8:27-29;
Matt. 16:13-16;
Luke 9:18-20;
Matt. 16:13

28   And they told Him, saying, "John the Baptist; and others *say* Elijah; but others, one of the prophets."

8:28
Mark 6:14; Luke
9:7,8

29   And He *continued* by questioning^m them, "But who do *you* say that I am?" Peter *answered and *said to Him, "*Thou* art the Christ."

8:29
John 6:68,69

30   And He warned them to tell[~] no one about Him.

8:30
Matt. 8:4; 16:20;
Luke 9:21

31   And He began to teach[~] them that the Son of Man must suffer^x *many things* and be rejected^x by the elders and the chief priests and the scribes, and be killed,^x and after three days rise^x again.

8:31
Mark 8:31-9:1;
Matt. 16:21-28;
Luke 9:22-27;
Matt. 16:21

32   And He was stating^m the matter *plainly.* And Peter took Him aside and began to rebuke[~] Him.

8:32
John 10:24;
11:14; 16:25,29;
18:20

33   But turning around and seeing His disciples, He rebuked Peter, and *said, "Get behind Me, Satan; for you are not setting your mind on ^wGod's interests, but man's."

8:33
Matt. 4:10

34   And He summoned the multitude with His disciples, and said to them, "If anyone wishes to come[~] after *Me,* let him deny^{xl1} himself, and take^{xl} up his cross, and follow^{~l} Me.

8:34
Matt. 10:38; Luke
14:27

35   "For whoever wishes to *save*^x his life shall lose it; but whoever loses his life for My sake and the gospel's shall save it.

8:35
Matt. 10:39; Luke
17:33; John 12:25

36   "For what does it profit a man to gain^x the *whole* world, and forfeit^x his [†]*soul?*

37   "For what shall a man give^x in exchange for his soul?

38   "For whoever is ashamed^x of Me and •My words^{43a} in *this adulterous* and *sinful* generation, the Son of Man will also be ashamed of him when He comes in the glory of His Father with the holy^{28a} angels."

8:38
Matt. 10:33; Luke
9:26; Heb. 11:16;
Matt. 8:20;
Matt. 16:27; Mark
13:26; Luke 9:26

The Transfiguration

9   And He was saying^m to them, "•Truly I say to you, there are some of those who are standing here who shall •*not* taste^x death until they see^x the kingdom of God after it has come⁺ with power."^{32a}

9:1
Matt. 16:28; Mark
13:26; Luke 9:27

^wLit., *the things of God*

9:2
Mark 9:2-8: Matt.
17:1-8; Luke
9:28-36;
Mark 5:37

2   And six days later, Jesus *took with Him Peter and James and John, and *brought them up to a high mountain by •themselves. And He was transfigured before them;

9:3
Matt. 28:3

3   and His garments became radiant and exceedingly white, as no launderer on earth can whiten˟ them.

4   And *Elijah* appeared to them along with *Moses;* and they were talking˜ with Jesus.

9:5
Matt. 23:7;
Matt. 17:4; Luke
9:33

5   And Peter answered and *said to Jesus, "Rabbi, it is good for us to be here; and let us make˟ three tabernacles, one for You, and one for Moses, and one for Elijah."

6   For he did not know what to answer;˟ for they became †terrified.¹

9:7
2 Pet. 1:17f.;
Matt. 3:17; Mark
1:11; Luke 3:22

7   Then a cloud formed, overshadowing them, and a voice came out of the cloud, "This is My *beloved* Son, listen˜ to Him!"

8   And all at once they looked around and saw no one with them anymore, except Jesus alone.

9:9
Mark 9:9-13:
Matt. 17:9-13;
Matt. 8:4; Mark
5:43; 7:36; 8:30

9   And as they were coming down from the mountain, He gave them orders not to relate˟ to anyone what they had seen, until the Son of Man should rise˟ from the dead.

10   And they seized upon *that statement,* discussing with one another what rising˟ from the dead might mean.

9:11
Mal. 4:5; Matt.
11:14

11   And they asked Him, saying, *"Why is it* that the scribes say that *Elijah* must come first?"

9:12
Mark 9:31;
Matt. 16:21;
26:24

12   And He said to them, "Elijah does first come and restore all things. And *yet* how is it written⁺ of the Son of Man that He should suffer˟ *many things* and be treated˟ with contempt?

13   "But I say to you, that Elijah has indeed come,⁺ and they did to him whatever they wished,ᵐ just as it is written⁺ of him."

All Things Possible

9:14
Mark 9:14-28:
Matt. 17:14-19;
Luke 9:37-42
9:15
Mark 14:33;
16:5, 6

14   And when they came *back* to the disciples, they saw a large crowd around them, and *some* scribes arguing with them.

15   And immediately, when the entire crowd saw Him, they were amazed,¹ and *began* runningᵐ up to greet Him.

16   And He asked them, "What are you discussing with them?"

17   And one of the crowd answered Him, "Teacher, I brought You my son, possessed with a spirit which makes him mute;

18   and whenever it seizes˟ him, it dashes him *to the ground* and he foams *at the mouth,* and grinds his teeth, and stiffens out. And I told Your disciples to cast˟ it out, and they could not *do it."*

19   And He *answered them and *said, "O unbelieving generation, how long shall I be with you? How long shall I put up with you? Bring him to Me!"

20 And they brought the boy to Him. And when he saw Him, immediately the spirit threw him into a convulsion, and falling to the ground, he *began* rolling^ᵐ about and foaming *at the mouth.*

21 And He asked his father, "How long has this been happening⁺ to him?" And he said, "From childhood.

22 "And it has often thrown him both into the *fire* and into the ⁺*water* to destroy^x him. But if You can do anything, take pity on us and help^{xᴵ} us!"

23 And Jesus said to him, " 'If You can!' All things are possible to him who believes."

9:23
Matt. 17:20; John 11:40

24 Immediately the boy's father cried out and *began* saying,^ᵐ "I do believe; help ~ᴵ my *unbelief.*"

25 And when Jesus saw that a crowd was rapidly gathering, He rebuked the unclean spirit, saying to it, "You deaf and dumb spirit, I command you, come^{xᴵ} out of him and do not enter[◦] him again."

9:25
Mark 9:15

26 And after crying out and throwing him into terrible convulsions, it came out; and *the boy* became so much like a corpse that most *of them* said, ~ "He is dead!"

27 But Jesus took him by the hand and raised him; and he got up.

28 And when He had come into *the* house, His disciples *began* questioning Him privately, "Why could *we* not cast^x it out?"

9:28
Mark 2:1; 7:17

29 And He said to them, "This kind cannot come^x out by anything but prayer^x."

Death and Resurrection Foretold

30 And from there they went out and *began* to go through Galilee, and He was unwilling^ᵐ for anyone to know^x *about it.*

9:30
Mark 9:30-32; Matt. 17:22,23; Luke 9:43-45
9:31
Matt. 16:21; Mark 8:31; 9:12

31 For He was teaching^ᵐ His disciples and telling^ᵐ them, "The Son of Man is to be ^ydelivered into the hands of men, and they will kill Him; and when He has been killed, He will rise three days later."

32 But they did not understand^ᵐ *this* statement, and they were afraid^ᵐ to ask^{x 9c} Him.

9:32
Luke 2:50; 9:45; 18:34; John 12:16

33 And they came to Capernaum; and when He was in the house, He *began* to question^ᵐ them, "What were you discussing^ᵐ on the way?"

9:33
Mark 9:33-37; Matt. 18:1-5; Luke 9:46-48; Mark 3:19

34 But they kept silent,^ᵐ for on the way they had discussed with one another which *of them was* the greatest.

9:34
Matt. 18:4; Mark 9:50; Luke 22:24

35 And sitting down, He called the twelve and *said to them, "If anyone wants to be first, he shall be *last* of all, and *servant*[38a] of all."

9:35
Matt. 20:26; 23:11; Mark 10:43,44; Luke 22:26

^xMany mss. add: *and fasting* ^yOr, *betrayed*

36 And taking a child, He set him before them, and taking him in His arms, He said to them,

9:37
Matt. 10:40; Luke
10:16; John 13:20

37 "Whoever receives[x] one child like this in My name receives *Me;* and whoever receives[~] *Me* does not receive *Me,* but Him who sent Me."

Dire Warnings

9:38
Mark 9:38-40:
Luke 9:49,50;
Num. 11:27-29

38 John said to Him, "Teacher, we saw someone casting out demons in Your name, and we tried to hinder[m] him because he was not following[m] us."

39 But Jesus said, "Do not hinder[o] him, for there is no one who shall perform a miracle in My name, and be able soon afterward to speak[x] evil of Me.

9:40
Matt. 12:30; Luke
11:23
9:41
Matt. 10:42

40 "For he who is not against us is [z]for us.

41 "For whoever gives[x] you a cup of water to drink because of your name as *followers* of [†]Christ, [•]truly I say to you, he shall [•]*not* lose[x] his reward.

9:42
Matt. 18:6; Luke
17:2; 1 Cor. 8:12

42 "And whoever causes one of these little ones who believe to stumble,[x] it would be better for him if, with a heavy millstone hung around his neck, he had been cast[•] into the sea.

9:43
Matt. 5:30; 18:8;
Matt. 5:22;
Matt. 3:12; 25:41

43 "And if your hand causes you to stumble,[~] cut[xl] it off; it is better for you to enter[x] life *crippled,* than having your *two hands,* to go[x] into hell,[27b] into the *unquenchable* fire,

44 [[a]where THEIR WORM DOES NOT DIE, AND THE FIRE IS NOT QUENCHED.]

9:45
Matt. 5:22

45 "And if your foot causes you to stumble,[~] cut[xl] it off; it is better for you to enter[x] life lame, than having your *two feet,* to be cast[x] into hell,[27b]

46 [[a]where THEIR WORM DOES NOT DIE, AND THE FIRE IS NOT QUENCHED.]

9:47
Matt. 5:29; 18:9;
Matt. 5:22

47 "And if your eye causes you to stumble,[~] cast[xl] it out; it is better for you to enter[x] the kingdom of God with *one* eye, than having *two* eyes, to be cast[x] into hell,[27b]

9:48
Is. 66:24;
Matt. 3:12; 25:41

48 where THEIR WORM DOES NOT DIE, AND THE FIRE IS NOT QUENCHED.

49 "For everyone will be salted with *fire.*

9:50
Matt. 5:13; Luke
14:34f.;
Col. 4:6;
Mark 9:34; Rom.
12:18; 2 Cor.
13:11; 1 Thess.
5:13

50 "Salt is good; but if the salt becomes *unsalty,* with what will you make it salty *again?* Have[~l] salt *in yourselves,* and be at peace[~l] with one another."

Jesus' Teaching about Divorce

10:1
Mark 10:1-12:
Matt. 19:1-9;
Matt. 4:23; 26:55;
Mark 1:21; 2:13;
4:2; 6:2,6,34;
12:35; 14:49

10 And rising up, He [*]went from there to the region of Judea, and beyond the Jordan; and crowds [*]gathered around

[z]Or, *on our side* [a]Vv. 44 and 46, which are identical with v. 48, are not found in the best ancient mss.

Him again, and, according to His custom, He once more *began* to teach them.

2   And *some* Pharisees came up to Him, testing Him, and *began* to question[m] Him whether it was lawful for a man to divorce[x] a wife.

3   And He answered and said to them, "What did *Moses* command you?"

4   And they said, "Moses permitted[6c] *a man* TO WRITE[x] A CERTIFICATE OF DIVORCE AND SEND[x] *her* AWAY."

> **10:4**
> Deut. 24:1,3;
> Matt. 5:31

5   But Jesus said to them, "Because of *your hardness of heart* he wrote you this commandment.

> **10:5**
> Matt. 19:8

6   "But from the beginning of creation, *God* MADE THEM *MALE AND FEMALE.*

> **10:6**
> Mark 13:19;
> 2 Pet. 3:4;
> Gen. 1:27; 5:2

7   "FOR THIS CAUSE A MAN SHALL LEAVE HIS FATHER AND MOTHER,[b]

> **10:7**
> Gen. 2:24

8   AND THE TWO SHALL BECOME ONE FLESH; consequently they are no longer two, but *one* flesh.

> **10:8**
> Gen. 2:24

9   "What therefore God has joined together, let no *man* separate."[o]

10   And in the house the disciples *began* questioning[m] Him about this again.

11   And He *said to them, "Whoever divorces[x] his wife and marries[x] another woman commits adultery against her;

> **10:11**
> Matt. 5:32

12   and if she herself divorces her husband and marries[x] another man, she is committing adultery."

> **10:12**
> 1 Cor. 7:11,13

Jesus Blesses Little Children

13   And they were bringing[m] children to Him so that He might touch[x] them; and the disciples rebuked them.

> **10:13**
> Mark 10:13-16:
> *Matt. 19:13-15;*
> *Luke 18:15-17*

14   But when Jesus saw this, He was indignant and said to them, "Permit[x16a] the children to come~ to Me; do not hinder[o] them; for the kingdom of God belongs to such as these.

> **10:14**
> Matt. 5:3

15   "•Truly I say to you, whoever does not receive[x] the kingdom of God like a child shall •*not* enter[x] it *at all.*"

> **10:15**
> Matt. 18:3; 19:14;
> Luke 18:17; 1
> Cor. 14:20; 1 Pet.
> 2:2

16   And He took them in His arms and *began* blessing[m] them, laying His hands upon them.

> **10:16**
> Mark 9:36

The Rich Young Ruler

17   And as He was setting out on a journey, a man ran up to Him and knelt before Him, and *began* asking[9c] Him, "Good[25a] Teacher, what shall I do[x19a] to inherit[x] *eternal life?*"

> **10:17**
> Mark 10:17-31:
> *Matt. 19:16-30;*
> *Luke 18:18-30;*
> Mark 1:40;
> Matt. 25:34; Luke
> 10:25; 18:18;
> Acts 20:32; Eph.
> 1:18; 1 Pet. 1:4

18   And Jesus said to him, "Why do you call Me good?[25a] No one is good except God alone.

---

[b]Some mss. add: *and shall cleave to his wife*

10:19
Ex. 20:12-16;
Deut. 5:16-20

19 "You know[29e] the commandments, 'DO NOT MURDER,° DO NOT COMMIT ADULTERY,° DO NOT STEAL,° DO NOT BEAR° FALSE WITNESS, Do not defraud,° HONOR[~1] YOUR FATHER AND MOTHER.' "

10:20
Matt. 19:20

20 And he said to Him, "Teacher, I have kept *all* these things from my youth up."

10:21
Matt. 6:20

21 And looking at him, Jesus felt a love[31a] for him, and said to him, "One thing you lack: go and sell[xi] *all you possess,* and give[xi] to the poor, and you shall have treasure in heaven; and come, follow[~1] Me."

22 But at these words his face fell, and he went away grieved, for he was one who owned *much* property.

10:23
Matt. 19:23

23 And Jesus, looking around, *said to His disciples, "How [†]*hard* it will be for those who are wealthy to enter the kingdom of God!"

10:24
Mark 1:27

24 And the disciples were amazed[m] at His words. But Jesus *answered again and *said to them, "Children, how [†]*hard* it is [c]to enter[x] the kingdom of God!

10:25
Matt. 19:24

25 "It is [†]*easier* for a camel to go[x] through the *eye of a needle* than for a rich man to enter[x] the kingdom of God."

26 And they were even more astonished[m1] and said to Him, "Then who can be saved?"[x]

10:27
Matt. 19:26

27 Looking upon them, Jesus *said, "With *men* it is impossible, but not with [†]*God;* for all things are possible with God."

10:28
Matt. 4:20-22

28 Peter began to say[~] to Him, "Behold, *we* have left everything and followed[+] You."

10:29
Matt. 6:33; 19:29;
Luke 18:29f.

29 Jesus said, "[•]*Truly* I say to you, there is no one who has left house or brothers or sisters or mother or father or children or farms, for My sake and for the gospel's sake,

10:30
Matt. 12:32

30 but that he shall receive[x] a hundred times as much *now* in the *present* age, houses and brothers and sisters and mothers and children and farms, along with persecutions; and in the age to *come,* eternal life.

10:31
Matt. 19:30;
20:16; Luke 13:30

31 "But many *who are first,* will be last; and the [†]*last,* first."

Jesus' Sufferings Foretold

10:32
Mark 10:32-34;
Matt. 20:17-19;
Luke 18:31-33;
Mark 1:27

32 And they were on the road, going[~] up to Jerusalem, and Jesus was walking[~] on ahead of them; and they were amazed,[m] and those who followed were fearful.[m] And again He took the twelve aside and began to tell[~] them what was going to happen to Him,

10:33
Mark 8:31; 9:12

33 *saying,* "Behold, we are going up to Jerusalem, and the Son of Man will be [d]delivered to the chief priests and the scribes; and

[c]Later mss. insert: *for those who trust in wealth*   [d]Or, *betrayed*

they will condemn Him to death, and will deliver Him to the Gentiles.

34 "And they will mock Him and spit upon Him, and scourge Him, and kill *Him,* and three days later He will rise again."

35 And James and John, the two sons of Zebedee, *came up to Him, saying to Him, "Teacher, we want You to do[x] for us whatever we ask[x] of You."

36 And He said to them, "What do you want Me to do[x] for you?"

37 And they said to Him, "Grant[xi] that we may sit[x] in Your glory, one on Your right, and one on *Your* left."

38 But Jesus said to them, "You do not know what you are asking for. Are you able to drink[x] the cup that *I* drink, or to be baptized[x] with the baptism with which *I* am baptized?"

39 And they said to Him, "We are able." And Jesus said to them, "The cup that *I* drink you *shall drink,* and you *shall be baptized* with the baptism with which *I* am baptized.

40 "But to sit[x] on My right or on *My* left, this is not Mine to give;[x] but it is for those for whom it has been prepared." +

41 And hearing this, the ten began to feel~ indignant with James and John.

42 And calling them to Himself, Jesus *said to them, "You know that those who are recognized as rulers of the Gentiles lord it over them; and their great men exercise authority over them.

43 "But it is not so among you, but whoever wishes~ to become †great[26a] among you shall be your *servant,* [38a]

44 and whoever wishes~ to be first among you shall be *slave* [38b] of all.

45 "For even the Son of Man did not come to be served,[x] [38a] but to serve,[x] and to give[x] His life a ransom for many."

Bartimaeus Receives His Sight

46 And they *came to Jericho. And as He was going out from Jericho with His disciples and a great multitude, a blind beggar *named* Bartimaeus, the son of Timaeus, was sitting[m] by the road.

47 And when he heard that it was Jesus the Nazarene, he began to cry~ out and say,~ "Jesus, Son of David, have mercy[xi] on me!"

48 And many were sternly telling[m] him to be quiet,[x] but he kept crying[m] out all the more, "Son of David, have mercy[xi] on me!"

49 And Jesus stopped and said, "Call[xi] him *here.*" And they *called the blind man, saying to him, "Take courage, arise! He is calling for you."

10:34
Matt. 16:21;
26:67; 27:30;
Mark 9:31; 14:65
10:35
Mark 10:35-45:
Matt. 20:20-28

10:37
Matt. 19:28

10:38
Matt. 20:22;
Luke 12:50

10:39
Acts 12:2; Rev.
1:9

10:40
Matt. 13:11

10:41
Mark 10:42-45;
Luke 22:25-27

10:43
Matt. 20:26;
23:11; Mark 9:35;
Luke 22:26

10:45
Matt. 20:28

10:46
Mark 10:46-52:
Matt. 20:29-34;
Luke 18:35-43;
Luke 18:35; 19:1

10:47
Mark 1:24;
Matt. 9:27

10:48
Matt. 9:27

10:49
Matt. 9:2

50   And casting aside his cloak, he jumped up, and came to Jesus.

10:51
Matt. 23:7; John 20:16

51   And answering him, Jesus said, "What do you want Me to do˟ for you?" And the blind man said to Him, "ᵉRabboni, *I want* to regain˟ my sight!"

10:52
Matt. 9:22

52   And Jesus said to him, "Go your way; your faith has made⁺ you well." And immediately he regained his sight and *began* following˟˟ Him on the road.

The Triumphal Entry

11:1
Mark 11:1-10;
Matt. 21:1-9;
Luke 19:29-38;
Matt. 21:17;
Matt. 21:1

11 And as they *approached Jerusalem, at Bethphage and Bethany, near the Mount of Olives, He *sent two of His disciples,

2   and *said to them, "Go into the village opposite you, and immediately as you enter it, you will find a colt tied⁺ *there*, on which no one yet has ever sat; untie˟ᴵ it and bring〜ᴵ it *here*.

3   "And if anyone says˟ to you, 'Why are you doing this?' you say,˟ᴵ 'The Lord has need of it'; and immediately he will send it back here."

4   And they went away and found a colt tied⁺ at the door outside in the street; and they *untied it.

5   And some of the bystanders were saying˟˟ to them, "What are you doing, untying the colt?"

6   And they spoke to them just as Jesus had told *them*, and they gave them permission.

11:7
Mark 11:7-10;
Matt. 21:4-9;
Luke 19:35-38;
John 12:12-15

7   And they *brought the colt to Jesus and put their garments on it; and He sat upon it.

8   And many spread *their garments* in the road, and others *spread* leafy branches which they had cut from the fields.

11:9
Ps. 118:26; Matt. 21:9

9   And those who went before, and those who followed after, were crying˟˟ out,

"Hosanna!
Blessed⁺ is He who comes in the name of the Lord;

11:10
Matt. 21:9

10   Blessed⁺ *is* the coming kingdom of our father David; Hosanna in the highest!"

11:11
Matt. 21:12;
Matt. 21:17

11   And He entered Jerusalem *and came* into the temple; and after looking all around, He departed for Bethany with the twelve, since it was already late.

11:12
Mark 11:12-14,
20-24; *Matt. 21:18-22*

12   And on the next day, when they had departed from Bethany, He became hungry.

13   And seeing at a distance a fig tree in leaf, He went *to see* if perhaps He would find anything on it; and when He came to it,

ᵉI.e., My Master

He found †nothing but leaves, for it was not the season for figs.

14   And He answered and said to it, "May no one *ever* eat^x fruit from you *again!*" And His disciples were listening.^{xx}

Jesus Drives Moneychangers from the Temple

15   And they *came to Jerusalem. And He entered the temple and began to cast~ out those who were buying and selling in the temple, and overturned the tables of the moneychangers and the seats of those who were selling doves;

16   and He would not permit^{xx} anyone to carry^x goods through the temple.

17   And He *began* to teach and say to them, "Is it not written, + 'MY HOUSE SHALL BE CALLED A *HOUSE OF PRAYER* FOR ALL THE NATIONS'? But *you* have made+ it a ROBBERS' DEN."

18   And the chief priests and the scribes heard *this*, and *began* seeking^{xx} how to destroy^x Him; for they were afraid^{xx} of Him, for all the multitude was astonished^{xx1} at His teaching.

19   And whenever evening came, they would go^{xx} out of the city.

20   And as they were passing by in the morning, they saw the fig tree withered+ from the roots *up*.

21   And being reminded, Peter *said to Him, "Rabbi, behold, the fig tree which You cursed has withered."+

22   And Jesus *answered saying to them, "Have~ faith in God.

23   "•Truly I say to you, whoever says^x to this mountain, 'Be taken^{xl} up and cast^{xl} into the sea,' and does not doubt^x in his heart, but believes~ that what he says is going to happen, it shall be *granted* him.

24   "Therefore I say to you, all things for which you pray and ask, ^{9a} believe~ that you have received^{5b} them, and they shall be *granted* you.

25   "And whenever you stand praying, forgive, ~^{121a} if you have anything against anyone; so that your Father also who is in heaven may forgive^x you your transgressions. ^{40b}

26   ["†But if you do not forgive,^{21a} neither will your Father who is in heaven forgive your transgressions."]

Jesus' Authority Questioned

27   And they *came again to Jerusalem. And as He was walking in the temple, the chief priests, and scribes, and elders *came to Him,

28   and *began* saying^{xx} to Him, "By what authority are You

11:15
Mark 11:15-18:
Matt. 21:12-16;
Luke 19:45-47;
John 2:13-16

11:17
Is. 56:7;
Jer. 7:11

11:18
Matt. 21:46; Mark
12:12; Luke
20:19; John 7:1;
Matt. 7:28

11:19
Matt. 21:17; Mark
11:11; Luke 21:37

11:20
Mark 11:12-14,
20-24: *Matt.
21:19-22*
11:21
Matt. 23:7

11:22
Matt. 17:20;
21:21f.

11:23
Matt. 17:20;
1 Cor. 13:2

11:24
Matt. 7:7f.

11:25
Matt. 6:5;
Matt. 6:14

11:26
Matt. 6:15; 18:35

11:27
Mark 11:27-33:
Matt. 21:23-27;
Luke 20:1-8

†Many mss. do not contain this verse

doing~ these things, or who gave *You* this authority to do these things?''

29   And Jesus said to them, ''I will ask you †one question, and you answer^{xl} Me, and *then* I will tell you by what authority I do these things.

30   ''Was the baptism of John from *heaven*, or from †men? Answer^{xl} Me.''

31   And they *began* reasoning ^m among themselves, saying, ''If we say,^x 'From heaven,' He will say, 'Then why did you not believe him?'

32   ''But shall we say,^x 'From men'?''—they were afraid^m of the multitude, for all considered^m John to have been a prophet *indeed.*

33   And answering Jesus, they *said, ''We do not know.'' And Jesus *said to them, ''Neither will *I* tell you by what authority I do these things.''

Parable of the Vine-growers

12:1
Mark 3:23; 4:2ff.;
Mark 12:1-12:
Matt. 21:33-46;
Luke 20:9-19;
Is. 5:1,2

12 And He began to speak~ to them in parables: ''A man PLANTED A VINEYARD, AND PUT A WALL AROUND IT, AND DUG A VAT UNDER THE WINE PRESS, AND BUILT A TOWER, and rented it out to ^gvine-growers and went on a journey.

2   ''And at the *harvest* time he sent a slave to the vine-growers, in order to receive^x *some* of the produce of the vineyard from the vine-growers.

3   ''And they took him, and beat him, and sent him away empty-handed.

4   ''And again he sent them another slave, and they wounded him in the head, and treated him shamefully.

5   ''And he sent *another,* and *that one* they killed; and *so with* many others, beating some, and killing others.

6   ''He had one more *to send,* a *beloved* son; he sent him last *of all* to them, saying, 'They will respect my son.'

7   ''But those vine-growers said to one another, 'This is the heir; come, let us kill^x him, and the inheritance will be *ours!'*

8   ''And they took him, and killed him, and threw him out of the vineyard.

9   ''What will the owner of the vineyard do? He will come and destroy the vine-growers, and will give the vineyard to others.

12:10
Ps. 118:22

10   ''Have you not even read this Scripture:

'THE STONE WHICH THE BUILDERS †REJECTED,

THIS BECAME THE CHIEF CORNER *stone;*

9Or, *tenant farmers,* also vv. 2, 7, 9

11   THIS CAME ABOUT *FROM THE LORD,*
    AND IT IS MARVELOUS IN OUR EYES'?''

12   And they were seeking[m] to seize[x] Him; and *yet* they feared the multitude; for they understood that He spoke the parable *against them.* And *so* they left Him, and went away.

Jesus Answers the Pharisees, Sadducees and Scribes

13   And they *sent some of the Pharisees and Herodians to Him, in order to trap[x] Him in a statement.

14   And they *came and *said to Him, ''Teacher, we know that You are [t]truthful, and defer to no one; for You are not partial to any, but teach the way of God in *truth.* Is it lawful to pay[x] a poll-tax to Caesar, or not?

15   ''Shall we pay,[x] or shall we not pay?''[x] But He, knowing their *hypocrisy,* said to them, ''Why are you testing Me? Bring Me a [h]denarius to look[x] at.''

16   And they brought *one.* And He *said to them, ''Whose likeness and inscription is this?'' And they said to Him, ''Caesar's.''

17   And Jesus said to them, ''Render[x] to Caesar the things that are *Caesar's,* and to God the things that are [t]*God's.''* And they were amazed[m1] at Him.

18   And *some* Sadducees (who say that there is no resurrection) *came to Him, and *began* questioning[m] Him, saying,

19   ''Teacher, Moses wrote for us that IF A MAN'S BROTHER DIES,[x] and leaves[x] behind a wife, AND LEAVES[x] NO CHILD, HIS BROTHER SHOULD TAKE[x] THE WIFE, AND RAISE[x] UP OFFSPRING TO HIS BROTHER.

20   ''There were *seven* brothers; and the first took a wife, and died, leaving no offspring.

21   ''And the second one took her, and died, leaving behind no offspring; and the third likewise;

22   and *so* all seven left no offspring. Last of all the woman died also.

23   ''In the resurrection, [i]when they rise[x] again, which one's wife will she be? For all seven had her as wife.''

24   Jesus said to them, ''Is this not the reason you are mistaken, that you do not understand[29e] the Scriptures, or the power[32a] of God?

25   ''For when they rise[x] from the dead, they neither marry, nor are given in marriage, but are like angels in heaven.

26   ''But regarding the fact that the dead rise again, have you not read in the book of Moses, in the *passage about the burning*

[h]The denarius was equivalent to one day's wage   [i]Most ancient mss. do not contain *when they rise again*

12:11
Ps. 118:23

12:12
Mark 11:18;
Matt. 22:22

12:13
Mark 12:13-17;
Matt. 22:15-22;
Luke 20:20-26;
Matt. 22:16;
Luke 11:54

12:17
Matt. 22:21

12:18
Mark 12:18-27;
Matt. 22:23-33;
Luke 20:27-38;
Acts 23:8
12:19
Deut. 25:5

12:26
Luke 20:37; Rom.
11:2;
Ex. 3:6

bush, how God spoke to him, saying, 'I AM THE GOD OF ABRA-
HAM, AND THE GOD OF ISAAC, AND THE GOD OF JACOB'?

12:27
Matt. 22:32; Luke
20:38

27 "He is not the God of the dead, but of the living; you are greatly mistaken."

12:28
Mark 12:28-34;
Matt. 22:34-40;
Luke 10:25-28;
20:39f.;
Matt. 22:34;
20:39
12:29
Deut. 6:4

28 And one of the scribes came and heard them arguing, and recognizing that He had answered them well, asked Him, "What commandment is the foremost of all?"

29 Jesus answered, "The foremost is, 'HEAR, ~ O ISRAEL! THE LORD OUR GOD IS *ONE* LORD;

12:30
Deut. 6:5

30 AND YOU SHALL LOVE[31a] THE LORD YOUR GOD WITH ALL YOUR HEART, AND WITH ALL YOUR SOUL,[30c] AND WITH ALL YOUR MIND,[33a] AND WITH ALL YOUR STRENGTH.'[32c]

12:31
Lev. 19:18

31 "The second is this, 'YOU SHALL LOVE YOUR NEIGHBOR AS YOURSELF.' There is no other commandment greater[26a] than these."

12:32
Deut. 4:35

32 And the scribe said to Him, "Right, Teacher, You have truly stated that HE IS †*ONE; AND THERE IS NO ONE ELSE BESIDES HIM;

12:33
Deut. 6:5;
1 Sam. 15:22;
Hos. 6:6; Mic.
6:6-8; Matt. 9:13;
12:7

33 AND TO LOVE~ HIM WITH ALL THE HEART AND WITH ALL THE UNDERSTANDING[29f] AND WITH ALL THE STRENGTH,[32c] AND TO LOVE~ ONE'S NEIGHBOR AS HIMSELF, is much more than all burnt offerings and sacrifices."

12:34
Matt. 22:46

34 And when Jesus saw that he had answered intelligently, He said to him, "You are not far from the kingdom of God." And after that, no one would venture[m] to ask[x] Him any more questions.

12:35
Mark 12:35-37;
Matt. 22:41-46;
Luke 20:41-44;
Matt. 26:55; Mark
10:1;
Matt. 9:27
12:36
Ps. 110:1

35 And Jesus answering *began* to say, as He taught in the temple, "How *is it that* the scribes say that the Christ is the *son of David?*

36 "David *himself* said in the Holy Spirit,
'THE LORD SAID TO MY LORD,
"SIT AT MY RIGHT HAND,
UNTIL I PUT[x] THINE ENEMIES BENEATH THY FEET." '

12:37
John 12:9

37 "David *himself* calls Him 'Lord'; and *so* in what sense is He *his* son?" And the great crowd enjoyed listening[m] to Him.

12:38
Mark 12:38-40;
Matt. 23:1-7;
Luke 20:45-47;
Matt. 23:7; Luke
11:43

38 And in His teaching He was saying:[m] "Beware~ of the scribes who like to walk~ around in long robes, and *like* respectful greetings in the market places,

39 and chief seats in the synagogues, and places of honor at banquets,

12:40
Luke 20:47

40 who devour[l] widows' houses, and for appearance's †sake offer long prayers; these will receive greater condemnation."

The Widow's Mite

41   And He sat down opposite the treasury, and *began* observing^m how the multitude were putting money into the treasury; and many rich people were putting^m in large sums.

42   And a poor widow came and put in two small copper coins, which amount to a cent.

43   And calling His disciples to Him, He said to them, "•Truly I say to you, this poor widow put in *more than all* the contributors to the treasury;

44   for they all put in out of their surplus, but she, out of her *poverty,* put in *all* she owned, all she had^m to live on."

12:41
Mark 12:41-44:
Luke 21:1-4;
John 8:20;
2 Kin. 12:9

12:44
Luke 8:43; 15:12,
30; 21:4

Things to Come

13   And as He was going out of the temple, one of His disciples *said to Him, "Teacher, behold ⁱwhat wonderful stones and what wonderful buildings!"

2   And Jesus said to him, "Do you see these great buildings? •*Not* one stone shall be left^x upon another which will •*not* be torn^x down."

3   And as He was sitting on the Mount of Olives opposite the temple, Peter and James and John and Andrew were questioning^m Him privately,

4   "Tell^x us, when will these things be, and what *will be* the sign when all these things are going to be fulfilled?"

5   And Jesus began to say~ to them, "See^{~i} to it that no one misleads^x you.

6   "Many will come in My name, saying, '*I* am *He!*' and will mislead *many.*

7   "And when you hear^x of wars and rumors of wars, do not be frightened;^θ *those things* must take place; but *that is* not [†]yet the end.

8   "For nation will arise against nation, and kingdom against kingdom; there will be earthquakes in various places; there will *also* be famines. These things are *merely* the *beginning of birth* [†]*pangs.*

9   "But be on your guard;^{~i} for they will deliver you to *the* courts, and you will be flogged in *the* synagogues, and you will stand before governors and kings for My sake, as a testimony to them.

10   "And the gospel must first be preached^x to *all the nations.*

11   "And when they arrest~ you and deliver you up, do not be anxious^θ beforehand about what you are to say,^x but say^{~i}

13:1
Mark 13:1-37:
*Matt. 24; Luke
21:5-36*

13:2
Luke 19:44

13:3
Matt. 21:1;
Matt. 17:1

13:6
John 8:24

13:9
Matt. 10:17

13:10
Matt. 24:14
13:11
Mark 13:11-13:
*Matt. 10:19-22;
Luke 21:12-17*

ⁱLit., *how great*

whatever is given[x] you in that hour; for it is not *you* who speak, but *it is* the Holy Spirit.

12 "And brother will deliver brother to death, and a father *his* child; and children will rise up against parents and have them put to death.

13:13
Matt. 10:22; John 15:21

13 "And you will be hated~ by all on account of My name, but the one who endures to the end, he shall be saved.

13:14
Matt. 24:15f.; Dan. 9:27; 11:31; 12:11

14 "But when you see[x] the ABOMINATION OF DESOLATION standing+ where it should not be (let the reader understand), ~[29d] then let those who are in Judea flee to the mountains.

13:15
Luke 17:31

15 "And let him who is on the housetop not go[θ] down, or enter[θ] in, to get[x] anything out of his house;

16 and let him who is in the field not turn[θ] back to get[x] his cloak.

17 "But woe to those who are with child and to those who nurse babes in those days!

18 "But pray~ that it may not happen in the winter.

13:19
Dan. 12:1; Mark 10:6

19 "For *those* days will be a *time of* tribulation such as has not occurred+ since the beginning of the creation which God created, until now, and •*never shall.*

20 "And unless the Lord had shortened *those* days, *no life* would have been saved; but for the sake of the elect whom He chose, He shortened the days.

21 "And then if anyone says[x] to you, 'Behold, here is the Christ'; or, 'Behold, *He is* there'; do not believe[θ] *him;*

13:22
Matt. 7:15; Matt. 24:24; John 4:48

22 for false Christs and false prophets will arise, and will show signs and wonders, in order, if possible, to lead the elect astray.~

23 "But take heed;~ behold, I have told+ you everything in advance.

The Return of Christ

13:24
Is. 13:10; Ezek. 32:7; Joel 2:10, 31; 3:15; Rev. 6:12
13:25
Is. 34:4; Rev. 6:13
13:26
Dan. 7:13; Rev. 1:7; Matt. 16:27; Mark 8:38
13:27
Deut. 30:4; Zech. 2:6

24 "But in those days, after *that* tribulation, THE SUN WILL BE DARKENED, AND THE MOON WILL NOT GIVE ITS LIGHT,

25 AND THE STARS WILL BE FALLING~ from heaven, and the powers that are in the heavens will be shaken.

26 "And then they will see THE SON OF MAN COMING IN CLOUDS with great[26b] power[32a] and glory.

27 "And then He will send forth the angels, and will gather together His elect from the four winds, from the farthest end of the earth, to the farthest end of heaven.

28 "Now learn[xl] the parable from the fig tree: when its branch has already become tender, and puts~ forth its leaves, you know[29a] that summer is *near.*

29 "Even so, you too, when you see[x] these things happening, recognize[~l] that He is near, *right* at the door.

30 "•Truly I say to you, this [k]generation will •*not* pass[x] away until all these things take place.

31 "Heaven and earth will pass away, but My words[43a] will •*not* pass away.

32 "But of *that* day or hour no one knows, not even the angels in heaven, nor the Son, but the Father *alone*.

33 "Take heed, [~l] keep on the alert; [~l] for you do not know[29e] when the *appointed* time is.

34 "*It is* like a man, away on a journey, *who* upon leaving his house and putting his slaves in charge, *assigning* to each one his task, also commanded the doorkeeper to stay[~] on the alert.

35 "Therefore, be on the alert[~l]—for you do not know when the master of the house is coming, whether in the evening, at midnight, at cockcrowing, or in the morning—

36 lest he come suddenly and find[x] you asleep.

37 "And what I say to you I say to *all*, 'Be on the alert!' "[~l]

Death Plot and Anointing

14 Now the Passover and Unleavened Bread was two days off; and the chief priests and the scribes were seeking[m] how to seize Him by *stealth*, and kill[x] *Him*;

2 for they were saying,[m] "Not during the festival, lest there be a riot of the people."

3 And while He was in Bethany at the home of Simon the leper, and reclining *at the table*, there came a woman with an alabaster vial of *very costly* perfume of *pure* nard; *and* she broke the vial and poured it over His *head*.

4 But some were indignantly *remarking* to one another, "Why has this perfume been wasted?

5 "For this perfume might[m] have been sold[x] for over three hundred [l]denarii, and *the money* given[x] to the poor." And they were scolding[m] her.

6 But Jesus said, "Let[xl] her alone; why do you bother her? She has done a *good*[25b] deed to Me.

7 "For the poor you always have with you, and whenever you wish, you can do[x] them good; but you do not always have *Me*.

8 "She has done what she could; she has anointed[x] My body beforehand for the burial.

9 "And •truly I say to you, wherever the gospel is preached[x] in the whole world, that also which *this woman* has done shall be spoken of in memory of her."

[k]Or, *race*   [l]The denarius was equivalent to one day's wage

---

13:32
Matt. 24:36; Acts 1:7

13:33
Eph. 6:18; Col. 4:2

13:34
Luke 12:36-38

13:35
Matt. 24:42; Mark 13:37;
Mark 14:30;
Matt. 14:25; Mark 6:48
13:36
Rom. 13:11
13:37
Matt. 24:42; Mark 13:35

14:1
Mark 14:1,2;
Matt. 26:2-5;
Luke 22:1,2;
Ex. 12:1-27; Mark 14:12; John 11:55; 13:1;
Matt. 12:14

14:3
Mark 14:3-9;
Matt. 26:6-13;
Luke 7:37-39;
John 12:1-8;
Matt. 21:17;
Matt. 26:6f.; John 12:3

14:7
Deut. 15:11; Matt. 26:11; John 12:8

14:8
John 19:40

14:9
Matt. 26:13

14:10
Mark 14:10,11;
Matt. 26:14-16;
Luke 22:3-6;
John 6:71
10 And Judas Iscariot, who was one of the twelve, went off to the chief priests, in order to betray[x] Him to them.

11 And they were glad when they heard *this*, and promised to give[x] him money. And he *began* seeking[xx] how to betray[x] Him at an opportune time.

The Last Passover

14:12
Mark 14:12-16;
Matt. 26:17-19;
Luke 22:7-13;
Matt. 26:17;
Deut. 16:5; Mark
14:1; Luke 22:7; 1
Cor. 5:7
12 And on the first day of Unleavened Bread, when the *Passover lamb* was being sacrificed,[x] His disciples *said to Him, "Where do You want us to go and prepare[xx] for You to eat[x] the Passover?"

13 And He *sent two of His disciples, and *said to them, "Go into the city, and a *man* will meet you carrying a pitcher of water; follow[xl] him;

14:14
Luke 22:11
14 and wherever he enters,[x] say[xl] to the owner of the house, 'The Teacher says, "Where is My guest room in which I may eat[x] the Passover with My disciples?" '

15 "And he himself will show you a large upper room furnished[+] *and* ready; and prepare[xl] for us *there.*"

16 And the disciples went out, and came to the city, and found *it* just as He had told them; and they prepared the Passover.

14:17
Mark 14:17-21;
Matt. 26:20-24;
Luke 22:14,
21-23; John
13:18ff.
17 And when it was evening He *came with the twelve.

18 And as they were reclining *at the table* and eating, Jesus said, "•Truly I say to you that one of you will betray Me—one who is eating with Me."

19 They began to be grieved[~] and to say[~] to Him one by one, "Surely not I?"

20 And He said to them, *"It is* one of the twelve, one who dips with Me in the bowl.

21 "For the Son of Man *is to* go, just as it is written[+] of Him; but woe to *that* man by whom the Son of Man is betrayed! *It would have been* good for *that* man if he had *not been born.*"

The Lord's Supper

14:22
Mark 14:22-25;
Matt. 26:26-29;
Luke 22:17-20;
1 Cor. 11:23-25;
Mark 10:16;
Matt. 14:19
22 And while they were eating, He took *some* bread, and after a blessing He broke *it;* and gave *it* to them, and said, "Take[xl] *it;* this is My body."

23 And when He had taken a cup, *and* given thanks, He gave *it* to them; and they all drank from it.

14:24
Ex. 24:8;
Jer. 31:31-34
24 And He said to them, "This is My blood of the covenant, which is poured out for many.

25 "•Truly I say to you, I shall •never again drink[x] of the fruit of

the vine until that day when I drink~ it new[34a] in the kingdom of God."

26 And after singing a hymn, they went out to the Mount of Olives.

27 And Jesus *said to them, "You will all fall away, because it is written,[+] 'I WILL STRIKE DOWN THE SHEPHERD, AND THE SHEEP SHALL BE SCATTERED.'

28 "But after I have been raised,[x] I will go before you to Galilee."

29 But Peter said[m] to Him, "*Even* though all may fall away, yet I will not."

30 And Jesus *said to him, "•Truly I say to you, that *you yourself* this very night, before a cock crows[x] twice, shall three times deny Me."

31 But *Peter* kept saying[m] insistently,[1] "*Even* if I have~ to die[x] with You, I will •*not* deny You!" And they all were saying[m] the same thing, too.

Jesus in Gethsemane

32 And they *came to a place named Gethsemane; and He *said to His disciples, "Sit[N] here until I have prayed."[x]

33 And He *took with Him Peter and James and John, and began to be very[1] distressed~ and troubled.~

34 And He *said to them, "My soul is *deeply*[1] grieved to the point of death; remain[N] here and keep watch."[M]

35 And He went a little beyond *them,* and fell[m] to the ground, and *began* to pray[m] that if it were possible, the hour might *pass[x] Him by.*

36 And He was saying,[m] "Abba! Father! All things are possible for Thee; remove[N] this cup from Me; yet not what *I* will, but what [+]*Thou* wilt."

37 And He *came and *found them sleeping, and *said to Peter, "Simon, are you asleep? Could you not keep[x] watch for *one* hour?

38 "Keep watching[M] and praying,[M] that you may not come into temptation; the spirit is willing, but the flesh is weak."

39 And again He went away and prayed, saying the same words.

40 And again He came and found them sleeping, for *their* eyes were~ very heavy; and they did not know what to answer[x] Him.

41 And He *came the third time, and *said to them, "Are you still sleeping[M] and taking[M] your rest? It is enough; the hour has

14:26
Matt. 26:30;
Matt. 21:1

14:27
Mark 14:27-31;
Matt. 26:31-35;
Zech. 13:7

14:28
Matt. 28:16

14:30
Matt. 26:34;
Mark 14:68,72;
John 13:38

14:32
Mark 14:32-42;
Matt. 26:36-46;
Luke 22:40-46
14:33
Mark 9:15; 16:5,6

14:34
Matt. 26:38; John
12:27

14:35
Matt. 26:45; Mark
14:41

14:36
Rom. 8:15; Gal.
4:6;
Matt. 26:39

14:38
Matt. 26:41

14:41
Mark 14:35

come; behold, the Son of Man is being betrayed into the hands of sinners.

42 "Arise, let us be going;~ behold, the one who betrays Me is at hand!"⁺

Betrayal and Arrest

14:43
Mark 14:43-50:
Matt. 26:47-56;
Luke 22:47-53;
John 18:3-11

43 And immediately while He was still speaking, Judas, one of the twelve, *came up, accompanied by a multitude with swords and clubs, from the chief priests and the scribes and the elders.

44 Now he who was betraying Him had given them a signal, saying, "Whomever I shall kiss,ˣ He is the one; seizeᵘ Him, and lead~ᵗ Him away under guard."

14:45
Matt. 23:7

45 And after coming, he immediately went to Him, saying, "Rabbi!" and kissed¹ Him.

46 And they laid hands on Him, and seized Him.

47 But a certain one of those who stood by drew his sword, and struck the slave of the high priest, and cut off his ear.

48 And Jesus answered and said to them, "Have you come out with swords and clubs to arrestˣ Me, as against a robber?

14:49
Mark 12:35; Luke
19:47; 21:37

49 "Every day I was with you in the temple teaching, ~ and you did not seize Me; but this has happened that the Scriptures might be fulfilled."ˣ

50 And they all left Him and fled.

51 And a certain young man was followingᵐ Him, wearing⁺ nothing but a linen sheet over his naked body; and they *seized him.

52 But he left the linen sheet behind, and escaped naked.

Jesus before His Accusers

14:53
Mark 14:53-65:
Matt. 26:57-68;
John 18:12f.,
19-24
14:54
Mark 14:68;
Matt. 26:3;
Mark 14:67; John
18:18
14:55
Matt. 5:22

53 And they led Jesus away to the high priest; and all the chief priests and the elders and the scribes *gathered together.

54 And Peter had followed Him at a distance, right into the courtyard of the high priest; and he was sitting~ with the officers, and warming~ himself at the fire.

55 Now the chief priests and the whole ᵐCouncil kept tryingᵐ to obtain testimony against Jesus to putˣ Him to death; and they were not findingᵐ any.

56 For many were givingᵐ false testimony against Him, and yet their testimony was not consistent.

57 And some stood up and began to giveᵐ false testimony against Him, saying,

14:58
Matt. 26:61; Mark
15:29; John 2:19

58 "We heard Him say, 'I will destroy this temple made with

ᵐOr, Sanhedrin

hands, and in *three* days I will build *another* made *without hands.'* "

59 And not even in *this respect* was their testimony *consistent.*

60 And the high priest stood up *and came* forward and questioned Jesus, saying, "Do You make no answer? What is it that these men are testifying against You?"

61 But He kept silent,[m] and made no answer. Again the high priest was questioning[m] Him, and saying to Him, "Are *You* the Christ, the Son of the Blessed *One?*"

62 And Jesus said, "I am; and you shall see THE SON OF MAN SITTING AT THE *RIGHT HAND* OF POWER,[32a] and COMING WITH THE CLOUDS OF HEAVEN."

63 And tearing his clothes, the high priest *said, "What further need do we have of witnesses?

64 "You have heard the blasphemy; how does it seem to you?" And they all condemned[14c] Him to be deserving of *death.*

65 And some began to spit~ at Him, and to blindfold~ Him, and to beat~ Him with their fists, and to say~ to Him, "Prophesy!"[x] And the officers received Him with *slaps in the face.*

Peter's Denials

66 And as Peter was below in the courtyard, one of the servant-girls of the high priest *came,

67 and seeing Peter warming himself, she looked at him, and *said, "*You, too,* were with Jesus the *Nazarene.*"

68 But he denied *it,* saying, "I neither know nor understand what you are talking about." And he went out onto the porch.[n]

69 And the maid saw him, and began once more to say~ to the bystanders, "This is *one* of *them!*"

70 But again he was denying[m] it. And after a little while the bystanders were again saying[m] to Peter, "Surely you are *one* of *them,* for you are a *Galilean too.*"

71 But he began to curse~ and swear,~ "I do not know *this* man you are talking about!"

72 And immediately a cock crowed a *second time.* And Peter remembered how Jesus had made the remark to him, "Before a cock crows[x] twice, you will deny Me three times." And he began to weep.[m]

Jesus before Pilate

15 And early in the morning the chief priests with the elders and scribes, and the whole °Council, immediately held a

14:61
Matt. 26:63;
Mark 14:61-63;
Matt. 26:63ff.;
Luke 22:67-71

14:62
Ps. 110:1; Mark
13:26;
Dan. 7:13

14:63
Num. 14:6; Matt.
26:65; Acts 14:14

14:64
Lev. 24:16

14:65
Matt. 26:67; Mark
10:34;
Esth. 7:8;
Matt. 26:68; Luke
22:64

14:66
Mark 14:66-72;
Matt. 26:69-75;
Luke 22:56-62;
John 18:16-18,
25-27;
Mark 14:54
14:67
Mark 14:54;
Mark 1:24
14:68
Mark 14:54

14:70
Mark 14:68;
Matt. 26:73; Luke
22:59

14:72
Mark 14:30,68

15:1
Matt. 27:1;
Matt. 5:22

[n]Later mss. add: *and a cock crowed*   °Or, *Sanhedrin*

consultation; and binding Jesus, they led Him away, and delivered Him up to Pilate.

15:2
Mark 15:2-5;
Matt. 27:11-14;
Luke 23:2,3; John
18:29-38

2 And Pilate questioned Him, "Are *You* the King of the Jews?" And answering He *said to him, "*It is as* you say."

3 And the chief priests *began* to accuse^m Him harshly.

4 And Pilate was questioning^m Him again, saying, "Do You make no answer? See how many charges they bring against You!"

15:5
Matt. 27:12

5 But Jesus made no further answer; so that Pilate was amazed. ~

15:6
Mark 15:6-15;
Matt. 27:15-26;
Luke 23:18-25;
John 18:39-19:16

6 Now at *the* feast he used to release^m for them *any* †one prisoner whom they requested.^m

7 And the man named Barabbas had been imprisoned⁺ with the insurrectionists who had committed murder in the insurrection.

8 And the multitude went up and began asking~ him *to do* as he had been accustomed to do^m for them.

9 And Pilate answered them, saying, "Do you want me to release^x for you the King of the Jews?"

10 For he was aware^m that the chief priests had delivered Him up because of *envy.*

15:11
Acts 3:14

11 But the chief priests stirred up¹ the multitude *to ask* him to release^x *Barabbas* for them instead.

12 And answering again, Pilate was saying^m to them, "Then what shall I do^x with Him whom you call the King of the Jews?"

13 And they shouted back, "Crucify^{xi} Him!"

14 But Pilate was saying^m to them, "Why, what evil¹⁰ᵃ has He done?" But they shouted all the more, "Crucify^{xi} Him!"

15:15
Matt. 27:26

15 And wishing to satisfy^x the *multitude,* Pilate released Barabbas for them, and after having Jesus scourged, he delivered *Him* to be crucified.^x

Jesus Is Mocked

15:16
Mark 15:16-20;
Matt. 27:27-31;
Matt. 26:3; 27:27;
Acts 10:1

16 And the soldiers took Him away into the palace (that is, the Praetorium), and they *called together the whole *Roman* ᴾcohort.

17 And they *dressed Him up in purple, and after weaving a crown of thorns, they put it on Him;

18 and they began to acclaim~ Him, "Hail, King of the Jews!"

19 And they kept beating^m His head with a ᑫreed, and spitting^m at Him, and kneeling and bowing^m before Him.

20 And after they had mocked Him, they took the purple off

ᴾOr, *battalion* ᑫOr, *staff* (made of a reed)

Him, and put His garments on Him. And they *led Him out to crucify[x] Him.

21   And they *pressed into service a passer-by coming from the country, Simon of Cyrene (the father of Alexander and Rufus), to bear[x] His cross.

15:21
Mark 15:21: Matt. 27:32; Luke 23:26; Rom. 16:13

The Crucifixion

22   And they *brought Him to the place Golgotha, which is translated, Place of a Skull.

23   And they tried to give[m] Him wine mixed[+] with myrrh; but He did not take it.

24   And they *crucified Him, and *divided up His garments among themselves, casting lots for them, *to decide* what each should take.[x]

25   And it was the [r]*third* hour when they crucified Him.

26   And the inscription of the charge against Him read,[+] "THE KING OF THE JEWS."

27   And they *crucified two robbers with Him, one on His right and one on His left.

28   [[s]And the Scripture was fulfilled which says, "And He was numbered with transgressors."]

29   And those passing by were hurling[m] abuse at Him, wagging their heads, and saying, "Ha! You who *are going to* destroy the temple and rebuild it in *three* days,

30   save[x] Yourself, and come down from the cross!"

31   In the same way the chief priests also, along with the scribes, were mocking *Him* among themselves and saying,[m] "He saved *others;* He cannot save[x] *Himself.*

32   "Let *this* Christ, the King of Israel, now come[x] down from the cross, so that we may see[x] and believe!"[x] And those who were crucified[+] with Him were casting[m] the same insult at Him.

33   And when the [t]*sixth* hour had come, darkness fell over the whole land until the [u]*ninth* hour.

34   And at the ninth hour Jesus cried out with a loud voice, "Eloi, Eloi, lama sabachthani?" which is translated, "My God, My God, why hast Thou forsaken Me?"

35   And when some of the bystanders heard it, they *began* saying,[m] "Behold, He is calling for *Elijah.*"

36   And someone ran and filled a sponge with sour wine, put it on a reed, and gave[m] Him a drink, saying, "Let us see[x] whether Elijah will come to take[x] Him down."

37   And Jesus uttered a loud cry, and breathed His last.

15:22
Mark 15:22-32; Matt. 27:33-44; Luke 23:33-43; John 19:17-24; Luke 23:33; John 19:17
15:23
Matt. 27:34
15:24
Ps. 22:18; John 19:24
15:25
Mark 15:33
15:26
Matt. 27:37
15:29
Ps. 22:7; 109:25; Matt. 27:39; Mark 14:58; John 2:19
15:31
Matt. 27:42; Luke 23:35
15:32
Matt. 27:42; Mark 15:26; Matt. 27:44; Mark 15:27; Luke 23:39-43
15:33
Mark 15:33-41; Matt. 27:45-56; Luke 23:44-49; Matt. 27:45f.; Mark 15:25; Luke 23:44
15:34
Matt. 27:45f.; Mark 15:25; Luke 23:44; Ps. 22:1; Matt. 27:46
15:37
Matt. 27:50; Luke 23:46; John 19:30

[r]I.e., 9 a.m.   [s]Many mss. do not contain this verse   [t]I.e., noon   [u]I.e., 3 p.m.

15:38
Ex. 26:31-33;
Matt. 27:51; Luke
23:45
38   And the veil of the temple was torn in two from top to bottom.

15:39
Matt. 27:54; Mark
15:45; Luke 23:47
39   And when the centurion, who was standing right in front of Him, saw the way He breathed His last, he said, "Truly this man was the *Son of God!*"

15:40
Mark 15:40,41;
Matt. 27:55f.;
Luke 23:49; John
19:25;
Luke 19:3;
Mark 16:1
40   And there were also *some* women looking~ on from a distance, among whom *were* Mary Magdalene, and Mary the mother of James the Less and Joses, and Salome.

15:41
Matt. 27:55f.
41   And when He was in Galilee, they used to follow™ Him and minister™ to Him; and *there were* many other women who had come up with Him to Jerusalem.

Jesus Is Buried

15:42
Mark 15:42-47;
Matt. 27:57-61;
Luke 23:50-56;
John 19:38-42;
Matt. 27:62
42   And when evening had already come, because it was the preparation day, that is, the day before the Sabbath,

15:43
Matt. 27:57; Luke
23:50,51; Acts
13:50; 17:12;
Matt. 27:57; Luke
2:25,38; 23:51;
John 19:38
43   Joseph of Arimathea came, a prominent member of the Council, who himself was waiting~ for the kingdom of God; and he gathered up courage and went in before Pilate, and asked for the body of Jesus.

44   And Pilate wondered if He was dead by this time, and summoning the centurion, he questioned him as to whether He was already dead.

15:45
Mark 15:39
45   And ascertaining this from the centurion, he granted the body to Joseph.

46   And *Joseph* bought a linen cloth, took Him down, wrapped Him in the linen cloth, and laid Him in a tomb which had been hewn⁺ out in the rock; and he rolled a stone against the entrance of the tomb.

15:47
Matt. 27:56; Mark
15:40; 16:1
47   And Mary Magdalene and Mary the *mother* of Joses were looking™ on *to see* where He was laid.⁺

The Resurrection

16:1
Mark 16:1-8;
Matt. 28:1-8;
Luke 24:1-10;
John 20:1-8;
Mark 15:47;
Luke 23:56; John
19:39f.
16 And when the Sabbath was over, Mary Magdalene, and Mary the *mother* of James, and Salome, bought spices, that they might come and anoint˟ Him.

2   And very early on the first day of the week, they *came to the tomb when the sun had risen.

16:3
Matt. 27:60; Mark
15:46; 16:4
3   And they were saying™ to one another, "Who will roll away the stone for us from the entrance of the tomb?"

4   And looking up, they *saw that the stone had *been rolled⁺ away*, although it was extremely large.

16:5
John 20:11,12;
Mark 9:15
5   And entering the tomb, they saw a young man sitting at the right, wearing⁺ a ⁺white robe; and they were amazed.¹

6 And he *said to them, "Do not be amazed;[01] you are looking for Jesus the Nazarene, who has been crucified.* He has risen; He is not here; behold, *here is* the place where they laid Him.

7 "But go, tell[xi] His disciples and Peter, 'He is going before you into Galilee; *there* you will see Him, just as He said to you.' "

8 And they went out and fled from the tomb, for *trembling and astonishment*[1] had[xx] gripped them; and they said nothing to anyone, for they were afraid.[xx]

9 [[v]Now after He had risen early on the first day of the week, He first appeared to Mary Magdalene, from whom He had cast out seven demons.

10 She went and reported to those who had been with Him, while they were mourning and weeping.

11 And when they heard that He was alive, and had been seen by her, they refused to believe it.

12 And after that, He appeared in a different form[22c] to two of them, while they were walking along on their way to the country.

13 And they went away and reported it to the others, but they did not believe *them either*.

The Disciples Commissioned

14 And afterward He appeared to the eleven themselves as they were reclining *at the table*; and He reproached them for their unbelief and hardness of heart, because they had not believed those who had seen Him after He had risen.*

15 And He said to them, "Go into *all* the world and preach[xi] the gospel to all creation.

16 "He who has believed and has been baptized shall be saved; but he who has disbelieved shall be condemned.[14c]

17 "And *these* signs will accompany[1] those who have believed: in My name they will cast out *demons*, they will speak with new[34a] *tongues*;

18 they will pick up *serpents*, and if they drink[x] any *deadly poison*, it shall •*not* hurt[x] them; they will lay hands on the *sick*, and they will recover."

19 So then, when the Lord Jesus had spoken[x] to them, He was received up into heaven, and sat down at the right hand of God.

[v]Some of the oldest mss. do not contain vv. 9-20

16:6
Mark 9:15;
Mark 1:24;
Matt. 28:6; Luke
24:6

16:7
Matt. 26:32; Mark
14:28

16:9
Matt. 27:56; John
20:14

16:10
John 20:18

16:11
Matt. 28:17; Mark
16:13,14; Luke
24:11,41; John
20:25
16:12
Mark 16:14; John
21:1,14;
Luke 24:13-35

16:13
Matt. 28:17; Mark
16:11,14; Luke
24:11,41; John
20:25

16:14
Mark 16:12; John
21:1,14;
Luke 24:36; John
20:19,26; 1 Cor.
15:5;
Matt. 28:17; Mark
16:11,13; Luke
24:11,41; John
20:25
16:15
Matt. 28:19; Acts
1:8
16:16
John 3:18,36;
Acts 16:31

16:17
Mark 9:38; Luke
10:17; Acts 5:16;
8:7; 16:18; 19:12;
Acts 2:4; 10:46;
19:6; 1 Cor.
12:10,28,30;
13:1; 14:2
16:18
Luke 10:19; Acts
28:3-5;
Mark 5:23

16:19
Acts 1:3;
Luke 9:51; 24:51;
John 6:62; 20:17;
Acts 1:2,9-11;
1 Tim. 3:16;
Ps. 110:1; Luke
22:69; Acts
7:55f.; Rom. 8:34;
Eph. 1:20; Col.
3:1; Heb. 1:3; 8:1;
10:12; 12:2; 1
Pet. 3:22

20   And they went out and preached everywhere, while the Lord worked with them, and confirmed the word by the signs that followed.]¹

ʷ[*And they promptly reported⁺ all these instructions to Peter and his companions. And after that, Jesus Himself sent out through them from east to west the sacred and imperishable proclamation of eternal salvation.*]

ʷA few later mss. and versions contain this paragraph, usually after verse 8; a few have it at the end of chapter.

The Gospel According to
Luke

Introduction

1 Inasmuch[2] as many have undertaken to compile[x] an account of the things accomplished[+] among us,

2 just as those who from the beginning were eyewitnesses and servants of the [a]word have handed them down to us,

3 it seemed fitting for me as well, having investigated[+1] everything *carefully* from the beginning, to write[x] *it* out for you in consecutive order, most excellent Theophilus;

4 so that you might know[x29b] the *exact truth* about the things you have been taught.

Birth of John the Baptist Foretold

5 In the days of Herod, king of Judea, there was a certain priest named Zacharias, of the division of [b]Abijah; and he had a wife [c]from the daughters of Aaron, and her name was Elizabeth.

6 And they were both righteous in the sight of God, walking blamelessly[11a] in all the commandments and requirements of the Lord.

7 And they had no child, because Elizabeth was barren, and they were both advanced in years.

8 Now it came about, while he was performing~ his priestly service before God in the *appointed* order of his division,

9 according to the custom of the priestly office, he was chosen by lot to enter the temple of the Lord and burn[x] incense.

10 And the whole multitude of the people were in prayer~ outside at the hour of the incense offering.

11 And an angel of the Lord appeared to him, standing to the right of the altar of incense.

12 And Zacharias was troubled when he saw *him*, and fear gripped him.

13 But the angel said to him, "Do not be afraid,[θ] Zacharias, for your petition has been heard, and your wife Elizabeth will bear you a son, and you will give him the name John.

14 "And you will have joy and gladness, and many will rejoice at *his birth*.

15 "For he will be great in the sight of the Lord, and he will

---

[a]i.e., gospel [b]Gr., *Abia* [c]i.e., of priestly descent

1:1
Rom. 4:21; 14:5; Col. 2:2; 4:12; 1 Thess. 1:5; 2 Tim. 4:17; Heb. 6:11; 10:22
1:2
John 15:27; Acts 1:21f.; 2 Pet. 1:16; 1 John 1:1; Acts 26:16; 1 Cor. 4:1; Heb. 2:3; Mark 4:14; 16:20; Acts 8:4; 14:25; 16:6; 17:11
1:3
1 Tim. 4:6; Acts 11:4; 18:23; Acts 23:26; 24:3; 26:25; Acts 1:1
1:4
Acts 18:25; Rom. 2:18; 1 Cor. 14:19; Gal. 6:6
1:5
Matt. 2:1; 1 Chr. 24:10
1:6
Gen. 7:1; Acts 2:25; 8:21; Phil. 2:15; 3:6; 1 Thess. 3:13
1:8
1 Chr. 24:19; 2 Chr. 8:14; 31:2
1:9
Ex. 30:7f.
1:10
Lev. 16:17
1:11
Luke 2:9; Acts 5:19
1:12
Luke 2:9
1:13
Matt. 14:27; Luke 1:30; Luke 1:60,63
1:15
Num. 6:3; Judg. 13:4; Matt. 11:18; Luke 7:33

drink[x] •*no wine* or *liquor;* and he will be filled with the *Holy Spirit,* while yet in his mother's womb.

1:16
Matt. 3:2,6; Luke 3:3

16 "And he will turn back *many of the sons of Israel* to the Lord their God.

1:17
Luke 1:76;
Matt. 11:14;
Mal. 4:6

17 "And it is *he* who will go *as a forerunner* before Him in the spirit and power of Elijah, TO TURN[x] THE HEARTS OF THE FATHERS BACK TO THE CHILDREN, and the disobedient to the attitude of the righteous; so as to make[x] ready a people prepared[+] for the Lord."

1:18
Gen. 17:17

18 And Zacharias said to the angel, "How shall I know this *for certain*? For [+]*I* am an old man, and my wife is advanced in years."

1:19
Dan. 8:16; 9:21;
Luke 1:26;
Matt. 18:10

19 And the angel answered and said to him, "[+]*I* am Gabriel, who stands[+] in the presence of God; and I have been sent to speak[x] to you, and to bring[x] you this good news.

20 "And behold, you shall be silent[~] and unable to speak[x] until the day when these things take place, because you did not believe my words, which shall be fulfilled in their proper time."

21 And the people were waiting[~] for Zacharias, and were wondering[m] at his delay[~] in the temple.

1:22
Luke 1:62

22 But when he came out, he was unable[m] to speak[x] to them; and they realized[1] that he had seen[+] a *vision* in the temple; and he kept making[~] signs to them, and remained[m] mute.

23 And it came about, when the days of his priestly service were ended, that he went back home.

24 And after these days Elizabeth his wife became pregnant; and she kept[m] herself in seclusion for five months, saying,

1:25
Gen. 30:23; Is.
4:1; 25:8

25 "This is the way the Lord has dealt[+] with me in the days when He looked *with favor* upon *me,* to take[x] away my disgrace among men."

Jesus' Birth Foretold

1:26
Luke 1:19;
Matt. 2:23

26 Now in the sixth month the angel Gabriel was sent from God to a city in Galilee, called Nazareth,

1:27
Matt. 1:18;
Matt. 1:16,20;
Luke 2:4

27 to a virgin engaged[+] to a man whose name was Joseph, of the descendants of David; and the virgin's name was Mary.

28 And coming in, he said to her, "Hail, favored[+] one! The Lord *is* with you."[d]

1:29
Luke 1:12
1:30
Matt. 14:27; Luke
1:13
1:31
Is. 7:14; Matt.
1:21,25; Luke
2:21
1:32
Mark 5:7; Luke
1:35,76; 6:35;
Acts 7:48;
2 Sam. 7:12,13,
16; Is. 9:7

29 But she was *greatly*[1] *troubled* at *this* statement, and kept pondering[m] what kind of salutation this might be.

30 And the angel said to her, "Do not be afraid,[◊] Mary; for you have found favor with God.

31 "And behold, you will conceive in your womb, and bear a son, and you shall name Him Jesus.

32 "He will be great, and will be called the *Son of the Most*

[d]Later mss. add: *you are blessed among women*

High; and the Lord God will give *Him* the throne of His father David;

33   and He will reign over the house of Jacob forever; and *His kingdom* will have no end."

34   And Mary said to the angel, "How can this be, since I am a *virgin?*"

35   And the angel answered and said to her, "The Holy[28a] Spirit will come upon you, and the power[32a] of the Most High will overshadow you; and for that reason the holy offspring shall be called the Son of God.

36   "And behold, even your relative Elizabeth has also conceived⁺ a son in her old age; and she who was called barren is now in her sixth month.

37   "For *nothing* will be impossible with God."

38   And Mary said, "Behold, the ᵉbondslave of the Lord; be it done to me according to your word."[43b] And the angel departed from her.

Mary Visits Elizabeth

39   Now at this time Mary arose and went with haste to the hill country, to a city of Judah,

40   and entered the house of Zacharias and greeted Elizabeth.

41   And it came about that when Elizabeth heard Mary's greeting, the baby leaped in her womb; and Elizabeth was filled with the *Holy Spirit.*

42   And she cried out with a loud voice, and said, "⁺Blessed⁺ among women *are* you, and ⁺blessed⁺ *is* the fruit of your womb!

43   "And how has it *happened* to me, that the mother of my Lord should come to •me?

44   "For behold, when the sound of your greeting reached my ears, the baby leaped in my womb for *joy.*

45   "And ⁺blessed *is* she who believed that there would be a fulfillment of what had been spoken⁺ to her by the Lord."

The Magnificat

46   And Mary said:
      "My soul[30c] exalts the Lord,

47   "And my spirit[30b] has rejoiced in God my Savior.

48   "For He has had regard for the humble state of His
            bondslave;
            For behold, from this time on all generations will
            count me blessed.

49   "For the Mighty One has done *great things* for me;

ᵉI.e., female slave

1:33
Matt. 1:1;
2 Sam. 7:13,16;
Ps. 89:36,37;
Dan. 2:44; 7:14,
18,27; Matt.
28:18

1:35
Matt. 1:18;
Luke 1:32;
Mark 1:24;
Matt. 4:3; John
1:34,49; 20:31

1:37
Gen. 18:14; Jer.
32:17; Matt.
19:26

1:39
Josh. 20:7; 21:11;
Luke 1:65

1:41
Luke 1:67; Acts
2:4; 4:8; 9:17

1:43
Luke 2:11

1:45
Luke 1:20,48

1:46
Luke 1:46-53;
1 Sam. 2:1-10;
Ps. 34:2f.
1:47
Ps. 35:9; Hab.
3:18;
1 Tim. 1:1; 2:3;
Titus 1:3; 2:10;
3:4; Jude 25
1:48
Ps. 138:6;
Luke 1:45

And *holy*[28a] is His name.

1:50
Ps. 103:17
50　"AND HIS MERCY IS UPON GENERATION AFTER
　　GENERATION
TOWARD THOSE WHO FEAR HIM.

1:51
Ps. 98:1; 118:15
51　"He has done mighty deeds with His arm;
　　He has scattered *those who were* proud in the
　　thoughts of their heart.

1:52
Job 5:11
52　"He has brought down rulers from *their* thrones,
　　And has exalted those who were humble.

1:53
Ps. 107:9
53　"HE HAS FILLED THE *HUNGRY* WITH GOOD THINGS;
　　And sent away the *rich* empty-handed.

54　"He has given help to Israel His servant,
　　In remembrance[x] of His mercy,

1:55
Gen. 17:19; Ps.
132:11; Gal. 3:16;
Gen. 17:7
55　As He spoke to our fathers,
　　To Abraham and his offspring forever."

56　And Mary stayed with her about three months, and *then* returned to her home.

John Is Born

57　Now the time had come for Elizabeth to give[x] birth, and she brought forth a son.

1:58
Gen. 19:19
58　And her neighbors and her relatives heard that the Lord had displayed[m] His great mercy toward her; and they were rejoicing[m] with her.

1:59
Gen. 17:12; Lev.
12:3; Luke 2:21;
Phil. 3:5
59　And it came about that on the eighth day they came to circumcise[x] the child, and they were going to call him Zacharias, after his father.

1:60
Luke 1:13,63
60　And his mother answered and said, "No •*indeed;* but he shall be called John."

61　And they said to her, "There is no one among your relatives who is called by †*that* name."

1:62
Luke 1:22
62　And they made[m] signs to his father, as to what he wanted him called. ~

1:63
Luke 1:13,60
63　And he asked for a tablet, and wrote as follows, "His name is *John.*" And they were all astonished.

1:64
Luke 1:20
64　And at *once* his mouth was opened and his tongue *loosed,* and he *began* to speak[m] in praise of God.

1:65
Luke 1:39
65　And *fear* came on all those living around them; and all these matters were being talked[m] about in all the hill country of Judea.

1:66
Acts 11:21
66　And all who heard them kept them in mind, saying, "What then will †*this* child *turn out to* be?" For the hand of the Lord was certainly with him.

Zacharias' Prophecy

67 And his father Zacharias was filled with the Holy Spirit, and prophesied, saying:

68   "†Blessed *be* the Lord God of Israel,
     For He has visited us and accomplished redemption
       for His people,
69   And has raised up a horn of salvation for us
     In the house of David His servant—
70   As He spoke by the mouth of His holy[28a] prophets
     from of old—
71   Salvation FROM OUR ENEMIES,
     And FROM THE HAND OF ALL WHO HATE US;
72   To show[x] mercy toward our fathers,
     And to remember[x] His holy[28a] covenant,
73   The oath which He swore to Abraham our father,
74   To grant[x] us that we, being delivered[18b] from the
     hand of our enemies,
     Might serve[~38c] Him without fear,
75   In holiness and righteousness before Him all our
     days.
76   "And *you,* child, will be called the *prophet of the*
     Most High;
     For you will go on BEFORE THE LORD TO PREPARE[x] HIS
     WAYS;
77   To give[x] to His people *the* knowledge of salvation
     By the forgiveness of their sins,
78   Because of the tender mercy of our God,
     With which the Sunrise from on high shall visit us,
79   TO SHINE[x] UPON THOSE WHO SIT IN DARKNESS AND
     THE SHADOW OF DEATH,
     To guide[x] our feet into the way of peace."

80 And the child continued to grow,[m] and to become[m] strong in spirit, and he lived in the deserts until the day of his public appearance to Israel.

Jesus' Birth in Bethlehem

2 Now it came about in those days that a decree went out from Caesar Augustus, that a census be taken[~] of all ᶠthe inhabited earth.

2 This was the first census taken while ⁹Quirinius was governor of Syria.

ᶠI.e., the Roman empire   ⁹Gr., *Kyrenios*

1:67
Luke 1:41; Acts 2:4,8; 9:17; Joel 2:28

1:68
1 Kin. 1:48; Ps. 41:13; 72:18; 106:48; Luke 1:71; 2:38; Heb. 9:12

1:69
1 Sam. 2:1,10; Ps. 18:2; 89:17; 132:17; Ezek. 29:21; Matt. 1:1

1:70
Rom. 1:2; Acts 3:21

1:71
Luke 1:68; Ps. 106:10

1:72
Mic. 7:20; Ps. 105:8f.,42; 106:45

1:73
Gen. 22:16ff.; Heb. 6:13

1:75
Eph. 4:24

1:76
Matt. 11:9; Luke 1:32; Mal. 3:1; Matt. 11:10; Mark 1:2; Luke 7:27; Luke 1:17

1:77
Jer. 31:34; Mark 1:4

1:78
Mal. 4:2; Eph. 5:14; 2 Pet. 1:19

1:79
Is. 9:2; Is. 59:8; Matt. 4:16

1:80
Luke 2:40

2:1
Matt. 22:17; Luke 3:1; Matt. 24:14

2:2
Matt. 4:24

3   And all were proceeding^m to register~ for the census, everyone to his own city.

2:4
Luke 1:27

4   And Joseph also went up from Galilee, from the city of Nazareth, to Judea, to the city of David, which is called Bethlehem, because he was of the house and family of David,

5   in order to register,ˣ along with Mary, who was engaged⁺ to him, and was with child.

6   And it came about that while they were there, the days were completed for her to giveˣ birth.

2:7
Matt. 1:25

7   And she gave birth to her *first-born* son; and she wrapped Him in cloths, and laid Him in a manger, because there was no room for them in the inn.

8   And in the *same* region there were *some* shepherds staying out in the fields, and keeping watch over their flock by night.

2:9
Luke 1:11; Acts
5:19;
Luke 24:4; Acts
12:7

9   And an angel of the Lord suddenly stood before them, and the glory of the Lord shone around them; and they were *terribly*⁴ frightened.

2:10
Matt. 14:27

10   And the angel said to them, "Do not be afraid;ᵒ for behold, I bring you good news of a great joy which shall be for all the people;

2:11
Matt. 1:21; John
4:42; Acts 5:31;
Matt. 1:16; 16:16,
20; John 11:27;
Luke 1:43; Acts
2:36; 10:36
2:12
1 Sam. 2:34;
2 Kin. 19:29;
20:8f.; Is. 7:11,14

11   for today in the city of David there has been born for you a *Savior*, who is ʰChrist the Lord.

12   "And this *will be* a sign for you: you will find a baby wrapped⁺ in cloths, and lying in a manger."

13   And suddenly there appeared with the angel a multitude of the heavenly host praising God, and saying,

2:14
Matt. 21:9; Luke
19:38;
Luke 3:22; Eph.
1:9; Phil. 2:13

14   "Glory to God in the highest,
And on earth peace among men ⁱwith whom He is
pleased."

15   And it came about when the angels had gone away from them into heaven, that the shepherds *began* saying to one another, "Let us goˣ straight² to Bethlehem then, and seeˣ this thing that has happened⁺ which the Lord has made known to us."

16   And they came in haste and found their way to Mary and Joseph, and the baby as He lay in the manger.

17   And when they had seen this, they made known the statement which had been told them about this Child.

18   And all who heard it wondered at the things which were told them by the shepherds.

2:19
Luke 2:51

19   But Mary treasured^{m1} up all *these things,*⁴³ᵇ pondering them in her heart.

2:20
Matt. 9:8

20   And the shepherds went back, glorifying and praising

ʰI.e., Messiah   ⁱLit., *of good pleasure;* or possibly, *of good will*

God for all that they had heard and seen, just as had been told them.

Jesus Presented at the Temple

21 And when eight days were completed before His circumcision,[x] His name was *then* called Jesus, the name given by the angel before He was conceived[x] in the womb.

22 And when the days for their purification according to the law of Moses were completed, they brought Him up to Jerusalem to present[x] Him to the Lord

23 (as it is written[*] in the Law of the Lord, "EVERY *first-born* MALE THAT OPENS THE WOMB SHALL BE CALLED HOLY[28a] TO THE LORD"),

24 and to offer[x] a sacrifice according to what was said[*] in the Law of the Lord, "A PAIR OF TURTLEDOVES, OR TWO YOUNG PIGEONS."

25 And behold, there was a man in Jerusalem whose name was Simeon; and this man was righteous and devout, looking for the consolation of Israel; and the *Holy* Spirit was upon him.

26 And it had been revealed[*] to him by the Holy Spirit that he would not see[x] death before he had seen[x] the Lord's Christ.

27 And he came *in the* [+]*Spirit* into the temple; and when the parents brought[x] in the child Jesus, to carry[x] out for Him the custom of the Law,

28 then he took Him into his arms, and blessed God, and said,

29   "Now Lord, Thou dost let Thy bond-servant depart
       In peace, according to Thy word;[43b]

30   For my eyes have seen Thy salvation,

31   Which Thou hast prepared in the presence of all
       peoples,

32   A LIGHT OF REVELATION TO THE GENTILES,
       And the glory of Thy people Israel."

33 And His father and mother were amazed[~] at the things which were being said about Him.

34 And Simeon blessed them, and said to Mary His mother, "Behold, this *Child* is appointed for the fall and rise of many in Israel, and for a sign to be opposed—

35 and a sword will pierce even *your own* soul—to the end that thoughts from *many hearts* may be revealed."[x]

36 And there was a prophetess, Anna the daughter of Phanuel, of the tribe of Asher. She was advanced in years, having lived with a husband seven years after her marriage,

37 and then as a widow to the age of eighty-four. And she

2:21
Gen. 17:12; Lev. 12:3; Luke 1:59; Matt. 1:21,25; Luke 1:31

2:22
Lev. 12:6-8

2:23
Ex. 13:2,12; Num. 3:13; 8:17

2:24
Lev. 5:11; 12:8

2:25
Luke 1:6; Mark 15:43; Luke 2:38; 23:51

2:26
Matt. 2:12; Ps. 89:48; John 8:51; Heb. 11:5

2:27
Luke 2:22

2:29
Luke 2:26

2:30
Ps. 119:166,174; Is. 52:10; Luke 3:6

2:32
Is. 9:2; 42:6; 49:6, 9; 51:4; 60:1-3; Matt. 4:16; Acts 13:47; 26:23

2:33
Matt. 12:46

2:34
Matt. 12:46; Matt. 21:44; 1 Cor. 1:23; 2 Cor. 2:16; 1 Pet. 2:8

2:36
Luke 2:38; Acts 21:9; Josh. 19:24; 1 Tim. 5:9

2:37
Luke 5:33; Acts 13:3; 14:23; 1 Tim. 5:5

never left the temple, serving night and day with fastings and prayers.

2:38
Luke 1:68; 2:25

38   And at that very moment she came up and *began* giving[m] thanks to God, and continued to speak[m] of Him to all those who were looking for the redemption of Jerusalem.

Return to Nazareth

2:39
Matt. 2:23; Luke 1:26; 2:51; 4:16

39   And when they had performed everything according to the Law of the Lord, they returned to Galilee, to their own city of Nazareth.

2:40
Luke 1:80; 2:52

40   And the Child continued to grow[m] and become[m] strong, increasing in wisdom; and the grace of God was upon Him.

Visit to Jerusalem

2:41
Ex. 12:11; 23:15; Deut. 16:1-6

41   And His parents used to go[m] to Jerusalem every year at the Feast of the Passover.

42   And when He became twelve, they went up *there* according to the custom of the Feast;

2:43
Ex. 12:15

43   and as they were returning,~ after spending the full number of days, the boy Jesus stayed behind in Jerusalem. And His parents were unaware of it,

44   but supposed Him to be in the caravan, and went a day's journey; and they *began* looking[m1] for Him among their relatives and acquaintances.

45   And when they did not find Him, they returned to Jerusalem, looking for Him.

46   And it came about that after three days they found Him in the temple, sitting in the midst of the teachers, both listening to them, and asking them questions.

2:47
Matt. 7:28; 13:54; 22:33; Mark 1:22; 6:2; 11:18; Luke 4:32; John 7:15
2:48
Matt. 12:46; Luke 2:49; 3:23; 4:22

47   And all who heard Him were amazed[m] at His understanding and His answers.

48   And when they saw Him, they were astonished;[m1] and His mother said to Him, "Son, why have You treated us *this way?* Behold, Your father and I have been anxiously looking[m] for You."

2:49
John 4:34; 5:36

49   And He said to them, "Why is it that you were looking[m] for Me? Did you not know that *I* had to be in *My Father's house?"*

2:50
Mark 9:32; Luke 9:45; 18:34

50   And they did not understand[29f] the statement which He had made to them.

2:51
Luke 2:39; Matt. 12:46; Luke 2:19

51   And He went down with them, and came to Nazareth; and He continued in subjection~ to them; and His mother treasured[m1] all *these* things in her heart.

2:52
Luke 2:40

52   And Jesus kept increasing[m] in wisdom and stature, and in favor with God and men.

John the Baptist Preaches

3 Now in the fifteenth year of the reign of Tiberius Caesar, when Pontius Pilate was governor of Judea, and Herod was tetrarch of Galilee, and his brother Philip was tetrarch of the region of Ituraea and Trachonitis, and Lysanias was tetrarch of Abilene,

2   in the high priesthood of Annas and Caiaphas, the *word*[43b] *of God* came to John, the son of Zacharias, in the wilderness.

3   And he came into all the district around the Jordan, preaching a baptism of repentance for the forgiveness of sins;

4   as it is written* in the book of the words of Isaiah the prophet,

> "THE VOICE OF ONE CRYING IN THE WILDERNESS,
> 'MAKE[xl] READY THE WAY OF THE LORD,
> MAKE[~l] HIS PATHS STRAIGHT.
>
> 5 'EVERY RAVINE SHALL BE FILLED UP,
> AND EVERY MOUNTAIN AND HILL SHALL BE BROUGHT
>   LOW;
> AND THE CROOKED SHALL BECOME STRAIGHT,
> AND THE ROUGH ROADS SMOOTH;
>
> 6 AND *ALL FLESH* SHALL SEE THE SALVATION OF GOD.' "

7   He therefore *began* saying to the multitudes who were going out to be baptized[x] by him, "You brood of vipers, who warned you to flee[x] from the wrath[7b] to come?

8   "Therefore bring[xl] forth fruits in keeping with repentance, and do not begin[ə] to say[~] to yourselves, 'We have *Abraham* for our father,' for I say to you that God is able from *these stones* to raise[x] up children to Abraham.

9   "And also the axe is already laid at the root of the trees; every tree therefore that does not bear good[25b] fruit is cut down and thrown into the *fire."*

10   And the multitudes were questioning[m] him, saying, "Then what shall we do?"[x]

11   And he would answer and say[m] to them, "Let the man who has *two* tunics share[xl] with him who has none; and let him who has food do[~l] likewise."

12   And *some* ¡tax-gatherers also came to be baptized,[x] and they said to him, "Teacher, what shall we do?"[x]

13   And he said to them, "Collect[~l] no ⁺more than what you have been ordered* to."

14   And *some* ᵏsoldiers were questioning[m] him, saying, "And *what about* us, what shall *we* do?"[x] And he said to them, "Do not

¡I.e., Collectors of Roman taxes for profit ᵏI.e., men in active military service

3:1
Matt. 27:2;
Matt. 14:1

3:2
John 18:13,24;
Acts 4:6;
Matt. 26:3;
Luke 3:3-10:
Matt. 3:1-10;
Mark 1:3-5
3:3
Matt. 3:5
3:4
Is. 40:3

3:5
Is. 40:4

3:6
Is. 40:5;
Luke 2:30
3:7
Matt. 12:34;
23:33

3:8
Luke 5:21; 13:25,
26; 14:9;
John 8:33

3:9
Matt. 7:19; Luke
13:6-9

3:10
Luke 3:12,14;
Acts 2:37,38

3:11
Is. 58:7; 1 Tim.
6:17,18; James
2:14-20

3:12
Luke 7:29

3:14
Ex. 20:16; 23:1;
Phil. 4:11

take° money from anyone by force,¹ or accuse° *anyone* falsely, and be content^ with your wages."

3:15
John 1:19f.

15 Now while the people were in a state of expectation and all were wondering in their hearts about John, as to whether *he* might be the Christ,

3:16
Luke 3:16,17;
Matt. 3:11,12;
Mark 1:7,8

16 John answered and said to them all, "As for me, *I* baptize you with *water;* but One is coming who is mightier than I, and I am not fit to untie^x the thong of His sandals; *He* will baptize you with the Holy Spirit and fire.

3:17
Is. 30:24;
Mark 9:43,48

17 "And His winnowing fork is in His hand to thoroughly¹ clear^x His threshing floor, and to gather^x the wheat into His barn; but He will burn up the chaff with *unquenchable* fire."

18 So with many other exhortations also he preached^m the gospel to the people.

3:19
Matt. 14:3; Mark
6:17;
Matt. 14:1; Luke
3:1

19 But when Herod the tetrarch was reproved by him on account of Herodias, his brother's wife, and on account of all the *wicked*[10b] *things* which Herod had done,

3:20
John 3:24

20 he added this also to them all, that he locked John up in prison.

Jesus Is Baptized

3:21
Luke 3:21,22;
Matt. 3:13-17;
Mark 1:9-11;
Matt. 14:23; Luke
5:16; 9:18,28f.

21 Now it came about when all the people were baptized,^x that *Jesus also* was baptized, and while He was praying, heaven was opened,^x

3:22
Ps. 2:7; Is. 42:1;
Matt. 3:17; 17:5;
Mark 1:11; Luke
9:35; 2 Pet. 1:17

22 and the Holy Spirit descended^x upon Him in bodily form[22a] like a dove, and a voice came out of heaven, *"Thou* art My *beloved* Son, in *Thee* I am well-pleased."

Genealogy of Jesus

3:23
Matt. 4:17; Acts
1:1;
Matt. 1:16; Luke
3:23-27

23 And when He began His ministry, Jesus Himself was about thirty years of age, being supposedly *the* son of Joseph, the son of Eli,

24 the *son* of Matthat, the *son* of Levi, the *son* of Melchi, the *son* of Jannai, the *son* of Joseph,

25 the *son* of Mattathias, the *son* of Amos, the *son* of Nahum, the *son* of Hesli, the *son* of Naggai,

26 the *son* of Maath, the *son* of Mattathias, the *son* of Semein, the *son* of Josech, the *son* of Joda,

3:27
Matt. 1:12

27 the *son* of Joanan, the *son* of Rhesa, the *son* of Zerubbabel, the *son* of Shealtiel, the *son* of Neri,

28 the *son* of Melchi, the *son* of Addi, the *son* of Cosam, the *son* of Elmadam, the *son* of Er,

29 the *son* of Joshua, the *son* of Eliezer, the *son* of Jorim, the *son* of Matthat, the *son* of Levi,

30   the *son* of Simeon, the *son* of Judah, the *son* of Joseph, the *son* of Jonam, the *son* of Eliakim,

31   the *son* of Melea, the *son* of Menna, the *son* of Mattatha, the *son* of Nathan, the *son* of David,

32   the *son* of Jesse, the *son* of Obed, the *son* of Boaz, the *son* of Salmon, the *son* of Nahshon,

33   the *son* of Amminadab, the *son* of Admin, the *son* of Ram, the *son* of Hezron, the *son* of Perez, the *son* of Judah,

34   the *son* of Jacob, the *son* of Isaac, the *son* of Abraham, the *son* of Terah, the *son* of Nahor,

35   the *son* of Serug, the *son* of Reu, the *son* of Peleg, the *son* of Heber, the *son* of Shelah,

36   the *son* of Cainan, the *son* of Arphaxad, the *son* of Shem, the *son* of Noah, the *son* of Lamech,

37   the *son* of Methuselah, the *son* of Enoch, the *son* of Jared, the *son* of Mahalaleel, the *son* of Cainan,

38   the *son* of Enosh, the *son* of Seth, the *son* of Adam, the *son* of God.

The Temptation of Jesus

4   And Jesus, full of the Holy Spirit, returned from the Jordan and was led[xx] about by the Spirit in the wilderness

2   for forty days, being tempted by the devil. And He ate nothing during those days; and when they had ended, He became hungry.

3   And the devil said to Him, "If You are the *Son* of God, tell[xl] this stone to become bread."

4   And Jesus answered him, "It is written, ✝ 'MAN SHALL NOT LIVE ON *BREAD ALONE.*'"

5   And he led Him up and showed Him all the kingdoms of the world in a moment of time.

6   And the devil said to Him, "I will give You *all* this domain and its glory; for it has been handed✝ over to *me,* and I give it to whomever I wish.

7   "Therefore if *You* worship[x44b] before me, it shall all be *Yours.*"

8   And Jesus answered and said to him, "It is written, ✝ 'YOU SHALL WORSHIP THE LORD YOUR GOD AND SERVE[38c] *HIM ONLY.*'"

9   And he led Him to Jerusalem and had Him stand on the pinnacle of the temple, and said to Him, "If You are the *Son* of God, throw[xl] Yourself down from here;

10   for it is written, ✝

     'HE WILL GIVE *HIS ANGELS* CHARGE CONCERNING YOU
       TO GUARD[x] YOU,'

3:32
Luke 3:32-34:
Matt. 1:1-6

3:34
Luke 3:34-36:
Gen. 11:26-30; 1
Chr. 1:24-27

3:36
Luke 3:36-38:
Gen. 5:3-32;
1 Chr. 1:1-4

4:1
Luke 4:1-13:
Matt. 4:1-11;
Mark 1:12,13;
Luke 3:3
4:2
Ex. 34:28; 1 Kin.
19:8

4:4
Deut. 8:3

4:5
Matt. 4:8-10;
Matt. 24:14

4:6
1 John 5:19

4:8
Deut. 6:13; 10:20;
Matt. 4:10

4:9
Matt. 4:5-7

4:10
Ps. 91:11

4:11
Ps. 91:12

11   and,

   'ON their HANDS THEY WILL BEAR YOU UP,

   LEST YOU STRIKE^x YOUR FOOT AGAINST A STONE.' "

4:12
Deut. 6:16

12   And Jesus answered and said to him, "It is said,* 'YOU SHALL NOT 'PUT THE LORD YOUR GOD TO THE TEST.' "1

13   And when the devil had finished every temptation, he departed from Him until an opportune time.

Jesus' Public Ministry

4:14
Matt. 4:12;
Matt. 9:26; Luke 4:37
4:15
Matt. 4:23

14   And Jesus returned to Galilee in the power32a of the Spirit; and news about Him spread through all the surrounding district.

15   And He *began* teaching in their synagogues and was praised by all.

4:16
Luke 2:39,51;
Matt. 13:54; Mark 6:1f.;
Acts 13:14-16

16   And He came to Nazareth, where He had been brought* up; and as was His custom, He entered the synagogue on the Sabbath, and stood up to read.^x

17   And the book of the prophet Isaiah was handed to Him. And He opened the book, and found the place where it was written,*

4:18
Is. 61:1; Matt. 11:5; 12:18; John 3:34

18   "THE SPIRIT OF THE LORD IS UPON ME,

   BECAUSE HE ANOINTED ME TO PREACH^x THE GOSPEL

     TO THE POOR.

   HE HAS SENT* ME TO PROCLAIM^x RELEASE TO THE

     CAPTIVES,

   AND RECOVERY OF SIGHT TO THE BLIND,

   TO SET^x FREE THOSE WHO ARE DOWNTRODDEN,*

4:19
Is. 61:2; Lev. 25:10
4:20
Luke 4:17;
Matt. 26:55

19   TO PROCLAIM^x THE FAVORABLE YEAR OF THE LORD."

20   And He closed the book, and gave it back to the attendant, and sat down; and the eyes of *all* in the synagogue were fixed~ upon Him.

21   And He began to say~ to them, "†Today *this Scripture* has been fulfilled* in your hearing."

4:22
Matt. 13:55; Mark 6:3; John 6:42

22   And all were speaking^m well of Him, and wondering^m at the gracious words which were falling from His lips; and they were saying,^m "Is this not *Joseph's* son?"

4:23
Matt. 4:13; Mark 1:21ff.; 2:1ff.;
Luke 4:35ff.; John 4:46ff.; Luke
Mark 6:1; Luke 2:39,51; 4:16
4:24
Matt. 13:57; Mark 6:4; John 4:44
4:25
1 Kin. 17:1; 18:1;
James 5:17

23   And He said to them, "No doubt you will quote this proverb to Me, 'Physician, heal^{xl} yourself! Whatever we heard was done at Capernaum, do^{xl} here in your home town as well.' "

24   And He said, "•Truly I say to you, no prophet is welcome in his home town.

25   "But I say to you in truth, there were many widows in *Israel* in the days of Elijah, when the sky was shut up for three years and six months, when a great famine came over all the land;

'Or, tempt . . . God

26   and yet Elijah was sent to *none of them,* but only to Zarephath, *in the land* of †Sidon, to a woman who was a widow.

27   "And there were many lepers in Israel in the time of Elisha the prophet; and none of them was cleansed, but only Naaman the †Syrian."

28   And *all* in the synagogue were filled with rage as they heard these things;

29   and they rose up and cast Him out of the city, and led Him to the brow of the hill on which their city had been built, in order to throw[x] Him down the cliff.

30   But passing through their midst, He went[m] His way.

31   And He came down to Capernaum, a city of Galilee. And He was teaching[~] them on the Sabbath;

32   and they were amazed[m1] at His teaching, for His message was with *authority.*

33   And there was a man in the synagogue possessed by the spirit of an unclean demon, and he cried out with a loud voice,

34   "Ha! What do we have to do with You, Jesus of Nazareth? Have You come to destroy[x] us? I know[29e] who You are—the Holy[28a] One of God!"

35   And Jesus rebuked him, saying, "Be quiet[x] and come[xl] out of him!" And when the demon had thrown him down in *their* midst, he came out of him without doing him any harm.

36   And amazement came upon them all, and they *began* discussing[m] with one another saying, "What is this message? For with *authority* and *power*[32a] He commands the unclean spirits, and they come out."

37   And the report about Him was getting[m] out into every locality in the surrounding district.

Many Are Healed

38   And He arose and *left* the synagogue, and entered Simon's home. Now Simon's mother-in-law was suffering[~] from a high fever; and they made request of Him on her behalf.

39   And standing over her, He rebuked the fever, and it left her; and she immediately arose and waited[m] on them.

40   And while the sun was setting, all who had[m] any sick with *various* diseases brought them to Him; and laying His hands on every one of them, He was healing[m] them.

41   And demons also were coming[m] out of many, crying out and saying, "*You* are the Son of God!" And rebuking them, He would not allow[m6b] them to speak,[~] because they knew Him to be the *Christ.*

42   And when day came, He departed and went to a lonely

4:26 1 Kin. 17:9; Matt. 11:21
4:27 2 Kin. 5:1-14
4:29 Num. 15:35; Acts 7:58; Heb. 13:12
4:30 John 10:39
4:31 Luke 4:31-37; Mark 1:21-28; Matt. 4:13; Luke 4:23
4:32 Matt. 7:28; Luke 4:36; John 7:46
4:34 Matt. 8:29; Mark 1:24
4:35 Matt. 8:26; Mark 4:39; Luke 4:39, 41; 8:24
4:36 Luke 4:32
4:37 Luke 4:14
4:38 Luke 4:38,39; Matt. 8:14,15; Mark 1:29-31; Matt. 4:24
4:39 Luke 4:35,41
4:40 Luke 4:40,41; Matt. 8:16,17; Mark 1:32-34; Mark 1:32; Mark 5:23; Matt. 4:23
4:41 Matt. 4:3; Luke 4:35; Matt. 8:16; Mark 1:34
4:42 Luke 4:42,43; Mark 1:35-38

place; and the multitudes were searching^m for Him, and came to Him, and tried^m to keep Him from going away from them.

4:43
Mark 1:38

43 But He said to them, "I *must* preach^x the kingdom of God to the *other cities also,* for I was sent for this purpose."

4:44
Matt. 4:23

44 And He kept on preaching ~ in the synagogues of ^mJudea.

The First Disciples

5:1
Matt. 4:18-22;
Mark 1:16-20;
Luke 5:1-11; John
1:40-42;
Num. 34:11;
Deut. 3:17; Josh.
12:3; 13:27; Matt.
4:18

5 Now it came about that while the multitude were pressing~ around Him and listening~ to the word of God, He was standing~ by the lake of Gennesaret;

2 and He saw two boats lying at the edge of the lake; but the fishermen had gotten out of them, and were washing^m their nets.

5:3
Matt. 13:2; Mark
3:9,10; 4:1

3 And He got into one of the boats, which was Simon's, and asked him to put^x out a little way from the land. And He sat down and *began* teaching the multitudes from the boat.

5:4
John 21:6

4 And when He had finished speaking, He said to Simon, "Put^{xl} out into the deep water and let^{xl} down your nets for a catch."

5:5
Luke 8:24; 9:33,
49; 17:13;
John 21:3

5 And Simon answered and said, "Master, we worked hard all night and caught †nothing, but *at Your bidding*^{43b} I will let down the nets."

5:6
John 21:6

6 And when they had done this, they enclosed a *great* quantity of fish; and their nets *began* to break;^m

7 and they signaled to their partners in the other boat, for them to come and help^x them. And they came, and filled both of the boats, so that they began to sink. ~

8 But when Simon Peter saw *that,* he fell down at Jesus' feet, saying, "Depart^{xl} from me, for I am a *sinful* man, O Lord!"

9 For amazement had seized him and all his companions because of the catch of fish which they had taken;

5:10
Matt. 14:27;
2 Tim. 2:26

10 and so also James and John, sons of Zebedee, who were partners with Simon. And Jesus said to Simon, "Do not fear,^o from now on you will be catching~ *men.*"

5:11
Matt. 4:20,22;
19:29; Mark 1:18,
20; Luke 5:28

11 And when they had brought their boats to land, they left everything and followed Him.

The Leper and the Paralytic

5:12
Luke 5:12-14;
Matt. 8:2-4; Mark
1:40-44

12 And it came about that while He was in one of the cities, behold, *there was* a man full of leprosy; and when he saw Jesus, he fell on his face and implored Him, saying, "Lord, if You are willing, ~ You can make^x me clean."

13 And He stretched out His hand, and touched him, saying,

^mI.e., the country of the Jews (including Galilee); some mss. read *Galilee*

"I am willing; be cleansed."[xi] And immediately the leprosy left him.

14 And He ordered him to tell[x] no one, "But go and show[xi] yourself to the priest, and make[xi] an offering for your cleansing, just as Moses commanded, for a testimony to them."

5:14
Lev. 13:49; 14:2ff.

15 But the news about Him was spreading[m] even farther, and *great multitudes* were gathering[m] to hear~ *Him* and to be healed~[15a] of their sicknesses.

5:15
Matt. 9:26

16 But He Himself would *often* slip~ away to the wilderness and pray.~

5:16
Matt. 14:23; Mark 1:35; Luke 6:12

17 And it came about one day that He was teaching;~ and there were *some* Pharisees and teachers of the law sitting~ *there*, who had come+ from every village of Galilee and Judea and *from* Jerusalem; and the power[32a] of the Lord was *present* for Him to ·perform~ healing.[15b]

5:17
Matt. 15:1; Luke 2:46; Mark 1:45; Mark 5:30; Luke 6:19; 8:46

18 And behold, *some* men *were* carrying on a bed a man who was paralyzed;+ and they were trying[m] to bring[x] him in, and to set[x] him down in front of Him.

5:18
Luke 5:18-26; *Matt. 9:2-8; Mark 2:3-12*

19 And not finding any *way* to bring[x] him in because of the crowd, they went up on the roof and let him down *through the tiles* with his stretcher, right in the center, in front of Jesus.

5:19
Matt. 24:17; Mark 2:4

20 And seeing their faith, He said, "Friend, your sins are forgiven+ you."

5:20
Matt. 9:2

21 And the scribes and the Pharisees began to reason,~ saying, "Who is this *man* who speaks blasphemies? Who can forgive[x] sins, but God alone?"

5:21
Luke 3:8; Luke 7:49; Is. 43:25

22 But Jesus, aware[1] of their reasonings, answered and said to them, "Why are you reasoning in your hearts?

23 "Which is easier, to say,[x] 'Your sins have been forgiven+ you,' or to say,[x] 'Rise and walk'?

24 "But in order that you may know[29e] that the Son of Man has authority on earth to forgive~[21a] sins,"—He said to the paralytic+—"I say to you, rise, and take up your stretcher and go home."

5:24
Matt. 4:24

25 And at once he rose up before them, and took up what he had been lying[m] on, and went home, glorifying God.

5:25
Matt. 9:8

26 And they were all seized with astonishment[1] and *began* glorifying[m] God; and they were filled with fear, saying, "We have seen remarkable things today."

5:26
Matt. 9:8; Luke 1:65; 7:16

Call of Levi (Matthew)

27 And after that He went out, and noticed a [n]tax-gatherer named Levi, sitting in the tax office, and He said to him, "Follow~[l] Me."

5:27
Luke 5:27-39; *Matt. 9:9-17; Mark 2:14-22;* Matt. 9:9

[n]I.e., Collector of Roman taxes for profit

5:28
Luke 5:11
28   And he left everything behind, and rose and *began* to follow[m] Him.

5:29
Matt. 9:9;
Luke 15:1
29   And Levi gave a big reception for Him in his house; and there was a great crowd of tax-gatherers and other *people* who were reclining~ *at the table* with them.

5:30
Mark 2:16; Luke
15:2; Acts 23:9
30   And the Pharisees and their scribes *began* grumbling[m] at His disciples, saying, "Why do you eat and drink with the *tax-gatherers* and *sinners?*"

5:31
Matt. 9:12,13;
Mark 2:17
31   And Jesus answered and said to them, "*It is* not those who are well who need a physician, but those who are sick.

32   "I have not come* to call[x] the righteous but sinners to repentance."

5:33
Matt. 9:14; Mark
2:18
33   And they said to Him, "The disciples of John often fast and offer prayers; the *disciples* of the Pharisees also do the same; but Yours eat and drink."

34   And Jesus said to them, "You cannot make[x] the attendants of the bridegroom fast[x] while the bridegroom is *with them,* can you?

5:35
Matt. 9:15; Mark
2:20; Luke 17:22
35   "But *the* days will come; and when the bridegroom is taken[x] away from them, then they will fast in those days."

36   And He was also telling them a parable: "No one tears a piece from a *new* garment and puts it on an *old* garment; otherwise he will both tear the new, and the piece from the new will *not match* the old.

37   "And no one puts †new wine into †old wineskins; otherwise the †new wine will burst the skins, and it will be spilled out, and the skins will be ruined.

38   "But †new wine must be put into †fresh wineskins.

39   "And no one, after drinking old *wine* wishes for new; for he says, 'The old is good *enough.*' "

Jesus Is Lord of the Sabbath

6:1
Luke 6:1-5; Matt.
12:1-8; Mark
2:23-28;
Deut. 23:25
6 Now it came about that on a *certain* Sabbath He was passing~ through *some* grainfields; and His disciples were picking[m] and eating the heads *of grain,* rubbing[m] them in their hands.

6:2
Matt. 12:2
2   But some of the Pharisees said, "Why do you do what is not lawful on the Sabbath?"

6:3
1 Sam. 21:6
3   And Jesus answering them said, "Have you not even read what *David* did when *he* was hungry, he and those who were with him,

6:4
Lev. 24:9
4   how he entered the house of God, and took and ate the °*consecrated* †*bread* which is not lawful for any to eat[x] except the priests alone, and gave it to his companions?"

°Or, *showbread,* lit., *loaves of presentation*

5   And He was saying to them, "The Son of Man is *Lord* of the Sabbath."

6   And it came about on another Sabbath, that He entered[x] the synagogue and was teaching;~ and there was a man there whose right hand was withered.

7   And the scribes and the Pharisees were watching[m] Him closely,[1] *to see* if He healed on the Sabbath, in order that they might find[x] *reason* to accuse~ Him.

8   But *He* knew what they were thinking, and He said to the man with the *withered* hand, "Rise and come[xl] forward!" And he rose and came forward.

9   And Jesus said to them, "I ask you, is it lawful on the Sabbath to do[x] good, or to do[x] harm, to save[x] a life, or to destroy[x] it?"

10   And after looking around at them all, He said to him, "Stretch[xl] out your hand!" And he did *so;* and his hand was restored.

11   But they themselves were filled with rage, and discussed[m] together what they might do[x] to Jesus.

Choosing the Twelve

12   And it was at this time that He went[x] off to the mountain to pray,[x] and He spent~ the whole night in prayer to God.

13   And when day came, He called His disciples to Him; and chose twelve of them, whom He also named as *apostles:*

14   Simon, whom He also named Peter, and Andrew his brother; and James and John; and Philip and Bartholomew;

15   and Matthew and Thomas; James *the son* of Alphaeus, and Simon who was called the Zealot;

16   Judas *the son* of James, and Judas Iscariot, who became a traitor.

17   And He descended with them, and stood on a level place; and *there was* a great multitude of His disciples, and a great throng of people from all Judea and Jerusalem and the coastal region of Tyre and Sidon,

18   who had come to hear[x] Him, and to be healed[x15b] of their diseases; and those who were troubled with unclean spirits were being cured.[m15a]

19   And all the multitude were trying[m] to touch~ Him, for power[32a] was coming[m] from Him and healing[m15b] *them* all.

The Beatitudes

20   And turning His gaze on His disciples, He *began* to say, "†Blessed *are* you *who are* poor, for *yours* is the kingdom of God.

6:6
Luke 6:6-11;
Matt. 12:9-14;
Mark 3:1-6;
Luke 6:1;
Matt. 4:23
6:7
Mark 3:2

6:8
Matt. 9:4

6:10
Mark 3:5

6:12
Matt. 5:1;
Matt. 14:23; Luke 5:16; 9:18,28
6:13
Luke 6:13-16;
Matt. 10:2-4;
Mark 3:16-19;
Acts 1:13;
Mark 6:30

6:15
Matt. 9:9

6:17
Luke 6:12;
Matt. 4:25; Mark 3:7,8;
Matt. 11:21

6:19
Matt. 9:21; 14:36;
Mark 3:10;
Luke 5:17

6:20
Matt. 5:3-12;
Luke 6:20-23;
Matt. 5:3

21 "⁺Blessed *are* you who hunger *now,* for you shall be satisfied. ⁺Blessed *are* you who weep *now,* for you shall laugh.

6:22
1 Pet. 4:14;
John 9:22; 16:2

22 "⁺Blessed are you when men hate˟ you, and ostracize˟ you, and cast˟ insults at you, and spurn˟ your name as evil, for the sake of the Son of Man.

6:23
Mal. 4;
2 Chr. 36:16; Acts
7:52

23 "Be glad˟ⁱ in that day, and leap˟ⁱ *for joy,* for behold, your reward is great²⁶ᵇ in heaven; for in the *same way their fathers* used˟ to treat the prophets.

6:24
Luke 16:25;
James 5:1;
Matt. 6:2

24 "But woe to you who are rich, for you are receiving your comfort in full.

25 "Woe to you who are well-fed⁺ *now,* for you shall be hungry. Woe *to you* who laugh *now,* for you shall mourn and weep.

6:26
Matt. 7:15

26 "Woe *to you* when *all men* speak˟ well of you, for in the *same way their fathers* used˟ to treat the false prophets.

6:27
Matt. 5:44; Luke
6:35

27 "But I say to you who hear, love˟³¹ᵃ your enemies, do˟ *good* to those who hate you,

6:28
Matt. 5:44; Luke
6:35

28 bless˟ those who curse you, pray˟ for those who mistreat you.

6:29
Luke 6:29,30:
Matt. 5:39-42

29 "Whoever hits you on the cheek, offer˟ him the other also; and whoever takes away your coat, do not withhold⁰ your shirt from him either.

30 "Give˟ to everyone who asks of you, and whoever takes away what is yours, do not demand⁰ it back.

6:31
Matt. 7:12

31 "And just as you want people to treat˜ ⁺*you,* treat˟ ⁺*them* in the same way.

6:32
Matt. 5:46

32 "And if you love those who love you, what credit is *that* to you? For even sinners love *those who love them.*

33 "And if you do˜ good to those who do good to you, what credit is *that* to you? For even sinners do *the same.*

6:34
Matt. 5:42

34 "And if you lend˟ to those from whom you expect to receive,˟ what credit is *that* to you? Even sinners lend to *sinners,* in order to receive˟ back the same *amount.*

6:35
Luke 6:27;
Matt. 5:9;
Luke 1:32

35 "But love˟³¹ᵃ your enemies, and do˟ good, and lend,˟ expecting nothing in return; and your reward will be *great,* ²⁶ᵇ and you will be sons of the Most High; for *He Himself* is kind to ungrateful and evil *men.*

36 "Be merciful,˟ just as your Father is merciful.

6:37
Luke 6:37-42:
Matt. 7:1-5;
Matt. 6:14; Luke
23:16; Acts 3:13

37 "And do not judge⁰ and you will •not be judged;˟ and do not condemn,⁰¹⁴ᵇ and you will •not be condemned;˟ pardon,˟ and you will be pardoned.

6:38
Mark 4:24;
Ps. 79:12; Is.
65:6,7; Jer. 32:18

38 "Give,˟ and it will be given to you; *good*²⁵ᵇ measure, *pressed⁺ down, shaken⁺ together, running over,* ¹ they will pour into your lap. For by your standard of measure it will be measured to you in return."

39 And He also spoke a parable to them: "A *blind man* cannot guide~ a *blind man,* can he? Will they not both fall into a *pit?*

40 "A pupil is not above his teacher; but everyone, after he has been fully trained,⁺ will be like his teacher.

41 "And why do you look at the speck that is in your brother's eye, but do not notice the *log* that is in your *own* eye?

42 "Or how can you say~ to your brother, 'Brother, letˣⁱ me takeˣ out the speck that is in your eye,' when you yourself do not see the *log* that is in your *own* eye? You hypocrite, first takeˣⁱ the log out of your own eye, and then you will see clearly¹ to takeˣ out the speck that is in your brother's eye.

43 "For there is no good²⁵ᵇ tree which produces ⁺bad¹⁰ᶜ fruit; nor, on the other hand, a ⁺bad¹⁰ᶜ tree which produces good²⁵ᵇ fruit.

44 "For each tree is known²⁹ᵃ by its *own fruit.* For men do not gather figs from *thorns,* nor do they pick grapes from a *briar bush.*

45 "The good²⁵ᵃ man out of the good treasure of his heart brings forth what is good; and the evil¹⁰ᵇ *man* out of the evil *treasure* brings forth what is evil; for his mouth speaks from that which *fills his heart.*

Builders and Foundations

46 "And why do you call Me, 'Lord, Lord,' and do not do what I say?

47 "Everyone who comes to Me, and hears *My* words,⁴³ᵃ and acts upon them, I will show you whom he is like:

48 he is like a man building a house, who dug deep and laid a foundation upon the rock; and when a *flood* rose, the torrent burst against that house and could not shakeˣ it, because it had been well built.⁺

49 "But the one who has heard, and has not acted *accordingly,* is like a man who built a house upon the ground without any foundation; and the torrent burst against it and immediately it collapsed, and the ruin of that house was *great.*"

Jesus Heals a Centurion's Servant

7 When He had completed all His discourse in the hearing of the people, He went to Capernaum.

2 And a certain centurion's slave, who was highly regarded by him, was sick and about to die.

3 And when he heard about Jesus, he sent some Jewish elders asking Him to come and saveˣ the life of his slave.

4 And when they had come to Jesus, they earnestly

6:39
Matt. 15:14

6:40
Matt. 10:24; John 13:16; 15:20

6:43
Luke 6:43,44;
Matt. 7:16,18,20

6:44
Matt. 7:16; 12:33

6:45
Matt. 12:35;
Matt. 12:34

6:46
Mal. 1:6; Matt. 7:21

6:47
Luke 6:47-49;
Matt. 7:24-27;
James 1:22ff.

7:1
Matt. 7:28;
Luke 7:1-10;
Matt. 8:5-13

7:3
Matt. 8:5

entreated^m Him, saying, "He is †*worthy* for You to grant this to him;

5 for he loves our nation, and it was he who built us our *synagogue.*"

6 Now Jesus *started* on His way with them; and when He was already not far from the house, the centurion sent friends, saying to Him, "Lord, do not trouble[◊] Yourself further, for I am *not* †*worthy* for You to come^x under my roof;

7 for this reason I did not even consider *myself* worthy to come to *You,* but *just* say^{xı} the word,^{43a} and my servant will be healed.^{15b}

8 "For *I, too,* am a man *under authority,* with soldiers under me; and I say to this one, 'Go!'^{xı} and he goes; and to another, 'Come!' and he comes; and to my slave, 'Do^{xı} this!' and he does it.''

9 Now when Jesus heard this, He marveled at him, and turned and said to the multitude that was following Him, "I say to you, not even in *Israel* have I found such great faith."

10 And when those who had been sent returned to the house, they found the slave in good health.

11 And it came about soon afterwards, that He went to a city called Nain; and His disciples were going^m along with Him, accompanied by a large multitude.

12 Now as He approached the gate of the city, behold, a dead man was being carried out, the only son of his mother, and she was a widow; and a *sizeable* crowd from the city was with her.

13 And when the Lord saw her, He felt compassion for her, and said to her, "Do not weep."[◊]

14 And He came up and touched the coffin; and the bearers came to a halt. And He said, "Young man, I say to you, arise!"^{xı}

15 And the dead man sat up, and began to speak. ~ And *Jesus* gave him back to his mother.

16 And fear gripped them all, and they *began* glorifying^m God, saying, "A great prophet has arisen among us!" and, "God has visited His people!"

17 And this report concerning Him went out all over Judea, and in all the surrounding district.

A Deputation from John

18 And the disciples of John reported to him about all these things.

19 And summoning two of his disciples, John sent them to the Lord, saying, "Are *You* the Expected One, or do we look for *someone else?*"

7:9
Matt. 8:10; Luke 7:50

7:13
Luke 7:19; 10:1; 11:1,39; 12:42; 13:15; 17:5,6; 18:6; 19:8; 22:61; 24:34; John 4:1; 6:23; 11:2

7:16
Luke 5:26; Matt. 9:8; Matt. 21:11; Luke 7:39

7:17
Matt. 9:26

7:18
Luke 7:18-35; Matt. 11:2-19
7:19
Luke 7:13; 10:1; 11:1,39; 12:42; 13:15; 17:5,6; 18:6; 19:8; 22:61; 24:34; John 4:1; 6:23; 11:2

20 And when the men had come to Him, they said, "John the Baptist has sent us to You, saying, 'Are *You* the Expected One, or do we look for *someone else?'* "

21 At that very time He cured many *people* of diseases and afflictions and evil spirits; and He granted sight~ to *many who were* blind.

7:21
Matt. 4:23;
Mark 3:10

22 And He answered and said to them, "Go and report^x to John what you have seen and heard: *the* BLIND RECEIVE SIGHT, *the* lame walk, *the* lepers are cleansed, and *the* deaf hear, *the* dead are raised up, *the* POOR HAVE THE GOSPEL PREACHED TO THEM.

7:22
Is. 35:5;
Is. 61:1

23 "And †blessed is he who keeps from stumbling^x over Me."

24 And when the messengers of John had left, He began to speak~ to the multitudes about John, "What did you go out into the wilderness to look^x at? A reed shaken by the wind?

25 "But what did you go out to see?^x A man dressed⁺ in soft clothing? Behold, those who are splendidly clothed and live in luxury are *found* in royal palaces.

26 "But what did you go out to see?^x A prophet? Yes, I say to you, and one who is more than a prophet.

27 "This is the one about whom it is written,⁺

7:27
Mal. 3:1; Matt.
11:10; Mark 1:2

'BEHOLD, I SEND MY MESSENGER BEFORE YOUR FACE,
WHO WILL PREPARE YOUR WAY BEFORE YOU.'

28 "I say to you, among those born of women, there is no one greater than John; yet he who is least in the kingdom of God is *greater than* †he."

29 And when all the people and the ᵖtax-gatherers heard *this,* they acknowledged God's justice, having been baptized with the baptism of John.

7:29
Luke 7:35;
Matt. 21:32; Luke
3:12;
Acts 18:25; 19:3

30 But the Pharisees and the �q lawyers *rejected* God's purpose for themselves, not having been baptized by John.

7:30
Matt. 22:35

31 "To what then shall I compare the men of this generation, and what are they like?

32 "They are like children who sit in the market place and call to one another; and they say, 'We played the flute for you, and you did not dance; we sang a dirge, and you did not weep.'

33 "For John the Baptist has come⁺ eating no bread and drinking no wine; and you say, 'He has a *demon!'*

7:33
Luke 1:15

34 "The Son of Man has come⁺ eating and drinking; and you say, 'Behold, a gluttonous man, and a drunkard, a friend of tax-gatherers and sinners!'

35 "Yet wisdom is vindicated by all her children."

7:35
Luke 7:29

36 Now one of the Pharisees was requesting^m Him to dine^x

ᵖI.e., Collectors of Roman taxes for profit   qI.e., experts in the Mosaic law

with him. And He entered the Pharisee's house, and reclined *at the table.*

7:37
Matt. 26:6-13;
Mark 14:3-9;
Luke 7:37-39;
John 12:1-8

37   And behold, there was a woman in the city who was a sinner; and when she learned that He was reclining *at the table* in the Pharisee's house, she brought an alabaster vial of perfume,

38   and standing behind *Him* at His feet, weeping, she began to wet~ His feet with her *tears,* and kept wiping^{xxx} them with the *hair of her head,* and kissing^{xxx1} His feet, and anointing^{xxx} them with the perfume.

7:39
Luke 7:16; John
4:19

39   Now when the Pharisee who had invited Him saw this, he said to himself, "If this man were a prophet He would know^{xxx29a} who and what sort of person this woman is who is touching Him, that she is a †*sinner.*"

Parable of Two Debtors

40   And Jesus answered and said to him, "Simon, I have something to say^x to you." And he replied, "Say^{xi} it, Teacher."

7:41
Matt. 18:28; Mark
6:37

41   "A certain moneylender had two debtors: one owed five hundred ʳdenarii, and the other fifty.

7:42
Matt. 18:25

42   "When they were unable to repay,^x he graciously forgave^{21b} them *both.* Which of them therefore will love^{31a} him †*more?*"

43   Simon answered and said, "I suppose the one whom he forgave *more.*" And He said to him, "You have judged correctly."

7:44
Gen. 18:4; 19:2;
43:24; Judg.
19:21; 1 Tim.
5:10

44   And turning toward the woman, He said to Simon, "Do you see this woman? I entered *your* house; you gave Me no water for My feet, but she has wet My feet with her *tears,* and wiped them with her *hair.*

7:45
2 Sam. 15:5

45   "You gave Me no kiss; but she, since the time I came in, has not ceased to kiss¹ My *feet.*

7:46
2 Sam. 12:20; Ps.
23:5; Eccl. 9:8;
Dan. 10:3

46   "You did not anoint My head with oil, but she anointed My feet with *perfume.*

47   "For this reason I say to you, her sins, which are *many,* have been *forgiven,*+ for she loved much; but he who is forgiven little, loves *little.*"

7:48
Matt. 9:2; Mark
2:5,9; Luke 5:20,
23
7:49
Luke 5:21
7:50
Matt. 9:22; Luke
17:19; 18:42;
Mark 5:34; Luke
8:48

48   And He said to her, "Your *sins* have been forgiven."+

49   And those who were reclining *at the table* with Him began to say~ to themselves, "Who is this *man* who even forgives *sins?*"

50   And He said to the woman, "Your faith has saved+ you; go in peace."

ʳThe denarius was equivalent to one day's wage

Ministering Women

8 And it came about soon afterwards, that He *began* going[m] about from one city and village to another, proclaiming and preaching the kingdom of God; and the twelve were with Him,

2   and *also* some women who had been healed[+] of evil spirits and sicknesses: Mary who was called Magdalene, from whom seven demons had gone out,

3   and Joanna the wife of Chuza, Herod's steward, and Susanna, and many others who were contributing[m] to their support out of their private means.

Parable of the Sower

4   And when a *great* multitude were coming together, and those from the various cities were journeying to Him, He spoke by way of a parable:

5   "The sower went out to sow[x] his seed; and as he sowed,[~] some fell beside the road; and it was trampled under foot, and the birds of the air ate it up.

6   "And other *seed* fell on rocky *soil,* and as soon as it grew up, it withered away, because it had no moisture.

7   "And other *seed* fell among the thorns; and the thorns grew up with it, and choked it out.

8   "And other *seed* fell into the [+]*good*[25a] soil, and grew up, and produced a crop a *hundred* times as great." As He said these things, He would call[m] out, "He who has ears to hear,[~] let him hear."[~!]

9   And His disciples *began* questioning[m] Him as to what this parable might be.

10   And He said, "To *you* it has been granted[+] to know[x29a] the mysteries of the kingdom of God, but to the rest *it is* in *parables,* in order that SEEING THEY MAY NOT SEE,[~] AND HEARING THEY MAY NOT UNDERSTAND.[~29f]

11   "Now the parable is *this:* the seed is the word of God.

12   "And those beside the road are those who have heard; then the *devil* comes and takes away the word from their heart, so that they may not believe and be saved.[x]

13   "And those on the rocky *soil are* those who, when they hear,[x] receive[5a] the word with joy; and these have no *firm* root; they believe *for a while,* and in time of temptation fall away.

14   "And the *seed* which fell among the thorns, these are the ones who have heard, and as they go on their way they are choked with *worries* and *riches* and *pleasures of this life,*[30a] and bring no fruit to maturity.

8:1
Matt. 4:23

8:2
Matt. 27:55; Mark 15:40,41; Luke 23:49,55;
Matt. 27:56; Mark 16:9
8:3
Matt. 14:1;
Matt. 20:8

8:4
Luke 8:4-8: *Matt. 13:2-9; Mark 4:1-9*

8:8
Matt. 11:15; Mark 7:16; Luke 14:35;
Rev. 2:7,11,17, 29; 3:6,13,22; 13:9

8:9
Luke 8:9-15:
Matt. 13:10-23; Mark 4:10-20
8:10
Matt. 13:11; Is. 6:9; Matt. 13:14; Acts 28:26

8:11
1 Pet. 1:23

15 "And the *seed* in the good[25b] soil, these are the ones who have heard the word in an honest[25b] and good[25a] heart, and hold it fast, and bear fruit with perseverance.

Parable of the Lamp

8:16
Matt. 5:15; Mark
4:21; Luke 11:33

16 "Now no one after lighting a lamp covers it over with a container, or puts it *under a bed;* but he puts it on a *lampstand,* in order that those who come in may see~ the light.

8:17
Matt. 10:26; Mark
4:22; Luke 12:2

17 "For nothing is hidden that shall not become[x] *evident,* nor *anything* secret that shall not be known and come *to light.*

8:18
Matt. 13:12;
25:29; Luke 19:26

18 "Therefore take care~ how you listen; for whoever has,~ to him shall *more* be given; and whoever does not have,~ even what he thinks he has shall be taken away from him."

8:19
Luke 8:19-21;
Matt. 12:46-50;
Mark 3:31-35

19 And His mother and brothers came to Him, and they were unable[m] to get[x] to Him because of the crowd.

20 And it was reported to Him, "Your mother and Your brothers are standing outside, wishing to see[x] You."

8:21
Luke 11:28

21 But He answered and said to them, "My mother and My brothers are these who hear the word of God and do it."

Jesus Stills the Sea

8:22
Luke 8:22-25;
Matt. 8:23-27;
Mark 4:36-41;
Luke 5:1f.; 8:23

22 Now it came about on one of *those* days, that He and His disciples got into a boat, and He said to them, "Let us go[x] over to the other side of the lake." And they launched out.

8:23
Luke 5:1f.; 8:22

23 But as they were sailing along He fell asleep; and a fierce gale of wind descended upon the lake, and they *began* to be swamped and to be in danger.

8:24
Luke 5:5;
Luke 4:39

24 And they came to Him and woke Him up, saying, "Master, Master, we are perishing!" And being aroused, He rebuked the wind and the surging waves, and they stopped, and it became calm.

25 And He said to them, "Where is your faith?" And they were fearful and amazed, saying to one another, "Who then is *this,* that He commands even the *winds* and the *water,* and they obey Him?"

The Demoniac Cured

8:26
Luke 8:26-37;
Matt. 8:28-34;
Mark 5:1-17

26 And they sailed to the country of the Gerasenes, which is opposite Galilee.

27 And when He had come out onto the land, He was met by a certain man from the city who was possessed with demons; and who had not put on any clothing for a long time, and was not living[m] in a *house,* but in the †*tombs.*

8:28
Matt. 8:29;
Mark 5:7

28 And seeing Jesus, he cried out and fell before Him, and

said in a loud voice, "What do I have to do with You, Jesus, Son of the Most High God? I beg You, do not torment me."⊗

29   For He had been commanding the unclean spirit to come^x out of the man. For it had seized him *many times;* and he was bound^ᵐ with chains and shackles and kept under guard; and *yet* he would burst his fetters and be driven^ᵐ by the demon into the desert.

30   And Jesus asked him, "What is your name?" And he said, "Legion"; for *many* demons had entered him.

31   And they were entreating^ᵐ Him not to command^x them to depart^x into the abyss.

32   Now there was a herd of many swine feeding there on the mountain; and *the demons* entreated Him to permit them to enter^x the swine. And He gave^x them permission.

33   And the demons came out from the man and entered the swine; and the herd rushed down the steep bank into the lake, and were drowned.

34   And when the herdsmen saw what had happened,⁺ they ran away and reported it in the city and *out* in the country.

35   And *the people* went out to see^x what had happened;⁺ and they came to Jesus, and found the man from whom the demons had gone out, sitting down at the feet of Jesus, clothed⁺ and in his right mind; and they became frightened.

36   And those who had seen it reported to them how the man who was demon-possessed had been made well.

37   And all the people of the country of the Gerasenes and the surrounding district asked Him to depart^x from them; for they were gripped^ᵐ with *great fear;* and He got into a boat, and returned.

38   But the man from whom the demons had gone out was begging^ᵐ Him that he might accompany Him; but He sent him away, saying,

39   "Return⌣ᶦ to your house and describe⌣ᶦ what great things God has done for you." And he went away, proclaiming throughout the whole city what great things *Jesus* had done for him.

Miracles of Healing

40   And as Jesus returned,⌣ the multitude welcomed Him, for they had all been waiting⌣ for Him.

41   And behold, there came a man named Jairus, and he was an official of the synagogue; and he fell at Jesus' feet, and *began* to entreat^ᵐ Him to come^x to his house;

42   for he had an *only* daughter, about twelve years old, and

8:30
Matt. 26:53

8:31
Rom. 10:7; Rev. 9:1f.,11; 11:7; 17:8; 20:1,3

8:33
Luke 5:1f.; 8:22

8:35
Luke 10:39

8:36
Matt. 4:24

8:38
Luke 8:38,39; Mark 5:18-20

8:40
Matt. 9:1; Mark 5:21

8:41
Luke 8:41-56; Matt. 9:18-26; Mark 5:22-43; Mark 5:22; Luke 8:49

she was dying.ᵐ But as He went, the multitudes were pressingᵐ against Him.

43 And a woman who had a hemorrhage for twelve years, ˢand could not be healedˣ by anyone,

44 came up behind Him, and touched the fringe of His cloak; and immediately her hemorrhage stopped.

8:45
Luke 5:5

45 And Jesus said, "Who is the one who touched Me?" And while they were all denying it, Peter said, "Master, the multitudes are crowding and pressing upon You."

8:46
Luke 5:17

46 But Jesus said, "Someone did touch Me, for *I* was aware that power³²ᵃ had gone⁺ out of Me."

47 And when the woman saw that she had not escaped notice, she came trembling and fell down before Him, and declared in the presence of all the people the reason why she had touched Him, and how she had been *immediately* healed.¹⁵ᵇ

8:48
Matt. 9:22;
Mark 5:34; Luke
7:50
8:49
Luke 8:41

48 And He said to her, "Daughter, your faith has made⁺ you well; go in peace."

49 While He was still speaking, someone *came from *the house of* the synagogue official, saying, "Your daughter has *died;* do not trouble⁰ the Teacher anymore."

8:50
Mark 5:36

50 But when Jesus heard *this,* He answered him, "Do not be afraid⁰ *any longer;* only believe,ˣ¹ and she shall be made well."

51 And when He had come to the house, He did not allow anyone to enterˣ with Him, except Peter and John and James, and the girl's father and mother.

8:52
Matt. 11:17; Luke
23:27;
John 11:13

52 Now they were all weepingᵐ and lamentingᵐ for her; but He said, "Stop weeping,⁰ for she has not died, but is asleep."

53 And they *began* laughingᵐ¹ at Him, knowing that she had died.

54 He, however, took her by the hand and called, saying, "Child, arise!"

55 And her spirit returned, and she rose *immediately;* and He gave orders for *something* to be givenˣ her to eat.ˣ

8:56
Matt. 8:4

56 And her parents were *amazed;* but He instructed them to tellˣ no one what had happened.⁺

Ministry of the Twelve

9:1
Matt. 10:5; Mark
6:7
9:2
Matt. 10:7
9:3
Luke 9:3-5: Matt.
10:9-15; Mark
6:8-11; Luke
10:4-12; 22:35;
Matt. 10:10;
Mark 6:8; Luke
22:35f.

9 And He called the twelve together, and gave them power³²ᵃ and authority over all the demons, and to heal~¹⁵ᵃ diseases.

2 And He sent them out to proclaim~ the kingdom of God, and to perform~ healing.¹⁵ᵇ

3 And He said to them, "Take~¹ nothing for *your* journey,

ˢSome mss. add *who had spent all her living upon physicians*

neither a staff, nor a bag, nor bread, nor money; and do not *even* have *two* tunics apiece.

4 "And whatever house you enter,[x] stay[m] there, and take your leave from there.

5 "And as for those who do not receive[~] you, as you go out from that city, shake[m] off the *dust from your feet* as a testimony against them."

6 And departing, they *began* going[m] about among the villages, preaching the gospel, and healing[15a] everywhere.

7 Now Herod the tetrarch heard of all that was happening; and he was greatly[1] perplexed,[m] because it was said[~] by some that John had risen from the dead,

8 and by some that Elijah had appeared, and by others, that one of the prophets of old had risen again.

9 And Herod said, "I myself had *John* beheaded; but who is this man about whom I hear such things?" And he kept trying[m] to see[x] Him.

10 And when the apostles returned, they gave an account to Him of all that they had done. And taking them with Him, He withdrew by Himself to a city called Bethsaida.

11 But the multitudes were aware of this and followed Him; and welcoming them, He *began* speaking[m] to them about the kingdom of God and curing[m][15b] those who had need of healing.[15a]

Five Thousand Fed

12 And the day began to decline,[~] and the twelve came and said to Him, "Send[xi] the multitude away, that they may go into the surrounding villages and countryside and find[x] lodging and get[x] something to eat; for here we are in a *desolate place.*"

13 But He said to them, *"You* give[xi] them *something* to eat!"[x] And they said, "We have no more than five loaves and two fish, unless perhaps *we* go and buy[x] food for all these people."

14 (For there were about five thousand men.) And He said to His disciples, "Have them recline[xi] *to eat* in groups of about fifty each."

15 And they did so, and had them all recline.

16 And He took the five loaves and the two fish, and looking up to heaven, He blessed them, and broke *them,* and kept giving[m] *them* to the disciples to set[x] before the multitude.

17 And they *all* ate and were satisfied; and the broken pieces which they had left over were picked up, twelve baskets *full.*

18 And it came about that while He was praying alone, the

9:5
Luke 10:11; Acts
13:51

9:6
Mark 6:12; Luke
8:1

9:7
Luke 9:7-9: Matt.
14:1,2; Mark
6:14f.;
Matt. 14:1; Luke
3:1; 13:31; 23:7;
Matt. 14:2
9:8
Matt. 16:14

9:9
Luke 23:8

9:10
Mark 6:30;
Luke 9:10-17;
Matt. 14:13-21;
Mark 6:32-44;
John 6:5-13;
Matt. 11:21

9:14
Mark 6:39

9:17
Matt. 14:20
9:18
Luke 9:18-20;
Matt. 16:13-16;
Mark 8:27-29;
Matt. 14:23; Luke
6:12; 9:28

disciples were with Him, and He questioned them, saying, "Who do the multitudes say that I am?"

19 And they answered and said, "John the Baptist, and others *say* Elijah; but others, that one of the prophets of old has risen again."

9:20
John 6:68f.

20 And He said to them, "But who do *you* say that I am?" And Peter answered and said, "The Christ of God."

9:21
Matt. 8:4; 16:20;
Mark 8:30

21 But He warned them, and instructed *them* not to tell~ this to anyone,

9:22
Luke 9:22-27:
Matt. 16:21-28;
Mark 8:31-9:1;
Matt. 16:21; Luke
9:44

22 saying, "The Son of Man must suffer^x *many things,* and be rejected^x by the elders and chief priests and scribes, and be killed,^x and be raised^x up on the third day."

9:23
Matt. 10:38; Luke
14:27

23 And He was saying^m to *them* all, "If anyone wishes to come~ after *Me,* let him deny^xⁱⁱ himself, and take^xⁱ up his cross daily, and follow~ⁱ Me.

9:24
Matt. 10:39; Luke
17:33; John 12:25

24 "For whoever wishes~ to *save*^x his life shall lose it, but whoever loses^x his life for My sake, *he*is the one who will save it.

9:25
Heb. 10:34

25 "For what is a man profited if he gains the *whole*world, and loses or forfeits *himself?*

9:26
Matt. 10:33; Luke
12:9

26 "For whoever is ashamed^x of Me and •My words, [43a] of *him* will the Son of Man be ashamed when He comes in His glory, and *the glory* of the Father and of the holy[28a] angels.

9:27
Matt. 16:28

27 "But I say to you truthfully, there are some of those standing here who shall •*not*taste^x death until they see^x the kingdom of God."

The Transfiguration

9:28
Luke 9:28-36:
Matt. 17:1-8;
Mark 9:2-8;
Matt. 17:1;
Matt. 5:1;
Luke 3:21; 5:16;
6:12; 9:18
9:29
Luke 3:21; 5:16;
6:12; 9:18; Mark 16:12

28 And some eight days after these sayings, it came about that He took along Peter and John and James, and went up to the mountain to pray.^x

29 And while He was praying,~ the appearance[22a] of His face became *different,* [8b] and His clothing *became* white *and* gleaming.

30 And behold, two men were talking^m with Him; and they were Moses and Elijah,

9:31
2 Pet. 1:15

31 who, appearing in glory, were speaking^m of His departure which He was about to accomplish at Jerusalem.

9:32
Matt. 26:43; Mark
14:40

32 Now Peter and his companions had been overcome⁺ with sleep; but when they were fully awake, they saw His glory and the two men standing with Him.

9:33
Luke 5:5; 9:49;
Matt. 17:4; Mark
9:5;
Mark 9:6

33 And it came about, as these were parting from Him, Peter said to Jesus, "Master, it is good for us to be here; and let us make^x three tabernacles: one for You, and one for Moses, and one for Elijah"—not realizing what he was saying.

34 And while he was saying this, a cloud formed and *began to*

overshadow them; and they were afraid as they entered[x] the cloud.

35   And a voice came out of the cloud, saying, "This is My Son, *My* Chosen[+] One; listen[◆] to *Him!*"

36   And when the voice had spoken, Jesus was found alone. And they kept silent, and reported to no one in those days any of the things which they had seen. [+]

37   And it came about on the next day, that when they had come down from the mountain, a great multitude met Him.

38   And behold, a man from the multitude shouted out, saying, "Teacher, I beg You to look[x] at my son, for he is my [†]*onlyboy,*

39   and behold, a spirit seizes him, and he suddenly screams, and it throws him into a convulsion with foaming *at the mouth,* and as it mauls him, it scarcely leaves him.

40   "And I begged Your disciples to cast[x] it out, and they could not."

41   And Jesus answered and said, "O unbelieving and perverted[+] generation, how long shall I be with you, and put up with you? Bring[xl] your son here."

42   And while he was still approaching, the demon dashed him *to the ground,* and threw him into a convulsion. But Jesus rebuked the unclean spirit, and healed[15b] the boy, and gave him back to his father.

43   And they were all amazed[ml1] at the greatness of God.

But while everyone was *marveling* at all that He was doing, He said[m] to His disciples,

44   "Let these words sink[xl] into your ears; for the Son of Man is going to be delivered into the hands of men."

45   But they did not understand[m] this statement, and it was concealed[+] from them so that they might not perceive[x] it; and they were afraid[m] to ask[x] Him about this statement.

The Test of Greatness

46   And an argument arose among them as to which of them might be the greatest.

47   But Jesus, knowing what they were thinking in their heart, took a child and stood him by His side,

48   and said to them, "Whoever receives[x] this child in My name receives *Me;* and whoever receives[x] *Me* receives Him who sent Me; for he who is least among you, this is the one who is great."

49   And John answered and said, "Master, we saw someone casting out demons in Your name; and we tried to hinder[m] him because he does not follow along with us."

9:35
2 Pet. 1:17f.;
Is. 42:1; Matt.
3:17; 12:18; Mark
1:11; Luke 3:22
9:36
Matt. 17:9; Mark
9:9f.

9:37
Luke 9:37-42:
Matt. 17:14-18;
Mark 9:14-27

9:43
2 Pet. 1:16;
Luke 9:43-45:
Matt. 17:22f.;
Mark 9:30-32
9:44
Luke 9:22

9:45
Mark 9:32

9:46
Luke 9:46-48:
Matt. 18:1-5;
Mark 9:33-37;
Luke 22:24
9:47
Matt. 9:4

9:48
Matt. 10:40; Luke
10:16; John
13:20;
Luke 22:26

9:49
Luke 9:49,50:
Mark 9:38-40;
Luke 5:5; 9:33

9:50
Matt. 12:30; Luke
11:23

50 But Jesus said to him, "Do not hinder⁰ *him;* for he who is not against you is for you."

9:51
Mark 16:19;
Luke 13:22;
17:11; 18:31;
19:11,28
9:52
Matt. 10:5; Luke
10:33; 17:16;
John 4:4

51 And it came about, when the days were approaching for His ascension, that He *resolutely* set His face to go to Jerusalem;

52 and He sent messengers on ahead of Him. And they went, and entered a village of the Samaritans, to make˟ arrangements for Him.

9:53
John 4:9

53 And they did not receive Him, because He was journeying~ with His face toward Jerusalem.

9:54
Mark 3:17;
2 Kin. 1:9-16

54 And when His disciples James and John saw *this,* they said, "Lord, do You want us to command˟ fire to come˟ down from heaven and consume˟ them?"

55 But He turned and rebuked them, [and said, "You do not know²⁹ᵉ what kind of spirit you are of;

56 for the Son of Man did not come to destroy men's lives, but to save them."] And they went on to another village.

Exacting Discipleship

9:57
Luke 9:51;
Luke 9:57-60;
Matt. 8:19-22
9:58
Matt. 8:20

57 And as they were going along the road, someone said to Him, "I will follow You wherever You go."~

58 And Jesus said to him, "The foxes have holes, and the birds of the air *have* †nests, but the Son of Man has nowhere to lay~ His head."

9:59
Matt. 8:22

59 And He said to another,⁸ᵇ "Follow~ᴵ Me." But he said, "†Permit˟ᴵ⁶ᶜ me first to go and bury˟ my father."

9:60
Matt. 4:23

60 But He said to him, "Allow˟ᴵ⁶ᵃ the dead to bury˟ their own dead; but as for you, go and proclaim~ᴵ everywhere the kingdom of God."

9:61
1 Kin. 19:20

61 And another⁸ᵇ also said, "I will follow You, Lord; but *first* permit˟ᴵ⁶ᶜ me to say˟ good-bye to those at home."

9:62
Phil. 3:13

62 But Jesus said to him, "No one, after putting his hand to the plow and looking back, is †*fit* for the kingdom of God."

The Seventy Sent Out

10:1
Luke 7:13;
Luke 9:1f.,52;
Mark 6:7

10 Now after this the Lord appointed seventy others, and sent them two and two ahead of Him to every city and place where He Himself was going to come.

10:2
Matt. 9:37,38;
John 4:35

2 And He was saying to them, "The harvest is plentiful, but the laborers are few; therefore beseech˟ᴵ the Lord of the harvest to send˟ out *laborers* into His harvest.

10:3
Matt. 10:16

3 "Go your ways; behold, I send you out as lambs in the midst of wolves.

†Some mss. add *Lord*

4 "Carry⁰ no purse, no bag, no shoes; and greet⁰ no one on the way.

5 "And whatever house you enter, first say, 'Peace *be* to †this house.'

6 "And if a man of peace is there, your peace will rest upon him; but if not, it will return to you.

7 "And stay~ˡ in *that house*, eating and drinking what they give you; for the laborer is worthy of his wages. Do not keep moving⁰ from house to house.

8 "And whatever city you enter,~ and they receive~ you, eat~ˡ what is set before you;

9 and heal~ˡ those in it who are sick, and say~ˡ to them, 'The kingdom of God has come⁺ near to you.'

10 "But whatever city you enter˟ and they do not receive~ you, go out into its streets and say,˟

11 '*Even the dust* of your city which clings to our feet, we wipe off *in protest* against you; yet be sure~ˡ of this, that the kingdom of God has come⁺ near.'

12 "I say to you, it will be more tolerable in that day for *Sodom,* than for that city.

13 "Woe to you, Chorazin! Woe to you, Bethsaida! For if the miracles had been performed in *Tyre* and *Sidon* which occurred in you, they would have repented *long ago,* sitting in sackcloth and ashes.

14 "But it will be more tolerable for *Tyre* and *Sidon* in the judgment, than for you.

15 "And you, Capernaum, will not be exalted to *heaven,* will you? You will be brought down to *Hades!*

16 "The one who listens to you listens to *Me,* and the one who rejects you rejects *Me;* and he who rejects Me rejects the One who sent Me."

The Happy Results

17 And the seventy returned with joy, saying, "Lord, even the *demons* are subject to us in Your name."

18 And He said to them, "I was watching Satan fall from heaven like lightning.

19 "Behold, I have given⁺ you authority to tread~ upon serpents and scorpions, and over all the power³²ᵃ of the enemy, and •*nothing* shall injure˟ you.

20 "Nevertheless do not rejoice⁰ in *this,* that the spirits are subject to you, but rejoice~ˡ that your names are recorded⁺ in heaven."

21 At that very time He rejoiced greatly in the Holy Spirit, and

10:4
Matt. 10:9-14;
Mark 6:8-11;
Luke 9:3-5;
10:4-12

10:7
Matt. 10:10;
1 Cor. 9:14; 1
Tim. 5:18

10:8
1 Cor. 10:27

10:9
Matt. 3:2; 10:7;
Luke 10:11

10:11
Matt. 10:14; Mark
6:11; Luke 9:5;
Acts 13:51;
Matt. 3:2; 10:7;
Luke 10:9
10:12
Gen. 19:24-28;
Matt. 10:15;
11:24;
Matt. 10:15
10:13
Luke 10:13-15:
Matt. 11:21-23;
Is. 23:1-18; Ezek.
26:1-28:26; Joel
3:4-8; Matt.
11:21;
Rev. 11:3
10:14
Matt. 11:21

10:15
Is. 14:13-15;
Matt. 4:13; 11:23

10:16
Matt. 10:40; Mark
9:37; Luke 9:48;
John 13:20; Gal.
4:14;
John 12:48; 1
Thess. 4:8

10:17
Mark 16:17

10:18
Matt. 4:10

10:19
Ps. 91:13; Mark
16:18
10:20
Ex. 32:32; Ps.
69:28; Is. 4:3;
Ezek. 13:9; Dan.
12:1; Phil. 4:3;
Heb. 12:23; Rev.
3:5; 13:8; 17:8;
20:12,15; 21:27
10:21
Luke 10:21,22:
Matt. 11:25-27

said, "I praise Thee, O Father, Lord of heaven and earth, that Thou didst hide these things from *the* wise and intelligent and didst reveal them to babes. Yes, Father, for thus it was well-pleasing in Thy sight.

10:22
John 3:35;
John 10:15

22 "All things have been handed over to Me by My Father, and no one knows[29a] who the Son is except the Father, and who the Father is except the Son, and anyone to whom the *Son* wills~ to reveal[x] *Him*."

10:23
Luke 10:23,24:
Matt. 13:16,17

23 And turning to the disciples, He said *privately*, "[†]Blessed *are* the eyes which see the things you see,

24 for I say to you, that many prophets and kings wished to see[x] the things which *you* see, and did not see *them*, and to hear[x] the things which you hear, and did not hear *them*."

10:25
Luke 10:25-28:
Matt. 22:34-40;
Mark 12:28-31;
Matt. 19:16-19;
Matt. 22:35

25 And behold, a certain lawyer stood up and put Him to the test,[1] saying, "Teacher, what shall I do to inherit *eternal life?*"

26 And He said to him, "What is written[+] in the Law? How does it read to you?"

10:27
Deut. 6:5; Lev.
19:18

27 And he answered and said, "YOU SHALL LOVE[31a] THE LORD YOUR GOD WITH ALL YOUR HEART, AND WITH ALL YOUR SOUL,[30c] AND WITH ALL YOUR STRENGTH,[32c] AND WITH ALL YOUR MIND;[33a] AND YOUR NEIGHBOR AS YOURSELF."

10:28
Lev. 18:5; Ezek.
20:11; Matt.
19:17

28 And He said to him, "You have answered correctly; DO ~[19a] THIS, AND YOU WILL LIVE."

10:29
Luke 16:15

29 But wishing to justify[x] himself, he said to Jesus, "And who is my *neighbor?*"

The Good Samaritan

10:30
Luke 18:31; 19:28

30 Jesus replied and said, "A certain man was going down from Jerusalem to Jericho; and he fell among robbers, and they stripped him and beat him, and went off leaving him half dead.

31 "And by chance a certain priest was going down on that road, and when he saw him, he passed by on the other side.

32 "And likewise a Levite also, when he came to the place and saw him, passed by on the other side.

10:33
Matt. 10:5; Luke
9:52

33 "But a certain Samaritan, who was on a journey, came upon him; and when he saw him, he felt compassion,

34 and came to him, and bandaged up his wounds, pouring oil and wine on *them*; and he put him on his •own beast, and brought him to an inn, and took care of him.

35 "And on the next day he took out two [u]denarii and gave them to the innkeeper and said, 'Take care[xi] of him; and whatever more you spend,[x] when I return, *I* will repay you.'

[u]The denarius was equivalent to one day's wage

36 "Which of these three do you think proved⁺ to be a *neighbor* to the man who fell into the robbers' *hands?*"

37 And he said, "The one who showed mercy toward him." And Jesus said to him, "Go and do⌃ the same."

Martha and Mary

38 Now as they were traveling along, He entered a certain village; and a woman named Martha welcomed Him into her home.

39 And she had a sister called Mary, who moreover was listening⌃ to the Lord's word, seated at His feet.

40 But Martha was distracted⌃ with all her preparations; and she came up *to Him*, and said, "Lord, do You not care that my sister has left me to do all the serving~ *alone?* Then tell⌃ her to help⌃ me."

41 But the Lord answered and said to her, "Martha, Martha, you are worried and bothered about so many things;

42 but *only* a *few things* are necessary, really *only one,* for Mary has chosen the *good part,* which shall not be taken away from her."

Instruction about Prayer

11 And it came about that while He was praying in a certain place, after He had finished, one of His disciples said to Him, "Lord, teach⌃ us to pray~ just as John also taught his disciples."

2 And He said to them, "When you pray,~ say:⌃
  'ᵛFather, hallowed⌃ be Thy name.
  Thy kingdom come.⌃

3 'Give⌃ us each day our *daily bread.*

4 'And forgive⌃²¹ᵃ us our sins,
  For we ourselves also forgive everyone who is
    indebted to us.
  And lead⊖ us not into temptation.' "

5 And He said to them, "Suppose one of you shall have a friend, and shall go to him at midnight, and say⌃ to him, 'Friend, lend⌃ me three loaves;

6 for a friend of mine has come to me from a journey, and I have nothing to set before him';

7 and from inside he shall answer and say,ˣ 'Do not bother⊖ me; the door has already been shut⁺ and my children and I are in *bed;* I cannot get up and give⌃ you *anything.*'

8 "I tell you, even though he will not get up and give him

ᵛSome mss. insert phrases from Matt. 6:9-13 to make the two passages closely similar

10:38
Luke 10:40f.;
John 11:1,5,19ff.,
30,39; 12:2

10:39
Luke 10:42; John
11:1f.,19f.,28,
31f.,45; 12:3;
Luke 8:35; Acts
22:3
10:40
Luke 10:38,41;
John 11:1,5,19ff.,
30,39; 12:2

10:41
Luke 10:38,40;
John 11:1,5,19ff.,
30,39; 12:2;
Matt. 6:25
10:42
Ps. 27:4; John
6:27;
Luke 10:39; John
11:1f.,19f.,28,
31f.,45; 12:3

11:2
Luke 11:2-4:
Matt. 6:9-13

11:3
Acts 17:11
11:4
Luke 13:4 mg.

11:8
Luke 18:1-5

anything because he is his friend, yet because[2] of his *persistence* he will get up and give him as much as he needs.

11:9
Luke 11:9-13:
Matt. 7:7-11

9 "And I say to you, ask,~[9a] and it shall be given to you; seek,~ and you shall find; knock,~ and it shall be opened to you.

10 "For everyone who asks, receives;[5b] and he who seeks, finds; and to him who knocks, it shall be opened.

11 "Now suppose one of you fathers is asked by his son for a fish; he will not give him a *snake* instead of a *fish,* will he?

12 "Or *if* he is asked for an egg, he will not give him a scorpion, will he?

11:13
Matt. 7:11; Luke
18:7f.

13 "If *you* then, being ✝*evil,* [10b] know how to give~ *good*[25a] *gifts* to your children, how much more shall *your* heavenly Father give the Holy Spirit to those who ask Him?"

Pharisees' Blasphemy

11:14
Luke 11:14,15:
Matt. 12:22,24;
Matt. 9:32-34

14 And He was casting~ out a demon, and it was dumb; and it came about that when the demon had gone out, the dumb man spoke; and the multitudes marveled.

11:15
Matt. 9:34;
Matt. 10:25

15 But some of them said, "He casts out demons by *Beelzebul,* the *ruler of the demons.*"

11:16
Matt. 12:38; 16:1;
Mark 8:11

16 And others, to test *Him,* were demanding[m] of Him a *sign from heaven.*

11:17
Luke 11:17-22:
Matt. 12:25-29;
Mark 3:23-27

17 But He knew their *thoughts,* and said to them, "Any kingdom divided *against itself* is laid waste; and a house *divided* against itself falls.

11:18
Matt. 4:10;
Matt. 10:25

18 "And if Satan also is divided *against himself,* how shall his kingdom stand? For you say that I cast~ out demons by *Beelzebul.*

11:19
Matt. 10:25

19 "And if I by *Beelzebul* cast out demons, by whom do your sons cast them out? Consequently *they* shall be *your* judges.

11:20
Ex. 8:19;
Matt. 3:2

20 "But if I cast out demons by the *finger of God,* then the kingdom of God has come upon you.

21 "When a strong *man,* fully[1] armed,✶ guards~ his own homestead, his possessions are *undisturbed;*

22 but when someone stronger than he attacks him and overpowers[x] him, he takes away from him all *his armor* on which he had relied, and distributes *his plunder.*

11:23
Matt. 12:30; Mark
9:40

23 "He who is not with Me is *against Me;* and he who does not gather with Me, scatters.

11:24
Luke 11:24-26:
Matt. 12:43-45

24 "When the unclean spirit goes[x] out of a man, it passes through waterless places seeking rest, and not finding any, it says, 'I will return to my house from which I came.'

25 "And when it comes, it finds it swept✶ and put✶ in order.

26 "Then it goes and takes *along seven* other spirits more evil

than itself, and they go in and live there; and the *last state* of that man becomes worse than the first."

27   And it came about while He said~ these things, one of the women in the crowd raised her voice, and said to Him, "†Blessed is the womb that bore You, and the breasts at which You nursed."

11:27
Luke 23:29

28   But He said, "On the contrary, †blessed are those who hear the word of God, and observe it."

11:28
Luke 8:21

The Sign of Jonah

29   And as the crowds were increasing, He began to say,~ "This generation is a *wicked* generation; it seeks[1] for a *sign,* and *yet* no sign shall be given to it but the sign of Jonah.

11:29
Luke 11:29-32;
Matt. 12:39-42;
Matt. 16:4; Mark
8:12;
Matt. 12:38; Luke
11:16

30   "For just as Jonah became a sign to the Ninevites, so shall the Son of Man be to this generation.

11:30
Jon. 3:4

31   "The Queen of the South shall rise up with the men of this generation at the judgment and condemn them, because she came from the ends of the earth to hear[x] the wisdom of Solomon; and behold, something greater[26b] than Solomon is here.

11:31
1 Kin. 10:1-10; 2
Chr. 9:1-12

32   "The men of Nineveh shall stand up with this generation at the judgment and condemn it, because they repented at the preaching of Jonah; and behold, something greater than Jonah is here.

11:32
Jon. 3:5

33   "No one, after lighting a lamp, puts it away in a *cellar,* nor under a peck-measure, but on the lampstand, in order that those who enter may see~ the light.

11:33
Matt. 5:15; Mark
4:21; Luke 8:16

34   "The lamp of your body is your eye; when your eye is clear, your whole body also is full of light; but when it is bad,[10b] your body also is full of †darkness.

11:34
Luke 11:34,35;
Matt. 6:22,23

35   "Then watch~[l] out that the light in you may not be *darkness.*

36   "If therefore your *whole* body is full of light, with *no dark* part in it, it shall be *wholly* illumined, as when the lamp illumines~ you with its rays."

Woes upon the Pharisees

37   Now when He had spoken,[x] a Pharisee *asked Him to have lunch with him; and He went in, and reclined *at the table.*

38   And when the Pharisee saw it, he was surprised that He had not first ceremonially washed before the meal.

11:38
Matt. 15:2; Mark
7:3f.

39   But the Lord said to him, "Now you Pharisees clean the *outside* of the cup and of the platter; but inside of you, you are full of robbery and wickedness.

11:39
Luke 7:13;
Matt. 23:25f.

11:40
Luke 12:20;
1 Cor. 15:36

40 "You foolish[20b] ones, did not He who made the outside make the *inside also?*

11:41
Luke 12:33; 16:9;
Mark 7:19; Titus
1:15

41 "But give[xi] that which is *within* as charity, and then all things are clean[13c] for you.

11:42
Matt. 23:23;
Lev. 27:30; Luke
18:12

42 "But woe to you Pharisees! For you pay tithe of mint and rue and every *kind of* garden herb, and *yet* disregard justice and the love of God; but *these* are the things you should[m] have done[x] without neglecting[x] the others.

11:43
Matt. 23:6f.; Mark
12:38f.; Luke
14:7; 20:46

43 "Woe to you Pharisees! For you love the front seats in the synagogues, and the respectful greetings in the market places.

11:44
Matt. 23:27

44 "Woe to you! For you are like *concealed* tombs, and the people who walk over *them* are unaware *of it.*"

11:45
Matt. 22:35; Luke
11:46,52

45 And one of the [w]lawyers *said to Him in reply, "Teacher, when You say this, You insult *us too.*"

11:46
Matt. 22:35; Luke
11:45,52;
Matt. 23:4

46 But He said, "Woe to you *lawyers as well!* For you weigh men down with burdens hard to bear, while *you yourselves* will not even touch the burdens with *one of your fingers.*

11:47
Matt. 23:29ff.

47 "Woe to you! For you build the tombs of the prophets, and *it was* your fathers *who* killed them.

48 "Consequently, you are witnesses and approve the deeds of your fathers; because it was *they* who killed them, and *you* build *their tombs.*

11:49
1 Cor. 1:24,30;
Col. 2:3;
Matt. 23:34-36

49 "For this reason also the wisdom of God said, 'I will send to them prophets and apostles, and *some* of them they will kill and *some* they will persecute,[1]

11:50
Matt. 25:34

50 in order that the blood of all the prophets, shed[+] since the foundation of the world, may be charged[x] against [†]*this* generation,

11:51
Gen. 4:8;
2 Chr. 24:20,21

51 from the blood of Abel to the blood of Zechariah, who perished between the altar and the house *of God;* yes, I tell you, it shall be charged against *this* generation.'

11:52
Matt. 22:35; Luke
11:45,46;
Matt. 23:13

52 "Woe to you lawyers! For you have taken away the key of knowledge; you did not enter in *yourselves,* and those who were entering in you *hindered.*"

53 And when He left there, the scribes and the Pharisees began to be very hostile[~] and to question[~] Him closely on many subjects,

11:54
Mark 3:2; Luke
20:20; Acts
23:21;
Mark 12:13

54 plotting against Him, to catch[x] *Him* in something He might say.

God Knows and Cares

12:1
Matt. 16:6,11f.;
Mark 8:15

12 Under these circumstances, after so many thousands of the multitude had gathered together that they were step-

[w]i.e., experts in the Mosaic law

ping~ on one another, He began saying~ to His disciples first *of all,* "Beware~ of the leaven of the Pharisees, which is hypocrisy.

2 "But there is nothing covered⁺ up that will not be revealed, and hidden that will not be known.

3 "Accordingly, whatever you have said in the *dark* shall be heard in the *light,* and what you have whispered in the inner rooms shall be proclaimed upon the housetops.

4 "And I say to you, My friends, do not be afraid⁶ of those who kill the body, and after that have no more that they can do.ˣ

5 "But I will warn you whom to fear:ˣ fearˣ¹ the One who after He has killedˣ has authority to castˣ into hell;²⁷ᵇ yes, I tell you, fearˣ¹ *Him!*

6 "Are not *five* sparrows sold for ⁺*two* cents? And *yet* not one of them is forgotten⁺ before God.

7 "Indeed, the very hairs of your head are *all* numbered.⁺ Do not fear;⁶ you are of more value than *many sparrows.*

8 "And I say to you, everyone who confessesˣ Me before men, the Son of Man shall confess him also before the angels of God;

9 but he who denies Me before men shall be denied¹ before the angels of God.

10 "And everyone who will speak a word against the Son of Man, it shall be forgiven him; but he who blasphemes against the Holy ⁺*Spirit,* it shall not be forgiven him.

11 "And when they bring~ you before the synagogues and the rulers and the authorities, do not become anxious⁶ about how or what you should speakˣ in your defense, or what you should say;ˣ

12 for the Holy Spirit will teach you in that very hour what you ought to say."ˣ

Covetousness Denounced

13 And someone in the crowd said to Him, "Teacher, tellˣ¹ my brother to divideˣ the *family* inheritance with me."

14 But He said to him, "Man, who appointed Me a judge or arbiter over you?"

15 And He said to them, "Beware, ~¹ and be on your guard~¹ against every form of greed; for not *even* when one has~ an *abundance* does his life³⁰ᵇ consist of his possessions."

16 And He told them a parable, saying, "The land of a certain rich man was *very productive.*

17 "And he began reasoningᵐ to himself, saying, 'What shall I do,ˣ since I have no place to storeˣ my crops?'

18 "And he said, 'This is what I will do: I will tear down *my*

12:2
Luke 12:2-9;
Matt. 10:26-33;
Matt. 10:26; Mark
4:22; Luke 8:17
12:3
Matt. 10:27;
24:17

12:4
John 15:13-15

12:5
Heb. 10:31;
Matt. 5:22

12:6
Matt. 10:29

12:7
Matt. 10:30

12:8
Matt. 10:32; Luke
15:10; Rom. 10:9

12:9
Matt. 10:33; Luke
9:26;
Luke 15:10
12:10
Matt. 12:31,32;
Mark 3:28-30

12:11
Matt. 10:17;
Matt. 6:25; 10:19;
Mark 13:11; Luke
12:22; 21:14

12:12
Matt. 10:20; Luke
21:15

12:14
Mic. 6:8; Rom.
2:1,3; 9:20

12:15
1 Tim. 6:6-10

barns and build *larger ones,* and there I will store all my grain and my goods.

12:19
Eccl. 11:9

19 'And I will say to my soul, "Soul, you have many goods laid up for *many* years *to come;* take your ease, ᴹ eat,ˣⁱ drinkˣⁱ *and* be merry." ' ᴹ

12:20
Jer. 17:11; Luke 11:40; Job 27:8; Ps. 39:6

20 "But *God* said to him, 'You fool!²⁰ᵇ This *very* night *your soul* is required of you; and *now* who will own what you have prepared?'

12:21
Luke 12:33

21 "So is the man who lays up treasure for himself, and is not rich toward *God.*"

12:22
Luke 12:22-31;
Matt. 6:25-33

22 And He said to His disciples, "For this reason I say to you, do not be anxiousᴼ for *your* life, ³⁰ᶜ *as to* what you shall eat;ˣ nor for your body, *as to* what you shall putˣ on.

23 "For life³⁰ᶜ is more than food, and the body than clothing.

12:24
Job 38:41;
Luke 12:18

24 "Considerˣⁱ the ravens, for they neither sow nor reap; and they have no storeroom nor barn; and *yet* God feeds them; how much more valuable *you* are than the birds!

12:25
Ps. 39:5

25 "And which of you by being anxious can addˣ a *single* ˣ cubit to his ʸlife's span?

26 "If then you cannot do even a *very*³ *little thing,* why are you anxious about *other matters?*

12:27
1 Kin. 10:4-7;
2 Chr. 9:3-6

27 "Considerˣⁱ the lilies, how they grow; they neither toil nor spin; but I tell you, even Solomon in all his glory did not clothe himself like one of these.

12:28
Matt. 6:30

28 "But if God so arrays the *grass* in the field, which is *alive* today and tomorrow is thrown into the furnace, how much more *will He clothe* you, O men of little faith!

12:29
Matt. 6:31

29 "And do not seekᴼ what you shall eat,ˣ and what you shall drink,ˣ and do not keep worrying.ᴼ

30 "For all these things the nations of the world eagerly¹ seek; but your *Father* knows that you need these things.

12:31
Matt. 6:33

31 "But seekᴹ for His kingdom, and these things shall be added to you.   •

12:32
Matt. 14:27;
John 21:15-17;
Eph. 1:5,9

32 "Do not be afraid,ᴼ little flock, for your Father has chosen gladly to giveˣ you the kingdom.

12:33
Matt. 19:21; Luke 11:41; 18:22; Matt. 6:20; Luke 12:21

33 "Sellˣⁱ your possessions and giveˣⁱ to charity; makeˣⁱ yourselves purses which do not wear out, an *unfailing* treasure in heaven, where no thief comes near, nor moth destroys.

12:34
Matt. 6:21

34 "For where your treasure is, there will your heart be also.

Be in Readiness

12:35
Matt. 25:1ff.;
Eph. 6:14; 1 Pet. 1:13

35 "Be dressed⁺ in readiness, and *keep* your lamps alight.

36 "And be like men who are waiting for their master when he

ˣI.e., One cubit equals approx. 18 in.   ʸOr, *height*

returns[x] from the wedding feast, so that they may immediately open[x] *the door* to him when he comes and knocks.

37 "[†]Blessed are [†]those slaves[38b] whom the master shall find on the alert when he comes; •truly I say to you, that he will gird himself *to serve,* and have them recline *at the table,* and will come up and wait on them.

12:37
Matt. 24:42;
Luke 17:8; John 13:4

38 "Whether he comes in the [z]second watch, or even in the [a]third, and finds[x] *them* so, [†]blessed are those *slaves.*[38b]

12:38
Matt. 24:43

39 "And be sure[~] of this, that if the head of the house had known at what hour the thief was coming, he would not have allowed his house to be broken[x] into.

12:39
Luke 12:39,40;
Matt. 24:43,44;
Matt. 6:19

40 "*You too,* be ready;[~] for the Son of Man is coming at an hour that you do not expect."

12:40
Mark 13:33; Luke 21:36

41 And Peter said, "Lord, are You addressing this parable to *us,* or to everyone *else* as well?"

12:41
Luke 12:47,48

42 And the Lord said, "Who then is the faithful and sensible[35b] steward, whom his master will put in charge of his servants, to give[~] them their rations at the proper time?

12:42
Luke 7:13;
Luke 12:42-46:
Matt. 24:45-51;
Matt. 24:45; Luke 16:1ff.

43 "[†]Blessed is *that* slave whom his master finds so doing when he comes.

12:43
Luke 12:42

44 "•Truly I say to you, that he will put him in charge of *all his possessions.*

45 "But if that slave says[x] in his heart, 'My master will be a long time in coming,'[~] and begins[x] to beat[~] the slaves, *both* men and women, and to eat[~] and drink[~] and get drunk;[~]

46 the master of that slave will come on a day when he does not expect *him,* and at an hour he does not know, and will cut him in pieces, and assign him a place with the *unbelievers.*

47 "And that slave who knew his master's will and did not get ready or act in accord with his will, shall receive many lashes,

12:47
Deut. 25:2;
James 4:17

48 but the one who did not know[29a] *it,* and committed deeds worthy of a flogging, will receive but few. And from everyone who has been given much shall much be required; and to whom they entrusted much, of him they will ask all the more.

12:48
Lev. 5:17; Num. 15:29f.;
Matt. 13:12

Christ Divides Men

49 "I have come to cast[x] *fire* upon the earth; and how I wish it were already kindled!

50 "But I have a *baptism* to undergo,[x] and how distressed I am until it is accomplished![x]

12:50
Mark 10:38

51 "Do you suppose that I came to grant[x] *peace* on earth? I tell you, •*no,* but rather division;

12:51
Luke 12:51-53:
Matt. 10:34-36

[z]I.e., 9 p.m. to midnight   [a]I.e., midnight to 3 a.m.

52   for from now on five *members* in one household will be divided, ⁺ three against two, and two against three.

12:53
Mic. 7:6; Matt.
10:21

53 "They will be divided, father against son, and son against father; mother against daughter, and daughter against mother; mother-in-law against daughter-in-law, and daughter-in-law against mother-in-law."

12:54
Matt. 16:2f.

54   And He was also saying to the multitudes, "When you see ˣ a cloud rising in the west, immediately you say, 'A shower is coming,' and so it turns out.

12:55
Matt. 20:12

55 "And when *you see* a south wind blowing, you say, 'It will be a hot day,' and it turns out *that way.*

12:56
Matt. 16:3

56 "You hypocrites! You know ²⁹ᵉ how to analyze~ the appearance of the *earth* and the *sky,* but why do you not analyze~ *this present time?*

12:57
Luke 21:30

57 "And why do you not even on your *own initiative* judge what is right?

12:58
Luke 12:58,59;
Matt. 5:25,26

58 "For while you are going with your opponent to appear before the magistrate, *on your way there* make ˣ¹ an effort to settle ⁺ with him, in order that he may not drag~ you before the judge, and the judge turn you over to the constable, and the constable throw you into prison.

12:59
Mark 12:42

59 "I say to you, you shall •not get ˣ out of there until you have paid ˣ the *very last cent.*"

Call to Repent

13:1
Matt. 27

13 Now on the same occasion there were some present who reported to Him about the Galileans, whose blood Pilate had mingled with their sacrifices.

13:2
John 9:2f.

2   And He answered and said to them, "Do you suppose that †these Galileans were *greater sinners* than all *other* Galileans, because they suffered ⁺ this *fate?*

3   "I tell you, •no, but, unless you repent, ~ you will all likewise perish.

13:4
Neh. 3:15; Is. 8:6;
John 9:7,11;
Matt. 6:12; Luke
11:4

4   "Or do you suppose that those eighteen on whom the tower in Siloam fell and killed them, were *worse culprits* than all the men who live in Jerusalem?

5   "I tell you, •no, but unless you repent, ~you will all likewise perish."

13:6
Matt. 21:19

6   And He *began* telling this parable: "A certain man had a fig tree which had been planted ⁺ in his vineyard; and he came looking for fruit on it, and did not find any.

13:7
Matt. 3:10; 7:19;
Luke 3:9

7   "And he said to the vineyard-keeper, 'Behold, for *three* years I have come looking for fruit on this fig tree without finding any. Cut ˣ¹ it down! Why does it even use up the ground?'

8 "And he answered and said to him, 'Let* it alone, sir, for this year too, until I dig* around it and put* in fertilizer;

9   and if it bears* fruit next year, *fine;* but if not, cut it down.' "

Healing on the Sabbath

10   And He was teaching~ in one of the synagogues on the Sabbath.

13:10
Matt. 4:23

11   And behold, there was a woman who for eighteen years had had a sickness caused by a *spirit;* and she was bent~ double, and could~ not straighten* up at all.

13:11
Luke 13:16

12   And when Jesus saw her, He called her over and said to her, "Woman, you are freed* from your sickness."

13   And He laid His hands upon her; and immediately she was made erect again, and *began* glorifying^m God.

13:13
Mark 5:23;
Matt. 9:8

14   And the synagogue official, indignant because Jesus had healed on the *Sabbath, began* saying to the multitude in response, "There are *six* days in which work should be done;~ therefore come during *them* and get healed,~15a and not on the Sabbath day."

13:14
Mark 5:22;
Matt. 12:2; Luke 14:3;
Ex. 20:9; Deut. 5:13

15   But the Lord answered him and said, "You hypocrites, does not each of you on the Sabbath untie his ox or his donkey from the stall, and lead him away to water *him?*

13:15
Luke 7:13;
Luke 14:5

16   "And this woman, a daughter of †Abraham as she is, whom Satan has bound for *eighteen long* years, should^m she not have been released* from this bond on the Sabbath day?"

13:16
Luke 19:9;
Matt. 4:10; Luke 13:11

17   And as He said this, all His opponents were being humiliated;^m and the entire multitude was rejoicing^m over all the glorious things being done by Him.

13:17
Luke 18:43

Parables of Mustard Seed and Leaven

18   Therefore He was saying, "What is the kingdom of God like, and to what shall I compare it?

13:18
Luke 13:18,19;
Matt. 13:31,32;
Mark 4:30-32;
Matt. 13:24; Luke 13:20

19   "It is like a mustard seed, which a man took and threw into his own garden; and it grew and became a tree; and THE BIRDS OF THE AIR NESTED IN ITS BRANCHES."

13:19
Ezek. 17:23

20   And again He said, "To what shall I compare the kingdom of God?

13:20
Matt. 13:24; Luke 13:18

21   "It is like leaven, which a woman took and hid in three pecks of meal, until it was all leavened."

13:21
Luke 13:20,21;
Matt. 13:33;
Matt. 13:33

Teaching in the Villages

22   And He was passing^m through from one city and village to another, teaching, and proceeding on His way to Jerusalem.

13:22
Luke 9:51

23   And someone said to Him, "Lord, are there *just* a few who are being saved?" And He said to them,

13:24
Matt. 7:13

24   "Strive~¹ to enter˟ by the narrow door; for many, I tell you, will seek to enter˟ and will not be able.

13:25
Matt. 25:10;
Matt. 7:22; 25:11;
Matt. 7:23; 25:12;
Luke 13:27

25   "Once the head of the house gets˟ up and shuts˟ the door, and you begin˟ to stand outside and knock~ on the door, saying, 'Lord, open˟ᶦ up to us!' then He will answer and say to you, 'I do not know where you are from.'

13:26
Luke 3:8

26   "Then you will begin to say,~ 'We ate and drank in Your presence, and You taught in our streets';

13:27
Luke 13:25;
Ps. 6:8; Matt.
25:41

27   and He will say, 'I tell you, I do not know²⁹ᵉ where you are from; DEPART˟ᶦ FROM ME, ALL YOU EVILDOERS.'

13:28
Matt. 8:12; 22:13;
25:30

28   "There will be weeping and gnashing of teeth there when you see Abraham and Isaac and Jacob and all the prophets in the kingdom of God, but yourselves being cast out.

13:29
Matt. 8:11

29   "And they will come from east and west, and from north and south, and will recline *at the table* in the kingdom of God.

13:30
Matt. 19:30;
20:16; Mark
10:31

30   "And behold, *some* are last who will be first and *some* are first who will be last."

13:31
Matt. 14:1; Luke
3:1; 9:7; 23:7

31   Just at that time some Pharisees came up, saying to Him, "Go˟ᶦ away and depart from here, for Herod wants to kill˟ You."

13:32
Heb. 2:10; 5:9;
7:28

32   And He said to them, "Go and tell˟ᶦ that fox, 'Behold, I cast out demons and perform cures today and tomorrow, and *the third day* I reach My goal.'

13:33
John 11:9;
Matt. 21:11

33   "Nevertheless I must journey~ on today and tomorrow and the next *day;* for it cannot be that a prophet should perish˟ outside of Jerusalem.

13:34
Luke 13:34,35;
Matt. 23:37-39;
Luke 19:41;
Matt. 23:37

34   "O Jerusalem, Jerusalem, *the city* that kills the prophets and stones those sent⁺ to her! How often I wanted to gather˟ your children together, just as a hen *gathers* her brood under her wings, and you would not *have it!*

13:35
Ps. 118:26; Matt.
21:9; Luke 19:38

35   "Behold, your house is left to you *desolate;* and I say to you, you shall •not see˟ Me until *the time* comes when you say,˟ '⁺*BLESSED*⁺ IS HE WHO COMES IN THE NAME OF THE LORD!' "

Jesus Heals on the Sabbath

14:1
Mark 3:2

14   And it came about when He went into the house of one of the leaders of the Pharisees on *the* Sabbath to eat˟ bread, that they were watching~ Him closely.¹

2   And there, in front of Him was a certain man suffering from dropsy.

14:3
Matt. 22:35;
Matt. 12:2; Luke
13:14

3   And Jesus answered and spoke to the lawyers and Pharisees, saying, "Is it lawful to heal˟ on the Sabbath, or not?"

4   But they kept silent. And He took hold of him, and healed[15b] him, and sent him away.

5   And He said to them, "Which one of you shall have a son or an ox fall into a well, and will not immediately pull him out on a Sabbath day?"

14:5
Matt. 12:11; Luke 13:15

6   And they could make no reply[x] to this.

14:6
Matt. 22:46; Luke 20:40

Parable of the Guests

7   And He *began* speaking a parable to the invited[+] guests when He noticed how they had been picking[m] out the *places of honor at the table;* saying to them,

14:7
Matt. 23:6

8   "When you are invited[x] by someone to a wedding feast, do not take[o] the place of honor, lest someone more distinguished than you may have been invited[+] by him,

14:8
Prov. 25:6,7

9   and he who invited you both shall come and say to you, 'Give[xi] place to this man,' and then in disgrace you proceed to occupy[~] the *last place.*

14:9
Luke 3:8

10   "But when you are invited,[x] go and recline[xi] at the last place, so that when the one who has invited[+] you comes, he may say to you, 'Friend, move[xi] up higher'; then you will have honor in the sight of all who are at the table with you.

14:10
Prov. 25:6,7

11   "For everyone who exalts himself shall be humbled, and he who humbles himself shall be exalted."

14:11
2 Sam. 22:28; Prov. 29:23; Matt. 23:12; Luke 1:52; 18:14; James 4:10

12   And He also went on to say to the one who had invited[+] Him, "When you give[~] a luncheon or a dinner, do not invite[o] your friends or your brothers or your relatives or rich neighbors, lest they also invite[x] you in return, and repayment come to you.

13   "But when you give[~] a reception, invite[m] *the* poor, *the* crippled, *the* lame, *the* blind,

14   and you will be [+]*blessed,* since they do not have *the means* to repay you;[x37a] for you will be repaid at the resurrection of the righteous."

14:14
John 5:29; Acts 24:15; Rev. 20:4, 5

15   And when one of those who were reclining *at the table* with Him heard this, he said to Him, "[+]Blessed is everyone who shall eat bread in the kingdom of God!"

14:15
Rev. 19:9

Parable of the Dinner

16   But He said to him, "A certain man was giving[m] a big dinner, and he invited many;

14:16
Matt. 22:2-14; Luke 14:16-24

17   and at the dinner hour he sent his slave to say[x] to those who had been invited,[+] 'Come;[m] for everything is ready now.'

18   "But they all alike began to make[~] excuses. The first one said to him, 'I have bought a *piece of land* and I need to go out and look[x] at it; please consider[m] me excused.'[+]

19 "And another one said, 'I have bought *five* yoke of oxen, and I am going to try^x them out; please consider^{~ı} me excused.'⁺

14:20
Deut. 24:5; 1 Cor.
7:33

20 "And another one said, 'I have married a *wife,* and for that reason I cannot come.'

21 "And the slave came *back* and reported this to his master. Then the head of the household became angry and said to his slave, 'Go^{xı} out at once into the streets and lanes of the city and bring^{xı} in here the *poor* and *crippled* and *blind* and *lame.'*

22 "And the slave said, 'Master, what you commanded has been done,⁺ and still there is *room.'*

23 "And the master said to the slave, 'Go^{xı} out into the highways and along the hedges, and compel^{xı} *them* to come^x in, that my house may be *filled.*^x

24 'For I tell you, none of those men who were invited⁺ shall taste of *my* dinner.' "

Discipleship Tested

25 Now *great multitudes* were going^{xx} along with Him; and He turned and said to them,

14:26
Matt. 10:37

26 "If anyone comes to Me, and does not ^bhate his own father and mother and wife and children and brothers and sisters, yes, and even his own life, he cannot be My disciple.

14:27
Matt. 10:38;
16:24; Mark 8:34;
Luke 9:23

27 "Whoever does not carry his *own* cross and come after Me cannot be My disciple.

28 "For which one of you, when he wants to build^x a tower, does not first sit down and calculate the cost, to see if he has enough to complete it?

29 "Otherwise, when he has laid a foundation, and is not able to finish,^{xı} all who observe it begin^x to ridicule[~] him,

30 saying, 'This man began to build[~] and was not able to finish.'^{xı}

14:31
Prov. 20:18

31 "Or what king, when he sets out to meet^x another king in battle, will not first sit down and take counsel whether he is strong enough with *ten* thousand *men* to encounter^x the one coming against him with *twenty* thousand?

32 "Or else, while the other is still far away, he sends a delegation and asks terms of peace.

14:33
Phil. 3:7; Heb.
11:26

33 "So therefore, no one of you can be My disciple who does not give up all his own possessions.

14:34
Matt. 5:13; Mark
9:50

34 "Therefore, salt is good; but if even salt has become^x tasteless, with what will it be seasoned?

14:35
Matt. 11:15

35 "It is ⁺useless either for the soil or for the manure pile; it is thrown out. He who has ears to hear,[~] let him hear." ^{~ı}

^bI.e., by comparison of his love for Me

The Lost Sheep

15 Now all the tax-gatherers and the sinners were coming~ near Him to listen~ to Him.

15:1
Luke 5:29

2   And both the Pharisees and the scribes *began* to grumble,ᵐ saying, "This man receives *sinners* and eats with them."

15:2
Matt. 9:11

3   And He told them this parable, saying, ˎ

4   "What man among you, if he has a *hundred* sheep and has lost *one* of them, does not leave the ninety-nine in the open pasture, and go after the one which is lost,⁺ until he finds˟ it?

15:4
Matt. 18:12-14;
Luke 15:4-7

5   "And when he has found it, he lays it on his shoulders, rejoicing.

6   "And when he comes home, he calls together his friends and his neighbors, saying to them, 'Rejoiceˣˡ with me, for I have found my sheep which was lost!'⁺

7   "I tell you that in the same way, there will be *more* joy in heaven over ⁺*one* sinner who repents, than over *ninety-nine* righteous persons who need no repentance.

The Lost Coin

8   "Or what woman, if she has ten silver coins and loses˟ one coin, does not light a lamp and sweep the house and search *carefully* until she finds˟ it?

9   "And when she has found it, she calls together her friends and neighbors, saying, 'Rejoiceˣˡ with me, for I have found the coin which I had lost!'

10   "In the same way, I tell you, there is joy in the presence of the angels of God over ⁺*one* sinner who repents."

15:10
Matt. 10:32; Luke
15:7

The Prodigal Son

11   And He said, "A certain man had two sons;

12   and the younger of them said to his father, 'Father, giveˣˡ me the share of the estate that falls to me.' And he divided his wealth between them.

15:12
Deut. 21:17;
Mark 12:44; Luke
15:30

13   "And not many days later, the younger son gathered everything together and went on a journey into a distant country, and there he squandered his estate with loose living.

14   "Now when he had spent everything, a severe famine occurred in that country, and he began to be in need. ~

15   "And he went and attached himself to one of the citizens of that country, and he sent him into his fields to feed~ swine.

16   "And he was longingᵐ to fillˣ his stomach with the pods that the swine were eating,ᵐ and no one was givingᵐ *anything* to him.

17   "But when he came to his senses, he said, 'How many of my

father's hired men have more than enough bread, but *I* am dying *here* with *hunger!*

18 'I will get up and go to my father, and will say to him, "Father, I have sinned against heaven, and in your sight;

19 I am no longer worthy to be called[x] your son; make[xi] me as one of your hired men." '

20 "And he got up and came to his father. But while he was still a *long way off*, his father saw him, and felt compassion *for him*, and ran and embraced him, and kissed[1] him.

21 "And the son said to him, 'Father, I have sinned against heaven and in your sight; I am no longer worthy to be called[x] your son.'

22 "But the father said to his slaves, '*Quickly* bring[xi] out the *best* robe and put[xi] it on him, and put[xi] a ring on his hand and sandals on his feet;

23 and bring[xi] the *fattened* calf, kill[xi] it, and let us eat and be merry;[x]

24 for this son of mine was [†]*dead*, and has come to life again; he was lost,[•] and has been found.' And they began to be merry. [~]

25 "Now his older son was in the field, and when he came and approached the house, he heard music and dancing.

26 "And he summoned one of the servants and *began* inquiring[m] what these things might be.

27 "And he said to him, 'Your brother has come, and your father has killed the *fattened* calf, because he has received him back safe and sound.'

28 "But he became angry, and was not willing[m] to go[x] in; and his father came out and *began* entreating[m] him.

29 "But he answered and said to his father, 'Look! For so many years I have been serving you, and I have never neglected a command of yours; and *yet* you have never given *me* a kid, that I might be merry[x] with *my friends*;

30 but when *this* son of yours came, who has devoured *your* wealth with harlots, you killed the fattened calf for him.'

31 "And he said to him, '*My* child, *you* have always been with me, and all that is mine is *yours*.

32 'But we *had* to be merry[x] and rejoice,[x] for this brother of yours was [†]*dead* and *has begun* to live, and *was* lost[•] and has been found.' "

The Unrighteous Steward

16 Now He was also saying to the disciples, "There was a certain rich man who had a steward, and this *steward* was reported to him as squandering his possessions.

2 "And he called him and said to him, 'What is this I hear about you? Give[xl] an account of your stewardship, for you can no longer be[~] steward.'

3 "And the steward said to himself, 'What shall I do,[x] since my master is taking the stewardship away from me? I am not strong enough to dig;[~] I am ashamed to beg. [~]

4 'I know what I shall do,[x] so that when I am removed[x] from the stewardship, they will receive[x] me into their homes.'

5 "And he summoned each one of his master's debtors, and he *began* saying to the first, 'How much do you owe my master?'

6 "And he said, 'A hundred measures of oil.' And he said to him, 'Take[xl] your bill, and sit down *quickly* and write[xl] [†]*fifty.*'

7 "Then he said to another, 'And how much do *you* owe?' And he said, 'A hundred measures of wheat.' He *said to him, 'Take[xl] your bill, and write[xl] [†]*eighty.*'

8 "And his master praised the unrighteous steward because he had acted shrewdly;[35b] for the sons of [†]*this* age are more shrewd[35b] in relation to their *own kind* than the sons of light.

9 "And I say to you, make[xl] friends *for yourselves* by means of the [c]mammon of unrighteousness; that when it fails,[x] they may receive[x] you into the [†]eternal dwellings.

10 "He who is faithful in a very[3] little [†]thing is faithful *also in much;* and he who is unrighteous in a very[3] little [†]thing is unrighteous *also in much.*

11 "If therefore you have not been faithful in the *use of unrighteous mammon,* who will entrust the *true riches* to you?

12 "And if you have not been faithful in *the use of* that which is *another's,* who will give you that which is your *own?*

13 "No servant can serve[~38b] *two* masters; for either he will hate the one, and love the other, or else he will hold to one, and despise the other. You cannot serve[~] *God* and mammon."

14 Now the Pharisees, who were lovers of money, were listening[xx] to all these things, and they were scoffing[xx1] at Him.

15 And He said to them, "You are those who justify yourselves in the sight of men, but God knows[29a] your hearts; for that which is highly esteemed among men is detestable in the sight of God.

16 "The Law and the Prophets *were proclaimed* until John; since then the gospel of the kingdom of God is preached, and everyone is *forcing* his way into it.

17 "But it is easier for heaven and earth to pass[x] away than for [†]*one* stroke of a letter of the *Law* to fail.[x]

18 "Everyone who divorces his wife and marries another

[c]Or, *riches*

16:8
Matt. 12:32; Luke 20:34;
John 12:36; Eph. 5:8; 1 Thess. 5:5

16:9
Matt. 19:21; Luke 11:41; 12:33;
Matt. 6:24; Luke 16:11,13;
Luke 16:4
16:10
Matt. 25:21,23

16:11
Luke 16:9

16:13
Matt. 6:24;
Luke 16:9

16:14
2 Tim. 3:2;
Luke 23:35

16:15
Luke 10:29; 18:9, 14;
1 Sam. 16:7;
Prov. 21:2; Acts 1:24; Rom. 8:27

16:16
Matt. 11:12f.;
Matt. 4:23

16:17
Matt. 5:18

16:18
Matt. 5:32; 1 Cor. 7:10,11

commits adultery; and he who marries one who is divorced[+] from a husband commits adultery.

The Rich Man and Lazarus

19 "Now there was a certain rich man, and he habitually dressed[m] in purple and fine linen, gaily living in splendor every day.

16:20
Acts 3:2

20 "And a certain poor man named Lazarus was laid at his gate, covered[+] with sores,

21 and longing[m] to be fed[x] with the *crumbs* which were falling from the rich man's table; besides, even the dogs were coming and licking his sores.

16:22
John 1:18; 13:23

22 "Now it came about that the poor man died[x] and he was carried[x] away by the angels to Abraham's bosom; and the rich man also died and was buried.

16:23
Matt. 11:23

23 "And in Hades he lifted up his eyes, being in *torment*, and *saw Abraham far away, and Lazarus in his bosom.

16:24
Luke 3:8; 16:30;
19:9;
Matt. 25:41

24 "And he cried out and said, 'Father Abraham, have mercy[xl] on me, and send[xl] Lazarus, that he may dip[x] the tip of his finger in water and cool[x] off my tongue; for I am in agony in this flame.'

16:25
Luke 6:24

25 "But Abraham said, 'Child, remember[xl] that during your life you received your good things, and likewise Lazarus bad things; but now he is being comforted here, and *you* are in agony.

26 'And besides all this, between *us* and *you* there is a great chasm fixed,[+] in order that those who wish to come[x] over from here to you may not be able,[~] and *that* none may cross[~] over from there to us.'

27 "And he said, 'Then I beg you, Father, that you send[x] him to my father's house—

16:28
Acts 2:40; 8:25;
10:42; 18:5;
20:21ff.; 23:11;
28:23; Gal. 5:3;
Eph. 4:17;
1 Thess. 2:11; 4:6

28 for I have *five* brothers—that he may warn[~1] them, lest *they also* come to this place of torment.'

16:29
Luke 4:17; John
5:45-47; Acts
15:21

29 "But Abraham *said, 'They have Moses and the Prophets; let them hear[xl] them.'

16:30
Luke 3:8; 16:24;
19:9

30 "But he said, '•*No*, Father Abraham, but if someone goes[x] to them from the *dead*, they will repent!'

31 "But he said to him, 'If they do not listen to *Moses* and the *Prophets*, neither will they be persuaded if someone[x] rises from the *dead*.'"

Instructions

17:1
Matt. 18:7; 1 Cor.
11:19; 1 Tim. 4:1

17 And He said to His disciples, "It is inevitable that stumbling blocks should come, but woe to him through whom they come!

17:2
Matt. 18:6; Mark
9:42; 1 Cor. 8:12

2 "It would be better for him if a millstone were hung around

his neck and he were thrown⁺ into the sea, than that he should cause one of these little ones to stumble.ˣ

3 "Be on your guard! ᴹ If your brother sins,ˣ rebukeˣⁱ him; and if he repents,ˣ forgiveˣⁱ²¹ᵃ him.

17:3
Matt. 18:15

4 "And if he sinsˣ against you seven times a day, and returnsˣ to you seven times, saying, 'I repent,' forgive²¹ᵃ him."

17:4
Matt. 18:21f.

5 And the apostles said to the Lord, "Increaseˣⁱ our faith!"

17:5
Mark 6:30;
Luke 7:13

6 And the Lord said, "If you had faith like a mustard seed, you would sayᵐ to this mulberry tree, 'Be uprootedˣⁱ and be plantedˣⁱ in the sea'; and it would obey you.

17:6
Luke 7:13;
Matt. 13:31;
17:20; Mark 4:31;
Luke 13:19;
Luke 19:4

7 "But which of you, having a *slave* plowing or tending sheep, will say to him when he has come in from the field, 'Come immediately and sitˣⁱ down to eat'?

8 "But will he not say to him, 'Prepareˣⁱ something for me to eat,ˣ and *properly* clothe yourself and serveᴹ me until I have eatenˣ and drunk;ˣ and afterward *you* will eat and drink'?

17:8
Luke 12:37

9 "He does not thank the slave because he did the things which were commanded, does he?

10 "So you too, when you doˣ all the things which are commanded you, say, ᴹ 'We are *unworthy* slaves;³⁸ᵇ we have doneˣ *only* that which we oughtᵐ to have done.' "⁺

Ten Lepers Cleansed

11 And it came about while He was on the way to Jerusalem, that He was passing between Samaria and Galilee.

17:11
Luke 9:51;
Luke 9:52ff.; John
4:3f.

12 And as He entered a certain village, *ten* leprous men who stood at a distance met Him;

17:12
Lev. 13:45f.

13 and they raised their voices, saying, "Jesus, Master, have mercyˣⁱ on us!"

17:13
Luke 5:5

14 And when He saw them, He said to them, "Go and showˣⁱ yourselves to the priests." And it came about that as they were ⁺going, they were cleansed.

17:14
Lev. 14:1-32;
Matt. 8:4; Luke
5:14

15 Now one of them, when he saw that he had been healed, ¹⁵ᵇ turned back, glorifying God with a loud voice,

17:15
Matt. 9:8

16 and he fell on his face at His feet, giving thanks to Him. And *he* was a Samaritan.

17:16
Matt. 10:5

17 And Jesus answered and said, "Were there not ten cleansed? But the *nine*—where are they?

18 "Was no one found who turned back to giveˣ glory to God, except this foreigner?"

17:18
Matt. 9:8

19 And He said to him, "Rise, and go your way; your faith ᵈhas made⁺ you well."

17:19
Matt. 9:22; Luke
18:42

20 Now having been questioned by the Pharisees as to when

17:20
Luke 19:11; Acts
1:6;
Luke 14:1

ᵈOr, *has saved you*

the kingdom of God was coming, He answered them and said, "The kingdom of God is not coming with signs to be observed;[1]

17:21
Luke 17:23

21 nor will they say, 'Look, here *it is!*' or, 'There *it is!*' For behold, the kingdom of God is *in your midst."*

Second Coming Foretold

17:22
Matt. 9:15; Mark
2:20; Luke 5:35

22 And He said to the disciples, "The days shall come when you will long to see[x] *one* of the days of the Son of Man, and you will not see it.

17:23
Matt. 24:23; Mark
13:21; Luke 21:8

23 "And they will say to you, 'Look there! Look here!' Do not go[⊙] away, and do not run[⊙] after *them.*

17:24
Matt. 24:27

24 "For just as the lightning, when it flashes out of one part of the sky, shines to the other part of the sky, so will the Son of Man be in His day.

17:25
Matt. 16:21; Luke
9:22

25 "But first He must suffer[x] *many things* and be rejected[x] by this generation.

17:26
Luke 17:26,27;
Matt. 24:37-39;
Gen. 6:5-8; 7

26 "And just as it happened in the days of Noah, so it shall be also in the days of the Son of Man:

27 they were eating,[m] they were drinking,[m] they were marrying,[m] they were being given[m] in marriage, until the day that Noah entered the ark, and the flood came and destroyed them all.

17:28
Gen. 19

28 "It was the same as happened in the days of Lot: they were eating,[m] they were drinking,[m] they were buying,[m] they were selling,[m] they were planting,[m] they were building;[m]

29 but on the day that Lot went out from Sodom it rained fire and brimstone from heaven and destroyed them all.

17:30
Matt. 16:27;
1 Cor. 1:7; Col.
3:4; 2 Thess. 1:7;
1 Pet. 1:7; 4:13;
1 John 2:28

30 "It will be just the same on the day that the Son of Man is revealed.

17:31
Matt. 24:17,18;
Mark 13:15f.;
Luke 21:21

31 "On that day, let not the one who is on the housetop and whose goods are in the house go[⊙] down to take[x] them away; and likewise let not the one who is in the field turn[⊙] back.

17:32
Gen. 19:26

32 "Remember[m] Lot's wife.

17:33
Matt. 10:39

33 "Whoever seeks[x] to *keep[x]* his life shall lose it, and whoever loses[x] *his life* shall preserve it.

34 "I tell you, on that night there will be two men in one bed; one will be taken, and the other will be left.

17:35
Matt. 24:41

35 "There will be two women grinding at the same place; one will be taken, and the other[8b] will be left.

17:36
Matt. 24:40

36 ["[e]Two men will be in the field; one will be taken and the other[8b] will be left."]

17:37
Matt. 24:28

37 And answering they *said to Him, "Where, Lord?" And

[e]Many mss. do not contain this verse

He said to them, "Where the body *is*, there also will the vultures be gathered."

Parables on Prayer

18 Now He was telling them a parable to show~ that at all times they ought to pray~ and not to lose~ heart,

2   saying, "There was in a certain city a judge who did not fear God, and did not respect man.

3   "And there was a widow in that city, and she kept coming^{xxx} to him, saying, 'Give^{xi} me legal protection from my opponent.'

4   "And for a while he was unwilling;^{xxx} but afterward he said to himself, 'Even though I do not fear God nor respect man,

5   yet because² this widow bothers~ me, I will give her legal protection, lest by continually coming she wear~ me out.' "

6   And the Lord said, "Hear^{xi} what the unrighteous judge *said;

7   now shall not *God* bring^x about justice for His elect, who cry to Him day and night, and will He delay long over them?

8   "I tell you that He will bring about justice for them speedily. However, when the Son of Man comes, will He find faith on the earth?"

The Pharisee and the Publican

9   And He also told this parable to certain ones who trusted⁺ in themselves that they were righteous, and viewed others with contempt:

10   "Two men went up into the temple to pray,^x one a Pharisee, and the other a tax-gatherer.

11   "The Pharisee stood and was praying^{xxx} thus to himself, 'God, I thank Thee that I am not like other people: swindlers, unjust, adulterers, or even like this tax-gatherer.

12   'I fast twice a week; I pay tithes of all that I get.'

13   "But the tax-gatherer, standing some distance away, was even unwilling^{xxx} to lift^x up his *eyes* to heaven, but was beating^{xxx} his breast, saying, 'God, be merciful^{xi} to me, the sinner!'

14   "I tell you, *this man* went down to his house justified⁺ rather than the ⁺other; for everyone who exalts himself shall be humbled, but he who humbles himself shall be exalted."

15   And they were bringing^{xxx} even their babies to Him so that He might touch~ them, but when the disciples saw it, they *began* rebuking^{xxx} them.

16   But Jesus called for them, saying, "Permit^{xi6a} the children to come~ to Me, and do not hinder^θ them, for the kingdom of God belongs to such as these.

18:1
Luke 11:5-10;
2 Cor. 4:1

18:2
Luke 18:4; 20:13;
Heb. 12:9

18:4
Luke 18:2; 20:13;
Heb. 12:9

18:5
Luke 11:8;
1 Cor. 9:27

18:6
Luke 7:13

18:7
Rev. 6:10;
Matt. 24:22; Rom.
8:33; Col. 3:12; 2
Tim. 2:10; Titus
1:1;
2 Pet. 3:9
18:8
Luke 17:26ff.

18:9
Luke 16:15;
Rom. 14:3,10

18:10
1 Kin. 10:5; 2 Kin.
20:5,8; Acts 3:1

18:11
Matt. 6:5; Mark
11:25; Luke 22:41

18:12
Matt. 9:14;
Luke 11:42
18:13
Matt. 6:5; Mark
11:25; Luke
22:41;
Ezra 9:6;
Luke 23:48
18:14
Matt. 23:12; Luke
14:11

18:15
Luke 18:15-17;
Matt. 19:13-15;
Mark 10:13-16

18:17
Matt. 18:3; 19:14;
Mark 10:15; 1
Cor. 14:20; 1 Pet.
2:2

17 "•Truly I say to you, whoever does not receive^x the kingdom of God like a child shall •*not* enter^x it *at all.*"

The Rich Young Ruler

18:18
Luke 18:18-30:
Matt. 19:16-29;
Mark 10:17-30;
Luke 10:25-28

18 And a certain ruler questioned Him, saying, "Good[25a] Teacher, what shall I do to inherit *eternal life?*"

19 And Jesus said to him, "Why do you call Me good?[25a] No one is good except God alone.

18:20
Ex. 20:12-16;
Deut. 5:16-20

20 "You know[29e] the commandments, 'Do NOT COMMIT ADUL- TERY,^⊗ DO NOT MURDER,^⊗ DO NOT STEAL,^⊗ DO NOT BEAR^⊗ FALSE WITNESS, HONOR^⌒ YOUR FATHER AND MOTHER.' "

21 And he said, "*All* these things I have kept from *my* youth."

18:22
Matt. 19:21;
12:33;
Matt. 6:20

22 And when Jesus heard *this,* He said to him, "One thing you still lack; sell^xi *all that you possess,* and distribute^xi it to the poor, and you shall have treasure in heaven; and come, follow^⌒ Me."

23 But when he had heard these things, he became *very*[1] *sad;* for he was extremely rich.

18:24
Matt. 19:23; Mark
10:23f.

24 And Jesus looked at him and said, "How †*hard* it is for those who are wealthy to enter the kingdom of God!

18:25
Matt. 19:24; Mark
10:25

25 "For it is †easier for a camel to go^x through the *eye of a needle,* than for a rich man to enter^x the kingdom of God."

26 And they who heard it said, "Then who can be saved?"^x

18:27
Matt. 19:26

27 But He said, "The things impossible with men are *possible with God."*

18:28
Luke 5:11

28 And Peter said, "Behold, we have left our own *homes,* and followed You."

18:29
Matt. 6:33; 19:29;
Mark 10:29f.

29 And He said to them, "•Truly I say to you, there is no one who has left house or wife or brothers or parents or children, for the sake of the kingdom of God,

18:30
Matt. 12:32

30 who shall not receive^x many times as much at †*this* time and in the age to *come,* eternal life."

18:31
Luke 18:31-33:
Matt. 20:17-19;
Mark 10:32-34;
Luke 9:51;
Ps. 22; Is. 53

31 And He took the twelve aside and said to them, "Behold, we are going up to Jerusalem, and all things which are written⁺ through the prophets about the Son of Man will be accom- plished.

18:32
Matt. 16:21

32 "For He will be delivered to the Gentiles, and will be mocked and mistreated and spit upon,

33 and after they have scourged Him, they will kill Him; and the third day He will rise again."

18:34
Mark 9:32; Luke
9:45

34 And *they* understood none of these things, and this saying was hidden⁺ from them, and they did not comprehend^m the things that were said.

Bartimaeus Receives Sight

35   And it came about that as He was approaching Jericho, a certain blind man was sitting™ by the road, begging.

36   Now hearing a multitude going by, he *began* to inquire™ what this might be.

37   And they told him that Jesus of Nazareth was passing by.

38   And he called out, saying, "Jesus, Son of David, have mercy˟ˡ on me!"

39   And those who led the way were sternly telling™ him to be quiet;˟ but he kept crying™ out all the more, "Son of David, have mercy˟ˡ on me!"

40   And Jesus stopped and commanded that he be brought˟ to Him; and when he had come near, He questioned him,

41   "What do you want Me to do˟ for you?" And he said, "Lord, *I want* to regain˟ my sight!"

42   And Jesus said to him, "Receive˟ˡ your sight; your faith has made⁺ you well."

43   And immediately he regained his sight, and *began* following™ Him, glorifying God; and when all the people saw it, they gave praise to God.

Zaccheus Converted

19   And He entered and was passing through Jericho.
2   And behold, there was a man called by the name of Zaccheus; and he was a chief tax-gatherer, and he was rich.

3   And he was trying™ to see˟ who Jesus was, and he was unable™ because of the crowd, for he was small in stature.

4   And he ran on ahead and climbed up into a sycamore tree in order to see Him, for He was about to pass through that way.

5   And when Jesus came to the place, He looked up and said to him, "Zaccheus, hurry and come˟ˡ down, for ⁺today I must stay˟ at your house."

6   And he hurried and came down, and received Him gladly.

7   And when they saw it, they all *began* to grumble,™ saying, "He has gone to be the guest of a man who is a *sinner.*"

8   And Zaccheus stopped and said to the Lord, "Behold, Lord, *half* of my possessions I will give to the poor, and if I have defrauded anyone of anything, I will give back four times as much."

9   And Jesus said to him, "Today salvation has come to *this house,* because *he, too,* is a son of Abraham.

10   "For the Son of Man has come to seek˟ and to save˟ that which was lost."⁺

18:35
Luke 18:35-43:
Matt. 20:29-34;
Mark 10:46-52;
Matt. 20:29; Mark
10:46; Luke 19:1

18:38
Matt. 9:27; Luke
18:39

18:39
Luke 18:38

18:42
Matt. 9:22

18:43
Matt. 9:8;
Luke 9:43; 13:17;
19:37

19:1
Luke 18:35

19:4
1 Kin. 10:27;
1 Chr. 27:28;
2 Chr. 1:15; 9:27;
Ps. 78:47; Is.
9:10; Luke 17:6

19:8
Luke 7:13;
Luke 3:14;
Ex. 22:1; Lev.
6:5; Num. 5:7; 2
Sam. 12:6

19:9
Luke 3:8; 13:16;
Rom. 4:16; Gal.
3:7
19:10
Matt. 18:11

Parable of Money Usage

19:11
Luke 9:51;
Luke 17:20
11 And while they were listening to these things, He went on to tell a parable, because He was near Jerusalem, and they supposed~ that the kingdom of God was going to appear *immediately.*

19:12
Matt. 25:14-30;
Luke 19:12-27
12 He said therefore, "A certain nobleman went to a distant country to receive[x] a kingdom for himself, and *then* return.[x]

13 "And he called ten of his slaves, and gave them ten ʰminas, and said to them, 'Do business[xl] *with this* until I come *back.*'

14 "But his citizens hated[xx] him, and sent a delegation after him, saying, 'We do not want this man to reign[x] over us.'

15 "And it came about that when he returned,[x] after receiving the kingdom, he ordered[x] that these slaves, to whom he had given the money, be called to him in order that he might know[x] what business they had done.

16 "And the first appeared, saying, 'Master, your mina has made *ten* minas more.'

19:17
Luke 16:10
17 "And he said to him, 'Well done, good[25a] slave, because you have been faithful in a *very*[3] *little thing,* be in authority over *ten* cities.'

18 "And the second came, saying, 'Your mina, master, has made *five* minas.'

19 "And he said to him also, 'And *you* are to be~ᴵ over *five* cities.'

20 "And another[8b] came, saying, 'Master, behold your mina, which I kept put away in a handkerchief;

21 for I was afraid[xx] of you, because you are an *exacting* man; you take up what you did not lay down, and reap what you did not sow.'

22 "He *said to him, '*By your own words* I will judge you, you worthless slave. Did you know that *I* am an *exacting* man, taking up what I did not lay down, and reaping what I did not sow?

23 'Then why did you not put the money in the bank, and having come, I would have collected it with interest?'

24 "And he said to the bystanders, 'Take[xl] the mina away from him, and give[xl] it to the one who has the ten minas.'

25 "And they said to him, 'Master, he has *ten* minas *already.'*

19:26
Matt. 13:12; Mark
4:25; Luke 8:18
26 "I tell you, that to everyone who has shall *more* be given, but from the one who does not have, even what he does have shall be taken away.

19:27
Luke 19:14;
Matt. 22:7; Luke
20:16
27 "But these *enemies of mine,* who did not want me to reign[x] over them, bring[xl] them here and slay[xl] them in my presence."

ʰA mina is equal to about 100 days' wages or nearly $20

Triumphal Entry

28   And after He had said these things, He was going[m] on ahead, ascending to Jerusalem.

29   And it came about that when He approached Bethphage and Bethany, near the mount that is called Olivet, He sent two of the disciples,

30   saying, "Go into the village opposite *you*, in which as you enter you will find a colt tied, on which no one yet has ever sat; untie it, and bring[xi] it *here*.

31   "And if anyone asks[~] you, 'Why are you untying it?' thus shall you speak, 'The Lord has need of it.' "

32   And those who were sent[+] went away and found it just as He had told them.

33   And as they were untying the colt, its owners said to them, "Why are you untying the colt?"

34   And they said, "The Lord has need of it."

35   And they brought it to Jesus, and they threw *their* garments on the colt, and put Jesus *on it*.

36   And as He was going, they were spreading[m] *their* garments in the road.

37   And as He was now approaching, near the descent of the Mount of Olives, the whole multitude of the disciples began to praise[~] God joyfully with a loud voice for all the *miracles* which they had seen,

38   saying,

> "BLESSED[+] IS THE King WHO COMES IN THE NAME OF
>   THE LORD;
> Peace in heaven and glory in the highest!"

39   And some of the Pharisees in the multitude said to Him, "Teacher, rebuke[xi] Your disciples."

40   And He answered and said, "I tell you, if these become silent, the stones will cry out!"

41   And when He approached, He saw the city and wept over it,

42   saying, "If you had known in †this day, *even you*, the things which make for peace! But now they have been hidden from your eyes.

43   "For the days shall come upon you when your enemies will throw up a bank before you, and surround you, and hem you in on every side,

44   and will level you to the ground and your children within you, and they will not leave in you one stone upon another, because you did not recognize the time of your visitation."

19:28
Mark 10:32;
Luke 9:51

19:29
Luke 19:29-38:
Matt. 21:1-9;
Mark 11:1-10;
Matt. 21:17;
Luke 21:37; Acts
1:12

19:35
Luke 19:35-38:
Matt. 21:4-9;
Mark 11:7-10;
John 12:12-15

19:37
Matt. 21:1; Luke
19:29;
Luke 18:43

19:38
Ps. 118:26;
Matt. 2:2; 25:34;
Matt. 21:9; Luke
2:14

19:39
Matt. 21:15f.

19:40
Hab. 2:11

19:41
Luke 13:34,35

19:43
Eccl. 9:14; Is.
29:3; 37:33; Jer.
6:6; Ezek. 4:2;
26:8;
Luke 21:20
19:44
Matt. 24:2; Mark
13:2; Luke 21:6;
1 Pet. 2:12

Traders Driven from the Temple

19:45
Luke 19:45,46;
Matt. 21:12,13;
Mark 11:15-17;
John 2:13-16
19:46
Is. 56:7; Jer. 7:11;
Matt. 21:13; Mark
11:17;
Jer. 7:11
19:47
Matt. 26:55; Luke
21:37;
Luke 20:19

45 And He entered the temple and began to cast~ out those who were selling,

46 saying to them, "It is written,⁺ 'AND MY HOUSE SHALL BE A HOUSE OF PRAYER,' but *you* have made it a ROBBERS' DEN."

47 And He was teaching~ daily in the temple; but the chief priests and the scribes and the leading men among the people were trying* to destroy* Him,

48 and they could not find* anything that they might do,* for *all* the people were hanging* upon His words.

Jesus' Authority Questioned

20:1
Luke 20:1-8;
Matt. 21:23-27;
Mark 11:27-33;
Matt. 26:55;
Luke 8:1;
Acts 4:1; 6:12

20 And it came about on one of the days while He was teaching the people in the temple and preaching the gospel, that the chief priests and the scribes with the elders confronted *Him*,

2 and they spoke, saying to Him, "Tell* us by what authority You are doing these things, or who is the one who gave You ⁺this authority?"

3 And He answered and said to them, "*I* shall *also* ask you a question, and you tell* Me:

4 "Was the baptism of John from *heaven* or from ⁺*men?*"

5 And they reasoned among themselves, saying, "If we say,* 'From heaven,' He will say, 'Why did you not believe him?'

20:6
Matt. 11:9; Luke
7:29,30

6 "But if we say,* 'From men,' all the people will stone us to death, for they are convinced⁺ that John was a *prophet.*"

7 And they answered that they did not know where *it came* from.

8 And Jesus said to them, "Neither will *I* tell you by what authority I do these things."

Parable of the Vine-growers

20:9
Luke 20:9-19;
Matt. 21:33-46;
Mark 12:1-12

9 And He began to tell~ the people this parable: "A man planted a vineyard and rented it out to vine-growers, and went on a journey for a long time.

10 "And at the *harvest* time he sent a slave to the vine-growers, in order that they might give him *some* of the produce of the vineyard; but the vine-growers beat him and sent him away *empty-handed.*

11 "And he proceeded to send* *another* slave; and they beat him also and treated him shamefully, and sent him away *empty-handed.*

12 "And he proceeded to send[x] a *third;* and this one also they wounded and cast out.

13 "And the owner of the vineyard said, 'What shall I do?[x] I will send my *beloved* son; perhaps they will respect *him.'*

20:13
Luke 18:2

14 "But when the vine-growers saw him, they reasoned[m] with one another, saying, 'This is the heir; let us kill[x] him that the inheritance may be *ours.'*

15 "And they threw him out of the vineyard and killed him. What, therefore, will the owner of the vineyard do to them?

16 "He will come and destroy these vine-growers and will give the vineyard to others." And when they heard it, they said, "May it never be!"

20:16
Matt. 21:41; Mark 12:9; Luke 19:27; Rom. 3:4,6,31; 6:2,15; 7:7,13; 9:14; 11:1,11; 2:17; 3:21; 6:14

17 But He looked at them and said, "What then is this that is written,[*]

20:17
Ps. 118:22; Eph. 2:20; 1 Pet. 2:6

'THE STONE WHICH THE BUILDERS [†]REJECTED,

THIS BECAME THE CHIEF CORNER *stone'*?

18 "Everyone who falls on that stone will be broken to pieces;[1] but on whomever it falls,[x] it will scatter him like dust."

20:18
Matt. 21:44

Tribute to Caesar

19 And the scribes and the chief priests tried to lay[x] hands on Him that very hour, and they feared the people; for they understood that He spoke this parable against *them.*

20:19
Luke 19:47

20 And they watched[1] Him, and sent spies who pretended to be righteous, in order that they might catch[x] Him in some statement, so as to deliver[x] Him up to the rule and the authority of the governor.

20:20
Luke 20:20-26; Matt. 22:15-22; Mark 12:13-17; Mark 3:2; Luke 11:54; 20:26; Matt. 27:2

21 And they questioned Him, saying, "Teacher, we know that You speak and teach correctly, and You are not partial to any, but teach the way of God in *truth.*

22 "Is it lawful for us to pay[x] taxes to *Caesar,* or not?"

20:22
Matt. 17:25; Luke 23:2

23 But He detected their *trickery* and said to them,

24 "Show[xi] Me a [g]denarius. Whose likeness and inscription does it have?" And they said, "Caesar's."

25 And He said to them, "Then render[xi] to Caesar the things that are Caesar's, and to God the things that are God's."

20:25
Matt. 22:21; Mark 12:17

26 And they were unable to catch[x] Him in a saying in the presence of the people; and marveling at His answer, they became silent.

20:26
Luke 11:54

Is There a Resurrection?

27 Now there came to Him some of the Sadducees (who say that there is no resurrection),

20:27
Luke 20:27-40; Matt. 22:23-33; Mark 12:18-27; Acts 23:8

[g]The denarius was equivalent to one day's wage

20:28
Deut. 25:5

28   and they questioned Him, saying, "Teacher, Moses wrote for us that IF A MAN'S BROTHER DIES,[x] having a wife, AND HE IS CHILDLESS, HIS BROTHER SHOULD TAKE[x] THE WIFE AND RAISE[x] UP OFFSPRING TO HIS BROTHER.

29   "Now there were *seven* brothers; and the first took a wife, and died childless;

30   and the second

31   and the third took her; and in the same way all seven died, leaving no children.

32   "Finally the woman died also.

33   "In the resurrection therefore, which one's wife will she be? For all seven had her as wife."

20:34
Matt. 12:32; Luke
16:8

34   And Jesus said to them, "The sons of [†]this age marry and are given in marriage,

20:35
Matt. 12:32; Luke
16:8

35   but those who are considered[1] worthy to attain[x] to *that* age and the resurrection from the dead, neither marry, nor are given in marriage;

20:36
Rom. 8:16f.;
1 John 3:1,2

36   for neither can they die[x] anymore, for they are like angels, and are sons of *God*, being sons of the *resurrection*.

20:37
Mark 12:26;
Ex. 3:6

37   "But that the dead are raised, even *Moses* showed, in the *passage about the burning* bush, where he calls the Lord THE GOD OF ABRAHAM, AND THE GOD OF ISAAC, AND THE GOD OF JACOB.

20:38
Matt. 22:32; Mark
12:27;
Rom. 14:8

38   "Now He is not the God of the dead, but of the living; for all live to Him."

39   And some of the scribes answered and said, "Teacher, You have spoken well."

20:40
Matt. 22:46; Luke
14:6

40   For they did not have[m] courage to question[~] Him any longer about anything.

20:41
Luke 20:41-44;
Matt. 22:41-46;
Mark 12:35-37;
Matt. 9:27

41   And He said to them, "How *is it that* they say [h]the Christ is *David's* son?

20:42
Ps. 110:1

42   "For David *himself* says in the book of Psalms,

'THE LORD SAID TO MY LORD,
    "SIT AT MY RIGHT HAND,

20:43
Ps. 110:1

43   UNTIL I MAKE[x] THINE ENEMIES A FOOTSTOOL FOR THY
            FEET." '

44   "David therefore calls Him '*Lord*,' and how is He *his* son?"

20:45
Luke 20:45-47;
Matt. 23:1-7;
Mark 12:38-40

45   And while all the people were listening, He said to the disciples,

20:46
Luke 11:43; 14:7

46   "Beware[~m] of the scribes, who like to walk[~] around in long robes, and love[31b] respectful greetings in the market places, and chief seats in the synagogues, and places of honor at banquets,

47   who devour[1] widows' houses, and for appearance's sake offer long prayers; these will receive greater condemnation."

[h]I.e., the Messiah

The Widow's Gift

21 And He looked up and saw the rich putting their gifts into the treasury.

21:1
Luke 21:1-4:
Mark 12:41-44

2   And He saw a certain poor widow putting in two small copper coins.

21:2
Mark 12:42

3   And He said, "Truly I say to you, this poor widow put in *more than all of them;*

4   for they all out of their surplus put into the offering; but she out of her *poverty* put in *all* that she had^m to *live on."*

21:4
Mark 12:44

5   And while some were talking about the temple, that it was adorned• with beautiful stones and votive gifts, He said,

21:5
Luke 21:5-36:
Matt. 24; Mark 13

6   *"As for* these things which you are looking at, the days will come in which there will not be left one stone upon another which will not be torn down."

21:6
Luke 19:44

7   And they questioned Him, saying, "Teacher, when therefore will these things be? And what *will be* the sign when these things are about to take place?"

8   And He said, "See ᵐ to it that you be not misled;ˣ for many will come in My name, saying, '†*I* am *He,'* and, 'The time is at hand';• do not goᵉ after them.

21:8
John 8:24;
Luke 17:23

9   "And when you hearˣ of wars and disturbances, do not be terrified;ᵉ for these things must take place first, but the end *does* not *follow* †immediately."

Things to Come

10   Then He continued by saying to them, "Nation will rise against nation, and kingdom against kingdom,

11   and there will be great earthquakes, and in various places plagues and famines; and there will be terrors and great signs from heaven.

12   "But before all these things, they will lay their hands on you and will persecute you, delivering you to the synagogues and prisons, bringing you before kings and governors for My name's sake.

21:12
Luke 21:12-17:
Matt. 10:19-22;
Mark 13:11-13

13   "It will lead to an opportunity for your testimony.

21:13
Phil. 1:12

14   "So makeˣⁱ up your minds not to prepare~ beforehand to defendˣ yourselves;

21:14
Luke 12:11

15   for *I* will give you utterance and wisdom which none of your opponents will be able to resistˣ or refute.ˣ

21:15
Luke 12:12

16   "But you will be delivered up even by parents and brothers and relatives and friends, and they will put *some* of you to death,

17   and you will be hated~ by all on account of My name.

18   "Yet •*not* a hair of your head will perish.ˣ

21:18
Matt. 10:30; Luke
12:7

21:19
Matt. 10:22;
24:13; Rom. 2:7;
5:3f.; Heb. 10:36;
James 1:3; 2 Pet.
1:6
21:20
Luke 19:43
21:21
Luke 17:31

19 "By your *endurance* you will gain your lives.

20 "But when you see* *Jerusalem* surrounded by armies, then recognize** that her desolation is at hand. ✦

21 "Then let those who are in Judea flee to the mountains, and let those who are in the midst of the city depart, and let not those who are in the country enter the city;

21:22
Is. 63:4; Dan.
9:24-27; Hos. 9:7

22 because these are *days of vengeance,* in order that all things which are written✦ may be fulfilled.*

21:23
Dan. 8:19; 1 Cor.
7:26

23 "Woe to those who are with child and to those who nurse babes in those days; for there will be *great distress* upon the land, and wrath to this people,

21:24
Gen. 34:26; Ex.
17:13; Heb.
11:34;
Is. 63:18; Dan.
8:13;
Rev. 11:2;
Rom. 11:25

24 and they will fall by the edge of the sword, and will be led captive into *all* the nations; and Jerusalem will be trampled~ under foot by the Gentiles until the times of the Gentiles be fulfilled.*

The Return of Christ

25 "And there will be signs in sun and moon and stars, and upon the earth dismay among nations, in perplexity at the roaring of the sea and the waves,

26 men fainting from fear and the expectation of the things which are coming upon the world; for the powers of the heavens will be shaken.

21:27
Matt. 16:27;
24:30; 26:64;
Mark 13:26;
Dan. 7:13; Rev.
1:7
21:28
Luke 18:7

27 "And then they will see THE SON OF MAN COMING IN A CLOUD with power and *great*[26b] glory.

28 "But when these things begin to take~ place, straighten** up and lift** up your heads, because your redemption is drawing near."

29 And He told them a parable: "Behold* the fig tree and all the trees;

21:30
Luke 12:57

30 as soon as they put* forth *leaves,* you see it and know for yourselves that summer is now *near.*

21:31
Matt. 3:2

31 "Even so you, too, when you see* these things happening, recognize~ that the kingdom of God is near.

32 "•Truly I say to you, this generation will •*not* pass* away until all things take place.

21:33
Matt. 5:18; Luke
16:17

33 "Heaven and earth will pass away, but My words will •*not* pass away.

21:34
Matt. 24:42-44;
Mark 4:19; Luke
12:40,45;
1 Thess. 5:2ff.

34 "Be on guard,~ that your hearts may not be *weighted*x *down* with dissipation and drunkenness and the worries of life, and that day come* on you *suddenly* like a trap;

35 for it will come upon all those who dwell on the face of all the earth.

21:36
Mark 13:33; Luke
12:40;
Luke 1:19; Rev.
7:9; 8:2; 11:4

36 "But keep on the alert~ at all times, praying in order that

you may have[x] strength to escape[x] all these things that are about to take place, and to stand[x] before the Son of Man."

37   Now during the day He was teaching~ in the temple, but at evening He would go out and spend[m] the night on the mount that is called Olivet.

21:37
Matt. 26:55; Luke
19:47;
Mark 11:19;
Matt. 21:1

38   And all the people would get[m] up early in the morning *to come* to Him in the temple to listen~ to Him.

21:38
John 8:2

Preparing the Passover

22 Now the Feast of Unleavened Bread, which is called the Passover, was approaching.

22:1
Luke 22:1,2: Matt.
26:2-5; Mark
14:1,2; Ex.
12:1-27;
John 11:55; 13:1

2   And the chief priests and the scribes were seeking[m] how they might put[x] Him to death; for they were afraid[m] of the people.

22:2
Matt. 12:14

3   And *Satan* entered into Judas who was called Iscariot, belonging to the number of the twelve.

22:3
Luke 22:3-6:
Matt. 26:14-16;
Mark 14:10,11;
Matt. 4:10; John
13:2,27

4   And he went away and discussed with the chief priests and officers how he might betray[x] Him to them.

22:4
1 Chr. 9:11; Neh.
11:11; Luke
22:52; Acts 4:1;
5:24,26

5   And they were glad, and agreed to give[x] him *money.*

6   And he consented, and *began* seeking[m] a good opportunity to betray[x] Him to them apart from the multitude.

7   Then came the *first* day of Unleavened Bread on which the Passover *lamb* had[m] to be sacrificed. ~

22:7
Luke 22:7-13:
Matt. 26:17-19;
Mark 14:12-16

8   And He sent Peter and John, saying, "Go and prepare[xi] the Passover for us, that we may eat[x] it."

22:8
Acts 3:1,11; 4:13,
19; 8:14; Gal. 2:9

9   And they said to Him, "Where do You want us to prepare[x] it?"

10   And He said to them, "Behold, when you have entered the city, a *man* will meet you carrying a pitcher of water; follow[x] him into the house that he enters.

11   "And you shall say to the owner of the house, 'The Teacher says to you, "Where is the guest room in which I may eat[x] the Passover with My disciples?" '

12   "And he will show you a large, furnished,[*] upper room; prepare[xi] it *there.*"

13   And they departed and found *everything* just as He had told them; and they prepared the Passover.

The Lord's Supper

14   And when the hour had come He reclined *at the table,* and the apostles with Him.

22:14
Matt. 26:20; Mark
14:17;
Mark 6:30

15   And He said to them, "I have *earnestly*[4] desired to eat[x] this Passover with you before I suffer;[x]

16　for I say to you, I shall •never again eat[x] it until it is fulfilled[x] in the kingdom of God."

17　And when He had taken a cup *and* given thanks, He said, "Take[xi] this and share[xi] it among yourselves;

18　for I say to you, I will •not drink[⊙] of the fruit of the vine from now on until the kingdom of God comes."

19　And when He had taken *some* bread *and* given thanks, He broke *it,* and gave *it* to them, saying, "This is My body [i]which is given for you; do[ᵐⁱ] this in remembrance of •*Me.*"

20　And in the same way *He took* the cup after they had eaten,[x] saying, "This cup which is poured out for you is the new[34a] covenant in My blood.

21　"But behold, the hand of the one betraying Me is with Me on the table.

22　"For indeed, the Son of Man is going as it has been *deter-mined;•* but woe to *that* man by whom He is betrayed!"

23　And they began to discuss[~] among themselves which one of them it might be who was going to do[19b] this thing.

Who Is Greatest

24　And there arose also a dispute among them *as to* which one of them was regarded to be greatest.

25　And He said to them, "The kings of the Gentiles lord it over them; and those who have authority over them are called 'Benefactors.'

26　"But not so with you, but let him who is the greatest among you become[ᵐⁱ] as the youngest, and the leader as the servant.[38a]

27　"For who is greater, the one who reclines *at the table,* or the one who serves? Is it not the one who reclines *at the table?* But [†]*I* am among you as the one who serves.

28　"And you are those who have stood[•] by Me in My trials;

29　and just as My Father has granted Me a kingdom, *I* grant you

30　that you may eat[~] and drink[~] at My table in My kingdom, and you will sit on thrones judging the twelve tribes of Israel.

31　"Simon, Simon, behold, Satan has demanded[1] *permission* to sift[x] you like wheat;

32　but *I* have prayed[9b] for you, that your faith may not fail;[x] and you, when once you have turned again, strengthen[xi] your brothers."

33　And he said to Him, "Lord, *with You* I am ready to go both to prison and to death!"

34　And He said, "I say to you, Peter, the cock will not crow

22:16
Luke 14:15;
22:18,30; Rev.
19:9
22:17
Luke 22:17-20:
Matt. 26:26-29;
Mark 14:22-25; 1
Cor. 11:23-25;
1 Cor. 10:16;
Matt. 14:19
22:18
Matt. 26:29; Mark
14:25
22:19
Matt. 14:19

22:20
Matt. 26:28; Mark
14:24;
Ex. 24:8; Jer.
31:31; 1 Cor.
11:25; 2 Cor. 3:6;
Heb. 8:8,13; 9:15
22:21
Luke 22:21-23:
Matt. 26:21-24;
Mark 14:18-21;
Ps. 41:9; John
13:18,21,22,26
22:22
Acts 2:23; 4:28;
10:42; 17:31

22:24
Mark 9:34; Luke
9:46

22:25
Luke 22:25-27:
Matt. 20:25-28;
Mark 10:42-45

22:26
Matt. 23:11; Mark
9:35; Luke 9:48;
1 Pet. 5:5
22:27
Luke 12:37;
Matt. 20:28; John
13:12-15

22:28
Heb. 2:18; 4:15
22:29
Matt. 5:3; 2 Tim.
2:12

22:30
Luke 22:16;
Matt. 5:3; 2 Tim.
2:12;
Matt. 19:28
22:31
Job 1:6-12; 2:1-6;
Matt. 4:10;
Amos 9:9
22:32
John 17:9,15;
John 21:15-17

22:33
Luke 22:33,34:
Matt. 26:33-35;
Mark 14:29-31;
John 13:37,38

[i]Some ancient mss. do not contain the remainder of v. 19 nor any of v. 20

today until you have denied[x] three times that you know[29e] Me."

35 And He said to them, "When I sent you out without purse and bag and sandals, you did not lack anything, did you?" And they said, "*No, nothing.*"

36 And He said to them, "But now, let him who has a purse take[xl] it along, likewise also a bag, and let him who has no sword sell[xl] his robe and buy[xl] one.

37 "For I tell you, that this which is written[*] must be fulfilled[x] in Me, 'AND HE WAS NUMBERED WITH *TRANSGRESSORS*'; for that which refers to Me has *its* fulfillment."

38 And they said, "Lord, look, here are two swords." And He said to them, "It is enough."

The Garden of Gethsemane

39 And He came out and proceeded as was His custom to the Mount of Olives; and the disciples also followed Him.

40 And when He arrived at the place, He said to them, "Pray[~] that you may not enter[x] into temptation."

41 And He withdrew from them about a stone's throw, and He knelt down and *began* to pray,[xxx]

42 saying, "Father, if Thou art willing, remove[xl] this cup from Me; yet not My will, but *Thine* be done."[~l]

43 Now an angel from heaven appeared to Him, strengthening Him.

44 And being in agony He was praying[xx] very[3] fervently; and His sweat became like drops of blood, falling down upon the ground.

45 And when He rose from prayer, He came to the disciples and found them sleeping from sorrow,

46 and said to them, "Why are you sleeping? Rise and pray[~l] that you may not enter[x] into temptation."

Jesus Betrayed by Judas

47 While He was still speaking, behold, a multitude *came*, and the one called Judas, one of the twelve, was preceding them; and he approached Jesus to kiss[x] Him.

48 But Jesus said to him, "Judas, are you betraying the Son of Man with a *kiss?*"

49 And when those who were around Him saw what was going to happen, they said, "Lord, shall we strike with the sword?"

50 And a certain one of them struck the slave of the high priest and cut off his right ear.

22:35
Matt. 10:9f.; Mark 6:8; Luke 9:3ff.; 10:4

22:37
Is. 53:12;
John 17:4; 19:30

22:38
Luke 22:36,49

22:39
Matt. 26:30; Mark 14:26; John 18:1; Luke 21:37; Matt. 21:1
22:40
Luke 22:40-46; Matt. 26:36-46; Mark 14:32-42; Matt. 6:13; Luke 22:46
22:41
Matt. 26:39; Mark 14:35; Luke 18:11
22:42
Matt. 20:22; Matt. 26:39
22:43
Matt. 4:11

22:44
Heb. 5:7

22:46
Luke 22:40

22:47
Luke 22:47-53; Matt. 26:47-56; Mark 14:43-50; John 18:3-11

22:49
Luke 22:38

51   But Jesus answered and said, "Stop! No more of this." And He touched his ear and healed[15b] him.

22:52
Luke 22:4;
Luke 22:37

52   And Jesus said to the chief priests and officers of the temple and elders who had come against Him, "Have you come out with swords and clubs as against a *robber?*

53   "While I was with you daily in the temple, you did not lay hands on Me; but this hour and the power[32b] of darkness are *yours.*"

Jesus' Arrest

22:54
Matt. 26:57; Mark
14:53;
Matt. 26:58; Mark
14:54; John 18:15

54   And having arrested Him, they led Him *away*, and brought Him to the house of the high priest; but Peter was following[m] at a *distance.*

22:55
Luke 22:55-62;
Matt. 26:69-75;
Mark 14:66-72;
John 18:16-18,
25-27;
Matt. 26:3

55   And after they had kindled a fire in the middle of the courtyard and had sat down together, Peter was sitting among them.

56   And a certain servant-girl, seeing him as he sat in the firelight, and looking intently at him, said, "This man was *with Him too.*"

57   But he denied *it*, saying, "Woman, I do not know Him."

22:58
John 18:26

58   And a little later, another[8b] saw him and said,[m] "*You* are *one of them too!*" But Peter said,[m] "Man, I am not!"

22:59
Matt. 26:73; Mark
14:70

59   And after about an hour had passed, another[8a] man *began* to insist,[m] saying, "*Certainly* this man *also was with Him*, for he is a *Galilean too.*"

60   But Peter said, "Man, I do not know what you are talking about." And immediately, while he was still speaking, a *cock* crowed.

22:61
Luke 7:13;
Luke 22:34

61   And the Lord turned and looked at Peter. And Peter *remembered* the word of the Lord, how He had told him, "Before a cock crows[x] today, you will deny Me three times."

62   And he went out and wept *bitterly.*

22:63
Matt. 26:67f.;
Mark 14:65; John
18:22f.
22:64
Matt. 26:68; Mark
14:65

63   And the men who were holding Jesus in custody were mocking[m] Him, and beating Him,

64   and they blindfolded Him and were asking[m9c] Him, saying, "Prophesy,[x] who is the one who hit You?"

22:65
Matt. 27:39

65   And they were saying[m] many other things against Him, blaspheming.

Jesus before the Sanhedrin

22:66
Matt. 27:1f.; Mark
15:1; John 18:28;
Acts 22:5;
Matt. 5:22

66   And when it was day, the ʲCouncil of elders of the people assembled, both chief priests and scribes, and they led Him away to their council *chamber*, saying,

ʲOr, *Sanhedrin*

67 "If *You* are the Christ, tell^{kl} us.^{kl}" But He said to them, "If I tell^x you, you will •not believe;^x

68   and if I ask^x a question, you will •not answer.^x

22:67
Matt. 26:63-66;
Mark 14:61-63;
Luke 22:67-71;
John 18:19-21

69 "But from now on THE SON OF MAN WILL BE SEATED AT THE RIGHT HAND of the power[32a] OF GOD."

22:69
Matt. 26:64; Mark
14:62; 16:19;
Ps. 110:1

70   And they all said, "Are *You* the Son of God, then?" And He said^m to them, "Yes, I am."

22:70
Matt. 4:3;
Matt. 26:64;
27:11; Luke 23:3

71   And they said, "What further need do we have of *testimony*? For we have heard it *ourselves* from His own mouth."

Jesus before Pilate

23 Then the whole body of them arose and brought Him before Pilate.

23:1
Matt. 27:2; Mark
15:1; John 18:28

2   And they began to accuse~ Him, saying, "We found this man misleading our nation and forbidding to pay~ *taxes to Caesar,* and saying that He Himself is *Christ,* a *King.*"

23:2
Luke 23:2,3; *Matt.
27:11-14; Mark
15:2-5; John
18:29-37;
Luke 23:14;*

3   And Pilate asked^{9c} Him, saying, "Are *You* the King of the Jews?" And He answered him and said,^m "*It is as* you say."

Luke 20:22; John
18:33ff.; 19:12;
Acts 17:7
23:3
Luke 22:70

4   And Pilate said to the chief priests and the multitudes, "I find no *guilt* in this man."

23:4
Matt. 27:23; Mark
15:14; Luke
23:14,22; John
18:38; 19:4,6

5   But they kept on insisting,^m saying, "He stirs up[1] the people, teaching all over Judea, starting from Galilee, even as far as this place."

23:5
Matt. 4:12

6   But when Pilate heard it, he asked^{9c} whether the man was a *Galilean.*

7   And when he learned that He belonged to *Herod's jurisdiction,* he sent Him to Herod, who himself also was in Jerusalem at that time.

23:7
Matt. 14:1; Mark
6:14; Luke 3:1;
9:7; 13:31

Jesus before Herod

8   Now Herod was very glad when he saw Jesus; for he had wanted~ to see^x Him for a long time, because he had been hearing~ about Him and was hoping^m to see^x some *sign* performed by Him.

23:8
Luke 9:9

9   And he questioned^m Him at some length; but *He* answered him †*nothing.*

23:9
Matt. 27:12,14;
Mark 15:5; John
19:9

10   And the chief priests and the scribes were standing there, accusing Him vehemently.

11   And Herod with his soldiers, after treating Him with contempt and mocking Him, dressed Him in a gorgeous robe and sent Him back to Pilate.

23:11
Matt. 27:28

12   Now Herod and Pilate became friends with one another that very day; for before they had^m been at enmity with each other.

23:12
Acts 4:27

Pilate Seeks Jesus' Release

23:13
Luke 23:35; John
7:26,48; 12:42;
Acts 3:17; 4:5,8;
13:27
23:14
Luke 23:2;
Luke 23:4

13   And Pilate summoned the chief priests and the rulers and the people,

14   and said to them, "You brought this man to me as one who incites the people to rebellion, and behold, having examined Him before ⁺you, I have found no *guilt* in this man regarding the charges which you make against Him.

23:15
Luke 9:9

15   "No, nor has Herod, for he sent Him back to us; and behold, nothing deserving *death* has been done⁺ by Him.

23:16
Matt. 27:26; Mark
15:15; Luke
23:22; John 19:1;
Acts 16:37

16   "I will therefore punish Him and release Him."

17   [ᵏNow he was obliged to release to them at the feast one prisoner.]

23:18
Luke 23:18-25;
Matt. 27:15-26;
Mark 15:6-15;
John 18:39-19:16

18   But they cried out all together, saying, "Away⁓ with this man, and release˟ˡ for us Barabbas!"

19   (He was one who had been thrown into prison for a certain insurrection made in the city, and for murder.)

20   And Pilate, wanting to release˟ Jesus, addressed them again,

21   but they kept on calling˟˟ out, saying, "Crucify, crucify Him!"

23:22
Luke 23:16

22   And he said to them the third time, "Why, what evil¹⁰ᵃ has this man done? I have found in Him no guilt *demanding death;* I will therefore punish Him and release Him."

23   But they were insistent,˟˟ with loud voices asking that He be crucified.˟ And their voices *began* to *prevail.*˟˟

24   And Pilate pronounced sentence that their demand should be granted.

25   And he released the man they were asking˟˟ for who had been thrown⁺ into prison for insurrection and ⁺murder, but he delivered *Jesus* to their will.

Simon Bears the Cross

23:26
Luke 23:26; Matt.
27:32; Mark
15:21; John
19:17;
Matt. 27:32
23:27
Luke 8:52

26   And when they led Him away, they laid hold of one Simon of Cyrene, coming in from the country, and placed on him the cross to carry⁓ behind Jesus.

27   And there were following˟˟ Him a great multitude of the people, and of women who were mourning˟˟ and lamenting˟˟ Him.

28   But Jesus turning to them said, "Daughters of Jerusalem, stop weeping⁰ for Me, but weep⁓ for *yourselves* and for your ⁺children.

23:29
Matt. 24:19; Luke
11:27; 21:23

29   "For behold, the days are coming when they will say,

ᵏMany mss. do not contain this verse

'†Blessed are the barren, and the wombs that never bore, and the breasts that never nursed.'

30 "Then they will begin TO SAY~ TO THE MOUNTAINS, 'FALL[xi] ON US,' AND TO THE HILLS, 'COVER[xi] US.'

23:30
Hos. 10:8; Is. 2:19,20; Rev. 6:16

31 "For if they do these things in the *green* tree, what will happen in the *dry?*"

32 And two others[8b] also, who were criminals, were being led[m] away to be put[x] to death with Him.

23:32
Matt. 27:38; Mark 15:27; John 19:18

The Crucifixion

33 And when they came to the place called The Skull, *there* they crucified Him and the criminals, one on the right and the other on the left.

23:33
Luke 23:33-43:
Matt. 27:33-44;
Mark 15:22-32;
John 19:17-24

34 But Jesus was saying,[m] "Father, forgive[xi21a] them; for they do not know[29e] what they are doing." And they cast lots, dividing up His garments among themselves.

23:34
Matt. 11:25; Luke 22:42;
Ps. 22:18; John 19:24

35 And the people stood by, looking on. And even the rulers were sneering[m1] at Him, saying, "He saved *others;* let Him save[xi] Himself if this is the Christ of God, His Chosen †One."

23:35
Luke 23:13;
Matt. 27:43

36 And the soldiers also mocked Him, coming up to Him, offering Him sour wine,

23:36
Matt. 27:48

37 and saying, "If *You* are the King of the Jews, save[xi] Yourself!"

23:37
Matt. 27:43

38 Now there was also an inscription above Him, "THIS IS THE KING OF THE JEWS."

23:38
Matt. 27:37; Mark 15:26; John 19:19

39 And one of the criminals who were hanged *there* was hurling[m] abuse at Him, saying, "Are *You* not the Christ? Save[xi] Yourself and us!"

23:39
Matt. 27:44; Mark 15:32; Luke 23:39-43;
Luke 23:35,37

40 But the other answered, and rebuking him said,[m] "Do *you* not even fear God, since you are under the same sentence of condemnation?

41 "And we indeed justly, for we are receiving what we deserve for our deeds; but *this man* has done nothing wrong."

42 And he was saying,[m] "Jesus, remember[xi] me when You come in Your kingdom!"

43 And He said to him, "•Truly I say to you, †*today* you shall be with *Me* in Paradise."

23:43
2 Cor. 12:4; Rev. 2:7

44 And it was now about ˡthe *sixth* hour, and darkness fell over the whole land until ᵐthe *ninth* hour,

23:44
Luke 23:44-49:
Matt. 27:45-56;
Mark 15:33-41;
John 19:14

45 the sun being *obscured;* and the veil of the temple was *torn* in two.

23:45
Ex. 26:31-33;
Matt. 27:51

46 And Jesus, crying out with a loud voice, said, "Father,

23:46
Matt. 27:50; Mark 15:37; John 19:30;
Ps. 31:5

ˡi.e., 12 noon   ᵐi.e., 3 p.m.

INTO THY HANDS I COMMIT MY SPIRIT." And having said this, He breathed His last.

23:47
Matt. 27:54; Mark
15:39;
Matt. 9:8

47   Now when the centurion saw what had happened, he *began* praising^m God, saying, "Certainly this man was *innocent.*"

23:48
Luke 8:52; 18:13

48   And all the multitudes who came together for this spectacle, when they observed what had happened, *began* to return,^m beating their breasts.

23:49
Matt. 27:55f.;
Mark 15:40f.;
Luke 8:2; John
19:25

49   And all His acquaintances and the women who accompanied Him from Galilee, were standing at a *distance,* seeing these things.

Jesus Is Buried

23:50
Luke 23:50-56:
Matt. 27:57-61;
Mark 15:42-47;
John 19:38-42;
Mark 15:43

50   And behold, a man named Joseph, who was a member of the †*Council,* a good²⁵ᵃ and righteous man

23:51
Mark 15:43; Luke
2:25

51   (he had not consented⁺ to their plan and action), *a man* from Arimathea, a city of the Jews, who was waiting^m for the kingdom of God;

52   this man went to Pilate and asked for the body of Jesus.

53   And he took it down and wrapped it in a linen cloth, and laid Him in a tomb cut into the rock, where no one had ever lain.

23:54
Matt. 27:62; Mark
15:42

54   And it was the *preparation* day, and the Sabbath was about to begin.

23:55
Luke 23:49

55   Now the women who had come⁺ with Him out of Galilee followed after, and saw the tomb and how His body was laid.

23:56
Mark 16:1; Luke
24:1;
Ex. 20:10f.; Deut.
5:14

56   And they returned and prepared spices and perfumes. And on the Sabbath they rested according to the commandment.

The Resurrection

24:1
Luke 24:1-10:
Matt. 28:1-8;
Mark 16:1-8;
John 20:1-8

24   But on the first day of the week, at early dawn, they came to the tomb, bringing the *spices* which they had prepared.

2   And they found the stone rolled⁺ away from the tomb,

24:3
Luke 7:13; Acts
1:21

3   but when they entered, they did not find the body of the Lord Jesus.

24:4
John 20:12;
Luke 2:9; Acts
12:7

4   And it happened that while they were perplexed~¹ about this, behold, two men suddenly stood near them in dazzling apparel;

5   and as *the women* were *terrified* and bowed their faces to the ground, *the men* said to them, "Why do you seek the living One among the dead?

24:6
Mark 16:6;
Matt. 17:22f.;
Mark 9:30f.; Luke
9:44; 24:44

6 "He is not here, but He has risen. Remember^{xl} how He spoke to you while He was still in Galilee,

24:7
Matt. 16:21; Luke
24:46

7   saying that the *Son of Man* must be delivered^x into the

hands of *sinful* men, and be crucified,ˣ and the third day riseˣ again."

8   And they remembered His words,

9   and returned from the tomb and reported all these things to the eleven and to all the rest.

10   Now they were Mary Magdalene and Joanna and Mary the *mother* of James; also the other women with them were tellingᵐ these things to the apostles.

11   And these words appeared to them as nonsense, and they would not believeᵐ them.

12   [ⁿBut Peter arose and ran to the tomb; stooping and looking in, he *saw the linen wrappings only; and he went away to his home, marveling at that which had happened.⁺]

The Road to Emmaus

13 And behold, two of them were going~ that very day to a village named Emmaus, which was ᵒabout seven miles from Jerusalem.

14   And they were conversingᵐ with each other about all these things which had taken⁺ place.

15   And it came about that while they were conversing~ and discussing,~ Jesus Himself approached, and *began* traveling with them.

16   But their eyes were preventedᵐ from recognizingˣ¹ Him.

17   And He said to them, "What are these words that you are exchanging with one another as you are walking?" And they stood still, looking sad.

18   And one of them, named Cleopas, answered and said to Him, "Are *You* the only one visiting Jerusalem and unaware of the things which have happened here in these days?"

19   And He said to them, "What things?" And they said to Him, "The things about Jesus the Nazarene, who was a prophet mighty in deed and word in the sight of God and all the people,

20   and how the chief priests and our rulers delivered Him up to the sentence of death, and crucified Him.

21   "But *we* were hopingᵐ that it was *He* who was going to redeem³⁶ᵇ Israel. Indeed, besides² all this, it is the third day since these things happened.

22   "But also some women among us amazed us. When they were at the tomb early in the morning,

23   and did not find His body, they came, saying that they had also seen⁺ a *vision of angels,* who said that He was alive.

24   "And some of those who were with us went to the tomb and

24:8
John 2:22

24:10
Matt. 27:56;
Mark 6:30

24:11
Mark 16:11

24:12
John 20:3-6;
John 20:10

24:13
Mark 16:12

24:16
Luke 24:31; John
20:14; 21:4

24:19
Mark 1:24;
Matt. 21:11

24:20
Luke 23:13

24:21
Luke 1:68

24:22
Luke 24:1ff.

ⁿSome ancient mss. do not contain v. 12   ᵒI.e., 60 stadia, one stadion was about 600 feet

found it just exactly as the women also had said; but *Him* they did not see."

24:25
Matt. 26:24
25 And *He* said to them, "O foolish[20a] men and slow of heart to believe~ in all that the prophets have spoken!

24:26
Luke 24:7,44ff.;
Heb. 2:10; 1 Pet.
1:11
26 "Was it not necessary for the Christ to suffer[x] *these things* and to enter[x] into His glory?"

24:27
Gen. 3:15; 12:3;
Num. 21:9 [John
3:14]; Deut. 18:15
[John 1:45]; John
5:46; 2 Sam.
7:12-16; Is. 7:14
[Matt. 1:23]; Is.
9:1f. [Matt.
4:15f.]; Is. 42:1
[Matt. 12:18ff.]; Is.
53:4 [Matt. 8:17;
Luke 22:37]; Dan.
7:13 [Matt.
24:30]; Mic. 5:2
[Matt. 2:6]; Zech.
9:9 [Matt. 21:5];
Acts 13:27
27 And beginning with Moses and with all the prophets, He explained to them the things concerning Himself in all the Scriptures.

24:28
Mark 6:48
28 And they approached the village where they were going, and He acted as though He would go farther.

24:30
Matt. 14:19
29 And they urged Him, saying, "Stay[xi] with us, for it is *getting* toward evening, and the day is now nearly over." And He went in to stay[x] with them.

24:31
Luke 24:16
30 And it came about that when He had reclined[x] *at the table* with them, He took the bread and blessed *it,* and breaking *it,* He *began* giving[m] *it* to them.

31 And *their* eyes were opened and they recognized[1] Him; and *He* vanished from their sight.

24:32
Luke 24:45
32 And they said to one another, "Were not our hearts *burning~* within us while He was speaking[m] to us on the road, while He was explaining[m] the Scriptures to us?"

24:33
Mark 16:13;
Acts 1:14
33 And they arose that very hour and returned to Jerusalem, and found gathered+ together the eleven and those who were with them,

24:34
Luke 24:6;
1 Cor. 15:5
34 saying, "The Lord has *really risen,* and has appeared to Simon."

24:35
Luke 24:30f.
35 And they *began* to relate[m] their experiences on the road and how He was recognized by them in the breaking of the bread.

Other Appearances

24:36
Mark 16:14
36 And while they were telling these things, *He Himself* stood in their midst. p

24:37
Matt. 14:26; Mark
6:49
37 But they were startled and frightened and thought[m] that they were seeing~ a *spirit.*

38 And He said to them, "Why are you troubled,+ and why do doubts arise in your hearts?

24:39
John 20:20,27;
1 John 1:1
39 "See[xi] My hands and My feet, that it is +*I Myself;* touch[xi] Me and see,[xi] for a spirit does not have *flesh* and *bones* as you see that *I* have."

40 [qAnd when He had said this, He showed them His hands and His feet.]

24:41
Luke 24:11;
John 21:5
41 And while they still could not believe *it* for joy and were

pSome ancient mss. insert *And He says to them, "Peace be to you."* qMany mss. do not contain this verse

marveling, He said to them, "Have you anything here to eat?"

42   And they gave Him a piece of a broiled fish;

43   and He took it and ate *it* before them.

44   Now He said to them, "These are My words which I spoke to you while I was still with you, that all things which are writ-ten⁺ about Me in the Law of Moses and the Prophets and the Psalms must be fulfilled."ˣ

45   Then He opened their *minds*³³ᵇ to understand~²⁹ᶠ the Scriptures,

46   and He said to them, "Thus it is written,⁺ that the Christ should *suffer*ˣ and riseˣ again from the dead the third day;

47   and that repentance for forgiveness of sins should be pro-claimedˣ in His name to all the nations, beginning from Jerusa-lem.

48   "You are witnesses of these things.

49   "And behold, *I* am sending forth the promise of My Father upon you; but *you* are to stayˣˡ in the city until you are clothedˣ with power³²ᵃ from on high."

The Ascension

50   And He led them out as far as Bethany, and He lifted up His hands and blessed them.

51   And it came about that while He was blessing~ them, He parted from them.ʳ

52   And theyˢ returned to Jerusalem with great joy,

53   and were continually in the temple, praising God.

ʳSome mss. add *and was carried up into heaven*   ˢSome mss. insert *worshiped Him, and*

24:43
Acts 10:41
24:44
Luke 9:22,44f.;
18:31-34; 22:37;
Luke 24:27;
Ps. 2:7ff. [Acts
13:33]; Ps. 16:10
[Acts 2:27]; Ps.
27:34-46]; Ps.
69:1-21 [John
19:28ff.]; Ps. 72;
110:1 [Matt.
22:43f.]; Ps.
118:22f. [Matt.
21:42]
24:45
Luke 24:32; Acts
16:14; 1 John
5:20
24:46
Luke 24:26,44;
Luke 24:7
24:47
Acts 5:31; 10:43;
13:38; 26:18;
Matt. 28:19
24:48
Acts 1:8,22; 2:32;
3:15; 4:33; 5:32;
10:39,41; 13:31;
1 Pet. 5:1
24:49
John 14:26;
Acts 1:4
24:50
Matt. 21:17; Acts
1:12

The Gospel According to
John

The Deity of Jesus Christ

1:1
Gen. 1:1; Col.
1:17; 1 John 1:1;
John 1:14; Rev.
19:13;
John 17:5; 1 John
1:2;
Phil. 2:6
1:3
John 1:10; 1 Cor.
8:6; Col. 1:16;
Heb. 1:2
1:4
John 5:26; 11:25;
14:6;
John 8:12; 9:5;
12:46
1:5
John 3:19

1 In the beginning was the Word,[43a] and the Word was with God, and the Word was *God.*

2 He was in the beginning with God.

3 All things came into being by Him, and apart from Him •*nothing* came into being that has come⁺ into being.

4 *In Him* was life,[30b] and the life was the light of men.

5 And the light shines in the darkness, and the darkness did not ᵃcomprehend it.

The Witness of John

1:6
Matt. 3:1

6 There ᵇcame a man, sent⁺ from God, whose name was John.

1:7
John 1:15,19,32;
3:26; 5:33;
John 1:12; Acts
19:4; Gal. 3:26
1:8
John 1:20

7 He came for a witness, that he might bearˣ witness of the light, that all might believeˣ through him.

8 *He* was not the light, but *came* that he might bearˣ witness of the light.

1:9
1 John 2:8

9 There was the true light ᶜwhich, coming into the world, enlightens every man.

1:10
1 Cor. 8:6; Col.
1:16; Heb. 1:2
1:12
John 11:52; Gal.
3:26;
John 1:7; 3:18; 1
John 3:23; 5:13
1:13
John 3:5f.; James
1:18; 1 Pet. 1:23;
1 John 2:29; 3:9
1:14
Rev. 19:13;
Rom. 1:3; Gal.
4:4; Phil. 2:7f.;
1 Tim. 3:16; Heb.
2:14; 1 John 1:1f.;
4:2; 2 John 7;
Rev. 21:3;
Luke 9:32; John
2:11; 17:22,24;
2 Pet. 1:16f.;
1 John 1:1;
John 1:17; Rom.
5:21; 6:14;
John 8:32; 14:6;
18:37
1:15
John 1:7;
Matt. 3:11; John
1:27,30;
John 1:30

10 He was in the world, and the world was made *through Him,* and the world did not know²⁹ᵃ Him.

11 He came to His ᵈown, and those who were His own did not receive Him.

12 But as many as received⁵ᵇ Him, to them He gave the right to become children of God, *even* to those who believe in His name,

13 who were born not of blood, nor of the will of the flesh, nor of the will of man, but of *God.*

The Word Made Flesh

14 And the Word[43a] became *flesh,* and dwelt among us, and we beheld His glory, glory as of the only begotten from the Father, full of grace and truth.

15 John *bore witness of Him, and cried⁺ out, saying, "This

ᵃOr, *overpower* ᵇOr, *came into being* ᶜOr, *which enlightens every man coming into the world* ᵈOr, *own things, possessions, domain*

182

was He of whom I said, 'He who comes after me has a *higher rank* than I, for He existed⁺ before me.' "

16 For of *His fulness* we have all received, and grace upon grace.

17 For the Law was given through Moses; grace and truth were realized through *Jesus Christ.*

18 No man has seen⁺ *God* at any time; the only begotten ᵉGod, who is in the bosom of the Father, *He* has explained *Him.*

The Testimony of John

19 And this is the witness of John, when the Jews sent to him priests and Levites from Jerusalem to askˣ him, "Who are you?"

20 And he confessed, and did not deny, and he confessed, "*I am not the Christ.*"

21 And they asked him, "What then? Are you *Elijah?*" And he *said, "I am not." "Are you the *Prophet?*" And he answered, "No."

22 They said then to him, "Who are you, so that we may giveˣ an answer to those who sent us? What do you say about yourself?"

23 He said, "I am A VOICE OF ONE CRYING IN THE WILDERNESS, 'MAKEˣⁱ STRAIGHT THE WAY OF THE LORD,' as Isaiah the prophet said."

24 Now they had been sent⁺ from the Pharisees.

25 And they asked him, and said to him, "Why then are you baptizing, if *you* are not the Christ, nor Elijah, nor the Prophet?"

26 John answered them saying, "*I* baptize ⁱin water, *but among you* stands⁺ One whom you do not know.²⁹ᵉ

27 "*It is* He who comes after me, the thong of whose sandal *I* am not worthy to untie."ˣ

28 These things took place in Bethany beyond the Jordan, where John was baptizing. ~

29 The next day he *saw Jesus coming to him, and *said, "Behold, the Lamb of God who takes away the sin of the world!

30 "This is He on behalf of whom I said, 'After me comes a Man who has a *higher rank* than I, for He existed⁺ before me.'

31 "And *I* did not recognize Him, but in order that He might be manifestedˣ to Israel, *I* came baptizing ⁱin *water.*"

32 And John bore witness saying, "I have beheld⁺ the Spirit descending as a dove out of heaven, and He remained upon Him.

33 "And *I* did not recognize Him, but *He* who sent me to baptize~ ⁱin water said to me, 'He upon whom you seeˣ the

ᵉSome later mss. read *Son*   ⁱThe Gr. here can be translated *in, with* or *by*

Cross-references (right margin):

1:16
Eph. 1:23; 3:19;
4:13; Col. 1:19;
2:9
1:17
John 7:19;
John 1:14; Rom.
5:21; 6:14;
John 8:32; 14:6;
18:37
1:18
Ex. 33:20; John
6:46; Col. 1:15; 1
Tim. 6:16; 1 John
4:12;
John 3:16,18;
1 John 4:9;
Luke 16:22; John
13:23;
John 3:11
1:19
John 1:7;
John 2:18,20;
5:10,15f.,18;
6:41,52; 7:1,11,
13,15,35; 8:22,
48,52,57; 9:18,
22; 10:24,31,33;
Matt. 15:1
1:20
Luke 3:15f.; John
3:28
1:21
Matt. 11:14;
16:14;
Deut. 18:15,18;
Matt. 21:11; John
1:25
1:23
Is. 40:3; Matt. 3:3;
Mark 1:3; Luke
3:4
1:25
Deut. 18:15,18;
Matt. 21:11; John
1:21
1:26
Matt. 3:11; Mark
1:8; Luke 3:16;
Acts 1:5
1:27
Matt. 3:11; John
1:30;
Matt. 3:11; Mark
1:7; Luke 3:16
1:28
John 3:26; 10:40
1:29
Is. 53:7; John
1:36; Acts 8:32; 1
Pet. 1:19; Rev.
5:6,8,12f.; 6:1;
Matt. 1:21; 1 John
3:5
1:30
Matt. 3:11; John
1:27;
John 1:15
1:32
John 1:7;
Matt. 3:16; Mark
1:10; Luke 3:22
1:33
Matt. 3:11; Mark
1:8; Luke 3:16;
Acts 1:5

Spirit descending and remaining upon Him, this is the one who baptizes in the Holy Spirit.'

1:34
Matt. 4:3; John
1:49

34 "And *I* have seen,* and have borne* witness that this is the Son of God."

Jesus' Public Ministry, First Converts

1:35
John 1:29

35 Again the next day John was standing with two of his disciples,

1:36
John 1:29

36 and he looked upon Jesus as He walked, and *said, "Behold, the Lamb of God!"

37 And the two disciples heard him speak, and they followed Jesus.

1:38
Matt. 23:7f.; John
1:49

38 And Jesus turned, and beheld them following, and *said to them, "What do you seek?" And they said to Him, "Rabbi (which translated means Teacher), where are You staying?".

1:40
Matt. 4:18-22;
Mark 1:16-20;
Luke 5:2-11; John
1:40-42

39 He *said to them, "Come, ~ and you will see." They came therefore and saw where He was staying; and they stayed with Him that day, for it was about the 9tenth hour.

1:41
Dan. 9:25; John
4:25

40 One of the two who heard John *speak,* and followed Him, was Andrew, Simon Peter's brother.

1:42
Matt. 16:17; John
21:15-17;
1 Cor. 1:12; 3:22;
9:5; 15:5; Gal.
1:18; 2:9,11,14;
Matt. 16:18

41 He *found †first his own brother Simon, and *said to him, "We have found* the Messiah" (which translated means Christ).

1:43
John 1:29,35;
Matt. 4:12; John
1:28; 2:11;

42 He brought him to Jesus. Jesus looked at him, and said, "You are Simon the son of John; you shall be called Cephas" (which is translated Peter).

Matt. 10:3; John
1:44-48; 6:5,7;
12:21f.; 14:8f.;
Matt. 8:22

43 The next day He purposed to go× forth into Galilee, and He *found Philip. And Jesus *said to him, "Follow ~ Me."

1:44
Matt. 10:3; John
1:44-48; 6:5,7;
12:21f.; 14:8f.;
Matt. 11:21

44 Now Philip was from Bethsaida, of the city of Andrew and Peter.

1:45
Matt. 10:3; John
1:44-48; 6:5,7;
12:21f.; 14:8f.;
John 1:46-49;
21:2;
Luke 24:27;
Matt. 2:23;
Luke 2:48; 3:23;
4:22; John 6:42

45 Philip *found Nathanael and *said to him, "We have found* Him of whom Moses in the Law and *also* the Prophets wrote, Jesus of Nazareth, the son of Joseph."

1:46
John 7:41,52;
Matt. 10:3; John
1:44-48; 6:5,7;
12:21f.; 14:8f.

46 And Nathanael *said to him, "Can any good 25a thing come out of *Nazareth?*" Philip *said to him, "Come and see." ×l

1:47
Rom. 9:4

47 Jesus saw Nathanael coming to Him, and *said of him, "Behold, an Israelite indeed, in whom is no guile!"

1:48
Matt. 10:3; John
1:44-48; 6:5,7;
12:21f.; 14:8f.

48 Nathanael *said to Him, "How do You know 29a me?" Jesus answered and said to him, "Before Philip called× you, when you were *under the fig tree,* I saw you."

1:49
John 1:38;
John 1:34;
Matt. 2:2; 27:42;
Mark 15:32; John
12:13

49 Nathanael answered Him, "Rabbi, *You* are the Son of God; *You* are the *King* of Israel."

50 Jesus answered and said to him, "Because I said to you

9Perhaps 10 a.m. (Roman time)

that I saw you under the fig tree, do you believe? You shall see *greater †things* than these."

51   And He *said to him, "•Truly, •truly, I say to you, you shall see the heavens opened,• and the angels of God ascending and descending on the Son of Man."

Miracle at Cana

2   And on the third day there was a wedding in Cana of Galilee, and the mother of Jesus was there;

2   and Jesus also was invited, and His disciples, to the wedding.

3   And when the wine gave out, the mother of Jesus *said to Him, "They have no wine."

4   And Jesus *said to her, "Woman, what do I have to do with you? My hour has not yet come."

5   His mother *said to the servants, "Whatever He says~ to you, do^{xi} it."

6   Now there were six stone waterpots set there for the Jewish custom of purification, containing twenty or thirty gallons each.

7   Jesus *said to them, "Fill^{xi} the waterpots with water." And they filled them up to the brim.

8   And He *said to them, "Draw^{xi} *some* out now, and take it to the ʰheadwaiter." And they took it *to him.*

9   And when the headwaiter tasted the water which had become• *wine,* and did not know where it came from (but the servants who had drawn• the water knew), the headwaiter *called the bridegroom,

10   and *said to him, "Every man serves the *good wine* first, and when *men* have drunk^x freely, *then* that which is poorer; *you* have kept• the good wine until now."

11   This beginning of *His* signs Jesus did in Cana of Galilee, and manifested His glory, and His disciples believed in Him.

12   After this He went down to Capernaum, He and His mother, and *His* brothers, and His disciples; and there they stayed a few days.

First Passover—Cleansing the Temple

13   And the Passover of the Jews was at hand, and Jesus went up to Jerusalem.

14   And He found in the temple those who were selling oxen and sheep and doves, and the moneychangers seated.

15   And He made a scourge of cords, and drove *them all* out of

ʰOr, *steward*

1:51
Ezek. 1:1; Matt.
3:16; Luke 3:21;
Acts 7:56; 10:11;
Rev. 19:11;
Gen. 28:12;
Matt. 8:20

2:1
John 1:29,35,43;
John 2:11; 4:46;
21:2;
Matt. 12:46
2:2
John 1:40-49;
2:12,17,22; 3:22;
4:2,8,27; 6:8,12,
16,22,24,60f.,66;
7:3; 8:31

2:4
John 19:26;
Matt. 8:29;
John 7:6,8,30;
8:20
2:5
Matt. 12:46

2:6
Mark 7:3f.; John
3:25

2:9
John 4:46

2:10
Matt. 24:49; Luke
12:45; Acts 2:15;
1 Cor. 11:21;
Eph. 5:18; 1
Thess. 5:7; Rev.
17:2,6
2:11
John 2:23; 3:2;
4:54; 6:2,14,26,
30; 7:31; 9:16;
10:41; 11:47;
12:18,37; 20:30;
John 1:43;
John 1:14
2:12
Matt. 4:13;
Matt. 12:46;
John 2:2
2:13
Deut. 16:1-6;
John 5:1; 6:4;
11:55;
Luke 2:41; John
2:23
2:14
John 2:14-16;
Matt. 21:12ff.;
Mark 11:15,17;
Luke 19:45f.; Mal.
3:1ff.

the temple, with the sheep and the oxen; and He poured out the coins of the moneychangers, and overturned their tables;

2:16
Matt. 21:12;
Luke 2:49

16 and to those who were selling the doves He said, "Take^{xl} these things away; stop making[○] My Father's house a house of merchandise."

2:17
John 2:2;
Ps. 69:9

17 His disciples remembered that it was written,⁺ "ZEAL FOR THY HOUSE WILL CONSUME ME."

2:18
John 1:19;
Matt. 12:38

18 The Jews therefore answered and said to Him, "What sign do You show to us, seeing that You do these things?"

2:19
Matt. 26:61;
27:40; Mark
14:58; 15:29;
Acts 6:14
2:20
John 1:19;
Ezra 5:16
2:21
1 Cor. 6:19
2:22
John 2:2;
Luke 24:8; John
2:17; 12:16;
14:26;
Ps. 16:10; Luke
24:26f.; John
20:9; Acts 13:33
2:23
John 2:13;
John 2:11

19 Jesus answered and said to them, "Destroy^{xl} this temple, and in *three* days I will raise it up."

20 The Jews therefore said, "It took *forty-six* years to build this temple, and will *You* raise it up in *three* days?"

21 But *He* was speaking of the temple of His body.

22 When therefore He was raised from the dead, His disciples remembered that He said^m this; and they believed the Scripture, and the word which Jesus had spoken.

23 Now when He was in Jerusalem at the Passover, during the feast, many believed in His name, beholding His signs which He was doing.^{xx}

2:24
Acts 1:24; 15:8

24 But Jesus, on His part, was not entrusting^m Himself to them, for He knew^{~29a} all men,

2:25
Matt. 9:4; John
1:42,47; 6:61,64;
13:11

25 and because He did not need anyone to bear^x witness concerning man for He Himself knew^m what was in man.

The New Birth

3:1
John 7:50; 19:39;
Luke 23:13; John
7:26,48

3 Now there was a man of the Pharisees, named Nicodemus, a ruler of the Jews;

3:2
Matt. 23:7; John
3:26;
John 2:11;
John 9:33; 10:38;
14:10f.; Acts
2:22; 10:38

2 this man came to Him by night, and said to Him, "Rabbi, we know that You have come⁺ from *God as* a teacher; for no one can do[~] these signs that You do unless *God* is with him."

3:3
2 Cor. 5:17;
1 Pet. 1:23;
Matt. 19:24;
21:31; Mark 9:47;
10:14f.; John 3:5

3 Jesus answered and said to him, "•Truly, •truly, I say to you, unless one is born^x *again,* he cannot see^x the kingdom of God."

4 Nicodemus *said to Him, "How can a man be born^x when he is old? He cannot enter^x a second time into his mother's womb and be born,^x can he?"

3:5
Ezek. 36:25-27;
Eph. 5:26; Titus
3:5;
Matt. 19:24;
21:31; Mark 9:47;
10:14f.; John 3:3

5 Jesus answered, "•Truly, •truly, I say to you, unless one is born^x of water and the Spirit, he cannot enter^x into the kingdom of God.

3:6
John 1:13; 1 Cor.
15:50

6 "That which is born⁺ of the flesh is *flesh,* and that which is born⁺ of the Spirit is *spirit.*

7 "Do not marvel[○] that I said to you, 'You must be born^x *again.'*

8 "The wind blows where it *wishes* and you hear the sound of it, but do not know where it comes from and where it is going; so is everyone who is born⁺ of the Spirit."

9 Nicodemus answered and said to Him, "How can these things be?"

10 Jesus answered and said to him, "Are *you* the teacher of Israel, and do not understand *these things?*

11 "•Truly, •truly, I say to you, we speak that which we know, and bear witness of that which we have seen;⁺ and you do not receive our witness.

12 "If I told you *earthly things* and you do not believe, how shall you believe if I tell* you *heavenly things?*

13 "And no one has ascended⁺ into heaven, but He who descended from heaven, *even* the Son of Man.

14 "And as Moses lifted up the serpent in the wilderness, even so must the Son of Man be lifted* up;

15 that whoever ⁱbelieves may in Him have~ ⁺eternal life.

16 "For God so loved³¹ᵃ the world, that He gave His *only begotten* Son, that whoever believes in Him should not perish,* but have~ ⁺eternal life.

17 "For God did not send the Son into the world to judge* the world, but that the world should be *saved* through Him.

18 "He who believes in Him is not judged; he who does not believe has been judged⁺ already, because he has not believed⁺ in the name of the only begotten Son of God.

19 "And this is the judgment, that the light is come⁺ into the world, and men loved the *darkness* rather than the light; for their deeds were *evil.* ¹⁰ᵇ

20 "For everyone who does¹⁹ᵇ evil¹⁰ᵈ hates the light, and does not come to the light, lest his deeds should be exposed.*

21 "But he who practices¹⁹ᵃ the truth comes to the light, that *his* deeds may be manifested* as having been wrought⁺ *in God."*

John's Last Testimony

22 After these things Jesus and His disciples came into the land of Judea, and there He was spending^ᵐ time with them and baptizing.^ᵐ

23 And John also was baptizing~ in Aenon near Salim, because there was much water there; and they were coming^ᵐ and were being baptized.^ᵐ

24 For John had not yet been thrown⁺ into prison.

25 There arose therefore a discussion on the part of John's disciples with a Jew about purification.

ⁱSome mss. read *believes in Him may have eternal life*

3:8
Ps. 135:7; Eccl. 11:5; Ezek. 37:9

3:10
Luke 2:46; 5:17; Acts 5:34

3:11
John 1:18; 7:16f.; 8:26,28; 12:49; 14:24; John 3:32

3:13
Deut. 30:12; Prov. 30:4; Acts 2:34; Rom. 10:6; Eph. 4:9; John 3:31; 6:38, 42; Matt. 8:20
3:14
Num. 21:9; Matt. 8:20; John 8:28; 12:34
3:15
John 20:31; 1 John 5:11-13
3:16
Rom. 5:8; Eph. 2:4; 2 Thess. 2:16; 1 John 4:10; Rev. 1:5; Rom. 8:32; 1 John 4:9; John 1:18; 3:18; John 3:36; 6:40; 11:25f.
3:17
John 3:34; 5:36, 38; 6:29,38,57; 7:29; 8:42; 10:36; 11:42; 17:3,8,18, 21,23,25; 20:21; Luke 19:10; John 8:15; 12:47; 1 John 4:14
3:18
Mark 16:16; John 5:24; John 1:18; 1 John 4:9
3:19
John 1:4; 8:12; 9:5; 12:46; John 7:7
3:20
John 3:20,21; Eph. 5:11,13
3:21
1 John 1:6
3:22
John 2:2; John 4:1,2

3:24
Matt. 4:12; 14:3; Mark 6:17; Luke 3:20
3:25
John 2:6

3:26
Matt. 23:7; John
3:2;
John 1:28;
John 1:7

26   And they came to John and said to him, "Rabbi, He who was with you beyond the Jordan, to whom you have borne⁺ witness, behold, He is baptizing, and all are coming to Him."

3:27
1 Cor. 4:7; Heb.
5:4;
James 1:17

27   John answered and said, "A man can receive~ •*nothing*, unless it has been given⁺ him from heaven.

3:28
John 1:20,23

28   "*You yourselves* bear me witness, that I said, '*I* am not the Christ,' but, 'I have been sent⁺ before Him.'

3:29
Matt. 9:15; 25:1;
John 15:11;
16:24; 17:13;
Phil. 2:2; 1 John
1:4; 2 John 12

29   "He who has the bride is the bridegroom; but the friend of the bridegroom, who stands and hears him, rejoices *greatly*⁴ because of the bridegroom's voice. And so this joy of mine has been made⁺ full.

30   "*He* must increase,~ but *I* must decrease.~

3:31
Matt. 28:18; John
3:13; 8:23;
1 Cor. 15:47; 1
John 4:5

31   "He who comes from above is above all, he who is of the earth is from the earth and speaks of the ⁺earth. He who comes from heaven is *above* ⁺*all*.

3:32
John 3:11

32   "What He has seen⁺ and heard, of that He bears witness; and no man receives His witness.

3:33
John 6:27; Rom.
4:11; 15:28; 1
Cor. 9:2; 2 Cor.
1:22; Eph. 1:13;
4:30; 2 Tim. 2:19;
Rev. 7:3-8
3:34
John 3:17;
Matt. 12:18; Luke
4:18; Acts 1:2;
10:38
3:35
Matt. 28:18; John
5:20; 17:2;
Matt. 11:27; Luke
10:22
3:36
John 3:16;
Acts 14:2; Heb.
3:18

33   "He who has received *His* witness has set his seal to *this*, that God is ⁺true.

34   "For He whom *God* has sent speaks the *words*⁴³ᵇ *of God;* for He gives the Spirit *without measure*.

35   "The Father loves³¹ᵃ the Son, and has given⁺ *all things* into His hand.

36   "He who believes in the Son has eternal life; but he who does not obey the Son shall not see life, but the wrath⁷ᵇ of God abides on him."

Jesus Goes to Galilee

4:1
Luke 7:13;
John 3:22,26; 1
Cor. 1:17

4   When therefore the Lord knew that the Pharisees had heard that Jesus was making and baptizing more disciples than John

4:2
John 3:22,26; 1
Cor. 1:17;
John 2:2

2   (although² Jesus Himself was not baptizing,ᵐ but His disciples were),

4:3
John 3:22;
John 2:11f.
4:4
Luke 9:52
4:5
Luke 9:52;
Gen. 33:19; Josh.
24:32;
Gen. 48:22; John
4:12

3   He left Judea, and departed again into Galilee.

4   And He had to pass through Samaria.

5   So He *came to a city of Samaria, called Sychar, near the parcel of ground that Jacob gave to his son Joseph;

6   and Jacob's well was there. Jesus therefore, being wearied⁺ from His journey, was sittingᵐ thus by the well. It was about ⁱthe sixth hour.

ⁱPerhaps 6 p.m. (Roman time)

The Woman of Samaria

7 There *came a woman of Samaria to draw[x] water. Jesus *said to her, "Give[xi] Me a drink."

8 For His disciples had gone away into the city to buy[x] food.

9 The Samaritan woman therefore *said to Him, "How is it that *You*, being a +*Jew*, ask *me* for a drink since I am a *Samaritan* +*woman?*" (For Jews have no dealings with Samaritans.)

10 Jesus answered and said to her, "If you knew the gift[24a] of God, and who it is who says to you, 'Give[xi] Me a drink,' you would have asked Him, and He would have given you *living* water."

11 She *said to Him, "Sir, You have nothing to draw with and the well is deep; where then do You get that *living* water?

12 "*You* are not +greater[26a] than our father Jacob, are You, who gave us the well, and drank of it himself, and his sons, and his cattle?"

13 Jesus answered and said to her, "Everyone who drinks of +*this* water shall thirst again;

14 but whoever drinks[x] of the water that *I* shall give him shall •never thirst; but the water that I shall give him shall become in him a well of water springing up to +eternal life."

15 The woman *said to Him, "Sir, give[xi] me this water, so I will not be thirsty,~ nor come~ all the way here to draw."~

16 He *said to her, "Go, call[xi] your husband, and come[xi] here."

17 The woman answered and said, "I have no husband." Jesus *said to her, "You have well said, 'I have no *husband'*;

18 for you have had *five* husbands, and the one whom you now have is not your *husband;* this you have said+ truly."

19 The woman *said to Him, "Sir, I perceive that You are a *prophet.*

20 "Our fathers worshiped in this mountain, and *you people* say that in *Jerusalem* is the place where men ought to worship."~

21 Jesus *said to her, "Woman, believe~ Me, an hour is coming when neither in this mountain, nor in Jerusalem, shall you worship the Father.

22 "*You* worship that which you do not know; *we* worship that which we know, for salvation is from the *Jews*.

23 "But an hour is coming, and now is, when the true worshipers shall worship the Father in spirit and truth; for *such people* the Father seeks to be His worshipers.

24 "God is *spirit,* and those who worship Him must worship~[44b] in *spirit* and *truth.*"

4:8
John 2:2;
John 4:5,39
4:9
Luke 9:52;
Ezra 4:3-6,11ff.;
Matt. 10:5; John
8:48; Acts 10:28
4:10
Jer. 2:13; John
4:14; 7:37f.; Rev.
7:17; 21:6; 22:1,
17

4:11
Jer. 2:13; John
4:14; 7:37f.; Rev.
7:17; 21:6; 22:1,
17
4:12
John 4:6

4:14
John 6:35; 7:38;
Matt. 25:46; John
6:27

4:15
John 6:35

4:19
Matt. 21:11; Luke
7:16,39; 24:19;
John 6:14; 7:40;
9:17
4:20
Gen. 33:20; John
4:12;
Deut. 11:29;
Josh. 8:33;
Luke 9:53
4:21
John 4:23; 5:25,
28; 16:2,32;
Mal. 1:11; 1 Tim.
2:8
4:22
2 Kin. 17:28-41;
Is. 2:3; Rom.
3:1f.; 9:4f.
4:23
John 4:21; 5:25,
28; 16:2,32;
Phil. 3:3
4:24
Phil. 3:3

4:25
Dan. 9:25; John
1:41;
Matt. 1:16; 27:17,
22; Luke 2:11

25 The woman *said to Him, "I know that Messiah is coming (He who is called Christ); when *that One* comes, He will declare all things to us."

4:26
John 8:24,28,58;
9:37; 13:19

26 Jesus *said to her, "⁺*I* who speak to you am *He.*"

4:27
John 4:8

27 And at this point His disciples came, and they marveled^ᵐ that He had been speaking^ᵐ with a woman; yet² no one said, "What do You seek?" or, "Why do You speak with her?"

28 So the woman left her waterpot, and went into the city, and *said to the men,

4:29
John 4:17f.;
Matt. 12:23; John
7:26,31

29 "Come, see^{ˣⁱ} a man who told me all the things that I *have* done; this is not the Christ, is it?"

30 They went out of the city, and were coming^ᵐ to Him.

4:31
Matt. 23:7; 26:25,
49; Mark 9:5;
11:21; 14:45;
John 1:38,49; 3:2,
26; 6:25; 9:2;
11:8

31 In the meanwhile the disciples were requesting^ᵐ Him, saying, "Rabbi, eat."^{ˣⁱ}

32 But He said to them, "*I* have food to eat^ˣ that *you* do not know about."

4:33
Luke 6:13-16;
John 1:40-49; 2:2

33 The disciples therefore were saying^ᵐ to one another, "No one brought Him *anything* to eat,^ˣ did he?"

4:34
John 5:30; 6:38;
John 5:36; 17:4;
19:28,30

34 Jesus *said to them, "•*My* food is to do^ˣ the will of Him who sent Me, and to accomplish^ˣ *His* work.

4:35
Matt. 9:37,38;
Luke 10:2

35 "Do you not say, 'There are yet four months, and *then* comes the harvest'? Behold, I say to you, lift^{ˣⁱ} up your eyes, and look^{ˣⁱ} on the fields, that they are ⁺white for harvest.

4:36
Prov. 11:18;
1 Cor. 9:17f.;
Rom. 1:13;
Matt. 19:29; John
3:36; 4:14; 5:24;
Rom. 2:7; 6:23

36 "Already he who reaps is receiving *wages,* and is gathering fruit for life ⁺eternal; that he who sows and he who reaps may *rejoice~ together.*

4:37
Job 31:8; Mic.
6:15

37 "For in this *case* the saying is true, 'One sows, and another reaps.'

38 "I sent you to reap~ that for which you have not labored;⁺ others have labored,⁺ and *you* have entered⁺ into *their labor.*"

The Samaritans

4:39
John 4:5,30;
John 4:29

39 And from that city many of the Samaritans believed in Him because of the word of the woman who testified, "He told me all the things that I *have* done."

40 So when the Samaritans came to Him, they were asking^ᵐ Him to stay^ˣ with them; and He stayed there two days.

41 And many more believed because of His word;

4:42
Matt. 1:21; Luke
2:11; John 1:29;
Acts 5:31; 13:23;
1 Tim. 4:10; 1
John 4:14

42 and they were saying^ᵐ to the woman, "It is no longer because of what *you* said that we believe, for we have heard⁺ for *ourselves* and know that this One is *indeed* the Savior of the world."

4:43
John 4:40

43 And after the two days He went forth from there into Galilee.

44   For Jesus Himself testified that a prophet has no honor in his *own* country.

4:44
Matt. 13:57; Mark
6:4; Luke 4:24

45   So when He came to Galilee, the Galileans received Him, having seen⁺ all the things that He did in Jerusalem at the feast; for they themselves also went to the feast.

4:45
John 2:23

Healing a Nobleman's Son

46   He came therefore again to Cana of Galilee where He had made the water wine. And there was a certain royal official, whose son was sickᵐ at Capernaum.

4:46
John 2:1;
John 2:9;
Luke 4:23; John
2:12

47   When he heard that Jesus had come out of Judea into Galilee, he went to Him, and was requestingᵐ *Him* to comeˣ down and healˣ¹⁵ᵇ his *son;* for he was at the point of death.

4:47
John 4:3,54

48   Jesus therefore said to him, "Unless you *people* seeˣ signs and wonders, you *simply* will •*not* believe."ˣ

4:48
Dan. 4:2f.; 6:27;
Matt. 24:24; Mark
13:22; Acts 2:19,
22,43; 4:30; 5:12;
6:8; 7:36; 14:3;
15:12; Rom.
15:19; 1 Cor.
1:22; 2 Cor.
12:12; 2 Thess.
2:9; Heb. 2:4

49   The royal official *said to Him, "Sir, comeˣⁱ down before my child dies."ˣ

50   Jesus *said to him, "Go your way; your son lives." The man *believed* the word that Jesus spoke to him, and he started off.

4:50
Matt. 8:13

51   And as he was now going down, *his* slaves met him, saying that his son was living.

52   So he inquired of them the hour when he began to get better. They said therefore to him, "Yesterday at the ᵏ*seventh* hour the fever left him."

53   So the father knew that *it was* at that hour in which Jesus said to him, "Your son lives"; and *he himself* believed, and his *whole* household.

4:53
Acts 11:14

54   This is again a second sign that Jesus performed, when He had come out of Judea into Galilee.

4:54
John 2:11;
John 4:45f.

The Healing at Bethesda

5   After these things there was ˡa feast of the Jews, and Jesus went up to Jerusalem.

5:1
Deut. 16:1; John
2:13

2   Now there is in Jerusalem by the sheep *gate* a pool, which is called in Hebrew Bethesda, having five ⁺porticoes.

5:2
Neh. 3:1,32;
12:39;
John 19:13,17,20;
20:16; Acts
21:40; Rev. 9:11;
16:16

3   In these layᵐ a multitude of those who were sick, blind, lame, and withered, [ᵐwaiting for the moving of the waters;

4   for an angel of the Lord went down at certain seasons into the pool, and stirred up the water; whoever then first, after the stirring up of the water, stepped in was made well from whatever disease with which he was afflicted.]

ᵏPerhaps 7 p.m. (Roman time)   ˡMany mss. read *the feast*, i.e., the Passover   ᵐMany mss. do not contain the remainder of v. 3 nor v. 4

5   And a certain man was there, who had been *thirty-eight* years in his sickness.

6   When Jesus saw him lying there, and knew that he had already been a long time *in that condition,* He *said to him, "Do you wish to get well?"

5:7
John 5:4

7   The sick man answered Him, "Sir, I have no man to put[x] me into the pool when the water is stirred[x] up, but while *I* am coming, another steps down *before me."*

5:8
Matt. 9:6; Mark
2:11; Luke 5:24
5:9
John 9:14

8   Jesus *said to him, "Arise, take[xi] up your pallet, and walk."

9   And immediately the man became well, and took up his pallet and *began* to walk.[xx]

Now it was the Sabbath on that day.

5:10
John 1:19; 5:15,
16,18;
Neh. 13:19; Jer.
17:21f.; Matt.
12:2; Luke 6:2;
John 7:23; 9:16

10   Therefore the Jews were saying[xx] to him who was cured,[+15a] "It is the Sabbath, and it is not permissible for you to carry[x] your pallet."

11   But he answered them, "He who made me well was the one who said to me, 'Take[xi] up your pallet and walk.' "

12   They asked him, "Who is the man who said to you, 'Take[xi] up *your pallet,* and walk'?"

13   But he who was healed[15b] did not know who it was; for Jesus had slipped away while there was a crowd in *that* place.

5:14
Mark 2:5; John
8:11;
Ezra 9:14

14   Afterward Jesus *found him in the temple, and said to him, "Behold, you have become[+] *well;* do not sin[θ] anymore, so that nothing worse may befall you."

5:15
John 1:19; 5:16,
18

15   The man went away, and told the Jews that it was [†]Jesus who had made him well.

5:16
John 1:19; 5:10,
15,18

16   And for this reason the Jews were persecuting[xx] Jesus, because He was doing[xx] these things on the Sabbath.

17   But He answered them, "My Father is working until now, and *I* Myself am working."

Jesus' Equality with God

5:18
John 1:19; 5:15,
16;
John 5:16; 7:1;
John 10:33; 19:7

18   For this cause therefore the Jews were seeking[xx] all the more to kill[x] Him, because He not only was breaking[xx] the Sabbath, but also was calling[xx] God His *own Father,* making Himself *equal* with God.

5:19
Matt. 26:39; John
5:30; 6:38; 8:28;
12:49; 14:10

19   Jesus therefore answered and was saying[xx] to them, "•Truly, •truly, I say to you, the Son can do[~19a] •*nothing* of Himself, unless *it is* something He sees[~] the Father doing; for whatever *the Father* does,[~] *these things* the Son also does in like manner.

5:20
Matt. 3:17; John
3:35; 2 Pet. 1:17;
John 14:12

20   "For the Father loves[31b] the Son, and shows Him *all things* that He Himself is doing; and *greater*[26a] works than these will He show Him, that you may marvel.[~]

21 "For just as the Father raises the dead and gives them life, even so the Son also gives life to whom *He wishes.*

5:21
Rom. 4:17; 8:11;
John 11:25

22 "For not even the Father judges anyone, but He has given⁺ *all* judgment to the Son,

5:22
John 5:27; 9:39;
Acts 10:42; 17:31

23 in order that all may honor~ the Son, even as they honor the Father. He who does not honor the Son does not honor the Father who sent Him.

5:23
Luke 10:16;
1 John 2:23

24 "•Truly, •truly, I say to you, he who hears My word,[43a] and believes Him who sent Me, has eternal life, and does not come into *judgment,* but has passed⁺ out of death into life.

5:24
John 3:18; 12:44;
20:31; 1 John
5:13;
John 3:18;
1 John 3:14

Two Resurrections

25 "•Truly, •truly, I say to you, an hour is coming and now is, when the dead shall hear the voice of the Son of God; and those who hear shall live.

5:25
John 4:21,23;
5:28;
Luke 15:24;
John 6:60; 8:43,
47; 9:27

26 "For just as the Father has life[30b] in Himself, even so He gave to the *Son also* to have life in Himself;

5:26
John 1:4; 6:57

27 and He gave Him *authority* to execute~ *judgment,* because He is *the* Son of ⁺Man.

5:27
John 9:39; Acts
10:42; 17:31

28 "Do not marvel⁰ at this; for an hour is coming, in which all who are in the tombs shall hear His voice,

5:28
John 4:21;
John 11:24;
1 Cor. 15:52

29 and shall come forth; those who did the good[25a] *deeds* to a resurrection of life, those who committed the evil[10d] *deeds* to a resurrection of judgment.

5:29
Dan. 12:2; Matt.
25:46; Acts 24:15

30 "*I* can do~ •*nothing* on My own initiative. As I hear, I judge; and My judgment is ⁺*just,* because I do not seek My own will, but the will of Him who sent Me.

5:30
John 5:19;
John 8:16;
John 4:34; 6:38

31 "If I *alone* bear~ witness of Myself, My testimony is not true.

5:31
John 8:14

32 "There is another[8a] who bears witness of Me, and I know that the testimony which He bears of Me is *true.*

5:32
John 5:37

Witness of John

33 "*You* have sent⁺ to John, and he has borne⁺ witness to the truth.

5:33
John 1:7,15,19,
32; 3:26-30

34 "But the witness which *I* receive is *not from man,* but I say these things that *you* may be saved.ˣ

5:34
John 5:32; 1 John
5:9

35 "He was the lamp that was burning and was shining and *you* were willing to rejoiceˣ for a while in his light.

5:35
2 Sam. 21:17;
2 Pet. 1:19;
Mark 1:5

Witness of Works

36 "But the witness which *I* have is greater than *that of* John; for the works which the *Father* has given⁺ Me to accomplish,ˣ the very works that I do, bear witness of Me, that the Father has sent⁺ Me.

5:36
Matt. 11:4; John
2:23; 10:25,38;
14:11; 15:24;
John 4:34;
John 3:17

Witness of the Father

5:37
Matt. 3:17; Mark
1:11; Luke 3:22;
24:27; John 8:18;
1 John 5:9

37 "And the Father who sent Me, *He* has borne⁺ witness of Me. You have neither heard⁺ *His voice* at any time, nor seen⁺ *His* form. [22a]

5:38
1 John 2:14;
John 3:17

38 "And you do not have *His word*[43a] abiding in you, for *you* do not believe Him whom *He* sent.

Witness of the Scripture

5:39
John 7:52; Rom.
2:17ff.;
Luke 24:25,27;
Acts 13:27

39 "ⁿYou search the Scriptures, because you think that *in them* you have eternal life; and it is *these* that bear witness of Me;

40 and you are unwilling to come to Me, that you may have~ life.

5:41
John 5:44; 7:18; 1
Thess. 2:6

41 "I do not receive *glory from men;*

42 but I know⁺ you, that you do not have the *love of God* in yourselves.

5:43
Matt. 24:5

43 "*I* have come⁺ in My Father's name, and you do not receive Me; if another shall come in his *own* name, you will receive *him.*

5:44
John 5:41;
Rom. 2:29;
John 17:3; 1 Tim.
1:17

44 "How can *you* believe,ˣ when you receive glory from one ⁺another, and you do not seek the glory that is from the *one and only God?*

5:45
John 9:28; Rom.
2:17ff.

45 "Do not think⁰ that *I* will accuse you before the Father; the one who accuses you is *Moses,* in whom you have set⁺ your hope.

5:46
Luke 24:27

46 "For if you believedᵐ Moses, you would believe •Me; for he wrote of *Me.*

5:47
Luke 16:29,31

47 "But if you do not believe *his* writings, how will you believe *My* words?"[43b]

Five Thousand Fed

6:1
John 6:1-13;
Matt. 14:13-21;
Mark 6:32-44;
Luke 9:10-17;
Matt. 4:18; Luke
5:1;
John 6:23; 21:1
6:2
John 2:11,23; 3:2;
6:14,30; 11:47;
12:18,37; 20:30
6:3
Matt. 5:1; Mark
3:13; Luke 6:12;
9:28; John 6:15
6:4
Deut. 16:1; John
2:13
6:5
John 1:43
6:6
2 Cor. 13:5; Rev.
2:2

6 After these things Jesus went away to the other side of the Sea of Galilee (or Tiberias).

2 And a great multitude was followingᵐ Him, because they were seeingᵐ the signs which He was performingᵐ on those who were sick.

3 And Jesus went up on the mountain, and there He sat with His disciples.

4 Now the Passover, the feast of the Jews, was at hand.

5 Jesus therefore lifting up His eyes, and seeing that a great multitude was coming to Him, *said to Philip, "Where are we to buyˣ bread, that *these* may eat?"ˣ

6 And this He was saying to test him; for He Himself knew what He was intending to do.

ⁿOr, (a command) *Search the Scriptures!*

7   Philip answered Him, *"Two hundred* °denarii worth of bread is not sufficient for them, for everyone to receive[x] a *little."*

6:7
John 1:43;
Mark 6:37

8   One of His disciples, Andrew, Simon Peter's brother, *said to Him,

6:8
John 2:2;
John 1:40

9   "There is a lad here who has *five* barley loaves and *two* fish, but what are *these* for so many people?"

6:9
John 6:11; 21:9,
10,13

10   Jesus said, "Have[xi] the people sit[x] down." Now there was much grass in the place. So the men sat down, in number about five thousand.

6:10
Mark 6:39;
Matt. 14:21

11   Jesus therefore took the loaves; and having given thanks, He distributed to those who were seated; likewise also of the fish as much as they wanted.[xx]

6:11
Matt. 15:36; John
6:23;
John 6:9; 21:9,10,
13

12   And when they were filled, He *said to His disciples, "Gather[xi] up the leftover fragments that nothing may be lost."[x]

6:12
John 2:2

13   And so they gathered them up, and filled *twelve* baskets with fragments from the five barley loaves, which were left over by those who had eaten.[+]

6:13
Matt. 14:20

14   When therefore the people saw the sign which He had performed, they said,[xx] "This is of a *truth* the Prophet who is to come into the world."

6:14
Matt. 11:3; 21:11;
John 1:21

Jesus Walks on the Water

15   Jesus therefore perceiving[29a] that they were intending to come and take Him by force, to make[x] Him king, withdrew again to the mountain by *Himself alone.*

6:15
John 18:36f.;
John 6:15-21:
Matt. 14:22-33;
Mark 6:45-51;
John 6:3

16   Now when evening came, His disciples went down to the sea,

6:16
John 2:2

17   and after getting into a boat, they *started to* cross the sea to Capernaum. And it had already become dark, and Jesus had not yet come to them.

6:17
Mark 6:45; John
6:24,59

18   And the sea *began* to be stirred[xx] up because a strong wind was blowing.

19   When therefore they had rowed[+] about three or four miles, they *beheld Jesus walking on the sea and drawing near to the boat; and they were frightened.

20   But He *said to them, "It is *I;* do not be afraid."[θ]

6:20
Matt. 14:27

21   They were willing therefore to receive[x] Him into the boat; and immediately the boat was at the land to which they were going.

22   The next day the multitude that stood on the other side of the sea saw that there was no other small boat there, except one, and that *Jesus* had not entered with His disciples into the boat, but *that* His disciples had gone away alone.

6:22
John 6:2;
John 6:15ff.

°The denarius was equivalent to one day's wage

6:23
John 6:1;
Luke 7:13;
John 6:11
6:24
Matt. 14:34; Mark
6:53; John 6:17,
59

6:25
Matt. 23:7

6:26
John 6:24;
John 6:2,14,30

6:27
Is. 55:2;
John 3:15f.; 4:14;
6:40,47,54;
10:28; 17:2f.;
Matt. 8:20; John
6:53,62;
John 3:33

6:29
1 Thess. 1:3;
James 2:22;
1 John 3:23; Rev.
2:26;
John 3:17
6:30
Matt. 12:38;
John 6:2,14,26

6:31
Ex. 16:4,15,21;
Num. 11:8; John
6:49,58;
Ps. 78:24; Ex.
16:4,15; Neh.
9:15; Ps. 105:40

6:33
John 6:41,50

6:34
John 4:15

6:35
John 6:48,51;
John 4:14
6:36
John 6:26
6:37
John 6:39; 17:2,
24
6:38
John 3:13;
Matt. 26:39;
John 4:34; 5:30;
John 6:29
6:39
John 6:37; 17:2,
24;
John 17:12; 18:9;
Matt. 10:15; John
6:40,44,54; 11:24
6:40
John 12:45;
14:17,19;
John 3:16;
Matt. 10:15; John
6:39,44,54;
11:24

23 There came other small boats from Tiberias near to the place where they ate the bread after the Lord had given thanks.

24 When the multitude therefore saw that Jesus was not there, nor His disciples, they themselves got into the small boats, and came to Capernaum, seeking Jesus.

25 And when they found Him on the other side of the sea, they said to Him, "Rabbi, when did You get⁺ here?"

Words to the People

26 Jesus answered them and said, "•Truly, •truly, I say to you, you seek Me, not because you saw signs, but because you ate of the loaves, and were filled.

27 "Do not work for the food which perishes, but for the food which endures to ⁺eternal life, which the Son of Man shall give to you, for on *Him* the Father, *even God,* has set His seal."

28 They said therefore to Him, "What shall we do,~ that we may work~ the works of God?"

29 Jesus answered and said to them, "This is the work of God, that you believe~ in Him whom *He* has sent."

30 They said therefore to Him, "What then do *You* do for a sign, that we may see,ˣ and believeˣ You? What work do You perform?

31 "Our fathers ate the manna in the wilderness; as it is written,⁺ 'HE GAVE THEM *BREAD OUT OF HEAVEN TO EAT.'* "ˣ

32 Jesus therefore said to them, "•Truly, •truly, I say to you, it is not Moses who has given⁺ you the bread out of heaven, but it is My Father who gives you the *true* bread out of heaven.

33 "For the bread of God is ᴾthat which comes down out of heaven, and gives *life* to the world."

34 They said therefore to Him, "Lord, *evermore* giveˣⁱ us ⁺this bread."

35 Jesus said to them, "⁺*I* am the bread of life;³⁰ᵇ he who comes to •*Me* shall •*not* hunger,ˣ and he who believes in Me shall *never* thirst.

36 "But I said to you, that you have seen⁺ Me, and yet do not believe.

37 "All that the Father gives Me shall come *to Me,* and the one who comes to Me I will certainly •*not* castˣ out.

38 "For I have come⁺ down from heaven, not to do~ My own will, but the will of Him who sent Me.

39 "And this is the will of Him who sent Me, that of all that He has given⁺ Me I loseˣ nothing, but raise it up on the last day.

40 "For this is the will of My Father, that everyone who be-

ᴾOr, *He who comes*

holds the Son and believes in Him, may have~ eternal life; and *I Myself* will raise him up on the last day."

Words to the Jews

41 The Jews therefore were grumbling^ᵐ about Him, because He said, "†*I* am the bread that came down out of heaven."

42 And they were saying,^ᵐ "Is not this Jesus, the son of Joseph, whose father and mother *we* know? How does He now say, 'I have come⁺ down out of *heaven*'?"

43 Jesus answered and said to them, "Do not grumble^θ among yourselves.

44 "No one can come to Me, unless the Father who sent Me draws^x him; and I will raise him up on the last day.

45 "It is written⁺ in the prophets, 'AND THEY SHALL ALL BE TAUGHT OF GOD.' Everyone who has heard and learned from the Father, comes to •*Me*.

46 "Not that any man has seen⁺ the Father, except the One who is from God; *He* has seen⁺ the Father.

47 "•Truly, •truly, I say to you, he who believes has eternal life.

48 "†*I* am the bread of life.

49 "Your fathers ate the manna in the wilderness, and they died.

50 "This is the bread which comes down out of heaven, so that one may eat^x of it and not die.^x

51 "†*I* am the *living* bread that came down out of heaven; if anyone eats^x of this bread, he shall live forever; and the bread also which *I* shall give for the life of the world is *My flesh*."

52 The Jews therefore *began* to argue^ᵐ with one another, saying, "How can *this man* give^x us *His* flesh to eat?"^x

53 Jesus therefore said to them, "•Truly, •truly, I say to you, unless you eat^x the flesh of the Son of Man and drink^x *His* blood, you have no life^{30b} in yourselves.

54 "He who eats *My* flesh and drinks *My* blood has eternal life, and *I* will raise him up on the last day.

55 "For My flesh is *true* food, and My blood is *true* drink.

56 "He who eats *My* flesh and drinks *My* blood abides in Me, and I in †him.

57 "As the living Father sent Me, and *I* live because of the Father, so he who eats Me, he also shall live because of Me.

58 "This is the bread which came down out of heaven; not as the fathers ate, and died, he who eats this bread shall live forever."

6:41
John 1:19; 6:52;
John 6:33,51,58

6:42
Luke 4:22;
John 7:27f.;
John 6:38,62

6:44
Jer. 31:3; Hos.
11:4; John 6:65;
12:32;
John 6:39

6:45
Acts 7:42; 13:40;
Heb. 8:11;
Is. 54:13; Jer.
31:34;
Phil. 3:15;
1 Thess. 4:9;
1 John 2:27

6:46
John 1:18

6:47
John 3:36; 5:24;
6:51,58; 11:26

6:48
John 6:35,51

6:49
John 6:31,58

6:50
John 6:33;
John 3:36; 5:24;
6:47,51,58; 11:26

6:51
John 6:35,48;
John 6:41,58;
John 3:36; 5:24;
6:47,58; 11:26;
John 1:29; 3:14f.;
Heb. 10:10; 1
John 4:10;
John 6:53-56

6:52
John 1:19; 6:41;
John 9:16; 10:19

6:53
Matt. 8:20; John
6:27,62

6:54
John 6:39

6:56
John 15:4f.;
17:23; 1 John
2:24; 3:24; 4:15f.

6:57
Matt. 16:16; John
5:26;
John 3:17; 6:29,
38

6:58
John 6:33,41,51;
John 6:31,49;
John 3:36; 5:24;
6:47,51; 11:26

Words to the Disciples

6:59
Matt. 4:23;
John 6:24

59   These things He said in the synagogue, as He taught in Capernaum.

6:60
John 2:2; 6:66;
7:3;
John 6:52

60   Many therefore of His disciples, when they heard *this* said, "This is a *difficult* statement; who can listen~ to it?"

6:61
John 6:64;
Matt. 11:6

61   But Jesus, conscious that His disciples grumbled at this, said to them, "Does this cause you to stumble?

6:62
Matt. 8:20; John
6:27,53;
Mark 16:19; John
3:13
6:63
2 Cor. 3:6;
John 6:68

62   *"What* then if you should behold~ the Son of Man ascending where He was before?

63   "It is the Spirit who gives life; the flesh profits •*nothing;* the words[43b] that *I* have spoken✝ to you are *spirit* and are *life.*

6:64
John 6:60,66;
John 2:25;
Matt. 10:4; John
6:71; 13:11

64   "But there are some of you who do not believe." For Jesus knew from the beginning who they were who did not believe, and who it was that would betray Him.

6:65
John 6:37,44;
Matt. 13:11; John
3:27

65   And He was saying,[m] "For this reason I have said✝ to you, that no one can come to Me, unless it has been granted✝ him from the Father."

Peter's Confession of Faith

6:66
John 2:2; 7:3;
John 6:60,64

66   As a result of this many of His disciples withdrew, and were not walking[m] with Him anymore.

6:67
Matt. 10:2; John
2:2; 6:70f.; 20:24

67   Jesus said therefore to the twelve, "*You* do not want to go away *also,* do you?"

6:68
Matt. 16:16;
John 6:63;
12:49f.; 17:8
6:69
Mark 1:24; 8:29;
Luke 9:20

68   Simon Peter answered Him, "Lord, to whom shall we go? You have *words*[43b] *of eternal life.*

69   "And *we* have believed✝ and have come to know✝[29a] that *You* are the Holy One of God."

6:70
John 15:16,19;
Matt. 10:2; John
2:2; 6:71; 20:24;
John 8:44; 13:2,
27; 17:12
6:71
John 12:4; 13:2,
26;
Mark 14:10;
Matt. 10:2; John
2:2; 6:70; 20:24

70   Jesus answered them, "Did *I Myself* not choose you, the twelve, and *yet* one of *you* is a devil?"

71   Now He meant Judas *the son* of Simon Iscariot, for he, one of the twelve, was going to betray Him.

Jesus Teaches at the Feast

7:1
John 4:3; 6:1;
11:54;
John 1:19; 7:11,
13,15,35;
John 5:18; 7:19;
8:37,40; 11:53
7:2
Lev. 23:34; Deut.
16:13,16; Zech.
14:16-19
7:3
Matt. 12:46; Mark
3:21; John 7:5,10;
John 6:60

7   And after these things Jesus was walking[m] in Galilee; for He was unwilling[m] to walk~ in Judea, because the Jews were seeking[m] to kill[x] Him.

2   Now the feast of the Jews, the Feast of Booths, was at hand.

3   His brothers therefore said to Him, "Depart[xl] from here, and go into Judea, that Your disciples also may behold Your works which You are doing.

4   "For no one does anything in secret, when he himself seeks

to be *known* publicly. If You do these things, show[xi] Yourself to the world."

5 For not even His *brothers* were believing[m] in Him.

6 Jesus therefore *said to them, "My time is not yet at hand, but *your* time is always opportune.

7 "The world cannot hate~ you; but it hates *Me* because *I* testify of it, that its deeds are †*evil.*

8 "Go[xi] up to the feast yourselves; *I* do not go up to †this feast because *My* time has not yet fully come."*

9 And having said these things to them, He stayed in Galilee.

10 But when His brothers had gone up to the feast, then He Himself also went up, not publicly, but as it were, in secret.

11 The Jews therefore were seeking[m] Him at the feast, and were saying,[m] "Where is He?"

12 And there was *much* grumbling among the multitudes concerning Him; some were saying,[m] "He is a good[25a] †man"; others were saying,[m] "No, on the contrary, He leads the multitude astray."

13 Yet[2] no one was speaking[m] openly of Him for fear of the Jews.

14 But when it was now the midst of the feast Jesus went up into the temple, and *began to* teach.

15 The Jews therefore were marveling,[m] saying, "How has this man become *learned,*+ having never been educated?"

16 Jesus therefore answered them, and said, *"My* teaching is not Mine, but His who sent Me.

17 "If any man is willing~ to do~ *His will,* he shall know[29a] of the teaching, whether it is of *God,* or *whether* I speak from *Myself.*

18 "He who speaks from himself seeks his *own* glory; but He who is seeking the glory of the one who sent Him, He is †true, and there is no unrighteousness *in Him.*

19 "Did not Moses give+ you the Law, and *yet* none of you carries out the Law? Why do you seek to kill[x] Me?"

20 The multitude answered, "You have a *demon!* Who seeks to kill[x] You?"

21 Jesus answered and said to them, "I did *one* deed, and you all marvel.

22 "On this account Moses has given+ you circumcision (not because it is from *Moses,* but from the fathers), and on *the* Sabbath you circumcise a man.

23 "If a man receives *circumcision* on *the* Sabbath that the Law

7:5
Matt. 12:46; Mark 3:21; John 7:3,10
7:6
Matt. 26:18; John 2:4; 7:8,30
7:7
John 15:18f.; John 3:19f.
7:8
John 7:6
7:10
Matt. 12:46; Mark 3:21; John 7:3,5
7:11
John 7:13,15,35; John 11:56
7:12
John 7:40-43
7:13
John 9:22; 12:42; 19:38; 20:19
7:14
Matt. 26:55; John 7:28
7:15
John 1:19; 7:11, 13,35; Acts 26:24
7:16
John 3:11
7:17
Ps. 25:9,14; Prov. 3:32; Dan. 12:10; John 3:21; 8:43f.
7:18
John 5:41; 8:50, 54; 12:43
7:19
John 1:17; Mark 11:18; John 7:1
7:20
Matt. 11:18; John 8:48f.,52; 10:20
7:21
John 5:2-9,16; 7:23
7:22
Lev. 12:3; Gen. 17:10ff.; 21:4; Acts 7:8
7:23
Matt. 12:2; John 5:9,10

of Moses may not be broken,ˣ are you angry with Me because I made an *entire man* well on *the* Sabbath?

24 "Do not judge° according to appearance, but judge~ with *righteous judgment.*"

25 Therefore some of the people of Jerusalem were saying,ᵐ "Is this not the man whom they are seeking to kill?ˣ

26 "And look, He is speaking publicly, and they are saying nothing to Him. The rulers do not really know²⁹ᵃ that this is the Christ, do they?

27 "However, we know²⁹ᵉ where *this man* is from; but whenever the Christ may come,~ no one knows²⁹ᵃ where He is from."

28 Jesus therefore cried out in the temple, teaching and saying, "You both know²⁹ᵉ Me and know where I am from; and I have not come⁺ of *Myself,* but He who sent Me is true, whom *you* do not know.

29 "*I* know Him; because I am from ⁺*Him,* and He sent Me."

30 They were seekingᵐ therefore to seizeˣ Him; and no man laid his hand on Him, because His hour had not yet ⁺come.

31 But many of the multitude believed in Him; and they were saying,ᵐ "When the Christ shall come, He will not perform *more signs* than those which this man has, will He?"

32 The Pharisees heard the multitude muttering these things about Him; and the chief priests and the Pharisees sent officers to seizeˣ Him.

33 Jesus therefore said, "For a little while longer I am with you, then I go to Him who sent Me.

34 "You shall seek Me, and shall not find Me; and where *I* am, *you* cannot come."

35 The Jews therefore said to one another, "Where does this man intend to go that *we* shall not find Him? He is not intending to go to the Dispersion among the *Greeks,* and teach the Greeks, is He?

36 "What is this statement that He said, 'You will seek Me, and will not find Me; and where *I* am, *you* cannot come'?"

37 Now on the last day, the great *day* of the feast, Jesus stood and cried out, saying, "If any man is thirsty,~ let him come~ to Me and drink.~

38 "He who believes in Me, as the Scripture said, 'From his innermost being shall flow rivers of *living water.*'"

39 But this He spoke of the Spirit, whom those who *believed in Him* were to receive; for the Spirit was not yet *given,* because Jesus was not yet glorified.

Division of People over Jesus

40 *Some* of the multitude therefore, when they heard these words, were saying,ᵐ "This *certainly* is the Prophet."

> **7:40**
> Matt. 21:11; John 1:21

41 Others were saying,ᵐ "This is the Christ." Still others were saying,ᵐ "Surely the Christ is not going to come from *Galilee*, is He?

> **7:41**
> John 1:46; 7:52

42 "Has not the Scripture said that the Christ comes from the *offspring of David*, and from *Bethlehem*, the village where David was?"

> **7:42**
> Ps. 89:4; Mic. 5:2; Matt. 1:1; 2:5f.; Luke 2:4ff.

43 So there arose a division in the multitude because of Him.

> **7:43**
> John 9:16; 10:19

44 And some of them wantedᵐ to seizeˣ Him, but no one laid hands on Him.

> **7:44**
> John 7:30

45 The officers therefore came to the chief priests and Pharisees, and they said to them, "Why did you not bring Him?"

> **7:45**
> John 7:32

46 The officers answered, "†Never did a man speak the way *this* man speaks."

> **7:46**
> John 7:32; Matt. 7:28

47 The Pharisees therefore answered them, "*You* have not *also* been led⁺ astray, have you?

> **7:47**
> John 7:12

48 "No one of the rulers or †Pharisees has believed in Him, has he?

> **7:48**
> John 12:42; Luke 23:13; John 7:26

49 "But this multitude which does not know the Law is †accursed."

50 Nicodemus *said to them (he who came to Him before, being one of *them*),

> **7:50**
> John 3:1; 19:39

51 "Our Law does not judge a man, unless it †first hearsˣ from him and knowsˣ what he is doing, does it?"

> **7:51**
> Ex. 23:1; Deut. 17:6; 19:15; Prov. 18:13; Acts 23:3

52 They answered and said to him, "You are not also from *Galilee*, are you? Search,ˣˡ and seeˣˡ that no prophet arises out of *Galilee*."

> **7:52**
> John 1:46; 7:41

53 [ᑫAnd everyone went to his home.

The Adulterous Woman

8 But Jesus went to the Mount of Olives.

> **8:1**
> Matt. 21:1

2 And early in the morning He came again into the temple, and all the people were comingᵐ to Him; and He sat down and *began* to teach them.

> **8:2**
> Matt. 26:55; John 8:20

3 And the scribes and the Pharisees *brought a woman caught⁺ in adultery, and having set her in the midst,

4 they *said to Him, "Teacher, this woman has been caught⁺ in adultery, in the very act.

5 "Now in the Law Moses commanded us to stone~ *such* women; what then do *You* say?"

> **8:5**
> Lev. 20:10; Deut. 22:22f.

ᑫJohn 7:53-8:11 is not found in most of the old mss.

8:6
Matt. 16:1; 19:3;
22:18,35; Mark
8:11; 10:2; 12:15;
Luke 10:25;
11:16;
Mark 3:2
8:7
John 8:10;
Matt. 7:1; Rom.
2:1;
Deut. 17:7

6 And they were saying^m this, testing Him, in order that they might have~ grounds for accusing~ Him. But Jesus stooped down, and with His finger wrote^m on the ground.

7 But when they persisted^m in asking Him, He straightened up, and said to them, "He who is without sin among you, let him *be the first* to throw^xl a stone at her."

8 And again He stooped down, and wrote^m on the ground.

9 And when they heard it, they *began* to go^m out one by one, beginning with the older ones, and He was left alone, and the woman, where she was, in the midst.

8:10
John 8:7

10 And straightening up, Jesus said to her, "Woman, where are they? Did no one condemn^14c you?"

8:11
John 3:17;
John 5:14

11 And she said, "No one, Lord." And Jesus said, "Neither do *I* condemn you; go your way. From now on sin^0 no more."]

Jesus Is the Light of the World

8:12
John 1:4; 9:5;
12:35;
Matt. 5:14

12 Again therefore Jesus spoke to them, saying, "†*I* am the light of the world; he who follows Me shall •*not* walk^x in the darkness, but shall have the light of life."^30b

8:13
John 5:31

13 The Pharisees therefore said to Him, "You are bearing witness of *Yourself;* Your witness is not true."

8:14
John 18:37; Rev.
1:5; 3:14;
John 8:42; 13:3;
16:28;
John 7:28; 9:29

14 Jesus answered and said to them, "*Even if I* bear~ witness of Myself, My witness is *true;* for I know where I came from, and where I am going; but *you* do not know where I come from, or where I am going.

8:15
1 Sam. 16:7;
John 7:24;
John 3:17
8:16
John 5:30

15 "You people judge according to the *flesh; I* am not judging •anyone.

16 "But even if *I* do judge,~ My judgment is †*true;* for I am not *alone in it*, but I and ʳHe who sent Me.

8:17
Deut. 17:6; 19:15;
Matt. 18:16

17 "Even in *your* law it has been written,⁺ that the testimony of *two* men is true.

8:18
John 5:37; 1 John
5:9

18 "I am He who bears witness of Myself, and the *Father who sent Me* bears witness of Me."

8:19
John 7:28; 8:55;
14:7,9; 16:3

19 And so they were saying^m to Him, "Where is Your Father?" Jesus answered, "You know^29e neither *Me*, nor *My* †*Father;* if you knew *Me*, you would know^29e *My Father also.*"

8:20
Mark 12:41,43;
Luke 21:1;
John 7:14; 8:2;
John 7:30

20 These words He spoke in the treasury, as He taught in the temple; and no one seized Him, because His hour had not yet come.

8:21
John 7:34;
John 8:24

21 He said therefore again to them, "I go away, and you shall seek Me, and shall die *in your sin;* where *I* am going, *you* cannot come."

8:22
John 1:19; 8:48,
52,57;
John 7:35

22 Therefore the Jews were saying,^m "Surely He will not kill

ʳMany ancient mss. read *the Father who sent Me*

Himself, will He, since He says, 'Where *I* am going, *you* cannot come'?"

23   And He was saying[m] to them, "*You* are from below, *I* am from above; *you* are of this world, *I* am not of †*this* world.

24   "I said therefore to you, that you shall die in your sins; for unless you believe[x] that I am *He,* you shall die in your sins."

25   And so they were saying[m] to Him, "Who are *You?*" Jesus said to them, "What have I been saying to you *from* the beginning?

26   "I have many things to speak~ and to judge~ concerning you, but He who sent Me is †*true;* and the things which I heard from Him, *these* I speak to the world."

27   They did not realize that He had been speaking[m] to them about the *Father.*

28   Jesus therefore said, "When you lift[x] up the Son of Man, then you will know[29a] that I am *He,* and I do *nothing* on My own initiative, but I speak these things as the *Father* taught Me.

29   "And He who sent Me is *with* †*Me;* He has not left Me alone, for I *always* do the things that are *pleasing to Him.*"

30   As He spoke these things, many came to believe in Him.

The Truth Shall Make You Free

31   Jesus therefore was saying[m] to those Jews who had believed† Him, "If *you* abide[x] in My word, *then* you are truly disciples of †Mine;

32   and you shall know[29a] the truth, and the truth shall make you free."

33   They answered Him, "We are Abraham's †offspring, and have *never yet* been enslaved† to anyone; how is it that *You* say, 'You shall become *free'?*"

34   Jesus answered them, "•Truly, •truly, I say to you, everyone who commits[19a] sin is the *slave* of sin.

35   "And the slave does not remain in the house forever; the son does remain forever.

36   "If therefore the Son shall make[x] you free, you shall be *free indeed.*

37   "I know that you are Abraham's offspring; yet you seek to kill[x] Me, because My word has no place in you.

38   "I speak the things which *I* have seen† with *My* Father; therefore *you* also do the things which you heard from *your* father."

39   They answered and said to Him, "*Abraham* is our father." Jesus *said to them, "If you are *Abraham's* †*children,* do the *deeds of Abraham.*

8:23
John 3:31;
1 John 4:5;
John 17:14,16
8:24
John 8:21;
Matt. 24:5; Mark
13:6; Luke 21:8;
John 4:26; 8:28,
58; 13:19

8:26
John 3:33; 7:28;
John 8:40; 12:49;
15:15

8:28
John 3:14; 12:32;
Matt. 24:5; Mark
13:6; Luke 21:8;
John 4:26; 8:24,
58; 13:19;
John 3:11; 5:19
8:29
John 8:16; 16:32;
John 4:34
8:30
John 7:31

8:31
John 15:7; 2 John
9;
John 2:2

8:32
John 1:14,17;
John 8:36; Rom.
8:2; 2 Cor. 3:17;
Gal. 5:1,13;
James 2:12; 1
Pet. 2:16
8:33
Matt. 3:9; Luke
3:8; John 8:37,39
8:34
Rom. 6:16; 2 Pet.
2:19
8:35
Gen. 21:10; Gal.
4:30;
Luke 15:31
8:36
John 8:32

8:37
Matt. 3:9; John
8:39;
John 7:1; 8:40
8:38
John 8:41,44

8:39
Matt. 3:9; John
8:37;
Rom. 9:7; Gal.
3:7

8:40
John 7:1; 8:37;
John 8:26

8:41
John 8:38,44;
Deut. 32:6; Is.
63:16; 64:8

8:42
1 John 5:1;
John 13:3; 16:28,
30; 17:8;
John 7:28;
John 3:17
8:43
John 8:33,39,41;
John 5:25

8:44
1 John 3:8;
John 8:38,41;
John 7:17;
Gen. 3:4; 1 John
3:8,15;
1 John 2:4;
Matt. 12:34

8:45
John 18:37
8:46
John 18:37

8:47
1 John 4:6

8:48
John 1:19;
Matt. 10:5; John
4:9;
John 7:20
8:49
John 7:20

8:50
John 5:41; 8:54

8:51
John 8:55; 14:23;
15:20; 17:6;
Matt. 16:28; Luke
2:26; John 8:52;
Heb. 2:9; 11:5
8:52
John 1:19;
John 7:20;
John 8:55; 14:23;
15:20; 17:6;
John 8:51
8:53
John 4:12

8:54
John 8:50;
John 7:39

8:55
John 8:19; 15:21;
John 7:29;
John 8:44;
John 8:51; 15:10

8:56
John 8:37,39;
Matt. 13:17; Heb.
11:13
8:57
John 1:19

40 "But as it is, you are seeking to kill[x] Me, a man who has told[+] you the *truth,* which I heard from God; this Abraham did not do.

41 "You are doing the deeds of your father." They said to Him, "*We* were not born[+] of *fornication;* we have *one* Father, *even* God."

42 Jesus said to them, "If God were your Father, you would love Me; for *I* proceeded forth and have come *from God,* for I have not even come[+] on My *own initiative,* but *He* sent Me.

43 "Why do you not understand what I am saying? *It is* because you cannot hear[~] My word.[43a]

44 "*You* are of *your* father the devil, and you want to do[~] the [†]desires of your father. *He* was a *murderer* from the beginning, and does not stand[m] in the truth, because there is no truth in him. Whenever he speaks[~] a lie, he speaks from his *own nature;* for he is a *liar,* and the father of lies.

45 "But because *I* speak the *truth,* you do not believe Me.

46 "Which one of you convicts Me of sin? If I speak *truth,* why do you not believe Me?

47 "He who is of God hears the *words*[43b] of God; for this reason *you* do not hear *them,* because you are not *of God.*"

48 The Jews answered and said to Him, "Do we not say rightly that You are a *Samaritan* and have a *demon?*"

49 Jesus answered, "*I* do not have a demon; but I honor My Father, and *you* dishonor Me.

50 "But *I* do not seek My glory; there is One who seeks and judges.

51 "•Truly, •truly, I say to you, if anyone keeps[x] *My* word[43a] he shall •never see[x] *death.*"

52 The Jews said to Him, "Now we know that You have a demon. Abraham died, and the prophets *also;* and *You* say, 'If anyone keeps[x] My word, he shall •never taste[x] of death.'

53 "Surely *You* are not greater than our father Abraham, who died? The prophets died too; whom do You make Yourself out to *be?*"

54 Jesus answered, "If *I* glorify[x] Myself, My glory is nothing; it is *My Father* who glorifies Me, of whom *you* say, 'He is our [†]God';

55 and you have not come to know[+29a] Him, but *I* know[29e] Him; and if I say[x] that I do not know[29e] Him, I shall be a *liar* like you, but I do know[29e] Him, and *keep* His word.[43a]

56 "Your father Abraham rejoiced to see[x] My day, and he saw *it* and was glad."

57 The Jews therefore said to Him, "You are not yet *fifty* years old, and have You seen[+] *Abraham?*"

58   Jesus said to them, "•Truly, •truly, I say to you, before Abraham was born, I am."

59   Therefore they picked up stones to throw[x] at Him; but Jesus hid Himself, and went out of the temple.

Healing the Man Born Blind

9 And as He passed by, He saw a man blind from birth.
2   And His disciples asked Him, saying, "Rabbi, who sinned, this man or his parents, that he should be born[x] blind?"

3   Jesus answered, "*It was* neither *that* this man sinned, nor his parents; but *it was* in order that the *works of God* might be displayed[x] in him.

4   "*We* must work~ the works of Him who sent Me, as long as it is day; night is coming, when no man can work. ~

5   "While I am in the world, I am the light of the world."

6   When He had said this, He spat on the ground, and made clay of the spittle, and applied the clay to his eyes,

7   and said to him, "Go, wash[x] in the pool of Siloam" (which is translated, Sent). And so he went away and washed, and came *back* seeing.

8   The neighbors therefore, and those who previously saw him as a beggar, were saying,[m] "Is not this the one who used to sit and beg?"

9   Others were saying,[m] "This is he," *still* others were saying,[m] "•No, but he is like him." He kept saying,[m] "I am the one."

10   Therefore they were saying[m] to him, "How then were your eyes opened?"

11   He answered, "The man who is called Jesus made clay, and anointed my eyes, and said to me, 'Go to Siloam, and wash';[x] so I went away and washed, and I received sight."

12   And they said to him, "Where is He?" He *said, "I do not know."

Controversy over the Man

13   They *brought to the Pharisees him who was formerly blind.

14   Now it was a Sabbath on the day when Jesus made the clay, and opened his eyes.

15   Again, therefore, the Pharisees also were asking[m] him how he received his sight. And he said to them, "He applied clay to my eyes, and I washed, and I see."

16   Therefore some of the Pharisees were saying,[m] "*This* man is not from *God,* because He does not keep the *Sabbath.*" But

8:58 Ex. 3:14; John 1:1; 17:5,24
8:59 Matt. 12:14; John 10:31; 11:8; John 12:36
9:2 Matt. 23:7; Luke 13:2; John 9:34; Acts 28:4; Ex. 20:5
9:3 John 11:4
9:4 John 7:33; 11:9; 12:35; Gal. 6:10
9:5 Matt. 5:14; John 1:4; 8:12; 12:46
9:6 Mark 7:33; 8:23
9:7 Neh. 3:15; Is. 8:6; Luke 13:4; John 9:11; 2 Kin. 5:13f.; Is. 29:18; 35:5; 42:7; Matt. 11:5; John 11:37
9:8 Acts 3:2,10
9:11 John 9:7
9:14 John 5:9
9:15 John 9:10
9:16 Matt. 12:2; Luke 13:14; John 5:10; 7:23; John 2:11; John 6:52; 7:12, 43; 10:19

others were saying,ᵐ "How can a man who is a *sinner* perform~ *such signs?"* And there was a division among them.

9:17
John 9:15;
Deut. 18:15; Matt.
21:11

17 They *said therefore to the blind man *again,* "What do *you* say about Him, since He opened your eyes?" And he said, "He is a †*prophet."*

9:18
John 1:19; 9:22

18 The Jews therefore did not believe *it* of him, that he had been blind, and had received sight, until they called the parents of the very one who had received his sight,

19 and questioned them, saying, "Is this your son, who *you* say was born *blind?* Then how does he now see?"

20 His parents answered them and said, "We know that this is our son, and that he was born blind;

21 but how he now sees, we do not know; or who opened his eyes, *we* do not know. Askˣⁱ *him;* he is of age, *he* shall speak for *himself."*

9:22
John 7:13;
John 7:45-52;
Luke 6:22; John
12:42; 16:2

22 His parents said this because they were afraidᵐ of the Jews; for the Jews had already agreed, that if anyone should confessˣ Him to be Christ, he should be put *out of the synagogue.*

9:23
John 9:21
9:24
Josh. 7:19; Ezra
10:11; Rev.
11:13;
John 9:16

23 For this reason his parents said, "He is of age; askˣⁱ *him."*

24 So a second time they called the man who had been blind, and said to him, "Giveˣ glory to God; *we* know that this man is a †*sinner."*

25 He therefore answered, "Whether He is a sinner, I do not know; *one thing* I do know, that, whereas I was blind, now I see."

26 They said therefore to him, "What did He do to you? How did He open your eyes?"

9:27
John 9:15;
John 5:25

27 He answered them, "I told you already, and you did not listen; why do you want to hear~ *it* again? *You* do not want to become *His* disciples *too,* do you?"

9:28
John 5:45; Rom.
2:17

28 And they reviled him, and said, "*You* are *His* disciple, but *we* are disciples of *Moses.*

9:29
John 8:14

29 "*We* know that God has spoken⁺ to *Moses;* but as for *this* man, we do not know where He is from."

30 The man answered and said to them, "Well, here is an amazing thing, that *you* do not know where He is from, and *yet* He opened my eyes.

9:31
Job 27:8f.; 35:13;
Ps. 34:15f.;
66:18; 145:19;
Prov. 15:29; 28:9;
Is. 1:15; James
5:16ff.
9:33
John 3:2; 9:16
9:34
John 9:2;
John 9:22,35;
3 John 10

31 "We know that God does not hear *sinners;* but if anyone is †*God-fearing,* and does~¹⁹ᵃ His will, He hears *him.*

32 "Since the *beginning of time* it has never been heard that anyone opened the eyes of a person born⁺ blind.

33 "If this man were not from God, He couldᵐ do~ •nothing."

34 They answered and said to him, "*You* were born *entirely* in sins, and are *you* teaching us?" And they put him out.

Jesus Affirms His Deity

35 Jesus heard that they had put him out; and finding him, He said, "Do *you* believe in the Son of Man?"

36 He answered and said, "And who is He, Lord, that I may believe[x] in Him?"

37 Jesus said to him, "You have both seen[+] Him, and He is the one who is talking with you."

38 And he said, "Lord, I believe." And he worshiped Him.

39 And Jesus said, "For *judgment* I came into this world, that those who do not see may see;[~] and that those who see may become blind."

40 Those of the Pharisees who were with Him heard these things, and said to Him, "*We* are not blind too, are we?"

41 Jesus said to them, "If you were blind, you would have[ᵐ] no sin; but since you say, 'We see,' your sin remains.

Parable of the Good Shepherd

10 "•Truly, •truly, I say to you, he who does not enter by the door into the fold of the sheep, but climbs up some other way, he is a thief and a †robber.

2 "But he who enters by the door is a *shepherd* of the sheep.

3 "To *him* the doorkeeper opens, and the sheep hear *his* voice, and he calls his own sheep by name, and leads them out.

4 "When he puts[x] forth all his own, he goes *before* them, and the sheep follow him because they know[29e] his voice.

5 "And a *stranger* they simply will •not follow, but will flee from him, because they do not know the voice of *strangers.*"

6 This figure of speech Jesus spoke to them, but they did not understand what those things were which He had been saying[ᵐ] to them.

7 Jesus therefore said to them again, "•Truly, •truly, I say to you, †*I* am the door of the sheep.

8 "All who came before Me are thieves and †robbers, but the sheep did not hear them.

9 "†*I* am the door; if anyone enters[x] through *Me,* he shall be saved, and shall go in and out, and find pasture.

10 "The thief comes only to steal,[x] and kill,[x] and destroy;[x] *I* came that they might have[~] *life,*[30b] and might have[~] *it* abundantly.

11 "†*I* am the good[25b] shepherd; the good shepherd lays down His life[30c] for the sheep.

12 "He who is a hireling, and *not* a shepherd, who is not the owner of the sheep, beholds the wolf coming, and leaves the

9:35
John 9:22,34; 3
John 10;
Matt. 4:3
9:36
Rom. 10:14

9:37
John 4:26

9:38
Matt. 8:2
9:39
John 3:19; 5:22,
27;
Luke 4:18;
Matt. 13:13;
15:14
9:40
Rom. 2:19

9:41
John 15:22,24;
Prov. 26:12

10:1
John 10:8

10:2
John 10:11f.
10:3
John 10:4f.,16,27;
John 10:9

10:4
John 10:5,16,27

10:5
John 10:4,16,27

10:6
John 16:25,29; 2
Pet. 2:22

10:7
John 10:1f.,9

10:8
Jer. 23:1f.; Ezek.
34:2ff.; John 10:1

10:9
John 10:1f.,9

10:10
John 5:40
10:11
Is. 40:11; Ezek.
34:11-16,23;
John 10:14; Heb.
13:20; 1 Pet. 5:4;
Rev. 7:17;
John 10:15,17,18;
15:13; 1 John
3:16
10:12
John 10:2

sheep, and flees, and the wolf snatches them, and scatters *them*.

13 *"He flees* because he is a †hireling, and is not concerned about the sheep.

10:14
John 10:11;
John 10:27

14 *"†I* am the good[25b] shepherd; and I know[29a] My own, and My own know[29a] Me,

10:15
Matt. 11:27; Luke
10:22;
John 10:11,17,18

15 even as the Father knows[29a] Me and I know[29a] the Father; and I lay down *My life* for the sheep.

10:16
Is. 56:8;
John 11:52;
17:20f.; Eph.
2:13-18; 1 Pet.
2:25;
Ezek. 34:23;
37:24

16 "And I have other sheep, which are not of this fold; I must bring[x] *them also,* and they shall hear *My voice;* and they shall become †one flock *with* †one shepherd.

10:17
John 10:11,15,18

17 "For this reason the Father loves[31a] Me, because *I* lay down My life that I may take[x] it again.

10:18
Matt. 26:53; John
2:19; 5:26;
John 10:11,15,17;
John 14:31;
15:10; Phil. 2:8;
Heb. 5:8

18 "No one ˢhas taken it away from Me, but *I* lay it down on My own initiative. I have *authority* to lay[x] it down, and I have *authority* to take[x] it up again. This commandment I received from My Father."

10:19
John 7:43; 9:16

19 There arose a division again among the Jews because of these words.

10:20
John 7:20;
Mark 3:21

20 And many of them were saying,ᵐ "He has a *demon* and is insane. Why do you listen to Him?"

10:21
Matt. 4:24;
Ex. 4:11; John
9:32f.

21 Others were saying,ᵐ "These are not the sayings of one demon-possessed. A demon cannot open[x] the eyes of the *blind,* can he?"

Jesus Asserts His Deity

22 At that time the Feast of the Dedication took place at Jerusalem;

10:23
Acts 3:11; 5:12

23 it was winter, and Jesus was walking in the temple in the portico of Solomon.

10:24
John 1:19; 10:31,
33;
Luke 22:67; John
16:25

24 The Jews therefore gathered around Him, and were saying ᵐ to Him, "How long will You keep us in suspense? If *You* are the Christ, tellᴺ us plainly."

10:25
John 8:56,58;
John 5:36; 10:38

25 Jesus answered them, "I told you, and you do not believe; the works that I do in My Father's name, these bear witness of Me.

10:26
John 8:47
10:27
John 10:4,16;
John 10:14

26 "But *you* do not believe, because you are not of My sheep.

27 "My sheep hear *My voice,* and *I* know[29a] them, and they follow Me;

10:28
John 17:2f.;
1 John 2:25; 5:11;
John 6:37,39

28 and I give eternal life to them, and they shall •*never* perish; and no †one shall snatch[x] them out of My hand.

29 "†‡My Father, who has given⁺ *them* to Me, is greater than †all; and no one is able to snatch~ *them* out of the Father's hand.

10:30
John 17:21ff.

30 "I and the Father are *one."*

ˢMany Gr. mss. read *takes* †Some early mss. read *What My Father has given Me is greater than all*

31 The Jews took up stones again to stone^x Him.

32 Jesus answered them, "I showed you many *good*[25b] works from the Father; for which of them are you stoning Me?"

33 The Jews answered Him, "For a *good work* we do not stone You, but for †*blasphemy;* and because You, being a man, make Yourself out *to be* God."

34 Jesus answered them, "Has it not been written⁺ in your Law, 'I SAID, YOU ARE GODS'?

35 "If he called *them* gods, to whom the word of God came (and the Scripture cannot be broken),ˣ

36 do you say of Him, whom the Father sanctified and sent into the world, 'You are blaspheming,' because I said, 'I am the *Son of* †*God'?*

37 "If I do not do the works of My Father, do not believe° Me;

38 but if I do them, though you do not believe~ *Me,* believe~⁺ the *works,* that you may know^{x29a} and understand~[29a] that the Father is in Me, and I in the Father."

39 Therefore they were seeking^m again to seize^x Him, and He eluded their grasp.

40 And He went away again beyond the Jordan to the place where John was first baptizing,~ and He was staying there.

41 And many came to Him and were saying,^m "While John performed *no* sign, yet everything John said about this man was †true."

42 And many believed in Him there.

The Death and Resurrection of Lazarus

11 Now a certain man was sick,~ Lazarus of Bethany, the village of Mary and her sister Martha.

2 And it was the Mary who anointed the Lord with ointment, and wiped His feet with her hair, whose brother Lazarus was sick.^m

3 The sisters therefore sent to Him, saying, "Lord, behold, he whom You love[31b] is sick."

4 But when Jesus heard it, He said, "This sickness is not unto death, but for the glory of God, that the Son of God may be glorified^x by it."

5 Now Jesus loved^{m31a} Martha, and her sister, and Lazarus.

6 When therefore He heard that he was sick, He stayed then two days *longer* in the place where He was.

7 Then after this He *said to the disciples, "Let us go~ to Judea again."

8 The disciples *said to Him, "Rabbi, the Jews were just now seeking^m to stone^x You, and are You going there again?"

10:31
John 8:59

10:33
Lev. 24:16;
John 5:18

10:34
John 8:17;
John 12:34;
15:25; Rom. 3:19;
1 Cor. 14:21;
Ps. 82:6

10:36
Jer. 1:5; John
6:69; John
John 3:17;
John 5:17f.; 10:30

10:37
John 10:25; 15:24
10:38
John 10:25;
14:11;
John 14:10f.,20;
17:21,23

10:39
John 7:30;
Luke 4:30; John
8:59
10:40
John 1:28

10:41
John 2:11;
John 1:27,30,34;
3:27-30

10:42
John 7:31

11:1
Matt. 21:17; John
11:18;
Luke 10:38; John
11:5,19ff.
11:2
Luke 7:38; John
12:3;
Luke 7:13; John
11:3,21,32;
13:13f.
11:3
Luke 7:13; John
11:2,21,32;
13:13f.;
John 11:5,11,36
11:4
John 9:3; 10:38;
11:40

11:5
John 11:1

11:7
John 10:40

11:8
Matt. 23:7;
John 8:59; 10:31

9   Jesus answered, "Are there not *twelve hours* in the day? If anyone walks~ in the day, he does not stumble, because he sees the light of this world.

10   "But if anyone walks~ in the night, he stumbles, because the light is not in him."

11   This He said, and after that He *said to them, "Our friend Lazarus has fallen⁺ asleep; but I go, that I may awaken^x him out of sleep."

12   The disciples therefore said to Him, "Lord, if he has fallen⁺ asleep, he will recover."

13   Now Jesus had spoken of his death, but they thought that He was speaking of literal sleep.

14   Then Jesus therefore said to them plainly, "Lazarus is dead,

15   and I am glad for your sakes that I was not there, so that you may believe;^x but let us go~ to him."

16   Thomas therefore, who is called Didymus, said to *his* fellow disciples, "Let us also go,~ that we may die^x with Him."

17   So when Jesus came, He found that he had already been in the tomb *four* days.

18   Now Bethany was near Jerusalem, about two miles off;

19   and many of the Jews had come to Martha and Mary, to console^x them concerning *their* brother.

20   Martha therefore, when she heard that Jesus was coming, went to meet Him; but Mary still sat in the house.

21   Martha therefore said to Jesus, "Lord, if You had been here, my brother would not have died.

22   "Even now I know²⁹ᵉ that whatever You ask^x of God, God will give You."

23   Jesus *said to her, "Your brother shall *rise again.*"

24   Martha *said to Him, "I know that he will rise again in the resurrection on the last day."

25   Jesus said to her, "⁺*I* am the resurrection and the life;³⁰ᵇ he who believes in Me shall live even if he dies,^x

26   and everyone who lives and believes in Me shall •*never* die.^x Do you believe this?"

27   She *said to Him, "Yes, Lord; I have believed⁺ that *You* are the Christ, the Son of God, *even* He who comes into the world."

28   And when she had said this, she went away, and called Mary her sister, saying secretly, "The Teacher is here, and is calling for you."

29   And when she heard it, she *arose quickly, and was coming to Him.

30 Now Jesus had not yet come into the village, but was still in the place where Martha met Him.

31 The Jews then who were with her in the house, and consoling her, when they saw that Mary rose up quickly and went out, followed her, supposing that she was going to the tomb to weep[x] there.

32 Therefore, when Mary came where Jesus was, she saw Him, and fell at His feet, saying to Him, "Lord, if You had been here, my *brother* would not have died."

33 When Jesus therefore saw her weeping, and the Jews who came with her, *also* weeping, He was deeply moved in spirit, and was troubled,

34 and said, "Where have you laid[+] him?" They *said to Him, "Lord, come and see."[xl]

35 Jesus *wept.*

36 And so the Jews were saying,[m] "Behold how He loved[m31b] him!"

37 But some of them said, "Could[m] not this man, who opened the eyes of him who was blind, have kept[x] this man also from dying?"[x]

38 Jesus therefore again being deeply moved within, *came to the tomb. Now it was a cave, and a stone was lying[m] against it.

39 Jesus *said, "Remove[xl] the stone." Martha, the sister of the deceased, *said to Him, "Lord, by this time there will be a stench, for he has been *dead [+]four* days."

40 Jesus *said to her, "Did I not say to you, if you believe,[x] you will see the glory of God?"

41 And so they removed the stone. And Jesus raised His eyes, and said, "Father, I thank Thee that Thou heardest Me.

42 "And I knew that Thou hearest Me always; but because of the people standing around I said it, that they may believe[x] that *Thou* didst send Me."

43 And when He had said these things, He cried out with a loud voice, "Lazarus, come forth."

44 He who had died came forth, bound[+] hand and foot with wrappings; and his face was wrapped around with a cloth. Jesus *said to them, "Unbind[xl] him, and let[xl] him go."

45 Many therefore of the Jews, who had come to Mary and beheld what He had done, believed in Him.

46 But some of them went away to the Pharisees, and told them the things which Jesus had done.

Conspiracy to Kill Jesus

47 Therefore the chief priests and the Pharisees convened a

11:30
John 11:20

11:31
John 11:19,33;
John 11:19

11:32
John 11:2;
John 11:21

11:33
John 11:19;
John 11:38;
John 12:27; 13:21

11:35
Luke 19:41; John
11:33
11:36
John 11:19;
John 11:3
11:37
John 9:7

11:38
Matt. 27:60; Mark
15:46; Luke 24:2;
John 20:1
11:39
John 11:17

11:40
John 11:4,23ff.

11:41
Matt. 27:60; Mark
15:46; Luke 24:2;
John 20:1;
John 17:1; Acts
7:55;
Matt. 11:25
11:42
John 12:30;
17:21;
John 3:17

11:44
John 19:40;
John 20:7

11:45
John 7:31;
John 11:19;
12:17f.;
John 2:23
11:46
John 7:32,45;
11:57
11:47
John 7:32,45;
11:57;
Matt. 26:3;
Matt. 5:22;
John 2:11

council, and were saying,ᵐ "What are we doing? For this man is performing *many* signs.

11:48
Matt. 24:15

48 "If we letˣ Him *go on* like this, all men will believe in Him, and the *Romans* will come and take away both our place and our nation."

11:49
Matt. 26:3;
John 11:51; 18:13

49 But a certain one of them, Caiaphas, who was high priest that year, said to them, "*You* know •nothing at all,

11:50
John 18:14

50 nor do you take into account that it is expedient for you that †one man should dieˣ for the people, and that the whole nation should not perish."ˣ

11:51
John 18:13

51 Now this he did not say on his *own initiative;* but being high priest *that* year, he prophesied that Jesus was going to die for the nation,

11:52
John 10:16

52 and not for the nation only, but that He might also gatherˣ together into one the children of God who are scattered⁺ abroad.

11:53
Matt. 26:4
11:54
John 7:1;
2 Chr. 13:19 mg.

53 So from that day on they planned together to killˣ Him.

54 Jesus therefore no longer continued to walkᵐ publicly among the Jews, but went away from there to the country near the wilderness, into a city called Ephraim; and there He stayed with the disciples.

11:55
Matt. 26:1f.; Mark
14:1; Luke 22:1;
John 2:13; 12:1;
13:1;
Num. 9:10; 2 Chr.
30:17f.; John
18:28
11:56
John 7:11

55 Now the Passover of the Jews was at hand, and many went up to Jerusalem out of the country before the Passover, to purifyˣ themselves.

56 Therefore they were seekingᵐ for Jesus, and were sayingᵐ to one another, as they stood in the temple, "What do you think; that He will not come to the feast at all?"

11:57
John 11:47

57 Now the chief priests and the Pharisees had given orders that if anyone knewˣ where He was, he should reportˣ it, that they might seizeˣ Him.

Mary Anoints Jesus

12:1
John 12:1-8;
Matt. 26:6-13;
Mark 14:3-9;
Luke 7:37-39;
John 11:55;
12:20;
Matt. 21:17; John
11:43f.
12:2
Luke 10:38
12:3
Luke 7:37f.; John
11:2;
Mark 14:3

12 Jesus, therefore, six days before the Passover, came to Bethany where Lazarus was, whom Jesus had raised *from the dead.*

2 So they made Him a supper there, and Martha was serving;ᵐ but Lazarus was one of those reclining *at the table* with Him.

3 Mary therefore took a pound of *very costly* perfume of *pure* nard, and anointed the feet of Jesus, and wiped His feet with her hair; and the house was filled with the fragrance of the perfume.

12:4
John 6:71

4 But Judas Iscariot, one of His disciples, who was intending to betray Him, *said,

5 "Why was this perfume not sold for ᵘ*three hundred* denarii, and given to poor *people*?"

6 Now he said this, not because he was concerned about the poor, but because he was a †*thief,* and as he had the money box, he used to pilferᵐ what was put into it.

12:6
John 13:29;
Luke 8:3

7 Jesus therefore said, "Letˣⁱ her alone, in order that she may keepˣ ᵛit for the *day of My burial.*

12:7
John 19:40

8 "For the *poor* you always have with you, but you do not always have *Me.*"

12:8
Deut. 15:11; Matt.
26:11; Mark 14:7

9 The great multitude therefore of the Jews learned that He was there; and they came, not for Jesus' sake only, but that they might also seeˣ *Lazarus,* whom He raised from the dead.

12:9
Mark 12:37; John
12:12 mg.;
John 11:43f.;
12:1,17f.

10 But the chief priests took counsel that they might putˣ *Lazarus* to death *also;*

11 because on account of *him* many of the Jews were going away, and were believingᵐ in Jesus.

12:11
John 11:45f.;
12:18;
John 7:31; 11:42

Jesus Enters Jerusalem

12 On the next day the great multitude who had come to the feast, when they heard that Jesus was coming to Jerusalem,

12:12
John 12:12-15:
Matt. 21:4-9;
Mark 11:7-10;
Luke 19:35-38;
John 12:1

13 took the branches of the palm trees, and went out to meet Him, and *began* to cryᵐ out, "Hosanna! BLESSED⁺ IS HE WHO COMES IN THE NAME OF THE LORD, even the *King of Israel.*"

12:13
Ps. 118:26;
John 1:49

14 And Jesus, finding a young donkey, sat on it; as it is written,⁺

15 "FEAR⁰ NOT, DAUGHTER OF ZION; BEHOLD, YOUR KING IS COMING, SEATED ON A DONKEY'S COLT."

12:15
Zech. 9:9

16 These things *His* disciples did not understand at the first; but when Jesus was *glorified,* then they remembered that these things were written⁺ of *Him,* and that they had done these things to Him.

12:16
Mark 9:32; John
2:22; 14:26;
John 7:39; 12:23

17 And so the multitude who were with Him when He called Lazarus out of the tomb, and raised him from the dead, were bearingᵐ Him witness.

12:17
John 11:42

18 For this cause also the multitude went and met Him, because they heard that He had performed⁺ *this* sign.

12:18
Luke 19:37; John
12:12;
John 12:11

19 The Pharisees therefore said to one another, "You see that you are not doing •any good; look, the world has gone after Him."

Greeks Seek Jesus

20 Now there were certain Greeks among those who were going up to worshipˣ at the feast;

12:20
John 7:35;
John 12:1

ᵘEquivalent to 11 months' wages ᵛI.e., The custom of anointing for burial

12:21
John 1:44;
Matt. 11:21

12:22
John 1:44

12:23
Matt. 26:45; Mark
14:35,41; John
13:1; 17:1;
John 7:39; 12:16;
13:32
12:24
Rom. 14:9; 1 Cor.
15:36

12:25
Matt. 10:39;
16:25; Mark 8:35;
Luke 9:24; 17:33;
Luke 14:26
12:26
John 14:3; 17:24;
2 Cor. 5:8; Phil.
1:23; 1 Thess.
4:17;
1 Sam. 2:30; Ps.
91:15; Luke 12:37

12:27
Matt. 26:38; Mark
14:34; John
11:33;
Matt. 11:25;
John 12:23
12:28
Matt. 11:25;
Matt. 3:17; 17:5;
Mark 1:11; 9:7;
Luke 3:22; 9:35
12:29
Acts 23:9

12:30
John 11:42
12:31
John 3:19; 9:39;
16:11;
John 14:30;
16:11; 2 Cor. 4:4;
Eph. 2:2; 6:12;
1 John 4:4; 5:19
12:32
John 3:14; 8:28;
12:34;
John 6:44
12:33
John 18:32; 21:19
12:34
John 10:34;
Ps. 110:4; Is. 9:7;
Ezek. 37:25; Dan.
7:14;
Matt. 8:20;
John 3:14; 8:28;
12:32
12:35
John 7:33; 9:4;
John 12:46;
1 John 2:10;
Gal. 6:10; Eph.
5:8;
1 John 1:6; 2:11
12:36
John 12:46;
Luke 16:8; John
8:12;
John 8:59

21   these therefore came to Philip, who was from Bethsaida of Galilee, and *began to* ask^m him, saying, "Sir, we wish to see^x Jesus."

22   Philip *came and *told Andrew; Andrew and Philip *came, and they *told Jesus.

23   And Jesus *answered them, saying, "The hour has come⁺ for the Son of Man to be glorified.^x

24   "•Truly, •truly, I say to you, unless a grain of wheat falls into the earth and dies,^x it remains by itself *alone;* but if it dies,^x it bears *much fruit.*

25   "He who loves^31b his life^30c loses it; and he who hates his life^30c in ⁺this world shall keep it to *life*^30b *eternal.*

26   "If anyone serves~ Me, let him follow^⌐ Me; and where *I* am, there shall My servant also be; if anyone serves~^38a Me, the *Father* will honor him.

Jesus Foretells His Death

27   "Now My soul has become troubled;⁺ and what shall I say,^x 'Father, save^xi Me from this hour'? But for this purpose I came to this hour.

28   "Father, glorify^xi *Thy* name." There came therefore a voice out of heaven: "I have both glorified it, and will glorify it again."

29   The multitude therefore, who stood by and heard it, were saying^xx that it had thundered;⁺ others were saying,^xx "An angel has spoken⁺ to Him."

30   Jesus answered and said, "This voice has not come⁺ for *My* sake, but for your sakes.

31   "Now judgment is upon this world; now the ruler of this world shall be cast out.

32   "And *I*, if I be lifted^x up from the earth, will draw *all men* to Myself."

33   But He was saying^m this to indicate the kind of death by which He was to die.

34   The multitude therefore answered Him, "We have heard out of the Law that the Christ is to remain forever; and how can *You* say, 'The Son of Man must be lifted^x up'? Who is this Son of Man?"

35   Jesus therefore said to them, "For a little while longer the light is among you. Walk^⌐ while you have the *light,* that darkness may not overtake^x you; he who walks in the darkness does not know where he goes.

36   "While you have the *light,* believe^⌐ in the light, in order that you may become *sons of light.*"

These things Jesus spoke, and He departed and hid Himself from them.

37   But though He had performed⁺ *so many* signs before them, *yet* they were not believing^m in Him;

38   that the word of Isaiah the prophet might be fulfilled,ˣ which he spoke, "LORD, WHO HAS BELIEVED OUR REPORT? AND TO WHOM HAS THE ARM OF THE LORD BEEN REVEALED?"

12:38
Is. 53:1; Rom.
10:16

39   For this cause they could^m not believe,~ for Isaiah said again,

40   "HE HAS BLINDED⁺ *THEIR* EYES, AND HE HARDENED *THEIR* HEART; LEST THEY SEEˣ WITH THEIR EYES, AND PERCEIVEˣ WITH THEIR HEART, AND BE CONVERTED,ˣ AND I HEAL^{15b} THEM."

12:40
Is. 6:10; Matt.
13:14f.;
Mark 6:52

41   These things Isaiah said, because he saw His glory, and he spoke of Him.

12:41
Is. 6:1ff.;
Luke 24:27

42   Nevertheless² many even of the *rulers* believed in Him, but because of the *Pharisees* they were not confessing^m *Him*, lest they should be put *out of the synagogue;*

12:42
John 7:48; 12:11;
Luke 23:13;
John 7:13;
John 9:22

43   for they loved the approval of men rather² than the approval of God.

12:43
John 5:41,44

44   And Jesus cried out and said, "He who believes in Me does not believe in Me, but in Him who sent Me.

12:44
Matt. 10:40; John
5:24

45   "And he who beholds •*Me* beholds the One who sent Me.

12:45
John 14:9

46   "*I* have come⁺ *as light* into the world, that everyone who believes in Me may not remainˣ in *darkness.*

12:46
John 1:4; 3:19;
8:12; 9:5; 12:35f.

47   "And if anyone hearsˣ *My* sayings, and does not keepˣ them, *I* do not judge him; for I did not come to judgeˣ the world, but to saveˣ the world.

12:47
John 3:17; 8:15f.

48   "He who rejects •Me, and does not receive My sayings, has one who judges him; the word I spoke is what will judge him at the last day.

12:48
Luke 10:16;
Deut. 18:18f.;
John 5:45ff.; 8:47;
Matt. 10:15; John
6:39; Acts 17:31;
1 Pet. 1:5; 2 Pet.
3:3,7; Heb. 10:25

49   "For *I* did not speak on My *own initiative,* but the Father *Himself* who sent Me has given⁺ Me commandment, what to say,ˣ and what to speak.ˣ

12:49
John 3:11; 7:16;
8:26,28,38;
14:10,24;
John 14:31; 17:8

50   "And I know that His commandment is eternal life; therefore the things *I* speak, I speak just as the *Father* has told⁺ Me."

12:50
John 6:68;
John 5:19; 8:28

The Lord's Supper

13 Now before the Feast of the Passover, Jesus knowing that His hour had come that He should depart out of this world to the Father, having loved His own who were in the world, He loved^{31a} them *to the end.*

13:1
John 2:13; 11:55;
John 12:23;
John 13:3; 16:28

2   And during supper, the devil having already put⁺ into the heart of Judas Iscariot, *the son* of Simon, to betrayˣ Him,

13:2
John 6:70; 13:27;
John 6:71
13:3
John 3:35;
John 8:42

3   *Jesus,* knowing that the Father had given *all things* into His

hands, and that He had come forth *from God,* and was going back *to God,*

13:4
Luke 12:37; 17:8

4 *rose from supper, and *laid aside His garments; and taking a towel, He girded Himself about.

Jesus Washes the Disciples' Feet

13:5
Gen. 18:4; 19:2;
43:24; Judg.
19:21; Luke 7:44;
1 Tim. 5:10

5 Then He *poured water into the basin, and began to wash~ the disciples' feet, and to wipe~ them with the towel with which He was girded.⁺

6 And so He *came to Simon Peter. He *said to Him, "Lord, do *You* wash *my* feet?"

13:7
John 13:12ff.

7 Jesus answered and said to him, "What I do you do not realize now, but you shall understand hereafter."

13:8
Ps. 51:2,7; Ezek.
36:25; Acts
22:16; 1 Cor.
6:11; Heb. 10:22;
Deut. 12:12;
2 Sam. 20:1;
1 Kin. 12:16

8 Peter *said to Him, "•Never shall You wash° *my* feet!" Jesus answered him, "If I do not wash^x you, you have no part with Me."

9 Simon Peter *said to Him, "Lord, not my feet only, but also my hands and my head."

13:10
John 15:3; Eph.
5:26

10 Jesus *said to him, "He who has bathed⁺ needs only to wash^x his feet, but is completely clean;¹³ᶜ and *you* are clean, but •*not* all *of you.*"

13:11
John 6:64; 13:2

11 For He knew the one who was betraying Him; for this reason He said, "•*Not* all of you are clean."¹³ᶜ

13:12
John 13:4
13:13
John 11:28;
John 11:2; 1 Cor.
12:3; Phil. 2:11
13:14
John 11:2; 1 Cor.
12:3; Phil. 2:11
13:15
1 Pet. 5:3
13:16
Matt. 10:24; Luke
6:40; John 15:20;
2 Cor. 8:23; Phil.
2:25
13:17
Matt. 7:24ff.; Luke
11:28; James
1:25
13:18
John 13:10f.;
John 6:70; 15:16,
19;
John 15:25;
17:12; 18:32;
19:24,36;
Ps. 41:9; Matt.
26:21ff.; Mark
14:18f.; Luke
22:21ff.; John
13:21,22,26
13:19
John 14:29; 16:4;
John 8:24
13:20
Matt. 10:40;
Mark 9:37; Luke
9:48; 10:16; Gal.
4:14

12 And so when He had washed their feet, and taken His garments, and reclined *at the table* again, He said to them, "Do you know what I have done⁺ to you?

13 "You call Me Teacher and Lord; and you are right, for *so* I am.

14 "If *I* then, the Lord and the Teacher, washed *your* feet, *you* also ought to wash~ one another's feet.

15 "For I gave you an example that *you also* should do~ as *I* did to you.

16 "•Truly, •truly, I say to you, a slave is not greater than his master; neither *is* one who is sent greater than the one who sent him.

17 "If you know these things, you are ⁺*blessed* if you do~ them.

18 "I do not speak of *all of* ⁺*you. I* know the ones I have chosen; but *it is* that the Scripture may be fulfilled,^x 'HE WHO EATS *MY* BREAD HAS LIFTED UP HIS HEEL AGAINST ME.'

19 "From now on I am telling you before *it* comes to pass, so that when it does occur, you may believe^x that I am *He.*

20 "•Truly, •truly, I say to you, he who receives whomever I

send[x] receives *Me;* and he who receives •Me receives Him who sent Me."

Jesus Predicts His Betrayal

21 When Jesus had said this, He became troubled in spirit, and testified, and said, "•Truly, •truly, I say to you, that one of you will betray Me."

22 The disciples *began* looking[m] at one another, at a loss *to know* of which one He was speaking.

23 There was reclining~ on Jesus' breast one of His disciples, whom Jesus loved.[m]

24 Simon Peter therefore *gestured to him, and *said to him, "Tell *us* who it is of whom He is speaking."

25 He, leaning back thus on Jesus' breast, *said to Him, "Lord, who is it?"

26 Jesus therefore *answered, "That is the one for whom I shall dip the morsel and give it to him." So when He had dipped the morsel, He *took and *gave it to Judas, *the son* of Simon Iscariot.

27 And after the morsel, *Satan* then entered into him. Jesus therefore *said to him, "What you do, do[x] quickly."[3]

28 Now no one of those reclining *at the table* knew for what purpose He had said this to him.

29 For some were supposing,[m] because Judas had[m] the money box, that Jesus was saying to him, "Buy[x] the things we have need of for the feast"; or else, that he should give[x] something to the poor.

30 And so after receiving the morsel he went out *immediately;* and it was night.

31 When therefore he had gone out, Jesus *said, "Now is the Son of Man glorified, and God is glorified in Him;

32 if God is glorified in Him, God will also glorify Him in Himself, and will glorify Him immediately.

33 "Little children, I am with you a little while longer. You shall seek Me; and as I said to the Jews, I now say to you also, 'Where *I* am going, *you* cannot come.'

34 "A *new*[34a] commandment I give to you, that you love~[31a] one another, even as I have loved you, that *you also* love~[31a] one another.

35 "By this all men will know[29a] that you are *My* disciples, if you have~ love[31a] for one another."

36 Simon Peter *said to Him, "Lord, where are You going?" Jesus answered, "Where I go, you cannot follow[x] Me *now;* but you shall follow *later.*"

13:21
John 11:33;
Matt. 26:21f.;
Mark 14:18ff.;
Luke 22:21ff.;
John 13:18,22,26
13:22
Matt. 26:21ff.;
Mark 14:18ff.;
Luke 22:21ff.;
John 13:18,21,26
13:23
John 1:18;
John 19:26; 20:2;
21:7,20

13:25
John 21:20

13:26
John 6:71

13:27
Matt. 4:10;
Luke 22:3; John 13:2

13:29
John 12:6;
John 13:1;
John 12:5

13:30
Luke 22:53

13:31
Matt. 8:20;
John 7:39;
John 14:13; 17:4;
1 Pet. 4:11
13:32
John 17:1
13:33
1 John 2:1;
John 7:33;
John 7:34
13:34
John 15:12,17; 1
John 2:7f.; 3:11,
23; 2 John 5;
Lev. 19:18; Matt.
5:44; Gal. 5:14;
1 Thess. 4:9;
Heb. 13:1; 1 Pet.
1:22; 1 John 4:7;
Eph. 5:2; 1 John
4:10f.
13:35
1 John 3:14; 4:20
13:36
John 13:33; 14:2;
16:5;
John 21:18f.;
2 Pet. 1:14

13:37
John 13:37,38;
Matt. 26:33-35;
Mark 14:29-31;
Luke 22:33-34
13:38
Mark 14:30; John
18:27

37   Peter *said to Him, "Lord, why can I not follow[x] You right now? I will lay down *my life* for You."

38   Jesus *answered, "Will you lay down *your life* for Me? •Truly, •truly, I say to you, a cock shall •not crow,[x] until you deny[x] Me three times.

Jesus Comforts His Disciples

14:1
John 14:27;
16:22,24

14 "Let not *your* heart be troubled;[⊙] [w]believe[ᴹ] in God, believe[ᴹ] also in *Me.*

14:2
John 13:33,36

2   "In My Father's house are *many* dwelling places; if it were not so, I would have told you; for I go to prepare[x] a place for you.

14:3
John 14:18,28;
John 12:26

3   "And if I go[x] and prepare[x] a place for you, I will come again, and receive you to Myself; that where *I* am, *there you* may be *also.*

4   "[x]And you know[29e] the way where *I* am going."

14:5
John 11:16

5   Thomas *said to Him, "Lord, we do not know where You are going, how do we know the way?"

14:6
John 10:9; Rom.
5:2; Eph. 2:18;
Heb. 10:20;
John 1:14;
John 1:4; 11:25; 1
John 5:20

6   Jesus *said to him, "[†]*I* am the way, and the truth, and the life; no one comes to the Father, but through Me.

Oneness with the Father

14:7
John 8:19;
1 John 2:13;
John 6:46

7   "If you had known[+29a] Me, you would have known[29e] My Father also; from now on you know[29a] Him, and have seen[+] Him."

14:8
John 1:43

8   Philip *said to Him, "Lord, show[xi] us the Father, and it is enough for us."

14:9
John 1:14; 12:45;
Col. 1:15; Heb.
1:3

9   Jesus *said to him, "Have I been so long with you, and *yet* you have not come to know[29a] Me, Philip? He who has seen[+] •Me has seen[+] the Father; how do *you* say, 'Show[xi] us the Father'?

14:10
John 10:38;
14:11,20;
John 5:19; 14:24

10   "Do you not believe that I am in the Father, and the Father is in Me? The words[43b] that I say to you I do not speak on My *own initiative,* but the Father abiding in Me does His works.

14:11
John 10:38;
14:10,20;
John 5:36

11   "Believe[ᴹ] Me that I am in the Father, and the Father in Me; otherwise believe[ᴹ] on account of the *works themselves.*

14:12
John 4:37f.; 5:20;
John 7:33; 14:28

12   "•Truly, •truly, I say to you, he who believes in Me, the works that *I* do shall *he* do *also;* and *greater*[26a] *works* than these shall he do; because I go to the *Father.*

14:13
Matt. 7:7;
John 13:31
14:14
John 15:16;
16:23f.

13   "And whatever you ask[x] in My name, that will I do, that the Father may be glorified[x] in the Son.

14   "If you ask[x] Me anything in My name, *I* will do *it.*

14:15
John 14:21,23;
15:10; 1 John
5:3; 2 John 6

15   "If you love[~31a] Me, you will keep My commandments.

[w]Or, *you believe in God*   [x]Many ancient authorities read *And where I go you know, and the way you know*

Role of the Spirit

16 "And *I* will ask[9c] the Father, and He will give you *another*[8a] *Helper,* that He may be with you forever;

17 *that is* the Spirit of truth, whom the world cannot receive,[x] because it does not behold Him or know[29a] Him, *but you* know Him because He abides *with you,* and will be *in you.*

18 "I will not leave you as orphans; I will come to you.

19 "After a little while the world will behold Me no more; but *you will* behold Me; because *I* live, *you* shall live also.

20 "In that day *you* shall know[29a] that I am in My Father, and you in Me, and I in you.

21 "He who has My commandments and keeps them, he it is who loves[31a] Me; and he who loves Me shall be loved by My Father, and *I* will love him, and will disclose Myself to him."

22 Judas (not Iscariot) *said to Him, "Lord, what then has happened• that You are going to disclose Yourself to us, and •*not* to the †world?"

23 Jesus answered and said to him, "If anyone loves~ Me, he will keep My word;[43a] and My Father will love him, and We will come to *him,* and make *Our abode* with *him.*

24 "He who does not love[31a] Me does not keep My words; and the word which you hear is not Mine, but the Father's who sent Me.

25 "These things I have spoken• to you, while abiding with you.

26 "But the Helper, the Holy Spirit, whom the Father will send in My name, *He* will teach you all things, and bring to your remembrance all that *I* said to you.

27 "*Peace* I leave with you; *My* peace I give to you; not as the world gives, do I give to you. Let not *your* heart be troubled,⊖ nor let it be fearful.⊖

28 "You heard that *I* said to you, 'I go away, and I will come to you.' If you loved[m] Me, you would have rejoiced, because I go to the Father; for the Father is greater than I.

29 "And now I have told• you before it comes to pass, that when it comes to pass, you may believe.[x]

30 "I will not speak much more with you, for the ruler of the world is coming, and he has •*nothing* in Me;

31 but that the world may know[x][29a] that I love the Father, and as the Father gave Me commandment, even so I do. Arise, let us go~ from here.

14:16
John 7:39; 14:26;
15:26; 16:7; Rom.
8:26; 1 John 2:1
14:17
John 15:26;
16:13; 1 John 4:6;
5:7;
1 Cor. 2:14

14:18
John 14:3,28
14:19
John 7:33;
John 16:16,22;
John 6:57
14:20
John 16:23,26;
John 10:38; 14:11

14:21
John 14:15,23;
15:10; 1 John 5:3;
2 John 6;
John 14:23;
16:27;
Ex. 33:18f.; Prov.
8:17
14:22
Luke 6:16; Acts
1:13;
Acts 10:40,41
14:23
John 14:15,21;
15:10; 1 John 5:3;
2 John 6;
John 8:51; 1 John
2:5;
John 14:21;
2 Cor. 6:16; Eph.
3:17; 1 John 2:24;
Rev. 3:20; 21:3
14:24
John 14:23;
John 7:16; 14:10

14:26
John 14:16;
Luke 24:49; John
1:33; 15:26; 16:7;
Acts 2:33;
John 16:13f.; 1
John 2:20,27;
John 2:22
14:27
John 16:33;
20:19; Phil. 4:7;
Col. 3:15;
John 14:1
14:28
John 14:2-4;
John 14:3,18;
John 14:12;
John 10:29; Phil.
2:6
14:29
John 13:19

14:30
John 12:31

14:31
John 10:18;
12:49;
John 13:1; 18:1

Jesus Is the Vine—Followers Are Branches

15:1
Ps. 80:8ff.; Is.
5:1ff.; Ezek.
19:10ff.; Matt.
21:33ff.;
Matt. 15:13; Rom.
11:17; 1 Cor. 3:9

15 "⁺*I* am the true vine, and My Father is the ⁺vinedresser.
2 "Every branch in Me that does not bear fruit, He takes away; and every *branch* that bears fruit, He ʸprunes it, that it may bear˜ *more* fruit.

15:3
John 13:10;
17:17; Eph. 5:26

3 "*You* are already clean¹³ᶜ because of the word⁴³ᵃ which I have spoken⁺ to you.

15:4
John 6:56;
15:4-7; 1 John
2:6

4 "Abideˣˡ in Me, and I in you. As the branch cannot bear˜ fruit of itself, unless it abides˜ in the vine, so neither *can* you, unless you abide˜ *in Me.*

15:5
John 15:16

5 "⁺*I* am the vine, you are the branches; he who abides in Me, and I in him, he bears *much* fruit; for *apart from Me* you can do˜ •*nothing.*

15:6
John 15:2

6 "If anyone does not abide˜ in Me, he is thrown away as a branch, and dries up; and they gather them, and cast them into the fire, and they are burned.

15:7
Matt. 7:7; John
15:16

7 "If you abideˣ in Me, and My words⁴³ᵇ abideˣ in you, askˣˡ whatever you wish, and it shall be done for you.

15:8
Matt. 5:16;
John 8:31

8 "By this is My Father glorified, that you bear˜ *much* fruit, and *so* prove to be *My* disciples.

15:9
John 3:35; 17:23,
24,26

9 "Just as the *Father* has loved³¹ᵃ Me, *I* have also loved *you;* abideˣˡ in My love.

15:10
John 14:15;
John 8:29

10 "If you keepˣ My commandments, you will abide in My love; just as *I* have kept⁺ My Father's commandments, and abide in *His* love.

15:11
John 17:13;
John 3:29

11 "These things I have spoken⁺ to you, that My joy may be in you, and *that* your joy may be made full.ˣ

Disciples' Relation to Each Other

15:12
John 13:34;
15:17; 1 John
3:23; 2 John 5
15:13
Rom. 5:7f.;
John 10:11

12 "This is My commandment, that you love˜³¹ᵃ one another, just as I have loved you.
13 "*Greater*²⁶ᵃ *love* has no one than this, that one layˣ down his *life*³⁰ᶜ for his friends.

15:14
Luke 12:4;
Matt. 12:50
15:15
John 8:26; 16:12

14 "You are My ⁺*friends,* if you do˜¹⁹ᵃ what *I* command you.
15 "No longer do I call you slaves, for the slave does not know what his master is doing; but I have called⁺ *you* friends, for all things that I have heard from My Father I have made known to you.

15:16
John 6:70; 13:18;
15:19;
John 15:5;
John 14:13; 15:7;
16:23

16 "*You* did not choose Me, but *I* chose you, and appointed you, that *you* should go and bear˜ *fruit,* and *that* your fruit should remain,˜ that whatever you askˣ of the Father in My name, He may giveˣ to you.

ʸLit., *cleanses*

17 "This I command you, that you love~[31a] one another.

15:17
John 15:12

Disciples' Relation to the World

18 "If the world hates you, you know that it has hated⁺ *Me* before *it hated* you.

15:18
John 7:7; 1 John 3:13

19 "If you were of the world, the world would love[31b] its *own;* but because you are not of the world, but I chose you out of the world, therefore the world *hates* you.

15:19
John 15:16;
Matt. 10:22; 24:9;
John 17:14

20 "Remember~ the word[43a] that I said to you, 'A slave is not greater than his master.' If they persecuted *Me,* they will *also* persecute *you;* if they kept *My word,* [43a] they will keep *yours also.*

15:20
Matt. 10:24; John 13:16;
1 Cor. 4:12;
2 Cor. 4:9; 2 Tim. 3:12;
John 8:51

21 "But all these things they will do to you for My name's sake, because they do not know the One who sent Me.

15:21
Matt. 10:22; 24:9;
Mark 13:13; Luke 21:12,17; Acts 4:17; 5:41; 9:14;
26:9; 1 Pet. 4:14;
Rev. 2:3;
John 8:19,55;
16:3; 17:25; Acts 3:17; 1 John 3:1

22 "If I had not come and spoken to them, they would not have[m] sin, but now they have *no excuse* for their sin.

15:22
John 9:41; 15:24

23 "He who hates Me hates *My Father also.*

24 "If I had not done among them the *works* which no one else did, they would not have[m] sin; but now they have both seen⁺ and hated⁺ Me and My Father as well.

15:24
John 9:41; 15:21;
John 5:36; 10:37

25 "But *they have done this* in order that the word[43a] may be *fulfilled*[x] that is written⁺ in their Law, 'THEY HATED ME *WITHOUT A CAUSE.'*

15:25
John 10:34;
Ps. 35:19; 69:4

26 "When the Helper comes, whom I will send to you from the Father, *that is* the Spirit of truth, who proceeds from the Father, *He* will bear witness of Me,

15:26
John 14:16;
John 14:26;
John 14:17;
1 John 5:7

27 and *you will* bear witness also, because you have been with Me from the beginning.

15:27
Luke 24:48; John 19:35; 21:24;
1 John 1:2; 4:14;
Luke 1:2

Jesus' Warning

16 "These things I have spoken⁺ to you, that you may be kept[x] from stumbling.

16:1
John 15:18-27;
Matt. 11:6

2 "They will make you outcasts from the synagogue, but an hour is coming for everyone who kills you to think[x] that he is offering~ *service* to God.

16:2
John 9:22;
John 4:21; 16:25;
Is. 66:5; Acts 26:9-11; Rev. 6:9

3 "And these things they will do, because they have not known[29a] the Father, or Me.

16:3
John 8:19,55;
15:21; 17:25;
Acts 3:17; 1 John 3:1

4 "But these things I have spoken⁺ to you, that when their hour comes, you may remember~ that I told you of them. And these things I did not say to you at the beginning, because I was with you.

16:4
John 13:19;
Luke 1:2

The Holy Spirit Promised

16:5
John 7:33; 16:10,
17,28;
John 13:36; 14:5
16:6
John 14:1; 16:22

5 "But now I am going to Him who sent Me; and none of you asks Me, 'Where are You going?'

6 "But because I have said⁺ these things to you, sorrow has filled⁺ your heart.

16:7
John 14:16;
John 14:26

7 "But I tell you the *truth*, it is to your advantage that I go^x away; for if I do not go^x away, the Helper shall •*not* come to you; but if I go,^x I will send Him to you.

8 "And *He*, when He comes, will convict the world concerning sin, and righteousness, and judgment;

16:9
John 15:22,24
16:10
Acts 3:14; 7:52;
17:31; 1 Pet.
3:18;
John 16:5
16:11
John 12:31

9 concerning sin, because they do not believe in Me;

10 and concerning righteousness, because I go to the Father, and you no longer behold Me;

11 and concerning judgment, because the ruler of this world has been judged.⁺

12 "I have many more things to say~ to you, but you cannot bear~ *them* now.

16:13
John 14:17;
John 14:26

13 "But when *He*, the Spirit of truth, comes, He will guide you into *all* the truth; for He will not speak on His own initiative, but whatever He hears, He will speak; and He will disclose to you what *is to come*.

16:14
John 7:39

14 "He shall glorify *Me;* for He shall take of *Mine*, and shall disclose *it* to you.

16:15
John 17:10

15 "All things that the Father has are *Mine;* therefore I said, that He takes of *Mine*, and will disclose *it* to you.

Jesus' Death and Resurrection Foretold

16:16
John 7:33;
John 14:18-24;
16:16-24
16:17
John 16:16;
John 16:5

16 "A little while, and you will no longer behold Me; and again a little while, and you will see Me."

17 *Some* of His disciples therefore said to one another, "What is this thing He is telling us, 'A little while, and you will not behold Me; and again a little while, and you will see Me'; and, 'because I go to the Father'?"

18 And so they were saying,^m "What is this that He says, 'A little while'? We do not know²⁹ᵉ what He is talking about."

16:19
Mark 9:32; John
6:61

19 Jesus knew that they wished^m to question~ Him, and He said to them, "Are you deliberating together about this, that I said, 'A little while, and you will not behold Me, and again a little while, and you will see Me'?

16:20
Mark 16:10; Luke
23:27;
John 20:20
16:21
Is. 13:8; 21:3;
26:17; 66:7; Hos.
13:13; Mic. 4:9; 1
Thess. 5:3

20 "•Truly, •truly, I say to you, that *you* will weep and lament, but the world will rejoice; *you* will be sorrowful, but your sorrow will be turned to *joy*.

21 "Whenever a woman is in travail~ she has sorrow, because

her hour has come; but when she gives[x] birth to the child, she remembers the anguish no more, for joy that a child has been born into the world.

22 "Therefore *you too* now have sorrow; but I will see you again, and your heart will *rejoice,* and no one takes *your joy* away from you.

Prayer Promises

23 "And in that day you will ask[9c] *Me* •no question. •Truly, •truly, I say to you, if you shall ask[x9a] the Father for anything, He will give it to you in My name.

24 "Until now you have asked[9a] for •nothing in My name; ask,[~!] and you will receive,[5b] that your joy may be made[+] †full.

25 "These things I have spoken[+] to you in figurative language; an hour is coming when I will speak no more to you in figurative language, but will tell you plainly of the *Father.*

26 "In that day you will ask *in My name,* and I do not say to you that *I* will request the Father on your behalf;

27 for the Father *Himself* loves[31b] you, because you have loved[+31b] *Me,* and have believed[+] that *I* came forth *from the Father.*

28 "I came forth from the Father, and have come[+] into the world; I am leaving the world again, and going to the Father."

29 His disciples *said, "Lo, now You are speaking *plainly,* and are not using a figure of speech.

30 "Now we know that You know all things, and have no need for anyone to question[~] You; by this we believe that You came from *God.*"

31 Jesus answered them, "Do you now believe?

32 "Behold, an hour is coming, and has *already* come,[+] for you to be scattered,[x] each to his own *home,* and to leave[x] *Me alone;* and *yet* I am not alone, because the Father is with Me.

33 "These things I have spoken[+] to you, that in Me you may have[~] *peace.* In the world you have *tribulation,* but take courage; *I* have overcome[+] the world."

The High Priestly Prayer

17 These things Jesus spoke; and lifting up His eyes to heaven, He said, "Father, the hour has come;[+] glorify[xi] Thy Son, that the Son may glorify[x] •Thee,

2 even as Thou gavest Him authority over all mankind, that to all whom Thou hast given[+] Him, He may give[x] eternal life.

3 "And this is eternal life, that they may know[~29a] Thee, the only true God, and Jesus Christ whom Thou hast sent.

16:22 John 16:6; John 16:16

16:23 John 14:20; 16:26; John 16:19,30; John 15:16

16:24 John 14:14; John 3:29; 15:11

16:25 Matt. 13:34; John 10:6; 16:29; John 16:2

16:26 John 14:20; 16:23; John 16:19,30

16:27 John 14:21,23; John 2:11; 16:30; John 8:42

16:28 John 8:42; 16:30; John 13:1,3; 16:5, 10,17

16:29 Matt. 13:34; John 10:6; 16:25

16:30 John 2:11; 16:27; John 8:42; 16:28

16:32 John 4:23; 16:2, 25; Zech. 13:7; Matt. 26:31; John 19:27; John 8:29

16:33 John 14:27; John 15:18ff.; Matt. 9:2; Rom. 8:37; 2 Cor. 2:14; 4:7ff.; 6:4ff.; Rev. 3:21; 12:11

17:1 John 11:41; John 7:39; 13:31f.

17:2 John 3:35; John 6:37,39; 17:6,9,24; John 10:28

17:3 John 5:44; John 3:17; 17:8, 21,23,25

17:4
John 13:31;
Luke 22:37; John
4:34
17:5
John 17:1;
John 1:1; 8:58;
17:24; Phil. 2:6
17:6
John 17:26;
John 6:37,39;
17:2,9,24;
John 8:51

4 "I glorified Thee on the earth, having †accomplished the work which Thou hast given⁺ Me to do.ˣ

5 "And now, glorifyˣ⁺ Thou Me together with Thyself, Father, with the glory which I hadᵐ with Thee before the world was.

6 "I manifested *Thy* name to the men whom Thou gavest Me out of the world; *Thine* they were, and Thou gavest them to Me, and they have kept⁺ *Thy word*. ⁴³ᵃ

7 "Now they have come to know⁺ that everything Thou hast given⁺ Me is from Thee;

17:8
John 6:68; 12:49;
John 15:15;
17:14,26;
John 8:42; 16:27,
30;
John 3:17; 17:18,
21,23,25
17:9
Luke 22:32; John
14:16;
Luke 23:34; John
17:20f.;
John 6:37,39;
17:2,6,24
17:10
John 16:15
17:11
John 13:1;
John 7:33; 17:13;
John 17:25;
John 17:6; Phil.
2:9; Rev. 19:12;
John 17:21f.;
Rom. 12:5; Gal.
3:28
17:12
John 17:6; Phil.
2:9; Rev. 19:12;
John 6:39; 18:9;
John 6:70;
Ps. 41:9; John
13:18

8 for the words⁴³ᵇ which Thou gavest Me I have given⁺ to them; and *they* received⁵ᵇ *them*, and truly understood²⁹ᵃ that I came forth from *Thee*, and they believed that *Thou* didst send Me.

9 "I ask⁹ᶜ on *their behalf;* I do not ask on behalf of the *world*, but of those whom Thou hast given⁺ Me; for they are †Thine;

10 and all things that are Mine are Thine, and Thine are Mine; and I have been glorified⁺ in them.

11 "And I am no more in the world; and *yet* they themselves are in the world, and *I* come to *Thee*. Holy²⁸ᵃ Father, keepˣ⁺ them in Thy name, *the name* which Thou hast given⁺ Me, that they may be one, even as We *are*.

12 "While I was with them, *I* was keepingᵐ them in Thy name which Thou hast given⁺ Me; and I guarded them, and not one of them perished but the son of perdition, that the Scripture might be fulfilled.ˣ

The Disciples in the World

17:13
John 7:33; 17:11;
John 15:11;
John 3:29
17:14
John 15:19;
John 8:23; 17:16

13 "But now I come to *Thee;* and these things I speak in the world, that they may have~ My joy made⁺ full in themselves.

14 "I have given⁺ them Thy word;⁴³ᵃ and the world has hated them, because they are not of the world, even as *I* am not of the world.

17:15
Matt. 5:37
17:16
John 17:14
17:17
John 15:3
17:18
John 3:17; 17:3,8,
21,23,25;
Matt. 10:5; John
4:38; 20:21
17:19
John 15:13;
John 15:3;
2 Cor. 7:14; Col.
1:6; 1 John 3:18
17:21
John 10:38;
17:11,23;
John 17:8;
John 3:17; 17:3,
8,18,23,25

15 "I do not ask⁹ᶜ Thee to takeˣ them out of the world, but to keepˣ them from the evil¹⁰ᵇ *one*.

16 "They are not *of the world,* even as *I* am not of the world.

17 "Sanctifyˣ⁺ them in the truth; Thy word⁴³ᵃ is truth.

18 "As Thou didst send Me into the world, I also have sent them into the world.

19 "And for *their sakes* I sanctify Myself, that *they themselves also* may be sanctified⁺ in truth.

20 "I do not ask in behalf of these †alone, but for those also who believe in Me through their word;

21 that they may all be *one;* even as Thou, Father, *art* in Me,

and I in Thee, that *they also* may be in Us; that the world may believe~ that *Thou* didst send Me.

Their Future Glory

22 "And the *glory* which *Thou* hast given⁺ *Me* I have given⁺ to them; that they may be one, just as We are one;

23 I in them, and Thou in Me, that they may be perfected⁺ in unity, that the world may know~ that *Thou* didst send Me, and didst love them, even as Thou didst love *Me*.

24 "Father, I desire that they also, whom Thou hast given⁺ Me, be with Me where *I* am, in order that they may behold~ My glory, which Thou hast given⁺ Me; for Thou didst love Me before the foundation of the world.

25 "O righteous Father, although the world has not known²⁹ᵃ Thee, yet *I* have known Thee; and these have known that *Thou* didst send Me;

26 and I have made Thy name known to them, and will make it known; that the love³¹ᵃ wherewith Thou didst love Me may be in them, and I in them."

Judas Betrays Jesus

18 When Jesus had spoken these words, He went forth with His disciples over the ravine of the Kidron, where there was a garden, into which He Himself entered, and His disciples.

2 Now Judas also, who was betraying Him, knew the place; for Jesus had often met there with His disciples.

3 Judas then, having received the *Roman* cohort, and officers from the chief priests and the Pharisees, *came there with lanterns and torches and weapons.

4 Jesus therefore, knowing all the things that were coming upon Him, went forth, and *said to them, "Whom do you seek?"

5 They answered Him, "Jesus the Nazarene." He *said to them, "I am *He*." And Judas also who was betraying Him, was standing with them.

6 When therefore He said to them, "I am *He*," they drew back, and fell to the ground.

7 Again therefore He asked⁹ᶜ them, "Whom do you seek?" And they said, "Jesus the Nazarene."

8 Jesus answered, "I told you that I am *He*; if therefore you seek *Me*, let×ⁱ these go their way,"

9 that the word⁴³ᵃ might be *fulfilled*ˣ which He spoke, "Of those whom Thou hast given⁺ Me I lost •*not one*."

10 Simon Peter therefore having a sword, drew it, and struck

17:22
John 1:14; 17:24

17:23
John 10:38;
17:11,21;
John 3:17; 17:3,8,
18,21,25;
John 16:27
17:24
John 17:2;
John 12:26;
John 1:14; 17:22;
Matt. 25:34; John
17:5

17:25
John 17:11;
1 John 1:9;
John 7:29; 15:21;
John 3:17; 17:3,8,
18,21,23
17:26
John 17:6;
John 15:9

18:1
Matt. 26:30,36;
Mark 14:26,32;
Luke 22:39;
2 Sam. 15:23; 1
Kin. 2:37; 15:13;
2 Kin. 23:4,6,12;
2 Chr. 15:16;
29:16; 30:14; Jer.
31:40; John 18:26
18:2
Luke 21:37; 22:39
18:3
John 18:3-11;
Matt. 26:47-56;
Mark 14:43-50;
Luke 22:47-53;
Acts 10:1;
John 7:32; 18:12,
18;
Matt. 25:1
18:4
John 6:64; 13:1,
11;
John 18:7

18:7
John 18:4

18:9
John 17:12
18:10
Matt. 26:51;
Mark 14:47

the high priest's slave, and cut off his right ear; and the slave's name was Malchus.

18:11
Matt. 20:22;
26:39; Mark
14:36; Luke 22:42

11 Jesus therefore said to Peter, "Put^{xi} the sword into the sheath; the cup which the *Father* has given⁺ Me, shall I not drink^x it?"

Jesus before the Priests

18:12
John 18:12f.:
Matt. 26:57ff.;
John 18:3

12 So the *Roman* cohort and the commander, and the officers of the Jews, arrested Jesus and bound Him,

18:13
Luke 3:2; John
18:24;
Matt. 26:3; John
11:49,51

13 and led Him to Annas first; for he was father-in-law of Caiaphas, who was high priest that year.

18:14
John 11:50

14 Now Caiaphas was the one who had advised the Jews that it was expedient for one man to die^x on behalf of the people.

18:15
Matt. 26:58; Mark
14:54; Luke
22:54;
Matt. 26:3; John
18:24,28

15 And Simon Peter was following^m Jesus, and *so was* another disciple. Now that disciple was known to the high priest, and entered with Jesus into the court of the high priest,

18:16
John 18:16-18:
Matt. 26:69f.;
Mark 14:66-68;
Luke 22:55-57

16 but Peter was standing at the door outside. So the other disciple, who was known to the high priest, went out and spoke to the doorkeeper, and brought in Peter.

18:17
Acts 12:13;
John 18:25

17 The slave-girl therefore who kept the door *said to Peter, "*You* are not *also one* of this man's *disciples,* are you?" He *said, "I am not."

18:18
John 18:3;
John 21:9;
Mark 14:54,67

18 Now the slaves and the officers were standing *there,* having made⁺ a charcoal fire, for it was cold and they were warming^m themselves; and Peter also was with them, standing~ and warming~ himself.

18:19
John 18:19-24:
Matt. 26:59-68;
Mark 14:55-65;
Luke 22:63-71

19 The high priest therefore questioned Jesus about His disciples, and about His teaching.

18:20
John 7:26; 8:26;
Matt. 4:23; John
6:59;
Matt. 26:55

20 Jesus answered him, "*I* have spoken⁺ ⁺*openly* to the world; *I* always taught in synagogues, and in the temple, where all the Jews come together; and I spoke *nothing in secret.*

21 "Why do you question ⁺Me? Question^{xi} those who have heard⁺ what I spoke to them; behold, these know what *I* said."

18:22
John 18:3;
John 19:3

22 And when He had said this, one of the officers standing by gave Jesus a blow, saying, "Is that the way You answer the high priest?"

18:23
Matt. 5:39; Acts
23:2-5

23 Jesus answered him, "If I have spoken wrongly, bear^{xi} witness of the wrong; but if rightly, why do you strike Me?"

18:24
John 18:13

24 Annas therefore sent Him bound⁺ to Caiaphas the high priest.

18:25
John 18:25-27:
Matt. 26:71-75;
Mark 14:69-72;
Luke 22:58-62;
John 18:18;
John 18:17

Peter's Denial of Jesus

25 Now Simon Peter was standing~ and warming~ himself.

They said therefore to him, "*You* are not *also one* of His disciples, are you?" He denied *it*, and said, "I am not."

26 One of the slaves of the high priest, being a relative of the one whose ear Peter cut off, *said, "Did *I* not see you in the garden with Him?"

27 Peter therefore denied *it* again; and immediately a cock crowed.

Jesus before Pilate

28 They *led Jesus therefore from Caiaphas into the ᶻPraetorium, and it was early; and they themselves did not enter into the Praetorium in order that they might not be defiled,ˣ but might eatˣ the Passover.

29 Pilate therefore went out to them, and *said, "What accusation do you bring against this Man?"

30 They answered and said to him, "If this Man were not an †evildoer, we would not have delivered Him up to you."

31 Pilate therefore said to them, "Takeˣ' Him *yourselves,* and judgeˣ' Him according to *your law.*" The Jews said to him, "*We* are not permitted to putˣ •anyone to death,"

32 that the word of Jesus might be fulfilled,ˣ which He spoke, signifying by what kind of death He was about to die.

33 Pilate therefore entered again into the ᶻPraetorium, and summoned Jesus, and said to Him, "Are *You* the King of the Jews?"

34 Jesus answered, "Are you saying this on your *own initiative,* or did others tell you about Me?"

35 Pilate answered, "*I* am not a *Jew,* am I? Your own nation and the chief priests delivered You up to me; what have You done?"

36 Jesus answered, "My kingdom is not of †this world. If My kingdom were of *this world,* then My servants would be fighting, that I might not be deliveredˣ up to the Jews; but as it is, My kingdom is not ᵃof this realm."

37 Pilate therefore said to Him, "So You are a *king?*" Jesus answered, "*You* say *correctly* that I am a king. For this *I* have been born,• and for this I have come• into the world, to bearˣ witness to the truth. Everyone who is of the truth hears *My* voice."

38 Pilate *said to Him, "What is truth?"

And when he had said this, he went out again to the Jews, and *said to them, "*I* find no *guilt* in Him.

39 "But you have a custom, that I should releaseˣ *someone* for

ᶻI.e., governor's official residence   ᵃLit., *from here*

18:26
John 18:10;
John 18:1

18:27
John 13:38

18:28
Matt. 27:2; Mark 15:1; Luke 23:1; John 18:13; Matt. 27:27; John 18:33; 19:9; John 11:55; Acts 11:3

18:29
John 18:29-38; Matt. 27:11-14; Mark 15:2-5; Luke 23:2,3

18:32
Matt. 20:19; 26:2; Mark 10:33f.; Luke 18:32f.; John 3:14; 8:28; 12:32f.

18:33
John 18:28,29; 19:9; Luke 23:3; John 19:12

18:36
Matt. 26:53; Luke 17:21; John 6:15

18:37
Matt. 27:11; Mark 15:2; Luke 22:70; 23:3; John 1:14; 3:32; 8:14; John 8:47; 1 John 4:6

18:38
John 18:33; Luke 23:4; John 19:4,6

18:39
John 18:39-19:16; Matt. 27:15-26; Mark 15:6-15; Luke 23:18-25

you at the Passover; do you wish then that I release˟ for you the King of the Jews?"

18:40
Acts 3:14

40   Therefore they cried out again, saying, "Not this Man, but Barabbas." Now Barabbas was a robber.

The Crown of Thorns

19:1
Matt. 27:26
19:2
Matt. 27:27-30;
Mark 15:16-19

19 Then Pilate therefore took Jesus, and scourged Him.

2   And the soldiers wove a crown of thorns and put it on His head, and arrayed Him in a purple robe;

19:3
Matt. 27:29; Mark
15:18;
John 18:22
19:4
John 18:33,38;
Luke 23:4; John
19:6

3   and they *began* to come˫˫ up to Him, and say,˫˫ "Hail, King of the Jews!" and to give˫˫ Him blows *in the face.*

4   And Pilate came out again, and *said to them, "Behold, I am bringing Him out to you, that you may know˟ that I find *no guilt* in Him."

19:5
John 19:2

5   Jesus therefore came out, wearing the crown of thorns and the purple robe. And *Pilate* *said to them, "Behold, the Man!"

19:6
Matt. 26:58; John
18:3;
Luke 23:4; John
18:38; 19:4

6   When therefore the chief priests and the officers saw Him, they cried out, saying, "Crucify,˟˫ crucify!"˟˫ Pilate *said to them, "Take˟˫ Him *yourselves,* and crucify˟˫ Him, for *I* find no *guilt* in Him."

19:7
Lev. 24:16; Matt.
26:63-66;
John 5:18; 10:33

7   The Jews answered him, "We have a *law,* and *by that law* He ought to die˟ because He made Himself out *to be* the *Son of God."

8   When Pilate therefore heard this statement, he was the more afraid;

19:9
John 18:33;
Matt. 26:63;
27:12,14; John
18:34-37

9   and he entered into the ᵇPraetorium again, and *said to Jesus, "Where are You from?" But Jesus gave him no answer.

10   Pilate therefore *said to Him, "You do not speak to *me?* Do You not know that I have authority to release˟ You, and I have authority to crucify˟ You?"

19:11
Rom. 13:1;
John 18:13f.,28ff.;
Acts 3:13

11   Jesus answered, "You would have *no* authority over Me, unless it had been given* you from above; for this reason he who delivered Me up to you has *the greater sin."*

19:12
Luke 23:2; John
18:33ff.

12   As a result of this Pilate made˫˫ efforts to release˟ Him, but the Jews cried out, saying, "If you release˟ *this Man,* you are no friend of Caesar; everyone who makes himself out *to be* a *king* opposes Caesar."

19:13
Matt. 27:19;
John 5:2; 19:17,
20

13   When Pilate therefore heard ⁺these words, he brought Jesus out, and sat down on the judgment seat at a place called The Pavement, but in Hebrew, Gabbatha.

19:14
Matt. 27:62; John
19:31,42;
Matt. 27:45; Mark
15:25;
John 19:19,21

14   Now it was the day of preparation for the Passover; it was about the ᶜsixth hour. And he *said to the Jews, "Behold, your King!"

ᵇI.e., governor's official residence   ᶜPerhaps 6 a.m. (Roman time)

15   They therefore cried out, "Away[xi] with *Him*, away[xi] with *Him*, crucify[xi] Him!" Pilate *said to them, "Shall I crucify[x] *your King?*" The chief priests answered, "We have no king but Caesar."

The Crucifixion

16   So he then delivered Him to them to be crucified.[x]

17   They took Jesus therefore, and He went out, bearing His own cross, to the place called the Place of a Skull, which is called in Hebrew, Golgotha.

18   There they crucified Him, and with Him two other men, one on either side, and Jesus in between.

19   And Pilate wrote an inscription also, and put it on the cross. And it was written,* "JESUS THE NAZARENE, THE KING OF THE JEWS."

20   Therefore *this inscription* many of the *Jews* read, for the place where Jesus was crucified was near the city; and it was written* in Hebrew, Latin, *and* in Greek.

21   And so the chief priests of the Jews were saying[m] to Pilate, "Do not write,[o] 'The King of the Jews'; but that *He* said, 'I am King of the Jews.' "

22   Pilate answered, "What I have written* I have written."*

23   The soldiers therefore, when they had crucified Jesus, took His outer garments and made four parts, a part to every soldier and *also* the [d]tunic; now the tunic was seamless, woven in one piece.

24   They said therefore to one another, "Let us not tear[x] it, but cast[x] lots for it, *to decide* whose it shall be"; that the Scripture might be fulfilled,[x] "THEY DIVIDED MY OUTER GARMENTS AMONG THEM, AND FOR MY CLOTHING THEY CAST LOTS."

25   Therefore the soldiers did these things. But there were standing by the cross of Jesus His mother, and His mother's sister, Mary the *wife* of Clopas, and Mary Magdalene.

26   When Jesus therefore saw His mother, and the disciple whom He loved[m31a] standing nearby, He *said to His mother, "Woman, behold, your son!"

27   Then He *said to the disciple, "Behold, your mother!" And from that hour the disciple took her into his own *household*.

28   After this, Jesus, knowing that all things had already been accomplished,* in order that the Scripture might be *fulfilled,*[x] *said, "I am thirsty."

29   A jar full of *sour wine* was standing there; so they put a

[d]Gr., *khiton*, the garment worn next to the skin

19:15
Luke 23:18

19:16
Matt. 27:26; Mark 15:15; Luke 23:25
19:17
John 19:17-24: Matt. 27:33-44; Mark 15:22-32; Luke 23:33-43;
Matt. 27:32; Mark 15:21; Luke 14:27; 23:26; John 19:13
19:18
Luke 23:32
19:19
Matt. 27:37; Mark 15:26; Luke 23:38;
John 19:14,21
19:20
John 19:13

19:21
John 19:14,19

19:22
Gen. 43:14; Esth. 4:16
19:23
Matt. 27:35; Mark 15:24; Luke 23:34; Acts 12:4

19:24
Ex. 28:32; Matt. 27:35; Mark 15:24; Luke 23:34; John 19:28,36f.; Ps. 22:18

19:25
Matt. 27:55f.; Mark 15:40f.; Luke 23:49; Matt. 12:46; Luke 24:18; John 8:2; John 20:1,18
19:26
John 13:23; John 2:4

19:27
Luke 18:28; John 1:11; 16:32; Acts 21:6
19:28
John 13:1; 17:4; John 19:24,36f.; Ps. 69:21
19:29
John 19:29,30; Matt. 27:48,50; Mark 15:36f.; Luke 23:36

sponge full of the sour wine upon *a branch of* hyssop, and brought it up to His mouth.

19:30
John 17:4;
Matt. 27:50; Mark
15:37; Luke 23:46

30 When Jesus therefore had received the sour wine, He said, "It is finished!"⁺ And He bowed His head, and gave up His spirit.

Care of the Body of Jesus

19:31
John 19:14,42;
Deut. 21:23;
Josh. 8:29;
10:26f.;
Ex. 12:16

31 The Jews therefore, because it was the *day of preparation,* so that the bodies should not remainˣ on the cross on the Sabbath (for that Sabbath was a high *day*), asked Pilate that their legs might be *broken,*ˣ and *that* they might be takenˣ away.

19:32
John 19:18

32 The soldiers therefore came, and broke the legs of the first man, and of the other man who was crucified with Him;

33 but coming to Jesus, when they saw that He was ⁺already dead, they did not break *His* legs;

19:34
1 John 5:6,8

34 but one of the soldiers pierced His side with a *spear,* and immediately there came out *blood and water.*

19:35
John 15:27; 21:24

35 And he who has seen⁺ has borne⁺ witness, and *his* witness is *true;* and he knows that he is telling the *truth,* so that *you also* may believe. ~

19:36
John 19:24,28;
Ex. 12:46; Num.
9:12; Ps. 34:20
19:37
Zech. 12:10; Rev.
1:7

36 For these things came to pass, that the Scripture might be fulfilled,ˣ "NOT A BONE OF HIM SHALL BE BROKEN."

37 And again another Scripture says, "THEY SHALL LOOK ON HIM WHOM THEY PIERCED."¹

19:38
John 19:38-42;
Matt. 27:57-61;
Mark 15:42-47;
Luke 23:50-56;
John 7:13

38 And after these things Joseph of ⁺Arimathea, being a disciple of Jesus, but a secret *one,* for fear of the Jews, asked Pilate that he might takeˣ away the body of Jesus; and Pilate granted permission. He came therefore, and took away His body.

19:39
John 3:1;
Mark 16:1;
Ps. 45:8; Prov.
7:17; Song 4:14;
Matt. 2:11;
John 12:3

39 And Nicodemus came also, who had first come to Him by night; bringing a mixture of myrrh and aloes, about a hundred pounds *weight.*

19:40
Matt. 26:12; Mark
14:8; John 11:44;
Luke 24:12; John
20:5,7

40 And so they took the body of Jesus, and bound it in linen wrappings with the spices, as is the burial custom of the Jews.

19:41
Matt. 27:60;
Luke 23:53

41 Now in the place where He was crucified there was a garden; and in the garden a ⁺*new* tomb, in which no one had yet been laid. ⁺

19:42
John 19:14,31;
John 19:20,41

42 Therefore on account of the Jewish day of preparation, because the tomb was nearby, they laid Jesus there.

The Empty Tomb

20:1
John 20:1-8;
Matt. 28:1-8;
Mark 16:1-8;
Luke 24:1-10;
John 19:25;
20:18;
Matt. 27:60,66;
Mark 15:46;
16:3f.; John
11:38

20 Now on the first *day* of the week Mary Magdalene *came early to the tomb, while it *was still dark, and *saw the stone *already* taken⁺ away from the tomb.

20:2
John 13:23;
John 20:13

2 And so she *ran and *came to Simon Peter, and to the other

disciple whom Jesus loved,[m31b] and *said to them, "They have
taken away the Lord out of the tomb, and we do not know where
they have laid Him."

3   Peter therefore went forth, and the other disciple, and they
were going to the tomb.

4   And the two were running together; and the other disciple
ran ahead faster than Peter, and came to the tomb first;

5   and stooping and looking in, he *saw the linen wrappings
lying *there*; but[2] he did not go in.

6   Simon Peter therefore also *came, following him, and entered the tomb; and he *beheld the linen wrappings lying *there*,

7   and the face-cloth, which had been on His head, not lying
with the linen wrappings, but rolled* up in a place by itself.

8   So the other disciple who had first come to the tomb entered then also, and he saw and believed.

9   For as yet they did not understand[29e] the Scripture, that He
must rise[x] again from the dead.

10   So the disciples went away again to their own homes.

11   But Mary was standing outside the tomb weeping; and so,
as she wept,[m] she stooped and looked into the tomb;

12   and she *beheld two angels in white sitting, one at the
head, and one at the feet, where the body of Jesus had been
lying.[m]

13   And they *said to her, "Woman, why are you weeping?"
She *said to them, "Because they have taken away my Lord, and
I do not know where they have laid Him."

14   When she had said this, she turned around, and *beheld
Jesus standing *there*, and did not know that it was [†]*Jesus*.

15   Jesus *said to her, "Woman, why are you weeping? Whom
are you seeking?" Supposing Him to be the [†]gardener, she *said
to Him, "Sir, if you have carried Him away, tell[x1] me where you
have laid Him, and *I* will take Him away."

16   Jesus *said to her, "Mary!" She *turned and *said to Him in
Hebrew, "Rabboni!" (which means, Teacher).

17   Jesus *said to her, "Stop clinging[O] to Me, for I have not yet
ascended* to the Father; but go to My brethren, and say[x1] to them,
'I ascend to My Father and your Father, and My God and your
God.' "

18   Mary Magdalene *came, announcing to the disciples, "I
have seen* the Lord," and *that* He had said these things to her.

Jesus among His Disciples

19   When therefore it was evening, on that day, the first *day* of
the week, and when the doors were *shut* * where the disciples

20:3
Luke 24:12; John
20:3-10

20:5
John 20:11;
John 19:40

20:7
John 11:44;
John 19:40

20:8
John 20:4

20:9
Matt. 22:29; John
2:22;
Luke 24:26ff.,46
20:10
Luke 24:12
20:11
Mark 16:5;
John 20:5

20:12
Matt. 28:2f.; Mark
16:5; Luke 24:4

20:13
John 20:15;
John 20:2

20:14
Matt. 28:9; Mark
16:9;
John 21:4
20:15
John 20:13

20:16
John 5:2;
Matt. 23:7; Mark
10:51
20:17
Matt. 28:10;
Mark 12:26;
16:19; John 7:33

20:18
John 20:1;
Mark 16:10; Luke
24:10,23

20:19
John 7:13;
Luke 24:36; John
14:27; 20:21,26

were, for fear of the Jews, Jesus came and stood in their midst, and *said to them, "Peace *be* with you."

20 And when He had said this, He showed them both His hands and His side. The disciples therefore *rejoiced* when they saw the Lord.

20:20
Luke 24:39,40;
John 19:34;
John 16:20,22

21 Jesus therefore said to them again, "Peace *be* with you; as the *Father* has sent⁺ Me, *I also* send you."

20:21
Luke 24:36; John
14:27; 20:19,26;
John 17:18

22 And when He had said this, He breathed on them, and *said to them, "Receive[xi] the Holy Spirit.

23 "If you forgive[x21a] the sins of any, *their sins* have been forgiven⁺ them; if you retain~ the *sins* of any, they have been retained."⁺

20:23
Matt. 16:19;
18:18

24 But Thomas, one of the twelve, called Didymus, was not with them when Jesus came.

20:24
John 11:16;
John 6:67

25 The other disciples therefore were saying[m] to him, "We have seen⁺ the Lord!" But he said to them, "Unless I shall see[x] in His hands the imprint of the nails, and put[x] my finger into the place of the nails, and put[x] *my* hand into His side, I will •*not* believe."[x]

20:25
John 20:20;
Mark 16:11

26 And after eight days again His disciples were inside, and Thomas with them. Jesus *came, the doors having been *shut,*⁺ and stood in their midst, and said, "Peace *be* with you."

20:26
Luke 24:36; John
14:27; 20:19,21

27 Then He *said to Thomas, "Reach here your finger, and see[xi] My hands; and reach here your hand, and put[xi] it into My side; and be⁶ not unbelieving, but believing."

20:27
Luke 24:40; John
20:25

28 Thomas answered and said to Him, "My Lord and my God!"

29 Jesus *said to him, "Because you have seen⁺ Me, have you believed?⁺ Blessed *are* they who did not see, and *yet* believed."

20:29
1 Pet. 1:8

Why This Gospel Was Written

30 *Many* other signs therefore Jesus also performed in the presence of the disciples, which are not written⁺ in this book;

20:30
John 21:25;
John 2:11

31 but these have been written⁺ that you may believe~ that Jesus is the Christ, the Son of God; and that believing you may have~ *life*[30b] in His name.

20:31
John 19:35;
Matt. 4:3;
John 3:15

Jesus Appears at the Sea of Galilee

21 After these things Jesus manifested Himself again to the disciples at the Sea of Tiberias, and He manifested *Himself* in this way.

21:1
Mark 16:12; John
21:14;
John 20:19,26;
John 6:1

2 There were together Simon Peter, and Thomas called Didymus, and Nathanael of Cana in Galilee, and the *sons* of Zebedee, and two others of His disciples.

21:2
John 11:16;
John 1:45ff.;
John 2:1;
Matt. 4:21; Mark
1:19; Luke 5:10

3 Simon Peter *said to them, "I am going fishing."~ They *said to him, "We will also come with you." They went out, and got into the boat; and that night they caught nothing.

4 But when the day was now breaking, Jesus stood on the beach; yet the disciples did not know that it was †Jesus.

5 Jesus therefore *said to them, "Children, you do not have any fish, do you?" They answered Him, "No."

6 And He said to them, "Castⁿ the net on the right-hand side of the boat, and you will find a catch." They cast therefore, and then they were not able^m to haul^x it in because of the great number of fish.

7 That disciple therefore whom Jesus loved^m *said to Peter, "It is the †Lord." And so when Simon Peter heard that it was the †Lord, he put his outer garment on (for he was stripped for work), and threw himself into the sea.

8 But the other disciples came in the little boat, for they were not far from the land, but about one hundred yards away, dragging the net full of fish.

9 And so when they got out upon the land, they *saw a charcoal fire already laid, and fish placed on it, and bread.

10 Jesus *said to them, "Bring^x some of the fish which you have now caught."

11 Simon Peter went up, and drew the net to land, full of †large fish, a hundred and fifty-three; and although there were so many, the net was not torn.

Jesus Provides

12 Jesus *said to them, "Come and have^x breakfast." None of the disciples ventured^m to question^x Him, "Who are You?" knowing that it was the †Lord.

13 Jesus *came and *took the bread, and *gave them, and the fish likewise.

14 This is now the third time that Jesus was manifested to the disciples, after He was raised from the dead.

The Love Motivation

15 So when they had finished breakfast, Jesus *said to Simon Peter, "Simon, son of John, do you love[31a] Me more than these?" He *said to Him, "Yes, Lord; You know that I love[31b] You." He *said to him, "Tend~ My lambs."

16 He *said to him again a second time, "Simon, son of John, do you love[31a] Me?" He *said to Him, "Yes, Lord; You know that I love[31b] You." He *said to him, "Shepherd~ My sheep."

17 He *said to him the third time, "Simon, son of John, do you

21:3
Luke 5:5

21:4
Luke 24:16; John 20:14

21:5
Luke 24:41

21:6
Luke 5:4ff.

21:7
John 13:23; 21:20

21:9
John 18:18;
John 6:9,11;
21:10,13
21:10
John 6:9,11; 21:9,
13

21:12
John 21:15

21:13
John 21:9;
John 6:9,11; 21:9,
10
21:14
John 20:19,26

21:15
John 21:12;
Matt. 26:33; Mark
14:29; John
13:37;
Luke 12:32

21:16
Matt. 2:6; Acts
20:28; 1 Pet. 5:2;
Rev. 7:17
21:17
John 13:38;
John 16:30;
John 21:15,16

love[31b] Me?" Peter was grieved because He said to him the third time, "Do you love[31b] Me?" And he said to Him, "Lord, You know[29e] *all things;* You know[29a] that I love[31b] You." Jesus *said to him, "Tend~ My sheep.

Our Times Are in His Hand

18 "•Truly, •truly, I say to you, when you were younger, you used to gird[m] yourself, and walk[m] wherever you wished;[m] but when you grow[x] old, you will stretch out your hands, and someone else will gird you, and bring you where you do not wish to *go.*"

19 Now this He said, signifying by what kind of death he would glorify God. And when He had spoken this, He *said to him, "Follow~ Me!"

20 Peter, turning around, *saw the disciple whom Jesus loved[m] following *them;* the one who also had leaned back on His breast at the supper, and said, "Lord, who is the one who betrays You?"

21 Peter therefore seeing him *said to Jesus, "Lord, and what about *this man?*"

22 Jesus *said to him, "If I want him to remain~ until I come, what *is that* to you? *You* follow~ Me!"

23 This saying therefore went out among the brethren that *that* disciple would not die; yet Jesus did *not say* to him that he would not die, but *only,* "If I want him to remain~ until I come, what *is that* to you?"

24 This is the disciple who bears witness of these things, and wrote these things; and we know that his witness is *true.*

25 And there are also *many* other things which Jesus did, which if they *were written~ in detail, I suppose that even the world *itself* *would not contain[x] the books which *were written.

21:19 John 12:33; 18:32; 2 Pet. 1:14; Matt. 8:22; 16:24; John 21:22
21:20 John 21:7; John 13:25
21:22 Matt. 16:27f.; 1 Cor. 4:5; 11:26; James 5:7; Rev. 2:25; Matt. 8:22; 16:24; John 21:19
21:23 Acts 1:15; Matt. 16:27f.; 1 Cor. 4:5; 11:26; James 5:7; Rev. 2:25
21:24 John 15:27
21:25 John 20:30

The Acts
of the Apostles

Introduction

1 The first account I composed, Theophilus, about all that Jesus began to do~ and teach,~

1:1
Luke 1:3;
Luke 3:23

2 until the day when He was taken up, after He had *by the Holy Spirit* given orders to the apostles whom He had chosen.

1:2
Mark 16:19; Acts
1:9,11,22;
Matt. 28:19f.;

3 To these He also presented Himself alive, after His suffering,ˣ by many convincing proofs, appearing to them over *a period of* forty days, and speaking of the things concerning the kingdom of God.

Mark 16:15; John
20:21f.; Acts
10:42;
Mark 6:30;
John 13:18; Acts
10:41
1:3
Matt. 28:17; Mark
16:12,14; Luke
24:34,36; John
20:19,26; 21:1,
14; 1 Cor. 15:5-7;
Acts 8:12; 19:8;
28:23,31
1:4

4 And gathering them together, He commanded them not to leave Jerusalem, but to wait~ for what the Father had promised, "Which," *He said,* "you heard of from Me;

Luke 24:49;
John 14:16,26;
15:26; Acts 2:33

5 for John baptized with water, but *you* shall be baptized with the Holy *Spirit* not many days from now."

1:5
Matt. 3:11; Mark
1:8; Luke 3:16;
John 1:33; Acts
11:16;
Acts 2:1-4

6 And so when they had come together, they were askingᵐ Him, saying, "Lord, is it at †*this* time You are restoring the kingdom to Israel?"

1:6
Matt. 17:11; Mark
9:12; Luke 17:20;
19:11

7 He said to them, "It is not for *you* to knowˣ times or epochs which the Father has fixed by His •own authority;

1:7
Matt. 24:36; Mark
13:32

8 but you shall receive power³²ᵃ when the Holy Spirit has come upon you; and you shall be *My* witnesses both in Jerusalem, and in all Judea and Samaria, and even to the remotest part of the earth."

1:8
Acts 2:1-4;
Luke 24:48; John
15:27;
Acts 8:1,5,14;
Matt. 28:19; Mark
16:15; Rom.
10:18; Col. 1:23

The Ascension

9 And after He had said these things, He was lifted up while they were looking on, and a cloud received Him out of their sight.

1:9
Luke 24:50,51;
Acts 1:2

10 And as they were gazing~ intently into the sky while He was departing, behold, two men in white clothing stood beside them;

1:10
Luke 24:4; John
20:12

11 and they also said, "Men of Galilee, why do you stand looking into the sky? This Jesus, who has been taken up from you into heaven, will come in just the same way as you have watched Him go into heaven."

1:11
Acts 2:7; 13:31;
Mark 16:19; Acts
1:9,22;
Matt. 16:27f.;
Acts 3:21

The Upper Room

1:12
Luke 24:52;
Matt. 21:1

12 Then they returned to Jerusalem from the mount called Olivet, which is near Jerusalem, a Sabbath day's journey away.

1:13
Mark 14:15; Luke
22:12; Acts 9:37,
39; 20:8;
Acts 1:13: Matt.
10:2-4; Mark
3:16-19; Luke
6:14-16;
John 14:22

13 And when they had entered, they went up to the upper room, where they were staying;[1]~ that is, Peter and John and James and Andrew, Philip and Thomas, Bartholomew and Matthew, James *the son* of Alphaeus, and Simon the Zealot, and Judas *the son* of James.

1:14
Acts 2:42; 6:4;
Rom. 12:12; Eph.
6:18; Col. 4:2;
Luke 8:2f.;
Matt. 12:46

14 These all with one mind were continually devoting~ themselves to prayer, along with *the* women, and Mary the mother of Jesus, and with His brothers.

1:15
John 21:23; Acts
6:3; 9:30; 10:23;
11:1,12,26,29;
12:17; 14:2; 15:1,
3,22,23,32f.,40;
16:2,40; 17:6,10,
14; 18:18,27;
21:7,17; 22:5;
28:14f.; Rom.
1:13

15 And at this time Peter stood up in the midst of the brethren (a gathering of about one hundred and twenty persons was there together), and said,

1:16
John 13:18;
17:12; Acts 1:20;
Matt. 26:47; Mark
14:43; Luke
22:47; John 18:3

16 "Brethren, the Scripture had to be fulfilled,[x] which the Holy †Spirit foretold by the mouth of David concerning Judas, who became a guide to those who arrested Jesus.

1:17
John 6:70f.;
Acts 1:25; 20:24;
21:19

17 "For he was counted✦ among us, and received his portion in this ministry."

1:18
Matt. 27:3-10;
Matt. 26:14f.

18 (Now this man acquired a field with the price of his wickedness; and falling headlong, he burst open in the middle and all his bowels gushed out.

1:19
Matt. 27:8; Acts
21:40

19 And it became known to all who were living in Jerusalem; so that in their own language that field was called[x] Hakeldama, that is, Field of Blood.)

1:20
Ps. 69:25;
Ps. 109:8

20 "For it is written✦ in the book of Psalms,

'LET HIS HOMESTEAD BE MADE[xi] DESOLATE,
AND LET NO MAN DWELL IN IT';

and,

'HIS OFFICE LET ANOTHER[8b] MAN TAKE.'[xi]

1:21
Luke 24:3

21 "It is therefore necessary that of the men who have accompanied us all the time that the Lord Jesus went in and out among us —

1:22
Matt. 3:16; Mark
1:1-4,9; Luke
3:21;
Mark 16:19; Acts
1:2;
Acts 1:8; 2:32

22 beginning with the baptism of John, until the day that He was taken up from us—one of *these* should become a witness with us of His resurrection."

1:23
Acts 1:26

23 And they put forward two men, Joseph called Barsabbas (who was also called Justus), and Matthias.

1:24
Acts 6:6; 13:3;
14:23;
1 Sam. 16:7; Jer.
17:10; Acts 15:8;
Rom. 8:27

24 And they prayed, and said, "Thou, Lord, who knowest the hearts of all men, show[xi] which one of these two Thou hast chosen

1:25
Acts 1:17;
Rom. 1:5; 1 Cor.
9:2; Gal. 2:8

25 to occupy[x] this ministry and apostleship from which Judas turned aside to go[x] to his *own* place."

26 And they drew lots for them, and the lot fell to Matthias; and he was numbered with the eleven apostles.

The Day of Pentecost

2 And when the day of Pentecost had come, they were all together in one place.

2 And suddenly there came from heaven a noise like a violent, rushing wind, and it filled the whole house where they were sitting.

3 And there appeared to them tongues as of fire distributing themselves, and they rested on each one of them.

4 And they were all filled with the Holy Spirit and began to speak~ with other tongues, as the Spirit was giving^m them utterance.~

5 Now there were Jews living~ in Jerusalem, devout men, from every nation under heaven.

6 And when this sound occurred, the multitude came together, and were bewildered, because they were each one hearing^m them speak in his *own* language.

7 And they were amazed^m and marveled,^m saying, "Why, are not all these who are speaking *Galileans*?

8 "And how is it that *we* each hear *them* in our own language to which we were born?

9 "Parthians and Medes and Elamites, and residents of Mesopotamia, Judea and Cappadocia, Pontus and Asia,

10 Phrygia and Pamphylia, Egypt and the districts of Libya around Cyrene, and visitors from Rome, both Jews and ^aproselytes,

11 Cretans and Arabs—we hear them in *our own* tongues speaking of the mighty deeds of God."

12 And they all continued in amazement^m and great¹ perplexity,^m saying^m to one another, "What does this mean?"

13 But others were mocking and saying,^m "They are full⁺ of *sweet wine.*"

Peter's Sermon

14 But Peter, taking his stand with the eleven, raised his voice and declared to them: "Men of Judea, and *all* you who live in Jerusalem, let this be known to you, and give heedⁿ to my words.

15 "For these men are not drunk, as you suppose, for it is *only* the ^b*third* hour of the day;

16 but this is what was spoken⁺ of through the prophet Joel:

17 'AND IT SHALL BE IN THE LAST DAYS,' God says,

a I.e., Gentile converts to Judaism   b I.e., 9 a.m.

1:26
Lev. 16:8; Josh. 14:2; 1 Sam. 14:41f.; Neh. 10:34; 11:1; Prov. 16:33; Acts 1:23; Acts 2:14
2:1
Lev. 23:15f.; Acts 20:16; 1 Cor. 16:8
2:2
Acts 4:31
2:4
Matt. 10:20; Acts 1:5,8; 4:8,31; 6:3, 5; 7:55; 8:17; 9:17; 11:15; 13:9, 52; Mark 16:17; 1 Cor. 12:10f.; 14:21
2:5
Luke 2:25; Acts 8:2
2:6
Acts 2:2
2:7
Acts 2:12; Matt. 26:73; Acts 1:11
2:9
1 Pet. 1:1; Acts 18:2; Acts 6:9; 16:6; 19:10; 20:4; 21:27; 24:18; 27:2; Rom. 16:5; 1 Cor. 16:19; 2 Cor. 1:8; 2 Tim. 1:15; Rev. 1:4
2:10
Acts 16:6; 18:23; Acts 13:13; 14:24; 15:38; 27:5; Matt. 27:32; Acts 17:21; Matt. 23:15
2:12
Acts 2:7
2:13
1 Cor. 14:23
2:14
Acts 1:26
2:15
1 Thess. 5:7
2:17
Joel 2:28-32

'THAT I WILL POUR FORTH OF MY SPIRIT UPON ALL
MANKIND;
AND YOUR SONS AND YOUR DAUGHTERS SHALL
†PROPHESY,
AND YOUR YOUNG MEN SHALL SEE VISIONS,
AND YOUR OLD MEN SHALL DREAM DREAMS;

18   EVEN[2] UPON MY BONDSLAVES, BOTH MEN AND WOMEN,
I WILL IN THOSE DAYS POUR FORTH OF MY SPIRIT
And they shall prophesy.

19   'AND I WILL GRANT WONDERS IN THE SKY ABOVE,
AND SIGNS ON THE EARTH BENEATH,
BLOOD, AND FIRE, AND VAPOR OF SMOKE.

20   'THE SUN SHALL BE TURNED INTO DARKNESS,
AND THE MOON INTO BLOOD,
BEFORE THE GREAT AND GLORIOUS DAY OF THE LORD
SHALL COME.

21   'AND IT SHALL BE, THAT EVERYONE WHO CALLS[x] ON
THE NAME OF THE LORD SHALL BE SAVED.'

22 "Men of Israel, listen[xi] to these words: Jesus the Nazarene, a man attested[*] to you by God with miracles and wonders and signs which *God* performed through Him in your midst, just as you yourselves know—

23 this *Man*, delivered up by the *predetermined[*] plan* and *foreknowledge of God,* you nailed to a cross by the *hands of godless men* and put *Him* to death.

24 "And God raised Him up again, putting an end to the agony of death, since it was impossible for Him to be held[~] in its power.

25 "For David says of Him,
'I WAS ALWAYS BEHOLDING[xii] THE LORD IN MY
PRESENCE;
FOR HE IS AT MY RIGHT HAND, THAT I MAY NOT BE
SHAKEN.[x]

26   'THEREFORE MY HEART WAS GLAD AND MY TONGUE
EXULTED;
MOREOVER MY FLESH ALSO WILL ABIDE IN HOPE;

27   BECAUSE THOU WILT NOT ABANDON MY SOUL TO
HADES,
NOR ALLOW[x] THY HOLY[28b] ONE TO UNDERGO DECAY.

28   'THOU HAST MADE KNOWN TO ME THE WAYS OF LIFE;
THOU WILT MAKE ME FULL OF GLADNESS WITH THY
PRESENCE.'

29 "Brethren, I may confidently say[x] to you regarding the patriarch David that he both died and was buried, and his tomb •*is* with us to †*this* day.

2:21
Rom. 10:13

2:22
Acts 3:6; 4:10;
10:38;
John 3:2;
John 4:48; Acts
2:19,43

2:23
Luke 22:22; Acts
3:18; 4:28; 1 Pet.
1:20;
Matt. 27:35; Mark
15:24; Luke
23:33; 24:20;
John 19:18; Acts
3:13
2:24
Matt. 28:5,6;
Mark 16:6; Luke
24:5,6; Acts 2:32;
3:15,26; 4:10;
5:30; 10:40;
13:30,33,34,37;
17:31; Rom. 4:24;
6:4; 8:11; 10:9;
1 Cor. 6:14;
15:15; 2 Cor.
4:14; Gal. 1:1;
Eph. 1:20; Col.
2:12; 1 Thess.
1:10; Heb. 13:20;
1 Pet. 1:21;
John 20:9
2:25
Ps. 16:8-11
2:27
Matt. 11:23; Acts
2:31;
Acts 13:35

2:29
Acts 7:8f.; Heb.
7:4;
Acts 13:36;
1 Kin. 2:10;
Neh. 3:16

30 "And so, because he was a prophet, and knew that GOD HAD SWORN TO HIM WITH AN *OATH* TO SEAT^x *one* OF HIS DESCENDANTS UPON HIS THRONE,

2:30
Matt. 22:43;
Ps. 132:11; 2
Sam. 7:12f.; Ps.
89:3f.

31 he looked ahead and spoke of the resurrection of ^cthe Christ, that HE WAS NEITHER ABANDONED TO HADES, NOR DID His flesh SUFFER DECAY.

2:31
Matt. 11:23; Acts
2:27

32 "This Jesus God *raised up again,* to which we are all witnesses.

2:32
Acts 2:24; 3:15,
26; 4:10; 5:30;
10:40; 13:30,33,
34,37; 17:31;
Rom. 4:24; 6:4;
8:11; 10:9; 1 Cor.
6:14; 15:15;
2 Cor. 4:14; Gal.
1:1; Eph. 1:20;
Col. 2:12; 1
Thess. 1:10; Heb.
13:20; 1 Pet.
1:21;
Acts 1:8

33 "Therefore having been exalted to the right hand of [†]God, and having received from the Father the promise of the Holy Spirit, He has poured forth this which *you* both see and hear.

2:33
Mark 16:19; Acts
5:31;
Acts 1:4;
John 7:39; Gal.
3:14;
Acts 2:17; 10:45

34 "For it was not David who ascended into heaven, but *he himself* says:

2:34
Ps. 110:1; Matt.
22:44f.

'THE LORD SAID TO MY LORD,

   "SIT AT MY RIGHT HAND,

35   UNTIL I MAKE^x THINE ENEMIES A FOOTSTOOL FOR THY FEET." '

36 "Therefore let all the house of Israel know^{~i} for [†]*certain* that God has made Him *both Lord* and *Christ*—this Jesus whom *you* crucified."

2:36
Ezek. 36:22,32,
37; 45:6;
Luke 2:11;
Acts 2:23

The Ingathering

37 Now when they heard *this,* they were pierced¹ to the heart, and said to Peter and the rest of the apostles, "Brethren, what shall we do?"^x

2:37
Luke 3:10,12,14

38 And Peter *said* to them, "Repent,^{xi} and let each of you be baptized^{xi} in the name of Jesus Christ for the forgiveness of your sins; and you shall receive the gift^{24a} of the Holy Spirit.

2:38
Mark 1:15; Luke
24:47; Acts 3:19;
5:31; 20:21;
Mark 16:16; Acts
8:12,16; 22:16

39 "For the promise is for you and your children, and for all who are far off, as many as the Lord our God shall call^x to Himself."

2:39
Is. 43:3; 54:13;
57:19; Joel 2:32;
Rom. 9:4; Eph.
2:12;
Eph. 2:13,17

40 And with *many* other words he solemnly¹ testified and kept^m on exhorting them, saying, "Be saved^{xi} from this perverse generation!"

2:40
Luke 16:28;
Deut. 32:5; Matt.
17:17; Phil. 2:15

41 So then, those who had received his word were baptized; and there were added that day about three thousand ^dsouls.

2:41
Acts 3:23; 7:14;
27:37; Rom. 13:1;
1 Pet. 3:20; Rev.
16:3

42 And they were continually devoting[~] themselves to the apostles' teaching and to fellowship, to the breaking of bread and to prayer.

2:42
Acts 1:14;
Luke 24:30; Acts
2:46; 20:7; 1 Cor.
10:16

43 And everyone kept feeling^m a *sense of awe;* and many wonders and signs were taking^m place through the ^eapostles.

2:43
Acts 2:22

^cI.e., the Messiah   ^dI.e., persons   ^eSome ancient mss. add *in Jerusalem; and great fear was upon all*

2:44
Acts 4:32,37; 5:2

2:45
Matt. 19:21; Acts
4:34

2:46
Acts 5:42;
Luke 24:30; Acts
2:42; 20:7; 1 Cor.
10:16

2:47
Acts 5:13;
Acts 2:41; 4:4;
5:14; 6:1,7; 9:31,
35,42; 11:21,24;
14:1,21; 16:5;
17:12;
1 Cor. 1:18

3:1
Luke 22:8; Acts
3:3,4,11;
Ps. 55:17; Matt.
27:45; Acts 10:30
3:2
Acts 14:8;
Luke 16:20;
John 9:8; Acts
3:10

3:3
Luke 22:8; Acts
3:1,4,11

3:4
Acts 10:4

3:6
Acts 2:22; 3:16;
4:10

3:8
Acts 14:10

3:9
Acts 4:16,21
3:10
John 9:8; Acts 3:2

3:11
Luke 22:8; Acts
3:3,4;
John 10:23; Acts
5:12

44 And all those who had believed ᶠwere together, and had all things in common;

45 and they *began* selling^m their property and possessions, and were sharing^m them with all, as anyone might have^m need.

46 And day by day continuing with one mind in the temple, and breaking bread from house to house, they were taking^m their meals together with gladness and sincerity of heart,

47 praising God, and having favor with all the people. And the Lord was adding^m to their number day by day those who were being saved.

Healing the Lame Beggar

3 Now Peter and John were going^m up to the temple at the ᵍninth *hour,* the hour of prayer.

2 And a certain man who had been lame from his mother's womb was being carried^m along, whom they used to set^m down every day at the gate of the temple which is called Beautiful, in order to beg~ ʰalms of those who were entering the temple.

3 And when he saw Peter and John about to go into the temple, he *began* asking^m to receive^x alms.

4 And Peter, along with John, fixed his gaze upon him and said, "Look^x at us!"

5 And he *began* to give them his attention, expecting to receive^x something from them.

6 But Peter said, "I do not possess *silver* and *gold,* but what I *do* have I give to you: In the name of Jesus Christ the Nazarene—walk!"

7 And seizing him by the right hand, he raised him up; and immediately his feet and his ankles were strengthened.

8 And with a leap, he stood upright and *began* to walk;^m and he entered the temple with them, walking and leaping and praising God.

9 And all the people saw him walking and praising God;

10 and they were taking^m note of him as being the one who used to sit at the Beautiful Gate of the temple to *beg* alms, and they were filled with wonder and amazement[1] at what had happened⁺ to him.

Peter's Second Sermon

11 And while he was clinging to Peter and John, all the people ran together to them at the so-called portico of Solomon, full[1] of amazement.

12 But when Peter saw *this,* he replied to the people, "Men of

ᶠSome ancient mss. do not contain *were*   ᵍI.e., 3 p.m.   ʰOr, *a gift of charity*

Israel, why do you marvel at this, or why do you gaze at *us,* as if by our *own* power or piety we had made⁺ him walk?˜

13 "The God of Abraham, Isaac, and Jacob, the God of our fathers, has glorified His servant Jesus, *the one* whom *you* delivered up, and disowned in the presence of Pilate, when he had decided to release˜ Him.

14 "But *you* disowned the *Holy* and *Righteous One,* and asked for a murderer to be granted˟ to you,

15 but put to death the *Prince of life, the one* whom God raised from the dead, *a fact* to which *we* are witnesses.

16 "And on the basis of faith in His name, *it is* the *name of Jesus* which has strengthened this man whom you see and know; and the faith which *comes through Him* has given him this perfect health in the presence of you all.

17 "And now, brethren, I know that you acted in *ignorance,* just as your rulers did also.

18 "But the things which God announced beforehand by the mouth of all the prophets, that His Christ should suffer,˟ He has thus fulfilled.

19 "Repent˟ˡ therefore and return,˟ˡ that your *sins* may be wiped˟ away, in order that times of refreshing may come from the presence of the Lord;

20 and that He may send˟ Jesus, the Christ appointed⁺ for you,

21 whom heaven must receive˟ until *the* period of restoration of all things about which God spoke by the mouth of His holy²⁸ᵃ prophets from ancient time.

22 "Moses said, 'THE LORD GOD SHALL RAISE UP FOR YOU A PROPHET LIKE ME FROM YOUR BRETHREN; TO *HIM* YOU SHALL GIVE HEED in everything He says˟ to you.

23 'And it shall be that every soul that does not heed˟ *that* prophet shall be utterly¹ destroyed from among the people.'

24 "And likewise, all the prophets who have spoken, from Samuel and *his* successors onward, also announced these days.

25 "It is ⁺*you* who are the sons of the prophets, and of the covenant which God made with your fathers, saying to Abraham, 'AND IN YOUR SEED ALL THE FAMILIES OF THE EARTH SHALL BE BLESSED.'

26 "For *you first,* God raised up His Servant, and sent Him to bless you by turning˜ every one *of you* from your wicked ways."

3:13
Matt. 22:32;
Ex. 3:13,15; Acts
5:30; 7:32; 22:14;
Acts 3:26; 4:27,
30;
Matt. 20:19; John
19:11; Acts 2:23;
Matt. 27:2;
Luke 23:4
3:14
Mark 1:24; Acts
4:27; 7:52; 2 Cor.
5:21;
Matt. 27:20; Mark
15:11; Luke
23:18,25
3:15
Acts 5:31; Heb.
2:10; 12:2;
Acts 2:24;
Luke 24:48
3:16
Acts 3:6

3:17
Luke 23:34; John
15:21; Acts
13:27; 26:9; Eph.
4:18;
Luke 23:13
3:18
Acts 2:23;
Luke 24:27; Acts
17:3; 26:23

3:19
Acts 2:38; 26:20;
2 Thess. 1:7;
Heb. 4:1ff.

3:21
Acts 1:11;
Matt. 17:11; Rom.
8:21;
Luke 1:70

3:22
Deut. 18:15,18;
Acts 7:37

3:23
Deut. 18:19;
Acts 2:41;
Lev. 23:29
3:24
Luke 24:27; Acts
17:3; 26:23
3:25
Acts 2:39;
Rom. 9:4f.;
Gen. 22:18

3:26
Matt. 15:24; John
4:22; Acts 13:46;
Rom. 1:16; 2:9f.;
Acts 2:24

Peter and John Arrested

4:1
Luke 22:4;
Matt. 3:7;
Luke 20:1; Acts
6:12

4 And as they were speaking to the people, the priests and the captain of the temple *guard*, and the Sadducees, came upon them,

4:2
Acts 3:15; 17:18

2 being greatly[1] disturbed because they were teaching~ the people and proclaiming~ in Jesus the resurrection from the dead.

4:3
Acts 5:18

3 And they laid hands on them, and put them in jail until the next day, for it was already evening.

4:4
Acts 2:41

4 But many of those who had heard the message believed; and the number of the men came to be about five thousand.

4:5
Luke 23:13; Acts
4:8

5 And it came about on the next day, that their rulers and elders and scribes were gathered[x] together in Jerusalem;

4:6
Luke 3:2;
Matt. 26:3

6 and Annas the high priest *was there*, and Caiaphas and John and Alexander, and all who were of high-priestly descent.

7 And when they had placed them in the center, they *began to* inquire,[m] "By what power, or in what name, have *you* done this?"

4:8
Acts 2:4; 13:9;
Luke 23:13; Acts
4:5

8 Then Peter, filled with the Holy Spirit, said to them, "Rulers and elders of the people,

4:9
Acts 3:7f.

9 if we are on trial today for a benefit done to a sick man, as to how this man has been made+ well,

4:10
Acts 2:22; 3:6;
Acts 2:24

10 let it be known to all of you, and to all the people of Israel, that by the name of Jesus Christ the Nazarene, whom *you* crucified, whom God raised from the dead—*by this name* this man stands here before you in good health.

4:11
Matt. 21:42;
Ps. 118:22;
Mark 9:12

11 "He is the STONE WHICH WAS REJECTED by you, THE BUILDERS, *but* WHICH BECAME THE VERY CORNER *stone*.

4:12
Matt. 1:21; Acts
10:43; 1 Tim. 2:5

12 "And there is salvation in *no one else;* for there is *no other* name under heaven that has been given+ among men, by which we must be saved."[x]

Threat and Release

4:13
Acts 4:31;
Luke 22:8; Acts
4:19;
John 7:15

13 Now as they observed the confidence of Peter and John, and understood that they were uneducated and +untrained men, they were marveling,[m] and *began* to recognize[m] them as having been with Jesus.

14 And seeing the man who had been *healed*+ standing with them, they had[m] nothing to say[x] in reply.

4:15
Matt. 5:22

15 But when they had ordered them to go[x] aside out of the Council, they *began* to confer[m] with one another,

4:16
John 11:47;
Acts 3:7-10

16 saying, "What shall we do[x] with these men? For the fact that a noteworthy miracle has taken+ place through them is +apparent to all who live in Jerusalem, and we cannot deny~ it.

17 "But in order that it may not spread^x any further among the people, let us warn^x them to speak~ no more to any man in †*this* name."

4:17
John 15:21

18 And when they had summoned them, they commanded them not to speak~ or teach~ at all in the name of Jesus.

4:18
Acts 5:28f.

19 But Peter and John answered and said to them, "Whether it is right in the sight of God to give heed~ to *you* rather than to †*God,* you be the judge;^{xl}

4:19
Acts 4:13;
Acts 5:28f.

20 for *we* cannot *stop speaking*~ what we have seen and heard."

4:20
1 Cor. 9:16

21 And when they had threatened them further, they let them go (finding no basis on which they might punish^x them) on account of the people, because they were all glorifying^{xxx} God for what had happened;†

4:21
Acts 5:26;
Matt. 9:8

22 for the man was more than forty years old on whom this miracle of healing^{15b} had been performed.

23 And when they had been released, they went to their own *companions,* and reported all that the chief priests and the elders had said to them.

24 And when they heard *this,* they lifted their voices to God with *one accord* and said, "O Lord, it is Thou who DIDST MAKE THE HEAVEN AND THE EARTH AND THE SEA, AND ALL THAT IS IN THEM,

4:24
Ex. 20:11; Neh.
9:6; Ps. 146:6

25 who by the Holy Spirit, *through* the mouth of our father David Thy servant, didst say,
    'WHY DID THE ⁱGENTILES RAGE,
    AND THE PEOPLES DEVISE FUTILE THINGS?

4:25
Acts 1:16;
Ps. 2:1

26   'THE KINGS OF THE EARTH TOOK THEIR STAND,
    AND THE RULERS WERE GATHERED TOGETHER
    AGAINST THE LORD, AND AGAINST HIS CHRIST.'

4:26
Ps. 2:2;
Dan. 9:24f.; Luke
4:18; Acts 10:38;
Heb. 1:9

27 "For truly in †this city there were gathered together against Thy holy servant Jesus, whom Thou didst anoint, both Herod and Pontius Pilate, along with the Gentiles and the peoples of Israel,

4:27
Acts 3:13; 4:30;
Matt. 14:1; Luke
23:7-11;
Matt. 27:2; Mark
15:1; Luke 23:1,
12; John 18:28,
29;

28 to do^x whatever Thy hand and Thy purpose predestined to occur.

Matt. 20:19
4:28
Acts 2:23

29 "And now, Lord, take^{xl} note of their threats, and grant^{xl} that Thy bond-servants may speak~ Thy word with *all* confidence,

4:29
Phil. 1:14;
Acts 4:13,31;
14:3

30 while Thou dost extend~ Thy hand to heal, and signs and wonders take~ place through the name of Thy holy servant Jesus."

4:30
John 4:48;
Acts 3:13; 4:27

31 And when they had prayed,^{9b} the place where they had gathered† together was *shaken,* and they were *all* filled with the

4:31
Acts 2:1;
Acts 2:4;
Phil. 1:14;
Acts 4:13; 14:3

ⁱOr, *nations*

Holy Spirit, and *began* to speak^m the word of God with boldness.

Sharing among Believers

4:32
Acts 2:44

32 And the congregation of those who believed were of *one* heart and soul; and not one *of them* claimed^m that anything belonging to him was his •*own;* but all things were common property to them.

4:33
Acts 1:8;
Luke 24:48

33 And with *great power*^{32a} the apostles were giving^m witness to the *resurrection* of the Lord Jesus, and abundant grace was upon them all.

4:34
Matt. 19:21

34 For there was not a needy person among them, for all who were owners of land or houses would sell them and bring^m the proceeds of the sales,

4:35
Acts 4:37; 5:2;
Acts 2:45; 6:1

35 and lay^m them at the apostles' feet; and they would be distributed^m to each, as any had^m need.

4:36
Acts 11:19f.;
13:4; 15:39; 21:3,
16; 27:4;
Acts 9:27; 11:22,
30; 12:25; 13:1,2,
7; 1 Cor. 9:6; Gal.
2:1,9,13; Col.
4:10;
Acts 2:40; 11:23;
13:15; 1 Cor.
14:3; 1 Thess. 2:3

36 And Joseph, a Levite of Cyprian birth, who was also called Barnabas by the apostles (which translated means, Son of Encouragement),

4:37
Acts 4:35; 5:2

37 and who owned a tract of land, sold it and brought the money and laid it at the apostles' feet.

Fate of Ananias and Sapphira

5 But a certain man named Ananias, with his wife Sapphira, sold a piece of property,

5:2
Acts 5:3;
Acts 4:35,37

2 and kept back *some* of the price for himself, with his wife's full knowledge,• and bringing a portion of it, he laid it at the apostles' feet.

5:3
Matt. 4:10; Luke
22:3; John 13:2,
27;
Acts 5:4,9;
Acts 5:2

3 But Peter said, "Ananias, why has *Satan* filled your heart to lie^x to the Holy Spirit, and to keep^x back *some* of the price of the land?

5:4
Acts 5:3,9

4 "While it remained *unsold,* did it not remain your †*own?* And after it was sold, was it not under •*your* control? Why is it that you have conceived this deed in your heart? You have not lied to men, but to God."

5:5
Ezek. 11:13; Acts
5:10;
Acts 2:43; 5:11

5 And as he heard these words, Ananias fell down and breathed his last; and great †fear came upon all who heard of it.

5:6
John 19:40

6 And the young men arose and covered him up, and after carrying him out, they buried him.

7 Now there elapsed an interval of about three hours, and his wife came in, not knowing what had happened.•

5:8
Acts 5:2

8 And Peter responded to her, "Tell^x me whether you sold the land for *such and such a price?"* And she said, "Yes, that was the price."

5:9
Acts 15:10;
Acts 5:3,4

9 Then Peter *said* to her, "Why is it that you have agreed

together to put[x] the Spirit of the Lord to the test? Behold, the feet of those who have buried your husband are at the door, and they shall carry you out *as well*."

10   And she fell *immediately* at his feet, and breathed her last; and the young men came in and found her dead, and they carried her out and buried her beside her husband.

11   And great [†]fear came upon the whole church, and upon all who heard of these things.

12   And at the hands of the apostles *many* signs and wonders were taking[m] place among the people; and they were all with *one accord* in Solomon's portico.

13   But none of the rest dared[m] to associate[~] with them; however, the people held[m] them in *high esteem*.

14   And all the more believers in the Lord, multitudes of men and women, were constantly added[m] to *their number*;

15   to such an extent that they even carried[~] the sick out into the *streets*, and laid[~] them on cots and pallets, so that when Peter came by, at least his shadow might fall[x] on any one of them.

16   And also the people from the cities in the vicinity of Jerusalem were coming[m] together, bringing people who were sick [j]or afflicted with unclean spirits; and they were *all* being healed.[m]

Imprisonment and Release

17   But the high priest rose up, along with all his associates (that is the sect of the Sadducees), and they were filled with jealousy;

18   and they laid hands on the apostles, and put them in a public jail.

19   But an angel of the Lord during the night opened the gates of the prison, and taking them out he said,

20   "Go your way, stand and speak[~] to the people in the temple the whole message of [†]*this* Life."

21   And upon hearing *this*, they entered into the temple about daybreak, and *began* to teach.[m] Now when the high priest and his associates had come, they called the Council together, even all the Senate of the sons of Israel, and sent *orders* to the prison house for them to be brought.[x]

22   But the officers who came did not find them in the prison; and they returned, and reported back,

23   saying, "We found the prison house locked[+] quite securely and the guards standing[+] at the doors; but when we had opened up, we found no one inside."

24   Now when the captain of the temple *guard* and the chief

[j]Lit., *and*

5:10
Ezek. 11:13; Acts 5:5

5:11
Acts 2:43; 5:5

5:12
John 4:48;
John 10:23; Acts 3:11

5:13
Acts 2:47; 4:21

5:14
2 Cor. 6:15;
Acts 2:47; 11:24

5:15
Acts 19:12

5:17
Acts 15:5;
Matt. 3:7; Acts 4:1

5:18
Acts 4:3

5:19
Matt. 1:20,24;
2:13,19; 28:2;
Luke 1:11; 2:9;
Acts 8:26; 10:3;
12:7,23; 27:23
5:20
John 6:63,68
5:21
John 8:2;
Acts 4:6;
Matt. 5:22; Acts 5:27,34,41

5:22
Matt. 26:58; Acts 5:26

5:24
Acts 4:1; 5:26

priests heard these words, they were greatly[1] perplexed[m] about them as to what would come of this.

25 But someone came and reported to them, "Behold, the men whom you put in prison are standing~ in the †temple and teaching~ the people!"

5:26
Acts 5:24;
Acts 5:22;
Acts 4:21; 5:13

26 Then the captain went along with the officers and *proceeded* to bring[m] them *back* without violence (for they were afraid[m] of the people, lest they should be stoned).[x]

5:27
Matt. 5:22; Acts
5:21,34,41

27 And when they had brought them, they stood them before the Council. And the high priest questioned them,

5:28
Acts 4:18;
Matt. 23:35;
27:25; Acts 2:23,
36; 3:14f.; 7:52

28 saying, "We gave you *strict*[4] orders not to continue teaching~ in †this name, and behold, you have filled[+] Jerusalem with your teaching, and intend to bring[x] this man's blood upon *us.*"

5:29
Acts 4:19

29 But Peter and the apostles answered and said, "We must obey~ *God* rather than †men.

5:30
Acts 3:13;
Acts 2:24;
Acts 10:39;
13:29; Gal. 3:13;
1 Pet. 2:24

30 "The God of our fathers raised up Jesus, whom *you* had put to death by hanging Him on a cross.

5:31
Acts 2:33;
Acts 3:15;
Luke 2:11;
Luke 24:47; Acts
2:38

31 "*He* is the one whom God exalted to His right hand as a *Prince* and a *Savior,* to grant[x] repentance to Israel, and forgiveness of sins.

5:32
Luke 24:48;
John 15:26; Acts
15:28; Rom. 8:16;
Heb. 2:4

32 "And *we* are [k]witnesses of these things; and *so is* the Holy Spirit, whom *God* has given to those who obey Him."

Gamaliel's Counsel

5:33
Acts 2:37; 7:54

33 But when they heard this, they were cut[m] to the quick and were intending[m] to slay[x] them.

5:34
Acts 22:3;
Luke 2:46; 5:17;
Acts 5:21

34 But a certain Pharisee named Gamaliel, a teacher of the Law, respected by all the people, stood up in the Council and gave orders to put[x] the men outside for a short time.

35 And he said to them, "Men of Israel, take care~[1] what you propose to do with †these men.

5:36
Acts 8:9; Gal. 2:6;
6:3

36 "For some time ago Theudas rose up, claiming to be somebody; and a group of about four hundred men joined up with him. And he was slain; and all who followed[m] him were dispersed and came to nothing.

5:37
Luke 2:2

37 "After this man Judas of Galilee rose up in the days of the census, and drew away *some* people after him, *he too* perished, and all those who followed[m] him were scattered.

5:38
Mark 11:30

38 "And so in the present case, I say to you, stay[xi] away from these men and let[xi] them alone, for if this plan or action should be of *men,* it will be overthrown;

5:39
Prov. 21:30; Acts
11:17

39 but if it is of *God,* you will not be able to overthrow[x] them; or else you may even be found[x] *fighting against God.*"

[k]Some mss. add *in Him,* or, *of Him*

40   And they took his advice; and after calling the apostles in, they flogged them and ordered them to speak~ no more in the name of Jesus, and *then* released them.

41   So they went on their way from the presence of the Council, rejoicing that they had been considered[1] worthy to suffer[x] shame *for His name.*

42   And every day, in the temple and from house to house, they kept[m] right on teaching and preaching Jesus *as* the Christ.

Choosing of the Seven

6   Now at this time while the disciples were increasing *in number,* a complaint arose on the part of the [l]Hellenistic *Jews* against the *native* Hebrews, because *their widows* were being overlooked[m] in the daily serving *of food.*

2   And the twelve summoned the congregation of the disciples and said, "It is not desirable for us to neglect the word[43a] of God in order to serve~ tables.

3   "But select[xi] from among you, brethren, seven men of good reputation, full of the Spirit and of wisdom, whom we may put in charge of this task.

4   "But *we* will devote ourselves to *prayer,* and to the *ministry of the word."*

5   And the statement found approval with the whole congregation; and they chose Stephen, a man full of faith and of the Holy Spirit, and Philip, Prochorus, Nicanor, Timon, Parmenas and Nicolas, a [m]proselyte from Antioch.

6   And these they brought before the apostles; and after praying, they laid their hands on them.

7   And the word of God kept on spreading;[m] and the number of the disciples continued to increase[m] greatly in Jerusalem, and a great many of the priests were becoming[m] obedient to the faith.

8   And Stephen, full of grace and power, was performing[m] great[26a] wonders and signs among the people.

9   But some men from what was called the Synagogue of the Freedmen, *including* both Cyrenians and Alexandrians, and some from Cilicia and Asia, rose up and argued with Stephen.

10   And *yet* they were unable[m] to cope[x] with the wisdom and the Spirit with which he was speaking.[m]

11   Then they secretly induced men to say, "We have heard[+] him speak *blasphemous* words against Moses and *against* God."

12   And they stirred up the people, the elders and the scribes, and they came upon him and dragged him away, and brought him before the Council.

5:40
Matt. 10:17

5:41
Acts 5:21;
1 Pet. 4:14,16;
John 15:21

5:42
Acts 2:46;
Acts 8:35; 11:20;
17:18; Gal. 1:16

6:1
Acts 11:26;
Acts 2:47; 6:7;
Acts 9:29; 11:20;
2 Cor. 11:22; Phil.
3:5;
Acts 9:39,41;
1 Tim. 5:3;
Acts 4:35; 11:29

6:3
John 21:23; Acts
1:15;
Acts 2:4

6:4
Acts 1:14

6:5
Acts 6:8ff.; 11:19;
22:20;
Acts 6:3; 11:24;
Acts 8:5ff.; 21:8;
Matt. 23:15;
Acts 11:19

6:6
Acts 1:24;
Num. 8:10; 27:18;
Deut. 34:9; Mark
5:23; Acts 8:17ff.;
9:17; 13:3; 19:6;
1 Tim. 4:14;
2 Tim. 1:6; Heb.
6:2
6:7
Acts 12:24;
19:20;
Acts 6:1;
Gal. 1:23; 6:10;
Jude 3,20
6:8
John 4:48
6:9
Matt. 27:32; Acts
2:10;
Acts 18:24;
Acts 15:23,41;
21:39; 22:3;
23:34; 27:5; Gal.
1:21;
Acts 16:6; 19:10;
21:27; 24:18
6:12
Luke 20:1; Acts
4:1;
Matt. 5:22

[l]i.e., non-Palestinian Jews who normally spoke Greek   [m]i.e., a Gentile convert to Judaism

6:13
Matt. 26:59-61;
Acts 7:58;
Matt. 24:15; Acts
21:28; 25:8
6:14
Matt. 26:61;
Acts 15:1; 21:21;
26:3; 28:17

6:15
Matt. 5:22

13   And they put forward *false* witnesses who said, "This man incessantly speaks against this holy place, and the Law;

14   for we have heard• him say that this Nazarene, Jesus, will destroy this place and alter the customs which *Moses* handed down to us."

15   And fixing their gaze on him, all who were sitting in the Council saw his face like the face of an angel.

Stephen's Defense

7   And the high priest said, "Are these things so?"

7:2
Acts 22:1;
Ps. 29:3; 1 Cor.
2:8;
Gen. 11:31; 15:7

7:3
Gen. 12:1

7:4
Gen. 11:31; 15:7;
Gen. 12:4,5

7:5
Gen. 12:7; 13:15;
15:18; 17:8

7:6
Gen. 15:13f.

7:7
Ex. 3:12

7:8
Gen. 17:10ff.;
Gen. 21:2-4;
Gen. 25:26;
Gen. 29:31ff.;
30:5ff.; 35:23ff.;
Acts 2:29

7:9
Gen. 37:11,28;
39:2,21f.; 45:4

7:10
Gen. 39:21;
41:40-46; Ps.
105:21

7:11
Gen. 41:54f.; 42:5

7:12
Gen. 42:2

7:13
Gen. 45:1-4;
Gen. 45:16

2   And he said, "Hear[xl] me, brethren and fathers! The God of glory appeared to our father Abraham when he was in Mesopotamia, before he lived[x] in Haran,

3   and said to him, 'DEPART[xl] FROM YOUR COUNTRY AND YOUR RELATIVES, AND COME INTO THE LAND THAT I WILL SHOW[x] YOU.'

4   "Then he departed from the land of the Chaldeans, and settled in Haran. And from there, after his father died,[x] *God* removed him into this country in which *you* are now living.

5   "And He gave him no inheritance in it, not even a foot of ground; and *yet,* even when he had *no* child, He promised that HE WOULD GIVE[x] IT TO HIM AS A POSSESSION, AND TO HIS OFFSPRING AFTER HIM.

6   "But God spoke to this effect, that his OFFSPRING WOULD BE ALIENS IN A FOREIGN LAND, AND THAT THEY WOULD BE ENSLAVED AND MISTREATED FOR FOUR HUNDRED YEARS.

7   " 'AND WHATEVER NATION TO WHICH THEY SHALL BE IN BONDAGE I MYSELF WILL JUDGE,' said God, 'AND AFTER THAT THEY WILL COME OUT AND [n]SERVE[3bc] ME IN THIS PLACE.'

8   "And He gave him the covenant of circumcision; and so *Abraham* became the father of Isaac, and circumcised him on the eighth day; and Isaac *became the father of* Jacob, and Jacob *of* the twelve patriarchs.

9   "And the patriarchs became jealous of Joseph and sold him into Egypt. And *yet God* was with him,

10   and rescued[18a] him from all his afflictions, and granted him favor and wisdom in the sight of Pharaoh, king of Egypt; and he made him governor over Egypt and all his household.

11   "Now a famine came over all Egypt and Canaan, and great affliction *with it;* and our fathers could find[m] no food.

12   "But when Jacob heard that there was grain in Egypt, he sent our fathers *there* the first time.

13   "And on the second *visit* Joseph made himself known to his brothers, and Joseph's family was disclosed to Pharaoh.

[n]Or, *worship*

14 "And Joseph sent *word* and invited Jacob his father and all his relatives to come to him, seventy-five persons *in all*.

15 "And Jacob went down to Egypt and *there* passed away, he and our fathers.

16 "And *from there* they were removed to Shechem, and laid in the tomb which Abraham had purchased for a sum of money from the sons of Hamor in Shechem.

17 "But as the time of the promise was approaching which God had assured to Abraham, the people increased and multiplied in Egypt,

18   until THERE AROSE ANOTHER[8b] KING OVER EGYPT WHO KNEW NOTHING ABOUT JOSEPH.

19 "It was he who took shrewd advantage of our race, and mistreated our fathers so that they would expose~ their infants and they would not survive.~

20 "And it was at this time that Moses was born; and he was lovely in the sight of God; and he was nurtured three months in his father's home.

21 "And after he had been exposed, Pharaoh's daughter took him away, and nurtured him as her own son.

22 "And Moses was educated in all the learning of the Egyptians, and he was a man of power in words and deeds.

23 "But when he was approaching[m] the age of forty, it entered his mind to visit[x] his brethren, the sons of Israel.

24 "And when he saw one *of them* being treated unjustly, he defended him and took vengeance for the oppressed[1] by striking down the Egyptian.

25 "And he supposed[m] that his brethren understood[29f] that God was granting them deliverance through him; but they did not understand.~

26 "And on the following day he appeared to them as they were fighting together, and he tried[m] to reconcile them in peace, saying, 'Men, you are brethren, why do you injure one another?'

27 "But the one who was injuring his neighbor pushed him away, saying, 'WHO MADE YOU A RULER AND JUDGE OVER US?

28 'YOU DO NOT MEAN TO KILL[x] ME AS YOU KILLED THE EGYPTIAN YESTERDAY, DO YOU?'

29 "And at this remark MOSES FLED, AND BECAME AN ALIEN IN THE LAND OF MIDIAN, where he became the father of two sons.

30 "And after forty years had passed, AN ANGEL APPEARED TO HIM IN THE WILDERNESS OF MOUNT Sinai, IN THE FLAME OF A BURNING THORN BUSH.

31 "And when Moses saw it, he *began* to marvel at the sight;

7:14
Gen. 45:9,10,17, 18;
Gen. 46:26f.; Ex. 1:5; Deut. 10:22; Acts 2:41
7:15
Gen. 46:1-7; 49:33; Ex. 1:6
7:16
Gen. 23:16; 33:19; 50:13; Josh. 24:32

7:17
Gen. 15:13; Ex. 1:7f.

7:18
Ex. 1:8

7:19
Ex. 1:10f.,16ff.; Ex. 1:22

7:20
Ex. 2:2; Heb. 11:23

7:21
Ex. 2:5f.,10

7:22
1 Kin. 4:30; Is. 19:11

7:23
Ex. 2:11f.; Heb. 11:24-26

7:26
Ex. 2:13f.

7:27
Ex. 2:14; Acts 7:35

7:28
Ex. 2:14

7:29
Ex. 2:15,22; Ex. 18:3,4

7:30
Ex. 3:1f.; Is. 63:9

and as he approached to look[x] *more* closely, there came the voice of the Lord:

7:32
Ex. 3:6; Matt.
22:32

32 'I AM THE GOD OF YOUR FATHERS, THE GOD OF ABRAHAM AND ISAAC AND JACOB.' And Moses shook with fear and would[m] not venture to look.[x]

7:33
Ex. 3:5;
Josh. 5:15

33 "But THE LORD SAID TO HIM, 'TAKE[xi] OFF THE SANDALS FROM YOUR FEET, FOR THE PLACE ON WHICH YOU ARE STANDING IS HOLY[28a] GROUND.

7:34
Ex. 3:7f.;
Ex. 3:10

34 'I HAVE *CERTAINLY*[4] SEEN THE OPPRESSION OF MY PEOPLE IN EGYPT, AND HAVE HEARD THEIR GROANS, AND I HAVE COME DOWN TO DELIVER[x18a] THEM; COME NOW, AND I WILL[x] SEND YOU TO EGYPT.'

7:35
Ex. 2:14; Acts
7:27

35 "This Moses whom they disowned, saying, 'WHO MADE YOU A RULER AND A JUDGE?' is the one whom God sent[•] *to be* both a ruler and a deliverer with the help of the angel who appeared to him in the thorn bush.

7:36
Ex. 12:41; 33:1;
Heb. 8:9;
Ex. 7:3; 14:21;
John 4:48;
Ex. 16:35; Num.
14:33; Ps.
95:8-10; Acts
7:42; 13:18; Heb.
3:8f.
7:37
Deut. 18:15,18;
Acts 3:22
7:38
Ex. 19:17;
Acts 7:53;
Deut. 32:47; Heb.
4:12;
Rom. 3:2; Heb.
5:12; 1 Pet. 4:11
7:39
Num. 14:3f.

36 "This man led them out, performing wonders and signs in the land of Egypt and in the Red Sea and in the wilderness for forty years.

37 "This is the Moses who said to the sons of Israel, 'GOD SHALL RAISE UP FOR YOU A *PROPHET LIKE ME* FROM YOUR BRETHREN.'

38 "This is the one who was in the congregation in the wilderness together with the angel who was speaking to him on Mount Sinai, and *who was* with our fathers; and he received living oracles to pass[x] on to you.

39 "And our fathers were unwilling to be obedient to him, but repudiated him and in their hearts turned back to Egypt,

7:40
Ex. 32:1,23

40 SAYING TO AARON, 'MAKE[xi] FOR US GODS WHO WILL GO BEFORE US; FOR THIS MOSES WHO LED US OUT OF THE LAND OF EGYPT—WE DO NOT KNOW WHAT HAPPENED TO HIM.'

7:41
Ex. 32:4,6;
Rev. 9:20

41 "And at that time they made a calf and brought a sacrifice to the idol, and were rejoicing[m] in the works of their hands.

7:42
Josh. 24:20; Is.
63:10; Jer. 19:13;
Ezek. 20:39;
Amos 5:25;
Acts 7:36

42 "But God *turned*[†]*away* and delivered them up to serve[~] the host of heaven; as it is written[•] in the book of the prophets, 'IT WAS NOT TO ME THAT YOU OFFERED *VICTIMS* AND *SACRIFICES* FORTY YEARS IN THE WILDERNESS, WAS IT, O HOUSE OF ISRAEL?

7:43
Amos 5:26,27

43 'YOU ALSO TOOK ALONG THE TABERNACLE OF MOLOCH AND THE STAR OF THE GOD ROMPHA, THE IMAGES WHICH YOU MADE TO WORSHIP[~] THEM. I ALSO WILL REMOVE YOU BEYOND BABYLON.'

7:44
Ex. 25:8,9; 38:21;
Ex. 25:40
7:45
Deut. 32:49;
Josh. 3:14ff.;
18:1; 23:9;
24:18; Ps. 44:2f.

44 "Our fathers had the tabernacle of testimony in the wilderness, just as He who spoke to Moses directed *him* to make[x] it according to the pattern which he had seen.

45 "And having received it in their turn, our fathers brought it

in with Joshua upon dispossessing the nations whom †*God* drove out before our fathers, until the time of David.

46 "And *David* found favor in God's sight, and asked that he might find^x a dwelling place for the ^oGod of Jacob.

47 "But it was Solomon who built a house for Him.

48 "However, the Most High does *not* dwell in *houses made by human hands;* as the prophet says:

49   'HEAVEN IS MY THRONE,
        AND EARTH IS THE FOOTSTOOL OF MY FEET;
        WHAT KIND OF HOUSE WILL YOU BUILD FOR ME?' says
           the Lord;
        'OR WHAT PLACE IS THERE FOR MY REPOSE?

50   'WAS IT NOT *MY* †*HAND* WHICH MADE ALL THESE
           THINGS?'

51 "*You men* who are stiff-necked and uncircumcised in heart and ears are always resisting the *Holy Spirit;* you are doing just as your fathers did.

52 "Which one of the prophets did your fathers *not persecute?* And they killed those who had previously announced the coming of the Righteous One, whose betrayers and murderers *you* have now become;

53   you who received the law as ordained by angels, and *yet* did not keep it."

Stephen Put to Death

54 Now when they heard this, they were cut^m to the quick, and they *began* gnashing^m their teeth at him.

55 But being full of the Holy †Spirit, he gazed intently into heaven and saw the glory of God, and Jesus standing⁺ at the right hand of God;

56 and he said, "Behold, I see the heavens opened⁺ up and the Son of Man standing⁺ at the *right hand* of God."

57 But they cried out with a loud voice, and covered their ears, and they rushed upon him with one impulse.

58 And when they had driven him out of the city, they *began* stoning^m *him,* and the witnesses laid aside their robes at the feet of a young man named Saul.

59 And they went on stoning^m Stephen as he called upon *the Lord* and said, "Lord Jesus, receive^{x¹} my spirit!"

60 And falling on his knees, he cried out with a loud voice, "Lord, do not hold[⊙] this sin against them!" And having said this, he fell asleep.

^oThe earliest mss. read *house* instead of *God;* the Septuagint reads *God*

7:46
2 Sam. 7:8ff.; Ps. 132:1-5; Acts 13:22;
2 Sam. 7:1-16; 1 Chr. 17:1-14
7:47
1 Kin. 6:1-38; 8:20; 2 Chr. 3:1-17
7:48
Luke 1:32
7:49
Is. 66:1; Matt. 5:34f.

7:50
Is. 66:2

7:51
Ex. 32:9; 33:3,5; Lev. 26:41; Num. 27:14; Is. 63:10; Jer. 6:10; 9:26
7:52
2 Chr. 36:15f.; Matt. 5:12; 23:31, 37; Acts 3:14; 22:14; 1 John 2:1; Acts 5:28
7:53
Deut. 33:2; Acts 7:38; Gal. 3:19; Heb. 2:2

7:54
Acts 5:33

7:55
Acts 2:4; John 11:41; Mark 16:19

7:56
John 1:51; Matt. 8:20
7:58
Lev. 24:14,16; Luke 4:29; Deut. 13:9f.; 17:7; Acts 6:13; Acts 22:20; Acts 8:1; 26:10
7:59
Acts 9:14,21; 22:16; Rom. 10:12-14; 1 Cor. 1:2; 2 Tim. 2:22
7:60
Luke 22:41; Matt. 5:44; Luke 23:34; Dan. 12:2; Matt. 27:52; John 11:11f.; Acts 13:36; 1 Cor. 15:6,18,20; 1 Thess. 4:13ff.; 2 Pet. 3:4

Saul Persecutes the Church

8:1
Acts 7:58; 22:20;
26:10;
Acts 9:31;
Acts 8:4; 11:19;
Acts 1:8; 8:5,14

8 And Saul was~ in hearty agreement with putting him to death.

And on that day a great persecution arose against the church in Jerusalem; and they were all scattered throughout the regions of Judea and Samaria, *except the apostles.*

2   And *some* devout men buried Stephen, and made loud lamentation over him.

8:3
Acts 9:1,13,21;
22:4,19; 26:10f.;
1 Cor. 15:9; Gal.
1:13; Phil. 3:6; 1
Tim. 1:13;
James 2:6

3   But Saul *began* ravaging^m the church, entering house after house; and dragging off men and women, he would put^m them in prison.

Philip in Samaria

8:4
Acts 8:1;
Acts 8:12; 15:35

4   Therefore, those who had been scattered went about preaching the word.

8:5
Acts 6:5; 8:26,30

5   And Philip went down to the city of Samaria and *began* proclaiming Christ to them.

6   And the multitudes with *one accord* were giving^m attention to what was said by Philip, as they heard~ and saw~ the signs which he was performing.^m

8:7
Mark 16:17;
Matt. 4:24

7   For *in the case of* many who had unclean spirits, they were coming^m out *of them* shouting with a loud voice; and many who had been paralyzed⁺ and lame were healed.

8:8
John 4:40-42;
Acts 8:39
8:9
Acts 8:11; 13:6;
Acts 5:36

8   And there was much rejoicing in that city.

9   Now there was a certain man named Simon, who formerly was practicing magic in the city, and astonishing the people of Samaria, claiming to be someone great;

8:10
Acts 14:11; 28:6

10   and they all, from smallest to greatest, were giving^m attention to him, saying, "This man is what is called the Great Power of God."

8:11
Acts 8:9; 13:6

11   And they were giving^m him attention because he had for a long time astonished them with his magic arts.

8:12
Acts 1:3; 8:4;
Acts 2:38

12   But when they believed Philip preaching the good news about the kingdom of God and the name of Jesus Christ, they were being baptized,^m men and women alike.

8:13
Acts 8:6;
Acts 19:11

13   And even Simon *himself* believed; and after being baptized, he continued~ on with Philip; and as he observed signs and great²⁶ᵃ miracles taking place, he was constantly amazed.^m

8:14
Acts 8:1;
Luke 22:8

14   Now when the apostles in Jerusalem heard that *Samaria* had received⁺⁵ᵃ the word of God, they sent them Peter and John,

8:15
Acts 2:38; 19:2

15   who came down and prayed for them, that they might receive^{x5b} the Holy Spirit.

16   For He had not yet fallen⁺ upon any of them; they had^m simply been baptized⁺ in the name of the Lord Jesus.

17   Then they *began* laying^m their hands on them, and they were receiving^m the Holy Spirit.

18   Now when Simon saw that the Spirit was bestowed through the *laying on of the apostles' hands,* he offered them money,

19   saying, "Give^xl ⁺*this* authority to me as well, so that everyone on whom I lay^x my hands may receive~ the Holy Spirit."

20   But Peter said to him, "May your silver perish with you, because you thought you could obtain~ the gift²⁴ᵃ of God with *money!*

21   "You have no part or portion in ⁺*this* matter, for your heart is not right before God.

22   "Therefore repent^xl of this wickedness of yours, and pray^xl⁹ᵇ the Lord that if possible, the intention of your heart may be forgiven you.

23   "For I see that you are in the *gall of bitterness* and in the *bondage of iniquity.*"

24   But Simon answered and said, "Pray^xl to the Lord for me *yourselves,* so that nothing of what you have said⁺ may come^x upon me."

An Ethiopian Receives Christ

25   And so, when they had solemnly[1] testified and spoken the word of the Lord, they started^m back to Jerusalem, and were preaching^m the gospel to many villages of the Samaritans.

26   But an angel of the Lord spoke to Philip saying, "Arise^xl and go south to the road that descends from Jerusalem to Gaza." (This is a desert *road.*)

27   And he arose and went; and behold, there was an Ethiopian eunuch, a court official of Candace, queen of the Ethiopians, who was in charge of all her treasure; and he had come to Jerusalem to worship.

28   And he was returning and sitting in his chariot, and was reading^m the prophet Isaiah.

29   And the ⁺*Spirit* said to Philip, "Go^xl up and join^xl ⁺*this* chariot."

30   And when Philip had run up, he heard him reading Isaiah the prophet, and said, "Do[2] you understand what you are reading?"

31   And he said, "Well, how could~ I, unless someone guides me?" And he invited Philip to come up and sit^x with him.

8:16
Matt. 28:19; Acts 19:2;
Acts 2:38; 10:48
8:17
Mark 5:23; Acts 6:6;
Acts 2:4

8:20
2 Kin. 5:16; Is. 55:1; Dan. 5:17;
Matt. 10:8; Acts 2:38

8:21
Deut. 10:9; 12:12;
Eph. 5:5;
Ps. 78:37
8:22
Is. 55:7

8:23
Is. 58:6

8:24
Gen. 20:7; Ex. 8:8; Num. 21:7;
James 5:16

8:25
Luke 16:28;
Acts 13:12;
Acts 8:40;
Matt. 10:5

8:26
Acts 5:19; 8:29;
Acts 8:5;
Gen. 10:19

8:27
Ps. 68:31; 87:4;
Is. 56:3ff.;
1 Kin. 8:41f.;
John 12:20

8:29
Acts 8:39; 10:19;
11:12; 13:2; 16:6, 7; 20:23; 21:11;
28:25; Heb. 3:7

8:32
Is. 53:7

32 Now the passage of Scripture which he was reading^m was this:

"HE WAS LED AS A SHEEP TO SLAUGHTER;
AND AS A LAMB BEFORE ITS SHEARER IS SILENT,
SO HE DOES NOT OPEN HIS MOUTH.

8:33
Is. 53:8

33 "IN *HUMILIATION* HIS JUDGMENT WAS TAKEN AWAY;
WHO SHALL RELATE *HIS GENERATION*?
FOR HIS LIFE IS REMOVED FROM THE EARTH."

34 And the eunuch answered Philip and said, "Please *tell me*, of whom does the prophet say this? Of himself, or of someone else?"

8:35
Matt. 5:2;
Luke 24:27; Acts
17:2; 18:28;
28:23;
Acts 5:42
8:36
Acts 10:47

35 And Philip opened his mouth, and beginning from this Scripture he preached Jesus to him.

36 And as they went^m along the road they came to some water; and the eunuch *said, "Look! Water! What prevents me from being baptized?"^x

37 [^pAnd Philip said, "If you believe with all your heart, you may." And he answered and said, "I believe that Jesus Christ is the Son of God."]

38 And he ordered the chariot to stop;^x and they both went down into the water, Philip as well as the eunuch; and he baptized him.

8:39
1 Kin. 18:12;
2 Kin. 2:16; Ezek.
3:12,14; 8:3;
11:1,24; 43:5;
2 Cor. 12:2
8:40
Josh. 11:22;
1 Sam. 5:1;
Acts 8:25;
Acts 9:30; 10:1,
24; 11:11; 12:19;
18:22; 21:8,16;
23:23,33; 25:1,4,
6,13

39 And when they came up out of the water, the Spirit of the Lord snatched Philip away; and the eunuch saw him no more, but went^m on his way rejoicing.

40 But Philip found himself at Azotus; and as he passed through he kept preaching^m the gospel to all the cities, until he came to Caesarea.

The Conversion of Saul

9:1
Acts 9:1-22;
22:3-16; 26:9-18;
Acts 8:3; 9:13-21
9:2
Acts 9:14,21;
22:5; 26:10;
Matt. 10:17;
Gen. 14:15;
2 Cor. 11:32; Gal.
1:17;
John 14:6; Acts
18:25f.; 19:9,23;
22:4; 24:14,22
9:3
1 Cor. 15:8
9:4
Acts 22:7; 26:14

9 Now Saul, still breathing threats and murder against the disciples of the Lord, went to the high priest,

2 and asked for letters from him to the synagogues at Damascus, so that if he found^x any belonging to the Way, both men and women, he might bring^x them bound* to Jerusalem.

3 And it came about that as he journeyed,[~] he was approaching Damascus, and suddenly a *light from heaven* flashed around him;

4 and he fell to the ground, and heard a voice saying to him, "Saul, Saul, why are you persecuting [†]Me?"

5 And he said, "Who art Thou, Lord?" And He *said*, "[†]*I* am Jesus whom *you* are persecuting,

^pMany mss. do not contain this verse

6   but rise,ˣˡ and enterˣˡ the city, and it shall be told you what you must do."∼

7   And the men who traveled with him stood speechless, hearing the voice, but seeing no one.

8   And Saul got up from the ground, and though his eyes were open,⁺ he could seeᵐ nothing; and leading him by the hand, they brought him into Damascus.

9   And he was three days without sight, and neither ate nor drank.

10   Now there was a certain disciple at Damascus, named Ananias; and the Lord said to him in a vision, "Ananias." And he said, "Behold, *here am* I, Lord."

11   And the Lord *said* to him, "Arise and goˣˡ to the street called Straight, and inquireˣˡ at the house of Judas for a man from Tarsus named Saul, for behold, he is praying,

12   and he has seen ᑫin a vision a man named Ananias come in and lay his hands on him, so that he might regainˣ his sight."

13   But Ananias answered, "Lord, I have heard from many about ⁺this man, how much harm he did to Thy saints at Jerusalem;

14   and here he has authority from the chief priests to bindˣ all who call upon Thy name."

15   But the Lord said to him, "Go, for he is a *chosen* ʳ*instrument* of Mine, to bearˣ My name before the Gentiles and kings and the sons of Israel;

16   for *I* will show him how much he must *suffer*ˣ for My name's sake."

17   And Ananias departed and entered the house, and after laying his hands on him said, "Brother Saul, the Lord Jesus, who appeared to you on the road by which you were coming, has sent⁺ me so that you may regainˣ your sight, and be filledˣ with the Holy Spirit."

18   And immediately there fell from his eyes something like scales, and he regained his sight, and he arose and was baptized;

19   and he took food and was strengthened.

Saul Begins to Preach Christ

Now for several days he was with the disciples who were at Damascus,

20   and immediately he *began* to proclaimᵐ Jesus in the synagogues, saying, "He is the Son of God."

21   And all those hearing him continued to be amazed,ᵐ and were saying,ᵐ "Is this not he who in Jerusalem destroyed those

ᑫSome mss. do not contain *in a vision*   ʳOr, *vessel*

9:6
Acts 9:16

9:7
Acts 26:14;
John 12:29f.; Acts
22:9
9:8
Acts 9:18; 22:11;
Gen. 14:15;
2 Cor. 11:32; Gal.
1:17

9:10
Gen. 14:15;
2 Cor. 11:32; Gal.
1:17;
Acts 22:12;
Acts 10:3,17,19;
11:5; 12:9; 16:9f.;
18:9
9:11
Acts 9:30; 11:25;
21:39; 22:3
9:12
Mark 5:23; Acts
6:6; 9:17
9:13
Acts 8:3;
Acts 9:32,41;
26:10; Rom. 1:7;
15:25,26,31;
16:2,15; 1 Cor.
1:2
9:14
Acts 9:2,21;
Acts 7:59
9:15
Acts 13:2; Rom.
1:1; 9:23; Gal.
1:15; Eph. 3:7;
Acts 22:21;
26:17; Rom. 1:5;
11:13; 15:16; Gal.
1:16; 2:7ff.; Eph.
3:1,8; 1 Tim. 2:7;
2 Tim. 4:17;
Acts 25:22f.;
26:1,32; 2 Tim.
4:17
9:16
Acts 20:23; 21:4,
11,13; 2 Cor.
6:4f.; 11:23-27;
1 Thess. 3:3
9:17
Mark 5:23; Acts
6:6; 9:12;
Acts 22:13;
Acts 2:4

9:19
Acts 26:20;
Acts 9:26,38;
11:26

9:20
Acts 13:5,14;
14:1; 16:13; 17:2,
10; 18:4,19; 19:8;
Matt. 4:3; Acts
9:22; 13:33
9:21
Acts 8:3; 9:13;
Gal. 1:13,23;
Acts 9:14

who called on this name, and *who* had come here for the purpose of bringing[x] them bound[+] before the chief priests?"

22   But Saul kept increasing[m] in strength and confounding[m] the Jews who lived at Damascus by proving that this *Jesus* is the Christ.

9:23
Gal. 1:17,18;
1 Thess. 2:16

23   And when *many* days had elapsed,[m] the Jews plotted together to do[x] away with him,

9:24
Acts 20:3,19;
23:12,30; 25:3;
2 Cor. 11:32f.

24   but their plot became known to Saul. And they were also watching[m][1] the gates day and night so that they might put[x] him to death;

25   but his disciples took him by night, and let him down through *an opening in* the *wall,* lowering him in a large basket.

9:26
Acts 22:17-20;
26:20

26   And when he had come to Jerusalem, he was trying[m] to associate[~] with the disciples; and they were all afraid[m] of him, not believing that he was a disciple.

9:27
Acts 4:36;
Acts 9:3-6;
Acts 9:20,22;
Acts 4:13,29;
9:29

27   But Barnabas took hold of him and brought him to the apostles and described to them how he had seen the Lord on the road, and that He had talked to him, and how at Damascus he had spoken out boldly in the name of Jesus.

9:28
Acts 4:13,29;
9:29

28   And he was with them moving[~] about freely in Jerusalem, speaking out boldly in the name of the Lord.

9:29
Acts 6:1

29   And he was talking[m] and arguing[m] with the Hellenistic *Jews;* but they were attempting[m] to put[x] him to death.

9:30
Acts 1:15;
Acts 8:40;
Gal. 1:21;
Acts 9:11
9:31
Acts 5:11; 8:1;
16:5

30   But when the brethren learned *of it,* they brought him down to Caesarea and sent him away to Tarsus.

31   So the church throughout all Judea and Galilee and Samaria enjoyed[m] peace, being built up; and, going on in the fear of the Lord and in the comfort of the Holy Spirit, it continued[m] to increase.

Peter's Ministry

9:32
Acts 9:13;
1 Chr. 8:12; Ezra
2:33; Neh. 7:37;
11:35

32   Now it came about that as Peter was traveling through all *those parts,* he came[x] down also to the saints who lived at Lydda.

33   And there he found a certain man named Aeneas, who had been bedridden eight years, for he was paralyzed.[+]

9:35
1 Chr. 8:12; Ezra
2:33; Neh. 7:37;
11:35;
1 Chr. 5:16;
27:29; Is. 33:9;
35:2; 65:10;
Acts 2:47; 9:42;
11:21
9:36
Josh. 19:46;
2 Chr. 2:16; Ezra
3:7; Jon. 1:3; Acts
9:38,42f.; 10:5,8,
23,32; 11:5,13
9:37
Acts 1:13; 9:39

34   And Peter said to him, "Aeneas, *Jesus Christ* heals[15b] you; arise,[xi] and make[xi] your bed." And immediately he arose.

35   And all who lived at Lydda and Sharon saw him, and they turned to the Lord.

36   Now in Joppa there was a certain disciple named Tabitha (which translated *in Greek* is called Dorcas); this woman was abounding with deeds of kindness[25a] and charity, which she continually did.[m]

37   And it came about at that time that she fell sick and died;[x]

and when they had washed her body, they laid it in an upper room.

38   And since Lydda was near Joppa, the disciples, having heard that Peter was there, sent two men to him, entreating him, "Do not delay⁹ to come˟ to us."

39   And Peter arose and went with them. And when he had come, they brought him into the upper room; and all the widows stood beside him weeping, and showing all the ˢtunics and garments that Dorcas used to makeᵐ while she was with them.

40   But Peter sent them all out and knelt down and prayed, and turning to the body, he said, "Tabitha, arise."ˣˡ And she opened her eyes, and when she saw Peter, she sat up.

41   And he gave her his hand and raised her up; and calling the saints and widows, he presented her alive.

42   And it became known all over Joppa, and *many* believed in the Lord.

43   And it came about that he stayed˟ many days in Joppa with a certain tanner, Simon.

Cornelius' Vision

10 Now *there was* a certain man at Caesarea named Cornelius, a centurion of what was called the Italian ᵗcohort,

2   a devout man, and one who feared God with all his household, and gave many ᵘalms to the *Jewish* people, and prayed⁹ᵇ to God continually.

3   About the ᵛninth hour of the day he clearly saw in a vision an angel of God who had *just* come in to him, and said to him, "Cornelius!"

4   And fixing his gaze upon him and being much alarmed, he said, "What is it, Lord?" And he said to him, "Your prayers and ʷalms have ascended as a memorial before God.

5   "And now dispatchˣˡ *some* men to Joppa, and sendˣˡ for a man *named* Simon, who is also called Peter;

6   he is staying with a certain tanner *named* Simon, whose house is by the sea."

7   And when the angel who was speaking to him had departed, he summoned two of his servants and a devout soldier of those who were in constant attendance upon him,

8   and after he had explained everything to them, he sent them to Joppa.

9   And on the next day, as they were on their way, and approaching the city, Peter went up on the housetop about the ˣsixth hour to pray.ˣ

ˢOr, *inner garments*   ᵗOr, *battalion*   ᵘOr, *gifts of charity*   ᵛI.e., 3 p.m.   ʷOr, *deeds of charity*   ˣI.e., noon

---

9:38
Josh. 19:46;
2 Chr. 2:16; Ezra
3:7; Jon. 1:3; Acts
9:36,42f.; 10:5,8,
23,32; 11:5,13;
Acts 11:26
9:39
Acts 1:13; 9:37;
Acts 6:1

9:40
Matt. 9:25;
Luke 22:41; Acts
7:60;
Mark 5:41

9:41
Acts 9:13,32;
Acts 6:1

9:42
Josh. 19:46;
2 Chr. 2:16; Jon.
1:3; Acts 9:38,
42f.; 10:5,8,23,
32; 11:5,13;
Acts 9:35
9:43
Josh. 19:46;
2 Chr. 2:16; Ezra
3:7; Jon. 1:3; Acts
9:38,42f.; 10:5,8,
23,32; 11:13,15;
Acts 10:6
10:1
Acts 8:40; 10:24;
Matt. 27:27; Mark
15:16; John 18:3,
12; Acts 21:31;
27:1
10:2
Acts 10:22,35;
13:16,26;
Luke 7:4f.
10:3
Acts 3:1;
Acts 9:10; 10:17,
19;
Acts 5:19
10:4
Acts 3:4;
Rev. 8:4;
Matt. 26:13; Phil.
4:18; Heb. 6:10
10:5
Acts 9:36

10:6
Acts 9:43

10:8
Acts 9:36

10:9
Acts 10:9-32;
11:5-14;
Jer. 19:13; 32:29;
Zeph. 1:5; Matt.
24:17;
Ps. 55:17; Acts
10:3

10:10
Acts 11:5; 22:17

10   And he became hungry,[1] and was desiring[m] to eat;[x] but while they were making preparations, he fell into a †trance;

10:11
John 1:51

11   and he *beheld the sky opened* up, and a certain ʸobject like a great sheet coming down, lowered by four corners to the ground,

12   and there were[m] in it all *kinds of* four-footed animals and ᶻcrawling creatures of the earth and birds of the air.

13   And a voice came to him, "Arise, Peter, kill[x] and eat!"[xl]

10:14
Matt. 8:2ff.; John
4:11ff.; Acts 9:5;
22:8;
Lev. 11:20-25;
Deut. 14:4-20;
Ezek. 4:14; Dan.
1:8; Acts 10:28

14   But Peter said, "By no means, Lord, for I have †never eaten anything unholy[41b] and unclean."

10:15
Matt. 15:11; Mark
7:19; Rom. 14:14;
1 Cor. 10:25ff.;
1 Tim. 4:4f.; Titus
1:15

15   And again a voice *came* to him a second time, "What God has cleansed, no *longer* consider⁰ unholy."[41b]

10:17
Acts 10:3;
Acts 10:8

16   And this happened three times; and immediately the object was taken up into the sky.

17   Now while Peter was greatly[1] perplexed[m] in mind as to what the vision which he had seen might be, behold, the men who had been sent* by Cornelius, having asked directions for Simon's house, appeared at the gate;

18   and calling out, they were asking[m] whether Simon, who was also called Peter, was staying there.

10:19
Acts 10:3;
Acts 8:29

19   And while Peter was reflecting[1] on the vision, the *Spirit* said to him, "Behold, three men are looking for you.

10:20
Acts 15:7-9

20   "But arise, go[x] downstairs, and accompany them without misgivings; for I have sent them *Myself.*"

21   And Peter went down to the men and said, "Behold, I am the one you are looking for; what is the reason for which you have come?"

10:22
Acts 10:2;
Matt. 2:12;
Mark 8:38; Luke
9:26; Rev. 14:10;
Acts 11:14

22   And they said, "Cornelius, a centurion, a righteous and God-fearing man well spoken of by the entire nation of the Jews, was *divinely* directed by a holy angel to send[x] for you *to come* to his house and hear[x] a message from you."

10:23
Acts 10:45;
11:12;
Acts 1:15;
Acts 9:36

23   And so he invited them in and gave them lodging.

Peter at Caesarea

And on the next day he arose and went away with them, and some of the brethren from Joppa accompanied him.

10:24
Acts 8:40; 10:1

24   And on the following day he entered Caesarea. Now Cornelius was waiting~ for them, and had called together his relatives and close friends.

10:25
Matt. 8:2

25   And when it came about that Peter entered,[x] Cornelius met him, and fell at his feet and worshiped *him.*

10:26
Acts 14:15; Rev.
19:10; 22:8f.

26   But Peter raised him up, saying, "Stand[x] up; *I too* am *just a man.*"

ʸOr, *vessel* ᶻOr possibly, *reptiles*

27   And as he talked with him, he entered, and found many people assembled.✦

28   And he said to them, "You yourselves know how †unlaw-ful it is for a man who is a Jew to associate~ with a foreigner or to visit~ him; and *yet* God has shown *me* that I should not call~ *any* man unholy⁴¹ᵇ or unclean.

29   "That is why I came without even raising any objection when I was sent for. And so I ask for what reason you have sent for me."

30   And Cornelius said, "Four days ago to this hour, I was praying~ in my house during the ᵃninth hour; and behold, a man stood before me in shining garments,

31   and he *said, 'Cornelius, your prayer has been heard and your alms have been remembered before God.

32   'Sendˣᶦ therefore to Joppa and inviteˣᶦ Simon, who is also called Peter, to come to you; he is staying at the house of Simon *the* tanner by the sea.'

33   "And so I sent to you immediately, and you have been kind enough to come. Now then, we are all here present before God to hearˣ all that you have been commanded✦ by the Lord."

Gentiles Hear Good News

34   And opening his mouth, Peter said:
"I most certainly understand *now* that *God* is not one to show partiality,

35   but in every nation the man who fears Him and does what is right, is *welcome to Him.*

36   "The word⁴³ᵃ which He sent to the sons of Israel, preaching peace through Jesus Christ (He is Lord of *all*)—

37   you yourselves know the thing which took place through-out all Judea, starting from Galilee, after the baptism which John proclaimed.

38   *"You know of* Jesus of Nazareth, how *God* anointed Him with the Holy Spirit and with power,³²ᵃ and *how* He went about doing good, and healing¹⁵ᵇ all who were oppressed by the devil; for God was with Him.

39   "And we are witnesses of all the things He did both in the land of the Jews and in Jerusalem. And they also put Him to death by hanging Him on a cross.

40   "God raised Him up on the third day, and granted that He should become *visible,*

41   not to all the people, but to witnesses who were chosen✦

ᵃI.e., 3 to 4 p.m.

10:27
Acts 10:24

10:28
John 4:9; 18:28;
Acts 11:3;
Acts 10:14f.,35;
15:9

10:30
Acts 10:9,22f.;
Acts 3:1;
Acts 10:3-6,30-32

10:32
John 4:9; 18:28;
Acts 11:3

10:34
Matt. 5:2;
Deut. 10:17;
2 Chr. 19:7; Rom.
2:11; Gal. 2:6;
Eph. 6:9; Col.
3:25; 1 Pet. 1:17
10:35
Acts 10:28;
Acts 10:2

10:36
Acts 13:32;
Luke 1:79; 2:14;
Rom. 5:1; Eph.
2:17;
Matt. 28:18; Acts
2:36; Rom. 10:12

10:38
Acts 2:22;
Acts 4:26;
Matt. 4:23;
John 3:2

10:39
Luke 24:48; Acts
10:41;
Acts 5:30
10:40
Acts 2:24
10:41
John 14:19,22;
15:27;
Luke 24:48; Acts
10:39;
Luke 24:43; Acts
1:4 mg.

beforehand by God, *that is,* to us, who ate and drank with Him after He arose^x from the dead.

10:42
Acts 1:2;
Luke 16:28;
Luke 22:22;
John 5:22,27;
Acts 17:31;
2 Tim. 4:1; 1 Pet.
4:5

42 "And He ordered us to preach^x to the people, and solemnly[1] to testify^x that this is the One who has been appointed⁺ by God as Judge of the living and the dead.

10:43
Acts 3:18;
Luke 24:47; Acts
2:38; 4:12

43 "Of *Him* all the prophets bear witness that through His name everyone who believes in Him receives^{x5b} *forgiveness of sins."*

10:44
Acts 11:15; 15:8

44 While Peter was still speaking ⁺these words,^{43b} the *Holy Spirit* fell upon all those who were listening to the message.

10:45
Acts 10:23;
Acts 2:33,38

45 And all the circumcised believers who had come with Peter were amazed, because the gift^{24a} of the Holy Spirit had been poured⁺ out upon the *Gentiles also.*

10:46
Mark 16:17; Acts
2:4; 19:6

46 For they were hearing^m them speaking with tongues and exalting God. Then Peter answered,

10:47
Acts 8:36;
Acts 2:4; 10:44f.;
11:17; 15:8

47 "Surely no one can *refuse*^x the water for these to be baptized^x who have received^{5b} the *Holy Spirit* just as ⁺we *did,* can he?"

10:48
1 Cor. 1:14-17;
Acts 2:38; 8:16;
19:5

48 And he ordered them to be baptized^x in the name of Jesus Christ. Then they asked him to stay^x on for a few days.

Peter Reports at Jerusalem

11:1
Acts 1:15

11 Now the apostles and the brethren who were throughout Judea heard that the Gentiles [~]also had received^{5a} the word of God.

11:2
Acts 10:45

2 And when Peter came up to Jerusalem, those who were circumcised took^m issue with him,

11:3
Matt. 9:11; Acts
10:28; Gal. 2:12

3 saying, "You went to uncircumcised men and ate with them."

11:4
Luke 1:3

4 But Peter began *speaking* and *proceeded* to explain to them in orderly sequence, saying,

11:5
Acts 10:9-32;
11:5-14;
Acts 9:10

5 "I was in the city of Joppa praying;[~] and in a trance I saw a vision, a certain object coming down like a great sheet lowered by four corners from the sky; and it came right down to me,

6 and when I had fixed my gaze upon it and was observing^m it I saw the four-footed animals of the earth and the wild beasts and the ^bcrawling creatures and the birds of the air.

7 "And I also heard a voice saying to me, 'Arise, Peter; kill^{xi} and eat.'^{xi}

8 "But I said, 'By no means, Lord, for nothing unholy^{41b} or unclean has ⁺ever entered my mouth.'

11:9
Acts 10:15

9 "But a voice from heaven answered a second time, 'What God has cleansed, no longer consider^o unholy.'^{41b}

^bOr possibly, *reptiles*

10 "And this happened three times, and everything was drawn back up into the sky.

11 "And behold, at that moment three men appeared before the house in which we were *staying,* having been sent+ to me from Caesarea.

12 "And the *Spirit* told me to go^x with them without misgivings. And these six brethren also went with me, and we entered the man's house.

13 "And he reported to us how he had seen the angel standing in his house, and saying, 'Send^xi to Joppa, and have Simon, who is also called Peter, brought^xi here;

14 and he shall speak words to you by which you will be saved, you and all your household.'

15 "And as I began^x to speak,~ the *Holy Spirit* fell upon them, just as *He did* upon us at the beginning.

16 "And I remembered the word[43b] of the Lord, how He used to say,^m 'John baptized with water, but *you* shall be baptized with the Holy Spirit.'

17 "If God therefore gave to them the *same gift*[24a] as *He gave* to us also after believing in the Lord Jesus Christ, who was *I* that I could stand^x in God's way?"

18 And when they heard this, they quieted down, and glorified God, saying, "Well then, God has granted to the *Gentiles also* the repentance *that leads* to life."

The Church at Antioch

19 So then those who were scattered because of the persecution that arose in connection with Stephen made their way to Phoenicia and Cyprus and Antioch, speaking the word[43a] to no one except to Jews alone.

20 But there were some of them, men of Cyprus and Cyrene, who came to Antioch and *began* speaking to the ^cGreeks also, preaching the Lord Jesus.

21 And the hand of the Lord was with them, and a large number who believed turned to the Lord.

22 And the news about them reached the ears of the church at Jerusalem, and they sent Barnabas off to Antioch.

23 Then when he had come and witnessed the grace of God, he rejoiced and *began* to encourage^m them all with resolute heart to remain~ *true* to the Lord;

24 for he was a good[25a] man, and full of the Holy Spirit and of faith. And considerable numbers were brought to the Lord.

25 And he left for Tarsus to look^xi for Saul;

^cSome mss. read *Greek-speaking Jews*

11:11
Acts 8:40

11:12
Acts 8:29;
Acts 15:9; Rom.
3:22;
Acts 10:23

11:14
Acts 10:22;
John 4:53; Acts
10:2; 16:15,
31-34; 18:8; 1
Cor. 1:16
11:15
Acts 10:44;
Acts 2:4
11:16
Acts 1:5

11:17
Acts 10:45,47;
Acts 5:39

11:18
Matt. 9:8;
2 Cor. 7:10

11:19
Acts 8:1,4;
Acts 15:3; 21:2;
Acts 4:36;
Acts 6:5; 11:20,
22,27; 14:26;
15:22f.,30,35;
18:22; Gal. 2:11
11:20
Acts 4:36;
Matt. 27:32; Acts
2:10; 6:9; 13:1;
Acts 6:5; 11:19,
22,27; 14:26;
15:22f.,30,35;
18:22; Gal. 2:11;
John 7:35;
Acts 5:42
11:21
Luke 1:66;
Acts 2:47
11:22
Acts 4:36;
Acts 6:5; 11:19,
20,27; 13:1;
18:22; Gal. 2:11
11:23
Acts 13:43;
14:26; 15:40;
20:24,32
11:24
Acts 2:4;
Acts 2:47; 5:14;
11:21
11:25
Acts 9:11

11:26
Acts 6:5; 11:20,
22,27;
John 2:2; Acts
1:15;
Acts 26:28; 1 Pet.
4:16

11:27
Luke 11:49; Acts
2:17; 13:1; 1 Cor.
12:10,28f.;
Acts 6:5; 11:20,
22,26; 14:26;
15:22f.,30,35;
18:22; Gal. 2:11
11:28
Acts 21:10;
Matt. 24:14;
Acts 18:2
11:29
John 2:2; Acts
1:15; 6:1f.; 9:19,
25,26,38; 11:26;
13:52; 14:20,22,
28;
Acts 11:1
11:30
Acts 12:25;
Acts 4:36;
Acts 14:23; 15:2,
4,6,22f.; 16:4;
20:17; 21:18;
1 Tim. 5:17,19;
Titus 1:5; James
5:14; 1 Pet. 5:1; 2
John 1; 3 John 1
12:2
Matt. 4:21; 20:23;
Mark 10:39

12:3
Acts 24:27; 25:9;
Ex. 12:15; 23:15;
Acts 20:6

12:4
John 19:23;
Ex. 12:1-27; Mark
14:1; Acts 12:3

12:6
Acts 21:33

12:7
Acts 5:19;
Luke 2:9; 24:4;
Acts 16:26

12:9
Acts 9:10

12:10
Acts 5:19; 16:26

26   and when he had found him, he brought him to Antioch. And it came about that for an *entire year* they met[x] with the church, and taught[x] considerable numbers; and the disciples were first called[x] Christians in Antioch.

27   Now at this time some *prophets* came down from Jerusalem to Antioch.

28   And one of them named Agabus stood up and *began* to indicate by the Spirit that there would certainly be a great famine all over the world. And this took place in the *reign* of Claudius.

29   And in the proportion that any of the disciples had means,[m] each of them determined to send[x] *a contribution* for the relief of the brethren living in Judea.

30   And this they did, sending it in charge of Barnabas and Saul to the elders.

Peter's Arrest and Deliverance

12   Now about that time Herod the king laid hands on some who belonged to the church, in order to mistreat[x] them.

2   And he had James the brother of John put to death with a sword.

3   And when he saw that it [†]*pleased* the Jews, he proceeded to arrest[x] Peter also. Now it was during the days of Unleavened Bread.

4   And when he had seized him, he put him in prison, delivering him to *four* squads of soldiers to guard[~] him, intending after the Passover to bring[x] him out before the people.

5   So Peter was kept in the prison, but prayer for him was being made[~] fervently by the church to God.

6   And on the very night when Herod was about to bring him forward, Peter was sleeping[~] between two soldiers, bound[*] with two chains; and guards in front of the door were watching[m] over the prison.

7   And behold, an angel of the Lord suddenly appeared, and a light shone in the cell; and he struck Peter's side and roused him, saying, "Get[x] up quickly." And his chains *fell off* his hands.

8   And the angel said to him, "Gird[x] yourself and put[x] on your sandals." And he did so. And he *said to him, "Wrap[x] your cloak around you and follow[m] me."

9   And he went out and continued to follow,[m] and he did not know that what was being done by the angel was [†]real, but thought[m] he was seeing[~] a *vision*.

10   And when they had passed the first and second guard, they came to the *iron* gate that leads into the city, which opened

for them by *itself;* and they went out and went along one street; and immediately the angel departed from him.

11   And when Peter came to himself, he said, "Now I know for *sure* that the *Lord* has sent forth His angel and rescued[18a] me from the hand of Herod and from all that the Jewish people were expecting."

12:11
Luke 15:17;
Dan. 3:28; 6:22

12   And when he realized *this,* he went to the house of Mary, the mother of John who was also called Mark, where many were gathered⁺ together and were praying. ~

12:12
Acts 12:25; 13:5,
13; 15:37,39; Col.
4:10; 2 Tim. 4:11;
Philem. 24; 1 Pet.
5:13;
Acts 12:5

13   And when he knocked at the door of the gate, a servant-girl named Rhoda came to answer.ˣ

12:13
John 18:16f.

14   And when she recognized Peter's voice, because of her *joy* she did not open the gate, but ran in and announced that *Peter* was standing in front of the gate.

12:14
Luke 24:41

15   And they said to her, "You are out of your mind!" But she kept insistingᵐ that it was so. And they kept saying,ᵐ "It is his ⁺*angel.*"

12:15
Matt. 18:10

16   But Peter continuedᵐ knocking; and when they had opened *the door,* they saw him and were amazed.

17   But motioning to them with his hand to be silent, ~ he described to them how the Lord had led him out of the prison. And he said, "Reportˣ these things to James and the brethren." And he departed and went to another place.

12:17
Acts 13:16;
19:33; 21:40;
Mark 6:3; Acts
15:13; 21:18;
1 Cor. 15:7; Gal.
1:19; 2:9,12;
Acts 1:15

18   Now when day came, there was no small disturbance among the soldiers *as to* what could have become of Peter.

19   And when Herod had searched¹ for him and had not found him, he examined the guards and ordered that they be ledˣ away *to execution.* And he went down from Judea to Caesarea and was spendingᵐ time there.

12:19
Acts 16:27;
27:42;
Acts 8:40

Death of Herod

20   Now he was very angry ~ with the people of Tyre and Sidon; and with one accord they cameᵐ to him, and having won over Blastus the king's chamberlain, they were askingᵐ for peace, because *their* country was fed ~ by the king's country.

12:20
Matt. 11:21;
1 Kin. 5:11; Ezra
3:7; Ezek. 27:17

21   And on an appointed day Herod, having put on his royal apparel, took his seat on the rostrum and *began* delivering an address to them.

22   And the people kept cryingᵐ out, "The voice of a *god* and not of a man!"

23   And immediately an angel of the Lord struck him because he did not give God the glory, and he was eaten by worms and died.

12:23
2 Sam. 24:16;
2 Kin. 19:35; Acts
5:19

12:24
Acts 6:7; 19:20

24 But the word of the Lord continued to grow^m and to be multiplied.^m

12:25
Acts 4:36; 13:1ff.;
Acts 11:30;
Acts 12:12

25 And Barnabas and Saul returned from Jerusalem when they had fulfilled their mission, taking along with *them* John, who was also called Mark.

First Missionary Journey

13:1
Acts 11:19;
Acts 11:26;
Acts 11:27;
15:32; 19:6; 21:9;
1 Cor. 11:4f.;
13:2,8f.; 14:29,
32,37;
Rom. 12:6f.;
1 Cor. 12:28f.;
Eph. 4:11; James
3:1;
Acts 4:36;
Matt. 27:32; Acts
11:20;
Matt. 14:1

13 Now there were at Antioch, in the church that was *there*, prophets and teachers: Barnabas, and Simeon who was called Niger, and Lucius of Cyrene, and Manaen who had been brought up with Herod the tetrarch, and Saul.

13:2
Acts 8:29; 13:4;
Acts 4:36;
Acts 9:15

2 And while they were ministering^{38d} to the Lord and fasting, the *Holy* †*Spirit* said, "Set^x apart [2] for Me Barnabas and Saul for the work to which I have called⁺ them."

13:3
Acts 1:24;
Acts 6:6;
Acts 13:4; 14:26

3 Then, when they had fasted and prayed and laid their hands on them, they sent them away.

13:4
Acts 13:2f.;
Acts 4:36

4 So, being sent out by the Holy Spirit, they went down to Seleucia and from there they sailed to Cyprus.

13:5
Acts 9:20; 13:14;
Acts 12:12

5 And when they reached Salamis, they *began* to proclaim^m the word of God in the synagogues of the Jews; and they also had^m John as their helper.

13:6
Acts 8:9;
Matt. 7:15

6 And when they had gone through the whole island as far as Paphos, they found a certain magician, a Jewish false prophet whose name was Bar-Jesus,

13:7
Acts 13:8,12;
18:12; 19:38

7 who was with the proconsul, Sergius Paulus, a man of intelligence. This man summoned Barnabas and Saul and sought[1] to hear^x the word of God.

13:8
Acts 8:9;
Acts 13:7,12;
18:12; 19:38;
Acts 6:7

8 But Elymas the magician (for thus his name is translated) was opposing^m them, seeking to turn^x the proconsul away from the faith.

13:9
Acts 2:4; 4:8

9 But Saul, who was also *known as* Paul, filled with the Holy Spirit, fixed his gaze upon him,

13:10
Matt. 13:38; John
8:44;
Hos. 14:9; 2 Pet.
2:15

10 and said, "You who are full of all deceit and fraud, you son of the devil, you enemy of all righteousness, will you not cease to make crooked the straight ways of the Lord?

13:11
Ex. 9:3; 1 Sam.
5:6f.; Job 19:21;
Ps. 32:4; Heb.
10:31

11 "And now, behold, the hand of the Lord is upon you, and you will be blind and not see the sun for a time." And immediately a mist and a darkness fell upon him, and he went about seeking^m those who would lead him by the hand.

13:12
Acts 13:7,8;
18:12; 19:38;
Acts 8:25; 13:49;
15:35f.; 19:10,20

12 Then the proconsul believed when he saw what had happened,⁺ being amazed[1] at the teaching of the Lord.

13:13
Acts 13:6;
Acts 14:25;
Acts 2:10; 14:24;
15:38; 27:5;
Acts 12:12

13 Now Paul and his companions put out to sea from Paphos and came to Perga in Pamphylia; and John left them and returned to Jerusalem.

14 But going on from Perga, they arrived at Pisidian Antioch, and on the Sabbath day they went into the synagogue and sat down.

15 And after the reading of the Law and the Prophets the synagogue officials sent to them, saying, "Brethren, if you have any word of exhortation for the people, say ᴹ it."

16 And Paul stood up, and motioning with his hand, he said, "Men of Israel, and you who fear God, listen:ˣ¹

17 "The God of this people Israel chose our fathers, and made the people great during their stay in the land of Egypt, and with an *uplifted* arm He led them out from it.

18 "And for a period of about *forty years* He put up with them in the wilderness.

19 "And when He had destroyed seven nations in the land of Canaan, He distributed their land as an inheritance—*all of which* took about four hundred and fifty years.

20 "And after these things He gave *them* judges until Samuel the prophet.

21 "And then they asked for a king, and God gave them Saul the son of Kish, a man of the tribe of Benjamin, for forty years.

22 "And after He had removed him, He raised up David to be their king, concerning whom He also testified and said, 'I HAVE FOUND DAVID the son of Jesse, A MAN AFTER MY HEART, who will do all My will.'

23 "From the offspring of *this man*, according to promise, God has brought to Israel a Savior, Jesus,

24 after John had proclaimed before His coming a baptism of repentance to all the people of Israel.

25 "And while John was completingᵐ his course, he kept saying,ᵐ 'What do you suppose that *I* am? *I* am not *He*. But behold, one is coming after me the sandals of whose feet I am not worthy to untie.'ˣ

26 "Brethren, sons of Abraham's family, and those among you who fear God, to *us* the word of ⁺this salvation is sent out.

27 "For those who live in Jerusalem, and their rulers, recognizing neither Him nor the utterances of the prophets which are read every Sabbath, fulfilled *these* by condemning *Him*.

28 "And though they found no ⁺ground for *putting Him to death*, they asked Pilate that He be executed.ˣ

29 "And when they had carried out all that was written⁺ concerning Him, they took Him down from the cross and laid Him in a tomb.

30 "But God raised Him from the dead;

31 and for many days He appeared to those who came up

13:14 Acts 14:24; Acts 14:19,21; 2 Tim. 3:11; Acts 13:42,44; 16:13; 17:2; 18:4; Acts 9:20; 13:5
13:15 Acts 15:21; 2 Cor. 3:14f.; Acts 13:27; Mark 5:22
13:16 Acts 12:17; Acts 10:2; 13:26
13:17 Ex. 6:1,6; 13:14, 16; Deut. 7:6-8; Acts 7:17ff.; Ex. 1:7; Ex. 12:51
13:18 Num. 14:34; Acts 7:36; Deut. 1:31
13:19 Acts 7:45; Deut. 7:1; Josh. 14:1; 19:51; Ps. 78:55; Judg. 11:26; 1 Kin. 6:1
13:20 Judg. 2:16; 1 Sam. 3:20; Acts 3:24
13:21 1 Sam. 8:5; 1 Sam. 9:1f.; 10:1,21
13:22 1 Sam. 15:23,26, 28; 16:1,13; 1 Sam. 13:14; Ps. 89:20; Acts 7:46
13:23 Matt. 1:1; Acts 13:32f.; Luke 2:11; John 4:42
13:24 Mark 1:1-4; Acts 1:22; 19:4; Luke 3:3
13:25 Acts 20:24; Matt. 3:11; Mark 1:7; Luke 3:16; John 1:20,27
13:26 John 6:68; Acts 4:12; 5:20; 13:46; 28:28
13:27 Luke 23:13; Acts 3:17; Luke 24:27; Acts 13:15
13:28 Matt. 27:22,23; Mark 15:13,14; Luke 23:21-23; John 19:15; Acts 3:14
13:29 Acts 26:22; Acts 5:30; Matt. 27:57-61; Mark 15:42-47; Luke 23:50-56; John 19:38-42
13:30 Acts 2:24; 13:33, 34,37
13:31 Acts 1:3; Luke 24:48

with Him from Galilee to Jerusalem, the very ones who are now His witnesses to the people.

13:32
Acts 5:42; 14:15;
Acts 13:23; 26:6;
Rom. 1:2; 4:13;
9:4

32 "And *we* preach to you the good news of the promise made to the fathers,

13:33
Acts 2:24; 13:30,
34,37;
Ps. 2:7

33 that God has fulfilled⁺¹ *this promise* to our children in that He raised up Jesus, as it is also written⁺ in the *second Psalm,* 'Thou art My Son; today I have begotten⁺ Thee.'

13:34
Acts 2:24; 13:30,
33,37;
Is. 55:3

34 "*And as for the fact that* He raised Him up from the dead, no more to return to decay, He has spoken⁺ in this way: 'I will give you the holy²⁸ᵇ *and* sure *blessings* of David.'

13:35
Ps. 16:10; Acts
2:27

35 "Therefore He also says in another *Psalm,* 'Thou wilt not allow Thy Holy²⁸ᵇ One to undergoˣ decay.'

13:36
Acts 2:29;
Acts 13:22;
20:27;
1 Kin. 2:10; Acts
8:1

36 "For David, after he had served the purpose of God in his own generation, fell asleep, and was laid among his fathers, and underwent decay;

13:37
Acts 2:24; 13:30,
33,34

37 but He whom God raised did not undergo decay.

13:38
Luke 24:47; Acts
2:38

38 "Therefore let it be known to you, brethren, that through *Him* forgiveness of sins is proclaimed to you,

13:39
Acts 10:43; Rom.
3:28; 10:4

39 and through *Him* everyone who believes is freedˣ from *all things,* from which you could not be freed through the Law of Moses.

13:40
Luke 24:44; John
6:45; Acts 7:42

40 "Take heed⁓¹ therefore, so that the thing spoken⁺ of in the Prophets may not comeˣ upon *you:*

13:41
Hab. 1:5

41   'Behold,ˣ¹ you scoffers, and marvel,ˣ¹ and perish;ˣ¹
        For *I* am accomplishing a work⁴ in your days,
        A work which you will ⁺never believe,ˣ though
        someone should describe⁓¹ it to you.' "

13:42
Acts 13:14

42 And as Paul and Barnabas were going out, the people kept begging˟ that these things might be spokenˣ to them the next Sabbath.

13:43
Acts 13:50;
16:14; 17:4,17;
18:7;
Matt. 23:15;
Acts 11:23

43 Now when *the meeting of* the synagogue had broken up, many of the Jews and of the God-fearing proselytes followed Paul and Barnabas, who, speaking to them, were urging˟ them to continue⁓ in the grace of God.

Paul Turns to the Gentiles

13:44
Acts 13:14

44 And the next Sabbath nearly the whole city assembled to hearˣ the word⁴³ᵃ of God.

13:45
Acts 13:50; 14:2,
4,5,19; 1 Thess.
2:16

45 But when the Jews saw the †crowds, they were filled with jealousy, and *began* contradicting˟ the things spoken by Paul, and were blaspheming.

13:46
Acts 3:26; 9:20;
13:5,14;
Acts 18:6; 19:9;
22:21; 26:20;
28:28

46 And Paul and Barnabas spoke out boldly and said, "It was necessary that the word of God should be spokenˣ to *you first;*

since you repudiate it, and judge yourselves *unworthy* of eternal life, behold, we are turning to the Gentiles.

47 "For thus the *Lord* has commanded⁺ us,
    'I HAVE PLACED⁺ YOU AS A LIGHT FOR THE GENTILES,
    THAT YOU SHOULD BRING SALVATION TO THE END OF
        THE EARTH.' "

48 And when the Gentiles heard this, they *began* rejoicing^m and glorifying^m the word of the Lord; and as many as had been appointed⁺ to eternal life *believed.*

49 And the word of the Lord was being spread^m through the whole region.

50 But the Jews aroused the devout women of prominence and the leading men of the city, and instigated a persecution against Paul and Barnabas, and drove them out of their district.

51 But they shook off the dust of their feet *in protest* against them and went to Iconium.

52 And the disciples were continually filled^m with joy and with the Holy Spirit.

Acceptance and Opposition

14 And it came about that in Iconium they entered^x the synagogue of the Jews together, and spoke^x in such a manner that a great multitude believed,^x both of Jews and of Greeks.

2 But the Jews who disbelieved stirred up the minds of the Gentiles, and embittered them against the brethren.

3 Therefore they spent a long time *there* speaking boldly *with reliance* upon the Lord, who was bearing witness to the word of His grace, granting that signs and wonders be done~ by their hands.

4 But the multitude of the city was divided; and some sided with the Jews, and some with the apostles.

5 And when an attempt was made by both the Gentiles and the Jews with their rulers, to mistreat^x and to stone^x them,

6 they became aware of it and fled to the cities of Lycaonia, Lystra and Derbe, and the surrounding region;

7 and there they continued to preach~ the gospel.

8 And at Lystra there was sitting^m a certain man, without strength in his feet, lame from his mother's womb, who had never walked.

9 This man was listening to Paul as he spoke, who, when he had fixed his gaze upon him, and had seen that he had faith to be made^x well,

10 said with a *loud* voice, "Stand^xl *upright* on your feet." And he leaped up and *began* to walk.

13:47 Is. 42:6; 49:6; Luke 2:32
13:48 Acts 13:12; Rom. 8:28ff.; Eph. 1:4f.,11
13:49 Acts 13:12
13:50 Acts 13:45; 14:2, 4,5,19; 1 Thess. 2:14ff.; Acts 13:43; 16:14; 17:4,17; 18:7; Mark 15:43
13:51 Matt. 10:14; Mark 6:11; Luke 9:5; 10:11; Acts 18:6; Acts 14:1,19,21; 16:2; 2 Tim. 3:11
13:52 Acts 2:4
14:1 Acts 13:51; 14:19,21; 16:2; 2 Tim. 3:11; Acts 13:5; Acts 2:47; John 7:35; Acts 18:4
14:2 Acts 13:45,50; 14:4,5,19; 1 Thess. 2:14ff.; John 3:36; Acts 1:15
14:3 Acts 4:29f.; 20:32; Heb. 2:4; John 4:48
14:4 Acts 17:4f.; 19:9; 28:24; Acts 13:45,50; 14:2,5,19; 1 Thess. 2:14ff.; Acts 14:14
14:5 Acts 13:45,50; 14:2,4,19; 1 Thess. 2:14ff.
14:6 Acts 14:11; Acts 14:8,21; 16:1f.; 2 Tim. 3:11; Acts 14:20; 20:4
14:7 Acts 14:15,21; 16:10
14:8 Acts 14:6,21; 16:1f.; 2 Tim. 3:11; Acts 3:2
14:9 Acts 3:4; 10:4; Matt. 9:28
14:10 Acts 3:8

14:11
Acts 14:6;
Acts 8:10; 28:6

14:13
Dan. 2:46
14:14
Acts 14:4;
Num. 14:6; Matt.
26:65; Mark
14:63
14:15
Acts 10:26;
James 5:17;
Acts 13:32; 14:7,
21;
Deut. 32:21;
1 Sam. 12:21;
Jer. 8:19; 14:22;
1 Cor. 8:4;
Matt. 16:16;
Ex. 20:11; Ps.
146:6; Acts 4:24;
17:24; Rev. 14:7
14:16
Acts 17:30;
Ps. 81:12; Mic.
4:5
14:17
Acts 17:26f.;
Rom. 1:19f.;
Deut. 11:14; Job
5:10; Ps. 65:10f.;
Ezek. 34:26f.;
Joel 2:23
14:19
Acts 13:45,50;
14:2,4,5; 1 Thess.
2:14ff.;
Acts 13:14;
14:21,26;
Acts 13:51; 14:1,
21; 2 Cor. 11:25;
2 Tim. 3:11
14:20
Acts 11:26;
14:22,28;
Acts 14:6
14:21
Acts 14:7;
Acts 2:47;
Acts 14:6;
Acts 13:51; 14:1,
19;
Acts 13:14;
14:19,26
14:22
Acts 11:26;
14:28;
Acts 6:7;
Mark 10:30; John
15:18,20; 16:33;
Acts 9:16; 1
Thess. 3:3; 2 Tim.
3:12; 1 Pet. 2:21;
Rev. 1:9
14:23
2 Cor. 8:19; Titus
1:5;
Acts 11:30;
Acts 1:24; 13:3;
Acts 20:32
14:24
Acts 13:14;
Acts 13:13
14:25
Acts 13:13
14:26
Acts 11:19;
Acts 13:3;
Acts 11:23;
15:40

11 And when the multitudes saw what Paul had done, they raised their voice, saying in the Lycaonian language, "The gods have become like men and have come down to us."

12 And they *began* calling Barnabas, Zeus, and Paul, Hermes, because he was the chief speaker.

13 And the priest of Zeus, whose *temple* was just outside the city, brought *oxen* and *garlands* to the gates, and wanted^m to offer~ sacrifice with the crowds.

14 But when the apostles, Barnabas and Paul, heard of it, they tore their robes and rushed out into the crowd, crying out

15 and saying, "Men, why are you doing these things? *We* are *also* men of the *same nature* as you, and preach the gospel to you in order that you should turn~ from these ^dvain things to a living God, WHO MADE THE HEAVEN AND THE EARTH AND THE SEA, AND ALL THAT IS IN THEM.

16 "And in the generations gone⁺ by He permitted^{6b} all the nations to go~ their own ways;

17 and yet He did not leave Himself *without witness,* in that He did good and gave you rains from heaven and fruitful seasons, satisfying your hearts with food and gladness."

18 And *even* saying these things, they with difficulty restrained the crowds from offering~ sacrifice to them.

19 But *Jews* came from Antioch and Iconium, and having won over the multitudes, they stoned Paul and dragged him out of the city, supposing him to be dead.

20 But while the disciples stood around him, he arose and entered the city. And the next day he went away with Barnabas to Derbe.

21 And after they had preached the gospel to that city and had made many disciples, they returned to Lystra and to Iconium and to Antioch,

22 strengthening the souls of the disciples, encouraging them to continue~ in the faith, and *saying,* 'Through *many tribulations* we must enter^x the kingdom of God."

23 And when they had appointed elders for them in every church, having prayed with fasting, they commended them to the Lord in whom they had believed.

24 And they passed through Pisidia and came into Pamphylia.

25 And when they had spoken the word in Perga, they went down to Attalia;

26 and from there they sailed to Antioch, from which they

^dI.e., idols

had been commended* to the grace of God for the work that they had accomplished.

27   And when they had arrived and gathered the church together, they *began* to report^m all things that *God* had done with them and how He had opened a door of faith to the *Gentiles*.

28   And they spent a long time with the disciples.

The Council at Jerusalem

15 And some men came down from Judea and *began* teaching^m the brethren, "Unless you are circumcised^x according to the custom of Moses, you cannot be saved."^x

2   And when Paul and Barnabas had great dissension and debate with them, *the brethren* determined that Paul and Barnabas and certain others of them should go up to Jerusalem to the apostles and elders concerning †*this* issue.

3   Therefore, being sent on their way by the church, they were passing^m through both Phoenicia and Samaria, describing in detail the conversion of the Gentiles, and were bringing^m great joy to all the brethren.

4   And when they arrived at Jerusalem, they were received by the church and the apostles and the elders, and they reported all that God had done with them.

5   But certain ones of the sect of the Pharisees who had believed,* stood up, saying, "It is necessary to circumcise~ them, and to direct~ them to observe~ the Law of Moses."

6   And the apostles and the elders came together to look^x into this matter.

7   And after there had been much debate, Peter stood up and said to them, "Brethren, you know^{29c} that in the early days God made a choice among you, that by my mouth the Gentiles should hear^x the word of the gospel and believe.^x

8   "And God, who knows the heart, bore witness to them, giving them the Holy Spirit, just as He also did to us;

9   and He made no †distinction between us and them, cleansing their hearts by *faith*.

10   "Now therefore why do you put God to the test by placing^x upon the neck of the disciples a yoke which neither our fathers nor *we* have been able to bear?^x

11   "But we believe that we are saved^x through the *grace of the Lord Jesus*, in the same way as they also are."

12   And all the multitude kept silent, and they were listening^m to Barnabas and Paul as they were relating what signs and wonders *God* had done through them among the Gentiles.

14:27
Acts 15:3,4,12;
21:19;
1 Cor. 16:9; 2
Cor. 2:12; Col.
4:3; Rev. 3:8
14:28
Acts 11:26; 14:22

15:1
Acts 15:24;
Acts 1:15; 15:3,
22,32;
Lev. 12:3; Acts
15:5; 1 Cor. 7:18;
Gal. 2:11,14;
5:2f.;
Acts 6:14
15:2
Acts 15:7;
Gal. 2:2;
Acts 11:30; 15:4,
6,22,23; 16:4
15:3
Acts 20:38; 21:5;
Rom. 15:24; 1
Cor. 16:6,11;
2 Cor. 1:16; Titus
3:13; 3 John 6;
Acts 11:19;
Acts 14:27; 15:4,
12;
Acts 1:15; 15:22,
32
15:4
Acts 11:30; 15:6,
22,23; 16:4
15:5
Acts 14:27; 15:12
Acts 5:17; 24:5,
14; 26:5; 28:22;
Matt. 3:7; 1 Cor.
7:18; Gal. 2:11,
14; 5:2f.
15:6
Acts 11:30; 15:4,
22,23; 16:4
15:7
Acts 15:2;
Acts 10:19f.;
Acts 20:24

15:8
Acts 1:24;
Acts 2:4; 10:44,
47
15:9
Acts 10:28,34;
11:12;
Acts 10:43
15:10
Acts 5:9;
Matt. 23:4; Gal.
5:1
15:11
Rom. 3:24; 5:15;
2 Cor. 13:14;
Eph. 2:5-8
15:12
Acts 14:27; 15:3,
4;
John 4:48

James' Judgment

15:13
Acts 12:17

13   And after they had stopped speaking,ˣ James answered, saying, "Brethren, listenˣⁱ to me.

15:14
Acts 15:7; 2 Pet. 1:1

14   "Simeon has related how God first concerned Himself about takingˣ from among the Gentiles a people for His name.

15:15
Acts 13:40

15   "And with this the words of the Prophets agree, just as it is written,⁺

15:16
Amos 9:11;
Jer. 12:15

16   'AFTER THESE THINGS I will return,
        AND I WILL REBUILD THE TABERNACLE OF DAVID
        WHICH HAS FALLEN,⁺
        AND I WILL REBUILD ITS RUINS,
        AND I WILL RESTORE IT,

15:17
Amos 9:12;
Deut. 28:10; Is. 63:19; Jer. 14:9; Dan. 9:19; James 2:7

17   IN ORDER THAT THE REST OF ⁺MANKIND MAY SEEKˣⁱ
        THE LORD,
        AND ALL THE GENTILES WHO ARE CALLED⁺ BY MY
        ⁺NAME,'

15:18
Amos 9:12;
Is. 45:21

18   SAYS THE LORD, WHO MAKES THESE THINGS KNOWN
        FROM OF OLD.

15:19
Acts 15:28; 21:25

19   "Therefore it is *my* judgment that we do not trouble~ⁱ those who are turning to God from among the Gentiles,

15:20
Ex. 34:15-17;
Dan. 1:8; Acts 15:29; 1 Cor. 8:7, 13; 10:7f.,14-28; Rev. 2:14,20; Lev. 18:6-23; Gen. 9:4; Lev. 3:17; 7:26; 17:10, 14; 19:26; Deut. 12:16,23; 15:23; 1 Sam. 14:33

20   but that we writeˣ to them that they abstain~ from things contaminated by idols and from fornication and from what is strangled and from blood.

15:21
Acts 13:15; 2 Cor. 3:14f.

21   "For Moses from ancient generations has in *every* ⁺*city* those who preach him, since he is read in the synagogues *every* ⁺*Sabbath."*

15:22
Acts 15:2;
Acts 11:20;
Acts 15:27,32,40; 16:19,25,29; 17:4,10,14f.; 18:5; 2 Cor. 1:19; 1 Thess. 1:1; 2 Thess. 1:1; 1 Pet. 5:12; Acts 15:1

22   Then it seemed good to the apostles and the elders, with the whole church, to choose men from among them to sendˣ to Antioch with Paul and Barnabas—Judas called Barsabbas, and Silas, leading men among the brethren,

23   and they sent this letter by them,

15:23
Acts 15:2;
Acts 15:1;
Acts 11:20;
Matt. 4:24; Acts 15:41; Gal. 1:21; Acts 6:9; Acts 23:26; James 1:1; 2 John 10f.

       "The apostles and the brethren who are elders, to the brethren in Antioch and Syria and Cilicia who are from the Gentiles, greetings.~

24   "Since we have heard that some of our number to whom we gave no instruction have disturbed you with *their* words, unsettling your souls,

15:24
Acts 15:1;
Gal. 1:7; 5:10

25   it seemed good to us, having become of one mind, to select men to sendˣ to you with our beloved Barnabas and Paul,

15:25
Acts 15:28

15:26
Acts 9:23ff.;
14:19

26   men who have risked⁺ their lives for the name of our Lord Jesus Christ.

15:27
Acts 15:22,32

27   "Therefore we have sent⁺ Judas and Silas, who

themselves will also report the same things by word *of mouth*.

28   "For it seemed good to the Holy Spirit and to us to lay~ upon you no greater burden than these essentials:

29   that you abstain~ from things sacrificed to idols and from blood and from things strangled and from fornication; if you keep¹ yourselves free from such things, you will do well. Farewell."

30   So, when they were sent away, they went down to Antioch; and having gathered the congregation together, they delivered the letter.

31   And when they had read it, they rejoiced because of its encouragement.

32   And Judas and Silas, also being prophets themselves, encouraged and strengthened the brethren with a *lengthy* message.

33   And after they had spent time *there*, they were sent away from the brethren in peace to those who had sent them out.

34   [ᵉBut it seemed good to Silas to remain there.]

35   But Paul and Barnabas stayed in Antioch, teaching and preaching, with many others also, the word of the Lord.

Second Missionary Journey

36   And after some days Paul said to Barnabas, "Let us return² and visitˣ the brethren in every city in which we proclaimed the word of the Lord, *and see* how they are."

37   And Barnabas was desirousᵐ of takingˣ John, called Mark, along with them also.

38   But Paul kept insistingᵐ that they should not take~ him along who had deserted them in Pamphylia and had not gone with them to the work.

39   And there arose such a sharp ᵗdisagreement that they separatedˣ from one another, and Barnabas took Mark with him and sailedˣ away to Cyprus.

40   But Paul chose Silas and departed, being committed by the brethren to the grace of the Lord.

41   And he was travelingᵐ through Syria and Cilicia, strengthening the churches.

The Macedonian Vision

16   And he came also to Derbe and to Lystra. And behold, a certain disciple was there, named Timothy, the son of a

ᵉMany mss. do not contain this verse

15:28
Acts 15:25;
Acts 5:32; 15:8;
Acts 15:19

15:29
Acts 15:20

15:30
Acts 15:22f.

15:32
Acts 15:22,27;
Acts 13:1;
Acts 15:1

15:33
Mark 5:34; Acts
16:36; 1 Cor.
16:11; Heb.
11:31;
Acts 15:22
15:35
Acts 12:25;
Acts 8:4;
Acts 13:12

15:36
Acts 13:4,13,14,
51; 14:6,24f.;
Acts 13:12

15:37
Acts 12:12

15:38
Acts 13:13
15:39
Acts 12:12;
15:37; Col. 4:10;
Acts 4:36
15:40
Acts 15:22;
Acts 11:23; 14:26
15:41
Matt. 4:24; Acts
15:23;
Acts 6:9
16:1
Acts 14:6;
Acts 17:14f.;
18:5; 19:22; 20:4;
Rom. 16:21; 1
Cor. 4:17; 16:10;
2 Cor. 1:1,19;
Phil. 1:1; 2:19;
Col. 1:1;
1 Thess. 1:1; 3:2,
6; 2 Thess. 1:1; 1
Tim. 1:2,18;
6:20; 2 Tim. 1:2;
Philem. 1; Heb.
13:23;
2 Tim. 1:5; 3:15

16:2
Acts 16:40;
Acts 14:6;
Acts 13:51
16:3
Gal. 2:3

Jewish woman who was a believer, but his father was a Greek,

2 and he was well spoken^m of by the brethren who were in Lystra and Iconium.

3 Paul wanted this man to go^x with him; and he took him and circumcised him because of the Jews who were in those parts, for they *all* knew that his father was a *Greek.*

16:4
Acts 15:28f.;
Acts 15:2;
Acts 11:30

4 Now while they were passing^m through the cities, they were delivering^m the decrees, which had been decided⁺ upon by the apostles and elders who were in Jerusalem, for them to observe.~

16:5
Acts 9:31;
Acts 2:47

5 So the churches were being strengthened^m in the faith, and were increasing^m in number daily.

16:6
Acts 2:10; 18:23;
Acts 18:23; 1 Cor.
16:1; Gal. 1:2;
3:1; 2 Tim. 4:10;
1 Pet. 1:1;
Acts 2:9

6 And they passed through the Phrygian and Galatian region, having been forbidden by the Holy Spirit to speak^x the word in Asia;

16:7
Acts 16:8;
1 Pet. 1:1;
Luke 24:49; Acts
8:29; Rom. 8:9;
Gal. 4:6; Phil.
1:19; 1 Pet. 1:11

7 and when they had come to Mysia, they were trying^m to go^x into Bithynia, and the *Spirit of Jesus* did not permit^{6b} them;

16:8
Acts 16:7;
Acts 16:11;
20:5f.; 2 Cor.
2:12; 2 Tim. 4:13

8 and passing by Mysia, they came down to Troas.

16:9
Acts 9:10;
Acts 16:10,12;
18:5; 19:21f.,29;
20:1,3; 27:2;
Rom. 15:26

9 And a vision appeared to Paul in the night: a certain man of Macedonia was standing~ and appealing~ to him, and saying,~ "Come over to Macedonia and help^{xi} us."

16:10
Acts 9:10;
[we] Acts
16:10-17;
20:5-15; 21:1-18;
27:1-28:16;
Acts 14:7

10 And when he had seen the *vision,* immediately we sought to go^x into Macedonia, concluding that *God* had called⁺ us to preach^x the gospel to them.

16:11
Acts 16:8; 20:5f.;
2 Cor. 2:12;
2 Tim. 4:13;
Acts 21:1

11 Therefore putting out to sea from Troas, we ran a straight course to Samothrace, and on the day following to Neapolis;

16:12
Acts 20:6; Phil.
1:1; 1 Thess. 2:2;
Acts 16:9,10;
18:5; 19:21f.,29;
20:1,3; 27:2;
Rom. 15:26;
Acts 16:21

12 and from there to Philippi, which is a leading city of the district of Macedonia, a *Roman* colony; and we were staying~ in this city for some days.

16:13
Acts 13:14
16:14
Rev. 1:11; 2:18,
24;
Acts 13:43; 18:7;
Luke 24:45

13 And on the Sabbath day we went outside the gate to a riverside, where we were supposing^m that there would be a place of prayer; and we sat down and began speaking to the women who had assembled.

First Convert in Europe

14 And a certain woman named Lydia, from the city of Thyatira, a seller of purple fabrics, a worshiper of God, was listening;^m and the Lord opened her heart to respond~ to the things spoken by Paul.

16:15
Acts 11:14
16:16
Acts 16:13;
Lev. 19:31; 20:6,
27; Deut. 18:11;
1 Sam. 28:3,7;
2 Kin. 21:6;
1 Chr. 10:13; Is.
8:19

15 And when she and her household had been baptized, she urged us, saying, "If you have judged⁺ me to be *faithful to the Lord,* come into my house and stay."^mᵗ And she prevailed upon us.

16 And it happened that as we were going to the place of

prayer, a certain slave-girl having a spirit of divination met[x] us, who was bringing[xx] her masters *much* profit by fortunetelling.

17 Following after Paul and us, she kept crying[xx] out, saying, "These men are *bond-servants*[38b] *of the Most High God,* who are proclaiming to you the way of salvation."

16:17
Mark 5:7

18 And she continued doing[xx] this for many days. But Paul was greatly[1] annoyed, and turned and said to the spirit, "I command you in the name of Jesus Christ to come[x] out of her!" And it came out at that very moment.

16:18
Mark 16:17

19 But when her masters saw that their hope of profit was gone, they seized Paul and Silas and dragged them into the market place before the authorities,

16:19
Acts 16:16;
19:25f.;
Acts 15:22,40;
16:25,29;
Acts 8:3; 17:6f.;
21:30; James 2:6

20 and when they had brought them to the chief magistrates, they said, "These men are throwing *our* city into confusion,[1] being [†]*Jews,*

21 and are proclaiming customs which it is not lawful for us to accept[~] or to observe,[~] being [†]*Romans.*"

16:21
Esth. 3:8;
Acts 16:12

Paul and Silas Imprisoned

22 And the crowd rose up together against them, and the chief magistrates tore their robes off them, and proceeded to order[xx] *them* to be beaten[~] with rods.

16:22
2 Cor. 11:25;
1 Thess. 2:2

23 And when they had inflicted *many* blows upon them, they threw them into prison, commanding the jailer to guard[~] them securely;

16:23
Acts 16:27,36

24 and he, having received *such a command,* threw them into the inner prison, and fastened their feet in the stocks.

16:24
Job 13:27; 33:11;
Jer. 20:2f.; 29:26

25 But about midnight Paul and Silas were praying and singing[xx] hymns of praise to God, and the prisoners were listening[xx] to them;

16:25
Acts 16:19;
Eph. 5:19

26 and suddenly there came a *great* earthquake, so that the foundations of the prison house were shaken;[x] and *immediately all* the doors were opened, and *everyone's* chains were unfastened.

16:26
Acts 4:31;
Acts 12:10;
Acts 12:7

27 And when the jailer had been roused out of sleep and had seen the prison doors opened,[*] he drew his sword and was about to kill himself, supposing that the prisoners had *escaped.*[*]

16:27
Acts 16:23,36;
Acts 12:19

28 But Paul cried out with a *loud* voice, saying, "Do[x] yourself no harm, for we are •*all* here!"

29 And he called for lights and rushed in and, trembling with [†]fear, he fell down before Paul and Silas,

16:29
Acts 16:19

30 and after he brought them out, he said,[xx] "Sirs, what must I do[~][19a] to be saved?"[x]

16:30
Acts 2:37; 22:10

The Jailer Converted

16:31
Mark 16:16;
Acts 11:14; 16:15

31 And they said, "Believe[xl] in the Lord Jesus, and you shall be saved, you and your household."

32 And they spoke the word of the Lord to him together with all who were in his house.

16:33
Acts 16:25

33 And he took them that *very* hour of the night and washed their wounds, and *immediately* he was baptized, he and all his *household*.

16:34
Acts 11:14; 16:15

34 And he brought them into his house and set food before them, and rejoiced greatly, having believed[*] in God with his whole household.

35 Now when day came, the chief magistrates sent their policemen, saying, "Release[xl] those men."

16:36
Acts 16:27;
Acts 15:33

36 And the jailer reported these words to Paul, *saying*, "The chief magistrates have sent[*] to release[x] you. Now therefore, come out and go in peace."

16:37
Acts 22:25-29

37 But Paul said[m] to them, "They have beaten us in public without trial, men who are *Romans,* and have thrown us into prison; and now are they sending us away *secretly?* No indeed! But let them come *themselves* and bring[xl] us out."

16:38
Acts 22:29

38 And the policemen reported *these* words to the chief magistrates. And they were afraid when they heard that they were [+]*Romans,*

16:39
Matt. 8:34

39 and they came and appealed to them, and when they had brought them out, they kept begging[m] them to leave[x] the city.

16:40
Acts 16:14;
Acts 1:15; 16:2

40 And they went out of the prison and entered *the house of* Lydia, and when they saw the brethren, they encouraged them and departed.

17:1
Acts 17:11,13;
20:4; 27:2; Phil.
4:16; 1 Thess.
1:1; 2 Thess. 1:1;
2 Tim. 4:10

Paul at Thessalonica

17 Now when they had traveled through Amphipolis and Apollonia, they came to Thessalonica, where there was a synagogue of the Jews.

17:2
Acts 9:20; 17:10,
17;
Acts 13:14;
Acts 8:35

2 And according to Paul's custom, he went to them, and for three Sabbaths reasoned with them from the Scriptures,

17:3
Acts 3:18;
John 20:9;
Acts 9:22; 18:5,
28

3 explaining and giving evidence that *the Christ* had[m] to suffer[x] and rise[x] again from the dead, and *saying,* "This Jesus whom *I* am proclaiming to you is the Christ."

17:4
Acts 14:4;
Acts 15:22,40;
17:10,14f.;
Acts 13:43;
17:17;
John 7:35;
Acts 13:50

4 And some of them were persuaded and joined Paul and Silas, along with a *great* multitude of the God-fearing Greeks and a *number* of the leading women.

17:5
Acts 17:13; 1
Thess. 2:14ff.;
Acts 17:6,7,9;
Rom. 16:21

5 But the Jews, becoming jealous and taking along some *wicked* men from the market place, formed a mob and set[m] the

city in an uproar; and coming upon the house of Jason, they were seeking^m to bring^x them out to the people.

6   And when they did not find them, they *began* dragging Jason and some brethren before the city authorities, shouting, "These men who have upset ᶠthe world have come here also;

7   and *Jason* has welcomed⁺ them, and they all act contrary to the *decrees of Caesar,* saying that there is *another*^{8b} king, *Jesus."*

8   And they stirred up the crowd and the city authorities who heard these things.

9   And when they had received a pledge from Jason and the others, they released them.

Paul at Berea

10   And the brethren immediately sent Paul and Silas away by night to Berea; and when they arrived, they went^m into the *synagogue of the Jews.*

11   Now these were more noble-minded than those in Thessalonica, for they received the word with great eagerness, examining the Scriptures *daily, to see* whether these things were˜ so.

12   Many of them therefore believed, along with a *number* of prominent Greek women and men.

13   But when the Jews of Thessalonica found out that the word of God had been proclaimed by Paul in *Berea also,* they came *there likewise,* agitating and stirring up the crowds.

14   And then immediately the brethren sent *Paul* out to go as far as the sea; and Silas and Timothy remained there.

15   Now those who conducted Paul brought him as far as Athens; and receiving a command for Silas and Timothy to come to him as soon³ as possible, they departed.^{xx}

Paul at Athens

16   Now while Paul was waiting for them at Athens, his spirit was being provoked^m within him as he was beholding the city full¹ of idols.

17   So he was reasoning^m in the synagogue with the Jews and the God-fearing *Gentiles,* and in the market place every day with those who happened to be present.

18   And also some of the Epicurean and Stoic philosophers were conversing^m with him. And some were saying,^{xx} "What would *this idle babbler* wish to say?"˜ Others, "He seems to be a proclaimer of *strange deities,"*— because he was preaching^{xx} *Jesus* and the *resurrection.*

19   And they took him and brought him to the Areopagus,

ᶠLit., *the inhabited earth*

17:6
Acts 16:19f.;
Matt. 24:14; Acts
17:31

17:7
Luke 10:38;
James 2:25;
Luke 23:2

17:9
Acts 17:5

17:10
Acts 1:15; 17:6,
14f.;
Acts 17:4;
Acts 17:13; 20:4;
Acts 17:1f.
17:11
Acts 17:1

17:12
Acts 2:47;
Mark 15:43;
Acts 13:50
17:13
Acts 17:1;
Acts 17:10; 20:4

17:14
Acts 1:15; 17:6,
10;
Acts 15:22; 17:4,
10;
Acts 16:1
17:15
Acts 15:3;
Acts 17:16,21f.;
18:1; 1 Thess.
3:1;
Acts 17:14;
Acts 18:5

17:16
Acts 17:15,21f.;
18:1; 1 Thess. 3:1

17:17
Acts 9:20; 17:2;
Acts 17:4

17:18
1 Cor. 1:20; 4:10;
Acts 4:2; 17:31f.

17:19
Acts 23:19;
Acts 17:22;
Mark 1:27

saying, "May we know[x] what this new teaching is which you are proclaiming?

20 "For you are bringing some *strange things* to our ears; we want to know[x] therefore what these things mean."

17:21
Acts 2:10

21 (Now all the Athenians and the strangers visiting there used to spend[m] their time in nothing other than telling[~] or hearing[~] something new.)

Sermon on Mars Hill

17:22
Acts 17:15;
Acts 25:19

22 And Paul stood in the midst of the Areopagus and said, "Men of Athens, I observe that you are *very*[3] *religious* in all respects.

17:23
2 Thess. 2:4;
John 4:22

23 "For while I was passing through and examining the objects of your worship, I also found an altar with this inscription, 'TO AN UNKNOWN GOD.' What therefore you worship in ignorance, this *I* proclaim to you.

17:24
Is. 42:5; Acts
14:15;
Deut. 10:14; Ps.
115:16; Matt.
11:25;
1 Kin. 8:27; Acts
7:48

24 "The God who made the world and all things in it, since He is *Lord* of heaven and earth, does not dwell in *temples made with hands;*

17:25
Job 22:2; Ps.
50:10-12

25 neither is He served by *human* hands, as though He needed anything, since He Himself gives to all life and breath and all things;

17:26
Mal. 2:10;
Deut. 32:8; Job
12:23

26 and He made from [g]one, every nation of mankind to live[~] on all the face of the earth, having determined[+] *their* appointed times, and the boundaries of their habitation,

17:27
Deut. 4:7; Jer.
23:23f.; Acts
14:17

27 that they should seek[~] God, if perhaps[2] they might grope[x] for Him and find[x] Him, though[2] He is not far from each one of us;

17:28
Job 12:10; Dan.
5:23

28 for in *Him* we live and move and exist, as even some of your own poets have said,[+] 'For we also are *His* offspring.'

17:29
Is. 40:18ff.; Rom.
1:23

29 "Being then the offspring of *God,* we ought not to think[~] that the Divine Nature is like gold or silver or stone, an image formed by the art and thought of man.

17:30
Acts 14:16; Rom.
3:25;
Acts 17:23;
Luke 24:47; Acts
26:20; Titus 2:11f.

30 "Therefore having overlooked the times of ignorance, God is now declaring to men that all everywhere[4] should repent,[~]

17:31
Matt. 10:15;
Ps. 9:8; 96:13;
98:9; John 5:22,
27; Acts 10:42;
Matt. 24:14; Acts
17:6;
Luke 22:22;
Acts 2:24

31 because He has fixed a day in which He will judge the world in righteousness through a Man whom He has appointed, having furnished [+]*proof* to all men by raising Him from the dead."

17:32
Acts 17:18,31

32 Now when they heard of the resurrection of the dead, some *began* to sneer,[m] but others said, "We shall hear you again concerning this."

33 So Paul went out of their midst.

17:34
Acts 17:19,22

34 But some men joined him and believed, among whom also

[g]Some later mss. read *one blood*

were Dionysius the Areopagite and a woman named Damaris and others with them.

Paul at Corinth

18 After these things he left Athens and went to Corinth. 2 And he found a certain Jew named Aquila, a native of Pontus, having recently come⁺ from Italy with his wife Priscilla, because Claudius had commanded⁺ all the Jews to leave Rome. He came to them,

3 and because he was of the same trade, he stayed^m with them and they were working;^m for by trade they were tentmakers.

4 And he was reasoning^m in the synagogue every Sabbath and trying^m to persuade Jews and Greeks.

5 But when Silas and Timothy came down from Macedonia, Paul *began devoting*^m *himself completely* to the word, solemnly¹ testifying to the Jews that *Jesus* was the Christ.

6 And when they resisted and blasphemed, he shook out his garments and said to them, "Your blood *be* upon your own heads! I am clean. From now on I shall go to the *Gentiles.*"

7 And he departed from there and went to the house of a certain man named Titius Justus, a worshiper of God, whose house was next to the synagogue.

8 And Crispus, the leader of the synagogue, believed in the Lord with all his household, and many of the Corinthians when they heard were believing^m and being baptized.^m

9 And the ⁺Lord said to Paul in the night by a vision, "Do not be afraid◦ *any longer*, but go on speaking~ and do not be silent;◦

10 for *I* am with you, and no man will attack you in order to harm^x you, for I have *many* people in this city."

11 And he settled *there* a year and six months, teaching the word⁴³ᵃ of God among them.

12 But while Gallio was *proconsul* of Achaia, the Jews with one accord rose up against Paul and brought him before the judgment seat,

13 saying, "This man persuades men to worship~⁴⁴ᶜ God *contrary to the law.*"

14 But when Paul was about to open~ his mouth, Gallio said to the Jews, "If it were a matter of ⁺wrong or of *vicious* ⁺crime, O Jews, it would be *reasonable* for me to put up with you;

15 but if there are questions about words and names and your own law, look after it yourselves; *I* am unwilling to be a judge of these matters."

16 And he drove them away from the judgment seat.

18:1
Acts 17:15;
Acts 18:8; 19:1; 1
Cor. 1:2; 2 Cor.
1:1,23; 6:11;
2 Tim. 4:20
18:2
Acts 18:18,26;
Rom. 16:3; 1 Cor.
16:19; 2 Tim.
4:19;
Acts 2:9;
Acts 27:1,6; Heb.
13:24;
Acts 11:28
18:3
Acts 20:34; 1 Cor.
4:12; 9:14f.; 2
Cor. 11:7; 12:13;
1 Thess. 2:9;
4:11; 2 Thess. 3:8
18:4
Acts 9:20; 18:19;
Acts 13:19;
Acts 14:1
18:5
Acts 15:22; 16:1;
17:14;
Acts 17:15;
Acts 16:9;
Luke 16:28; Acts
20:21;
Acts 17:3; 18:28
18:6
Neh. 5:13; Acts
13:51;
2 Sam. 1:16;
1 Kin. 2:33; Ezek.
18:13; 33:4,6,8;
Matt. 27:25; Acts
20:26;
Acts 13:46
18:7
Acts 13:43; 16:14
18:8
1 Cor. 1:14;
Mark 5:22;
Acts 11:14;
Acts 18:1; 19:1; 1
Cor. 1:2; 2 Cor.
1:1,23; 6:11;
2 Tim. 4:20
18:9
Acts 9:10

18:12
Acts 13:7;
Acts 18:27;
19:21; Rom.
15:26; 1 Cor.
16:15; 2 Cor. 1:1;
9:2; 1 Thess. 1:7f.;
1 Thess. 1:7f.;
1 Thess. 2:14ff.;
Matt. 27:19
18:13
John 19:7; Acts
18:15
18:14
Matt. 5:2

18:15
Acts 23:29; 25:19

18:16
Matt. 27:19

18:17
1 Cor. 1:1;
Acts 18:8;
Matt. 27:19

18:18
Mark 6:46;
Acts 1:15; 18:27;
Matt. 4:24;
Acts 18:2,26;
Rom. 16:1;
Num. 6:2,5,9,18;
Acts 21:24
18:19
Acts 18:21,24;
19:1,17,26,28,
34f.; 20:16f.;
21:29; 1 Cor.
15:32; 16:8; Eph.
1:1; 1 Tim. 1:3;
2 Tim. 1:18; 4:12;
Rev. 1:11; 2:1;
Acts 18:4
18:21
Mark 6:46;
Rom. 1:10; 15:32;
1 Cor. 4:19; 16:7;
Heb. 6:3; James
4:15; 1 Pet. 3:17;
Acts 18:19,24;
19:1,17,26,28,
34f.; 20:16f.;
21:29; 1 Cor.
15:32; 16:8; Eph.
1:1; 1 Tim. 1:3;
2 Tim. 1:18; 4:12;
Rev. 1:11; 2:1
18:22
Acts 8:40;
Acts 11:19
18:23
Acts 16:6
18:24
Acts 19:1; 1 Cor.
1:12; 3:5,6,22;
4:6; 16:12; Titus
3:13;
Acts 6:9;
Acts 18:19
18:25
Acts 9:2; 18:26;
Luke 7:29; Acts
19:3
18:26
Acts 18:2,18;
Acts 18:25

18:27
Acts 18:12; 19:1;
Acts 18:18;
Acts 11:26

18:28
Acts 8:35;
Acts 18:5
19:1
1 Cor. 1:12; 3:5,6,
22; 4:6; 16:12;
Titus 3:13;
Acts 18:1;
Acts 18:23;
Acts 18:21,24;
19:17,26,28,34f.;
20:16f.; 21:29;
1 Cor. 15:32;
16:8; Eph. 1:1;
1 Tim. 1:3; 2 Tim.
1:18; 4:12; Rev.
1:11; 2:1
19:2
Acts 8:15f.;
11:16f.;
John 7:39

17 And they all took hold of Sosthenes, the leader of the synagogue, and *began* beating^m him in front of the judgment seat. And Gallio was not concerned^m about any of these things.

18 And Paul, having remained many days longer, took leave of the brethren and put^m out to sea for Syria, and with him were Priscilla and Aquila. In Cenchrea he had his hair cut, for he was keeping^m a vow.

19 And they came to Ephesus, and he left them there. Now he himself entered the synagogue and reasoned with the Jews.

20 And when they asked him to stay^x for a longer time, he did not consent,

21 but taking leave of them and saying, "I will return to you again if *God* wills," he set sail from Ephesus.

22 And when he had landed at Caesarea, he went up and greeted the church, and went down to Antioch.

Third Missionary Journey

23 And having spent some time *there*, he departed and passed successively through the Galatian region and Phrygia, strengthening all the disciples.

24 Now a certain Jew named Apollos, an Alexandrian by birth, an eloquent man, came to Ephesus; and he was mighty in the Scriptures.

25 This man had been instructed* in the way of the Lord; and being fervent in spirit, he was speaking^xx and teaching^m accurately the things concerning Jesus, being acquainted only with the baptism of John;

26 and he began to speak~ out boldly in the synagogue. But when Priscilla and Aquila heard him, they took him aside and explained to him the way of God more †accurately.

27 And when he wanted to go^x across to Achaia, the brethren encouraged him and wrote to the disciples to welcome^x him; and when he had arrived, he helped greatly those who had believed* through grace;

28 for he *powerfully* refuted^m1 the Jews in public, demonstrating by the Scriptures that *Jesus* was the Christ.

Paul at Ephesus

19 And it came about that while Apollos was at Corinth, Paul having passed through the upper country came^x to Ephesus, and found^x some disciples,

2 and he said to them, "Did you receive the *Holy Spirit* when you believed?" And they *said* to him, "No, we have not even heard whether there *is* a Holy Spirit."

3   And he said, "Into what then were you baptized?" And they said, "Into †John's baptism."

4   And Paul said, "John baptized with the baptism of repentance, telling the people to believe[x] in Him who was coming *after him*, that is, in Jesus."

5   And when they heard this, they were baptized in the name of the Lord Jesus.

6   And when Paul had laid his hands upon them, the Holy Spirit came on them, and they *began* speaking[m] with tongues and prophesying.[m]

7   And there were in all about twelve men.

8   And he entered the synagogue and continued speaking[m] out boldly for three months, reasoning and persuading *them* about the kingdom of God.

9   But when some were becoming hardened[m] and disobedient,[m] speaking evil of the Way before the multitude, he withdrew from them and took away the disciples, reasoning daily in the school of Tyrannus.

10   And this took place for two years, so that all who lived in Asia heard[x] the word of the Lord, both Jews and Greeks.

Miracles at Ephesus

11   And God was performing[m] *extraordinary* miracles by the hands of Paul,

12   so that *handkerchiefs or aprons* were even carried[~] from his body to the sick, and the diseases left[~] them and the evil †spirits went[~] out.

13   But also some of the Jewish exorcists, who went from place to place, attempted to name[~] over those who had the evil spirits the name of the Lord Jesus, saying, "I adjure you by Jesus whom Paul preaches."

14   And *seven* sons of one Sceva, a Jewish chief priest, were doing this.

15   And the evil spirit answered and said to them, "I recognize[29a] *Jesus,* and I know[29c] about *Paul,* but who are *you?*"

16   And the man, in whom was the evil spirit, leaped on them and subdued all of them and overpowered them, so that they fled[x] out of that house naked and wounded.[+]

17   And this became known to all, both Jews and Greeks, who lived in Ephesus; and *fear* fell upon them all and the name of the Lord Jesus was being *magnified.*[m]

18   Many also of those who had believed[+] kept coming,[m] confessing[1] and disclosing their practices.

19   And many of those who practiced magic brought their

19:3
Luke 7:29; Acts 18:25

19:4
Matt. 3:11; Mark 1:4,7,8; Luke 3:16; John 1:26, 27; Acts 13:24; John 1:7

19:5
Acts 8:12,16; 10:48

19:6
Acts 6:6; 8:17; Mark 16:17; Acts 2:4; 10:46; Acts 13:1

19:8
Acts 9:20; 18:26; Acts 1:3

19:9
Acts 14:4; Acts 9:2; 19:23; Acts 11:26; 19:30

19:10
Acts 19:8; 20:31; Acts 16:6; 19:22, 26,27; Acts 13:12; 19:20

19:11
Acts 8:13

19:12
Acts 5:15; Mark 16:17

19:13
Matt. 12:27; Luke 11:19

19:17
Acts 18:19

19:19
Luke 15:8

books together and *began* burning[xx1] them in the sight of all; and they counted up the price of them and found it fifty thousand pieces of silver.

19:20
Acts 19:10;
Acts 6:7; 12:24

20 So the word of the Lord was growing[xx] *mightily*[32d] and prevailing.[xx32c]

19:21
Acts 20:16,22;
21:15; Rom.
15:25; 2 Cor.
1:16;
Acts 20:1; 1 Cor.
16:5;
Acts 16:9; 19:22,
29; Rom. 15:26; 1
Thess. 1:7f.;
Acts 18:12;
Acts 23:11; Rom.
15:24,28

21 Now after these things were finished, Paul purposed in the spirit to go to Jerusalem after he had passed through Macedonia and Achaia, saying, "After I have been there, I must also see[x] *Rome.*"

19:22
Acts 16:9; 19:21,
29;
Acts 13:5; 20:34;
2 Cor. 8:19;
Acts 16:1;
Rom. 16:23;
2 Tim. 4:20;
Acts 19:10

22 And having sent into Macedonia two of those who ministered to him, Timothy and Erastus, he himself stayed in Asia for a while.

19:23
Acts 19:9
19:24
Acts 16:16,19f.

23 And about that time there arose *no small* disturbance concerning the Way.

24 For a certain man named Demetrius, a silversmith, who made silver shrines of Artemis, was bringing[xx] no little business to the craftsmen;

25 these he gathered together with the workmen of similar *trades,* and said, "Men, you know[29c] that our prosperity depends *upon this business.*

19:26
Acts 18:19;
Acts 19:10;
Deut. 4:28; Ps.
115:4; Is.
44:10-20; Jer.
10:3ff.; Acts
17:29; 1 Cor. 8:4;
10:19; Rev. 9:20
19:27
Acts 19:10;
Matt. 24:14

26 "And you see and hear that not only in Ephesus, but in almost all of Asia, this Paul has persuaded and turned away a considerable number of people, saying that gods made with hands are no gods *at all.*

27 "And not only is there danger that this trade of ours fall into *disrepute,* but also that the temple of the great goddess Artemis be regarded[x] as [+]*worthless*[~] and that she whom all of Asia and the world worship[44c] should even be *dethroned* from her magnificence."

19:28
Acts 18:19

28 And when they heard *this* and were filled with rage, they *began* crying[xx] out, saying, "[+]*Great* is Artemis of the Ephesians!"

19:29
Acts 20:4; 27:2;
Col. 4:10; Philem.
24;
Acts 13:5; 19:22;
20:34; 2 Cor.
8:19;
Acts 16:9; 19:22
19:30
Acts 19:9

29 And the city was filled with the confusion, and they rushed with one accord into the theater, dragging along Gaius and Aristarchus, Paul's traveling companions from Macedonia.

30 And when Paul wanted to go[x] into the assembly, the disciples would not let[xx] him.

31 And also some of the [h]Asiarchs who were friends of his sent to him and repeatedly urged[xx] him not to venture[x] into the theater.

19:32
Acts 21:34

32 So then, some were shouting[xx] one thing and some another, for the assembly was in *confusion,*[+] and the majority did not know[29e] for what cause they had come together.

19:33
Acts 12:17

33 And some of the crowd concluded *it was* Alexander, since

[h]I.e., political or religious officials of the province of Asia

the Jews had put him forward; and having motioned with his hand, Alexander was intending^m to make$^~$ a defense to the assembly.

34   But when they recognized that he was a †Jew, a *single outcry* arose from them all as they shouted for about two hours, "$^†Great$ is Artemis of the Ephesians!"

35   And after quieting the multitude, the town clerk *said, "Men of Ephesus, what man is there after all who does not know that the city of the Ephesians is †guardian of the temple of the great Artemis, and of the *image* which fell down from heaven?

19:35
Acts 18:19

36   "Since then these are undeniable facts, you ought to keep calm$^•$ and to do$^~$ nothing rash.

37   "For you have brought these men *here* who are neither robbers of temples nor blasphemers of our goddess.

19:37
Rom. 2:22

38   "So then, if Demetrius and the craftsmen who are with him have a complaint against any man, the courts are in session and proconsuls are *available*; let them bring$^{~l}$ charges against one another.

19:38
Acts 13:7

39   "But if you want anything beyond this, it shall be settled in the *lawful assembly.*

40   "For indeed we are in danger of being accused$^~$ of a riot in connection with today's affair, since there is no *real* cause *for it*; and in this connection we shall be unable to account^x for this disorderly gathering."

41   And after saying this he dismissed the assembly.

Paul in Macedonia and Greece

20 And after the uproar had ceased,^{x} Paul sent for the disciples and when he had exhorted them and taken his leave of them, he departed to go$^~$ to Macedonia.

20:1
Acts 11:26;
Acts 19:21;
Acts 16:9; 20:3

2   And when he had gone through those districts and had given them much exhortation, he came to Greece.

20:3
Acts 9:23f.;
20:19;
Matt. 4:24;
Acts 16:9; 20:1

3   And *there* he spent three months, and when a plot was formed against him by the Jews as he was about to set sail for Syria, he determined to return$^~$ through Macedonia.

20:4
Acts 17:10;
Acts 19:29;
Acts 17:1;
Acts 14:6;
Acts 16:1;

4   And he was accompanied^m by Sopater of Berea, *the son* of Pyrrhus; and by Aristarchus and Secundus of the Thessalonians; and Gaius of Derbe, and Timothy; and Tychicus and Trophimus of Asia.

Eph. 6:21; Col.
4:7; 2 Tim. 4:12;
Titus 3:12;
Acts 21:29; 2
Tim. 4:20;
Acts 16:6; 20:16,
18

5   But these had gone on ahead and were waiting^m for us at Troas.

20:5
Acts 16:10;
20:5-15;
Acts 16:8

6   And we sailed from Philippi after the days of Unleavened Bread, and came to them at Troas within five days; and there we stayed seven days.

20:6
Acts 16:10;
20:5-15;
Acts 16:12;
Acts 12:3;
Acts 16:8

20:7
1 Cor. 16:2; Rev.
1:10;
Acts 16:10;
20:5-15;
Acts 2:42

7   And on the first day of the week, when we were gathered⁺ together to break˟ bread, Paul *began* talking™ to them, intending to depart the next day, and he prolonged his message until midnight.

20:8
Matt. 25:1;
Acts 1:13

8   And there were many lamps in the upper room where we were gathered⁺ together.

9   And there was a certain young man named Eutychus sitting on the window sill, sinking into a *deep* sleep; and as Paul kept on talking, he was overcome by sleep and fell down from the third floor, and was picked up dead.

20:10
1 Kin. 17:21;
2 Kin. 4:34;
Matt. 9:23f.; Mark
5:39
20:11
Acts 2:42; 20:7

10   But Paul went down and fell upon him and after embracing him, he said, "Do not be troubled,⁰ for his life³⁰ᶜ is in him."

11   And when he had gone *back* up, and had broken the bread and eaten, he talked with them a long while, until daybreak, and so departed.

12   And they took away the boy alive, and were *greatly* comforted.

Troas to Miletus

20:13
Acts 16:10;
20:5-15

13   But we, going ahead to the ship, set sail for Assos, intending from there to take Paul on board; for thus he had arranged⁺ it, intending himself to go by land.

14   And when he met us at Assos, we took him on board and came to Mitylene.

20:15
Acts 20:17; 2
Tim. 4:20

15   And sailing from there, we arrived the following day opposite Chios; and the next day we crossed over to Samos; and the day following we came to Miletus.

20:16
Acts 18:19;
Acts 16:6; 20:4,
18;
Acts 19:21; 20:6,
22; 1 Cor. 16:8;
Acts 2:1

16   For Paul had decided to sail˟ past Ephesus in order that he might not have to spend˟ time in Asia; for he was hurrying™ to be in Jerusalem, if possible, on the day of Pentecost.

Farewell to Ephesus

20:17
Acts 18:19;
Acts 11:30

17   And from Miletus he sent to Ephesus and called to him the elders of the church.

20:18
Acts 18:19; 19:1,
10; 20:4,16

18   And when they had come to him, he said to them, "You yourselves know,²⁹ᶜ from the first day that I set foot in Asia, how I was with you the whole time,

20:19
Acts 20:3
20:20
Acts 20:27
20:21
Luke 16:28; Acts
18:5; 20:23,24;
Acts 2:38; 11:18;
26:20;
Acts 24:24;
26:18; Eph. 1:15;
Col. 2:5;
Philem. 5

19   serving³⁸ᵇ the Lord with all humility²³ᶜ and with tears and with trials which came upon me through the plots of the Jews;

20   how I did not shrink from declaring˟ to you anything that was profitable, and teaching˟ you publicly and from house to house,

21   solemnly¹ testifying to both Jews and Greeks of repentance toward God and faith in our Lord Jesus Christ.

22 "And now, behold, bound⁺ *in spirit,* I am on my way to Jerusalem, not knowing what will happen to me there,

23 except that the Holy Spirit solemnly¹ testifies to me in every city, saying that bonds and afflictions await me.

24 "But I do not consider my life of *any account* as dear to myself, in order that I may finishˣ my course, and the ministry which I received from the Lord Jesus, to testifyˣ solemnly¹ of the gospel of the grace of God.

25 "And now, behold, I know that *all of you,* among whom I went about preaching the kingdom, will see my face no more.

26 "Therefore I testify to you this day, that I am innocent of the blood of all men.

27 "For I did not shrink from declaringˣ to you the whole purpose of God.

28 "Be on guard⁓ for yourselves and for all the flock, among which the Holy Spirit has made you overseers, to shepherd⁓ the church of God which He purchased with His *own* blood.

29 "I know that after my departure *savage* wolves will come in among you, not sparing the flock;

30 and from among *your own selves* men will arise, speaking perverse⁺ things, to draw⁓ away the disciples after them.

31 "Therefore be on the alert,⁓ remembering that night and day for a period of three years I did not cease to admonish each one with tears.

32 "And now I commend you to God and to the word of His grace, which is able to buildˣ *you* up and to giveˣ *you* the inheritance among *all* those who are sanctified.⁺

33 "I have coveted no one's *silver* or *gold* or *clothes.*

34 "You yourselves know²⁹ᵃ that *these hands* ministered to my *own* needs and to the men who were with me.

35 "In everything I showed you that by working hard in this manner you must help⁓ the weak and remember⁓ the words of the Lord Jesus, that He Himself said, 'It is more ⁺blessed to give⁓ than to receive.' "⁓

36 And when he had said these things, he knelt down and prayed with them all.

37 And they *began* to weepᵐ aloud and embraced Paul, and repeatedly¹ kissedᵐ him,

38 grieving especially over the word which he had spoken, that they should see his face no ⁺more. And they were accompanyingᵐ him to the ship.

20:22
Acts 17:16; 20:16

20:23
Acts 8:29;
Luke 16:28; Acts 18:5; 20:21,24;
Acts 9:16; 21:33
20:24
Acts 21:13;
Acts 13:25;
2 Tim. 4:7;
Acts 1:17;
Luke 16:28; Acts 18:5; 20:21;
Acts 11:23; 20:32
20:25
Matt. 4:23; Acts 28:31

20:26
Acts 18:6

20:27
Acts 20:20;
Acts 13:36

20:28
Luke 12:32; John 21:15-17; Acts 20:29; 1 Pet. 5:2f.;
Matt. 16:18; Rom. 16:16; 1 Cor. 10:32;
Eph. 1:7,14; Titus 2:14; 1 Pet. 1:19; 2:9; Rev. 5:9
20:29
Ezek. 22:27;
Matt. 7:15;
Luke 12:32; John 21:15-17; Acts 20:28; 1 Pet. 5:2f.
20:30
Acts 11:26
20:31
Acts 19:8,10;
24:17;
Acts 20:19
20:32
Acts 14:23;
Acts 14:3; 20:24;
Acts 9:31;
Acts 26:18; Eph. 1:14; 5:5; Col. 1:12; 3:24; Heb. 9:15; 1 Pet. 1:4
20:33
1 Cor. 9:4-18;
2 Cor. 11:7-12;
12:14-18;
1 Thess. 2:5f.
20:34
Acts 18:3;
Acts 19:22

20:36
Acts 9:40; 21:5;
Luke 22:41

20:37
Luke 15:20

20:38
Acts 20:25;
Acts 15:3

Paul Sails from Miletus

21 And when it came about that we had parted from them and had set[x] sail, we ran a straight course to Cos and the next day to Rhodes and from there to Patara;

2 and having found a ship crossing over to Phoenicia, we went aboard and set sail.

3 And when we had come in sight of Cyprus, leaving it on the left, we kept sailing to Syria and landed at Tyre; for there the ship was to unload~ its cargo.

4 And after looking up the disciples, we stayed there seven days; and they kept telling[m] Paul through the Spirit not to set foot in Jerusalem.

5 And when it came about that our days there were ended,[x1] we departed and started on our journey, while they all, with wives and children, escorted us until *we were* out of the city. And after kneeling down on the beach and praying, we said farewell to one another.

6 Then we went on board the ship, and they returned home again.

7 And when we had finished the voyage from Tyre, we arrived at Ptolemais; and after greeting the brethren, we stayed with them for a day.

8 And on the next day we departed and came to Caesarea; and entering the house of Philip the evangelist, who was one of the seven, we stayed with him.

9 Now this man had four virgin daughters who were prophetesses.

10 And as we were staying there for some days, a certain prophet named Agabus came down from Judea.

11 And coming to us, he took Paul's belt and bound his own feet and hands, and said, "This is what the *Holy Spirit* says: 'In this way the Jews at Jerusalem will bind the man who owns [t]this belt and deliver him into the hands of the Gentiles.' "

12 And when we had heard this, *we* as well as the *local residents began* begging[m] him not to go up to Jerusalem.

13 Then Paul answered, "What are you doing, weeping and breaking[1] my *heart?* For *I* am ready not only to be bound,[x] but even to *die*[x] at Jerusalem for the name of the Lord Jesus."

14 And since he would not be persuaded, we fell silent, remarking, "The will of the Lord be done!"[m1]

Cross references:
21:1 [we] Acts 16:10; 21:1-18; Acts 16:11
21:2 Acts 11:19; 21:3
21:3 Acts 4:36; 21:16; Matt. 4:24; Acts 12:20; 21:7; Acts 21:2
21:4 Acts 11:26; 21:16; Acts 20:23; 21:11
21:5 Acts 15:3; Luke 22:41; Acts 9:40; 20:36
21:6 John 19:27
21:7 Acts 12:20; 21:3; Acts 1:15; 21:17
21:8 Acts 8:40; 21:16; Acts 6:5; 8:5; Eph. 4:11; 2 Tim. 4:5
21:9 Luke 2:36; Acts 13:1; 1 Cor. 11:5
21:10 Acts 11:28
21:11 1 Kin. 22:11; Is. 20:2; Jer. 13:1-11; 19:1,11; John 18; Acts 8:29; Acts 9:16; 21:33; Matt. 20:19
21:12 Acts 21:15
21:13 Acts 20:24; Acts 5:41; 9:16
21:14 Luke 22:42

Paul at Jerusalem

15   And after these days we got ready and started^m on our way up to Jerusalem.

21:15
Acts 21:12

16   And *some* of the disciples from Caesarea also came with us, taking us to Mnason of Cyprus, a disciple of long standing with whom we were to lodge.^x

21:16
Acts 21:4;
Acts 8:40;
Acts 4:36; 21:3;
Acts 15:7

17   And when we had come to Jerusalem, the brethren received us gladly.

21:17
Acts 1:15; 21:7

18   And now the following day Paul went^m in with us to James, and all the elders were present.

21:18
Acts 12:17;
Acts 11:30

19   And after he had greeted them, he *began* to relate^m one by one the things which *God* had done among the Gentiles through his ministry.

21:19
Acts 14:27;
Acts 1:17

20   And when they heard it they *began* glorifying^m God; and they said to him, "You see, brother, how many thousands there are among the Jews of those who have believed,[*] and they are all zealous for the Law;

21:20
Matt. 9:8;
Acts 15:1; 22:3;
Rom. 10:2; Gal.
1:14

21   and they have been told about you, that you are teaching all the Jews who are among the Gentiles to *forsake* Moses, telling them *not to circumcise*[~] their children nor to walk^{~42a} according to the *customs*.

21:21
Acts 21:28;
Acts 15:19ff.; 1
Cor. 7:18f.;
Acts 6:14

22   "What, then, is *to be done?* They will certainly hear that you have come.[*]

23   "Therefore do^x this that we tell you. We have four men who are under a *vow;*

21:23
Num. 6:13-21;
Acts 18:18

24   take them and purify^x yourself along with them, and pay^x their expenses in order that they may shave their heads; and *all* will know that there is nothing to the things which they have been told[*] about you, but that *you yourself also* walk^{42b} orderly, keeping the Law.

21:24
John 11:55; Acts
21:26; 24:18;
Acts 18:18

25   "But concerning the Gentiles who have believed,[*] *we* wrote, having decided that they should abstain[~] from meat sacrificed to idols and from blood and from what is strangled and from fornication."

21:25
Acts 15:19f.,29

26   Then Paul took the men, and the next day, purifying himself along with them, went^m into the temple, giving notice of the completion of the days of purification, until the sacrifice was offered for each one of them.

21:26
John 11:55; Acts
21:24; 24:18;
Num. 6:13

Paul Seized in the Temple

27   And when the seven days were almost over, the Jews from Asia, upon seeing him in the temple, *began* to stir^m up all the multitude and laid hands on him,

21:27
Num. 6:9,13-20;
Acts 20:19;
24:18;
Acts 16:6

21:28
Matt. 24:15; Acts
6:13f.; 24:6

28 crying out, "Men of Israel, come~ to our aid! This is the man who preaches to all men †everywhere⁴ against our people, and the Law, and this place; and besides he has even brought *Greeks* into the temple and has defiled⁺¹⁷ᵃ this holy place."

21:29
Acts 20:4;
Acts 18:19

29 For they had previously seen⁺ Trophimus the Ephesian in the city with him, and they supposedᵐ that Paul had brought him *into the temple.*

21:30
2 Kin. 11:15; Acts
16:19; 26:21

30 And *all* the city was aroused, and the people rushed together; and taking hold of Paul, they dragged him out of the temple; and immediately the doors were shut.

21:31
Acts 10:1

31 And while they were seeking to killˣ him, a report came up to the ᶦcommander of the *Roman* cohort that *all* Jerusalem was in confusion.

21:32
Acts 23:27

32 And at once he took along *some* soldiers and centurions, and ran down to them; and when they saw the commander and the soldiers, they stopped beating Paul.

21:33
Acts 20:23;
21:11; 22:29;
26:29; 28:20;
Eph. 6:20; 2 Tim.
1:16; 2:9;
Acts 12:6
21:34
Acts 19:32;
Acts 21:37;
22:24; 23:10,16,
32

33 Then the commander came up and took hold of him, and ordered him to be boundˣ with two chains; and he *began* askingᵐ who he was and what he had done.⁺

34 But among the crowd some were shoutingᵐ one thing *and* some another, and when he could not findˣ out the facts on account of the uproar, he ordered him to be brought~ into the barracks.

21:35
Acts 21:40

35 And when he got to the stairs, it so happened that he was carried~ by the soldiers because of the violence of the mob;

21:36
Luke 23:18; John
19:15; Acts 22:22

36 for the multitude of the people kept followingᵐ behind, crying out, "Away~ with him!"

21:37
Acts 21:34;
22:24; 23:10,16,
32

37 And as Paul was about to be brought into the barracks, he said to the commander, "May I sayˣ something to you?" And he *said, "Do you know *Greek?*

21:38
Acts 5:36;
Matt. 24:26

38 "Then *you* are not the Egyptian who some time ago stirred up a revolt and led the four thousand men of the Assassins out into the wilderness?"

21:39
Acts 9:11; 22:3;
Acts 6:9

39 But Paul said, "*I* am a *Jew* of Tarsus in Cilicia, a citizen of *no insignificant city;* and I beg you, allowˣˡ me to speakˣ to the people."

21:40
Acts 21:35;
Acts 12:17;
John 5:2; Acts
1:19; 22:2; 26:14

40 And when he had given him permission, Paul, standing on the stairs, motioned to the people with his hand; and when there was a *great hush,* he spoke to them in the Hebrew dialect, saying,

ᶦI.e., chiliarch, in command of one thousand troops

Paul's Defense before the Jews

22 "Brethren and fathers, hear^x my defense which I •now *offer* to you."

2   And when they heard that he was addressing^m them in the *Hebrew dialect,* they became even more quiet; and he *said,

3   "†*I* am a Jew, born* in Tarsus of Cilicia, but brought* up in †*this* city, educated* under †Gamaliel, strictly according to the law of our fathers, being zealous for God, just as *you* all are today.

4   "And I persecuted this Way to the death, binding and putting both men and women into prisons,

5   as also the high priest and all the Council of the elders can testify. From them I also received letters to the brethren, and started off for Damascus in order to bring even those who were *there* to Jerusalem as prisoners to be punished.^x

6   "And it came about that as I was on my way, approaching Damascus about noontime, a *very bright light* suddenly flashed^x from heaven all around me,

7   and I fell to the ground and heard a voice saying to me, 'Saul, Saul, why are you persecuting †Me?'

8   "And I answered, 'Who art Thou, Lord?' And He said to •*me,* '†*I* am Jesus the Nazarene, whom *you* are persecuting.'

9   "And those who were with me beheld the light, to be sure, but did not understand the *voice* of the One who was speaking to me.

10   "And I said, 'What shall I do,^x Lord?' And the Lord said to me, 'Arise and go on into Damascus; and there you will be told of all that has been appointed* for you to do.'^x

11   "But since I could not see^m because of the brightness of that light, I was led by the hand by those who were with me, and came into Damascus.

12   "And a certain Ananias, a man who was devout by the standard of the Law, *and* well spoken of by all the Jews who lived there,

13   came to •me, and standing near said to me, 'Brother Saul, receive^x your sight!' And at that very time I looked up at him.

14   "And he said, 'The God of our fathers has appointed you to know^{x29a} His will, and to see^x the Righteous One, and to hear^x an utterance from His mouth.

15   'For you will be a witness for Him to all men of what you have seen* and heard.

16   'And now why do you delay? Arise, and be baptized,^x and wash^x away your sins, calling on His name.'

22:1
Acts 7:2

22:2
Acts 21:40

22:3
Acts 9:1-22;
22:3-16; 26:9-18;
Acts 21:39;
Acts 9:11;
Acts 6:9;
Acts 5:34;
Acts 23:6; 26:5;
Phil. 3:6;
Acts 21:20
22:4
Acts 8:3; 22:19f.;
26:9-11;
Acts 9:2
22:5
Acts 9:1;
Luke 22:66; Acts
5:21; 1 Tim. 4:14;
Acts 9:2;
Acts 2:29; 3:17;
13:26; 23:1;
28:17,21; Rom.
9:3
22:6
Acts 22:6-11;
Acts 9:3-8;
26:12-18

22:8
Acts 26:9

22:9
Acts 26:13;
Acts 9:7

22:10
Acts 16:30

22:11
Acts 9:8

22:12
Acts 9:10;
Acts 6:3; 10:22

22:13
Acts 9:17;
Acts 9:18
22:14
Acts 3:13;
Acts 9:15; 26:16;
Acts 9:17; 1 Cor.
9:1; 15:8;
Acts 7:52
22:15
Acts 23:11;
26:16;
Acts 22:14
22:16
Acts 9:18;
Acts 2:38; 1 Cor.
6:11; Eph. 5:26;
Heb. 10:22;
Acts 7:59

22:17
Acts 9:26; 26:20;
Acts 10:10
17 "And it came about when I returned to Jerusalem and was praying in the temple, that I fell into a trance,

22:18
Acts 9:29
18   and I saw[x] Him saying to me, 'Make haste,[xl] and get[xl] out of Jerusalem quickly, because they will not accept *your* testimony about Me.'

22:19
Acts 8:3; 22:4;
Matt. 10:17; Acts
26:11
19 "And I said, 'Lord, they themselves understand[29c] that in one synagogue after another *I* used to imprison[~] and beat[~] those who believed in Thee.

22:20
Acts 7:58f.; 8:1;
26:10
20 'And when the blood of Thy witness Stephen was being shed,[m] *I also* was standing[~] by approving,[~] and watching[~] out for the cloaks of those who were slaying him.'

22:21
Acts 9:15
21 "And He said to me, 'Go! For *I* will send you far away to the *Gentiles.*' "

22:22
Acts 21:36; 1
Thess. 2:16;
Acts 25:24
22   And they listened[m] to him up to this statement, and *then* they raised their voices and said, "Away[~l] with such a fellow from the earth, for he should not be allowed[m] to live!"[~]

22:23
Acts 7:58;
2 Sam. 16:13
23   And as they were crying out and throwing off their cloaks and tossing dust into the air,

22:24
Acts 21:34;
Acts 22:29
24   the ¹commander ordered him to be brought[~] into the barracks, stating that he should be examined[~] by *scourging* so that he might find[x] out the reason why they were shouting[m] against him that way.

22:25
Acts 16:37
25   And when they stretched him out with thongs, Paul said to the centurion who was standing by, "Is it lawful for you to scourge[~] a man who is a *Roman* and *uncondemned?*"

26   And when the centurion heard *this*, he went to the commander and told him, saying, "What are you about to do? For †this man is a *Roman.*"

27   And the commander came and said to him, "Tell me, are you a *Roman?*" And he said, "Yes."

28   And the commander answered, "*I* acquired this citizenship with a *large sum of money.*" And Paul said, "But *I* was actually born* *a citizen.*"

22:29
Acts 22:24;
Acts 16:38;
Acts 21:33
29   Therefore those who were about to examine him immediately let go of him; and the commander also was afraid when he found out that he was a †*Roman,* and because he had put* him in chains.

22:30
Acts 23:28;
Acts 21:33;
Matt. 5:22
30   But on the next day, wishing to know[x] for certain why he had been accused by the Jews, he released him and ordered the chief priests and all the Council to assemble,[x] and brought Paul down and set him before them.

¹I.e., chiliarch, in command of one thousand troops

Paul before the Council

23 And Paul, looking intently at the Council, said, "Brethren, I have lived⁺ my life with a perfectly good conscience before God up to this day."

2 And the high priest Ananias commanded those standing beside him to strike~ him on the mouth.

3 Then Paul said to him, "God is going to *strike~ you,* you *whitewashed⁺* wall! And do *you* sit to try me according to the Law, and in violation of the Law order me to be struck?"~

4 But the bystanders said, "Do you revile *God's high priest?"*

5 And Paul said, "I was not aware, brethren, that he was high priest; for it is written,⁺ 'YOU SHALL NOT SPEAK EVIL OF A RULER OF YOUR PEOPLE.' "

6 But perceiving²⁹ᵃ that one part were Sadducees and the other Pharisees, Paul *began* crying™ out in the Council, "Brethren, I am a *Pharisee,* a son of Pharisees; I am on trial for the *hope and resurrection of the dead!"*

7 And as he said this, there arose a dissension between the Pharisees and Sadducees; and the assembly was divided.

8 For the Sadducees say that there is no resurrection, nor an angel, nor a spirit; but the Pharisees acknowledge them all.

9 And there arose a great uproar; and some of the scribes of the Pharisaic party stood up and *began* to argue™ heatedly,¹ saying, "We find *nothing wrong* with this man; suppose a spirit or an angel has spoken to him?"

10 And as a great dissension was developing, the ᵏcommander was afraid Paul would be tornˣ to pieces by them and ordered the troops to go down and takeˣ him away from them by force, and bring him into the barracks.

11 But on the night *immediately* following, the †Lord stood at his side and said, "Take courage; for as you have solemnly¹ witnessed to My cause at Jerusalem, so you must witnessˣ at Rome also."

A Conspiracy to Kill Paul

12 And when it was day, the Jews formed a conspiracy and bound themselves under an oath, saying that they would neither eatˣ nor drinkˣ until they had killedˣ Paul.

13 And there were more than forty who formed this plot.

14 And they came to the chief priests and the elders, and said,

ᵏI.e., chiliarch, in command of one thousand troops

23:1
Acts 22:30; 23:6,
15,20,28;
Acts 22:5;
Acts 24:16; 2 Cor.
1:12; 2 Tim. 1:3
23:2
Acts 24:1;
John 18:22
23:3
Matt. 23:27;
Lev. 19:15; Deut.
25:2; John 7:51
23:5
Ex. 22:28
23:6
Matt. 3:7; 22:23;
Acts 22:30; 23:1,
15,20,28;
Acts 22:5;
Acts 26:5; Phil.
3:5;
Acts 24:15,21;
26:8
23:8
Matt. 22:23; Mark
12:18; Luke 20:27
23:9
Mark 2:16; Luke
5:30;
Acts 23:29;
John 12:29; Acts
22:6ff.
23:10
Acts 21:34;
23:16,32
23:11
Acts 18:9;
Matt. 9:2;
Acts 19:21;
Luke 16:28; Acts
28:23
23:12
Acts 9:23; 23:30;
1 Thess. 2:16;
Acts 23:14,21
23:14
Acts 23:12,21

"We have bound ourselves under a *solemn*[4] oath to taste[x] nothing until we have killed[x] Paul.

23:15
Acts 22:30; 23:1,
6,20,28

15 "Now, therefore, *you* and the Council notify[xl] the commander to bring[x] him down to you, as though you were going to determine[1] his case by a more[3] thorough investigation; and *we* for our part are ready to slay[x] him *before he comes*[x] *near the place.*"

23:16
Acts 21:34;
23:10,32

16 But the son of Paul's sister heard of their ambush, and he came and entered the barracks and told Paul.

17 And Paul called one of the centurions to him and said, "Lead[xl] this young man to the commander, for he has something to report[x] to him."

23:18
Eph. 3:1

18 So he took him and led him to the commander and *said, "Paul the prisoner called me to him and asked me to lead[x] this young man to you since he has something to tell[x] you."

19 And the commander took him by the hand and stepping aside, *began* to inquire of him privately, "What is it that you have to report[x] to me?"

23:20
Acts 23:14f.;
Acts 22:30; 23:1,
6,15,28

20 And he said, "The Jews have agreed to ask[x] you to bring[x] *Paul* down tomorrow to the Council, as though they were going to inquire somewhat more[3] thoroughly about him.

23:21
Luke 11:54;
Acts 23:12,14

21 "So do not listen[e] to them, for *more than forty* of them are lying in wait for him who have bound themselves under a curse not to eat[x] or drink[x] until they slay[x] him; and now they are ready and waiting for the promise from you."

22 Therefore the commander let the young man go, instructing him, "Tell[x] *no* [†]*one* that you have notified •*me* of these things."

Paul Moved to Caesarea

23:23
Acts 8:40; 23:33

23 And he called to him two of the centurions, and said, "Get[xl] two hundred soldiers ready by [l]the third hour of the night to proceed[x] to Caesarea, with seventy horsemen and two hundred spearmen."

23:24
Acts 23:26,33;
24:1,3,10; 25:14

24 *They were* also to provide[x] mounts to put Paul on and bring[x] him safely to Felix the governor.

25 And he wrote a letter having this form:

23:26
Luke 1:3; Acts
24:3; 26:25;
Acts 15:23

26 "Claudius Lysias, to the most excellent governor Felix, greetings.

23:27
Acts 21:32f.;
Acts 22:25-29

27 "When this man was arrested by the Jews and was about to be slain by them, I came upon them with the troops and rescued[18a] him, having learned that he was a [†]*Roman.*

[l]I.e., 9 p.m.

28   "And wanting to ascertain[x] the charge for which
      they were accusing[m] him, I brought him down to
      their Council;

29   and I found him to be accused over questions
      about their Law, but under no accusation *deserv-
      ing death* or *imprisonment.*

30   "And when I was informed that there would be a
      plot against the man, I sent him to you at once, also
      instructing his accusers to bring~ charges against
      him before you."

31 So the soldiers, in accordance with their orders, took Paul
and brought him by night to Antipatris.

32   But the next day, leaving the horsemen to go on with him,
they returned to the barracks.

33   And when these had come to Caesarea and delivered the
letter to the governor, they also presented Paul to him.

34   And when he had read it, he asked from what province he
was; and when he learned that he was from Cilicia,

35   he said, "I will give you a hearing after your accusers
arrive[x] also," giving orders for him to be kept~ in *Herod's* [m]*Praetorium.*

Paul before Felix

24 And after *five* days the high priest Ananias came down
with some elders, with a certain attorney *named* Tertullus;
and they brought charges to the governor against Paul.

2   And after *Paul* had been summoned, Tertullus began to
accuse~ him, saying *to the governor,*
"Since we have through you attained much peace, and since by
•*your* providence reforms are being carried out for [t]this nation,

3   we acknowledge *this* in *every way* and *everywhere,* most
excellent Felix, with all thankfulness.

4   "But, that I may not weary~ you any further, I beg you to
grant[x] us, by •*your* kindness,[23a] a brief hearing.

5   "For we have found this man a real pest and a fellow who
stirs up dissension among all the Jews throughout [n]the world,
and a ringleader of the sect of the Nazarenes.

6   "And he even tried to desecrate[x] the *temple;* and then we
arrested him. [[o]And we wanted to judge him according to our
•*own* Law.

7   "But Lysias the commander came along, and with much
violence took him out of our hands,

23:28
Acts 22:30;
Acts 23:10;
Acts 23:1

23:29
Acts 18:15;
25:19;
Acts 23:9; 25:25;
26:31; 28:18

23:30
Acts 23:20f.;
Acts 9:24; 23:12;
Acts 23:35;
24:19; 25:16

23:32
Acts 23:23;
Acts 23:10

23:33
Acts 8:40; 23:23;
Acts 23:24,26;
24:1,3,10; 25:14
23:34
Acts 25:1;
Acts 6:9; 21:39

23:35
Acts 23:30;
24:19; 25:16;
Acts 24:27

24:1
Acts 24:11;
Acts 23:2;
Acts 23:24

24:3
Acts 23:26; 26:25

24:5
Acts 15:5; 24:14

24:6
Acts 21:28

[m]I.e., governor's official residence   [n]Lit., *the inhabited earth*   [o]Many mss. do not contain the remainder of
v. 6, v. 7, nor the first part of v. 8

8   ordering his accusers to come before you.] And by examining him yourself concerning all these matters, you will be able to ascertain^x the things of which we accuse him."

24:9
1 Thess. 2:16

9   And the Jews also joined in the attack, asserting that these things were so.

24:10
Acts 23:24

10   And when the governor had nodded for him to speak,~ Paul responded:

"Knowing[29c] that for many years you have been a judge to †this nation, I cheerfully make my defense,

24:11
Acts 21:18,27;
24:1

11   since you can take note[x] of the fact that no more than twelve days ago I went up to Jerusalem to worship.

24:12
Acts 25:8;
Acts 24:18

12   "And neither in the *temple,* nor in the †*synagogues,* nor in the †*city itself* did they find me carrying on a discussion with anyone or causing a *riot.*

24:13
Acts 25:7

13   "Nor can they *prove*[x] to you *the charges* of which they •now accuse me.

24:14
Acts 9:2; 24:22;
Acts 15:5; 24:5;
Acts 3:13;
Acts 25:8; 26:4ff.,
22f.; 28:23

14   "But this I admit to you, that according to the Way which they call a sect I do serve[38c] the God of our fathers, believing everything that is in accordance with the Law, and that is writ-ten[✦] in the Prophets;

24:15
Dan. 12:2; John
5:28f.; 11:24;
Acts 23:6

15   having a *hope* in God, which these men cherish *themselves,* that there shall certainly be a resurrection of both the righteous and the wicked.

24:16
Acts 23:1

16   "In view of this, I also do my best to maintain always a *blameless conscience both* before God and before men.

24:17
Acts 20:31;
Acts 11:29f.;
Rom. 15:25-28;
1 Cor. 16:1-4;
2 Cor. 8:1-4; 9:1,
2,12; Gal. 2:10

17   "Now after several years I came to bring Palms to my nation and to present offerings;

24:18
Acts 21:26;
Acts 24:12;
Acts 21:27

18   in which they found me *occupied* in the temple, having been purified,[✦] without *any* crowd or uproar. But *there were* cer-tain Jews from Asia—

24:19
Acts 23:30

19   who ought[m] to have been *present*~ before you, and to make~ accusation, if they should have~ anything against me.

24:20
Matt. 5:22

20   "Or else let these men *themselves* tell[xi] what misdeed they found when I stood before the Council,

24:21
Acts 23:6; 24:15

21   other than for this one statement which I shouted out while standing among them, 'For the *resurrection of the dead* I am on trial before you today.' "

24:22
Acts 24:14

22   But Felix, having a more[1] exact knowledge about the Way, *put them off,* saying, "When Lysias the qcommander comes[x] down, I will decide[1] your case."

24:23
Acts 23:35;
Acts 28:16;
Acts 23:16; 27:3

23   And he gave orders to the centurion for him to be kept~ in custody and *yet* have *some* freedom, and not to prevent~ any of his friends from ministering~ to him.

POr, *gifts to charity*   qI.e., chiliarch, in command of one thousand troops

24   But some days later, Felix arrived with Drusilla, his wife who was a Jewess, and sent for Paul, and heard him *speak* about faith in Christ Jesus.

24:24
Acts 20:21

25   And as he was discussing righteousness, self-control and the judgment to come, Felix became †*frightened* and said, "Go away for the present, and when I find †time, I will summon you."

24:25
Titus 2:12;
Gal. 5:23; Titus
1:8; 2 Pet. 1:6;
Acts 10:42

26   At the same time too, he was hoping that money would be given him by Paul; therefore he also used to send for him quite †often[3] and converseᵐ with him.

24:26
Acts 24:17

27   But after *two years* had passed, Felix was succeeded by Porcius Festus; and wishing to do the Jews a *favor,* Felix leftˣ Paul imprisoned.⁺

24:27
Acts 25:1,4,9,12;
26:24f.,32;
Acts 12:3;
Acts 23:35; 25:14

Paul before Festus

25   Festus therefore, having arrived in the province, *three* days later went up to Jerusalem from Caesarea.

25:1
Acts 23:34;
Acts 8:40; 25:4,6,
13
25:2
Acts 24:1; 25:15

2   And the chief priests and the leading men of the Jews brought charges against Paul; and they were urgingᵐ him,

3   requesting a concession against Paul, that he might have him broughtˣ to Jerusalem (*at the same time,* setting an ambush to killˣ him on the way).

25:3
Acts 9:24

4   Festus then answered that Paul was being kept˜ in custody at Caesarea and that he himself was about to leave shortly.

25:4
Acts 25:16;
Acts 24:23;
Acts 8:40; 25:1,6,
13

5   "Therefore," he ˣsaid, "let the influential men among you go there with me, and if there is anything *wrong* about the man, let them prosecute˜ⁱ him."

6   And after he had spent not more than eight or ten days among them, he went down to Caesarea; and on the next day he took his seat on the tribunal and ordered Paul to be brought.ˣ

25:6
Acts 8:40; 25:1,4,
13;
Matt. 27:19; Acts
25:10,17

7   And after he had arrived, the Jews who had come⁺ down from Jerusalem stood around him, bringing many and serious charges against him which they couldᵐ not prove;ˣ

25:7
Acts 24:5f.;
Acts 24:13

8   while Paul said in *his own defense,* "I have committed no offense either against the *Law* of the Jews or against the *temple* or against *Caesar.*"

25:8
Acts 6:13; 24:12;
28:17

9   But Festus, wishing to do the Jews a *favor,* answered Paul and said, "Are you willing to goˣ up to *Jerusalem* and standˣ trial before me on these *charges?*"

25:9
Acts 12:3; 24:27;
Acts 25:20

10   But Paul said, "I am standing⁺ before *Caesar's tribunal,* where I ought to be tried.˜ I have done no wrong to *the Jews,* as *you* also very[3] well know.²⁹ᵇ

25:10
Matt. 27:19; Acts
25:6,17

11   "If then I am a wrongdoer, and have committed⁺ anything worthy of death, I do not refuse to die;ˣ but if †*none* of those

25:11
Acts 25:21,25;
26:32; 28:19

things is *true* of which these men accuse me, no one can hand^x me over to *them*. I appeal to *Caesar*."

12   Then when Festus had conferred with his council, he answered, "You have appealed⁺ to *Caesar, to Caesar* you shall go."

25:13
Acts 8:40; 25:1,4, 6

13   Now when several days had elapsed, King Agrippa and Bernice arrived at Caesarea, and paid their respects to Festus.

25:14
Acts 24:27

14   And while they were spending^m many days there, Festus laid Paul's case before the king, saying, "There is a certain man left⁺ a prisoner by Felix;

25:15
Acts 24:1; 25:2

15   and when I was at Jerusalem, the chief priests and the elders of the Jews brought charges against him, asking for a sentence of condemnation upon him.

25:16
Acts 25:4f.;
Acts 23:30

16   "And I answered them that it is not the custom of the Romans to hand~ over any man before the accused meets~ his accusers *face to face,* and has an *opportunity* to make^x his *defense* against the charges.

25:17
Matt. 27:19; Acts 25:6,10

17   "And so after they had assembled here, I made no delay, but on the next day took my seat on the tribunal, and ordered the man to be brought.^x

18   "And when the accusers stood up, they *began* bringing^m charges against him *not of such crimes* as I was expecting;^m

25:19
Acts 18:15;
23:29;
Acts 17:22

19   but they *simply* had^m some points of disagreement with him about their *own* religion and about a certain dead man, Jesus, whom Paul asserted^m to be alive. ~

25:20
Acts 25:9

20   "And being at a loss how to investigate such matters, I asked^m whether he was willing~ to go~ to Jerusalem and there stand~ trial on these matters.

25:21
Acts 25:11f.

21   "But when Paul *appealed* to be held^x in custody for ʳthe ⁺*Emperor's* decision, I ordered him to be kept~ in custody until I send^x him to Caesar."

25:22
Acts 9:15

22   And Agrippa *said* to Festus, "I also would like to hear^x the man myself." "Tomorrow," he *said, "you shall hear him."

Paul before Agrippa

25:23
Acts 25:13; 26:30

23   And so, on the next day when Agrippa had come together with Bernice, amid great pomp, and had entered the auditorium ˢaccompanied by the commanders and the prominent men of the city, at the command of Festus, Paul was brought in.

25:24
Acts 25:2,7;
Acts 22:22

24   And Festus *said, "King Agrippa, and all you gentlemen here present with us, you behold this man about whom all the people of the Jews appealed to me, both at Jerusalem and here, loudly declaring that he ought~ not to live~ any longer.

25:25
Luke 23:4; Acts 23:29;
Acts 25:11f.

25   "But *I* found that he had committed⁺ nothing worthy of

ʳLit., *the Augustus'* (in this case Nero) ˢLit., *and with*

death; and since *he himself* appealed to the Emperor, I decided to send~ him.

26 "Yet I have *nothing definite* about him to write[x] to my lord. Therefore I have brought him before you *all* and especially before you, King Agrippa, so that after the investigation has taken place, I may have[x] something to write.[x]

27 "For it seems *absurd* to me in sending a prisoner, not to indicate[x] also the *charges against him.*"

Paul's Defense before Agrippa

26 And Agrippa said to Paul, "You are permitted to speak~ for yourself." Then Paul stretched out his hand and *proceeded* to make his defense:

2 "In regard to all the things of which I am accused by the Jews, I consider myself fortunate, King Agrippa, that I am about to make my defense *before you* today;

3 especially because you are an *expert* in all customs and questions among *the* Jews; therefore I beg you to listen[x] to me patiently.

4 "So then, all Jews know *my manner of life* from my youth up, which from the beginning was spent among my *own* nation and at Jerusalem;

5 since they have known about me for a long time previously, if they are willing to testify,~ that I lived *as* a Pharisee according to the *strictest sect of our religion.*

6 "And now I am standing⁺ trial for the hope of the *promise made by God to our fathers;*

7 *the promise* to which our twelve tribes hope to attain,[x] as they earnestly serve[38c] *God* night and day. And for this hope, O King, I am being accused by Jews.

8 "Why is it considered *incredible* among you *people* if God does raise the *dead?*

9 "So then, I thought to myself that I had~ to do[x19b] many things *hostile* to the name of Jesus of Nazareth.

10 "And this is just what I did in Jerusalem; not only did I lock up many of the saints in *prisons,* having received authority from the chief priests, but also when they were being put to death I cast my vote against them.

11 "And as I punished them often in all the synagogues, I tried to force[m] them to blaspheme;~ and being furiously enraged at them, I kept pursuing[m] them even to *foreign cities.*

12 "While thus engaged as I was journeying to Damascus with the authority and commission of the chief priests,

13 at midday, O King, I saw on the way a *light* from heaven,

26:1
Acts 9:15

26:3
Acts 6:14; 25:19;
26:7

26:4
Gal. 1:13f.; Phil.
3:5

26:5
Acts 23:6; Phil.
3:5;
Acts 22:3;
Acts 15:5

26:6
Acts 24:15;
28:20;
Acts 13:32
26:7
James 1:1;
Acts 24:15;
28:20;
Acts 26:2

26:8
Acts 23:6

26:9
John 16:2; 1 Tim.
1:13;
John 15:21
26:10
Acts 8:3; 9:13;
Acts 9:1f.;
Acts 22:20

26:11
Matt. 10:17; Acts
22:19;
Acts 9:1;
Acts 22:5

26:12
Acts 26:12-18;
9:3-8; 22:6-11

brighter than the sun, shining all around me and those who were journeying with me.

26:14
Acts 9:7;
Acts 21:40

14 "And when we had all fallen to the ground, I heard a voice saying to me in the Hebrew dialect, 'Saul, Saul, why are you persecuting ᵗMe? It is hard for you to kick~ against the goads.'

15 "And I said, 'Who art Thou, Lord?' And the Lord said, 'ᵗI am Jesus whom you are persecuting.

26:16
Ezek. 2:1; Dan.
10:11;
Acts 22:14;
Luke 1:2;
Acts 22:15

16 'But arise,ˣ¹ and standˣ¹ on your feet; for this purpose I have appeared to you, to appointˣ you a minister and a witness not only to the things which you have seen, but also to the things in which I will appear to you;

26:17
Jer. 1:8,19;
1 Chr. 16:35; Acts
9:15
26:18
Is. 35:5; 42:7,16;
Col. 1:13; 1 Pet.
2:9;
John 1:5; Eph.
5:8; Col. 1:12f.; 1
Thess. 5:5; 1 Pet.
2:9;
Matt. 4:10;
Luke 24:47; Acts
2:38;
Acts 20:32;
Acts 20:21

17 delivering¹⁸ᵃ you from the Jewish people and from the Gentiles, to whom I am sending you,

18 to openˣ their eyes so that they may turnˣ from darkness to light and from the dominion of Satan to God, in order that they may receiveˣ⁵ᵇ forgiveness of sins and an inheritance among those who have been sanctified⁺ by faith in Me.'

19 "Consequently, King Agrippa, I did not prove disobedient to the heavenly vision,

26:20
Acts 9:19ff.;
Acts 9:26-29;
22:17-20;
Acts 9:15; 13:46;
Acts 3:19;
Matt. 3:8; Luke
3:8
26:21
Acts 21:27,30;
Acts 21:31
26:22
Luke 16:28;
Acts 10:43; 24:14

20 but kept declaringˣˣ both to those of Damascus first, and also at Jerusalem and then throughout all the region of Judea, and even to the Gentiles, that they should repent~ and turn~ to God, performing¹⁹ᵇ deeds appropriate to repentance.

21 "For this reason some Jews seized me in the temple and triedˣˣ to putˣ me to death.

22 "And so, having obtained help from ᵗGod, I stand⁺ to this day testifying both to small and great, stating nothing but what the Prophets and Moses said was going to take place;

26:23
Matt. 26:24; Acts
3:18;
1 Cor. 15:20,23;
Col. 1:18; Rev.
1:5;
Is. 42:6; 49:6;
Luke 2:32; 2 Cor.
4:4
26:24
John 7:15; 2 Tim.
3:15
26:25
Acts 23:26; 24:3

23 that the Christ was to suffer, and that by reason of His resurrection from the dead He should be the first to proclaim light both to the Jewish people and to the Gentiles."

24 And while Paul was saying this in his defense, Festus *said in a loud voice, "Paul, you are out of your mind! Your great learning is driving you mad."

25 But Paul *said, "I am not out of my mind, most excellent Festus, but I utter words of sober truth.

26:26
Acts 26:3

26 "For the king knows²⁹ᶜ about these matters, and I speak to him also with confidence, since I am persuaded that none of these things escape~ his notice; for this has not been done⁺¹⁹ᵇ in a corner.

27 "King Agrippa, do you believe the Prophets? I know²⁹ᵉ that you do."

26:28
Acts 11:26

28 And Agrippa replied to Paul, "In a short time you will persuade ᵗme to becomeˣ a Christian."

29   And Paul *said*, "I would* to God, that whether in a short or long time, not only you, but also all who hear me this day, might become such as *I* am, except for these chains."

30   And the king arose and the governor and Bernice, and those who were sitting with them,

31   and when they had drawn aside, they *began* talking™ to one another, saying, "This man is not doing anything worthy of *death* or *imprisonment.*"

32   And Agrippa said to Festus, "This man might have been set⁺ *free* if he had not appealed to Caesar."

Paul Is Sent to Rome

27   And when it was decided that we should sail~ for Italy, they proceeded to deliver™ Paul and some other prisoners to a centurion of the Augustan ʰcohort named Julius.

2   And embarking in an Adramyttian ship, which was about to sail to the regions along the coast of Asia, we put out to sea, accompanied by Aristarchus, a Macedonian of Thessalonica.

3   And the next day we put in at Sidon; and Julius treated Paul with consideration and allowed him to go to his friends and receive* care.

4   And from there we put out to sea and sailed under the shelter of Cyprus because the winds were contrary.

5   And when we had sailed through the sea along the coast of Cilicia and Pamphylia, we landed at Myra in Lycia.

6   And there the centurion found an Alexandrian ship sailing for Italy, and he put us aboard it.

7   And when we had sailed slowly for a good many days, and with difficulty had arrived off Cnidus, since the wind did not permit us *to go* farther, we sailed under the shelter of Crete, off Salmone;

8   and with difficulty sailing past it we came to a certain place called Fair Havens, near which was the city of Lasea.

9   And when considerable time had passed and the voyage was *now* dangerous, since even the ᵘfast was already over, Paul *began* to admonish™ them,

10   and said to them, "Men, I perceive that the voyage will certainly be *attended* with damage and great loss, not only of the cargo and the ship, but also of *our lives.*"

11   But the centurion was more persuaded™ by the *pilot* and the *captain* of the ship, than by what was being said by Paul.

12   And because the harbor was *not suitable* for wintering, the majority reached a decision to put* out to sea from there, if

ᵗOr, *battalion*   ᵘI.e., Day of Atonement in September or October

26:29
Acts 21:33

26:30
Acts 25:23

26:31
Acts 23:29

26:32
Acts 28:18;
Acts 25:11

27:1
[we] Acts 16:10;
27:1-28;
Acts 25:12,25;
Acts 18:2;
Acts 10:1
27:2
Acts 2:9;
Acts 19:29;
Acts 16:9;
Acts 17:1

27:3
Matt. 11:21;
Acts 27:43;
Acts 24:23

27:4
Acts 4:36;
Acts 27:7

27:5
Acts 6:9;
Acts 13:13

27:6
Acts 28:11;
Acts 18:2; 27:1

27:7
Acts 27:4;
Acts 2:11;
27:12f.,21; Titus
1:5,12

27:8
Acts 27:13

27:9
Lev. 16:29-31;
23:27-29; Num.
29:7

27:10
Acts 27:21

27:11
Rev. 18:17

27:12
Acts 2:11; 27:13,
21; Titus 1:5,12

somehow they could~ reach Phoenix, a harbor of Crete, facing southwest and northwest, and spend* the winter *there.*

27:13
Acts 27:8;
Acts 2:11;
27:12f.,21; Titus
1:5,12

13   And when a moderate south wind came up, supposing that they had gained⁺ their purpose, they weighed anchor and *began* sailing along Crete, close ³ *inshore.*

Shipwreck

27:14
Mark 4:37

14   But before very long there rushed down from the land a *violent* wind, called ᵛEuraquilo;

15   and when the ship was caught *in it,* and could not face~ the wind, we gave way *to it,* and let ourselves be driven™ along.

16   And running under the shelter of a small island called Clauda, we were scarcely able to get the *ship's* boat under control.

27:17
Acts 27:26,29

17   And after they had hoisted it up, they used™ supporting cables in undergirding the ship; and fearing that they might run* aground on *the shallows* of Syrtis, they let down the sea anchor, and so let themselves be driven™ along.

27:18
Jon. 1:5; Acts
27:38

18   The next day as we were being violently storm-tossed, they began to jettison™ the cargo;

19   and on the third day they threw the *ship's tackle* overboard with their own hands.

20   And since neither sun nor stars appeared for many days, and no small storm was assailing *us,* from then on *all* hope of our being saved~ was gradually abandoned.™

27:21
Acts 27:10;
Acts 27:7

21   And when they had gone a long time without food, then Paul stood up in their midst and said, "Men, you ought™ to have followed my advice and not to have set* sail from Crete, and incurred~ ⁺*this* damage and loss.

27:22
Acts 27:25,36

22   "And *yet* now I urge you to keep~ up your courage, for there shall be *no* loss of life among you, but *only* of the ship.

27:23
Acts 5:19;
Rom. 1:9;
Acts 18:9; 23:11;
2 Tim. 4:17

23   "For this very night an *angel of the God* to whom I belong and whom I serve³⁸ᶜ stood before me,

27:24
Acts 23:11;
Acts 27:31,42,44

24   saying, 'Do not be afraid,⁰ Paul; you must stand* before *Caesar;* and behold, God has granted⁺ *you* all those who are sailing with you.'

27:25
Acts 27:22,36

25   "Therefore, keep™ up your courage, men, for I believe God, that it will turn out exactly as I have been told.⁺

27:26
Acts 27:17,29;
Acts 28:1

26   "But we must run* aground on a certain island."

27   But when the fourteenth night had come, as we were being driven about in the Adriatic Sea, about midnight the sailors *began* to surmise that they were approaching~ some land.

28   And they took soundings, and found *it to be* twenty fath-

ᵛI.e., a northeaster

oms; and a little farther on they took another sounding and found *it to be* fifteen fathoms.

29   And fearing that we might run[x] aground somewhere on the rocks, they cast four anchors from the stern and wished[m] for daybreak.

27:29
Acts 27:17,26

30   And as the sailors were trying to escape[x] from the ship, and had let down the *ship's* boat into the sea, on the *pretense* of intending to lay out anchors from the bow,

27:30
Acts 27:16

31   Paul said to the centurion and to the soldiers, "Unless *these men* remain[x] in the ship, *you* yourselves *cannot* be saved."[x]

32   Then the soldiers *cut away* the ropes of the *ship's* boat, and let it fall[x] away.

27:32
John 2:15

33   And until the day was about to dawn, Paul was encouraging[m] them all to take[x] some food, saying, "Today is the *fourteenth* day that you have been constantly watching and going *without eating,* having taken nothing.

34   "Therefore I encourage you to take[x] some food, for this is for *your* preservation; for not a hair from the head of any of [†]you shall perish."

27:34
Matt. 10:30

35   And having said this, he took bread and gave thanks to God in the presence of all; and he broke it and began to eat. [~]

27:35
Matt. 14:19

36   And all of them were encouraged, and they themselves also took food.

27:36
Acts 27:22,25

37   And all of us in the ship were two hundred and seventy-six persons.

27:37
Acts 2:41

38   And when they had eaten enough, they *began* to lighten[m] the ship by throwing out the wheat into the sea.

27:38
Jon. 1:5; Acts 27:18

39   And when day came, they could not recognize[m] the land; but they did observe[m] a certain bay with a beach, and they resolved[m] to [w]drive[x] the ship onto it if they could. [~]

27:39
Acts 28:1

40   And casting off the anchors, they left them in the sea while at the same time they were loosening the ropes of the rudders, and hoisting the foresail to the wind, they were heading[m] for the beach.

27:40
Acts 27:29

41   But striking a reef where two seas met, they ran the vessel aground; and the prow stuck fast and remained immovable, but the stern *began* to be broken[m] up by the force *of the waves.*

42   And the *soldiers'* plan was to *kill* [x] the prisoners, that none *of them* should swim away and escape;[x]

27:42
Acts 12:19

43   but the centurion, wanting to bring[x] Paul safely through, kept them from their intention, and commanded that those who could swim[~] should jump overboard first and get[~] to land,

27:43
Acts 27:3

[w]Some ancient mss. read *bring the ship safely ashore*

27:44
Acts 27:22,31

44   and the rest *should follow*, some on planks, and others on various things from the ship. And thus it happened that they all were brought[x] safely to land.

Safe at Malta

28:1
[we] Acts 16:10;
27:1;
Acts 27:39;
Acts 27:26
28:2
Acts 28:4; Rom.
1:14; 1 Cor.
14:11; Col. 3:11;
Rom. 14:1

28 And when they had been brought safely through, then we found out that the island was called Malta.

2   And the natives showed[m] us extraordinary kindness; for because of the rain that had set[+] in and because of the cold, they kindled a fire and received us all.

3   But when Paul had gathered a bundle of *sticks* and laid them on the fire, a viper came out because of the heat, and fastened on his hand.

28:4
Acts 28:2;
Luke 13:2,4

4   And when the natives saw the creature *hanging* from his hand, they *began* saying[m] to one another, "Undoubtedly this man is a *murderer,* and though he has been saved from the sea, justice has not allowed him to *live.*"[~]

28:5
Mark 16:18

5   However he shook the creature off into the fire and suffered no harm.

28:6
Acts 14:11

6   But they were expecting[m] that he was about to swell up or *suddenly* fall down dead. But after they had waited a *long time* and had seen nothing unusual happen to him, they changed their minds and *began* to say[m] that he was a god.

7   Now in the neighborhood of that place were[m] lands belonging to the leading man of the island, named Publius, who welcomed us and entertained us courteously three days.

28:8
Acts 9:40; James
5:14f.;
Matt. 9:18; Mark
5:23; 6:5

8   And it came about that the father of Publius was lying[~] *in bed* afflicted with *recurrent* fever and dysentery; and Paul went in *to see* him and after he had prayed, he laid his hands on him and healed[15b] him.

9   And after *this* had happened, the rest of the people on the island who had diseases were coming[m] to him and getting[m] cured.[15a]

10   And they also honored us with *many marks of respect;* and when we were setting sail, they supplied *us* with all we needed.

Paul Arrives at Rome

28:11
Acts 27:6

11   And at the end of *three* months we set sail on an Alexandrian ship which had wintered[+] at the island, and which had the Twin Brothers for its figurehead.

12   And after we put in at Syracuse, we stayed there for three days.

13   And from there we sailed around and arrived at Rhegium,

and a day later a south wind sprang up, and on the second day we came to Puteoli.

14   There we found *some* brethren, and were invited to stay[x] with them for seven days; and thus we came to *Rome*.

28:14
John 21:23; Acts
1:15; 6:3; 9:30;
Rom. 1:13; 28:15

15   And the brethren, when they heard about us, came from there as far as the Market of Appius and Three Inns to meet us; and when Paul saw them, he thanked God and took courage.

28:15
Acts 1:15; 10:23;
11:1,12,29; 12:17

16   And when we entered Rome, Paul was allowed[6c] to stay[~] by himself, with the soldier who was guarding him.

28:16
Acts 24:23

17   And it happened that after three days he called[x] together those who were the leading men of the Jews, and when they had come together, he *began* saying to them, "Brethren, though I had done nothing against our people, or the customs of our fathers, yet I was delivered prisoner from Jerusalem into the hands of the Romans.

28:17
Acts 13:50; 25:2;
Acts 22:5;
Acts 25:8;
Acts 6:14

18   "And when they had examined me, they were willing[m] to release[x] me because there was no ground for putting me to death.

28:18
Acts 22:24;
Acts 26:32;
Acts 23:29;
25:25; 26:31

19   "But when the Jews objected, I was forced to appeal[x] to Caesar; not that I had[~] any accusation against my nation.

28:19
Acts 25:11,21,25;
26:32

20   "For this reason therefore, I requested to see[x] you and to speak[x] with you, for I am wearing this chain for the sake of the *hope of Israel*."

28:20
Acts 21:33;
Acts 26:6f.

21   And they said to him, "We have neither received letters from Judea concerning you, nor have any of the brethren come here and reported or spoken anything bad about you.

28:21
Acts 3:17; 22:5;
28:14; Rom. 9:3

22   "But we desire to hear[x] from *you* what your views are; for concerning this sect, it is known to us that it is spoken against everywhere."

28:22
Acts 24:14;
1 Pet. 2:12; 3:16;
4:14,16

23   And when they had set a day for him, they came to him at his lodging in large numbers; and he was explaining[m] to them by solemnly[1] testifying about the kingdom of God, and trying to persuade them concerning Jesus, from both the Law of Moses and from the Prophets, from morning until evening.

28:23
Philem. 22;
Luke 16:28; Acts
1:3; 23:11;
Acts 8:35

24   And some were being persuaded[m] by the things spoken, but others would not believe.[m]

28:24
Acts 14:4

25   And when they did not agree with one another, they *began* leaving[m] after Paul had spoken one *parting* word, "The Holy Spirit [†]rightly spoke through Isaiah the prophet to your fathers,

26   saying,

'GO[x1] TO THIS PEOPLE AND SAY,[x1]
"YOU WILL KEEP[4] ON HEARING,[4] BUT WILL [•]NOT
UNDERSTAND;[x29f]

28:26
Is. 6:9;
Matt. 13:14f.

AND YOU WILL KEEP[4] ON SEEING,[4] BUT WILL •NOT
PERCEIVE;[x]

28:27
Is. 6:10

27   FOR THE HEART OF THIS PEOPLE HAS BECOME DULL,
AND WITH THEIR EARS THEY SCARCELY HEAR,
AND THEY HAVE CLOSED THEIR EYES;
LEST THEY SHOULD SEE[x] WITH THEIR EYES,
AND HEAR[x] WITH THEIR EARS,
AND UNDERSTAND[x] WITH THEIR HEART AND RETURN,[x]
AND I SHOULD HEAL[15b] THEM." '

28:28
Ps. 98:3; Luke
2:30; Acts 13:26;
Acts 9:15; 13:46

28   "Let it be known to you therefore, that this salvation of God has been sent to the *Gentiles; they* will also listen."

29   [[x]And when he had spoken these words, the Jews departed, having a great dispute among themselves.]

30   And he stayed two full years in his own rented quarters, and was welcoming[m] all who came to him,

28:31
Matt. 4:23; Acts
20:25; 28:23;
2 Tim. 2:9

31   preaching the kingdom of God, and teaching concerning the Lord Jesus Christ with all openness, unhindered.

[x]Many mss. do not contain this verse

The Epistle of Paul to the
Romans

The Gospel Exalted

1 Paul, a bond-servant[38b] of Christ Jesus, called *as* an apostle, set* apart for the gospel of God,

2 which He promised beforehand through His prophets in the holy Scriptures,

3 concerning His Son, who was born of a descendant of David according to the flesh,

4 who was declared the Son of God with power[32a] [a]by the resurrection from the dead, according to the spirit of holiness, Jesus Christ our Lord,

5 through whom we have received grace and apostleship to bring about *the* obedience of faith among all the Gentiles, for His name's sake,

6 among whom *you also* are the called of Jesus Christ;

7 to all who are beloved of God in Rome, called *as* saints: Grace to you and peace from God our Father and the Lord Jesus Christ.

8 First, I thank my God through Jesus Christ for you all, because your faith is being proclaimed throughout the whole world.

9 For *God,* whom I serve[38c] in my spirit in the *preaching of the* gospel of His Son, is my witness *as to* how unceasingly I make mention of you,

10 always in my prayers making request, if perhaps now at last[2] by the will of God I may succeed in coming to you.

11 For I long to see[x] you in order that I may impart[x] some *spiritual* gift[24c] to you, that you may be established;[x]

12 that is, that I may be encouraged[x] together with you *while* among you, each of us by the other's faith, both yours and mine.

13 And I do not want you to be unaware,[~] brethren, that often I have planned to come to you (and have been prevented thus far) in order that I might obtain[x] some fruit among you also, even as among the rest of the Gentiles.

14 I am [b]under obligation both to Greeks and to barbarians, both to the wise[35a] and to the foolish.[20a]

aOr, *as a result of* bLit., *debtor*

1:1
1 Cor. 1:1; 9:1;
2 Cor. 1:1;
Acts 9:15; 13:2;
Gal. 1:15;
Mark 1:14; Rom.
15:16
1:2
Titus 1:2;
Luke 1:70; Rom.
3:21; 16:26
1:3
Matt. 1:1;
John 1:14; Rom.
4:1; 9:3,5; 1 Cor.
10:18
1:4
Matt. 4:3
1:5
Acts 1:25; Gal.
1:16;
Acts 6:7; Rom.
16:26;
Acts 9:15
1:6
Jude 1; Rev.
17:14
1:7
Rom. 5:5ff.; 8:39;
Acts 9:13; Rom.
8:28ff.; 1 Cor. 1:2,
24;
Num. 6:25f.;
1 Cor. 1:3; 2 Cor.
1:2; Gal. 1:3;
Eph. 1:2; Phil.
1:2; Col. 1:2;
1 Thess. 1:1;
2 Thess. 1:2
1:8
1 Cor. 1:4; Eph.
1:15f.; Phil. 1:3f.;
Col. 1:3f.;
1 Thess. 1:2;
2:13;
Acts 28:22; Rom.
16:19
1:9
Rom. 9:1;
Acts 24:14;
2 Tim. 1:3;
Eph. 1:16; Phil.
1:3f.
1:10
Acts 18:21; Rom.
15:32
1:11
Acts 19:21; Rom.
15:23
1:13
Rom. 11:25;
1 Cor. 10:1; 12:1;
2 Cor. 1:8;
1 Thess. 4:13;
Acts 1:15; Rom.
7:1; 1 Cor. 1:10;
14:20,26; Gal.
3:15;
Acts 19:21; Rom.
15:22f.;
John 4:36; 15:16;
Phil. 1:22; Col.
1:6
1:14
1 Cor. 9:16;
Acts 28:2

1:15
Rom. 15:20

15 Thus, for my part, I am eager to preach[x] the gospel to you also who are in Rome.

1:16
Mark 8:38; 2 Tim.
1:8,12,16;
1 Cor. 1:18,24;
Acts 3:26; Rom.
2:9;
John 7:35

16 For I am not ashamed of the gospel, for it is the *power of* [†]*God* for salvation to everyone who believes, to the Jew first and also to the Greek.

1:17
Rom. 3:21; 9:30;
Phil. 3:9;
Hab. 2:4; Gal.
3:11; Heb. 10:38

17 For in *it the* righteousness of God is revealed from faith to faith; as it is written,[*] "BUT THE RIGHTEOUS *man* SHALL LIVE BY FAITH."

Unbelief and Its Consequences

1:18
Rom. 5:9; Eph.
5:6; Col. 3:6;
2 Thess. 2:6f.

18 For the *wrath* [7b] *of God* is revealed from heaven against all ungodliness and unrighteousness of men, who suppress the truth in unrighteousness,

1:19
Acts 14:17;
17:24ff.

19 because that which is known about God is *evident* within them; for God made it evident to them.

1:20
Mark 10:6;
Job 12:7-9; Ps.
19:1-6; Jer. 5:21f.

20 For since the creation of the world His invisible attributes, His eternal power[32a] and divine nature, have been clearly seen, being understood[29d] through what has been made, so that they are without excuse.

1:21
2 Kin. 17:15; Jer.
2:5; Eph. 4:17f.

21 For even though they knew[29a] God, they did not [c]honor Him *as God,* or give thanks; but they became futile in their speculations, and their foolish heart was *darkened.*

1:22
Jer. 10:14; 1 Cor.
1:20
1:23
Deut. 4:16-18;
Ps. 106:20; Jer.
2:11; Acts 17:29

22 Professing to be wise,[35a] they became fools,

23 and exchanged the glory of the incorruptible God for an image[22b] in the form[22d] of corruptible man and of birds and ed animals and [d]crawling creatures.

1:24
Rom. 1:26,28;
Eph. 4:19;
Eph. 2:3

24 Therefore God *gave them over* in the lusts of their hearts to impurity, that their bodies might be dishonored[~] among them.

1:25
Is. 44:20; Jer.
10:14; 13:25;
16:19;
Rom. 9:5; 2 Cor.
11:31

25 For they exchanged the truth of God for a lie, and worshiped and served the creature rather than the Creator, who is blessed forever. Amen.

1:26
Rom. 1:24;
1 Thess. 4:5

26 For this reason God *gave them over* to degrading passions; for their women exchanged the natural function for that which is unnatural,

1:27
Lev. 18:22; 20:13;
1 Cor. 6:9

27 and in the same way also the men abandoned the natural function of the woman and burned in their desire toward one another, men with men committing indecent acts and receiving in their own persons the *due penalty* of their error.

1:28
Rom. 1:24

28 And just as they did not see fit to acknowledge[29b] God any longer, God *gave them over* to a depraved mind,[33b] to do[~] those things which are not proper,

1:29
2 Cor. 12:20

29 being filled[*] with all unrighteousness, wickedness, greed,

[c]Lit., *glorify*   [d]Or possibly, *reptiles*

evil; full of envy, murder, strife, deceit, malice;[10e] *they are* gossips,

30   slanderers, haters of God, insolent, arrogant, boastful, inventors of evil,[10a] disobedient to parents,

31   without understanding, untrustworthy, unloving, unmerciful;

32   and, although they know[29b] the ordinance of God, that those who practice such things are *worthy of death,* they not only do the same, but also give hearty approval to those who practice[19b] them.

The Impartiality of God

2   Therefore you are without excuse, every man *of you* who passes judgment, for in that you judge another, you condemn[14c] *yourself;* for you who judge practice[19b] the *same things.*

2   And we know that the judgment of God rightly falls upon those who practice[19b] such things.

3   And do you suppose this, O man, when you pass judgment upon those who practice[19b] such things and do[19a] the same *yourself,* that *you* will escape the judgment of God?

4   Or do you think lightly of the riches of His kindness and forbearance and patience, not knowing that the kindness of God leads you to *repentance?*

5   But because of your stubbornness and unrepentant heart you are storing up wrath[7b] for yourself in the day of wrath and revelation of the righteous judgment of God,

6   who WILL RENDER TO EVERY MAN ACCORDING TO HIS DEEDS:

7   to those who by perseverance in doing good[25a] seek for glory and honor and immortality, eternal life;

8   but to those who are selfishly ambitious and do not obey the truth, but obey unrighteousness, wrath and indignation.

9   *There will be* tribulation and distress for every soul of man who does evil,[10a] of the Jew first and also of the Greek,

10   but glory and honor and peace to every man who does good,[25a] to the Jew first and also to the Greek.

11   For there is no partiality with God.

12   For all who have sinned without the Law will also perish without the Law; and all who have sinned under the Law will be judged by the Law;

13   for not the hearers of the Law are just before God, but the doers of the Law will be justified.

14   For when Gentiles who do not have the Law do~ instinctively the things of the Law, these, not having the Law, are a law *to themselves,*

1:30
Ps. 5:5;
2 Tim. 3:2

1:31
2 Tim. 3:3

1:32
Rom. 6:21;
Luke 11:48; Acts
8:1; 22:20

2:1
Rom. 1:20;
Luke 12:14; Rom.
2:3; 9:20;
2 Sam. 12:5-7;
Matt. 7:1; Luke
6:37; Rom. 14:22
2:3
Luke 12:14; Rom.
2:1; 9:20
2:4
Rom. 9:23; 11:33;
2 Cor. 8:2; Eph.
1:7,18; 2:7; Phil.
4:19; Col. 1:27;
2:2; Titus 3:6;
Rom. 11:22;
Rom. 3:25;
Ex. 34:6; Rom.
9:22; 1 Tim. 1:16;
1 Pet. 3:20; 2 Pet.
3:9,15
2:5
Deut. 32:34f.;
Prov. 1:18;
Ps. 110:5; 2 Cor.
5:10; 2 Thess.
1:5; Jude 6
2:6
Ps. 62:12; Prov.
24:12; Matt.
16:27
2:7
Luke 8:15; Heb.
10:36;
Rom. 2:10; Heb.
2:7; 1 Pet. 1:7;
1 Cor. 15:42,50,
53f.; Eph. 6:24;
2 Tim. 1:10;
Matt. 25:46
2:8
2 Cor. 12:20; Gal.
5:20; Phil. 1:17;
2:3; James 3:14,
16;
2 Thess. 2:12
2:9
Rom. 8:35;
Acts 3:26; Rom.
1:16; 1 Pet. 4:17
2:10
Rom. 2:7; Heb.
2:7; 1 Pet. 1:7;
Rom. 2:9
2:11
Deut. 10:17; Acts
10:34
2:12
Acts 2:23; 1 Cor.
9:21
2:13
Matt. 7:21,24ff.;
John 13:17;
James 1:22f.,25
2:14
Acts 10:35; Rom.
1:19; 2:15

2:15
Rom. 2:14,27
15 in that they show the work of the Law written in their hearts, their *conscience* bearing witness, and their thoughts alternately accusing or else defending them,

2:16
Rom. 16:25;
1 Cor. 15:1; Gal.
1:11; 1 Tim. 1:11;
2 Tim. 2:8;
Acts 10:42;
17:31; Rom. 3:6;
14:10
16 on the day when, according to my gospel, *God* will judge the secrets of men through Christ Jesus.

The Jew Is Condemned by the Law

2:17
Mic. 3:11; John
5:45; Rom. 2:23;
9:4
17 But if you bear the name *"Jew,"* and rely upon the Law, and boast in God,

2:18
Phil. 1:10
18 and know[29a] *His* will, and approve the things that are essential, being instructed out of the Law,

19 and are confident* that you yourself are a guide to the blind, a light to those who are in darkness,

2:20
Rom. 3:31; 2 Tim.
1:13
20 a corrector of the foolish, a teacher of the immature, having in the Law the embodiment of knowledge and of the truth,

2:21
Matt. 23:3ff.
21 you, therefore, who teach another, do you not teach *yourself ?* You who preach that one should not steal,~ do you steal?

2:22
Acts 19:37
22 You who say that one should not commit~ adultery, do you commit adultery? You who abhor idols, do you rob temples?

2:23
Mic. 3:11; John
5:45; Rom. 2:17;
9:4
23 You who *boast* in the Law, through your †*breaking*[40a] the Law, do you dishonor God?

2:24
Is. 52:5; Ezek.
36:20ff.;
2 Pet. 2:2
24 For "THE NAME OF GOD IS BLASPHEMED AMONG THE GENTILES BECAUSE OF YOU," just as it is written.*

2:25
Rom. 2:13f.,27;
Jer. 4:4; 9:25f.
25 For indeed circumcision is of value, if you *practice*~ [19b] the Law; but if you are a *transgressor* of the Law, your circumcision has become* *uncircumcision.*

2:26
1 Cor. 7:19;
Rom. 3:30; Eph.
2:11;
Rom. 2:25,27; 8:4
26 If therefore the uncircumcised man keeps~ the requirements of the Law, will not his uncircumcision be regarded as *circumcision?*

2:27
Rom. 3:30; Eph.
2:11;
Matt. 12:41
27 And will not he who is physically uncircumcised, if he keeps the Law, will he not judge •*you* who though having the letter *of the Law* and circumcision are a transgressor of the Law?

2:28
John 8:39; Rom.
2:17; 9:6; Gal.
6:15
28 For he is not a Jew who is one outwardly; neither is circumcision that which is outward in the flesh.

2:29
Phil. 3:3; Col.
2:11;
Deut. 30:6;
Rom. 2:27; 7:6;
2 Cor. 3:6;
John 5:44; 12:43;
1 Cor. 4:5; 2 Cor.
10:18
29 But he is a Jew who is one †*inwardly;* and circumcision is that which is of the heart, by the Spirit, not by the letter; and his praise is not from men, but from God.

All the World Guilty

3 Then what advantage has the Jew? Or what is the benefit of circumcision?

3:2
Deut. 4:8; Ps.
147:19; Rom. 9:4;
Acts 7:38
2 Great[26b] in every respect. First of all, that they were entrusted with the oracles of God.

3   What then? If some did not believe, their unbelief will not
nullify the *faithfulness of God,* will it?

3:3
Rom. 10:16; Heb.
4:2

4   May it never be! Rather, let God be found~¹ true, though
every man *be found* a liar, as it is written,⁺

3:4
Luke 20:16; Rom.
3:6,31;
Ps. 116:11; Rom.
3:7;
Ps. 51:4

"THAT THOU MIGHTEST BE JUSTIFIEDˣ IN THY WORDS,
AND MIGHTEST PREVAIL WHEN THOU ART JUDGED."~

5   But if our unrighteousness demonstrates the righteousness of *God,* what shall we say? The God who inflicts wrath⁷ᵇ is
not ⁺*unrighteous,* is He? (I am speaking in human terms.)

3:5
Rom. 5:8; 2 Cor.
6:4; 7:11;
Rom. 4:1; 7:7;
8:31; 9:14,30;
Rom. 6:19; 1 Cor.
9:8; 15:32; Gal.
3:15

6   May it never be! For otherwise how will God *judge* the
world?

3:6
Luke 20:16; Rom.
3:4,31;
Rom. 2:16

7   But if through *my* lie the truth of God abounded to His
glory, why am I also still being judged as a *sinner?*

3:7
Rom. 3:4;
Rom. 9:19

8   And why not *say* (as we are slanderously reported and as
some affirm that we say),~ "Let us doˣ evil¹⁰ᵃ that *good*²⁵ᵃ may
come"? Their condemnation is *just.*

3:8
Rom. 6:1

9   What then? Are we better than they? Not at all; for we have
already charged that both Jews and Greeks are *all under sin;*
10   as it is written,⁺

3:9
Rom. 3:1;
Rom. 2:1-29;
Rom. 1:18-32;
Rom. 3:19,23;
11:32; Gal. 3:22

3:10
Ps. 14:1-3; 53:1-3

"THERE IS NONE RIGHTEOUS, *NOT EVEN ONE;*
11   THERE IS NONE WHO UNDERSTANDS,²⁹ᶠ
THERE IS NONE WHO SEEKS FOR GOD;
12   ALL HAVE TURNED ASIDE, TOGETHER THEY HAVE
BECOME USELESS;
THERE IS NONE WHO DOES GOOD,
THERE IS NOT EVEN ONE."
13   "THEIR THROAT IS AN *OPEN* ⁺ *GRAVE,*
WITH THEIR TONGUES THEY KEEP DECEIVING,"ˣˣ
"THE POISON OF ASPS IS UNDER THEIR LIPS";

3:13
Ps. 5:9;
Ps. 140:3

14   "WHOSE MOUTH IS FULL OF CURSING AND BITTERNESS";
15   "THEIR FEET ARE SWIFT TO SHEDˣ BLOOD,
16   DESTRUCTION AND MISERY ARE IN THEIR PATHS,
17   AND THE *PATH OF PEACE* HAVE THEY NOT KNOWN."
18   "THERE IS NO FEAR OF GOD BEFORE THEIR EYES."

3:14
Ps. 10:7
3:15
Is. 59:7f.

3:18
Ps. 36:1

19   Now we know that whatever the Law says, it speaks to
those who are under the Law, that every mouth may be closed,ˣ
and all the world may become *accountable* to God;

3:19
John 10:34;
Rom. 2:12;
Rom. 3:9

20   because by the works of the Law no flesh will be justified in
His sight; for through the Law *comes* the knowledge²⁹ᵇ of sin.

3:20
Ps. 143:2; Acts
13:39; Gal. 2:16;
Rom. 4:15; 5:13,
20; 7:7

Justification by Faith

21   But •now *apart from the Law the* righteousness of God has
been manifested,⁺ being witnessed by the Law and the Prophets,

3:21
Rom. 1:17; 9:30;
Acts 10:43; Rom.
1:2

3:22
Rom. 1:17; 9:30;
Rom. 4:5;
Acts 3:16; Gal.
2:16,20; 3:22;
Eph. 3:12;
Rom. 4:11,16;
10:4;
Rom. 10:12; Gal.
3:28; Col. 3:11
3:23
Rom. 3:9
3:24
Rom. 4:4f.,16;
Eph. 2:8;
1 Cor. 1:30; Eph.
1:7; Col. 1:14;
Heb. 9:15
3:25
1 John 2:2; 4:10;
1 Cor. 5:7; Heb.
9:14,28; 1 Pet.
1:19; Rev. 1:5;
Rom. 2:4;
Acts 14:16; 17:30
3:27
Rom. 2:17,23;
4:2; 1 Cor. 1:29ff.;
Rom. 9:31
3:28
Acts 13:39; Rom.
3:20,21; Eph. 2:9;
James 2:20,24,26
3:29
Acts 10:34f.;
Rom. 9:24; 10:12;
15:9; Gal. 3:28
3:30
Rom. 10:12; Gal.
3:20;
Rom. 3:22; 4:11f.,
16; Gal. 3:8;
Deut. 6:4
3:31
Luke 20:16;
Matt. 5:17; Rom.
3:4,6; 8:4
4:1
Rom. 1:3
4:2
1 Cor. 1:31
4:3
Gen. 15:6; Rom.
4:9,22; Gal. 3:6;
James 2:23
4:4
Rom. 11:6
4:5
John 6:29; Rom.
3:22
4:7
Ps. 32:1
4:8
Ps. 32:2;
2 Cor. 5:19
4:9
Rom. 3:30;
Rom. 4:3;
Gen. 15:6

22   even *the* righteousness of God through faith in Jesus Christ for all those who believe; for there is no distinction;

23   for all have sinned and fall short of the glory of God,

24   being justified as a gift[24a] by His *grace* through the redemption which is in Christ Jesus;

25   whom God displayed publicly as a propitiation in His *blood* through faith. *This was* to demonstrate His righteousness, because in the forbearance of God He passed over the sins previously committed;*

26   for the demonstration, *I say,* of His righteousness at the present time, that He might be just and the justifier of the one who has faith in Jesus.

27   Where then is boasting? It is excluded. By what kind of law? Of works? *No, but by a law of faith.

28   For we maintain that a man is justified~ by *faith* apart from works of the Law.

29   Or is God *the God* of *Jews only?* Is He not *the God* of Gentiles also? Yes, of Gentiles also,

30   since indeed[2] God who will justify the circumcised by faith and the uncircumcised through faith is *one.*

31   Do we then *nullify* the Law through faith? May it never be! On the contrary, we *establish* the Law.

Justification by Faith Evidenced in Old Testament

4 What then shall we say that Abraham, our forefather according to the flesh, has found?*

2   For if Abraham was justified by *works,* he has something to boast about; but not before God.

3   For what does the Scripture say? "AND ABRAHAM ⁺BE-LIEVED GOD, AND IT WAS RECKONED TO HIM AS RIGHTEOUSNESS."

4   Now to the one who works, his wage is not reckoned as a favor, but as what is due.

5   But to the one who does not work, but believes in Him who justifies the ungodly, *his faith* is reckoned as righteousness,

6   just as David also speaks of the blessing upon the man to whom God reckons righteousness apart from works:

7   "⁺BLESSED ARE THOSE WHOSE LAWLESS DEEDS HAVE
        BEEN FORGIVEN,
    AND WHOSE SINS HAVE BEEN COVERED.

8   "⁺BLESSED IS THE MAN WHOSE SIN THE LORD WILL *NOT
        TAKE[X] INTO ACCOUNT."

9   Is this blessing then upon the circumcised, or upon the uncircumcised also? For we say, "FAITH WAS RECKONED TO *ABRA-HAM* AS RIGHTEOUSNESS."

10   How then was it reckoned? While he was circumcised, or uncircumcised? Not while circumcised, but while uncircumcised;

11   and he received the *sign* of circumcision, a seal of the righteousness of the faith which he had while ᵗ*uncircumcised,* that he might be the father of all who believe without being circumcised, that *righteousness* might be reckonedˣ to them,

4:11
Gen. 17:10f.;
John 3:33;
Luke 19:9; Rom.
4:16f.;
Rom. 3:22

12   and the father of circumcision to those who not only are of the circumcision, but who also follow⁴²ᵇ in the steps of the faith of our father Abraham which he had while uncircumcised.

13   For the promise to Abraham or to his descendants that he would be heir of the world was *not through the Law,* but through the righteousness of faith.

4:13
Rom. 9:8; Gal.
3:16,29;
Gen. 17:4-6;
22:17f.

14   For if those who are of the Law are heirs, faith is made⁺ *void* and the promise is *nullified;*⁺

4:14
Gal. 3:18

15   for the Law brings about *wrath,* ⁷ᵇ but where there is no law, neither is there violation.

4:15
Rom. 7:7,10-25; 1
Cor. 15:56; Gal.
3:10;
Rom. 3:20

16   For this reason *it is* by faith, that *it might be* in accordance with grace, in order that the promise may be ᵗ*certain* to all the descendants, not only to those who are of the Law, but also to those who are of the faith of Abraham, who is the father of us all,

4:16
Rom. 3:24;
Rom. 4:11; 9:8;
15:8;
Gal. 3:7;
Luke 19:9

17   (as it is written,⁺ "A FATHER OF MANY NATIONS HAVE I MADE⁺ YOU") in the sight of Him whom he believed, *even* God, who gives life to the dead and calls into being that which does not exist.

4:17
Gen. 17:5;
John 5:21;
Is. 48:13; 51:2;
1 Cor. 1:28

18   *In hope against hope* he believed, in order that he might become a father of many nations, according to that which had been spoken,⁺ "So SHALL YOUR DESCENDANTS BE."

4:18
Rom. 4:17;
Gen. 15:5

19   And without becoming weak in faith he contemplated his own body, now as good as dead since he was about a hundred years old, and the deadness of Sarah's womb;

4:19
Heb. 11:12;
Gen. 17:17;
Gen. 18:11

20   yet, with respect to the promise of God, he did not waver in unbelief, but grew strong in faith, giving glory to God,

4:20
Matt. 9:8
4:21
Rom. 14:5;
Gen. 18:14; Heb.
11:19

21   and being fully assured that what He had promised,⁺ He was *able* also to perform.ˣ

4:22
Gen. 15:6; Rom.
4:3

22   Therefore also IT WAS RECKONED TO HIM AS RIGHTEOUSNESS.

4:23
Rom. 15:4; 1 Cor.
9:9f.; 10:11; 2
Tim. 3:16f.

23   Now not for his sake only was it written, that it was reckoned to him,

24   but for our sake also, to whom it will be reckoned, as those who believe in Him who raised Jesus our Lord from the dead,

4:24
Rom. 10:9; 1 Pet.
1:21;
Acts 2:24

25   *He* who was delivered up because of our transgressions,⁴⁰ᵇ and was raised because of our justification.

4:25
Is. 53:4,5; Rom.
5:6,8; 8:32; Gal.
2:20; Eph. 5:2;
Rom. 5:18; 1
Cor. 15:17; 2
Cor. 5:15

Results of Justification

5:1
Rom. 3:28;
Rom. 5:11

5:2
Eph. 2:18; 3:12;
Heb. 10:19f.;
1 Pet. 3:18;
1 Cor. 15:1

5:3
Rom. 5:11; 8:23;
9:10; 2 Cor. 8:19;
Matt. 5:12; James
1:2f.;
Luke 21:19

5:4
Luke 21:19;
Phil. 2:22; James
1:12

5:5
Ps. 119:116;
Rom. 9:33; Heb.
6:18f.;
Acts 2:33; 10:45;
Gal. 4:6; Titus 3:6

5:6
Rom. 5:8,10;
Gal. 4:4;
Rom. 4:25; 8:32;
Gal. 2:20; Eph.
5:2

5:8
Rom. 3:5;
John 3:16; 15:13;
Rom. 8:39;
Rom. 4:25; 5:6;
8:32; Gal. 2:20;
Eph. 5:2

5:9
Rom. 3:25;
Rom. 1:18;
1 Thess. 1:10

5:10
Rom. 11:28;
2 Cor. 5:18f.;
Eph. 2:3; Col.
1:21f.;
Rom. 8:34; Heb.
7:25; 1 John 2:1

5:11
Rom. 5:3; 8:23;
9:10; 2 Cor. 8:19;
Rom. 5:10; 11:15;
2 Cor. 5:18f.

5:12
Gen. 2:17; 3:6,19;
Rom. 5:15-17;
1 Cor. 15:21f.;
Rom. 6:23; 1 Cor.
15:56; James
1:15;
Rom. 5:14,19,21;
1 Cor. 15:22

5:13
Rom. 4:15

5:14
Hos. 6:7;
1 Cor. 15:45

5:15
Rom. 5:12,18,19;
Acts 15:11

5:16
1 Cor. 11:32

5 Therefore having been justified by faith, we have *peace* with God through our Lord Jesus Christ,

2 through whom also we have obtained⁺ our introduction by faith into this grace in which we stand;⁺ and we exult in hope of the glory of God.

3 And not only this, but we also exult in our tribulations, knowing that tribulation brings about *perseverance;*

4 and perseverance, *proven* †*character;* and proven character, †*hope;*

5 and hope does not disappoint,³⁹ᶜ because the love of God has been poured⁺ out within our hearts through the Holy Spirit who was given to us.

6 For while we were still helpless, at the right time *Christ died* for the ungodly.

7 For² one will hardly die for a righteous man; though perhaps for the good man someone would dare even to die.ˣ

8 But *God* demonstrates His own love³¹ᵃ toward us, in that while we were *yet sinners,* Christ died *for us.*

9 Much more then, having now been justified by His blood, we shall be saved from the wrath⁷ᵇ *of God* through Him.

10 For if while we were †*enemies,* we were reconciled to God through the death of His Son, much more, having been reconciled, we shall be saved by His life.

11 And not only this, but we also exult in God through our Lord Jesus Christ, through whom we have now received the *reconciliation.*

12 Therefore, just as through *one* man sin entered into the world, and death through sin, and so death spread to *all men,* because all sinned—

13 for until the Law sin was in the world; but sin is not imputed when there is no law.

14 Nevertheless death *reigned* from Adam until Moses, even over those who had not sinned in the likeness²²ᵈ of the offense⁴⁰ᵃ of Adam, who is a ᵉtype of Him who was to come.

15 But the free gift²⁴ᶜ is not like the transgression.⁴⁰ᵇ For if by the transgression of the one the many died, much more did the grace of God and the gift²⁴ᵃ by the *grace* of the one Man, Jesus Christ, abound to the many.

16 And the gift is *not* like *that which came* through the one who sinned; for on the one hand the judgment *arose* from one *transgression* resulting in †condemnation, but on the other hand the

ᵉOr, *foreshadowing*

free gift[24c] *arose* from many transgressions[40b] resulting in †*justifi-*
cation.

17   For if by the transgression of the one, death reigned
through the one, much more those who receive[5b] the abundance
of grace and of the gift[24a] of righteousness will reign *in life*
through the One, Jesus Christ.

18   So then as through *one* †*transgression* there resulted condemnation to all men, even so through *one act of* †*righteousness*
there resulted justification of life to all men.

19   For as through the one man's disobedience the many were
made *sinners,* even so through the obedience of the One the
many will be made *righteous.*

20   And the Law came in that the transgression might increase;[x] but where sin increased, grace *abounded all the more,*[1]

21   that, as sin reigned in death, even so *grace* might reign[x]
through righteousness to eternal life through Jesus Christ our
Lord.

Believers Are Dead to Sin, Alive to God

6   What shall we say then? Are we to continue~ in sin that
grace might increase?[x]

2   May it never be! How shall we who died to sin still live
in it?

3   Or do you not know that all of us who have been baptized
into Christ Jesus have been baptized into His *death?*

4   Therefore we have been buried with Him through baptism
into death, in order that as Christ was raised from the dead
through the glory of the Father, so *we too* might walk[x42a] in
newness of life.[30b]

5   For if we have become⁺ united with *Him* in the likeness of
His death, certainly we shall be also *in the likeness* of His *resurrec-*
tion,

6   knowing this, that our old self was crucified with *Him,* that
our body of sin might be *done*[x] *away with,* that we should no
longer be slaves~ to sin;

7   for he who has died is freed⁺ from sin.

8   Now if we have died with Christ, we believe that we shall
also live with Him,

9   knowing that Christ, having been raised from the dead, is
never to die again; death no longer is master over *Him.*

10   For the death that He died, He died to sin, *once for all;* but
the life that He lives, He lives to God.

11   Even so consider~¹ yourselves to be dead to sin, but alive
to God in Christ Jesus.

5:17
Gen. 2:17; 3:6,19;
Rom. 5:12,15,16;
1 Cor. 15:21f.;
2 Tim. 2:12; Rev.
22:5

5:18
Rom. 5:12,15;
Rom. 3:25;
Rom. 4:25

5:19
Rom. 5:15,18;
Rom. 5:12; 11:32;
Phil. 2:8

5:20
Rom. 3:20; 7:7f.;
Gal. 3:19;
Rom. 6:1; 1 Tim.
1:14
5:21
Rom. 5:12,14;
John 1:17; Rom.
6:23

6:1
Rom. 3:5;
Rom. 3:8; 6:15

6:2
Luke 20:16; Rom.
6:15;
Rom. 6:11; 7:4,6;
Gal. 2:19; Col.
2:20; 3:3; 1 Pet.
2:24
6:3
Matt. 28:19;
Acts 2:38; 8:16;
19:5; Gal. 3:27
6:4
Col. 2:12;
Acts 2:24; Rom.
6:9;
John 11:40;
2 Cor. 13:4;
Rom. 7:6; 2 Cor.
5:17; Gal. 6:15;
Eph. 4:23f.; Col.
3:10
6:5
2 Cor. 4:10; Phil.
3:10f.; Col. 2:12;
3:1
6:6
Eph. 4:22; Col.
3:9;
Gal. 2:20; 5:24;
6:14;
Rom. 7:24
6:7
1 Pet. 4:1
6:8
Rom. 6:4; 2 Cor.
4:10; 2 Tim. 2:11
6:9
Acts 2:24; Rom.
6:4;
Rev. 1:18
6:11
Rom. 6:2; 7:4,6;
Gal. 2:19; Col.
2:20; 3:3; 1 Pet.
2:24

6:12
Rom. 6:14

6:13
Rom. 6:16,19;
7:5; Col. 3:5;
Rom. 12:1; 2 Cor.
5:14f.; 1 Pet. 2:24

6:14
Rom. 8:2,12;
Rom. 6:12;
Rom. 5:18; 7:4,6;
Gal. 4:21;
Rom. 5:17,21
6:15
Rom. 6:1;
Luke 20:16; Rom.
6:2
6:16
Rom. 11:2; 1 Cor.
3:16; 5:6; 6:2,3,9,
15,16,19; 9:13,
24;
John 8:34; 2 Pet.
2:19;
Rom. 6:21,23
6:17
Rom. 1:8; 2 Cor.
2:14;
2 Tim. 1:13
6:18
John 8:32; Rom.
6:22; 8:2

6:19
Rom. 3:5;
Rom. 6:13

6:20
Matt. 6:24; Rom.
6:16
6:21
Jer. 12:13; Ezek.
16:63; Rom. 7:5;
Rom. 1:32; 5:12;
6:16,23; 8:6,13;
Gal. 6:8
6:22
John 8:32; Rom.
6:18; 8:2;
1 Cor. 7:22;
1 Pet. 2:16;
Rom. 7:4;
1 Pet. 1:9
6:23
Rom. 1:32; 5:12;
6:16,21; 8:6,13;
Gal. 6:8;
Matt. 25:46; Rom.
5:21; 8:38,39

7:1
Rom. 1:13

7:2
1 Cor. 7:39

12 Therefore do not let sin reign⁰ in your mortal body that you should obey~ its lusts,

13 and do not go on presenting⁰ the members of your body to sin *as* instruments of unrighteousness; but present ˣⁱ yourselves to God as those alive from the dead, and your members *as* instruments of righteousness to God.

14 For sin shall not be master over *you,* for you are not under law, but under grace.

15 What then? Shall we sinˣ because we are not under law but under grace? May it never be!

16 Do you not know that when you present yourselves to someone *as* slaves for obedience, you are †*slaves* ³⁸ᵇ of the one whom you obey, either of sin resulting in death, or of obedience resulting in righteousness?

17 But thanks be to God that though you were slaves³⁸ᵇ of sin, you became obedient from the heart to *that form of teaching* to which you were committed,

18 and having been freed from sin, you became slaves³⁸ᵇ of righteousness.

19 I am speaking in human terms because of the weakness of your flesh. For just as you presented your members *as* slaves to impurity and to lawlessness, resulting in *further* lawlessness, so now present ˣⁱ your members *as* slaves to righteousness, resulting in sanctification.

20 For when you were *slaves* of sin, you were *free* in regard to righteousness.

21 Therefore what benefit were you then deriving ᵐ from the things of which you are now ashamed? For the outcome of those things is death.

22 But •*now* having been freed from sin and enslaved to God, you derive your benefit, resulting in sanctification, and the outcome, eternal life.

23 For the wages of sin is death, but the free gift²⁴ᶜ of God is eternal life in Christ Jesus our Lord.

Believers United to Christ

7 Or do you not know, brethren (for I am speaking to those who know²⁹ᵃ the law), that the law has jurisdiction over a person as long as he lives?

2 For the married woman is bound⁺ by law to her husband while he is living; but if her husband *dies,*ˣ she is released⁺ from the law concerning the husband.

3 So then if, while her husband is living, she is joined to another man, she shall be called an *adulteress;* but if her husband

dies,[x] she is [†]*free* from the law, so that she is not an adulteress, though she is joined to another man.

4   Therefore, my brethren, *you also* were made to die to the Law through the body of Christ, that you might be joined to another, to Him who was raised from the dead, that we might bear[x] fruit for God.

5   For while we were in the flesh, the sinful passions, which were *aroused by the Law*, were at work[m] in the members of our body to bear[x] fruit for death.

6   But •*now* we have been released from the Law, having died to that by which we were bound,[m] so that we serve[~38b] in newness of the [f]Spirit and not in oldness of the letter.

7   What shall we say then? Is the Law sin? May it never be! On the contrary, I would not have come to *know*[29a] sin except through the Law; for I would not have known[29e] about *coveting* if the Law had not said,[m] "YOU SHALL NOT COVET."

8   But sin, taking opportunity *through the commandment*, produced in me coveting of every kind; for *apart from the Law* sin *is* dead.

9   And *I* was once alive apart from the Law; but when the commandment came, sin became alive, and *I* died;

10   and this commandment, which was to result in life, proved to result in death for me;

11   for sin, taking opportunity *through the commandment*, deceived[16a] me, and through it killed me.

12   So then, the Law is holy,[28a] and the commandment is holy and righteous and good.[25a]

13   Therefore did that which is good become *a cause of* death for me? May it never be! Rather it was sin, in order that it might be shown[x] to be sin by effecting my death through that which is [†]*good*,[25a] that through the commandment sin might become *utterly sinful*.

The Conflict of Two Natures

14   For we know[29e] that the Law is *spiritual;* but *I* am of *flesh*, sold[•] into bondage to sin.

15   For that which I am doing, I do not understand; for I am not practicing[19b] what I *would* like to *do*, but I am doing the very thing I hate.

16   But if I do[19a] the very thing I do not wish *to do*, I agree with the Law, *confessing* that it is good.[25b]

17   So •*now*, no longer am *I* the one doing it, but sin which indwells me.

[†]Or, *spirit*

7:4
Rom. 6:2; 7:6;
Rom. 8:2; Gal.
2:19; 5:18;
Col. 1:22

7:5
Rom. 8:8f.; 2 Cor.
10:3;
Rom. 7:7f.;
Rom. 6:13,21,23

7:6
Rom. 7:2;
Rom. 6:2;
Rom. 6:4;
Rom. 2:29

7:7
Rom. 3:5;
Luke 20:16;
Rom. 3:20; 4:15;
5:20;
Ex. 20:17; Deut.
5:21

7:8
Rom. 7:11;
Rom. 3:20;
1 Cor. 15:56

7:10
Lev. 18:5; Luke
10:28; Rom. 10:5;
Gal. 3:12
7:11
Rom. 7:8;
Rom. 3:20;
Gen. 3:13
7:12
Rom. 7:16; 1 Tim.
1:8

7:13
Luke 20:16

7:14
1 Cor. 3:1;
1 Kin. 21:20,25;
2 Kin. 17:17;
Rom. 6:6; Gal.
4:3;
Rom. 3:9
7:15
John 15:15;
Rom. 7:19; Gal.
5:17
7:16
Rom. 7:12; 1 Tim.
1:8
7:17
Rom. 7:20

7:18
John 3:6; Rom.
7:25; 8:3

18   For I know[29e] that nothing good[25a] dwells in me, that is, in my flesh; for the wishing~ is present in me, but the doing~ of the good[25b] *is* not.

7:19
Rom. 7:15

19   For the good[25a] that I wish, I do not do;[19a] but I practice[19b] the *very evil*[10a] that I do not wish.

7:20
Rom. 7:17

20   But if I am doing the very thing *I* do not wish, *I* am no longer the one doing it, but sin which dwells in me.

7:21
Rom. 7:23,25; 8:2

21   I find then the principle that evil[10a] is present in •*me,* the one who wishes to do~[19a] good.[25b]

7:22
2 Cor. 4:16; Eph.
3:16; 1 Pet. 3:4
7:23
Rom. 6:19; Gal.
5:17; James 4:1;
1 Pet. 2:11;
Rom. 7:21,25; 8:2
7:24
Rom. 6:6; Col.
2:11;
Rom. 8:2
7:25
1 Cor. 15:57;
Rom. 7:21,23; 8:2

22   For I joyfully concur with the law of God in the inner man,

23   but I see a different law in the members of my body, waging war against the law of my mind,[33b] and making me a prisoner of the law of sin which is in my members.

24   *Wretched* man that I am! Who will set me free from the body of †this death?

25   Thanks be to God through Jesus Christ our Lord! So then, on the one hand *I myself* with my mind[33b] am serving[38b] the law of God, but on the other, with my flesh the law of sin.

Deliverance from Bondage

8:1
Rom. 5:16; 8:34;
Rom. 8:9f.;
Rom. 8:2,11,39;
16:3
8:2
1 Cor. 15:45;
Rom. 8:1,11,39;
16:3;
John 8:32,36;
Rom. 6:14,18; 7:4
8:3
Acts 13:39; Heb.
10:1ff.;
Rom. 7:18f.; Heb.
7:18;
Phil. 2:7; Heb.
2:14,17; 4:15
8:4
Luke 1:6; Rom.
2:26;
Gal. 5:16,25
8:5
Gal. 5:19-21;
Gal. 5:22-25

8   There is therefore now no condemnation for those who are in Christ Jesus.

2   For the law of the Spirit of life in Christ Jesus has set [9]you free from the law of sin and of death.

3   For what the Law could not do, weak[xx] as it was through the flesh, God *did:* sending His *own Son* in the likeness of sinful flesh and *as an offering* for sin, He condemned[14c] sin in the flesh,

4   in order that the requirement of the Law might be fulfilled[x] in us, who do not walk[42a] according to the flesh, but according to the †*Spirit.*

5   For those who are according to the flesh set their minds[33c] on the things of the *flesh,* but those who are according to the Spirit, the things of the †*Spirit.*

8:6
Gal. 6:8;
Rom. 6:21; 8:13

6   For the mind[33c] set on the flesh is death, but the mind set on the Spirit is life[30b] and peace,

8:7
James 4:4

7   because the mind[33c] set on the flesh is hostile toward God; for it does *not subject itself* to the law of God, for it is not even able *to do so;*

8:8
Rom. 7:5
8:9
Rom. 7:5;
John 14:23; Rom.
8:11; 1 Cor. 3:16;
6:19; 2 Cor. 6:16;
Gal. 4:6; Phil.
1:19; 2 Tim. 1:14;
1 John 4:13;
John 14:17

8   and those who are in the flesh *cannot* please[x] God.

9   However, *you* are not in the flesh but in the Spirit, if indeed[2] the Spirit of God dwells in you. But if anyone does not have the *Spirit of Christ,* he does not belong to Him.

[9]Some ancient mss. read *me*

10   And if Christ is in you, though the body is dead because of sin, yet the spirit is alive because of righteousness.

11   But if the Spirit of Him who raised Jesus *from the dead* dwells in you, He who raised Christ Jesus *from the dead* will also give life to your mortal bodies hthrough His Spirit who indwells you.

12   So then, brethren, we are under obligation, not to the flesh, to live~ according to the *flesh*—

13   for if you are living according to the *flesh,* you must die; but if by the *Spirit* you are putting to death the deeds of the body, you will live.

14   For all who are being led by the *Spirit of God,* these are *sons* of God.

15   For you have not received a spirit of slavery leading to fear again, but you have received a spirit of adoption as sons by which we cry out, "Abba! Father!"

16   The Spirit Himself bears witness with our spirit that we are children of God,

17   and if children, heirs also, heirs of God and fellow heirs with Christ, if indeed[2] we suffer with *Him* in order that we may also be glorified[x] with *Him.*

18   For I consider that the sufferings of this present time are *not worthy* to be compared with the glory that is to be revealed[x] to us.

19   For the anxious longing of the creation waits eagerly[1] for the *revealing of the sons of God.*

20   For the creation was subjected to *futility,* not of its own will, but because of Him who subjected it, iin hope

21   that the *creation itself* also will be set free from its slavery to corruption into the freedom of the glory of the children of God.

22   For we know that the whole creation groans and suffers the pains of childbirth together until now.

23   And not only this, but also we ourselves, having the first fruits of the Spirit, *even we ourselves* groan within ourselves, waiting eagerly[1] for *our* tadoption as sons, the redemption of our body.

24   For in *hope* we have been saved, but hope that is seen is not hope; for jwhy does one also hope for what he sees?

25   But if we hope for what we do not see, with *perseverance* we wait eagerly[1] for it.

hSome ancient mss. read *because of*   iSome ancient mss. read *in hope; because the creation*   jSome ancient mss. read *who hopes for what he sees?*

8:10
John 17:23; Gal. 2:20; Eph. 3:17; Col. 1:27
8:11
Acts 2:24; John 5:21; Rom. 6:4; 8:1,2,39; 16:3
8:13
Rom. 8:6; Col. 3:5
8:14
Gal. 5:18; Hos. 1:10; Matt. 5:9; John 1:12; Rom. 8:16,19; 9:8,26; 2 Cor. 6:18; Gal. 3:26; 1 John 3:1; Rev. 21:7
8:15
2 Tim. 1:7; Heb. 2:15; Rom. 8:23; Gal. 4:5f.; Mark 14:36; Gal. 4:6
8:16
Acts 5:32; Hos. 1:10; Matt. 5:9; John 1:12; Rom. 8:14,19; 9:8,26; 2 Cor. 6:18; Gal. 3:26; 1 John 3:1; Rev. 21:7
8:17
Acts 20:32; Gal. 3:29; 4:7; Eph. 3:6; Titus 3:7; Heb. 1:14; Rev. 21:7; 2 Cor. 1:5,7; Phil. 3:10; Col. 1:24; 2 Tim. 2:12; 1 Pet. 4:13
8:18
2 Cor. 4:17; Col. 3:4; Titus 2:13; 1 Pet. 1:5; 4:13; 5:1
8:19
Phil. 1:20; Rom. 8:18; 1 Cor. 1:7f.; Col. 3:4; 1 Pet. 1:7,13;
8:20
1 John 3:2; Hos. 1:10; Matt. 5:9; John 1:12; Rom. 8:14,16; 9:8,26; 2 Cor. 6:18; Gal. 3:26; 1 John 3:1; Rev. 21:7
8:20
Gen. 3:17-19; 5:29; Ps. 39:5f.; Eccl. 1:2
8:21
Acts 3:21; 2 Pet. 3:13; Rev. 21:1
8:22
Jer. 12:4,11
8:23
Rom. 5:3; 8:16; 2 Cor. 1:22; 5:2,4; Rom. 8:15,19,25; Gal. 5:5; Rom. 7:24
8:24
Rom. 8:20; 1 Thess. 5:8; Titus 3:7; Rom. 4:18; 2 Cor. 5:7; Heb. 11:1
8:25
1 Thess. 1:3

8:26
Matt. 20:22;
2 Cor. 12:8;
John 14:16; Rom.
8:15f.; Eph. 6:18
8:27
Ps. 139:1f.; Luke
16:15; Acts 1:24;
Rev. 2:23;
Rom. 8:6;
Rom. 8:34
8:28
Rom. 8:32;
Rom. 8:30; 9:24;
11:29; 1 Cor. 1:9;
Gal. 1:6,15; 5:8;
Eph. 1:11; 3:11;
2 Thess. 2:14;
Heb. 9:15; 1 Pet.
2:9; 3:9
8:29
Rom. 11:2; 1 Cor.
8:3; 2 Tim. 1:9;
1 Pet. 1:2,20;
Rom. 9:23; 1 Cor.
2:7; Eph. 1:5,11;
1 Cor. 15:49; Phil.
3:21;
Col. 1:18; Heb.
1:6
8:30
Rom. 9:23; 11:29;
1 Cor. 2:7; Eph.
1:5,11;
Rom. 8:28; 9:24;
1 Cor. 1:9; Gal.
1:6,15; 5:8; Eph.
1:11; 3:11;
2 Thess. 2:14;
Heb. 9:15; 1 Pet.
2:9; 3:9;
1 Cor. 6:11;
John 17:22; Rom.
8:21
8:31
Rom. 3:5; 4:1;
Ps. 118:6; Matt.
1:23
8:32
John 3:16; Rom.
5:8;
Rom. 4:25
8:33
Luke 18:7;
Is. 50:8f.
8:34
Rom. 8:1;
Rom. 5:6f.;
Acts 2:24;
Mark 16:19;
Rom. 8:27; Heb.
7:25
8:35
Rom. 8:37f.;
Rom. 2:9; 2 Cor.
4:8;
1 Cor. 4:11; 2
Cor. 11:26f.
8:36
Ps. 44:22; Acts
20:24; 1 Cor. 4:9;
15:30f.; 2 Cor.
1:9; 4:10f.; 6:9;
11:23
8:37
John 16:33;
1 Cor. 15:57;
Gal. 2:20; Eph.
5:2; Rev. 1:5
8:38
1 Cor. 3:22;
1 Cor. 15:24;
Eph. 1:21; 1 Pet.
3:22
8:39
Rom. 5:8;
Rom. 8:1

Our Victory in Christ

26   And in the same way the Spirit also helps our weakness; for we do not know how to pray[x] as we should, but the Spirit Himself intercedes for *us* with groanings *too deep for words;*

27   and He who searches the hearts knows what the mind[33c] of the Spirit is, because He intercedes for the saints *according to the will of God.*

28   And we know that [k]God causes all things to work together for good[25a] to those who love[31a] God, to those who are called according to *His* purpose.

29   For whom He foreknew, He also predestined *to become* conformed to the image[22b] of His Son, that He might be the first-born among many brethren;

30   and whom He predestined, these He also called; and whom He called, these He also justified; and whom He justified, these He also glorified.

31   What then shall we say to these things? If God *is* for us, who *is* against us?

32   He who[2] did not spare His *own Son,* but delivered Him up for us all, how will He not also with Him freely give us *all things?*

33   Who will bring a charge against God's elect? God is the one who justifies;

34   who is the one who condemns?[14c] Christ Jesus is He who died, yes, rather who was [l]raised, who is at the right hand of God, who also intercedes for us.

35   Who shall separate *us* from the love[31a] of [m]Christ? Shall tribulation, or distress, or persecution, or famine, or nakedness, or peril, or sword?

36   Just as it is written,[+]

> "FOR THY SAKE WE ARE BEING PUT TO DEATH ALL DAY
>   LONG;
> WE WERE CONSIDERED AS SHEEP TO BE SLAUGHTERED."

37   But in *all* these things we overwhelmingly[1] conquer through Him who loved us.

38   For I am convinced[+] that neither death, nor life, nor angels, nor principalities, nor things present, nor things to come, nor powers,[32a]

39   nor height, nor depth, nor any other created thing, shall be able to separate[x] us from the love[31a] of God, which is in Christ Jesus our Lord.

---

[k]Some ancient mss. read *all things work together for good*   [l]Some ancient mss. read *raised from the dead*
[m]Some ancient mss. read *God*

Solicitude for Israel

9 I am telling the truth in Christ, I am not lying, my conscience bearing me witness in the Holy Spirit,

2   that I have *great* sorrow and unceasing grief in my heart.

3   For I could wish that *I myself* were accursed, *separated* from Christ for the sake of my brethren, my kinsmen according to the flesh,

4   who are Israelites, to whom belongs the adoption as sons and the glory and the covenants and the giving of the Law and the *temple* service and the promises,

5   whose are the fathers, and from whom is the Christ according to the flesh, who is over all, God blessed forever. Amen.

6   But *it is* not as though the word[43a] of God has failed. For they are not all Israel who are *descended* from Israel;

7   neither are they all children because they are Abraham's descendants, but: "THROUGH *ISAAC* YOUR DESCENDANTS WILL BE NAMED."

8   That is, it is not the children of the flesh who are children of God, but the children of the promise are regarded as descendants.

9   For this is a word of *promise:* "AT THIS TIME I WILL COME, AND SARAH SHALL HAVE A *SON.*"

10   And not only this, but there was Rebekah also, when she had conceived *twins* by one man, our father Isaac;

11   for though *the twins* were not yet born, and had not done[19b] anything good[25a] or bad,[10d] in order that God's purpose according to *His* choice might stand, not because of works, but because of Him who calls,

12   it was said to her, "THE OLDER WILL SERVE THE YOUNGER."

13   Just as it is written, "JACOB I *LOVED,* BUT ESAU I *HATED.*"

14   What shall we say then? There is no injustice with God, is there? May it never be!

15   For He says to Moses, "I WILL HAVE MERCY ON WHOM I HAVE MERCY, AND I WILL HAVE COMPASSION ON WHOM I HAVE COMPASSION."

16   So then it *does* not *depend* on the man who wills or the man who runs, but on God who has mercy.

17   For the Scripture says to Pharaoh, "FOR THIS VERY PURPOSE I RAISED YOU UP, TO DEMONSTRATE[x] MY POWER[32a] IN YOU, AND THAT MY NAME MIGHT BE PROCLAIMED[x] THROUGHOUT THE WHOLE EARTH."

18   So then He has mercy on *whom He desires,* and He hardens *whom He desires.*

9:1
2 Cor. 11:10; Gal. 1:20; 1 Tim. 2:7

9:3
Ex. 32:32; 1 Cor. 12:3; 16:22; Gal. 1:8f.; Rom. 1:3; 11:14; Eph. 6:5
9:4
Deut. 7:6; 14:1f.; Rom. 9:6; Ex. 4:22; Rom. 8:15; Ex. 40:34; 1 Kin. 8:11; Ezek. 1:28; Heb. 9:5; Gen. 17:2; Deut. 29:14; Luke 1:72; Acts 3:25; Eph. 2:12; Deut. 4:13f.; Ps. 147:19; Heb. 9:1,6; Acts 2:39; 13:32
9:5
Acts 3:13; Rom. 11:28; Matt. 1:1-16; Rom. 1:3; Col. 1:16-19; John 1:1; Rom. 1:25
9:6
Num. 23:19; John 1:47; Rom. 2:28f.; Gal. 6:16
9:7
John 8:33,39; Gal. 4:23; Gen. 21:12; Heb. 11:18
9:8
Rom. 8:14; Rom. 4:13,16; Gal. 3:29; 4:28; Heb. 11:11
9:9
Gen. 18:10
9:10
Rom. 5:3; Gen. 25:21
9:11
Rom. 4:17; 8:28
9:12
Gen. 25:23
9:13
Mal. 1:2f.
9:14
Rom. 3:5; 2 Chr. 19:7; Rom. 2:11; Luke 20:16
9:15
Ex. 33:19
9:16
Gal. 2:2; Eph. 2:8
9:17
Ex. 9:16
9:18
Ex. 4:21; 7:3; 9:12; 10:20,27; 11:10; 14:4,17; Deut. 14; Josh. 11:20; John 12:40; Rom. 11:7,25

9:19
Rom. 11:19;
1 Cor. 15:35;
James 2:18;
Rom. 3:7;
2 Chr. 20:6; Job
9:12; Dan. 4:35
9:20
Rom. 2:1;
Job 33:13;
Is. 29:16; 45:9;
64:8; Jer. 18:6;
Rom. 9:22f.;
2 Tim. 2:20

9:22
Rom. 2:4;
Prov. 16:4; 1 Pet.
2:8

9:23
Rom. 2:4; Eph.
3:16;
Acts 9:15;
Rom. 8:29f.

9:24
Rom. 8:28;
Rom. 3:29

9:25
Hos. 2:23; 1 Pet.
2:10

9:26
Hos. 1:10;
Matt. 16:16

9:27
Is. 10:22;
Gen. 22:17; Hos.
1:10;
Rom. 11:5

9:28
Is. 10:23

9:29
Is. 1:9;
James 5:4;
Deut. 29:23; Is.
13:19; Jer. 49:18;
50:40; Amos 4:11

9:30
Rom. 9:14;
Rom. 1:17; 3:21f.;
10:6; Gal. 2:16;
3:24; Phil. 3:9;
Heb. 11:7
9:31
Is. 51:1; Rom.
9:30; 10:2f.,20;
11:7;
Gal. 5:4
9:32
Is. 8:14; 1 Pet.
2:6,8
9:33
Is. 28:16;
Is. 8:14;
Rom. 10:11;
Rom. 5:5

19 You will say to me then, "Why does He still find fault? For who resists[*] *His will?*"

20 On the contrary,[2] who are *you*, O man, who answers back to God? The thing molded will not say to the molder, "Why did you make me *like this,*" will it?

21 Or does not the potter have *a right* over the clay, to make[x] from the same lump one vessel for *honorable use,* and another for *common* [†]*use?*

22 What if God, although willing to demonstrate[x] His wrath[7b] and to make His power known,[x] endured with much patience vessels of wrath prepared[*] for destruction?

23 And *He did so* in order that He might make known[x] the riches of His glory upon vessels of mercy, which He prepared beforehand for glory,

24 *even* us, whom He also called, not from among Jews only, but also from among Gentiles.

25 As He says also in Hosea,

"I WILL CALL THOSE WHO WERE NOT MY PEOPLE, 'MY
    PEOPLE,'
    AND HER WHO WAS NOT BELOVED,[*] 'BELOVED.' "[*]

26 "AND IT SHALL BE THAT IN THE PLACE WHERE IT WAS
    SAID TO THEM, 'YOU ARE NOT MY PEOPLE,'
    THERE THEY SHALL BE CALLED SONS OF THE LIVING
    GOD."

27 And Isaiah cries out concerning Israel, "THOUGH THE NUM-BER OF THE SONS OF ISRAEL BE AS THE SAND OF THE SEA, IT IS THE [†]REMNANT THAT WILL BE SAVED;

28 FOR THE LORD WILL EXECUTE HIS WORD UPON THE EARTH, THOROUGHLY[1] AND QUICKLY."[1]

29 And just as Isaiah foretold,[*]

"EXCEPT THE LORD OF SABAOTH HAD LEFT TO US A
    POSTERITY,
    WE WOULD HAVE BECOME AS SODOM, AND WOULD
    HAVE RESEMBLED GOMORRAH."

30 What shall we say then? That Gentiles, who did not pursue righteousness, attained righteousness; even the righteousness which is by faith;

31 but Israel, pursuing a law of righteousness, did *not arrive* at *that* law.

32 Why? Because *they did* not *pursue it* by faith, but as though *it were* by works. They stumbled over the stumbling stone,

33 just as it is written,[*]

"BEHOLD, I LAY IN ZION A STONE OF STUMBLING AND A
    ROCK OF OFFENSE,

AND HE WHO BELIEVES IN HIM WILL NOT BE
DISAPPOINTED."

The Word of Faith Brings Salvation

10 Brethren, •*my* heart's desire and my prayer to God for them is for *their* salvation.

2   For I bear them witness that they have a zeal for God, but not in accordance with knowledge.[29b]

3   For not knowing about †*God's* righteousness, and seeking to establish[x] their *own,* they did not subject themselves to the *righteousness of God.*

4   For *Christ* is the end of the law for righteousness to everyone who believes.

5   For Moses writes that the man who practices the righteousness which is based on law shall live by that righteousness.

6   But the righteousness *based on* †*faith* speaks thus, "Do NOT SAY[Θ] IN YOUR HEART, 'WHO WILL ASCEND INTO HEAVEN?' (that is, to bring[x] Christ down),

7   or 'WHO WILL DESCEND INTO THE ABYSS?' (that is, to bring[x] Christ up from the dead)."

8   But what does it say? "THE WORD[43b] IS *NEAR YOU,* IN YOUR MOUTH AND IN YOUR HEART"—that is, the word[43b] of faith which we are preaching,

9   that if you confess[x] with your mouth Jesus *as* Lord, and believe[x] in your heart that God raised Him from the dead, you shall be saved;

10   for with the heart man believes, resulting in righteousness, and with the mouth he confesses, resulting in salvation.

11   For the Scripture says, "WHOEVER BELIEVES IN HIM WILL NOT BE DISAPPOINTED."

12   For there is no distinction between Jew and Greek; for the same *Lord* is Lord of all, abounding in riches for all who call upon Him;

13   for "WHOEVER WILL CALL[x] UPON THE NAME OF THE LORD WILL BE SAVED."

14   How then shall they call[x] upon Him in whom they have not believed? And how shall they believe[x] in Him whom they have not heard? And how shall they hear[x] without a preacher?

15   And how shall they preach[x] unless they are sent?[x] Just as it is written,⁺ "How †BEAUTIFUL ARE THE FEET OF THOSE WHO BRING GLAD TIDINGS OF GOOD[25a] THINGS!"

16   However, they did not all heed the glad tidings; for Isaiah says, "LORD, WHO HAS BELIEVED OUR REPORT?"

10:2
Acts 21:20

10:3
Rom. 1:17;
Is. 51:1; Rom.
10:2f.,20; 11:7

10:4
Rom. 7:1-4; Gal.
3:24; 4:5;
Rom. 3:22

10:5
Lev. 18:5; Neh.
9:29; Ezek.
20:11,13,21;
Rom. 7:10

10:6
Rom. 9:30;
Deut. 30:12

10:7
Luke 8:31;
Heb. 13:20

10:8
Deut. 30:14

10:9
Matt. 10:32; Luke
12:8; Rom. 14:9;
1 Cor. 12:3; Phil.
2:11;
Acts 16:31; Rom.
4:24;
Acts 2:24

10:11
Is. 28:16; Rom.
9:33

10:12
Rom. 3:22,29;
Acts 10:36

10:13
Joel 2:32; Acts
2:21

10:14
Eph. 2:17; 4:21;
Acts 8:31; Titus
1:3

10:15
Is. 52:7;
Rom. 1:15; 15:20

10:16
Rom. 3:3;
Is. 53:1; John
12:38

10:17
Gal. 3:2,5;
Col. 3:16
17 So faith *comes* from hearing, and hearing by the word[43b] of Christ.

10:18
Ps. 19:4; Rom.
1:8; Col. 1:6,23;
1 Thess. 1:8
18 But I say, surely they have never heard, have they? Indeed[2] they have;

"THEIR VOICE HAS GONE OUT INTO *ALL THE EARTH,*
AND THEIR WORDS[43b] TO THE *ENDS OF THE WORLD.*"

10:19
Deut. 32:21;
Rom. 11:11,14
19 But I say, surely Israel did not know,[29a] did they? At the first Moses says,

"*I* WILL MAKE YOU JEALOUS BY THAT WHICH IS NOT A
NATION,
BY A NATION WITHOUT UNDERSTANDING WILL I ANGER
YOU."

10:20
Is. 65:1; Rom.
9:30
20 And Isaiah is very[1] bold and says,

"I WAS FOUND BY THOSE WHO SOUGHT ME NOT,
I BECAME †*MANIFEST* TO THOSE WHO DID NOT ASK[9c]
FOR ME."

10:21
Is. 65:2
21 But as for Israel He says, "ALL THE DAY LONG I HAVE STRETCHED OUT MY HANDS TO A DISOBEDIENT AND OBSTINATE PEOPLE."

Israel Is Not Cast Away

11:1
1 Sam. 12:22;
Jer. 31:37;
33:24-26;
Luke 20:16; Phil.
3:5
11 I say then, God has not *rejected* His people, has He? May it never be! For *I too* am an *Israelite,* a descendant of Abraham, of the tribe of Benjamin.

11:2
Ps. 94:14;
Rom. 8:29;
Rom. 6:16
2 God has *not rejected* His people whom He foreknew. Or do you not know what the Scripture says in *the passage about* Elijah, how he pleads with God against Israel?

11:3
1 Kin. 19:10,14
3 "Lord, THEY HAVE KILLED THY PROPHETS, THEY HAVE TORN DOWN THINE ALTARS, AND *I* ALONE AM LEFT, AND THEY ARE SEEKING MY LIFE."

11:4
1 Kin. 19:18
4 But what is the divine response to him? "I HAVE KEPT for Myself *SEVEN THOUSAND* MEN WHO HAVE NOT BOWED THE KNEE TO BAAL."

11:5
2 Kin. 19:4; Rom.
9:27
5 In the same way then, there has also come to be⁺ at the present time a remnant according to *God's gracious choice.*

11:6
Rom. 4:4
6 But if it is by grace, it is no longer on the basis of works, otherwise grace is no longer grace.

11:7
Rom. 9:31;
Mark 6:52; Rom.
9:18; 11:25;
2 Cor. 3:14
7 What then? That which Israel is seeking[1] for, it has *not* †*obtained,* but those who were chosen obtained it, and the rest were hardened;

11:8
Deut. 29:4; Is.
29:10; Matt.
13:13f.
8 just as it is written, ⁺

"GOD GAVE THEM A SPIRIT OF STUPOR,
EYES TO SEE ~ NOT AND EARS TO HEAR ~ NOT,
DOWN TO THIS VERY DAY."

9   And David says,

"LET THEIR TABLE BECOME[xi] A SNARE AND A TRAP,
AND A STUMBLING BLOCK AND A RETRIBUTION TO
      THEM.

10   "LET THEIR EYES BE DARKENED[xi] TO SEE ~ NOT,
AND BEND[xi] THEIR BACKS FOREVER."

11   I say then, they did not stumble so as to fall,[x] did they? May it never be! But by *their* transgression[40b] salvation *has come* to the Gentiles, to make[x] them jealous.

12   Now if their transgression be riches for the world and their failure be riches for the Gentiles, how much more will their fulfillment be!

13   But I am speaking to you who are Gentiles. Inasmuch then as *I* am an apostle of *Gentiles,* I magnify *my ministry,*

14   if somehow I might move to jealousy *my* fellow countrymen and save some of them.

15   For if their rejection be the reconciliation of the world, what will *their* acceptance be but life from the dead?

16   And if the first piece *of dough* be holy, [28a] the lump is also; and if the root be holy, the branches are too.

17   But if some of the branches were broken off, and *you,* being a wild olive, were grafted in among them and became *partaker* with them of the rich root of the olive tree,

18   do not be arrogant[o] toward the branches; but if you are arrogant, *remember that* it is not *you* who supports the root, but the root *supports* •*you.*

19   You will say then, "Branches were broken off so that *I* might be grafted[x] in."

20   Quite right, they were broken off for their *unbelief,* but *you* stand+ by your *faith.* Do not be conceited,[o] but fear; [~I]

21   for if God did not spare the *natural branches,* neither will He spare *you.*

22   Behold[xi] then the kindness and severity of God; to those who fell, *severity,* but to you, *God's kindness,* if you continue ~ in His kindness; otherwise *you also* will be cut off.

23   And they also, if they do not continue ~ in their unbelief, will be grafted in; for God is *able* to graft[x] them in again.

24   For if *you* were cut off from what is by nature a *wild olive tree,* and were grafted contrary to nature into a cultivated olive tree, how much more shall these who are the natural *branches* be grafted into their •*own* olive tree?

25   For I do not want you, brethren, to be uninformed~ of this mystery, lest you be wise [35b] in your own estimation, that a partial

---

11:9
Ps. 69:22

11:10
Ps. 69:23

11:11
Rom. 11:1;
Luke 20:16;
Acts 28:28;
Rom. 11:14

11:12
Rom. 11:25

11:13
Acts 9:15

11:14
Rom. 11:11;
Gen. 29:14;
2 Sam. 19:12f.;
Rom. 9:3;
1 Cor. 1:21; 7:16;
9:22; 1 Tim. 1:15;
2:4; 2 Tim. 1:9;
Titus 3:5
11:15
Rom. 5:11;
Luke 15:24,32
11:16
Num. 15:18ff.;
Neh. 10:37; Ezek.
44:30
11:17
Jer. 11:16; John
15:2;
Eph. 2:11ff.
11:18
John 4:22

11:19
Rom. 9:19

11:20
Rom. 5:2; 1 Cor.
10:12; 2 Cor.
1:24;
Rom. 12:16;
1 Tim. 6:17;
1 Pet. 1:17

11:22
Rom. 2:4;
1 Cor. 15:2; Heb.
3:6,14;
John 15:2

11:23
2 Cor. 3:16

11:25
Rom. 1:13;
Matt. 13:11; Rom.
16:25; 1 Cor.
2:7-10; Eph.
3:3-5,9;
Rom. 12:16;
Rom. 11:7;
Luke 21:24; John
10:16; Rom.
11:12

hardening has happened⁺ to Israel until the fulness of the Gentiles has come˟ in;

11:26
Is. 59:20

11:27
Is. 59:21; Jer.
31:33,34; Heb.
8:10;
Is. 27:9; Heb.
8:12

11:28
Rom. 5:10;
Deut. 7:8; 10:15;
Rom. 9:5

11:29
Rom. 8:28; 1 Cor.
1:26; Eph. 1:18;
4:1,4; Phil. 3:14;
2 Thess. 1:11; 2
Tim. 1:9; Heb.
3:1; 2 Pet. 1:10;
Heb. 7:21

11:32
Rom. 3:9; Gal.
3:22f.

11:33
Rom. 2:4; Eph.
3:8;
Eph. 3:10; Col.
2:3;
Job 5:9; 11:7;
15:8

11:34
Is. 40:13f.; 1 Cor.
2:16

11:35
Job 35:7; 41:11

11:36
1 Cor. 8:6; 11:12;
Col. 1:16; Heb.
2:10;
Rom. 16:27; Eph.
3:21; Phil. 4:20;
1 Tim. 1:17;
2 Tim. 4:18;
1 Pet. 4:11; 5:11;
2 Pet. 3:18; Jude
25; Rev. 1:6;
5:13; 7:12

12:1
1 Cor. 1:10;
2 Cor. 10:1-4;
Eph. 4:1; 1 Pet.
2:11;
Rom. 6:13,16,19;
1 Cor. 6:20; Heb.
13:15; 1 Pet. 2:5

12:2
1 Pet. 1:14;
Matt. 13:22; Gal.
1:4; 1 John 2:15;
Eph. 4:23; Titus
3:5;
Eph. 5:10,17; Col.
1:9

12:3
Rom. 1:5; 15:15;
1 Cor. 3:10;
15:10; Gal. 2:9;
Eph. 3:7f.;
Rom. 11:20;
12:16;
1 Cor. 7:17;
2 Cor. 10:13;
Eph. 4:7; 1 Pet.
4:11

12:4
1 Cor. 12:12-14;
Eph. 4:4,16

12:5
1 Cor. 10:17,33;
1 Cor. 12:20,27;
Eph. 4:12,25

26 and thus all Israel will be saved; just as it is written,⁺
 "THE DELIVERER WILL COME FROM ZION,
   HE WILL REMOVE UNGODLINESS FROM JACOB."

27 "AND THIS IS MY COVENANT WITH THEM,
   WHEN I TAKE˟ AWAY THEIR SINS."

28 From the standpoint of the gospel they are enemies for your sake, but from the standpoint of *God's* choice they are beloved for the sake of the fathers;

29 for the gifts²⁴ᶜ and the calling of God are *irrevocable.*

30 For just as you once were disobedient to God, but now have been shown mercy because of *their* disobedience,

31 so these also now have been disobedient, in order that because of the mercy shown to •you *they also* may now be shown˟ mercy.

32 For God has *shut up* all in disobedience that He might show˟ *mercy* to all.

33 Oh, the depth of the riches both of the wisdom and knowledge of God! How †*unsearchable* are His judgments and †*unfathomable* His ways!

34 For WHO HAS KNOWN THE MIND³³ᵇ OF THE LORD, OR WHO BECAME HIS COUNSELOR?

35 Or WHO HAS FIRST GIVEN TO HIM THAT IT MIGHT BE PAID BACK TO HIM AGAIN?

36 For *from Him* and *through Him* and *to Him* are all things. To †*Him be* the glory forever. Amen.

Dedicated Service

12 I urge you therefore, brethren, by the mercies of God, to present˟ your bodies a †living and †holy²⁸ᵃ sacrifice, †acceptable to God, *which is* your spiritual service of worship.⁴⁴ᵃ

2 And do not be conformed⊖ to †*this* world, but be transformed~¹ by the renewing of your mind,³³ᵇ that you may prove~ what the will of God is, that which is †good²⁵ᵃ and †acceptable and †perfect.

3 For through the grace given to me I say to every man among you not to think~ more highly of himself than he ought to think;~ but to think~ so as to have~ sound judgment, as God has allotted to *each* a measure of faith.

4 For just as we have many members in one body and all the members do not have the same *function,*

5 so we, who are many, are *one* body in Christ, and individually members *one of another.*

6   And since we have gifts[24c] that *differ* according to the grace given to us, *let each exercise them accordingly:* if prophecy, according to the proportion of his faith;

7   if service, in his serving; or he who teaches, in his teaching;

8   or he who exhorts, in his exhortation; he who gives, with [n]liberality; he who leads, with diligence; he who shows mercy, with cheerfulness.

9   Let love[31a] be without hypocrisy. Abhor what is evil;[10b] cling to what is good.[25a]

10   Be devoted to one another in brotherly love; give preference to one another in honor;

11   not lagging behind in diligence, fervent in spirit, serving[38b] the Lord;

12   rejoicing in hope, persevering in tribulation, devoted to prayer,

13   contributing to the needs of the saints, practicing hospitality.

14   Bless[~I] those who persecute [o]you; bless[~I] and curse not.[o]

15   Rejoice[~] with those who rejoice, and weep[~] with those who weep.

16   Be of the same [t]mind[33c] toward one another; do not be haughty in mind,[33c] but associate with the lowly. Do not be[o] wise[35b] in your own estimation.

17   Never pay back evil[10a] for [t]evil to anyone. Respect what is right[25b] in the sight of all men.

18   If possible, so far as it depends on you, be at peace with all men.

19   Never take your own revenge, beloved, but leave[xI] room for the wrath[7b] *of God,* for it is written,[+] "VENGEANCE IS *MINE, I* WILL REPAY,"[37a] says the Lord.

20   "BUT IF YOUR ENEMY IS HUNGRY,[~] FEED[~I] HIM, AND IF HE IS THIRSTY,[~] GIVE[~I] HIM A DRINK; FOR IN SO DOING YOU WILL HEAP *BURNING COALS* UPON HIS HEAD."

21   Do not be overcome[o] by evil,[10a] but overcome[~I] evil *with good.*[25a]

Be Subject to Government

13   Let every person be in subjection[~I] to the governing authorities. For there is no authority except from God, and those which exist are established[+] by God.

2   Therefore he who resists authority has opposed[+] the ordinance of God; and they who have opposed[+] will receive condemnation upon themselves.

[n]Or, *simplicity*   [o]Some ancient mss. do not contain *you*

13:3
1 Pet. 2:14

13:4
1 Thess. 4:6
13:5
Eccl. 8; 1 Pet.
2:13,19
13:7
Matt. 22:21; Mark
12:17; Luke
20:25;
Luke 20:22; 23:2;
Matt. 17:25
13:8
Matt. 7:12;
22:39f.; John
13:34; Rom.
13:10; Gal. 5:14;
James 2:8
13:9
Ex. 20:13ff.; Deut.
5:17ff.;
Lev. 19:18; Matt.
19:19
13:10
Matt. 7:12;
22:39f.; John
13:34; Rom. 13:8;
Gal. 5:14; James
2:8
13:11
1 Cor. 7:29f.;
10:11; James 5:8;
1 Pet. 4:7; 2 Pet.
3:9,11; 1 John
2:18; Rev. 1:3;
22:10;
Mark 13:37;
1 Cor. 15:34;
Eph. 5:14;
1 Thess. 5:6
13:12
1 Cor. 7:29f.;
10:11; James 5:8;
1 Pet. 4:7; 2 Pet.
3:9,11; 1 John
2:18; Rev. 1:3;
22:10;
Heb. 10:25;
1 John 2:8; Rev.
1:3; 22:10;
Eph. 5:11;
2 Cor. 6:7; 10:4;
Eph. 6:11,13;
1 Thess. 5:8
13:13
1 Thess. 4:12;
Luke 21:34; Gal.
5:21; Eph. 5:18; 1
Pet. 4:3
13:14
Job 29:14; Gal.
3:27; Eph. 4:24;
Col. 3:10,12;
Gal. 5:16; 1 Pet.
2:11
14:1
Acts 28:2; Rom.
11:15; 14:3; 15:7;
Rom. 14:2; 15:1;
1 Cor. 8:9ff.; 9:22
14:2
Rom. 14:14;
Rom. 14:1; 15:1;
1 Cor. 8:9ff.; 9:22
14:3
Luke 18:9; Rom.
14:10;
Rom. 14:10,13;
Col. 2:16;
Acts 28:2; Rom.
11:15; 14:1; 15:7
14:4
Rom. 9:20;
James 4:12

3   For rulers are not a cause of fear for good behavior, but for evil. Do you want to have~ no fear of authority? Do ᴹ what is *good,* and you will have praise from the same;

4   for it is a minister of *God* to you for good. But if you do ~ what is *evil,* be afraid; ᴹ for it does not bear the *sword for nothing;* for it is a minister of *God,* an avenger who brings wrath ⁷ᵇ upon the one who practices ¹⁹ᵇ evil.

5   Wherefore it is necessary to be in subjection,~ not only because of wrath, but also for conscience' sake.

6   For because of this you also pay taxes, for *rulers* are servants of God, devoting themselves to this very thing.

7   Render ˣᴵ to all what is due them: tax to whom tax *is due;* custom to whom custom; fear to whom fear; honor to whom honor.

8   Owe ᴹ nothing⁴ to anyone except to love ~ one another; for he who loves his neighbor has fulfilled⁺ *the* law.

9   For this, "You shall not commit adultery, You shall not murder, You shall not steal, You shall not covet," and if there is any other commandment, it is summed up in ⁺*this* saying, "You shall love ³¹ᵃ your neighbor as yourself."

10   Love ³¹ᵃ does no *wrong* to a neighbor; love therefore is the *fulfillment* of *the* law.

11   And this *do,* knowing the time, that it is already the hour for you to awaken˟ from sleep; for now ᴾsalvation is *nearer* to us than when we believed.

12   The night is almost gone, and the day is at hand.⁺ Let us therefore lay ˣ aside the deeds of darkness and put ˣ on the armor of light.

13   Let us behave ˣ properly as in the day, not in carousing and drunkenness, not in sexual promiscuity and sensuality, not in strife and jealousy.

14   But put ˣᴵ on the Lord Jesus Christ, and make ⁰ no provision for the *flesh* in regard to *its* lusts.

Principles of Conscience

14   Now accept ᴹ the one who is *weak in faith, but* not for *the purpose of* passing judgment on his opinions.

2   One man has faith that he may eat˟ all things, but he who is weak eats vegetables *only.*

3   Let not him who eats regard⁰ with contempt him who does not eat, and let not him who does not eat judge⁰ him who eats, for God has accepted him.

4   Who are *you* to judge the servant of *another?* To his *own*

ᴾOr, *our salvation is nearer than when*

master he stands or falls; and stand he will, for the *Lord* is able to make him stand. [x]

5   One man regards one day above another, another regards every day *alike*. Let each man be *fully convinced* [~] in his •own mind. [33b]

14:5
Gal. 4:10;
Luke 1:1; Rom.
4:21; 14:23

6   He who observes the day, observes it for the Lord, and he who eats, does so for the Lord, for he gives thanks to God; and he who eats not, for the Lord he does not eat, and gives thanks to God.

14:6
Matt. 14:19;
15:36; 1 Cor.
10:30; 1 Tim.
4:3f.

7   For not one of us lives *for himself,* and not one dies *for himself;*

14:7
Rom. 8:38f.;
2 Cor. 5:15; Gal.
2:20; Phil. 1:20f.

8   for if we live, [~] we live *for the Lord,* or if we die, [~] we die *for the Lord;* therefore whether we live [~] or die, [~] we are the *Lord's.*

14:8
Luke 20:38; Phil.
1:20; 1 Thess.
5:10; Rev. 14:13

9   For to this end Christ died and lived *again,* that He might be [x] Lord both of the dead and of the living.

14:9
Rev. 1:18; 2:8;
Matt. 28:18; John
12:24; Phil. 2:11;
1 Thess. 5:10

10   But you, why do *you* judge your brother? Or you again, why do *you* regard your brother with contempt? For we shall all stand before the judgment seat of God.

14:10
Luke 18:9; Rom.
14:3;
Rom. 2:16; 2 Cor.
5:10

11   For it is written, [+]

14:11
Is. 45:23;
Phil. 2:10f.

"As I live, says the Lord, every knee shall bow to Me,

And every tongue shall give praise to God."

12   So then each one of us shall give account of *himself* to God.

14:12
Matt. 12:36;
16:27; 1 Pet. 4:5

13   Therefore let us not judge [~] *one another* anymore, but rather determine [x] this—not to put [~] an obstacle or a stumbling block in a brother's way.

14:13
Matt. 7:1; Rom.
14:3;
1 Cor. 8:13

14   I know and am convinced [+] in the Lord Jesus that nothing is unclean [41b] in itself; but to him who thinks anything to be unclean, to him it is unclean.

14:14
Acts 10:15; Rom.
14:2,20;
1 Cor. 8:7

15   For if because of *food* your brother is hurt, you are no longer walking [42a] according to *love.* Do not destroy [⊙] with your *food* him for whom Christ died.

14:15
Eph. 5:2;
Rom. 14:20;
1 Cor. 8:11

16   Therefore do not let what is for you a *good* [25a] thing be spoken [⊙] of as evil;

14:16
1 Cor. 10:30;
Titus 2:5

17   for the kingdom of God is not eating and drinking, but righteousness and peace and joy in the Holy Spirit.

14:17
1 Cor. 8:8;
Rom. 15:13; Gal.
5:22

18   For he who in this *way* serves [38b] Christ is acceptable to God and approved by men.

14:18
Rom. 16:18;
2 Cor. 8:21; Phil.
4:8; 1 Pet. 2:12

19   So then [q] let us pursue [~] the things which make for peace and the building [†] up of one another.

14:19
Ps. 34:14; Rom.
12:18; 1 Cor.
7:15; 2 Tim. 2:22;
Heb. 12:14;
Rom. 15:2; 1 Cor.
10:23; 14:3f.,26;
2 Cor. 12:19;
Eph. 4:12,29

20   Do not tear [⊙] down the work of God for the *sake of food.* All

14:20
Rom. 14:15;
Acts 10:15; Rom.
14:2,14;
1 Cor. 8:9-12

[q] Many ancient mss. read *we pursue*

things indeed are clean, [13c] but they are evil for the man who eats and gives offense.

14:21
1 Cor. 8:13

21 It is good[25b] not to eat[x] meat or to drink[x] wine, or *to do anything* by which your brother stumbles.

14:22
1 John 3:21

22 The faith which *you* have, have[~I] as your own conviction before God. Happy is he who does not condemn himself in what he approves.

14:23
Rom. 14:5

23 But he who doubts is condemned[+] if he eats,[x] because *his eating is* not from faith; and whatever is not from faith is *sin*.

Self-denial on Behalf of Others

15:1
Rom. 14:1; Gal.
6:2; 1 Thess. 5:14

15 Now *we* who are *strong* ought to bear[~] the weaknesses of those without strength and not *just* please[~] *ourselves*.

15:2
1 Cor. 9:22;
10:24,33; 2 Cor.
13:9;
Rom. 14:19;
1 Cor. 10:23;
14:3f.,26; 2 Cor.
12:19; Eph. 4:12,
29

2 Let each of us please[~I] his *neighbor* for his good, to his edification.

15:3
2 Cor. 8:9;
Ps. 69:9

3 For even *Christ* did not please *Himself;* but as it is written,[+] "THE REPROACHES OF THOSE WHO REPROACHED THEE FELL UPON ME."

15:4
Rom. 4:23f.;
2 Tim. 3:16

4 For whatever was written in earlier times was written for •*our* instruction, that through perseverance and the encouragement of the Scriptures we might have[~] *hope.*

15:5
2 Cor. 1:3;
Rom. 12:16

5 Now may the God who gives perseverance and encouragement grant[x] you to be[~] of the *same* [+]*mind* [33c] with one another according to Christ Jesus;

15:6
Rev. 1:6

6 that with *one accord* you may with *one voice* glorify[~] the God and Father of our Lord Jesus Christ.

15:7
Rom. 14:1

7 Wherefore, accept[~I] one another, just as Christ also accepted us to the glory of God.

15:8
Matt. 15:24; Acts
3:26;
Rom. 4:16; 2 Cor.
1:20

8 For I say that Christ has become[+] a servant to the circumcision on behalf of the truth of God to confirm[x] the promises *given* to the fathers,

15:9
Rom. 3:29;
11:30f.;
Matt. 9:8;
2 Sam. 22:50; Ps.
18:49

9 and for the [+]Gentiles to glorify[x] God for His *mercy;* as it is written,[+]

"THEREFORE I WILL GIVE PRAISE TO THEE AMONG THE
GENTILES,
AND I WILL SING TO THY NAME."

15:10
Deut. 32:43

10 And again he says,
"REJOICE,[xI] O GENTILES, WITH HIS PEOPLE."

15:11
Ps. 117:1

11 And again,
"PRAISE[~I] THE LORD ALL YOU GENTILES,
AND LET ALL THE PEOPLES PRAISE[xI] HIM."

15:12
Is. 11:10;
Rev. 5:5; 22:16;
Matt. 12:21

12 And again Isaiah says,
"THERE SHALL COME THE ROOT OF JESSE,
AND HE WHO ARISES TO RULE[~] OVER THE GENTILES,

IN *HIM* SHALL THE GENTILES HOPE."

13   Now may the God of hope fill[x] you with all joy and peace in believing,[~] that you may abound[~] in hope by the power[32a] of the Holy Spirit.

14   And concerning you, my brethren, *I myself* also am convinced[+] that *you yourselves* are full of goodness, filled[+] with all knowledge, and able also to admonish[~] one another.

15   But I have written very boldly to you on some points, so as to remind you again, because of the grace that was given me from God,

16   to be a minister of Christ Jesus to the Gentiles, ministering as a priest the gospel of God, that *my* offering of the Gentiles might become acceptable, sanctified[+] by the Holy Spirit.

17   Therefore in Christ Jesus I have found reason for boasting in things pertaining to God.

18   For I will not presume to speak[~] of anything except what *Christ* has accomplished through me, resulting in the obedience of the Gentiles by word and deed,

19   in the power of signs and wonders, in the power of the Spirit; so that from Jerusalem and round about as far as Illyricum I have fully preached[+] the gospel of Christ.

20   And thus I aspired to preach[~] the gospel, not where Christ was *already named,* that I might not build[~] upon *another man's* foundation;

21   but as it is written,[+]

"THEY WHO HAD NO NEWS OF HIM SHALL SEE,
AND THEY WHO HAVE NOT HEARD[+] SHALL
    UNDERSTAND."[29f]

22   For this reason I have often been hindered[m] from coming to you;

23   but •now, with no further place for me in ⁺these regions, and since I have had for many years a longing to come to you

24   whenever I go[~] to Spain—for I hope to see[x] you in passing, and to be helped[x] on my way there by you, when I have first enjoyed[x] your company for a while—

25   but •now, I am going to Jerusalem serving[38a] the saints.

26   For Macedonia and Achaia have been pleased to make[x] a contribution for the poor among the saints in Jerusalem.

27   Yes, they were pleased *to do so,* and they are indebted to them. For if the Gentiles have shared in their *spiritual things,* they are indebted to minister[x] to them also in *material things.*

28   Therefore, when I have finished this, and have put my seal on this fruit of theirs, I will go on by way of you to Spain.

15:13
Rom. 14:17;
Rom. 15:19;
1 Cor. 2:4;
1 Thess. 1:5

15:14
Eph. 5:9;
2 Thess. 1:11;
1 Cor. 1:5; 8:1,7,
10; 12:8; 13:2

15:15
Rom. 12:3

15:16
Acts 9:15; Rom.
11:13;
Rom. 1:1; 15:19,
20;
Rom. 12:1; Eph.
5:2; Phil. 2:17
15:17
Phil. 3:3;
Heb. 2:17; 5:1
15:18
Acts 15:12;
21:19; Rom. 1:5;
2 Cor. 3:5

15:19
John 4:48;
Rom. 15:13;
1 Cor. 2:4; 1
Thess. 1:5;
Acts 22:17-21;
Acts 20:1f.
15:20
Rom. 1:15; 10:15;
15:16;
1 Cor. 3:10;
2 Cor. 10:15f.
15:21
Is. 52:15

15:22
Rom. 1:13;
1 Thess. 2:18

15:23
Acts 19:21; Rom.
1:10f.; 15:29,32

15:24
Rom. 15:28;
Acts 15:3;
Rom. 1:12

15:25
Acts 19:21;
Acts 24:17
15:26
Acts 16:9; 1 Cor.
16:5; 2 Cor. 1:16;
2:13; 7:5; 8:1;
9:2,4; 11:9; Phil.
4:15; 1 Thess.
1:7f.; 4:10; 1 Tim.
1:3;
Acts 18:12; 19:21
15:27
1 Cor. 9:11
15:28
John 3:33;
Rom. 15:24

15:29
Acts 19:21; Rom.
1:10f.; 15:23,32

15:30
Gal. 5:22; Col.
1:8;
2 Cor. 1:11; Col.
4:12

15:31
2 Cor. 1:10;
2 Thess. 3:2;
2 Tim. 3:11; 4:17;
Rom. 15:25f.;
2 Cor. 8:4; 9:1;
Acts 9:13,15
15:32
Rom. 15:23;
Acts 18:21; Rom.
1:10
15:33
Rom. 16:20;
2 Cor. 13:11; Phil.
4:9; 1 Thess.
5:23; 2 Thess.
3:16; Heb. 13:20
16:1
2 Cor. 3:1;
Acts 18:18
16:2
Phil. 2:29;
Acts 9:13,15

16:3
Acts 18:2;
Rom. 8:11ff.;
16:7,9,10; 2 Cor.
5:17; 12:2; Gal.
1:22;
Rom. 8:1
16:5
1 Cor. 16:19; Col.
4:15; Philem. 2;
1 Cor. 16:15;
Acts 16:6
16:7
Rom. 9:3; 16:11,
21;
Col. 4:10; Philem.
23;
Rom. 8:11ff.;
16:3,9,10; 2 Cor.
5:17; 12:2; Gal.
1:22
16:9
Rom. 8:11ff.;
16:3,7,10; 2 Cor.
5:17; 12:2; Gal.
1:22
16:10
Rom. 8:11ff.;
16:3,7,9; 2 Cor.
5:17; 12:2; Gal.
1:22
16:11
Rom. 9:3; 16:7,21

16:13
Mark 15:21

16:15
Rom. 16:2,14

29   And I know that when I come to you, I will come in the *fulness* of the *blessing of Christ.*

30   Now I urge you, brethren, by our Lord Jesus Christ and by the love of the Spirit, to strive[x] together with me in your prayers to God for me,

31   that I may be delivered[x18b] from those who are disobedient in Judea, and *that* my service for Jerusalem may prove[x] acceptable to the saints;

32   so that I may come to you in joy by the will of God and find[x] *refreshing* rest in your company.

33   Now the God of peace be with you all. Amen.

Greetings and Love Expressed

16   I commend to you our sister Phoebe, who is a servant of the church which is at Cenchrea;

2   that you receive[x] her in the Lord in a manner worthy of the saints, and that you help[x] her in whatever matter she may have need~ of you; for she herself has also been a helper of many, and of myself as well.

3   Greet[xi] Prisca and Aquila, my fellow workers in Christ Jesus,

4   who for my life risked *their own necks,* to whom not *only* do *I* give thanks, but also all the churches of the Gentiles;

5   also *greet* the church that is in their house. Greet[xi] Epaenetus, my beloved, who is the first convert to Christ from Asia.

6   Greet[xi] Mary, who has worked hard for you.

7   Greet[xi] Andronicus and Junias, my kinsmen, and my fellow prisoners, who are outstanding among the apostles, who also were⁺ in Christ *before me.*

8   Greet[xi] Ampliatus, my beloved in the Lord.

9   Greet[xi] Urbanus, our fellow worker in Christ, and Stachys my beloved.

10   Greet[xi] Apelles, the approved in Christ. Greet[xi] those who are of the *household* of Aristobulus.

11   Greet[xi] Herodion, my kinsman. Greet[xi] those of the *household* of Narcissus, who are in the Lord.

12   Greet[xi] Tryphaena and Tryphosa, workers in the Lord. Greet Persis the beloved, who has worked hard in the Lord.

13   Greet[xi] Rufus, a choice man in the Lord, also his mother and mine.

14   Greet[xi] Asyncritus, Phlegon, Hermes, Patrobas, Hermas and the brethren with them.

15   Greet[xi] Philologus and Julia, Nereus and his sister, and Olympas, and all the saints who are with them.

16   Greet[xl] one another with a holy[28a] kiss. All the churches of Christ greet you.

17   Now I urge you, brethren, keep[~] your eye on those who cause dissensions and hindrances contrary to the teaching which *you* learned, and turn[~l] away from them.

18   For such men are slaves, not of *our Lord Christ* but of their *own* [t]*appetites;* and by their smooth and flattering speech they deceive[16a] the hearts of the unsuspecting.

19   For the report of your obedience has reached to *all;* therefore I am rejoicing over you, but I want you to be *wise* in what is good,[25a] and [t]*innocent* in what is evil.[10a]

20   And the God of peace will [t]*soon* crush Satan under your feet.

The grace of our Lord Jesus be with you.

21   Timothy my fellow worker greets you, and *so do* Lucius and Jason and Sosipater, my kinsmen.

22   *I, Tertius,* who write this letter, greet you in the Lord.

23   Gaius, host to me and to the whole church, greets you. Erastus, the city treasurer greets you, and Quartus, the brother.

24   [[r]The grace of our Lord Jesus Christ be with you all. Amen.]

25   Now to Him who is able to establish[x] you according to my gospel and the preaching of Jesus Christ, according to the revelation of the mystery which has been kept[t] secret for long ages [t]past,

26   but *now* is manifested, and by the Scriptures of the prophets, according to the commandment of the eternal God, has been made known to *all the nations, leading* to obedience of faith;

27   to the only wise God, through Jesus Christ, be the glory forever. Amen.

[r]Many mss. do not contain this verse

16:16
1 Cor. 16:20;
2 Cor. 13:12; 1
Thess. 5:26; 1
Pet. 5:14
16:17
1 Tim. 1:3; 6:3;
Matt. 7:15; Gal.
1:8f.; 2 Thess.
3:6,14; Titus 3:10;
2 John 10
16:18
Rom. 14:18;
Phil. 3:19;
Col. 2:4; 2 Pet.
2:3
16:19
Rom. 1:8;
Jer. 4:22; Matt.
10:16; 1 Cor.
14:20
16:20
Rom. 15:33;
Matt. 4:10;
1 Cor. 16:23;
2 Cor. 13:14; Gal.
6:18; Phil. 4:23;
1 Thess. 5:28;
2 Thess. 3:18;
Rev. 22:21
16:21
Acts 16:1;
Acts 13:1 [?];
Acts 17:5 [?];
Acts 20:4 [?];
Rom. 9:3; 16:7,11
16:22
1 Cor. 16:21; Gal.
6:11; Col. 4:18;
2 Thess. 3:17;
Philem. 19
16:23
Acts 19:29; 20:4
[?]; 1 Cor. 1:14;
Acts 19:22;
2 Tim. 4:20
16:25
Eph. 3:20; Jude
24;
Rom. 2:16;
Matt. 13:35; Rom.
11:25; 1 Cor. 2:1,
7; 4:1; Eph. 1:9;
3:3,9; 6:19; Col.
1:26f.; 2:2; 4:3;
1 Tim. 3:16;
2 Tim. 1:9; Titus
1:2
16:26
Rom. 1:2;
Rom. 1:5
16:27
Rom. 11:36

The First Epistle of Paul to the
Corinthians

Appeal to Unity

1:1
Rom. 1:1;
Rom. 1:10; 2 Tim.
1:1;
Acts 18:17;
Acts 1:15
1:2
1 Cor. 10:32;
Acts 18:1;
Rom. 1:7; 8:28;
Acts 7:59

1 Paul, called *as* an apostle of Jesus Christ by the will of God, and Sosthenes our brother,

2 to the church of God which is at Corinth, to those who have been sanctified⁺ in Christ Jesus, saints by calling, with all who in every place call upon the name of our Lord Jesus Christ, their *Lord* and ours:

1:3
Rom. 1:7

3 Grace to you and peace from God our Father and the Lord Jesus Christ.

1:4
Rom. 1:8

4 I thank ᵃmy God always concerning you, for the grace of God which was given you in Christ Jesus,

1:5
2 Cor. 9:11;
Rom. 15:14;
2 Cor. 8:7

5 that in everything you were enriched in Him, in all speech and all knowledge,

1:6
2 Thess. 1:10;
1 Tim. 2:6; 2 Tim.
1:8; Rev. 1:2

6 even as the testimony concerning Christ was confirmed in you,

1:7
Luke 17:30; Rom.
8:19,23; Phil.
3:20; 2 Pet. 3:12

7 so that you are not lacking~ in any gift,²⁴ᶜ awaiting eagerly¹ the revelation of our Lord Jesus Christ,

1:8
Rom. 8:19; Phil.
1:6; Col. 2:7;
1 Thess. 3:13;
5:23;

8 who shall also confirm you to the end, blameless¹¹ᶜ in the day of our Lord Jesus Christ.

Luke 17:24,30; 1
Cor. 5:5; 2 Cor.
1:14; Phil. 1:6,10;
2:16; 1 Thess.
5:2; 2 Thess. 2:2

9 God is faithful, through whom you were called into fellowship with His Son, Jesus Christ our Lord.

1:9
Deut. 7:9; Is.
49:7; 1 Cor.
10:13; 2 Cor.
1:18; 1 Thess.
5:24; 2 Thess.
3:3;
Rom. 8:28;
1 John 1:3

10 Now I exhort you, brethren, by the name of our Lord Jesus Christ, that you all *agree*,~ and there be no *divisions* among you, but you be made complete⁺ in the same mind³³ᵇ and in the same judgment.

1:10
Rom. 12:1;
Rom. 1:13;
1 Cor. 11:18;
Rom. 12:16; Phil.
1:27

11 For I have been informed concerning you, my brethren, by Chloe's *people,* that there are quarrels among you.

1:12
Matt. 23:8-10; 1
Cor. 3:4;
Acts 18:24; 1 Cor.
3:22;
John 1:42; 1 Cor.
3:22; 9:5; 15:5

12 Now I mean this, that each one of you is saying, "I am of Paul," and "I of Apollos," and "I of Cephas," and "I of Christ."

13 Has Christ been ⁺*divided?*⁺ Paul was not crucified for you, was he? Or were you baptized in the name of *Paul?*

1:13
Matt. 28:19; Acts
2:38

14 ᵇI thank God that I baptized none of you except Crispus and Gaius,

1:14
Acts 18:8;
Rom. 16:23

15 that no man should sayˣ you were baptized in *my* name.

1:16
1 Cor. 16:15,17

16 Now I did baptize also the household of *Stephanas;* beyond that, I do not know whether I baptized any other.

ᵃSome ancient mss. do not contain *my* ᵇSome ancient mss. read *I give thanks that*

17   For Christ did not send me to baptize,~ but to preach~ the †gospel, not in cleverness of speech, that the cross of Christ should not be made void.ˣ

The Wisdom of God

18   For the word⁴³ᵃ of the cross is to those who are perishing *foolishness,* but to us who are being saved it is the *power*³²ᵃ *of God.*

19   For it is written,⁺

"I WILL DESTROY THE WISDOM OF THE WISE,³⁵ᵃ
AND THE CLEVERNESS OF THE CLEVER I WILL SET
ASIDE."

20   Where is the wise³⁵ᵃ man? Where is the scribe? Where is the debater of this age? Has not God made *foolish*²⁰ᶜ the wisdom of the world?

21   For since in the wisdom of God the world through *its wisdom* did not *come to* know²⁹ᵃ God, God was well-pleased through the foolishness of the message preached to saveˣ those who believe.

22   For indeed Jews ask for *signs,* and Greeks search for *wisdom;*

23   but *we* preach ᶜChrist †*crucified,*⁺ to Jews a stumbling block, and to Gentiles foolishness,

24   but to those who are the called, both Jews and Greeks, Christ the power of *God* and the wisdom of *God.*

25   Because the foolishness of God is wiser than men, and the weakness of God is stronger than men.

26   For consider~ˡ your calling, brethren, that there were not many wise according to the flesh, not many mighty, not many noble;

27   but God has chosen the *foolish*²⁰ᶜ *things* of the world to shame~³⁹ᶜ the wise, and God has chosen the *weak things* of the world to shame~ the things which are strong,

28   and the *base things* of the world and the *despised,*⁺ God has chosen, the things that are not, that He might nullifyˣ the things that are,

29   that *no man* should boastˣ before God.

30   But by *His doing* you are in Christ Jesus, who became to us wisdom from God, and righteousness and sanctification, and redemption,

31   that, just as it is written,⁺ "LET HIM WHO BOASTS, BOAST~ˡ IN THE LORD."

ᶜI.e., Messiah

1:17
John 4:2; Acts 10:48;
1 Cor. 2:1,4,13;
2 Cor. 10:10; 11:6

1:18
Acts 2:47; 2 Cor. 2:15; 4:3;
2 Thess. 2:10;
1 Cor. 1:21,23,25;
2:14; 4:10;
Rom. 1:16; 1 Cor. 1:24
1:19
Is. 29:14
1:20
Job 12:17; Is. 19:11f.; 33:18;
Matt. 13:22;
1 Cor. 2:6,8; 3:18, 19;
Rom. 1:20ff.;
John 12:31;
1 Cor. 1:27f.; 6:2;
11:32; James 4:4
1:21
John 12:31;
1 Cor. 1:27f.; 6:2;
11:32; James 4:4;
Luke 12:32; Gal. 1:15; Col. 1:19;
1 Cor. 1:18,23,25;
2:14; 4:10;
Rom. 11:14;
James 5:20
1:22
Matt. 12:38
1:23
1 Cor. 2:2; Gal. 3:1; 5:11;
Luke 2:34; 1 Pet. 2:8;
1 Cor. 1:18,21,25;
2:14; 4:10
1:24
Rom. 8:28;
Rom. 1:16; 1 Cor. 1:18;
Luke 11:49;
1 Cor. 1:30
1:25
1 Cor. 1:18,21,23;
2:14; 4:10;
2 Cor. 13:4
1:26
Rom. 11:29;
Matt. 11:25;
1 Cor. 1:20; 2:8
1:27
James 2:5;
1 Cor. 1:20
1:28
1 Cor. 1:20;
Rom. 4:17;
Job 34:19; 1 Cor. 2:6; 2 Thess. 2:8;
Heb. 2:14
1:29
Eph. 2:9
1:30
Rom. 8:1; 1 Cor. 4:15;
1 Cor. 1:24;
Jer. 23:5f.; 33:16;
2 Cor. 5:21; Phil. 3:9;
1 Cor. 1:2; 6:11;
1 Thess. 5:23;
Rom. 3:24; Eph. 1:7,14; Col. 1:14
1:31
Jer. 9:23f.; 2 Cor. 10:17

Paul's Reliance upon the Spirit

2 And when I came to you, brethren, I did not come with superiority of speech or of wisdom, proclaiming to you the ᵈtestimony of God.

2 For I determined to know nothing among you except Jesus Christ, and Him crucified.⁺

3 And *I* was with you in weakness and in fear and in *much* trembling.

4 And my message and my preaching were not in persuasive *words* of wisdom, but in †*demonstration* of the Spirit and of power,

5 that your faith should not rest on the wisdom of men, but on the power of God.

6 Yet we do speak wisdom among those who are mature; a wisdom, however, not of †*this* age, nor of the rulers of this age, who are passing away;

7 but we speak *God's* wisdom in a mystery, the hidden⁺ *wisdom*, which *God* predestined before the ages to our glory;

8 *the wisdom* which none of the rulers of this age has understood;⁺²⁹ᵃ for if they had understood it, they would not have crucified the *Lord of glory;*

9 but just as it is written,⁺

"THINGS WHICH EYE HAS NOT SEEN AND EAR HAS NOT HEARD,
AND *which* HAVE NOT ENTERED THE HEART OF MAN,
ALL THAT GOD HAS PREPARED FOR THOSE WHO LOVE³¹ᵃ HIM."

10 ᵉFor to us God *revealed them* through the Spirit; for the Spirit searches *all things,* even the depths of God.

11 For who among men knows²⁹ᵉ the *thoughts* of a man except the spirit of the man, which is in him? Even so the *thoughts* of *God* no one knows⁺²⁹ᵃ except the Spirit of God.

12 Now *we* have received,⁵ᵇ not the spirit of the *world,* but the Spirit who is from †*God,* that we might know²⁹ᵉ the things freely given to us by God,

13 which things we also speak, not in words taught by *human wisdom,* but in those taught by the †*Spirit,* combining spiritual *thoughts* with spiritual *words.*

14 But a natural man does not accept⁵ᵃ the things of the Spirit of God; for they are foolishness to him, and he cannot understand˟²⁹ᵃ them, because they are spiritually appraised.

ᵈSome ancient mss. read *mystery* ᵉSome ancient mss. use *But*

2:1 1 Cor. 1:17; 2:4, 13; 1 Cor. 2:7
2:2 1 Cor. 1:23; Gal. 6:14
2:3 1 Cor. 4:10; 2 Cor. 11:30; 12:5,9f.; 13:9; Is. 19:16; 2 Cor. 7:15; Eph. 6:5
2:4 1 Cor. 1:17; 2:1, 13; Rom. 15:19; 1 Cor. 4:20
2:5 2 Cor. 4:7; 6:7; 12:9
2:6 Eph. 4:13; Phil. 3:15; Heb. 5:14; 6:1; Matt. 13:22; 1 Cor. 1:20; 1 Cor. 1:28
2:7 Rom. 11:25; 16:25f.; 1 Cor. 2:1; Rom. 8:29f.; Heb. 1:2; 11:3
2:8 1 Cor. 1:26; 2:6; Matt. 13:22; 1 Cor. 1:20; Acts 7:2; James 2:1
2:9 Is. 64:4; 65:17
2:10 Matt. 11:25; 13:11; 16:17; Gal. 1:12; Eph. 3:3,5; John 14:26; Rom. 11:33ff.
2:11 Prov. 20:27
2:12 Rom. 8:15; 1 Cor. 1:27
2:13 1 Cor. 1:17; 2:1,4
2:14 1 Cor. 15:44,46; James 3:15; Jude 19 mg.; John 14:17; 1 Cor. 1:18

15   But he who is spiritual appraises all things, yet *he himself* is appraised by no man.

16   For WHO HAS KNOWN[29a] THE MIND[33b] OF THE LORD, THAT HE SHOULD INSTRUCT HIM? But *we* have the *mind*[33b] *of Christ*.

Foundations for Living

3   And I, brethren, could not speak[x] to you as to spiritual men, but as to men of flesh, as to babes in Christ.

2   I gave you *milk* to drink, not solid food; for you were not yet able[m] *to receive it*. Indeed, even now you are not yet able,

3   for you are still *fleshly*. For since there is jealousy and strife among you, are you not fleshly, and are you not walking like *mere men*?

4   For when one says, ~ "I am of Paul," and another, "I am of Apollos," are you not *mere* [†]men?

5   What then is Apollos? And what is Paul? Servants through whom you believed, even as the Lord gave *opportunity* to *each one*.

6   I planted, Apollos watered, but God was causing[m] the growth.

7   So then neither the one who plants nor the one who waters is anything, but *God* who causes the growth.

8   Now he who plants and he who waters are *one;* but each will receive his *own* reward according to his *own* [†]labor.

9   For we are *God's* fellow workers; you are *God's* field, *God's* building.

10   According to the grace of God which was given to me, as a wise master builder I laid a foundation, and another is building upon it. But let each man be careful[m] how he builds upon it.

11   For no man can lay[x] a foundation other than the one which is laid, which is Jesus Christ.

12   Now if any man builds upon the foundation with gold, silver, precious stones, wood, hay, straw,

13   *each man's* work will become evident; for the day will show it, because it is *to be* revealed with *fire;* and the fire itself will test the quality of *each man's* work.

14   If any man's work which he has built upon it remains, he shall receive a *reward*.

15   If any man's work is burned up, he shall suffer loss; but *he himself* shall be saved, yet so as through fire.

16   Do you not know that you are a *temple of* [†]*God*, and *that* the Spirit of God dwells *in you?*

17   If any man *destroys* the temple of God, *God* will destroy him, for the temple of God is *holy*,[28a] and that is what *you* are.

2:15
1 Cor. 3:1; 14:37; Gal. 6:1

2:16
Is. 40:13; Rom. 11:34; John 15:15

3:1
1 Cor. 2:15; 14:37; Gal. 6:1; Rom. 7:14; 1 Cor. 2:14;
3:2
Heb. 5:12f.; 1 Pet. 2:2; John 16:12
3:3
Rom. 13:13; 1 Cor. 1:10f.; 11:18; 1 Cor. 3:4
3:4
1 Cor. 1:12; 1 Cor. 3:3
3:5
Rom. 15:16; 2 Cor. 3:3,6; 4:1; 5:18; 6:4; Eph. 3:7; Col. 1:25; 1 Tim. 1:12; Rom. 12:6; 1 Cor. 3:10
3:6
1 Cor. 4:15; 9:1; 15:1; 2 Cor. 10:14f.; Acts 18:24-27; 1 Cor. 1:12; 1 Cor. 15:10
3:8
1 Cor. 3:14; 4:5; 9:17; Gal. 6:4
3:9
Mark 16:20; 2 Cor. 6:1; Is. 61:3; Matt. 15:13; 1 Cor. 3:16; Eph. 2:20-22; Col. 2:7; 1 Pet. 2:5
3:10
Rom. 12:3; 1 Cor. 15:10; Rom. 15:20; 1 Cor. 3:11f.; 1 Thess. 3:2
3:11
Is. 28:16; Eph. 2:20; 1 Pet. 2:4ff.
3:13
1 Cor. 4:5; Matt. 10:15; 1 Cor. 1:8; 2 Thess. 1:7-10; 2 Tim. 1:12,18; 4:8
3:14
1 Cor. 3:8; 4:5; 9:17; Gal. 6:4
3:15
Job 23:10; Ps. 66:10,12; Jude 23
3:16
Rom. 6:16; Rom. 8:9; 1 Cor. 6:19; 2 Cor. 6:16; Eph. 2:21f.

3:18
Is. 5:21;
1 Cor. 8:2; Gal.
6:3;
1 Cor. 1:20

18 Let no man deceive~¹¹⁶ᵃ †himself. If any man among you thinks that he is wise in this age, let him become*ˡ *foolish* that he may become wise.

3:19
1 Cor. 1:20;
Job 5:13

19 For the wisdom of this world is *foolishness* before God. For it is written,⁺ *"He is* THE ONE WHO CATCHES THE WISE IN THEIR CRAFTINESS";

3:20
Ps. 94:11

20 and again, "THE LORD KNOWS THE REASONINGS of the wise, THAT THEY ARE USELESS."

3:21
1 Cor. 4:6;
Rom. 8:32

21 So then let no one boast~ˡ in men. For all things belong to you,

3:22
1 Cor. 1:12; 3:5,6;
Rom. 8:38

22 whether Paul or Apollos or Cephas or the world or life or death or things present or things to come; all things belong to you,

3:23
1 Cor. 15:23;
2 Cor. 10:7; Gal.
3:29;
1 Cor. 11:3; 15:28

23 and you belong to Christ; and Christ belongs to God.

Servants of Christ

4:1
Luke 1:2;
1 Cor. 9:17; Titus
1:7; 1 Pet. 4:10;
Rom. 11:25;
16:25

4 Let a man regard~ *us* in this manner, as servants of Christ, and stewards of the mysteries of God.

2 In this case, moreover, it is required of stewards that one be foundˣ trustworthy.

3 But to me it is a *very*³ *small thing* that I should be examinedˣ by you, or by *any* human court; in fact, I do not even examine *myself.*

4:4
Acts 23:1; 2 Cor.
1:12;
Ps. 143:2; Rom.
2:13
4:5
Matt. 7:1; Rom.
2:1;
John 21:22; Rom.
2:16;
1 Cor. 3:13;
Rom. 2:29; 1 Cor.
3:8; 2 Cor. 10:18

4 For I am conscious⁺ of nothing against myself, yet I am not *by this* acquitted;⁺ but the one who examines me is the *Lord.*

5 Therefore do not go on passing judgment⁰ *before* †the *time, but wait* until the Lord comes who will both bring to light the things hidden in the darkness and disclose the motives of *men's* hearts; and then each man's praise will come to him from God.

4:6
1 Cor. 1:19,31;
3:19f.;
1 Cor. 4:18f.; 8:1;
13:4;
1 Cor. 1:12; 3:4

6 Now these things, brethren, I have figuratively applied to myself and Apollos for your sakes, that in us you might learnˣ not to exceed what is written,⁺ in order that no one of you might become arrogant~ in behalf of one against the other.

4:7
John 3:27; Rom.
12:3,6; 1 Pet.
4:10

7 For who regards you as superior? And what do you have that you did not receive? But if you did receive it, why do you boast as if you had not received it?

4:8
Rev. 3:17f.

8 You are already filled,⁺ you have already become rich, you have become kings *without us;* and *I* would indeed² that you had become kings so that *we also* might reignˣ with you.

4:9
Rom. 8:36; 1 Cor.
15:31; 2 Cor.
11:23;
Heb. 10:33

9 For, I think, God has exhibited *us apostles* last of all, as men condemned to death; because we have become a *spectacle* to the world, both to angels and to men.

†I.e., the appointed time of judgment

10   We are fools for Christ's sake, but you are prudent[35b] in Christ; we are weak, but you are strong; you are distinguished, but we are without honor.

11   To this present hour we are both hungry and thirsty, and are poorly clothed, and are roughly treated, and are homeless;

12   and we toil, working with our own hands; when we are reviled, we bless; when we are persecuted, we endure;

13   when we are slandered, we try to conciliate; we have become as the *scum of the world*, the *dregs* of all things, *even* until now.

14   I do not write these things to shame you, but to admonish you as my *beloved* children.

15   For if you were to have~ *countless tutors* in Christ, yet *you would* not *have* many fathers; for in Christ Jesus *I* became your father through the gospel.

16   I exhort you therefore, be~ᴵ *imitators of me.*

17   For this reason I have sent to you Timothy, who is my beloved and faithful child in the Lord, and he will remind you of my ways which are in Christ, just as I teach everywhere in every church.

18   Now some have become arrogant, as though I were not coming to you.

19   But I will come to you soon, if the Lord wills,ˣ and I shall find out, not the words of those who are arrogant,⁺ but their power.

20   For the kingdom of God does not consist in *words,* but in ⁺*power.* [32a]

21   What do you desire? Shall I come to you with a *rod* or with love and a spirit of gentleness?[23b]

Immorality Rebuked

5   It is actually reported that there is *immorality* among you, and immorality of such a kind as does not exist even among the *Gentiles,* that someone has his *father's* wife.

2   And *you* have become arrogant,⁺ and have •not mourned instead, in order that the one who had done[19b] this deed might be removedˣ from your midst.

3   For *I,* on my part, though absent in body but present in spirit, have already judged⁺ him who has so committed this, as though I were present.

4   In the name of our Lord Jesus, when you are assembled, and •I with you in spirit, with the power[32a] of our Lord Jesus,

5   *I have decided* to deliverˣ such a one to Satan for the

4:10
Acts 17:18;
26:24; 1 Cor.
1:18;
1 Cor. 1:19f.;
3:18; 2 Cor.
11:19;
1 Cor. 2:3; 2 Cor.
13:9
4:11
Rom. 8:35; 2 Cor.
11:23-27
4:12
Acts 18:3;
1 Pet. 3:9;
John 15:20; Rom.
8:35
4:13
Lam. 3:45

4:14
1 Cor. 6:5; 15:34;
2 Cor. 6:13;
12:14; 1 Thess.
2:11; 1 John 2:1;
3 John 4
4:15
Gal. 3:24f.;
1 Cor. 1:30;
Num. 11:12;
1 Cor. 3:8; Gal.
4:19; Philem. 10;
1 Cor. 9:12,14,18,
23; 15:1
4:16
1 Cor. 11:1; Phil.
3:17; 4:9; 1
Thess. 1:6; 2
Thess. 3:9
4:17
1 Cor. 16:10;
Acts 16:1;
1 Cor. 4:14;
1 Tim. 1:2,18; 2
Tim. 1:2;
1 Cor. 7:17;
14:33; 16:1; Titus
1:5
4:18
1 Cor. 4:6;
1 Cor. 4:21
4:19
Acts 19:21; 20:2;
1 Cor. 11:34;
16:5f.; 16:7-9;
2 Cor. 1:15f.;
Acts 18:21;
1 Cor. 4:6
4:20
1 Cor. 2:4
4:21
2 Cor. 1:23; 2:1,3;
12:20; 13:2,10
5:1
Lev. 18:8; Deut.
22:30; 27:20

5:2
1 Cor. 4:6;
2 Cor. 7:7-10;
1 Cor. 5:13
5:3
Col. 2:5; 1 Thess.
2:17
5:4
2 Thess. 3:6;
John 20:23;
2 Cor. 2:10; 13:3,
10
5:5
Prov. 23:14;
Luke 22:31; 1
Tim. 1:20;
Matt. 4:10;
1 Cor. 1:8

destruction of his flesh, that his spirit may be saved[x] in the day of the Lord [9]Jesus.

6 Your boasting is not good.[25b] Do you not know that a little leaven leavens the *whole lump of dough*?

7 Clean[xl] out the old leaven, that you may be a new[34b] lump, just as you are *in fact* unleavened. For *Christ* our Passover also has been sacrificed.

8 Let us therefore celebrate~ the feast, not with *old* leaven, nor with the leaven of malice[10e] and wickedness,[10b] but with the unleavened bread of sincerity and truth.

9 I wrote you in my letter not to associate~ with immoral people;

10 I *did* not at all *mean* with the immoral people of this world, or with the covetous and swindlers, or with idolaters; for then you would have to go[x] *out of the world*.

11 But actually, I wrote to you not to associate~ with any so-called brother if he should be an immoral person, or covetous, or an idolater, or a reviler, or a drunkard, or a swindler—not even *to eat*~ with such a one.

12 For what have I to do with judging~ *outsiders*? Do *you* not judge those who are *within the church*?

13 But those who are *outside*, God judges. REMOVE[xl] THE WICKED MAN FROM AMONG YOURSELVES.

Lawsuits Discouraged

6 Does any one of you, when he has a case against his neighbor, [†]dare to go~ to law before the unrighteous, and •*not* before the saints?

2 Or do you not know that the saints will judge the *world*? And if the world is judged by *you*, are you not competent *to* constitute the *smallest*[3] law courts?

3 Do you not know that we shall judge *angels*? How much more, matters of this life?

4 If then you have~ law courts dealing with matters of this life, do you appoint *them as judges* who are of no account[†] in the church?

5 I say *this* to your *shame*. Is it *so*, *that* there is not among you one wise man who will be able to decide[x] between his brethren,

6 but brother goes to law with brother, and that before [†]un-*believers*?

7 Actually, then, it is already a defeat for you, that you have *lawsuits* with one another. Why not rather be wronged? Why not rather be defrauded?

[9]Some ancient mss. do not contain *Jesus*

5:6
1 Cor. 5:2; James 4:16;
Rom. 6:16;
Hos. 7:4; Matt. 16:6,12; Gal. 5:9
5:7
Mark 14:12;
1 Pet. 1:19

5:8
Ex. 12:19; 13:7;
Deut. 16:3

5:9
2 Cor. 6:14; Eph. 5:11; 2 Thess. 3:6

5:10
1 Cor. 10:27

5:11
Acts 1:15;
2 Thess. 3:6;
1 Cor. 10:7,14, 20f.

5:12
Mark 4:11;
1 Cor. 5:3-5;
6:1-4
5:13
Deut. 13:5; 17:7, 12; 21:21; 22:21;
1 Cor. 5:2

6:1
Matt. 18:17

6:2
Rom. 6:16;
Dan. 7:18,22,27;
Matt. 19:28;
1 Cor. 1:20

6:3
Rom. 6:16

6:5
1 Cor. 4:14;
15:34;
Acts 1:15; 9:13;
1 Cor. 6:1
6:6
2 Cor. 6:14f.;
1 Tim. 5:8
6:7
Matt. 5:39f.

8   On the contrary, *you yourselves* wrong and defraud, and that *your* †brethren.

9   Or do you not know that the unrighteous shall not inherit the kingdom of *God*? Do not be deceived;[916b] neither fornicators, nor idolaters, nor adulterers, nor heffeminate, nor homosexuals,

10   nor thieves, nor *the* covetous, nor drunkards, nor revilers, nor swindlers, shall inherit the kingdom of God.

11   And such were some of you; but you were washed, but you were sanctified, but you were justified in the name of the Lord Jesus Christ, and in the Spirit of our God.

The Body Is the Lord's

12   All things are lawful for me, but not all things are profitable. All things are lawful for me, but I will *not* be mastered by anything.

13   Food is for the stomach, and the stomach is for food; but God will do away with *both of them*. Yet the body is not for immorality, but for the Lord; and the Lord is for the body.

14   Now God has not only raised the *Lord*, but will also raise *us* up through His power.[32a]

15   Do you not know that your bodies are *members of Christ*? Shall I then take away the members of Christ and make[x] them members of a *harlot*? May it never be!

16   Or do you not know that the one who joins himself to a harlot is *one body with her*? For He says, "THE TWO WILL BECOME ONE FLESH."

17   But the one who joins himself to the Lord is *one spirit with Him*.

18   Flee[~] immorality. Every *other* sin that a man commits[x] is *outside* the body, but the immoral man sins *against his own body*.

19   Or do you not know that your body is a *temple of the Holy †Spirit* who is in you, whom you have from God, and that you are not your own?

20   For you have been bought with a price: therefore[2] glorify[xl] God in your body.

Advice on Marriage

7 Now concerning the things about which you wrote, it is good for a man not to touch~ a woman.

2   But because of immoralities, let each man have[~] his own wife, and let each woman have[~] her *own* husband.

hI.e., effeminate by perversion

6:8
1 Thess. 4:6
6:9
Rom. 6:16;
Acts 20:32; 1 Cor.
15:50; Gal. 5:21;
Eph. 5:5;
Luke 21:8; 1 Cor.
15:33; Gal. 6:7;
James 1:16; 1
John 3:7;
Rom. 13:13;
1 Cor. 5:11; Gal.
5:19-21; Eph. 5:5;
1 Tim. 1:10; Rev.
21:8; 22:15
6:10
Acts 20:32; 1 Cor.
15:50; Gal. 5:21;
Eph. 5:5
6:11
1 Cor. 12:2; Eph.
2:2f.; Col. 3:5-7;
Titus 3:3-7;
Acts 22:16; Eph.
5:26;
1 Cor. 1:2,30;
Rom. 8:30
6:12
1 Cor. 10:23
6:13
Matt. 15:17;
Col. 2:22;
1 Cor. 6:15,19;
Gal. 5:24; Eph.
5:23
6:14
Acts 2:24;
John 6:39f.;
1 Cor. 15:23
6:15
1 Cor. 6:3;
Rom. 12:5; 1 Cor.
6:13; 12:27; Eph.
5:30;
Luke 20:16
6:16
1 Cor. 6:3;
Gen. 2:24; Matt.
19:5; Mark 10:8;
Eph. 5:31
6:17
John 17:21-23;
Rom. 8:9-11;
1 Cor. 6:15; Gal.
2:20
6:18
1 Cor. 6:9; 2 Cor.
12:21; Eph. 5:3;
Col. 3:5; Heb.
13:4
6:19
1 Cor. 6:3;
John 2:21; 1 Cor.
3:16; 2 Cor. 6:16;
Rom. 14:7f.
6:20
Acts 20:28; 1 Cor.
7:23; 1 Pet.
1:18f.; 2 Pet. 2:1;
Rev. 5:9;
Rom. 12:1; Phil.
1:20
7:1
1 Cor. 7:8,26

3 Let the husband fulfill~¹ *his duty* to his wife, and likewise also the wife to her husband.

4 The wife does not have authority *over her own body,* but the husband *does;* and likewise also the husband does not have authority *over his own body,* but the wife *does.*

7:5
Ex. 19:15; 1 Sam. 21:5; Matt. 4:10

5 Stop depriving⁰ one another, except by agreement for a time that you may devoteˣ yourselves to prayer, and come together again lest Satan tempt~ you because of your lack of self-control.

7:6
2 Cor. 8:8
7:7
1 Cor. 7:8; 9:5; Matt. 19:11f.; Rom. 12:6; 1 Cor. 12:4,11

6 But this I say by way of concession, not of command.

7 ¹Yet I wish that all men were even as I myself am. However, each man has his *own* gift²⁴ᶜ from God, one in this manner and another in that.

7:8
1 Cor. 7:1,26; 1 Cor. 7:7; 9:5

8 But I say to the unmarried and to widows that it is good for them if they remainˣ even as I.

7:9
1 Tim. 5:14

9 But if they do not have self-control, let them marry;ˣ¹ for it is better to marryˣ than to burn.~

7:10
Mal. 2:16; Matt. 5:32; 19:3-9; Mark 10:2-12; Luke 16:18; 1 Cor. 7:6

10 But to the married⁺ I give instructions, not I, but the Lord, that the wife should *not leave*ˣ her husband

11 (but if she does leave,ˣ let her remain~¹ unmarried, or else be reconciledˣ¹ to her husband), and that the husband should *not send~ his wife away.*

7:12
1 Cor. 7:6; 2Cor. 11:17

12 But to the rest *I* say, not the Lord, that if any brother has a wife who is an *unbeliever,* and she consents to live~ with him, let him not send⁰ her away.

13 And a woman who has an unbelieving husband, and he consents to live~ with her, let her not send⁰ her husband away.

7:14
Ezra 9:2; Mal. 2:15

14 For the unbelieving husband is *sanctified*⁺ through his wife, and the unbelieving wife is *sanctified*⁺ through her believing husband; for otherwise your children are unclean, but now they are *holy.*²⁸ᵃ

7:15
Rom. 14:19

15 Yet if the unbelieving one leaves, let him leave; the brother or the sister is *not under bondage*⁺ in such *cases,* but God has called⁺ ʲus to *peace.*

7:16
Rom. 11:14; 1 Pet. 3:1

16 For how do you know, O wife, whether you will *save* your husband? Or how do you know, O husband, whether you will *save* your wife?

7:17
Rom. 12:3; 1 Cor. 4:17; 1 Cor. 11:16; 14:33; 2 Cor. 8:18; 11:28; Gal. 1:22; 1 Thess. 2:14; 2 Thess. 1:4

17 Only, as the Lord has assigned to *each one,* as God has called⁺ *each,* in this manner let him walk. ~¹⁴²ᵃ And thus I direct in *all* the churches.

7:18
Acts 15:1ff.

18 Was any man called *already circumcised?*⁺ Let him not become uncircumcised. Has anyone been called⁺ *in uncircumcision?* Let him not be circumcised.

ⁱSome ancient mss. read *For*   ʲSome ancient mss. read *you*

19   Circumcision is nothing, and uncircumcision is nothing, but *what matters is* the keeping of the commandments of God.

7:19
Rom. 2:27,29;
Gal. 3:28; 5:6;
6:15; Col. 3:11;
Rom. 2:25

20   Let each man remain⌐ in that condition in which he was called.

7:20
1 Cor. 7:24

21   Were you called while a slave? Do not worry⁰ about it; but if you are able also to become free, rather do^x that.

22   For he who was called in the Lord while a slave, is the *Lord's freedman;* likewise he who was called while free, is Christ's *slave.* ³⁸ᵇ

7:22
John 8:32,36;
Philem. 16;
Eph. 6:6; Col.
3:24; 1 Pet. 2:16

23   You were bought with a *price;* do not become⁰ slaves of men.

7:23
1 Cor. 6:20

24   Brethren, let each man remain⌐ with God in that *condition* in which he was called.

7:24
1 Cor. 7:20

25   Now concerning virgins I have no command of the Lord, but I give an opinion as one who by the mercy⁺ of the Lord is trustworthy.

7:25
1 Cor. 7:6;
2 Cor. 4:1; 1 Tim.
1:13,16

26   I think then that this is good in view of the present distress, that it is good for a man to remain as he is.

7:26
Luke 21:23;
2 Thess. 2:2;
1 Cor. 7:1,8

27   Are you bound⁺ to a wife? Do not seek⁰ to be released. Are you released⁺ from a wife? Do not seek⁰ a wife.

28   But if you should marry,^x you have not sinned; and if a virgin should marry,^x she has not sinned. Yet such will have *trouble in this life,* and I am trying to spare you.

29   But this I say, brethren, the time has been shortened,⁺ so that from now on those who have wives should be as though they *had none;*

7:29
Rom. 13:11f.;
1 Cor. 7:31

30   and those who weep, as though they did not weep; and those who rejoice, as though they did not rejoice; and those who buy, as though they did not possess;

31   and those who use the world, as though they did not make full use of it; for the form of this world is passing away.

7:31
1 Cor. 9:18;
1 Cor. 7:29;
1 John 2:17

32   But I want you to be *free from concern.* One who is unmarried is concerned about the things of the Lord, how he may please^x the Lord;

7:32
1 Tim. 5:5

33   but one who is married is concerned about the things of the world, how he may please^x his ᵏwife,

34   and *his interests* are divided.⁺ And the woman who is unmarried, and the virgin, is concerned about the things of the Lord, that she may be holy²⁸ᵃ both in body and spirit; but one who is married is concerned about the things of the world, how she may please^x her husband.

35   And this I say for your *own benefit;* not to put^x a *restraint*

ᵏSome mss. read *wife. And there is a difference also between the wife and the virgin. One who is unmarried is concerned . . .*

upon you, but to promote what is seemly, and *to secure undistracted* devotion to the Lord.

36 But if any man thinks that he is acting~ *unbecomingly* toward his virgin *daughter,* if she should be of full age, and if it must be~ so, let him do^ what he wishes, he does not sin; let her marry.^

37 But he who stands⁺ *firm* in his heart, being under no constraint, but has *authority* over his·own will, and has decided⁺ this in his ·own heart, to keep~ his own virgin *daughter,* he will do well.

38 So then both he who gives his own virgin *daughter* in marriage does well, and he who does not give her in marriage will do better.

39 A wife is bound⁺ as long as her husband lives; but if her husband is dead,ˣ she is free to be marriedˣ to whom she wishes, only in the Lord.

40 But in·my opinion she is happier if she remainsˣ as she is; and I think that I also have the Spirit of God.

Take Care with Your Liberty

8 Now concerning things sacrificed to idols, we know²⁹ᵉ that we all have knowledge. Knowledge makes arrogant, but love edifies.

2 If anyone supposes that he knows⁺²⁹ᵃ anything, he has not yet known as he ought to know;ˣ

3 but if anyone loves³¹ᵃ God, he is known⁺²⁹ᵃ by Him.

4 Therefore concerning the eating of things sacrificed to idols, we know²⁹ᵉ that ¹there is no such thing as an idol in the world, and that there is no God but one.

5 For even² if there are so-called gods whether in heaven or on earth, as indeed there are *many* gods and *many* lords,

6 yet for *us* there is but⁺*one* God, the Father, from whom are all things, and we *exist* for Him; and ⁺*one* Lord, Jesus Christ, by whom are all things, and we *exist* through Him.

7 However not all men have this knowledge; but some, being accustomed to the idol until now, eat *food* as if it were *sacrificed to an idol;* and their conscience being weak is defiled.¹⁷ᶜ

8 But food will not commend us to God; we are neither the worse if we do not eat,ˣ nor the better if we do eat.ˣ

9 But take care^ lest this liberty of yours somehow become a stumbling ⁺block to the weak.

10 For if someone seesˣ you, who have knowledge, dining in

7:39
Rom. 7:2;
2 Cor. 6:14

7:40
1 Cor. 7:6,25
8:1
Acts 15:20; 1 Cor.
8:4,7,10;
Rom. 15:14;
1 Cor. 8:7,10;
10:15;
1 Cor. 4:6;
Rom. 14:19
8:2
1 Cor. 3:18;
1 Cor. 13:8-12; 1
Tim. 6:4
8:3
Ps. 1:6; Jer. 1:5;
Amos 3:2; Rom.
8:29; 11:2; Gal.
4:9
8:4
Acts 15:20; 1 Cor.
8:1,7,10;
Acts 14:15; 1 Cor.
10:19; Gal. 4:8;
Deut. 4:35,39;
6:4; 1 Cor. 8:6
8:5
2 Thess. 2:4
8:6
Deut. 4:35,39;
6:4; 1 Cor. 8:4;
10:6,7; 1 Cor. 8:4;
Mal. 2:10; Eph.
4:6;
Rom. 11:36;
John 13:13;
1 Cor. 1:2; Eph.
4:5; John 1:3; Col.
1:16
8:7
1 Cor. 8:4ff.;
Rom. 14:14,22f.
8:8
Rom. 14:17
8:9
Rom. 14:13,21;
1 Cor. 10:28; Gal.
5:13;
Rom. 14:1;
1 Cor. 8:10f.
8:10
1 Cor. 8:4ff.;
Acts 15:20;
1 Cor. 8:1,4,7

ˡI.e., has no real existence

an idol's temple, will not his conscience, if he is weak, be strengthened to eat~ things sacrificed to idols?

11 For through *your knowledge he who is weak is *ruined,* the brother for whose sake Christ died.

12 And thus, by sinning against the brethren and wounding their conscience when it is weak, you sin *against Christ.*

13 Therefore,[2] if food causes my brother to stumble, I will *never eat[x] meat again, that I might not cause my brother to stumble.[x]

Paul's Use of Liberty

9 Am I not free? Am I not an apostle? Have I not seen* *Jesus our Lord?* Are you not *my work* in the Lord?

2 If to *others* I am not an apostle, at least[2] I am to *you;* for you are the seal of *my* apostleship in the Lord.

3 *My defense to those who examine *me is this:

4 Do we not have a right to eat[x] and drink?[x]

5 Do we not have a right to take~ along a believing wife, even as the rest of the apostles, and the brothers of the Lord, and Cephas?

6 Or do only Barnabas and I not have a right to refrain~ from working?

7 Who at any time serves as a soldier at his own expense? Who plants a vineyard, and does not eat the *fruit* of it? Or who tends a flock and does not use the *milk of the flock?*

8 I am not speaking these things according to human judgment, am I? Or does not the *Law* also say these things?

9 For it is written* in the Law of †*Moses,* "YOU SHALL NOT MUZZLE THE OX WHILE HE IS THRESHING." God is not concerned about *oxen,* is He?

10 Or is He speaking altogether for our sake? Yes, for *our sake* it was written, because the plowman ought to plow~ in hope, and the thresher *to thresh* in hope of sharing~ *the crops.*

11 If we sowed *spiritual things* in you, is it too much if we should reap *material things* from you?

12 If others share the right over *you,* do we not more? Nevertheless, we did not use this right, but we endure all things, that we may cause[x] *no hindrance* to the gospel of Christ.

13 Do you not know that those who perform sacred services eat the *food* of the *temple, and* those who attend regularly to the altar have their share with the *altar?*

14 So also the Lord directed those who proclaim the gospel to get~ their living from the *gospel.*

15 But *I* have used* none of these things. And I am not

8:11
1 Cor. 8:4ff.;
Rom. 14:15,20
8:12
Matt. 18:6; Rom. 14:20;
Matt. 25:45
8:13
Rom. 14:21;
1 Cor. 10:32;
2 Cor. 6:3; 11:29
9:1
1 Cor. 9:19;
10:29;
Acts 14:14; Rom. 1:1; 2 Cor. 12:12;
1 Thess. 2:6; 1 Tim. 2:7; 2 Tim. 1:11;
Acts 9:3,17; 18:9; 22:14,18; 23:11;
1 Cor. 15:8;
9:2
1 Cor. 3:6; 4:15
John 3:33; 2 Cor. 3:2f.;
9:4
Acts 1:25
1 Cor. 9:14;
1 Thess. 2:6,9;
2 Thess. 3:8f.
9:5
1 Cor. 7:7f.;
Matt. 12:46;
Matt. 8:14; John 1:42
9:6
Acts 4:36
9:7
2 Cor. 10:4;
1 Tim. 1:18; 2 Tim. 2:3f.;
Deut. 20:6; Prov. 27:18; 1 Cor. 3:6, 8
9:8
Rom. 3:5
9:9
Deut. 25:4; 1 Tim. 5:18;
Deut. 22:1-4; Prov. 12:10
9:10
Rom. 4:23f.;
2 Tim. 2:6
9:11
Rom. 15:27;
1 Cor. 9:14
9:12
Acts 18:3; 20:33;
1 Cor. 9:15,18;
2 Cor. 6:3; 11:12;
1 Cor. 4:15; 9:14, 16,18,23; 2 Cor. 2:12
9:13
Rom. 6:16;
Lev. 6:16,26; 7:6, 31ff.; Num. 5:9f.;
18:8-20,31; Deut. 18:1
9:14
Matt. 10:10; Luke 10:7; 1 Tim. 5:18;
1 Cor. 4:15; 9:12, 16,18,23; 2 Cor. 2:12;
Luke 10:8; 1 Cor. 9:4
9:15
Acts 18:3; 20:33;
1 Cor. 9:12,18;
2 Cor. 11:10

writing these things that it may be done so in my case; for it would be better for me to die^x than have any man make my boast an empty one.

16   For if I preach~ the gospel, I have nothing to boast of, for I am under compulsion; for woe is me if I do not preach^x the gospel.

17   For if I do^{19b} this voluntarily, I have a *reward;* but if against my †will, I have a *stewardship* entrusted⁺ to me.

18   What then is my reward? That, when I preach the gospel, I may offer^x the gospel *without charge,* so as not to make full use^x of my right in the gospel.

19   For though I am free from all *men,* I have made myself a *slave* to all, that I might win^x *the more.*

20   And to the Jews I became as a Jew, that I might win^x *Jews;* to those who are under the Law, as under the Law, though not being myself under the Law, that I might win^x those who are *under the Law;*

21   to those who are without law, as without law, though not being without the law of God but under the law of Christ, that I might win^x those who are without law.

22   To the weak I became weak, that I might win^x the *weak;* I have become⁺ all things to *all men,* that I may by all means save^x some.

23   And I do^{19a} *all things* for the sake of the gospel, that I may become a *fellow* †*partaker* of it.

24   Do you not know that those who run in a race all run, but *only* one receives¹ the prize? Run~ in such a way that you may win.^x

25   And everyone who competes in the games exercises self-control in *all things.* They then *do it* to receive^x a *perishable wreath,* but we an †*imperishable.*

26   Therefore *I* run in such a way, as not without aim; I box in such a way, as not beating the air;

27   but I buffet my body and make it my slave, lest possibly, after I have preached to others, *I myself* should be disqualified.

Avoid Israel's Mistakes

10   For I do not want you to be unaware,~ brethren, that our fathers were all under the cloud, and all passed through the sea;

2   and all ᵐwere baptized into Moses in the cloud and in the sea;

3   and all ate the same spiritual food;

ᵐSome ancient mss. read *received baptism*

9:16
Acts 9:15; Rom. 1:14;
1 Cor. 4:15; 9:12,
14,18,23; 2 Cor. 2:12
9:17
John 4:36; 1 Cor. 3:8; 9:18;
1 Cor. 4:1; Gal. 2:7; Eph. 3:2;
Phil. 1:16; Col. 1:25
9:18
John 4:36; 1 Cor. 3:8; 9:17;
Acts 18:3; 2 Cor. 11:7; 12:13;
1 Cor. 7:31; 9:12
9:19
1 Cor. 9:1;
2 Cor. 4:5; Gal. 5:13;
Matt. 18:15;
1 Pet. 3:1
9:20
Acts 16:3;
21:23-26; Rom. 11:14;
Gal. 2:19
9:21
Rom. 2:12,14;
Gal. 2:3; 3:2;
1 Cor. 7:22; Gal. 6:2
9:22
Rom. 14:1; 15:1;
2 Cor. 11:29;
1 Cor. 10:33;
Rom. 11:14

9:24
1 Cor. 9:13;
Phil. 3:14; Col. 2:18;
Gal. 2:2; 2 Tim. 4:7; Heb. 12:1
9:25
Eph. 6:12; 1 Tim. 6:12; 2 Tim. 2:5;
4:7;
2 Tim. 4:8; James 1:12; 1 Pet. 5:4;
Rev. 2:10; 3:11
9:26
Gal. 2:2; 2 Tim. 4:7; Heb. 12:1;
1 Cor. 14:9
9:27
Rom. 8:13

10:1
Rom. 1:13;
Ex. 13:21; Ps. 105:39;
Ex. 14:22,29;
Neh. 9:11; Ps. 66:6
10:2
Rom. 6:3; 1 Cor. 1:13; Gal. 3:27
10:3
Ex. 16:4,35; Deut. 8:3; Neh. 9:15,20;
Ps. 78:24f.; John 6:31

4   and all drank the same spiritual drink, for they were drink-ing^m from a spiritual rock which followed them; and the rock was Christ.

10:4
Ex. 17:6; Num.
20:11; Ps. 78:15

5   Nevertheless, with *most of them* God was not well-pleased; for they were laid low in the wilderness.

10:5
Num. 14:29ff.,37;
26:65; Heb. 3:17;
Jude 5

6   Now these things happened as *examples for us,* that we should not crave evil^{10a} things, as they also craved.

10:6
1 Cor. 10:11;
Num. 11:4,34; Ps.
106:14

7   And do not be^o *idolaters,* as some of them were; as it is written,⁺ "The people sat down to eat^x and drink,^x and stood up to play."~

10:7
Ex. 32:4; 1 Cor.
5:11; 10:14;
Ex. 32:6;
Ex. 32:19

8   Nor let us act~ immorally, as some of them did, and *twenty-three thousand* fell in one day.

10:8
Num. 25:1ff.;
Num. 25:9

9   Nor let us try~1 the Lord, as some of them did, and were *destroyed*^m by the serpents.

10:9
Num. 21:5f.

10   Nor grumble,^o as some of them did, and were destroyed by the destroyer.

10:10
Num. 16:41; 17:5,
10;
Num. 16:49;
Ex. 12:23; 2 Sam.
24:16; 1 Chr.
21:15; Heb. 11:28

11   Now these things happened^m to them as an example, and they were written for our instruction, upon whom the ends of the ages have come.⁺

10:11
1 Cor. 10:6;
Rom. 4:23;
Rom. 13:11

12   Therefore let him who thinks he stands⁺ take heed~1 lest he fall.^x

10:12
Rom. 11:20;
2 Pet. 3:17

13   No temptation has overtaken⁺ you but such as is common to man; and God is *faithful,* who will not allow^{6b} you to be tempted^x beyond what you are able, but with the temptation will provide the way of escape also, that you may be able~ to endure^x it.

10:13
1 Cor. 1:9;
2 Pet. 2:9

14   Therefore,² my beloved, flee~1 from idolatry.

10:14
Heb. 6:9;
1 Cor. 10:7,19f.;
1 John 5:21

15   I speak as to wise^{35b} men; *you* judge^{xi} what I say.

16   Is not the cup of blessing which we bless a sharing in the blood of Christ? Is not the bread which we break a sharing in the body of Christ?

10:16
Matt. 26:27f.;
Mark 14:23f.;
Luke 22:20;
1 Cor. 11:25;
Matt. 26:26; Luke
22:19; Acts 2:42;
1 Cor. 11:23f.

17   Since there is *one* bread, we who are many are *one* body; for we all partake of the *one* bread.

10:17
Rom. 12:5; 1 Cor.
12:12f.,27; Eph.
4:4,16; Col. 3:15

18   Look~1 at the nation Israel; are not those who eat the sacrifices sharers in the altar?

10:18
Rom. 1:3;
Lev. 7:6,14f.;
Deut. 12:17f.

19   What do I mean then? That a thing sacrificed to idols is anything, or that an idol is anything?

10:19
1 Cor. 8:4

20   *No,* but *I say* that the things which the Gentiles sacrifice, they sacrifice to *demons,* and *not to God;* and I do not want you to become~ *sharers in demons.*

10:20
Deut. 32:17; Ps.
106:37; Gal. 4:8;
Rev. 9:20

21   You cannot drink~ the cup of the Lord and the cup of demons; you cannot partake~ of the table of the Lord and the table of demons.

10:21
2 Cor. 6:16;
Is. 65:11

10:22
Deut. 32:21;
Eccl. 6:10; Is.
45:9
10:23
1 Cor. 6:12;
Rom. 14:19
10:24
Rom. 15:2; 1 Cor.
10:33; 13:5;
2 Cor. 12:14; Phil.
2:21
10:25
Acts 10:15; 1 Cor.
8:7
10:26
Ps. 24:1; 50:12;
1 Tim. 4:4
10:27
1 Cor. 5:10;
Luke 10:8
10:28
1 Cor. 8:7,10-12

10:29
Rom. 14:16;
1 Cor. 9:19

10:30
1 Cor. 9:1;
Rom. 14:6

10:31
Col. 3:17; 1 Pet.
4:11

10:32
Acts 24:16; 1 Cor.
8:13;
Acts 20:28; 1 Cor.
1:2; 7:17; 11:22;
15:9; 2 Cor. 1:1;
Gal. 1:13; Phil.
3:6; 1 Tim. 3:5,15
10:33
Rom. 15:2; 1 Cor.
9:22; Gal. 1:10;
Rom. 15:2; 1 Cor.
13:5; 2 Cor.
12:14; Phil. 2:21;
Rom. 11:14; 1
Thess. 2:16
11:1
1 Cor. 4:16; Phil.
3:17
11:2
1 Cor. 11:17,22;
1 Cor. 4:17; 15:2;
1 Thess. 1:6; 3:6;
2 Thess. 2:15; 3:6
11:3
Eph. 1:22; 4:15;
5:23; Col. 1:18;
2:19;
Gen. 3:16; Eph.
5:23;
1 Cor. 3:23
11:4
Acts 13:1;
1 Thess. 5:20
11:5
Luke 2:36; Acts
21:9; 1 Cor.
14:34;
Deut. 21:12

11:7
Gen. 1:26; 5:1;
9:6; James 3:9

22 Or do we provoke the Lord to jealousy? We are not stronger than He, are we?

23 All things are lawful, but not all things are profitable. All things are lawful, but not all things edify.

24 Let no one seek~ *his own good,* but that of his neighbor.

25 Eat~ anything that is sold in the meat market, without asking questions for conscience' sake;

26 FOR THE EARTH IS THE LORD'S, AND ALL IT CONTAINS.

27 If one of the unbelievers invites you, and you wish to go, eat~ anything that is set before you, without asking questions for conscience' sake.

28 But if anyone should say^x to you, "This is meat *sacrificed to idols,"* do not eat^o it, for the sake of the one who informed *you,* and for conscience' sake;

29 I mean not your own conscience, but the other *man's;* for why is my freedom judged by another's conscience?

30 If *I* partake with thankfulness, why am I slandered concerning that for which *I* give thanks?

31 Whether, then, you eat or drink or whatever you do, do~ *all* to the glory of God.

32 Give~ *no offense* either to Jews or to Greeks or to the church of God;

33 just as *I also* please *all men* in *all things,* not seeking my own profit, but the *profit* of the many, that they may be saved.^x

Christian Order

11 Be~ *imitators of me,* just as I also am of Christ.
2 Now I praise you because you remember^+ me in everything, and hold firmly to the traditions, just as I delivered them to you.

3 But I want you to understand that *Christ* is the head of every man, and the +*man* is the head of a woman, and +*God* is the head of Christ.

4 Every man who has *something* on his head while praying or prophesying, disgraces his head.

5 But every woman who has her head uncovered while praying or prophesying, disgraces her head; for she is one and the same with her whose head is shaved.^+

6 For if a woman does not cover her head, let her also have her hair cut^xi off; but if it is disgraceful for a woman to have her hair cut^x off or her head shaved,~ let her cover~ her head.

7 For a man ought not to have his head covered,~ since he is the image^22b and glory of +God; but the woman is the glory of +man.

8   For man does not originate from woman, but woman from man;

9   for indeed man was not created for the woman's sake, but woman for the man's sake.

10   Therefore the woman ought to have *a symbol of* authority on her head, because of the angels.

11   However, in the Lord, neither is woman independent of man, nor is man independent of woman.

12   For as the woman originates from the man, so also the man *has his birth* through the woman; and all things originate from God.

13   Judge[xi] *for yourselves:* is it proper for a woman to pray[~] to God *with head uncovered?*

14   Does not even nature itself teach you that if a man has long hair, it is a [†]dishonor to him,

15   but if a woman has long hair, it is a [†]glory to her? For her hair is given[*] to her for a covering.

16   But if one is inclined to be contentious, *we* have *no other practice,* nor have the churches of God.

17   But in giving this instruction, I do not praise you, because you come together not for the better but for the *worse.*

18   For, in the first place, when you come together as a church, I hear that divisions exist[~] among you; and in part, I believe it.

19   For there must also be factions among you, in order that those who are approved may have become *evident* among you.

20   Therefore when you meet together, it is not to eat[x] the *Lord's Supper,*

21   for in your eating[x] each one takes his •*own* supper first; and one is hungry and another is drunk.

22   What! Do you not have *houses* in which to eat[~] and drink?[~] Or do you despise the *church of God,* and shame[39c] those who have nothing? What shall I say[x] to you? Shall I praise[x] you? In this I will not praise you.

The Lord's Supper

23   For *I* received from the Lord that which I also delivered to you, that the Lord Jesus in the night in which He was betrayed[m] took bread;

24   and when He had given thanks, He broke it, and said, "This is *My* body, which [n]is for you; do[~] this in remembrance of •Me."

25   In the same way *He took* the cup also, after supper, saying,

[n]Some ancient mss. read *is broken*

11:8
Gen. 2:21-23;
1 Tim. 2:13

11:9
Gen. 2:18

11:12
2 Cor. 5:18;
Rom. 11:36

11:13
Luke 12:57

11:16
1 Cor. 4:5; 9:1-3,
6;
1 Cor. 7:17
11:17
1 Cor. 11:2,22

11:18
1 Cor. 1:10; 3:3

11:19
Matt. 18:7; Luke
17:1; 1 Tim. 4:1;
2 Pet. 2:1;
Deut. 13:3; 1
John 2:19

11:21
Jude 12

11:22
1 Cor. 10:32;
James 2:6;
1 Cor. 11:2,17

11:23
1 Cor. 15:3; Gal.
1:12; Col. 3:24;
1 Cor. 11:23-25;
Matt. 26:26-28;
Mark 14:22-24;
Luke 22:17-20;
1 Cor. 10:16

11:25
1 Cor. 10:16;
Ex. 24:6-8; Luke
22:20; 2 Cor. 3:6

11:26
John 21:22;
1 Cor. 4:5

11:27
Heb. 10:29

11:28
Matt. 26:22;
2 Cor. 13:5; Gal.
6:4

11:30
Acts 7:60
11:32
2 Sam. 7:14; Ps.
94:12; Heb.
12:7-10; Rev.
3:19;
1 Cor. 1:20
11:34
1 Cor. 11:21;
1 Cor. 11:22;
1 Cor. 4:17; 7:17;
16:1;
1 Cor. 4:19
12:1
1 Cor. 12:4; 14:1;
Rom. 1:13
12:2
1 Cor. 6:11; Eph.
2:11f.; 1 Pet. 4:3;
1 Thess. 1:9;
Ps. 115:5; Is.
46:7; Jer. 10:5;
Hab. 2:18f.
12:3
Matt. 22:43;
1 John 4:2f.; Rev.
1:10;
Rom. 9:3;
John 13:13; Rom.
10:9
12:4
Rom. 12:6f.;
1 Cor. 12:11;
Eph. 4:4ff.,11;
Heb. 2:4
12:6
1 Cor. 15:28;
Eph. 1:23; 4:6
12:7
1 Cor. 12:12-30;
14:26; Eph. 4:12
12:8
1 Cor. 2:6; 2 Cor.
1:12;
Rom. 15:14;
1 Cor. 2:11,16; 2
Cor. 2:14; 4:6;
8:7; 11:6
12:9
1 Cor. 13:2;
2 Cor. 4:13;
1 Cor. 12:28,30
12:10
1 Cor. 12:28f.;
Gal. 3:5;
1 Cor. 11:4; 13:2,
8;
1 Cor. 14:29;
1 John 4:1;
Mark 16:17;
1 Cor. 13:1;
14:2ff.;
1 Cor. 12:30;
14:26

"This cup is the new[34a] covenant in •My blood; do⌣ this, as often as you drink~ it, in remembrance of •Me."

26   For as often as you eat~ this bread and drink~ the cup, you proclaim the Lord's death until He comes.

27   Therefore whoever eats~ the bread or drinks~ the cup of the Lord in an unworthy manner, shall be guilty of the body and the blood of the Lord.

28   But let a man examine⌣ himself, and so let him eat⌣ of the bread and drink⌣ of the cup.

29   For he who eats and drinks, eats and drinks judgment to himself, if he does not judge the body rightly.

30   For this reason many among you are weak and sick, and a number sleep.

31   But if we judged ourselves rightly, we should not be judged.

32   But when we are judged, we are disciplined by the Lord in order that we may not be condemned[x] along with the world.

33   So then, my brethren, when you come together to eat,[x] wait ⌣ for one another.

34   If anyone is hungry, let him eat⌣ at home, so that you may not come~ together for judgment. And the remaining matters I shall arrange when I come.

The Use of Spiritual Gifts

12 Now concerning spiritual gifts, brethren, I do not want you to be unaware. ~

2   You know that when you were pagans, you were led~ astray to the dumb idols, however you were led.[xx]

3   Therefore I make known to you, that no one speaking by the Spirit of God says, "Jesus is accursed"; and no one can say,[x] "Jesus is Lord," except by the Holy Spirit.

4   Now there are varieties of gifts,[24c] but the same Spirit.

5   And there are varieties of ministries, and the same Lord.

6   And there are varieties of effects, but the same God who works all things in all persons.

7   But to each one is given the manifestation of the Spirit for the common good.

8   For to one is given the word of wisdom through the Spirit, and to another[8a] the word of †knowledge according to the same Spirit;

9   to another[8b] †faith by the same Spirit, and to another[8a] gifts[24c] of †healing by the one Spirit,

10   and to another the effecting of †miracles, and to another †prophecy, and to another[8a] the distinguishing of †spirits, to

another[8b] *various kinds of*[†]*tongues,* and to another[8a] the *interpretation of* [†]*tongues.*

11　But one and the same Spirit works *all these things,* distributing to each one individually just as He wills.

12　For even as the body is *one* and *yet* has *many* members, and all the members of the body, though they are many, are *one* body, so also is *Christ.*

13　For by *one* Spirit we were all baptized into *one* body, whether Jews or Greeks, whether slaves or free, and we were all made to drink of *one* Spirit.

14　For the body is not one member, but many.

15　If the foot should say,[x] "Because I am not a hand, I am not *a part* of the body," it is not for this reason any the less *a part* of the body.

16　And if the ear should say,[x] "Because I am not an eye, I am not *a part* of the body," it is not for this reason any the less *a part* of the body.

17　If the whole body were an eye, where would the hearing be? If the whole were hearing, where would the sense of smell be?

18　But now God has placed the members, each one of them, in the body, just as He desired.

19　And if they were *all* one member, where would the body be?

20　But now there are many members, but [†]one body.

21　And the eye cannot say[x] to the hand, "I have no need of you"; or again the head to the feet, "I have no need of you."

22　On the contrary, it is much truer that the members of the body which seem to be weaker are [†]*necessary;*

23　and those *members* of the body, which we deem less honorable, on these we bestow *more abundant* honor, and our unseemly *members come to* have *more abundant* seemliness,

24　whereas our seemly *members* have no need *of it.* But God has *so* composed the body, giving *more abundant* honor to that *member* which lacked,

25　that there should be no division in the body, but *that* the members should have the *same care*~ for one another.

26　And if one member suffers, *all the members* suffer with it; if *one* member is honored, all the members rejoice with it.

27　Now you are Christ's body, and individually members of it.

28　And *God* has appointed in the church, first apostles, second prophets, third teachers, then miracles, then gifts[24c] of healings, helps, administrations, *various* kinds of tongues.

12:11
1 Cor. 12:4

12:12
Rom. 12:4f.;
1 Cor. 10:17;
1 Cor. 12:27

12:13
Rom. 3:22; Gal.
3:28; Eph.
2:13-18; Col.
3:11;
John 7:37-39
12:14
1 Cor. 12:20

12:18
1 Cor. 12:28;
Rom. 12:6; 1 Cor.
12:11

12:20
1 Cor. 12:12,14

12:27
1 Cor. 1:2; 12:12;
Eph. 1:23; 4:12;
Col. 1:18,24;
2:19;
Rom. 12:5; Eph.
5:30
12:28
1 Cor. 12:18;
1 Cor. 10:32;
Eph. 4:11;
Acts 13:1; Eph.
2:20; 3:5;
1 Cor. 12:10,29;
1 Cor. 12:9,30;
Rom. 12:8

29 All are not apostles, are they? All are not prophets, are they? All are not teachers, are they? All are not *workers of* miracles, are they?

12:30
1 Cor. 12:10;

30 All do not have gifts[24c] of healings, do they? All do not speak with tongues, do they? All do not interpret, do they?

12:31
1 Cor. 14:1,39;

31 But earnestly desire ~ the *greater*[26a] gifts. [24c]

And I show you a still *more excellent way.*

The Excellence of Love

13:1
1 Cor. 12:10;
2 Cor. 12:4; Rev.
14:2;
Ps. 150:5

13 If I speak ~ with the tongues of men and of angels, but do not have ~ *love,* [31a] I have become⁺ a noisy gong or a clanging cymbal.

13:2
Matt. 7:22; Acts
13:1; 1 Cor. 11:4;
13:8; 14:1,39;
1 Cor. 14:2;
15:51;
Rom. 15:14;
1 Cor. 12:9;
Matt. 17:20;
21:21; Mark
11:23

2 And if I have~ *the gift of* prophecy, and know[29e] all mysteries and all knowledge; and if I have~ all faith, so as to remove ~ *mountains,* but do not have ~ *love,* I am †*nothing.*

13:3
Matt. 6:2;
Dan. 3:28

3 And if I give[x] all my possessions to feed *the poor,* and if I deliver[x] my body °to be burned,[x] but do not have~ *love,* it profits me †*nothing.*

13:4
Prov. 10:12; 17:9;
1 Thess. 5:14; 1
Pet. 4:8;
Acts 7:9;
1 Cor. 4:6

4 Love[31a] is patient, love is kind, *and* is not jealous; love does not brag *and* is not arrogant,

13:5
1 Cor. 10:24; Phil.
2:21;
2 Cor. 5:19

5 does not act unbecomingly; it does not seek its own, is not provoked, does not take into account a wrong *suffered,*

13:6
2 Thess. 2:12;
2 John 4; 3 John
3f.

6 does not rejoice in unrighteousness, but rejoices with the truth;

13:7
1 Cor. 9:12

7 bears all things, believes all things, hopes all things, endures all things.

13:8
1 Cor. 13:2;
1 Cor. 13:1

8 Love[31a] never fails; but if *there are gifts of* prophecy, they will be done away; if *there are* tongues, they will cease; if *there is* knowledge, it will be done away.

13:9
1 Cor. 8:2; 13:12

9 For we know[29a] in *part,* and we prophesy in *part;*

10 but when *the perfect* comes, the partial will be done away.

11 When I was a child, I used to speak[m] as a child, think[m] as a child, reason[m] as a child; when I became⁺ a man, I did⁺away with childish things.

13:12
2 Cor. 5:7; Phil.
3:12; James 1:23;
Gen. 32:30; Num.
12:8; 1 John 3:2;
1 Cor. 8:3

12 For now we see in a mirror dimly, but then face to face; now I know[29a] in part, but then I shall know[29b] fully just as I also have been fully known. [29b]

13:13
Gal. 5:6

13 But •now abide faith, hope, love,[31a] these three; but the greatest of these is love.

Prophecy a Superior Gift

14:1
1 Cor. 16:14;
1 Cor. 12:31;
14:39;
1 Cor. 12:1;
1 Cor. 13:2

14 Pursue ~ love, [31a] yet desire ~ earnestly spiritual *gifts,* but especially that you may prophesy. ~

°Some ancient mss. read *that I may boast*

2   For one who speaks in a tongue does not speak to *men*, but to †*God*; for no one understands, but in *his spirit* he speaks mysteries.

3   But one who prophesies speaks to *men* for edification and exhortation and consolation.

4   One who speaks in a tongue edifies *himself*, but one who prophesies edifies the *church*.

5   Now I wish that you all spoke ~in tongues, but *even* more that you would prophesy; ~ and greater is one who prophesies than one who speaks in tongues, unless he interprets, ~ so that the church may receive ˣ *edifying*.

6   But now, brethren, if I come to you speaking in tongues, what shall I profit you, unless I speakˣ to you either by way of revelation or of knowledge or of prophecy or of teaching?

7   Yet *even* lifeless things, either flute or harp, in producing a sound, if they do not produceˣ a *distinction* in the tones, how will it be known what is played on the flute or on the harp?

8   For if the bugle producesˣ an *indistinct* sound, who will prepare himself for battle?

9   So *also you*, unless you utterˣ by the tongue speech that is *clear*, how will it be known what is spoken? For you will be speaking~ into the air.

10   There are, perhaps, a great many kinds of languages in the world, and no *kind* is without meaning.

11   If then I do not know the meaning of the language, I shall be to the one who speaks a barbarian, and the one who speaks will be a barbarian to me.

12   So *also you*, since you are zealous of spiritual *gifts*, seek ᴹ to abound ~ for the *edification of the church*.

13   Therefore let one who speaks in a tongue pray ᴹ that he may interpret. ~

14   For if I pray ~in a tongue, my spirit prays, but my mind [33b] is unfruitful.

15   What is *the outcome* then? I shall pray with the spirit and I shall pray with the mind[33b] also; I shall sing with the spirit and I shall sing with the mind also.

16   Otherwise if you bless ~in the spirit *only*, how will the one who fills the place of the ungifted say the "Amen" at •your giving of thanks, since he does not know what you are saying?

17   For *you* are giving thanks well enough, but the other man is not edified.

18   I thank God, I speak in tongues *more than you all*;

19   however, in the church I desire to speakˣ *five* words with

14:2
Mark 16:17;
1 Cor. 12:10,28,
30; 13:1; 14:18ff.;
1 Cor. 13:2

14:3
Rom. 14:19;
1 Cor. 14:5,12,17,
26;
Acts 4:36
14:4
Mark 16:17;
1 Cor. 12:10,28,
30; 13:1; 14:18ff.,
26f.;
Rom. 14:19;
1 Cor. 14:5,12,17,
26;
1 Cor. 13:2
14:5
Mark 16:17;
1 Cor. 12:10,28,
30; 13:1; 14:18ff.,
26f.;
Num. 11:29;
Rom. 14:19;
1 Cor. 14:4,12,17,
26
14:6
1 Cor. 14:26;
Eph. 1:17;
1 Cor. 12:8;
1 Cor. 13:2;
Acts 2:42; Rom.
6:17
14:8
Num. 10:9; Jer.
4:19; Ezek.
33:3-6; Joel 2:1
14:9
1 Cor. 9:26

14:11
Acts 28:2

14:12
Rom. 14:19;
1 Cor. 14:4,5,17,
26

14:15
Acts 21:22; 1 Cor.
14:26;
Eph. 5:19; Col.
3:16

14:16
Deut. 27:15-26;
1 Chr. 16:36;
Neh. 5:13; 8:6;
Ps. 106:48; Rev.
11:5; 28:6; Rev.
5:14; 7:12;
Matt. 15:36
14:17
Rom. 14:19;
1 Cor. 14:4,5,12,
26

my mind, that I may instruct[x] *others also,* rather than *ten thousand* words in a tongue.

Instruction for the Church

20 Brethren, do not be[o] *children* in your thinking; yet in *evil*[10e] be[M] babes, but in your thinking be[M] *mature.*

21 In the Law it is written,[+] "BY MEN OF *STRANGE TONGUES* AND BY THE *LIPS OF STRANGERS* I WILL SPEAK TO THIS PEOPLE, AND EVEN SO THEY WILL NOT LISTEN TO ME," says the Lord.

22 So then tongues are for a sign, not to those who believe, but to unbelievers; but prophecy *is for a sign,* not to unbelievers, but to those who believe.

23 If therefore the *whole* church should assemble[x] together and all speak[~] in tongues, and ungifted men or unbelievers enter,[x] will they not say that you are mad?

24 But if all prophesy,[~] and an unbeliever or an ungifted man enters,[x] he is convicted by all, he is called to account by all;

25 the secrets of his heart are *disclosed;* and so he will fall on his face and worship[44b] God, declaring that God is *certainly* among you.

26 What is *the outcome* then, brethren? When you assemble,[~] each one has a *psalm,* has a *teaching,* has a *revelation,* has a *tongue,* has an *interpretation.* Let *all things* be done[M] for *edification.*

27 If anyone speaks in a tongue, *it should be* by two or at the most three, and *each* in turn, and let one interpret;[M]

28 but if there is no interpreter, let him keep silent[M] in the church; and let him speak[M] to *himself* and to God.

29 And let two or three prophets speak,[M] and let the others pass judgment.[M]

30 But if a revelation is made[x] to another who is seated, let the first keep silent.[M]

31 For you can *all* prophesy[~] one by one, so that all may learn[~] and all may be exhorted;[~]

32 and the spirits of prophets are *subject* to prophets;

33 for God is not *a God* of *confusion* but of [+]*peace,* as in all the churches of the saints.

34 Let the women keep silent[M] in the churches; for they are not permitted to speak,[~] but let them subject[M] themselves, just as the Law also says.

35 And if they desire to learn[x] anything, let them ask[M] [9c] their own husbands at *home;* for it is improper for a woman to speak[~] in church.

36   Was it from *you* that the word of God *first* went forth? Or has it come to *you only?*

37   If anyone thinks he is a prophet or spiritual, let him recognize~¹ that the things which I write to you are the *Lord's* commandment.

38   But if anyone ᴾdoes not recognize *this,* he is not recognized.

39   Therefore, my brethren, desire~ earnestly to prophesy,~ and do *not forbid* ⁰ to speak~ in tongues.

40   But let all things be done~ *properly* and in an *orderly* manner.

The Fact of Christ's Resurrection

15   Now I make known to you, brethren, the gospel which I preached to you, which also you received, in which also you stand,⁺

2   by which also you are saved, if you hold fast the word which I preached to you, unless you believed in vain.

3   For I delivered to you as of first importance what I also received, that Christ died for our sins according to the Scriptures,

4   and that He was buried, and that He was raised⁺ on the third day according to the Scriptures,

5   and that He appeared to Cephas, then to the twelve.

6   After that He appeared to more than *five hundred* brethren at one time, most of whom remain until now, but some have fallen asleep;

7   then He appeared to James, then to all the apostles;

8   and last of all, as it were to one untimely born, He appeared to me also.

9   For †I am the least of the apostles, who am not fit to be called~ an apostle, because I persecuted the church of God.

10   But by the *grace of God* I am what I am, and His grace toward me did not prove *vain;* but I labored even more than *all of them,* yet not I, but the grace of God with me.

11   Whether then *it was* I or they, so we preach and so you believed.

12   Now if Christ is preached, that He has been raised⁺ *from the dead,* how do some among you say that there is no resurrection of the dead?

13   But if there is no resurrection of the dead, not even *Christ* has been raised;⁺

14   and if Christ has not been raised,⁺ then our preaching is *vain,* your faith also is *vain.*

ᴾSome ancient mss. read *is ignorant, let him be ignorant*

14:37
2 Cor. 10:7;
1 Cor. 2:15;
1 John 4:6

14:39
1 Cor. 12:31;
1 Cor. 13:2; 14:1

14:40
1 Cor. 14:33

15:1
Rom. 2:16; Gal.
1:11;
Rom. 2:16; 1 Cor.
3:6; 4:15;
Rom. 5:2; 11:20;
2 Cor. 1:24
15:2
Rom. 11:22;
Gal. 3:4
15:3
1 Cor. 11:23;
John 1:29; Gal.
1:4; Heb. 5:1,3;
1 Pet. 2:24;
Is. 53:5-12; Matt.
26:24; Luke
24:25-27; Acts
8:32f.; 17:2f.;
26:22
15:4
Matt. 16:21; John
2:20ff.; Acts 2:24;
Ps. 16:8ff.; Acts
2:31; 26:22f.
15:5
Luke 24:34;
1 Cor. 1:12;
Mark 16:14; Luke
24:36; John 20:19
15:6
Acts 7:60; 1 Cor.
15:18,20
15:7
Acts 12:17;
Luke 24:33,36f.;
Acts 1:3f.
15:8
Acts 9:3-8;
22:6-11;
26:12-18; 1 Cor.
9:1
15:9
2 Cor. 12:11;
Eph. 3:8; 1 Tim.
1:15;
Acts 8:3
15:10
Rom. 12:3;
2 Cor. 11:23; Col.
1:29; 1 Tim. 4:10;
1 Cor. 3:6; 2 Cor.
3:5; Phil. 2:13
15:12
Acts 17:32; 23:8;
2 Tim. 2:18
15:14
1 Thess. 4:14

15:15
Acts 2:24

15 Moreover we are even found *to be* false witnesses of God, because we witnessed against God that He raised qChrist, whom He did not raise, if 2in fact the dead are not raised.

16 For if the dead are not raised, not even *Christ* has been raised; ✦

15:17
Rom. 4:25

17 and if Christ has not been raised, ✦your faith is *worthless;* you are still in your sins.

15:18
1 Cor. 15:6;
1 Thess. 4:16;
Rev. 14:13
15:19
1 Cor. 4:9; 2 Tim.
3:12

18 Then those also who have fallen asleep in Christ have perished.

19 If we have hoped✦in Christ in this life *only,* we are of all men most to be pitied.

The Order of Resurrection

15:20
Acts 2:24; 1 Pet.
1:3;
Acts 26:23; 1 Cor.
15:23; Rev. 1:5;
1 Cor. 15:6;
1 Thess. 4:16;
Rev. 14:13
15:21
Rom. 5:12
15:22
Rom. 5:14-18
15:23
Acts 26:23; 1 Cor.
15:20; Rev. 1:5;
1 Cor. 6:14;
15:52; 1 Thess.
4:16;
1 Thess. 2:19
15:24
Dan. 2:44; 7:14,
27; 2 Pet. 1:11;
Eph. 5:20;
Rom. 8:38
15:25
Ps. 110:1; Matt.
22:44
15:26
2 Tim. 1:10; Rev.
20:14; 21:4
15:27
Ps. 8:6;
Matt. 11:27;
28:18; Eph. 1:22;
Heb. 2:8

20 But •nowChrist has been raised✦from the dead, the first fruits of those who are asleep.✦

21 For since by a man *came* death, by a man also *came* the resurrection of the dead.

22 For as *in Adam*all die, so also *in Christ*all shall be made alive.

23 But each in his own order: Christ the first fruits, after that those who are Christ's at His coming,

24 then *comes* the end, when He delivers~ up the kingdom to the God and Father, when He has abolishedˣ all rule and all authority and power.

25 For He must reign ~ until He has putˣ all His enemies under His feet.

26 The last enemy that will be abolished is *death.*

27 For HE HAS PUT *ALL THINGS*IN SUBJECTION UNDER HIS FEET. But when He says,ˣ "All things are put in subjection," ✦ it is evident that He is excepted who put all things in subjection to Him.

15:28
Phil. 3:21;
1 Cor. 3:23; 12:6

28 And when all things are subjected ˣto Him, then the Son Himself also will be subjected to the One who subjected all things to Him, that *God*may be all in all.

29 Otherwise, what will those do who are baptized for the dead? If the dead are not raised at all, why then are they baptized for them?

15:30
2 Cor. 11:26
15:31
Rom. 8:36

30 Why are *we*also in danger every hour?

31 I protest, brethren, by the boasting in •you, which I have in Christ Jesus our Lord, I die *daily.*

15:32
2 Cor. 1:8;
Acts 18:19; 1 Cor.
16:8;
Is. 22:13; 56:12;
Luke 12:19

32 If from human motivesI fought with wild beasts at Ephesus, what does it profit me? If the dead are not raised, LET US EATˣ AND DRINK,ˣ FOR TOMORROW WE DIE.

qI.e., the Messiah

33   Do not be deceived:[616b] *"Bad*[10a] company corrupts *good* morals."

34   Become[xi] sober-minded as you ought, and stop sinning;[6] for some have *no knowledge of God.* I speak *this* to your *shame.*

35   But someone will say, "How are the *dead* raised? And with what kind of body do they come?"

36   You fool! That which *you* sow does not come to life unless it dies;[x]

37   and that which you sow, you do not sow the *body which is to be,* but a bare grain, perhaps of wheat or of something else.

38   But God gives it a body just as He wished, and to each of the seeds a body of its own.

39   All flesh is not the same flesh, but there is one *flesh* of men, and another flesh of beasts, and another flesh of birds, and another of fish.

40   There are also *heavenly* bodies and *earthly* bodies, but the glory of the heavenly is one, and the *glory* of the earthly is another.[8b]

41   There is one glory of the sun, and another[8a] glory of the moon, and another glory of the stars; for star differs from star in glory.

42   So also is the resurrection of the dead. It is sown a perishable *body,* it is raised an imperishable *body;*

43   it is sown in dishonor, it is raised in glory; it is sown in weakness, it is raised in power;

44   it is sown a *natural* body, it is raised a *spiritual* body. If there is a *natural* body, there•*is* also a †*spiritual body.*

45   So also it is written,⁺ "The first MAN, Adam, BECAME A LIVING SOUL." The last Adam *became* a †*life-giving* spirit.

46   However, the spiritual is not first, but the natural; then the spiritual.

47   The first man is from the earth, earthy; the second man is from heaven.

48   As is the earthy, so also are those who are earthy; and as is the heavenly, so also are those who are heavenly.

49   And just as we have borne the image of the earthy, ʳ we shall also bear the image[22b] of the heavenly.

The Mystery of Resurrection

50   Now I say this, brethren, that flesh and blood *cannot* inherit[x] the kingdom of God; nor does the perishable inherit the *imperishable.*

ʳSome ancient mss. read *let us also*

15:33
1 Cor. 6:9

15:34
Rom. 13:11;
Matt. 22:29; Acts
26:8;
1 Cor. 6:5
15:35
Rom. 9:19;
Ezek. 37:3
15:36
Luke 11:40;
John 12:24

15:38
Gen. 1:11

15:42
Dan. 12:3; Matt.
13:43;
Rom. 8:21; 1 Cor.
15:50; Gal. 6:8;
Rom. 2:7
15:43
Phil. 3:21; Col.
3:4
15:44
1 Cor. 2:14;
1 Cor. 15:50
15:45
Gen. 2:7;
Rom. 5:14;
John 5:21; 6:57f.;
Rom. 8:2

15:47
John 3:31;
Gen. 2:7; 3:19

15:48
Phil. 3:20f.

15:49
Gen. 5:3;
Rom. 8:29

15:50
Matt. 16:17; John
3:5f.;
1 Cor. 6:9;
Rom. 2:7

15:51
1 Cor. 13:2;
2 Cor. 5:2,4

51 Behold, I tell you a mystery; we shall not all sleep, but we shall all be changed,

15:52
Matt. 24:31;
John 5:28;
1 Thess. 4:15,17

52 in a moment, in the twinkling of an eye, at the last trumpet; for the trumpet will sound, and the dead will be raised imperishable, and *we* shall be changed.

15:53
Rom. 2:7;
2 Cor. 5:4

53 For this perishable must put[x] on the imperishable, and this mortal must put[x] on immortality.

15:54
Is. 25:8

54 But when this perishable will have put[x] on the imperishable, and this mortal will have put[x] on immortality, then will come about the saying that is written,* "DEATH IS SWALLOWED UP in victory.

15:55
Hos. 13:14

55 "O DEATH, WHERE IS YOUR VICTORY? O DEATH, WHERE IS YOUR STING?"

15:56
Rom. 5:12;
Rom. 3:20; 4:15;
7:8
15:57
Rom. 7:25; 2 Cor.
2:14;
Rom. 8:37; Heb.
2:14f.; 1 John 5:4;
Rev. 21:4
15:58
2 Pet. 3:14;
1 Cor. 16:10

56 The sting of death is sin, and the power of sin is the law;

57 but thanks be to *God,* who gives us the victory through our Lord Jesus Christ.

58 Therefore, my beloved brethren, be[~l] steadfast, immovable, always abounding in the work of the Lord, knowing that your toil is not *in* vain in the Lord.

Instructions and Greetings

16:1
Acts 24:17; Rom.
15:25f.;
Acts 9:13;
1 Cor. 4:17;
Acts 16:6
16:2
Acts 20:7;
2 Cor. 9:4f.

16 Now concerning the collection for the saints, as I directed the churches of Galatia, so do[xl] *you also.*

2 On the first day of every week let each one of you put[~l] aside and save, as he may prosper,~ that no collections be made~ when I come.

16:3
2 Cor. 3:1; 8:18f.

3 And when I arrive,[x] whomever you may approve,[x] I shall send them with letters to carry[x] your gift to Jerusalem;

4 and if it is fitting for me to go also, they will go with me.

16:5
1 Cor. 4:19;
Rom. 15:26;
Acts 19:21
16:6
Acts 15:3; 1 Cor.
16:11
16:7
2 Cor. 1:15f.;
Acts 18:21
16:8
Acts 18:19;
Acts 2:1
16:9
Acts 14:27;
Acts 19:9
16:10
Acts 16:1; 1 Cor.
4:17; 2 Cor. 1:1;
1 Cor. 15:58
16:11
1 Tim. 4:12; Titus
2:15;
Acts 15:3; 1 Cor.
16:6;
Acts 15:33
16:12
Acts 18:24;
1 Cor. 1:12; 3:5f.

5 But I shall come to you after I go[x] through *Macedonia,* for I am going through *Macedonia;*

6 and perhaps I shall stay with you, or even spend the winter, that *you* may send[x] me on my way wherever I may go.~

7 For I do not wish to see you now *just* in passing; for I hope to remain[x] with you for *some time,* if the Lord permits.[x6c]

8 But I shall remain in Ephesus until Pentecost;

9 for a *wide* door for *effective service* has opened* to me, and there are *many* adversaries.

10 Now if Timothy comes, see[~l] that he is with you without cause to be afraid; for he is doing the *Lord's work,* as I also am.

11 Let no one therefore despise[o] him. But send[xl] him on his way in peace, so that he may come to me; for I expect him with the brethren.

12 But concerning Apollos our brother, I encouraged him

greatly to come to you with the brethren; and it was not at all *his* desire to come now, but he will come when he has[x] opportunity.

13　Be on the alert,[m] stand[m] firm in the faith, act[m] like men, be strong.[m]

14　Let all that you do be done[m] *in love.*[31a]

15　Now I urge you, brethren (you know the household of Stephanas, that they were the first fruits of Achaia, and that they have devoted themselves for ministry[38a] to the saints),

16　that *you also* be in subjection[~] to such men and to everyone who helps in the work and labors.

17　And I rejoice over the coming of Stephanas and Fortunatus and Achaicus; because they have supplied what was lacking on *your* part.

18　For they have refreshed •my spirit and yours. Therefore acknowledge[m129b] such men.

19　The churches of Asia greet you. Aquila and Prisca greet you heartily in the Lord, with the church that is in their house.

20　All the brethren greet you. Greet[x] one another with a holy[28a] kiss.

21　The greeting is in my •own hand—Paul.

22　If anyone does not love[31b] the Lord, let him be accursed. Maranatha.

23　The grace of the Lord Jesus be with you.

24　My love be with you all in Christ Jesus. Amen.

16:13
Matt. 24:42;
1 Cor. 15:1; Gal.
5:1; Phil. 1:27;
4:1; 1 Thess. 3:8;
2 Thess. 2:15;
1 Sam. 4:9;
2 Sam. 10:12;
Ps. 31:24; Eph.
3:16; 6:10; Col.
1:11
16:14
1 Cor. 14:1
16:15
1 Cor. 1:16;
Rom. 16:5;
Acts 18:12;
Rom. 16:5;
1 Cor. 16:1
16:16
1 Thess. 5:12;
Heb. 13:17
16:17
2 Cor. 7:6f.;
2 Cor. 11:9; Phil.
2:30
16:18
2 Cor. 7:13;
Philem. 7,20;
Phil. 2:29;
1 Thess. 5:12
16:19
Acts 16:6;
Acts 18:2;
Rom. 16:5
16:20
Rom. 16:16
16:21
Rom. 16:22; Gal.
6:11; Col. 4:18;
2 Thess. 3:17;
Philem. 19
16:22
Rom. 9:3;
Phil. 4:5; Rev.
22:20
16:23
Rom. 16:20

The Second Epistle of Paul to the
Corinthians

Introduction

1:1
Rom. 1:1; Gal.
1:1; Eph. 1:1; Col.
1:1; 2 Tim. 1:1;
Titus 1:1;
Gal. 3:26;
1 Cor. 1:1;
Acts 16:1; 1 Cor.
16:10; 2 Cor.
1:19;
1 Cor. 10:32;
Acts 18:1;
Acts 18:12
1:2
Rom. 1:7
1:3
Eph. 1:3; 1 Pet.
1:3;
Rom. 15:5
1:4
Is. 51:12; 66:13;
2 Cor. 7:6,7,13
1:5
2 Cor. 4:10; Phil.
3:10; Col. 1:24
1:6
2 Cor. 4:15;
12:15; Eph. 3:1,
13; 2 Tim. 2:10
1:7
Rom. 8:17
1:8
Rom. 1:13;
Acts 19:23; 1 Cor.
15:32;
Acts 16:6
1:10
Rom. 15:31;
1 Tim. 4:10
1:11
Rom. 15:30; Phil.
1:19; Philem. 22;
2 Cor. 4:15; 9:11f.
1:12
Acts 23:1; 1
Thess. 2:10; Heb.
13:18;
2 Cor. 2:17;
1 Cor. 1:17;
James 3:15

1 Paul, an apostle of Christ Jesus by the will of God, and Timothy *our* brother, to the church of God which is at Corinth with all the saints who are throughout Achaia:

2 Grace to you and peace from God our Father and the Lord Jesus Christ.

3 Blessed *be* the God and Father of our Lord Jesus Christ, the Father of mercies and God of all comfort;

4 who comforts us in all our affliction so that we may be able~ to comfort~ those who are in any affliction with the comfort with which we ourselves are comforted by God.

5 For just as the *sufferings of Christ* are ours in abundance, so *also our comfort* is abundant through Christ.

6 But if we are afflicted, it is for *your* comfort and salvation; or if we are comforted, it is for *your* comfort, which is effective in the patient enduring of the same sufferings which *we also* suffer;

7 and our hope for you is firmly grounded, knowing that as you are sharers of our sufferings, so also you are *sharers* of our comfort.

8 For we do not want you to be unaware,~ brethren, of our affliction which came *to us* in Asia, that we were burdened *excessively, beyond our strength*, so that we despaired^{X1} even of life;

9 indeed, we had⁺ the sentence of death *within ourselves* in order that we should not trust⁺ *in ourselves*, but in ⁺*God* who raises the dead;

10 who delivered^{18b} us from so great a *peril of* death, and will deliver *us*, He on whom we have set⁺ our hope. And He will yet deliver^{18b} us,

11 you also joining in helping us through your prayers, that thanks may be given^x by many persons on our behalf for the favor^{24c} bestowed upon us through *the prayers of* many.

Paul's Integrity

12 For our proud confidence is this, the testimony of our conscience, that in holiness and godly sincerity, not in *fleshly* wisdom but in the grace of God, we have conducted ourselves in the world, and especially toward you.

356

13   For we write nothing else to you than what you read and understand,[29b] and I hope you will understand[29b] *until the end;*

14   just as you also partially did understand us, that we are your reason to be proud as you also are ours, in the day of our Lord Jesus.

15   And in *this* †*confidence* I intended[m] at first to come to you, that you might *twice* receive[x] a blessing;

16   that is, to pass[x] *your* way into Macedonia, and again from Macedonia to come to you, and by you to be helped[x] on my journey to Judea.

17   Therefore, I was not *vacillating* when I intended to do this, was I? Or that which I purpose, do I purpose according to the *flesh,* that with me there should be yes, yes and no, no *at the same time?*

18   But as God is faithful, our word to you is not yes and no.

19   For the Son of *God,* Christ Jesus, who was preached among you by us—by me and Silvanus and Timothy—was not yes and no, but is⁺ *yes in Him.*

20   For as many as may be the promises of God, in Him they are *yes;* wherefore also by Him is our *Amen* to the glory of God through us.

21   Now He who establishes us with you in Christ and anointed us is God,

22   who also sealed us and gave *us* the Spirit in our hearts as a pledge.

23   But I call God *as witness* to •my soul, that to spare you I came no more to Corinth.

24   Not that we lord it over your *faith,* but are workers with you for your joy; for in your *faith* you are standing⁺ firm.

Reaffirm Your Love

2   But I determined this for my own sake, that I would not come to you in sorrow again.

2   For if *I* cause you sorrow, who then makes me glad but the one whom I made sorrowful?

3   And this is the very thing I wrote you, lest, when I came, I should have[x] sorrow from those who ought[m] to make me rejoice;~ having confidence⁺ in you all, that •my joy would be *the joy* of you all.

4   For out of *much affliction* and *anguish of heart* I wrote to you with many tears; not that you should be made[x] sorrowful, but that you might know[x29a] the *love* which I have especially for you.

5   But if any has caused⁺ sorrow, he has caused⁺ sorrow not

1:13
1 Cor. 1:8
1:14
1 Cor. 1:8
1:15
1 Cor. 4:19;
Rom. 1:11; 15:29
1:16
Acts 19:21; 1 Cor.
16:5-7;
Acts 19:21; Rom.
15:26;
Acts 15:3; 1 Cor.
16:6,11
1:17
2 Cor. 10:2f.;
11:18
1:18
1 Cor. 1:9;
2 Cor. 2:17
1:19
Matt. 4:3; 16:16;
26:63;
Acts 15:22; 1
Thess. 1:1; 2
Thess. 1:1; 1 Pet.
5:12;
Acts 18:5; 2 Cor.
1:1;
Heb. 13:8
1:20
Rom. 15:8;
Heb. 13:8;
1 Cor. 14:16;
Rev. 3:14
1:21
1 Cor. 1:8;
1 John 2:20,27
1:22
John 3:33;
Rom. 8:16; 2 Cor.
5:5; Eph. 1:14
1:23
Rom. 1:9; Gal.
1:20;
1 Cor. 4:21;
2 Cor. 2:1,3;
2 Cor. 1:1
1:24
2 Cor. 4:5; 11:20;
1 Pet. 5:3;
Rom. 11:20;
1 Cor. 15:1
2:1
1 Cor. 4:21;
2 Cor. 12:21
2:2
2 Cor. 7:8
2:3
2 Cor. 2:9; 7:8,12;
1 Cor. 4:21;
2 Cor. 12:21;
Gal. 5:10;
2 Thess. 3:4;
Philem. 21
2:4
2 Cor. 2:9; 7:8,12
2:5
1 Cor. 5:1f.

to *me,* but in some degree—in order not to say~ too much—to *all of you.*

6 Sufficient for such a one is this punishment which was *inflicted by* the majority,

7 so that on the contrary you should rather forgive[x21b] and comfort[x] *him,* lest somehow such a one be *overwhelmed* [x1] by excessive[1] sorrow.

8 Wherefore I urge you to reaffirm[x] *your* love[31a] for him.

9 For to this end also I wrote that I might put[x] you to the test, whether you are *obedient* in all things.

10 But whom you forgive[21b] anything, I *forgive* also; for indeed what I have forgiven,[+] if I have forgiven[+] anything, *I did it* for your sakes in the presence of Christ,

11 in order that no advantage be taken[x] of us by Satan; for we are not ignorant of his schemes.

12 Now when I came to Troas for the gospel of Christ and when a door was *opened* [+] for me in the Lord,

13 I had[+] no rest for my spirit, not finding[x] Titus my brother; but taking my leave of them, I went on to Macedonia.

14 But thanks be to God, who always leads us in His triumph in Christ, and manifests through us the sweet aroma of the knowledge of Him in every place.

15 For we are a fragrance of *Christ* to God among those who are being saved and among those who are perishing;

16 to the one an aroma from death to death, to the other an aroma from life to life. And who is adequate for these things?

17 For we are not like many, [a]peddling the word of God, but as from sincerity, but as from *God,* we speak *in Christ* in the sight[1] of God.

Ministers of a New Covenant

3 Are we beginning to commend~ *ourselves* again? Or do we need, as some, letters of commendation to you or from you?

2 *You* are our letter, written[+] in our hearts, known and read[+] by all men;

3 being manifested that you are a letter of Christ, cared for by us, written[+] not with ink, but with the Spirit of the living God, not on tablets of *stone,* but on tablets of *human hearts.*

4 And *such* confidence we have through Christ toward God.

5 Not that we are adequate in *ourselves* to consider[x] anything as *coming* from ourselves, but our adequacy is from God,

6 who also made us adequate *as* servants of a new[34a] cove-

[a]Or, *corrupting*

2:6
1 Cor. 5:4f.;
2 Cor. 7:11
2:7
Gal. 6:1; Eph.
4:32
2:9
2 Cor. 2:3f.;
2 Cor. 8:2; Phil.
2:22;
2 Cor. 7:15; 10:6
2:10
1 Cor. 5:4; 2 Cor.
4:6
2:11
Matt. 4:10;
Luke 22:31;
2 Cor. 4:4; 1 Pet.
5:8
2:12
Acts 16:8;
Rom. 1:1; 2 Cor.
4:3,4; 8:18; 9:13;
10:14; 11:4,7; 1
Thess. 3:2;
Acts 14:27
2:13
2 Cor. 7:5;
2 Cor. 7:6,13f.;
8:6,16,23; 12:18;
Gal. 2:1,3; 2 Tim.
4:10; Titus 1:4;
Mark 6:46;
Rom. 15:26
2:14
Rom. 1:8; 6:17; 1
Cor. 15:57; 2 Cor.
8:16; 9:15;
Col. 2:15;
Song 1:3; Ezek.
20:41; Eph. 5:2;
Phil. 4:18;
1 Cor. 12:8
2:15
Song 1:3; Ezek.
20:41; Eph. 5:2;
Phil. 4:18;
1 Cor. 1:18
2:16
Luke 2:34; John
9:39; 1 Pet. 2:7f.;
2 Cor. 3:5f.
2:17
2 Cor. 4:2; Gal.
1:6-9;
1 Cor. 5:8; 2 Cor.
1:12; 1 Thess.
2:4; 1 Pet. 4:11;
2 Cor. 12:19
3:1
2 Cor. 5:12;
10:12,18; 12:11;
Acts 18:27; 1 Cor.
16:3
3:2
1 Cor. 9:2
3:3
2 Cor. 3:6;
Matt. 16:16;
Ex. 24:12; 31:18;
32:15f.; 2 Cor.
3:7;
Prov. 3:3; 7:3;
Jer. 17:1;
Jer. 31:33; Ezek.
11:19; 36:26
3:4
Eph. 3:12
3:5
1 Cor. 15:10
3:6
1 Cor. 3:5;
Jer. 31:31; Luke
22:20; Rom. 2:29;
John 6:63; Rom.
7:6

nant, not of the letter, but of the Spirit; for the letter kills, but the Spirit gives life.

7 But if the ministry of death, in letters engraved* on stones, came with glory, so that the sons of Israel could~ not look˟ intently at the face of Moses because of the glory of his face, fading *as* it was,

8 how shall the ministry of the Spirit fail to be even more with glory?

9 For if the ministry of condemnation has glory, much more does the *ministry of righteousness* abound in glory.

10 For indeed what had glory,* in this case has no glory* on account of the glory that surpasses *it*.

11 For if that which fades away *was* with glory, much more that which remains *is* in glory.

12 Having therefore such a hope, we use *great boldness* in *our* speech,

13 and *are* not as Moses, *who* used to put˟ a veil over his face that the sons of Israel might not look˟ intently at the end of what was fading away.

14 But their minds were *hardened;* for until this very day at the reading of the old covenant the same veil *remains* unlifted, because it is removed *in Christ.*

15 But to this day whenever Moses is read,~ a veil lies over their heart;

16 but whenever a man turns˟ to the Lord, the veil is *taken away.*

17 Now the Lord is the †*Spirit;* and where the Spirit of the Lord is, *there* is liberty.

18 But we all, with unveiled* face beholding as in a mirror the glory of the Lord, are being transformed into the *same image* [22b] from glory to glory, just as from the Lord, the Spirit.

Paul's Apostolic Ministry

4 Therefore, since we have †this ministry, as we received mercy, we do not lose heart,

2 but we have renounced the things hidden because of shame, not walking in craftiness or adulterating the word of God, but by the manifestation of truth commending ourselves to every man's conscience in the sight of God.

3 And even if our gospel *is veiled,* it is veiled* to those who are perishing,

4 in whose case the god of †this world has blinded the minds of the unbelieving, that they might not see˟ the light of the gospel of the glory of Christ, who is the image [22b] of God.

3:7
Rom. 4:15; 5:20;
7:5f.; 2 Cor. 3:9;
Gal. 3:10,21f.;
Ex. 24:12; 31:18;
32:15f.; 2 Cor.
3:3;
Ex. 34:29-35;
2 Cor. 3:13

3:9
Deut. 27:26;
2 Cor. 3:7; Heb.
12:18-21;
Rom. 1:17; 3:21f.

3:12
2 Cor. 7:4;
Acts 4:13,29; 2
Cor. 7:4; Eph.
6:19; 1 Thess. 2:2
3:13
Ex. 34:33-35; 2
Cor. 3:7

3:14
Rom. 11:7; 2 Cor.
4:4;
Acts 13:15;
2 Cor. 3:6

3:16
Ex. 34:34; Rom.
11:23
3:17
Is. 61:1f.; Gal.
4:6;
John 8:32; Gal.
5:1,13
3:18
1 Cor. 13:12;
John 17:22,24; 2
Cor. 4:4,6;
Rom. 8:29;
2 Cor. 3:17
4:1
1 Cor. 3:5;
1 Cor. 7:25;
Luke 18:1; 2 Cor.
4:16; Gal. 6:9;
Eph. 3:13; 2
Thess. 3:13
4:2
Rom. 6:21; 1 Cor.
4:5;
2 Cor. 2:17;
2 Cor. 5:11f.
4:3
2 Cor. 2:12;
1 Cor. 2:6ff.;
2 Cor. 3:14;
1 Cor. 1:18;
2 Cor. 2:15
4:4
John 12:31;
Matt. 13:22;
2 Cor. 3:14;
Acts 26:18; 2
Cor. 4:6;
2 Cor. 3:18; 4:6;
John 1:18; Phil.
2:6; Col. 1:15;
Heb. 1:3

4:5
1 Cor. 4:15f.;
1 Thess. 2:6f.

4:6
Gen. 1:3;
2 Pet. 1:19;
Acts 26:18; 2 Cor.
4:4

4:7
Job 4:19; 10:9;
33:6; Lam. 4:2;
2 Cor. 5:1; 2 Tim.
2:20;
Judg. 7:2; 1 Cor.
2:5
4:8
2 Cor. 1:8; 7:5;
2 Cor. 6:12;
Gal. 4:20
4:9
John 15:20; Rom.
8:35f.;
Ps. 129:2; Heb.
13:5;
Ps. 37:24; Prov.
24:16; Mic. 7:8
4:10
Rom. 6:5; 8:36;
Gal. 6:17;
Rom. 6:8

4:13
1 Cor. 12:9;
Ps. 116:10

4:14
Acts 2:24;
1 Thess. 4:14;
Luke 21:36; Eph.
5:27; Col. 1:22;
Jude 24
4:15
Rom. 8:28; 2 Cor.
1:6;
1 Cor. 9:19; 2
Cor. 1:11
4:16
2 Cor. 4:1;
Rom. 7:22;
Is. 40:29,31; Col.
3:10
4:17
Rom. 8:18
4:18
Rom. 8:24; 2 Cor.
5:7; Heb. 11:1,13

5:1
Job 4:19; 1 Cor.
15:47; 2 Cor. 4:7;
2 Pet. 1:13f.;
Mark 14:58; Acts
7:48; Heb. 9:11,
24
5:2
Rom. 8:23; 2 Cor.
5:4;
1 Cor. 15:53f.;
2 Cor. 5:4
5:4
2 Cor. 5:2;
1 Cor. 15:53f.;
2 Cor. 5:2;
1 Cor. 15:54

5 For we do not preach *ourselves* but Christ Jesus as Lord, and ourselves as your bond-servants[38b] for Jesus' sake.

6 For God, who said, "Light shall shine *out of darkness,*" is the One who has shone in our hearts to give the light of the knowledge of the glory of God in the face of Christ.

7 But we have this treasure in earthen vessels, that the surpassing greatness of the power may be of God and not from ourselves;

8 *we are* afflicted in every way, but *not* crushed; perplexed, but *not* despairing;[1]

9 persecuted, but *not* forsaken; struck down, but *not* destroyed;

10 always carrying about in the body the *dying of Jesus,* that the *life*[30b] *of Jesus* also may be manifested[x] in our body.

11 For we who live are constantly being delivered over to death for Jesus' sake, that the life of Jesus also may be manifested[x] in our mortal flesh.

12 So death works in us, but life in you.

13 But having the same spirit of faith, according to what is written, [+] "I BELIEVED, THEREFORE I SPOKE," *we* also believe, therefore also we speak;

14 knowing that He who raised the Lord Jesus will raise *us* also with Jesus and will present us with you.

15 For all things *are* for your sakes, that the grace which is spreading to more and more people may cause the giving of thanks to abound[x] to the glory of God.

16 Therefore we do not lose heart, but though our outer man is decaying, yet our inner man is being renewed day by day.

17 For momentary, light affliction is producing[1] for us an eternal weight of glory *far beyond*[4] *all comparison,*

18 while we look not at the things which are seen, but at the things which are not seen; for the things which are seen are temporal, but the things which are not seen are eternal.

The Temporal and Eternal

5 For we know that if the earthly tent which is our house is torn[x] down, we have a *building from God,* a house *not made with hands,* eternal in the heavens.

2 For indeed in this *house* we groan, [†]longing to be clothed[x1] with our *dwelling from heaven;*

3 inasmuch[2] as we, having put it on, shall not be found *naked.*

4 For indeed while we are in this tent, we groan, being burdened, because we do not want to be unclothed,[x] but to be

clothed,ˣ¹ in order that what is mortal may be swallowedˣ up¹ by life.

5 Now He who prepared us for this very purpose is *God,* who gave to us the Spirit as a pledge.

6 Therefore, being always of good courage, and knowing that while we are at home in the body we are absent from the Lord—

7 for we walk⁴²ᵃ by *faith,* not by sight—

8 we are of good courage, I say, and prefer rather to be absentˣ from the body and to be at homeˣ with the Lord.

9 Therefore also we have as our ambition, whether at home or absent, to be †*pleasing* to Him.

10 For we must *all* appearˣ before the judgment seat of Christ, that *each one* may be recompensedˣ for his deeds in the body, according to what he has done,¹⁹ᵇ whether good²⁵ᵃ or bad.¹⁰ᵈ

11 Therefore knowing the fear of the Lord, we persuade men, but we are made manifest⁺ to *God;* and I hope that we are made manifest⁺ also in *your consciences.*

12 We are not again commending ourselves to you but *are* giving you an occasion to be proud of us, that you may have~ *an answer* for those who take pride in appearance, and not in heart.

13 For if we are beside ourselves, it is for God; if we are of sound mind, it is for you.

14 For the love of Christ controls us, having concluded this, that one died *for all,* therefore all died;

15 and He died *for all,* that they who live should no longer live~ *for themselves,* but for Him who died and rose again on their behalf.

16 Therefore from now on we recognize no man according to the flesh; even though we have known⁺²⁹ᵃ *Christ* according to the flesh, yet now we know *Him thus* no longer.

17 Therefore if any man is in Christ, *he is* a new³⁴ᵃ creature; the old things passed away; behold, new³⁴ᵃ *things* have come.⁺

18 Now all *these* things are from God, who reconciled us to Himself through Christ, and gave us the ministry of reconciliation,

19 namely, that God was in Christ reconciling the world to Himself, not counting their trespasses⁴⁰ᵇ against them, and He has committed to us the word of reconciliation.

20 Therefore, we are ambassadors for *Christ,* as though *God* were entreating through us; we beg you on behalf of Christ, be reconciledˣ¹ to God.

21 He made Him who knew²⁹ᵃ *no sin to be sin* on our behalf, that *we* might become the righteousness of God in Him.

5:5
Rom. 8:23; 2 Cor. 1:22

5:6
Heb. 11:13f.

5:7
1 Cor. 13:12; 2 Cor. 4:18
5:8
Phil. 1:23; John 12:26; Phil. 1:23
5:9
Rom. 14:18; Col. 1:10; 1 Thess. 4:1
5:10
Matt. 16:27; Acts 10:42; Rom. 2:16; 14:10,12; Eph. 6:8

5:11
Heb. 10:31; 12:29; Jude 23; 2 Cor. 4:2

5:12
2 Cor. 3:1; 2 Cor. 1:14; Phil. 1:26

5:13
Mark 3:21; 2 Cor. 11:1,16ff.; 12:11

5:14
Acts 18:5; Rom. 5:15; 6:6f.; Gal. 2:20; Col. 3:3
5:15
Rom. 14:7-9
5:16
John 8:15; 2 Cor. 11:18; Phil. 3:4
5:17
Rom. 16:7; John 3:3; Rom. 6:4; Gal. 6:15; Is. 43:18f.; 65:17; Eph. 4:24; Rev. 21:4f.
5:18
1 Cor. 11:12; Rom. 5:10; Col. 1:20; 1 Cor. 3:5
5:19
Col. 2:9; Rom. 4:8; 1 Cor. 13:5
5:20
Mal. 2:7; Eph. 6:20; 2 Cor. 6:1; Rom. 5:10; Col. 1:20
5:21
Acts 3:14; Heb. 4:15; 7:26; 1 Pet. 2:22; 1 John 3:5; Rom. 3:25; 4:25; 8:3; Gal. 3:13; Rom. 1:17; 3:21f.; 1 Cor. 1:30

6:1
1 Cor. 3:9;
2 Cor. 5:20;
Acts 11:23
6:2
Is. 49:8
6:3
1 Cor. 8:9,13;
9:12
6:4
Rom. 3:5;
1 Cor. 3:5; 2 Tim.
2:24f.;
Acts 9:16; 2 Cor.
4:8-11; 6:4ff.;
11:23-27; 12:10
6:5
Acts 16:23;
Acts 19:23ff.;
1 Cor. 4:11
6:6
1 Cor. 12:8;
2 Cor. 11:6;
2 Cor. 1:23; 2:10;
13:10;
1 Cor. 2:4;
1 Thess. 1:5;
Rom. 12:9
6:7
2 Cor. 2:17; 4:2;
1 Cor. 2:5;
Rom. 13:12;
2 Cor. 10:4; Eph.
6:11ff.
6:8
1 Cor. 4:10;
Rom. 3:8; 1 Cor.
4:13; 2 Cor. 12:16;
Matt. 27:63;
2 Cor. 1:18; 4:2; 1
Thess. 2:3f.
6:9
Rom. 8:36;
2 Cor. 1:8,10;
4:11
6:10
John 16:22;
2 Cor. 7:4; Phil.
2:17; 4:4; Col.
1:24; 1 Thess.
1:6;
1 Cor. 1:5; 2 Cor.
8:9; Acts 3:6;
Rom. 8:32; 1 Cor.
3:21
6:11
Ezek. 33:22; Eph.
6:19;
Is. 60:5; 2 Cor.
7:3
6:12
2 Cor. 7:2
6:13
Gal. 4:12;
1 Cor. 4:14
6:14
Deut. 22:10;
1 Cor. 5:9f.;
1 Cor. 6:6;
Eph. 5:7,11;
1 John 1:6
6:15
1 Cor. 10:21;
Acts 5:14; 1 Pet.
1:21; 1 Cor. 6:6
6:16
1 Cor. 10:21;
1 Cor. 3:16; 6:19;
Matt. 16:16;
Ex. 29:45; Lev.
26:12; Jer. 31:1;
Ezek. 37:27;
Ex. 25:8; John
14:23; Rev. 2:1
6:17
Is. 52:11;
Rev. 18:4

Their Ministry Commended

6 And working together *with Him,* we also urge you not to receive[x5a] the grace of God in *vain*—

2 for He says,

"AT THE ACCEPTABLE TIME I LISTENED TO YOU,
AND ON THE DAY OF SALVATION I HELPED YOU";

behold, now is "THE ACCEPTABLE TIME," behold, now is "THE DAY OF †SALVATION"—

3 giving no cause for offense in anything, in order that the ministry be not *discredited,*[x]

4 but in everything commending ourselves as servants of *God,* in much endurance, in afflictions, in hardships, in distresses,

5 in beatings, in imprisonments, in tumults, in labors, in sleeplessness, in hunger,

6 in purity, in knowledge, in patience, in kindness, in the Holy Spirit, in genuine love,[31a]

7 in the word[43a] of truth, in the power of God; by the weapons of righteousness for the right hand and the left,

8 by glory and dishonor, by evil report and good report; *regarded* as deceivers and yet true;

9 as unknown yet well-known,[29b] as dying yet behold, we live; as punished yet not put to death,

10 as sorrowful yet always rejoicing, as poor yet making many rich, as having nothing yet possessing all things.

11 Our mouth has spoken✦ freely to you, O Corinthians, our heart is opened✦ wide.

12 You are not restrained by us, but you are restrained in your own affections.

13 Now in a like exchange—I speak as to children—open[xi] wide *to us* also.

14 Do not be⊙ bound together with unbelievers; for what partnership have righteousness and lawlessness, or what fellowship has light with darkness?

15 Or what harmony has Christ with Belial, or what has a believer in common with an unbeliever?

16 Or what agreement has the temple of God with idols? For *we* are the temple of the *living* God; just as God said,

"I WILL DWELL IN THEM AND WALK AMONG THEM;
AND I WILL BE THEIR GOD, AND *THEY* SHALL BE MY PEOPLE.

17 "Therefore, COME[xi] OUT FROM THEIR MIDST AND BE SEPARATE,"[xi] says the Lord.

"AND DO *NOT TOUCH*° WHAT IS UNCLEAN;
And *I* will welcome you.

18   "And I will be a father to you,
And *you* shall be sons and daughters to Me,"
Says the Lord Almighty.

6:18
2 Sam. 7:14;
1 Chr. 17:13; Is.
43:6; Hos. 1:10;
Rom. 8:14

Paul Reveals His Heart

7 Therefore, having *these* promises, beloved, let us cleanse[x] ourselves from all defilement of flesh and spirit, perfecting holiness in the fear of God.

7:1
Heb. 6:9;
1 Pet. 1:15f.

2   Make room[xi] for us *in your hearts;* we wronged no one, we corrupted no one, we took advantage of no one.

7:2
2 Cor. 6:12f.;
12:15

3   I do not speak to condemn you; for I have said[+] before that you are *in our hearts* to die[x] together and to live[~] together.

7:3
2 Cor. 6:11f.;
Phil. 1:7

4   Great is my confidence in you, great is my boasting on your behalf; I am filled[+] with comfort. I am overflowing with joy in all our affliction.

7:4
2 Cor. 3:12;
2 Cor. 7:14; 8:24;
9:2f.; 10:8; Phil.
1:26; 2 Thess.
1:4;
2 Cor. 1:4;
2 Cor. 6:10

5   For even when we came into Macedonia our flesh had[+] no rest, but we were afflicted on every side: conflicts without, fears within.

7:5
Rom. 15:26;
2 Cor. 2:13;
2 Cor. 4:8;
Deut. 32:25

6   But *God,* who comforts the depressed, comforted us by the coming of Titus;

7:6
2 Cor. 1:3f.;
2 Cor. 7:13;
2 Cor. 2:13; 7:13f.

7   and not only by his coming, but also by the comfort with which he was comforted in you, as he reported to us your longing, your mourning, your zeal for me; so that I rejoiced[x] even more.

8   For though I caused you sorrow by my letter, I do not regret it; though I did regret it—*for* I see that that letter caused you sorrow, though only for a while—

7:8
2 Cor. 2:2

9   I now rejoice, not that you were made sorrowful, but that you were made sorrowful to *the point of* repentance; for you were made sorrowful according to *the will of* God, in order that you might not suffer[x] loss in anything through us.

10   For the sorrow that is according to *the will of* God produces[1] a repentance *without regret, leading* to salvation; but the sorrow of the world produces[1] *death.*

7:10
Acts 11:18

11   For behold what earnestness this very thing, this godly sorrow, has produced in you: what vindication of yourselves, what indignation, what fear, what longing, what zeal, what avenging of wrong! In everything you demonstrated yourselves to be innocent[13a] in the matter.

7:11
2 Cor. 7:7;
2 Cor. 2:6;
Rom. 3:5

12   So although I wrote to you *it was* not for the sake of the offender, nor for the sake of the one offended, but that your

7:12
2 Cor. 2:3,9; 7:8;
1 Cor. 5:1f.

earnestness on our behalf might be made known[x] to you in the sight of God.

13   For this reason we have been comforted.[+]

And besides our comfort, we rejoiced even much more for the joy of Titus, because his spirit has been refreshed[+] by you all.

14   For if in anything I have boasted[+] to him about you, I was not put to shame;[39c] but as we spoke all things to you in truth, so also our boasting before Titus proved to be *the* truth.

15   And his affection abounds all the more toward you, as he remembers the obedience of you all, how you received him with fear and trembling.

16   I rejoice that in everything I have confidence in you.

Great Generosity

8   Now, brethren, we *wish to* make known to you the grace of God which has been given[+] in the churches of Macedonia,

2   that in a great ordeal of affliction their abundance of joy and their deep poverty overflowed in the wealth of their liberality.

3   For I testify that according to their ability, and beyond their ability *they gave* of their own accord,

4   begging us with much entreaty for the favor of participation in the support of the saints,

5   and *this*, not as we had expected, but they [†]first gave *themselves* to the Lord and to us by the will of God.

6   Consequently we urged[x] Titus that as he had previously made a beginning, so he would also complete[x] in you this gracious work as well.

7   But just as you abound in everything, in faith and utterance and knowledge and in all earnestness and in the [b]love we inspired in you, *see* that you abound[~] in this gracious work also.

8   I am not speaking *this* as a command, but as proving through the earnestness of *others* the sincerity of [•]*your* love also.

9   For you know[29a] the grace of our Lord Jesus Christ, that though He was rich, yet for your sake He became poor, that *you* through *His poverty* might become[x] rich.

10   And I give *my* opinion in this matter, for this is to your advantage, who were the first to begin a year ago not only to do[x] *this*, but also to desire *to do it*.

11   But [•]*now* finish[u] *doing* [x] it also; that just as *there was* the readiness to desire it, so *there may be* also the completion[x] of it by your ability.

12   For if the readiness is present, it is acceptable according

bLit., *love from us in you*; some ancient mss. read *your love for us*

7:13
2 Cor. 7:6;
2 Cor. 2:13; 7:6,
14;
1 Cor. 16:18

7:14
2 Cor. 7:4; 8:24;
9:2f.; 10:8; Phil.
1:26; 2 Thess.
1:4;
2 Cor. 2:13; 7:6,
13

7:15
2 Cor. 2:9;
1 Cor. 2:3; Phil.
2:12

7:16
2 Cor. 2:3

8:1
2 Cor. 8:5;
Acts 16:9

8:2
Rom. 2:4

8:3
1 Cor. 16:2;
2 Cor. 8:11

8:4
Acts 24:17; Rom.
15:25f.;
Rom. 15:31;
2 Cor. 8:19f.; 9:1,
12f.

8:5
2 Cor. 8:1;
1 Cor. 1:1

8:6
2 Cor. 8:17;
12:18;
2 Cor. 2:13; 8:16,
23;
2 Cor. 8:10;
Acts 24:17; Rom.
15:25f.

8:7
2 Cor. 9:8;
Rom. 15:14;
1 Cor. 1:5; 12:8

8:8
1 Cor. 7:6

8:9
2 Cor. 13:14;
Matt. 20:28;
2 Cor. 6:10; Phil.
2:6f.

8:10
1 Cor. 7:25,40;
1 Cor. 16:2f.; 2
Cor. 9:2

8:11
2 Cor. 8:12,19;
9:2

8:12
Mark 12:43f.;
Luke 21:3,4;
2 Cor. 9:7

to what *a man* has,~ not according to what he does not have.

13   For *this* is not for the ease of others *and* for your affliction, but by way of equality—

14   at this present time *your* abundance *being a supply* for †*their* want, that †*their* abundance also may become *a supply* for *your* want, that there may be *equality;*

15   as it is written, ✦ "HE WHO *gathered* MUCH DID NOT HAVE TOO MUCH, AND HE WHO *gathered* LITTLE HAD NO LACK."

16   But thanks be to God, who puts the same earnestness on your behalf in the heart of Titus.

17   For he not only accepted our appeal, but being himself very[3] earnest, he has gone to you of his *own accord.*

18   And we have sent along with him the brother whose fame in *the things of* the gospel *has spread* through all the churches;

19   and not only *this,* but he has also been appointed by the churches to travel with us in this gracious work, which is being administered by us for the glory of the Lord Himself, and *to show* our readiness,

20   taking precaution that no one should discredit[x] us in our administration of this generous gift;

21   for we have regard for what is honorable,[25b] not only in the sight of the Lord, but also in the sight of men.

22   And we have sent with them our brother, whom we have often tested and found diligent in many[4] things, but •now even more[4] diligent, because of *his* great confidence in you.

23   As for Titus, *he is* •my partner and fellow worker among you; as for our brethren, *they are* messengers of the churches, a glory to Christ.

24   Therefore openly before the churches show them the *proof* of your love and of our reason for boasting about you.

God Gives Most

9 For it is superfluous for me to write~ to you about this ministry to the saints;

2   for I know your readiness, of which I boast about you to the Macedonians, *namely,* that Achaia has been prepared✦ since last year, and your zeal has stirred up most of them.

3   But I have sent the brethren, that our boasting about you may not be made[x] empty in this case, that, as I was saying,[m] you may be prepared;✦

4   lest if any Macedonians come with me and find[x] you unprepared, *we* (not to speak~ of †*you*) should be put to shame[x39c] by this confidence.

5   So I thought it necessary to urge[x] the brethren that they

---

8:14
Acts 4:34; 2 Cor.
9:12

8:15
Ex. 16:18

8:16
2 Cor. 2:14;
Rev. 17:17;
2 Cor. 2:13; 8:6,
23
8:17
2 Cor. 8:6; 12:18

8:18
1 Cor. 16:3;
2 Cor. 12:18;
2 Cor. 2:12;
1 Cor. 4:17; 7:17
8:19
Rom. 5:3;
Acts 14:23; 1 Cor.
16:3f.;
2 Cor. 8:4,6;
2 Cor. 8:11,12;
9:2

8:21
Rom. 12:17;
Prov. 3:4; Rom.
14:18

8:23
2 Cor. 8:6;
Philem. 17;
2 Cor. 8:18,22;
John 13:16; Phil.
2:25;
1 Cor. 11:7
8:24
2 Cor. 7:4

9:1
1 Thess. 4:9;
2 Cor. 8:4

9:2
2 Cor. 7:4;
Rom. 15:26;
Acts 18:12;
2 Cor. 8:10

9:3
2 Cor. 7:4;
1 Cor. 16:2

9:4
Rom. 15:26
9:5
2 Cor. 9:3;
Gen. 33:11;
Judg. 1:15; 2
Cor. 9:6;
Phil. 4:17;
2 Cor. 12:17f.

would go[x] on ahead to you and arrange[x] beforehand your previously[4] promised[+] bountiful gift, that the same might be *ready* as a bountiful gift, and not affected by covetousness.

9:6
Prov. 11:24f.;
22:9; Gal. 6:7,9

6 Now this *I say,* he who sows sparingly shall also reap *sparingly;* and he who sows bountifully shall also reap *bountifully.*

9:7
Deut. 15:10;
1 Chr. 29:17;
Rom. 12:8; 2 Cor.
8:12;
Ex. 25:2

7 Let each one *do* just as he has purposed[+] in his heart; not grudgingly or under compulsion; for God loves a *cheerful giver.*

9:8
Eph. 3:20

8 And God is *able* to make *all grace* abound[x] to you, that *always* having *all sufficiency* in *everything,*[4] you may have[~] an abundance for every good[25a] deed;

9:9
Ps. 112:9

9 as it is written,[+]

"HE SCATTERED ABROAD, HE GAVE TO THE POOR,
HIS RIGHTEOUSNESS ABIDES FOREVER."

9:10
Is. 55:10;
Hos. 10:12

10 Now He who supplies seed to the sower and bread for food, will supply and multiply your seed for sowing and increase the harvest of your righteousness;

9:11
1 Cor. 1:5;
2 Cor. 1:11

11 you will be enriched in everything for all liberality, which through us is producing[1] thanksgiving to God.

9:12
2 Cor. 8:14;
2 Cor. 1:11

12 For the ministry of this service is not only fully supplying[~] the needs of the saints, but is also overflowing[~] through many thanksgivings to God.

9:13
Rom. 15:31;
2 Cor. 8:4;
Matt. 9:8;
1 Tim. 6:12f.;
Heb. 3:1; 4:14;
10:23;
2 Cor. 2:12

13 Because of the proof given by this ministry they will glorify God for *your* obedience to your confession of the gospel of Christ, and for the liberality of your contribution to them and to all,

14 while they also, by prayer on your behalf, yearn for you because of the surpassing grace of God in you.

9:15
2 Cor. 2:14;
Rom. 5:15f.

15 Thanks be to God for His indescribable gift![24a]

Paul Describes Himself

10:1
Gal. 5:2; Eph.
3:1; Col. 1:23;
Rom. 12:1;
Matt. 11:29;
1 Cor. 4:21; Phil.
4:5;
1 Cor. 2:3f.;
2 Cor. 10:10

10 Now *I,* Paul, *myself* urge you by the meekness[23b] and gentleness[23a] of Christ—I who am meek when face to face with you, but bold toward you when absent!

10:2
1 Cor. 4:21;
2 Cor. 13:2,10;
1 Cor. 4:18f.;
Rom. 8:4; 2 Cor.
1:17

2 I ask[9b] that when I am present I may not be bold[x] with the confidence with which I propose to be courageous[x] against some, who regard us as if we walked according to the flesh.

10:3
Rom. 8:4; 2 Cor.
1:17

3 For though we walk in the flesh, we do not *war* according to the flesh,

10:4
1 Cor. 9:7; 2 Cor.
6:7; 1 Tim. 1:18;
Jer. 1:10; 2 Cor.
10:8; 13:10

4 for the weapons of our warfare are not of the flesh, but divinely powerful for the destruction of fortresses.

10:5
Is. 2:11f.;
2 Cor. 9:13

5 *We are* destroying speculations and every lofty thing raised up against the knowledge of God, and *we are* taking every thought captive to the obedience of Christ,

6   and we are ready to punish[x] all disobedience, whenever *your* obedience is complete.[x]

7   You are looking at things as they are outwardly. If anyone is confident[+] in himself that he is Christ's, let him consider[~] this again within himself, that just as he is Christ's, so also are we.

8   For even if I should boast[x] somewhat further about our authority, which the *Lord* gave for building you up and not for destroying you, I shall not be put to shame,[39a]

9   for I do not wish to seem[x] as if I would terrify[~1] you by my letters.

10   For they say, "His letters are weighty and strong, but his personal presence is unimpressive, and his speech contemptible."[+]

11   Let such a person consider[~] this, that what we are in word by letters when absent, such persons *we are* also *in deed* when present.

12   For we are not bold to class[x] or compare[x] ourselves with some of those who commend themselves; but when they measure themselves *by themselves,* and compare themselves *with* [+]*themselves,* they are without understanding.[29f]

13   But *we* will not boast beyond *our* measure, but within the measure of the sphere which *God* apportioned to us as a measure, to reach[x] even as far as you.

14   For we are not overextending[1] ourselves, as if we did not reach to you, for we were the *first* to come even as far as *you* in the gospel of Christ;

15   not boasting beyond *our* measure, *that is,* in other men's labors, but with the hope that as your faith grows, we shall be, within our sphere, enlarged[x] even more by you,

16   so as to preach[x] the gospel even to the regions beyond you, *and* not to boast[x] in what has been accomplished in the sphere of [+]another.

17   But HE WHO BOASTS, LET HIM BOAST[~1] IN THE LORD.

18   For not he who commends himself is approved, but whom the Lord commends.

Paul Defends His Apostleship

11   I wish that you would bear with me in a little foolishness; but indeed you are bearing with me.

2   For I am jealous for you with a *godly* jealousy; for I betrothed you to one husband, that to Christ I might present[x] you *as a pure*[13a] virgin.

3   But I am afraid, lest as the serpent deceived[16a] Eve by his

10:6 2 Cor. 2:9

10:7 John 7:24; 2 Cor. 5:12; 1 Cor. 1:12; 14:37; 1 Cor. 9:1; 2 Cor. 11:23; Gal. 1:12
10:8 2 Cor. 7:4; 2 Cor. 13:10

10:10 1 Cor. 2:3; 2 Cor. 12:7; Gal. 4:13f.; 1 Cor. 1:17; 2 Cor. 11:6

10:12 2 Cor. 3:1; 10:18

10:13 2 Cor. 10:15; Rom. 12:3; 2 Cor. 10:15f.

10:14 1 Cor. 3:6; 2 Cor. 2:12

10:15 2 Cor. 10:13; Rom. 15:20; 2 Thess. 1:3; Acts 5:13

10:16 2 Cor. 11:7; Acts 19:21; Rom. 15:20

10:17 Jer. 9:24; 1 Cor. 1:31
10:18 2 Cor. 10:12; Rom. 2:29; 1 Cor. 4:5
11:1 Matt. 17:17; 2 Cor. 11:4,16, 19f.; 2 Cor. 5:13; 11:17,21
11:2 Hos. 2:19f.; Eph. 5:26f.; 2 Cor. 4:14
11:3 Gen. 3:4,13; John 8:44; 1 Thess. 3:5; 1 Tim. 2:14; Rev. 12:9,15

craftiness, your minds should be *led* ˣ *astray* from the simplicity and purity *of devotion* to Christ.

4 For if one comes and preaches another[8a] Jesus whom we have not preached, or you receive a *different*[8b] spirit which you have not received, or a *different*[8b] †gospel which you have not accepted, you bear *this* †beautifully.

5 For I consider myself not in the least inferior⁺ to the most eminent apostles.

6 But even if I am unskilled in speech, yet I am not *so* in knowledge; in fact, in every way we have made *this* evident to you in all things.

7 Or did I commit a *sin* in humbling myself that *you* might be exalted,ˣ because I preached the gospel of *God* to you *without charge?*

8 I robbed *other churches,* taking wages *from them* to serve *you;*

9 and when I was present with you and was in need, I was not a burden to anyone; for when the brethren came from Macedonia, *they* fully supplied my need, and in *everything* I kept myself from being a burden to you, and will continue to do so.

10 As the truth of Christ is in me, this boasting of mine will not be stopped in the regions of Achaia.

11 Why? Because I do not love you? God knows *I do!*

12 But what I am doing, I will continue to do, that I may cutˣ off opportunity from those who desire an opportunity to be regardedˣ just as we are in the matter about which they are boasting.

13 For such men are false apostles, *deceitful* workers, disguising themselves as apostles of Christ.

14 And no wonder, for even *Satan* disguises himself as an angel of light.

15 Therefore it is not surprising if his servants also disguise themselves as servants of righteousness; whose end shall be according to their deeds.

16 Again I say, let no one thinkᵒ me foolish; but if *you do,* receiveˣˡ me *even as foolish,* [20b] that *I also* may boastˣ a little.

17 That which I am speaking, I am not speaking as the *Lord* would, but as in †*foolishness,* in this confidence of boasting.

18 Since many boast according to the flesh, *I* will boast *also.*

19 For you, being *so* wise, bear with the foolish gladly.

20 For you bear with anyone if he enslaves[1] you, if he †devours you, if he takes †advantage of you, if he exalts †himself, if he hits you in the face.

21 To *my shame* I *must* say that *we* have been weak⁺ *by compar-*

ison. But in whatever respect anyone *else* is bold~ (I speak in *foolishness),* I am just as bold *myself.*

22   Are they Hebrews? So am I. Are they Israelites? So am I. Are they descendants of Abraham? So am I.

23   Are they servants of Christ? (I speak as if insane) I *more so;* in far more labors, in far more imprisonments, beaten times without number, often in danger of death.

24   Five times I received from the Jews thirty-nine *lashes.*

25   Three times I was beaten with rods, once I was stoned, three times I was shipwrecked, a night and a day I have spent⁺ in the deep.

26   *I have been* on frequent journeys, in dangers⁴ from rivers, dangers from robbers, dangers from *my* countrymen, dangers from the Gentiles, dangers in the city, dangers in the wilderness, dangers on the sea, dangers among false brethren;

27   *I have been* in labor and hardship, through many sleepless nights, in hunger and thirst, often without food, in cold and exposure.

28   Apart from *such* external things, there is the daily pressure upon me *of* concern for all the churches.

29   Who is weak without my being weak? Who is led into sin without my intense concern?

30   If I *have* to boast,~ I will boast of what pertains to *my* weakness.

31   The God and Father of the Lord Jesus, He who is blessed forever, knows that I am not lying.

32   In Damascus the ethnarch under Aretas the king was guardingᵐ the city of the Damascenes in order to seizeˣ me,

33   and I was let down in a *basket* through a window in the wall, and *so* escaped his hands.

Paul's Vision

12   Boasting~ is *necessary,* though it is not profitable; but I will go on to visions and revelations of the Lord.

2   I know a man in Christ who fourteen years ago—whether in the body I do not know, or out of the body I do not know, God knows—such a man was caught up to the third heaven.

3   And I know how such a man—whether in the body or apart from the body I do not know, God knows—

4   was caught up into Paradise, and heard inexpressible words, which a man is not permitted to speak.ˣ

5   On *behalf of such a man* will I boast; but on my *own behalf* I will not boast, except in regard to *my* weaknesses.

6   For if I do wishˣ to boastˣ I shall not be foolish,²⁰ᵇ for I shall

11:22
Acts 6:1;
Phil. 3:5;
Rom. 9:4;
Gal. 3:16;
Rom. 11:1
11:23
1 Cor. 3:5; 2 Cor.
3:6; 10:7;
1 Cor. 15:10;
2 Cor. 6:5;
Acts 16:23; 2 Cor.
6:5;
Rom. 8:36
11:24
Deut. 25:3
11:25
Acts 16:22;
Acts 14:19
11:26
Acts 9:23; 13:45,
50; 14:5; 17:5,13;
18:12; 20:3,19;
21:27; 23:10,12;
25:3; 1 Thess.
2:15;
Acts 14:5,19;
19:23ff.; 27:42;
Acts 21:31;
Gal. 2:4
11:27
1 Thess. 2:9;
2 Thess. 3:8;
1 Cor. 4:11; Phil.
4:12;
2 Cor. 6:5;
1 Cor. 4:11
11:28
1 Cor. 7:17
11:29
1 Cor. 8:9,13;
9:22
11:30
1 Cor. 2:3
11:31
Rom. 1:25;
2 Cor. 11:11
11:32
Acts 9:2;
Acts 9:24
11:33
Acts 9:25
12:1
2 Cor. 11:16,18,
30; 12:5,9;
1 Cor. 14:6;
2 Cor. 12:7; Gal.
1:12; 2:2; Eph.
3:3
12:2
Rom. 16:7;
2 Cor. 11:11;
Ezek. 8:3; Acts
8:39; 2 Cor. 12:4;
1 Thess. 4:17;
Rev. 12:5;
Deut. 10:14; Ps.
148:4; Eph. 4:10;
Heb. 4:14
12:3
2 Cor. 11:11
12:4
Ezek. 8:3; Acts
8:39; 2 Cor. 12:2;
1 Thess. 4:17;
Rev. 12:5;
Luke 23:43
12:5
2 Cor. 12:1;
1 Cor. 2:3; 2 Cor.
12:9f.
12:6
2 Cor. 5:13;
11:16f.; 12:11;
2 Cor. 7:14

12:7
2 Cor. 12:1;
Num. 33:55;
Ezek. 28:24; Hos.
2:6;
Job 2:6; Matt.
4:10; 1 Cor. 5:5
12:8
Matt. 26:44
12:9
1 Cor. 2:5; Eph.
3:16; Phil. 4:13;
1 Cor. 2:3; 2 Cor.
12:5
12:10
Rom. 5:3; 8:35;
2 Cor. 6:4;
2 Thess. 1:4;
2 Tim. 3:11;
2 Cor. 5:15,20;
2 Cor. 13:4
12:11
2 Cor. 5:13;
11:16f.; 12:6;
1 Cor. 15:10;
2 Cor. 11:5;
1 Cor. 3:7; 13:2;
15:9
12:12
John 4:48; Rom.
15:19; 1 Cor. 9:1
12:13
1 Cor. 9:12,18; 2
Cor. 11:9; 12:14;
2 Cor. 11:7
12:14
2 Cor. 1:15; 13:1,
2;
1 Cor. 9:12,18;
2 Cor. 11:9;
12:13;
1 Cor. 10:24,33;
1 Cor. 9:19;
1 Cor. 4:14f.; Gal.
4:19;
Prov. 19:14;
Ezek. 34:2
12:15
Rom. 9:3; 2 Cor.
1:6; Phil. 2:17;
Col. 1:24;
1 Thess. 2:8;
2 Tim. 2:10;
2 Cor. 11:11
12:16
2 Cor. 11:9;
2 Cor. 11:20
12:17
2 Cor. 9:5
12:18
2 Cor. 8:6;
2 Cor. 2:13;
2 Cor. 8:18;
1 Cor. 4:21;
Rom. 4:12
12:19
Rom. 9:1; 2 Cor.
2:17;
Rom. 14:19;
2 Cor. 10:8; 1
Thess. 5:11;
Heb. 6:9
12:20
1 Cor. 4:21;
2 Cor. 2:1-4;
1 Cor. 1:11; 3:3;
Gal. 5:20;
Rom. 2:8; 1 Cor.
11:19;
Rom. 1:30;
James 4:11;
1 Pet. 2:1;
Rom. 1:29;
1 Cor. 4:6,18;
5:2;
1 Cor. 14:33

be speaking the truth; but I refrain *from this,* so that no one may credit[x] me with more than he sees *in* me or hears from me.

A Thorn in the Flesh

7　And because of the surpassing greatness of the revelations, for this reason, to keep me from exalting~ myself, there was given me a thorn in the flesh, a messenger of Satan to buffet~ me—to keep me from exalting~ myself![4]

8　Concerning this I entreated the Lord *three times* that it might depart[x] from me.

9　And He has said[+] to me, *"My grace* is sufficient for you, for [c]power[32a] is perfected in *weakness."* Most[3] gladly, therefore, I will rather boast about my weaknesses, that the *power of Christ* may dwell[x] in me.

10　Therefore I am well content with weaknesses, with insults, with distresses, with persecutions, with difficulties, for Christ's sake; for when I am weak,~ then I am *strong.*

11　I have become[+] foolish;[20b] *you yourselves* compelled me. Actually I should[m] have been *commended*~ by you, for in no respect was I inferior to the most eminent apostles, even though I am a nobody.

12　The signs of a true apostle were performed among you with all perseverance, by signs and wonders and miracles.

13　For in what respect were you treated as inferior to the rest of the churches, except that *I myself* did not become a burden to you? Forgive[xi] me [+]*this* wrong!

14　Here for this third time I am ready to come to you, and I will not be a burden to you; for I do not seek what is yours, but you; for children are not responsible to save~ up for *their parents,* but parents for *their* children.

15　And I will most[3] gladly spend and be expended for your souls. If I love you the more, am I to be loved the [+]less?

16　But be that as it may, I did not burden you myself; nevertheless, *crafty fellow* that I am, I took you in by *deceit.*

17　*Certainly* I have not taken advantage of you through any of those whom I have sent[+] to you, have I?

18　I urged Titus *to go,* and sent the brother with him. *Titus* did not take any advantage of you, did he? Did we not conduct ourselves in the *same spirit and walk* in the *same [+]steps?*

19　All this time you have been thinking that we are defending ourselves to you. *Actually,* it is in the *sight*[1] *of God* that we have been speaking *in Christ;* and all for *your* upbuilding, beloved.

20　For I am afraid that perhaps when I come I may find[x] you

[c]Later mss. read *My power*

to be not what *I wish* and may be found[x] by you to be not what you wish; that perhaps *there may be* strife, jealousy, angry tempers, disputes, slanders, gossip, arrogance, disturbances;

21   I am afraid that when I come again my God may humiliate[x] me before you, and I may mourn[x] over many of those who have sinned[+] in the past and not repented of the impurity, immorality and sensuality which they have practiced.

Examine Yourselves

13 This is the third time I am coming to you. EVERY FACT IS TO BE CONFIRMED BY THE TESTIMONY OF *TWO OR THREE WITNESSES.*

2   I have previously said[+] when present the second time, and though now absent I say in advance to those who have sinned[+] in the past and to all the rest as well, that if I come again, I will not spare *anyone,*

3   since you are seeking for *proof* of the Christ who speaks in me, and who is not weak toward you, but mighty in you.

4   For indeed He was crucified because of weakness, yet He lives because of the power[32a] of God. For *we also* are weak [d]in Him, yet we shall live with Him because of the power of God *directed* toward you.

5   *Test*[~l] yourselves *to see* if you are in the faith; *examine*[~l] yourselves! Or do you not recognize[29b] this about yourselves, that Jesus Christ is in you—unless indeed you *fail the test?*

6   But I trust that you will realize that we ourselves do not fail the test.

7   Now we pray to God that you do[x] *no* wrong; not that we ourselves may appear[x] *approved,* but that you may do[~] what is *right,* [25b] even though we should appear *unapproved.*

8   For we can do nothing against the truth, but *only* for the truth.

9   For we rejoice when we ourselves are weak[~] but *you* are strong; this we also pray for, that *you* be made complete.

10   For this reason I am writing these things while absent, in order that when present I may not use[x] severity, in accordance with the authority which the Lord gave me, for building up and not for tearing down.

11   Finally, brethren, rejoice,[~l] be made complete,[~l] be comforted,[~l] be like-minded,[~l] live in peace;[~l] and the God of love and peace shall be with you.

12   Greet[xl] one another with a holy[28a] kiss.

13   All the saints greet you.

[d]Some early mss. read *with Him*

12:21
2 Cor. 13:2;
1 Cor. 6:9,18;
Gal. 5:19; Col.
3:5

13:1
2 Cor. 12:14;
Deut. 17:6; 19:15;
Matt. 18:16

13:2
2 Cor. 12:21;
1 Cor. 4:21;
2 Cor. 13:10;
2 Cor. 1:23; 10:11

13:3
2 Cor. 10:1,10;
Matt. 10:20;
1 Cor. 5:4; 7:40;
2 Cor. 9:8; 10:4
13:4
Phil. 2:7f.; 1 Pet.
3:18;
Rom. 1:4; 6:4;
1 Cor. 6:14;
1 Cor. 2:3; 2 Cor.
13:9;
Rom. 6:8
13:5
John 6:6;
1 Cor. 11:28;
1 Cor. 9:27

13:9
2 Cor. 12:10;
13:4;
1 Cor. 1:10;
2 Cor. 13:11;
Eph. 4:12;
1 Thess. 3:10
13:10
2 Cor. 2:3;
Titus 1:13;
1 Cor. 5:4; 2 Cor.
10:8
13:11
1 Thess. 4:1;
2 Thess. 3:1;
1 Cor. 1:10;
2 Cor. 13:9; Eph.
4:12; 1 Thess.
3:10;
Rom. 12:16;
Mark 9:50;
Rom. 15:33; Eph.
6:23
13:12
Rom. 16:16
13:13
Phil. 4:22

13:14
Rom. 16:20;
2 Cor. 8:9;
Rom. 5:5; Jude
21;
Phil. 2:1

14 The grace of the Lord Jesus Christ, and the love of God, and the fellowship of the Holy Spirit, be with you all.

The Epistle of Paul to the
Galatians

Introduction

1 Paul, an apostle (not *sent* from men, nor through the agency of man, but through Jesus Christ, and God the Father, who raised Him from the dead),

2 and all the brethren who are with me, to the churches of Galatia:

3 Grace to you and peace from God our Father, and the Lord Jesus Christ,

4 who gave Himself for our sins, that He might deliver[x18a] us out of this *present evil* age, according to the will of our God and Father,

5 to whom *be* the glory forevermore. Amen.

Perversion of the Gospel

6 I am amazed that you are so quickly deserting Him who called you by the grace of Christ, for a different[8b] gospel;

7 which is *really* not another,[8a] only there are some who are disturbing you, and want to distort[x] the gospel of Christ.

8 But even though *we*, or an angel from heaven, should preach~ to you a gospel contrary to that which we have preached to you, let him be *accursed*.

9 As we have said+ before, so I say again now, if any man is preaching to you a gospel contrary to that which you received, let him be *accursed*.

10 For am I now seeking the favor of *men*, or of †*God*? Or am I striving to please~ *men*? If I were still trying to please *men*, I would not be a bond-servant[38b] of *Christ*.

Paul Defends His Ministry

11 For I would have you know, brethren, that the gospel which was preached by me is not according to man.

12 For I neither received it from *man*, nor was I taught it, but *I received it* through a revelation of Jesus Christ.

13 For you have heard of •my former manner of life in Judaism, how I used to persecute[xx] the church of God beyond measure, and tried to destroy[xx] it;

14 and I was advancing[xx] in Judaism beyond many of my

1:1
2 Cor. 1:1.;
Gal. 1:11f.;
Acts 9:15; Gal.
1:15f.;
Acts 2:24
1:2
Phil. 4:21;
Acts 16:6; 1 Cor.
16:1
1:3
Rom. 1:7
1:4
Gal. 2:20;
Matt. 13:22; Rom.
12:2; 2 Cor. 4:4;
Phil. 4:20
1:5
Rom. 11:36
1:6
Rom. 8:28; Gal.
1:15; 5:8;
2 Cor. 11:4; Gal.
1:7,11; 2:2,7;
5:14; 1 Tim. 1:3
1:7
Acts 15:24; Gal.
5:10
1:8
2 Cor. 11:14;
Rom. 9:3
1:9
Acts 18:23;
Rom. 16:17;
Rom. 9:3
1:10
1 Cor. 10:33; 1
Thess. 2:4;
Rom. 1:1; Phil.
1:1
1:11
Rom. 2:16; 1 Cor.
15:1;
1 Cor. 3:4; 9:8
1:12
1 Cor. 11:23; Gal.
1:1;
1 Cor. 2:10;
2 Cor. 12:1; Gal.
1:16; 2:2
1:13
Acts 26:4f.;
Acts 8:3; 22:4,5;
1 Cor. 10:32;
Acts 9:21
1:14
Acts 22:3;
Jer. 9:14; Matt.
15:2; Mark 7:3;
Col. 2:8

contemporaries among my countrymen, being more extremely zealous for my ancestral traditions.

15　But when He who had set me apart, *even* from my mother's womb, and called me through His grace, was pleased

16　to reveal[x] His Son in me, that I might preach~ Him among the Gentiles, I did not immediately consult with flesh and blood,

17　nor did I go up to Jerusalem to those who were apostles before me; but I went away to Arabia, and returned once more to Damascus.

18　Then *three* years later I went up to Jerusalem to become acquainted[x] with Cephas, and stayed with him fifteen days.

19　But I did not see any other of the apostles except James, the Lord's brother.

20　(Now in what I am writing to you, I assure you before God that I am not lying.)

21　Then I went into the regions of Syria and Cilicia.

22　And I was *still* unknown~ by sight to the churches of Judea which were in Christ;

23　but only, they kept hearing,~ "He who once persecuted us is now preaching the faith which he once tried to destroy."[xxx]

24　And they were glorifying[xxx] God because of me.

The Council at Jerusalem

2　Then after an interval of *fourteen* years I went up again to Jerusalem with Barnabas, taking Titus along also.

2　And it was because of a revelation that I went up; and I submitted to them the gospel which I preach among the Gentiles, but I *did so* in private to those who were of reputation, for fear that I might be running,~ or had run, in *vain*.

3　But not even Titus who was with me, though he was a †*Greek*, was compelled to be circumcised.[x]

4　But *it was* because of the false brethren who had sneaked in to spy[x] out our liberty which we have in Christ Jesus, in order to bring us into bondage.

5　But we did not yield in subjection to them for *even an hour,* so that the truth of the gospel might remain[x] with you.

6　But from those who were of high reputation (what they were makes no difference to me; God shows *no partiality)*—well, those who were of reputation contributed nothing to me.

7　But on the contrary, seeing that I had been entrusted+ with the gospel to the uncircumcised, just as Peter *had been* to the circumcised

8　(for He who effectually worked for Peter in *his* apostleship to the circumcised effectually worked for me also to the Gentiles),

---

1:15
Is. 49:1,5; Jer. 1:5; Acts 9:15; Rom. 1:1; Gal. 1:6
1:16
Acts 9:15; Gal. 2:9; Acts 9:20; Matt. 16:17
1:17
Acts 9:19-22; Acts 9:2
1:18
Acts 9:22f.; Acts 9:26; John 1:42; Gal. 2:9,11,14
1:19
Matt. 12:46; Acts 12:17
1:20
Rom. 9:1; 2 Cor. 1:23; 11:31
1:21
Acts 9:30; Acts 15:23,41; Acts 6:9
1:22
1 Cor. 7:17; 1 Thess. 2:14; Rom. 16:7
1:23
Acts 6:7; Gal. 6:10; Acts 9:21
1:24
Matt. 9:8
2:1
Acts 15:2; Acts 4:36; Gal. 2:9,13; 2 Cor. 2:13; Gal. 2:3
2:2
Acts 15:2; Gal. 1:12; Gal. 1:6; Rom. 9:16; 1 Cor. 9:24ff.; Gal. 5:7; Phil. 2:16; 2 Tim. 4:7; Heb. 12:1
2:3
2 Cor. 2:13; Gal. 2:1; Acts 16:3; 1 Cor. 9:21
2:4
Acts 15:1,24; 2 Cor. 11:13,26; Gal. 1:7; 2 Pet. 2:1; Jude 4; Gal. 5:1,13; James 1:25; Rom. 8:15; 2 Cor. 11:20
2:5
Gal. 1:6; 2:14; Col. 1:5
2:6
2 Cor. 11:5; 12:11; Gal. 2:9; 6:3; Acts 10:34
2:7
1 Cor. 9:17; 1 Thess. 2:4; 1 Tim. 1:11; Acts 9:15; Gal. 1:16; Gal. 1:18; 2:9,11,14
2:8
Acts 1:25

9 and recognizing[29a] the grace that had been given to me, James and Cephas and John, who were reputed to be pillars, gave to me and Barnabas the right hand of *fellowship*, that we *might go* to the Gentiles, and they to the circumcised.

10 *They* only *asked* us to remember~ the *poor*—the very thing I also was eager to do.[x]

Peter (Cephas) Opposed by Paul

11 But when Cephas came to Antioch, I opposed him to his face, because he stood †*condemned*.✦ [14a]

12 For prior to the coming of certain men from James, he used to eat[ᵒᵒ] with the Gentiles; but when they came, he *began* to withdraw and hold himself aloof, fearing the party of the circumcision.

13 And the rest of the Jews joined him in hypocrisy, with the result that even *Barnabas* was carried away by their *hypocrisy*.

14 But when I saw that they were not straightforward about the truth of the gospel, I said to Cephas in the presence of all, "If *you*, being a Jew, live like the Gentiles and not like the Jews, how *is it that* you compel the *Gentiles* to live~ like Jews?

15 "We *are* Jews by nature, and not sinners from among the Gentiles;

16 nevertheless knowing that a man is not justified by the works of the Law but through faith in Christ Jesus, even *we* have believed *in Christ Jesus,* that we may be justified[x] by faith in Christ, and not by the works of the Law; since by the works of the Law shall *no flesh* be justified.

17 "But if, while seeking to be justified[x] in Christ, we ourselves have also been found sinners, is Christ then a minister of *sin?* May it never be!

18 "For if I rebuild what I have *once* destroyed, I prove myself to be a *transgressor.*

19 "For through the Law *I* died *to the Law,* that I might live[x] *to* God.

20 "I have been *crucified*✦ with Christ; and it is no longer *I* who live, but *Christ* lives in me; and the *life* which I now live in the flesh I live by *faith* in the Son of God, who loved me, and delivered Himself up for me.

21 "I do not nullify the grace of God; for if righteousness *comes through the Law,* then Christ died needlessly."

2:9
Rom. 12:3;
Acts 12:17; Gal.
2:12;
Luke 22:8; Gal.
1:18; 2:7,11,14;
2 Cor. 11:5;
12:11; Gal. 2:2,6;
6:3;
1 Tim. 3:15; Rev.
3:12;
Acts 4:36; Gal.
2:1,13;
2 Kin. 10:15;
Gal. 1:16
2:10
Acts 24:17

2:11
Gal. 1:18; 2:7,9,
14;
Acts 11:19; 15:1

2:12
Acts 12:17; Gal.
2:9;
Acts 11:3;
Acts 11:2

2:13
Acts 4:36; Gal.
2:1,9

2:14
Heb. 12:13;
Gal. 1:6; 2:5; Col.
1:5;
Gal. 1:18; 2:7,9,
11;
Acts 10:28; Gal.
2:12

2:15
Phil. 3:4f.;
1 Sam. 15:18;
Luke 24:7

2:16
Acts 13:39; Gal.
3:11;
Rom. 3:22; 9:30;
Ps. 143:2; Rom.
3:20

2:17
Gal. 2:15;
Luke 20:16; Gal.
3:21

2:18
Rom. 3:5

2:19
Rom. 6:2; 7:4;
1 Cor. 9:20

2:20
Rom. 6:6; Gal.
5:24; 6:14;
Rom. 8:10;
Matt. 4:3;
Rom. 8:37;
Gal. 1:4

2:21
Gal. 3:21

Faith Brings Righteousness

3:1
Gal. 1:2;
1 Cor. 1:23; Gal.
5:11

3 You foolish[20a] Galatians, who has bewitched you, before whose eyes Jesus Christ was publicly portrayed *as* crucified?*

3:2
Rom. 10:17

2 This is the only thing I want to find[x] out from you: did you receive the Spirit by the *works of the Law,* or by *hearing with* †*faith?*

3 Are you so †foolish?[20a] Having begun by the Spirit, are you now being perfected by the flesh?

3:4
1 Cor. 15:2

4 Did you suffer so many things in *vain* — if indeed[2] it was in vain?

3:5
2 Cor. 9:10; Phil.
1:19;
1 Cor. 12:10;
Rom. 10:17

5 Does He then, who provides you with the Spirit and works miracles among you, do it by the works of the Law, or by hearing with faith?

3:6
Rom. 4:3;
Gen. 15:6

6 Even so Abraham BELIEVED GOD, AND IT WAS RECKONED TO HIM AS RIGHTEOUSNESS.

3:7
Rom. 4:16; Gal.
3:9;
Luke 19:9; Gal.
6:16

7 Therefore, be sure~~1~~ that it is those who are of faith who are sons of *Abraham.*

3:8
Gen. 12:3

8 And the Scripture, foreseeing that God would justify the Gentiles by *faith,* preached the gospel beforehand to Abraham, *saying,* "ALL THE NATIONS SHALL BE BLESSED IN YOU."

3:9
Gal. 3:7

9 So then those who are of faith are blessed with Abraham, the believer.

3:10
Deut. 27:26

10 For as many as are of the works of the Law are under a †*curse;* for it is written,* "†CURSED IS EVERYONE WHO DOES NOT ABIDE BY ALL THINGS WRITTEN* IN THE BOOK OF THE LAW, TO PERFORM[x] THEM."

3:11
Gal. 2:16;
Hab. 2:4; Rom.
1:17; Heb. 10:38
3:12
Lev. 18:5; Rom.
10:5

11 Now that no one is justified by the *Law* before God is evident; for, "THE RIGHTEOUS MAN SHALL LIVE BY *FAITH.*"

12 However, the Law is not of faith; on the contrary, "HE WHO PRACTICES THEM SHALL LIVE BY THEM."

3:13
Gal. 4:5;
Deut. 21:23;
Acts 5:30

13 Christ redeemed[36a] us from the curse of the Law, having become a *curse* for us—for it is written,* "†CURSED IS EVERYONE WHO HANGS ON A TREE"—

3:14
Rom. 4:9,16; Gal.
3:28;
Gal. 3:2;
Acts 2:33; Eph.
1:13

14 in order that in Christ Jesus the blessing of Abraham might come to the *Gentiles,* so that we might receive[x] the *promise of the Spirit* through faith.

Intent of the Law

3:15
Acts 1:15; Rom.
1:13; Gal. 6:18;
Rom. 3:5;
Heb. 6:16
3:16
Luke 1:55; Rom.
4:13,16; 9:4;
Acts 3:25

15 Brethren, I speak in terms of human relations: even though it is *only* a *man's* covenant, yet when it has been ratified,* no one sets it aside or adds conditions to it.

16 Now the promises were spoken to Abraham and to his

†seed. He does not say, "And to seeds," as *referring* to many, but *rather* to one, "And to your seed," that is, Christ.

17 What I am saying is this: the Law, which came *four hundred and thirty* years later, does *not invalidate* a covenant previously ratified⁺ by God, so as to nullifyˣ the promise.

18 For if the inheritance is based on *law*, it is no longer based on a promise; but God has granted⁺ it to Abraham by means of a *promise.*

19 Why the Law then? It was added *because of transgressions,* ⁴⁰ª having been ordained through angels by the agency of a mediator, until the seed should come to whom the promise had been made. ⁺

20 Now a mediator is not for one *party only;* whereas God is *only* †one.

21 Is the Law then contrary to the promises of God? May it never be! For if a law had been given which was able to impartˣ life, then righteousness would indeed have been based on *law.*

22 But the Scripture has shut up all men under sin, that the promise by *faith in Jesus Christ* might be givenˣ to those who believe.

23 But before faith came, we were keptˣˣ in custody *under the law,* being shut up to the faith which was later to be revealed. ˣ

24 Therefore the Law has become⁺ our †tutor *to lead us* to Christ, that we may be justifiedˣ by *faith.*

25 But now that faith has come, we are no longer under a tutor.

26 For you are all *sons of God* through faith in Christ Jesus.

27 For all of you who were baptized *into Christ* have clothed yourselves *with Christ.*

28 There is neither Jew nor Greek, there is neither slave nor free man, there is neither male nor female; for you are all *one* in Christ Jesus.

29 And if you belong to Christ, then you are *Abraham's* offspring, *heirs* according to promise.

Sonship in Christ

4 Now I say, as long as the heir is a child, he does not differ at all from a slave although he is owner of †everything,

2 but he is under guardians and managers until the date set by the father.

3 So also we, while we were children, were held⁺ in bondage under the elemental things of the world.

4 But when the fulness of the †time came, God sent forth His Son, born of a woman, born under the Law,

3:17
Gen. 15:13f.; Ex. 12:40; Acts 7:6

3:18
Rom. 4:14; Heb. 6:14

3:19
Rom. 5:20; Acts 7:53; Ex. 20:19; Deut. 5:5; Gal. 3:16

3:20
1 Tim. 2:5; Heb. 8:6; 9:15; 12:24

3:21
Luke 20:16; Gal. 2:17; Gal. 2:21

3:22
Rom. 11:32

3:23
Rom. 11:32
3:24
1 Cor. 4:15; Gal. 2:16
3:25
1 Cor. 4:15
3:26
Rom. 8:14; Gal. 4:5; Rom. 8:1; Gal. 3:28; 4:14; 5:6, 24; Eph. 1:1; Phil. 1:1; Col. 1:4; 1 Tim. 1:12; 2 Tim. 1:1; Titus 1:4
3:27
Matt. 28:19; Rom. 6:3; 1 Cor. 10:2; Rom. 13:14
3:28
Rom. 3:22; 1 Cor. 12:13; Col. 3:11; John 17:11; Eph. 2:15; Rom. 8:1; Gal. 3:26; 4:14; 5:6, 24; Eph. 1:1; Phil. 1:1; Col. 1:4; 1 Tim. 1:12; 2 Tim. 1:1; Titus 1:4
3:29
Rom. 4:13; 1 Cor. 3:23; Rom. 9:8; Gal. 3:18; 4:28
4:3
Gal. 2:4; 4:8f., 24f.; Gal. 4:9; Col. 2:8, 20; Heb. 5:12
4:4
Mark 1:15; John 1:14; Rom. 1:3; 8:3; Phil. 2:7; Luke 2:21f.,27

4:5
Rom. 8:14; Gal.
3:26

4:6
Acts 16:7; Rom.
5:5; 8:9,16; 2 Cor.
3:17;
Mark 14:36; Rom.
8:15
4:7
Rom. 8:17
4:8
1 Cor. 1:21; Eph.
2:12; 1 Thess.
4:5; 2 Thess. 1:8;
Gal. 4:3;
2 Chr. 13:9; Is.
37:19; Jer. 2:11;
1 Cor. 8:4f.; 10:20
4:9
1 Cor. 8:3;
Col. 2:20;
Gal. 4:3
4:10
Rom. 14:5; Col.
2:16

4:12
Gal. 6:18;
2 Cor. 6:11,13

4:14
Matt. 10:40;
1 Thess. 2:13;
Gal. 3:26

4:16
Amos 5:10

4:18
Gal. 4:13f.

4:19
1 John 2:1;
1 Cor. 4:15;
Eph. 4:13
4:20
2 Cor. 4:8

4:21
Luke 16:29
4:22
Gen. 16:15;
Gen. 21:2
4:23
Rom. 9:7; Gal.
4:29;
Gen. 17:16ff.;
18:10ff.; 21:1;
Gal. 4:28; Heb.
11:11
4:24
1 Cor. 10:11;
Deut. 33:2;
Gal. 4:3

5   in order that He might *redeem*ˣ ³⁶ᵃ those who were under the Law, that we might receiveˣ the *adoption as sons.*

6   And because you are sons, God has sent forth the Spirit of His Son into our hearts, crying, "Abba! Father!"

7   Therefore you are no longer a slave, but a son; and if a son, then an heir through God.

8   However at that time, when you did not know²⁹ᵉ God, you were slaves to those which by nature are no gods.

9   But now that you have come to know²⁹ᵃ God, or rather to be known²⁹ᵃ by God, how is it that you turn back *again* to the weak and worthless elemental things, to which you desire to be enslaved~ *all over again?*

10   You observe¹ days and months and seasons and years.

11   I fear for you, that perhaps I have labored⁺ over you in vain.

12   I beg of you, brethren, become~¹ as I *am,* for I also *have become* as you *are.* You have done me no wrong;

13   but you know that it was because of a bodily illness that I preached the gospel to you the first time;

14   and that which was a trial to you in my bodily condition you did not despise or loathe, but you received me as an angel of God, as Christ Jesus *Himself.*

15   Where then is that sense of blessing you had? For I bear you witness, that if possible, you would have plucked out your †eyes and given them to me.

16   Have I therefore become⁺ your *enemy* by telling you the truth?

17   They eagerly seek you, not commendably, but they wish to shutˣ you out, in order that you may seek *them.*

18   But it is good always to be eagerly sought~ in a commendable manner, and not only when I am present~ with you.

19   My children, with whom I am again in labor until *Christ* is formedˣ in you—

20   but I could wish to be present~ with you now and to changeˣ my tone, for I am perplexed about you.

Bond and Free

21   Tell~¹ me, you who want to be under law, do you not *listen* to the law?

22   For it is written⁺ that Abraham had two sons, one by the bondwoman and one by the free woman.

23   But the son by the bondwoman was born⁺ according to the *flesh,* and the son by the free woman through the †*promise.*

24   This is allegorically speaking: for these *women* are two

covenants, one *proceeding* from Mount Sinai bearing children who are to be †*slaves;* she is Hagar.

25   Now this Hagar is Mount Sinai in Arabia, and corresponds to the present Jerusalem, for she is in slavery with her children.

26   But the Jerusalem above is †*free;* she is our mother.

27   For it is written, ✦

"REJOICE,ˣⁱ BARREN WOMAN WHO DOES NOT BEAR;
BREAKˣⁱ FORTH AND SHOUT,ˣⁱ YOU WHO ARE NOT IN
    LABOR;
FOR MORE ARE THE CHILDREN OF THE DESOLATE
THAN OF THE ONE WHO HAS A HUSBAND."

28   And *you* brethren, like Isaac, are children of *promise.*

29   But as at that time he who was born according to the flesh persecutedˣˣ him *who was born* according to the Spirit, so it is now also.

30   But what does the Scripture say?

"CASTˣⁱ OUT THE BONDWOMAN AND HER SON,
FOR THE SON OF THE BONDWOMAN SHALL •NOT BE AN
    HEIR WITH THE SON OF THE FREE WOMAN."

31   So then, brethren, we are not children of a *bondwoman,* but of the *free* †*woman.*

Walk by the Spirit

5 It was for *freedom* that Christ set us free; therefore keep standingᵐⁱ firm and do not be subjectᵒ again to a *yoke of slavery.*

2   Behold *I, Paul,* say to you that if you receive~ circumcision, Christ will be of no benefit to you.

3   And I testify again to every man who receives circumcision, that he is under obligation to keepˣ the *whole Law.*

4   You have been severed from Christ, you who are seeking to be justified by *law;* you have fallen from *grace.*

5   For *we* through the Spirit, by faith, are waiting[1] for the *hope of righteousness.*

6   For in Christ Jesus neither circumcision nor uncircumcision means anything, but faith working *through love.* [31a]

7   You were runningᵐˣ well; who hindered you from obeying~ the truth?

8   This persuasion *did* not *come* from Him who calls you.

9   A little leaven leavens the *whole lump of dough.*

10   I have confidence in you in the Lord, that you will adopt no other †view; but the one who is disturbing you shall bear his judgment, whoever he is.

11   But *I,* brethren, if I still preach *circumcision,* why am I still

4:26
Heb. 12:22; Rev. 3:12; 21:2,10
4:27
Is. 54:1

4:28
Gal. 4:23;
Rom. 9:7ff.; Gal. 3:29
4:29
Gal. 4:23;
Gen. 21:9;
Gal. 5:11
4:30
Gen. 21:10,12;
John 8:35

5:1
John 8:32,36;
Rom. 8:15; 2 Cor. 3:17; Gal. 2:4;
5:13;
1 Cor. 16:13;
Acts 15:10
5:2
2 Cor. 10:1;
Acts 15:1; Gal. 5:3,6,11
5:3
Luke 16:28;
Acts 15:1; Gal. 5:2,6,11;
Rom. 2:25
5:4
Heb. 12:15;
2 Pet. 3:17
5:5
Rom. 8:23; 1 Cor. 1:7
5:6
Gal. 3:26;
1 Cor. 7:19; Gal. 6:15;
Col. 1:4f.;
1 Thess. 1:3;
James 2:18,20,22
5:7
Gal. 2:2
5:8
Rom. 8:28; Gal. 1:6
5:9
1 Cor. 5:6
5:10
2 Cor. 2:3;
Gal. 5:7; Phil. 3:15;
Gal. 1:7; 5:12
5:11
Gal. 4:29; 6:12;
Rom. 9:33; 1 Cor. 1:23

persecuted? Then the stumbling block of the cross has been abolished. +

5:12
Gal. 2:4; 5:10;
Deut. 23:1

12   Would that those who are troubling you would even *muti-late themselves.*

5:13
Gal. 5:1;
1 Cor. 8:9; 1 Pet.
2:16;
1 Cor. 9:19; Eph.
5:21

13   For you were called to *freedom,* brethren; only *do* not *turn* your freedom into an opportunity for the flesh, but through love[31a] serve [138b] one another.

5:14
Matt. 7:12; 22:40;
Rom. 13:8,10;
Gal. 6:2;
Lev. 19:18; Matt.
19:19; John 13:34

14   For the whole Law is fulfilled + in one word, in the *state-ment,* "YOU SHALL LOVE[31a] YOUR NEIGHBOR AS YOURSELF."

5:15
Gal. 5:20; Phil.
3:2

15   But if you bite and devour[1] one another, take care [M] lest you be consumed[x] by one another.

5:16
Rom. 8:4; 13:14;
Gal. 5:24f.;
Eph. 2:3

16   But I say, walk [142a] by the *Spirit,* and you will •*not* carry[x] out the *desire of the flesh.*

5:17
Rom. 7:18,23;
8:5ff.;
Rom. 7:15ff.

17   For the flesh sets its desire against the Spirit, and the Spirit against the flesh; for these are in opposition to one another, so that you may not do [19a] the things that you please.

5:18
Rom. 8:14;
Rom. 6:14; 7:4; 1
Tim. 1:9

18   But if you are led by the *Spirit,* you are not under the Law.

5:19
1 Cor. 6:9,18;
2 Cor. 12:21

19   Now the deeds of the flesh are *evident,* which are: immo-rality, impurity, sensuality,

5:20
Rev. 21:8;
2 Cor. 12:20;
Rom. 2:8; James
3:14ff.;
1 Cor. 11:19

20   idolatry, sorcery, enmities, strife, jealousy, outbursts of anger,[7a] disputes, dissensions, factions,

5:21
Rom. 13:13;
1 Cor. 6:9

21   envying, drunkenness, carousing, and things like these, of which I forewarn you just as I have forewarned you that those who practice[19b] such things shall not inherit the *kingdom of God.*

5:22
Matt. 7:16ff.; Eph.
5:9;
Rom. 5:1-5;
1 Cor. 13:4; Col.
3:12-15

22   But the fruit of the Spirit is love,[31a] joy, peace, patience, kindness, goodness, faithfulness,

5:23
Acts 24:25;
Gal. 5:18

23   gentleness,[23b] self-control; against such things there is no law.

5:24
Gal. 3:26;
Rom. 6:6; Gal.
2:20; 6:14;
Gal. 5:16f.

24   Now those who belong to Christ Jesus have *crucified* the flesh with its passions and desires.

5:25
Gal. 5:16

25   If we live by the Spirit, let us also *walk* [42b] by the Spirit.

5:26
Phil. 2:3

26   Let us not become [~] boastful, challenging one another, envying one another.

Bear One Another's Burdens

6:1
Gal. 6:18;
1 Thess. 4:1;
1 Cor. 2:15;
2 Cor. 2:7;
2 Thess. 3:15;
Heb. 12:13;
James 5:19f.;
1 Cor. 4:21

6   Brethren, even if a man is *caught*[x] in any trespass,[40b] you who are spiritual, restore [M] such a one in a spirit of gentle-ness;[23b] *each one* looking to yourself, lest *you too* be tempted.[x]

6:2
Rom. 15:1;
Rom. 8:2; 1 Cor.
9:21; James 1:25;
2:12; 2 Pet. 3:2

2   Bear [M] *one another's* burdens,[12a] and thus fulfill the law of Christ.

6:3
Acts 5:36; 1 Cor.
3:18; 2 Cor.
12:11

3   For if anyone thinks he is something when he is nothing, he deceives himself.

6:4
1 Cor. 11:28;
Phil. 1:26

4   But let each one examine [M] his *own* work, and then he will

have *reason for* boasting in regard to *himself alone,* and not in regard to another.

5   For each one shall bear his *own* load.[12b]

6   And let the one who is taught the word share[~] all good[25a] things with him who teaches.

7   Do not be deceived,[Ο16b] God is not mocked; for whatever a man sows,[~] this he will also *reap.*

8   For the one who sows to his own flesh shall *from the flesh* reap corruption, but the one who sows to the Spirit shall *from the Spirit* reap eternal life.

9   And let us not lose[~] heart in doing good,[25b] for in *due* time we shall reap if we do not grow weary.

10   So then, while we have opportunity, let us do[~] good[25a] to all men, and especially to those who are of the household of the faith.

11   See[xl] with what large letters I am writing to you with my •own hand.

12   Those who desire to make[x] a good showing in the flesh try to compel you to be circumcised,[~] simply that they may not be persecuted[~] for the cross of Christ.

13   For those who [a]are circumcised do not even keep the Law *themselves,* but they desire to have [†]*you* circumcised,[~] that they may boast[x] in *your* flesh.

14   But may it never be that I should boast,[~] except in the cross of our Lord Jesus Christ, through which the world has been crucified[†] *to me,* and I to the world.

15   For neither is circumcision anything, nor uncircumcision, but a new[34a] creation.

16   And those who will walk[42b] by *this rule,* peace and mercy *be* upon them, and upon the Israel of God.

17   From now on let no one cause[~] trouble for me, for *I* bear on my body the *brand-marks* of Jesus.

18   The grace of our Lord Jesus Christ be with your spirit, brethren. Amen.

[a]Some ancient mss. read *have been*

6:5
Prov. 9:12; Rom. 14:12; 1 Cor. 3:8
6:6
1 Cor. 9:11,14; 2 Tim. 4:2
6:7
1 Cor. 6:9; Job 13:9; 2 Cor. 9:6
6:8
Job 4:8; Hos. 8:7; Rom. 6:21; 1 Cor. 15:42; Rom. 8:11; James 3:18
6:9
1 Cor. 15:58; 2 Cor. 4:1; Matt. 10:22; Heb. 12:3,5; James 5:7f.
6:10
Prov. 3:27; John 12:35; Eph. 2:19; Heb. 3:6; 1 Pet. 2:5; 4:17; Acts 6:7; Gal. 1:23
6:11
1 Cor. 16:21
6:12
Matt. 23:27f.; Acts 15:1; Gal. 5:11
6:13
Rom. 2:25; Phil. 3:3
6:14
Luke 20:16; Gal. 2:17; 3:21; 1 Cor. 2:2; Gal. 2:20; Col. 2:20; Rom. 6:2,6; Gal. 2:19f.; 5:24
6:15
Rom. 2:26,28; 1 Cor. 7:19; Gal. 5:6; 2 Cor. 5:17; Eph. 2:10,15; 4:24; Col. 3:10
6:16
Rom. 9:6; Gal. 3:7,29; Phil. 3:3
6:17
Is. 44:5; Ezek. 9:4; 2 Cor. 4:10; 11:23; Rev. 13:16
6:18
Rom. 16:20; 2 Tim. 4:22; Acts 1:15; Rom. 1:13; Gal. 3:15; 4:12,28,31

The Epistle of Paul to the

Ephesians

1:1
2 Cor. 1:1;
Rom. 8:1;
1 Cor. 1:1;
Acts 9:13;
Acts 18:19;
Col. 1:2
1:2
Rom. 1:7
1:3
2 Cor. 1:3;
Eph. 1:20; 2:6;
3:10; 6:12
1:4
Eph. 2:10;
2 Thess. 2:13f.;
Matt. 25:34;
Eph. 5:27; Col.
1:22;
Eph. 4:2,15,16;
5:2
1:5
Acts 13:48; Rom.
8:29f.;
Rom. 8:14ff.;
Phil. 2:13; Col.
1:19
1:6
Eph. 1:12,14;
Matt. 3:17
1:7
Col. 1:14;
Rom. 3:24; 1 Cor.
1:30; Eph. 1:14;
Acts 20:28; Rom.
3:25;
Acts 2:38;
Rom. 2:4; Eph.
1:18; 2:7; 3:8,16
1:9
Rom. 11:25; Eph.
3:3;
1 Cor. 1:21; Gal.
1:15;
Rom. 8:28; Eph.
1:11
1:10
Mark 1:15;
Eph. 3:15; Phil.
2:9f.; Col. 1:16,20
1:11
Deut. 4:20; Eph.
1:14; Titus 2:14;
Eph. 1:5;
Rom. 8:28f.; Eph.
3:11;
Rom. 9:11; Heb.
6:17
1:12
Eph. 1:6,14
1:13
Eph. 4:21; Col.
1:5;
Eph. 4:30;
Acts 2:33
1:14
2 Cor. 1:22;
Acts 20:32;
Eph. 1:7;
Eph. 1:11;
Eph. 1:6,12
1:15
Col. 1:4; Philem.
5;
Eph. 1:1; 3:18

The Blessings of Redemption

1 Paul, an apostle of Christ Jesus by the will of God, to the saints who are [a]at Ephesus, and *who are* faithful in Christ Jesus:

2 Grace to you and peace from God our Father and the Lord Jesus Christ.

3 †Blessed *be* the God and Father of our Lord Jesus Christ, who has blessed us with every †*spiritual* blessing in the heavenly *places* in Christ,

4 just as He chose us in Him before the foundation of the world, that we should be holy[28a] and blameless[11b] before[1] [b]Him. *In love*[31a]

5 He predestined us to adoption as sons through Jesus Christ to Himself, according to the kind intention of His will,

6 to the praise of the glory of His grace, which He freely bestowed on us in the Beloved.⁺

7 In Him we have redemption through His blood, the forgiveness of our trespasses,[40b] according to the riches of His grace,

8 which He lavished upon us. In all wisdom and insight

9 He made known to us the mystery of His will, according to His kind intention which He purposed in Him

10 with a view to an administration suitable to the fulness of the times, *that is*, the summing[x] up of all things in Christ, things in the heavens and things upon the earth. In Him

11 also we have obtained an inheritance, having been predestined according to His purpose who works all things after the counsel of His will,

12 to the end that we who were the first to hope⁺ in [c]Christ should be to the praise of His glory.

13 In Him, you also, after listening to the message of truth, the gospel of your salvation—having also believed, you were sealed in Him with the Holy Spirit of *promise,*

14 who is given as a pledge of our inheritance, with a view to the redemption of *God's own* possession, to the praise of His glory.

15 For this reason I too, having heard of the faith in the Lord

---

[a]Some ancient mss. do not contain *at Ephesus.* [b]Or, *Him, in love.* [c]i.e., the Messiah

Jesus which *exists* among you, and ᵈyour love for all the saints,

16   do not cease giving thanks for you, while making mention *of you* in my prayers;

17   that the God of our Lord Jesus Christ, the Father of glory, may giveˣ to you a spirit of wisdom and of revelation in the knowledge¹ of Him.

18   *I pray that* the eyes of your heart may be enlightened,⁺ so that you may know what is the hope of His calling, what are the riches of the glory of His inheritance in the saints,

19   and what is the surpassing greatness of His power³²ᵃ toward us who believe. *These are* in accordance with the working of the strength³²ᵈ of His might³²ᶜ

20   which He brought about in Christ, when He raised Him from the dead, and seated Him at His right hand in the heavenly *places,*

21   far above all rule and authority and power and dominion, and every name that is named, not only in this age, but also in the one to come.

22   And He put *all things* in subjection under His feet, and gave *Him* as head over all things to the church,

23   which is His body, the fulness of Him who fills all in all.⁴

Made Alive in Christ

2   And you were dead in your trespasses⁴⁰ᵇ and sins,

2   in which you formerly walked according to the course of †this world, according to the prince of the power³²ᵇ of the air, of the spirit that is now working in the sons of disobedience.

3   Among them *we too* all formerly lived in the lusts of our flesh, indulging the desires of the flesh and of the mind,³³ᵃ and were by *nature* children of wrath,⁷ᵇ even as the rest.

4   But God, being rich in mercy, because of His great²⁶ᵇ love with which He loved us,

5   even when we were *dead* in our transgressions,⁴⁰ᵇ made us alive together ᵉwith Christ (by †grace you have been saved),⁺

6   and raised us up with Him, and seated us with Him in the heavenly *places*, in Christ Jesus,

7   in order that in the ages *to come* He might showˣ the surpassing riches of His grace in kindness toward us in Christ Jesus.

8   For by †grace you have been saved⁺ through faith; and that not of yourselves, *it is* the gift of *God;*

9   not as a result of works, that no one should boast.ˣ

10   For we are †*His* workmanship, created in Christ Jesus for

ᵈMany ancient mss. do not contain *your love*   ᵉSome ancient mss. read *in Christ*

1:16
Rom. 1:8f.; Col. 1:9; Rom. 1:9
1:17
John 20:17; Rom. 15:6;
Acts 7:2; 1 Cor. 2:8; Col. 1:9;
1 Cor. 14:6
1:18
Acts 26:18; 2 Cor. 4:6; Heb. 6:4;
Eph. 4:4;
Rom. 11:29;
Eph. 1:7;
Eph. 1:11;
Col. 1:12
1:19
Col. 1:29;
Eph. 3:7; 6:10
1:20
Acts 2:24;
Mark 16:19;
Eph. 1:3
1:21
Matt. 28:18; Col. 1:16;
Phil. 2:9; Rev. 19:12;
Matt. 12:32
1:22
Ps. 8:6; 1 Cor. 15:27;
1 Cor. 11:3; Eph. 4:15; Col. 1:18
1:23
1 Cor. 12:27;
Eph. 4:12; Col. 1:18,24;
John 1:16; Eph. 3:19; 4:10;
Col. 3:11
2:1
Eph. 2:5; Col. 2:13
2:2
1 Cor. 6:11; Eph. 2:3; Eph. 1:21;
John 12:31; Eph. 6:12;
Eph. 5:6
2:3
Eph. 2:2;
Gal. 5:16f.;
Rom. 2:14; Gal. 2:15;
Rom. 5:9; Col. 1:21; 2 Pet. 2:14;
Rom. 5:12
2:4
Eph. 1:7;
John 3:16
2:5
Eph. 2:1;
Acts 15:11
2:6
Col. 2:12;
Eph. 1:20;
Eph. 1:3;
Eph. 1:1; 2:10,13
2:7
Rom. 2:4; Eph. 1:7; Titus 3:4
2:8
Acts 15:11; Eph. 2:5; 1 Pet. 1:5;
John 4:10
2:9
Rom. 3:28;
2 Tim. 1:9;
1 Cor. 1:29
2:10
Eph. 2:15; 4:24;
Col. 3:10;
Eph. 1:1; 2:6,13;
Titus 2:14;
Eph. 1:4; 4:1

good[25a] works, which *God* prepared beforehand, that we should walk[x42a] in *them*.

11   Therefore remember,[ᵐ] that formerly you, the Gentiles in the flesh, who are called "Uncircumcision" by the so-called "Circumcision," *which is* performed in the flesh by human hands—

12   *remember* that you were at that time separate from Christ, excluded[*] from the commonwealth of Israel, and strangers to the covenants of promise, having no hope and without God in the world.

13   But •*now* in Christ Jesus you who formerly were far off have been brought near by the blood of Christ.

14   For *He* [†]*Himself* is our peace, who made both *groups into* one, and broke down the barrier of the dividing [†]wall,

15   by abolishing in His flesh the enmity, *which is* the Law of commandments *contained* in ordinances, that in Himself He might make[x] the *two* into [†]*one* new[34a] man, *thus* establishing peace,

16   and might reconcile[x1] them both in [†]*one* body to God through the cross, by it having put to death the enmity.

17   AND HE CAME AND PREACHED PEACE TO YOU WHO WERE FAR AWAY, AND PEACE TO THOSE WHO WERE NEAR;

18   for through Him we *both* have our access in [†]*one* Spirit to the Father.

19   So then you are no longer strangers and aliens, but you are fellow citizens with the saints, and are of God's household,

20   having been built upon the foundation of the apostles and prophets, Christ Jesus *Himself* being the corner *stone*,

21   in whom the whole building, being fitted together is growing into a [†]*holy*[28a] temple in the Lord;

22   in whom *you also* are being built together into a dwelling of God in the Spirit.

Paul's Stewardship

3   For this reason I, Paul, the prisoner of Christ Jesus for the sake of you Gentiles—

2   if indeed[ꜰ] you have heard of the stewardship of God's grace which was given to me for you;

3   that by *revelation* there was made known to me the mystery, as I wrote before in brief.

4   And by referring to this, when you read you can understand[x29d] my insight into the mystery of Christ,

5   which in other generations was not made known to the sons of men, as it has now been revealed to His holy[28a] apostles and prophets in the Spirit;

6 *to be specific*, that the Gentiles are fellow heirs and fellow members of the body, and fellow partakers of the promise in Christ Jesus through the gospel,

7 of which I was made a minister, according to the gift[24a] of God's grace which was given to me according to the working of His power.

8 To *me*, the very[3] least of all saints, this grace was given, to preach[x] to the *Gentiles* the unfathomable riches of Christ,

9 and to bring[x] to light what is the administration of the mystery which for ages has been hidden[*] in God, who created all things;

10 in order that the *manifold wisdom of God* might *now* be made known[x] through the church to the rulers and the authorities in the heavenly *places*.

11 *This was* in accordance with the eternal purpose which He carried out in Christ Jesus our Lord,

12 in whom we have boldness and confident access through faith in Him.

13 Therefore I ask you not to lose[~] heart at my tribulations on your behalf, for they are your glory.

14 For this reason, I bow my knees before the Father,

15 from whom every family in heaven and on earth derives its name,

16 that He would grant[x] you, according to the riches of His glory, to be strengthened[x] with power[32a] through His Spirit in the inner man;

17 so that *Christ* may dwell[x] in your hearts through faith; *and* that you, being rooted[*] and grounded[*] in [+]love,

18 may be able[x1] to comprehend[x1] with all the saints what is the breadth and length and height and depth,

19 and to know[x29a] the love of Christ which surpasses knowledge, that you may be filled[x] up to all the fulness of God.

20 Now to Him who is able to do[x19a] *exceeding abundantly beyond* all that we ask[9a] or think, according to the power[32a] that works within us,

21 to[+]*Him be* the glory in the church and in Christ Jesus to all generations forever and ever. Amen.

Unity of the Spirit

4 *I*, therefore, the prisoner of the Lord, entreat you to walk[x42a] in a manner *worthy* of the calling with which you have been called,

2 with all humility[23c] and gentleness,[23b] with patience, showing forbearance to one another in love,[31a]

3:4
2 Cor. 11:6;
Rom. 11:25;
16:25; Eph. 3:3,
9; 6:19; Col.
1:26f.; 4:3
3:5
1 Cor. 12:28;
Eph. 2:20
3:6
Gal. 3:29;
Eph. 2:16; 5:7;
Gal. 5:24
3:7
Col. 1:23,25;
1 Cor. 3:5;
Acts 9:15; Rom.
12:3; Eph. 3:2;
Eph. 1:19; 3:20
3:8
1 Cor. 15:9;
Acts 9:15;
Rom. 2:4; Eph.
1:7; 3:1f.; 3:16
3:9
Rom. 11:25;
16:25; Eph. 3:3,4;
6:19; Col. 1:26f.;
4:3; Col. 3:3;
Rev. 4:11
3:10
Rom. 11:33;
1 Cor. 2:7;
Eph. 1:23; 1 Pet.
1:12;
Eph. 1:21; 6:12;
Col. 2:10,15;
Eph. 1:3
3:11
Gal. 5:24; Eph.
1:11; 3:1
3:12
2 Cor. 3:4; Heb.
4:16; 10:19,35; 1
John 2:28; 3:21;
Eph. 2:18
3:13
2 Cor. 4:1;
Eph. 3:1
3:14
Phil. 2:10
3:16
Eph. 1:18; 3:8;
1 Cor. 16:13; Phil.
4:13; Col. 1:11;
Rom. 7:22
3:17
John 14:23; Rom.
8:9f.; 2 Cor. 13:5;
Eph. 2:22;
1 Cor. 3:6; Col.
2:7; Col. 1:23
3:18
Eph. 1:15;
Job 11:8f.
3:19
Rom. 8:35,39;
Phil. 4:7;
Col. 2:10;
Eph. 1:23
3:20
Rom. 16:25;
2 Cor. 9:8;
Eph. 3:7
3:21
Rom. 11:36
4:1
Eph. 3:1;
Rom. 12:1;
Eph. 2:10; Col.
1:10; 2:6;
1 Thess. 2:12;
Rom. 11:29;
Rom. 8:28f.
4:2
Col. 3:12f.;
Eph. 1:4

4:3
Col. 3:14f.

3 being diligent to preserve~ the unity of the Spirit in the bond of peace.

4:4
1 Cor. 12:4ff.;
Eph. 2:16,18;
Eph. 1:18
4:5
1 Cor. 8:6
4:6
Rom. 11:36

4 *There is* †one body and †one Spirit, just as also you were called in †one hope of your calling;

5 †one Lord, †one faith, †one baptism,

6 †one God and Father of all who is over all and through all and in all.

4:7
1 Cor. 12:7,11;
Eph. 3:2;
Rom. 12:3
4:8
Ps. 68:18;
Col. 2:15

7 But to *each one* of us grace was given according to the measure of Christ's gift. [24a]

8 Therefore it says,

"WHEN HE ASCENDED ON HIGH,
HE LED CAPTIVE A HOST OF CAPTIVES,
AND HE GAVE GIFTS TO MEN."

4:9
John 3:13;
Is. 44:23
4:10
Eph. 1:20f.; Heb.
4:14; 7:26;
Eph. 1:23
4:11
Eph. 4:8;
Acts 13:1; 1 Cor.
12:28;
Acts 21:8;
Acts 13:1
4:12
2 Cor. 13:9;
1 Cor. 12:27;
Eph. 1:23
4:13
Eph. 4:3,5;
John 6:69; Eph.
1:17; Phil. 3:10;
1 Cor. 14:20; Col.
1:28; Heb. 5:14;
John 1:16; Eph.
1:23
4:14
1 Cor. 14:20;
James 1:6; Jude
12;
1 Cor. 3:19;
2 Cor. 4:2; 11:3;
Eph. 6:11
4:15
Eph. 1:4;
Eph. 2:21;
Eph. 1:22
4:16
Rom. 12:4f.; Col.
2:19;
Eph. 1:4
4:17
Col. 2:4;
Eph. 2:2; 4:22;
Rom. 1:21; Col.
2:18; 1 Pet. 1:18;
2 Pet. 2:18
4:18
Rom. 1:21;
Eph. 2:1,12;
Acts 3:17; 17:30;
1 Cor. 2:8; Heb.
5:2; 9:7; 1 Pet.
1:14;
Mark 3:5; Rom.
11:7,25; 2 Cor.
3:14
4:19
1 Tim. 4:2;
Rom. 1:24;
Col. 3:5

9 (Now this *expression,* "He ascended," what does it mean except that He also had descended into the lower parts of the earth?

10 He who descended is Himself also He who ascended far above all the heavens, that He might[x] fill all things.)

11 And *He* gave some *as* apostles, and some *as* prophets, and some *as* evangelists, and some *as* pastors and teachers,

12 for the equipping of the saints for the work of service, to the building up of the body of Christ;

13 until we *all* attain[x] to the unity of the faith, and of the knowledge[29b] of the Son of God, to a *mature* man, to the measure of the stature which belongs to the fulness of Christ.

14 As a result, we are no longer to be children, tossed here and there by waves, and carried about by every wind of doctrine, by the trickery of men, by craftiness in deceitful scheming;

15 but speaking the truth in love,[31a] we are to grow[x] up in all *aspects* into Him, who is the head, *even* Christ,

16 from whom the whole body, being fitted and held together by that which every joint supplies, according to the proper working of each individual part, causes the *growth of the body* for the building up of itself in love.

The Christian's Walk

17 This I say therefore, and affirm together with the Lord, that *you* walk no longer just as the Gentiles also walk, ~[42a] in the futility of their mind,[33b]

18 being darkened⁺ in their understanding,[33a] excluded⁺ from the life of God, because of the ignorance that is in them, because of the hardness of their heart;

19 and they, having become⁺ callous, have given *themselves*

over to sensuality, for the practice of every kind of impurity with greediness.

20   But *you* did not learn Christ in this way,

21   if indeed[2] you have heard *Him* and have been taught *in Him,* just as truth is in Jesus,

22   that, in reference to your former manner of life, you lay[x] aside the old self, which is being corrupted in accordance with the lusts of deceit,

23   and that you be renewed~ in the spirit of your mind,[33b]

24   and put[x] on the new[34a] self, which in *the likeness of* [†]God has been created in righteousness and holiness of the truth.

25   Therefore, laying aside falsehood, SPEAK[~ℓ] TRUTH, EACH ONE *of you,* WITH HIS NEIGHBOR, for we are members of *one another.*

26   BE ANGRY,[~ℓ] AND *yet* DO NOT SIN;[⊖] do not let the *sun go*[⊖] *down* on your anger,[1]

27   and do not give[⊖] the devil an opportunity.

28   Let him who steals steal[⊖] no longer; but rather let him labor,[~ℓ] performing with his own hands what is good,[25a] in order that he may have~ *something* to share~ with him who has need.

29   Let no unwholesome[10c] word proceed[⊖] from your mouth, but only such *a word* as is good for edification according to the need *of the moment,* that it may give[x] grace to those who hear.

30   And do not grieve[⊖] the Holy Spirit of God, by whom you were sealed for the day of redemption.

31   Let all bitterness and wrath[7a] and anger and clamor and slander be *put*[xℓ] *away* from you, along with all malice.[10e]

32   And be[~ℓ] kind to one another, tender-hearted, forgiving each other, just as God *in Christ* also has forgiven [†]you.

Be Imitators of God

5 Therefore be[~ℓ] imitators of God, as beloved children;

2   and walk[~42a] in love,[31a] just as Christ also loved [†] you, and gave Himself up for us, an offering and a sacrifice to God as a fragrant aroma.

3   But do not let immorality or any impurity or greed even *be named*[⊖] among you, as is proper among saints;

4   and *there must be no* filthiness and silly talk, or coarse jesting, which are not fitting, but rather giving of thanks.

5   For this you know~ with certainty, that no immoral or impure person or covetous man, who is an idolater, has an inheritance in the kingdom of Christ and God.

6   Let no one deceive[⊖16a] you with empty words, for because

[†]Some ancient mss. read *us*

4:20
Matt. 11:29
4:21
Rom. 10:14; Eph.
1:13; 2:17; Col.
1:5; Col. 2:7
4:22
Eph. 4:25,31; Col.
3:8; Heb. 12:1;
James 1:21; 1
Pet. 2:1; Rom. 6:6;
2 Cor. 11:3; Heb.
3:13
4:23
Rom. 12:2
4:24
Rom. 13:14;
Rom. 6:4; 7:6;
12:2; 2 Cor. 5:17;
Col. 3:10;
Eph. 2:10
4:25
Eph. 4:22,31; Col.
3:8; Heb. 12:1;
James 1:21;
1 Pet. 2:1;
Zech. 8:16; Eph.
4:15; Col. 3:9;
Rom. 12:5
4:26
Ps. 4:4
4:27
Rom. 12:19;
James 4:7
4:28
Acts 20:35; 1 Cor.
4:12; Gal. 6:10;
1 Thess. 4:11;
2 Thess. 3:8,11f.;
Titus 3:8,14;
Luke 3:11; 1
Thess. 4:12
4:29
Matt. 12:34; Eph.
5:4; Col. 3:8;
Eccl. 10:12; Rom.
14:19; Col. 4:6
4:30
Is. 63:10; 1
Thess. 5:19;
John 3:33; Eph.
1:13
4:31
Rom. 3:14; Col.
3:8,19; Eph. 4:22;
1 Pet. 2:1
4:32
1 Cor. 13:4; Col.
3:12f.; 1 Pet. 3:8;
Matt. 6:14f.;
2 Cor. 2:10
5:1
Matt. 5:48; Luke
6:36; Eph. 4:32
5:2
Rom. 4:25; 8:37;
14:15;
John 6:51; 13:34;
Col. 3:14; Gal.
2:20; Eph. 5:25
Heb. 7:27; 9:14;
10:10,12;
Ex. 29:18,25;
2 Cor. 2:14
5:3
Col. 3:5
5:4
Matt. 12:34; Eph.
4:29; Col. 3:8;
Rom. 1:28;
Eph. 5:20
5:5
1 Cor. 6:9; Col.
3:5; Col. 1:13
5:6
Col. 2:8; 3:6; Rom.
1:18; Eph. 2:2

of these things the *wrath*[7b] *of God* comes upon the sons of disobedience.

7 Therefore do not be° partakers with them;

8 for you were formerly darkness, but now you are light in the Lord; walk~[42a] as *children of light*

9 (for the fruit of the light *consists* in all goodness and righteousness and truth),

10 trying to learn what is pleasing to the Lord.

11 And do not participate° in the *unfruitful* deeds of darkness, but instead even *expose*~ them;

12 for it is disgraceful even to *speak*~ of the things which are done by them in secret.

13 But all things become visible when they are exposed by the light, for everything that becomes visible is light.

14 For this reason it says,

"Awake,~ sleeper,
And arise[xi] from the dead,
And *Christ* will shine on you."

15 Therefore be careful~ how you walk, not as unwise men, but as wise,

16 making the most of your time, because the days are [†]evil.[10b]

17 So then do not be° foolish,[20b] but understand~[29f] what the will of the Lord is.

18 And do not get drunk° with wine, for that is dissipation, but be filled~ with the Spirit,

19 speaking to one another in psalms and hymns and spiritual songs, singing and making melody with your heart to the Lord;

20 always giving thanks for all things in the name of our Lord Jesus Christ to God, even the Father;

21 and be subject to one another in the fear of Christ.

Marriage Like Christ and the Church

22 Wives, *be subject* to your own husbands, as to the Lord.

23 For the husband is the head of the wife, as Christ also is the head of the church, He Himself *being* the Savior of the body.

24 But as the church is subject to Christ, so also the wives *ought to be* to their husbands in everything.

25 Husbands, love~[31a] your wives, just as Christ also loved[31a] the church and gave *Himself* up for her;

26 that He might sanctify[x] her, having cleansed her by the washing of water with the word,[43b]

27 that *He* might present[x] to [†]*Himself* the church in all her

glory, having no spot or wrinkle or any such thing; but that she should be holy[28a] and blameless.[11b]

28   So husbands ought also to love[~31a] their own wives as their own bodies. He who loves[31a] his own wife loves himself;

29   for no one ever hated his *own flesh,* but nourishes[1] and cherishes it, just as Christ also *does* the church,

30   because we are *members* of His body.

31   FOR THIS CAUSE A MAN SHALL LEAVE HIS FATHER AND MOTHER, AND SHALL CLEAVE TO HIS WIFE; AND THE TWO SHALL BECOME ONE FLESH.

32   †*This* mystery is *great;* but I am speaking with reference to Christ and the church.

33   Nevertheless let each individual among you also love[~31a] his own wife even as himself; and *let* the wife *see to it* that she respect[~] her husband.

Family Relationships

6 Children, obey[~1] your parents in the Lord, for this is right.
    2   HONOR[~1] YOUR FATHER AND MOTHER (which is the first commandment with a promise),

3   THAT IT MAY BE WELL WITH YOU, AND THAT YOU MAY LIVE LONG ON THE EARTH.

4   And, fathers, do not provoke[θ] your children to anger; but bring[~1] them up in the discipline and instruction of the Lord.

5   Slaves, be obedient[~1] to those who are your masters according to the flesh, with fear and trembling, in the sincerity of your heart, as to Christ;

6   not by way of eyeservice, as men-pleasers, but as slaves of Christ, doing the will of God from the heart.[30c]

7   With good will render service, as to the Lord, and not to men,

8   knowing that whatever good[25a] thing each one does,[x] this he will receive back from the Lord, whether slave or free.

9   And, masters, do[~1] the *same things* to them, and give up threatening, knowing that both *their* Master *and yours* is in heaven, and there is no partiality with Him.

The Armor of God

10   Finally, be strong[~1] in the Lord, and in the strength[32d] of His might.[32c]

11   Put[x1] on the full armor of God, that you may be able[~] to stand[x] firm against the schemes of the devil.

12   For our struggle is not against flesh and blood, but against the rulers, against the powers,[32b] against the world forces of this

5:28
Eph. 5:25,33; 1
Pet. 3:7

5:30
1 Cor. 6:15;
12:27;
Eph. 1:23
5:31
Gen. 2:24; Matt.
19:5; Mark 10:7f.

5:33
Eph. 5:25,28;
1 Pet. 3:7;
1 Pet. 3:2,5f.

6:1
Prov. 6:20; 23:22;
Col. 3:20
6:2
Ex. 20:12; Deut.
5:16
6:4
Col. 3:21;
Gen. 18:19; Deut.
6:7; 11:19; Ps.
78:4; Prov. 22:6;
2 Tim. 3:15
6:5
Col. 3:22; 1 Tim.
6:1; Titus 2:9;
1 Cor. 2:3;
Eph. 5:22
6:6
Col. 3:22;
Gal. 1:10;
1 Cor. 7:22;
Mark 3:35
6:7
Col. 3:23
6:8
Col. 3:24;
Matt. 16:27;
2 Cor. 5:10; Col.
3:24f.;
1 Cor. 12:13; Col.
3:11
6:9
Lev. 25:43;
Job 31:13ff.; John
13:13; Col. 4:1;
Deut. 10:17; Acts
10:34; Col. 3:25
6:10
1 Cor. 16:13;
2 Tim. 2:1;
Eph. 1:19
6:11
Rom. 13:12; Eph.
6:13;
Eph. 4:14
6:12
1 Cor. 9:25;
Matt. 16:17;
Eph. 1:21; 2:2;
3:10;
John 12:31;
Acts 26:18; Col.
1:13;
Eph. 3:10;
Eph. 1:3

6:13
Eph. 6:11;
James 4:7;
Eph. 5:16
6:14
Is. 11:5; Luke
12:35; 1 Pet.
1:13;
Is. 59:17; Rom.
13:12; Eph. 6:13;
1 Thess. 5:8
6:15
Is. 52:7; Rom.
10:15
6:16
1 Thess. 5:8;
Ps. 7:13; 120:4;
Matt. 5:37
6:17
Is. 59:17;
Is. 49:2; Hos. 6:5;
Heb. 4:12;
Eph. 5:26; Heb.
6:5
6:18
Phil. 4:6;
Luke 18:1; Col.
1:3; 4:2; 1 Thess.
5:17;
Rom. 8:26f.;
Mark 13:33;
Acts 1:14;
1 Tim. 2:1
6:19
Col. 4:3; 1 Thess.
5:25;
2 Cor. 6:11;
2 Cor. 3:12;
Eph. 3:3
6:20
2 Cor. 5:20;
Philem. 9 mg.;
Acts 21:33;
28:20; Eph. 3:1;
Phil. 1:7; Col. 4:3;
2 Cor. 3:12;
Col. 4:4
6:21
Eph. 6:21,22: Col.
4:7-9;
Acts 20:4; 2 Tim.
4:12;
Col. 4:7
6:22
Col. 4:8;
Col. 2:2; 4:8
6:23
Rom. 15:33; Gal.
6:16; 2 Thess.
3:16; 1 Pet. 5:14;
Gal. 5:6;
1 Thess. 5:8

darkness, against the spiritual *forces* of wickedness in the heaven-ly *places.*

13   Therefore, take[xl5b] up the full armor of God, that you may be able[x] to resist[x] in the +*evil*[10b] day, and having done everything, to stand[x] firm.

14   Stand[xl] firm therefore, HAVING GIRDED YOUR LOINS WITH TRUTH, and HAVING PUT ON THE BREASTPLATE OF RIGHTEOUSNESS,

15   and having shod YOUR FEET WITH THE PREPARATION OF THE GOSPEL OF PEACE;

16   in addition to all, taking[5b] up the shield of faith with which you will be able to extinguish[x] all the flaming+ missiles of the evil *one.*

17   And take[xl5a] THE HELMET OF SALVATION, and the sword of the Spirit, which is the word[43b] of God.

18   With all prayer and petition pray at all times in the Spirit, and with this in view, be on the alert with all perseverance and petition for all the saints,

19   and *pray* on my behalf, that utterance may be given[x] to me in the opening of my mouth, to make known[x] with *boldness* the mystery of the gospel,

20   for which I am an ambassador in chains; that 9in *proclaiming* it I may speak[x] boldly, as I ought to speak.[x]

21   But that you also may know about my circumstances, how I am doing, Tychicus, the beloved brother and faithful minister in the Lord, will make everything known to you.

22   And I have sent him to you for this very purpose, so that you may know[x] about us, and that he may comfort[x] your hearts.

23   Peace be to the brethren, and love[31a] with faith, from God the Father and the Lord Jesus Christ.

24   Grace be with all those who love[31a] our Lord Jesus Christ with *a love* incorruptible.

9Some ancient mss. read *I may speak it boldly*

The Epistle of Paul to the
Philippians

Thanksgiving

1 Paul and Timothy, bond-servants[38b] of Christ Jesus, to all the saints in Christ Jesus who are in Philippi, including the overseers and deacons:

2 Grace to you and peace from God our Father and the Lord Jesus Christ.

3 I thank my God in all my remembrance of you,

4 always offering prayer with †joy in my every prayer for you all,

5 in view of your participation in the gospel from the first day until now.

6 *For I am* confident⁺ of this very thing, that He who began a good[25a] work in you will perfect[1] it until the day of Christ Jesus.

7 For it is only right for me to feel~ this way about you all, because I have you in my heart, since both in my imprisonment and in the defense and confirmation of the gospel, you all are partakers of grace with me.

8 For *God* is my witness, how I long for you all with the affection of Christ Jesus.

9 And this I pray, that your love[31a] may abound~ still more and more in real[1] knowledge and all discernment,

10 so that you may approve~ the things that are excellent, in order to be sincere and blameless until the day of Christ;

11 having been filled⁺ with the fruit of righteousness which *comes* through Jesus Christ, to the glory and praise of God.

The Gospel Is Preached

12 Now I want you to know,~ brethren, that my circumstances have turned⁺ out for the *greater progress* of the gospel,

13 so that my imprisonment in *the cause of* Christ has become *well known* throughout the whole ᵃpraetorian guard and to everyone else,

14 and that most of the brethren, trusting⁺ in the Lord because of my imprisonment, have~ far more courage to speak~ the word[43a] of God without †fear.

ᵃOr, *governor's palace*

1:1
2 Cor. 1:1;
Acts 16:1;
Rom. 1:1; Gal.
1:10;
Gal. 3:26;
2 Cor. 1:1; Col.
1:2;
Acts 9:13;
Acts 16:12;
Acts 20:28; 1
Tim. 3:1f.; Titus
1:7;
1 Tim. 3:8ff.
1:2
Rom. 1:7
1:3
Rom. 1:8
1:4
Rom. 1:9
1:5
Acts 2:42; Phil.
4:15;
Phil. 1:7; 2:22;
4:3,15;
Acts 16:12-40;
Phil. 2:12; 4:15
1:6
1 Cor. 1:8; Phil.
1:10; 2:16
1:7
2 Pet. 1:13;
2 Cor. 7:3;
Acts 21:33; Eph.
6:20; Phil. 1:13f.,
17;
Phil. 1:16;
Phil. 1:5,12,16,
27; 2:22; 4:3,15
1:8
Rom. 1:9;
Gal. 3:26
1:9
1 Thess. 3:12;
Col. 1:9
1:10
Rom. 2:18;
1 Cor. 1:8; Phil.
1:6; 2:16
1:11
James 3:18

1:12
Luke 21:13;
Phil. 1:5,7,16,27;
2:22; 4:3,15
1:13
Phil. 1:7; 2 Tim.
2:9;
Acts 28:30

1:14
Phil. 1:7; 2 Tim.
2:9;
Acts 4:31; 2 Cor.
3:12; 7:4; Phil.
1:20

1:15
2 Cor. 11:13

1:16
Phil. 1:5,7,12,27;
2:22; 4:3,15

1:17
Rom. 2:8; Phil.
2:3;
Phil. 1:7; 2 Tim.
2:9

1:19
2 Cor. 1:11;
Acts 16:7

1:20
Rom. 8:19;
Rom. 5:5; 1 Pet.
4:16;
Acts 4:31; 2 Cor.
3:12; 7:4; Phil.
1:14;
1 Cor. 6:20;
Rom. 14:8

1:21
Gal. 2:20
1:22
Rom. 1:13

1:23
2 Cor. 5:8; 2 Tim.
4:6;
John 12:26

1:25
Phil. 2:24

1:26
2 Cor. 5:12; 7:4;
Phil. 2:16

1:27
Eph. 4:1;
Phil. 1:5;
1 Cor. 16:13; Phil.
4:1;
Acts 4:32;
Jude 3

1:28
2 Thess. 1:5

1:29
Matt. 5:11,12;
Acts 14:22
1:30
Col. 1:29; 2:1; 1
Thess. 2:2; 1 Tim.
6:12; 2 Tim. 4:7;
Heb. 10:32; 12:1;
Acts 16:19-40;
Phil. 1:13

15   Some, to be sure, are preaching Christ even from *envy* and *strife,* but some also from good will;

16   ᵇthe latter *do it* out of love, knowing that I am appointed for the defense of the gospel;

17   the former proclaim Christ out of *selfish ambition,* rather than from pure motives, thinking to cause~ me *distress* in my imprisonment.

18   What then? Only that in every way, whether in pretense or in truth, Christ is proclaimed; and in this I rejoice, yes, and I will rejoice.

19   For I know that this shall turn out for my deliverance through your prayers and the provision of the Spirit of Jesus Christ,

20   according to my earnest expectation and hope, that I shall not be put to shame³⁹ᵃ in anything, but *that* with all boldness, *Christ* shall even now, as always, be exalted in my body, whether by life or by death.

To Live Is Christ

21   For to me, to live~ is Christ, and to dieˣ is gain.

22   But if *I am* to live~ *on* in the flesh, this *will mean* fruitful labor for me; and I do not know which to choose.

23   But I am hard-pressed from both *directions,* having the desire to departˣ and be *with Christ,* for *that* is very³ much better;

24   yet to remain~ on in the flesh is more necessary for your sake.

25   And convinced⁺ of this, I know that I shall remain and continue with you all for *your* progress and joy in the faith,

26   so that your proud confidence in me may abound~ in Christ Jesus through •my coming to you again.

27   Only conduct~ᴵ yourselves in a manner *worthy* of the *gospel of Christ;* so that whether I come and see you or remain absent, I may hear~ of you that you are standing firm in ⁺*one* spirit, with ⁺*one* mind³⁰ᶜ striving together for the faith of the gospel;

28   in no way alarmed by *your* opponents—which is a sign of destruction for them, but of *salvation* for you, and that *too,* from God.

29   For to you it has been granted for Christ's sake, not only to ⁺believe~ in Him, but also to *suffer* ~ for His sake,

30   experiencing the same conflict which you saw in me, and now hear *to be* in me.

ᵇSome later mss. reverse the order of vv. 16 and 17

Be Like Christ

2 If therefore there is any encouragement in Christ, if there is any consolation of love, if there is any fellowship of the Spirit, if any affection and compassion,

2 make[xi] my *joy* complete by being~ of the same †mind,[33c] maintaining the same †love, united in spirit, intent on one purpose.

3 Do nothing from selfishness or empty conceit, but with humility[23c] of mind let each of you regard one another as more important than himself;

4 do not *merely* look out for your own personal interests, but also for the interests of *others*.

5 Have[~1] this attitude[33c] in yourselves which was also in Christ Jesus,

6 who, although He existed in the *form*[22c] *of God*, did not regard equality with God a thing to be grasped,

7 but [c]*emptied* Himself, taking the form[22c] of a †bond-servant,[38b] *and* being made in the likeness of †men.

8 And being found in appearance[22e] as a man, He humbled Himself by becoming obedient to the point of death, even death on a cross.

9 Therefore also God highly[1] exalted Him, and bestowed on Him the name which is above every name,

10 that at the *name of Jesus* EVERY KNEE SHOULD BOW,[x] of those who are in heaven, and on earth, and under the earth,

11 and that every tongue should confess[x1] that Jesus Christ is *Lord*, to the glory of God the Father.

12 So then, my beloved, just as you have always obeyed, not as in my presence only, but now much more in my absence, *work*[~1] *out*[1] your salvation with *fear* and *trembling*;

13 for it is God who is at work in you, both to will~ and to work~ for *His* good pleasure.

14 Do[~1] all things without grumbling or disputing;

15 that you may prove yourselves to be blameless[11a] and innocent, children of God above reproach[11b] in the midst of a crooked and perverse ✦ generation, among whom you appear as lights in the world,

16 holding fast the word[43a] of life, so that in the day of Christ I may have cause to glory because I did not run in *vain* nor toil in *vain*.

17 But even if I am being poured out as a drink offering upon

[c]i.e., laid aside His privileges

2:1
2 Cor. 13:14;
Col. 3:12

2:2
John 3:29;
Rom. 12:16; Phil. 4:2

2:3
Rom. 2:8; Phil. 1:17;
Gal. 5:26;
Rom. 12:10; Eph. 5:21

2:4
Rom. 15:1f.

2:5
Matt. 11:29; Rom. 15:3;
Phil. 1:1

2:6
John 1:1;
2 Cor. 4:4;
John 5:18; 10:33; 14:28

2:7
2 Cor. 8:9;
Matt. 20:28;
John 1:14; Rom. 8:3; Gal. 4:4;
Heb. 2:17

2:8
2 Cor. 8:9;
Matt. 26:39; John 10:18; Rom. 5:19;
Heb. 5:8;
Heb. 12:2

2:9
Heb. 1:9;
Matt. 28:18; Acts 2:33; Heb. 2:9;
Eph. 1:21

2:10
Is. 45:23; Rom. 14:11;
Eph. 1:10

2:11
John 13:13; Rom. 10:9; 14:9

2:12
Phil. 1:5,6; 4:15;
Heb. 5:9;
2 Cor. 7:15

2:13
Rom. 12:3; 1 Cor. 12:6; 15:10; Heb. 13:21;
Eph. 1:5

2:14
1 Cor. 10:10;
1 Pet. 4:9

2:15
Luke 1:6; Phil. 3:6;
Matt. 5:45; Eph. 5:1;
Deut. 32:5; Acts 2:40;
Matt. 5:14-16

2:16
Phil. 1:6;
Gal. 2:2;
Is. 49:4; Gal. 4:11; 1 Thess. 3:5

2:17
2 Cor. 12:15;
2 Tim. 4:6;
Num. 28:6,7;
Rom. 15:16

the sacrifice and service of your faith, I rejoice and share my joy with you all.

18   And you too, *I urge you*, rejoice ᵐ in the same way and share ᵐ your joy with me.

Timothy and Epaphroditus

2:19
Phil. 2:23;
Phil. 1:1

19   But I hope in the Lord Jesus to sendˣ Timothy to you shortly, so that *I also* may be encouraged~ when I learn of your condition.

2:20
1 Cor. 16:10;
2 Tim. 3:10

20   For I have no one *else* of *kindred spirit* who will *genuinely* be concerned for your welfare.

2:21
1 Cor. 10:24;
13:5; Phil. 2:4

21   For they all seek after their *own interests,* not those of Christ Jesus.

2:22
Rom. 5:4; Acts
16:2;
Acts 16:3; 1 Cor.
16:10; 2 Tim.
3:10;
1 Cor. 4:17
2:23
Phil. 2:19
2:24
Phil. 1:25

22   But you know of his proven worth that he served³⁸ᵇ with me in the furtherance of the gospel like a child *serving* his father.

23   Therefore I hope to sendˣ him *immediately,* as soon as I seeˣ how things *go* with me;

24   and I trust in the Lord that I myself also shall be coming shortly.

2:25
Phil. 4:18;
Rom. 16:3,9,21;
Phil. 4:3; Philem.
1,24;
Philem. 2;
John 13:16;
2 Cor. 8:23

25   But I thought it necessary to sendˣ to you Epaphroditus, my brother and fellow worker and fellow soldier, who is also your messenger and minister to my need;

26   because he was *longing*~ ᵈfor you all and was distressed ~ because you had heard that he was sick.

27   For indeed he was sick to the point¹ of death, but God had mercy on him, and not on him only but also on me, lest I should haveˣ sorrow upon sorrow.

28   Therefore I have sent him all the more ³ eagerly in order that when you see him again you may rejoiceˣ and I may be less concerned *about you.*

2:29
Rom. 16:2;
1 Cor. 16:18

29   Therefore receive ᵐ him in the Lord with all joy, and hold ᵐ men like him in *high regard;*

2:30
Acts 20:24;
1 Cor. 16:17; Phil.
4:10

30   because he came close to death for the *work of Christ,* risking his life to completeˣ what was deficient in your service to me.

The Goal of Life

3:1
Phil. 2:18; 4:4
3:2
Ps. 22:16,20; Gal.
5:15; Rev. 22:15;
2 Cor. 11:13
3:3
Rom. 2:29; 9:6;
Gal. 6:15;
Gal. 5:25;
Rom. 15:17; Gal.
6:14;
Rom. 8:39; Phil.
1:1; 3:12

3   Finally, my brethren, rejoice ᵐ in the Lord. To write~ the same things *again* is no trouble to me, and it is a safeguard for you.

2   Beware ᵐ of the dogs, beware ᵐ of the evil¹⁰ᵃ workers, beware ᵐ of the false circumcision;

3   for †we are the *true* circumcision, who worship³⁸ᶜ in the

ᵈSome ancient mss. read *to see you all*

Spirit of †*God* and glory in Christ Jesus and put⁺ no confidence in the flesh,

4   although² I myself might have confidence even in the flesh. If *anyone else* has a mind to put⁺ confidence in the flesh, †*I* far more:

5   circumcised the eighth day, of the nation of Israel, of the tribe of Benjamin, a Hebrew of Hebrews; as to the Law, a Pharisee;

6   as to zeal, a persecutor of the church; as to the righteousness which is in the Law, found blameless. ¹¹ᵃ

7   But whatever things were †gain to me, those things I have counted⁺ as *loss* for the sake of Christ.

8   •*More*² than that, I count all things to be *loss* in view of the surpassing value of knowing Christ Jesus my Lord, for whom I have suffered the loss of *all things,* and count them but rubbish in order that I may gainˣ *Christ,*

9   and may be foundˣ in Him, not having a righteousness of *my* •*own* derived from *the* Law, but that which is through faith in Christ, the righteousness which *comes* from †*God* on the basis of faith,

10   that I may knowˣ ²⁹ᵃ Him, and the power ³²ᵃ of His resurrection and the fellowship of His sufferings, being conformed to His death;

11   in order that I may attainˣ to the resurrection¹ from the dead.

12   Not that I have already obtained *it,* or have already become⁺ perfect, but I press on in order that I may lay holdˣ¹ of that for which also I was laid hold of by Christ Jesus.

13   Brethren, I do not regard myself as having laid hold⁺¹ of *it* yet; but one thing *I do*: forgetting what *lies* behind and reaching forward¹ to what *lies ahead,*

14   I press on toward the *goal* for the prize of the upward call of God in Christ Jesus.

15   Let us therefore, as many as are perfect, have~ this attitude; and if in anything you have a different attitude, God will reveal that also to you;

16   however, let us keep living ~⁴²ᵇ by that same *standard* to which we have attained.

17   Brethren, join ~ᵐ in following *my example,* and observe ~ᵐ those who walk ⁴²ᵃ according to the pattern you have in us.

18   For many walk, of whom I often told ᵐ you, and now tell you even weeping, *that they are* enemies of the cross of Christ,

19   whose end is destruction, whose god is *their* appetite, and

3:4
2 Cor. 5:16; 11:18

3:5
Luke 1:59;
Rom. 11:1; 2 Cor. 11:22;
Rom. 11:1;
Acts 22:3; 23:6; 26:5
3:6
Acts 8:3; 22:4,5; 26:9-11;
Phil. 3:9;
Phil. 2:15
3:7
Luke 14:33
3:8
Jer. 9:23f.; John 17:3; Eph. 4:13;
Phil. 3:10; 2 Pet. 1:3;
Rom. 8:39; Phil. 1:1; 3:12
3:9
Rom. 10:5; Phil. 3:6;
Rom. 9:30; 1 Cor. 1:30
3:10
Jer. 9:23f.; John 17:3; Eph. 4:13;
Phil. 3:8; 2 Pet. 1:13;
Rom. 6:5;
Rom. 8:17;
Rom. 6:5; 8:36;
Gal. 6:17
3:11
Acts 26:7; 1 Cor. 15:23; Rev. 20:5f.
3:12
1 Cor. 9:24f.;
1 Tim. 6:12,19;
1 Cor. 13:10;
1 Tim. 6:12,19;
Acts 9:5f.;
Rom. 8:39; Phil. 1:1; 3:3,8
3:13
Luke 9:62
3:14
1 Cor. 9:24; Heb. 6:1;
Rom. 8:28; 11:29;
2 Tim. 1:9;
Phil. 3:3
3:15
Matt. 5:48; 1 Cor. 2:6;
Gal. 5:10;
John 6:45; Eph. 1:17; 1 Thess. 4:9
3:16
Gal. 6:16
3:17
1 Cor. 4:16; 11:1;
Phil. 4:9;
1 Pet. 5:3
3:18
2 Cor. 11:13;
Acts 20:31;
Gal. 6:14
3:19
Rom. 16:18;
Titus 1:12;
Rom. 6:21; Jude 13;
Rom. 8:5f.; Col. 3:2

whose glory is in their shame, who set their minds[33c] on earthly things.

20　For our citizenship is in heaven, from which also we eagerly[1] wait for a *Savior,* the Lord Jesus Christ;

21　who will transform the body of our humble state into conformity with the body of His glory, by the exertion of the power that He has~ even to *subject*[x] all things to Himself.

Think of Excellence

4　Therefore, my beloved brethren whom I long *to see,* my joy and crown, so stand~ firm in the Lord, my beloved.

2　I *urge* Euodia and I urge Syntyche to live~ in harmony in the Lord.

3　Indeed, true comrade, I ask you also to help~ these women who have shared my struggle in *the cause of* the gospel, together with Clement also, and the rest of my fellow workers, whose names are in the book of life.

4　Rejoice~ in the Lord *always;* again I will say, rejoice!~

5　Let[x] your *forbearing*[23a] *spirit* be known[29a] to all men. The Lord is near.

6　Be anxious° for nothing, but in everything by prayer and supplication with thanksgiving let your requests be made~ known to God.

7　And the peace of God, which surpasses all comprehension,[33b] shall guard your hearts and your minds in Christ Jesus.

8　Finally, brethren, whatever is true, whatever is honorable, whatever is right, whatever is pure,[13a] whatever is lovely, whatever is of good repute, if there is any excellence and if anything worthy of praise, let your mind dwell~ on these things.

9　The things you have learned and received and heard and seen in me, practice~[19b] these things; and the God of peace shall be with you.

God's Provisions

10　But I rejoiced in the Lord greatly, that now at last you have revived your concern~ for me; indeed, you were concerned[xx] *before,* but you lacked[xx] opportunity.

11　Not that I speak from want; for I have learned to be *content* in whatever circumstances I am.

12　I know how to get~ along with humble means, and I also know how to live~ in prosperity; in *any* and *every circumstance* I have learned+ the secret of being filled~ and going hungry, ~ both of having~ abundance and suffering~ need.

13　I can do *all things* through Him who strengthens me.

3:20
Eph. 2:19; Phil.
1:27; Col. 3:1;
Heb. 12:22;
1 Cor. 1:7
3:21
1 Cor. 15:43-53;
Rom. 8:29; Col.
3:4;
1 Cor. 15:43,49;
Eph. 1:19;
1 Cor. 15:28

4:1
Phil. 1:8;
1 Cor. 16:13; Phil.
1:27
4:2
Phil. 2:2

4:3
Phil. 2:25;
Luke 10:20

4:4
Phil. 3:1
4:5
1 Cor. 16:22 mg.;
Heb. 10:37;
James 5:8f.
4:6
Matt. 6:25;
Eph. 6:18; 1 Tim.
2:1; 5:5

4:7
Is. 26:3; John
14:27; Phil. 4:9;
Col. 3:15;
1 Pet. 1:5;
2 Cor. 10:5;
Phil. 1:1; 4:19,21
4:8
Rom. 14:18;
1 Pet. 2:12

4:9
Phil. 3:17;
Rom. 15:33

4:10
2 Cor. 11:9; Phil.
2:30

4:11
2 Cor. 9:8; 1 Tim.
6:6,8; Heb. 13:5

4:12
1 Cor. 4:11;
2 Cor. 11:9

4:13
2 Cor. 12:9; Eph.
3:16; Col. 1:11

14 Nevertheless, you have done well to share *with me* in my affliction.

15 And you yourselves also know, Philippians, that at the first preaching of the gospel, after I departed from Macedonia, no church shared with me in the matter of giving and receiving but you alone;

16 for even in *Thessalonica* you sent *a gift more than once* for my needs.

17 Not that I seek the gift itself, but I seek for the profit which increases to your account.

18 But I have received everything in full, and have an abundance; I am amply supplied, * having received from Epaphroditus what you have sent, a fragrant aroma, an acceptable sacrifice, well-pleasing to God.

19 And my God shall supply all your needs according to His riches in glory in Christ Jesus.

20 Now to our God and Father *be* the glory forever and ever. Amen.

21 Greetᵛ every saint in Christ Jesus. The brethren who are with me greet you.

22 All the saints greet you, especially those of Caesar's household.

23 The grace of the Lord Jesus Christ be with your spirit.

4:14
Heb. 10:33; Rev. 1:9

4:15
Phil. 1:5;
Rom. 15:26;
2 Cor. 11:9

4:16
Acts 17:1;
1 Thess. 2:9

4:17
1 Cor. 9:11f.;
2 Cor. 9:5

4:18
Phil. 2:25;
Ex. 29:18; 2 Cor. 2:14; Eph. 5:2

4:19
2 Cor. 9:8;
Rom. 2:4

4:20
Gal. 1:4;
Rom. 11:36

4:21
Gal. 1:2

4:22
2 Cor. 13:13;
Acts 9:13

4:23
Rom. 16:20;
2 Tim. 4:22

The Epistle of Paul to the

Colossians

Thankfulness for Spiritual Attainments

1:1
Phil. 1:1;
1 Cor. 1:1;
2 Cor. 1:1; 1
Thess. 3:2

1 Paul, an apostle of Jesus Christ by the will of God, and Timothy our brother,

1:2
Acts 9:13;
Rom. 1:7

2 to the saints and faithful brethren in Christ *who are* at Colossae: Grace to you and peace from God our Father.

1:3
Rom. 1:8;
Rom. 15:6; 2 Cor.
1:3

3 We give thanks to God, the Father of our Lord Jesus Christ, praying always for you,

1:4
Eph. 1:15;
Gal. 5:6;
Eph. 6:18

4 since we heard of your faith in Christ Jesus and the love which you have for all the saints;

1:5
Acts 23:6;
2 Tim. 4:8;
Eph. 1:13

5 because of the hope laid up for you in heaven, of which you previously heard in the word[43a] of truth, the gospel,

1:6
Rom. 10:18;
Rom. 1:13;
Eph. 4:21

6 which has come to you, just as in all the world also it is constantly bearing~ fruit and increasing,~ even as *it has been doing* in you also since the day you heard *of it* and understood[29b] the grace of God in truth;

1:7
Col. 4:12;
Col. 4:7

7 just as you learned *it* from Epaphras, our beloved fellow bond-servant, who is a faithful servant of Christ on ᵃour behalf,

1:8
Rom. 15:30

8 and he also informed us of your love in the Spirit.

1:9
Col. 1:4;
Eph. 1:16;
Phil. 1:9;
Eph. 1:17

9 For this reason also, since the day we heard *of it*, we have not ceased to pray for you and to ask[9a] that you may be filled[x] with the knowledge[29b] of His will in all spiritual wisdom and understanding,

1:10
Eph. 4:1;
Eph. 5:10;
Rom. 1:13

10 so that you may walk[x42a] in a manner worthy of the Lord, to please *Him* in all respects, bearing fruit in every good[25a] work and increasing in the knowledge[29b] of God;

1:11
1 Cor. 16:13;
Eph. 4:2

11 strengthened[4] with all power,[32a] according to His glorious might,[32d] for the attaining of all steadfastness and patience; joyously

1:12
Eph. 2:18;
Acts 20:32;
Acts 26:18

12 giving thanks to the Father, who has qualified us to share in the inheritance of the saints in light.

The Incomparable Christ

1:13
Eph. 6:12;
Eph. 1:6

13 For He delivered[18b] us from the domain of darkness, and transferred us to the kingdom of His beloved Son,

1:14
Rom. 3:24

14 in whom we have redemption, the forgiveness of sins.

ᵃSome later mss. read *your*

15   And He is the image[22b] of the invisible God, the first-born of all creation.

1:15
2 Cor. 4:4;
John 1:18;;
Rom. 8:29

16   For *by Him* all things were created, *both* in the heavens and on earth, visible and invisible, whether thrones or dominions or rulers or authorities—all things have been created[+] *by Him* and *for Him.*

1:16
Eph. 1:10;
Eph. 1:20f.; Col.
2:15;
John 1:3 Rom.
11:36; 1 Cor. 8:6

17   And *He* is before all things, and *in Him* all things hold[+] together.

1:17
John 1:1; 8:58

18   *He* is also head of the body, the church; and He is the beginning, the first-born from the dead; so that *He Himself* might come to have first place in *everything.*

1:18
Eph. 1:22;
Eph. 1:23; Col.
1:24; 2:19;
Rev. 3:14;
Acts 26:23

19   For it was the *Father's* good pleasure for all the fulness to dwell[x] *in Him,*

1:19
Eph. 1:5;
John 1:16

20   and *through Him* to reconcile[x1] all things to Himself, having made peace through the blood of His cross; *through* [+]*Him, I say,* whether things on earth or things in heaven.

1:20
2 Cor. 5:18; Eph.
2:16;
Rom. 5:1; Eph.
2:14;
Eph. 2:13;
Col. 1:16

21   And although you were formerly alienated[+] and hostile in mind,[33a] *engaged* in evil deeds,

1:21
Rom. 5:10; Eph.
2:3,12

22   yet He has •now reconciled[1] you in His fleshly body through death, in order to present[x] you before[1] Him holy[28a] and blameless[11b] and beyond reproach—[11c]

1:22
2 Cor. 5:18; Eph.
2:16;
Rom. 7:4;
Eph. 5:27; Col.
1:28;
Eph. 1:4

23   if indeed[2] you continue in the faith firmly established[+] and steadfast, and not moved away from the hope of the gospel that you have heard, which was proclaimed in all creation under heaven, and of which *I,* Paul, was made a minister.

1:23
Eph. 3:17; Col.
2:7;
Col. 1:5;
Mark 16:15; Acts
2:5; Col. 1:6;
Eph. 3:7; Col.
1:25;
1 Cor. 3:5

24   Now I rejoice in my sufferings for your sake, and in my flesh I do my share on behalf of His body (which is the church) in filling up that which is lacking in Christ's afflictions.

1:24
Rom. 8:17; 2 Cor.
1:5; 12:15; Phil.
2:17;
2 Tim. 1:8; 2:10;
Col. 1:18

25   Of *this church* I was made a minister according to the stewardship from God bestowed on me for your benefit, that I might fully carry[x] out the *preaching of* the word of God,

1:25
Col. 1:23;
Eph. 3:2

26   *that is,* the mystery which has been hidden[+] from the *past* ages and generations; but has now been manifested to His saints,

1:26
Rom. 16:25f.;
Eph. 3:3f.; Col.
2:2; 4:3

27   to whom *God* willed to make known[x] what is the riches of the glory of this mystery among the Gentiles, which is Christ in you, the hope of glory.

1:27
Matt. 13:11;
Eph. 1:7,18; 3:16;
Rom. 8:10;
1 Tim. 1:1

28   And we proclaim Him, admonishing every man and teaching every man with all wisdom, that we may present[x] every man complete in Christ.

1:28
Acts 20:31; Col.
3:16;
1 Cor. 2:6f.; Col.
2:3;
Col. 1:22;
Matt. 5:48; Eph.
4:13

29   And for this purpose also I labor, striving according to His power, which mightily works within me.

1:29
1 Cor. 15:10;
Col. 2:1; 4:12;
Eph. 1:19; Col.
2:12

You Are Built Up in Christ

2:1
Col. 1:29; 4:12;
Col. 4:13,15f.;
Rev. 1:11

2 For I want you to know how great a struggle I have on your behalf, and for those who are at Laodicea, and for all those who have not personally seen⁺ my face,

2:2
1 Cor. 14:31;
Eph. 6:22; Col.
4:8;
Col. 2:19;
Eph. 1:7,18; 3:16;
Matt. 13:11;
Rom. 16:25f.;
Eph. 3:3f.; Col.
1:26; 4:3
2:3
Is. 11:2; Rom.
11:33
2:4
Eph. 4:17;
Rom. 16:18
2:5
1 Cor. 5:3;
1 Cor. 14:40;
1 Pet. 5:9

2 that their hearts may be encouraged,ˣ having been knit together in love, and *attaining* to all the wealth that comes from the full assurance of understanding, *resulting* in a true¹ knowledge of God's mystery, *that is,* Christ *Himself,*

3 in whom are *hidden* all the treasures of wisdom and knowledge.

4 I say this in order that no one may delude˜ you with persuasive argument.

5 For even though I am absent in body, nevertheless I am with you in spirit, rejoicing to see your good discipline and the stability of your faith in Christ.

2:6
Gal. 3:26;
Col. 1:10

6 As you therefore have received Christ Jesus the Lord, *so* walk ˜¹⁴²ᵃ *in Him,*

2:7
Eph. 3:17;
1 Cor. 3:9; Eph.
2:20;
1 Cor. 1:8;
Eph. 4:21

7 having been firmly rooted⁺ *and now* being built up in Him and established ᵇin your faith, just as you were instructed, *and* overflowing with gratitude.

2:8
1 Cor. 8:9; 10:12;
Gal. 5:15; Heb.
3:12;
Eph. 5:6; Col.
2:23; 1 Tim. 6:20;
Gal. 4:3; Col.
2:20

8 See ˜ to it that no one takes you captive through philosophy and empty deception, according to the tradition of men, according to the elementary principles of the world, rather than according to Christ.

2:9
2 Cor. 5:19; Col.
1:19
2:10
Eph. 3:19;
Eph. 1:21f.;
1 Cor. 15:24;
Eph. 3:10; Col.
2:15

9 For *in Him* all the fulness of Deity dwells in *bodily form,*

10 and *in Him* you have been made complete,⁺ and He is the head over all rule and authority;

2:11
Rom. 2:29; Eph.
2:11;
Rom. 6:6; 7:24;
Gal. 5:24; Col.
3:5

11 and in Him you were also circumcised with a circumcision made without hands, in the removal of the body of the flesh by the circumcision of Christ;

2:12
Rom. 6:4f.;
Rom. 6:5; Eph.
2:6; Col. 2:13;
3:1;
Acts 2:24

12 having been buried with Him in baptism, in which you were also raised up with Him through faith in the working of God, who raised Him from the dead.

2:13
Eph. 2:1;
Eph. 2:5; Col.
2:12

13 And when you were dead in your transgressions⁴⁰ᵇ and the uncircumcision of your flesh, He made you alive together with Him, having forgiven us all our transgressions,

2:14
Eph. 2:15; Col.
2:20;
1 Pet. 2:24

14 having canceled out the certificate of debt consisting of decrees against us *and* which was hostile to us; and He has taken⁺ it out of the way, having nailed it to the cross.

2:15
John 12:31;
1 Cor. 15:24;
Eph. 3:10; Col.
2:10; Eph. 4:8;
2 Cor. 2:14

15 When He had disarmed¹ the rulers and authorities, He made a public display of them, having triumphed over them through Him.

ᵇOr, *by*

16　Therefore let no one act° as *your* judge in regard to food or drink or in respect to a festival or a new moon or a Sabbath day—

17　things which are a *mere* shadow of what is to come; but the substance belongs to Christ.

18　Let no one keep defrauding° you of your prize by delighting in self-abasement and the worship of the angels, taking his stand on *visions* he has seen,⁺ inflated without cause by his fleshly mind, 33b

19　and *not* holding fast to the head, from whom the entire body, being supplied and held together by the joints and ligaments, grows with a growth which is from God.

20　If you have died with Christ to the elementary principles of the world, why, as if you were living in the world, do you submit yourself to decrees, such as,

21　"Do not handle,° do not taste,° do not touch!"°

22　(which all *refer to* things destined to perish with the using)—in accordance with the commandments and teachings of men?

23　These are matters which have, to be sure, the appearance of wisdom in self-made religion and self-abasement and severe treatment of the body, *but are* of no value against fleshly indulgence.

Put On the New Self

3　If then you have been raised up with Christ, keep seeking ᴹ the *things above,* where Christ is, seated at the *right hand of God.*

2　Set ᴹ your mind 33c on the things above, not on the things that are on earth.

3　For you have died and your life 30b is hidden⁺ with Christ in God.

4　When Christ, who is our life, is revealed,ˣ then *you also* will be revealed with Him in glory.

5　Therefore considerˣ the members of your earthly body as dead to immorality, impurity, passion, evil 10a desire, and greed, which amounts to idolatry.

6　For it is on account of these things that the *wrath* 7b *of God* will ᶜcome,

7　and in them you also once walked, when you were living ˣˣ in them.

8　But •*now* you also, putˣ them all aside: anger, wrath, 7a malice, 10e slander, *and* abusive speech from your mouth.

ᶜSome early mss. add *upon the sons of disobedience*

2:16
Rom. 14:3;
Mark 7:19; Rom.
14:17; Heb. 9:10;
Lev. 23:2; Rom.
14:5;
1 Chr. 23:31; 2
Chr. 31:3; Neh.
10:33;
Mark 2:27f.; Gal.
4:10
2:17
Heb. 8:5; 10:1
2:18
1 Cor. 9:24; Phil.
3:14;
Col. 2:23;
1 Cor. 4:6;
Rom. 8:7
2:19
Eph. 1:22;
Eph. 1:23; 4:16
2:20
Rom. 6:2;
Col. 2:8;
Gal. 4:9;
Col. 2:14,16

2:22
1 Cor. 6:13;
Is. 29:13; Matt.
15:9; Titus 1:14

2:23
Col. 2:18;
1 Tim. 4:3;
Rom. 13:14;
1 Tim. 4:8

3:1
Col. 2:12;
Ps. 110:1; Mark
16:19

3:2
Matt. 16:23; Phil.
3:19,20

3:3
Rom. 6:2; 2 Cor.
5:14; Col. 2:20

3:4
John 11:25; Gal.
2:20;
1 Cor. 1:7; Phil.
3:21; 1 Pet. 1:13;
1 John 2:28; 3:2
3:5
Rom. 8:13;
Col. 2:11;
Mark 7:21f.;
1 Cor. 6:9f.,18;
2 Cor. 12:21; Gal.
5:19f.; Eph. 4:19;
5:3,5
3:6
Rom. 1:18; Eph.
5:6
3:7
Eph. 2:2
3:8
Eph. 4:22;
Eph. 4:31;
Eph. 4:29

3:9
Eph. 4:25;
Eph. 4:22
3:10
Eph. 4:24;
Rom. 12:2; 2 Cor.
4:16; Eph. 4:23;
Gen. 1:26; Rom.
8:29;
Eph. 2:10
3:11
Rom. 10:12;
1 Cor. 12:13; Gal.
3:28;
1 Cor. 7:19; Gal.
5:6;
Acts 28:2;
Eph. 6:8;
Eph. 1:23
3:12
Luke 18:7;
Eph. 4:24;
Luke 1:78; Gal.
5:22f.; Phil. 2:1;
Eph. 4:2; Phil.
2:3;
1 Cor. 13:4; 2
Cor. 6:6
3:13
Eph. 4:2;
Rom. 15:7; Eph.
4:32
3:14
Eph. 4:3;
John 17:23; Heb.
6:1
3:15
John 14:27;
Eph. 2:16
3:16
Rom. 10:17; Eph.
5:26; 1 Thess.
1:8;
Col. 1:28;
Eph. 5:19;
1 Cor. 14:15
3:17
1 Cor. 10:31;
Eph. 5:20; Col.
3:15
3:18
Col. 3:18-4:1;
Eph. 5:22-6:9
3:19
Eph. 5:25; 1 Pet.
3:7
3:20
Eph. 6:1
3:21
Eph. 6:4
3:22
Eph. 6:5;
Eph. 6:6
3:23
Eph. 6:7
3:24
Eph. 6:8;
Acts 20:32; 1 Pet.
1:4;
1 Cor. 7:22
3:25
Eph. 6:8;
Deut. 10:17; Acts
10:34; Eph. 6:9

9 Do not lie[o] to one another, since you laid aside[1] the old self with its *evil* practices,

10 and have put on the new[34b] self who is being renewed to a true[1] knowledge according to the image[22b] of the One who created him

11 —*a renewal* in which there is no *distinction between* Greek and Jew, circumcised and uncircumcised, barbarian, Scythian, slave and freeman, but *Christ* is all, and in all.

12 And so, as those who have been chosen of God, holy[28a] and beloved,[*] put[xi] on a heart of compassion, kindness, humility,[23c] gentleness[23b] and patience;

13 bearing with one another, and forgiving each other, whoever has[~] a complaint against anyone; just as the Lord forgave you, so also should you.

14 And beyond all these things *put on* love,[31a] which is the perfect bond of unity.

15 And let the peace of Christ *rule*[~] in your hearts, to which indeed you were called in one body; and be[~] *thankful.*

16 Let the word[43a] of [d]Christ *richly dwell*[~] *within you,* with all wisdom teaching and admonishing one another with psalms *and* hymns *and* spiritual songs, singing with thankfulness in your hearts to God.

17 And whatever you do[~] in word or deed, *do* all in the name of the Lord Jesus, giving thanks through Him to God the Father.

Family Relations

18 Wives, be subject[~] to your husbands, as is fitting[m] in the Lord.

19 Husbands, love[~][31a] your wives, and do not be embittered[o] against them.

20 Children, be obedient[~] to your parents in all things, for this is [†]well-pleasing to the Lord.

21 Fathers, do not [e]exasperate[o] your children, that they may not lose[~] heart.

22 Slaves, in all things obey[~] those who are your masters on earth, not with external service, as those who *merely* please men, but with sincerity of heart, fearing the Lord.

23 Whatever you do,[~] do[~] your work *heartily,* [30c] as for the Lord rather than for men;

24 knowing that from the *Lord* you will receive the reward of the inheritance. It is the *Lord Christ* whom you serve.[38b]

25 For he who does wrong will receive the consequences of the wrong which he has done, and that without partiality.

[d]Some mss. read *the Lord;* others read *God* [e]Some early mss. read *provoke to anger*

Fellow Workers

4 Masters, grant~ᴵ to your slaves justice and fairness, knowing that *you* too have a Master in heaven.

2   *Devote*~ᴵ yourselves to prayer, keeping alert in it with *an attitude of* thanksgiving;

3   praying at the same time for us as well, that God may openˣ up to us a door for the word, so that we may speakˣ forth the mystery of Christ, for which I have also been imprisoned;⁺

4   in order that I may makeˣ it clear in the way I ought to speak.ˣ

5   Conduct~ᴵ yourselves with *wisdom* toward outsiders, making the most of the opportunity.

6   Let your speech always be with grace, seasoned,⁺ *as it were,* with salt, so that you may know how you should respond~ to each person.

7   As to all my affairs, Tychicus, *our* beloved brother and faithful servant and fellow bond-servant in the Lord, will bring you information.

8   For I have sent him to you for this very purpose, that you may knowˣ *about* our circumstances and that he may encourageˣ your hearts;

9   and with him Onesimus, *our* faithful and beloved brother, who is one of your *number.* They will inform you about the whole situation here.

10   Aristarchus, my fellow prisoner, sends you his greetings; and *also* Barnabas' cousin Mark (about whom you received instructions: if he comes to you, welcomeˣᴵ him);

11   and *also* Jesus who is called Justus; these are the only fellow workers for the kingdom of God who are from the circumcision; and they have proved to be an encouragement to me.

12   Epaphras, who is one of your number, a bondslave³⁸ᵇ of Jesus Christ, sends you his greetings, always laboring earnestly for you in his prayers, that you may standˣ perfect and fully assured⁺ in all the will of God.

13   For I bear him witness that he has a deep concern for you and for those who are in Laodicea and Hierapolis.

14   Luke, the beloved physician, sends you his greetings, and *also* Demas.

15   Greetˣᴵ the brethren who are in Laodicea and also ᶠNympha and the church that is in her house.

16   And when this letter is readˣ among you, haveˣᴵ it also

ᶠOr, *Nymphas* (masc.)

4:1
Eph. 6:9

4:2
Acts 1:14; Eph. 6:18

4:3
Eph. 6:19;
Acts 14:27;
2 Tim. 4:2;
Eph. 3:3,4
Eph. 6:20

4:4
Eph. 6:20

4:5
Eph. 5:15;
Mark 4:11;
Eph. 5:16

4:6
Eph. 4:29;
Mark 9:50;
1 Pet. 3:15

4:7
Col. 4:7-9: *Eph.* 6:21,22;
Acts 20:4; 2 Tim. 4:12;
Col. 1:7

4:8
Eph. 6:22;
Col. 2:2

4:9
Philem. 10;
Col. 1:7;
Col. 4:12

4:10
Acts 19:29; 27:2;
Philem. 24;
Rom. 16:7;
Acts 4:36; 12:12, 25; 15:37,39;
2 Tim. 4:11

4:11
Rom. 16:3;
Acts 11:2

4:12
Col. 1:7; Philem. 23;
Col. 4:9;
Rom. 15:30;
Col. 1:28

4:13
Col. 2:1; 4:15f.

4:14
2 Tim. 4:11;
Philem. 24;
2 Tim. 4:10

4:15
Col. 2:1; 4:13,16;
Rom. 16:5

4:16
1 Thess. 5:27;
2 Thess. 3:14;
Col. 2:1; 4:13,15

4:17
Philem. 2;
2 Tim. 4:5
read[x] in the church of the Laodiceans; and you, for your part read[x] my letter *that is coming* from Laodicea.

4:18
1 Cor. 16:21;
Heb. 13:3;
Phil. 1:7; Col. 4:3;
1 Tim. 6:21; 2
Tim. 4:22; Titus
3:15; Heb. 13:25
17   And say[xi] to Archippus, "Take heed[~] to the ministry which you have received in the Lord, that you may fulfill[~] it."

18   I, Paul, write this greeting with my •own hand. Remember[~] my imprisonment. Grace be with you.

The First Epistle of Paul to the

Thessalonians

Thanksgiving for These Believers

1 Paul and Silvanus and Timothy to the church of the Thessalonians in God the Father and the Lord Jesus Christ: Grace to you and peace.

2 We give thanks to God always for all of you, making mention *of you* in our prayers;

3 constantly bearing in mind your work of faith and labor of love[31a] and steadfastness of hope in our Lord Jesus Christ in the presence of our God and Father,

4 knowing, brethren beloved⁺ by God, *His* choice of you;

5 for our gospel did not come to you in word only, but also in power[32a] and in the Holy Spirit and with *full*[26b] conviction; just as you know what kind of men we proved to be among you for your sake.

6 You also became *imitators of us* and of the ⁺*Lord,* having received the word in *much* tribulation with the joy of the Holy Spirit,

7 so that you became an example to all the believers in Macedonia and in Achaia.

8 For the word of the Lord has sounded⁺ forth *from you,* not only in Macedonia and Achaia, but also in every place your faith toward God has gone⁺ forth, so that we have no need to say~ anything.

9 For they themselves report about us what kind of a reception we had with you, and how you turned to God from idols to serve~[38b] a living and true God,

10 and to wait~[1] for His Son from heaven, whom He raised from the dead, *that is* Jesus, who delivers[18b] us from the wrath[7b] to come.

Paul's Ministry

2 For you yourselves know, brethren, that our coming to you was not in vain,

2 but after we had already suffered and been mistreated in Philippi, as you know, we had the boldness in our God to speak[x] to you the gospel of God amid much opposition.

1:1
2 Thess. 1:1;
2 Cor. 1:19;
Acts 16:1;
Acts 17:1;
Rom. 1:7
1:2
Rom. 1:8;
2 Thess. 1:3;
Rom. 1:9
1:3
John 6:29;
1 Cor. 13:13;
Rom. 8:25; 15:4;
Gal. 1:4
1:4
Rom. 1:7;
2 Thess. 2:13;
2 Pet. 1:10
1:5
1 Cor. 9:14;
Rom. 15:19;
Luke 1:1; Col.
2:2;
1 Thess. 2:10
1:6
1 Cor. 4:16;
11:1f.;
Acts 17:5-10;
2 Tim. 4:2;
Acts 13:52; 2 Cor.
6:10; Gal. 5:22
1:7
Rom. 15:26;
Acts 18:12
1:8
Col. 3:16;
2 Thess. 3:1;
Rom. 10:18;
Rom. 15:26;
Acts 18:12;
Rom. 1:8; 16:19;
2 Cor. 2:14
1:9
1 Thess. 2:1;
Acts 14:15;
1 Cor. 12:2;
Matt. 16:16
1:10
Matt. 16:27f.;
1 Cor. 1:7;
Acts 2:24;
Rom. 5:9;
Matt. 3:7; 1
Thess. 2:16; 5:9
2:1
1 Thess. 1:9;
2 Thess. 1:10
2:2
Acts 14:5;
16:19-24; Phil.
1:30;
Acts 16:22-24;
Acts 17:1-9;
Rom. 1:1;
Phil. 1:30

2:3
Acts 13:15;
2 Thess. 2:11;
1 Thess. 4:7;
2 Cor. 4:2
2:4
2 Cor. 2:17;
Gal. 2:7;
Gal. 1:10;
Rom. 8:27
2:5
Acts 20:33; 2 Pet.
2:3; Rom. 1:9; 1
Thess. 2:10
2:6
John 5:41,44;
2 Cor. 4:5;
1 Cor. 9:1f.
2:7
2 Tim. 2:24;
Gal. 4:19; 1
Thess. 2:11
2:8
2 Cor. 12:15;
1 John 3:16;
Rom. 1:1
2:9
Phil. 4:16;
2 Thess. 3:8;
Acts 18:3;
1 Cor. 9:4f.;
2 Cor. 11:9;
Rom. 1:1
2:10
1 Thess. 2:5;
2 Cor. 1:12;
1 Thess. 1:5
2:11
1 Thess. 5:14;
Luke 16:28;
1 Thess. 4:6;
1 Cor. 4:14;
1 Thess. 2:7
2:12
Eph. 4:1;
Rom. 8:28; 1
Thess. 5:24; 2
Thess. 2:14;
2 Cor. 4:6; 1 Pet.
5:10
2:13
Rom. 1:8;
1 Thess. 1:2;
Rom. 10:17; Heb.
4:2;
Matt. 10:20; Gal.
4:14; Heb. 4:12
2:14
1 Thess. 1:6;
1 Cor. 7:17;
10:32; Gal. 1:22;
Acts 17:5; 1
Thess. 3:4; 2
Thess. 1:4f.;
Heb. 10:33f.
2:15
Luke 24:20; Acts
2:23;
Matt. 5:12; Acts
7:52
2:16
Acts 9:23; 13:45,
50; 14:2,5,19;
17:5,13; 18:12;
21:21f.,27; 25:2,
7; 1 Cor. 10:33;
Gen. 15:16; Dan.
8:23; Matt. 23:32;
1 Thess. 1:10
2:17
1 Cor. 5:3;
1 Thess. 3:10
2:18
Rom. 15:22;
Phil. 4:16;
Matt. 4:10;
Rom. 1:13; 15:22

3   For our exhortation does not *come* from error or impurity or by way of deceit;

4   but just as we have been approved⁺ by God to be entrusted˟ with the gospel, so we speak, not as pleasing men but ⁺*God,* who examines our hearts.

5   For we never came with flattering speech, as you know, nor with a pretext for greed—God is witness—

6   nor did we seek glory from *men,* either from you or from others, even though as *apostles* of Christ we might have asserted our authority.

7   But we proved to be ᵃgentle among you, as a nursing *mother* tenderly cares˜ for her own children.

8   Having thus a fond affection for you, we were well-pleasedᵐ to impart˟ to you not only the gospel of God but also our own lives, because you had become *very dear to us.*

9   For you recall, brethren, our labor and hardship, *how* working night and day so as not to be˟ a burden to any of you, we proclaimed to you the gospel of God.

10   You are witnesses, and *so is* God, how devoutly and uprightly and blamelessly we behaved toward you believers;

11   just as you know how we *were* exhorting and encouraging and imploring each one of you as a father *would* his own children,

12   so that you may walk˜ in a manner worthy of the God who calls you into His own kingdom and glory.

13   And for this reason we also constantly thank God that when you received from us the word of *God's* message, you accepted *it* not *as* the word of men, but *for* what it really is, the word⁴³ᵃ of God, which also performs its work in you who believe.

14   For you, brethren, became imitators of the churches of God in Christ Jesus that are in Judea, for *you also* endured the same sufferings at the hands of your •own countrymen, even as they *did* from the Jews,

15   who both killed the *Lord* Jesus and the prophets, and drove us out. They are not pleasing to God, but hostile to all men,

16   hindering us from speaking˟ to the Gentiles that they might be saved;˟ with the result that they *always* fill˟ up the measure of *their* sins. But wrath⁷ᵇ has come upon them ᵇto the utmost.

17   But we, brethren, having been bereft of you for a short while—in person, not in spirit—were all the more eager with great desire to see˟ your face.

18   For we wanted to come to you—I, Paul, more than once —and *yet Satan* thwarted us.

ᵃSome ancient mss. read *babes*   ᵇOr, *forever;* or, *altogether*

19   For who is our hope or joy or crown of exultation? Is it not even *you*, in the presence of our Lord Jesus at His coming?

20   For †*you* are our glory and joy.

Encouragement of Timothy's Visit

3 Therefore when we could endure *it* no longer, we thought it best to be left[x] behind at Athens alone;

2   and we sent Timothy, our brother and God's fellow worker in the gospel of Christ, to strengthen[x] and encourage[x] you as to your faith,

3   so that no man may be disturbed ~ by these afflictions; for you yourselves know that we have been destined for *this*.

4   For indeed when we were with you, we *kept* telling[xx] you in advance that we were going to suffer affliction; and so it came to pass, as you know.

5   For this reason, when I could endure *it* no longer, I also sent to find[x] out about your faith, for fear that the tempter might have tempted you, and our labor should be in *vain*.

6   But now that Timothy has come to us from you, and has brought us good news of your faith and love, and that you always think kindly of us, longing to see[x] us just as we also long to see you,

7   for this reason, brethren, in all our distress and affliction we were comforted about you through *your* faith;

8   for now we *really* live, if *you* stand firm in the Lord.

9   For what thanks can we render[x] to God for you in return for all the joy with which we rejoice before our God on your account,

10   as we night and day keep praying[9b] most earnestly that we may see[x] your face, and may complete[x] what is lacking in your faith?

11   Now may our God and Father Himself and Jesus our Lord direct[x] our way to you;

12   and may the Lord cause *you* to increase[x] and abound[x] in love for one another, and for all men, just as we also *do* for you;

13   so that He may establish[x] your hearts unblamable[11a] in holiness before our God and Father at the coming of our Lord Jesus with all His saints.

Sanctification and Love

4 Finally then, brethren, we request and exhort you in the Lord Jesus, that, as you received from us *instruction* as to

2:19
Phil. 4:1;
Matt. 16:27; Mark 8:38; John 21:22;
1 Thess. 3:13;
4:15; 5:23
2:20
2 Cor. 1:14

3:1
1 Thess. 3:5;
Acts 17:15f.

3:2
2 Cor. 1:1; Col. 1:1

3:3
Acts 9:16; 14:22

3:4
1 Thess. 2:14

3:5
Phil. 2:19;
1 Thess. 3:1;
1 Thess. 3:2;
Matt. 4:3;
2 Cor. 6:1; Phil. 2:16
3:6
Acts 18:5;
1 Thess. 1:3;
1 Cor. 11:2

3:8
1 Cor. 6:13
3:9
1 Thess. 1:2
3:10
2 Tim. 1:3;
1 Thess. 2:17;
2 Cor. 13:9
3:11
Gal. 1:4; 1 Thess. 3:13;
1 Thess. 4:16;
5:23; 2 Thess. 2:16; 3:16; Rev. 21:3;
2 Thess. 3:5
3:12
Phil. 1:9; 1 Thess. 4:1,10; 2 Thess. 1:3
3:13
1 Cor. 1:8; 1 Thess. 3:2;
Luke 1:6;
Gal. 1:4; 1 Thess. 3:11;
1 Thess. 2:19;
Matt. 25:31; Mark 8:38; 1 Thess. 4:17; 2 Thess. 1:7
4:1
2 Cor. 13:11;
2 Thess. 3:1;
Gal. 6:1; 1 Thess. 5:12; 2 Thess. 1:3; 2:1;
3:1,13;
Eph. 4:1;
2 Cor. 5:9;
Phil. 1:9;
1 Thess. 3:12;
4:10

how you ought to walk~ and please~ God (just as you actually do
ᶜwalk), that you may excel~ *still more.*

2   For you know what commandments we gave you ᵈby *the
authority of* the Lord Jesus.

3   For this is the will of God, your sanctification; *that is,* that
you abstain~ from sexual immorality;

4   that each of you know how to possess~ his own ᵉvessel in
sanctification and honor,

5   not in lustful passion, like the Gentiles who do not know
God;

6   *and* that no man transgress~ and defraud~ his brother in
the matter because the Lord is *the avenger* in all these things, just
as we also told you before and solemnly[1] warned *you.*

7   For God has not called us for the purpose of impurity, but
in †*sanctification.*

8   Consequently,[2] he who rejects *this* is not rejecting *man* but
the †*God* who gives His *Holy* Spirit to you.

9   Now as to the love of the brethren, you have no need for
anyone to write~ to you, for *you yourselves* are *taught by* †*God* to
love~[31a] one another;

10   for indeed you do practice it toward all the brethren who
are in all Macedonia. But we urge you, brethren, to excel~ *still
more,*

11   and to make~ it your ambition to lead~ a quiet life and
attend~ to your own business and work~ with your hands, just
as we commanded you;

12   so that you may behave~ properly toward outsiders and
not be~ in any need.

Those Who Died in Christ

13   But we do not want you to be uninformed,~ brethren,
about those who are asleep, that you may not grieve,~ as do the
rest who have no hope.

14   For if we believe that Jesus died and rose again, even so
God will bring with Him those who have fallen asleep in Jesus.

15   For this we say to you by the word of the Lord, that we
who are alive, and remain until the coming of the Lord, shall •*not*
precedeˣ those who have fallen asleep.

16   For the Lord Himself will descend from heaven with a
shout, with the voice of *the* archangel, and with the trumpet of
God; and the dead in Christ shall †first.

17   Then we who are alive and remain shall be caught up

4:3
1 Cor. 6:18
4:4
1 Cor. 7:2,9;
2 Cor. 4:7; 1 Pet.
3:7;
Rom. 1:24
4:5
Rom. 1:26;
Gal. 4:8
4:6
1 Cor. 6:8;
2 Cor. 7:11;
Rom. 12:19; 13:4;
Heb. 13:4;
Luke 16:28;
1 Thess. 2:11;
Heb. 2:6
4:7
1 Pet. 1:15;
1 Thess. 2:3
4:8
Rom. 5:5; 2 Cor.
1:22; Gal. 4:6;
1 John 3:24
4:9
John 13:34; Rom.
12:10;
2 Cor. 9:1;
1 Thess. 5:1;
Jer. 31:33f.; John
6:45; 1 John 2:27
4:10
1 Thess. 1:7;
1 Thess. 3:12
4:11
1 Pet. 4:15;
Acts 18:3; Eph.
4:28; 2 Thess.
3:10-12
4:12
Rom. 13:13; Col.
4:5;
Mark 4:11;
Eph. 4:28
4:13
Rom. 1:13;
Acts 7:60;
Eph. 2:3;
1 Thess. 5:6;
Eph. 2:12
4:14
Rom. 14:9; 2 Cor.
4:14;
1 Cor. 15:18;
1 Thess. 4:13
4:15
1 Kin. 13:17f.;
20:35; 2 Cor.
12:1; Gal. 1:12;
1 Cor. 15:52;
1 Thess. 5:10;
1 Thess. 2:19;
1 Cor. 15:18;
1 Thess. 4:13
4:16
1 Thess. 3:11;
1 Thess. 1:10;
2 Thess. 1:7;
Joel 2:11;
Jude 9;
Matt. 24:31;
1 Cor. 15:23;
2 Thess. 2:1;
Rev. 14:13
4:17
1 Cor. 15:52;
1 Thess. 5:10;
2 Cor. 12:2;
Dan. 7:13; Acts
1:9; Rev. 11:12;
John 12:26

ᶜOr, *conduct yourselves*   ᵈLit., *through the Lord*   ᵉI.e., body; or possibly, wife

together with them in the clouds to meet the Lord in the air, and thus we shall *always be with the Lord.*

18   Therefore comfort[m] one another with these words.

The Day of the Lord

5 Now as to the times and the epochs, brethren, you have no need of anything to be written[~] to you.

2   For you yourselves know full well that the day of the Lord will come just like a thief in the night.

3   While they are saying,[~] "Peace and safety!" then destruction will come upon them *suddenly* like birth pangs upon a woman with child; and they shall •*not* escape.[x]

4   But *you,* brethren, are not in darkness, that the day should overtake[x] *you* like a thief;

5   for *you* are all sons of light and sons of day. We are not of night nor of darkness;

6   so then let us not sleep[~] as others do, but let us be alert[~] and ᶠsober.[~]

7   For those who sleep do their sleeping at night, and those who get drunk get drunk at night.

8   But since we are of *the* day, let us be ᶠsober,[~] having put on the breastplate of faith and love,[31a] and as a helmet, the hope of salvation.

9   For God has not destined us for wrath,[7b] but for obtaining salvation through our Lord Jesus Christ,

10   who died for us, that whether we are awake[~] or asleep,[~] we may live[x] *together with Him.*

11   Therefore encourage[m] one another, and build[m] up one another, just as you also are doing.

Christian Conduct

12   But we request of you, brethren, that you appreciate[29e] those who diligently labor among you, and have charge over you in the Lord and give you instruction,

13   and that you esteem[~] them *very highly* in love[31a] because of their work. Live in peace[m] with one another.

14   And we urge you, brethren, admonish[m] the unruly, encourage[m] the fainthearted, help[m] the weak, be patient[m] with all men.

15   See[m] that no one repays[x] another with evil[10a] for evil, but always seek[m] after that which is *good*[25a] for one another and for all men.

16   Rejoice[m] always;

ᶠOr, *self-controlled*

5:1
Acts 1:7;
1 Thess. 4:9

5:2
1 Cor. 1:8;
Luke 21:34;
1 Thess. 5:4;
2 Pet. 3:10; Rev. 3:3; 16:15

5:3
Jer. 6:14; 8:11;
Ezek. 13:10;
2 Thess. 1:9;
John 16:21

5:4
Acts 26:18; 1 John 2:8;
Luke 21:34;
1 Thess. 5:2;
2 Pet. 3:10; Rev. 3:3; 16:15

5:5
Luke 16:8;
Acts 26:18;
1 John 2:8

5:6
Rom. 13:11;
1 Thess. 5:10;
Eph. 2:3; 1 Thess. 4:13;
1 Pet. 1:13

5:7
Acts 2:15; 2 Pet. 2:13

5:8
1 Thess. 5:5;
1 Pet. 1:13;
Is. 59:17; Eph. 6:14;
Eph. 6:23;
Eph. 6:17;
Rom. 8:24

5:9
1 Thess. 1:10;
2 Thess. 2:13f.

5:10
Rom. 14:9

5:11
Eph. 4:29

5:12
1 Cor. 16:18;
1 Tim. 5:17;
Rom. 16:6,12;
1 Cor. 15:10; 16:16;
Heb. 13:17

5:13
Mark 9:50

5:14
2 Thess. 3:6,7,11;
Is. 35:4;
Rom. 14:1f.;
1 Cor. 8:7ff.;
Rom. 15:1;
1 Cor. 13:4

5:15
Matt. 5:44; Rom. 12:17; 1 Pet. 3:9;
Rom. 12:9; Gal. 6:10; 1 Thess. 5:21

5:16
Phil. 4:4

5:17
Eph. 6:18
5:18
Eph. 5:20
5:19
Eph. 4:30
5:20
Acts 13:1; 1 Cor.
14:31
5:21
1 Cor. 14:29;
1 John 4:1;
Rom. 12:9; Gal.
6:10; 1 Thess.
5:15
5:23
Rom. 15:33;
1 Thess. 3:11;
Luke 1:46f.; Heb.
4:12;
James 1:4; 2 Pet.
3:14;
1 Thess. 2:19
5:24
1 Cor. 1:9;
2 Thess. 3:3;
1 Thess. 2:12
5:25
Eph. 6:19; 2
Thess. 3:1; Heb.
13:18
5:26
Rom. 16:16
5:27
Col. 4:16;
Acts 1:15
5:28
Rom. 16:20;
2 Thess. 3:18

17   pray^ᴹ without ceasing;

18   in everything give^ᴹ thanks; for this is God's will for you in Christ Jesus.

19   Do *not quench*^ᴼ the Spirit;

20   do *not despise*^ᴼ prophetic ᵍutterances.

21   But *examine*^ᴹ everything *carefully*; hold^ᴹ *fast* to that which is good;²⁵ᵇ

22   abstain^ᴹ from every ʰform²²ᵃ of evil.¹⁰ᵇ

23   Now may the God of peace Himself sanctify^ˣ you entirely; and may your spirit and soul and body be preserved^ˣ *complete, without blame* at the coming of our Lord Jesus Christ.

24   Faithful is He who calls you, and He also will bring it to pass.

25   Brethren, pray^ᴹ for us^ⁱ.

26   Greet^ˣ all the brethren with a holy²⁸ᵃ kiss.

27   I adjure you by the Lord to have this letter read^ˣ to all the brethren.

28   The grace of our Lord Jesus Christ be with you.

ᵍOr, *gifts* ʰOr, *appearance* ⁱSome mss. add *also*

The Second Epistle of Paul to the
Thessalonians

Thanksgiving for Faith and Perseverance

1 Paul and Silvanus and Timothy to the church of the Thessalonians in God our Father and the Lord Jesus Christ:

2 Grace to you and peace from God the Father and the Lord Jesus Christ.

3 We ought always to give~ *thanks* to God for you, brethren, as is *only* fitting, because your faith is greatly enlarged, and the love of each one of you toward one another grows *ever* greater;

4 therefore, we ourselves speak~ proudly of you among the churches of God for your perseverance and faith in the midst of all your persecutions and afflictions which you endure.

5 *This is* a plain indication of God's righteous judgment so that you may be considered[x1] worthy of the kingdom of God, for which indeed you are suffering.

6 For after all[2] it is *only* just for God to repay[x37a] with *affliction* those who afflict you,

7 and *to give relief* to you who are afflicted and to us as well when the Lord Jesus shall be revealed from heaven with His mighty angels in flaming fire,

8 dealing out retribution to those who do not know God and to those who do not obey the gospel of our Lord Jesus.

9 And these will pay the *penalty* of eternal destruction, away from the presence of the Lord and from the glory of His power,[32c]

10 when He comes to be glorified[x1] in His saints on that day, and to be marveled[x] at among all who have believed—for our testimony to you was believed.

11 To this end also we pray for you always that our God may count[x] you *worthy* of your calling, and fulfill[x] every desire for goodness and the work of faith with power;[32a]

12 in order that the name of our Lord Jesus may be glorified[*1] in you, and you in Him, according to the grace of our God and the Lord Jesus Christ.

Man of Lawlessness

2 Now we request you, brethren, with regard to the coming of our Lord Jesus Christ, and our *gathering* together to Him,

2:2
1 Cor. 14:32;
1 John 4:1;
1 Thess. 5:2; 2
Thess. 2:15;
2 Thess. 3:17;
1 Cor. 1:8;
1 Cor. 7:26
2:3
Eph. 5:6;
1 Tim. 4:1;
Dan. 7:25; 8:25;
11:36; 2 Thess.
2:8; Rev. 13:5ff.;
John 17:12
2:4
1 Cor. 8:5;
Is. 14:14; Ezek.
28:2
2:5
1 Thess. 3:4

2:6
2 Thess. 2:7

2:7
Rev. 17:5,7;
2 Thess. 2:6

2:8
Dan. 7:25; 8:25;
11:36; 2 Thess.
2:3; Rev. 13:5ff.;
Is. 11:4; Rev.
2:16; 19:15;
1 Tim. 6:14; 2
Tim. 1:10; 4:1,8;
Titus 2:13
2:9
Matt. 4:10;
Matt. 24:24; John
4:48
2:10
1 Cor. 1:18;
2 Thess. 2:12,13

2:11
1 Kin. 22:22;
Rom. 1:28;
1 Thess. 2:3; 2
Tim. 4:4
2:12
Rom. 2:8; 1 Cor.
13:6
2:13
2 Thess. 1:3;
1 Thess. 1:4;
Eph. 1:4ff.;
1 Cor. 1:21;
1 Thess. 2:12;
5:9; 1 Pet. 1:5;
1 Thess. 4:7;
1 Pet. 1:2
2:14
1 Thess. 2:12;
1 Thess. 1:5
2:15
1 Cor. 16:13;
1 Cor. 11:2;
2 Thess. 3:6;
2 Thess. 2:2

2:16
1 Thess. 3:11;
John 3:16;
Titus 3:7; 1 Pet.
1:3

2:17
1 Thess. 3:2,13;
2 Thess. 3:3

2   that you may not be quickly shaken[x] from your composure or be disturbed[~] either by a spirit or a message or a letter as if from us, to the effect that the day of the Lord *has come.*[*]

3   Let no one in any way deceive[⊙16a] you, for *it will not come* unless the ªapostasy comes *first,* and the man of lawlessness is revealed,[x] the son of destruction,

4   who opposes and exalts[1] himself above every so-called god or object of worship, so that he takes[x] his seat in the *temple of God,* displaying himself as being God.

5   Do you not remember that while I was still with you, I was telling[m] you these things?

6   And you know *what restrains* him now, so that in his time he may be revealed.[x]

7   For the mystery of lawlessness is already at work; only he who now restrains *will do so* until he is taken out of the way.

8   And then that lawless one will be revealed whom the Lord will slay with the breath of His mouth and bring to an end by the appearance of His coming;

9   *that is,* the one whose coming is in accord with the activity of Satan, with all power and signs and false wonders,

10   and with all the deception of wickedness for those who perish, because they did not receive[5a] the *love of the truth* so as to be saved.[x]

11   And for this reason God will send upon them a deluding influence so that they might believe[x] what is false,

12   in order that they all may be judged[x] who did not believe the truth, but took pleasure in wickedness.

13   But *we* should always give thanks[~] to God for you, brethren beloved[*] by the Lord, because God has *chosen you* ᵇfrom the beginning for salvation through sanctification by the Spirit and faith in the truth.

14   And it was for this He called you through our gospel, that you may gain the glory of our Lord Jesus Christ.

15   So then, brethren, stand[~] firm and hold[~] to the traditions which you were taught, whether by word *of mouth* or by letter from us.

16   Now may our Lord Jesus Christ Himself and God our Father, who has loved us and given us eternal comfort and good hope by grace,

17   comfort[x] and strengthen[x] your *hearts* in every good[25a] work and word.

ªOr, *falling away* from the faith   ᵇSome ancient mss. read *first fruits*

Exhortation

3 Finally, brethren, pray^m! for us that the word of the Lord may spread~ rapidly and be glorified,~ just as *it did* also with you;

2 and that we may be delivered^x18b from perverse and evil men; for *not all* have faith.

3 But the Lord is faithful, and He will strengthen and protect you from the evil *one*.

4 And we have confidence* in the Lord concerning you, that you are doing and will *continue to* do what we command.

5 And may the Lord direct^x your *hearts* into the love of God and into the steadfastness of Christ.

6 Now we command you, brethren, in the name of our Lord Jesus Christ, that you keep~ aloof from every brother who leads an unruly life and not according to the tradition which you received from us.

7 For you yourselves know how you ought to follow~ our example, because we did not act in an undisciplined manner among you,

8 nor did we eat anyone's bread *without paying for it*, but with labor and hardship we *kept* working night and day so that we might not be^x a burden to any of you;

9 not because we do not have the right *to this*, but in order to offer^x *ourselves as a model* for you, that you might follow~ our example.

10 For even when we were with you, we used to give^m you this order: if anyone will not work,~ neither let him eat.^θ

11 For we hear that some among you are leading an *undisciplined life*, doing no work at all, but acting like busybodies.

12 Now such persons we command and exhort in the Lord Jesus Christ to work in quiet fashion and eat~ their *own bread*.

13 But as for you, brethren, do not grow^θ weary of doing good.

14 And if anyone does not obey our instruction in this letter, take^m! special note of *that man* and do not associate~ with him, so that he may be put^x to shame.^39b

15 And *yet* do not regard^θ him as an *enemy*, but admonish^m! him as a brother.

16 Now may the Lord of peace Himself continually grant^x you peace in every^4 circumstance. The Lord be with you all!

17 I, Paul, write this greeting with my •own hand, and this is a distinguishing mark in every letter; this is the way I write.

18 The grace of our Lord Jesus Christ be with you all.

3:1
1 Thess. 4:1;
1 Thess. 5:25;
1 Thess. 1:8

3:2
Rom. 15:31

3:3
1 Cor. 1:9;
1 Thess. 5:24;
Matt. 5:37
3:4
2 Cor. 2:3;
1 Thess. 4:10

3:5
1 Thess. 3:11

3:6
1 Cor. 5:4;
Rom. 16:17;
1 Cor. 5:11;
2 Thess. 3:14;
1 Thess. 5:14;
2 Thess. 3:7,11;
1 Cor. 11:2;
2 Thess. 2:15
3:7
1 Thess. 1:6;
2 Thess. 3:9

3:8
1 Cor. 9:4;
1 Thess. 2:9;
Acts 18:3; Eph.
4:28

3:9
1 Cor. 9:4ff.;
2 Thess. 3:7

3:10
1 Thess. 3:4;
1 Thess. 4:11

3:11
2 Thess. 3:6;
1 Tim. 5:13;
1 Pet. 4:15
3:12
1 Thess. 4:1;
1 Thess. 4:11

3:13
1 Thess. 4:1;
2 Cor. 4:1; Gal.
6:9
3:14
Col. 4:16;
2 Thess. 3:6;
1 Cor. 4:14

3:15
Gal. 6:1;
1 Thess. 5:14;
2 Thess. 3:6,13
3:16
Rom. 15:33;
1 Thess. 3:11;
Ruth 2:4
3:17
1 Cor. 16:21
3:18
Rom. 16:20; 1
Thess. 5:28

1:1
2 Cor. 1:1;
1 Tim. 1:12;
Titus 1:3;
Col. 1:27
1:2
2 Tim. 1:2;
Rom. 1:7; Titus
1:4;
1 Tim. 1:12
1:3
Rom. 15:26;
Acts 18:19;
Rom. 16:17;
2 Cor. 11:4; Gal.
1:6f.; 1 Tim. 6:3
1:4
1 Tim. 4:7; 2 Tim.
4:4; Titus 1:14; 2
Pet. 1:16;
Titus 3:9;
2 Tim. 2:23;
Eph. 3:2
1:5
1 Tim. 1:18;
2 Tim. 2:22;
1 Tim. 1:19; 3:9;
2 Tim. 1:3; 1 Pet.
3:16,21;
2 Tim. 1:5
1:6
Titus 1:10
1:7
James 3:1;
Luke 2:46
1:8
Rom. 7:12,16
1:9
Gal. 5:23;
Titus 1:6,10;
1 Pet. 4:18; Jude
15;
1 Tim. 4:7; 6:20;
Heb. 12:16
1:10
1 Cor. 6:9;
Lev. 18:22;
Ex. 21:16; Rev.
18:13;
Rev. 21:8,27;
22:15;
Matt. 5:33;
1 Tim. 4:6; 6:3;
2 Tim. 4:3; Titus
1:9,13; 2:1,2
1:11
2 Cor. 4:4;
1 Tim. 6:15;
Gal. 2:7
1:12
Gal. 3:26;
Acts 9:22; Phil.
4:13; 2 Tim. 4:17;
Acts 9:15
1:13
Acts 8:3;
1 Cor. 7:25;
Acts 26:9
1:14
Rom. 5:20;
1 Cor. 3:10;
2 Cor. 4:15; Gal.
1:13-16;
1 Thess. 1:3; 1
Tim. 2:15; 4:12;
6:11; 2 Tim.
1:13; 2:22; Titus
2:2
1:15
1 Tim. 3:1; 4:9; 2
Tim. 2:11; Titus
3:8;
Mark 2:17; Luke
15:2ff.; 19:10;
Rom. 11:14;
1 Cor. 15:9; Eph.
3:8

The First Epistle of Paul to
Timothy

Misleadings in Doctrine and Living

1 Paul, an apostle of Christ Jesus according to the command-ment of God our Savior, and of Christ Jesus, *who is* our hope;

2 to Timothy, *my* true child in *the* faith: Grace, mercy *and* peace from God the Father and Christ Jesus our Lord.

3 As I urged you upon my departure for Macedonia, remain[x] on at Ephesus, in order that you may instruct[x] certain men not to teach[~] strange doctrines,

4 nor to pay[~] attention to myths and endless genealogies, which give rise to *mere speculation* rather than *furthering* the administration of God which is by faith.

5 But the goal of our instruction is love[31a] from a pure[13c] heart and a good[25a] conscience and a sincere faith.

6 For some men, straying from these things, have turned aside to fruitless discussion,

7 wanting to be teachers of the Law, even though they do not understand[29d] either what they are saying or the matters about which they make confident[1] assertions.

8 But we know that the Law is good,[25b] if one uses[~] it law-fully,

9 realizing the fact that law is not made for a *righteous man,* but for those who are lawless and rebellious, for the ungodly and sinners, for the unholy[41a] and profane, for those who kill their fathers or mothers, for murderers

10 and immoral men and homosexuals and kidnappers and liars and perjurers, and whatever else is contrary to sound teach-ing,

11 according to the glorious gospel of the blessed God, with which *I* have been entrusted.

12 I thank Christ Jesus our Lord, who has strengthened me, because He considered me *faithful,* putting me into service;

13 even though I was formerly a blasphemer and a persecutor and a violent aggressor. And yet I was shown mercy, because I acted ignorantly in unbelief;

14 and the grace of our Lord was *more*[1] *than abundant,* with the faith and love[31a] which are *found* in Christ Jesus.

15 It is a trustworthy statement, deserving *full acceptance,*

that Christ Jesus came into the world to save[x] *sinners,* among whom I am *foremost of all.*

16   And yet for this reason I found mercy, in order that in *me* as the *foremost,* Jesus Christ might demonstrate[x] His perfect patience, as an example for those who would believe in Him for eternal life.

17   Now to the King eternal, immortal, invisible, the only God, *be* honor and glory forever and ever. Amen.

18   This command I entrust to you, Timothy, my son, in accordance with the prophecies previously made concerning you, that by them you may fight[~] the good[25b] fight,

19   keeping faith and a good[25a] conscience, which some have rejected and suffered shipwreck in regard to their faith.

20   Among these are Hymenaeus and Alexander, whom I have delivered over to Satan, so that they may be taught[x] not to blaspheme.[~]

A Call to Prayer

2   First of all, then, I urge that entreaties *and* prayers, petitions *and* thanksgivings, be made[~] on behalf of all men,

2   for kings and all who are in authority, in order that we may lead[~] a tranquil and quiet life in all godliness and dignity.

3   This is good[25b] and acceptable in the sight of God our Savior,

4   who desires *all men* to be saved[x] and to come to the *knowledge*[29b] *of the truth.*

5   For there is *one* God, *and one* mediator also between God and men, *the* man Christ Jesus,

6   who gave Himself as a ransom for all, the testimony *borne* at the *proper* time.

7   And for this I was appointed a preacher and an apostle (I am telling the truth, I am not lying) as a teacher of the Gentiles in faith and truth.

8   Therefore I want the men in every place to *pray,* [~] lifting up holy[28b] hands, without wrath and dissension.

Women Instructed

9   Likewise, *I want* women to adorn [~] themselves with *proper* clothing, *modestly* and *discreetly,* not with braided hair and gold or pearls or *costly* garments;

10   but rather by means of good[25a] works, as befits women making a claim to godliness.

11   Let a woman quietly receive[~] instruction with entire submissiveness.

1:16
1 Cor. 7:25;
1 Tim. 1:13;
Eph. 2:7
1:17
Rev. 15:3;
1 Tim. 6:16;
Col. 1:15;
John 5:44; 1 Tim.
6:15; Jude 25;
Rom. 2:7,10;
11:36; Heb. 2:7
1:18
1 Tim. 1:5;
1 Tim. 1:2;
1 Tim. 4:14;
2 Cor. 10:4;
1 Tim. 6:12;
2 Tim. 2:3f.; 4:7
1:19
1 Tim. 1:5;
1 Tim. 6:12,21;
2 Tim. 2:18
1:20
2 Tim. 2:17;
2 Tim. 4:14;
1 Cor. 5:5;
1 Cor. 11:32;
Heb. 12:5ff.
2:1
Eph. 6:18
2:2
Ezra 6:10; Rom.
13:1
2:3
Luke 1:47; 1 Tim.
1:1; 4:10
2:4
Ezek. 18:23,32;
John 3:17; 1 Tim.
4:10; Titus 2:11; 2
Pet. 3:9;
Rom. 11:14;
2 Tim. 2:25; 3:7;
Titus 1:1; Heb.
10:26
2:5
Rom. 3:30; 10:12;
1 Cor. 8:4;
1 Cor. 8:6; Gal.
3:20;
Matt. 1:1; Rom.
1:3
2:6
Matt. 20:28; Gal.
1:4;
1 Cor. 1:6;
Mark 1:15; Gal.
4:4; 1 Tim. 6:15;
Titus 1:3
2:7
Eph. 3:8; 1 Tim.
1:11; 2 Tim. 1:11;
1 Cor. 9:1;
Rom. 9:1;
Acts 9:15
2:8
Phil. 1:12; 1 Tim.
5:14; Titus 3:8;
John 4:21; 1 Cor.
1:2; 2 Cor. 2:14;
1 Thess. 1:8;
Ps. 63:4; Luke
24:50;
Ps. 24:4; James
4:8
2:9
1 Pet. 3:3
2:11
1 Cor. 14:34;
Titus 2:5

2:12
1 Cor. 14:34;
Titus 2:5
2:13
Gen. 2:7,22; 3:16;
1 Cor. 11:8ff.
2:14
Gen. 3:6,13;
2 Cor. 11:3
2:15
1 Tim. 1:14

12   But I do not allow a woman to *teach*~ or exercise~ authority over a †man, but to remain quiet.

13   For it was Adam who was first created, *and* then Eve.

14   And *it was* not Adam *who* was deceived,[16a] but the woman being quite[1] deceived, fell* into transgression.[40a]

15   But *women* shall be preserved through the bearing of children if they continue[x] in faith and love[31a] and sanctity with self-restraint.

Overseers and Deacons

3:1
1 Tim. 1:15;
Acts 20:28; Phil.
1:1
3:2
1 Tim. 3:2-4;
Titus 1:6-8;
Luke 2:36f.;
1 Tim. 5:9; Titus
1:6;
1 Tim. 3:8,11;
Titus 2:2;
Rom. 12:13; Titus
1:8; Heb. 13:2; 1
Pet. 4:9;
2 Tim. 2:24
3:3
Titus 1:7;
1 Tim. 3:8; 6:10;
Titus 1:7; Heb.
13:5
3:4
1 Tim. 3:12
3:5
1 Cor. 10:32;
1 Tim. 3:15
3:6
1 Tim. 6:4; 2 Tim.
3:4;
1 Tim. 3:7
3:7
2 Cor. 8:21;
Mark 4:11;
1 Tim. 6:9; 2 Tim.
2:26
3:8
Phil. 1:1; 1 Tim.
3:12;
1 Tim. 5:23; Titus
2:3;
1 Tim. 3:3; Titus
1:7; 1 Pet. 5:2
3:9
1 Tim. 1:5,19
3:10
1 Tim. 5:22
3:11
2 Tim. 3:3; Titus
2:3;
1 Tim. 3:2
3:12
Phil. 1:1; 1 Tim.
3:8;
1 Tim. 3:2;
1 Tim. 3:4
3:13
Matt. 25:21
3:15
1 Cor. 3:16;
2 Cor. 6:16; Eph.
2:21f.; 1 Pet. 2:5;
4:17;
1 Tim. 3:5;
Matt. 16:16;
1 Tim. 4:10;
Gal. 2:9; 2 Tim.
2:19

3   It is a trustworthy statement: if any man aspires to the office of overseer, it is a *fine work* he desires *to do.*

2   An overseer, then, must be above †reproach,[11d] the husband of one wife, temperate, prudent, respectable, hospitable, able to teach,

3   not addicted to wine or pugnacious, but gentle,[23a] uncontentious, free from the love of money.

4   *He must be* one who manages his *own* household well, keeping his children under control with all dignity

5   (but if a man does not know how to manage[x] his *own* household, how will he take care of the *church of God?*);

6   *and* not a new convert, lest he become conceited and fall[k] into the condemnation incurred by the *devil.*

7   And he must have a *good*[25b] reputation with those outside *the church,* so that he may not fall[k] into reproach and the snare of the devil.

8   Deacons likewise *must be* men of dignity, not double-tongued, or addicted to *much* wine or fond of sordid gain,

9   *but* holding to the mystery of the faith with a clear conscience.

10   And let these also first be tested;~ then let them serve~[38a] as deacons if they are beyond reproach.[11c]

11   Women *must* likewise *be* dignified, not malicious gossips, but temperate, faithful in all things.

12   Let deacons be husbands of *only* one wife, *and* good managers of *their* children and their *own households.

13   For those who have served well as deacons obtain for themselves a *high*[25b] standing and great[26b] confidence in the faith that is in Christ Jesus.

14   I am writing these things to you, hoping to come to you before long;

15   but in case I am delayed,~ *I write* so that you may know how one ought to conduct~ himself in the household of God,

which is the church of the living God, the pillar and support of the truth.

16   And by common confession great[26a] is the mystery of godliness:

> [a]He who was revealed in the flesh,
> Was vindicated in the Spirit,
> Beheld by angels,
> Proclaimed among the nations,
> Believed on in the world,
> Taken up in glory.

Apostasy

4   But the Spirit explicitly says that in later times some will fall away from the faith, paying attention to deceitful spirits and doctrines of demons,

2   by means of the hypocrisy of liars seared[+] in their •own conscience as with a branding iron,

3   *men* who forbid marriage~ *and advocate* abstaining~ from foods, which God has created to be gratefully shared in by those who believe and know[+29b] the truth.

4   For everything created by God is good,[25b] and nothing is to be rejected, if it is received with gratitude;

5   for it is sanctified by means of the word of God and prayer.

A Good Minister's Discipline

6   In pointing out these things to the brethren, you will be a good[25b] servant of Christ Jesus, *constantly* nourished on the words of the faith and of the sound doctrine which you have been following.[+1]

7   But have nothing to do~ with worldly fables fit only for old women. On the other hand, discipline~ yourself for the purpose of godliness;

8   for bodily discipline is only of little profit, but godliness is profitable for *all things,* since it holds promise for the present life and *also* for the *life* to come.

9   It is a trustworthy statement deserving *full acceptance.*

10   For it is for [+]this we labor and strive, because we have fixed[+] our hope on the living God, who is the Savior of all men, especially of believers.

11   Prescribe~ and teach~ these things.

12   Let no one look~ down on your *youthfulness,* but *rather* in speech, conduct, love, faith *and* purity, show~ yourself an *example* of those who believe.

[a]Some later mss. read *God*

3:16
Rom. 16:25;
John 1:14; 1 Pet.
1:20; 1 John
3:5, 8;
Rom. 3:4;
Luke 2:13; 24:4;
1 Pet. 1:12;
Rom. 16:26;
2 Cor. 1:19; Col.
1:23;
2 Thess. 1:10;
Mark 16:19; Acts
1:9

4:1
John 16:13; Acts
20:23; 21:11;
1 Cor. 2:10f.;
2 Thess. 2:3ff.;
2 Tim. 3:1; 2 Pet.
3:3; Jude 18;
1 John 4:6;
James 3:15
4:2
Eph. 4:19
4:3
Heb. 13:4;
Col. 2:16,23;
Gen. 1:29; 9:3;
Rom. 14:6; 1 Cor.
10:30f.; 1 Tim.
4:4
4:4
1 Cor. 10:26;
Rom. 14:6; 1 Cor.
10:30f.; 1 Tim.
4:3
4:5
Gen. 1:25,31;
Heb. 11:3
4:6
Acts 1:15;
2 Cor. 11:23;
1 Tim. 1:10;
Luke 1:3; Phil.
2:20,22; 2 Tim.
3:10
4:7
1 Tim. 1:9;
1 Tim. 1:4;
1 Tim. 4:8; 6:3,
5f.; 2 Tim. 3:5
4:8
Col. 2:23;
1 Tim. 4:7; 6:3,
5f.; 2 Tim. 3:5;
Ps. 37:9,11; Prov.
19:23; 22:4; Matt.
6:33;
Matt. 6:33; 12:32;
Mark 10:30
4:9
1 Tim. 1:15
4:10
2 Cor. 1:10;
1 Tim. 6:17;
1 Tim. 3:15;
John 4:42; 1 Tim.
2:4
4:11
1 Tim. 5:7; 6:2
4:12
1 Cor. 16:11;
Titus 2:15;
1 Tim. 1:14;
Titus 2:7; 1 Pet.
5:3

4:13
1 Tim. 3:14;
2 Tim. 3:15ff.

4:14
1 Tim. 1:18;
Acts 6:6; 1 Tim.
5:22; 2 Tim. 1:6;
Acts 11:30

4:16
Acts 20:28;
1 Cor. 1:21

5:1
Lev. 19:32;
Titus 2:2;
Titus 2:6

5:3
Acts 6:1; 9:39,41;
1 Tim. 5:5,16
5:4
Eph. 6:2;
1 Tim. 2:3

5:5
Acts 6:1; 9:39,41;
1 Tim. 5:3,16;
1 Cor. 7:34;
1 Pet. 3:5;
Luke 2:37; 1 Tim.
2:1; 2 Tim. 1:3
5:6
James 5:5;
Luke 15:24;
2 Tim. 3:6; Rev.
3:1
5:7
1 Tim. 4:11
5:8
2 Tim. 2:12; Titus
1:16; 2 Pet. 2:1;
Jude 4

5:9
1 Tim. 5:16;
1 Tim. 3:2

5:10
Acts 9:36; 1 Tim.
6:18; Titus 2:7;
3:8; 1 Pet. 2:12;
1 Tim. 3:2;
Luke 7:44; John
13:14;
1 Tim. 5:16
5:11
Rev. 18:7

5:13
3 John 10;
2 Thess. 3:11;
Titus 1:11

13   Until I come, give attention ⌣ to the *public* reading *of Scripture*, to exhortation and teaching.

14   Do not neglect⊖ the spiritual gift[24c] within you, which was bestowed upon you through prophetic utterance with the laying on of hands by the presbytery.

15   Take pains ⌣ with these things; be *absorbed* in them, so that your *progress* may be evident to all.

16   Pay close attention ⌣ to yourself and to your teaching; persevere ⌣ in these things; for as you do this you will insure salvation both for yourself and for those who hear you.

Honor Widows

5   Do not sharply rebuke⊖ an older man, but *rather* appeal ⌣ to *him* as a father, *to* the younger men as brothers,

2   the older women as mothers, *and* the younger women as sisters, in all purity.

3   Honor ⌣ widows who are widows indeed;

4   but if any widow has children or grandchildren, let them first learn ⌣ to practice ~ piety in regard to their *own* family, and to make~ some return to their parents; for this is acceptable in the sight of God.

5   Now she who is a widow indeed, and who has been left⁺ alone has fixed⁺ her hope on God, and continues in entreaties and prayers night and day.

6   But she who gives herself to wanton pleasure is dead even while she lives.

7   Prescribe ⌣ these things as well, so that they may be above †reproach. [11d]

8   But if anyone does not provide for his own, and especially for those of his household, he has denied⁺ the faith, and is worse than an unbeliever.

9   Let a widow be put ⌣ on the list only if she is not less than sixty years old, *having been* the wife of one man,

10   having a reputation for *good*[25b] works; *and* if she has brought up children, if she has shown hospitality to strangers, if she has washed the *saints'* feet, if she has assisted *those in distress, and* if she has devoted herself to every good[25a] work.

11   But refuse ⌣ *to put* younger widows *on the list*, for when they feelˣ sensual desires in disregard of Christ, they want to get married, ~

12   *thus* incurring condemnation, because they have set aside their *previous pledge.*

13   And at the same time they also learn *to be idle,* as they go around from house to house; and not merely idle, but also gos-

sips and busybodies, talking about things not proper *to mention.*

14   Therefore, I want younger *widows* to get married,~ bear~ children, keep~ house, *and* give~ the enemy no occasion for reproach;

15   for some have already turned aside to follow Satan.

16   If any woman who is a believer has *dependent* widows, let her assist[~] them, and let not the church be burdened,^θ so that it may assist^x those who are widows indeed.

Concerning Elders

17   Let the elders who rule◆ well be considered ~ worthy of double honor, especially those who work hard at preaching and teaching.

18   For the Scripture says, "YOU SHALL NOT MUZZLE THE OX WHILE HE IS THRESHING," and "The laborer is *worthy* of his wages."

19   Do not receive^θ an accusation against an *elder* except on the basis of two or three witnesses.

20   Those who continue in sin, rebuke[~] in the *presence of all,* so that the rest also may be ~ *fearful of sinning.*

21   I solemnly[1] charge you in the presence of God and of Christ Jesus and of *His* chosen angels, to maintain^x these *principles* without bias, doing nothing in a *spirit of* partiality.

22   Do not lay^θ hands upon anyone *too hastily* and thus share ~ *responsibility for* the sins of others; keep ~ *yourself* free from sin.

23   No longer drink^θ water *exclusively*, but use[~] a *little* wine for the sake of your stomach and your frequent ailments.

24   The sins of *some men* are quite evident, going before them to judgment; for others, their *sins* follow[1] after.

25   Likewise also, deeds that are *good*[25b] are quite evident, and those which are otherwise *cannot* be concealed. ^x

Instructions to Those Who Minister

6   Let all who are under the yoke as slaves regard[~] their own masters as worthy of all honor so that the name of God and *our* doctrine may not be spoken~ against.

2   And let those who have *believers* as their masters not be disrespectful^θ to them because they are †*brethren*, but let them serve ~ them all the more, because those who partake of the benefit are believers and beloved. Teach ~ and preach ~ these *principles.*

3   If anyone advocates a different doctrine, and does not

5:14
1 Cor. 7:9; 1 Tim. 4:3; Titus 2:5; 1 Tim. 6:1

5:15
1 Tim. 1:20; Matt. 4:10

5:16
1 Tim. 5:4; 1 Tim. 5:10; 1 Tim. 5:3

5:17
Acts 11:30; 1 Tim. 4:14; 5:19; Rom. 12:8; 1 Thess. 5:12

5:18
Deut. 25:4; 1 Cor. 9:9; Lev. 19:13; Deut. 24:15; Matt. 10:10; Luke 10:7; 1 Cor. 9:14

5:19
Acts 11:30; 1 Tim. 4:14; 5:17; Deut. 17:6; 19:15; Matt. 18:16

5:20
Gal. 2:14; Eph. 5:11; 2 Tim. 4:2; 2 Cor. 7:11

5:21
Luke 9:26; 1 Tim. 6:13; 2 Tim. 2:14; 4:1

5:22
1 Tim. 3:10; 4:14; Eph. 5:11; 1 Tim. 3:2-7

5:23
1 Tim. 3:8

5:24
Rev. 14:13

5:25
Prov. 10:9

6:1
Eph. 6:5; Titus 2:9; 1 Pet. 2:18; Titus 2:5

6:2
Acts 1:15; Gal. 3:28; Philem. 16; 1 Tim. 4:11

6:3
1 Tim. 1:3; 1 Tim. 1:10; Titus 1:1

agree with sound words, those of our Lord Jesus Christ, and with the doctrine conforming to godliness,

4   he is conceited[+] *and* understands[29c] nothing; but he has a morbid interest in controversial questions and disputes about words, out of which arise envy, strife, abusive language, evil suspicions,

5   and constant[1] friction between men of depraved[+] mind[33b] and deprived[+] of the truth, who suppose that godliness is a *means of gain.*

6   But godliness *actually* •*is* a means of great gain, when accompanied by contentment.

7   For we have brought nothing into the world, [b]so we can-not *take*[x] *anything out* of it either.

8   And if we have food and covering, with these we shall be content.

9   But those who want to get[~] rich fall into temptation and a snare and many foolish[20a] and harmful desires which plunge men into ruin and destruction.

10   For *the love of money* is a root of all sorts of evil,[10a] and some by longing for it have wandered away from the faith, and pierced themselves with *many* a pang.

11   But flee[~] from these things, you man of God; and pur-sue[~] righteousness, godliness, faith, love,[31a] perseverance *and* gentleness.

12   Fight[~] the good[25b] fight[4] of faith; take hold[x] of the eternal life to which you were called, and you made the good[25b] confes-sion in the presence of many witnesses.

13   I charge you in the presence of God, who gives life to all things, and of Christ Jesus, who testified the good confession before Pontius Pilate,

14   that you keep[x] the commandment without stain or re-proach[11d] until the appearing of our Lord Jesus Christ,

15   which He will bring about at the *proper* time—He who is the blessed and only Sovereign, the King of kings and Lord of lords;

16   who alone possesses immortality and dwells in *unap-proachable* light; whom *no man* has seen or *can* see.[x] To Him *be* honor and eternal dominion![32d] Amen.

17   Instruct[~] those who are rich in this present world not to be conceited[~] or to fix[+] their hope on the uncertainty of *riches,* but on [†]*God,* who richly supplies us with all things to enjoy.

18   *Instruct them* to do[~] good, to be[~] rich in good[25b] works, to be generous and ready to share,

[b]Later mss. read *it is clear that*

19   storing up for themselves the treasure of a good[25b] foundation for the future, so that they may take hold[x] of that which is life
indeed.

20   O Timothy, guard[x] what has been *entrusted* to you, avoid-
ing worldly *and* empty chatter *and* the opposing arguments of
what is falsely called "knowledge"—

21   which some have professed and thus gone astray from the
faith.

Grace be with you.

6:19
Matt. 6:20;
1 Tim. 6:12

6:20
1 Tim. 1:2;
2 Tim. 1:12,14;
1 Tim. 1:9; 2 Tim.
2:16

6:21
2 Tim. 2:18;
1 Tim. 1:19;
Col. 4:18

The Second Epistle of Paul to
Timothy

1:1
2 Cor. 1:1;
Gal. 3:26;
1 Cor. 1:1;
1 Tim. 6:19
1:2
Acts 16:1; 1 Tim.
1:2;
2 Tim. 2:1; Titus
1:4;
Rom. 1:7
1:3
Rom. 1:8;
Acts 24:14;
Acts 23:1; 24:16;
1 Tim. 1:5;
Rom. 1:9
1:4
2 Tim. 4:9,21;
Acts 20:37
1:5
1 Tim. 1:5;
Acts 16:1; 2 Tim.
3:15
1:6
1 Tim. 4:14
1:7
John 14:27; Rom.
8:15
1:8
Mark 8:38; Rom.
1:16; 2 Tim. 1:12,
16;
1 Cor. 1:6;
Eph. 3:1;
2 Tim. 2:3,9; 4:5;
2 Tim. 1:10; 2:8
1:9
Rom. 11:14;
Rom. 8:28ff.;
Rom. 11:29;
Eph. 2:9;
Rom. 16:25; Eph.
1:4; Titus 1:2
1:10
Rom. 16:26;
2 Thess. 2:8; 2
Tim. 4:1,8; Titus
2:11;
2 Tim. 1:1;
1 Cor. 15:26;
Heb. 2:14f.
1:11
1 Tim. 2:7
1:12
2 Tim. 1:8,16;
Titus 3:8;
1 Tim. 6:20;
2 Tim. 1:14;
1 Cor. 1:8; 3:13;
2 Tim. 1:18; 4:8
1:13
2 Tim. 3:14; Titus
1:9;
Rom. 2:20; 6:17;
1 Tim. 1:10;
2 Tim. 2:2;
1 Tim. 1:14;
2 Tim. 1:1
1:14
Rom. 8:9;
1 Tim. 6:20; 2
Tim. 1:12
1:15
Acts 2:9;
2 Tim. 4:10,11,
16

Timothy Charged to Guard His Trust

1 Paul, an apostle of Christ Jesus by the will of God, according to the promise of life in Christ Jesus,

2 to Timothy, my beloved son: Grace, mercy *and* peace from God the Father and Christ Jesus our Lord.

3 I thank God, whom I serve[38c] with a clear conscience the way my forefathers did, as I constantly remember you in my prayers night and day,

4 longing to see[x] you, even as I recall[+] your tears, so that I may be filled[x] with *joy.*

5 For I am mindful of the sincere faith within you, which first dwelt in your grandmother Lois, and your mother Eunice, and I am sure[+] that *it is* in you as well.

6 And for this reason I remind you to kindle[~] afresh the gift[24c] of God which is in you through the laying on of my hands.

7 For God has not given us a spirit of timidity, but of power and love[31a] and discipline.

8 Therefore do not be ashamed[⊙] of the testimony of our Lord, or of me His prisoner; but join[xi] with *me* in suffering for the gospel according to the power[32a] of God,

9 who has saved us, and called us with a holy[28a] calling, not according to our works, but according to His •own purpose and grace which was granted us in Christ Jesus from all eternity,

10 but now has been revealed by the appearing of our Savior Christ Jesus, who abolished death, and brought life and immortality to light through the gospel,

11 for which I was appointed a preacher and an apostle and a teacher.

12 For this reason I also suffer these things, but I am not ashamed; for I know[29e] whom I have believed[+] and I am convinced[+] that He is *able* to guard[x] what I have entrusted to Him until that day.

13 Retain[~] the *standard* of sound words[43a] which you have heard from me, in the faith and love which are in Christ Jesus.

14 Guard,[xi] through the Holy Spirit who dwells in us, the *treasure* which has been entrusted to *you.*

15 You are aware of the fact that all who are in Asia turned

away from me, among whom are Phygelus and Hermogenes.

16   The Lord grant[x] mercy to the house of Onesiphorus for he often refreshed me, and was not ashamed of my chains;

17   but when he was in Rome, he eagerly searched for me, and found me—

18   the Lord grant[x] to him to find[x] mercy from the Lord on that day—and *you* know *very[3] well* what services he rendered at Ephesus.

1:16
2 Tim. 4:19;
2 Tim. 1:8;
Eph. 6:20

1:18
1 Cor. 1:8; 3:13;
2 Tim. 1:12; 4:8;
Acts 18:19;
1 Tim. 1:3

Be Strong

2   You therefore, my son, be strong[~l] in the grace that is in Christ Jesus.

2   And the things which you have heard from me in the presence of many witnesses, these entrust[xl] to faithful men, who will be able to teach[x] *others also.*

3   Suffer[xl] hardship with *me,* as a good[25b] soldier of Christ Jesus.

4   No soldier in active service entangles himself in the affairs of everyday life, so that he may please[x] the *one who enlisted him* as a soldier.

5   And also if anyone competes[~] as an athlete, he does not win the prize unless he competes[x] according to the rules.

6   The *hard-working farmer* ought to be the first to receive[~] his share of the crops.

7   Consider[~l] what I say, for the Lord will give you understanding in everything.

8   Remember[~l] Jesus Christ, risen[*] from the dead, descendant of David, according to my gospel,

9   for which I suffer hardship even to imprisonment as a criminal; but the word of God is not imprisoned.[*]

10   For this reason I endure all things for the sake of those who are chosen, that *they also* may obtain[x] the salvation which is in Christ Jesus *and* with *it* eternal glory.

11   It is a trustworthy statement:

> For if we died with Him, we shall also live with
>   Him;

12   If we endure, we shall also reign with Him;
     If we deny Him, He also will deny us;

13   If we are faithless, He remains *faithful;* for He
     cannot *deny*[x] *Himself.*

2:1
2 Tim. 1:2;
Eph. 6:10;
2 Tim. 1:1
2:2
2 Tim. 1:13;
1 Tim. 6:12;
1 Tim. 1:18;
1 Tim. 1:12;
2 Cor. 2:14ff.; 3:5
2:3
2 Tim. 1:8;
1 Cor. 9:7; 1 Tim.
1:18;
2 Tim. 1:1
2:4
2 Pet. 2:20

2:5
1 Cor. 9:25

2:6
1 Cor. 9:10
2:8
Acts 2:24;
Matt. 1:1;
Rom. 2:16
2:9
2 Tim. 1:8; 2:3;
Phil. 1:7;
Luke 23:32;
1 Thess. 1:8;
Acts 28:31; 2
Tim. 4:17
2:10
Col. 1:24;
Luke 18:7; Titus
1:1;
2 Cor. 1:6;
1 Thess. 5:9;
1 Cor. 1:21;
2 Tim. 1:1; 2:1,3;
2 Cor. 4:17;
1 Pet. 5:10
2:11
1 Tim. 1:15;
Rom. 6:8;
1 Thess. 5:10
2:12
Matt. 19:28; Luke
22:29; Rom. 5:17;
8:17;
Matt. 10:33; Luke
12:9; 1 Tim. 5:8
2:13
Rom. 3:3; 1 Cor.
1:9;
Num. 23:19;
Titus 1:2
2:14
1 Tim. 5:21;
2 Tim. 4:1;
1 Tim. 6:4; 2 Tim.
2:23; Titus 3:9

An Unashamed Workman

14   Remind[~l] *them* of these things, and solemnly[1] charge *them*

in the presence of God not to wrangle~ about words, which is useless, *and leads* to the ruin of the hearers.

2:15
Rom. 6:13;
James 1:12;
Eph. 1:13; James
1:18

15 Be diligent[xl] to present[x] yourself *approved* to God as a workman who does not need to be ashamed, handling accurately the word[43a] of truth.

2:16
Titus 3:9;
1 Tim. 1:9; 6:20

16 But avoid~ worldly *and* empty chatter, for it will lead to *further* ungodliness,

2:17
1 Tim. 1:20

17 and their talk will spread like [a+]gangrene. Among them are Hymenaeus and Philetus,

2:18
1 Cor. 15:12;
1 Tim. 1:19; Titus
1:11

18 *men* who have gone astray from the truth saying that the resurrection has already taken+ place, and thus they upset the faith of some.

2:19
Is. 28:16f.; 1 Tim.
3:15;
John 3:33;
John 10:14;
1 Cor. 8:3;
Luke 13:27;
1 Cor. 1:2

19 Nevertheless,[2] the firm foundation of God stands,+ having +*this* seal, "The Lord +knows[29a] those who are His," and, "Let everyone who names the name of the Lord abstain[xl] from wickedness."

2:20
Rom. 9:21

20 Now in a large house there are not only gold and silver vessels, but also vessels of wood and of earthenware, and some to honor and some to dishonor.

2:21
1 Tim. 6:11;
2 Tim. 2:16-18;
2 Cor. 9:8; Eph.
2:10; 2 Tim. 3:17

21 Therefore, if a man cleanses[xl] himself from these *things*, he will be a vessel for honor, sanctified,+ useful to the Master, prepared+ for every good[25a] work.

2:22
1 Tim. 6:11;
1 Tim. 1:14;
Acts 7:59;
1 Tim. 1:5

22 Now flee~ from youthful lusts, and pursue~ righteousness, faith, love *and* peace, with those who call on the Lord from a pure[13c] heart.

2:23
1 Tim. 6:4; 2 Tim.
2:14; Titus 3:9;
James 4:1

23 But refuse~ foolish[20c] and ignorant speculations, knowing that they produce quarrels.

2:24
1 Tim. 3:3; Titus
1:7;
1 Tim. 3:2

24 And the *Lord's bond-servant*[38b] must not be quarrelsome,~ but be kind to all, able to teach, patient when wronged,

2:25
Gal. 6:1; Titus
3:2; 1 Pet. 3:15;
Acts 8:22;
1 Tim. 2:4

25 with gentleness[23b] correcting those who are in opposition, if perhaps God may grant[x] them repentance leading to the knowledge[29b] of the truth,

2:26
1 Tim. 3:7;
Luke 5:10

26 and they may come[x] to their senses *and escape* from the snare of the devil, having been held+ captive by him to do •*his* will.

"Difficult Times Will Come"

3:1
1 Tim. 4:1
3:2
Phil. 2:21;
Luke 16:14;
1 Tim. 3:3; 6:10;
Rom. 1:30;
2 Pet. 2:10-12;
Luke 6:35;
1 Tim. 1:9
3:3
Rom. 1:31;
1 Tim. 3:11;
Titus 1:8

3 But realize~ this, that in the last days *difficult* times will come.

2 For men will be lovers of self, lovers of money, boastful, arrogant, revilers, disobedient to parents, ungrateful, unholy,[41a]

3 unloving, irreconcilable, malicious gossips, without self-control, brutal, haters of good,

aOr, *cancer*

4   treacherous, reckless, conceited,⁺ lovers of pleasure rather than lovers of God;

5   holding to a form of godliness, although they have denied⁺ its *power;* and avoid◠ such men as these.

6   For among them are those who enter into households and captivate weak women weighed⁺ down with sins, led on by various impulses,

7   always learning and never able to come to the *knowl-edge*²⁹ᵇ *of the truth.*

8   And just as Jannes and Jambres opposed Moses, so these *men* also oppose the truth, men of depraved⁺ mind,³³ᵇ rejected as regards the faith.

9   But they will not make further progress; for their folly will be obvious¹ to all, as also that of those *two* came to be.

10   But *you* followed¹ my teaching, conduct, purpose, faith, patience, love,³¹ᵃ perseverance,

11   persecutions, *and* sufferings, such as happened to me at Antioch, at Iconium *and* at Lystra; what persecutions I endured, and *out of them all* the Lord delivered¹⁸ᵇ me!

12   And indeed, all who desire to live◠ godly in Christ Jesus will be persecuted.

13   But evil men and impostors will proceed *from bad* to worse, deceiving¹⁶ᵇ and being deceived.

14   *You,* however, continue◠ in the things you have learned and become convinced of, knowing from whom you have learned *them;*

15   and that from childhood you have known the *sacred writings* which are able to give˟ you the wisdom that leads to salvation through faith which is in Christ Jesus.

16   ᵇAll Scripture is inspired by God and profitable for teaching, for reproof, for correction, for training in righteousness;

17   that the man of God may be *adequate,* equipped⁺¹ for every good²⁵ᵃ †work.

"Preach the Word"

4   I solemnly¹ charge *you* in the presence of God and of Christ Jesus, who is to judge the living and the dead, and by His appearing and His kingdom:

2   preach˟ the word; be ready˟ in season *and* out of season; reprove,˟ rebuke,˟ exhort,˟ with great patience and instruction.

3   For the time will come when they will not endure sound doctrine; but *wanting* to have their ears tickled, they will accumulate for *themselves* teachers in accordance to their •own desires;

ᵇOr possibly, *Every Scripture inspired by God is also profitable*

3:4
Acts 7:52;
Acts 19:36;
1 Tim. 3:6;
Phil. 3:19
3:5
1 Tim. 4:7;
1 Tim. 5:8;
Matt. 7:15; 2
Thess. 3:6
3:6
Jude 4;
1 Tim. 5:6; Titus
3:3
3:7
2 Tim. 2:25

3:8
Ex. 7:11;
Acts 13:8;
1 Tim. 6:5

3:9
Luke 6:11;
Ex. 7:11,12; 8:18;
9:11
3:10
Phil. 2:20,22;
1 Tim. 4:6;
1 Tim. 6:11
3:11
2 Cor. 12:10;
2 Cor. 1:5,7;
Acts 13:14,45,50;
Acts 14:1-7,19;
Acts 14:8-20;
2 Cor. 11:23-27;
Rom. 15:31
3:12
John 15:20; Acts
14:22; 2 Cor. 4:9f.
3:13
2 Tim. 2:16;
Titus 3:3
3:14
2 Tim. 1:13; Titus
1:9

3:15
2 Tim. 1:5;
John 5:47; Rom.
2:27;
Ps. 119:98f.;
1 Cor. 1:21;
2 Tim. 1:1
3:16
Rom. 4:23f.; 15:4;
2 Pet. 1:20f.
3:17
1 Tim. 6:11;
2 Tim. 2:21; Heb.
13:21

4:1
1 Tim. 5:21;
2 Tim. 2:14;
Acts 10:42;
2 Thess. 2:8; 2
Tim. 1:10; 4:8
4:2
Gal. 6:6; Col. 4:3;
1 Thess. 1:6;
1 Tim. 5:20; Titus
1:13; 2:15;
2 Tim. 3:10
4:3
2 Tim. 3:1;
1 Tim. 1:10;
2 Tim. 1:13

4:4
2 Thess. 2:11;
Titus 1:14;
1 Tim. 1:4
4:5
1 Pet. 1:13;
2 Tim. 1:8;
Acts 21:8;
Eph. 4:12; Col.
4:17
4:6
Phil. 1:23; 2:17;
2 Pet. 1:14
4:7
1 Cor. 9:25f.; Phil.
1:30; 1 Tim. 1:18;
6:12;
Acts 20:24; 1 Cor.
9:24; 2 Tim. 3:10
4:8
Col. 1:5; 1 Pet.
1:4; 1 Cor. 9:25; 2
Tim. 2:5; James
1:12; 2 Tim. 1:12;
Phil. 3:11;
2 Tim. 4:1
4:9
2 Tim. 1:4; 4:21;
Titus 3:12
4:10
Col. 4:14;
1 Tim. 6:17;
Acts 16:6; 17:1;
2 Cor. 2:13; 8:23;
Gal. 2:3; Titus 1:4
4:11
2 Tim. 1:15;
Col. 4:14; Philem.
24; Acts 12:12,25;
15:37-39; Col.
4:10; 2 Tim. 2:21
4:12
Acts 20:4; Eph.
6:21,22; Col.
4:7f.; Acts 18:19
4:13
Acts 16:8
4:14
Acts 19:33;
1 Tim. 1:20;
Ps. 62:12; Rom.
2:6; 12:19
4:16
Acts 7:60; 1 Cor.
13:5
4:17
1 Tim. 1:12;
2 Tim. 2:1; 4:5;
Titus 1:3;
Acts 9:15; Phil.
1:12ff.; Rom. 15:31;
2 Tim. 3:11;
1 Sam. 17:37; Ps.
22:21
4:18
1 Cor. 1:21;
1 Cor. 15:50;
2 Tim. 4:1; Heb.
11:16; 12:22;
Rom. 11:36;
2 Pet. 3:18
4:19
Acts 18:2;
2 Tim. 1:16
4:20
Acts 18:1; 19:22;
20:4; 20:15; 21:29;
Rom. 16:23
4:21
2 Tim. 4:9;
Titus 3:12
4:22
Gal. 6:18; Phil.
4:23; Philem. 25;
Col. 4:18

4　and will turn away their ears from the *truth,* and will turn aside to *myths.*

5　But *you,* be sober ⁓ᴵ in all things, endure ˣᴵ hardship, do ˣᴵ the work of an *evangelist,* fulfill ˣᴵ your ministry.

6　For *I* am already being poured out as a drink offering, and the time of my departure has come. ⁺

7　I have fought ⁺ the *good* ²⁵ᵇ fight, I have *finished* ⁺ the course, I have *kept* ⁺ the faith;

8　in the future there is laid up for me the crown of righteousness, which the Lord, the *righteous Judge,* will award to me on that day; and not only to me, but also to all who have loved ⁺ His appearing.

Personal Concerns

9　Make ˣᴵ every effort to come to me soon;

10　for Demas, having loved this present world, has deserted me and gone to Thessalonica; Crescens *has gone* to Galatia, Titus to Dalmatia.

11　Only Luke is with me. Pick up Mark and bring him with you, for he is useful to me for service.

12　But Tychicus I have sent to Ephesus.

13　When you come *bring* the cloak which I left at Troas with Carpus, and the books, especially the parchments.

14　Alexander the coppersmith did me *much harm;* the Lord will repay him according to his deeds.

15　Be on guard ⁓ᴵ against him *yourself,* for he vigorously opposed •our teaching.

16　At my first defense no one supported me, but all deserted me; may it not be counted ˣ against them.

17　But the Lord stood with me, and strengthened me, in order that through me the proclamation might be fully accomplished, ˣ and that all the Gentiles might hear; ˣ and I was delivered out of the lion's mouth.

18　The *Lord* will deliver ¹⁸ᵇ me from every evil ¹ᵇ deed, and will bring me safely to His †heavenly kingdom; to Him *be* the glory forever and ever. Amen.

19　Greet ˣᴵ Prisca and Aquila, and the household of Onesiphorus.

20　Erastus remained at Corinth, but Trophimus I left sick at Miletus.

21　Make ˣᴵ every effort to come before winter. Eubulus greets you, also Pudens and Linus and Claudia and all the brethren.

22　The Lord be with your spirit. Grace be with you.

The Epistle of Paul to
Titus

Salutation

1 Paul, a bond-servant[38b] of God, and an apostle of Jesus Christ, for the faith of those chosen of God and the knowledge[29b] of the truth which is according to godliness,

2 in the hope of eternal life, which *God,* who *cannot lie,* promised long ages ago,

3 but at the proper time manifested, *even* His word, in the proclamation with which *I* was entrusted according to the commandment of God our Savior;

4 to Titus, my true child in a common faith: Grace and peace from God the Father and Christ Jesus our Savior.

Qualifications of Elders

5 For this reason I left you in Crete, that you might set[x] in order what remains, and appoint[x] elders in every city as I directed you,

6 *namely,* if any man be above reproach,[11c] the husband of one wife, having children who believe, not accused of dissipation or rebellion.

7 For the overseer must be above reproach[11c] as *God's* steward, not self-willed, not quick-tempered, not addicted to wine, not pugnacious, not fond of sordid gain,

8 but hospitable, loving what is good, sensible, just, devout, self-controlled,

9 holding fast the faithful word[43a] which is in accordance with the teaching, that he may be able both to exhort~ in *sound* doctrine and to refute~ those who contradict.

10 For there are many rebellious men, empty talkers and deceivers, especially those of the circumcision,

11 who must be silenced~ because they are upsetting *whole families,* teaching things they should not *teach,* for the sake of sordid gain.

12 One of themselves, a prophet of *their own,* [4] said, "Cretans are always liars, evil beasts, *lazy* gluttons."

13 This testimony is true. For this cause reprove~ them severely that they may be sound~ in the faith,

1:1
Rom. 1:1; James 1:1; Rev. 1:1;
2 Cor. 1:1;
Luke 18:7;
1 Tim. 2:4;
1 Tim. 6:3
1:2
2 Tim. 1:1; Titus 3:7;
2 Tim. 2:13; Heb. 6:18;
Rom. 1:2;
2 Tim. 1:9
1:3
1 Tim. 2:6;
Rom. 16:25;
2 Tim. 4:17;
1 Tim. 1:11;
Luke 1:47; 1 Tim. 1:1; Titus 2:10;
3:4
1:4
2 Cor. 2:13; 8:23;
Gal. 2:3; 2 Tim. 4:10;
2 Tim. 1:2;
2 Pet. 1:1;
Rom. 1:7;
1 Tim. 1:12; 2 Tim. 1:1
1:5
Acts 27:7; Titus 1:12;
Acts 14:23;
Acts 11:30
1:6
1 Tim. 3:2-4;
Titus 1:6-8;
Eph. 5:18;
Titus 1:10
1:7
1 Tim. 3:2;
1 Cor. 4:1;
2 Pet. 2:10;
1 Tim. 3:3,8
1:8
1 Tim. 3:2;
2 Tim. 3:3
1:9
2 Thess. 2:15;
1 Tim. 1:19;
2 Tim. 1:13;
1 Tim. 1:10; Titus 2:1
1:10
2 Cor. 11:13;
Titus 1:6;
1 Tim. 1:6;
Acts 11:2
1:11
1 Tim. 5:4; 2 Tim. 3:6;
1 Tim. 5:13;
1 Tim. 6:5
1:12
Acts 2:11; 27:7
1:13
1 Tim. 5:20;
2 Tim. 4:2; Titus 2:15;
2 Cor. 13:10;
Titus 2:2

1:14
1 Tim. 1:4;
Col. 2:22;
2 Tim. 4:4
1:15
Luke 11:41; Rom.
14:20;
Rom. 14:14,23;
1 Tim. 6:5
1:16
1 John 2:4;
1 Tim. 5:8;
Rev. 21:8;
Titus 3:3;
2 Tim. 3:8;
2 Tim. 3:17; Titus
3:1

14   not paying attention to Jewish myths and commandments of men who turn away from the truth.

15   To the pure,[13c] all things are pure; but to those who are defiled[+17b] and unbelieving, nothing is pure, but both their mind[33b] and their *conscience* are defiled.[+]

16   They profess to know God, but by *their deeds* they deny *Him*, being detestable and disobedient, and *worthless* for any good[25a] deed.

Duties of the Older and Younger

2:1
Titus 1:9

2 But as for *you*, speak[~l] the things which are fitting for sound doctrine.

2:2
Philem. 9;
1 Tim. 3:2;
Titus 1:13;
1 Tim. 1:2,14
2:3
1 Tim. 3:11;
1 Tim. 3:8

2   Older men are to be temperate, dignified, sensible, sound in faith, in love,[31a] in perseverance.

3   Older women likewise are to be reverent in their behavior, not malicious gossips, nor enslaved[+] to *much* wine, teaching what is good,

4   that they may encourage[~] the young women to love their †husbands, to love their children,

2:5
1 Tim. 5:14;
Eph. 5:22;
1 Tim. 6:1

5   *to be* sensible, pure,[13a] workers at home, kind,[25a] being subject to their own husbands, that the word[43a] of God may not be dishonored.[~]

2:6
1 Tim. 5:1
2:7
1 Tim. 4:12
2:8
2 Thess. 3:14;
1 Pet. 2:12
2:9
Eph. 6:5; 1 Tim.
6:1
2:10
Titus 1:3
2:11
2 Tim. 1:10; Titus
3:4;
1 Tim. 2:4
2:12
1 Tim. 6:9; Titus
3:3;
2 Tim. 3:12;
1 Tim. 6:17
2:13
2 Thess. 2:8;
1 Tim. 1:1; 2 Tim.
1:2; Titus 1:4;
2 Pet. 1:1
2:14
1 Tim. 2:6;
Ps. 130:8; 1 Pet.
1:18f.;
Ezek. 37:23; Heb.
1:3; 9:14; 1 John
1:7;
Ex. 19:5; Deut.
4:20; 7:6; 14:2;
Eph. 1:11; 1 Pet.
2:9;
Eph. 2:10; Titus
3:8; 1 Pet. 3:13
2:15
1 Tim. 4:13;
5:20; 2 Tim. 4:2;
1 Tim. 4:12

6   Likewise urge[~l] the young men to be sensible;[~]

7   in all things show *yourself* to be an example of good[25b] deeds, *with* purity in doctrine, dignified,

8   sound *in* speech which is beyond reproach, in order that the opponent may be put[x] to shame,[39b] having nothing *bad*[10d] to say[~] about us.

9   *Urge* bondslaves to be subject[~] to their own masters in everything, to be well-pleasing, not argumentative,

10   not pilfering, but showing all *good*[25a] faith that they may adorn[~] the doctrine of God our Savior in every respect.

11   For the grace of God has appeared, bringing salvation to all men,

12   instructing us to deny ungodliness and worldly desires and to live[x] sensibly, righteously and godly in the present age,

13   looking for the blessed hope and the appearing of the glory of our great God and Savior, Christ Jesus;

14   who gave Himself for us, that He might redeem[x36b] us from every lawless deed and purify[x] for Himself a people for His own possession, zealous for good[25b] deeds.

15   These things speak[~l] and exhort[~l] and reprove[~l] with all authority. Let no one disregard[~l] you.

Godly Living

3 Remind ᴹ them to be subject~ to rulers, to authorities, to be obedient,~ to be ready for every good[25a] deed,

2 to malign~ no one, to be uncontentious, gentle,[23a] showing every consideration[23b] for all men.

3 For *we also* once were foolish[20a] ourselves, disobedient, deceived, enslaved[38b] to various lusts and pleasures, spending our life in malice and envy, hateful, hating one another.

4 But when the kindness of God our Savior and *His* love for mankind appeared,

5 He saved us, not on the basis of deeds which *we* have done in righteousness, but according to *His* mercy, by the washing of regeneration and renewing by the Holy Spirit,

6 whom He poured out upon us *richly* through Jesus Christ our Savior,

7 that being justified by His grace we might be made *heirs* according to *the* hope of eternal life.

8 This is a trustworthy statement; and concerning these things I want you to speak~ confidently,[1] so that those who have believed+ God may be~ careful to engage~ in good[25b] deeds. These things are good and profitable for men.

9 But shun ᴹ foolish[20c] controversies and genealogies and strife and disputes about the Law; for they are unprofitable and worthless.

10 Reject ᴹ a *factious man* after a first and second warning,

11 knowing that such a man is perverted+ and is sinning, being self-condemned.

Personal Concerns

12 When I send ˣ Artemas or Tychicus to you, make ˣᴵ every effort to come to me at Nicopolis, for I have decided+ to spend ˣ the winter there.

13 *Diligently* help ˣᴵ Zenas the lawyer and Apollos on their way so that nothing is lacking~ for them.

14 And let our *people* also learn ᴹ to engage~ in *good*[25b] *deeds* to meet pressing needs, that they may not be unfruitful.

15 All who are with me greet you. Greet ˣᴵ those who love[31b] us in *the* faith.

Grace be with you all.

3:1
2 Tim. 2:14;
Rom. 13:1;
2 Tim. 2:21
3:2
1 Tim. 3:3; 1 Pet.
2:18;
2 Tim. 2:25
3:3
Rom. 11:30; Col.
3:7;
Titus 1:16;
2 Tim. 3:13;
Rom. 6:6,12;
2 Tim. 3:6; Titus
2:12;
Rom. 1:29
3:4
Rom. 2:4; Eph.
2:7; 1 Pet. 2:3;
Titus 2:10;
Titus 2:11
3:5
Rom. 11:14;
2 Tim. 1:9;
Eph. 2:9;
Eph. 2:4; 1 Pet.
1:3;
John 3:5; Eph.
5:26; 1 Pet. 3:21;
Rom. 12:2
3:6
Rom. 5:5;
Rom. 2:4; 1 Tim.
6:17
3:7
Matt. 25:34; Mark
10:17; Rom. 8:17,
24; Titus 1:2
3:8
1 Tim. 1:15;
1 Tim. 2:8;
2 Tim. 1:12;
Titus 2:7,14; 3:14
3:9
2 Tim. 2:16;
1 Tim. 1:4; 2 Tim.
2:23;
James 4:1;
2 Tim. 2:14
3:10
2 John 10;
Rom. 16:17;
Matt. 18:15f.
3:11
Titus 1:14
3:12
Acts 20:4; Eph.
6:21f.; Col. 4:7f.;
2 Tim. 4:12;
2 Tim. 4:9;
2 Tim. 4:21
3:13
Matt. 22:35;
Acts 18:24; 1 Cor.
16:12
3:14
Titus 2:8;
Titus 3:8;
Rom. 12:13; Phil.
4:16;
Matt. 7:19; Phil.
1:11; Col. 1:10
3:15
Acts 20:34;
1 Tim. 1:2;
Col. 4:18

The Epistle of Paul to
Philemon

Salutation

1 Paul, a prisoner of Christ Jesus, and Timothy our brothe Philemon our beloved *brother* and fellow worker,

2 and to Apphia our sister, and to Archippus our fellow soldier, and to the church in your house:

3 Grace to you and peace from God our Father and the Lord Jesus Christ.

Philemon's Love and Faith

4 I thank my God always, making mention of you in my prayers,

5 because I hear of your love, and of the faith which you have toward the Lord Jesus, and toward all the saints;

6 *and I pray* that the fellowship of your faith may become effective ªthrough the knowledge²⁹ᵇ of every good²⁵ᵃ thing which is in ᵇyou for Christ's sake.

7 For I have come to have *much* joy and comfort in your love, because the hearts of the saints have been refreshed* through you, brother.

8 Therefore, though I have enough confidence in Christ to order~ you *to do* that which is proper,

9 yet for *love's*³¹ᵃ *sake* I rather appeal *to you*—since I am such a person as Paul, the aged, and •now also a prisoner of Christ Jesus—

Plea for Onesimus, a Free Man

10 I appeal to you for •*my* child, whom I have begotten in my imprisonment, ᶜOnesimus,

11 who formerly was useless to you, but •*now* is useful both to you and to me.

12 And I have sent him back to you in person, that is, *sending* •*my* very heart,

13 whom I wishedᵐ to keep~ with me, that in *your behalf* he might minister~ to me in my imprisonment for the gospel;

14 but without •your consent I did not want to doˣ anything,

ªOr, *in* ᵇSome ancient mss. read *us* ᶜi.e., useful

430

that your goodness should not be as it were by compulsion, but of your own free will.

15 For perhaps he was for this reason parted *from you* for a while, that you should have~ him back *forever,*

16 no longer as a slave, but more than a slave, a *beloved* †*brother,* especially to me, but how much more to you, both in the flesh and in the Lord.

17 If then you regard †*me* a partner, accept^{xl} him as *you would* me.

18 But if he has wronged you in any way, or owes you anything, charge~ that to *my* account;

19 *I,* Paul, am writing this with my •own hand, *I* will repay^{37b} it (lest I should mention~ to you that you owe to me even your *own self* as well).

20 Yes, brother, let me benefit^x from you in the Lord; refresh^{xl} *my* heart in Christ.

21 Having confidence⁺ in your obedience, I write to you, since I know that you will do even *more* than what I say.

22 And at the same time also prepare~ me a lodging; for I hope that through your prayers I shall be given to you.

23 Epaphras, my fellow prisoner in Christ Jesus, greets you,

24 *as do* Mark, Aristarchus, Demas, Luke, my fellow workers.

25 The grace of the Lord Jesus Christ be with your ᵈspirit.

dSome ancient mss. add *Amen*

1:15
Gen. 45:5,8

1:16
1 Cor. 7:22;
Matt. 23:8; 1 Tim.
6:2;
Eph. 6:5; Col.
3:22
1:17
2 Cor. 8:23

1:19
1 Cor. 16:21;
2 Cor. 10:1; Gal.
5:2;
2 Cor. 9:4
1:20
Philem. 7
1:21
2 Cor. 2:3
1:22
Acts 28:23;
Phil. 1:25; 2:24;
2 Cor. 1:11;
Acts 27:24; Heb.
13:19
1:23
Col. 1:7; 4:12;
Rom. 16:7;
Philem. 1
1:24
Acts 12:12,25;
15:37-39; Col.
4:10;
Acts 19:29; 27:2;
Col. 4:14; 2 Tim.
4:10f.;
Philem. 1
1:25
Gal. 6:18;
2 Tim. 4:22

The Epistle to the
Hebrews

God's Final Word in His Son

1:1
John 9:29; 16:13;
Heb. 2:2f.; 3:5;
4:8; 5:5; 11:18;
12:25;
Acts 2:30; 3:21;
Num. 12:6,8; Joel
2:28
1:2
Matt. 13:39;
1 Pet. 1:20;
John 9:29;
John 5:26,27;
Heb. 3:6; 5:8;
7:28;
Ps. 2:8; Matt.
28:18; Mark 12:7;
Rom. 8:17; Heb.
2:8;
John 1:3; 1 Cor.
8:6; Col. 1:16;
1 Cor. 2:7; Heb.
11:3
1:3
2 Cor. 4:4;
Col. 1:17;
Titus 2:14; Heb.
9:14;
Mark 16:19; Heb.
8:1; 10:12; 12:2;
2 Pet. 1:17
1:4
Eph. 1:21
1:5
Ps. 2:7; Acts
13:33; Heb. 5:5;
2 Sam. 7:14
1:6
Heb. 10:5;
Matt. 24:14;
Ps. 97:7
1:7
Ps. 104:4

1:8
Ps. 45:6

1:9
Ps. 45:7;
John 10:17; Phil.
2:9; Heb. 2:9;
Is. 61:1,3

1:10
Ps. 102:25

1 God, after He spoke long ago to the fathers in the prophets in many portions and in many ways,

2 in these last days has spoken to us in *His* Son, whom He appointed heir of all things, through whom also He made the world.

3 And He is the radiance of His glory and the exact representation of His nature, and upholds all things by the word[43b] of His power. When He had made purification of sins, He sat down at the right hand of the Majesty on high;

4 having become as much better than the angels, as He has inherited[+] a *more excellent* name than they.

5 For to which of the *angels* did He ever say,

"Thou art *My Son*,
Today *I* have begotten[+] Thee"?

And again,

"*I* will be a Father to Him,
And *He* shall be a Son to Me"?

6 And when He again brings[x] the first-born into the world, He says,

"And let all the angels of God worship Him."[x144b]

7 And of the angels He says,

"Who makes His angels winds,
And His ministers a flame of fire."

8 But of the Son *He says,*

"Thy throne, O God, is forever and ever,
And the righteous scepter is the scepter of [a]His kingdom.

9 "Thou hast loved righteousness and hated lawlessness;
Therefore God, Thy God, hath anointed Thee
With the oil of gladness above Thy companions."

10 And,

"*Thou*, Lord, in the beginning didst lay the foundation of the *earth*,

[a]Some mss. read *Thy*

432

AND THE *HEAVENS* ARE THE WORKS OF THY HANDS;

11   *THEY* WILL PERISH, BUT *THOU* REMAINEST;
      AND THEY ALL WILL BECOME OLD AS A GARMENT,

12   AND AS A MANTLE THOU WILT ROLL THEM UP;
      AS A GARMENT THEY WILL ALSO BE CHANGED.
      BUT *THOU* ART THE SAME,
      AND THY YEARS WILL *NOT COME TO AN* †END."

13   But to which of the angels has He ever said,✦

      "SIT AT MY RIGHT HAND,
      UNTIL I MAKEˣ THINE ENEMIES
      A FOOTSTOOL FOR THY FEET"?

14   Are they not all ministering[38a] spirits, sent out to *render
service* for the sake of those who will inherit salvation?

Give Heed

2   For this reason we must pay~ much closer attention to what
    we have heard, lest we driftˣ away *from it.*

    2   For if the word spoken through angels proved unalterable,
and every transgression[40a] and disobedience received a just recompense,

    3   how shall *we* escape if we neglect *so great* a salvation?
After it was at the first spoken~ through the Lord, it was confirmed to us by *those who heard,*

    4   God also bearing witness with them, both by signs and
wonders and by various miracles and by gifts of the Holy Spirit
according to *His own* will.

Earth Subject to Man

    5   For He did not subject to *angels* the world to come, con-
cerning which we are speaking.

    6   But one has testified[1] somewhere, saying,

      "WHAT IS MAN, THAT THOU REMEMBEREST HIM?
      OR THE SON OF MAN, THAT THOU ART CONCERNED
        ABOUT HIM?

7   "THOU HAST MADE HIM FOR A LITTLE WHILE LOWER
        THAN THE ANGELS;
      THOU HAST CROWNED HIM WITH *GLORY* AND *HONOR,*
      bAND HAST APPOINTED HIM OVER THE WORKS OF THY
        HANDS;

8   THOU HAST PUT *ALL THINGS* IN SUBJECTION UNDER HIS
        FEET."

For in subjectingˣ all things to him, He left †*nothing* that is not

bSome ancient mss. do not contain *And . . . hands*

Cross references (right column):

1:11
Ps. 102:26;
Is. 51:6; Heb.
8:13

1:12
Ps. 102:26,27;
Heb. 13:8

1:13
Ps. 110:1; Matt.
22:44; Heb. 1:3;
Josh. 10:24; Heb.
10:13

1:14
Ps. 103:20f.; Dan.
7:10;
Matt. 25:34; Mark
10:17; Titus 3:7;
Heb. 6:12;
Rom. 11:14;
1 Cor. 1:21; Heb.
2:3; 5:9; 9:28
2:1
Prov. 3:21

2:2
Heb. 1:1;
Acts 7:53;
Heb. 10:28;
Heb. 10:35; 11:26

2:3
Heb. 10:29;
12:25;
Rom. 11:14;
1 Cor. 1:21; Heb.
1:14; 5:9; 9:28;
Heb. 1:1;
Mark 16:20; Luke
1:2; 1 John 1:1
2:4
John 4:48;
Mark 6:14;
1 Cor. 12:4,11;
Eph. 4:7;
Eph. 1:5

2:5
Matt. 24:14; Heb.
6:5

2:6
Heb. 4:4;
Ps. 8:4

2:7
Ps. 8:5,6

2:8
Ps. 8:6; 1 Cor.
15:27;
1 Cor. 15:25

subject to him. But now we do not yet see all things subjected* to him.

Jesus Briefly Humbled

2:9
Heb. 2:7;
Phil. 2:9; Heb.
1:9;
Acts 2:33; 3:13;
1 Pet. 1:21;
John 3:16;
Matt. 16:28; John
8:52;
Heb. 7:25
2:10
Luke 24:26;
Rom. 11:36;
Heb. 5:9; 7:28;
Acts 3:15; 5:31
2:11
Heb. 13:12;
Heb. 10:10;
Acts 17:28;
Matt. 25:40; Mark
3:34f.; John 20:17
2:12
Ps. 22:22

9 But we do see Him who has been made* for a little while lower than the angels, *namely,* Jesus, because of the suffering of death crowned* with *glory* and *honor,* that by the grace of God He might taste^x death *for everyone.*

10 For it was fitting for Him, for whom are all things, and through whom are all things, in bringing many sons to glory, to perfect^x the author of their salvation *through sufferings.*

11 For both He who sanctifies and those who are sanctified are all from *one Father;* for which reason He is not ashamed to call~ them *brethren,*

12 saying,

"I will proclaim Thy name to My brethren,
In the midst of the congregation I will sing Thy praise."

2:13
Is. 8:17;
Is. 8:18

13 And again,

"I will put* My trust in Him."

And again,

"Behold, I and the children whom God has given Me."

2:14
Matt. 16:17;
John 1:14;
1 Cor. 15:54-57;
2 Tim. 1:10;
John 12:31;
1 John 3:8

14 Since then the children share* in flesh and blood, *He Himself* likewise[1] also partook of the same, that *through death* He might render^x powerless him who had the power[32d] of death, that is, the devil;

2:15
Rom. 8:15

15 and might deliver^x those who through *fear of death* were subject to slavery all their lives.

16 For assuredly He does not give help to *angels,* but He gives help to the *descendant of Abraham.*

2:17
Phil. 2:7; Heb.
2:14;
Heb. 4:15f.; 5:2;
Heb. 3:1; 4:14f.;
5:5,10; 6:20;
7:26,28; 8:1,3;
9:11; 10:21;
Rom. 15:17; Heb.
5:1;
Dan. 9:24; 1 John
2:2; 4:10
2:18
Heb. 4:15
3:1
Acts 1:15; Heb.
2:11; 3:12; 10:19;
13:22;
Phil. 3:14;
John 17:3;
Heb. 2:17; 4:14f.;
5:5,10; 6:20;
7:26,28; 8:1,3;
9:11; 10:21;
2 Cor. 9:13; Heb.
4:14; 10:23

17 Therefore, He had^m to be made^x *like His brethren* in all things, that He might become a merciful and faithful high priest in things pertaining to God, to make~ propitiation for the sins of the people.

18 For since *He Himself* was tempted in that which He has suffered,* He is able to come^x to the aid of those who are tempted.

Jesus Our High Priest

3 Therefore, holy[28a] brethren, partakers of a *heavenly* calling, consider^xl Jesus, the Apostle and High Priest of our confession.

2   He was faithful to Him who appointed Him, as Moses also was in all His house.

3   For He has been counted* worthy of *more* glory than Moses, by just so much as the builder of the house has more honor than the house.

4   For every house is built by someone, but the builder of all things is God.

5   Now Moses was faithful in all His house as a servant, for a testimony of those things which were to be spoken later;

6   but Christ *was faithful* as a Son over His house whose house *we* are, if we hold* fast our confidence and the boast of our hope firm until the end.

7   Therefore, just as the Holy Spirit says,
"TODAY IF YOU HEAR* *HIS VOICE*,

8   DO NOT HARDEN⊙ YOUR HEARTS AS WHEN THEY
            PROVOKED ME,
        AS IN THE DAY OF TRIAL IN THE WILDERNESS,

9   WHERE YOUR FATHERS TRIED *Me* BY TESTING *Me*,
        AND SAW MY WORKS FOR FORTY YEARS.

10   "THEREFORE I WAS ANGRY WITH THIS GENERATION,
        AND SAID, 'THEY ALWAYS GO ASTRAY IN THEIR HEART;
        AND *THEY* DID NOT KNOW MY WAYS';

11   AS I SWORE IN MY WRATH,[7b]
        'THEY SHALL NOT ENTER MY REST.' "

The Peril of Unbelief

12   Take care,~ brethren, lest there should be in any one of you an *evil,* [10b] *unbelieving heart,* in falling* away from the living God.

13   But encourage~ one another day after day, as long as it is *still* called *"Today,"* lest any one of you be *hardened*ˣ by the deceitfulness of sin.

14   For we have become* partakers of Christ, if[2] we hold* fast the beginning of our assurance firm *until the end;*

15   while it is said,~
"TODAY IF YOU HEAR* *HIS VOICE*,
        DO NOT HARDEN⊙ YOUR HEARTS, AS WHEN THEY
            PROVOKED ME."

16   For who provoked *Him* when they had heard? Indeed, did not all those who came out of Egypt *led* by Moses?

17   And with whom was He angry for *forty* years? Was it not with those who sinned, whose bodies fell in the wilderness?

18   And to whom did He swear that they should not enter His rest, but to those who were disobedient?

3:2
Ex. 40:16; Num.
12:7; Heb. 3:5

3:3
2 Cor. 3:7-11

3:5
Ex. 40:16; Num.
12:7; Heb. 3:2;
Ex. 14:31
Deut. 18:18f.;
Heb. 1:1
3:6
Heb. 1:2;
1 Cor. 3:16;
1 Tim. 3:15;
Rom. 11:22; Heb.
3:14; 4:14;
Eph. 3:12; Heb.
4:16; 10:19,35;
Heb. 6:11; 7:19;
10:23; 11:1;
1 Pet. 1:3
3:7
Acts 28:25; Heb.
9:8; 10:15;
Ps. 95:7; Heb.
3:15; 4:7
3:8
Ps. 95:8
3:9
Ps. 95:9-11;
Acts 7:36
3:10
Ps. 95:10

3:11
Ps. 95:11; Heb.
4:3,5

3:12
Col. 2:8; Heb.
12:25;
Matt. 16:16; Heb.
9:14; 10:31;
12:22
3:13
Heb. 10:24f.;
Eph. 4:22

3:14
Heb. 3:6;
Heb. 11:1

3:15
Ps. 95:7f.; Heb.
3:7; 4:7

3:16
Jer. 32:29; 44:3,
8;
Num. 14:2,11,30;
Deut. 1:35,36,38
3:17
Num. 14:29;
1 Cor. 10:5
3:18
Num. 14:23;
Deut. 1:34f.; Heb.
4:2;
Rom. 11:30-32;
Heb. 4:6,11

19 And *so* we see that they were not able to enter[x] because of unbelief.

The Believer's Rest

4 Therefore, let us fear[x] lest, while a promise remains of entering[x] His rest, any one of you should seem~ to have come⁺ short of it.

2 For indeed we have had good news preached⁺ to us, just as they also; but the word they heard did *not profit* them, because it was not united⁺ by faith in those who heard.

3 ᶜFor we who have *believed* enter that rest, just as He has said,⁺

"As I swore in My wrath,[7b]
They shall not enter My rest,"

although His works were finished from the foundation of the world.

4 For He has thus said⁺ somewhere concerning the seventh *day*, "And God rested on the seventh day from all His works";

5 and again in this *passage*, "They shall not enter My rest."

6 Since therefore it remains for some to enter[x] it, and those who formerly had good news preached to them failed to enter because of disobedience,

7 He again fixes a certain day, "Today," saying through David after so long a time just as has been said⁺ before,

"Today if you hear[x] *His voice*,
Do not harden° your hearts."

8 For if Joshua had given *them* rest, He would not have spoken[m] of *another* day after that.

9 There *remains* therefore a Sabbath rest for the people of God.

10 For the one who has entered His rest has himself also rested from his works, as *God* did from His.

11 Let us therefore be diligent[x] to enter[x] that rest, lest anyone fall[x] through *following* the *same* example of disobedience.

12 For the word[43a] of God is *living* and active and sharper than any two-edged sword, and piercing as far as the division of soul and spirit, of both joints and marrow, and able to judge the thoughts and intentions of the heart.

13 And there is no creature hidden from His sight, but all things are open and laid⁺ bare to the eyes of Him with whom we have to do.

ᶜSome ancient mss. read *Therefore*

14 Since then we have a great high priest who has passed⁺ through the heavens, Jesus the Son of God, let us hold~ fast our confession.

15 For we do not have a high priest who cannot sympathize˟ with our weaknesses, but one who has been tempted⁺ in all things as *we are, yet* without sin.

16 Let us therefore draw~ near with confidence to the throne of grace, that we may receive˟ mercy and may find˟ *grace* to help in time of need.

The Perfect High Priest

5 For every high priest taken from among men is appointed on behalf of men in things pertaining to God, in order to offer~ both gifts and sacrifices for sins;

2 he can deal~ gently with the ignorant and misguided, since *he himself also* is beset with weakness;

3 and because of it he is obligated to offer~ *sacrifices* for sins, as for the people, so also for himself.

4 And no one takes the honor to himself, but *receives it* when he is called by God, even as Aaron was.

5 So also Christ did not glorify *Himself* so as to become a high priest, but He who said to Him,

"Tʜᴏᴜ ᴀʀᴛ *Mʏ Sᴏɴ*,
Tᴏᴅᴀʏ *I* ʜᴀᴠᴇ ʙᴇɢᴏᴛᴛᴇɴ⁺ Tʜᴇᴇ";

6 just as He says also in another *passage*,

"Tʜᴏᴜ ᴀʀᴛ ᴀ ᴘʀɪᴇsᴛ ꜰᴏʀᴇᴠᴇʀ
Aᴄᴄᴏʀᴅɪɴɢ ᴛᴏ ᴛʜᴇ ᴏʀᴅᴇʀ ᴏꜰ Mᴇʟᴄʜɪᴢᴇᴅᴇᴋ."

7 In the days of His flesh, He offered up both prayers and supplications with *loud* crying and tears to the One able to save~ Him from death, and He was heard because of His piety.

8 Although[2] He was a Son, He learned obedience from the things which *He suffered.*

9 And having been made perfect, He became to all those who obey Him the source of eternal salvation,

10 being designated by God as a high priest according to the order of Melchizedek.

11 Concerning ᵈhim we have much to say, and *it is* hard to explain, ~ since you have become⁺ *dull* of hearing.

12 For though by this time you ought to be teachers, you have need again for someone to teach~ you the elementary principles of the oracles of God, and you have come⁺ to need milk and not solid food.

ᵈOr, *Him;* or, *this*

4:14
Heb. 2:17;
Eph. 4:10; Heb.
6:20; 8:1; 9:24;
Matt. 4:3; Heb.
1:2; 6:6; 7:3;
10:29;
Heb. 3:1
4:15
Heb. 2:17;
Heb. 2:18;
2 Cor. 5:21; Heb.
7:26
4:16
Heb. 7:19;
Heb. 3:6

5:1
Ex. 28:1;
Heb. 2:17; 8:3f.;
9:9; 10:11;
1 Cor. 15:3; Heb.
7:27; 10:12
5:2
Heb. 2:18; 4:15;
Eph. 4:18; Heb.
9:7 mg.;
James 5:19;
1 Pet. 2:25;
Heb. 7:28
5:3
1 Cor. 15:3; Heb.
7:27; 10:12;
Lev. 9:7; 16:6;
Heb. 9:7
5:4
Num. 16:40; 18:7;
2 Chr. 26:18;
Ex. 28:1; 1 Chr.
23:13
5:5
John 8:54;
Heb. 2:17; 5:10;
Heb. 1:1,5;
Ps. 2:7
5:6
Ps. 110:4; Heb.
7:17;
Heb. 5:10; 6:20;
7:11
5:7
Matt. 26:39,42,
44; Mark 14:36,
39; Luke 22:41,
44;
Matt. 27:46,50;
Mark 15:34,37;
Luke 23:46;
Mark 14:36;
Heb. 11:7; 12:28
5:8
Heb. 1:2;
Phil. 2:8
5:9
Heb. 2:10
5:10
Heb. 2:17; 5:5;
Heb. 5:6

5:12
Gal. 4:3;
Heb. 6:1;
Acts 7:38;
1 Cor. 3:2; 1 Pet.
2:2

5:13
1 Cor. 3:1; 14:20;
1 Pet. 2:2

13   For everyone who partakes *only* of milk is not accustomed to the word of righteousness, for he is a †*babe.*

5:14
1 Cor. 2:6; Eph.
4:13; Heb. 6:1;
1 Tim. 4:7;
Rom. 14:1ff.

14   But solid food is for the *mature,* who because of practice have their senses trained✝ to discern good25b and evil. 10a

The Peril of Falling Away

6:1
Phil. 3:13f.;
Heb. 5:12;
Heb. 5:14;
Heb. 9:14

6   Therefore leaving the elementary teaching about the Christ, let us press~ on to *maturity,* not laying again a foundation of repentance from dead works and of faith toward God,

6:2
John 3:25; Acts
19:3f.;
Acts 6:6;
Acts 17:31f.
6:3
Acts 18:21
6:4
2 Cor. 4:4,6; Heb.
10:32;
John 4:10; Eph.
2:8;
Gal. 3:2; Heb. 2:4
6:5
1 Pet. 2:3;
Eph. 6:17;
Heb. 2:5
6:6
Matt. 19:26; Heb.
10:26f.; 2 Pet.
2:21; 1 John 5:16;
Heb. 10:29
6:7
2 Tim. 2:6

2   of instruction about washings, and laying on of hands, and the resurrection of the dead, and eternal judgment.

3   And this we shall do, if2 God permits. ~6c

4   For in the case of those who have once been enlightened and have tasted of the *heavenly* gift24a and have been made partakers of the *Holy Spirit,*

5   and have tasted the good word43b of *God* and the powers32a of the age to come,

6   and *then* have fallen away, it is *impossible* to renew~ them again to repentance, since they again crucify to themselves the Son of God, and put Him to open shame.

7   For ground that drinks the rain which often falls upon it and brings forth vegetation useful to those for whose sake it is also tilled, receives a blessing from God;

6:8
Gen. 3:17f.; Deut.
29:22ff.

8   but if it yields thorns and thistles, it is worthless and close to being *cursed,* and it ends up being burned.

Better Things for You

6:9
1 Cor. 10:14;
2 Cor. 7:1; 12:19;
1 Pet. 2:11; 2 Pet.
3:1; 1 John 2:7;
Jude 3
6:10
Prov. 19:17; Matt.
10:42; 25:40;
Acts 10:4;
1 Thess. 1:3;
Rom. 15:25; Heb.
10:32-34
6:11
Heb. 10:22;
Heb. 3:6
6:12
Heb. 13:7;
2 Thess. 1:4;
James 1:3; Rev.
13:10;
Heb. 1:14
6:13
Gal. 3:15,18;
Gen. 22:16; Luke
1:73
6:14
Gen. 22:17
6:15
Gen. 12:4; 21:5
6:16
Gal. 3:15;
Ex. 22:11

9   But, beloved, we are convinced✝ of better things concerning you, and things that accompany salvation, though we are speaking in this way.

10   For God is *not unjust* so as to forgetˣ your work and the love which you have shown toward His name, in having ministered38a and in still ministering to the saints.

11   And we desire that each one of you show~ the *same* diligence so as to realize the full assurance of hope until the end,

12   that you may not be †*sluggish,* but imitators of those who through faith and patience inherit the promises.

13   For when God made the promise to Abraham, since He couldᵐ swearˣ by no one greater, 26a He swore by Himself,

14   saying, "I WILL SURELY4 BLESS YOU, AND I WILL SURELY4 MULTIPLY YOU."

15   And thus, having patiently waited, he obtained the promise.

16   For men swear by one greater *than themselves,* and with

them an oath *given* as confirmation is an end of every dispute.

17   In the same way God, desiring even more to show[x] to the heirs of the promise the unchangeableness of His purpose, interposed with an oath,

18   in order that by *two unchangeable* things, in which it is impossible for God to lie,[x] we may have[~] *strong encouragement,* we who have fled for refuge in laying hold[x] of the hope set before us.

19   This hope we have as an *anchor* of the soul, a *hope* both sure and steadfast and one which enters within the veil,

20   where Jesus has entered as a forerunner *for us,* having become a high priest forever according to the order of Melchizedek.

Melchizedek's Priesthood Like Christ's

7 For this Melchizedek, king of Salem, priest of the Most High God, who met Abraham as he was returning from the slaughter of the kings and blessed him,

2   to whom also Abraham apportioned a *tenth part* of all *the spoils,* was first of all, by the translation *of his name,* king of righteousness, and then also king of Salem, which is king of peace.

3   Without father, without mother, without genealogy, having neither beginning of days nor *end* of life, but made[*] like the Son of God, he abides a priest perpetually.

4   Now observe[⌐] how great this man was to whom Abraham, the *patriarch,* gave a *tenth* of the choicest spoils.

5   And those indeed of the sons of Levi who receive the priest's office have commandment in the Law to collect[~] a tenth from the people, that is, from their brethren, although[2] these are descended[*] from Abraham.

6   But the one whose genealogy is not traced from them collected[*] a tenth from Abraham, and blessed[*] the one who had the promises.

7   But without any dispute the lesser is blessed by the greater.

8   And in this case •mortal men receive tithes, but in that case one *receives them,* of whom it is witnessed that he lives on.

9   And, so to speak,[x] through Abraham *even Levi,* who received[*] tithes, paid tithes,

10   for he was still in the loins of his father when Melchizedek met him.

11   Now if perfection was through the *Levitical priesthood* (for on the basis of it the people received[*] the Law), what further

---

6:17
Heb. 11:9;
Ps. 110:4; Prov.
19:21; Heb. 6:18

6:18
Num. 23:19; Titus
1:2;
Heb. 3:6; 7:19

6:19
Ps. 39:7; 62:5;
Acts 23:6; Rom.
4:18; 5:4,5; 1 Cor.
13:13; Col. 1:27;
1 Pet. 1:3;
Lev. 16:2,15;
Heb. 9:3,7
6:20
John 14:2; Heb.
4:14;
Ps. 110:4; Heb.
2:17; 5:6

7:1
Gen. 14:18-20;
Heb. 7:6;
Mark 5:7

7:3
Heb. 7:6;
Matt. 4:3; Heb.
7:1,28

7:4
Acts 2:29; 7:8f.;
Gen. 14:20

7:5
Num. 18:21,26;
2 Chr. 31:4f.

7:6
Heb. 7:3;
Heb. 7:1f.;
Rom. 4:13

7:8
Heb. 5:6; 6:20

7:11
Heb. 7:18f.; 8:7;
Heb. 9:6; 10:1;
Heb. 5:6; 7:17

need *was there* for *another*[8b] priest to arise~ according to the order of Melchizedek, and not be designated~ according to the order of Aaron?

12   For when the priesthood is changed, of necessity there takes place a change of *law* also.

7:13
Heb. 7:14;
Heb. 7:11

13   For the one concerning whom these things are spoken belongs[+] to *another*[8b] tribe, from which no one has officiated[+] at the altar.

7:14
Num. 24:17; Is.
11:1; Mic. 5:2;
Matt. 2:6; Rev.
5:5

14   For it is evident that our Lord was descended[+] from *Judah,* a tribe with reference to which Moses spoke nothing concerning priests.

15   And this is *clearer still,*[1] if *another*[8b] priest arises according to the likeness of Melchizedek,

7:16
Heb. 9:10;
Heb. 9:14

16   who has become[+] *such* not on the basis of a law of *physical* requirement, but according to the power[32a] of an *indestructible* life.[30b]

7:17
Ps. 110:4; Heb.
5:6; 6:20; 7:21

17   For it is witnessed *of Him,*

     "THOU ART A PRIEST FOREVER

     ACCORDING TO THE ORDER OF MELCHIZEDEK."

7:18
Rom. 8:3; Gal.
3:21; Heb. 7:11

18   For, on the one hand, there is a setting aside of a former commandment because of its weakness and uselessness

7:19
Acts 13:39; Rom.
3:20; 7:7f.; Gal.
2:16; 3:21; Heb.
9:9;
Heb. 3:6;
Lam. 3:57; Heb.
4:16; 7:25; 10:1,
22; James 4:8

19   (for the *Law* made nothing perfect), and on the other hand there is a bringing in of a better hope, through which we draw near to God.

20   And inasmuch as *it was* not without an oath

7:21
Ps. 110:4; Heb.
5:6; 7:17;
Num. 23:19;
1 Sam. 15:29;
Rom. 11:29;
Heb. 7:23f.,28

21   (for they indeed became[+] priests without an oath, but He *with an* [†]*oath* through the One who said to Him,

     "THE LORD HAS SWORN

     AND WILL NOT CHANGE HIS MIND,

     'THOU ART A PRIEST FOREVER' ");

7:22
Ps. 119:122; Is.
38:14;
Heb. 8:6

22   so much the more also *Jesus* has become[+] the guarantee of a better covenant.

7:24
Is. 9:7; John
12:34; Rom. 9:5;
Heb. 7:23f.,28

23   And the *former* priests, on the one hand, existed[+] in greater numbers, because they were prevented~ by [†]*death* from continuing,~

7:25
1 Cor. 1:21;
Heb. 7:19;
Rom. 8:34; Heb.
9:24

24   but He, on the other hand, because He abides~ forever, holds His priesthood *permanently.*

7:26
Heb. 2:17;
2 Cor. 5:21; Heb.
4:15;
1 Pet. 2:22;
Heb. 4:14

25   Hence, also, He is able to *save*~ *forever* those who draw near to God through Him, since He always lives to make~ intercession for them.

7:27
Heb. 5:1;
Lev. 9:7; Heb.
5:3;
Heb. 9:12;
Eph. 5:2; Heb.
9:14,28; 10:10,
12

26   For it was fitting that we should have such a high priest, holy,[28b] innocent, undefiled, separated[+] from sinners and exalted above the heavens;

27   who does not need daily, like those high priests, to offer~

up sacrifices, first for His •*own* sins, and then for the *sins* of the people, because this He did *once for all* when He offered up †*Himself.*

28   For the Law appoints men as high priests who are weak, but the word of the oath, which came after the Law, *appoints* a †*Son,* made⁺ perfect forever.

A Better Ministry

8 Now the main point in what has been said *is this*: we have such a high priest, who has taken His seat at the right hand of the throne of the Majesty in the heavens,

2   a minister in the *sanctuary,* and in the *true* tabernacle, which the *Lord* pitched, not man.

3   For every high priest is appointed to offer~ both gifts and sacrifices; hence it is necessary that *this high priest* also have something to offer.ˣ

4   Now if He were on earth, He would not be a priest at all, since there are those who offer the gifts according to the Law;

5   who serve a *copy* and *shadow* of the heavenly things, just as Moses was warned⁺ *by God* when he was about to erect the tabernacle; for, "SEE,"ᴹ He says, "THAT YOU MAKE all things ACCORDING TO THE PATTERN WHICH WAS SHOWN YOU ON THE MOUNTAIN."

6   But now He has obtained⁺ a *more excellent* ministry, by as much as He is also the mediator of a *better* covenant, which has been enacted⁺ on *better promises.*

A New Covenant

7   For if that †first *covenant* had been faultless, there would have been no occasion sought for a *second.*

8   For finding fault with them, He says,

"BEHOLD, DAYS ARE COMING, SAYS THE LORD,
WHEN I WILL EFFECT A NEW³⁴ᵃ COVENANT
WITH THE HOUSE OF ISRAEL AND WITH THE HOUSE OF
    JUDAH;

9   NOT LIKE THE COVENANT WHICH I MADE WITH THEIR
    FATHERS
ON THE DAY WHEN I TOOK THEM BY THE HAND
TO LEADˣ THEM OUT OF THE LAND OF EGYPT;
FOR *THEY* DID NOT CONTINUE IN MY COVENANT,
AND *I* DID NOT CARE FOR THEM, SAYS THE LORD.

10   "FOR THIS IS THE COVENANT THAT I WILL MAKE WITH
    THE HOUSE OF ISRAEL
AFTER THOSE DAYS, SAYS THE LORD:

7:28
Heb. 5:2;
Heb. 1:2;
Heb. 2:10

8:1
Col. 3:1; Heb.
2:17; 3:1;
Ps. 110:1; Heb.
1:3

8:2
Heb. 10:11;
Heb. 9:11,24;
Ex. 33:7

8:3
Heb. 2:17;
Rom. 4:25; 5:6,8;
Gal. 2:20; Eph.
5:2; Heb. 5:1; 8:4

8:4
Heb. 5:1; 7:27;
8:3; 9:9; 10:11

8:5
Heb. 9:23;
Col. 2:17; Heb.
10:1;
Matt. 2:12; Heb.
11:7; 12:25;
Ex. 25:40

8:6
1 Tim. 2:5;
Luke 22:20; Heb.
7:22; 8:8; 9:15;
12:24

8:7
Heb. 7:11

8:8
Jer. 31:31;
Luke 22:20;
2 Cor. 3:6; Heb.
7:22; 8:6,13;
9:15; 12:24

8:9
Ex. 19:5; 24:6-8;
Deut. 5:2,3; Jer.
31:32

8:10
Jer. 31:33; Rom.
11:27; Heb.
10:16;
2 Cor. 3:3

I WILL PUT MY LAWS INTO THEIR MINDS,[33a]
AND I WILL WRITE THEM UPON THEIR HEARTS.
AND I WILL BE THEIR GOD,
AND *THEY* SHALL BE MY PEOPLE.

11   "AND THEY SHALL •NOT TEACH[x] EVERYONE HIS FELLOW
CITIZEN,
AND EVERYONE HIS BROTHER, SAYING, 'KNOW[xl29a] THE
LORD,'
FOR †ALL SHALL KNOW[29e] ME,
FROM THE LEAST TO THE GREATEST OF THEM.

12   "FOR I WILL BE MERCIFUL TO THEIR INIQUITIES,
AND I WILL REMEMBER[x] *THEIR SINS NO MORE.*"

13   When He said,[x] "A new[34a] *covenant,*" He has made• the
first obsolete. But whatever is becoming obsolete and growing
old is ready to disappear.

The Old and the New

9   Now even the first *covenant* had[m] regulations of divine worship[44a] and the earthly sanctuary.

2   For there was a tabernacle prepared, the outer one, in
which *were* the lampstand and the table and the sacred bread;
this is called the holy place.

3   And behind the second veil, there was a tabernacle which
is called the Holy of Holies,

4   having a golden altar of incense and the ark of the covenant covered• on all sides with gold, in which *was* a golden jar
holding the manna, and Aaron's rod which budded, and the
tables of the covenant.

5   And above it *were* the cherubim of glory overshadowing
the mercy seat; but of these things we cannot now speak~ in
detail.

6   Now when these things have been thus prepared,• the
priests are continually entering the outer tabernacle, performing
the divine worship,[44a]

7   but into the second only the high priest *enters, once a year,*
not without *taking* blood, which he offers for himself and for the
sins of the people committed in ignorance.

8   The Holy Spirit *is* signifying this, that the way into the holy
place has not yet been disclosed,• while the outer tabernacle is
still standing,

9   which *is* a symbol for the *present* time. Accordingly both
gifts and sacrifices are offered which cannot make[x] the worshiper
perfect in conscience,

10   since they *relate* only to food and drink and various wash-

ings, regulations for the body imposed until a time of reformation.

11   But when Christ appeared *as* a high priest of the good[25a] things ᵉto come, *He entered* through the greater and more perfect tabernacle, not made with hands, that is to say, not of this creation;

12   and not through the blood of goats and calves, but through His *own blood,* He entered the holy place *once for all,* having obtained eternal ᵗredemption.

13   For if the blood of goats and bulls and the ashes of a heifer sprinkling those who have been defiled,⁺[17a] sanctify for the cleansing of the flesh,

14   how much more will the blood of Christ, who through the eternal Spirit offered *Himself* without blemish[11b] to God, cleanse your conscience from dead works to serve~[38c] the living God?

15   And for this reason He is the mediator of a *new*[34a] covenant, in order that since a *death* has taken place for the redemption of the transgressions[40a] that were *committed* under the first covenant, those who have been called⁺ may receiveˣ the promise of the *eternal inheritance.*

16   For where a covenant is, there must of necessity be the *death* of the one who made it.

17   For a covenant is valid *only* when men are dead, ᶠfor it is never in force while the one who made it lives.

18   Therefore even the first *covenant* was not inaugurated⁺ without ᵗblood.

19   For when every commandment had been spoken by Moses to all the people according to the Law, he took the blood of the calves and the goats, with water and scarlet wool and hyssop, and sprinkled both the book itself and all the people,

20   saying, "THIS IS THE BLOOD OF THE COVENANT WHICH *GOD* COMMANDED YOU."

21   And in the same way he sprinkled both the tabernacle and all the vessels of the ministry with the blood.

22   And according to the Law, *one may* almost *say,* all things are cleansed *with blood,* and without shedding of blood there is *no forgiveness.*

23   Therefore it was necessary for the copies of the things in the heavens to be cleansed~ with these, but the heavenly things themselves with better sacrifices than these.

24   For Christ did not enter a holy place made *with hands,* a *mere* copy of the true one, but into heaven itself, now to appearˣ in the presence of God for us;

ᵉSome ancient mss. read *that have come*   ᶠSome ancient mss. read *for is it then . . . lives?*

9:11
Heb. 2:17;
Heb. 10:1;
Heb. 8:2; 9:24;
Mark 14:58;
2 Cor. 5:1;
2 Cor. 4:18; Heb.
12:27; 13:14
9:12
Lev. 4:3; 16:6,15;
Heb. 9:19;
Heb. 9:14; 13:12;
Heb. 9:24;
Heb. 7:27;
Heb. 5:9; 9:15
9:13
Lev. 16:15; Heb.
9:19; 10:4;
Num. 19:9,17f.

9:14
Heb. 9:12; 13:12;
1 Cor. 15:45;
1 Pet. 3:18;
Eph. 5:2; Heb.
7:27; 10:10,12;
Acts 15:9; Titus
2:14; Heb. 1:3;
10:2,22;
Heb. 6:1;
Matt. 16:16; Heb.
3:12
9:15
Rom. 3:24;
1 Tim. 2:5; Heb.
8:6; 12:24;
Heb. 8:8;
Matt. 22:3ff.;
Rom. 8:28f.; Heb.
3:1;
Heb. 6:15; 10:36;
11:39;
Acts 20:32

9:19
Heb. 1:1;
Ex. 24:6ff.;
Heb. 9:12;
Lev. 14:4,7; Num.
19:6,18;
Ex. 24:7

9:20
Ex. 24:8; Matt.
26:28

9:21
Ex. 24:6; 40:9;
Lev. 8:15,19;
16:14-16
9:22
Lev. 5:11f.;
Lev. 17:11

9:23
Heb. 8:5

9:24
Heb. 4:14; 9:12;
Heb. 8:2;
Heb. 9:12;
Matt. 18:10; Heb.
7:25

9:25
Heb. 9:7;
Heb. 9:2; 10:19

9:26
Matt. 25:34; Heb.
4:3;
Heb. 7:27; Heb.
13:39; Heb.
1:2;
1 John 3:5,8;
Heb. 9:12,14

9:27
Gen. 3:19;
2 Cor. 5:10; 1
John 4:17

9:28
Heb. 7:27;
Is. 53:12; 1 Pet.
2:24;
Acts 1:11;
Heb. 5:9;
Heb. 4:15;
1 Cor. 1:7; Titus
2:13

10:1
Heb. 8:5;
Heb. 9:11;
Rom. 8:3; Heb.
9:9; 10:4,11;
Heb. 7:19

10:2
1 Pet. 2:19

10:3
Heb. 9:7

10:4
Heb. 10:1,11;
Heb. 9:12f.

10:5
Heb. 1:6;
Ps. 40:6;
Heb. 2:14; 5:7;
1 Pet. 2:24

10:6
Ps. 40:6

10:7
Ps. 40:7,8;
Ezra 6:2; Jer.
36:2; Ezek. 2:9;
3:1f.

10:8
Ps. 40:6; Heb.
10:5f.;
Mark 12:33;
Rom. 8:3

10:9
Ps. 40:7,8; Heb.
10:7

10:10
John 17:19; Eph.
5:26; Heb. 2:11;
10:14,29; 13:12;
John 6:51; Eph.
5:2; Heb. 7:27;
9:14,28; 10:12;
Heb. 2:14; 5:7; 1
Pet. 2:24

10:11
Heb. 5:1;
Mic. 6:6-8; Heb.
10:1,4

25　nor was it that He should offer~ Himself often, as the high priest enters the holy place year by year with blood not his own.

26　Otherwise, He would^m have needed to suffer^x often since the foundation of the world; but •now *once* at the consummation[1] of the ages He has been manifested* to put away sin by the sacrifice of Himself.

27　And inasmuch as it is appointed for men to die^x once and after this *comes* judgment,

28　so Christ also, having been offered once to bear^x the sins of *many*, shall appear a second time for salvation without *reference to* sin, to those who eagerly[1] await Him.

One Sacrifice of Christ Is Sufficient

10　For the Law, since it has *only* a *shadow* of the good things to come *and* not the very form[22b] of things, 9can never by the *same sacrifices* year by year, which they offer continually, make^x perfect those who draw near.

2　Otherwise, would they not have ceased to be offered, because the worshipers, having once been cleansed,* would no longer have had consciousness of sins?

3　But in those *sacrifices* there is a reminder of sins year by year.

4　For it is impossible for the blood of bulls and goats to take~ away sins.

5　Therefore, when He comes into the world, He says,

"SACRIFICE AND OFFERING THOU HAST NOT DESIRED,
BUT A *BODY* THOU HAST PREPARED FOR ME;

6　IN WHOLE BURNT OFFERINGS AND *sacrifices* FOR SIN
THOU HAST TAKEN NO PLEASURE.

7　"THEN I SAID, 'BEHOLD, I HAVE COME
(IN THE ROLL OF THE BOOK IT IS WRITTEN* OF ME)
TO DO^x THY †WILL, O GOD.'"

8　After saying above, "SACRIFICES AND OFFERINGS AND WHOLE BURNT OFFERINGS AND *sacrifices* FOR SIN THOU HAST NOT DESIRED, NOR HAST THOU TAKEN PLEASURE *in them*" (which are offered according to the Law),

9　then He said,* "BEHOLD, I HAVE COME TO DO^x THY WILL." He takes away the first in order to establish^x the second.

10　By this will we have been sanctified* through the offering of the body of Jesus Christ *once for all*.

11　And every priest stands daily ministering[38d] and offering time after time the *same* sacrifices, which can never take^x away sins;

9Some ancient mss. read *they can*

12　but He, having offered *one* sacrifice for sins for *all time,* SAT DOWN AT THE RIGHT HAND OF GOD,

13　waiting from that time onward UNTIL HIS ENEMIES BE MADE[x] A FOOTSTOOL FOR HIS FEET.

14　For by *one* offering He has perfected[+] for all time those who are sanctified.

15　And the *Holy Spirit also* bears witness to us; for after saying,[+]

16　"THIS IS THE COVENANT THAT I WILL MAKE WITH THEM
AFTER THOSE DAYS, SAYS THE LORD:
I WILL PUT MY LAWS UPON THEIR HEART,
AND UPON THEIR MIND[33a] I WILL WRITE THEM,"

He then says,

17　"AND THEIR SINS AND THEIR LAWLESS DEEDS
I WILL REMEMBER *NO MORE.*"

18　Now where there is forgiveness of these things, there is no longer *any* offering for sin.

A New and Living Way

19　Since therefore, brethren, we have confidence to enter the holy place by the blood of Jesus,

20　by a new and living way which He inaugurated for us through the veil, that is, His flesh,

21　and since *we have* a great priest over the house of God,

22　let us draw~ near with a sincere heart in full assurance of faith, having our hearts sprinkled[+] *clean* from an evil conscience and our bodies washed[+] with pure[13c] water.

23　Let us hold~ fast the confession of our hope *without wavering,* for He who promised is *faithful;*

24　and let us consider~ how to stimulate one another to love[31a] and good[25b] deeds,

25　not forsaking our own assembling together, as is the habit of some, but encouraging *one another*; and all the more, as you see the day drawing near.

Christ or Judgment

26　For if we go on sinning willfully after receiving[x] the knowledge[29b] of the truth, there no longer remains a *sacrifice* for sins,

27　but a certain terrifying expectation of judgment, and THE FURY OF A FIRE WHICH WILL CONSUME THE ADVERSARIES.

28　Anyone who has set aside the Law of Moses dies without mercy on *the testimony of* two or three witnesses.

29　How much *severer* punishment do you think he will deserve who has trampled under foot the Son of God, and has

regarded as ✝unclean[41b] the blood of the covenant by which he was sanctified, and has insulted the Spirit of ✝grace?

30 For we know Him who said, "VENGEANCE IS ✝MINE, I WILL REPAY."[37a] And again, "THE LORD WILL JUDGE HIS PEOPLE."

31 It is a terrifying thing to fall[x] into the hands of the living God.

32 But remember[m] the former days, when, after being enlightened, you endured a great[26b] conflict of sufferings,

33 partly, by being made a public spectacle through reproaches and tribulations, and partly by becoming sharers with those who were so treated.

34 For you showed sympathy to the prisoners, and accepted joyfully the seizure of your property, knowing that you have for yourselves a better possession and an abiding one.

35 Therefore, do not throw[o] away your confidence, which has a great[26a] reward.

36 For you have need of *endurance*, so that when you have done[19a] the will of ✝God, you may receive[x] what was promised.

37 FOR YET IN A VERY LITTLE WHILE,
HE WHO IS COMING WILL COME, AND WILL NOT DELAY.

38 BUT MY RIGHTEOUS ONE SHALL LIVE BY *FAITH*;
AND IF HE SHRINKS[x] BACK, MY SOUL HAS NO PLEASURE
    IN HIM.

39 But *we* are not of those who shrink back to destruction, but of those who have faith to the preserving of the soul.

The Triumphs of Faith

11 Now faith is the *assurance* of *things* hoped for, the *conviction* of things *not* seen.

2 For by it the men of old *gained approval.*

3 By *faith* we understand[29d] that the worlds were prepared[+] by the word[43b] of God, so that what is seen was not made[+] out of things which are visible.

4 By *faith* Abel offered to God a *better sacrifice* than Cain, through which he obtained the testimony that he was righteous, God testifying about his gifts, and through faith, though he is dead, he still speaks.

5 By *faith* Enoch was taken up so that he should not see[x] death; AND HE WAS NOT FOUND[xxx] BECAUSE GOD TOOK HIM UP; for he obtained[+] the witness that before his being taken up he was pleasing[+] to God.

6 And without faith it is impossible to please[x] *Him*, for he who comes to God must believe[x] that He is, and *that* He is a *rewarder* of those who seek Him.

10:30
Deut. 32:35;
Rom. 12:19;
Deut. 32:36
10:31
2 Cor. 5:11;
Matt. 16:16; Heb.
3:12
10:32
Heb. 5:12;
Heb. 6:4;
Phil. 1:30
10:33
1 Cor. 4:9; Heb.
12:4;
Phil. 4:14; 1
Thess. 2:14

10:34
Heb. 13:3;
Matt. 5:12;
Heb. 9:15; 11:16;
13:14; 1 Pet. 1:4f.

10:35
Heb. 10:19;
Heb. 2:2

10:36
Luke 21:19; Heb.
12:1;
Mark 3:35;
Heb. 9:15
10:37
Hab. 2:3; Heb.
10:25; Rev.
22:20;
Matt. 11:3
10:38
Hab. 2:4; Rom.
1:17; Gal. 3:11

11:1
Heb. 3:14;
Heb. 3:6;
Rom. 8:24; 2 Cor.
4:18; 5:7; Heb.
11:7,27
11:2
Heb. 1:1;
Heb. 11:4,39
11:3
John 1:3; Heb.
1:2;
Gen. ch. 1; Ps.
33:6,9; Heb. 6:5;
2 Pet. 3:5;
Rom. 4:17
11:4
Gen. 4:4; Matt.
23:35; 1 John
3:12;
Heb. 11:2;
Heb. 5:1;
Gen. 4:8-10; Heb.
12:24
11:5
Gen. 5:21-24;
Luke 2:26; John
8:51; Heb. 2:9
11:6
Heb. 7:19

7   By *faith* Noah, being warned *by God* about things not yet seen, in reverence prepared an ark for the salvation of his household, by which he condemned [14c] the world, and became an heir of the *righteousness* which is *according to faith.*

8   By *faith* Abraham, when he was called, obeyed by going[x] out to a place which he was to receive for an inheritance; and he went out, not knowing where he was going.

9   By *faith* he lived as an alien in the land of promise, as in a foreign *land*, dwelling in tents with Isaac and Jacob, fellow heirs of the same promise;

10   for he was looking[m] for the city which has foundations, whose architect and builder is *God.*

11   By *faith* even Sarah herself received *ability* to conceive, even beyond the proper time of life, since she considered Him *faithful* who had promised;

12   therefore, also, there was born of *one man,* and him as good as dead at that, *as many descendants* AS THE STARS OF HEAVEN IN NUMBER, AND INNUMERABLE AS THE SAND WHICH IS BY THE SEASHORE.

13   All these died *in faith,* without receiving the promises, but having seen them and having welcomed them from a distance, and having confessed that they were *strangers* and *exiles* on the earth.

14   For those who say such things make it clear that they are seeking[1] a *country of their own.*

15   And indeed if they had been thinking[m] of that *country* from which they went out, they would have had opportunity to return.[x]

16   But as it is, they desire a *better country*, that is a [†]*heavenly* one. Therefore God is not ashamed to be called[~] *their* God; for He has prepared a city for them.

17   By *faith* Abraham, when he was tested, offered[+] up Isaac; and he who had received the promises was offering[m] up his *only begotten son*;

18   *it was he* to whom it was said, " IN ISAAC YOUR DESCENDANTS SHALL BE CALLED."

19   He considered that God is able to raise[~] *men even from the dead;* from which he also received him back as a *type.*

20   By *faith* Isaac blessed Jacob and Esau, even regarding things to come.

21   By *faith* Jacob, as he was dying, blessed each of the sons of Joseph, and worshiped, *leaning* on the top of his staff.

22   By *faith* Joseph, when he was dying, made mention of the

11:7
Gen. 6:13-22;
Heb. 8:5;
Heb. 11:1;
Heb. 5:7;
1 Pet. 3:20;
Gen. 6:9; Ezek.
14:14,20; Rom.
4:13; 9:30
11:8
Gen. 12:1-4; Acts
7:2-4;
Gen. 12:7
11:9
Acts 7:5;
Gen. 12:8; 13:3,
18; 18:1,9;
Heb. 6:17
11:10
Heb. 12:22;
13:14;
Rev. 21:14ff.;
Heb. 11:16
11:11
Gen. 17:19;
18:11-14; 21:2;
Heb. 10:23
11:12
Rom. 4:19;
Gen. 15:5; 22:17;
32:12
11:13
Matt. 13:17;
Heb. 11:39;
John 8:56; Heb.
11:27;
Gen. 23:4; 47:9; 1
Chr. 29:15; Ps.
39:12; Eph. 2:19;
1 Pet. 1:1; 2:11
11:15
Gen. 24:6-8
11:16
2 Tim. 4:18;
Mark 8:38; Heb.
2:11;
Gen. 26:24;
28:13; Ex. 3:6,15;
4:5;
Heb. 11:10; Rev.
21:2
11:17
Gen. 22:1-10;
James 2:21;
Heb. 11:13
11:18
Gen. 21:12; Rom.
9:7
11:19
Rom. 4:21;
Heb. 9:9
11:20
Gen. 27:27-29,
39f.
11:21
Gen. 48:1,5,16,
20;
Gen. 47:31;
1 Kin. 1:47
11:22
Gen. 50:24f.; Ex.
13:19

exodus of the sons of Israel, and gave orders concerning his bones.

11:23
Ex. 2:2;
Ex. 1:16,22

23 By *faith* Moses, when he was born, was hidden for three months by his parents, because they saw he was a beautiful child; and they were not afraid of the king's edict.

11:24
Ex. 2:10,11ff.
11:25
Heb. 11:37
11:26
Luke 14:33; Phil.
3:7f.;
Heb. 2:2
11:27
Ex. 2:15; 12:50f.;
13:17f.;
Ex. 2:14; 10:28f.;
Col. 1:15; Heb.
11:1,13
11:28
Ex. 12:21ff.;
Ex. 12:23,29f.; 1
Cor. 10:10
11:29
Ex. 14:22-29
11:30
Josh. 6:20;
Josh. 6:15f.
11:31
Josh. 2:9ff.; 6:23;
James 2:25
11:32
Judg. ch. 6-8;
Judg. ch. 4,5;
Judg. ch. 13-16;
Judg. ch. 11,12;
1 Sam. 16:1,13;
1 Sam. 1:20
11:33
Judg. ch. 4,7,11,
14; 2 Sam.
5:17-20; 8:1f.;
10:12;
1 Sam. 12:4;
2 Sam. 8:15;
2 Sam. 7:11f.;
Judg. 14:6;
1 Sam. 17:34ff.;
Dan. 6:22
11:34
Dan. 3:23ff.;
Ex. 18:4; 1 Sam.
18:11; 19:10;
1 Kin. ch. 19;
2 Kin. ch. 6; Ps.
144:10;
Judg. 7:21; 15:8,
15f.; 1 Sam.
17:51f.; 2 Sam.
8:1-6; 10:15ff.
11:35
1 Kin. 17:23;
2 Kin. 4:36f.
11:36
Gen. 39:20; 1
Kin. 22:27; 2 Chr.
18:26; Jer. 20:2;
37:15
11:37
1 Kin. 21:13;
2 Chr. 24:21;
2 Sam. 12:31;
1 Chr. 20:3;
1 Kin. 19:10; Jer.
26:23;
1 Kin. 19:13,19;
2 Kin. 2:8,13f.;
Zech. 13:4;
Heb. 11:25; 13:3
11:38
1 Kin. 18:4,13;
19:9

24 By *faith* Moses, when he had grown up, refused to be called~ the son of Pharaoh's daughter;

25 choosing rather to endure~ ill-treatment with the people of God, than to enjoy the passing pleasures of *sin;*

26 considering the reproach of Christ *greater riches* than the treasures of Egypt; for he was looking^m to the reward.

27 By *faith* he left Egypt, not fearing the wrath[7a] of the king; for he endured, as seeing *Him* who is *unseen.*

28 By *faith* he kept+ the Passover and the sprinkling of the blood, so that he who destroyed the first-born might not touch^x them.

29 By *faith* they passed through the Red Sea as though *they were passing* through dry land; and the Egyptians, when they attempted it, were drowned.

30 By *faith* the walls of Jericho fell down, after they had been encircled for seven days.

31 By *faith* Rahab the harlot did not perish along with those who were disobedient, after she had welcomed the spies in peace.

32 And what more shall I say?~ For time will *fail me* if I tell of Gideon, Barak, Samson, Jephthah, of David and Samuel and the prophets,

33 who *by faith* conquered kingdoms, performed *acts of* righteousness, obtained promises, shut the mouths of lions,

34 quenched the power of fire, escaped the edge of the sword, from weakness were made strong, became mighty in war, put foreign *armies* to flight.

35 Women received *back* their dead by *resurrection;* and others were tortured, *not* accepting their release, in order that they might obtain^x a *better resurrection;*

36 and others experienced *mockings* and *scourgings,* yes, also chains and imprisonment.

37 They were stoned, they were sawn in two, ^hthey were tempted, they were put to death with the sword; they went about in sheepskins, in goatskins, being destitute, afflicted, ill-treated

38 (*men* of whom the world *was not worthy),* wandering in deserts and mountains and caves and holes in the ground.

^hSome mss. do not contain *they were tempted*

39 And all these, having gained approval through their faith, did not receive what was promised,

11:39
Heb. 11:2;
Heb. 10:36; 11:13

40 because God had *provided something better* for us, so that apart from †us they should not be made[x] perfect.

11:40
Heb. 11:16;
Rev. 6:11

Jesus, the Example

12 Therefore,[2] since we have so great a cloud of witnesses surrounding us, let us also lay aside *every* encumbrance, and the sin which so easily entangles us, and let us run[~] with *endurance* the race that is set before us,

12:1
Rom. 13:12; Eph. 4:22;
1 Cor. 9:24; Gal. 2:2;
Heb. 10:36

2 fixing our eyes on *Jesus,* the author and perfecter of faith, who for the joy set before Him endured the cross, despising the shame, and has sat[+] down at the right hand of the throne of God.

12:2
Heb. 2:10;
Phil. 2:8f.; Heb. 2:9;
1 Cor. 1:18,23;
Heb. 13:13;
Heb. 1:3

3 For consider[xi] Him who has endured[+] *such* hostility by sinners against Himself, so that you may not grow[x] weary and lose heart.

12:3
Rev. 2:3;
Gal. 6:9; Heb. 12:5

A Father's Discipline

4 You have not yet resisted to the point of shedding blood in your striving against sin;

12:4
Heb. 10:32ff.;
13:13;
Phil. 2:8

5 and you have forgotten[+] the exhortation which is addressed to you as sons,

12:5
Job 5:17; Prov. 3:11;
Heb. 12:3

"MY SON, DO NOT REGARD[0] LIGHTLY THE DISCIPLINE OF
THE LORD,
NOR FAINT[0] WHEN YOU ARE REPROVED BY HIM;

6 FOR THOSE WHOM THE LORD †LOVES[31a] HE
DISCIPLINES,
AND HE SCOURGES EVERY SON WHOM HE RECEIVES."

12:6
Prov. 3:12;
Ps. 119:75; Rev. 3:19

7 It is for discipline that you endure; God deals with you as with *sons;* for what son is there whom *his* father does not discipline?

12:7
Deut. 8:5; 2 Sam. 7:14; Prov. 13:24;
19:18; 23:13f.

8 But if you are without discipline, of which *all* have become[+] partakers, then you are *illegitimate children* and *not sons.*

12:8
1 Pet. 5:9

9 Furthermore, we had earthly fathers to discipline us, and we respected[m] them; shall we not much rather be subject to the Father of spirits, and live?

12:9
Luke 18:2;
Num. 16:22;
27:16; Rev. 22:6;
Is. 38:16

10 For they disciplined[m] us for a short time as seemed best to them, but He *disciplines us* for *our* good, that we may share[x] His holiness.

12:10
2 Pet. 1:4

11 All discipline for the moment seems not to be joyful, but †*sorrowful;* yet to those who have been trained[+] by it, afterwards it yields the *peaceful* fruit of *righteousness.*

12:11
1 Pet. 1:6;
Is. 32:17; 2 Tim. 4:8; James 3:17f.

12 Therefore, *strengthen*[xi] the hands that are weak[+] and the knees that are feeble,[+]

12:12
Is. 35:3

12:13
Prov. 4:26; Gal.
2:14;
Gal. 6:1; James
5:16

12:14
Rom. 14:19;
Rom. 6:22; Heb.
12:10;
Matt. 5:8; Heb.
9:28
12:15
2 Cor. 6:1; Gal.
5:4; Heb. 4:1;
Deut. 29:18;
Titus 1:15
12:16
Heb. 13:4;
1 Tim. 1:9;
Gen. 25:33f.
12:17
Gen. 27:30-40

12:18
2 Cor. 3:7-13;
Heb. 12:18ff.;
Ex. 19:12,16ff.;
20:18; Deut. 4:11;
5:22
12:19
Ex. 19:16,19;
20:18; Matt.
24:31;
Deut. 4:12;
Ex. 20:19; Deut.
5:25; 18:16
12:20
Ex. 19:12f.
12:21
Deut. 9:19
12:22
Rev. 14:1;
Eph. 2:19; Phil.
3:20; Heb. 11:10;
Rev. 21:2;
Heb. 3:12;
Gal. 4:26; Heb.
11:16;
Rev. 5:11
12:23
Ex. 4:22; Heb.
2:12;
Luke 10:20;
Gen. 18:25; Ps.
50:6; 94:2;
Heb. 11:40; Rev.
6:9,11
12:24
1 Tim. 2:5; Heb.
8:6; 9:15;
Heb. 9:19; 10:22;
1 Pet. 1:2;
Gen. 4:10; Heb.
11:4
12:25
Heb. 3:12;
Heb. 1:1;
Heb. 2:2f.;
10:28f.;
Heb. 12:19;
Ex. 20:22; Heb.
8:5; 11:7
12:26
Ex. 19:18; Judg.
5:4f.;
Hag. 2:6
12:27
Is. 34:4; 54:10;
65:17; Rom. 8:19,
21; 1 Cor. 7:31;
Heb. 1:10ff.
12:28
Dan. 2:44;
Heb. 13:15,21

13   and make ~ᴵ *straight* paths for your feet, so that *the limb* which is lame may not be put* out of joint, but rather be *healed.* ˣ ¹⁵ᵇ

14   Pursue ~ᴵ peace with all men, and the sanctification without which no one will see the Lord.

15   See to it that no one comes short of the grace of God; that no root of bitterness springing up causes~ trouble, and by it many be defiled;ˣ ¹⁷ᵇ

16   that *there be* no immoral or godless person like Esau, who sold his own birthright for a *single meal.*

17   For you know that even *afterwards,* when he desired to inheritˣ the blessing, he was rejected, for he found no place for *repentance,* though² he sought¹ for it with *tears.*

Contrast of Sinai and Zion

18   For you have not come⁺ to *a mountain* that may be touched and to a blazing⁺ fire, and to darkness and gloom and whirlwind,

19   and to the blast of a trumpet and the sound of words ⁴³ᵇ which *sound was such that* those who heard begged that no further word ⁴³ᵃ should be spokenˣ to them.

20   For they could not bear ᵐ the command, "Iꜰ ᴇᴠᴇɴ ᴀ ʙᴇᴀꜱᴛ ᴛᴏᴜᴄʜᴇꜱˣ ᴛʜᴇ ᴍᴏᴜɴᴛᴀɪɴ, ɪᴛ ᴡɪʟʟ ʙᴇ ꜱᴛᴏɴᴇᴅ."

21   And *so terrible* was the sight, *that* Moses said, "I ᴀᴍ ꜰᴜʟʟ ¹ ᴏꜰ ꜰᴇᴀʀ and trembling."

22   But you have come⁺ to Mount Zion and to the city of the living God, the *heavenly* Jerusalem, and to myriads of angels,

23   to the general assembly and church of the first-born who are enrolled⁺ in heaven, and to God, the Judge of *all,* and to the spirits of righteous men made⁺ perfect,

24   and to Jesus, the mediator of a *new* covenant, and to the sprinkled blood, which speaks better than *the blood* of Abel.

The Unshaken Kingdom

25   See ~ᴵ to it that you do not refuse⁰ Him who is speaking. For if those did not escape when they refused him who warned *them* on earth, much less *shall* we *escape* who turn away from Him who *warns* from heaven.

26   And His voice shook the earth *then,* but now He has promised, ⁺ saying, "Yᴇᴛ ᴏɴᴄᴇ ᴍᴏʀᴇ I ᴡɪʟʟ ꜱʜᴀᴋᴇ ɴᴏᴛ ᴏɴʟʏ ᴛʜᴇ ᴇᴀʀᴛʜ, ʙᴜᴛ ᴀʟꜱᴏ ᴛʜᴇ ʜᴇᴀᴠᴇɴ."

27   And this *expression,* "Yet once more," denotes the removing of those things which can be shaken, as of created things, in order that those things which cannot be shaken may remain.ˣ

28   Therefore, since we receive a kingdom which *cannot be*

shaken, let us show ~ gratitude, by which we may offer ~ to God an acceptable service [38c] with reverence and awe;

29   for our God is a *consuming* fire.

The Changeless Christ

13 Let *love of the brethren* continue. [~]

2   Do not neglect [o] to show *hospitality* to strangers, for by this some have entertained angels without knowing it.

3   Remember [~] the prisoners, as though in prison with them, and those who are ill-treated, since you yourselves also are in the body.

4   *Let* marriage *be held* in *honor* among all, and let the *marriage* bed *be* undefiled; for *fornicators* and *adulterers* God will judge.

5   Let your character be free from the *love of money,* being content with what you have; for He Himself has said, [+] "I WILL •*NEVER* DESERT[x] YOU, NOR WILL I •*EVER* FORSAKE[x] YOU,"

6   so that we confidently say, [~]

"THE LORD IS MY HELPER, I WILL NOT BE AFRAID.
WHAT SHALL [†]*MAN* DO TO ME?"

7   Remember [~] those who led you, who spoke the word [43a] of God to you; and considering the result of their conduct, imitate [~] their faith.

8   Jesus Christ *is* the *same* yesterday and today, *yes* and forever.

9   Do not be carried [o] away by *varied* and *strange* teachings; for it is good for the heart to be strengthened ~ by *grace,* not by foods, through which those who were thus occupied were not benefited.

10   We have an altar, from which those who serve the tabernacle have *no right* to eat.[x]

11   For the *bodies* of those animals whose *blood* is brought into the holy place by the high priest *as an offering* for sin, are burned outside the camp.

12   Therefore Jesus also, that He might sanctify[x] the people through *His own blood,* suffered *outside* the gate.

13   Hence, let us go ~ out to Him outside the camp, bearing His reproach.

14   For here we do not have a lasting city, but we are seeking [1] *the city* which is to *come.*

God-pleasing Sacrifices

15   *Through Him* then, let us continually offer ~ up a sacrifice of praise to God, that is, the fruit of lips that give thanks to His name.

12:29
Deut. 4:24; 9:3;
Is. 33:14; 2
Thess. 1:7; Heb.
10:27,31

13:1
Rom. 12:10; 1
Thess. 4:9; 1 Pet.
1:22
13:2
Matt. 25:35; Rom.
12:13; 1 Pet. 4:9;
Gen. 18:1ff.;
19:1f.
13:3
Col. 4:18;
Matt. 25:36; Heb.
10:34
13:4
1 Cor. 7:38;
1 Tim. 4:3;
1 Cor. 6:9; Gal.
5:19,21; 1 Thess.
4:6
13:5
Eph. 5:3; Col. 3:5;
1 Tim. 3:3;
Phil. 4:11;
Deut. 31:6,8;
Josh. 1:5
13:6
Ps. 118:6

13:7
Heb. 13:17,24;
Luke 5:1;
Heb. 6:12

13:8
2 Cor. 1:19; Heb.
1:12

13:9
Eph. 4:14; 5:6;
Jude 12;
2 Cor. 1:21; Col.
2:7;
Col. 2:16;
Heb. 9:10

13:10
1 Cor. 10:18;
Heb. 8:5

13:11
Ex. 29:14; Lev.
4:12,21; 9:11;
16:27; Num. 19:3,
7

13:12
Eph. 5:26; Heb.
2:11;
Heb. 9:12;
John 19:17
13:13
Luke 9:23; Heb.
11:26; 12:2
13:14
Heb. 10:34;
12:27;
Eph. 2:19; Heb.
2:5; 11:10,16;
12:22

13:15
1 Pet. 2:5;
Lev. 7:12;
Is. 57:19; Hos.
14:2

13:16
Rom. 12:13;
Phil. 4:18

13:17
1 Cor. 16:16;
Heb. 13:7,24;
Is. 62:6; Ezek.
3:17; Acts 20:28

13:18
1 Thess. 5:25;
Acts 24:16;
1 Tim. 1:5
13:19
Philem. 22
13:20
Rom. 15:33;
Acts 2:24; Rom.
10:7;
Is. 63:11; John
10:11; 1 Pet.
2:25;
Zech. 9:11; Heb.
10:29;
Is. 55:3; Jer.
32:40; Ezek.
37:26
13:21
1 Pet. 5:10;
Phil. 2:13;
Heb. 12:28;
1 John 3:22;
Rom. 11:36
13:22
Acts 13:15; Heb.
3:13; 10:25; 12:5;
13:19;
Heb. 3:1;
1 Pet. 5:12
13:23
Acts 16:1; Col.
1:1
13:24
1 Cor. 16:16;
Heb. 13:7,17;
Acts 9:13;
Acts 18:2
13:25
Col. 4:18

16   And do not neglect⁶ *doing good* and *sharing;* for with such sacrifices God is *pleased*.

17   Obey~ᴵ your leaders, and submit~ᴵ *to them;* for *they* keep watch over your souls,³⁰ᶜ as those who will give an account. Let them do~ this *with joy* and not with grief, for this would be *unprofitable for you*.

18   Pray~ᴵ for us, for we are sure that we have a good²⁵ᵇ conscience, desiring to conduct~ ourselves honorably in all things.

19   And I urge *you* all the more to do˟ this, that I may be restored˟ to you the sooner.

Benediction

20   Now the God of peace, who brought up from the dead the great²⁶ᵃ Shepherd of the sheep through the blood of the ✝eternal covenant, *even* Jesus our Lord,

21   equip˟ you in every good²⁵ᵃ thing to do˟ His will, working in us that which is pleasing in His sight, through Jesus Christ, to whom *be* the glory forever and ever. Amen.

22   But I urge you, brethren, bear~ᴵ with this word of exhortation, for I have written to you briefly.

23   Take~ᴵ notice that our brother Timothy has been released,✦ with whom, if he comes~ soon, I shall see you.

24   Greet˟ᴵ all of your leaders and all the saints. Those from Italy greet you.

25   Grace be with you all.

The Epistle of
James

Testing Your Faith

1 James, a bond-servant[38b] of God and of the Lord Jesus Christ, to the twelve tribes who are dispersed abroad, greetings.

2 Consider[xi] it all joy, my brethren, when you encounter[x] various *trials,*

3 knowing[29a] that the testing of your faith produces[1] endurance.

4 And let endurance have[ʍi] *its perfect* result, that you may be perfect and complete, lacking in nothing.

5 But if any of you lacks wisdom, let him ask[ʍi9a] of *God,* who gives to all men generously and without reproach, and it will be given to him.

6 But let him ask[ʍi] in faith without any doubting, for the one who doubts is like⁺ the surf of the sea driven and tossed by the wind.

7 For let not *that* man expect[ᶿ] that he will receive anything from the Lord,

8 *being* a double-minded man, unstable in all his ways.

9 But let the brother of humble circumstances glory[ʍi] in his high position;

10 and *let* the rich man *glory* in his humiliation, because *like flowering grass* he will pass away.

11 For the sun rises with a scorching wind, and withers the grass; and its flower falls off, and the beauty of its appearance is destroyed; so too the rich man in the midst of his pursuits will fade away.

12 †Blessed is a man who perseveres under trial; for once he has been †*approved,* he will receive[5b] the crown of life, which *the Lord* has promised to those who love[31a] Him.

13 Let no one say[ᶿ] when he is tempted, "I am being tempted by *God";* for God *cannot be tempted* by evil,[10a] and He Himself does not tempt *anyone.*

14 But each one is tempted when he is carried away and enticed by his •*own* lust.

15 Then when lust has conceived, it gives birth to sin; and when sin is accomplished,[1] it brings forth death.

1:1
Acts 12:17;
Titus 1:1;
Rom. 1:1;
Luke 22:30;
John 7:35;
Acts 15:23
1:2
Matt. 5:12; James 1:12; 5:11;
1 Pet. 1:6
1:3
1 Pet. 1:7;
Heb. 6:12;
Luke 21:19
1:4
Luke 21:19;
Matt. 5:48; Col. 4:12
1:5
1 Kin. 3:9ff.;
James 3:17;
Matt. 7:7
1:6
Matt. 21:21;
Mark 11:23; Acts 10:20;
Matt. 14:28-31;
Eph. 4:14
1:8
James 4:8;
2 Pet. 2:14
1:9
Luke 14:11
1:10
1 Cor. 7:31;
1 Pet. 1:24
1:11
Matt. 20:12;
Ps. 102:4,11; Is. 40:7f.
1:12
Luke 6:22; James 5:11; 1 Pet. 3:14;
4:14;
1 Cor. 9:25;
Ex. 20:6; James 2:5;
1 Cor. 2:9; 8:3
1:13
Gen. 22:1
1:15
Job 15:35; Ps. 7:14; Is. 59:4;
Rom. 5:12; 6:23

1:16
1 Cor. 6:9;
Acts 1:15; James
1:2,19; 2:1,5,14;
3:1,10; 4:11;
5:12,19
1:17
John 3:3; James
3:15,17;
Ps. 136:7; 1 John
1:5; Mal. 3:6
1:18
John 1:13;
James 1:15;
1 Pet. 1:3,23;
2 Cor. 6:7; Eph.
1:13; 2 Tim. 2:15;
Jer. 2:3; Rev.
14:4
1:19
1 John 2:21;
Acts 1:15; James
1:2,16; 2:1,5,14;
3:1,10; 4:11;
5:12,19;
Prov. 10:19;
16:32; 17:27;
Eccl. 7:9
1:20
Matt. 5:22; Eph.
4:26
1:21
Eph. 4:22; 1 Pet.
2:1;
Eph. 1:13; 1 Pet.
1:22f.
1:22
Matt. 7:24-27;
Luke 6:46-49;
Rom. 2:13;
James 1:22-25;
2:14-20
1:23
1 Cor. 13:12
1:25
John 8:32; Rom.
8:2; Gal. 2:4; 6:2;
James 2:12;
1 Pet. 2:16;
John 13:17
1:26
Ps. 39:1; 141:3;
James 3:2-12
1:27
Rom. 2:13; Gal.
3:11; Matt. 25:36;
Deut. 14:29; Job
31:16,17,21; Ps.
146:9; Is. 1:17,23;
Matt. 12:32; Eph.
2:2; Titus 2:12;
James 4:4; 2 Pet.
1:4; 2:20; 1 John
2:15-17
2:1
James 1:16;
Heb. 12:2;
Acts 7:2; 1 Cor.
2:8; Acts 10:34;
James 2:9
2:2
Luke 23:11;
James 2:3;
Zech. 3:3f.
2:3
Luke 23:11
2:4
Luke 18:6; John
7:24
2:5
James 1:16;
Job 34:19; 1 Cor.
1:27f.;
Luke 12:21; Rev.
2:9;
Matt. 5:3; 25:34;
James 1:12

16   Do not be deceived,°16b my beloved brethren.

17   Every †good25a thing bestowed and every perfect gift is *from above,* coming~ down from the Father of lights, with whom there is no variation, or *shifting* shadow.

18   In the exercise of His will He brought us forth by the word43a of truth, so that we might be, as it were, the first fruits among *His* creatures.

19   ªThis you know, my beloved brethren. But let everyone be quick to hear,ˣ slow to speakˣ *and* slow to anger;

20   for the anger of man does not achieve the *righteousness of God.*

21   Therefore putting aside all filthiness and *all* that remains of wickedness, in *humility*23b receiveˣˡ5a the word43a implanted, which is able to saveˣ your souls.

22   But prove~ˡ yourselves doers of the word,43a and not merely hearers who delude themselves.

23   For if anyone is a hearer of the word and not a doer, he is like⁺ a man who looks at his natural face in a mirror;

24   for *once* he has looked at himself and gone⁺ away, he has immediately forgotten what kind of person he was.

25   But one who looks intently at the perfect law, the *law* of liberty, and abides by it, not having become a forgetful hearer but an effectual †doer, this man shall be *blessed* in what he does.

26   If anyone thinks himself to be religious, and yet does not bridle his tongue but deceives16a his *own* heart, this man's religion is *worthless.*

27   This is pure13c and †undefiled religion in the sight of *our* God and Father, to visit~ orphans and widows in their distress, *and* to keep~ oneself *unstained* by the world.

The Sin of Partiality

2   My brethren, do not hold° your faith in our glorious Lord Jesus Christ with *an attitude of* personal favoritism.

2   For if a man comesˣ into your assembly with a gold ring and dressed in fine clothes, and there also comesˣ in a poor man in dirty clothes,

3   and you payˣ special attention to the one who is wearing the fine clothes, and say,ˣ "*You* sit here in a good place," and you sayˣ to the poor man, "*You* standˣˡ over there, or sit down by my footstool,"

4   have you not made distinctions among yourselves, and become judges with evil10b motives?

5   Listen,ˣˡ my beloved brethren: did not God choose the poor

ªOr, *Know* this

of this world *to be* rich in faith and heirs of the kingdom which He promised to those who love[31a] Him?

6   But *you* have dishonored the poor man. Is it not the rich who oppress you and personally drag you into court?

7   Do *they* not blaspheme the fair name by which you have been called?

8   If, however, you are fulfilling the *royal* law, according to the Scripture, "YOU SHALL LOVE[31a] YOUR NEIGHBOR AS YOURSELF," you are doing well.

9   But if you show partiality, you are committing *sin and* are convicted by the law as transgressors.

10   For whoever keeps[x] the *whole law* and yet stumbles[x] in one *point*, he has become[+] guilty of *all*.

11   For He who said, "DO NOT COMMIT ADULTERY,"[⊙] also said, "DO NOT COMMIT MURDER."[⊙] Now if you do not commit adultery, but do commit murder, you have become[+] a transgressor of the law.

12   So speak[~] and so act,[~] as those who are to be judged by *the law of liberty.*

13   For judgment *will be* merciless to one who has shown no mercy; mercy *triumphs* over judgment.

Faith and Works

14   What use is it, my brethren, if a man says[~] he has faith, but he has[~] no works? Can *that faith* save[x] him?

15   If a brother or sister is[~] without clothing and in need of daily food,

16   and one of you says[x] to them, "Go in peace, be warmed[~] and be filled,"[~] and yet you do not give[x] them what is necessary for *their* body, what use is that?

17   Even so faith, if it has[~] no works, is [+]*dead, being* by itself.

18   But someone may *well* say, "*You* have faith, and *I* have works; show[xl] me your faith without the works, and *I* will show you my faith *by my works.*"

19   *You* believe that [b]God is *one.* You do well; the *demons also* believe, and shudder.

20   But are you willing to recognize,[x] you foolish fellow, that faith without works is *useless?*

21   Was not Abraham our father justified by works, when he offered up Isaac his son on the altar?

22   You see that faith was working[m] with his works, and as a result of the *works,* faith was perfected;

23   and the Scripture was fulfilled which says, "AND

[b]Or, *there is one God*

2:6
Acts 8:3; 16:19

2:7
Acts 11:26; 1 Pet. 4:16

2:8
Matt. 7:12; Lev. 19:18

2:9
Acts 10:34; James 2:1

2:10
James 3:2; 2 Pet. 1:10; Jude 24; Matt. 5:19; Gal. 5:3

2:11
Ex. 20:14; Deut. 5:18; Ex. 20:13; Deut. 5:17

2:12
James 1:25

2:13
Prov. 21:13; Matt. 5:7; 18:32-35; Luke 6:37f.

2:14
James 1:22ff.; James 1:16

2:15
Matt. 25:35f.; Luke 3:11

2:16
1 John 3:17f.

2:17
Gal. 5:6; James 2:20,26

2:18
Rom. 9:19; Rom. 3:28; 4:6; Heb. 11:33; James 3:13; Matt. 7:16f.; Gal. 5:6

2:19
Deut. 6:4; Mark 12:29; James 2:8; Matt. 8:29; Mark 1:24; 5:7; Luke 4:34; Acts 19:15

2:20
Rom. 9:20; 1 Cor. 15:36; Gal. 5:6; James 2:17,26

2:21
Gen. 22:9,10,12, 16-18

2:22
John 6:29; Heb. 11:17; 1 Thess. 1:3

2:23
Gen. 15:6; Rom. 4:3; 2 Chr. 20:7; Is. 41:8

ABRAHAM BELIEVED GOD, AND IT WAS RECKONED TO HIM AS RIGHT-
EOUSNESS," and he was called the *friend of God*.

24   You see that a man is justified by *works*, and not by faith
alone.

2:25
Heb. 11:31;
Josh. 2:4,6,15

25   And in the same way was not Rahab the harlot also justified by works, when she received the messengers and sent them
out by another way?

2:26
Gal. 5:6; James
2:17,20

26   For just as the body without *the* spirit is dead, so also faith
without works is dead.

The Tongue Is a Fire

3:1
Matt. 23:8; Rom.
2:20f.; 1 Tim. 1:7;
James 1:16; 3:10
3:2
James 2:10;
Matt. 12:34-37;
James 3:2-12;
James 1:4;
James 1:26
3:3
Ps. 32:9

3 Let not *many of you* become° *teachers*, my brethren, knowing that as such we shall incur a stricter judgment.

2   For we *all* stumble in many *ways*. If anyone does not stumble in what he *says*, he is a perfect man, able to bridle[x] the whole
body as well.

3   Now if we put the bits into the horses' *mouths* so that they
may obey[~] us, we direct their *entire body* as well.

4   Behold, the ships also, though they are so †great and are
driven by strong winds, are still directed by a very[3] small rudder,
wherever the inclination of the pilot desires.

3:5
Ps. 12:3f.; 73:8f.;
Prov. 26:20f.

5   So also the tongue is a small part of the body, and *yet* it
boasts of *great things*. Behold, how *great a forest* is set aflame by
such a small fire!

3:6
Ps. 120:2,3; Prov.
16:27;
Matt. 12:36f.;
15:11,18f.;
Matt. 5:22

6   And the tongue is a fire, the *very* world of iniquity; the
tongue is set among our members as that which defiles the entire
body, and sets on fire the course of *our* life, and is set on fire by
hell.

7   For every species of beasts and birds, of reptiles and creatures of the sea, is tamed, and has been tamed⁺ by the human
race.

3:8
Ps. 140:3; Eccl.
10:11; Rom. 3:13

8   But no one can tame[x] the *tongue; it is* a restless evil[10a] *and*
full of *deadly* poison.

3:9
James 1:27;
Gen. 1:26; 1 Cor.
11:7

9   With it we bless *our* Lord and Father; and with it we curse
men, who have been made⁺ in the likeness of †God;

10   from the same mouth come *both* blessing and cursing. My
brethren, these things ought not to be[~] this way.

11   Does a fountain send out from the *same opening both* fresh
and bitter *water*?

3:12
Matt. 7:16

12   Can a fig tree, my brethren, produce[x] *olives*, or a vine
produce †*figs? Neither can* salt water produce[x] *fresh*.

Wisdom from Above

3:13
James 2:18;
1 Pet. 2:12

13   Who among you is wise[35a] and understanding? Let him

show[xi] by his good[25b] behavior his deeds in the gentleness[23b] of wisdom.

14 But if you have *bitter* jealousy and selfish ambition in your heart, do not be arrogant[θ] and *so* lie[θ] against the truth.

15 This wisdom is not that which comes down from above, but is earthly, natural, demonic.

16 For where jealousy and selfish ambition exist, there is disorder and every evil[10b] thing.

17 But the wisdom from above is first pure,[13a] then peaceable, gentle,[23a] reasonable, full of mercy and good[25a] fruits, unwavering, without hypocrisy.

18 And the seed whose fruit is righteousness is sown in peace by those who make peace.

Things to Avoid

4 What is the source of quarrels and conflicts among you? Is not the source your pleasures that wage war in your members?

2 You lust and do not have; *so* you commit murder. And you are envious and cannot obtain;[x] *so* you fight and quarrel. You do not have because you do not ask.[~9a]

3 You ask and do not receive, because you ask with wrong motives, so that you may spend[x] *it* on *your pleasures.*

4 You adulteresses, do you not know that friendship with the world is *hostility toward God?* Therefore whoever wishes[x] to be a friend of the world makes himself an *enemy of God.*

5 Or do you think that the Scripture speaks to no purpose: "[c]He *jealously* desires the Spirit which He has made to dwell in us"?

6 But He gives a *greater*[26a] grace. Therefore *it* says, "GOD IS OPPOSED TO THE *PROUD*, BUT GIVES GRACE TO THE *HUMBLE.*"

7 Submit[xi] therefore to God. Resist[xi] the devil and he will flee from you.

8 Draw[xi] near to God and He will draw near to you. Cleanse[xi] your hands, you sinners; and purify[xi] your hearts, you double-minded.

9 Be miserable[xi] and mourn[xi] and weep;[xi] let your laughter be turned[xi] into *mourning*, and your joy to [†]gloom.

10 Humble[xi] yourselves in the presence of the Lord, and He will exalt you.

11 Do not speak[θ] against one another, brethren. He who speaks against a brother, or judges his brother, speaks against

[c]Or, *The Spirit which He has made to dwell in us jealously desires us*

3:14
Rom. 2:8; 2 Cor. 12:20;
1 Tim. 2:4; James 1:18; 3:16; 5:19
3:15
James 1:17;
1 Cor. 2:6; 3:19;
2 Cor. 1:12; Jude 19; 2 Thess. 2:9f.;
1 Tim. 4:1; Rev. 2:24
3:16
Rom. 2:8; 2 Cor. 12:20; James 3:14
3:17
James 1:17;
2 Cor. 7:11;
James 4:8;
Matt. 5:9; Heb. 12:11; Titus 3:2;
Luke 6:36; James 2:13; James 2:4;
Rom. 12:9; 2 Cor. 6:6
3:18
Prov. 11:18; Is. 32:17; Hos. 10:12; Amos 6:12; Gal. 6:8;
Phil. 1:11
4:1
Titus 3:9;
Rom. 7:23
4:2
James 5:6;
1 John 3:15
4:3
1 John 3:22; 5:14
4:4
Jer. 2:2; Ezek. 16:32;
James 1:27;
Rom. 8:7; 1 John 2:15; Matt. 6:24;
John 15:19
4:5
Num. 23:19;
1 Cor. 6:19;
2 Cor. 6:16
4:6
Is. 54:7f.; Matt. 13:12;
Ps. 138:6; Prov. 3:34; Matt. 23:12;
1 Pet. 5:5
4:7
1 Pet. 5:6;
Eph. 4:27; 6:11f.;
1 Pet. 5:8f.
4:8
2 Chr. 15:2; Zech. 1:3; Mal. 3:7;
Heb. 7:19;
Job 17:9; Is. 1:16;
1 Tim. 2:8;
Jer. 4:14; James 3:17; 1 Pet. 1:22;
1 John 3:3;
James 1:8
4:9
Neh. 8:9; Prov. 14:13; Luke 6:25
4:10
Job 5:11; Ezek. 21:26; Luke 1:52;
James 4:6
4:11
2 Cor. 12:20;
James 5:9;
1 Pet. 2:1;
James 1:16; 5:7, 9,10; Matt. 7:1;
Rom. 14:4;
James 2:8;
James 1:22

the law, and judges the law; but if you judge the law, you are not a doer of the law, but a judge *of it.*

4:12
Is. 33:22; James
5:9;
Matt. 10:28;
Rom. 14:4

12   There is *only* one Lawgiver and Judge, the One who is able to save[x] and to destroy;[x] but who are *you* who judge your neighbor?

4:13
James 5:1;
Prov. 27:1; Luke
12:18-20

13   Come[~] now, you who say, "Today or tomorrow, we shall go to such and such a city, and spend a year there and engage in business and make a profit."

4:14
Job 7:7; Ps. 39:5;
102:3; 144:4

14   Yet you do not know[29c] what your life will be like *tomorrow.* You are *just* a [+]vapor that appears for a little while and then vanishes away.

4:15
Acts 18:21

15   Instead, *you ought* to say,[~] "If the Lord wills,[x] we shall live and also do this or that."

4:16
1 Cor. 5:6

16   But as it is, you boast in your arrogance; all such boasting is [+]*evil.* [10b]

4:17
Luke 12:47; John
9:41; 2 Pet. 2:21

17   Therefore, to one who knows[29e] *the* right thing to do,[~] and does not do it, to him it is *sin.*

Misuse of Riches

5:1
James 4:13;
Luke 6:24; 1 Tim.
6:9;
Is. 13:6; 15:3;
Ezek. 30:2

5   Come[~] now, you rich, weep[xi] and howl for your miseries which are coming upon you.

5:2
Job 13:28; Is.
50:9; Matt. 6:19f.

2   Your riches have rotted[+] and your garments have become[+] moth-eaten.

5:3
James 5:7,8

3   Your gold and your silver have rusted;[+] and their rust will be a *witness against you* and will consume your flesh like fire. It is in the last days that you have stored up your treasure!

5:4
Lev. 19:13; Job
24:10f.; Jer.
22:13; Mal. 3:5;
Ex. 2:23; Deut.
24:15; Job
31:38f.;
Rom. 9:29

4   Behold, the pay of the laborers who mowed your fields, *and* which has been withheld[+] by you, cries out *against you;* and the outcry of those who did the harvesting has reached[+] the *ears of the Lord of Sabaoth.*

5:5
Ezek. 16:49; Luke
16:19; 1 Tim. 5:6;
2 Pet. 2:13;
Jer. 12:3; 25:34

5   You have lived luxuriously on the earth and led a life of wanton pleasure; you have fattened your hearts in a day of slaughter.

5:6
James 4:2;
Heb. 10:38;
1 Pet. 4:18

6   You have condemned[14b] and put to death the righteous *man;* he does not resist you.

Exhortation

5:7
James 4:11; 5:9,
10;
John 21:22;
1 Thess. 2:19;
Gal. 6:9;
Deut. 11:14; Jer.
5:24; Joel 2:23

7   Be patient,[xi] therefore, brethren, until the coming of the Lord. Behold, the farmer waits for the precious produce of the soil, being patient about it, until it gets[x] the early and late rains.

5:8
Luke 21:19;
1 Thess. 3:13;
John 21:22;
1 Thess. 2:19;
Rom. 13:11,12;
1 Pet. 4:7

8   *You too* be patient;[xi] strengthen[xi] your hearts, for the coming of the Lord is at hand.[+]

5:9
James 4:11;
James 5:7,10;
1 Cor. 4:5;
James 4:12;
1 Pet. 4:5;
Matt. 24:33;
Mark 13:29

9   Do not complain,[○] brethren, against one another, that you

yourselves may not be judged;ˣ behold, the Judge is standing *right at the door.*

10   As an *example,* brethren, of suffering and patience, takeˣⁱ the prophets who spoke in the name of the Lord.

11   Behold, we count those blessed who endured. You have heard of the endurance of Job and have seen the *outcome of the Lord's dealings,* that the Lord is full of compassion and *is* merciful.

12   But above all, my brethren, do not swear,° either by heaven or by earth or with any other oath; but let your yes be yes, and your no, no; so that you may not fallˣ under judgment.

13   Is anyone among you suffering? Let him pray. ᷃ Is anyone cheerful? Let him sing᷃ praises.

14   Is anyone among you sick? Let him callˣⁱ for the elders of the church, and let them prayˣⁱ over him, anointing him with oil in the name of the Lord;

15   and the prayer offered in faith will ᵈrestore the one who is sick, and the *Lord* will raise him up, and if he has committed⁺ *sins,* they will be forgiven him.

16   Therefore, confess᷃ⁱ your sins to one another, and pray᷃ⁱ for one another, so that you may be healed.ˣ¹⁵ᵇ The effective prayer of a righteous man can *accomplish much.*

17   Elijah was a man with a *nature like ours,* and he prayed *earnestly*⁴ that it might not rain;ˣ and it did not rain on the earth for three years and six months.

18   And he prayed again, and the sky poured rain, and the earth produced its fruit.

19   My brethren, if any among you straysˣ from the truth, and one turnsˣ him back,

20   let him know᷃¹²⁹ᵃ that he who turns a sinner from the error of his way will save his soul from death, and will cover a multitude of sins.

ᵈOr, *save*

5:10
James 4:11; 5:7,
9;
Matt. 5:12
5:11
Matt. 5:10; 1 Pet.
3:14;
Job 1:21f.; 2:10;
Job 42:10,12;
Ex. 34:6; Ps.
103:8
5:12
James 1:16;
Matt. 5:34-37
5:13
James 5:10;
Ps. 50:15;
1 Cor. 14:15; Col.
3:16
5:14
Acts 11:30;
Mark 6:13; 16:18
5:15
James 1:6;
1 Cor. 1:21;
James 5:20;
John 6:39; 2 Cor.
4:14
5:16
Matt. 3:6; Mark
1:5; Acts 19:18;
Heb. 12:13;
1 Pet. 2:24;
Gen. 18:23-32;
John 9:31
5:17
Acts 14:15;
1 Kin. 17:1; 18:1;
Luke 4:25
5:18
1 Kin. 18:42;
1 Kin. 18:45
5:19
Matt. 18:15; Gal.
6:1;
James 3:14
5:20
Rom. 11:14;
1 Cor. 1:21;
James 1:21;
Prov. 10:12;
1 Pet. 4:8

The First Epistle of

Peter

A Living Hope, and a Sure Salvation

1:1
2 Pet. 1:1;
1 Pet. 2:11;
James 1:1;
Acts 2:9;
Acts 16:6;
Acts 16:7;
Matt. 24:22; Luke
18:7
1:2
Rom. 8:29; 1 Pet.
1:20;
2 Thess. 2:13;
1 Pet. 1:14,22;
Heb. 10:22;
12:24;
2 Pet. 1:2
1:3
2 Cor. 1:3;
Gal. 6:16; Titus
3:5;
James 1:18;
1 Pet. 1:23;
1 Pet. 1:13,21;
3:5,15; 1 John
3:3;
1 Cor. 15:20;
1 Pet. 3:21
1:4
Acts 20:32; Rom.
8:17; Col. 3:24;
1 Pet. 5:4;
2 Tim. 4:8
1:5
John 10:28; Phil.
4:7;
Eph. 2:8;
1 Cor. 1:21;
2 Thess. 2:13;
1 Pet. 4:13; 5:1
1:6
Rom. 5:2;
1 Pet. 5:10;
1 Pet. 3:17;
James 1:2; 1 Pet.
4:12
1:7
James 1:3;
1 Cor. 3:13;
Rom. 2:7;
Luke 17:30;
1 Pet. 1:13; 4:13
1:8
John 20:29;
Eph. 3:19
1:9
Rom. 6:22
1:10
Matt. 13:17; Luke
10:24;
Matt. 26:24;
1 Pet. 1:13
1:11
2 Pet. 1:21;
Matt. 26:24
1:12
1 Pet. 1:25; 4:6;
Acts 2:2-4;
1 Tim. 3:16

1 Peter, an apostle of Jesus Christ, to those who reside as aliens, scattered throughout Pontus, Galatia, Cappadocia, Asia, and Bithynia, who are chosen

2 according to the foreknowledge of God the Father, by the sanctifying work of the Spirit, that you may obey Jesus Christ and be sprinkled with His blood: May grace and peace be[x] yours in fullest measure.

3 †Blessed be the God and Father of our Lord Jesus Christ, who according to His great[26b] mercy has caused us to be born again to a †living hope through the resurrection of Jesus Christ from the dead,

4 to *obtain* an inheritance *which is* imperishable and undefiled and will not fade away, reserved+ in heaven for you,

5 who are protected by the power[32a] of God through faith for a salvation ready to be revealed[x] in the *last* time.

6 In this you greatly rejoice, even though now for a little while, if necessary, you have been distressed by various trials,

7 that the proof of your faith, *being* more precious than gold which is perishable, even though tested by fire, may be found[x] to result in praise and glory and honor at the revelation of Jesus Christ;

8 and though you have *not* seen Him, you love Him, and though you do not see Him now, but believe in Him, you greatly rejoice with joy inexpressible and full+ of glory,

9 obtaining as the outcome of your faith the salvation of [a]your souls.

10 As to this salvation, the prophets who prophesied of the grace that *would come* to you made careful[1] search and inquiry,

11 seeking to know what person or time the Spirit of Christ within them was indicating[m] as He predicted the sufferings of Christ and the glories to follow.

12 It was revealed to them that they were not serving[m] *themselves,* but *you,* in these things which now have been announced to you through those who preached the gospel to you by the

aSome ancient mss. do not contain *your*

460

Holy Spirit sent from heaven—things into which *angels* long to look.ˣ

13 Therefore, gird your minds[33a] for action, keep sober *in spirit*, fix[xi] your hope completely on the grace to be brought to you at the revelation of Jesus Christ.

14 As obedient children, do not be conformed to the former lusts *which were yours* in your ignorance,

15 but like the Holy[28a] One who called you, be[xi] *holy* yourselves also *in all your behavior;*

16 because it is written,⁺ "YOU SHALL BE HOLY, FOR I AM HOLY."

17 And if you address as *Father* the One who impartially judges according to each man's work, conduct[xi] yourselves in *fear* during the time of your stay *upon earth;*

18 knowing that you were not redeemed[36b] with perishable things like silver or gold from your futile way of life inherited from your forefathers,

19 but with *precious* ⁺*blood,* as of a lamb unblemished and spotless, *the blood* of Christ.

20 For He was foreknown⁺ before the foundation of the world, but has appeared in these last times for the sake of you

21 who through Him are believers in God, who raised Him from the dead and gave Him glory, so that your faith and hope are in God.

22 Since you have in obedience to the truth purified⁺ your souls for a sincere love of the brethren, fervently love[xi31a] one another *from* ᵇ*the heart,*

23 for you have been born⁺ again not of seed which is perishable but ⁺*imperishable, that is,* through the living and abiding word[43a] of God.

24 For,

"ALL FLESH IS LIKE GRASS,
AND ALL ITS GLORY LIKE THE FLOWER OF GRASS.
THE GRASS WITHERS,
AND THE FLOWER FALLS OFF,

25 BUT THE WORD[43b] OF THE LORD ABIDES FOREVER."

And this is the word[43b] which was preached to you.

As Newborn Babes

2 Therefore, putting aside all malice and all guile and hypocrisy and envy and all slander,

2 like newborn babes, long[xi] for the *pure milk of the word,* that by *it* you may grow[x] in respect to salvation,

ᵇSome mss. read *a clean heart*

1:13
Eph. 6:14;
1 Thess. 5:6,8;
2 Tim. 4:5; 1 Pet.
4:7; 5:8;
1 Pet. 1:3;
1 Pet. 1:10;
1 Pet. 1:7
1:14
1 Pet. 1:2;
Rom. 12:2; 1 Pet.
4:2f.;
Eph. 4:18
1:15
1 Thess. 4:7;
1 John 3:3;
2 Cor. 7:1;
James 3:13
1:16
Lev. 11:44f.; 19:2;
20:7
1:17
Ps. 89:26; Jer.
3:19; Matt. 6:9;
Acts 10:34;
Matt. 16:27;
2 Cor. 7:1; Heb.
12:28; 1 Pet.
3:15;
1 Pet. 2:11
1:18
Is. 52:3; 1 Cor.
6:20; Titus 2:14;
Heb. 9:12;
Eph. 4:17
1:19
Acts 20:28; 1 Pet.
1:2;
John 1:29
1:20
Acts 2:23; Eph.
1:4; 1 Pet. 1:2;
Rev. 13:8;
Matt. 25:34;
Heb. 9:26;
Heb. 2:14
1:21
Rom. 4:24; 10:9;
John 17:5,24;
1 Tim. 3:16; Heb.
2:9;
1 Pet. 1:3
1:22
1 Pet. 1:2;
James 4:8;
John 13:34; Rom.
12:10; Heb. 13:1;
1 Pet. 2:17; 3:8
1:23
John 3:3; 1 Pet.
1:3;
John 1:13;
Heb. 4:12
1:24
Is. 40:6ff.; James
1:10f.
1:25
Is. 40:8;
Heb. 6:5

2:1
Eph. 4:22,25,31;
James 1:21;
James 4:11
2:2
Matt. 18:3; 19:14;
Mark 10:15; Luke
18:17; 1 Cor.
14:20;
1 Cor. 3:2;
Eph. 4:15f.

2:3
Heb. 6:5;
Ps. 34:8; Titus
3:4

2:4
1 Pet. 2:7

2:5
1 Cor. 3:9;
Gal. 6:10; 1 Tim.
3:15;
Is. 61:6; 66:21; 1
Pet. 2:9; Rev. 1:6;
Rom. 15:16; Heb.
13:15
2:6
Is. 28:16; Rom.
9:32,33; 10:11; 1
Pet. 2:8;
Eph. 2:20

2:7
2 Cor. 2:16;
1 Pet. 2:7,8;
Ps. 118:22; Matt.
21:42; Luke 2:34;
1 Pet. 2:4

2:8
Is. 8:14;
1 Cor. 1:23; Gal.
5:11;
Rom. 9:22
2:9
Is. 43:20f.; Deut.
10:15;
Is. 61:6; 66:21;
1 Pet. 2:5; Rev.
1:6;
Ex. 19:6; Deut.
7:6;
Ex. 19:5; Deut.
4:20; 14:2; Titus
2:14;
Is. 9:2; 42:16;
Acts 26:18; 2 Cor.
4:6
2:10
Hos. 1:10; 2:23;
Rom. 9:25; 10:19
2:11
Heb. 6:9; 1 Pet.
4:12;
Rom. 12:1;
Lev. 25:23; Ps.
39:12; Eph. 2:19;
Heb. 11:13;
1 Pet. 1:17;
Rom. 13:14; Gal.
5:16,24;
James 4:1
2:12
2 Cor. 8:21; Phil.
2:15; Titus 2:8;
1 Pet. 2:15; 3:16;
Acts 28:22;
Matt. 5:16; 9:8;
John 13:31;
1 Pet. 4:11,16;
Is. 10:3; Luke
19:44
2:13
Rom. 13:1
2:14
Rom. 13:4;
Rom. 13:3
2:15
1 Pet. 3:17;
1 Pet. 2:12

3   if you have tasted the kindness of the Lord.

As Living Stones

4   And coming to Him as to a *living* stone, rejected* by men, but choice and precious in the sight of God,

5   you also, as *living stones,* are being built up as a *spiritual* house for a *holy*[28a] priesthood, to offer[x] up spiritual sacrifices acceptable to God through Jesus Christ.

6   For *this* is contained in Scripture:

"BEHOLD I LAY IN ZION A †CHOICE STONE, A †PRECIOUS
CORNER *stone,*
AND HE WHO BELIEVES IN HIM SHALL •NOT BE
DISAPPOINTED."[x]

7   This precious value, then, is for you who believe. But for those who disbelieve,

"THE STONE WHICH THE BUILDERS †REJECTED,
THIS BECAME THE VERY CORNER *stone,"*

8   and,

"A STONE OF STUMBLING AND A ROCK OF OFFENSE";
for they stumble because they are disobedient to the word, and to this *doom* they were also appointed.

9   But †*you* are A CHOSEN RACE, A royal PRIESTHOOD, A HOLY NATION, A PEOPLE FOR *God's* OWN POSSESSION, that you may proclaim[x] the *excellencies* of Him who has called you out of darkness into His marvelous light;

10   for you once were NOT A PEOPLE, but now you are THE PEOPLE OF GOD; you had NOT RECEIVED* MERCY, but now you have RECEIVED MERCY.

11   Beloved, I urge you as aliens and strangers to abstain~ from fleshly lusts, which wage war against the soul.

12   Keep your behavior excellent among the Gentiles, so that in the thing in which they slander you as evildoers, they may on account of your good[25b] deeds, as they observe *them,* glorify[x] God in the day of ᶜvisitation.

Honor Authority

13   Submit[xl] yourselves for the Lord's sake to every human institution, whether to a king as the one in authority,

14   or to governors as sent by him for the punishment of evildoers and the praise of those who do right.

15   For such is the will of God that by doing right you may silence~ the ignorance of foolish[20b] men.

ᶜI.e., Christ's coming again in judgment

16   *Act* as free men, and do not use your freedom as a covering for evil,[10e] but *use it* as bondslaves[38b] of *God*.

17   *Honor*[xl] all men; *love*[~l] the brotherhood, *fear*[~l] God, *honor*[~l] the king.

18   Servants, be submissive to your masters with all respect, not only to those who are good[25a] and gentle,[23a] but also to those who are unreasonable.

19   For this *finds* favor, if for the sake of *conscience toward God* a man bears up under sorrows when suffering *unjustly*.

20   For what credit is there if, when you sin and are harshly treated, you endure it with patience? But if when you do what is right and suffer *for it* you patiently endure it, this *finds* favor with God.

Christ Is Our Example

21   For you have been called for this purpose, since Christ also suffered for you, leaving you an example for you to follow[xl] in His steps,

22   WHO COMMITTED[11a] NO *SIN*, NOR WAS ANY *DECEIT* FOUND IN HIS MOUTH;

23   and while being reviled, He did not revile[m] in return; while suffering, He uttered[m] no threats, but kept entrusting[m] *Himself* to Him who judges *righteously*;

24   and *He Himself* bore *our sins* in His body on the cross, that we might die to *sin* and live[x] to *righteousness*; for *by His wounds* you were healed.[15b]

25   For you were continually straying[~16b] like sheep, but *now* you have returned to the Shepherd and Guardian of your souls.

Godly Living

3   In the same way, you wives, be submissive to your own husbands so that even if any *of them* are disobedient to the word, they may be won without a word by the behavior of their wives,

2   as they observe your chaste and respectful behavior.

3   And let not your adornment be *merely* external—braiding the hair, and wearing gold jewelry, or putting on dresses;

4   but *let it be* the hidden person of the †heart, with the imperishable quality of a gentle[23b] and quiet spirit, which is *precious* in the sight of God.

5   For in this way in former times the holy[28a] women also, who hoped in God, used to adorn[m] themselves, being submissive to their own husbands.

6   Thus Sarah obeyed Abraham, calling him lord, and you

2:16
John 8:32; James 1:25;
Rom. 6:22; 1 Cor. 7:22
2:17
Rom. 12:10; 13:7; 1 Pet. 1:22;
Prov. 24:21; Matt. 22:21;
1 Pet. 2:13
2:18
Eph. 6:5; James 3:17
2:19
Rom. 13:5; 1 Pet. 3:14,16f.
2:20
1 Pet. 3:17
2:21
Acts 14:22; 1 Pet. 3:9;
1 Pet. 3:18; 4:1, 13;
Matt. 11:29; 16:24
2:22
Is. 53:9; 2 Cor. 5:21
2:23
Is. 53:7; Heb. 12:3; 1 Pet. 3:9
2:24
Is. 53:4,11; 1 Cor. 15:3; Heb. 9:28;
Acts 5:30;
Rom. 6:2,13;
Is. 53:5;
Heb. 12:13; James 5:16
2:25
Is. 53:6;
John 10:11; 1 Pet. 5:4
3:1
1 Pet. 3:7;
Eph. 5:22; Col. 3:18;
1 Cor. 9:19
3:3
Is. 3:18ff.; 1 Tim. 2:9
3:4
Rom. 7:22
3:5
1 Tim. 5:5; 1 Pet. 1:3
3:6
Gen. 18:12;
1 Pet. 3:14

have become her children if you do what is right without being frightened by any fear.

3:7
Eph. 5:25; Col.
3:19;
1 Thess. 4:4

7   You husbands likewise, live with *your wives* in an understanding way, as with a weaker vessel, since she is a woman; and grant her honor as a fellow heir of the grace of life, so that your prayers may not be †hindered. ~

3:8
Rom. 12:16;
1 Pet. 1:22;
Eph. 4:32;
Eph. 4:2; Phil.
2:3; 1 Pet. 5:5
3:9
Rom. 12:17;
1 Thess. 5:15;
1 Pet. 2:23;
Luke 6:28; Rom.
12:14; 1 Cor.
4:12;
1 Pet. 2:21;
Gal. 3:14; Heb.
6:14; 12:17
3:10
Ps. 34:12,13

8   To sum up, let all be harmonious, sympathetic, brotherly, kindhearted, and humble in spirit;

9   not returning evil[10a] for evil, or insult for insult, but giving a blessing instead; for you were called for the very purpose that you might inherit[x] a *blessing.*

10   For,
> "LET HIM WHO MEANS TO LOVE~ LIFE AND SEE[x] GOOD[25a]
> DAYS
> REFRAIN[xi] HIS TONGUE FROM EVIL AND HIS LIPS FROM
> SPEAKING[x] GUILE.

3:11
Ps. 34:14

11   "AND LET HIM TURN[xi] AWAY FROM EVIL AND DO[xi] GOOD;
LET HIM SEEK[xi] PEACE AND PURSUE[xi] IT.

3:12
Ps. 34:15,16

12   "FOR THE EYES OF THE LORD ARE UPON THE RIGHTEOUS,
AND HIS EARS ATTEND TO THEIR PRAYER,
BUT THE FACE OF THE LORD IS AGAINST THOSE WHO DO
EVIL."

3:13
Prov. 16:7
3:14
Matt. 5:10; 1 Pet.
2:19ff.; 4:15f.;
James 5:11;
Is. 8:12f.; 1 Pet.
3:6
3:15
1 Pet. 1:3;
Col. 4:6;
2 Tim. 2:25;
1 Pet. 1:17
3:16
1 Tim. 1:5; Heb.
13:18; 1 Pet.
3:21;
1 Pet. 2:12,15
3:17
1 Pet. 2:20;
4:15f.;
Acts 18:21; 1 Pet.
1:6; 2:15; 4:19
3:18
1 Pet. 2:21;
Heb. 9:26,28;
10:10;
Rom. 5:2; Eph.
3:12;
Col. 1:22; 1 Pet.
4:1;
1 Pet. 4:6
3:19
1 Pet. 4:6
3:20
Rom. 2:4;
Gen. 6:3,5,13f.;
Heb. 11:7;
Gen. 8:18; 2 Pet.
2:5;
Acts 2:41; 1 Pet.
1:9,22; 2:25;
4:19

13   And who is there to harm you if you prove zealous for what is *good?*[25a]

14   But even if you should suffer~ for the sake of righteousness, *you are* blessed. AND DO NOT FEAR⊙ THEIR INTIMIDATION, AND DO NOT BE TROUBLED,⊙

15   but ᵈsanctify[xi] Christ *as Lord* in your hearts, always *being* ready to make a defense to everyone who asks you to give an account for the hope that is in you, yet with gentleness[23b] and reverence;

16   and keep a good[25a] conscience so that in the thing in which you are slandered, those who revile your *good*[25a] behavior in Christ may be put[x] to shame.[39c]

17   For it is better, if God should will it so, that you suffer~ for doing what is right rather than for doing what is wrong.

18   For Christ also died *for sins* once for all, *the* just for *the* unjust, in order that He might bring[x] us to God, having been put to death in the flesh, but made alive in the spirit;

19   in which also He went and made proclamation to the spirits *now* in prison,

20   who once were disobedient, when the *patience of God* kept waiting[m] in the days of Noah, during the construction of the

ᵈi.e., set apart

ark, in which a few, that is, *eight* persons, were brought safely through *the* water.

21   And corresponding to that, baptism now saves *you*—not the removal of dirt from the *flesh,* but an appeal to God for a *good conscience*—through the resurrection of Jesus Christ,

22   who is at the right hand of God, having gone into heaven, after angels and authorities and powers had been subjected to Him.

Keep Fervent in Your Love

4   Therefore, since *Christ* has ᵉsuffered in the flesh, armˣˡ yourselves also with the *same purpose,* because he who has suffered in the flesh has ceased⁺ from sin,

2   so as to liveˣ the rest of the time in the flesh no longer for the lusts of men, but for the will of ⁺God.

3   For the time already past is sufficient *for you* to have carried⁺ out the *desire of the Gentiles,* having pursued⁺ a course of sensuality, lusts, drunkenness, carousals, drinking parties and abominable idolatries.

4   And in *all* this, they are surprised that you do not run with *them* into the same excess of dissipation, and they malign *you;*

5   but they shall give account to Him who is ready to judgeˣ the living and the dead.

6   For the gospel has for this purpose been preached even to those who are *dead,* that though they are judgedˣ in the *flesh* as men, they may live~ in the ⁺spirit according to *the will of* God.

7   The end of *all things* is at hand;⁺ therefore, be of sound judgmentˣˡ and soberˣˡ *spirit* for the purpose of prayer.

8   Above all, keep fervent in your love³¹ᵃ for one another, because love covers a multitude of sins.

9   Be hospitable to one another without complaint.

10   As *each one* has received a *special* gift,²⁴ᶜ employ it in serving³⁸ᵃ one another, as good²⁵ᵇ stewards of the manifold grace of God.

11   Whoever speaks, *let him speak,* as it were, the utterances of God; whoever serves, *let him do so* as by the strength³² which *God* supplies; so that in all things God may be *glorified*~ through Jesus Christ, to whom belongs the glory and dominion³²ᵈ forever and ever. Amen.

Share the Sufferings of Christ

12   Beloved, do not be surprisedᶿ at the fiery ordeal among

ᵉI.e., suffered death

3:21
Acts 16:33; Titus 3:5;
Heb. 9:14; 10:22;
1 Tim. 1:5; Heb. 13:18; 1 Pet. 3:16;
1 Pet. 1:3
3:22
Mark 16:19;
Heb. 4:14; 6:20;
Rom. 8:38f.; Heb. 1:6

4:1
1 Pet. 2:21;
Eph. 6:13;
Rom. 6:7

4:2
Rom. 6:2; Col. 3:3;
1 Pet. 1:14;
Mark 3:35
4:3
1 Cor. 12:2;
Rom. 13:13; Eph. 2:2; 4:17ff.

4:4
Eph. 5:18;
1 Pet. 3:16

4:5
Acts 10:42; Rom. 14:9; 2 Tim. 4:1

4:6
1 Pet. 1:12; 3:19

4:7
Rom. 13:11; Heb. 9:26; James 5:8;
1 John 2:18;
1 Pet. 1:13
4:8
1 Pet. 1:22;
Prov. 10:12;
1 Cor. 13:4ff.;
James 5:20
4:9
1 Tim. 3:2; Heb. 13:2;
Phil. 2:14
4:10
Rom. 12:6f.;
1 Cor. 4:1
4:11
1 Thess. 2:4;
Titus 2:1,15; Heb. 13:7;
Acts 7:38;
Eph. 1:19; 6:10;
1 Cor. 10:31;
1 Pet. 2:12;
Rom. 11:36;
1 Pet. 5:11; Rev. 1:6; 5:13

4:12
1 Pet. 2:11;
1 Pet. 1:6f.

4:13
Rom. 8:17; 2 Cor.
1:5; 4:10; Phil.
3:10;
1 Pet. 1:7; 5:1;
2 Tim. 2:12
4:14
John 15:21; Heb.
11:26; 1 Pet.
4:16;
Matt. 5:11; Luke
6:22; Acts 5:41;
2 Cor. 4:10f.,16
4:15
1 Pet. 2:19f.;
3:17;
1 Thess. 4:11;
2 Thess. 3:11;
1 Tim. 5:13
4:16
Acts 5:41; 28:22;
James 2:7;
1 Pet. 4:11
4:17
Jer. 25:29; Ezek.
9:6; Amos 3:2;
1 Tim. 3:15; Heb.
3:6; 1 Pet. 2:5;
Rom. 2:9;
2 Thess. 1:8;
Rom. 1:1
4:18
Prov. 11:31; Luke
23:31;
1 Tim. 1:9
4:19
1 Pet. 3:17
5:1
Acts 11:30;
2 John 1; 3 John
1;
Luke 24:48; Heb.
12:1;
1 Pet. 1:5,7; 4:13;
Rev. 1:9
5:2
John 21:16; Acts
20:28;
Philem. 14;
1 Tim. 3:8
5:3
Ezek. 34:4; Matt.
20:25f.;
John 13:15; Phil.
3:17; 1 Thess.
1:7; 2 Thess. 3:9;
1 Tim. 4:12; Titus
2:7
5:4
1 Pet. 2:25;
1 Pet. 1:4;
1 Cor. 9:25
5:5
Luke 22:26;
1 Tim. 5:1;
Eph. 5:21;
1 Pet. 3:8;
Prov. 3:34;
James 4:6
5:6
Matt. 23:12; Luke
14:11; 18:14;
James 4:10
5:7
Ps. 55:22; Matt.
6:25
5:8
1 Pet. 1:13;
Matt. 24:42;
James 4:7;
2 Tim. 4:17
5:9
James 4:7;
Col. 2:5;
Acts 14:22

you, which comes upon you for your testing, as though *some strange*[4] *thing* were happening to you;

13 but to the degree that you share the sufferings of †Christ, keep on rejoicing;^ so that also at the *revelation of His glory,* you may rejoice^x with exultation.

14 If you are reviled for the name of Christ, you are blessed, because the Spirit of glory and of God rests *upon you.*

15 By no means let *any of you* suffer^⊙ as a murderer, or thief, or evildoer, or a troublesome meddler;

16 but if *anyone suffers* as a Christian, let him not feel ashamed,^⊙ but in †*that* name let him glorify^ God.

17 For *it is* time for judgment to begin^x with the household of God; and if *it begins* with us first, what *will be* the outcome for those who do not obey the gospel of God?

18 AND IF IT IS WITH DIFFICULTY THAT THE RIGHTEOUS IS SAVED, WHAT WILL BECOME OF THE GODLESS MAN AND THE SINNER?

19 Therefore, let those also who suffer according to the will of God entrust^ their souls to a *faithful Creator* in doing what is right.

Serve God Willingly

5 Therefore, I exhort the elders among you, as *your* fellow elder and witness of the sufferings of Christ, and a partaker also of the glory that is to be revealed,

2 shepherd^xı the flock of God among you, exercising oversight not under compulsion, but voluntarily, according to *the will of* God; and not for sordid gain, but with eagerness;

3 nor yet as lording it over those allotted to your charge, but proving to be *examples* to the flock.

4 And when the Chief Shepherd appears, you will receive the unfading crown of glory.

5 You younger men, likewise, be subject^xı to your elders; and all of you, clothe^xı yourselves with *humility*[23c] toward one another, for GOD IS OPPOSED TO THE PROUD, BUT GIVES GRACE TO THE HUMBLE.

6 Humble^xı yourselves, therefore, under the mighty hand of God, that He may exalt^x you at the proper time,

7 casting *all your anxiety* upon Him, because He cares for you.

8 Be of sober *spirit,*^xı be on the alert.^xı Your adversary, the devil, prowls about like a roaring lion, seeking someone to devour.^x1

9 But resist^xı him, firm in *your* faith, knowing that the same

experiences of suffering are being accomplished~ by your brethren who are in the world.

10   And after you have suffered for a little while, the God of all
grace, who called you to His eternal glory in Christ, will Himself
perfect, confirm, strengthen *and* establish you.

11   To †*Him be* dominion[32d] forever and ever. Amen.

12   Through Silvanus, our faithful brother (for so I regard
him), I have written to you briefly, exhorting and testifying that
this is the true grace of God. Stand[xl] firm in it!

13   †She who is in Babylon, chosen together with you, sends
you greetings, and *so does* my son, Mark.

14   Greet[xl] one another with a kiss of love.[31a]

Peace be to you all who are in Christ.

†Some mss. read *The church which*

5:10
1 Pet. 1:6;
1 Pet. 4:10;
1 Cor. 1:9;
1 Thess. 2:12;
2 Cor. 4:17;
2 Tim. 2:10;
1 Cor. 1:10; Heb.
13:21;
Rom. 16:25;
2 Thess. 2:17; 3:3
5:11
Rom. 11:36;
1 Pet. 4:11
5:12
2 Cor. 1:19;
Heb. 13:22;
Acts 11:23; 1 Pet.
1:13; 4:10;
1 Cor. 15:1
5:13
Acts 12:12,25;
15:37,39; Col.
4:10; Philem. 24
5:14
Rom. 16:16;
Eph. 6:23

The Second Epistle of
Peter

Growth in Christian Virtue

1 ªSimon Peter, a bond-servant[38b] and apostle of Jesus Christ, to those who have received a faith of the same kind as ours, by the righteousness of our God and Savior, Jesus Christ:

2 Grace and peace be multiplied[x] to you in the knowledge[29b] of God and of Jesus our Lord;

3 seeing that His divine power[32a] has granted[+] to us *everything* pertaining to life and godliness, through the true[1] knowledge of Him who called us by His own glory and excellence.

4 For by these He has granted[+] to us His precious and magnificent promises, in order that by them you might become partakers of *the divine* nature, having escaped the corruption that is in the world by lust.

5 Now for this very reason also, applying *all* diligence, in your faith supply[xl] moral excellence, and in *your* moral excellence, knowledge;

6 and in *your* knowledge, self-control, and in *your* self-control, perseverance, and in *your* perseverance, godliness;

7 and in *your* godliness, brotherly kindness, and in *your* brotherly kindness, love.[31a]

8 For if these *qualities* are yours and are increasing, they render you neither useless nor unfruitful in the true[1] knowledge of our Lord Jesus Christ.

9 For he who lacks these *qualities* is blind *or* short-sighted, having forgotten *his* purification from his former sins.

10 Therefore, brethren, be all the more diligent[xl] to make~ *certain* about His calling and choosing you; for as long as you practice[19a] these things, you will *never* stumble;[x]

11 for in this way the entrance into the eternal kingdom of our Lord and Savior Jesus Christ will be *abundantly supplied* to you.

12 Therefore, I shall always be ready to remind you of these things, even though[2] you *already* know *them*, and have been established[+] in the truth which is present with *you*.

13 And I consider it right, as long as I am in this *earthly* dwelling, to stir~ you up by way of reminder,

14 knowing that the laying aside of my *earthly* dwelling is

ªMost early mss. read *Simeon*

imminent, as also our Lord Jesus Christ has made clear to me.

15   And I will also be diligent that at any time after *my* departure you may be able to call~ these things to mind.

Eyewitnesses

16   For we did not follow cleverly devised⁺ tales when we made known to you the power³²ᵃ and coming of our Lord Jesus Christ, but we were *eyewitnesses* of His majesty.

17   For when He received honor and glory from God the Father, such² an utterance as this was made to Him by the Majestic Glory, "This is *My beloved Son* with whom *I* am well-pleased"—

18   and *we ourselves* heard this utterance made from heaven when we were with Him on the holy mountain.

19   And *so* we have the prophetic word *made more* ⁺*sure,* to which you do well to pay attention as to a lamp shining in a dark place, until the day dawnsˣ and the morning star arisesˣ in your hearts.

20   But know this first of all, that no prophecy of Scripture is *a matter* of one's *own* interpretation,

21   for no prophecy was ever made by an act of *human will,* but men moved by the *Holy* ⁺*Spirit* spoke from *God.*

The Rise of False Prophets

2   But false prophets also arose among the people, just as there will also be false teachers among *you,* who will secretly introduce destructive heresies, even denying the Master who bought ⁺them, bringing swift destruction upon themselves.

2   And many will follow their sensuality, and because of them the way of the truth will be maligned;

3   and in *their greed* they will exploit you with *false words;* their judgment from long ago is not idle, and their destruction is not asleep.

4   For if God did not spare *angels* when they sinned, but cast them into ⁺hell and committed them to pits of darkness, reserved for judgment;

5   and did not spare the *ancient world,* but preserved Noah, a preacher of *righteousness,* with seven others, when He brought a flood upon the world of the ungodly;

6   and *if* He condemned the cities of *Sodom and Gomorrah* to destruction by reducing *them* to ashes, having made⁺ them an ⁺*example* to those who would live~ ungodly thereafter;

7   and *if* He rescued¹⁸ᵇ *righteous Lot,* oppressed¹ by the sensual conduct of unprincipled men

1:15
Luke 9:31

1:16
1 Tim. 1:4; 2 Pet. 2:3;
Mark 13:26;
14:62; 1 Thess. 2:19;
Matt. 17:1ff.;
Mark 9:2ff.; Luke 9:28ff.
1:17
Matt. 17:5; Mark 9:7; Luke 9:35;
Heb. 1:3
1:18
Ex. 3:5; Josh. 5:15
1:19
1 Pet. 1:10f.;
Heb. 2:2;
Ps. 119:105;
Luke 1:78;
Rev. 22:16;
2 Cor. 4:6
1:20
2 Pet. 3:3;
Rom. 12:6
1:21
Jer. 23:26; 2 Tim. 3:16;
2 Sam. 23:2;
Luke 1:70; Acts 1:16; 3:18; 1 Pet. 1:11
2:1
Deut. 13:1ff.; Jer. 6:13;
2 Cor. 11:13;
Matt. 7:15; 1 Tim. 4:1;
Gal. 2:4; Jude 4;
1 Cor. 11:19; Gal. 5:20;
Rev. 6:10;
1 Cor. 6:20
2:2
Gen. 19:5ff.;
2 Pet. 2:7,18;
Jude 4;
Acts 16:17; 22:4; 24:14;
Rom. 2:24
2:3
1 Tim. 6:5; 2 Pet. 2:14; Jude 16;
2 Cor. 2:17;
1 Thess. 2:5;
Rom. 16:18;
2 Pet. 1:16;
Deut. 32:35
2:4
Jude 6;
Rev. 20:1f.
2:5
Ezek. 26:20;
2 Pet. 3:6;
Gen. 6:8,9; 1 Pet. 3:20
2:6
Gen. 19:24;
Jude 7;
Is. 1:9; Matt. 10:15; 11:23;
Rom. 9:29;
Jude 15
2:7
Gen. 19:16,29;
Gen. 19:5ff.;
2 Pet. 2:2,18;
Jude 4;
2 Pet. 3:17

2:8
Heb. 11:4

2:9
1 Cor. 10:13;
Rev. 3:10;
Matt. 10:15; Jude
6

2:10
2 Pet. 3:3; Jude
16,18;
Ex. 22:28; Jude
8;
Titus 1:7
2:11
Jude 9

2:12
Jude 10;
Jer. 12:3; Col.
2:22

2:13
2 Pet. 2:15;
Rom. 13:13;
1 Thess. 5:7;
1 Cor. 11:21;
Jude 12

2:14
2 Pet. 2:18;
James 1:8; 2 Pet.
3:16;
2 Pet. 2:3;
Eph. 2:3
2:15
Acts 13:10;
Num. 22:5,7;
Deut. 23:4; Neh.
13:2; Jude 11;
Rev. 2:14;
2 Pet. 2:13
2:16
Num. 22:21,23,
28,30ff.

2:17
Jude 12;
Jude 13

2:18
Jude 16;
Eph. 4:17;
2 Pet. 2:14;
2 Pet. 2:2;
2 Pet. 1:4; 2:20
2:19
John 8:34; Rom.
6:16

2:20
2 Pet. 2:18;
2 Pet. 1:2;
2 Pet. 1:11; 3:18;
2 Tim. 2:4;
Matt. 12:45; Luke
11:26

2:21
Ezek. 18:24; Heb.
6:4ff.; 10:26f.;
James 4:17;
Gal. 6:2; 1 Tim.
6:14; 2 Pet. 3:2;
Jude 3

8 (for by what he saw and heard *that* righteous man, while living among them, felt *his righteous* soul tormented[m] day after day with *their* lawless deeds),

9 *then* the Lord knows how to rescue[~18b] the *godly from temptation,* and to keep[~] the *unrighteous* under punishment for the day of judgment,

10 and especially those who indulge the flesh in *its* corrupt desires and despise [†]authority. Daring, *self-willed,* they do not tremble when they revile angelic majesties,

11 whereas angels who are [†]*greater* in might[32c] and power[32a] do not bring a reviling judgment against them before the Lord.

12 But these, like unreasoning animals, born[*] as creatures of instinct to be captured and killed, reviling where they have no knowledge, will in the destruction of those creatures also be destroyed,

13 suffering wrong as the wages of doing wrong. They count it a pleasure to revel in the daytime. They are stains and blemishes, reveling in their [b]deceptions, as they carouse with you,

14 having eyes full of adultery and that never cease from sin, enticing unstable souls, having a heart trained[*] in [†]greed, *accursed* children;

15 forsaking the right way they have gone astray, having followed the way of Balaam, the *son* of Beor, who loved the *wages of unrighteousness,*

16 but he received a rebuke for his own transgression; *for* a *dumb* donkey, speaking with a voice of a *man,* restrained the madness of the prophet.

17 These are springs *without water,* and mists driven by a storm, for whom the black darkness has been reserved.[*]

18 For speaking out arrogant *words* of vanity they entice by fleshly desires, by sensuality, those who barely escape from the ones who live in error,

19 promising them [†]freedom while they themselves are *slaves* of corruption; for by what a man is overcome,[*] by this he is enslaved.[*]

20 For if after they have escaped the defilements of the world by the knowledge[29b] of the Lord and Savior Jesus Christ, they are again entangled in them and are overcome,[*] the *last state* has become[*] worse for them than the first.

21 For it would be better for them not to have known[*29b] the way of righteousness, than having known[29b] it, to turn[x] away from the holy[28a] commandment delivered to them.

[b]Some ancient mss. read *love feasts,* (cf. Jude 12)

22   It has happened⁺ to them according to the true proverb, "A DOG RETURNS TO ITS OWN VOMIT," and, "A sow, after washing, *returns* to wallowing in the mire."

Purpose of This Letter

3   This is now, beloved, the second letter I am writing to you in which I am stirring up your sincere mind³³ᵃ by way of reminder,

2   that you should remember˟ the words⁴³ᵇ spoken⁺ beforehand by the holy prophets and the commandment of the Lord and Savior *spoken* by your apostles.

The Coming Day of the Lord

3   Know this first of all, that in the last days *mockers* will come with *their* mocking, following after their own ⁺lusts,

4   and saying, "Where is the promise of His coming? For *ever* since the fathers fell asleep, all continues just as it was from the beginning of creation."

5   For when they maintain this, it escapes their notice that by the word⁴³ᵃ of ⁺*God the* heavens existed long ago and *the* earth was formed out of water and by water,

6   through which the world at that time was destroyed, being flooded with water.

7   But the present heavens and earth by His ⁺word are being reserved⁺ for ⁺fire, kept for the day of judgment and destruction of ungodly men.

8   But do not let this one *fact* escape⁰ your notice, beloved, that with the Lord *one* day is as a *thousand* years, and a *thousand* years as ⁺*one* day.

9   The Lord is *not slow* about His promise, as some count slowness, but is patient toward you, not wishing for any to perish˟ but for all to come˟ to *repentance.*

A New Heaven and Earth

10   But the day of the Lord will come like a thief, in which the heavens will pass away with a roar and the elements will be destroyed with intense heat, and the earth and its works will be ᶜburned up.

11   Since *all* these things are to be destroyed in this way, what sort of people ought you to be~ in holy²⁸ᵃ conduct and godliness,

12   looking for and hastening the coming of the day of ⁺*God,* on account of which the heavens will be destroyed by burning, and the elements will melt with intense heat!

ᶜSome ancient mss. read *discovered*

2:22
Prov. 26:11

3:1
1 Pet. 2:11; 2 Pet. 3:8,14,17;
2 Pet. 1:13

3:2
Jude 17;
Luke 1:70; Acts 3:21; Eph. 3:5;
Gal. 6:2; 1 Tim. 6:14; 2 Pet. 2:21

3:3
2 Pet. 1:20;
1 Tim. 4:1; Heb. 1:2;
Jude 18;
2 Pet. 2:10
3:4
Is. 5:19; Jer. 17:15; Ezek. 11:3; 12:22,27;
Mal. 2:17; Matt. 24:48;
1 Thess. 2:19;
2 Pet. 3:12;
Acts 7:60;
Mark 10:6
3:5
Gen. 1:6,9; Heb. 11:3;
Ps. 24:2; 136:6
3:6
2 Pet. 2:5;
Gen. 7:11,12,21f.
3:7
2 Pet. 3:10,12;
Is. 66:15; Dan. 7:9f.; 2 Thess. 1:7; Heb. 12:29;
Matt. 10:15;
1 Cor. 3:13;
Jude 7
3:8
2 Pet. 3:1;
Ps. 90:4
3:9
Hab. 2:3; Rom. 13:11; Heb. 10:37;
Rom. 2:4; Rev. 2:21;
1 Tim. 2:4; Rev. 2:21
3:10
1 Cor. 1:8;
Matt. 24:43; Luke 12:39; 1 Thess. 5:2; Rev. 3:3; 16:15;
Is. 34:4; 2 Pet. 3:7,12;
Matt. 24:35; Rev. 21:1;
Is. 24:19; Mic. 1:4;
2 Pet. 3:7
3:12
1 Cor. 1:7;
2 Pet. 3:7,10;
Is. 24:19; 34:4;
Mic. 1:4

3:13
Is. 65:17; 66:22;
Rom. 8:21; Rev.
21:1;
Is. 60:21; 65:25;
Rev. 21:27
3:14
1 Cor. 15:58;
2 Pet. 1:10;
2 Pet. 3:1;
1 Pet. 1:7;
Phil. 2:15; 1
Thess. 5:23; 1
Tim. 6:14; James
1:27
3:15
2 Pet. 3:9;
Acts 9:17; 15:25;
2 Pet. 3:2;
1 Cor. 3:10; Eph.
3:3
3:16
2 Pet. 3:14;
Heb. 5:11;
2 Pet. 2:14;
2 Pet. 3:2
3:17
2 Pet. 3:1;
1 Cor. 10:12;
2 Pet. 2:18;
2 Pet. 2:7;
Rev. 2:5
3:18
2 Pet. 1:2;
2 Pet. 1:11; 2:20;
Rom. 11:36;
2 Tim. 4:18; Rev.
1:6

13 But according to His promise we are looking for *new heavens* and a *new earth,* in which righteousness dwells.

14 Therefore, beloved, since you look for these things, be diligent[xl] to be found[x] by Him in peace, *spotless* and *blameless,*

15 and regard[m] the patience of our Lord *to be salvation;* just as also our beloved brother Paul, according to the wisdom given him, wrote to you,

16 as also in all *his* letters, speaking in them of these things, in which are some things hard to †understand, which the untaught and unstable distort, as *they do* also the rest of the Scriptures, to their •own destruction.

17 You therefore, beloved, knowing this beforehand, be on your guard[m] lest, being carried away by the error of unprincipled men, you fall[x] from your own steadfastness,

18 but grow[m] in the grace and knowledge of our Lord and Savior Jesus Christ. To †*Him be* the glory, both now and to the day of eternity. Amen.

The First Epistle of

John

1:1
John 1:1f.; 1 John
2:13,14;
Acts 4:20; 1 John
1:3;
John 19:35;
2 Pet. 1:16;
1 John 1:2;
John 1:14; 1 John
4:14;
Luke 24:39; John
20:27;
John 1:1,4
1:2
John 1:4; 1 John
3:5,8; 5:20;
John 19:35;
1 John 1:1;
John 15:27;
1 John 4:14;
John 10:28; 17:3;
1 John 2:25; 5:11,
13,20;
John 1:1
1:3
John 19:35;
2 Pet. 1:16;
1 John 1:1;
Acts 4:20; 1 John
1:1;
John 17:3,21; 1
Cor. 1:9
1:4
1 John 2:1;
John 3:29
1:5
John 1:19; 1 John
3:11;
1 Tim. 6:16;
James 1:17
1:6
John 8:12; 1 John
2:11;
John 8:55; 1 John
2:4; 4:20;
John 3:21
1:7
Is. 2:5;
1 Tim. 6:16;
Titus 2:14
1:8
Job 15:14; Prov.
20:9; Rom.
3:10ff.; James
3:2;
John 8:44; 1 John
2:4
1:9
Ps. 32:5; Prov.
28:13;
Titus 2:14
1:10
Job 15:14;
John 3:33; 1 John
5:10;
1 John 2:14
2:1
John 13:33; Gal.
4:19; 1 John 2:12,
28; 3:7,18; 4:4;
5:21;
1 John 1:4;
Rom. 8:34;
1 Tim. 2:5; Heb.
7:25; 9:24;
John 14:16
2:2
Rom. 3:25; Heb.
2:17; 1 John
4:10;
John 4:42;
11:51f.; 1 John
4:14

Introduction The Incarnate Word

1 What was from the beginning, what we have heard, what we have seen with our eyes, what we beheld and our hands handled, concerning the Word[43a] of Life—

2   and the life was manifested, and we have seen and bear witness and proclaim to you the eternal life, which was with the Father and was manifested to us—

3   what we have seen and heard we proclaim to you also, that you also may have~ *fellowship* with us; and indeed *our* fellowship is with the Father, and with His Son Jesus Christ.

4   And these things *we* write, so that our joy may be made[+] complete.

God Is Light

5   And this is the message we have heard from Him and announce to you, that God is [+]*light,* and in Him there is no darkness *at all.*

6   If we say[x] that we have fellowship with Him and *yet* walk~ in the *darkness,* we lie and do not practice the truth;

7   but if we walk~ in the light as *He Himself* is in the light, we have *fellowship* with one another, and the blood of Jesus His Son cleanses us from all sin.

8   If we say[x] that we have no sin, we are deceiving[16b] *our-selves,* and the truth is not in us.

9   If we confess~ our sins, He is faithful and righteous to forgive[x21a] us our sins and to cleanse[x] us from all unrighteous-ness.

10   If we say[x] that we have not sinned,[+] we make Him a *liar,* and His word[43a] is not in us.

Christ Is Our Advocate

2 My little children, I am writing these things to you that you may not sin.[x] And if anyone sins,[x] we have an [a]*Advocate* with the Father, Jesus Christ the righteous;

2   and He Himself is the [+]*propitiation* for our sins; and not for ours only, but also for *those of* the whole world.

[a]Gr., *Parácletos,* one called alongside to help

2:3
1 John 2:5; 3:24;
4:13; 5:2;
1 John 2:4; 3:6;
4:7f.;
John 14:15;
15:10; 1 John
3:22,24; 5:3; Rev.
12:17; 14:12
2:4
Titus 1:10;
1 John 3:6; 4:7f.;
1 John 1:6; 1:8
2:5
John 14:23;
1 John 4:12;
1 John 2:3; 3:24;
4:13; 5:2
2:6
John 15:4;
John 13:15;
15:10; 1 Pet. 2:21
2:7
Heb. 6:9; 1 John
3:2,21; 4:1,7,11;
John 13:34;
1 John 3:11,23;
4:21; 2 John 5;
1 John 2:24; 3:11;
2 John 5,6
2:8
John 13:34;
Rom. 13:12; Eph.
5:8; 1 Thess.
5:4f.; John 1:9
2:9
1 John 2:11; 3:15;
4:20;
Acts 1:15; 1 John
3:10,16; 4:20f.
2:10
John 11:9; 1 John
2:10,11
2:11
1 John 1:6; 2:9;
3:15; 4:20;
John 12:35;
2 Cor. 4:4; 2 Pet.
1:9
2:12
1 John 2:1;
Acts 13:38; 1 Cor.
6:11
2:13
1 John 1:1;
John 16:33;
1 John 2:14; 4:4;
5:4f.; Rev. 2:7;
Matt. 5:37; 1 John
2:14; 3:12; 5:18f.;
John 14:7; 1 John
2:3
2:14
1 John 1:1;
Eph. 6:10;
John 5:38; 8:37;
1 John 1:10;
1 John 2:13
2:15
Rom. 12:2;
James 1:27; 4:4
2:16
Rom. 13:14; Eph.
2:3; 1 Pet. 2:11;
Prov. 27:20;
James 4:16
2:17
1 Cor. 7:31;
Mark 3:35
2:18
Rom. 13:11;
1 Tim. 4:1; 1 Pet.
4:7; Matt. 24:5,24;
1 John 2:22; 4:3;
2 John 7;
Mark 13:22;
1 John 4:1,3

3   And by this we know that we have come to know⁺²⁹ᵃ Him, if we keep~ His commandments.

4   The one who says, "I have come to know⁺²⁹ᵃ Him," and does not keep His commandments, is a †liar, and the truth is not in him;

5   but whoever keeps~ His *word*, ⁴³ᵃ in him the love of God has truly been perfected.⁺ By this we know that we are in †Him:

6   the one who says he abides~ in Him ought *himself* to walk~ in the same manner as *He* walked.

7   Beloved, I am not writing a *new* commandment to you, but an †old commandment which you have had꜒ from the beginning; the †old commandment is the word which you have heard.

8   On the other hand, I am writing a *new*³⁴ᵃ commandment to you, which is true in Him and in you, because the darkness is passing away, and the *true* light is already shining.

9   The one who says he is in the light and *yet* hates his brother is in the *darkness* until now.

10   The one who loves³¹ᵃ his brother abides in the *light* and there is *no cause for stumbling* in him.

11   But the one who hates his brother is in the darkness and walks in the darkness, and does not know where he is going because the darkness has blinded his eyes.

12   I am writing to you, little children, because your sins are *forgiven*⁺ you for His name's sake.

13   I am writing to you, fathers, because you know⁺²⁹ᵃ Him who has been from the beginning. I am writing to you, young men, because you have overcome⁺ the evil one. I have written to you, children, because you know⁺ the Father.

14   I have written to you, fathers, because you know⁺ Him who has been from the beginning. I have written to you, young men, because you are †strong, and the word⁴³ᵃ of God abides in you, and you have overcome⁺ the evil one.

Do Not Love the World

15   Do not love⁰ the world, nor the things in the world. If anyone loves~ the world, the love of the Father is not in him.

16   For all that is in the world, the lust of the flesh and the lust of the eyes and the boastful pride of life, ³⁰ᵃ is not from the Father, but is from the *world*.

17   And the world is passing away, and *also* its lusts; but the one who does the will of God abides forever.

18   Children, it is the last hour; and just as you heard that antichrist is coming, even *now* many antichrists have arisen;⁺ from this we know that it is the last hour.

19   They went out from us, but they were not *really* of us; for if they had been *of us,* they would have remained with us; but *they went out,* in order that it might be shown[x] that they *all* are not of us.

20   But you have an *anointing* from the Holy One, and you *all* know.

21   I have not written to you because you do not know the truth, but because you do know it, and because no lie is of the truth.

22   Who is the liar but the one who denies that Jesus is the Christ? This is the antichrist, the one who denies the Father and the Son.

23   Whoever denies the Son does not have the Father; the one who confesses the Son has the *Father also.*

24   As for you, let that abide[~] in you which you heard from the beginning. If what you heard from the beginning *abides*[x] in you, you also will abide *in the Son* and *in the Father.*

The Promise Is Eternal Life

25   And this is the promise which He Himself made to us: eternal life.

26   These things I have written to you concerning those who are trying to deceive[16b] you.

27   And as for you, the anointing which you received from Him abides in you, and you have no need for anyone to teach[~] you; but as *His* anointing teaches you about all things, and is true and is not a lie, and just as it has taught you, you abide[~] in Him.

28   And now, little children, abide[~] in Him, so that when He appears,[x] we may have[x] confidence and not shrink[x] away from Him in shame at His coming.

29   If you know[29e] that He is righteous, you know[29a] that everyone also who practices righteousness is born[+] *of Him.*

Children of God Love One Another

3   See[xl] how great a love the Father has bestowed[+] upon us, that we should be called[x] *children of God;* and *such* we are. For this reason the world does not know[29a] us, because it did not know[29a] Him.

2   Beloved, now we are children of [+]God, and it has not appeared as yet what we shall be. We know[29e] that, when He appears,[x] we shall be *like Him,* because we shall see Him just as He is.

3   And everyone who has [+]*this* hope *fixed* on Him purifies himself, just as *He* is pure. [13a]

2:19
Acts 20:30;
1 Cor. 11:19
2:20
2 Cor. 1:21;
1 John 2:27;
Mark 1:24; Acts
10:38;
Prov. 28:5; Matt.
13:11; John
14:26; 1 Cor.
2:15f.; 1 John
2:27
2:21
James 1:19;
2 Pet. 1:12; Jude
5;
John 8:44; 18:37;
1 John 3:19
2:22
1 John 4:3; 2
John 7;
Matt. 24:5,24; 1
John 2:18; 4:3;
2 John 7
2:23
John 8:19; 16:3;
17:3; 1 John 4:15;
5:1; 2 John 9
2:24
1 John 2:7;
John 14:23;
1 John 1:3;
2 John 9
2:25
John 3:15; 6:40;
1 John 1:2
2:26
1 John 3:7;
2 John 7
2:27
John 14:16;
1 John 2:20;
John 14:26;
1 Cor. 2:12; 1
Thess. 4:9;
John 14:17
2:28
1 John 2:1;
Luke 17:30; Col.
3:4; 1 John 3:2;
Eph. 3:12; 1 John
3:21; 4:17; 5:14;
Mark 8:38;
1 Thess. 2:19
2:29
John 7:18; 1 John
3:7;
John 1:13; 3:3;
1 John 3:9; 4:7;
5:1,4,18; 3 John 11
3:1
John 3:16; 1 John
4:10;
John 1:12; 11:52;
Rom. 8:16;
1 John 3:2,10;
John 15:18,21;
16:3
3:2
1 John 2:7;
John 1:12; 11:52;
Rom 8:16; 1 John
3:1,10;
Rom. 8:19,23f.;
Luke 17:30; Col.
3:4; 1 John 2:28;
Rom. 8:29; 2 Pet.
1:4;
John 17:24;
2 Cor. 3:18
3:3
Rom. 15:12;
1 Pet. 1:3;
John 17:19;
2 Cor 7:1; 2 Pet.
3:13f.; 1 John 2:6

3:4
Rom. 4:15;
1 John 5:17
3:5
1 John 1:2; 3:8;
John 1:29; 1 Pet.
1:18-20; 1 John
2:2; 2 Cor. 5:21;
1 John 2:29
3:6
1 John 2:3; 3:9;
3 John 11
3:7
1 John 2:1;
2:26; 2:29
3:8
Matt. 13:38; John
8:44; 1 John 3:10;
Matt. 4:3;
1 John 3:5;
John 12:31; 16:11
3:9
John 1:13; 3:3;
1 John 2:29; 4:7;
5:1,4,18; 3 John
11; 1 Pet. 1:23;
1 John 3:6; 5:18
3:10
John 1:12; 11:52;
Rom. 8:16;
1 John 3:1,2;
Matt. 13:38; John
8:44; 1 John 3:8;
Rom. 13:8ff.; Col.
3:14; 1 Tim 1:5;
1 John 4:8;
1 John 2:9
3:11
1 John 1:5; 2:7;
John 13:34f.;
15:12; 1 John 4:7,
11f.,21; 2 John 5
3:12
Gen. 4:8;
Matt. 5:37; 1 John
2:13f.;
Ps. 38:20; Prov.
29:10; John 8:40,
41
3:13
John 15:18; 17:14
3:14
John 5:24; 13:35;
1 John 2:10
3:15
Matt. 5:21f.; John
8:44; Gal. 5:20f.;
Rev. 21:8
3:16
John 10:11;15:13;
Phil. 2:17;
1 Thess. 2:8;
1 John 2:9
3:17
James 2:15f.;
Deut. 15:7;
1 John 4:20
3:18
1 John 2:1; 3:7;
2 John 1; 3 John
1
3:19
1 John 2:21
3:21
1 John 3:2;
1 John 2:28; 5:14
3:22
Job 22:26f.; Matt.
7:7; 21:22; John
9:31; 1 John 2:3;
John 8:29; Heb.
13:21
3:23
John 1:12; 2:23;
3:18; 6:29;
John 13:34;
15:12; 1 John 2:8

4   Everyone who practices sin also practices *lawlessness;* and sin is lawlessness.

5   And you know that He appeared in order to take[x] away *sins;* and *in Him* there is no sin.

6   No one who abides in Him sins; no one who sins has seen[+] Him or knows[+29a] Him.

7   Little children, let no one deceive[~] you; the one who practices righteousness is righteous, just as *He* is righteous;

8   the one who practices sin is of the devil; for the devil has sinned *from the beginning.* The Son of God appeared for this purpose, that He might destroy[x] the works of the devil.

9   No one who is born[+] of God practices *sin,* because His seed abides in him; and he cannot sin,[~] because he is born[+] *of God.*

10   By this the children of God and the children of the devil are obvious: anyone who does not practice righteousness is not of God, nor the one who does not love[31a] his brother.

11   For this is the message which you have heard from the beginning, that we should love[~31a] one another;

12   not as Cain, *who* was of the evil one, and slew his brother. And for what reason did he slay him? Because his deeds were evil,[10b] and his brother's were [+]righteous.

13   Do not marvel,[θ] brethren, if the world hates you.

14   We know that we have passed[+] out of death into life,· because we love[31a] the brethren. He who does not love abides in death.

15   Everyone who hates his brother is a murderer; and you know that no murderer has eternal life abiding in him.

16   We know[+29a] love by this, that He laid down *His life* for us; and *we* ought to lay[x] down *our lives* for the brethren.

17   But whoever has[~] the world's goods, and beholds[~] his brother in need and closes[x] his heart against him, how does the love of God abide in him?

18   Little children, let us not love[~] with word or with tongue, but in deed and truth.

19   We shall know by this that we are of the truth, and shall assure our heart before Him,

20   in whatever our *heart* condemns[~14a] us; for *God* is greater than our heart, and knows[29a] all things.

21   Beloved, if our heart does not condemn[~14a] us, we have *confidence* before God;

22   and whatever we ask[~] we receive from Him, because we keep *His commandments* and do[19a] the things that are *pleasing in His sight.*

23   And this is His commandment, that we believe[x] in the

name of His Son Jesus Christ, and love~[31a] one another, just as He commanded us.

24   And the one who keeps His commandments abides in Him, and He in †him. And we know[29a] by this that He abides in us, by the Spirit whom He has given us.

Testing the Spirits

4 Beloved, do not believe⁰ every spirit, but test~ᵗ the spirits to see whether they are from *God;* because many false prophets have gone⁺ out into the world.

2   By this you know[29a] the Spirit of God: every spirit that confesses that Jesus Christ has come⁺ in the flesh is *from God;*

3   and every spirit that does not confess Jesus is *not* from God; and this is the *spirit* of the antichrist, of which you have heard⁺ that it is coming, and now it is *already* in the world.

4   *You* are from God, little children, and have overcome⁺ them; because *greater*[26a] is He who is in you than he who is in the world.

5   *They* are from the world; therefore they speak *as from the world,* and the world listens to them.

6   *We* are from God; he who knows[29a] God listens to us; he who is not from God does not listen to us. By this we know[29a] the spirit of truth and the spirit of error.

God Is Love

7   Beloved, let us love~[31a] one another, for love is *from God;* and everyone who loves is born⁺ *of God* and knows[29a] God.

8   The one who does not love does not know God, for God is †*love.*

9   By this the love of God was manifested in us, that God has sent⁺ His *only begotten Son* into the world so that we might liveˣ through Him.

10   In this is love, not that *we* loved⁺ God, but that *He* loved us and sent His Son *to be* the propitiation for our sins.

11   Beloved, if God *so* loved[31a] us, *we also* ought to love~[31a] one another.

12   No one has beheld⁺ *God* at any time; if we love~ one another, God abides in us, and His love is *perfected*⁺ in us.

13   By this we know that we abide in Him and He in †us, because He has given⁺ us *of His Spirit.*

14   And *we* have beheld⁺ and bear witness that the Father has sent⁺ the Son *to be* the Savior of the world.

15   Whoever confessesˣ that Jesus is the Son of God, God abides in him, and he in God.

3:24
1 John 2:3;
John 6:56; 10:38;
1 John 2:6,24;
4:15;
John 14:17; Rom.
8:9,14,16;
1 Thess. 4:8;
1 John 4:13;
1 John 2:5
4:1
3 John 11;
Jer. 29:8; 1 Cor.
12:10; 1 Thess.
5:20f.; 2 Thess.
2:2;
Jer. 14:14; 2 Pet.
2:1; 1 John 2:18
4:2
1 Cor. 12:3;
1 John 2:23;
John 1:14; 1 John
1:2
4:3
1 John 2:22;
2 John 7;
1 John 2:18,22;
2 Thess. 2:3-7;
1 John 2:18
4:4
1 John 2:1;
1 John 2:13;
Rom. 8:31;
1 John 3:20;
John 12:31
4:5
John 15:19;
17:14,16
4:6
John 8:23; 1 John
4:4;
John 8:47; 10:3ff.;
18:37;
1 Cor. 14:37;
John 14:17;
1 Tim. 4:1
4:7
1 John 2:7;
1 John 3:11;
1 John 5:1;
1 John 2:29;
1 Cor. 8:3; 1 John
2:3
4:8
1 John 4:7,16
4:9
John 9:3; 1 John
4:16;
John 3:16f.;
1 John 4:10; 5:11
4:10
Rom. 5:8,10;
1 John 4:19;
John 3:16f.;
1 John 4:9; 5:11;
1 John 2:2
4:11
1 John 2:7;
1 John 4:7
4:12
John 1:18; 1 Tim.
6:16; 1 John 4:20;
1 John 2:5; 4:17f.
4:13
Rom. 8:9; 1 John
3:24
4:14
John 15:27;
1 John 1:2;
John 3:17; 4:42; 1
John 2:2
4:15
1 John 2:23;
Rom. 10:9;
1 John 3:23; 4:2;
5:1,5;
1 John 2:24; 3:24

4:16
John 6:69;
John 9:3; 1 John
4:9;
1 John 4:7,8;
1 John 4:12f.
4:17
1 John 2:5; 4:12;
1 John 2:28;
Matt. 10:15;
John 17:22;
1 John 2:6; 3:1,7,
16
4:18
Rom. 8:15;
1 John 4:12

4:19
1 John 4:10
4:20
1 John 1:6,8,10;
2:4;
1 John 2:9,11;
1 John 1:6;
1 John 3:17;
1 Pet. 1:8; 1 John
4:12
4:21
Lev. 19:18; Matt.
5:43f.; 22:37ff.;
John 13:34;
1 John 3:11

5:1
1 John 2:22f.; 4:2,
15;
John 1:3; 3:3;
1 John 2:29; 5:4,
18;
John 8:42
5:2
1 John 2:5;
1 John 3:14
5:3
John 14:15;
2 John 6;
1 John 2:3;
Matt. 11:30; 23:4
5:4
John 1:13; 3:3;
1 John 2:29; 5:1,
18;
1 John 2:13; 4:4
5:5
1 John 4:15; 5:1
5:6
John 19:34
5:7
Matt. 3:16f.; John
15:26; 16:13-15

5:8
Matt. 18:16

5:9
John 5:34,37;
8:18;
Matt. 3:17; John
5:32,37

5:10
Rom. 8:16; Gal.
4-6; Rev. 12:17;
John 3:18,33;
1 John 1:10

5:11
John 3:36; 1 John
1:2; 2:25; 4:9;
5:13,20;
John 1:4

16   And *we* have come to know ⁺²⁹ᵃ and have believed ⁺ the love which God has for us. God is ⁺*love,* ³¹ᵃ and the one who abides in love abides *in God,* and God abides *in him.*

17   By this, love is *perfected* ⁺ with us, that we may have ~ *confidence* in the day of judgment; because as *He* is, so also are *we* in ⁺*this* world.

18   There is no fear in love; ³¹ᵃ but perfect love casts out fear, because fear involves punishment, and the one who fears is not perfected ⁺ in love.

19   *We* love, ~ because *He* first loved us.

20   If someone says, ˣ "I love God," and hates ~ his brother, he is a ⁺*liar;* for the one who does not love his brother whom he has seen, ⁺ cannot love ~ God whom he has not seen. ⁺

21   And *this commandment* we have from Him, that the one who loves God should love ~ his brother also.

Overcoming the World

5   Whoever believes that Jesus is the ᵇChrist is born ⁺ of God; and whoever loves the Father loves the *child* born ⁺ of Him.

2   By this we know that we love the children of God, when we love ~ God and observe ~ His commandments.

3   For this is the love of God, that we keep ~ His commandments; and His commandments are not burdensome.

4   For whatever is born ⁺ of God overcomes the world; and this is the victory that has overcome the world—our faith.

5   And who is the one who overcomes the world, but he who believes that Jesus is the Son of God?

6   This is the one who came by water and blood, Jesus Christ; not with the water only, but with the water and with the blood.

7   And it is the Spirit who bears witness, because the Spirit is the truth.

8   For there are *three* that bear witness, ᶜthe Spirit and the water and the blood; and the three are in *agreement.*

9   If we receive the witness of men, the witness of God is *greater;* for the witness of God is this, that He has borne ⁺ witness concerning His Son.

10   The one who believes in the Son of God has the witness in himself; the one who does not believe God has made⁺ Him a *liar,* because he has not believed⁺ in the witness that *God* has borne ⁺ concerning His Son.

11   And the witness is this, that God has given us *eternal life,* ³⁰ᵇ and this life is *in His Son.*

ᵇI.e., Messiah   ᶜA few late mss. read *in heaven, the Father, the Word, and the Holy Spirit, and these three are one. And there are three that bear witness on earth, the Spirit*

12   He who has the Son has the life; he who does not have the Son of God does *not have* the life.

This Is Written That You May Know

13   These things I have written to you who believe in the name of the Son of God, in order that you may know [29e] that you have *eternal* life.

14   And this is the confidence which we have before Him, that, if we ask [~9a] anything according to His will, He hears us.

15   And if we know [29e] that He hears us *in* whatever we ask, [~] we know that we have the requests which we have asked [*] from Him.

16   If anyone sees [x] his brother committing a sin not *leading* to death, he shall ask and *God* will for him give life to those who commit sin not *leading* to death. There is a sin *leading* to death; I do not say that he should make [x] request for this.

17   All unrighteousness is sin, and there is a sin not *leading* to death.

18   We know [29e] that no one who is born [*] of God sins; but He who was born of God keeps him and the evil one does not touch him.

19   We know that we are of God, and the *whole* world lies in *the power of* the *evil one*.

20   And we know that the Son of God has come, and has given [*] us understanding, in order that we might know [~29a] Him who is true, and we are in Him who is true, in His Son Jesus Christ. This is the true God and eternal life.

21   Little children, guard [xi] yourselves from idols.

5:12
John 3:15f.,36

5:13
John 20:31;
1 John 3:23;
1 John 1:2; 2:25;
4:9; 5:11,20
5:14
1 John 2:28;
3:21f.;
Matt. 7:7; John
14:13; 1 John
3:22
5:15
1 John 5:18-20
5:16
James 5:15;
Num. 15:30; Heb.
6:4-6; 10:26;
Jer. 7:16; 14:11
5:17
1 John 3:4;
1 John 2:1f.; 5:16
5:18
1 John 5:15,19,
20;
1 John 3:9;
James 1:27; Jude
21;
1 John 2:13;
John 14:30;
1 John 5:15,18,20
5:19
1 John 4:6;
John 12:31;
17:15; Gal. 1:4
5:20
1 John 5:15,18,
19;
John 8:42; 1 John
5:5;
Luke 24:45;
John 17:3; Rev.
3:7;
John 1:18; 14:9;
1 John 2:23; Rev.
3:7;
1 John 1:2;
1 John 5:11
5:21
1 John 2:1;
1 Cor. 10:7,14;
1 Thess. 1:9

The Second Epistle of
John

Walk According to His Commandments

1:1
Acts 11:30; 1 Pet.
5:1; 3 John 1
Rom. 16:13;
1 Pet. 5:13; 2
John 13;
2 John 5;
1 John 3:18; 2
John 3; 3 John 1;
John 8:32; 1 Tim.
2:4
1:2
2 Pet. 1:12;
1 John 1:8;
John 14:16
1:3
Rom. 1:7; 1 Tim.
1:2
1:4
3 John 3f.
1:5
1 John 2:7;
John 13:34,35;
15:12,17; 1 John
3:11; 4:7,11

1:6
1 John 2:5; 5:3;
1 John 2:24;
1 John 2:7

1:7
1 John 2:26;
1 John 2:19; 4:1;
1 John 4:2f.;
1 John 2:18

1:8
Mark 13:9;
1 Cor. 3:8; Heb.
10:35
1:9
John 7:16; 8:31;
1 John 2:23

1:10
1 Kin. 13:16f.;
Rom. 16:17; 2
Thess. 3:6,14;
Titus 3:10

1:11
Eph. 5:11; 1 Tim.
5:22; Jude 23

1:12
3 John 13,14;
John 3:29; 1 John
1:4

1:13
2 John 1

1 The elder to the chosen lady and her children, whom I love in truth; and not only I, but also all who know⁺ the truth,

2 for the sake of the truth which abides in us and will be *with us* forever:

3 Grace, mercy *and* peace will be with us, from God the Father and from Jesus Christ, the Son of the Father, in truth and love.

4 I was very glad to find⁺ *some* of your children walking in truth, just as we have received *commandment to do* from the Father.

5 And now I ask you, lady, not as writing to you a *new* commandment, but the one which we have had™ from the beginning, that we love~ one another.

6 And this is love,³¹ᵃ that we walk~ according to His commandments. This is the commandment, just as you have heard from the beginning, that you should walk~ in it.

7 For many deceivers have gone out into the world, those who do not acknowledge Jesus Christ *as* coming in the flesh. This is the deceiver and the antichrist.

8 Watch^ᵐ! yourselves, that you might not lose˟ what we have accomplished, but that you may receive˟ a *full* reward.

9 Anyone who goes too far and does not abide in the teaching of Christ, does not have *God;* the one who abides in the teaching, he has *both* the *Father* and the *Son.*

10 If anyone comes to you and does not bring this teaching, do not receive⁰ him into *your* house, and do *not give⁰* him a greeting;

11 for the one who gives him a greeting participates in his ⁺evil¹⁰ᵇ deeds.

12 Having many things to write~ to you, I do not want to do *so* with paper and ink; but I hope to come to you and speak˟ face to face, that your joy may be made⁺ full.

13 The children of your chosen sister greet you.

The Third Epistle of
John

You Walk in the Truth

1 The elder to the beloved Gaius, whom I love in truth.
2 Beloved, I pray that in all respects you may prosper ~ and be ~ in good health, just as your *soul* prospers.

3 For I was very glad when brethren came and bore witness to your truth, *that is,* how *you* are walking *in truth.*

4 I have *no greater* joy than *this,* to hear ~ of •my children walking in the truth.

5 Beloved, you are acting faithfully in whatever you accomplishˣ for the brethren, and especially *when they are* strangers;

6 and they bear witness to your love before the church; and you will do well to send them on their way in a manner worthy of God.

7 For they went out for the *sake of the Name,* accepting nothing from the Gentiles.

8 Therefore *we* ought to support ~ such men, that we may be ~ *fellow workers* with the truth.

9 I wrote something to the church; but Diotrephes, who loves to be first among them, does not accept what we say.

10 For this reason, if I come, I will call attention to his *deeds* which he does, unjustly accusing us with *wicked* words; and not satisfied with this, neither does he himself receive the brethren, and he forbids *those who desire to do so,* and puts *them out of the church.*

11 Beloved, do not imitate⁰ what is evil,¹⁰ᵃ but what is good. ²⁵ᵃ The one who does good is *of God;* the one who does evil has not seen⁺ God.

12 *Demetrius* has received⁺ a *good* testimony from everyone, and from the truth itself; and *we also* bear witness, and you know that our witness is †true.

13 I hadᵂ many things to write ~ to you, but I am not willing to writeˣ *them* to you with pen and ink;

14 but I hope to see ~ you shortly, and we shall speak face to face. Peace *be* to you. The friends greet you. Greet ~ the friends by name.

1:1
2 John 1;
Acts 19:29; 20:4;
Rom. 16:23;
1 Cor. 1:14;
1 John 3:18;
2 John 1
1:3
2 John 4;
Acts 1:15; Gal.
6:10; 3 John 5,10
1:4
1 Cor. 4:14f.;
2 Cor. 6:13; Gal.
4:19; 1 Thess.
2:11; 1 Tim. 1:2;
2 Tim. 1:2;
Philem. 10; 1
John 2:1;
2 John 4
1:5
Acts 1:15; Gal.
6:10; 3 John 10;
Rom. 12:13; Heb.
13:2
1:6
Acts 15:3; Titus
3:13;
Col. 1:10;
1 Thess. 2:12
1:7
John 15:21; Acts
5:41; Phil. 2:9;
Acts 20:33,35
1:9
2 John 9
1:10
2 John 12;
2 John 10; 3 John
5;
Acts 1:15; Gal.
6:10; 3 John 3,5;
John 9:34

1:11
Ps. 34:14; 37:27;
1 John 2:29; 3:10;
1 John 3:6

1:12
Acts 6:3; 1 Tim.
3:7;
John 19:35; 21:24

1:13
2 John 12

1:14
John 20:19,21,26;
Eph. 6:23; 1 Pet.
5:14;
John 10:3

The Epistle of

Jude

1:1
Rom. 1:1;
Rom. 1:6f.;
John 17:11f.;
1 Pet. 1:5; Jude
21
1:2
Gal. 6:16; 1 Tim.
1:2;
1 Pet. 1:2; 2 Pet.
1:2
1:3
Heb. 6:9; Jude 1,
17,20;
Titus 1:4;
1 Tim. 6:12;
Acts 6:7; Jude 20;
2 Pet. 2:21;
Acts 9:13
1:4
Gal. 2:4; 2 Tim.
3:6;
1 Pet. 2:8;
Acts 11:23;
2 Pet. 2:7;
2 Tim. 2:12; Titus
1:16; 2 Pet. 2:1;
1 John 2:22
1:5
2 Pet. 1:12f.;
3:1f.;
1 John 2:20;
Ex. 12:51; 1 Cor.
10:5-10; Heb.
3:16f.
1:6
2 Pet. 2:4;
2 Pet. 2:9
1:7
Gen. 19:24f.;
2 Pet. 2:6;
Deut. 29:23; Hos.
11:8;
2 Pet. 2:2;
2 Pet. 2:6;
Matt. 25:41;
2 Thess. 1:8f.;
2 Pet. 3:7
1:8
2 Pet. 2:10
1:9
Dan. 10:13,21;
12:1; Rev. 12:7;
1 Thess. 4:16;
2 Pet. 2:11;
Deut. 34:6;
Zech. 3:2
1:10
2 Pet. 2:12;
Phil. 3:19
1:11
Gen. 4:3-8; Heb.
11:4; 1 John 3:12;
Num. 31:16;
2 Pet. 2:15; Rev.
2:14;
Num. 16:1-3,
31-35

1 Jude, a bond-servant[38b] of Jesus Christ, and brother of James, to those who are the called, beloved[+] in God the Father, and kept[+] for Jesus Christ:

2 May mercy and peace and love be multiplied[x] to you.

3 Beloved, while I was making every effort to write[~] you about our common salvation, I felt the necessity to write[x] to you appealing that you contend[~] earnestly for the faith which was once for all delivered to the saints.

4 For certain persons have crept in unnoticed, those who were long beforehand marked[+] out for this condemnation, ungodly persons who turn the grace of our God into licentiousness and deny our only Master and Lord, Jesus Christ.

5 Now I desire to remind[x] you, though you know all things once for all, that [a]the Lord, after saving a people out of the land of Egypt, subsequently *destroyed* those who did not believe.

6 And angels who did not keep their own domain, but abandoned their proper abode, He has kept[+] in eternal bonds under darkness for the *judgment of the great day.*

7 Just as Sodom and Gomorrah and the cities around them, since they in the same way as these indulged in gross immorality and went after strange[8b] flesh, are exhibited as an example, in undergoing the punishment of *eternal fire.*

8 Yet in the same manner these men, also by dreaming, defile[17b] the flesh, and reject authority, and revile angelic majesties.

9 But Michael the archangel, when he disputed with the devil and argued[xx] about the body of Moses, did not dare pronounce[x] against him a railing judgment, but said, "The *Lord* rebuke[x] you."

10 But these men revile the things which they do not understand; and the things which they know[29c] by instinct, like unreasoning animals, by these things they are destroyed.

11 Woe to them! For they have gone the *way of Cain,* and for pay they have rushed headlong into the *error of Balaam,* and perished in the *rebellion of Korah.*

aSome ancient mss. read *Jesus*

12   These men are those who are hidden reefs in your love feasts when they feast with you without fear, caring for †themselves; clouds without water, carried along by winds; autumn trees without fruit, doubly dead, uprooted;

13   wild waves of the sea, casting up their own shame like foam; wandering stars, for whom the black darkness has been reserved⁺ *forever.*

14   And about these *also Enoch, in* the seventh *generation* from Adam, prophesied, saying, "Behold, the Lord came with many thousands of His holy ones,

15   to execute˟ judgment upon all, and to convict˟ all the ungodly of all their ungodly deeds which they have done in an ungodly way, and of all the harsh things which *ungodly* sinners have spoken against Him."

16   These are grumblers, finding fault, following after their *own* lusts; they speak arrogantly, flattering people for the sake of *gaining an* advantage.

Keep Yourselves in the Love of God

17   But you, beloved, ought to remember˟ˡ the words that were spoken⁺ beforehand by the apostles of our Lord Jesus Christ,

18   that they were saying˟˟ to you, "In the last time there shall be mockers, following after their own *ungodly* lusts."

19   These are the ones who cause divisions, worldly-minded, devoid of the Spirit.

20   But you, beloved, building yourselves up on your most holy²⁸ᵃ faith; praying in the Holy †Spirit;

21   keep˟ˡ yourselves in the *love of God,* waiting anxiously for the mercy of our Lord Jesus Christ to eternal life.

22   And have mercy˟ˡ on some, who are doubting;

23   save˟ˡ others, snatching them out of the fire; and on some have mercy˟ˡ with fear, hating even the garment polluted⁺ by the flesh.

24   Now to Him who is able to keep˟ you from stumbling, and to make˟ you stand in the presence of His glory blameless¹¹ᵇ with great joy,

25   to the only God our Savior, through Jesus Christ our Lord, *be* glory, majesty, dominion and authority, before all time and now and forever. Amen.

1:12
1 Cor. 11:20ff.;
2 Pet. 2:13 and mg.;
Ezek. 34:2,8,10;
Prov. 25:14;
2 Pet. 2:17;
Eph. 4:14;
Matt. 15:13
1:13
Is. 57:20;
Phil. 3:19;
2 Pet. 2:17; Jude 6
1:14
Gen. 5:18,21ff.;
Deut. 33:2; Dan. 7:10; Matt. 16:27;
Heb. 12:22
1:15
2 Pet. 2:6ff.;
1 Tim. 1:9
1:16
Num. 16:11,41;
1 Cor. 10:10;
2 Pet. 2:10; Jude 18;
2 Pet. 2:18;
2 Pet. 2:3
1:17
Jude 3;
2 Pet. 3:2;
Heb. 2:3
1:18
Acts 20:29;
1 Tim. 4:1; 2 Tim. 3:1f.; 4:3; 2 Pet. 3:3;
Jude 4,16
1:19
1 Cor. 2:14f.;
James 3:15
1:20
Jude 3;
Col. 2:7; 1 Thess. 5:11;
Eph. 6:18
1:21
Titus 2:13; Heb. 9:28; 2 Pet. 3:12
1:23
Amos 4:11; Zech. 3:2; 1 Cor. 3:15;
Zech. 3:3f.; Rev. 3:4
1:24
Rom. 16:25;
2 Cor. 4:14;
1 Pet. 4:13
1:25
John 5:44; 1 Tim. 1:17;
Luke 1:47;
Rom. 11:36;
Heb. 13:8

The Revelation

to John

1:1
John 17:8; Rev.
5:7;
Rev. 22:6;
Dan. 2:28f.; Rev.
1:19;
Rev. 17:1; 19:9f.;
21:9; 22:16;
Rev. 1:4,9; 22:8
1:2
Rev. 1:9; 6:9;
12:17; 20:4;
1 Cor. 1:6; Rev.
12:17
1:3
Luke 11:28; Rev.
22:7;
Rom. 13:11; Rev.
3:11; 22:7,10,12
1:4
Rev. 1:1,9; 22:8;
Rev. 1:11,20;
Acts 2:9;
Rom. 1:7;
Rev. 1:8,17; 4:8;
16:5;
Is. 11:2; Rev. 3:1;
4:5; 5:6; 8:2
1:5
Rev. 3:14; 19:11;
1 Cor. 15:20; Col.
1:18;
Rev. 17:14;
19:16;
Rom. 8:37
1:6
Rev. 5:10; 20:6;
Rom. 15:6;
Rom. 11:36
1:7
Dan. 7:13;
1 Thess. 4:17;
Zech. 12:10-14;
John 19:37;
Luke 23:28
1:8
Is. 41:4; Rev.
21:6; 22:13;
Rev. 4:8; 11:17;
Rev. 1:4
1:9
Rev. 1:1;
Acts 1:15;
Matt. 20:23; Acts
14:22; 2 Cor. 1:7;
Phil. 4:14;
2 Tim. 2:12; Rev.
1:6;
2 Thess. 3:5;
Rev. 3:10;
Rev. 1:2
1:10
Matt. 22:43; Rev.
4:2; 17:3; 21:10;
Acts 20:7;
Rev. 4:1
1:11
Rev. 1:2,19;
Rev. 1:4,20;
Rev. 2:1;
Rev. 2:8;
Rev. 2:12;
Acts 16:14; Rev.
2:18,24;
Rev. 3:1,4;
Rev. 3:7;
Col. 2:1; Rev.
3:14

The Revelation of Jesus Christ

1 The Revelation of Jesus Christ, which †God gave Him to show[x] to His bond-servants, [38b] the things which must shortly take place; and He sent and communicated *it* by His angel to His bond-servant[38b] John,

2 who bore witness to the word of God and to the testimony of Jesus Christ, *even* to all that he saw.

3 †Blessed is he who reads and those who hear the words of the prophecy, and heed the things which are written+ in it; for the time is near.

Message to the Seven Churches

4 John to the seven churches that are in Asia: Grace to you and peace, from Him who is and who was and who is to come; and from the seven Spirits who are before His throne;

5 and from Jesus Christ, the faithful witness, the first-born of the dead, and the ruler of the kings of the earth. To Him who loves us, and released us from our sins by His blood,

6 and He has made us *to be* a kingdom, priests to His God and Father; to †*Him be* the glory and the dominion[32d] forever and ever. Amen.

7 BEHOLD, HE IS COMING WITH THE CLOUDS, and *every eye* will see Him, even those who †pierced[1] Him; and all the tribes of the †earth will mourn over Him. Even so. Amen.

8 "†*I* am the Alpha and the Omega," says the Lord God, "who is and who was and who is to come, the Almighty."

The Patmos Vision

9 I, John, your brother and fellow partaker in the tribulation and kingdom and perseverance *which are* in Jesus, was on the island called Patmos, because of the word of God and the testimony of Jesus.

10 I was [a]in the Spirit on the Lord's day, and I heard behind me a loud voice like *the sound* of a trumpet,

11 saying, "Write[x] in a book what you see, and send[x] *it* to the seven churches: to Ephesus and to Smyrna and to Pergamum

aOr, *in spirit*

484

and to Thyatira and to Sardis and to Philadelphia and to Laodicea."

12   And I turned to see~ the voice that was speaking ᵐ with
me. And having turned I saw *seven* †golden lampstands;

13   and in the middle of the lampstands one like ᵇa son of
man, clothed⁺ in a robe reaching to the feet, and girded⁺ across
His breast with a †golden girdle.

14   And His head and His hair were white like white wool, like
snow; and His eyes were like a flame of fire;

15   and His feet *were* like burnished bronze, when it has been
caused to glow⁺ in a furnace, and His voice *was* like the sound of
many waters.

16   And in His right hand He held seven stars; and out of His
mouth came a sharp two-edged †sword; and His face was *like the
†sun* shining in its strength. 32a

17   And when I saw Him, I fell at His feet as a dead man. And
He laid His right hand upon me, saying, "Do not be afraid;⁰ †*I* am
the first and the last,

18   and the living~ One; and I was dead, and behold, I am
alive forevermore, and I have the keys of death and of Hades. 27a

19   "Write ˣˡ therefore the things which you have seen, and the
things which are, and the things which shall take place after
these things.

20   "As for the mystery of the seven stars which you saw in My
right hand, and the seven golden lampstands: the seven stars are
the *angels* of the *seven churches,* and the *seven* lampstands are
the *seven churches.*

Message to Ephesus

2   "To the angel of the church in Ephesus write: ˣˡ
      The One who holds the seven stars in His right hand, the
One who walks among the seven golden lampstands, says this:

2   'I know your deeds and your toil and perseverance, and
that you cannot endure ˣ evil men, and you put to the test those
who call themselves apostles, and they are not, and you found
them *to be* false;

3   and you have perseverance and have endured for My
name's sake, and have not grown⁺ weary.

4   'But I have *this* against you, that you have left your *first
love.*

5   'Remember ᵐˡ therefore from where you have fallen,⁺ and
repent ˣˡ and do ˣˡ the deeds you did at *first* or else I am coming to

ᵇOr, *the Son of Man*

1:12
Ex. 25:37; 37:23;
Zech. 4:2; Rev.
1:20; 2:1
1:13
Rev. 2:1;
Ezek. 1:26; Dan.
7:13; 10:16; Rev.
14:14;
Dan. 10:5;
Rev. 15:6
1:14
Dan. 7:9; 10:6;
Rev. 2:18; 19:12
1:15
Ezek. 1:7; Dan.
10:6; Rev. 2:18;
Ezek. 1:24; 43:2;
Rev. 14:2; 19:6
1:16
Rev. 1:20; 2:1;
3:1;
Is. 49:2; Heb.
4:12; Rev. 2:12,
16; 19:15;
Matt. 17:2; Rev.
10:1;
Judg. 5:31
1:17
Dan. 8:17; 10:9,
10,15;
Dan. 8:18; 10:10,
12;
Matt. 14:27; 17:7;
Is. 41:4; 44:6;
48:12; Rev. 2:8;
22:13
1:18
Luke 24:5; Rev.
4:9f.;
Rom. 6:9; Rev.
2:8; 10:6; 15:7;
Job 38:17; Matt.
11:23; 16:19;
Rev. 9:1; 20:1
1:19
Rev. 1:11;
Rev. 1:12-16;
Rev. 4:1
1:20
Rom. 11:25;
Rev. 1:16; 2:1;
3:1;
Ex. 25:37; 37:23;
Zech. 4:2; Rev.
1:12;
Rev. 1:4,11;
Matt. 5:14f.
2:1
Rev. 1:11;
Rev. 1:16;
Rev. 1:12f.
2:2
Rev. 2:19; 3:1,8,
15;
John 6:6; 1 John
4:1;
2 Cor. 11:13
2:3
John 15:21
2:4
Jer. 2:2; Matt.
24:12
2:5
Rev. 2:16,22; 3:3,
19;
Heb. 10:32; Rev.
2:2;
Matt. 5:14ff.;
Phil. 2:15; Rev.
1:20

you, and will remove your lampstand out of its place—unless you repent.ˣ

2:6
Rev. 2:15

6 'Yet this you do have, that you hate the deeds of the Nicolaitans, which *I also* hate.

2:7
Matt. 11:15; Rev.
3:6,13,22; 13:9;
Rev. 2:11,17,26;
3:5,12,21; 21:7;
Gen. 2:9; 3:22;
Prov. 3:18; 11:30;
13:12; 15:4; Rev.
22:2,14;
Ezek. 28:13;
31:8f.; Luke 23:43

7 'He who has an ear, let him hearˣˡ what the Spirit says to the churches. To him who *overcomes*, I will grant to eatˣ of the tree of life, which is in the Paradise of God.'

Message to Smyrna

2:8
Rev. 1:11;
Is. 44:6; 48:12;
Rev. 1:17; 22:13;
Rev. 1:18

8 "And to the angel of the church in Smyrna write:ˣˡ

The first and the last, who was dead, and has come to life, says this:

2:9
Rev. 1:9;
2 Cor. 6:10; 8:9;
James 2:5;
Rev. 3:9;
Matt. 4:10; Rev.
2:13,24

9 'I know your tribulation and your poverty (but you are *rich*), and the blasphemy by those who say they are Jews and are not, but are a synagogue of Satan.

2:10
Rev. 3:10;
13:14ff.;
Dan. 1:12,14;
Rev. 2:13; 12:11;
17:14;
1 Cor. 9:25; Rev.
3:11

10 'Do not fearᵒ what you are about to suffer. Behold, the devil is about to cast some of you into prison, that you may be tested,ˣ and you will have tribulation ten days. Beᴺ! faithful until death, and I will give you the crown of life.

2:11
Matt. 11:15; Rev.
2:29; 3:6,13,22;
13:9;
Rev. 2:7,17,26;
3:5,12,21; 21:7;
Rev. 20:6,14;
21:8

11 'He who has an ear, let him hearˣˡ what the Spirit says to the churches. He who overcomes shall •*not* be hurtˣ by the †*second* death.'

Message to Pergamum

2:12
Rev. 1:11;
Rev. 1:16; 2:16

12 "And to the angel of the church in Pergamum write:ˣˡ

The One who has the sharp two-edged sword says this:

2:13
Matt. 4:10; Rev.
2:24;
1 Tim. 5:8; Rev.
14:12;
Acts 22:20; Rev.
1:5; 11:3; 17:6;
Rev. 2:10; 12:11;
17:14;
Rev. 2:9

13 'I know where you dwell, where Satan's throne is; and you hold fast My name, and did not deny My faith, even in the days of Antipas, My witness, My faithful one, who was killed among you, where Satan dwells.

2:14
Num. 31:16;
2 Pet. 2:15;
Num. 25:1f.; Acts
15:29; 1 Cor.
10:20; Rev. 2:20

14 'But I have a few things against you, because you have there some who hold the teaching of Balaam, who kept teachingᵐ Balak to putˣ a stumbling block before the sons of Israel, to eatˣ things sacrificed to idols, and to commitˣ *acts of* immorality.

2:15
Rev. 2:6

15 'Thus *you also* have some who in the *same way* hold the teaching of the Nicolaitans.

2:16
Rev. 2:5;
Rev. 22:7,20;
2 Thess. 2:8;
Rev. 1:16

16 'Repentᴺ! therefore; or else I am coming to you quickly, and I will make war against them with the sword of My mouth.

2:17
Rev. 2:7;
Ex. 16:33; John
6:49f.;
Is. 56:5; 62:2;
65:15;
Rev. 14:3; 19:12

17 'He who has an ear, let him hearˣˡ what the Spirit says to the churches. To him who *overcomes*, to him I will give *some* of the †hidden⁺ manna, and I will give him a †white stone, and a †new³⁴ᵃ name written⁺ on the stone which no one knows but he who receives it.'

Message to Thyatira

18 "And to the angel of the church in Thyatira write:[xi] The Son of God, who has eyes like a flame of fire, and His feet are like burnished bronze, says this:

19 'I know your deeds, and your love and faith and service and perseverance, and that your deeds of late are greater[26b] than at first.

20 'But I have *this* against you, that you tolerate the woman Jezebel, who calls herself a prophetess, and she teaches and leads •My bond-servants astray, so that they commit[x] *acts of immorality* and eat[x] things sacrificed to idols.

21 'And I gave her time to repent;[x] and she does not want to repent[x] of her immorality.

22 'Behold, I will cast her upon a bed *of sickness*, and those who commit adultery with her into great[26a] tribulation, unless they repent[x] of [c]her deeds.

23 'And I will kill her children with pestilence; and all the [t]churches will know[29a] that I am He who searches the minds and hearts; and I will give to each one of you according to your deeds.

24 'But I say to you, the rest who are in Thyatira, who do not hold this teaching, who have not known[29a] the deep things of Satan, as they call them—I place no other burden on you.

25 'Nevertheless what you have, hold[xi] fast until I come.[x]

26 'And he who overcomes, and he who keeps My deeds *until the end*, TO HIM I WILL GIVE AUTHORITY OVER THE NATIONS;

27 AND HE SHALL RULE THEM WITH A ROD OF [t]IRON, AS THE VESSELS OF THE POTTER ARE BROKEN TO PIECES, as *I also* have received* *authority* from My Father;

28 and I will give him the morning star.

29 'He who has an ear, let him hear[xi] what the Spirit says to the churches.'

Message to Sardis

3 "And to the angel of the church in Sardis write:[xi] He who has the seven Spirits of God, and the seven stars, says this: 'I know your deeds, that you have a *name* that you are alive, but you are *dead*.

2 'Wake[~i] up, and strengthen[xi] the things that remain, which were about to die; for I have not found* your deeds completed* in the sight of My God.

3 'Remember[~i] therefore what you have received and heard; and keep[~i] *it*, and repent.[xi] If therefore you will not wake[x] up, I

[c]Some mss. read *their*

2:18
Rev. 1:11; 2:24;
Matt. 4:3;
Rev. 1:14f.

2:19
Rev. 2:2

2:20
Rev. 2:14;
1 Kin. 16:31;
21:25; 2 Kin. 9:7,
22,30;
Acts 15:29; 1 Cor.
10:20

2:21
Rom. 2:4; 2 Pet.
3:9;
Rom. 2:5; Rev.
9:20f.; 16:9,11
2:22
Rev. 17:2; 18:9

2:23
Ps. 7:9; 26:2;
139:1; Jer. 11:20;
17:10; Matt.
16:27; Luke
16:15; Acts 1:24;
Rom. 8:27;
Ps. 62:12
2:24
Rev. 2:18;
1 Cor. 2:10;
Acts 15:28
2:25
Rev. 3:11;
John 21:22
2:26
Rev. 2:7;
Matt. 10:22; Heb.
3:6;
Ps. 2:8; Rev.
3:21; 20:4
2:27
Ps. 2:9; Rev.
12:5; 19:15;
Is. 30:14; Jer.
19:11
2:28
1 John 3:2; Rev.
22:16
2:29
Rev. 2:7

3:1
Rev. 1:11;
Rev. 1:4;
Rev. 1:16;
Rev. 2:2; 3:8,15;
1 Tim. 5:6

3:3
Rev. 2:5;
1 Thess. 5:2; 2
Pet. 3:10; Rev.
16:15;
Matt. 24:43; Luke
12:39f.

will come like a thief, and you will •*not*know^x at what hour I will come upon you.

3:4
Rev. 11:13;
Rev. 1:11;
Jude 23;
Eccl. 9:8; Rev.
3:5,18; 4:4; 6:11;
7:9,13f.; 19:8,14
3:5
Rev. 2:7;
Rev. 3:4;
Ex. 32:32f.; Ps.
69:28; Luke
10:20; Rev. 13:8;
17:8; 20:12,15;
21:27;
Matt. 10:32; Luke
12:8
3:6
Rev. 2:7

4 'But you have a few people in Sardis who have not soiled [17c] their garments; and they will walk with Me in white; for they are worthy.

5 'He who overcomes shall thus be clothed in †white garments; and I will •*not*erase^x his name from the book of life, and I will confess his name before My Father, and before His angels.

6 'He who has an ear, let him hear^{xi} what the Spirit says to the churches.'

Message to Philadelphia

3:7
Rev. 1:11;
Rev. 6:10;
1 John 5:20; Rev.
3:14; 19:11;
Job 12:14; Is.
22:22; Matt.
16:19; Rev. 1:18
3:8
Rev. 3:1;
Acts 14:27;
Rev. 2:13

7 "And to the angel of the church in Philadelphia write:^{xi}

He who is holy, [28a] who is true, who has the key of David, who opens and no one will shut, and who shuts and no one opens, says this:

8 'I know [29e] your ^ddeeds. Behold, I have put⁺ before you an open⁺ door which no one can shut, ^x because you have a little power, and have kept My word, [43a] and have not denied My name.

3:9
Rev. 2:9;
Is. 45:14; 49:23;
60:14;
Is. 43:4; John
17:23
3:10
John 17:6; Rev.
3:8;
Rev. 1:9;
2 Tim. 2:12;
2 Pet. 2:9;
Rev. 2:10;
Matt. 24:14; Rev.
16:14;
Rev. 6:10; 8:13;
11:10; 13:8,14;
17:8

9 'Behold, I will cause *those* of the synagogue of Satan, who say that they are Jews, and are not, but lie—behold, I will make them to come and bow down at your feet, and to know^x[29a] that *I* have loved [31a] you.

10 'Because you have kept the word of My perseverance, *I also* will keep you from the hour of testing, that *hour* which is about to come upon the whole world, to test^x those who dwell upon the earth.

3:11
Rev. 1:3; 22:7,12,
20;
Rev. 2:25;
Rev. 2:10
3:12
Rev. 3:5;
1 Kin. 7:21; Jer.
1:18; Gal. 2:9;
Rev. 14:1; 22:4;
Ezek. 48:35; Rev.
21:2;
Gal. 4:26; Heb.
13:14; Rev. 21:2,
10;
Is. 62:2; Rev.
2:17

11 'I am coming quickly; hold fast ~ what you have, in order that no one take^x your crown.

12 'He who overcomes, I will make him a pillar in the temple of My God, and he will •not go^x *out*from it anymore; and I will write upon him the name of My God, and the name of the city of My God, the new Jerusalem, which comes down out of heaven from My God, and My †new name.

3:13
Rev. 3:6
3:14
Rev. 1:11;
2 Cor. 1:20;
Rev. 1:5; 3:7;
Gen. 49:3; Deut.
21:17; Prov. 8:22;
John 1:3; Col.
1:18; Rev. 21:6;
22:13

13 'He who has an ear, let him hear^{xi} what the Spirit says to the churches.'

Message to Laodicea

14 "And to the angel of the church in Laodicea write:^{xi}

The Amen, the faithful and true Witness, the ^eBeginning of the creation of God, says this:

^dOr, *deeds (behold . . . shut), that you* ^ei.e., origin or source

15 'I know your deeds, that you are neither cold nor hot; I would that you were cold or hot.

16 'So because you are *lukewarm*, and neither hot nor cold, I will spit you out of My mouth.

17 'Because you say, "I am †*rich*, and have become⁺ wealthy, and have need of nothing," and you do not know that you are wretched and miserable and poor and blind and naked,

18 I advise you to buyˣ from Me gold refined⁺ by fire, that you may becomeˣ rich, and †white garments, that you may clotheˣ yourself, and *that* the shame of your nakedness may not be revealed ;ˣ and eye salve to anointˣ your eyes, that you may see. ~

19 'Those whom I *love*,~ ³¹ᵇ I reprove and discipline; be zealous~ᵛⁱ therefore, and repent.ˣⁱ

20 'Behold, I stand⁺ at the door and knock; if anyone hearsˣ My voice and opensˣ the door, I will come in to him, and will dine with him, and he with Me.

21 'He who overcomes, I will grant to him to sitˣ down with Me on My throne, as *I also* overcame and sat down with My Father on His throne.

22 'He who has an ear, let him hearˣⁱ what the Spirit says to the churches.' "

Scene in Heaven

4 After these things I looked, and behold, a door *standing* open⁺ in heaven, and the first voice which I had heard, like *the sound* of a trumpet speaking with me, said, "Comeˣⁱ up here, and I will show you what must take place after these things."

2 Immediately I was ʲin the Spirit; and behold, a throne was standingᵐ in heaven, and One sitting on the throne.

3 And He who was sitting *was* like a jasper stone and a sardius in appearance; and *there was* a rainbow around the throne, like an emerald in appearance.

4 And around the throne *were* twenty-four thrones; and upon the thrones I *saw twenty-four* elders sitting, clothed⁺ in †white garments, and †golden crowns on their heads.

The Throne and Worship of the Creator

5 And from the throne proceed flashes of lightning and sounds and peals of thunder. And *there were seven* lamps of fire burning before the throne, which are the seven Spirits of God;

6 and before the throne *there was*, as it were, a sea of glass like crystal; and in the center and around the throne, four living creatures full of eyes in front and behind.

†Or, *in spirit*

3:15
Rev. 3:1;
Rom. 12:11

3:17
Hos. 12:8; Zech.
11:5; Matt. 5:3;
1 Cor. 4:8

3:18
Is. 55:1; Matt.
13:44;
1 Pet. 1:7;
Rev. 3:4;
Rev. 16:15

3:19
Prov. 3:12; 1 Cor.
11:32; Heb. 12:6;
Rev. 2:5
3:20
Matt. 24:33;
James 5:9;
Luke 12:36; John
10:3;
John 14:23
3:21
Rev. 2:7;
Matt. 19:28;
2 Tim. 2:12; Rev.
2:26; 20:4;
John 16:33; Rev.
5:5; 6:2; 17:14
3:22
Rev. 2:7

4:1
Rev. 1:12ff.,19;
Ezek. 1:1; Rev.
19:11;
Rev. 1:10;
Rev. 11:12;
Rev. 1:19; 22:6
4:2
Rev. 1:10;
1 Kin. 22:19; Is.
6:1; Ezek. 1:26;
Dan. 7:9; Rev.
4:9f.
4:3
Rev. 21:11;
Rev. 21:20;
Ezek. 1:28; Rev.
10:1;
Rev. 21:19
4:4
Rev. 4:6; 5:11;
7:11;
Rev. 11:16;
Rev. 4:10; 5:6,8,
14; 19:4;
Matt. 19:28; Rev.
20:4;
Rev. 3:18
4:5
Ex. 19:16; Rev.
8:5; 11:19; 16:18;
Ex. 25:37; Zech.
4:2;
Rev. 1:4
4:6
Ezek. 1:22; Rev.
15:2; 21:18,21;
Rev. 4:4;
Ezek. 1:5; Rev.
4:8f.; 5:6; 6:1,6;
7:11; 14:3; 15:7;
19:4;
.Ezek. 1:18;
10:12

4:7
Ezek. 1:10; 10:14

7 And the first creature *was* like a lion, and the second creature like a calf, and the third creature had a face like that of a man, and the fourth creature *was* like a flying eagle.

4:8
Ezek. 1:5; Rev.
4:6,9; 5:6; 6:1,6;
7:11; 14:3; 15:7;
19:4;
Is. 6:2;
Ezek. 1:18;
10:12;
Rev. 14:11;
Is. 6:3;
Rev. 1:8;
Rev. 1:4

8 And the four living creatures, each one of them having six wings, are full of eyes around and within; and day and night they do *not cease* to say,

"HOLY, [28a] HOLY, HOLY, *is* THE LORD GOD, THE
ALMIGHTY, who was and who is and who is to
come."

4:9
Ps. 47:8; Is. 6:1;
Rev. 4:2;
Deut. 32:40; Dan.
4:34; 12:7; Rev.
10:6; 15:7

9 And when the living [t]creatures give glory and honor and thanks to Him who sits on the throne, to Him who lives forever and ever,

4:10
Rev. 4:4;
Rev. 5:8,14; 7:11;
11:16; 19:4;
Ps. 47:8; Is. 6:1;
Rev. 4:2;
Deut. 32:40; Dan.
4:34; 12:7;
Rev. 10:6; 15:7

10 the twenty-four elders will *fall down* before Him who sits on the throne, and will worship [44b] Him who lives forever and ever, and will cast their crowns before the throne, saying,

4:11
Rev. 1:6; 5:12;
Acts 14:15; Rev.
10:6; 14:7

11 " *Worthy* art Thou, our Lord and our God, to receive[x]
glory and honor and power; [32a]for *Thou* didst create all
things, and because of Thy will they existed, and were
created."

The Book with Seven Seals

5:1
Rev. 4:9; 5:7,13;
Ezek. 2:9,10;
Is. 29:11; Dan.
12:4

5 And I saw in the right hand of Him who sat on the throne a book written[+] inside and on the back, sealed[+] up with seven seals.

5:2
Rev. 10:1; 18:21

2 And I saw a strong angel proclaiming with a loud voice, "Who is worthy to open[x] the book and to break[x] its seals?"

5:3
Phil. 2:10; Rev.
5:13

3 And no one in heaven, or on the earth, or under the earth, was able[m] to open[x] the book, or to look[~] into it.

4 And I *began* to weep greatly, because no one was found *worthy* to open[x] the book, or to look[~] into it;

5:5
Gen. 49:9;
Heb. 7:14;
Is. 11:1,10; Rom.
15:12; Rev. 22:16

5 and one of the elders *said to me, "Stop weeping;[o] behold, the Lion that is from the tribe of Judah, the Root of David, has overcome so as to open[x] the book and its seven seals."

5:6
Rev. 4:4; 5:8,14;
John 1:29; Rev.
5:9,12; 13:8;
Dan. 8:3f.;
Zech. 3:9; 4:10;
Rev. 1:4

6 And I saw [g]between the throne (with the four living creatures) and the elders a Lamb standing, as if slain, [+]having seven horns and seven eyes, which are the seven Spirits of God, sent [+] out into all the earth.

5:7
Rev. 5:1

7 And He came, and He took *it* out of the right hand of Him who sat on the throne.

5:8
Rev. 4:6; 5:6,11,
14;
Rev. 4:4; 5:14;
Rev. 4:10;
John 1:29; Rev.
5:6,12f.; 13:8;
Rev. 14:2; 15:2;
Rev. 15:7;
Ps. 141:2; Rev.
8:3f.

8 And when He had taken the book, the four living creatures and the twenty-four elders fell down before the Lamb, having each one a harp, and [t]golden bowls full of incense, which are the prayers of the saints.

[g]Lit., *in the middle of the throne and of the four living creatures, and in the middle of the elders*

9   And they *sang a †new song, saying,
      " Worthy art Thou to take[x] the book, and to break[x] its
      seals; for Thou wast slain, and didst purchase for God
      with Thy blood *men* from every tribe and tongue and
      people and nation.
10   "And Thou hast made them *to be* a kingdom and priests
      to our God; and they will reign upon the earth."

Angels Exalt the Lamb

11   And I looked, and I heard the voice of many angels around
the throne and the living creatures and the elders; and the number of them was myriads of myriads, and thousands of thousands,
12   saying with a loud voice,
      " Worthy is the Lamb that was slain † to receive[x] pow-
      er [32a] and riches and wisdom and might [32c] and honor
      and glory and blessing."
13   And every created thing which is in heaven and on the
earth and under the earth and on the sea, and all things in them,
I heard saying,
      "To Him who sits on the †throne, and to the †Lamb, *be*
      blessing and honor and glory and dominion [32d] forever
      and ever."
14   And the four living creatures kept saying, [m]"Amen." And
the elders fell down and worshiped. [44b]

The Book Opened
The First Seal—False Christ

6   And I saw when the Lamb broke one of the seven seals, and
    I heard one of the four living creatures saying as with a voice
of thunder, "Come."
2   And I looked, and behold, a †white horse, and he who sat
on it had a bow; and a †crown was given to him; and he went out
conquering, and to conquer.[x]

The Second Seal—War

3   And when He broke the second seal, I heard the second
living creature saying, "Come."
4   And another, a †red horse, went out; and to him who sat
on it, it was granted to take[x] peace from the earth, and that *men*
should slay *one another*, and a great †sword was given to him.

The Third Seal—Famine

5   And when He broke the third seal, I heard the third living

5:9 Ps. 33:3; 40:3; 98:1; 149:1; Is. 42:10; Rev. 15:3; Rev. 4:11; Rev. 5:6,12; 13:8; 1 Cor. 6:20; Rev. 14:3f.; Dan. 3:4; 5:19; Rev. 7:9; 10:11; 11:9; 13:7; 14:6; 17:15
5:10 Rev. 1:6; Rev. 3:21; 20:4
5:11 Rev. 4:4; Rev. 4:6; 5:6,8, 14; Dan. 7:10; Heb. 12:22; Jude 14; Rev. 9:16
5:12 Rev. 1:6; 4:11; 5:9; John 1:29; Rev. 5:6,13; 13:8
5:13 Phil. 2:10; Rev. 5:3; Rev. 5:1; John 1:29; Rev. 5:6,12f.; 13:8; Rom. 11:36; Rev. 1:6
5:14 Rev. 4:6; 5:6,8, 11; 1 Cor. 14:16; Rev. 7:12; 19:4; Rev. 4:4; Rev. 4:10
6:1 John 1:29; Rev. 5:6,12f.; 13:8; Rev. 5:1; Rev. 4:6; 5:6,8, 11,14; Rev. 14:2; 19:6
6:2 Zech. 1:8; 6:3f.; Rev. 19:11; Zech. 6:11; Rev. 9:7; 14:14; 19:12; Rev. 3:21
6:3 Rev. 4:7
6:4 Zech. 1:8; 6:2; Matt. 10:34
6:5 Rev. 4:7; Zech. 6:2,6; Ezek. 4:16

creature saying, "Come." And I looked, and behold, a †black horse; and he who sat on it had a pair of scales in his hand.

6 And I heard as it were a voice in the center of the four living creatures saying, "A ʰquart of wheat for a ⁱdenarius, and three quarts of barley for a denarius; and do not harm⁹ the oil and the wine."

The Fourth Seal—Death

7 And when He broke the fourth seal, I heard the voice of the fourth living creature saying, "Come."

8 And I looked, and behold, an†ashen horse; and he who sat on it had the name Death; and Hades²⁷ᵃ was following^ᵐ with him. And†authority was given to them over a fourth of the earth, to kill^ˣ with sword and with famine and with pestilence and by the wild beasts of the earth.

The Fifth Seal—Martyrs

9 And when He broke the fifth seal, I saw underneath the altar the souls of those who had been slain* because of the word of God, and because of the testimony which they had maintained;^ᵐ

10 and they cried out with a loud voice, saying, "How long, O Lord, holy²⁸ᵃ and true, wilt Thou refrain from judging and avenging our blood on those who dwell on the earth?"

11 And there was given to each of them a white †robe; and they were told that they should rest for a little while longer, until the number of their fellow servants and their brethren who were to be killed even as they had been, should be completed^ˣ also.

The Sixth Seal—Terror

12 And I looked when He broke the sixth seal, and there was a great earthquake; and the sun became black as sackcloth made of hair, and the whole moon became like blood;

13 and the stars of the sky fell to the earth, as a fig tree casts its unripe figs when shaken by a great wind.

14 And the sky was split apart like a scroll when it is rolled up; and every mountain and island were moved out of their places.

15 And the kings of the earth and the great men and the ⁱcommanders and the rich and the strong and every slave and free man, hid themselves in the caves and among the rocks of the mountains;

16 and they *said to the mountains and to the rocks, "Fall^ˣⁱ on

ʰGr., choenix; i.e., a dry measure almost equal to a quart ⁱThe denarius was equivalent to one day's wage ʲI.e., chiliarchs, in command of one thousand troops

6:6
Rev. 4:6f.;
Rev. 7:3; 9:4

6:7
Rev. 4:7

6:8
Zech. 6:3;
Prov. 5:5; Hos.
13:14; Matt.
11:23; Rev. 1:18;
20:13f.;
Jer. 14:12; 15:2f.;
24:10; 29:17f.;
Ezek. 5:12,17;
14:21; 29:5

6:9
Ex. 29:12; Lev.
4:7; John 16:2;
Rev. 14:18; 16:7;
Rev. 20:4;
Rev. 1:2,9;
Rev. 12:17

6:10
Zech. 1:12;
Luke 2:29; 2 Pet.
2:1;
Rev. 3:7;
Deut. 32:43; Ps.
79:10; Luke 18:7;
Rev. 19:2;
Rev. 3:10

6:11
Rev. 3:4,5; 7:9;
2 Thess. 1:7;
Heb. 4:10; Rev.
14:13;
Heb. 11:40;
Acts 20:24;
2 Tim. 4:7

6:12
Matt. 24:7; Rev.
8:5; 11:13; 16:18;
Is. 13:10; Joel
2:10,31; 3:15;
Matt. 24:29; Mark
13:24;
Is. 50:3; Matt.
11:21

6:13
Matt. 24:29; Mark
13:25; Rev. 8:10;
9:1;
Is. 34:4

6:14
Is. 34:4; 2 Pet.
3:10; Rev. 20:11;
21:1;
Is. 54:10; Jer.
4:24; Ezek.
38:20; Nah. 1:5;
Rev. 16:20

6:15
Is. 2:10f.,19,21;
24:21; Rev. 19:18

6:16
Hos. 10:8; Luke
23:30; Rev. 9:6;
Rev. 4:9; 5:1;
Mark 3:5

us and hide[xi] us from the presence of Him who sits on the throne, and from the wrath[7b] of the Lamb;

17   for the great day of their wrath[7b] has come; and who is able to stand?"[x]

An Interlude

7   After this I saw four angels standing at the four corners of the earth, holding back the four winds of the earth, so that no wind should †blow ~ on the earth or on the sea or on any tree.

2   And I saw another angel ascending from the rising of the sun, having the seal of the living God; and he cried out with a loud voice to the four angels to whom it was granted to harm[x] the earth and the sea,

3   saying, "Do not harm° the earth or the sea or the trees, until we have sealed[x] the bond-servants[38b] of our God on their foreheads."

A Remnant of Israel—144,000

4   And I heard the number of those who were sealed,* one hundred and forty-four thousand sealed* from every tribe of the sons of Israel:

5   from the tribe of Judah, twelve thousand *were* sealed,* from the tribe of Reuben twelve thousand, from the tribe of Gad twelve thousand,

6   from the tribe of Asher twelve thousand, from the tribe of Naphtali twelve thousand, from the tribe of Manasseh twelve thousand,

7   from the tribe of Simeon twelve thousand, from the tribe of Levi twelve thousand, from the tribe of Issachar twelve thousand,

8   from the tribe of Zebulun twelve thousand, from the tribe of Joseph twelve thousand, from the tribe of Benjamin, twelve thousand *were* sealed.*

A Multitude from the Tribulation

9   After these things I looked, and behold, a great multitude, which no one could count,[x] from every nation and *all* tribes and peoples and tongues, standing before the throne and before the Lamb, clothed* in †white robes, and palm branches *were* in their hands;

10   and they cry out with a loud voice, saying,

"Salvation to our God who sits on the throne, and to the Lamb."

11   And all the angels were standing around the throne and

6:17
Is. 63:4; Jer. 30:7;
Joel 1:15; 2:1f.,
11,31; Zeph.
1:14f.; Rev.
16:14;
Ps. 76:7; Nah.
1:6; Mal. 3:2;
Luke 21:36
7:1
Rev. 9:14;
Is. 11:12; Ezek.
7:2; Rev. 20:8;
Jer. 49:36; Dan.
7:2; Zech. 6:5;
Matt. 24:31;
Rev. 7:3; 8:7; 9:4
7:2
Is. 41:2;
Rev. 7:3; 9:4;
Matt. 16:16;
Rev. 9:14
7:3
Rev. 6:6;
John 3:33; Rev.
7:3-8;
Ezek. 9:4,6; Rev.
13:16; 14:1,9;
20:4; 22:4

7:4
Rev. 9:16;
Rev. 14:1,3

7:9
Rev. 5:9;
Rev. 7:15;
Rev. 22:3;
Rev. 6:11; 7:14;
Lev. 23:40

7:10
Ps. 3:8; Rev.
12:10; 19:1;
Rev. 22:3
7:11
Rev. 4:4;
Rev. 4:6;
Rev. 4:10

around the elders and the four living creatures; and they fell on their faces before the throne and worshiped[44b] God,

12   saying,

"**A**men, blessing and glory and wisdom and thanksgiving and honor and power[32a] and might, [32c] *be* to our God forever and ever. Amen."

13   And one of the elders answered, saying to me, "These who are clothed[+] in the [†]white robes, who are they, and from where have they come?"

14   And I said to him, "My lord, *you* know." And he said to me, "These are the ones who come out of the great[26a] tribulation, and they have washed their robes and made them white in the blood of the Lamb.

15   "For this reason, they are before the throne of God; and they serve[38c] Him day and night in His temple; and He who sits on the throne shall spread His tabernacle over them.

16   "They shall hunger no more, neither thirst anymore; •*neither* shall the sun beat[x] down on them, nor any heat;

17   for the Lamb in the center of the throne shall be their shepherd, and shall guide them to springs of the water of *life;* and God shall wipe every tear from their eyes."

The Seventh Seal—the Trumpets

8 And when He broke the seventh seal, there was silence in heaven for about half an hour.

2   And I saw the seven angels who stand[+] before God; and *seven* trumpets were given to them.

3   And another angel came and stood at the altar, holding a [†]golden censer; and much [†]incense was given to him, that he might add it to the prayers of all the saints upon the [†]golden altar which was before the throne.

4   And the smoke of the incense, with the prayers of the saints, went up before God out of the angel's hand.

5   And the angel took the censer; and he filled it with the fire of the altar and threw it to the earth; and there followed peals of thunder and sounds and flashes of lightning and an earthquake.

6   And the seven angels who had the seven trumpets prepared themselves to sound[x] them.

7   And the first sounded, and there came hail and fire, mixed[+] with blood, and they were thrown to the earth; and a third of the earth was burned up, and a third of the trees were burned up, and all the green grass was burned up.

8   And the second angel sounded, and *something* like a great

7:12
Rev. 5:14;
Rev. 5:12

7:13
Acts 3:12;
Rev. 7:9

7:14
Dan. 12:1; Matt.
24:21; Mark
13:19;
Zech. 3:3-5; Rev.
22:14;
Rev. 6:11; 7:9;
Heb. 9:14; 1 John
1:7

7:15
Rev. 7:9;
Rev. 4:8f.; 22:3;
Rev. 11:19;
21:22;
Rev. 4:9;
Lev. 26:11; Ezek.
37:27; John 1:14;
Rev. 21:3

7:16
Ps. 121:5f.; Is.
49:10

7:17
Ps. 23:1f.; Matt.
2:6; John 10:11;
John 4:14; Rev.
21:6; 22:1;
Is. 25:8; Matt. 5:4;
Rev. 21:4

8:1
Rev. 5:1; 6:1,3,5,
7,9,12

8:2
Rev. 1:4; 8:6-13;
9:1,13; 11:15;
1 Cor. 15:52; 1
Thess. 4:16

8:3
Rev. 7:2;
Amos 9:1; Rev.
6:9;
Heb. 9:4;
Ex. 30:1; Rev.
5:8;
Ex. 30:3; Num.
4:11; Rev. 8:5;
9:13

8:4
Ps. 141:2

8:5
Lev. 16:12;
Ezek. 10:2;
Ex. 19:16; Rev.
4:5; 11:19; 16:18;
Rev. 6:12

8:6
Rev. 8:2

8:7
Ex. 9:23ff.; Is.
28:2; Ezek.
38:22; Joel 2:30;
Zech. 13:8,9;
Rev. 8:7-12; 9:15,
18; 12:4;
Rev. 9:4

8:8
Jer. 51:25;
Zech. 13:8,9;
Rev. 8:7-12;
9:15,18; 12:4;
Ex. 7:17ff.; Rev.
11:6; 16:3

mountain burning with fire was thrown into the sea; and a third of the sea became blood;

9   and a third of the creatures, which were in the sea and had life, [30c] died; and a †third of the ships were destroyed.

10   And the third angel sounded, and a great star fell from heaven, burning like a torch, and it fell on a third of the rivers and on the springs of waters;

11   and the name of the star is called Wormwood; and a third of the waters became wormwood; and many men died from the waters, because they were made bitter.

12   And the fourth angel sounded, and a third of the sun and a third of the moon and a third of the stars were smitten, so that a third of them might be darkened[x] and the day might not shine[x] for a third of it, and the night in the same way.

13   And I looked, and I heard an eagle flying in midheaven, saying with a loud voice, "Woe, woe, woe, to those who dwell on the earth, because of the remaining blasts of the trumpet of the three angels who are about to sound!"

The Fifth Trumpet—the Bottomless Pit

9   And the fifth angel sounded, and I saw a star from heaven which had fallen⁺ to the earth; and the key of the bottomless †pit was given to him.

2   And he opened the bottomless pit; and smoke went up out of the pit, like the smoke of a great furnace; and the sun and the air were darkened by the smoke of the pit.

3   And out of the smoke came forth *locusts* upon the earth; and †power[32b] was given them, as the scorpions of the earth have power. [32b]

4   And they were told that they should not hurt the grass of the earth, nor any green thing, nor any tree, but only the men who do not have the seal of God on their foreheads.

5   And they were not permitted to kill[x] anyone, but to torment for five months; and their torment was like the torment of a scorpion when it stings[x] a man.

6   And in those days men will seek death and will •*not* find it; and they will long to die[x] and death flees from them.

7   And the appearance of the locusts was like horses prepared⁺ for battle; and on their heads, as it were, crowns like gold, and their faces were like the faces of men.

8   And they had hair like the hair of women, and their teeth were like *the teeth* of lions.

9   And they had breastplates like breastplates of iron; and the

8:9
Zech. 13:8,9;
Rev. 8:7-12; 9:15,
18; 12:4;
Is. 2:16
8:10
Is. 14:12; Rev.
6:13; 9:1;
Zech. 13:8,9;
Rev. 8:7-12; 9:15,
18; 12:4;
Rev. 14:7; 16:4
8:11
Zech. 13:8,9;
Rev. 8:7-12; 9:15,
18; 12:4;
Jer. 9:15; 23:15
8:12
Zech. 13:8,9;
Rev. 8:7-12; 9:15,
18; 12:4;
Ex. 10:21ff.; Is.
13:10; Ezek.
32:7; Joel 2:10,
31; 3:15; Rev.
6:12f.
8:13
Rev. 14:6; 19:17;
Rev. 9:12; 11:14;
12:12;
Rev. 3:10;
Rev. 8:2

9:1
Rev. 8:2;
Rev. 8:10;
Rev. 1:18;
Luke 8:31; Rev.
9:2,11
9:2
Gen. 19:28; Ex.
19:18;
Joel 2:2,10

9:3
Ex. 10:12-15;
Rev. 9:7;
2 Chr. 10:11,14;
Ezek. 2:6; Rev.
9:5,10
9:4
Rev. 6:6;
Rev. 8:7;
Ezek. 9:4; Rev.
7:2,3
9:5
2 Chr. 10:11,14;
Ezek. 2:6; Rev.
9:3,10
9:6
Job 3:21; 7:15;
Jer. 8:3; Rev.
6:16
9:7
Joel 2:4

9:8
Joel 1:6
9:9
Jer. 47:3; Joel
2:5

sound of their wings was like the sound of chariots, of many horses rushing to battle.

10   And they have tails like scorpions, and stings; and in their tails is their power[32b] to hurt[x] men for five months.

11   They have as king over them, the angel of the abyss; his name in Hebrew is [k]Abaddon, and in the Greek he has the name Apollyon.

12   The first woe is past; behold, two woes are still coming after these things.

The Sixth Trumpet—Army from the East

13   And the sixth angel sounded, and I heard a voice from the [l]four horns of the golden altar which is before God,

14   one saying to the sixth angel who had the trumpet, "Release[xl] the four angels who are bound* at the great river Euphrates."

15   And the four angels, who had been prepared* for the hour and day and month and year, were released, so that they might kill[x] a third of mankind.

16   And the number of the armies of the horsemen was two hundred million; I heard the number of them.

17   And this is how I saw in the vision the horses and those who sat on them: *the riders* had breastplates *the color* of fire and of hyacinth and of brimstone; and the heads of the horses are like the heads of lions; and out of their mouths proceed fire and smoke and brimstone.

18   A third of mankind was killed by these three plagues, by the fire and the smoke and the brimstone, which proceeded out of their mouths.

19   For the power[32b] of the horses is in their mouths and in their tails; for their tails are like serpents and have heads; and with them they do harm.

20   And the rest of mankind, who were not killed by these plagues, did not repent of the works of their hands, so as not to worship demons, and the idols of gold and of silver and of brass and of stone and of wood, which can neither see~ nor hear~ nor walk;~

21   and they did not repent of their murders nor of their sorceries nor of their immorality nor of their thefts.

The Angel and the Little Book

10   And I saw another strong angel coming down out of heaven, clothed* with a cloud; and the rainbow was upon

[k]i.e., destruction   [l]Some ancient mss. do not contain *four*

his head, and his face was like the sun, and his feet like pillars of fire;

2   and he had in his hand a little book which was open.⁺ And he placed his right foot on the sea and his left on the land;

3   and he cried out with a loud voice, as when a lion roars; and when he had cried out, the seven peals of thunder uttered their voices.

4   And when the seven peals of thunder had spoken, I was about to write; and I heard a voice from heaven saying, "Seal* up the things which the seven peals of thunder have spoken, and do not write⁶ them."

5   And the angel whom I saw standing on the sea and on the land lifted up his right hand to heaven,

6   and swore by Him who lives forever and ever, WHO CREAT-ED HEAVEN AND THE THINGS IN IT, AND THE EARTH AND THE THINGS IN IT, AND THE SEA AND THE THINGS IN IT, that there shall be delay no longer,

7   but in the days of the voice of the seventh angel, when he is about to sound, then the mystery of God is finished, as He preached to His servants the prophets.

8   And the voice which I heard from heaven, *I heard* again speaking with me, and saying, "Go, take* the book which is open⁺ in the hand of the angel who stands on the sea and on the land."

9   And I went to the angel, telling him to give* me the little book. And he *said to me, "Take* it, and eat* it; and it will make your *stomach* bitter, but in your mouth it will be sweet as honey."

10   And I took the little book out of the angel's hand and ate it, and it was in my mouth sweet as honey; and when I had eaten it, my stomach was made bitter.

11   And they *said to me, "You must prophesy* again con-cerning many peoples and nations and tongues and kings."

The Two Witnesses

11   And there was given me a measuring rod like a staff; and someone said, "Rise and measure* the temple of God, and the altar, and those who worship in it.

2   "And leave* out the *court* which is *outside⁴ the temple,* and do not measure⁶ it, for it has been given to the nations; and they will tread under foot the *holy city* for forty-two months.

3   "And I will grant *authority* to my two witnesses, and they will prophesy for twelve hundred and sixty days, clothed⁺ in sackcloth."

10:2
Rev. 5:1; 10:8-10;
Rev. 10:5

10:3
Is. 31:4; Hos.
11:10;
Ps. 29:3-9; Rev.
4:5

10:4
Rev. 1:11,19;
Rev. 10:8;
Dan. 8:26; 12:4,9;
Rev. 22:10

10:5
Deut. 32:40; Dan.
12:7

10:6
Gen. 14:22; Ex.
6:8; Num. 14:30;
Ezek. 20:5;
Rev. 4:9;
Ex. 20:11; Rev.
4:11;
Rev. 6:11; 12:12;
16:17; 21:6
10:7
Rev. 11:15;
Amos 3:7; Rom.
16:25

10:8
Rev. 10:4;
Rev. 10:2

10:9
Jer. 15:16; Ezek.
2:8; 3:1-3

10:11
Rev. 11:1;
Ezek. 37:4,9;
Rev. 5:9;
Rev. 17:10,12
11:1
Ezek. 40:3-42:20;
Zech. 2:1; Rev.
21:15f.;
Rev. 10:11
11:2
Ezek. 40:17,20;
Luke 21:24;
Is. 52:1; Matt. 4:5;
27:53; Rev. 21:2,
10; 22:19;
Dan. 7:25; 12:7;
Rev. 12:6; 13:5
11:3
Rev. 1:5; 2:13;
Dan. 7:25; 12:7;
Rev. 12:6; 13:5;
Gen. 37:34;
2 Sam. 3:31;
1 Kin. 21:27;
2 Kin. 19:1f.;
Neh. 9:1; Esth.
4:1; Ps. 69:11;
Joel 1:13; Jon.
3:5f.,8

11:4
Ps. 52:8; Jer.
11:16; Zech. 4:3,
11,14
11:5
2 Kin. 1:10-12;
Jer. 5:14; Rev.
9:17f.;
Num. 16:29,35
11:6
1 Kin. 17:1; Luke
4:25;
Rev. 11:3;
Ex. 7:17ff.; Rev.
8:8;
1 Sam. 4:8
11:7
Rev. 13:1ff.; 17:8;
Rev. 9:1;
Dan. 7:21; Rev.
13:7
11:8
Rev. 14:8; 16:19;
17:18; 18:2,10,
16,18,19,21;
Is. 1:9,10; 3:9;
Jer. 23:14; Ezek.
16:46,49;
Ezek. 23:3,8,19,
27
11:9
Rev. 5:9; 10:11;
1 Kin. 13:22; Ps.
79:2f.
11:10
Rev. 3:10;
Neh. 8:10,12;
Esth. 9:19,22
11:11
Ezek. 37:5,9,10,
14
11:12
Rev. 4:1;
2 Kin. 2:11; Acts
1:9
11:13
Rev. 6:12; 8:5;
11:19; 16:18;
John 9:24; Rev.
14:7; 16:9; 19:7;
Rev. 16:11
11:14
Rev. 8:13; 9:12
11:15
Rev. 8:2; 10:7;
Rev. 16:17; 19:1;
Rev. 12:10;
Ps. 2:2; Acts
4:26;
Ex. 15:18; Dan.
2:44; 7:14,27;
Luke 1:33
11:16
Matt. 19:28; Rev.
4:4;
Rev. 4:10
11:17
Rev. 1:8;
Rev. 19:6

4 These are the two olive trees and the two lampstands that stand* before the Lord of the earth.

5 And if anyone desires to harm[x] them, fire proceeds out of their mouth and devours[1] their enemies; and if anyone would desire[x] to harm[x] them, in this manner he must be killed.[x]

6 These have the power[32b] to shut[x] up the sky, in order that rain may not fall~ during the days of their prophesying; and they have *power*[32b] over the waters to turn~ them into blood, and to smite[x] the earth with every plague, as often as they desire.[x]

7 And when they have finished[x] their testimony, the beast that comes up out of the abyss will make war with them, and overcome them and kill them.

8 And their dead [m]bodies *will lie* in the street of the great city which [n†]mystically is called Sodom and Egypt, where also their Lord was crucified.

9 And those from the peoples and tribes and tongues and nations *will* look at their dead [m]bodies for three and a half days, and will not permit their dead bodies to be laid[x] in a tomb.

10 And those who dwell on the earth *will* rejoice over them and make merry; and they will send *gifts* to one another, because these two prophets tormented those who dwell on the earth.

11 And after the three and a half days the breath of life from God came into them, and they stood on their feet; and great fear fell upon those who were beholding them.

12 And they heard a loud voice from heaven saying to them, "Come[xi] up here." And they went up into heaven in the cloud, and their enemies beheld them.

13 And in that hour there was a great †earthquake, and a tenth of the city fell; and seven thousand people were killed in the earthquake, and the rest were terrified and gave glory to the God of heaven.

14 The second woe is past; behold, the third woe is coming quickly.

The Seventh Trumpet—Christ's Reign Foreseen

15 And the seventh angel sounded; and there arose loud voices in heaven, saying,

"The kingdom of the world has become *the kingdom* of our Lord, and of His [o]Christ; and He will reign forever and ever."

16 And the twenty-four elders, who sit on their thrones before God, fell on their faces and worshiped[44b] God,

17 saying,

"We give Thee thanks, O Lord God, the Almighty, who art and

[m]Some ancient mss. read *body*   [n]Lit., *spiritually*   [o]I.e., Messiah

who wast, because Thou hast taken⁺ Thy great power and hast begun to reign.

18 "And the nations were enraged, and Thy wrath⁷ᵇ came, and the time *came* for the dead to be judged,ˣ and *the time* to giveˣ their reward to Thy bond-servants the prophets and to the saints and to those who fear Thy name, the small and the great, and to destroyˣ those who destroy the earth."

19 And the temple of God which is in heaven was opened; and the ark of His covenant appeared in His temple, and there were flashes of lightning and sounds and peals of thunder and an earthquake and a great hailstorm.

The Woman, Israel

12 And a great sign appeared in heaven: a woman clothed⁺ with the sun, and the moon under her feet, and on her head a crown of twelve stars;

2 and she was with child; and she *cried out, being in labor and in pain to giveˣ birth.

The Red Dragon, Satan

3 And another sign appeared in heaven: and behold, a great red dragon having seven heads and ten horns, and on his heads *were seven* diadems.

4 And his tail *swept away a third of the stars of heaven, and threw them to the earth. And the dragon stood before the woman who was about to giveˣ birth, so that when she gaveˣ birth he might devourˣ *her child.*

The Male Child, Christ

5 And she gave birth to a son, a male *child*, who is to rule all the nations with a rod of ⁺iron; and her child was *caught up* to God and to His throne.

6 And the woman fled into the wilderness where she *had a place prepared⁺ by God, so that there she might be nourished ~ for one thousand two hundred and sixty days.

The Angel, Michael

7 And there was war in heaven, Michael and his angels wagingˣ war with the dragon. And the dragon and his angels waged war,

8 and they were not strong enough, and there was no longer a place found for them in heaven.

9 And the great dragon was thrown down, the serpent of old who is called the devil and Satan, who deceives the whole

11:18
Ps. 2:1;
Ps. 2:5; 110:5;
Dan. 7:10; Rev.
20:12;
Rev. 10:7; 16:6;
Ps. 115:13; Rev.
13:16; 19:5

11:19
Rev. 4:1; 15:5;
Heb. 9:4;
Rev. 4:5; 8:5;
16:18;
Rev. 16:21

12:1
Matt. 24:30; Rev.
12:3;
Rev. 11:19;
Gal. 4:26;
Ps. 104:2; Song
6:10
12:2
Is. 26:17; 66:6-9;
Mic. 4:9f.

12:3
Rev. 12:1; 15:1;
Is. 27:1; Rev.
12:4,7,9,13,16f.;
13:2,4,11; 16:13;
20:2;
Rev. 17:3,7,9ff.;
Dan. 7:7,20,24;
Rev. 17:12,16;
Rev. 13:1; 19:12
12:4
Rev. 8:7,12;
Dan. 8:10;
Is. 27:1; Rev.
12:3,7,9,13,16f.;
13:2,4,11; 16:13;
20:2;
Matt. 2:16
12:5
Is. 66:7;
Ps. 2:9; Rev.
2:27;
2 Cor. 12:2ff.

12:6
Rev. 11:3; 13:5

12:7
Dan. 10:13,21;
12:1; Jude 9;
Rev. 12:3;
Matt. 25:41
12:9
Rev. 12:3;
Gen. 3:1; 2 Cor.
11:3; Rev. 12:15;
20:2;
Matt. 4:10;
25:41;
Rev. 13:14; 20:3,
8,10;
Luke 10:18; John
12:31

world; he was thrown down to the earth, and his angels were thrown down with him.

10   And I heard a loud voice in heaven, saying,

"Now the salvation, and the power,[32a] and the kingdom of our God and the authority of His Christ have come, for the accuser of our brethren has been thrown down, who accuses them before our God day and night.

11   "And *they* overcame him because of the blood of the Lamb and because of the word of their testimony, and they did not love their life[30c] even to death.

12   "For this reason, rejoice,[⌐] O heavens and you who dwell in them. Woe to the earth and the sea, because the devil has come down to you, having great wrath,[7a] knowing that he has *only* a *short time*."

13   And when the dragon saw that he was thrown down to the earth, he persecuted the woman who gave birth to the male *child*.

14   And the two [†]wings of the great eagle were given to the woman, in order that she might fly[~] into the wilderness to her place, where she *was nourished for a time and times and half a time, from the presence of the serpent.

15   And the serpent poured water like a river out of his mouth after the woman, so that he might cause[x] her to be *swept away* with the flood.

16   And the earth helped the woman, and the earth opened its mouth and drank up the river which the dragon poured out of his mouth.

17   And the dragon was *enraged* with the woman, and went off to make[x] war with the rest of her offspring, who keep the commandments of God and hold to the testimony of Jesus.

The Beast from the Sea

13   And he stood on the sand of the seashore.

And I saw a beast coming up out of the sea, having ten horns and seven heads, and on his horns *were ten* diadems, and on his heads *were* blasphemous names.

2   And the beast which I saw was like a leopard, and his feet were *like those* of a bear, and his mouth like the mouth of a lion. And the [†]*dragon* gave him his power and his throne and great authority.

3   And *I saw* one of his heads as if it had been slain,[*] and his fatal wound was healed.[15a] And the *whole* earth was amazed *and followed* after the beast;

4   and they worshiped the dragon, because he gave his authority to the beast; and they worshiped the beast, saying, "Who

is like the beast, and who is able to wage[x] war with him?"

5   And there was given to him a mouth speaking arrogant words and blasphemies; and authority to act[x] for forty-two months was given to him.

6   And he opened his mouth in blasphemies against God, to blaspheme[x] His name and His tabernacle, *that is*, those who dwell in heaven.

7   And it was given to him to make[x] war with the saints and to overcome[x] them; and authority over every tribe and people and tongue and nation was given to him.

8   And all who dwell on the earth will worship him, *everyone* whose name has not been ᵖwritten⁺ from the foundation of the world in the book of life of the Lamb who has been slain.⁺

9   If anyone has an ear, let him hear.ˣˡ

10   If anyone �q*is destined* for captivity, to captivity he goes; if anyone kills[x] with the sword, with the sword he must be killed.[x] Here is the perseverance and the faith of the saints.

The Beast from the Earth

11   And I saw another beast coming up out of the earth; and he had[m] two horns like a lamb, and he spoke[m] as a dragon.

12   And he exercises *all* the authority of the first beast in his presence. And he makes the earth and those who dwell in it to worship the first beast, whose fatal wound was healed.

13   And he performs great signs, so that he even makes~ *fire* come down out of heaven to the earth in the presence of men.

14   And he deceives[16b] those who dwell on the earth because of the signs which it was given him to perform[x] in the presence of the beast, telling those who dwell on the earth to make[x] an image to the beast who *had the wound of the sword and has come to life.

15   And there was given to him to give[x] breath to the image of the beast, that the image of the beast might even ʳspeak[x] and cause[x] as many as do not worship[x] the image of the beast to be killed.[x]

16   And he causes all, the small and the great, and the rich and the poor, and the free men and the slaves, to be given[x] a mark on their right hand, or on their forehead,

17   and *he provides* that no one should be able~ to buy[x] or to sell,[x] except the one who has the mark, *either* the name of the beast or the number of his name.

18   Here is wisdom. Let him who has understanding

13:5
Dan. 7:8,11,20, 25; 11:36;
2 Thess. 2:3f.;
Rev. 11:2

13:6
Rev. 7:15; 12:12

13:7
Dan. 7:21; Rev. 11:7;
Rev. 5:9

13:8
Rev. 3:10; 13:12, 14;
Rev. 3:5;
Matt. 25:34; Rev. 17:8;
Ps. 69:28;
Rev. 5:6

13:9
Rev. 2:7

13:10
Is. 33:1; Jer. 15:2; 43:11;
Gen. 9:6; Matt. 26:52; Rev. 11:18;
Heb. 6:12; Rev. 14:12

13:11
Rev. 13:1; 16:13;
Dan. 8:3;
Rev. 13:4

13:12
Rev. 13:4;
Rev. 13:14; 19:20;
Rev. 13:8;
Rev. 13:15; 14:9, 11; 16:2; 20:4;
Rev. 13:3

13:13
Matt. 24:24; Rev. 16:14; 19:20;
1 Kin. 18:38;
Luke 9:54; Rev. 11:5; 20:9

13:14
Rev. 12:9;
Rev. 13:8;
2 Thess. 2:9f.;
Rev. 13:12;
19:20;
Rev. 13:3

13:15
Dan. 3:3ff.;
Rev. 13:12; 14:9, 11; 16:2; 19:20;
20:4

13:16
Rev. 11:18; 19:5, 18;
Gal. 6:17; Rev. 7:3; 14:9; 20:4

13:17
Gal. 6:17; Rev. 7:3; 14:9; 20:4;
Rev. 14:11;
Rev. 15:2

13:18
Rev. 17:9;
Rev. 21:17

ᵖOr, *written in the book . . . slain from the foundation of the world*   qOr, leads *into captivity*   ʳSome ancient mss. read *speak, and he will cause*

calculate[xi] the number of the beast, for the number is that of a
†man, and his number is ˢsix hundred and sixty-six.

The Lamb and the 144,000 on Mount Zion

14:1
Rev. 5:6;
Ps. 2:6; Heb.
12:22;
Rev. 7:4; 14:3;
Rev. 3:12;
Ezek. 9:4; Rev.
7:3

14 And I looked, and behold, the Lamb *was* standing on
Mount Zion, and with Him *one hundred and forty-four*
thousand, having His name and the name of His Father written ⁺
on their foreheads.

14:2
Rev. 1:15;
Rev. 6:1;
Rev. 5:8

2 And I heard a voice from heaven, like the sound of many
waters and like the sound of loud thunder, and the voice which
I heard *was* like *the sound* of harpists playing on their harps.

14:3
Rev. 5:9;
Rev. 4:6;
Rev. 4:4;
Rev. 2:17;
Rev. 7:4; 14:1

3 And they *sang a †new song before the throne and before
the four living creatures and the elders; and no one could[m] learn[x]
the song except the one hundred and forty-four thousand who
had been purchased ⁺from the earth.

14:4
Matt. 19:12;
2 Cor. 11:2; Eph.
5:27; Rev. 3:4;
7:17; 17:14;
Rev. 5:9;
Heb. 12:23;
James 1:18

4 These are the ones who have not been defiled[17c] with
women, for they †have kept themselves †chaste. These *are* the
ones who follow the Lamb wherever He goes. These have been
purchased from among men as first fruits to God and to the
Lamb.

14:5
Ps. 32:2; Zeph.
3:13; Mal. 2:6;
John 1:47; 1 Pet.
2:22;
Heb. 9:14; 1 Pet.
1:19; Jude 24

5 And no *lie* was found in their mouth; they are †blame-
less. [11b]

Vision of the Angel with the Gospel

14:6
Rev. 8:13;
1 Pet. 1:25; Rev.
10:7;
Rev. 3:10;
Rev. 5:9

6 And I saw another angel flying in midheaven, having an
eternal gospel to preach[x] to those who live on the earth, and to
every nation and tribe and tongue and people;

14:7
Rev. 15:4;
Rev. 11:13;
Rev. 4:11;
Rev. 8:10

7 and he said with a loud voice, "Fear [xi]God, and give [xi]Him
glory, because the hour of His judgment has come; and worship [xi]
Him who made the heaven and the earth and sea and springs of
waters."

14:8
Is. 21:9; Jer. 51:8;
Rev. 18:2;
Dan. 4:30; Rev.
16:19; 17:5;
18:10;
Jer. 51:7;
Rev. 17:2,4; 18:3

8 And another angel, a second one, followed, saying, " *Fall-
en, fallen* is Babylon the great, she who has made all the nations
drink⁺ of the wine of the passion of her immorality."

Doom for Worshipers of the Beast

14:9
Rev. 13:12;
14:11;
Rev. 13:14f.;
Rev. 13:16

9 And another angel, a third one, followed them, saying
with a loud voice, "If anyone worships the beast and his image,
and receives a mark on his forehead or upon his hand,

14:10
Is. 51:17; Jer.
25:15f.,27; Rev.
16:19; 19:15;
Ps. 75:8; Rev.
18:6;
Gen. 19:24; Ezek.
38:22; 2 Thess.
1:7; Rev. 19:20;
20:10,14f.; 21:8;
Mark 8:38

10 *he also* will drink of the wine of the wrath [7a]of God, which
is mixed⁺ in full †strength in the cup of His anger; [7b]and he will be
tormented with fire and brimstone in the presence of the holy
angels and in the presence of the Lamb.

ˢSome mss. read 616   †Lit., *are chaste men*

11 "And the smoke of their torment goes up *forever and ever,* and they have no rest day and night, those who worship the beast and his image, and whoever receives the mark of his name."

12 Here is the perseverance of the saints who keep the commandments of God and their faith in Jesus.

13 And I heard a voice from heaven, saying, "Write,ˣᴵ '†Blessed are the dead who die in the †Lord from now on!' " "Yes," says the Spirit, "that they may rest from their labors, for their deeds follow with them."

The Reapers

14 And I looked, and behold, a white cloud, and sitting on the cloud *was* one like ᵘa son of man, having a golden crown on His head, and a sharp sickle in His hand.

15 And another angel came out of the temple, crying out with a loud voice to Him who sat on the cloud, "Putˣᴵ in your sickle and reap,ˣᴵ because the hour to reapˣ has come, because the harvest of the earth is ripe."

16 And He who sat on the cloud swung His sickle over the earth; and the earth was reaped.

17 And another angel came out of the temple which is in heaven, and he also had a sharp sickle.

18 And another angel, the one who has power ³²ᵇ over fire, came out from the altar; and he called with a loud voice to him who had the sharp sickle, saying, "Putˣᴵ in your sharp sickle, and gatherˣᴵ the clusters from the vine of the earth, because her grapes are ripe."

19 And the angel swung his sickle to the earth, and gathered *the clusters from* the vine of the earth, and threw them into the great wine press of the wrath ⁷ᵃof God.

20 And the wine press was trodden outside the city, and †bloodcame out from the wine press, up to the horses' bridles, for a distance of ᵛtwo hundred miles.

A Scene of Heaven

15 And I saw another sign in heaven, great and †marvelous, seven angels who had seven plagues, *which are* the last, because in them the wrath ⁷ᵃof God is finished.

2 And I saw, as it were, a sea of glass mixed⁺ with fire, and those who had come off victorious from the beast and from his image and from the number of his name, standing on the sea of glass, holding harps of God.

ᵘOr, *the Son of Man* ᵛLit., *sixteen hundred stadia*. A stadion was about six hundred feet.

14:11
Is. 34:8-10; Rev. 18:9,18; 19:3; Rev. 4:8; Rev. 13:12; 14:9; Rev. 13:17

14:12
Rev. 13:10; Rev. 12:17; Rev. 2:13
14:13
Rev. 20:6; 1 Cor. 15:18; 1 Thess. 4:16; Rev. 2:7; 22:17; Heb. 4:9ff.; Rev. 6:11; 1 Tim. 5:25

14:14
Matt. 17:5; Dan. 7:13; Rev. 1:13; Ps. 21:3; Rev. 6:2

14:15
Rev. 11:19; 14:17; 15:6; 16:17; Joel 3:13; Mark 4:29; Rev. 14:18; Jer. 51:33; Matt. 13:39-41

14:17
Rev. 11:19; 14:15; 15:6; 16:17
14:18
Rev. 16:8; Rev. 6:9; 8:3; Joel 3:13; Mark 4:29; Rev. 14:15

14:19
Is. 63:2f.; Rev. 19:15

14:20
Is. 63:3; Lam. 1:15; Rev. 19:15; Heb. 13:12; Rev. 11:8; Gen. 49:11; Deut. 32:14

15:1
Rev. 12:1,3; Rev. 15:6-8; 16:1; 17:1; 21:9; Lev. 26:21; Rev. 9:20
15:2
Rev. 4:6; Rev. 12:11; Rev. 13:1; Rev. 13:14f.; Rev. 13:17; Rev. 5:8

15:3
Ex. 15:1ff.;
Josh. 22:5; Heb.
3:5;
Rev. 5:9f.,12f.;
Deut. 32:3f.; Ps.
111:2; 139:14;
Hos. 14:9; Rev.
1:8;
1 Tim. 1:17

3   And they *sang the song of Moses the bond-servant of
God and the song of the Lamb, saying,

"Great[26a] and *marvelous* are Thy works,
O Lord God, the Almighty;
Righteous and *true* are Thy ways,
Thou King of the ᵂnations.

15:4
Jer. 10:7; Rev.
14:7;
Ps. 86:9; Is.
66:23;
Rev. 19:8

4   "Who will •not fear,ˣ O Lord, and glorify Thy name?
For Thou alone art holy;[28b]
For ALL THE NATIONS WILL COME AND WORSHIP
BEFORE THEE,
For Thy righteous acts have been revealed."

15:5
Rev. 11:19;
Ex. 38:21; Num.
1:50; Heb. 8:5;
Rev. 13:6
15:6
Rev. 15:1;
Rev. 14:15;
Rev. 1:13

5   After these things I looked, and the temple of the tabernacle of testimony in heaven was opened,

6   and the seven angels who had the seven plagues came out
of the temple, clothed⁺ in ˣlinen, clean *and* bright, and girded⁺
around their breasts with golden girdles.

15:7
Rev. 4:6;
Rev. 5:8;
Rev. 14:10; 15:1;
Rev. 4:9

7   And one of the four living creatures gave to the seven
angels *seven* golden bowls full of the wrath[7a] of God, who lives
forever and ever.

15:8
Ex. 19:18;
40:34f.; Lev. 16:2;
1 Kin. 8:10f.;
2 Chr. 5:13f.; Is.
6:4

8   And the temple was filled with smoke from the glory of
God and from His power; and no one was ableᵐ to enterˣ the
temple until the seven plagues of the seven angels were fin-
ished.ˣ

Six Bowls of Wrath

16:1
Rev. 11:19;
Rev. 15:1;
Ps. 79:6; Jer.
10:25; Ezek.
22:31; Zeph. 3:8;
Rev. 16:2ff.
16:2
Rev. 8:7;
Ex. 9:9-11; Deut.
28:35; Rev.
16:11;
Rev. 13:15-17;
14:9

16   And I heard a *loud* voice from the temple, saying to the
seven angels, "Go and pourᵐ out the seven bowls of the
wrath[7a] of God into the earth."

2   And the first *angel* went and poured out his bowl into the
earth; and it became a loathsome and ⁺malignant sore upon the
men who had the mark of the beast and who worshiped his
image.

16:3
Ex. 7:17-21; Rev.
8:8f.; 11:6

3   And the second *angel* poured out his bowl into the sea, and
it became blood like *that* of a dead man; and every living ʸthing in
the sea died.

16:4
Rev. 8:10;
Ex. 7:17-20; Ps.
78:44; Rev. 11:6
16:5
John 17:25;
Rev. 11:17;
Rev. 15:4;
Rev. 6:10

4   And the third *angel* poured out his bowl into the rivers and
the springs of waters; and ᶻthey became blood.

5   And I heard the angel of the waters saying, "⁺*Righteous*
art Thou, who art and who wast, O Holy[28b] One, because Thou
didst judge these things;

16:6
Rev. 17:6; 18:24;
Is. 49:26; Luke
11:49-51

6   for they poured out *the blood of saints and prophets,* and
Thou hast given⁺ them *blood* to drink.ˣ They ⁺*deserve* it."

ᵂSome ancient mss. read *ages*   ˣSome mss. read *stone*   ʸLit., *soul.* Some ancient mss. read *thing, the
things in the sea.*   ᶻSome ancient mss. read *it became*

7   And I heard the altar saying, "Yes, O Lord God, the Almighty, *true* and *righteous* are Thy judgments."

8   And the fourth *angel* poured out his bowl upon the sun; and it was given to it to scorch^x men with fire.

9   And men were scorched with *fierce heat* 4 and they blasphemed the name of God who has the power 32b over these plagues; and they did not repent, so as to give^x Him glory.

10   And the fifth *angel* poured out his bowl upon the throne of the beast; and his kingdom became⁺ darkened; and they gnawed^{xx} their tongues because of pain,

11   and they blasphemed the God of heaven because of their pains and their sores; and they did not repent of their deeds.

12   And the sixth *angel* poured out his bowl upon the great river, the Euphrates; and its water was dried up, that the way might be prepared^x for the kings from the east.

Armageddon

13   And I saw *coming* out of the mouth of the dragon and out of the mouth of the beast and out of the mouth of the false prophet, three unclean spirits like frogs;

14   for they are spirits of demons, performing signs, which go out to the kings of the whole world, to gather^x them together for the war of the great day of God, the Almighty.

15   ("Behold, I am coming like a thief. ⁺Blessed is the one who stays awake and keeps his garments, lest he walk~ about ⁺*naked* and men see~ his shame.")

16   And they gathered them together to the place which in Hebrew is called ᵃHar-Magedon.

Seventh Bowl of Wrath

17   And the seventh *angel* poured out his bowl upon the air; and a loud voice came out of the temple from the throne, saying, "It is done." ⁺

18   And there were flashes of lightning and sounds and peals of thunder; and there was a great earthquake, such as there had not been since man came to be upon the earth, so great an earthquake *was it, and* so mighty.

19   And the great city was split into *three* parts, and the cities of the nations fell. And Babylon the great was remembered before God, to give^x her the cup of the wine of His fierce wrath. 7b

20   And every island fled away, and the mountains were not found.

21   And huge hailstones, about ᵇone hundred pounds each,

ᵃSome authorities read *Armageddon* ᵇLit., *the weight of a talent*

16:7
Rev. 6:9; 14:18;
Rev. 1:8;
Rev. 15:3; 19:2
16:8
Rev. 6:12;
Rev. 14:18
16:9
Rev. 16:11,21;
Rev. 2:21;
Rev. 11:13
16:10
Rev. 13:2;
Ex. 10:21f.; Is.
8:22; Rev. 8:12;
9:2
16:11
Rev. 16:9,21;
Rev. 11:13;
Rev. 16:2;
Rev. 2:21
16:12
Rev. 9:14;
Is. 11:15f.; 44:27;
Jer. 51:36;
Is. 41:2,25; 46:11;
Rev. 7:2
16:13
Rev. 12:3;
Rev. 13:1;
Rev. 13:11,14;
19:20; 20:10;
Rev. 18:2;
Ex. 8:6
16:14
1 Tim. 4:1;
Rev. 13:13;
Rev. 3:10;
1 Kin. 22:21-23;
Rev. 17:14;
19:19; 20:8;
Rev. 6:17
16:15
Matt. 24:43f.;
Luke 12:39f.;
Rev. 3:3,11;
Luke 12:37;
Rev. 3:18
16:16
Rev. 19:19;
Rev. 9:11;
Judg. 5:19; 2 Kin.
23:29f.; 2 Chr.
35:22; Zech.
12:11
16:17
Eph. 2:2;
Rev. 11:15;
Rev. 14:15;
Rev. 10:6; 21:6
16:18
Rev. 4:5;
Rev. 6:12;
Dan. 12:1; Matt.
24:21
16:19
Rev. 11:8; 17:18;
18:10,18f.,21;
Rev. 14:8;
Rev. 18:5;
Rev. 14:10
16:20
Rev. 6:14; 20:11
16:21
Rev. 8:7; 11:19;
Rev. 16:9,11;
Ex. 9:18-25

*came down from heaven upon men; and men blasphemed God because of the plague of the hail, because its plague *was *extremely severe*.

The Doom of Babylon

17:1
Rev. 1:1; 21:9;
Rev. 15:1;
Rev. 15:7;
Rev. 16:19;
Is. 1:21; Jer. 2:20;
Nah. 3:4; Rev.
17:5,15f.; 19:2;
Jer. 51:13
17:2
Rev. 2:22; 18:3,9;
Rev. 3:10; 17:8;
Rev. 14:8

17 And one of the seven angels who had the seven bowls came and spoke with me, saying, "Come here, I shall show you the judgment of the great harlot who sits on many waters,

2   with whom the kings of the earth committed *acts of* immorality, and those who dwell on the earth were made drunk with the wine of her immorality."

17:3
Rev. 21:10;
Rev. 1:10;
Rev. 12:6,14;
Matt. 27:28; Rev.
18:12,16;
Rev. 13:1;
Rev. 12:3; 17:7,9,
12,16

3   And he carried me away ᶜin the Spirit into a wilderness; and I saw a woman sitting on a†scarlet beast, full of blasphemous names, having seven heads and ten horns.

17:4
Ezek. 28:13; Rev.
18:12,16;
Jer. 51:7; Rev.
18:6

4   And the woman was clothed† in purple and †scarlet, and adorned† with gold and precious stones and pearls, having in her hand a†gold cup full of abominations and of the unclean things of her immorality,

17:5
2 Thess. 2:7;
Rev. 1:20; 17:7;
Rev. 14:8; 16:19;
Rev. 17:2

5   and upon her forehead a name *was* written,† a mystery, "BABYLON THE GREAT, THE MOTHER OF HARLOTS AND OF THE ABOMINATIONS OF THE EARTH."

17:6
Rev. 16:6

6   And I saw the woman drunk with the blood of the saints, and with the blood of the witnesses of Jesus. And when I saw her, I *wondered*[4] *greatly*.

17:7
2 Thess. 2:7;
Rev. 1:20; 17:5;
Rev. 17:3

7   And the angel said to me, "Why do you wonder? *I* shall tell you the mystery of the woman and of the beast that carries her, which has the seven heads and the ten horns.

17:8
Dan. 7:7;
Rev. 13:3,12,14;
17:11;
Rev. 11:7; 13:1;
Rev. 9:1;
Rev. 13:10;
17:11;
Rev. 3:10;
Rev. 13:3;
Ps. 69:28; Rev.
3:5;
Matt. 25:34; Rev.
13:8

8   "The beast that you saw was and is not, and is about to come up out of the abyss and ᵈto go to *destruction*. And those who dwell on the earth will wonder, whose name has not been written† in the book of life from the foundation of the world, when they see the beast, that he was and is not and will come.

17:9
Rev. 13:18;
Rev. 17:3

9   "Here is the mind which has wisdom. The seven heads are *seven mountains* on which the woman sits,

17:10
Rev. 10:11

10   and they are *seven kings;* five have fallen, one is, the other has not yet come; and when he comes, he must remainˣ a little while.

17:11
Rev. 13:3,12,14;
Rev. 13:10; 17:8

11   "And the beast which was and is not, is *himself* also an *eighth,* and is *one of the seven,* and he goes to *destruction*.

17:12
Dan. 7:24; Rev.
12:3; 13:1; 17:16;
Rev. 18:10,17,19

12   "And the ten horns which you saw are *ten kings,* who have *not yet received* a kingdom, but they receive authority as kings with the beast for *one hour*.

ᶜOr, *in spirit*   ᵈSome ancient mss. read *he goes*

13 "These have *one purpose* and they give their power and authority to the *beast*.

Victory for the Lamb

14 "These will wage war *against the Lamb*, and the Lamb will overcome them, because He is Lord of lords and King of kings, and those who are with Him *are the* called and chosen and faithful."

15 And he *said to me, "The waters which you saw where the harlot sits, are peoples and multitudes and nations and tongues.

16 "And the ten horns which you saw, and the beast, these will hate the harlot and will make her †desolate◦ and naked, and will eat *her flesh* and will burn her †up with fire.

17 "For God has put it in their hearts to execute[x] His purpose by having[x] a common purpose, and by giving[x] their kingdom to the beast, until the words[43b] of God should be fulfilled.

18 "And the woman whom you saw ◦*is* the great city, which reigns over the kings of the earth."

Babylon Is Fallen

18 After these things I saw another angel coming down from heaven, having great authority, and the earth was illumined with his glory.

2 And he cried out with a mighty voice, saying, *"Fallen, fallen* is Babylon the great! And she has become a dwelling place of demons and a prison of every unclean spirit, and a prison of every unclean and hateful◦ bird.

3 "For all the nations [e]have drunk◦ of the wine of the passion of her immorality, and the kings of the earth have committed *acts of* †immorality with her, and the merchants of the earth have become rich by the wealth of her sensuality."

4 And I heard another voice from heaven, saying, "Come[xl] out of her, my people, that you may not participate[x] in her sins and that you may not receive[x] of *her plagues;*

5 for *her sins* have piled up as high as heaven, and God has remembered her iniquities.

6 "Pay[xl] her back even as *she* has paid, and give[xl] back *to her* double[d] according to her deeds; in the cup which she has mixed, mix[xl] twice as much for her.

7 "To the degree that she glorified herself and lived sensuously, to the same degree give[xl] her torment and mourning; for she says in her heart, 'I SIT *as* A QUEEN AND I AM NOT A *WIDOW*, and will ◦*never* see[x] *mourning.*'

[e]Many ancient mss. read *have fallen by*

17:13
Rev. 17:17

17:14
Rev. 16:14;
Rev. 3:21;
1 Tim. 6:15; Rev.
19:16;
Rev. 2:10f.;
Matt. 22:14

17:15
Is. 8:7; Jer. 47:2;
Rev. 17:1;
Rev. 5:9
17:16
Rev. 17:12;
Rev. 18:17,19;
Ezek. 16:37,39;
Rev. 19:18;
Rev. 18:8
17:17
2 Cor. 8:16;
Rev. 17:13;
Rev. 10:7

17:18
Rev. 11:8; 16:19

18:1
Rev. 17:1,7;
Rev. 10:1;
Ezek. 43:2

18:2
Is. 21:9; Jer. 51:8;
Rev. 14:8;
Is. 13:21f.; 34:11,
13-15; Jer. 50:39;
51:37; Zeph.
2:14f.;
Rev. 16:13
18:3
Jer. 51:7; Rev.
14:8;
Rev. 17:2;
Ezek. 27:9-25;
Rev. 18:11,15,19,
23;
1 Tim. 5:11; Rev.
18:7,9
18:4
Is. 52:11; Jer.
50:8; 51:6,9,45;
2 Cor. 6:17

18:5
Jer. 51:9;
Rev. 16:19

18:6
Ps. 137:8; Jer.
50:15,29;
Rev. 17:4

18:7
Ezek. 28:2-8;
1 Tim. 5:11; Rev.
18:3,9;
Is. 47:7f.; Zeph.
2:15

18:8
Is. 47:9; Jer.
50:31f.; Rev.
18:10;
Rev. 17:16;
Jer. 50:34; Rev.
11:17f.

8 "For this reason in *one day* her plagues will come, pestilence and mourning and famine, and she will be burned up with fire; for the Lord God who judges her is †strong.

Lament for Babylon

18:9
Rev. 17:2;
1 Tim. 5:11; Rev.
18:3,7;
Ezek. 26:16f.;
27:35;
Rev. 14:11;
18:18; 19:3
18:10
Rev. 18:15,17;
Rev. 11:8; 16:19;
18:16,18,19,21;
Rev. 17:12; 18:8,
17,19
18:11
Ezek. 27:9-25;
Rev. 18:3,15,19,
23;
Ezek. 27:27-34
18:12
Ezek. 27:12-22;
Rev. 17:4

9 "And the kings of the earth, who committed *acts of* immorality and lived sensuously with her, will weep and lament over her when they see~ the smoke of her burning,

10 standing at a distance because of the fear of her torment, saying, 'Woe, woe, the great city, Babylon, the strong city! For in *one hour* your judgment has come.'

11 "And the merchants of the earth weep and mourn over her, because no one buys *their cargoes* any more;

12 cargoes of gold and silver and precious stones and pearls and fine linen and purple and silk and scarlet, and every *kind of* citron wood and every article of ivory and every article *made* from very³ †costly wood and bronze and iron and marble,

18:13
1 Chr. 5:21; Ezek.
27:13; 1 Tim.
1:10

13 and cinnamon and spice and incense and perfume and frankincense and wine and olive oil and fine flour and wheat and cattle and sheep, and *cargoes* of horses and chariots and slaves and human lives.

14 "And the fruit you long for has gone from you, and all things that were luxurious and splendid have passed away from you and *men* will •*no longer* find them.

18:15
Rev. 18:3;
Rev. 18:12,13;
Rev. 18:10

15 "The merchants of these things, who became rich from her, will stand at a distance because of the fear of her torment, weeping and mourning,

18:16
Rev. 18:10,18,19,
21;
Rev. 17:4

16 saying, 'Woe, woe, the great city, she who was clothed✦in fine linen and purple and scarlet, and adorned✦ with gold and precious stones and pearls;

18:17
Rev. 18:10;
Rev. 17:16;
18:19;
Ezek. 27:28f.
18:18
Ezek. 27:30;
Rev. 18:9;
Ezek. 27:32; Rev.
13:4;
Rev. 18:10
18:19
Josh. 7:6; Job
2:12; Lam. 2:10;
Rev. 18:10;
Rev. 18:3,15;
Rev. 17:16; 18:17
18:20
Jer. 51:48; Rev.
12:12;
Luke 11:49f.;
Rev. 6:10; 18:6ff.;
19:2
18:21
Rev. 5:2; 10:1;
Jer. 51:63f.;
Rev. 18:10;
Ezek. 26:21

17 for in *one hour* such great wealth has been laid waste!' And every shipmaster and every passenger and sailor, and as many as make their living by the sea, stood at a distance,

18 and were crying ᵐ out as they saw the smoke of her burning, saying, 'What *city* is like the great city?'

19 "And they threw dust on their heads and were crying ᵐ out, weeping and mourning, saying, 'Woe, woe, the great city, in which all who had ships at sea became rich by her wealth, for in *one hour* she has been laid waste!'

20 "Rejoice~ᴵ over her, O heaven, and you saints and apostles and prophets, because God has pronounced judgment for you against her."

21 And a strong angel took up a stone like a great millstone and threw it into the sea, saying, "Thus will Babylon, the great

city, be thrown down with *violence,* and will •*not*be found^x any longer.

22 "And the sound of harpists and musicians and flute-players and trumpeters will •*not* be heard^x in you any longer; and no craftsman of any craft will be found^x in you any longer; and the sound of a mill will •*not*be heard^x in you any longer;

23   and the light of a lamp will •*not* shine^x in you any longer; and the voice of the bridegroom and bride will •*not*be heard^x in you any longer; for your merchants were the great men of the earth, because all the nations were deceived[16b] by your sorcery.

24 "And in *her* was found the blood of prophets and of saints and of all who have been slain+ on the earth."

The Fourfold Hallelujah

19 After these things I heard, as it were, a loud voice of a great multitude in heaven, saying,

"**H**allelujah! Salvation and glory and power[32a] belong to our God;

2   BECAUSE HIS JUDGMENTS ARE *TRUE* AND *RIGHTEOUS;* for He has judged the great harlot who was corrupting the earth with her immorality, and HE HAS AVENGED THE BLOOD OF HIS BOND-SERVANTS ON HER."

3   And a second time they said, "Hallelujah! HER SMOKE RISES UP FOREVER AND EVER."

4   And the *twenty-four* elders and the four living creatures fell down and worshiped[44b] God who sits on the throne saying, "Amen. Hallelujah!"

5   And a voice came from the throne, saying,

"Give ~ praise to our God, all you His bond-servants, you who fear Him, the small and the great."

6   And I heard, as it were, the voice of a great multitude and as the sound of many waters and as the sound of mighty peals of thunder, saying,

"**H**allelujah! For the Lord our God, the Almighty, *reigns.*

Marriage of the Lamb

7 "Let us rejoice ~ and be glad ~ and give^x the glory to Him, for the *marriage of the Lamb* has come and His bride has made herself ready."

8   And it was given to her to clothe^x herself in fine linen, †bright *and* †clean; for the fine linen is the *righteous acts of the saints.*

9   And he *said to me, "Write,^x '†Blessed are those who are

18:22
Is. 24:8; Ezek.
26:13; Matt. 9:23;
Eccl. 12:4; Jer.
25:10

18:23
Jer. 7:34; 16:9;
Is. 23:8; Rev.
6:15; 18:3;
Nah. 3:4; Rev.
9:21

18:24
Rev. 16:6; 17:6;
Matt. 23:35

19:1
Jer. 51:48; Rev.
11:15;
Ps. 104:35; Rev.
19:3,4,6;
Rev. 7:10;
Rev. 4:11

19:2
Ps. 19:9;
Rev. 6:10;
Rev. 16:7;
Rev. 17:1;
Deut. 32:43;
2 Kin. 9:7; Rev.
16:6; 18:20

19:3
Ps. 104:35; Rev.
19:1,4,6;
Is. 34:10; Rev.
14:11

19:4
Rev. 4:4,10;
Rev. 4:6;
Ps. 106:48; Rev.
5:14;
Ps. 104:35; Rev.
19:3,6

19:5
Ps. 22:23;
115:13; 134:1;
135:1;
Rev. 11:18

19:6
Jer. 51:48; Rev.
11:15; 19:1;
Ezek. 1:24; Rev.
1:15;
Rev. 6:1;
Ps. 93:1; 97:1;
99:1; Rev. 1:8

19:7
Rev. 11:13;
Matt. 22:2; 25:10;
Luke 12:36; John
3:29; Eph. 5:23,
32; Rev. 19:9;
Matt. 1:20; Rev.
21:2,9

19:8
Rev. 15:6; 19:14;
Rev. 15:4

19:9
Rev. 17:1; 19:10;
Rev. 1:19;
Matt. 22:2f.; Luke
14:15;
Rev. 17:17; 21:5;
22:6

invited⁺ to the marriage supper of the Lamb.' " And he *said to me, "These are *true words of God.*"

19:10
Rev. 22:8;
Acts 10:26; Rev.
22:9;
Rev. 1:1f.;
Rev. 12:17

10   And I fell at his feet to worship[x44b] him. And he *said to me, "Do not do[θ] that; I am a *fellow* ⁺servant of yours and your brethren who hold the testimony of Jesus; worship[xl] *God.* For the testimony of Jesus is the spirit of prophecy."

The Coming of Christ

19:11
Ezek. 1:1; John
1:51; Rev. 4:1;
Rev. 6:2; 19:19,
21;
Rev. 3:14;
Ps. 96:13; Is.
11:4
19:12
Dan. 10:6; Rev.
1:14;
Rev. 6:2; 12:3;
Rev. 2:17; 19:16
19:13
Is. 63:3;
John 1:1
19:14
Rev. 3:4; 19:8

11   And I saw heaven opened;⁺ and behold, a ⁺white horse, and He who sat upon it *is* called Faithful and True; and in *righteousness* He judges and wages war.

12   And His eyes *are* a flame of fire, and upon His head *are* many diadems; and He has a name written⁺ *upon Him* which no one knows except Himself.

13   And *He is* clothed⁺ with a robe dipped⁺ in blood; and His name is called⁺ The Word[43a] of God.

14   And the armies which are in heaven, clothed⁺ in fine linen, ⁺white *and* ⁺clean, were following[m] Him on white horses.

19:15
Rev. 1:16; 19:21;
Is. 11:4; 2 Thess.
2:8;
Ps. 2:9; Rev.
2:27;
Is. 63:3; Joel
3:13; Rev. 14:19,
20
19:16
Rev. 2:17; 19:12;
Rev. 17:14

15   And from His mouth comes a sharp sword, so that with it He may smite[x] the nations; and *He* will rule them with a rod of ⁺iron; and *He* treads the wine press of the fierce[7a] wrath[7b] of God, the Almighty.

16   And on His robe and on His thigh He has a name written,⁺ "KING OF KINGS, AND LORD OF LORDS."

19:17
Rev. 19:21;
Rev. 8:13;
1 Sam. 17:44;
Jer. 12:9; Ezek.
39:17
19:18
Ezek. 39:18-20;
Rev. 6:15;
Rev. 11:18;
13:16; 19:5

17   And I saw an angel standing in the sun; and he cried out with a loud voice, saying to all the birds which fly in midheaven, "Come, assemble[xl] for the great supper of God;

18   in order that you may eat[x] the flesh of kings and the flesh of ᶠcommanders and the flesh of mighty men and the flesh of horses and of those who sit on them and the flesh of all men, both free men and slaves, and small and great."

19:19
Rev. 11:7; 13:1;
Rev. 16:14,16;
Rev. 19:11,21

19   And I saw the beast and the kings of the earth and their armies, assembled⁺ to make[x] war against Him who sat upon the horse, and against His army.

Doom of the Beast and False Prophet

19:20
Rev. 16:13;
Rev. 13:13;
Rev. 13:14;
Rev. 13:16f.;
Rev. 13:12,15;
Rev. 20:10,14f.;
21:8;
Is. 30:33; Dan.
7:11; Rev. 14:10
19:21
Rev. 19:15;
Rev. 19:11,19;
Rev. 19:17

20   And the beast was seized, and with him the false prophet who performed the signs in his presence, by which he deceived[16b] those who had received the mark of the beast and those who worshiped his image; these two were thrown *alive* into the lake of fire which burns with brimstone.

21   And the rest were killed with the sword which came from

ᶠI.e., chiliarchs, in command of one thousand troops

the mouth of Him who sat upon the horse, and all the birds were filled with their flesh.

Satan Bound

20 And I saw an angel coming down from heaven, having the key of the abyss and a great chain in his hand.

2   And he laid hold of the dragon, the serpent of old, who is the devil and Satan, and bound him for a *thousand* years,

3   and threw him into the abyss, and shut *it* and sealed *it* over him, so that he should not deceive[x16b] the nations any longer, until the thousand years were completed;[x] after these things he must be released[x] for a short time.

4   And I saw thrones, and they sat upon them, and judgment was given to them. And I *saw* the souls of those who had been beheaded[*] because of the testimony of Jesus and because of the word of God, and those who had not worshiped the beast or his image, and had not received the mark upon their forehead and upon their hand; and they came to life and reigned with Christ for a *thousand* years.

5   The rest of the dead did not come to life until the thousand years were completed.[x] This is the *first* resurrection.

6   Blessed and holy[28a] is the one who has a part in the *first* resurrection; over these the second death has no power,[32b] but they will be priests of God and of Christ and will reign with Him for a thousand years.

Satan Freed, Doomed

7   And when the thousand years are completed,[x] Satan will be *released* from his prison,

8   and will come out to deceive[x16b] the nations which are in the four corners of the earth, Gog and Magog, to gather[x] them together for the war; the number of them is like the sand of the seashore.

9   And they came up on the broad plain of the earth and surrounded the camp of the saints and the beloved[*] city, and fire came down from heaven and devoured them.

10   And the devil who deceived them was thrown into the lake of fire and brimstone, where the beast and the false prophet are also; and they will be tormented day and night forever and ever.

Judgment at the Throne of God

11   And I saw a great white throne and Him who sat upon it,

20:1
Rev. 10:1;
Rev. 1:18; 9:1
20:2
Gen. 3:1; Rev. 12:9;
Is. 24:22; 2 Pet. 2:4; Jude 6
20:3
Rev. 20:1;
Dan. 6:17; Matt. 27:66;
Rev. 12:9; 20:8, 10
20:4
Dan. 7:9;
Matt. 19:28;
Dan. 7:22; 1 Cor. 6:2;
Rev. 6:9;
Rev. 1:9;
Rev. 13:12,15;
Rev. 13:16f.;
John 14:19;
Rev. 3:21; 5:10;
20:6; 22:5
20:5
Luke 14:14; Phil. 3:11; 1 Thess. 4:16
20:6
Rev. 14:13;
Rev. 2:11; 20:14;
Rev. 1:6;
Rev. 3:21; 5:10;
20:4; 22:5
20:7
Rev. 20:2f.
20:8
Rev. 12:9; 20:3, 10;
Ezek. 7:2; Rev. 7:1;
Ezek. 38:2; 39:1, 6;
Rev. 16:14;
Heb. 11:12
20:9
Ezek. 38:9,16;
Deut. 23:14;
Ps. 87:2;
Ezek. 38:22;
39:6; Rev. 13:13
20:10
Rev. 20:2f.;
Rev. 19:20;
20:14,15;
Rev. 16:13;
Rev. 14:10f.
20:11
Rev. 4:2;
Rev. 6:14; 21:1;
Dan. 2:35; Rev. 12:8

from whose presence earth and heaven fled away, and no place was found for them.

20:12
Rev. 11:18;
Dan. 7:10;
Rev. 3:5; 20:15;
Matt. 16:27; Rev.
2:23; 20:13

12   And I saw the dead, the great and the small, standing before the throne, and books were opened; and another book was opened, which is *the book* of life; and the dead were judged from the things which were written⁺ in the books, according to their deeds.

20:13
1 Cor. 15:26;
Rev. 1:18; 6:8;
21:4;
Is. 26:19;
Matt. 16:27; Rev.
2:23; 20:12
20:14
1 Cor. 15:26;
Rev. 1:18; 6:8;
21:4;
Rev. 19:20;
20:10,15;
Rev. 20:6
20:15
Rev. 3:5; 20:12

13   And the ⁺sea gave up the dead which were in it, and death and Hades²⁷ᵃ gave up the dead which were in them; and they were judged, every one *of them* according to their deeds.

14   And death and Hades²⁷ᵃ were thrown into the lake of fire. This is the *second death,* the lake of fire.

15   And if anyone's name was not found written⁺ in the book of life, he was thrown into the lake of fire.

The New Heaven and Earth

21:1
Is. 65:17; 66:22;
2 Pet. 3:13;
2 Pet. 3:10; Rev.
20:11
21:2
Is. 52:1; Rev.
11:2; 22:19;
Rev. 3:12; 21:10;
Heb. 11:10,16;
Is. 61:10; Rev.
19:7; 21:9; 22:17
21:3
Lev. 26:11f.;
Ezek. 37:27;
48:35; Heb. 8:2;
Rev. 7:15;
John 14:23;
2 Cor. 6:16
21:4
Is. 25:8; Rev.
7:17;
1 Cor. 15:26;
Rev. 20:14;
Is. 35:10; 51:11;
65:19;
2 Cor. 5:17; Heb.
12:27
21:5
Rev. 4:9; 20:11;
2 Cor. 5:17; Heb.
12:27;
Rev. 19:9; 22:6
21:6
Rev. 10:6; 16:17;
Rev. 1:8; 22:13;
Is. 55:1; John
4:10; Rev. 7:17;
22:17;
Rev. 7:17
21:7
Rev. 2:7;
2 Sam. 7:14; Ps.
89:26f.; 2 Cor.
6:16,18; Rev.
21:3
21:8
1 Cor. 6:9; Gal.
5:19-21; Rev.
9:21; 21:27;
22:15;
Rev. 19:20;
Rev. 2:11
21:9
Rev. 17:1;
Rev. 15:7;
Rev. 15:1;
Rev. 19:7; 21:2

21 And I saw a ⁺*new* heaven and a ⁺*new* earth; for the first heaven and the first earth passed away, and there is no longer *any* sea.

2   And I saw the *holy city, new Jerusalem,* coming down out of heaven from God, made ready⁺ as a bride adorned⁺ for her husband.

3   And I heard a loud voice from the throne, saying, "Behold, the tabernacle of God is among men, and He shall dwell among them, and *they* shall be *His people,* and God Himself shall be ⁹*among them,*

4   and He shall wipe away every tear from their eyes; and there shall no longer be *any* death; there shall no longer be *any* mourning, or crying, or pain; the first things have passed away."

5   And He who sits on the throne said, "Behold, I am making all things *new."* And He *said, "Write,*ˣ for these words are faithful and true."

6   And He said to me, "It is done.⁺ I am the Alpha and the Omega, the beginning and the end. *I* will give to the one who *thirsts* from the spring of the water of life *without cost.*

7   "He who overcomes shall inherit these things, and I will be his God and *he* will be My son.

8   "But for the cowardly and unbelieving and abominable⁺ and murderers and immoral persons and sorcerers and idolaters and all liars, their part *will be* in the lake that burns with fire and brimstone, which is the *second* death."

9   And one of the seven angels who had the seven bowls full of the seven last plagues, came and spoke with me, saying,

⁹Some ancient mss. add, and be *their God*

"Come here, I shall show you the bride, the wife of the Lamb."

The New Jerusalem

10   And he carried me away ʰin the Spirit to a great and ⁺high mountain, and showed me the holy city, Jerusalem, coming down out of heaven from God,

11   having the glory of God. Her brilliance was like a *very*³ ⁺*costly* stone, as a stone of crystal-clear jasper.

12   It had a great and ⁺high wall, with twelve gates, and at the gates twelve angels; and names *were* written⁺ on them, which are *those* of the twelve tribes of the sons of Israel.

13   *There were* three gates on the east and three gates on the north and three gates on the south and three gates on the west.

14   And the wall of the city had twelve foundation stones, and on them *were* the *twelve* names of the twelve apostles of the Lamb.

15   And the one who spoke with me had a gold measuring rod to measureˣ the city, and its gates and its wall.

16   And the city is laid out as a square, and its length is as great as the width; and he measured the city with the rod, ⁱfifteen hundred miles; its length and width and height are equal.

17   And he measured its wall, ʲseventy-two yards, *according to* human measurements, which are *also* angelic *measurements.*

18   And the material of the wall was jasper; and the city was pure¹³ᶜ gold, like clear¹³ᶜ glass.

19   The foundation stones of the city wall were adorned⁺ with every kind of precious stone. The first foundation stone was jasper; the second, sapphire; the third, chalcedony; the fourth, emerald;

20   the fifth, sardonyx; the sixth, sardius; the seventh, chrysolite; the eighth, beryl; the ninth, topaz; the tenth, chrysoprase; the eleventh, jacinth; the twelfth, amethyst.

21   And the twelve gates were *twelve* pearls; each one of the gates was a ⁺*single* pearl. And the street of the city was pure¹³ᶜ gold, like transparent glass.

22   And I saw *no temple* in it, for the Lord God, the Almighty, and the Lamb, are its temple.

23   And the city has no need of the sun or of the moon to shine~ upon it, for the glory of God has illumined it, and its lamp *is* the Lamb.

24   And the nations shall walk by its light, and the kings of the earth shall bring their glory into it.

ʰOr, *in spirit* ⁱLit., *twelve thousand stadia;* a stadion was about 600 ft. ʲLit., *one hundred forty-four cubits*

21:10
Ezek. 40:2; Rev. 17:3;
Rev. 1:10;
Rev. 21:2

21:11
Is. 60:1f.; Ezek. 43:2; Rev. 15:8; 21:23; 22:5;
Rev. 4:3; 21:18, 19;
Rev. 4:6

21:12
Ezek. 48:31-34;
Rev. 21:15,21,25; 22:14

21:14
Heb. 11:10;
Acts 1:26

21:15
Ezek. 40:3; Rev. 11:1;
Rev. 21:12,21,25

21:17
Deut. 3:11; Rev. 13:18;
Rev. 21:9

21:18
Rev. 21:11;
Rev. 21:21;
Rev. 4:6

21:19
Ex. 28:17-20; Is. 54:11f.; Ezek. 28:13;
Rev. 21:11;
Rev. 4:3

21:20
Rev. 4:3

21:21
Rev. 21:12,15,25;
Rev. 17:4;
Rev. 21:18;
Rev. 4:6

21:22
Matt. 24:2; John 4:21;
Rev. 1:8;
Rev. 5:6; 7:17; 14:4

21:23
Is. 24:23; 60:19, 20; Rev. 21:25; 22:5;
Rev. 21:11;
Rev. 5:6; 7:17; 14:4

21:24
Is. 60:3,5;
Ps. 72:10f.; Is. 49:23; 60:16;
Rev. 21:26

21:25
Zech. 14:7; Rev.
21:23; 22:5;
Rev. 21:12,15;
Is. 60:11
21:26
Ps. 72:10f.; Is.
49:23; 60:16
21:27
Is. 52:1; Ezek.
44:9; Zech.
14:21; Rev.
22:14f.;
Rev. 3:5

25   And in the daytime (for there shall be no night there) its gates shall •*never* be closed;[x]

26   and they shall bring the glory and the honor of the nations into it;

27   and *nothing unclean*[17a] and no one who practices abomination and lying, shall •*ever* come[x] into it, but only those whose names are written• in the Lamb's book of life.

The River and the Tree of Life

22:1
Rev. 1:1; 21:9;
22:6;
Ps. 46:4; Ezek.
47:1;
Zech. 14:8; Rev.
7:17; 22:17;
Rev. 4:6
22:2
Rev. 21:21;
Ezek. 47:12;
Gen. 2:9; Rev.
2:7; 22:14,19
22:3
Zech. 14:11;
Rev. 21:3;
Rev. 7:15

22   And he showed me a river of the water of life, clear as crystal, coming from the throne of God and of [k]the Lamb,

2   in the middle of its street. And on either side of the river was the tree of life, bearing twelve [l]*kinds of* fruit, yielding its fruit every month; and the leaves of the tree were for the healing of the nations.

3   And there shall no longer be any curse; and the throne of God and of the Lamb shall be in it, and His bond-servants[38b] shall serve[38c] Him;

22:4
Ps. 17:15; 42:2;
Matt. 5:8;
Rev. 14:1;
Rev. 7:3
22:5
Zech. 14:7; Rev.
21:25;
Is. 60:19; Rev.
21:23;
Dan. 7:18,27;
Matt. 19:28; Rom.
5:17; Rev. 20:4
22:6
Rev. 1:1; 21:9;
Rev. 19:9; 21:5;
1 Cor. 14:32;
Heb. 12:9;
Rev. 1:1; 22:16

4   and they shall see His face, and His name *shall be* on their foreheads.

5   And there shall no longer be *any* night; and they shall not have need of the light of a lamp nor the light of the sun, because the Lord God shall illumine them; and they shall reign forever and ever.

6   And he said to me, "These words[43a] are faithful and true"; and the Lord, the God of the spirits of the prophets, sent His angel to show[x] to His bond-servants the things which must shortly take place.

22:7
Rev. 1:3; 3:3,11;
16:15; 22:12,20;
Rev. 16:15;
Rev. 1:11; 22:9,
10,18f.
22:8
Rev. 1:1;
Rev. 19:10

7   "And behold, I am coming quickly. †Blessed is he who heeds the words of the prophecy of this book."

8   And I, John, am the one who heard and saw these things. And when I heard and saw, I fell down to worship[x] at the feet of the angel who showed me these things.

22:9
Rev. 19:10;
Rev. 1:1;
Rev. 1:11; 22:10,
18f.

9   And he *said to me, "Do not do[θ] that; I am a *fellow* †*servant* of yours and of your brethren the prophets and of those who heed the words of this book; worship[xl] *God.*"

The Final Message

22:10
Dan. 8:26; Rev.
10:4;
Rev. 1:11; 22:9,
18f.;
Rev. 1:3
22:11
Ezek. 3:27; Dan.
12:10

10   And he *said to me, "Do not seal[θ] up the words of the prophecy of this book, for the time is near.

11   "Let the one who does wrong, still do wrong;[xl] and let the one who is filthy, still be filthy;[xl] and let the one who is righteous,

[k]Or, *the Lamb. In the middle of its street, and on either side of the river, was*   [l]Or, *crops of fruit*

still practice[xl] righteousness; and let the one who is holy,[28a] still keep[xl] himself holy."

12 "Behold, I am coming quickly, and My reward *is* with Me, to render[x] to every man according to what he has done.

13 "I am the Alpha and the Omega, the first and the last, the beginning and the end."

14 †Blessed are those who wash their robes, that they may have the right[32b] to the tree of life, and may enter[x] by the gates into the city.

15 Outside are the dogs and the sorcerers and the immoral persons and the murderers and the idolaters, and everyone who loves[31b] and practices lying.

16 "I, Jesus, have sent My angel to testify[x] to you these things for the churches. †I am the root and the offspring of David, the bright morning star."

17 And the Spirit and the bride say, "Come."[~l] And let the one who hears say,[xl] "Come."[~l] And let the one who is thirsty come;[~l] let the one who wishes take[xl] the water of life *without cost.*

18 *I* testify to everyone who hears the words of the prophecy of this book: if anyone adds[x] to them, *God* shall add to him the plagues which are written† in this book;

19 and if anyone takes[x] away from the words of the book of this prophecy, *God* shall take away his part from the tree of life and from the †holy city, which are written† in this book.

20 He who testifies to these things says, "Yes, I am coming quickly." Amen. Come, Lord Jesus.

21 The grace of the Lord Jesus be with [m]all. Amen.

[m]Some ancient mss. read *the saints*

22:12
Rev. 22:7;
Is. 40:10; 62:11;
Ps. 28:4; Jer.
17:10; Matt.
16:27; Rev. 2:23
22:13
Rev. 1:8;
Is. 44:6; 48:12;
Rev. 1:17; 2:8;
Rev. 21:6
22:14
Rev. 7:14;
Gen. 2:9; 3:22;
Rev. 22:2;
Rev. 21:27;
Rev. 21:12
22:15
Matt. 8:12; 1 Cor.
6:9f.; Gal. 5:19ff.;
Rev. 21:8;
Deut. 23:18; Matt.
7:6; Phil. 3:2
22:16
Rev. 1:1; 22:6;
Rev. 1:4,11; 3:22;
Rev. 5:5;
Matt. 1:1;
Matt. 2:2; Rev.
2:28
22:17
Rev. 2:7; 14:13;
Rev. 21:2,9;
Is. 55:1; Rev.
21:6;
Rev. 7:17; 22:1
22:18
Rev. 22:7;
Deut. 4:2; 12:32;
Prov. 30:6;
Rev. 15:6-16:21
22:19
Deut. 4:2; 12:32;
Prov. 30:6;
Rev. 22:7;
Rev. 22:2;
Rev. 21:10-22:5
22:20
Rev. 1:2;
Rev. 22:7;
1 Cor. 16:22
22:21
Rom. 16:20

EXPLANATION OF THE SUPERIOR
NUMBERS

The meaning of the superior numbers 1, 2, 3, and 4

The superior numbers 1 (intensive compounds), 2 (intensive particles), 3 (elatives), or 4 (emphatic repetitions) basically mean "for further study." The interested reader who enjoys consulting extra study tools such as Greek grammars, lexicons, and so forth, will find in these exceptional occurrences an added, rewarding dimension of understanding.

The meaning of the superior number 1—intensive compounds

One of the fascinating features of the Greek New Testament is its ability to charge a word with a stronger or intensified meaning by assigning to it a particular prefix (namely the Greek prepositions *apo, dia, ek, epi, kata, para, huper,* and *sun*). Certain of these prefixed words function as *intensive compounds.*[1] Noticing these intensive compounds and their charged meaning will often bring to the reader a new dimension of understanding and appreciation of a given verse in Scripture. Indeed, such compounds are often more intensive than an English translation can convey (cf. 2 Timothy 3:7, where the meaning of "adequate" or "full" knowledge from *epignōsis* is not conveyed in most modern translations). Referring to the standard commentaries concerning these words we find that more often than not the prefix adds the thought "thoroughly," "completely," "fully," "utterly," or "adequately" (each intensive compound must be studied individually to avoid simplistic generalities).[2]

When an intensive compound is translated by the *New American Standard Bible* (NASB) as a simplex (i.e., without an auxiliary word) the superior number 1 appears at the upper right corner of that word; when the NASB supplies an auxiliary or help word such as "completely" or "fully" the superior

---

1. For a full discussion of these see Moulton, *Grammar of New Testament Greek,* 2:294–328; A. T. Robertson, pp. 571–634; Moule, pp. 87–92.
2. Below is the list of New Testament compounds regarded as having intensive or perfective force and marked with a superior number 1 in *The Discovery Bible.* For the convenience of the English reader, they are identified by their corresponding numbers as found in the *New American Standard Exhaustive Concordance,* Holman Bible Publishers, Nashville, 1981 (NASEC). The NASEC numbers also correspond to *Strong's Exhaustive Concordance* numbering system with corrections: 604, 1226, 1227, 1231, 1245b, 1246, 1254, 1259, 1263, 1264, 1278, 1280, 1286, 1298, 1301, 1326, 1331, 1552, 1555, 1559, 1567a, 1568, 1569a, 1571, 1592, 1598, 1603, 1605, 1611, 1613, 1615, 1629, 1630, 1815, 1818, 1820, 1822, 1827, 1830, 1840, 1864, 1872, 1878, 1901, 1902, 1921, 1922, 1934, 2005, 2606, 2612, 2614, 2615, 2650, 2660, 2661, 2666, 2669, 2684, 2705, 2710, 2712, 2714, 2716, 2719, 2728, 3859, 3877, 3897, 3898, 3906, 3907, 4917, 4919, 4930, 4932, 4933, 5229, 5232, 5239b, 5240, 5245, 5248, 5250, 5251.

number 1 appears at the upper right corner of that auxiliary word (see Acts 3:23, "utterly[1] destroyed" translating *exolethreuthesetai).*

In the New Testament, a word compounded with a preposition can have several different kinds of resultant meanings. In general, compounds having a local or directive sense have not been identified; rather, only those whose prefix gives an intensification in meaning were marked.

The meaning of the superior number 2—intensive particles

The superior number 2 signals the reader that a particular conclusion or condition is being introduced in a special way. Another feature of the Greek New Testament is its ability to give *extra force* and *clarity* to a verse or paragraph in Scripture through the use of intensive particles. Intensive particles are primarily those conjunctions that bring a stronger meaning to a condition or conclusion. The delicate touch that these particles lend is often untranslatable. As F. W. Farrar states regarding these emphatic particles in Homer, "They sustain and articulate the pulses of emotion. By them alone we can perceive that Greek was the language of a witty . . . and passionate people."[3] For example, the first word in Hebrews 12:1, "Therefore[2]" (translating the intensive Greek particle *toigaroun)* implies "consequently, therefore." The importance of the use of this intensive particle is that it shows that the conclusion about to be drawn has been firmly grounded in the preceding verses.

The meaning of the superior number 3—elatives

Elatives are those special word forms in the Greek language that are used to express a *very high degree of quality or intensity.* They are usually translated with the accompanying word "very." An example of this occurs in Mark 4:1 (note the elative form for "great"), "And such a very[3] great multitude gathered. . . ." The reader then is to take special notice of any words marked by a superior 3 and not to merely regard the exceptional degree of quality or intensity as a loose or exaggerated translation. Observe for example how important the elative form for "little" is in Luke 16:10, "He who is faithful in a very[3] little thing is faithful also in much; and he who is unrighteous in a very[3] little thing is unrighteous also in much."

The meaning of the superior number 4—emphatic repetitions

Special stress and emphasis is sometimes brought to a word or idea in the Greek New Testament by deliberately repeating a word where a single mention is all that is needed or expected. This is usually done through the use of cognates (words derived from the same root).[4] For example, the words of

3. A. T. Robertson, *A Grammar of the Greek New Testament in the Light of Historical Research* (Nashville: Broadman, 1934), p. 1145.
4. This kind of emphasis in the New Testament is at times probably a conscious imitation of the Hebrew infinitive absolute construction. For more details see Gesenius-Kautzsch, K., *Gesenius' Hebrew Grammar* (Oxford: Clarendon), pp. 339–47.

Luke 2:9, "they were *terribly*⁴ frightened" (describing the shepherds when an an angel of the Lord appeared to them) are really a translation of the emphatic, literal Greek text, "they feared a great fear." The device of repeating cognate words for the sake of emphasis occurs numerous times throughout the Greek New Testament. Because these occurrences are often not apparent in translation, the superior has been supplied to signal the reader so that special notice may be taken. The following verses illustrate this important device for achieving emphasis:

• Luke 22:15, "I have *earnestly*⁴ desired to eat *this Passover* with you" (literal Greek text, "With a desire I desired to").

• Acts 23:14, "We have bound ourselves under *solemn*⁴ oath to taste nothing until" (literal Greek text, "With a curse we cursed ourselves to taste nothing").

SELECTIVE GLOSSARY OF THE SYNONYMS OF THE GREEK NEW TESTAMENT

New Testament synonyms relate to Greek words closely associated in meaning but often not distinguished in translation. That is, two different Greek words may be translated by the same English word, even though they each have their own distinctive color and shade of meaning. Words in English, for example, such as slender and skinny or statesman and politician are related in meaning, but each word leaves a distinctly different impression. Regarding such words as merely interchangeable can often mean missing the point and the fuller meaning of what the Scripture writer is really saying. These distinctions, often "hidden" or blurred to the English reader, can easily be uncovered by simply comparing the superior number in *The Discovery Bible* text with its corresponding number in this glossary. For example, if you are reading in John 15 and wish to discover the distinction between the English term *word* in verses 3 and 7, you would simply refer to the glossary under number 43 (43a—*logos;* 43b—*rhēma*).

A grasp and appreciation of such delicate turns and variations in thought will often significantly "open up" understanding of a passage with fresh insight and meaning. When a particular synonym occurs more than once in the same verse or passage, usually only its first occurrence is marked by a superior number. The reader can assume that the subsequent occurrences are translating the same Greek word unless a change of number appears on that word (e.g., "holy" in 1 Pet. 1:15 and 1:16). Richard Trench aptly described the Greek language when he wrote that it was a "language spoken by a people who saw distinctions where others saw none; who divided out to different words what others were content to huddle confusedly under a common term; who were singularly alive to its value, diligently cultivating the art of synonymous distinction."[1] William Barclay (p. 17) adds, "Greek is one of the richest of all languages and it has an unrivalled power to express shades of meaning. It therefore often happens that Greek has a whole series of words to express different shades of meaning in one conception, while English has only one."

This glossary does not attempt to be a comprehensive lexicon or to show the full range of a word's meaning in its classical or New Testament usage. Rather, the following comments and summaries show the distinction that may at times exist between the synonyms (contiguous relations) involved

1. Richard Trench, *Synonyms of the New Testament* (Grand Rapids: Eerdmans, 1953), p. 3 of preface.

521

and thus shed light on those references marked in *The Discovery Bible* with a superior number.

Because the glossary words overlap in meaning to some extent, an effort was made to mark only those occurrences that contextually indicated the described distinctive shade or nuance of meaning. Several works (listed below) have been quoted freely in the preparation of this glossary. To avoid misunderstanding that may result from oversimplification, the following list of works is recommended to the reader for further study.

Arndt, William F., and Gingrich, F. Wilbur. *A Greek-English Lexicon of the New Testament* (Chicago: University of Chicago, 1957).

Barclay, William. *New Testament Words* (Philadelphia: Westminster, 1974).

Berry, George Ricker. *Dictionary of New Testament Greek Synonyms* (Grand Rapids: Zondervan, 1979).

Brown, Colin, ed. *The New International Dictionary of New Testament Theology* (DNTT). 3 vols. (Grand Rapids: Zondervan, 1967).

Cremer, Heinrich. *Biblico-Theological Lexicon of New Testament Greek* (Edinburgh: T. & T. Clark, 1880).

Green, S. G. *Handbook to the Grammar of the Greek New Testament* (London: Religious Tract Society, 1907).

Kittel, Gerhard, and Friedrich, Gerhard. *Theological Dictionary of the New Testament* (TDNT). 9 vols. (Grand Rapids: Eerdmans, 1964).

New American Standard Exhaustive Concordance (NASEC). (Nashville: Holman Bible Publishers, 1981).

Silva, Moses. *Biblical Words and Their Meanings* (Grand Rapids: Zondervan, 1983).

Thayer, Joseph Henry. *Thayer's Greek-English Lexicon of the New Testament* (New York: American Book Co., 1889).

Trench, Robert. *Synonyms of the New Testament* (Grand Rapids: Eerdmans, 1953).

Unger, Merril F. *Beyond the Crystal Ball* (Chicago: Moody, 1973).

Vine, W. E. *An Expository Dictionary of New Testament Words* (Chicago: Moody, 1985).

Walvoord, John F. *The Revelation of Jesus Christ* (Chicago: Moody, 1966).

Note: The synonyms begin with the number 5 because the numbers 1, 2, 3, and 4 appear in *The Discovery Bible* text at those occurrences where the reader who enjoys using additional study tools will find points of exegetical interest.

English Word	Greek Word	NASEC or Strong's Number	Comments and Summaries
5. **Accept**	5a *dechomai* (δέχομαι)	1209	passively accept; *receiving* something because it is offered
	5b *lambanō* (λαμβάνω)	2983	actively accept; *taking* something that is available

English Word	Greek Word	NASEC or Strong's Number	Comments and Summaries

Summary: 5b can often be a "self-prompted *taking*" (Thayer), involving more initiative or aggressiveness than 5a; 5a can highlight the initiative of the *giver*, 5b the initiative of the *receiver*.

6. Allow

	6a *aphiēmi* (ἀφίημι)	863	to let something go loose; release; remit
	6b *eaō* (ἐάω)	1439	to permit without attempting to hinder or restrain (often reluctantly)
	6c *epitrepō* (ἐπιτρέπω)	2010	to turn over to someone the authority to act

Summary: 6c requires a transfer of authority and a more formal consent than 6a or 6b; 6b is often done with a reluctance or unwillingness, whereas 6a is done voluntarily and without "red tape."

7. Anger

	7a *thumos* (θυμός)	2372	the anger of "impulse and passion" (Green); a "boiling agitation of the feelings" (Trench)
	7b *orgē* (ὀργή)	3709	the anger usually of a settled attitude of disapproval

Summary: 7a is an anger of passion when someone "sees red" as contrasted to 7b, the anger that stems from a settled, righteous indignation. The anger of 7b often "arises gradually" (Thayer) and is "guided by reason" (Trench); it can be a very valuable quality in a believer's life. Such righteous indignation is used of God, "who would not love good unless He hated evil" (Trench) and is encouraged for believers by Scripture itself (Eph. 4:26). There can be "no surer and sadder token of an utterly prostrate moral condition than not being able to be angry with sin!" (Trench).

English Word	Greek Word	NASEC or Strong's Number	Comments and Summaries
8. **Another**	8a *allos* (ἄλλος)	243	another of the same kind
	8b *heteros* (ἕτερος)	2087	another of a different kind

Summary: 8a is "one more" of a *similar* kind; 8b is "another" that is "qualitatively different" (Cremer) in nature or quality.

9. **Ask**	9a *aiteō* (αἰτέω)	154	usually to ask for something "to be *given*, rather than done" (Thayer); interestingly enough, 9a is never used of Jesus' own requests or prayers, but rather always 9b or 9c.
	9b *deomai* (δέομαι)	1189a	the "request of need" (Cremer); to ask for someone's *help*, often arising from some distress or pressing need; to beseech or ask for a favor
	9c *erōtaō* (ἐρωτάω)	2065	to ask for information; to ask or question someone on a more intimate basis than 9a (DNTT, TDNT)
	9d *eperōtaō* (ἐπερωτάω)	1905	to question or interrogate; usually a more in-depth probing in order to "get under the surface"; an intensified form of 9c

Summary: 9a gives "prominence to the thing asked for" (Thayer); 9b is often more pressing, specific, and problem centered; 9c is an asking that occurs on a more intimate level and a more equal footing than 9a; 9d is an intensive questioning or probing.

10. **Bad**	10a *kakos* (κακός)	2556	"evil in nature and purpose" (Cremer, p. 326); that which is inherently evil but not always

English Word	Greek Word	NASEC or Strong's Number	Comments and Summaries
			outwardly expressed; the "antithesis to [25a] (*agathos*) in the Septuagint" (Trench)
10b *ponēros* (πονηρός)		4190	the deliberate defiance of the moral law for personal gain, without regard to the pain or suffering brought to others by it; selfish greed often with malevolent and criminal intentions; the active outworking of 10a; "[10a] is content to perish in its own corruption, but [10b] is not content unless he is corrupting others as well" (Trench); used of Satan (cf. Eph. 6:16)
10c *sapros* (σαπρός)		4550	rotten; corrupt; of poor quality; used of over-ripe fruit that is useless and to be discarded; "no longer fit for use" (Thayer)
10d *phaulos* (φαῦλος)		5337	a very strong word meaning "rotten to the very core"; internally corrupt; "good for nothing" (Trench); that which is impossible for "any true gain" to come from it (Trench)
10e *kakia* (κακία)		2549	the stooping to unscrupulous means to malign or injure someone; the "evil habit of the mind" (Trench); that which takes pleasure in the misery or pain of another person, or in general an attitude of ill will

Summary: "[10a] describes the quality (of evil) according to its *nature*, [10b] according to its *effects*" (Cremer); "[10e] denotes the vicious disposition, [10b] the active exercise of the same" (Thayer); 10c is what is useless because it is rotten; 10d is internally corrupt and rotten through and through.

English Word	Greek Word	NASEC or Strong's Number	Comments and Summaries
11. **Blameless**	11a amemptos (ἄμεμπτος)	273	having a character deserving no censure or accusation; literally, without stain
	11b amōmos (ἄμωμος)	299b	being without defect or blemish; able to meet the requirements and prerequisites for sacred service to God; acceptable and without fault in the inner man as well as the outward man
	11c anegklētos (ἀνέγκλητος)	410	having a character able to stand under attack or formal censure
	11d anepilēmptos (ἀνεπίλημπτος)	423	used of a proved character of such good reputation as to be considered undeserving of unwarranted suspicion or unfounded criticism; not reprehensible

Summary: "[11a] is strictly unblamed . . . particularly in the verdict of others; [11b] is without blemish . . . free from imperfections; [11c] designates one against whom there is no (justified) accusation; [11d] designates one who affords nothing upon which an adversary might seize" (Berry).

English Word	Greek Word	NASEC or Strong's Number	Comments and Summaries
12. **Burden**	12a baros (βάρος)	922	a burden or weight that is transferrable and thus can be shared by someone else
	12b phortion (φορτίον)	5413	a burden that may be non-transferrable and is the personal responsibility of the particular person to whom it is assigned

Summary: 12a "points to the load of which a man may fairly rid himself when occasion serves"; 12b is "a load which he

English Word	Greek Word	NASEC or Strong's Number	Comments and Summaries

is expected to bear" (J. B. Lightfoot); 12a is "the pressure of a weight, which may be relieved or transferred"; 12b is "the load which each man must bear for himself" (Green).

13. **Clean**

	13a *hagnos* (ἀγνός)	53	free from moral or spiritual defilement; thoroughly pure from contamination; unadulterated; pure internally as well as externally
	13b *athōos* (ἀθῶος)	121	free from guilt; innocent
	13c *katharos* (καθαρός)	2513	free from impurities and undesirable elements; purged; clean; unmixed (Barclay); free from admixture

Summary: "Wine mixed with water may be [13a], not being contaminated; it is not [13c] however when there is the admixture of any element" (Vine); 13b means clean from guilt.

14. **Condemn**

	14a *kataginōskō* (καταγινώσκω)	2607	to find someone at fault or blameworthy on the basis of personal acquaintance or observation; to decide in someone's disfavor
	14b *katadikazō* (καταδικάζω)	2613a	to pass sentence upon someone for the purpose of appropriate punishment being meted out to him
	14c *katakrinō* (κατακρίνω)	2632	to find in the wrong or at fault and therefore worthy of punishment or rejection

Summary: 14a lays a certain stress on the personal involvement of the critic himself, which led to his unfavorable verdict; 14b on the desire to see the penalty carried out; 14c on

English Word	Greek Word	NASEC or Strong's Number	Comments and Summaries
			the final status of guilty and fully deserving its consequences.
15. **Cure**	15a *therapeuō* (θεραπεύω)	2323	the actual reversing of a condition of illness itself; healing possibly with the employment of medical treatment
	15b *iaomai* (ἰάομαι)	2390	cure, healing that not only reverses the condition but also draws attention to the divine power that performed it (Luke 5:17; 6:19; 8:46–47; Acts 9:34), so as to prompt those who witness it to glorify God (Luke 9:42–43; Acts 28:8–9)

Summary: The result of 15a is the healing itself; whereas 15b in the New Testament also draws attention to the display and exercise of divine power.

English Word	Greek Word	NASEC or Strong's Number	Comments and Summaries
16. **Deceive**	16a *apataō* (ἀπατάω)	538	to deceive by giving a distorted impression or false sense of reality; to trick; to cheat; to beguile
	exapataō (ἐξαπατάω)	1818	Note: an intensified form of 16a found in Rom. 7:11; 16:18; 1 Cor. 3:18; 2 Cor. 11:3; 2 Thess. 2:3; 1 Tim. 2:14; it means "to beguile *thoroughly*; to deceive *wholly*" (Vine); to deceive *completely*
	16b *planaō* (πλανάω)	4105	to lead astray; passive; wander from the truth into error, falsity, and delusion

Summary: 16a vividly brings out the *means* by which deception often occurs; 16b the inevitable pain and confusion that always *results* from trusting false promises or believing a lie.

English Word	Greek Word	NASEC or Strong's Number	Comments and Summaries
17. **Defile**	17a koinoō (κοινόω)	2840	literally, "make common"; to strip something of its special or sacred status by treating it as common or ordinary
	17b miainō (μιαίνω)	3392	to "pollute," contaminate, soil, "defile" (Vine); usually an infecting influence; not so much the effect of wickedness upon the evil-doer as on others around him (Cremer)
	17c molunō (μολύνω)	3435	to "stain, soil" (Arndt/Gingrich); to become mucky, dirty, filthy

Summary: 17a is to profane by not giving something its proper respect and place; 17b particularly brings out the contaminating effect of that which is defiled *upon others;* 17c is the actual filth or soiling result itself.

18. **Deliver**	18a exaireō (ἐξαιρέω)	1807	to remove or separate from danger and bring into safety
	18b rhuomai (ῥύομαι)	4506	to rescue or deliver from a hostile power that seeks to enslave

Summary: 18a lays stress on the power to *bring out of* and hence also bring to a place of safety; 18b lays stress on the superior exertion and demonstration of power that brings the rescue.

19. **Do**	19a poieō (ποιέω)	4160	to make, produce, or accomplish; to perform or carry out an act for a definite result
	19b prassō (πράσσω)	4238	"to practice" (Trench); "to do continually or repeatedly" (Berry); "habitual performance" (Thayer); a process

English Word	Greek Word	NASEC or Strong's Number	Comments and Summaries

Summary: 19a brings out more "the *end* of an act," whereas 19b is the continual practice or *"means* by which the object is attained" (Trench).

20. **Foolish**	20a *anoētos* (ἀνόητος)	453	lacking normal intelligence; mindless; dense; exhibiting a "lack of brains"
	20b *aphrōn* (ἄφρων)	878	showing poor judgment; irresponsibly stupid; failing to use one's thinking abilities
	20c *mōros* (μωρός)	3474	lacking the maturity to be discriminating; infantile; mentally or psychologically immature; easily deceived

Summary: 20a reveals a lack of reasoning abilities; 20b a poor use of reasoning abilities; 20c a low development or deficient use of reasoning abilities.

21. **Forgive**	21a *aphiēmi* (ἀφίημι)	863	the "undeserved releasing of the man from something that might justly have been inflicted upon him or exacted from him" (Barclay); to let go or send away; to remit (a sin or debt)
	21b *charizomai* (χαρίζομαι)	5483	an act of grace that willingly pardons without any requirement of merit or recompense

Summary: 21a centers on the act of unmerited favor or pardon from a debt, and so forth, whereas 21b centers on the attitude of kindness that prompts free and voluntary pardon.

22. **Form**	22a *eidos* (εἶδος)	1491b	the "outward appearance" of something (Arndt/Gingrich); literally "that which is seen" (Vine); "that which is exposed to view" (Thayer); a species or type

English Word	Greek Word	NASEC or Strong's Number	Comments and Summaries
	22b eikōn (εἰκών)	1504	an exact replica, representation, or "picture" of an original; 22b "always assumes a prototype, that which it not merely resembles, but from which it is drawn" (Trench)
	22c morphē (μορφή)	3444	the outward expression of the inward characteristics and essential nature of an original; that which reflects the true, inner identity of an original
	22d homoiōma (ὁμοίωμα)	3667	a likeness, similarity, or basic resemblance of an original
	22e schēma (σχῆμα)	4976	that which has the same shape, manner, or appearance as the original

Summary: 22a is "appearance, that may or may not have a basis in (physical) reality; [22b] denotes the exact representation, 'image'; [22c], the form as indicative of the interior nature; [22e], the form, *externally* regarded" (Green); with 22c, the "outward form expresses the inner essence, an idea which is absent from [22e]" (Berry); 22d is basic analogy or *resemblance*, not an exact copy.

English Word	Greek Word	NASEC or Strong's Number	Comments and Summaries
23. **Gentleness**	23a epieikeia (ἐπιείκεια)	1932	"The Greeks themselves explained this word as 'Justice and something better than justice.' They said that [23a] ought to come in when strict justice became unjust because of its generality. . . . A man has the quality of [23a] if he knows when *not* to apply the strict letter of the law, and when to relax justice and introduce mercy" (Barclay)
	23b prautēs (πραΰτης)	4240	the meekness which is "strength under control" (Barclay); a fruit of the Holy Spirit

English Word	Greek Word	NASEC or Strong's Number	Comments and Summaries
			(Gal. 5:23) that enables the believer to place the will of God before personal rights; the opposite of a "clutching" or "grabbing" spirit; 23b insists only on what is necessary; enables a person to be "always angry at the right time, and never angry at the wrong time" (Barclay)
	23c *tapeinophrosunē* (ταπεινοφροσύνη)	5012a	the humble recognition of personal unworthiness before God (or even before man); not a false modesty but rather an accurate self-perception; the opposite of inner spiritual pride, arrogance, or inflated ego, yet does not involve self-rejection or a poor self-image as such

Summary: 23a is the "relaxing of strict legal requirements concerning others . . . to carry out the real spirit of the law" (Berry); 23b is an "inwrought grace of the soul" (Trench) and the laying aside of personal rights to achieve the will of God; 23c is to "behave in an unassuming manner devoid of all haughtiness" (Thayer) or self-conceit.

English Word	Greek Word	NASEC or Strong's Number	Comments and Summaries
24. **Gift**	24a *dōrea* (δωρεά)	1431	always a gift freely given by God, to bring to the believer "bounty, honor, or privilege" (Westcott)
	24b *dōron* (δῶρον)	1435	often a sacrificial gift given to God by the believer; gift in general
	24c *charisma* (χάρισμα)	5486	(literally, "grace-gift") a gift that "comes from God and which could never have been achieved or attained or pos-

English Word	Greek Word	NASEC or Strong's Number	Comments and Summaries

sessed by a man's own effort" (Barclay); often the divine impartation of a particular grace to perform a Spirit-empowered service for the church

Summary: 24a gives prominence to God's beneficent act of giving; 24b to the gift itself, and 24c to divinely imparted grace that enables believers for service.

25. Good

25a
agathos
(ἀγαθός)

18

inwardly good; "of a good constitution or nature" (Thayer); hence, that which produces benefit and genuinely good effects and results; (25a has its focus on the inward character and thus carries the idea of "morally" or "inherently" virtuous or brave; *worthy* of admiration and respect.)

25b
kalos
(καλός)

2570

good in appearance; beautiful; aesthetically satisfying and pleasing; that which evokes admiration and a sense of the lovely and beautiful; praiseworthy; "good" as having the *perceived* value and outward impression of charm and attractiveness; useful ("The basic idea of [25b] is the idea of *winsome* beauty" [Barclay]; "excellent in its characteristics . . . therefore well adapted to its ends" [Thayer])

Summary: 25a is that which is *practically* and *morally* good; "[25b] is that which is . . . also aesthetically good . . . lovely and pleasing to the eye. . . . [25a] appeals to the moral sense, but [25b] appeals also to the eye" (Barclay); "[25b] is what is good as seen, as making a direct impression on those who come in contact with it—not only *good in result,* which would be 25a" (Hort); 25a

English Word	Greek Word	NASEC or Strong's Number	Comments and Summaries
			stresses the essence or reality of something; 26a its appearance and recognition
26. **Great**	26a *megas* (μέγας)	3173	great in rank, stature, level, or order
	26b *polus* (πολύς)	4183	great in amount, extent, number, or quantity

Summary: 26a stresses greatness in *comparison* to other things; 26b stresses greatness in terms of number and "muchness."

English Word	Greek Word	NASEC or Strong's Number	Comments and Summaries
27. **Hades**	27a *hadēs* (ᾅδης)	86	the present dwelling place for all the *un*believing dead; formerly the abode of all the deceased prior to Christ's resurrection; those unsaved who are in this "intermediate hell" are presently in a "discarnate state (soul and spirit separated from the body) but in conscious torment" (Unger, p. 156–57); 27a never refers to the eternal state of punishment where the wicked dead are given resurrection bodies suited for eternal punishment (Walvoord, pp. 307–8)
	27b *geenna* (γέεννα)	1067	the place of future punishment after the last judgment ... both body and soul are tormented in it (Mark 9:43, 45, 47); to be distinguished from 27a, which houses only the souls of the dead *before* the last judgment (DNTT); is not simply the state of the lost after death, but their post-resurrection condition, where both soul and body suffer destruction [Matt. 10:28]; the grim re-

English Word	Greek Word	NASEC or Strong's Number	Comments and Summaries
			ality for the unbelieving dead in 27b is summed up· in the words of C. H. Spurgeon, "Thy body will join thy soul, and then thou wilt have twin hells . . . thy body will lie, asbestos like, forever unconsumed, all thy veins roads for the feet of pain to travel on, every nerve—the string, on which the devil shall forever play his diabolical tune in Hell's unutterable lament")

Summary: 27b unlike 27a, includes the everlasting punishment of both soul *and* resurrection body.

English Word	Greek Word	NASEC or Strong's Number	Comments and Summaries
28. **Holy**	28a hagios (ἅγιος)	40	"the basic meaning of [28a] is *different* or *separate*. A thing that is [28a] is *different* from other things. A person who is [28a] is *separate* from other people. So a temple is [28a] because it is *different* from other buildings." (Note: "saint" is the same Greek word as 28a and "holiness" [*hagiosmos*] is from 28a and carries the same essential meaning.)
	28b hosios (ὅσιος)	3741	that which is committed to God; "religiously observing every moral obligation, pure, holy, pious" (Thayer)

Summary: 28a describes people or things that are *set apart* for God's purpose and will; 28b usually describes the *character* of the people who have thoroughly committed themselves to being 28a.

English Word	Greek Word	NASEC or Strong's Number	Comments and Summaries
29. **Know**	29a ginōskō (γινώσκω)	1097	to know through experience; to perceive through the senses; "subjective knowl-

English Word	Greek Word	NASEC or Strong's Number	Comments and Summaries
			edge" (Green); the knowing comes from "an active *relation* between the one who knows and the person or thing known" (Vine); effectively *coming to* know, or the *entering into* knowing through first-hand or personal interaction; knowledge usually gained through personal acquaintance or some relationship of intimacy or connection
	29b *epiginōskō* (ἐπιγινώσκω)	1921	to know (or its noun form *epignōsis*, no. 1922, "true knowledge") *adequately;* to come to a "fuller, clearer, and more thorough knowledge" (Berry); an adequate or valid knowledge; an intensified form of 29a
	29c *epistamai* (ἐπίσταμαι)	1987	to understand or know in a particularly informed or accurate way; to know the inner reality of something with intuitional depth, often due to extensive or prolonged acquaintance
	29d *noeō* (νοέω)	3539	to have a mental grasp of something by weighing and reasoning the matter in an appropriate manner; often relates to a knowledge that is inductive and logical; "to perceive with the mind" (Thayer)
	29e *oida* (οἶδα)	3609a	to know intellectually; to gain knowledge by observation (versus by experience or through the senses); to know something on the basis of an

English Word	Greek Word	NASEC or Strong's Number	Comments and Summaries
			absolute or achieved knowledge; to know *about* something without necessarily standing in any personal relation or connection with it
	29f *suniēmi* (συνίημι)	4920	to wisely discriminate and evaluate (Barclay); to comprehend; to gain an insight as a result of putting various facts together

Summary: 29a carries the idea of knowing on the basis of some sort of intimate or personal relation, unlike 29e, which requires no such connection; 29d differs from 29f in that it involves a greater degree of mental activity or reasoning; 29b suggests a knowledge that is particularly full and thorough yet not necessarily the result of the specialized or extended acquaintance inherent in 29c.

English Word	Greek Word	NASEC or Strong's Number	Comments and Summaries
30. **Life**	30a *bios* (βίος)	979	"the period or duration of earthly life . . . in a secondary sense, the *means* by which life is sustained; and thirdly, the *manner* in which that life is spent" (Trench)
	30b *zōē* (ζωή)	2222	that inextinguishable and indestructible quality that is self-existent in God and shared with animate creation; God's gift to man animating him both physically and spiritually and making him an eternal being; "the absolute fullness of life . . . which belongs to God" (Thayer)
	30c *psuchē* (ψυχή)	5590	(from which our English word *psychology* is derived); "the point of contact between man's bodily and spiritual na-

English Word	Greek Word	NASEC or Strong's Number	Comments and Summaries
			ture" (Green); "the inner life of man, equivalent to the ego, person, or personality" (DNTT); man's individual distinctiveness and identity before God

Summary: "[30a] is life in its earthly *manifestations,* life extrinsic; [30b] is life in its *principle,* life intrinsic" (Green); "[30c] is the seat of the feelings, desires, affections, aversions" (Thayer).

English Word	Greek Word	NASEC or Strong's Number	Comments and Summaries
31. **Love**	31a agapaō (ἀγαπάω)	25	(noun, *agapē*) In biblical and ecclesiastical usage *agapaō* and its associated noun, *agapē,* refer to an unselfish, outgoing affection or tenderness for another without necessarily expecting anything in return. It seeks a person's *highest good* on the basis of a decision of *will* and an inclination of heart. This verb "to love" rarely occurs in secular Greek in the B.C. period, although the Greek Old Testament uses it often for the Hebrew *'aheb,* which in some other contexts is translated *phileō,* number 31b.
	31b phileō (φιλέω)	5368	This verb connotes an inclination of mind or emotion that arouses favorable interest or approval. It often involves a shared interest or commitment to a common cause or to cherished ideals; in general it connotes the idea of *friendship* and cordially *liking* a person because of his congeniality or

English Word	Greek Word	NASEC or Strong's Number	Comments and Summaries
			desirable characteristics; unlike 31a, 31b can be alienated by an unworthy or ungrateful response. In some passages there appears to be a degree of overlap, as for example in John 21:15–17, where there is an interplay between the two verbs—possibly because the two different Greek terms bring out different connotations of the one and same Hebrew/Aramaic verb, reḥam, which was probably used in their actual conversation. But it is clear that Jesus was leading Peter from a human level to a higher divine level of loving commitment as a shepherd of Christ's sheep.

Summary: 31a denotes a *self-giving* personal commitment irrespective of grateful response; 31b denotes a loving *friendship* based on common interests, often accompanied by warm feelings and affection; "[31b] denotes the love of natural inclination, affection—love, so to say, originally spontaneous, involuntary; [31a], on the other hand, love as a direction of the will" (Cremer).

English Word	Greek Word	NASEC or Strong's Number	Comments and Summaries
32. **Might**	32a dunamis (δύναμις)	1411	inherent *ability*; "inherent capacity of someone or something to carry something out" (DNTT); power by virtue of one's own ability and resources (Vine)
	32b exousia (ἐξουσία)	1849	delegated power (Thayer); *authority*; "power to act . . . by virtue of the position he holds" (DNTT); "the right to act or use power" (Vine)

English Word	Greek Word	NASEC or Strong's Number	Comments and Summaries
	32c ischus (ἰσχύς)	2479	"inherent *strength*" (Lange); strength as an endowment (Green); strength that is resident in a person
	32d kratos (κράτος)	2904	*manifested* power (Thayer); dodominion; might; power that is exercised or applied, and hence that which prevails; mastery; force

Summary: 32a is *ability* resulting from inherent power; 32b is *authority* resulting from delegated power; 32c relates to inherent strength; 32d relates to "strength as *exerted*" (Green).

33. **Mind**	33a dianoia (διάνοια)	1271	That part of the intellect capable of abstract reasoning and moral reflection; that "faculty of the mind which understands, feels, and desires" (Thayer)
	33b nous (νοῦς)	3563	"the highest knowing power in man ... the organ by which divine things are comprehended and known" (Trench); "the seat of reflective consciousness" (Vine); the power of philosophical reasoning and logic; that exercise of the mind that considers and makes moral judgments
	33c phronēma (φρόνημα)	5427	the actual output of the mind as it achieves mental focus and attention; the focal point of one's moral preference and world view; the reflection of one's priorities, convictions, and beliefs; "what one has in his mind" (Thayer)

Summary: 33a denotes the activity of moral reasoning, reflection,

English Word	Greek Word	NASEC or Strong's Number	Comments and Summaries

and musing; whereas 33b is the actual faculty that makes 33a possible; 33c on the other hand reflects the settled or resultant views of 33a.

34. New	34a kainos (καινός)	2537	new in quality; new and different; 34a usually involves bringing in a superior innovation or advance and corresponds to 8b *(heteros)*, another of a different kind
	34b neos (νέος)	3501b	new in time; recent; young; unlike 34a, 34b may have exactly the same ingredients as that which it replaces; corresponds to 8a *(allos)*, "another of the same kind"

Summary: "[34a] is new in reference to *quality*; [34b] is new in reference to *time*, having recently come into existence" (Green).

35. Prudent	35a sophos (σοφός)	4680	manifesting a theoretical wisdom dealing essentially with a man's mind and thought (Barclay)
	35b phronimos (φρόνιμος)	5429	characterized by a practical wisdom that sees what must be done and what must not be done in any given situation; "quick and correct perceptions, hence 'discreet,' 'circumspect'" (Thayer); descriptive of one who is in practical touch with life and reality (Barclay)

Summary: 35a deals more in the theoretical and abstract, whereas 35b has more to do with the practical and concrete situations of life.

English Word	Greek Word	NASEC or Strong's Number	Comments and Summaries
36. **Redeem**	36a *exagorazō* (ἐξαγοράζω)	1805	to buy up or to purchase, "especially of purchasing a slave with a view to his freedom" (Vine)
	36b *lutroō* (λυτρόω)	3084	(akin to *lutron*, "a ransom") "to bring forward a ransom"; "to release on receipt of ransom" (Vine); "to get something back into the possession of its rightful owner, rescuing something from the power and possession of an alien possessor" (Barclay)

Summary: "[36a] does not signify the actual redemption, but the *price paid* with a view to it; [36b] signifies the *actual deliverance*, the setting at liberty" (Vine).

English Word	Greek Word	NASEC or Strong's Number	Comments and Summaries
37. **Repay**	37a *antapodidōmi* (ἀνταποδίδωμι)	467	"to give back as an equivalent; to requite, recompense (a complete return)" (Vine)
	37b *apotinō* (ἀποτίνω)	661	to repay by way of a fine or punishment (Vine); in suffering the just consequence of a wrong committed

Summary: The repayment of 37a differs from 37b in that 37b includes the added idea of a fine or punishment (Vine).

English Word	Greek Word	NASEC or Strong's Number	Comments and Summaries
38. **Serve**	38a *diakoneō* (διακονέω)	1247	to wait on others and care for their needs; to place the needs and comfort of someone else above our own in active work and service
	38b *douleuō* (δουλεύω)	1398	to completely and absolutely assign all personal rights over to the authority and will of another person; to be in a "permanent relation of servitude to another, his (the slave's)

English Word	Greek Word	NASEC or Strong's Number	Comments and Summaries
			will altogether swallowed up in the will of another" (Trench); the permanent surrender of personal rights in an attitude of total submission
	38c *latreuō* (λατρεύω)	3000	to serve; often in the capacity of officiating as priest or public official; used also as the sacred service and priestly ministering performed by believers through their heartfelt worship and prayer to God
	38d *leitourgeō* (λειτουργέω)	3008	literally, the service performed by priests and Levites in the Temple (Arndt/Gingrich); figuratively, of the priestly service offered by each believer whose life becomes a living sacrifice to God

Summary: In 38b the relation of dependence upon a master and state of servitude is the main thought, whereas in 38a the main reference is to the service or advantage rendered to another (Cremer); 38a represents the servant in his activity for the work, not in his relation to his master as in 38b (Thayer); 38c and 38d relate to the sacred ministering and priestly service that every believer can offer to God through prayer and personal adoration.

English Word	Greek Word	NASEC or Strong's Number	Comments and Summaries
39. **Shame**	39a *aischunē* (αἰσχύνη)	152	the feeling of *disgrace*, which results from doing an unworthy thing (Berry), or receiving rejection or contempt from others
	39b *entrepō* (ἐντρέπω)	1788	"The *wholesome shame* which leads a man to consideration of his condition if it is unworthy, and to a change of conduct for the better" (Berry)

English Word	Greek Word	NASEC or Strong's Number	Comments and Summaries
	39c kataischunō (καταισχύνω)	2617b	the feeling of inflicting disgrace with the added idea of *disappointment* or *humiliation before others*; a compounded form of 39a

Summary: 39b conveys the positive effect of shame of turning one back to his senses; 39c has the same basic meaning as 39a, but particularly brings out the humiliation or disappointment in the opinion of others.

English Word	Greek Word	NASEC or Strong's Number	Comments and Summaries
40. **Transgression**	40a parabasis (παράβασις)	3847	an "overstepping" (Arndt/ Gingrich); a deliberate breaking of the moral law; the willful overstepping of the clearly drawn line or boundary
	40b paraptōma (παράπτωμα)	3900	literally, "to fall to one side"; "a lapse or deviation from truth and uprightness; a misdeed" (Thayer); a failure, fault, or lapse

Summary: "[40a] is the passing beyond some assigned limit. It is the breaking of a distinctly recognized commandment; [40b] is used . . . sometimes in a milder sense, denoting an error, a mistake, a fault" (Berry); 40a lays stress on the engagement of the will and the intentional disobedience involved in sin; 40b differs from 40a by referring "directly to the disruption of a man's relation to God through his fault" (TDNT); 40a relates to the willful act of disobedience; 40b relates to the unhappy results of guilt or "subjective suffering" (Cremer) of sin even when it is "accidental" or "inadvertent."

English Word	Greek Word	NASEC or Strong's Number	Comments and Summaries
41. **Unholy**	41a anosios (ἀνόσιος)	462	"impious; wicked" (Thayer); disrespectful and irreverent to things that are holy
	41b koinos (κοινός)	2839	(literally "common") profane; ordinary (Arndt/Gingrich), secular

English Word	Greek Word	NASEC or Strong's Number	Comments and Summaries

Summary: 41a describes the unholiness that results from the blatant disregard and open disrespect of sacred things; 41b that which results from treating the sacred and special as common and ordinary.

42. **Walk**	42a *peripateō* (περιπατέω)	4043	used figuratively of the "walk of life" (Arndt/Gingrich); implying motion, direction, or progress
	42b *stoicheō* (στοιχέω)	4748	(from the root "to line up") an ancient military word meaning "in rank" (TDNT); "to walk in line" (Vine); to keep in step; to keep rank; to walk in strict accordance with

Summary: When used of the moral or spiritual walk of the believer, 42a means "to make one's way, make progress" (Thayer); 42b involves the disciplined, goal-oriented following of a prescribed course where one is expected to keep in step and keep rank.

43. **Word**	43a *logos* (λόγος)	3056	when used in reference to God, 43a means "God's word, command, commission," as well as "of the divine revelation through Christ and His messengers" (Arndt/Gingrich); the essence, reason, or cause of a matter, having particular reference to the "thought to which it is connected" (Cremer); "reasoned speech" (Vine)
	43b *rhēma* (ῥῆμα)	4487	the *spoken* word; "that which is or has been uttered by the living voice" (Thayer); an utterance, or spoken word in a specific situation (often

English Word	Greek Word	NASEC or Strong's Number	Comments and Summaries
			associated with dynamic or miraculous effects when spoken by God or Christ)

Summary: 43a is a broader term embracing the entire scope of the gospel message and divine revelation; 43b is more specific and "usually relates to individual words and utterances" (DNTT).

English Word	Greek Word	NASEC or Strong's Number	Comments and Summaries
44. Worship	44a *latreia* (λατρεία)	2999	sacred service performed by priests and Levites in the Temple; also the priestly service offered by any believer whose life becomes a living sacrifice to God
	44b *proskuneō* (προσκυνέω)	4352	"to fall down, prostrate oneself, adore on one's knees" (DNTT); to "do obeisance" (Arndt/Gingrich)
	44c *sebō* (σέβω)	4576	to show respect, "to revere" (Thayer); to be God-fearing

Summary: 44a relates to the worship by priestly service that every believer can now offer to God through prayer and personal adoration; 44b relates particularly to the recognition of authority and bodily expression (such as prostrating oneself) involved in such worship; 44c relates especially to the attitude of respect or reverence of the worshipers.

APPENDIX 1

PROCEDURAL STEPS FOLLOWED IN THE PREPARATION
OF THE DISCOVERY BIBLE NEW TESTAMENT

Throughout the project certain basic principles were observed in the process of examining which words were intended to be emphatic in the original text. Our policy was to follow a uniform procedure for each part of the Greek sentence that exhibited both a "normal" and "emphatic" position or arrangement. The procedure was:

1. to do a comparative study of the part of speech or sentence-function in question for the different periods of the Greek language; that is, to define what was the normal and what was the emphatic position in each phase of the development of the language from classical (Attic prose) up through Hellenistic, Koine, and modern Greek.
2. to do thorough research in all material in print pertinent to Greek word order (see bibliography in the Glossary).
3. to conduct an exhaustive statistical analysis of the New Testament corpus. This was achieved by two means: (a) manually going through all the citations of a given word or phrase with the help of the *Moulton-Geden Concordance to the Greek Testament* and marking each citation with a specific designation ("pre-posed," "post-posed," "attributive position," "trajected," etc.); (b) analysis of computerized printouts through GRAMCORD to determine relative frequencies for each author and book of the New Testament.
4. to give careful study to the individual style of each New Testament author. Prime importance was given to the determination of the level and extent of Semitic influence on each author (here we are particularly indebted to Dr. Nigel Turner's extensive research in *Grammar of New Testament Greek* [Edinburgh; 1963, 1976], volumes 3 and 4).
5. to put appropriate markings for (a) primary and secondary emphasis, intensive compounds and particles, and elative comparatives and superlatives; (b) mode of action (aspect) in non-indicative modes and tense-distinction in certain tenses of the indicative as well; and (c) selected Greek synonyms of special importance in the Greek text (as edited by Aland, Black, Martini, Metzger, and Wikgren).
6. to correlate and transfer the above data onto the text of the *New American Standard Bible*, coded for computer typesetting.

APPENDIX 2

Word Order Norms

The following is not intended to be a discussion of word order in general, but rather at determining which particular word orders were employed by the New Testament authors when special stress or emphasis was desired. To speak of emphatic ("marked") word orders naturally implies that there existed a more neutral, unstressed ("unmarked") alternative word order. This is certainly true in the case of the Greek language. Determining word order *norms* ("normal," "unmarked") for Koine Greek, then, of necessity is a preliminary step to laying down any principles concerning *emphatic* word order. It is vital to realize that it does not follow that a word is automatically to be understood as emphatic when it is out of its "normal" position; neither is it correct to say that a word was never intended to be stressed merely because it is in its normal position.[1] Several factors could account for a word to appear out of its normal position yet without emphasis—the logic of the sentence, the presence of a negative compound, relative pronoun, enclitic or interrogative particles, to mention just a few. For a word to qualify as highlighted or emphatic it had to appear in a marked (i.e., unusual, deliberately altered) position, which was free from syntactical constraints such as the ones just mentioned. It is an underlying presupposition of this work that the word order in the Greek New Testament was well constrained and that deviations from the normal word order (except when syntactical constraints made the order invariant) were often for the purpose of conveying emphasis and not always a matter of "free variation." To notice such cases is to pick up the original feeling, emotion, and effect for which the words were written.

Determining word order norms for Koine Greek involved weighing a number of factors together. Word order norms for classical, Hellenistic, and modern Greek were a vital base of comparison to see New Testament word order in light of the historical sweep of the Greek language.[2] A study of each

1. Greek speakers (like English) would at times give stress to a word by voice intonation rather than by use of its position in the sentence. Since the New Testament writings were before the use of recording devices, we lack any way of knowing which words were originally stressed by the speaking voice. For this reason, our study of emphasis is entirely concerned with emphasis achieved by variation in word order.
2. A special word of thanks and acknowledgment here is given to those experts in the departments of classics and linguistics at the University of Chicago and Harvard University for their helpful contributions. We have had the counsel and encouragement of many eminent scholars in America and the United Kingdom as we have drawn up this work. Among those are Dr. Nigel Turner of Cambridge, England; Dr. Bruce Metzger of Princeton University; Dr. Julian Hills of Harvard Divinity School; and Dr. Kostas Kazozis of the classics department of the University of Chicago.

individual writer of the New Testament as well as the extent of Semitic influence on each one was also required for responsible analysis. Extensive computer analysis for word order frequencies in the New Testament provided by GRAMCORD was also vitally important. Studies exclusively devoted to Greek word order in French and German (such as G. Cuendet and M. Frisk) as well as those in English (C. Short, T. Friberg, and others) gave valuable information and insight; however, we found that there was no substitute for the patient and exhaustive empirical method of studying each New Testament occurrence of a given word in its own context.

Though each of the following constructions is discussed in more detail later in the appendix, a summary listing of the *unmarked* (normal) word orders is given here to provide a basis for comparison in discussing emphatic or marked word orders. (These represent only general principles; many exceptions can and do occur.)

The unmarked word order or *word order norms* for the Greek New Testament would be as follows:

1. Direct objects follow the subjects and verbs.
2. Genitive nouns and pronouns follow the nouns they modify.
3. Attributive adjectives (both when anarthrous and definite) precede their nouns.
4. Predicate adjectives and predicate nominatives follow their verbs (i.e., the copula).
5. Imperatives precede their subjects or objects.
6. Subjects precede their verbs (except in cases in which Semitic influence, such as Old Testament quotations, etc., causes inversion).
7. Participles precede their subjects in genitive absolute constructions.
8. The participle in circumstantial clauses comes last.
9. Cardinal numerals follow their anarthrous nouns; ordinals precede their anarthrous nouns.
10. Attributive demonstrative pronouns precede their definite nouns.
11. Adverbs (except for "position adverbs") precede their verbs.
12. Adverbial phrases (when not "time" or "place") follow their verbs.
13. Dative modifiers and predicate complements follow their subjects (both in verbal and verbless clauses).
14. Nominative pronouns precede their finite verbs.
15. Adjectival material comes between the definite article and its coordinating participle in bracketing order.
16. Pronoun subjects and objects of infinitives follow their infinitives (in that order).
17. Complementary infinitives follow the verbs upon which they depend.
18. The verb "to be" precedes its coordinating present participle in periphrastic constructions.
19. Indirect objects follow their verbs.
20. Final, local, and causal clauses follow the main clause.
21. Temporal clauses precede the main clause.

APPENDIX 3

Emphasized words normally belong to the following classes:

1. accusative objects preceding the subject and the verb
2. genitive nouns preceding the noun they modify
3. genitive pronouns intervening between the noun they modify and its definite article or else preceding both of them
4. attributive adjectives (whether anarthrous or definite) following their noun
5. predicate adjectives and predicate nominatives preceding their subject and/or copula verb
6. imperatives following their subject and/or object
7. subjects following their verbs
8. participles following their subjects in genitive absolute constructions
9. ordinal numerals following their nouns (whether definite or anarthrous); cardinal numerals preceding their anarthrous nouns
10. attributive demonstrative pronouns following their nouns
11. adverbs following their verbs (the reverse is true in the case of positional adverbs)
12. adverbial phrases (except for those of time or place) preceding their verbs
13. dative modifiers and predicate complements preceding their subject
14. nominative pronouns used with a finite verb that already contains the pronoun involved
15. pronoun subjects and objects of infinitives when they precede their infinitive
16. complementary infinitives preceding their verbs
17. present participles preceding their copula verb in periphrastic constructions

*It is important to remember that these are only *general principles* and *not strict rules* to be rigidly applied in every circumstance. For each of the eighteen principles above, *many* instances occur where emphasis is not assigned, due to many possible mitigating syntactical factors.

18. Regardless of word order, the following "strengthened" or "intensified" forms are inherently emphatic:
    a. emphatic personal pronouns *(emou, emoi, eme, etc.)*
    b. emphatic possessive adjectives *(emos, sos, hēmeteros, etc.)*
    c. substantival use of *houtos* and *ekeinos* with a finite verb
    d. *ouchi, nuni,* and *oumē* (versus *ouk, nun, ou,* and *mē)*
    e. ascensive use of *kai* (i.e., when it means "even" or "also")
    f. the intensive pronoun *(autos, autē)*

H.E.L.P.S. STUDY SYSTEM BIBLIOGRAPHY

GRAMMARS

Blass, F. *Grammar of New Testament Greek*. New York: Macmillan, 1898.

Blass, F., and Debrunner, A. *A Greek Grammar of the New Testament*. Chicago: University of Chicago, 1961.

Gildersleeve, B. L. *Syntax of Classical Greek from Homer to Demosthenes*. 2 vols. New York: American Book Co., 1900, 1911.

Jannaris, A. N. *An Historical Greek Grammar*. London: Macmillan, 1897.

Kühner, R. *Ausführliche Grammatik der griechischen Sprache*, II. vols. 1 and 2, 3d ed. by B. Gerth. Hanover and Leipzig: Hahn, Goteschalk, Hueber, 1898–1904.

Mayser, E. *Grammatik der griechischen Papyri aus der Ptolemäerzeit*, II, vol. 2. Berlin: W. deGruyter, 1934.

Radermacher, L. *Neutestamentliche Grammatik*. Tübingen: n.p., 1925.

Robertson, A. T. *A Grammar of the Greek New Testament in the Light of Historical Research*. New York: Broadman, 1931.

Turner, N. *Grammar of New Testament Greek: III, Syntax*. Edinburgh: T & T Clark, 1963.

Turner, N. *Grammar of New Testament Greek: IV, Style*. Edinburgh: T & T Clark, 1976.

OTHER WRITTEN WORKS CONSULTED RELATING TO GREEK WORD ORDER

Abbott, E. A. *Johannine Grammar*. London: Adam and Charles Black, 1906.

Archer, G., and Chirichigno, G. C. *Old Testament Quotations in the New Testament: A Complete Survey*. Chicago: Moody, 1983.

Brown, Colin. *New International Dictionary of New Testament Theology*. 3 vols. Grand Rapids: Zondervan, 1967.

Cuendet, G. *L'ordre des mots dans le texte grec et dans les versions gotique . . . des Evangiles, I. Les groupes nominaux*. Paris: n.p., 1929.

Frisk, H. *Studien zur griechische Worstellung*. Goteborg: n.p., 1932; repr. University Microfilms International, Ann Arbor, Mich.

Hawkins, J. *Word Order Universals*. Orlando, Fla.: Academic, 1983.

Kittel, Gerhard, and Friedrich, Gerhard. *Theological Dictionary of the New Testament*. 10 vols. Grand Rapids: Eerdmans, 1964, 1974 (Vol. 1976)

Lampe, G. W. H. *A Patristic Greek Lexicon*. Oxford, 1961.

Liddell, H. G., and Scott, R. *A Greek-English Lexicon*. 9th ed. Revised by H. S. Jones. Oxford, 1925–1940.

Moule, C. F. D. *An Idiom Book of NT Greek*. Cambridge, Eng.: Cambridge Press, 1953.

Moulton, W. F., and Geden, A. S. *A Concordance to the Greek Testament*. Edinburgh: T & T Clark, 1897.

(NASEC) *New American Standard Exhaustive Concordance*. (Nashville: Holman Bible Publishers, 1981).

Rengstorf, K. H. *A Complete Concordance to Flavius Josephus*. 4 vols. Leiden: Brill, 1973.

H.E.L.P.S. Study System Bibliography

Short, C. *The Order of Words in Attic Greek Prose* (pp. xv to cxv, preface of *Yonge's English Greek Lexicon*). New York: Harper, 1870.
Sophocles, E. A. *Greek Lexicon of the Roman and Byzantine Periods* (from B.C. 146–A.D. 1100). 2 vols. New York: Doubner, 1887.
Strong, James, ed. *Strong's Exhaustive Concordance of the Bible*. Nashville: Nelson, 1977.
Thumb, A. *Handbook of the Modern Greek Vernacular*. London: T & T Clark, 1912.
Weil, H. *Order of Words in the Ancient Languages*. Translated by C. Super. Boston: Ginn and Co., 1887.
Winter, Ralph. *Word Study New Testament and Concordance*. Carol Stream, Ill., Tyndale, 1978.

PERIODICALS
Goodell, T. D. "The Order of Words in Greek." *Trans. and Proc. Amer. Phil. Assn.*, XX1.5 (21.214).
Norden, E. *Agnostos Theos*, Leipzig 1913, 365f, "Stellung des Verbums in NT Griechischen."
Rife, J. M. "The Mechanics of Translation Greek." *JBL*, 52, 1933, 244ff.
Roberts, W. Rhys. "A Point of Greek and Latin Word Order." *Class. Rev.*, 1912, 177–9.
Wilson, A. J. "Emphasis in the New Testament." *Journal of Theological Studies*, VIII, 75–85.

COMMENTARIES PAYING PARTICULAR ATTENTION TO GREEK WORD ORDER AND EMPHASIS
Alford, H. *Alford's Greek Testament*. Cambridge: n.p. 1844.
Ellicott, C. J. *St. Paul's Epistle to the Galatians*. London: Longman's, Green, and Co., 1889.
_____. *Ellicott's Commentaries on Philippians, Colossians, Philemon, 1 Timothy, 2 Timothy, Titus*. Boston: Draper Halliday, 1866.
_____. *Commentary on the Epistle to the Thessalonians*. Grand Rapids: Zondervan.
Lenski, R. *Commentary on the New Testament*. 12 vols. Minneapolis: Augsburg, 1961.
Meyer, H. A. W. *Meyer's Commentary on the New Testament*. London: T & T Clark, 1883.
Nicoll, W. Robertson, ed. *Expositor's Greek Testament*. Grand Rapids: Eerdmans, repr. 1979.
Rienecker, F., and Rogers, C. *Linguistic Key to the Greek New Testament*. Grand Rapids: Zondervan, 1976.
Robertson, A. T. *Word Pictures in the New Testament*. Nashville: Broadman, 1930.
Westcott, B. F. *Gospel According to John*. Grand Rapids: Baker, repr., 1980.
_____. *Epistle to the Hebrews*. Grand Rapids: Eerdmans, repr., 1974.
_____. *Epistles of St. John*. Grand Rapids: Eerdmans, repr., 1966.

COMPUTER DATA BASE
GRAMCORD. *Grammatical Concordance Computer Data Base of the Greek New Testament*. Deerfield, Ill.: Trinity Evangelical Divinity School.

The New American Standard
CONCORDANCE
to the New Testament

This is a collection of the principal **proper nouns** and **key words** in Scripture. The following format is used: Descriptive phrases and references are listed under each **proper noun**. If the descriptive phrases are numbered, this indicates different individuals or identities. **Key words** are immediately followed by explanatory words or synonyms. Under each **key word** examples are listed with text and reference. The **key word** is abbreviated in the text to its first letter, e.g., "abide" is "**a**". Variants add suffixes, e.g., "abides" appears as "**a-s**" and "abiding" appears as "**a-ing**".

A

AARON
rod of — Heb 9:4
ABADDON
angel of bottomless pit — Rev 9:11
ABANDON *leave*
a my soul to Hades — Acts 2:27
ABBA *father*
A! Father — Mark 14:36
we cry out, A! — Rom 8:15
ABEL
called righteous — Matt 23:35
a man of faith — Heb 11:4
ABHOR *despise, detest*
You who a idols — Rom 2:22
A what is evil — Rom 12:9
ABIDE *remain, stay*
wrath of God a-s — John 3:36
a in My word — John 8:31
If you a in Me — John 15:7
a in My love — John 15:9
now a faith — 1 Cor 13:13
word...LORD a-s — 1 Pet 1:25
love of God a — 1 John 3:17
God a-s in us — 1 John 4:12
ABILITY *power, strength*
according to his own a — Matt 25:15
a to conceive — Heb 11:11
ABLE *qualified*
a from these stones — Matt 3:9
I am a to do — Matt 9:28
Him who is a — Matt 10:28
a to separate us — Rom 8:39
what you are a — 1 Cor 10:13
a to comprehend — Eph 3:18
be a to teach — 2 Tim 2:2
a to save Him — Heb 5:7
One who is a — James 4:12
a to open — Rev 5:3
ABODE *habitation*
Our a with him — John 14:23
their proper a — Jude 6
ABOLISH
not come to a — Matt 5:17
a-ing in His flesh — Eph 2:15
who a-ed death — 2 Tim 1:10
ABOMINABLE *detestable*
a idolatries — 1 Pet 4:3
unbelieving and a — Rev 21:8
ABOMINATION *hated things*
a of desolation — Matt 24:15
a-s of the earth — Rev 17:5
ABOUND *excel, plentiful*
a in hope — Rom 15:13
a-ing in the work — 1 Cor 15:58
affection a-s — 2 Cor 7:15
all grace a — 2 Cor 9:8
ABOVE *over*
disciple is not a — Matt 10:24
I am from a — John 8:23
a every name — Phil 2:9
exalts himself a — 2 Thess 2:4
gift is from a — James 1:17
ABRAHAM
righteousness of — Rom 4:3-9
a man of faith — Heb 11:8,17
ABRAHAM'S BOSOM
rabbinic terminology for Paradise — Luke 16:22
ABSENT *being away*
a in body — 1 Cor 5:3
a from the Lord — 2 Cor 5:6
a from the body — 2 Cor 5:8
ABSTAIN *refrain from*
a-ing from foods — 1 Tim 4:3
a from wickedness — 2 Tim 2:19

a from fleshly lusts — 1 Pet 2:11
ABUNDANCE *plenty, surplus*
one has an a — Luke 12:15
the a of grace — Rom 5:17
ABUNDANT *enough, plenteous*
a grace was upon — Acts 4:33
comfort is a — 2 Cor 1:5
ABUSE (n) *insulting speech*
hurling a at Him — Matt 27:39
was hurling a — Luke 23:39
ABUSIVE *filthy, vulgar*
a speech from your — Col 3:8
strife, a language — 1 Tim 6:4
ABYSS *deep, depth*
depart into the a — Luke 8:31
descend into the a — Rom 10:7
angel of the a — Rev 9:11
key of the a — Rev 20:1
ACCEPT *receive*
hear the word and a — Mark 4:20
God has a-ed him — Rom 14:3
a one another — Rom 15:7
ACCEPTABLE *pleasing*
sacrifice, a to God — Rom 12:1
a to the saints — Rom 15:31
now is the a time — 2 Cor 6:2
to God an a service — Heb 12:28
sacrifices a to God — 1 Pet 2:5
ACCESS *approach, entry*
our a in one Spirit — Eph 2:18
confident a through faith — Eph 3:12
ACCOMPANY *attach to, follow*
that he might a Him — Luke 8:38
that a salvation — Heb 6:9
ACCOMPLISH *perform, realize*
a-ed redemption — Luke 1:68
a His work — John 4:34
I am a-ing a work — Acts 13:41
when sin is a-ed — James 1:15
man can a much — James 5:16
ACCORD *agreement, union*
voices...with one a — Acts 4:24
one a in Solomon's — Acts 5:12
multitudes with one a — Acts 8:6
one a they came — Acts 12:20
ACCORDING
a to his deeds — Matt 16:27
a to the revelation — Rom 16:25
heirs a to promise — Gal 3:29
a to His riches — Phil 4:19
ACCOUNT (n) *reckoning*
settled a with — Matt 25:19
who will give an a — Heb 13:17
ACCURATELY *correctly*
teaching a...things — Acts 18:25
handling a...word — 2 Tim 2:15
ACCURSED *damned*
Depart...a ones — Matt 25:41
let him be a — Gal 1:8
in greed, a children — 2 Pet 2:14
ACCUSATION *charge of wrong*
What a do you — John 18:29
a against my nation — Acts 28:19
Do not receive an a — 1 Tim 5:19
ACCUSE *testify against*
He was being a-d — Matt 27:12
a-ing...vehemently — Luke 23:10
a you before the — John 5:45
alternately a-ing — Rom 2:15
not a-d of dissipation — Titus 1:6
unjustly a-ing us — 3 John 10
ACCUSER *complainant*
instructing his a-s — Acts 23:30
when the a stood — Acts 25:18
a of our brethren — Rev 12:10

ACHAIA
province of Greece — Acts 18:12; Rom 15:26; 1 Cor 16:15
ACKNOWLEDGE *confess*
Pharisees a them all — Acts 23:8
see fit to a God — Rom 1:28
ACQUAINTANCE *friend*
relatives and a-s — Luke 2:44
And all His a-s — Luke 23:49
ACQUIRE *get, purchase*
Do not a gold — Matt 10:9
ACT (v) *behave*
I a-ed ignorantly — 1 Tim 1:13
So speak and so a — James 2:12
are a-ing faithfully — 3 John 5
ACTION *behavior, work*
plan or a should be — Acts 5:38
gird your minds for a — 1 Pet 1:13
ADAM
type of Christ — Rom 5:14
compared to Jesus — 1 Cor 15:22
ADD
can a a *single* cubit — Matt 6:27
if anyone a-s to them — Rev 22:18
ADJURE *charge solemnly*
I a you by Jesus — Acts 19:13
I a you by the Lord — 1 Thess 5:27
ADMINISTRATION
healings, helps, a-s — 1 Cor 12:28
in our a of this — 2 Cor 8:20
a of the mystery — Eph 3:9
ADMONISH *warn*
not cease to a each — Acts 20:31
able also to a one — Rom 15:14
a-ing one another — Col 3:16
a the unruly — 1 Thess 5:14
a him as a brother — 2 Thess 3:15
ADOPTION *acceptance*
spirit of a as sons — Rom 8:15
to whom belongs...a — Rom 9:4
receive the a as sons — Gal 4:5
predestined us to a — Eph 1:5
ADORN *array, clothe*
a-ed with beautiful — Luke 21:5
women to a — 1 Tim 2:9
a the doctrine of God — Titus 2:10
a-ed with gold — Rev 17:4
as a bride a-ed — Rev 21:2
ADULTERER
a-s, nor effeminate — 1 Cor 6:9
a-s God will judge — Heb 13:4
ADULTERESS
shall be called an a — Rom 7:3
ADULTERY
committed a with her — Matt 5:28
woman commits a — Matt 5:32
Do not commit a — Luke 18:20
eyes full of a — 2 Pet 2:14
ADVANCE *ahead, beyond*
have told you in a — Matt 24:25
both a-d in years — Luke 1:7
a-ing in Judaism — Gal 1:14
ADVANTAGE *benefit, profit*
a that I go away — John 16:7
what a has the Jew — Rom 3:1
no a be taken of us — 2 Cor 2:11
sake of *gaining* an a — Jude 16
ADVERSARY *foe, opponent*
there are many a-ies — 1 Cor 16:9
consume the a-ies — Heb 10:27
Your a, the devil — 1 Pet 5:8
ADVICE *counsel*
they took his a — Acts 5:40
have followed my a — Acts 27:21

ADVOCATE *defender, witness*
A with the Father 1 John 2:1
AFFECTION *devotion, love*
in your own **a-s** 2 Cor 6:12
a of Christ Jesus Phil 1:8
fond **a** for you 1 Thess 2:8
AFFLICT (v) *oppress, trouble*
were sick or **a-ed** Acts 5:16
are **a-ed** in every 2 Cor 4:8
those who **a** you 2 Thess 1:6
a-ed, ill-treated Heb 11:37
AFFLICTION *oppression*
a or persecution Mark 4:17
healed of her **a** Mark 5:29
a-s await me Acts 20:23
out of much **a** 2 Cor 2:4
great ordeal of **a** 2 Cor 8:2
to suffer **a** 1 Thess 3:4
AFRAID *dreading, fearful*
a to take Mary Matt 1:20
were **a** of Him Mark 11:18
Do not be **a,** Mary Luke 1:30
a of those who kill Luke 12:4
a of the people Luke 22:2
a, lest as the serpent 2 Cor 11:3
Do not be **a** Rev 1:17
AGABUS
prophet Acts 11:28;21:10
AGE *period, year*
either in this **a** Matt 12:32
the end of the **a** Matt 13:40
sons of this **a** are Luke 16:8
in the **a-s** to come Eph 2:7
hidden…*past* **a-s** Col 1:26
in the present **a** Titus 2:12
AGED *old*
Paul, the **a** Philem 9
AGONY *anguish*
in **a** in this flame Luke 16:24
in **a** He was praying Luke 22:44
the **a** of death Acts 2:24
AGREE *consent*
if two of you **a** Matt 18:19
did you not **a** Matt 20:13
Jews had already **a-d** John 9:22
have **a-d** together Acts 5:9
words…Prophets **a** Acts 15:15
a with sound words 1 Tim 6:3
AGREEMENT *accord*
Saul was in hearty **a** Acts 8:1
a has the temple 2 Cor 6:16
three are in **a** 1 John 5:8
AGRIPPA
see **Herod**
AIR *breeze, sky*
birds of the **a** Matt 6:26
not beating the **a** 1 Cor 9:26
speaking into the **a** 1 Cor 14:9
power of the **a** Eph 2:2
the Lord in the **a** 1 Thess 4:17
ALABASTER *whitish stone*
a vial of very costly Matt 26:7
brought an **a** vial Luke 7:37
ALARM (v) *frighten, warn*
being much **a-ed** Acts 10:4
in no way **a-ed** by Phil 1:28
ALERT (n) *watch*
be on the **a** Matt 24:42
be **a** and sober 1 Thess 5:6
ALERT (v) *be watchful*
keeping **a** in it Col 4:2
let us be **a** 1 Thess 5:6
ALEXANDER
1 *son of Simon of Cyrene* Mark 15:21
2 *of priestly family* Acts 4:6
3 *Ephesian Jew* Acts 19:33
4 *apostate teacher* 1 Tim 1:20
5 *enemy of Paul* 2 Tim 4:14
ALEXANDRIAN
1 *of Alexandria* Acts 6:9
2 *ship* Acts 27:6;28:11
3 *Apollos* Acts 18:24
ALIEN *foreigner, stranger*
a-s in a foreign land Acts 7:6
no longer…**a-s** Eph 2:19
he lived as an **a** Heb 11:9
I urge you as **a-s** 1 Pet 2:11
ALIENATE *estrange*
were formerly **a-d** Col 1:21
ALIVE
when He was…**a** Matt 27:63
heard…He was **a** Mark 16:11
presented Himself **a** Acts 1:3
yet the spirit is **a** Rom 8:10
all shall be made **a** 1 Cor 15:22
made us **a** together Eph 2:5
a in the spirit 1 Pet 3:18
I am **a** forevermore Rev 1:18
ALLOT *apportion, divide*
a-ted to each…faith Rom 12:3
a-ted to your charge 1 Pet 5:3
ALLOW *permit*
Nor **a** Thy Holy One Acts 2:27
not be **a-ed** to live Acts 22:22
a you to be tempted 1 Cor 10:13
not **a** a woman 1 Tim 2:12
ALMIGHTY *all-powerful*
Lord God, the **A** Rev 4:8
the **A,** reigns Rev 19:6
ALMS *charity*
therefore you give **a** Matt 6:2
a may be in secret Matt 6:4
a to the *Jewish* Acts 10:2
bring **a** to my nation Acts 24:17
ALONE
not live on bread **a** Matt 4:4
He was praying **a** Luke 9:18
I am not **a** *in it* John 8:16
receiving but you **a** Phil 4:15
and not by faith **a** James 2:24
ALOUD *joyful, piercing*
began to weep **a** Acts 20:37
ALPHA
first letter of Gr. alphabet Rev 1:8
title of Jesus Christ Rev 21:6
expresses eternalness of God Rev 22:13
ALTAR *place of sacrifice*
offering at the **a** Matt 5:23
a that sanctifies Matt 23:19
golden **a** of incense Heb 9:4
we have an **a** Heb 13:10
horns of the golden **a** Rev 9:13
ALWAYS *ever, forever*
I am with you **a** Matt 28:20
poor you **a** have Mark 14:7
Rejoice in the Lord **a** Phil 4:4
a be with…Lord 1 Thess 4:17
I shall **a** be ready 2 Pet 1:12
AMAZED *astonished, astounded*
a at His teaching Mark 1:22
heard Him were **a** Luke 2:47
were **a** and marveled Acts 2:7
whole earth was **a** Rev 13:3
AMAZEMENT *astonishment*
a came upon them Luke 4:36
with wonder and **a** Acts 3:10
AMBASSADOR *envoy*
a-s for Christ 2 Cor 5:20
an **a** in chains Eph 6:20
AMBITION *design, intention*
out of selfish **a** Phil 1:17
a to lead a quiet 1 Thess 4:11
jealousy…selfish **a** James 3:14
AMEN *so be it*
glory forever…**A** Phil 4:20
the **A,** the faithful Rev 3:14
A, Come, Lord Jesus Rev 22:20
ANANIAS
1 *deceived Jerusalem church* Acts 5:1-5
2 *Damascus Christian* Acts 9:10,17
3 *high priest* Acts 23:2
ANCHOR
they weighed **a** Acts 27:13
they cast four **a-s** Acts 27:29
an **a** of the soul Heb 6:19
ANCIENT *aged, old*
the **a-s** were told Matt 5:21
from **a** generations Acts 15:21
not spare the **a** world 2 Pet 2:5
ANDREW
fisherman Matt 4:18
brother of Peter Matt 4:18
receives Jesus John 1:40-42
apostle Luke 6:14
ANGEL *divine messenger*
give His **a-s** charge Matt 4:6
a Gabriel was sent Luke 1:26
they are like **a-s** Luke 20:36
two **a-s** in white John 20:12
like the face of an **a** Acts 6:15
as an **a** of light 2 Cor 11:14
worship of the **a-s** Col 2:18
entertained **a-s** Heb 13:2
God did not spare **a-s** 2 Pet 2:4
a of the church Rev 2:1
ANGEL OF THE LORD
a commanded him Matt 1:24
a appeared to Joseph Matt 2:13
a…opened the gates Acts 5:19
ANGER *indignation, wrath*
sun go down…**a** Eph 4:26
put…aside: **a** Col 3:8
slow to **a** James 1:19
ANGRY *enraged, indignant*
a with his brother Matt 5:22
Be **a**…do not sin Eph 4:26
a with this generation Heb 3:10
ANGUISH *distress, pain*
remembers the **a** no more John 16:21
and **a** of heart 2 Cor 2:4
ANIMAL *beast, creature*
four-footed **a-s** Acts 10:12
like unreasoning **a-s** 2 Pet 2:12
ANNA
prophetess Luke 2:36
ANNAS
high priest Luke 3:2; John 18:13ff
ANNOUNCE *proclaim*
a-ing to…disciples John 20:18
a-d…the Righteous Acts 7:52
ANNUL *dismiss, make void*
a-s one of the least Matt 5:19
ANOINT (v) *sprinkle oil upon*
has **a-ed** My body Mark 14:8
did not **a** My head Luke 7:46
and **a-ed** my eyes John 9:11
a-ed…feet of Jesus John 12:3
a-ed Him…Holy Spirit Acts 10:38
a-ing him with oil James 5:14
ANOINTING (n) *consecration*
a from the Holy 1 John 2:20
His **a** teaches you 1 John 2:27
ANSWER (n) *response*
gave him no **a** John 19:9
amazed at…His **a-s** Luke 2:47
ANSWER (v) *respond*
Jesus **a-ing** said Matt 3:15
who **a-s** back to God Rom 9:20
ANTICHRIST *foe of Christ*
a-s have arisen 1 John 2:18
This is the **a** 1 John 2:22
the *spirit* of the **a** 1 John 4:3
deceiver and the **a** 2 John 7
ANTIOCH
1 *city in Syria* Acts 6:5;11:19,26
2 *city in Galatia* Acts 13:14; 14:19
ANTIPAS
Pergamum martyr Rev 2:13
ANXIETY *sorrow*
casting all your **a** 1 Pet 5:7
ANXIOUS *concern, worry*
not be **a** for your life Matt 6:25
not be **a** for tomorrow Matt 6:34
be **a** beforehand Mark 13:11
a can add a *single* Luke 12:25
Be **a** for nothing Phil 4:6
APART *separate*
a from your Father Matt 10:29
a from Him nothing John 1:3
a from Me you can John 15:5
faith **a** from works Rom 3:28
APOLLOS
Alexandrian Jew Acts 18:24
taught at Ephesus Acts 18:24
taught at Corinth 1 Cor 3:4,6
APOSTASY *faithlessness*
unless the **a** comes 2 Thess 2:3
APOSTLE *sent with authority*
the twelve **a-s** Matt 10:2
named as **a-s** Luke 6:13
called *as* an **a** Rom 1:1
an **a** of Gentiles Rom 11:13
fit to be called an **a** 1 Cor 15:9
men are false **a-s** 2 Cor 11:13
He gave some *as* **a-s** Eph 4:11
Jesus, the **A** and Heb 3:1
a-s of the Lamb Rev 21:14
APOSTLESHIP *office of apostle*
received grace and **a** Rom 1:5
seal of my **a** 1 Cor 9:2
Peter in *his* **a** to Gal 2:8
APPAREL *clothing, garment*
men…in dazzling **a** Luke 24:4
put on his royal **a** Acts 12:21
APPEAL *ask, entreat*
standing and **a-ing** Acts 16:9
I **a** to Caesar Acts 25:11
Paul **a-ed** to be held Acts 25:21
a-ed to…Emperor Acts 25:25
a to *him* as a father 1 Tim 5:1
love's sake I…**a** Philem 9
APPEAR *become visible*
and **a-ed** to many Matt 27:53
first **a-ed** to Mary Mark 16:9
who, **a-ing** in glory Luke 9:31
a-ed to them tongues Acts 2:3
we must all **a** before 2 Cor 5:10
a-ing of the glory Titus 2:13
shall **a** a second time Heb 9:28
Chief Shepherd **a-s** 1 Pet 5:4
not **a-ed** as yet 1 John 3:2
APPEARANCE *countenance*
they neglect their **a** Matt 6:16
judge according to **a** John 7:24
a of His coming 2 Thess 2:8
a of the locusts Rev 9:7
APPETITE *desire, hunger*
whose god is *their* **a** Phil 3:19

APPOINT *assign, commission*
a-ed elders for them	Acts 14:23
a-ed a preacher and	1 Tim 2:7
For the Law **a-s** men	Heb 7:28

APPROPRIATE *suitable*
a to repentance	Acts 26:20

APPROVAL *consent*
loved the **a** of men	John 12:43
give hearty **a** to	Rom 1:32
men of old gained **a**	Heb 11:2

APPROVE *accept, attest*
standing by **a-ing**	Acts 22:20
and **a-d** by men	Rom 14:18
present yourself **a-d**	2 Tim 2:15

AQUILA
a native of Pontus
Corinthian Christian	Acts 18:18
co-worker with Paul	Rom 16:3

ARABIA
land SE of Israel / Judah | Gal 1:17;4:25

ARABS
Cretans and **A-**we hear	Acts 2:11

ARAM
ancestor of Jesus, shortened to Ram
Matt 1:3; Luke 3:33

ARCHANGEL
voice of *the* **a**	1 Thess 4:16
But Michael the **a**	Jude 9

ARCHELAUS *see* **HEROD**

ARCHIPPUS
Colossian Christian	Col 4:17
co-worker with Paul	Philem 2

AREOPAGUS
hill and council in Athens | Acts 17:19,22

ARGUE *dispute, question*
Pharisees...**a** with	Mark 8:11
scribes **a-ing** with	Mark 9:14
a-ing with the...*Jews*	Acts 9:29

ARGUMENT *disagreement*
a arose among them	Luke 9:46

ARISE *rise, stand*
a-n anyone greater	Matt 11:11
false prophets will **a**	Matt 24:11
arose from the dead	Acts 10:41
A, and be baptized	Acts 22:16
a from the dead	Eph 5:14
arose loud voices	Rev 11:15

ARISTARCHUS
Thessalonian Christian	Acts 20:4; Acts 27:2
co-worker with Paul	Col 4:10; Philem 24

ARK *chest, vessel*
Noah entered the **a**	Matt 24:38
a of His covenant	Rev 11:19

ARM (n) *part of body*
took...in His **a-s**	Mark 10:16
with an uplifted **a**	Acts 13:17

ARM (v) *mobilize*
a yourselves also	1 Pet 4:1

ARMOR *protective device*
all his **a** on which	Luke 11:22
put on...**a** of light	Rom 13:12
full **a** of God	Eph 6:11

ARMY *host, war*
a-ies in heaven	Rev 19:14
and against His **a**	Rev 19:19

AROMA *odor*
through us...sweet **a**	2 Cor 2:14
a from life to life	2 Cor 2:16
as a fragrant **a**	Eph 5:2

AROUSE *raise, stir*
And being **a-d**	Mark 4:39
Jews **a-d** the devout	Acts 13:50

ARRANGE *set in order*
thus he had **a-d** it	Acts 20:13
ahead to you and **a**	2 Cor 9:5

ARRAY (v) *adorn, clothe*
God so **a-s** the grass	Matt 6:30
a-ed Him in a purple	John 19:2

ARREST *restrain*
Herod had John **a-ed**	Matt 14:3
and clubs to **a** Me	Matt 26:55
proceeded to **a** Peter	Acts 12:3

ARROGANCE *pride*
slanders, gossip, **a**	2 Cor 12:20
you boast in your **a**	James 4:16

ARROGANT *proud*
Knowledge makes **a**	1 Cor 8:1
boastful, **a,** revilers	2 Tim 3:2
speaking...*a words*	2 Pet 2:18

ARTEMIS
Greek goddess | Acts 19:24ff

ARTICLE *object, vessel*
every **a** of ivory	Rev 18:12

ASCEND *go up*
has **a-ed** into heaven	John 3:13
Son of Man **a-ing**	John 6:62
a-ed to the Father	John 20:17
who **a-ed** far above	Eph 4:10

ASH
sackcloth and **a-es**	Luke 10:13
a-es of a heifer	Heb 9:13

ASHAMED *embarrassed*
a of Me...My words	Mark 8:38
a when He comes	Luke 9:26
not **a** of the gospel	Rom 1:16
a of the testimony	2 Tim 1:8
God is not **a**	Heb 11:16
let him not feel **a**	1 Pet 4:16

ASHER
tribe of Israel | Rev 7:6

ASIA
Roman province of Asia Minor
Acts 6:9; Rom 16:5; Rev 1:4

ASK *appeal, beg, inquire*
Give to him who **a-s**	Matt 5:42
A, and it shall be	Matt 7:7
a...believing	Matt 21:22
pray and **a,** believe	Mark 11:24
Jews **a** for signs	1 Cor 1:22
let him **a** of God	James 1:5

ASLEEP *death, rest*
not died, but is **a**	Matt 9:24
in the stern, **a**	Mark 4:38
Lazarus...fallen **a**	John 11:11
said this, he fell **a**	Acts 7:60
fallen **a** in Jesus	1 Thess 4:14

ASSAIL *attack*
storm was **a-ing** us	Acts 27:20

ASSEMBLE *gather*
whole city are **a-d**	Acts 13:44
a-d to make war	Rev 19:19

ASSEMBLY *congregation*
the **a** was divided	Acts 23:7
general and church	Heb 12:23
comes into your **a**	James 2:2

ASSOCIATE (n) *colleague*
high priest and...**a-s**	Acts 5:21

ASSOCIATE (v) *identify with*
dared to **a** with them	Acts 5:13
but **a** with the lowly	Rom 12:16
not **a** with him	2 Thess 3:14

ASSURANCE *confirmation*
a of understanding	Col 2:2
full **a** of hope	Heb 6:11
full **a** of faith	Heb 10:22
a of *things* hoped for	Heb 11:1

ASSURE *confirm*
I **a** you before God	Gal 1:20
shall **a** our heart	1 John 3:19

ASTONISHED *amazed*
a at His teaching	Matt 22:33
listeners were **a**	Mark 6:2
were utterly **a**	Mark 7:37
they were all **a**	Luke 1:63

ASTOUNDED *astonished*
were completely **a**	Mark 5:24

ASTRAY *erring, wandering*
lead the elect **a**	Mark 13:22
a from the faith	1 Tim 6:21
go **a** in their heart	Heb 3:10
My bond-servants **a**	Rev 2:20

ATHENS
leading Greek city | Acts 17:15ff

ATTACK (n) *assault*
joined in the **a**	Acts 24:9

ATTACK (v) *assault, fall upon*
no man will **a** you	Acts 18:10

ATTAIN *acquire*
worthy to **a** to that	Luke 20:35
a-ed righteousness	Rom 9:30
a to the resurrection	Phil 3:11

ATTEND *pay attention to*
who **a** regularly	1 Cor 9:13
a to...business	1 Thess 4:11
ears **a** to their prayer	1 Pet 3:12

ATTENDANT *helper, servant*
a-s of...bridegroom	Mark 2:19
gave it back to the **a**	Luke 4:20

ATTENTION *heed, regard*
pay **a** to myths	1 Tim 1:4
a to...reading	1 Tim 4:13

ATTITUDE *frame of mind*
a of the righteous	Luke 1:17
Have this **a** in	Phil 2:5
have a different **a**	Phil 3:15

AUGUSTUS
name of Caesar Octavianus | Luke 2:1

AUTHOR *source*
a of their salvation	Heb 2:10
a...perfecter of faith	Heb 12:2

AUTHORITY *power, right*
as *one* having **a**	Matt 7:29
a on earth to forgive	Matt 9:6
a over unclean spirits	Matt 10:1
All **a...**given to Me	Matt 28:18
Son of Man has **a**	Luke 5:24
no **a** except from God	Rom 13:1

majesty, dominion...**a**	Jude 25
give **a** over...nations	Rev 2:26

AVENGE *revenge*
a-ing our blood	Rev 6:10
He has **a-ed** the blood	Rev 19:2

AVENGER *revenger*
God, an **a** who brings	Rom 13:4
Lord is *the* **a**	1 Thess 4:6

AVOID *refuse*
a-ing...empty chatter	1 Tim 6:20
a such men	2 Tim 3:5

AWAIT *wait*
afflictions **a** me	Acts 20:23
a-ing...the revelation	1 Cor 1:7
who eagerly **a** Him	Heb 9:28

AWAKE *be attentive, watch*
that I may **a-n** him	John 11:11
hour for you to **a-n**	Rom 13:11

AWARE *know, understand*
But Jesus, **a** of *this*	Matt 12:15
I was **a** that power	Luke 8:46

AWE *fear, reverence*
feeling a sense of **a**	Acts 2:43
with reverence and **a**	Heb 12:28

AXE *cutting tool*
a is already laid	Luke 3:9

B

BABES *infants*
woe...who nurse **b**	Matt 24:19
as to **b** in Christ	1 Cor 3:1
like newborn **b**	1 Pet 2:2

BABY *infant*
b leaped...her womb	Luke 1:41
b wrapped in cloths	Luke 2:12
b as He lay	Luke 2:16

BABYLON *city*
symbolic of godlessness | Rev 14:8;17:5

BAD *evil, wrong*
if your eye is **b**	Matt 6:23
b tree bears **b** fruit	Matt 7:18
B company corrupts	1 Cor 15:33

BAG *sack*
b for *your* journey	Matt 10:10
Carry no purse, no **b**	Luke 10:4

BALAAM
heresy | Rev 2:14

BANK *slope*
herd rushed down...**b**	Luke 8:33

BANQUET *dinner, feast*
place of honor at **b-s**	Matt 23:6
Herod...gave a **b**	Mark 6:21

BAPTISM *symbolic washing*
Sadducees coming...**b**	Matt 3:7
b of repentance	Mark 1:4
b with which I am	Mark 10:38
with the **b** of John	Luke 7:29
a **b** to undergo	Luke 12:50
through **b** into death	Rom 6:4
one baptism, one **b**	Eph 4:5
buried with Him in **b**	Col 2:12

BAPTIZE *symbolic washing*
b... Holy Spirit	Matt 3:11
tax-gatherers...**b-d**	Luke 3:12
Jesus also was **b-d**	Luke 3:21
sent me to **b** in water	John 1:33
b-ing more disciples	John 4:1
b-d with the Holy	Acts 1:5
each of you be **b-d**	Acts 2:38
he arose and was **b-d**	Acts 9:18
household...been **b-d**	Acts 16:15
John **b-d** with the	Acts 19:4
b-d into Christ Jesus	Rom 6:3
b-d into Moses	1 Cor 10:2
b-d into one body	1 Cor 12:13
b-d for the dead	1 Cor 15:29

BARABBAS
robber	Matt 27:16; Luke 23:18
released by Pilate	Matt 27:26

BARBARIAN *non-Hellenic*
obligation...to **b-s**	Rom 1:14
who speaks a **b**	1 Cor 14:11
b, Scythian, slave	Col 3:11

BARE (v) *expose, uncover*
open and laid **b**	Heb 4:13

BAR-JESUS
magician | Acts 13:6

BARLEY *grain*
has five **b** loaves	John 6:9

BARN *farm building*
wheat into the **b**	Matt 3:12
nor gather into **b-s**	Matt 6:26
tear down my **b-s**	Luke 12:18

BARNABAS
Cyprian by birth	Acts 4:36
introduced Paul	Acts 9:27
co-worker with Paul	Acts 13:2,7
separated from Paul	Acts 15:39

the sea became **b**	Rev 8:8
b of the saints	Rev 17:6
BLOW *forcible stroke*	
gave Jesus a **b**	John 18:22
give Him **b-s**	John 19:3
inflicted many **b-s**	Acts 16:23
BOANERGES	
name of James and John	Mark 3:17
BOAST (n) *bragging*	
make my **b** an empty	1 Cor 9:15
the **b** of our hope	Heb 3:6
BOAST (v) *brag, glory*	
b in God	Rom 2:17
who **b** in the Law	Rom 2:23
b...my weaknesses	2 Cor 12:9
it **b-s** of great things	James 3:5
BOASTFUL *proud*	
insolent, arrogant, **b**	Rom 1:30
b pride of life	1 John 2:16
BOASTING *bragging*	
Where then is **b**	Rom 3:27
our **b** about you	2 Cor 9:3
all such **b** is evil	James 4:16
BOAT *watercraft*	
left the **b** and their	Matt 4:22
Peter got out of...**b**	Matt 14:29
filled both of the **b-s**	Luke 5:7
disciples into the **b**	John 6:22
BODY *corpse, flesh*	
lamp of the **b**	Matt 6:22
perfume upon My **b**	Matt 26:12
this is My **b**	Mark 14:22
did not find His **b**	Luke 24:23
b of sin...done away	Rom 6:6
redemption of our **b**	Rom 8:23
present your **b-ies**	Rom 12:1
b-ies are members	1 Cor 6:15
b is a temple	1 Cor 6:19
you are Christ's **b**	1 Cor 12:27
b to be burned	1 Cor 13:3
absent from the **b**	2 Cor 5:8
one **b** and one Spirit	Eph 4:4
building up of the **b**	Eph 4:12
wives as...own **b-ies**	Eph 5:28
transform the **b**	Phil 3:21
b be preserved	1 Thess 5:23
bore...sins in His **b**	1 Pet 2:24
BOLD *brave, fearless*	
I may not be **b**	2 Cor 10:2
I am just as **b** myself.	2 Cor 11:21
BOLDNESS *confidence*	
word of God with **b**	Acts 4:31
b and...access	Eph 3:12
with **b** the mystery	Eph 6:19
BOND *band, restraint*	
in the **b** of peace	Eph 4:3
eternal **b-s** under	Jude 6
BONDAGE *servitude, slavery*	
the **b** of iniquity	Acts 8:23
sold into **b** to sin	Rom 7:14
BOND-SERVANT *servant, slave*	
b-s of...Most High	Acts 16:17
Paul, a **b** of Christ	Rom 1:1
ourselves as your **b-s**	2 Cor 4:5
b...be quarrelsome	2 Tim 2:24
b of God...apostle	Titus 1:1
His **b-s**...serve Him	Rev 22:3
BONDSLAVE *servant, slave*	
state of His **b**	Luke 1:48
a **b** of Jesus Christ	Col 4:12
Urge **b-s** to be subject	Titus 2:9
use it as **b-s** of God	1 Pet 2:16
BONE	
dead men's **b-s**	Matt 23:27
Not a **b**...be broken	John 19:36
BOOK *scroll*	
not contain the **b-s**	John 21:25
names are in the **b**	Phil 4:3
worthy to open the **b**	Rev 5:2
Lamb's **b** of life	Rev 21:27
BOOK OF LIFE	
God's book with names of righteous	
	Phil 4:3; Rev 13:8;17:8;20:15
BOOTHS, FEAST OF	
see FEASTS	
BORN *brought into life*	
b King of the Jews	Matt 2:2
those **b** of women	Luke 7:28
b not of blood	John 1:13
unless one is **b** again	John 3:3
b of the Spirit	John 3:6
to one untimely **b**	1 Cor 15:8
b...to a living hope	1 Pet 1:3
loves is **b** of God	1 John 4:7
BORROW *use temporarily*	
wants to **b** from you	Matt 5:42
BOSOM *breast*	
to Abraham's **b**	Luke 16:22
the **b** of the Father	John 1:18

BOTHER *pester*	
you **b** the woman	Matt 26:10
worried and **b-ed**	Luke 10:41
this widow **b-s** me	Luke 18:5
BOTTOMLESS *without bottom*	
key of the **b** pit	Rev 9:1
he opened the **b** pit	Rev 9:2
BOUND (adj) *fastened, tied*	
on earth shall be **b** in heaven	Matt 16:19
A wife is as **b** as long	1 Cor 7:39
BOW (v) *bend, worship*	
He **b-ed** His head	John 19:30
every knee shall **b**	Rom 14:11
BOWELS *entrails, innards*	
b gushed out	Acts 1:18
BOWL *dish, jug*	
dips with Me in...**b**	Mark 14:20
b-s full of the wrath	Rev 15:7
BOX *container*	
as he had the money **b**	John 12:6
Judas had the...**b**	John 13:29
BOY *child, lad*	
b was cured at once	Matt 17:18
they took away the **b** alive	Acts 20:12
BRANCH *bough*	
birds...in its **b-es**	Luke 13:19
b-es of the palm	John 12:13
b...not bear fruit	John 15:2
you are the **b-es**	John 15:5
be holy, the **b-es**	Rom 11:16
BREAD *food*	
not live on **b** alone	Matt 4:4
Give us...daily **b**	Matt 6:11
gives you the true **b**	John 6:32
I am the **b** of life	John 6:35
BREAK *divide, shatter*	
waves were **b-ing**	Mark 4:37
she **broke** the vial	Mark 14:3
their nets *began* to **b**	Luke 5:6
b-ing the Sabbath	John 5:18
did not **b** His legs	John 19:33
your **b-ing** the Law	Rom 2:23
BREAST *bosom*	
b-s...never nursed	Luke 23:29
reclining on Jesus' **b**	John 13:23
girded about His **b**	Rev 1:13
BREASTPLATE *breast armor*	
b of faith and love	1 Thess 5:8
like **b-s** of iron	Rev 9:9
BREATH *air, spirit, wind*	
all life and **b** and all things	Acts 17:25
give **b** to the image	Rev 13:15
BREATHE *inhale and exhale*	
He **b-d** His last	Mark 15:39
He **b-d** on them	John 20:22
BRETHREN *brothers*	
b, why do you injure	Acts 7:26
sinning against...**b**	1 Cor 8:12
dangers...false **b**	2 Cor 11:26
Peace be to the **b**	Eph 6:23
faithful **b** in Christ	Col 1:2
the love of the **b**	1 Thess 4:9
b...not grow weary	2 Thess 3:13
my **b**, do not swear	James 5:12
our lives for the **b**	1 John 3:16
accuser of our **b**	Rev 12:10
BRIAR *thistle, thorn*	
grapes from a **b** bush	Luke 6:44
BRIDE *newlywed*	
He who has the **b**	John 3:29
b...of the Lamb	Rev 21:9
BRIDEGROOM *newlywed*	
attendants of the **b**	Matt 9:15
out to meet the **b**	Matt 25:1
BRIDLE (n) *head harness*	
up to the horses' **b-s**	Rev 14:20
BRIDLE (v) *control*	
not **b** his tongue	James 1:26
man, able to **b**	James 3:2
BRIGHT *shining*	
b cloud...them	Matt 17:5
b light...flashed	Acts 22:6
the **b** morning star	Rev 22:16
BRIMSTONE *sulfur*	
rained fire and **b**	Luke 17:29
tormented with...**b**	Rev 14:10
lake of fire and **b**	Rev 20:10
BRING *carry, lead*	
b-ing...a paralytic	Matt 9:2
not...to **b** peace	Matt 10:34
brought forth a son	Luke 1:57
I **b** you good news	Luke 2:10
Law **b-s** about wrath	Rom 4:15
b-ing salvation	Titus 2:11
BROAD *wide*	
way is...that leads to	Matt 7:13
they came up on the **b** plain	Rev 20:9

BROKEN *crushed, separated*	
Scripture...be **b**	John 10:35
Not a bone...**b**	John 19:36
Branches were **b** off	Rom 11:19
BRONZE *metal*	
His feet are like burnished **b**,	Rev 2:18
costly wood and **b**	Rev 18:12
BROOD *group, offspring*	
You **b** of vipers	Matt 3:7
hen *gathers* her **b**	Luke 13:34
BROTHER *male relative*	
reconciled to your **b**	Matt 5:24
b will deliver up **b**	Matt 10:21
behold, His...**b-s**	Matt 12:46
not forgive his **b**	Matt 18:35
My **b** and sister	Mark 3:35
b of yours was dead	Luke 15:32
left...wife or **b-s**	Luke 18:29
not even His **b-s**	John 7:5
b shall rise again	John 11:23
b goes to law with **b**	1 Cor 6:6
my **b** to stumble	1 Cor 8:13
yet hates his **b**	1 John 2:9
BROTHERHOOD	
love the **b**, fear god	1 Pet 2:17
BRUTAL *fierce, vicious*	
b, haters of good	2 Tim 3:3
BUFFET *beat*	
I **b** my body	1 Cor 9:27
Satan to **b** me	2 Cor 12:7
BUILD *construct, form*	
built his house upon	Matt 7:24
I will **b** My church	Matt 16:18
able to **b** you up	Acts 20:32
being **built** together	Eph 2:22
stones...being **built**	1 Pet 2:5
BUILDER *fashioner, maker*	
the **b-s** rejected	Matt 21:42
as a wise master **b**	1 Cor 3:10
architect and **b** is	Heb 11:10
BUILDING *structure*	
what wonderful **b-s**	Mark 13:1
you are...God's **b**	1 Cor 3:9
have a **b** from God	2 Cor 5:1
whole **b**, being fitted	Eph 2:21
BULL *animal*	
blood of **b-s** and	Heb 10:4
BUNDLE *package*	
in **b-s** to burn	Matt 13:30
Paul had gathered a **b**	Acts 28:3
BURDEN (n) *load, weight*	
b-s hard to bear	Luke 11:46
Bear one another's **b-s**	Gal 6:2
BURDEN (v) *weigh down*	
were **b-ed** excessively	2 Cor 1:8
not **b** you myself	2 Cor 12:16
the church be **b-ed**	1 Tim 5:16
BURIAL *interment*	
to prepare Me for **b**	Matt 26:12
b custom of the Jews	John 19:40
BURN (v) *consume, kindle*	
will **b** up the chaff	Luke 3:17
b-ed in their desire	Rom 1:27
my body to be **b-ed**	1 Cor 13:3
works will be **b-ed**	2 Pet 3:10
lake of fire...**b-s**	Rev 19:20
BURNISHED *polished*	
feet...like **b** bronze	Rev 1:15
BURNT OFFERINGS	
see OFFERINGS	
BURST *break*	
wine will **b** the skins	Luke 5:37
b his fetters	Luke 8:29
he **b** open	Acts 1:18
BURY *place in earth*	
go and **b** my father	Matt 8:21
dead to **b** their own	Matt 8:22
devout...**b-ied** Stephen	Acts 8:2
that He was **b-ied**	1 Cor 15:4
b-ied...in baptism	Col 2:12
BUSINESS *occupation, work*	
another to his **b**	Matt 22:5
attend to your...**b**	1 Thess 4:11
engage in **b**	James 4:13
BUSYBODIES *meddlers*	
no work...like **b**	2 Thess 3:11
gossips and **b**	1 Tim 5:13
BYSTANDERS *onlookers*	
b...said to Peter	Matt 26:73
the **b** heard it	Mark 15:35

C

CAESAR
1 *Roman emperor*
    Matt 22:17,21; Mark 12:14; John 19:12
2 *Augustus*   Luke 2:1
3 *Tiberius*   Luke 3:1; John 19:12
4 *Claudius*   Acts 11:28;17:7;18:2
5 *Nero*   Acts 25:12;26:32; Phil 4:22

CAESAREA
Roman coastal city   Acts 8:40;10:1;21:16;25:4
CAESAREA PHILIPPI
city at base of Mt. Hermon
          Matt 16:13; Mark 8:27
CAIAPHAS
high priest
      Matt 26:57; Luke 3:2; John 11:49ff;
                  Acts 4:6
CAIN
son of Adam
      Heb 11:4; 1 John 3:12; Jude 1:11
CALCULATE *count*
c the cost   Luke 14:28
c the...beast   Rev 13:18
CALF *animal*
bring the fattened c   Luke 15:23
blood of...c-ves   Heb 9:12
CALL *address, summon, name*
who is c-ed Christ   Matt 1:16
to c the righteous   Matt 9:13
c-s his own sheep   John 10:3
c Me Teacher and   John 13:13
God has not c-ed   1 Thess 4:7
c-s...a prophetess   Rev 2:20
CALLING *summoning*
the c of God   Rom 11:29
For consider your c   1 Cor 1:26
with a holy c   2 Tim 1:9
His c and choosing   2 Pet 1:10
CALM *still*
it became perfectly c   Matt 8:26
you ought to keep c   Acts 19:36
CAMEL *animal*
a garment of c-'s hair   Matt 3:4
c...eye of a needle   Matt 19:24
clothed with c-'s hair   Mark 1:6
CAMP (n) *lodging area*
are burned outside the c   Heb 13:11
the c of the saints   Rev 20:9
CANA
Galilean town
          John 2:1,11;4:46
CANAAN
Syro-Palestine   Acts 7:11;13:19
CAPERNAUM
city on Sea of Galilee
  Matt 4:13; Luke 4:23; John 6:24,59
CAPPADOCIA
province in Asia Minor   Acts 2:9; 1 Pet 1:1
CAPTAIN *leader*
the c of the temple *guard*   Acts 5:24
the c of the ship   Acts 27:11
CAPTIVE *prisoner*
release to the c-s   Luke 4:18
every thought c   2 Cor 10:5
having been held c   2 Tim 2:26
CAPTIVITY *imprisonment*
destined for c   Rev 13:10
to c he goes; if   Rev 13:10
CARE (n) *concern*
friends and receive c   Acts 27:3
c for one another   1 Cor 12:25
CARE (v) *have concern for*
and took c of him   Luke 10:34
take c of the church   1 Tim 3:5
he c-s for you   1 Pet 5:7
CAREFUL *watchful, on guard*
make c search for the Child   Matt 2:8
be c how you walk   Eph 5:15
CARELESS *thoughtless*
that every c word   Matt 12:36
CARGO *merchandise*
to unload its c   Acts 21:3
no one buys...c-es   Rev 18:11
CARPENTER *craftsman*
this the c-'s son   Matt 13:55
c, the son of Mary   Mark 6:3
CARRY *bear*
c-ied away...diseases   Matt 8:17
C no purse, no bag   Luke 10:4
the cross to c   Luke 23:26
c out the desire of   Gal 5:16
CAST *throw*
c-ing...insult   Mark 15:32
will c out demons   Mark 16:17
c Him out of...city   Luke 4:29
c fire upon...earth   Luke 12:49
clothing they c lots   John 19:24
c-ing all your anxiety   1 Pet 5:7
but c them into hell   2 Pet 2:4
c their crowns before   Rev 4:10
CATCH *seize, trap*
will be c-ing men   Luke 5:10
unable to c Him   Luke 20:26
caught in adultery   John 8:3
who c-es the wise   1 Cor 3:19
if a man is **caught**   Gal 6:1
child was **caught** up   Rev 12:5

CAUSE (n) *purpose, reason*
c a man shall leave   Matt 19:5
hated...without a c   John 15:25
CAUSE (v) *make*
who c dissensions   Rom 16:17
was c-ing the growth   1 Cor 3:6
CAVE *shelter*
mountains and c-s   Heb 11:38
hid...in the c-s   Rev 6:15
CEASE *stop*
c-d to kiss My feet   Luke 7:45
tongues, they will c   1 Cor 13:8
pray without c-ing   1 Thess 5:17
CENSER *incense container*
holding a golden c   Rev 8:3
angel took the c   Rev 8:5
CENSUS *population roll*
the first c taken   Luke 2:2
in the days of the c   Acts 5:37
CENT *money*
paid up the last c   Matt 5:26
sparrows...for a c   Matt 10:29
amount to a c   Mark 12:42
CENTURION *captain*
Jesus said to the c   Matt 8:13
summoning the c   Mark 15:44
soldiers and c-s   Acts 21:32
gave orders to the c   Acts 24:23
CEPHAS
apostle Peter
      John 1:42; 1 Cor 1:12;15:5; Gal 2:11
CERTAINTY *sureness*
you know with c   Eph 5:5
CERTIFICATE *permit, record*
a c of divorce   Matt 5:31
c of debt   Col 2:14
CHAFF *husk*
burn up the c   Matt 3:12; Luke 3:17
CHAIN *band*
was bound with c-s   Luke 8:29
c-s fell off his hands   Acts 12:7
great c in his hand   Rev 20:1
CHANGE (n) *alteration*
a c of law   Heb 7:12
CHANGE (v) *alter, transform*
shall all be c-d   1 Cor 15:51
And will not c His mind   Heb 7:21
CHARACTER
and proven c, hope   Rom 5:4
Let your c be free   Heb 13:5
CHARGE (n) *responsibility*
c of his household   Matt 24:45
allotted to your c   1 Pet 5:3
CHARGE (n) *accusation*
bring c-s against   Acts 19:38
c against God's elect   Rom 8:33
CHARGE (n) *cost*
gospel without c   1 Cor 9:18
to you without c   2 Cor 11:7
CHARGE (v) *command*
c-d against this generation   Luke 11:50
I solemnly c you   1 Tim 5:21
CHARGE (v) *exact a price*
c that to my account   Philem 18
CHARIOT *wagon*
and sitting in his c   Acts 8:28
like the sound of c-s   Rev 9:9
CHARITY *alms*
give that...as c   Luke 11:41
and give to c   Luke 12:33
deeds of...c   Acts 9:36
CHASTE *pure*
c...behavior   1 Pet 3:2
kept themselves c   Rev 14:4
CHATTER *babbling*
worldly...empty c   1 Tim 6:20
avoid...empty c   2 Tim 2:16
CHEEK *part of face*
slaps you on your right c   Matt 5:39
hits you on the c   Luke 6:29
CHEERFUL
God loves a c giver   2 Cor 9:7
Is anyone c   James 5:13
CHERISH *love*
men c themselves   Acts 24:15
c-es it, just as Christ   Eph 5:29
CHIEF *head, prominent*
c priests *began* to accuse   Mark 15:3
C Shepherd appears   1 Pet 5:4
CHILD
with c by the Holy   Matt 1:18
take the C and His   Matt 2:13
He called a c to   Matt 18:2
saying, C, arise   Luke 8:54
a woman with c   1 Thess 5:3
CHILDBIRTH
suffers the pains of c   Rom 8:22
CHILDLESS
and died c   Luke 20:29

CHILDREN
slew all the male c   Matt 2:16
stones to raise up c   Matt 3:9
c...against parents   Matt 10:21
and become like c   Matt 18:3
bringing c to Him   Mark 10:13
if c, heirs   Rom 8:17
C, obey your parents   Eph 6:1
My little c   1 John 2:1
kill her c with   Rev 2:23
CHOICE *option or best*
God made a c among   Acts 15:7
God's gracious c   Rom 11:5
His c of you   1 Thess 1:4
CHOKE *stifle*
riches c the word   Matt 13:22
began to c him   Matt 18:28
thorns...c-d it   Mark 4:7
c-d with worries   Luke 8:14
CHOOSE *select, take*
You did not c Me   John 15:16
not God c the poor   James 2:5
CHOSE *selected*
c twelve of them   Luke 6:13
has c-n the weak   1 Cor 1:27
He c us in Him   Eph 1:4
CHOSEN *elected, selected*
My Son, *My* C One   Luke 9:35
c of God, holy and   Col 3:12
of *His* c angels   1 Tim 5:21
you are a c race   1 Pet 2:9
CHRIST *Messiah*
birth of Jesus C was   Matt 1:18
C should suffer and   Luke 24:46
both Lord and C   Acts 2:36
fellow heirs with C   Rom 8:17
are one body in C   Rom 12:5
preach C crucified   1 Cor 1:23
judgment seat of C   2 Cor 5:10
ambassadors for C   2 Cor 5:20
faith in C Jesus   Gal 2:16
as sons through Jesus C   Eph 1:5
to live is C   Phil 1:21
C, who is our life   Col 3:4
dead in C shall   1 Thess 4:16
coming of...C   2 Thess 2:1
C...high priest   Heb 9:11
Advocate...Jesus C   1 John 2:1
with C for a thousand   Rev 20:4
CHRISTIAN *follower of Christ*
first called C-s in   Acts 11:26
me to become a C   Acts 26:28
suffers as a C   1 Pet 4:16
CHURCH *a called out assembly*
I will build my c   Matt 16:18
tell it to the c   Matt 18:17
shepherd the c   Acts 20:28
c-es of the Gentiles   Rom 16:4
together as a c   1 Cor 11:18
woman...speak in c   1 Cor 14:35
to the c-es of Judea   Gal 1:22
Christ...head of the c   Eph 5:23
persecutor of the c   Phil 3:6
c of the living God   1 Tim 3:15
Spirit says to the c-es   Rev 2:11
CILICIA
region in SE Asia Minor Acts 15:41;21:39;27:5
CINNAMON *spice*
and c and spice   Rev 18:13
CIRCUMCISE *be pure or cut off*
came to c the child   Luke 1:59
c-d the eighth day   Phil 3:5
CIRCUMCISION *act of purity*
c is...of the heart   Rom 2:29
if you receive c   Gal 5:2
if I still preach c   Gal 5:11
we are the *true* c   Phil 3:3
c made without hands   Col 2:11
those of the c   Titus 1:10
CIRCUMSTANCE *condition*
may know...my c-s   Eph 6:21
peace in every c   2 Thess 3:16
of humble c-s   James 1:9
CITIZEN *resident*
c-s hated him   Luke 19:14
c of no insignificant   Acts 21:39
fellow c-s with the   Eph 2:19
CITY
a c called Nazareth   Matt 2:23
into the holy c   Matt 4:5
the c was stirred   Matt 21:10
c, shake off the dust   Luke 9:5
c, has prepared a c   Heb 11:16
I saw the holy c   Rev 21:2
CLAIM *demand*
c-ing to be someone   Acts 8:9
making a c to godliness   1 Tim 2:10
CLAUDIA
Roman Christian   2 Tim 4:21

CLAUDIUS
Roman Emperor Acts 11:28;18:2
see CAESAR
CLAUDIUS LYSIAS
Roman tribune Acts 23:26
CLAY
the c to his eyes John 9:6
have a right over the c Rom 9:21
CLEAN *cleansed, washed*
You can make me c Matt 8:2
things are c for you Luke 11:41
c because of the word John 15:3
CLEANSE *purify, wash*
I am willing; be c-d Matt 8:3
the lepers are c-d Matt 11:5
not eat unless they c Mark 7:4
let us c ourselves 2 Cor 7:1
C…you sinners James 4:8
blood…c-s us 1 John 1:7
CLEAR *make free or plain*
c His threshing floor Matt 3:12
Christ had made c 2 Pet 1:14
river…c as crystal Rev 22:1
CLEAVE *cling, divide*
shall c to his wife Eph 5:31
CLEOPAS
disciple of Christ Luke 24:18
CLEVER *smart*
cleverness of the c 1 Cor 1:19
CLIMB *ascend*
c-ed…a sycamore Luke 19:4
c-s up…other way John 10:1
CLING *cleave*
Stop c-ing to Me John 20:17
c to what is good Rom 12:9
CLOAK *coat, mantle*
fringe of His c Matt 9:20
Wrap your c around Acts 12:8
CLOSE *shut, stop*
have c-d their eyes Acts 28:27
every mouth…c-d Rom 3:19
c-s his heart 1 John 3:17
CLOTH *fabric*
unshrunk c on an old Matt 9:16
in the linen c Mark 15:46
CLOTHE *array, dress*
naked…you c-d Me Matt 25:36
are splendidly c-d Luke 7:25
c-d with power Luke 24:49
c…with humility 1 Pet 5:5
c-d in the white robes Rev 7:13
CLOTHES *garments*
without wedding c Matt 22:12
And tearing his c Mark 14:63
CLOTHING *clothes, raiment*
and the body than c Matt 6:25
in sheep's c Matt 7:15
His c *became* white Luke 9:29
sister is without c James 2:15
CLOUD *mist*
voice came out…c Mark 9:7
Son…coming in c-s Mark 13:26
in a c with power Luke 21:27
and a c received Him Acts 1:9
CLUB *weapon*
with swords and c-s Matt 26:47
c-s as against a robber Luke 22:52
CLUSTER *collection*
gather the c Rev 14:18
COAL *charcoal*
heap burning c-s Rom 12:20
COAST
along the c of Asia Acts 27:2
COAT *cloak*
have your c also Matt 5:40
takes away your c Luke 6:29
COCK *bird*
before a c crows Matt 26:34
c shall not crow John 13:38
COFFIN *bier*
and touched the c Luke 7:14
COHORT *military unit*
the whole *Roman* c Matt 27:27
called the Italian c Acts 10:1
of the Augustan c Acts 27:1
COIN *money*
Show Me the c Matt 22:19
woman…loses one c Luke 15:8
He poured out…c-s John 2:15
COLD *cool*
cup of c water Matt 10:42
love will grow c Matt 24:12
neither c nor hot Rev 3:15
COLLECT *exact, take*
C no more than Luke 3:13
c-ed a tenth from Heb 7:6
COLLECTION *acquisition*
no c-s be made 1 Cor 16:2

COLOSSAE
city in Asia Minor Col 1:2
COLT *foal*
and a c with her Matt 21:2
on a donkey's c John 12:15
COME
Thy kingdom c Matt 6:10
C to Me, all who Matt 11:28
children to c to Me Mark 10:14
not c…temptation Mark 14:38
Son of Man c-ing Luke 21:27
Father…hour has c John 17:1
His judgment has c Rev 14:7
I am c-ing quickly Rev 22:20
COMFORT (n) *consolation*
c of the Holy Spirit Acts 9:31
and God of all c 2 Cor 1:3
your c and salvation 2 Cor 1:6
COMFORT (v) *console, cheer*
he is being c-ed Luke 16:25
c one another 1 Thess 4:18
COMING (n) *arrival*
be the sign of Your c Matt 24:3
c of the Son of Man Matt 24:37
Christ's at His c 1 Cor 15:23
c of the Lord is James 5:8
the promise of His c 2 Pet 3:4
COMMAND (n) *order*
no c of the Lord 1 Cor 7:25
could not bear the c Heb 12:20
COMMAND (v) *declare, order*
the angel…c-ed Matt 1:24
c that these stones Matt 4:3
c-s even the winds Luke 8:25
c-ing the jailer Acts 16:23
COMMANDER *captain, general*
to the c of the Acts 21:31
and the flesh of c-s Rev 19:18
COMMANDMENT *instruction*
which is the great c Matt 22:36
A new c I give John 13:34
will keep My c-s John 14:15
I have kept…c-s John 15:10
not writing a new c 1 John 2:7
keep the c-s of God Rev 14:12
COMMEND *praise, present*
I c you to God Acts 20:32
food will not c us 1 Cor 8:8
to c ourselves again 2 Cor 3:1
COMMIT *entrust, practice*
Do not c adultery Luke 18:20
I c My spirit Luke 23:46
everyone who c-s sin John 8:34
who c-ted no sin 1 Pet 2:22
COMMON *ordinary, shared*
had all things in c Acts 2:44
about our c salvation Jude 3
COMMONWEALTH *nation*
from the c of Israel Eph 2:12
COMMOTION *disturbance*
Why make a c and Mark 5:39
COMPANION *comrade, friend*
he and his c-s Matt 12:3
Paul and his c-s Acts 13:13
COMPANY *assembly, group*
your c for a while Rom 15:24
Bad c corrupts 1 Cor 15:33
COMPARE *contrast, like*
to what shall I c Matt 11:16
c the kingdom of Luke 13:20
be c-d with the glory Rom 8:18
COMPASSION *concern, love*
He felt c for them Matt 9:36
his father…felt c Luke 15:20
put on a heart of c Col 3:12
Lord is full of c James 5:11
COMPEL *force, press*
c them to come in Luke 14:23
c…to be circumcised Gal 6:12
COMPETE *strive*
everyone who c-s 1 Cor 9:25
c-s as an athlete 2 Tim 2:5
COMPLAIN *murmur*
Do not c, brethren James 5:9
COMPLAINT *grumbling*
a c against anyone Col 3:13
hospitable…without c 1 Pet 4:9
COMPLETE (adj) *full, total*
you have been made c Col 2:10
be perfect and c James 1:4
joy may be made c 1 John 1:4
COMPLETE (v) *finish, fulfill*
were c-d for her Luke 2:6
thousand years are c-d Rev 20:7
COMPOSE *write*
The first account I c-d Acts 1:1
COMPREHEND *understand*
and they did not c Luke 18:34
darkness did not c John 1:5

COMPULSION *coercion*
as it were by c Philem 14
not under c, but 1 Pet 5:2
CONCEAL *cover, hide*
was c-ed from them Luke 9:45
cannot be c-ed 1 Tim 5:25
CONCEIT *pride*
selfishness or empty c Phil 2:3
he is c-ed 1 Tim 6:4
c-ed, lovers of 2 Tim 3:4
CONCEIVE *become pregnant*
will c in your womb Luke 1:31
when lust has c-d James 1:15
CONCERN *have care*
c-ed about the poor John 12:6
is married is c-ed 1 Cor 7:33
not c-ed about oxen 1 Cor 9:9
CONDEMN *discredit, judge*
will c Him to death Mark 10:33
do not c, and you Luke 6:37
you c yourself Rom 2:1
he stood c-ed Gal 2:11
our heart c-s us 1 John 3:20
CONDEMNATION *judgment*
receive greater c Mark 12:40
same sentence of c Luke 23:40
Their c is just Rom 3:8
no c…in Christ Rom 8:1
c upon themselves Rom 13:2
c…by the devil 1 Tim 3:6
CONDITION *state, stipulation*
c in which…called 1 Cor 7:20
or adds c-s to it Gal 3:15
CONDUCT (n) *behavior*
sensual c of…men 2 Pet 2:7
holy c and godliness 2 Pet 3:11
CONDUCT (v) *behave*
c…same spirit 2 Cor 12:18
C…with wisdom Col 4:5
c yourselves in fear 1 Pet 1:17
CONFESS *acknowledge*
c Me before men Matt 10:32
c-ing their sins Mark 1:5
c with your mouth Rom 10:9
If we c our sins 1 John 1:9
I will c his name Rev 3:5
CONFESSION *admission*
your c of the gospel 2 Cor 9:13
testified the good c 1 Tim 6:13
the c of our hope Heb 10:23
CONFIDENCE *boldness, trust*
proud c is this 2 Cor 1:12
c in me may abound Phil 1:26
no c in the flesh Phil 3:3
CONFIRM *establish, strengthen*
c-ed…by the signs Mark 16:20
who shall also c you 1 Cor 1:8
CONFIRMATION *verification*
and c of the gospel Phil 1:7
an oath *given* as c Heb 6:16
CONFLICT *contention*
experiencing…c Phil 1:30
source of…c-s James 4:1
CONFORMED *being like*
c…image of His Son Rom 8:29
not be c to…world Rom 12:2
being c to His death Phil 3:10
CONFOUND *confuse*
c-ing the Jews Acts 9:22
CONFRONT *challenge, face*
the elders c-ed Him Luke 20:1
CONFUSION *disorder*
Jerusalem was in c Acts 21:31
not *a* God *of* c 1 Cor 14:33
CONGREGATION *assembly*
the c of the disciples Acts 6:2
In the midst of the c Heb 2:12
CONQUER *be victorious*
c through Him Rom 8:37
out c-ing, and to c Rev 6:2
CONSCIENCE *moral obligation*
always a blameless c Acts 24:16
also for c' sake Rom 13:5
their c being weak is 1 Cor 8:7
faith with a clear c 1 Tim 3:9
seared in their own c 1 Tim 4:2
keep a good c 1 Pet 3:16
CONSECRATED (adj) *sanctified*
ate the c bread Matt 12:4
CONSENT *agree*
c-s to live with him 1 Cor 7:12
without your c Philem 14
CONSIDER *observe, think*
C the ravens, for Luke 12:24
c your calling 1 Cor 1:26
He c-ed me faithful 1 Tim 1:12
c how to stimulate Heb 10:24
c-ed…God is able Heb 11:19

CONSIST *composed of*
life c of his	Luke 12:15
does not c in words	1 Cor 4:20
c-ing of decrees	Col 2:14

CONSOLATION *comfort*
for the c of Israel	Luke 2:25
is any c of love	Phil 2:1

CONSOLE *soothe*
c them concerning	John 11:19

CONSTRUCTION *structure*
the c of the ark	1 Pet 3:20

CONSULT *confer*
not…c with flesh	Gal 1:16

CONSUME *destroy, devour*
Zeal…will c	John 2:17
c your flesh like fire	James 5:3

CONSUMING (adj) *destroying*
our God is a c fire	Heb 12:29

CONTAIN *hold*
c-ing twenty…gallons	John 2:6
not c the books	John 21:25
is c-ed in Scripture	1 Pet 2:6

CONTEMPT *scorn*
treating Him with c	Luke 23:11
your brother with c	Rom 14:10

CONTEND *strive*
c…for the faith	Jude 3

CONTENT *satisfied*
c with your wages	Luke 3:14
c with weaknesses	2 Cor 12:10
have learned to be c	Phil 4:11
c with what you have	Heb 13:5

CONTENTIOUS *quarrelsome*
inclined to be c	1 Cor 11:16

CONTINUE *persevere, persist*
c in the grace of	Acts 13:43
Are we to c in sin	Rom 6:1
you c in the faith	Col 1:23
love of the brethren c	Heb 13:1

CONTRARY *against*
for the wind was c	Matt 14:24
grafted c to nature	Rom 11:24
c to the teaching	Rom 16:17
a gospel c to that	Gal 1:8
c to sound teaching	1 Tim 1:10

CONTRIBUTE *give*
c-ing to their support	Luke 8:3
c-ing to…the saints	Rom 12:13

CONTRIBUTION *gift, offering*
a c for the poor	Rom 15:26
liberality of your c	2 Cor 9:13

CONTROL (n) *order, rule*
was it not under…c	Acts 5:4
children under c	1 Tim 3:4

CONTROVERSY *dispute*
interest in c-ial questions	1 Tim 6:4
shun foolish c-ies	Titus 3:9

CONVERSE *discuss*
they were c-ing	Luke 24:15
Stoic…were c-ing	Acts 17:18
and c with him	Acts 24:26

CONVERSION *change*
c of the Gentiles	Acts 15:3

CONVERTED *changed*
unless you are c	Matt 18:3
perceive…and be c	John 12:40

CONVICT *condemn, judge*
one of you c-s Me	John 8:46
c…concerning sin	John 16:8
he is c-ed by all	1 Cor 14:24
to c all the ungodly	Jude 15

CONVINCED *persuaded*
c that John was a	Luke 20:6
c that neither death	Rom 8:38
c in the Lord Jesus	Rom 14:14
c of better things	Heb 6:9

CONVULSION *paroxysm*
threw him into a c	Mark 9:20
a c with foaming	Luke 9:39

COPPER *metal*
not acquire…c	Matt 10:9
widow…c coins	Luke 21:2

COPY *facsimile*
a c and shadow	Heb 8:5
mere c of the true	Heb 9:24

CORBAN *offering*
C (that is…)	Mark 7:11

CORD *band, rope*
a scourge of c-s	John 2:15

CORINTH
city in Greece
N.T. church site	Acts 18:1
	1 Cor 1:1,2

CORNELIUS
centurion, believer
	Acts 10:1ff

CORNER *angle, intersection*
on the street c-s	Matt 6:5
the chief c stone	Mark 12:10
four c-s of the earth	Rev 7:1

CORPSE *dead body*
boy…like a c	Mark 9:26

CORRECT *reprove*
gentleness c-ing	2 Tim 2:25

CORRECTION *improvement*
for reproof, for c	2 Tim 3:16

CORRUPT (v) *make evil*
Bad company c-s	1 Cor 15:33
harlot who was c-ing	Rev 19:2

CORRUPTION *decay, evil*
from the flesh reap c	Gal 6:8
c that is in the world	2 Pet 1:4
slaves of c	2 Pet 2:19

COST *expense, price*
calculate the c	Luke 14:28
water…without c	Rev 22:6

COSTLY *expensive*
vial of…c perfume	Mark 14:3
pearls or c garments	1 Tim 2:9

COUNCIL *assembly*
to their c chamber	Luke 22:66
conferred with his c	Acts 25:12

COUNCIL
Sanhedrin
	Matt 26:59
Jewish governing body
	Mark 15:1,43; Luke 23:50

COUNSEL (n) *advice, opinion*
chief priests took c	John 12:10
the c of His will	Eph 1:11

COUNSELOR *adviser*
who became His c	Rom 11:34

COUNT *consider, number*
was c-ed among us	Acts 1:17
I c all…loss	Phil 3:8
as some c slowness	2 Pet 3:9

COUNTRY *land, region*
prophet has no honor…c	John 4:44
they are seeking a c	Heb 11:14

COUNTRYMAN
my fellow c-men and	Rom 11:14
hands of your own c-men	1 Thess 2:14

COURAGE *heart, valor*
Take c, My son	Matt 9:2
Take c, it is I	Matt 14:27
c; I have overcome	John 16:33
we are of good c	2 Cor 5:8

COURAGEOUS *brave*
I purpose to be c	2 Cor 10:2

COURSE *area, extent, way*
I have finished the c	2 Tim 4:7
the c of our life	James 3:6

COURT *area, hall, tribunal*
then you have law c-s	1 Cor 6:4
drag you into c	James 2:6

COURTYARD *compound*
c of the high priest	Matt 26:58
Peter…in the c	Mark 14:66

COVENANT *agreement*
cup…is the new c	Luke 22:20
c which God made	Acts 3:25
this is My c with	Rom 11:27
servants of a new c	2 Cor 3:6
strangers to the c-s	Eph 2:12
guarantee…better c	Heb 7:22
blood of the…c	Heb 13:20
ark of His c	Rev 11:19

COVER (v) *hide, protest*
to the hills, C us	Luke 23:30
c a multitude of sins	James 5:20
love c-s a multitude	1 Pet 4:8

COVERING *canopy*
given to her for a c	1 Cor 11:15
freedom as a c	1 Pet 2:16

COVET *crave, desire*
c-ed no one's silver	Acts 20:33
You shall not c	Rom 7:7

COVETOUS *desirous*
the c and swindlers	1 Cor 5:10
c, nor drunkards	1 Cor 6:10

CRAFTINESS *shrewdness*
the wise in their c	1 Cor 3:19
not walking in c	2 Cor 4:2
by c in deceitful	Eph 4:14

CRAFTSMAN *artisan*
business to…c-men	Acts 19:24
c of any craft will	Rev 18:22

CRAVE *covet, desire*
generation c-s for	Matt 12:39
should not c evil	1 Cor 10:6

CRAWLING *creeping*
beasts and the c	Acts 11:6
and c creatures	Rom 1:23

CREATE *form, make*
c-d…for good works	Eph 2:10
c-d in righteousness	Eph 4:24
Thou didst c all	Rev 4:11

CREATION
beginning of c	Mark 10:6
preach…to all c	Mark 16:15

whole c groans	Rom 8:22
beginning of c	2 Pet 3:4

CREATOR *Maker*
rather than the C	Rom 1:25
to a faithful C	1 Pet 4:19

CREATURE *created being*
and crawling c-s	Rom 1:23
in Christ…new c	2 Cor 5:17
as c-s of instinct	2 Pet 2:12

CRETANS
inhabitants of Crete	Acts 2:11; Titus 1:12

CRETE
Mediterranean island	Acts 27:7,21; Titus 1:5

CRIME *vice*
not of such c-s	Acts 25:18

CRIMINAL *lawbreaker*
crucified…the c-s	Luke 23:33
imprisonment as a c	2 Tim 2:9

CRIPPLED *lame*
enter life c or lame	Matt 18:8
bring…c and blind	Luke 14:21

CRISPUS
Corinthian Christian
	Acts 18:8; 1 Cor 1:14

CROOKED *evil, twisted*
make c the straight	Acts 13:10
c and perverse	Phil 2:15

CROP *yield of produce*
and yielded a c	Matt 13:8
share of the c-s	2 Tim 2:6

CROSS (n) *execution device*
take his c and	Matt 10:38
down from the c	Matt 27:40
to bear His c	Mark 15:21
take up his c daily	Luke 9:23
standing by the c	John 19:25
hanging Him on a c	Acts 5:30
c of Christ should	1 Cor 1:17
word of the c is	1 Cor 1:18
boast, except in the c	Gal 6:14
even death on a c	Phil 2:8
enemies of the c	Phil 3:18
blood of His c	Col 1:20
endured the c	Heb 12:2

CROSS (v) *pass over*
Jesus had c-ed over	Mark 5:21
c-ing over to	Acts 21:2

CROWD *multitude*
because of the c	Mark 2:4
c of tax-gatherers	Luke 5:29
they stirred up the c	Acts 17:8

CROWN (n) *royal emblem or top*
a c of thorns	Matt 27:29
receive the c of life	James 1:12
c-s before the throne	Rev 4:10
golden c on His head	Rev 14:14

CROWN (v) *to place crown on*
c-ed him with glory	Heb 2:7

CRUCIFY *to execute on a cross*
scourge and c-ied	Matt 20:19
Let Him be c-ied	Matt 27:22
Jesus…been c-ied	Matt 28:5
c your King	John 19:15
Paul was not c-ied	1 Cor 1:13
preach Christ c-ied	1 Cor 1:23
not have c-ied the	1 Cor 2:8
c-ied with Christ	Gal 2:20
world…c-ied to me	Gal 6:14
their Lord was c-ied	Rev 11:8

CRUMBS *morsels*
dogs feed on the c	Matt 15:27
on the children's c	Mark 7:28

CRUSH *demolish, destroy*
c Satan under…feet	Rom 16:20

CRY (n) *scream, sob*
Jesus uttered a…c	Mark 15:37

CRY (v)
His elect, who c	Luke 18:7
stones will c out	Luke 19:40
Jesus stood and c-ied	John 7:37

CRYSTAL *glass*
sea of glass like c	Rev 4:6
water…clear as c	Rev 22:1

CUBIT *linear measure*
add a single c to	Matt 6:27

CUMMIN *plant for seasoning*
mint and dill and c	Matt 23:23

CUP *container*
c of cold water	Matt 10:42
let this c pass	Matt 26:39
washing of c-s and	Mark 7:4
gives you a c of	Mark 9:41
c…new covenant	Luke 22:20
c of blessing	1 Cor 10:16
eat…drink the c	1 Cor 11:26
c full of abominations	Rev 17:4

CURE *heal*
they could not c him	Matt 17:16
that…time He c-d	Luke 7:21

CURSE (n) *condemning oath*
become a c for us — Gal 3:13
no longer be any c — Rev 22:3
CURSE (v) *verbally condemn*
began to c and — Mark 14:71
bless and c not — Rom 12:14
with it we c men — James 3:9
CURSED (adj) *under a curse*
C...who hangs — Gal 3:13
CUSTODY *prison, protection*
John...taken into c — Matt 4:12
holding Jesus in c — Luke 22:63
CUSTOM *manner or tax*
c, He entered the — Luke 4:16
burial c of the Jews — John 19:40
c-s...not lawful — Acts 16:21
c-s of our fathers — Acts 28:17
whom tax *is due*; c — Rom 13:7
CUT *destroy, divide*
were c-ting branches — Matt 21:8
and c off his ear — Matt 26:51
were c to the quick — Acts 7:54
you...will be c off — Rom 11:22
CYMBAL *musical instrument*
or a clanging c — 1 Cor 13:1
CYPRUS
Mediterranean island — Acts 11:19;15:39;21:16
CYRENE
NW African port
Mark 15:21; Luke 23:26; Acts 2:10;11:20

D

DAMAGE (n) *destruction*
d and great loss — Acts 27:10
incurred this d and — Acts 27:21
DAMASCUS
city of Aram (Syria) — Acts 9:3,27;26:20
DANCE (n) *rhythmic movement*
music and d-ing — Luke 15:25
DANCE (v) *move rhythmically*
Herodias d-d before — Matt 14:6
DANGER *peril*
not only is there d — Acts 19:27
often in d of death — 2 Cor 11:23
d-s from...Gentiles — 2 Cor 11:26
DARE *presume, risk*
d from that day — Matt 22:46
did not d pronounce — Jude 9
DARK *dim, shadow*
it was still d — John 20:1
shining in a d place — 2 Pet 1:19
DARKEN *obscure*
sun will be d-ed — Mark 13:24
their eyes be d-ed — Rom 11:10
DARKNESS *gloom, shadow*
into the outer d — Matt 22:13
those who sit in d — Luke 1:79
men loved the d — John 3:19
turn from d to light — Acts 26:18
has light with d — 2 Cor 6:14
unfruitful deeds of d — Eph 5:11
in Him there is no d — 1 John 1:5
brother is in the d — 1 John 2:9
DAUGHTER
loves son or d more — Matt 10:37
mother against d — Luke 12:53
DAVID *king of Israel*
Jesus Christ, the son of D — Matt 1:1
the Root of D — Rev 5:5
DAWN (v) *become light*
a light d-ed — Matt 4:16
d toward the first — Matt 28:1
until the day d-s — 2 Pet 1:19
DAY *light*
Give us this d — Matt 6:11
raise...the last d — John 6:39
judge...the last d — John 12:48
the d of salvation — 2 Cor 6:2
perfect it until the d — Phil 1:6
d of the Lord — 1 Thess 5:2
d is as a thousand — 2 Pet 3:8
tormented d...night — Rev 20:10
DAZZLING *blinding, bright*
near...in d apparel — Luke 24:4
DEACONS *officer, server*
overseers and d — Phil 1:1
D likewise *must be* — 1 Tim 3:8
let them serve as d — 1 Tim 3:10
Let d be husbands — 1 Tim 3:12
served well as d — 1 Tim 3:13
DEAD *without life*
rising from the d — Mark 9:10
d shall hear the — John 5:25
resurrection of the d — Acts 23:6
d in your trespasses — Eph 2:1
first-born from the d — Col 1:18
living and the d — 2 Tim 4:1
repentance...d works — Heb 6:1
to those who are d — 1 Pet 4:6
I was d...I am alive — Rev 1:18

Hades gave up the d — Rev 20:13
DEAF *without hearing*
and *the* d hear — Matt 11:5
the d to hear — Mark 7:37
d and dumb spirit — Mark 9:25
DEAL *allot, barter, treat*
has d-t with me — Luke 1:25
he can d gently — Heb 5:2
DEALINGS *actions, relations*
no d with Samaritans — John 4:9
of the Lord's d — James 5:11
DEAR *beloved*
my life...as d to — Acts 20:24
had become very d — 1 Thess 2:8
DEATH *cessation of life*
let him be put to d — Matt 15:4
shall not taste d — Matt 16:28
to the point of d — Mark 14:34
passed out of d — John 5:24
he shall never see d — John 8:51
sickness is not unto d — John 11:4
the agony of d — Acts 2:24
d by hanging Him — Acts 10:39
d reigned from Adam — Rom 5:14
wages of sin is d — Rom 6:23
the law of sin and of d — Rom 8:2
proclaim...Lord's d — 1 Cor 11:26
d, where...victory — 1 Cor 15:55
even d on a cross — Phil 2:8
He might taste d — Heb 2:9
it brings forth d — James 1:15
passed out of d — 1 John 3:14
Be faithful until d — Rev 2:10
had the name D — Rev 6:8
second d...no power — Rev 20:6
DEBATE *dispute*
d-d...themselves — Mark 1:27
dissension and d — Acts 15:2
had been much d — Acts 15:7
DEBT *obligation*
forgive us our d-s — Matt 6:12
the certificate of d — Col 2:14
DEBTOR *borrower*
forgiven our d-s — Matt 6:12
had two d-s — Luke 7:41
his master's d-s — Luke 16:5
DECAY *corruption*
Holy One to...d — Acts 2:27
did not undergo d — Acts 13:37
DECEASED *dead*
the sister of the d — John 11:39
DECEIT *falsehood, deception*
d, sensuality, envy — Mark 7:22
full of envy...d — Rom 1:29
the lusts of d — Eph 4:22
nor was any d found — 1 Pet 2:22
DECEITFUL *false*
false apostles, d — 2 Cor 11:13
attention to d spirits — 1 Tim 4:1
DECEIVE *cheat, mislead*
they keep d-ing — Rom 3:13
Let no one d you — Eph 5:6
d-ing and being d-d — 2 Tim 3:13
DECEIVER *liar*
as d-s and yet true — 2 Cor 6:8
d and the antichrist — 2 John 7
DECEPTION *falsehood*
last d will be worse — Matt 27:64
philosophy and empty d — Col 2:8
reveling in their d-s — 2 Pet 2:13
DECISION *judgment, resolution*
for the Emperor's d — Acts 25:21
majority reached a d — Acts 27:12
DECLARE *explain, proclaim*
He will d all things — John 4:25
d-d the Son of God — Rom 1:4
DECREASE *abate, subside*
increase...I must d — John 3:30
DECREE (n) *judgment, order*
delivering the d-s — Acts 16:4
to the d-s of Caesar — Acts 17:7
DEDICATION, FEAST OF
see FEASTS
DEED *action or document*
prophet mighty in d — Luke 24:19
their d-s were evil — John 3:19
d-s of the flesh are — Gal 5:19
for every good d — Titus 3:1
I know your d-s — Rev 2:2
DEEP (adj) *far ranging*
the well is d — John 4:11
and their d poverty — 2 Cor 8:2
DEFEND *protect*
d-ed him and took — Acts 7:24
or else d-ing them — Rom 2:15
are d-ing ourselves — 2 Cor 12:19
DEFENSE *protection*
should speak in your d — Luke 12:11
a d to the assembly — Acts 19:33

the d...of the gospel — Phil 1:7
DEFILE *pollute, profane*
those d the man — Matt 15:18
is what d-s the man — Mark 7:20
conscience...is d-d — 1 Cor 8:7
d-s the entire body — James 3:6
DEFILEMENT *filth*
from all d of flesh — 2 Cor 7:1
DEFRAUD *deprive, wrong*
Do not d — Mark 10:19
no one keep d-ing — Col 2:18
DEITY *God, gods*
of strange d-ies — Acts 17:18
fulness of D dwells — Col 2:9
DELAY *hinder, linger, stall*
bridegroom...d-ing — Matt 25:5
Do not d to come — Acts 9:38
now why do you d — Acts 22:16
in case I am d-ed — 1 Tim 3:15
DELIGHT (v) *desire*
d-ing...self-abasement — Col 2:18
DELIVER *give, rescue, save*
d us from evil — Matt 6:13
d Him up to you — Matt 26:15
d-ed over to death — 2 Cor 4:11
The Lord will d me — 2 Tim 4:18
d-ed to the saints — Jude 3
DELIVERANCE *salvation*
them d through him — Acts 7:25
d through...prayers — Phil 1:19
DELIVERER *savior*
both a ruler and a d — Acts 7:35
D...come from Zion — Rom 11:26
DELUDE *lead astray*
no one may d you — Col 2:4
who d themselves — James 1:22
DEMAND *order, require*
do not d it back — Luke 6:30
d-ing of Him a sign — Luke 11:16
DEMETRIUS
1 *Ephesian smith* — Acts 19:24,38
2 *a Christian* — 3 John 12
DEMON *devil*
after the d was cast — Matt 9:33
sacrifice to d-s — 1 Cor 10:20
d-s also believe — James 2:19
not to worship d-s — Rev 9:20
DEMONIACS *possessed ones*
d, epileptics — Matt 4:24
the *incident* of the d — Matt 8:33
DEMON-POSSESSED
many who were d — Matt 8:16
a dumb man, d — Matt 9:32
to the d man — Mark 5:16
sayings of one d — John 10:21
DEMONSTRATE *show*
God d-s His own love — Rom 5:8
to d His wrath — Rom 9:22
d-d yourselves to be — 2 Cor 7:11
d His...patience — 1 Tim 1:16
DEMONSTRATION *a showing*
for the d, *I say* — Rom 3:26
in d of the Spirit — 1 Cor 2:4
DEN *abode*
it a robbers' d — Mark 11:17
DENARIUS
Roman silver coin — Matt 20:2,9
a day's wage — Luke 20:24
Denarii (pl) — John 6:7;12:5
DENY *conceal, refuse*
whoever shall d Me — Matt 10:33
has d-ied the faith — 1 Tim 5:8
deeds they *Him* — Titus 1:16
us to d ungodliness — Titus 2:12
d-ies the Son — 1 John 2:23
DEPART *leave*
I never knew you; d — Matt 7:23
d from Me, all you — Luke 13:27
D from your country — Acts 7:3
d and be with Christ — Phil 1:23
DEPARTURE *death or leaving*
speaking of His d — Luke 9:31
time of my d has — 2 Tim 4:6
any time after my d — 2 Pet 1:15
DEPEND *rely, rest*
d the whole Law — Matt 22:40
DEPORTATION *exile*
after the d to — Matt 1:12
to the d to Babylon — Matt 1:17
DEPRAVED *degenerate*
over to a d mind — Rom 1:28
men of d mind — 2 Tim 3:8
DEPRIVE *take away*
d-ing one another — 1 Cor 7:5
d-d of the truth — 1 Tim 6:5
DEPTH *abyss, deep*
drowned in the d — Matt 18:6
it had no d of soil — Mark 4:5
nor height, nor d — Rom 8:39

the **d** of the riches	Rom 11:33
even the **d-s** of God	1 Cor 2:10
DESCEND *go down*	
shall **d** to Hades	Matt 11:23
Spirit **d-ing**...dove	John 1:32
d into the abyss	Rom 10:7
who **d-ed**...ascended	Eph 4:10
DESCENDANT *seed, offering*	
So shall your **d-s** be	Rom 4:18
to the **d** of Abraham	Heb 2:16
DESCENT *hill or heritage*	
the **d** of the Mount	Luke 19:37
were of high-priestly **d**	Acts 4:6
DESCRIBE *explain*	
should **d** it to you	Acts 13:41
who had seen it **d-d**	Mark 5:16
DESECRATE *defile*	
tried to **d** the temple	Acts 24:6
DESERT (n) *wilderness*	
he lived in the **d-s**	Luke 1:80
this is a **d** road	Acts 8:26
DESERT (v) *abandon, forsake*	
who had **d-ed** them	Acts 15:38
so quickly **d-ing** Him	Gal 1:6
but all **d-ed** me	2 Tim 4:16
I will never **d** you	Heb 13:5
DESERVE *earn, merit*	
He is **d-ing** of death	Matt 26:66
receiving what we **d**	Luke 23:41
DESIGNATE *appoint*	
being **d-d** by God	Heb 5:10
not be **d-d** according to	Heb 7:11
DESIRE (n) *appetite, craving*	
d and my prayer	Rom 10:1
d-s of the flesh	Eph 2:3
d to depart and be	Phil 1:23
evil **d**, and greed	Col 3:5
DESIRE (v) *crave, wish*	
righteous men **d-d**	Matt 13:17
d the greater gifts	1 Cor 12:31
d...a good showing	Gal 6:12
d a better *country*	Heb 11:16
DESOLATE *lonely, waste*	
loaves in a **d** place	Matt 15:33
homestead be made **d**	Acts 1:20
children of the **d**	Gal 4:27
DESOLATION *ruin, waste*	
the abomination of **D**	Matt 24:15
her **d** is at hand	Luke 21:20
DESPAIR (v) *grieve*	
we **d-ed** even of life	2 Cor 1:8
but not **d-ing**	2 Cor 4:8
DESPISE *reject, scorn*	
not **d** one of these	Matt 18:10
hold to one, and **d**	Luke 16:13
do you **d**...church	1 Cor 11:22
DESTINE *appoint*	
things **d-d** to perish	Col 2:22
not **d-d** us for wrath	1 Thess 5:9
DESTITUTE *deprived, in need*	
being **d**, afflicted	Heb 11:37
DESTROY *abolish, ruin, waste*	
moth and rust **d**	Matt 6:19
who is able to **d**	Matt 10:28
You come to **d** us	Mark 1:24
seeking...to **d** Him	Mark 11:18
d the temple and	Mark 15:29
flood...**d-ed** them	Luke 17:27
D this temple, and	John 2:19
not for **d-ing** you	2 Cor 10:8
to save and to **d**	James 4:12
heavens will be **d-ed**	2 Pet 3:12
d the works of the	1 John 3:8
DESTRUCTION *calamity, ruin*	
broad that leads to **d**	Matt 7:13
whose end is **d**	Phil 3:19
d will come	1 Thess 5:3
penalty of eternal **d**	2 Thess 1:9
bringing swift **d** upon	2 Pet 2:1
DETERMINE *decide*	
d-d *their* appointed	Acts 17:26
but rather **d** this	Rom 14:13
d-d to know nothing	1 Cor 2:2
DETESTABLE *abominable*	
d...sight of God	Luke 16:15
being **d** and disobedient	Titus 1:16
DEVIL *demon, Satan*	
tempted by the **d**	Matt 4:1
one of you is a **d**	John 6:70
you son of the **d**	Acts 13:10
firm against...the **d**	Eph 6:11
render powerless...**d**	Heb 2:14
serpent...the **d**	Rev 12:9
d...into the lake	Rev 20:10
DEVISE *design, scheme, plot*	
d futile things	Acts 4:25
DEVOTE *commit, dedicate*	
d-ing...to prayer	Acts 1:14
d-d to one another	Rom 12:10

D yourselves to prayer	Col 4:2
DEVOUR *consume, swallow*	
d widows' houses	Mark 12:40
bite...**d** one another	Gal 5:15
DEVOUT *God-fearing*	
was righteous and **d**	Luke 2:25
d men, from every	Acts 2:5
the **d** women	Acts 13:50
DIALECT *language*	
in the Hebrew **d**	Acts 21:40
the Hebrew **d**	Acts 22:2
DIE *decease, expire*	
to **d** with You	Matt 26:35
child has not **d-d**	Mark 5:39
live even if he **d-s**	John 11:25
grain of wheat...**d-s**	John 12:24
she fell sick and **d-d**	Acts 9:37
d-d for the ungodly	Rom 5:6
we who **d-d** to sin	Rom 6:2
for whom Christ **d-d**	Rom 14:15
I **d** daily	1 Cor 15:31
I **d-d** to the Law	Gal 2:19
to **d** is gain	Phil 1:21
Jesus **d-d** and rose	1 Thess 4:14
to **d** once and after	Heb 9:27
these **d-d** in faith	Heb 11:13
who **d** in the Lord	Rev 14:13
DIFFICULT *hard*	
this is a **d** statement	John 6:60
last days **d** times	2 Tim 3:1
DIG *excavate, till*	
dug a wine press	Matt 21:33
until I **d** around it	Luke 13:8
DIGNITY *majesty*	
all godliness and **d**	1 Tim 2:2
must be men of **d**	1 Tim 3:8
DILIGENCE *effort*	
lagging behind in **d**	Rom 12:11
show the same **d**	Heb 6:11
DILIGENT *persistent*	
d to present	2 Tim 2:15
d to enter that rest	Heb 4:11
I will also be **d**	2 Pet 1:15
DINE *eat*	
came and were **d-ing**	Matt 9:10
will **d** with	Rev 3:20
DINNER *meal*	
I have prepared...**d**	Matt 22:4
because of...**d** guests	Mark 6:26
was giving a **d**	Luke 14:16
DIP *plunge*	
d-ped...with Me	Matt 26:23
who **d-s** with Me	Mark 14:20
robe **d-ped** in blood	Rev 19:13
DIRECT *arrange, guide, order*	
I **d-ed** the churches	1 Cor 16:1
d their entire body	James 3:3
DIRGE *lament*	
we sang a **d**	Matt 11:17; Luke 7:32
DISAPPEAR *vanish*	
old is ready to **d**	Heb 8:13
DISAPPOINT *frustrate*	
hope does not **d**	Rom 5:5
shall not be **d-ed**	1 Pet 2:6
DISBELIEVE *doubt*	
Jews who **d-d** stirred	Acts 14:2
for those who **d**	1 Pet 2:7
DISCERN *understand, recognize*	
d the...sky	Matt 16:3
to **d** good and evil	Heb 5:14
DISCERNMENT *judgment*	
knowledge and **d**	Phil 1:9
DISCIPLE *student, learner*	
His twelve **d-s**	Matt 10:1
d is not above his	Matt 10:24
d-s rebuked them	Matt 19:13
d-s left Him...fled	Matt 26:56
make **d-s** of all	Matt 28:19
Your **d-s** do not fast	Mark 2:18
Passover...My **d-s**	Mark 14:14
gaze on His **d-s**	Luke 6:20
he cannot be My **d**	Luke 14:26
d-s believed in Him	John 2:11
His **d-s** withdrew	John 6:66
wash the **d-s** feet	John 13:5
d whom He loved	John 19:26
d-s were first called	Acts 11:26
DISCIPLINE (n) *chastisement*	
to see your good **d**	Col 2:5
d...of little profit	1 Tim 4:8
DISCIPLINE (v) *chastise*	
d-d by the Lord	1 Cor 11:32
father does not **d**	Heb 12:7
DISCLOSE *reveal*	
will **d** Myself to him	John 14:21
the motives of **d**	1 Cor 4:5
secrets...are **d-d**	1 Cor 14:25
DISCUSS *converse, reason*	
d among themselves	Matt 16:7

What were you **d-ing**	Mark 9:33
d-ed together what	Luke 6:11
DISEASE *sickness*	
various **d-s** and pains	Matt 4:24
power...to heal **d-s**	Luke 9:1
DISGRACEFUL *shameful*	
d for a woman to	1 Cor 11:6
is **d** even to speak	Eph 5:12
DISGUISE *pretend*	
d-ing...as apostles	2 Cor 11:13
DISHONOR (v) *disgrace, shame*	
and you **d** Me	John 8:49
bodies might be **d-ed**	Rom 1:24
do you **d** God	Rom 2:23
DISMISS *release, send away*	
he **d-ed** the assembly	Acts 19:41
DISOBEDIENCE *rebellion*	
the one man's **d**	Rom 5:19
in the sons of **d**	Eph 2:2
d received a just	Heb 2:2
same example of **d**	Heb 4:11
DISOBEDIENT *rebellious*	
hardened and **d**	Acts 19:9
d to parents	Rom 1:30
d...obstinate people	Rom 10:21
DISPERSE *spread*	
who are **d-d** abroad	James 1:1
DISPLAY *declare, show*	
works of God...**d-ed**	John 9:3
DISPOSSESS *remove*	
d-ing the nations	Acts 7:45
DISPUTE (n) *controversy*	
a great **d** among	Acts 28:29
DISPUTE (v) *contend, debate*	
without...**d-ing**	Phil 2:14
He **d-d** with the devil	Jude 9
DISSENSION *division*	
great **d** and debate	Acts 15:2
d between the	Acts 23:7
those who cause **d-s**	Rom 16:17
without wrath and **d**	1 Tim 2:8
DISSIPATION *intemperance*	
weighted...with **d**	Luke 21:34
wine, for that is **d**	Eph 5:18
not accused of **d**	Titus 1:6
DISTANCE *far away*	
following...at a **d**	Matt 26:58
welcomed...from a **d**	Heb 11:13
DISTINCTION *difference*	
He made no **d**	Acts 15:9
for there is no **d**	Rom 3:22
d-s among yourselves	James 2:4
DISTINGUISH (v) *discern*	
d-ing of spirits	1 Cor 12:10
DISTINGUISHING (adj)	
this is a **d** mark	2 Thess 3:17
DISTORT *pervert*	
d the gospel of Christ	Gal 1:7
DISTRESS *adversity, trouble*	
d upon the land	Luke 21:23
d for every soul	Rom 2:9
assisted those in **d**	1 Tim 5:10
widows in their **d**	James 1:27
DISTRIBUTE *apportion*	
d it to the poor	Luke 18:22
d-ing to each one	1 Cor 12:11
DISTRICT *area, province*	
d around the Jordan	Matt 3:5
d of Galilee	Mark 1:28
the **d-s** of Libya	Acts 2:10
DISTURB *annoy, bother*	
being greatly **d-ed**	Acts 4:2
one who is **d-ing** you	Gal 5:10
DISTURBANCE *turmoil*	
hear of wars and **d-s**	Luke 21:9
d among the soldiers	Acts 12:18
arrogance, **d-s**	2 Cor 12:20
DIVIDE *apportion, separate*	
d-d up His garments	Matt 27:35
d-d his wealth	Luke 15:12
DIVINATION *witchcraft*	
a spirit of **d** met us	Acts 16:16
DIVINE (adj) *pertaining to deity*	
D Nature...gold	Acts 17:29
power and **d** nature	Rom 1:20
is the **d** response	Rom 11:4
DIVISION *dissension, segment*	
d in the multitude	John 7:43
no **d-s** among you	1 Cor 1:10
d of soul and spirit	Heb 4:12
DIVORCE (v) *separate*	
man to **d** his wife	Matt 19:3
Whoever **d-s** his	Mark 10:11
DIVORCED (adj) *separated*	
marries a **d** woman	Matt 5:32
marries...who is **d**	Luke 16:18
DOCTRINE *teaching*	
Teaching as **d-s** the	Matt 15:9

every wind of **d** — Eph 4:14
to teach strange **d-s** — 1 Tim 1:3
to exhort in sound **d** — Titus 1:9
DOER *workman*
d-s of the Law will — Rom 2:13
d-s of the word — James 1:22
not a **d** of the law — James 4:11
DOG *animal, scavenger*
Beware of the **d** — Phil 3:2
d-s and the sorcerers — Rev 22:15
DOMAIN *estate*
give You all this **d** — Luke 4:6
the **d** of darkness — Col 1:13
keep their own **d** — Jude 6
DOMINION *authority, rule*
and power and **d** — Eph 1:21
thrones or **d-s** or — Col 1:16
glory and the **d** forever — Rev 1:6
DONKEY *ass*
you will find a **d** — Matt 21:2
and mounted on a **d** — Matt 21:5
a dumb **d**, speaking — 2 Pet 2:16
DOOR *entrance, opening*
shut your **d**, pray — Matt 6:6
I am the **d** — John 10:9
right at the **d** — James 5:9
before you an open **d** — Rev 3:8
I stand at the **d** — Rev 3:20
DOORKEEPER *guard*
commanded the **d** — Mark 13:34
To him the **d** opens — John 10:3
DORCAS
Tabitha, a Joppa Christian — Acts 9:36-43
DOUBT (n) *unbelief*
why do **d-s** arise — Luke 24:38
DOUBT (v) *disbelieve*
why did you **d** — Matt 14:31
not **d** in his heart — Mark 11:23
d-s is condemned — Rom 14:23
who **d-s** is like the — James 1:6
DOVE *bird*
descending as a **d** — Matt 3:16
descending as a **d** — John 1:32
selling the **d-s** — John 2:16
DRACHMA
Greek silver coin — Matt 17:24
DRAG *draw, pull*
Paul and **d-ged** — Acts 14:19
d you into court — James 2:6
DRAGON *monster, serpent*
d stood before the — Rev 12:4
he laid hold of the **d** — Rev 20:2
DRAW *haul, pull*
redemption is **d-ing** — Luke 21:28
d all men to Myself — John 12:32
D near to God — James 4:8
DREAM (n) *vision*
to Joseph in a **d** — Matt 2:13
men shall dream **d-s** — Acts 2:17
DRESS (n) *clothing*
or putting on **d-es** — 1 Pet 3:3
DRESS (v) *array, clothe*
d-ed Him...purple — Mark 15:17
DRINK (n) *refreshment*
thirsty...gave Me a — Matt 25:35
My blood is true **d** — John 6:55
thirsty, give him a **d** — Rom 12:20
DRINK (v)
they all **drank** from — Mark 14:23
after **d-ing** old *wine* — Luke 5:39
who eats and **d-s** — 1 Cor 11:29
ground that **d-s** the — Heb 6:7
DRIVE *chase, defeat*
drove *them* all out — John 2:15
to **d** the ship — Acts 27:39
DROP (n) *drip*
like **d-s** of blood — Luke 22:44
DROWNED *suffocated*
he be **d** in the depth — Matt 18:6
were **d** in the sea — Mark 5:13
DRUNK *intoxicated*
not get **d** with wine — Eph 5:18
I saw the woman **d** — Rev 17:6
DRUNKARD *intoxicated person*
man, and a **d** — Luke 7:34
a reviler, or a **d** — 1 Cor 5:11
DRUNKENNESS *intoxicated*
weighted down...**d** — Luke 21:34
in carousing and **d** — Rom 13:13
envying, **d**, carousing — Gal 5:21
DRY
happen in the **d** — Luke 23:31
through **d** land — Heb 11:29
DUE (adj) *proper, right*
d penalty of their — Rom 1:27
for in **d** time — Gal 6:9
DULL *heavy, stupid*
people...become **d** — Matt 13:15
become **d** of hearing — Heb 5:11

DUMB *silent*
behold, a **d** man — Matt 9:32
and the **d** to speak — Mark 7:37
astray to the **d** idols — 1 Cor 12:2
DUST *dirt, earth*
shake off the **d** of — Matt 10:14
the **d** of your city — Luke 10:11
d on their heads — Rev 18:19
DUTY *responsibility*
his **d** to his wife — 1 Cor 7:3
DWELL *abide, live*
flesh, and **d-t** among — John 1:14
of God **d-s** in you — 1 Cor 3:16
Christ may **d** in your — Eph 3:17
mind **d** on these things — Phil 4:8
DWELLING *habitation*
into the eternal **d-s** — Luke 16:9
might find a **d** place — Acts 7:46

E

EAGLE *bird*
was like a flying **e** — Rev 4:7
I heard an **e** flying — Rev 8:13
EAR *hearing*
He who has **e-s** to — Matt 11:15
and cut off his **e** — Matt 26:51
fingers into his **e-s** — Mark 7:33
if he should say — 1 Cor 12:16
their **e-s** tickled — 2 Tim 4:3
He who has an **e** — Rev 2:7
EARLY *beforetime, soon*
e on the first day — Mark 16:2
at the tomb — Luke 24:22
the **e** and late rains — James 5:7
EARTH *land, world*
shall inherit the **e** — Matt 5:5
you shall bind on **e** — Matt 16:19
on **e** peace among — Luke 2:14
glorified...on the **e** — John 17:4
man is from the **e** — 1 Cor 15:47
heavens and a new **e** — 2 Pet 3:13
e and heaven fled — Rev 20:11
EARTHENWARE *pottery*
vessels of ... — 2 Tim 2:20
EARTHQUAKE *temblor*
be famines and **e-s** — Matt 24:7
will be great **e-s** — Luke 21:11
there was a great **e** — Rev 6:12
killed in the **e** — Rev 11:13
EARTHY *mortal*
man is...**e** — 1 Cor 15:47
those who are **e** — 1 Cor 15:48
EAST *direction of compass*
saw His star in the **e** — Matt 2:2
lightning...the **e** — Matt 24:27
kings from the **e** — Rev 16:12
EASY *without difficulty*
My yoke is **e**, and — Matt 11:30
EAT *consume, dine, feast*
what you shall **e** — Matt 6:25
e with unwashed — Matt 15:20
Take, **e**; this is My — Matt 26:26
sinners and **e-s** with — Luke 15:2
e...at My table — Luke 22:30
He took it and **ate** — Luke 24:43
e the flesh of...Son — John 6:53
Peter, kill and **e** — Acts 10:13
kingdom...not **e-ing** — Rom 14:17
ate...spiritual food — 1 Cor 10:3
e-s...judgment — 1 Cor 11:29
EDICT *decree*
afraid of the king's **e** — Heb 11:23
EDIFICATION *building up*
his good, to his **e** — Rom 15:2
speaks to men for **e** — 1 Cor 14:3
all things...for **e** — 1 Cor 14:26
EDIFY *build up*
but love **e-ies** — 1 Cor 8:1
not all things **e** — 1 Cor 10:23
man is not **e-ied** — 1 Cor 14:17
EDUCATED *taught*
Moses was **e** in all — Acts 7:22
e under Gamaliel — Acts 22:3
EFFEMINATE *womanlike*
e, nor homosexuals — 1 Cor 6:9
EGG
is asked for an **e** — Luke 11:12
EGYPT
country in NE Africa — Matt 2:13,14
— Acts 7:9,10; Heb 3:16
ELDER *aged, older*
tradition of the **e-s** — Matt 15:2
chief priests and **e-s** — Matt 27:12
scribes...**e-s** came — Mark 11:27
Council of **e-s** of — Luke 22:66
e-s of the church — Acts 20:17
I saw twenty-four **e-s** — Rev 4:4
ELEAZAR
ancestor of Jesus — Matt 1:15

ELECT *chosen*
sake of the **e** — Matt 24:22
to lead the **e** astray — Mark 13:22
justice for His **e** — Luke 18:7
against God's **e** — Rom 8:33
ELEMENTARY *basic*
e principles of the — Col 2:8
e principles of the — Heb 5:12
e teaching about the — Heb 6:1
ELEMENTS *physical matter*
e will be destroyed — 2 Pet 3:10
the **e** will melt with — 2 Pet 3:12
ELIAKIM
ancestor of Jesus — Matt 1:13
ancestor of Jesus — Luke 3:30,31
ELIEZER
ancestor of Jesus — Luke 3:29
ELIJAH
prophet — Matt 11:14;17:3,4;
— Mark 15:35,36; James 5:17
ELISHA
prophet — Luke 4:27
ELIMINATE *remove*
stomach, and is **e-d** — Matt 15:17; Mark 7:19
ELIZABETH
mother of John the Baptist — Luke 1:7,13,41,57
ELOQUENT *persuasive*
Apollos...an **e** man — Acts 18:24
ELYMAS
magician — Acts 13:8
also **Bar-Jesus**
EMBITTERED *resentful*
e them against the — Acts 14:2
not be **e** against them — Col 3:19
EMBRACE *clasp, hug*
ran and **e-d** him — Luke 15:20
aloud and **e-d** Paul — Acts 20:37
EMERALD *precious stone*
throne, like an **e** — Rev 4:3
the fourth **e** — Rev 21:19
EMINENT *renowned*
the most **e** apostles — 2 Cor 11:5
inferior to...**e** — 2 Cor 12:11
EMMAUS
village by Jerusalem — Luke 24:13
EMPTY (adj) *containing nothing*
deceive you with **e** — Eph 5:6
avoid...**e** chatter — 2 Tim 2:16
EMPTY (v) *remove contents*
but **e-ied** Himself — Phil 2:7
ENCIRCLED
been **e** for seven days — Heb 11:30
ENCOURAGE *strengthen*
Paul was **e-ing** them — Acts 27:33
e one another — 1 Thess 5:11
e the young women — Titus 2:4
ENCOURAGEMENT *support*
God who gives...**e** — Rom 15:5
is any **e** in Christ — Phil 2:1
we may have strong **e** — Heb 6:18
END (n) *extremity, goal, result*
who endures to...**e** — Matt 24:13
to the **e** of the age — Matt 28:20
kingdom...no **e** — Luke 1:33
He loved...to the **e** — John 13:1
Christ...**e** of the law — Rom 10:4
beginning and the **e** — Rev 21:6
END (v) *complete, stop*
days there were **e-ed** — Acts 21:5
it **e-s** up being burned — Heb 6:8
ENDLESS *limitless*
and **e** genealogies — 1 Tim 1:4
ENDURANCE *patience*
in much **e**, in — 2 Cor 6:4
you have need of **e** — Heb 10:36
let us run with **e** — Heb 12:1
of the **e** of Job — James 5:11
ENDURE *persevere*
the one who has **e-d** — Matt 10:22
who **e-s** to the end — Mark 13:13
e-s all things — 1 Cor 13:7
discipline that you **e** — Heb 12:7
blessed who **e-d** — James 5:11
ENEMY *foe*
love your **e-ies**, and — Matt 5:44
e of all righteousness — Acts 13:10
e is hungry, feed — Rom 12:20
e...be abolished — 1 Cor 15:26
an **e** of God — James 4:4
ENGAGE *be involved, betroth*
e-d to...Joseph — Luke 1:27
to **e** in good deeds — Titus 3:8
ENGRAVE *inscribe*
letters **e-d** on stones — 2 Cor 3:7
ENLIGHTEN *illumine*
eyes...may be **e-ed** — Eph 1:18
who have...been **e-ed** — Heb 6:4
ENMITY *hostility*
at **e** with each other — Luke 23:12

sorcery, **e-ies**, strife | Gal 5:20
abolishing...the **e** | Eph 2:15
ENOCH
Methuselah's father | Heb 11:5; Jude 1:14
ENRAGE *anger*
he became very **e-d** | Matt 2:16
dragon was **e-d** with | Rev 12:17
ENROLLED *recorded*
e in heaven | Heb 12:23
ENSLAVE *subjugate*
e-d and mistreated | Acts 7:6
if he **e-s** you | 2 Cor 11:20
e-d to various lusts | Titus 3:3
ENTANGLE *ensnare*
No soldier...**e-s** | 2 Tim 2:4
sin which...**e-s** us | Heb 12:1
ENTER *go in*
not **e** the kingdom | Matt 5:20
E by the narrow gate | Matt 7:13
to **e** life crippled | Matt 18:8
afraid as they **e-ed** | Luke 9:34
e into the kingdom | John 3:5
not **e** by the door | John 10:1
shall not **e** My rest | Heb 3:11
ENTICE *deceive, seduce*
e-d by his own lust | James 1:14
e-ing unstable souls | 2 Pet 2:14
ENTRANCE *doorway*
stone against the **e** | Matt 27:60
e into the eternal | 2 Pet 1:11
ENTREAT *appeal, ask*
centurion...**e-ing** Him | Matt 8:5
demons began to **e** | Matt 8:31
they were **e-ing** Him | Luke 8:31
I **e-ed** the Lord | 2 Cor 12:8
e you to walk in a | Eph 4:1
ENTRUST *assign, commit*
to whom they **e-ed** | Luke 12:48
not **e-ing** Himself to | John 2:24
ENVIOUS *covetous*
is your eye **e** | Matt 20:15
And you are **e** | James 4:2
ENVIRONS *outskirts, suburbs*
Bethlehem...its **e** | Matt 2:16
ENVY (n) *jealousy*
full of **e**, murder | Rom 1:29
preaching...from **e** | Phil 1:15
out of which arise **e** | 1 Tim 6:4
life in malice and **e** | Titus 3:3
e and all slander | 1 Pet 2:1
ENVY (v) *be discontent, jealous*
e-ing one another | Gal 5:26
EPAPHRAS
Colossian Christian | Col 1:7; 4:12
colleague of Paul | Philem 23
EPAPHRODITUS
Philippian Christian | Phil 2:25
colleague of Paul | Phil 4:18
EPHESUS
city of Asia Minor
Acts 18:19; 1 Cor 16:8; Rev 1:11;2:1
EPHRAIM
city | John 11:54
EPICUREAN
a Greek philosophy | Acts 17:18
EPOCHS *ages, seasons*
to know times or **e** | Acts 1:7
EQUAL *same*
have made them **e** | Matt 20:12
Himself **e** with God | John 5:18
EQUIP *furnish, provide*
e-ped for...work | 2 Tim 3:17
e you in every good | Heb 13:21
ERASTUS
Corinthian Christian | Acts 19:22;
Rom 16:23; 2 Tim 4:20
ERROR *mistake, sin*
e of unprincipled | 2 Pet 3:17
the spirit of **e** | 1 John 4:6
rushed...into the **e** | Jude 11
ESAU
son of Isaac | Rom 9:13; Heb 11:20
ESCAPE (n) *deliverance, refuge*
provide...**e** | 1 Cor 10:13
ESCAPE (v) *elude*
had not **e-d** notice | Luke 8:47
how shall we **e** if | Heb 2:3
it **e-s** their notice | 2 Pet 3:5
ESTABLISH *confirm, found*
we **e** the Law | Rom 3:31
may **e** your hearts | 1 Thess 3:13
e-ed in the truth | 2 Pet 1:12
ESTATE *domain or standard*
share of the **e** | Luke 15:12
squandered his **e** | Luke 15:13
ESTEEM (n) *honor*
held them in high **e** | Acts 5:13
ESTEEM (v) *have high regard*
e-ed among men | Luke 16:15

e them...in love | 1 Thess 5:13
ETERNAL *everlasting*
cast into the **e** fire | Matt 18:8
guilty of an **e** sin | Mark 3:29
to inherit **e** life | Luke 10:25
He may give **e** life | John 17:2
gift of God is **e** life | Rom 6:23
e weight of glory | 2 Cor 4:17
with the **e** purpose | Eph 3:11
Now to the King **e** | 1 Tim 1:17
source of **e** salvation | Heb 5:9
through the **e** Spirit | Heb 9:14
kept us in **e** bonds | Jude 6
an **e** gospel to preach | Rev 14:6
ETERNITY *perpetuity*
Jesus from all **e** | 2 Tim 1:9
to the day of **e** | 2 Pet 3:18
EUNICE
mother of Timothy | 2 Tim 1:5
EUNUCH *chamberlain official*
made **e-s** by men | Matt 19:12
an Ethiopian **e** | Acts 8:27
EUPHRATES
river of Mesopotamia | Rev 9:14;16:12
EVANGELIST *proclaimer*
house of Philip the **e** | Acts 21:8
and some as **e-s** | Eph 4:11
do the work of an **e** | 2 Tim 4:5
EVE
wife of Adam | 2 Cor 11:3; 1 Tim 2:13
EVENING *dusk, darkness*
when **e** had come | Matt 8:16
from morning until **e** | Acts 28:23
EVIDENCE *facts, testimony*
and giving **e** | Acts 17:3
EVIDENT *obvious, plain*
the tares became **e** | Matt 13:26
for God made it **e** | Rom 1:19
work will become **e** | 1 Cor 3:13
Law before God is **e** | Gal 3:11
it is **e** that our Lord | Heb 7:14
EVIL *bad, wicked, wrong*
deliver us from **e** | Matt 6:13
what **e** has He | Matt 27:23
If you then, being **e** | Luke 11:13
who does **e** hates the | John 3:20
Never...**e** for **e** | Rom 12:17
love of money is...**e** | 1 Tim 6:10
tongue...restless **e** | James 3:8
EVILDOER *wicked one*
depart...you **e-s** | Luke 13:27
punishment of **e-s** | 1 Pet 2:14
EXACT (adj) *certain, correct*
know the **e** truth | Luke 1:4
a more **e** knowledge | Acts 24:22
EXALT *extol, honor, lift*
humbles...be **e-ed** | Matt 23:12
e-ed to...right hand | Acts 2:33
be **e-ed** in my body | Phil 1:20
He will **e** you | James 4:10
EXAMINE *investigate, search*
e-ing the Scriptures | Acts 17:11
e-d by scourging | Acts 22:24
a man **e** himself | 1 Cor 11:28
EXAMPLE *model, pattern*
I gave you an **e** | John 13:15
e of those who | 1 Tim 4:12
e of disobedience | Heb 4:11
be **e-s** to the flock | 1 Pet 5:3
made them an **e** | 2 Pet 2:6
EXCEL *be superior*
you may **e**...more | 1 Thess 4:1
EXCELLENCE *perfection*
if there is any **e** | Phil 4:8
proclaim the **e-ies** of | 1 Pet 2:9
EXCELLENT *outstanding*
e governor Felix | Acts 23:26
a still more **e** way | 1 Cor 12:31
a more **e** name | Heb 1:4
EXCESS *too much*
overwhelmed by **e-ive** sorrow | 2 Cor 2:7
same **e** of dissipation | 1 Pet 4:4
EXCHANGE *trade, transfer*
in **e** for his soul | Mark 8:37
e-d the truth of God | Rom 1:25
EXCLUDE *refuse to admit*
e-d from the life of | Eph 4:18
EXCUSE *justification*
began to make **e-s** | Luke 14:18
no **e** for their sin | John 15:22
they are without **e** | Rom 1:20
EXECUTE *carry out*
Lord will **e** His word | Rom 9:28
e judgment upon all | Jude 15
EXERCISE *perform*
e authority over | Matt 20:25
e-s self-control in all | 1 Cor 9:25
EXHORT *admonish, urge*
and kept on **e-ing** | Acts 2:40

e, with...patience | 2 Tim 4:2
e in sound doctrine | Titus 1:9
e and reprove | Titus 2:15
e-ing and testifying | 1 Pet 5:12
EXHORTATION *urging*
with many other **e-s** | Luke 3:18
given them much **e** | Acts 20:2
who exhorts, in his **e** | Rom 12:8
this word of **e** | Heb 13:22
EXIST *be, live, occur*
live and move and **e** | Acts 17:28
authority...which **e** | Rom 13:1
EXODUS *departure*
e of...Israel | Heb 11:22
EXPECT *await*
lend, **e-ing** nothing | Luke 6:35
an hour you do not **e** | Luke 12:40
EXPECTATION *anticipation*
to my earnest **e** | Phil 1:20
e of judgment | Heb 10:27
EXPECTED *awaited*
Are You the **E** One | Matt 11:3
Are You the **E** One | Luke 7:20
EXPERIENCE *undergo*
began to relate their **e-s** | Luke 24:35
e-d mockings and | Heb 11:36
EXPERT *very skillful*
an **e** in all customs | Acts 26:3
EXPLAIN *make clear*
E the parable to us | Matt 15:15
e-ing the Scriptures | Luke 24:32
e-ed to him the way | Acts 18:26
EXPOSE *disclose, reveal*
deeds should be **e-d** | John 3:20
would **e** their infants | Acts 7:19
are **e-d** by the light | Eph 5:13
EXTENT *amount or degree*
e that you did it to | Matt 25:40
such an **e** that Jesus | Mark 1:45
EXTERNAL *outward*
not with **e** service | Col 3:22
adornment be...**e** | 1 Pet 3:3
EXTINGUISH *put out*
e all the flaming | Eph 6:16
EXTRAORDINARY *exceptional*
e miracles by | Acts 19:11
showed us **e** kindness | Acts 28:2
EXULT *rejoice*
e in our tribulations | Rom 5:3
EXULTATION *jubilation*
joy or crown of **e** | 1 Thess 2:19
may rejoice with **e** | 1 Pet 4:13
EYE *sight*
e for an **e**, and a | Matt 5:38
e...you to stumble | Matt 18:9
lamp...is your **e** | Luke 11:34
the clay to his **e-s** | John 9:6
which **e** has not seen | 1 Cor 2:9
e-s of your heart may | Eph 1:18
e-s full of adultery | 2 Pet 2:14
the lust of the **e-s** | 1 John 2:16
God, who has **e-s** like | Rev 2:18
His **e-s** *are* a flame | Rev 19:12
EYEWITNESSES *observers*
e...of the word | Luke 1:2
e of His majesty | 2 Pet 1:16

F

FACE *countenance*
fast...wash your **f** | Matt 6:17
they spat in His **f** | Matt 26:67
like the **f** of an angel | Acts 6:15
natural **f** in a mirror | James 1:23
His **f** was like the sun | Rev 1:16
FACT *truth*
f may be confirmed | Matt 18:16
are undeniable **f-s** | Acts 19:36
f is to be confirmed | 2 Cor 13:1
FACTIONS *divisions*
be **f** among you | 1 Cor 11:19
dissensions, **f** | Gal 5:20
FADE *wither*
rich man...will **f** | James 1:11
will not **f** away | 1 Pet 1:4
FAIL *be spent or fall short*
faith may not **f** | Luke 22:32
Love never **f-s** | 1 Cor 13:8
FAINT *languish, swoon*
men **f-ing** from fear | Luke 21:26
f when...reproved | Heb 12:5
FAINTHEARTED *weak*
encourage the **f** | 1 Thess 5:14
FAIR HAVENS
harbor in Crete | Acts 27:8
FAITH *believe, trust*
Jesus seeing their **f** | Matt 9:2
f as a mustard seed | Matt 17:20
Your **f** has saved you | Luke 7:50
Increase our **f** | Luke 17:5

your f may not fail	Luke 22:32
man full of f	Acts 6:5
of f to the Gentiles	Acts 14:27
sanctified by f in Me	Acts 26:18
justified by f	Rom 5:1
f...from hearing	Rom 10:17
if I have all f	1 Cor 13:2
your f also is vain	1 Cor 15:14
we walk by f	2 Cor 5:7
live by f in the Son	Gal 2:20
saved through f	Eph 2:8
one Lord, one f	Eph 4:5
joy in the f	Phil 1:25
stability of your f	Col 2:5
breastplate of f	1 Thess 5:8
for not all have f	2 Thess 3:2
fall away from the f	1 Tim 4:1
conduct, love, f	1 Tim 4:12
they upset the f	2 Tim 2:18
sound in the f	Titus 1:13
showing all good f	Titus 2:10
full assurance of f	Heb 10:22
By f Enoch was taken	Heb 11:5
perfecter of f	Heb 12:2
ask in f	James 1:6
prayer offered in f	James 5:15
power of God...f	1 Pet 1:5
the f of the saints	Rev 13:10

FAITHFUL *loyal, trustworthy*

Well done...f	Matt 25:23
God is f	1 Cor 1:9
F is He who calls	1 Thess 5:24
He considered me f	1 Tim 1:12
entrust to f men	2 Tim 2:2
souls to a f Creator	1 Pet 4:19
He is f... to forgive	1 John 1:9
Be f until death	Rev 2:10
called F and True	Rev 19:11

FAITHFULNESS *loyalty*

and mercy and f	Matt 23:23
nullify the f of God	Rom 3:3
kindness, goodness, f	Gal 5:22

FAITHLESS *unbelieving*

If we are f	2 Tim 2:13

FALL *descend or fail*

will f into a pit	Matt 15:14
f-ing on his knees	Mark 1:40
all may f...I will	Mark 14:29
appointed for the f	Luke 2:34
watching Satan f	Luke 10:18
house divided...f-s	Luke 11:17
f-ing headlong	Acts 1:18
sinned and f short	Rom 3:23
have f-en asleep	1 Cor 15:6
f-en from grace	Gal 5:4
rich f into temptation	1 Tim 6:9
rocks, F on us	Rev 6:16

FALSE *deceitful, dishonest*

not bear f witness	Matt 19:18
f Christs and f	Matt 24:24
men are f apostles	2 Cor 11:13
the f circumcision	Phil 3:2
and the f prophet	Rev 20:10

FALSEHOOD *deception*

laying aside f	Eph 4:25

FAME *greatness*

f in *the things of*	2 Cor 8:18

FAMILY *household, relatives*

every f in heaven	Eph 3:15
upsetting whole f-ies	Titus 1:11

FAMINE *shortage of food*

f-s and earthquakes	Matt 24:7
plagues and f-s	Luke 21:11
Now a f came	Acts 7:11
mourning and f	Rev 18:8

FAR *distant*

heart is f away from	Matt 15:8
f from the kingdom	Mark 12:34
glory f beyond all	2 Cor 4:17
f above all rule	Eph 1:21

FARM *agricultural land*

one to his own f	Matt 22:5
or f-s, for My sake	Mark 10:29

FARMER *husbandman*

hard-working f ought	2 Tim 2:6
the f waits for	James 5:7

FAST (n) *food abstinence*

f was already over	Acts 27:9

FARMER *husbandman*

hard-working f ought	2 Tim 2:6
the f waits for	James 5:7

FAST (v) *abstain from food*

had f-ed forty days	Matt 4:2
whenever you f	Matt 6:16
disciples do not f	Mark 2:18
I f twice a week	Luke 18:12
had f-ed and prayed	Acts 13:3

FASTING *food abstinence*

to be seen f by men	Matt 6:16
by prayer and f	Matt 17:21

Pharisees were f	Mark 2:18

FATHER *God or parent*

F who sees in secret	Matt 6:4
Our F who art in	Matt 6:9
does the will of My F	Matt 7:21
in My F-'s kingdom	Matt 26:29
in the glory of His F	Mark 8:38
be in my F-'s house	Luke 2:49
F, hallowed be Thy	Luke 11:2
F, forgive them	Luke 23:34
begotten from the F	John 1:14
my F-'s house a	John 2:16
F...bears witness	John 8:18
the f of lies	John 8:44
I and the F are one	John 10:30
In my F-'s house are	John 14:2
F is the vinedresser	John 15:1
ask the F for	John 16:23
I ascend to My F	John 20:17
one God and F of all	Eph 4:6

FATHER-IN-LAW

f of Caiaphas	John 18:13

FAULT *error, offense*

does He still find f	Rom 9:19
grumblers, finding f	Jude 16

FAVOR *kind regard*

found f with God	Luke 1:30
in f with God and	Luke 2:52
seeking the f of men	Gal 1:10

FEAR (n) *awe, dread, reverence*

they cried out for f	Matt 14:26
guards shook for f	Matt 28:4
men fainting for f	Luke 21:26
for f of the Jews	John 7:13
no f of God before	Rom 3:18
in weakness and in f	1 Cor 2:3
knowing the f of the	2 Cor 5:11
with f and trembling	Eph 6:5
through f of death	Heb 2:15
love casts out f	1 John 4:18

FEAR (v) *be afraid, revere*

do not f them	Matt 10:26
f-ed the multitude	Matt 14:5
who did not f God	Luke 18:2
slavery leading to f	Rom 8:15
I f for you	Gal 4:11
let us f lest	Heb 4:1

FEARFUL *terrifying*

were f and amazed	Luke 8:25
may be f of sinning	1 Tim 5:20

FEAST *celebration*

a wedding f	Matt 22:2
seeking Him at the f	John 7:11
celebrate the f	1 Cor 5:8
f with you without	Jude 12

FEASTS

1 Feast of Dedication	John 10:22
2 Feast of Passover	Luke 2:41
3 Feast of Unleavened Bread	Luke 22:1
4 Feast of Pentecost	Acts 2:1; 20:16; 1 Cor 16:8
5 Feast of Booths	John 7:2

FEEBLE *weak*

knees that are f	Heb 12:12

FEED *eat, supply*

dogs f on the	Matt 15:27
hungry, and f You	Matt 25:37
fed...the crumbs	Luke 16:21
enemy is hungry, f	Rom 12:20

FEEL *sense, touch*

He felt compassion	Matt 9:36
she felt...was healed	Mark 5:29
Jesus felt a love for	Mark 10:21
f-ing a sense of awe	Acts 2:43
f sensual desires	1 Tim 5:11

FELIX

Roman procurator	Acts 23:26; 24:25; 25:14

FELL *collapse, come upon*

seeds f beside the	Matt 13:4
He f asleep	Luke 8:23
he f to the ground	Acts 9:4
Holy Spirit f upon	Acts 10:44
star f from heaven	Rev 8:10

FELLOW *companion*

beat his f slaves	Matt 24:49
f heirs with Christ	Rom 8:17
f citizens with the	Eph 2:19
Gentiles are f heirs	Eph 3:6
brother and f worker	Phil 2:25
f worker in the	1 Thes 3:2
I am a f servant of	Rev 22:9

FELLOWSHIP *companionship*

f...Holy Spirit	2 Cor 13:14
right hand of f	Gal 2:9
f of His sufferings	Phil 3:10
f is with the Father	1 John 1:3
f with one another	1 John 1:7

FEMALE *girl, woman*

made them male and f	Matt 19:4
neither male nor f	Gal 3:28

FERVENT *ardent*

being f in spirit	Acts 18:25
in spirit, serving	Rom 12:11
keep f in your love	1 Pet 4:8

FESTIVAL *celebration*

during the f, lest	Matt 26:5
in respect to a f	Col 2:16

FESTUS, PORCIUS

Roman procurator of Judea	Acts 24:27; 25:14,23; 26:25

FETTERS *chains*

he would burst his f	Luke 8:29

FEVER *inflammation*

in bed with a f	Matt 8:14
from a high f	Luke 4:38
He rebuked the f	Luke 4:39
the f left him	John 4:52

FIELD *productive land*

the lilies of the f	Matt 6:28
the f is the world	Matt 13:38
shepherds...in the f-s	Luke 2:8
Two men...in the f	Luke 17:36
f-s...white for	John 4:35
F of Blood	Acts 1:19

FIERCE *violent*

a f gale of wind	Mark 4:37
scorched with f heat	Rev 16:9
f wrath of God	Rev 19:15

FIERY *burning*

into the f hell	Matt 5:22
f ordeal among you	1 Pet 4:12

FIG *fruit*

nor f-s from thistles	Matt 7:16
the f tree withered	Matt 21:19
f-s from thorns	Luke 6:44
under the f tree	John 1:48
Can a f tree	James 3:12

FIGHT *struggle*

f-ing against God	Acts 5:39
fought the good f	2 Tim 4:7
so you f and quarrel	James 4:2

FIGURATIVE *metaphorical*

in f language	John 16:25
I have f-ly applied	1 Cor 4:6

FIGURE *shape, type*

using a f of speech	John 16:29

FILL (v) *make full*

hall was f-ed	Matt 22:10
God of hope f you	Rom 15:13

FILTHY *offensive*

let the one who is f	Rev 22:11

FILTHINESS *disgustingly foul*

no f and silly talk	Eph 5:4
putting aside all f	James 1:21

FIND *discover, uncover*

few...who f it	Matt 7:14
has found his life	Matt 10:39
f rest for your souls	Matt 11:29
f-ing one pearl	Matt 13:46
f a colt tied	Mark 11:2
found...sleeping	Mark 14:40
seek, and you shall f	Luke 11:9
found the Messiah	John 1:41
was found worthy	Rev 5:4

FINGER *part of hand*

tip of his f in water	Luke 16:24
with His f wrote	John 8:6
Reach here your f	John 20:27

FINISH *complete*

It is f-ed	John 19:30
I may f my course	Acts 20:24
f doing it also	2 Cor 8:11
wrath of God is f-ed	Rev 15:1

FIRE *burning or flame*

the Holy Spirit and f	Matt 3:11
with unquenchable f	Matt 3:12
tongues as of f	Acts 2:3
lake that burns with f	Rev 21:8

FIRM *establish, steadfast*

stand f in the faith	1 Cor 16:13
f foundation of God	2 Tim 2:19
hope f until the end	Heb 3:6

FIRST *number*

seek f His kingdom	Matt 6:33
f take the log out	Matt 7:5
f will be last	Matt 19:30
f called Christians	Acts 11:26
to the Jew f	Rom 2:10
f fruits of the Spirit	Rom 8:23
He f loved us	1 John 4:19
I am the F and the	Rev 1:17
left your f love	Rev 2:4
f things have passed	Rev 21:4

FIRST-BORN *oldest*

birth to her f son	Luke 2:7
church of the f	Heb 12:23
f of the dead	Rev 1:5

FISH

loaves and two f	Matt 14:17
snake instead of a f	Luke 11:11

net *full* of **f** — John 21:8
FISHERMEN *fishers*
for they were **f** — Matt 4:18
the **f** had gotten out — Luke 5:2
FISHERS *fishermen*
make you **f** of men — Matt 4:19
become **f** of men — Mark 1:17
FIT *be suitable, worthy*
f to remove His — Matt 3:11
f for the kingdom — Luke 9:62
f to be…apostle — 1 Cor 15:9
body, being **f-ted** — Eph 4:16
f-ting in the Lord — Col 3:18
FIX *make firm, secure*
f-ed her hope on God — 1 Tim 5:5
f-ing…eyes on Jesus — Heb 12:2
f your hope — 1 Pet 1:13
FIXED *established*
is a great chasm **f** — Luke 16:26
Father has **f** by His — Acts 1:7
FLAME *fire*
f of a burning thorn — Acts 7:30
eyes *are* a **f** of fire — Rev 19:12
FLAMING *burning*
the **f** missiles of — Eph 6:16
angels in a **f** fire — 2 Thess 1:7
FLASH *reflect, sparkle*
light suddenly **f-ed** — Acts 22:6
FLASK *utensil*
took oil in **f-s** — Matt 25:4
FLATTERING
their smooth and **f** speech — Rom 16:18
we never came with **f** speech — 1 Thess 2:5
FLEE *escape, run away*
f to Egypt — Matt 2:13
left Him and **fled** — Matt 26:56
fled from the tomb — Mark 16:8
f from idolatry — 1 Cor 10:14
f from youthful lusts — 2 Tim 2:22
and heaven **fled** — Rev 20:11
FLESH *body, meat*
the **f** is weak — Matt 26:41
spirit…not have **f** — Luke 24:39
the Word became **f** — John 1:14
born of the **f** is **f** — John 3:6
who eats My **f** — John 6:56
children of the **f** — Rom 9:8
thorn in the **f** — 2 Cor 12:7
desires of the **f** — Eph 2:3
polluted by the **f** — Jude 23
filled with their **f** — Rev 19:21
FLESHLY *carnal*
not in **f** wisdom — 2 Cor 1:12
His **f** body — Col 1:22
abstain from **f** lusts — 1 Pet 2:11
FLIGHT *departure*
f may not be in — Matt 24:20
foreign armies to **f** — Heb 11:34
FLOCK *goats, sheep*
over their **f** by night — Luke 2:8
shall become one **f** — John 10:16
f of God among you — 1 Pet 5:2
FLOOD *overflowing of water*
the **f-s** came — Matt 7:25
f…destroyed — Luke 17:27
FLOOR *ground, level*
His threshing **f** — Matt 3:12
fell…from the third **f** — Acts 20:9
FLOW *pour forth*
f of her blood — Mark 5:29
f…living waters — John 7:38
FLOWER *blossom*
like **f-ing** grass — James 1:10
glory like the **f** — 1 Pet 1:24
FLUTE *musical instrument*
the **f** or on the harp — 1 Cor 14:7
musicians…**f-players** — Rev 18:22
FLY *soar*
heard an eagle **f-ing** — Rev 8:13
the birds which **f** — Rev 19:17
FOAL *colt*
f of a beast of burden — Matt 21:5
FOLD *animal pen*
not of this **f** — John 10:16
FOLLOW *imitate, pursue*
He said to them, **F** — Matt 4:19
left…and **f-ed** — Matt 4:20
his cross, and **f** Me — Matt 16:24
multitude was **f-ing** — Mark 5:24
allowed no one to **f** — Mark 5:37
and they **f** Me — John 10:27
Peter…**f-ing** Jesus — John 18:15
f-ing after…lusts — Jude 16
ones who **f** the Lamb — Rev 14:4
FOLLOWERS *disciples*
His **f**…*began* asking — Mark 4:10
FOOD *bread, meat*
his **f** was locusts — Matt 3:4
life more than **f** — Matt 6:25

f is to do the will — John 4:34
My flesh is true **f** — John 6:55
milk…not solid **f** — 1 Cor 3:2
FOOL *unwise person*
shall say, You **f** — Matt 5:22
f-s and blind men — Matt 23:17
wise, they became **f-s** — Rom 1:22
f-s for Christ's sake — 1 Cor 4:10
FOOLISH *silly, unwise*
f took their lamps — Matt 25:3
O **f** men and slow — Luke 24:25
let him become **f** — 1 Cor 3:18
You **f** Galatians — Gal 3:1
do not be **f** — Eph 5:17
FOOLISHNESS *folly*
f of God is wiser — 1 Cor 1:25
is **f** before God — 1 Cor 3:19
FOOT *part of body*
dust of your **feet** — Matt 10:14
Bind…hand and **f** — Matt 22:13
f causes you to — Mark 9:45
kissing His **feet** — Luke 7:38
anointed the **feet** — John 12:3
the disciples' **feet** — John 13:5
beautiful…the **feet** — Rom 10:15
Satan under…**feet** — Rom 16:20
worship at the **feet** — Rev 22:8
FOOTSTOOL *foot support*
enemies a **f** for thy feet — Luke 20:43
sit down by my **f** — James 2:3
FORBEARANCE *restraint*
in the **f** of God — Rom 3:25
showing **f** to one — Eph 4:2
FORBID *prohibit*
f-ding to pay taxes — Luke 23:2
do not **f** to speak — 1 Cor 14:39
men who **f** marriage — 1 Tim 4:3
he **f-s** those who — 3 John 10
FORCE (v) *compel*
f you to go one mile — Matt 5:41
not take…by **f** — Luke 3:14
f them to blaspheme — Acts 26:11
f-d to appeal to — Acts 28:19
FOREFATHER *ancestor*
Abraham, our **f** — Rom 4:1
the way my **f-s** did — 2 Tim 1:3
FOREHEAD *brow*
seal of God on their **f-s** — Rev 9:4
upon her **f** a name — Rev 17:5
FOREIGN *alien, strange*
as in a **f** land — Heb 11:9
f armies to flight — Heb 11:34
FOREKNEW *know beforehand*
whom He **f**, He also — Rom 8:29
people whom he **f** — Rom 11:2
He was **foreknown** — 1 Pet 1:20
FOREKNOWLEDGE
plan and **f** of God — Acts 2:23
f of God the Father — 1 Pet 1:2
FOREMOST *first*
f commandment — Matt 22:38
among whom I am **f** — 1 Tim 1:15
FORERUNNER *goes before*
Jesus…as a **f** for — Heb 6:20
FOREST *woods*
a **f** is set aflame — James 3:5
FORETOLD *predicted*
the Holy Spirit **f** — Acts 1:16
just as Isaiah **f** — Rom 9:29
FOREVER *always, eternal*
Christ is to remain **f** — John 12:34
He…with you **f** — John 14:16
He is able to save **f** — Heb 7:25
Son, made perfect **f** — Heb 7:28
they shall reign **f** — Rev 22:5
FORFEIT *lose*
and **f-s** his soul — Matt 16:26
and loses or **f-s** himself? — Luke 9:25
FORGET *forsake, neglect*
f-ing what *lies* behind — Phil 3:13
f your work and — Heb 6:10
FORGIVE *pardon*
f us our debts — Matt 6:12
authority…to **f** sins — Matt 9:6
f-gave him the debt — Matt 18:27
can **f** sins but God — Mark 2:7
he who is **f-n** little — Luke 7:47
Father, **f** them — Luke 23:34
whom you **f** — 2 Cor 2:10
f-ing each other — Eph 4:32
f-n us all our — Col 2:13
righteous to **f** us — 1 John 1:9
FORGIVENESS *pardon*
poured out…for **f** — Matt 26:28
repentance for **f** — Luke 24:47
receives of sins — Acts 10:43
of our trespasses — Eph 1:7
the **f** of sins — Col 1:14
there is no **f** — Heb 9:22

FORK *instrument*
His winnowing **f** — Matt 3:12
FORM (n) *appearance, shape*
in a different **f** — Mark 16:12
bodily **f** like a dove — Luke 3:22
f of corruptible man — Rom 1:23
existed in the **f** of God — Phil 2:6
FORM (v) *fashion, shape*
plot was **f-ed** against — Acts 20:3
Christ is **f-ed** in you — Gal 4:19
FORNICATION
f-s, thefts, false — Matt 15:19
were not born of **f** — John 8:41
strangled and from **f** — Acts 15:29
FORNICATORS
neither **f**, nor — 1 Cor 6:9
f…God will judge — Heb 13:4
FORSAKE
hast Thou **f-n** Me — Matt 27:46
persecuted…not **f-n** — 2 Cor 4:9
f-ing…assembling — Heb 10:25
nor will I ever **f** you — Heb 13:5
FORTRESS
for the destruction of **f-es** — 2 Cor 10:4
FORTY *number*
fasted **f** days and **f** — Matt 4:2
f days being tempted — Mark 1:13
FOUNDATION *establishment*
a **f** upon the rock — Luke 6:48
the firm **f** of God — 2 Tim 2:19
didst lay the **f** — Heb 1:10
a **f** of repentance — Heb 6:1
FOUNDED *established*
f upon the rock — Matt 7:25
FOUNTAIN
Does a **f** send out from the — James 3:11
FOX *small animal*
The **f-es** have holes — Matt 8:20
Go and tell that **f** — Luke 13:32
FRAGMENTS *pieces*
Gather up the…**f** — John 6:12
twelve baskets with **f** — John 6:13
FRAGRANCE *pleasant aroma*
with the **f** of the perfume — John 12:3
we are a **f** of Christ — 2 Cor 2:15
FRANKINCENSE *spice*
gold and **f** and myrrh — Matt 2:11
perfume and **f** and wine — Rev 18:13
FREE *at liberty*
shall make you **f** — John 8:32
who has died is **f-d** — Rom 6:7
the **f** gift of God — Rom 6:23
f from the law — Rom 8:2
Christ set us **f** — Gal 5:1
whether slave or **f** — Eph 6:8
FREEDOM *liberty*
f of the glory — Rom 8:21
you were called to **f** — Gal 5:13
do not use your **f** as — 1 Pet 2:16
FRESH *new, recently prepared*
new wine into **f** — Mark 2:22
f and bitter *water* — James 3:11
FRIEND *companion, comrade*
f of tax-gatherers — Matt 11:19
F, your sins are — Luke 5:20
f of the bridegroom — John 3:29
his life for his **f-s** — John 15:13
You are My **f-s**, if — John 15:14
FRIENDSHIP
f with the world — James 4:4
FRIGHTEN *terrify*
Him and were **f-ed** — Mark 6:50
wars, do not be **f-ed** — Mark 13:7
FRINGE *edge*
touched the **f** of His — Matt 9:20
just touch the **f** of His cloak; — Matt 14:36
FROGS
unclean spirits like **f** — Rev 16:13
FRUIT *growth, produce*
know…by their **f-s** — Matt 7:16
bad tree bears bad **f** — Matt 7:17
f for eternal life — John 4:36
the **f** of the Spirit — Gal 5:22
f in every good work — Col 1:10
FRUITFUL *productive*
f labor for me — Phil 1:22
from heaven and **f** seasons, — Acts 14:17
FULFILL *complete*
the prophet was **f-ed** — Matt 2:17
to abolish, but to **f** — Matt 5:17
The time is **f-ed** — Mark 1:15
f-ed in the kingdom — Luke 22:16
Scripture…be **f-ed** — John 13:18
husband **f** his duty — 1 Cor 7:3
the **f** law of Christ — Gal 6:2
f your ministry — 2 Tim 4:5
FULFILLMENT *completion*
f of what had been — Luke 1:45
f of *the* law — Rom 13:10

569

FULL *complete, whole*

twelve f baskets	Matt 14:20
f of dead…bones	Matt 23:27
f of the Holy Spirit	Luke 4:1
also is f of light	Luke 11:34
f of grace and truth	John 1:14
f of the Spirit	Acts 6:3
f armor of God	Eph 6:11
f of compassion	James 5:11

FULNESS *completeness*

His f we…received	John 1:16
the f of the Gentiles	Rom 11:25
f of the time came	Gal 4:4
all the f of God	Eph 3:19
f to dwell in Him	Col 1:19
the f of Deity dwells	Col 2:9

FURIOUS

being **f-ly** enraged at them	Acts 26:11

FURNACE *oven*

cast them into the f	Matt 13:42
to glow in a f	Rev 1:15

FURNISH *supply*

upper room **f-ed**	Mark 14:15
having **f-ed** proof to all men	Acts 17:31

FURY *anger*

the f of a fire	Heb 10:27

FUTILE *useless, vain*

devise f things	Acts 4:25
f in…speculations	Rom 1:21

FUTURE *that which is ahead*

foundation for the f	1 Tim 6:19
in the f there is laid up	2 Tim 4:8

G

GABRIEL

angel of high rank	Luke 1:19,26

GAD *tribe* — Rev 7:5

GAIN (n) *profit, increase*

to die is g	Phil 1:21
fond of sordid g	1 Tim 3:8

GAIN (v) *acquire*

g-s the whole world	Matt 16:26
that I may g Christ	Phil 3:8
may g the glory	2 Thess 2:14

GAIUS

1 *Macedonian*	Acts 19:29
2 *companion of Paul*	Acts 20:4
3 *Corinthian believer*	1 Cor 1:14
4 *addressee of 3 John*	3 John 1

GALATIA

Roman province in Asia Minor	1 Cor 16:1;
	2 Tim 4:10

GALE *storm*

a fierce g of wind	Mark 4:37; Luke 8:23

GALILEE

1 *district in N Palestine*	
	Matt 2:22; Acts 10:37
2 *Sea of*	Matt 4:18; Mark 7:31
also Lake of Gennesaret	

GALL *bitter herb, bitterness*

drink…with g	Matt 27:34
the g of bitterness	Acts 8:23

GALLIO

governor of Achaia	Acts 18:12,17

GAMALIEL

Pharisee	Acts 5:34;22:3

GARDEN *planted area*

in the g with Him	John 18:26
the g a new tomb	John 19:41

GARLAND *ornament*

brought…**g-s** to the	Acts 14:13

GARMENT *clothing, dress*

g of camel's hair	Matt 3:4
g as white as snow	Matt 28:3
I just touch His **g-s**	Mark 5:28
spread their **g-s**	Mark 11:8
dividing up His **g-s**	Luke 23:34
put his outer g on	John 21:7
become old as a g	Heb 1:11
clothed in white **g-s**	Rev 3:5

GATE *entry way*

Enter…narrow g	Matt 7:13
g-s of Hades shall	Matt 16:18
did not open the g	Acts 12:14

GATES OF JERUSALEM
see **Beautiful Gate**

GATEWAY

when he had gone out to the g	Matt 26:71

GATHER *assemble, collect*

hen **g-s** her chicks	Matt 23:37
elders…were **g-ed**	Matt 26:3
g…His elect	Mark 13:27
G up the leftover	John 6:12

GAZA

descends from Jerusalem to G	Acts 8:26

GAZE (n) *view, glance*

turning His g on His	Luke 6:20
fixed his g upon him	Acts 3:4

GAZE (v) *look, stare*

g-ing…into the sky	Acts 1:10
he **g-ed** intently into heaven	Acts 7:55

GENEALOGY *family record*

g of Jesus Christ	Matt 1:1
and endless **g-ies**	1 Tim 1:4
whose g is not traced	Heb 7:6

GENERATION *age, period*

this g seek for a sign	Mark 8:12
g-s…not made known	Eph 3:5
and perverse g	Phil 2:15

GENEROUS *bountiful*

because I am g	Matt 20:15
g…ready to share	1 Tim 6:18

GENNESARET

1 *lake*	Luke 5:1
2 *land or district*	Matt 14:34; Mark 6:53

GENTILES *foreigners, non-Jews*

Galilee of the G	Matt 4:15
deliver…to the G	Matt 20:19
revelation to the G	Luke 2:32
Why did the G rage	Acts 4:25
salvation…to the G	Rom 11:11
preach…among the G	Gal 1:16

GENTLE *compassionate, mild*

Blessed are the g	Matt 5:5
G, and mounted on	Matt 21:5
a g and quiet spirit	1 Pet 3:4

GENTLENESS *kindness*

and a spirit of g	1 Cor 4:21
and g of Christ	2 Cor 10:1
g, self-control	Gal 5:23
humility and g, with	Eph 4:2

GETHSEMANE

garden on Mount of Olives	Matt 26:36;
	Mark 14:32

GHOST *spirit*

saying, It is a g	Matt 14:26
it was a g	Mark 6:49

GIFT *present*

to Him **g-s**	Matt 2:11
g of the Holy Spirit	Acts 2:38
impart…spiritual g	Rom 1:11
g of God is eternal	Rom 6:23
desire…greater **g-s**	1 Cor 12:31
perfect g is from	James 1:17

GIRD *bind*

g-ed…with truth	Eph 6:14
g your minds for	1 Pet 1:13
g-ed across His breast	Rev 1:13

GIRDLE *belt, waistband*

with a golden g	Rev 1:13
with golden **g-s**	Rev 15:6

GIRL *maiden*

the g has not died	Matt 9:24
the king said to the g	Mark 6:22

GIVE *bestow, yield*

gave birth to a Son	Matt 1:25
G us this day	Matt 6:11
g-ing thanks, He	Matt 15:36
g you the keys	Matt 16:19
authority…been **g-n**	Matt 28:18
what shall a man g	Mark 8:37
body which is **g-n**	Luke 22:19
gave His only…Son	John 3:16
not as the world **g-s**	John 14:27
gave up His spirit	John 19:30
what I do have I g	Acts 3:6
g-n among men	Acts 4:12
more blessed to g	Acts 20:35
was **g-n** me a thorn	2 Cor 12:7
always **g-ing** thanks	Eph 5:20
who gave Himself	1 Tim 2:6
g-s a greater grace	James 4:6
g-n us eternal life	1 John 5:11
to be **g-n** a mark	Rev 13:16

GLAD *pleased*

Rejoice, and be g	Matt 5:12
Be g in that day	Luke 6:23
who bring g tidings	Rom 10:15

GLADNESS *joy*

g and sincerity of	Acts 2:46
With the oil of g	Heb 1:9

GLASS *crystal*

sea of g like crystal	Rev 4:6
pure gold, like clear g	Rev 21:18

GLOOM *darkness*

darkness and g and	Heb 12:18
and your joy to g	James 4:9

GLORIFY *honor, worship*

g your Father	Matt 5:16
shepherds…**g-ing**	Luke 2:20
Jesus…not yet **g-ied**	John 7:39
Father, g Thy name	John 12:28
God is **g-ied** in Him	John 13:31
were all **g-ing** God	Acts 4:21
Gentiles to g God	Rom 15:9
g God in your body	1 Cor 6:20
did not g Himself	Heb 5:5

GLORIOUS *exalted, great*

the g things being done	Luke 13:17
g gospel of…God	1 Tim 1:11

GLORY (n) *honor, splendor*

Solomon in all his g	Matt 6:29
g of the Lord shone	Luke 2:9
G…in the highest	Luke 2:14
He comes in His g	Luke 9:26
do not seek My g	John 8:50
short of the g of God	Rom 3:23
all to the g of God	1 Cor 10:31
eternal weight of g	2 Cor 4:17
body of His g	Phil 3:21
crowned Him with g	Heb 2:7
unfading crown of g	1 Pet 5:4

GLORY (v) *exalt*

I…have cause to g	Phil 2:16
bringing many sons to g	Heb 2:10

GLUTTON *excessive eater*

Behold, a **g-ous** man	Matt 11:19
evil beasts, lazy **g-s**	Titus 1:12

GNASH *grind*

weeping and **g-ing** of	Matt 8:12
g-ing their teeth	Acts 7:54

GNAT *insect*

strain out a g and	Matt 23:24

GO *move, proceed*

g one mile, g…two	Matt 5:41
G into all…world	Mark 16:15
I g to prepare a	John 14:2
night is almost **gone**	Rom 13:12

GOADS *inducements*

kick against the g	Acts 26:14

GOAL *end, object*

press on toward the g	Phil 3:14
g…is love	1 Tim 1:5

GOAT *animal*

sheep from the **g-s**	Matt 25:32
blood of **g-s**…bulls	Heb 9:13

GOD *Deity, Eternal One*

G descending…dove	Matt 3:16
they shall see G	Matt 5:8
What…G has joined	Matt 19:6
kingdom of G is at	Mark 1:15
My G, why hast	Mark 15:34
You the Son of G	Luke 22:70
the Word was G	John 1:1
No man has seen G	John 1:18
the Lamb of G	John 1:29
G so loved the world	John 3:16
G is spirit	John 4:24
voice of…Son of G	John 5:25
obey G rather than	Acts 5:29
judgment of G	Rom 2:2
bear fruit for G	Rom 7:4
we are children of G	Rom 8:16
are a temple of G	1 Cor 3:16
full armor of G	Eph 6:11
one G…one mediator	1 Tim 2:5
is inspired by G	2 Tim 3:16
word of G is…sharper	Heb 4:12
impossible…G to lie	Heb 6:18
G is love	1 John 4:8
great supper of G	Rev 19:17

GODDESS *female deity*

great g Artemis	Acts 19:27
blasphemers of…g	Acts 19:37

GODLESS *pagan, without God*

hands of g men	Acts 2:23
become of the g	1 Pet 4:18

GODLINESS *holiness*

in all g and dignity	1 Tim 2:2
the mystery of g	1 Tim 3:16
g is profitable	1 Tim 4:8
a form of g	2 Tim 3:5
g, brotherly kindness	2 Pet 1:7

GODLY *holy*

and g sincerity	2 Cor 1:12
to live g in Christ	2 Tim 3:12
rescue the g from	2 Pet 2:9

GOD(S) *false deity, idols*

The voice of a g	Acts 12:22
g-s…become like	Acts 14:11
the g of this world	2 Cor 4:4

GOD, SON OF
see **SON OF GOD**

GOG

symbol of godless nations	Rev 20:8

GOLD *precious metal*

to Him gifts of g	Matt 2:11
Do not acquire g	Matt 10:9
Divine nature…g	Acts 17:29
coveted no…g	Acts 20:33
city was pure g	Rev 21:18

GOLGOTHA

site of Crucifixion	
	Matt 27:33; Mark 15:22; John 19:17

GOMORRAH

probably S of Dead Sea	Matt 10:15; 2 Pet 2:6

HORSE *animal*
behold, a black **h** — Rev 6:5
Him on white **h** — Rev 19:14
HORSEMEN *cavalry, horse rider*
armies of the **h** — Rev 9:16
leaving the **h** — Acts 23:32
HOSANNA *acclamation of praise*
H to the Son of — Matt 21:9
H in the highest — Mark 11:10
H! Blessed is He — John 12:13
HOSEA
prophet, book — Rom 9:25
HOSPITABLE *friendly*
h, able to teach — 1 Tim 3:2
h, loving what is — Titus 1:8
h to one another — 1 Pet 4:9
HOSPITALITY *open to guests*
practicing **h** — Rom 12:13
show **h** to strangers — Heb 13:2
HOST *army, multitude*
of the heavenly **h** — Luke 2:13
the **h** of heaven — Acts 7:42
led captive a **h** — Eph 4:8
HOSTILE *antagonistic*
h to...Jesus — Acts 26:9
set on the flesh is **h** — Rom 8:7
h to all men — 1 Thess 2:15
HOT *very warm, violent*
will be a **h** day — Luke 12:55
neither cold nor **h** — Rev 3:15
HOUR *time*
healed that *very* **h** — Matt 8:13
watch...for one **h** — Matt 26:40
the **h** is at hand — Matt 26:45
ninth **h** Jesus cried — Mark 15:34
save Me from this **h** — John 12:27
the **h** has come — John 17:1
the **h** of testing — Rev 3:10
HOUSE *home or temple*
his **h** upon the rock — Matt 7:24
My **h**...a **h** of — Matt 21:13
devour widow's **h-s** — Mark 12:40
left **h** or wife or — Luke 18:29
In My Father's **h** — John 14:2
h not made...hands — 2 Cor 5:1
h for a holy — 1 Pet 2:5
HOUSEHOLD *family, home*
like a head of a **h** — Matt 13:52
are of God's **h** — Eph 2:19
manages his own **h** — 1 Tim 3:4
in the **h** of God — 1 Tim 3:15
HOUSETOP *roof*
upon the **h-s** — Matt 10:27
Peter went...the **h** — Acts 10:9
HUMAN *mankind, person*
tablets of **h** hearts — 2 Cor 3:3
terms of **h** relations — Gal 3:15
HUMBLE (adj) *gentle, modest*
gentle and **h** in — Matt 11:29
along with **h** means — Phil 4:12
grace to the **h** — James 4:6
HUMBLE (v) *modest*
h-s...as this child — Matt 18:4
H yourselves — 1 Pet 5:6
HUMILIATE *embarrass*
His opponents...**h-d** — Luke 13:17
may **h** me before — 2 Cor 12:21
HUMILIATION *embarrassment*
In **h** His judgment — Acts 8:33
HUMILITY *self-abasement*
with **h** of mind — Phil 2:3
clothe...with **h** — 1 Pet 5:5
HUNDRED *number or many*
in companies of **h-s** — Mark 6:40
five **h** brethren — 1 Cor 15:6
HUNGER (n) *craving, starvation*
sleeplessness, in **h** — 2 Cor 6:5
h and thirst — 2 Cor 11:27
HUNGER (v) *crave, need food*
are those who **h** — Matt 5:6
to Me shall not **h** — John 6:35
They shall **h** no more — Rev 7:16
HUNGRY *empty, needing food*
He then became **h** — Matt 4:2
disciples became **h** — Matt 12:1
For I was **h** — Matt 25:35
if your enemy is **h** — Rom 12:20
HUNT *pursue, seek*
companions **h-ed** for — Mark 1:36
HURT (n) *damage, harm, wound*
your brother is **h** — Rom 14:15
HURT (v) *cause pain, wound*
not **h** them — Mark 16:18
their power to **h** men — Rev 9:10
HUSBAND *family head, spouse*
divorces her **h** and — Mark 10:12
have had five **h-s** — John 4:18
if her **h** dies — Rom 7:2
have her own **h** — 1 Cor 7:2

unbelieving **h** is — 1 Cor 7:14
h is the head of — Eph 5:23
H-s, love your wives — Eph 5:25
h-s of...one wife — 1 Tim 3:12
adorned for her **h** — Rev 21:2
HYMENAEUS
heretical teacher at Ephesus
— 1 Tim 1:20; 2 Tim 2:17
HYMN *song of praise*
after singing a **h** — Matt 26:30
singing **h-s** of praise — Acts 16:25
psalms and **h-s** and — Eph 5:19
HYPOCRISY *pretense*
full of **h** and — Matt 23:28
love be without **h** — Rom 12:9
without **h** — James 3:17
HYPOCRITE *a pretender*
as the **h-s** do — Matt 6:2
and Pharisees, **h-s** — Matt 23:13
You **h**, first take — Luke 6:42
HYSSOP *fragrant plant*
upon *a branch of* **h** — John 19:29
scarlet wool and **h** — Heb 9:19

I

I AM
I the Son of God — Matt 27:43
Jesus said, **I** — Mark 14:62
believe that **I** *He* — John 8:24
will know that **I** *He* — John 8:28
before Abraham...**I** — John 8:58
believe that **I** *He* — John 13:19
I the Alpha and — Rev 1:8
I the first and — Rev 1:17
ICONIUM
city of Asia Minor
— Acts 14:1,19; 16:2; 2 Tim 3:11
IDLE *unemployed, uninvolved*
been standing here **i** — Matt 20:6
this **i** babbler — Acts 17:18
IDOL *false deity, image*
abstain from...**i-s** — Acts 15:20
guard...from **i-s** — 1 John 5:21
IDOLATER *idol worshiper*
covetous, or an **i** — 1 Cor 5:11
do not be **i-s** — 1 Cor 10:7
sorcerers and **i-s** — Rev 21:8
IDOLATRY *idol worship*
flee from **i** — 1 Cor 10:14
i, sorcery, enmities — Gal 5:20
and abominable **i-ies** — 1 Pet 4:3
IGNORANCE *lack of knowledge*
you worship in **i** — Acts 17:23
i that is in them — Eph 4:18
silence the **i** of — 1 Pet 2:15
IGNORANT *without knowledge*
not **i** of his schemes — 2 Cor 2:11
and **i** speculations — 2 Tim 2:23
ILL *unhealthy, sick*
lunatic, and is...**i** — Matt 17:15
healed many...**i** — Mark 1:34
ILLEGITIMATE *bastard*
you are **i** children — Heb 12:8
ILLNESS *infirmity, sickness*
because of a bodily **i** — Gal 4:13
ILLUMINE *light up*
glory of God has **i-d** — Rev 21:23
God shall **i** them — Rev 22:5
IMAGE *copy, likeness*
i and glory of God — 1 Cor 11:7
i of the invisible — Col 1:15
the **i** of the beast — Rev 13:15
IMITATORS *followers*
be **i** of me — 1 Cor 4:16
be **i** of God — Eph 5:1
i of the churches — 1 Thess 2:14
IMMANUEL
title of Jesus — Matt 1:23
IMMORAL *lewd, unchaste*
with **i** people — 1 Cor 5:9
the **i** man sins — 1 Cor 6:18
i men...liars — 1 Tim 1:10
i or godless person — Heb 12:16
and **i** persons — Rev 21:8
IMMORALITY *immoral acts*
except for **i** — Matt 19:9
Flee **i** — 1 Cor 6:18
abstain from...**i** — 1 Thess 4:3
the wine of her **i** — Rev 17:2
IMMORTALITY *everlasting life*
must put on **i** — 1 Cor 15:53
alone possess **i** — 1 Tim 6:16
life and **i** to light — 2 Tim 1:10
IMPERISHABLE *indestructable*
wreath, but we an **i** — 1 Cor 9:25
will be raised **i** — 1 Cor 15:52
inheritance...is **i** — 1 Pet 1:4
IMPLORE *ask, beseech*
I i You by God — Mark 5:7
face and **i-ed** Him — Luke 5:12

IMPOSE *force upon*
i-d until a time of — Heb 9:10
IMPOSSIBLE *cannot be done*
With men this is **i** — Matt 19:26
i for God to lie — Heb 6:18
without faith it is **i** — Heb 11:6
IMPRISON *jail, restrict*
I used to **i** and beat — Acts 22:19
word of God is not **i-ed** — 2 Tim 2:9
IMPRISONMENT *confinement*
in **i-s**, in tumults — 2 Cor 6:5
Remember my **i** — Col 4:18
even to **i** as a — 2 Tim 2:9
IMPURE *unclean*
eating...with **i** hands — Mark 7:2
no immoral or **i** person — Eph 5:5
IMPURITY *uncleanness*
as slaves to **i** — Rom 6:19
of **i** with greediness — Eph 4:19
INCENSE *fragrant substance*
golden altar of **i** — Heb 9:4
the smoke of the **i** — Rev 8:4
INCITE *stir up*
who **i-s** the people — Luke 23:14
INCORRUPTIBLE *not impure*
glory of the **i** God — Rom 1:23
Christ with a *love* **i** — Eph 6:24
INCREASE (v) *multiply*
i-ing in wisdom — Luke 2:52
i-ng in...knowledge — Col 1:10
Lord cause...to **i** — 1 Thess 3:12
INDIGNANT *be angry*
the ten became **i** — Matt 20:24
Jesus...was **i** — Mark 10:14
i because Jesus had — Luke 13:14
INDWELLS *inhabits*
but sin which **i** me — Rom 7:17
His Spirit who **i** you — Rom 8:11
INFANT *child*
the mouth of **i-s** — Matt 21:16
would expose their **i-s** — Acts 7:19
INFERIOR *lower in status*
i to...apostles — 2 Cor 12:11
i to...churches — 2 Cor 12:13
INFLICT *strike, impose*
i-ed many blows — Acts 16:23
God who **i-s** wrath — Rom 3:5
INHERIT *receive a legacy*
gentle...**i** the earth — Matt 5:5
do to **i** the earth — Luke 10:25
not **i** the kingdom — 1 Cor 6:9
might **i** a blessing — 1 Pet 3:9
who overcomes shall **i** — Rev 21:7
INHERITANCE *bequest, legacy*
the **i** will be ours — Mark 12:7
we...obtained an **i** — Eph 1:11
the **i** of the saints — Col 1:12
i...imperishable — 1 Pet 1:4
INIQUITY *injustice, wickedness*
the bondage of **i** — Acts 8:23
the *very* world of **i** — James 3:6
remembered her **i-ies** — Rev 18:5
INJURE *harm, wrong*
nothing shall **i** you — Luke 10:19
do you **i** one another — Acts 7:26
INJUSTICE *inequity, unfairness*
is no **i** with God — Rom 9:14
INK *writing liquid*
not with **i**, but with the Spirit — 2 Cor 3:3
with pen and **i** — 3 John 13
INN *lodge for travelers*
no room...in the **i** — Luke 2:7
brought him to...**i** — Luke 10:34
INNKEEPER *traveler's host*
gave them to the **i** — Luke 10:35
INNOCENT *blameless*
and **i** as doves — Matt 10:16
betraying **i** blood — Matt 27:4
i of this Man's — Matt 27:24
holy, **i**, undefiled — Heb 7:26
INQUIRE *ask, seek*
i...where the Christ — Matt 2:4
i-d of them the hour — John 4:52
INSANE *mad*
a demon and is **i** — John 10:20
I speak as if **i** — 2 Cor 11:23
INSCRIPTION *writing*
Pilate wrote an **i** — John 19:19
i, To An Unknown — Acts 17:23
INSIGHT *discernment*
not gained any **i** — Mark 6:52
In all wisdom and **i** — Eph 1:8
INSIGNIFICANT *unimportant*
citizen of no **i** city — Acts 21:39
INSOLENT *arrogant*
haters of God, **i** — Rom 1:30
INSPIRED *stimulated*
the love we **i** in you — 2 Cor 8:7
All Scripture is **i** — 2 Tim 3:16

INSTINCT *natural tendency*
as creatures of i — 2 Pet 2:12
they know by i — Jude 10
INSTRUCT *teach*
i-ed out of the Law — Rom 2:18
just as you were i-ed — Col 2:7
may i certain men — 1 Tim 1:3
INSTRUCTION *teaching*
i-s to His twelve — Matt 11:1
written for our i — Rom 15:4
i of the Lord — Eph 6:4
goal of our i is love — 1 Tim 1:5
i about washings — Heb 6:2
INSTRUMENT *object, vessel*
he is a chosen i — Acts 9:15
i-s of unrighteousness — Rom 6:13
INSULT (n) *affront, indignity*
casting the same i — Matt 27:44
and cast i-s at you — Luke 6:22
evil, or i for i — 1 Pet 3:9
INSULT (v) *treat with scorn*
when You say this, You i us too — Luke 11:45
i-ed the Spirit of — Heb 10:29
INTELLIGENCE *mental ability*
Paulus, a man of i — Acts 13:7
INTELLIGENT *bright, smart*
from *the* wise and i — Matt 11:25; Luke 10:21
INTEND *purpose*
i-ing to betray Him — John 12:4
i-ing...to take Paul — Acts 20:13
INTENTION *aim, goal*
i of your heart — Acts 8:22
kind i of His will — Eph 1:5
INTERCEDE *plead, mediate*
Spirit Himself i-s — Rom 8:26
who also i for us — Rom 8:34
INTEREST *concern or usury*
mind on God's i-s — Matt 16:23
money...with i — Matt 25:27
he has a morbid i — 1 Tim 6:4
INTERPRET *explain, translate*
unless he i-s — 1 Cor 14:5
pray that he may i — 1 Cor 14:13
INTERPRETATION *explain*
the i of tongues — 1 Cor 12:10
of one's own i — 2 Pet 1:20
INVALIDATE *nullify*
i-d the word of God — Matt 15:6
i-ing the word of God — Mark 7:13
does not i a covenant — Gal 3:17
INVESTIGATE *examine*
having i-d everything — Luke 1:3
at a loss how to i such matters — Acts 25:20
INVISIBLE *unseen*
His i attributes — Rom 1:20
image of the i God — Col 1:15
visible and i — Col 1:16
eternal, immortal, i — 1 Tim 1:17
INVITE *request*
did not i Me in — Matt 25:43
i *the* poor — Luke 14:13
IRON *metal*
conscience as with a branding i — 1 Tim 4:2
rule...rod of i — Rev 19:15
ISAAC *son of Abraham* — Matt 1:2; Gal 4:28
offered for sacrifice — Heb 11:17; James 2:21
ISAIAH *prophet of Judah*
Matt 3:3; Mark 7:6; Luke 4:17; Acts 8:28
ISCARIOT
geographical identity of Judas — Mark 3:19;
John 12:4; 13:26
ISLAND *surrounded by water*
i was called Malta — Acts 28:1
every i fled away — Rev 16:20
ISRAEL
under Roman rule
Luke 2:32; John 1:49; Rom 9:6
ISSACHAR
tribe — Rev 7:7
ISSUE (n) *subject at hand*
those who were circumcised took i
Acts 11:2
concerning this i — Acts 15:2
ITALY
S European country
Acts 18:2;27:1,6; Heb 13:24
ITURAEA
region N of Palestine — Luke 3:1
IVORY *elephant tusk*
every article of i — Rev 18:12

J

JACINTH *precious stone*
the eleventh, j — Rev 21:20
JACOB
son of Isaac
brother of Esau
father of Joseph — Matt 1:15,16; Mark 12:26;
Luke 13:28; Rom 9:13; Heb 11:21

JAIL *place of confinement*
put them in j until the next day — Acts 4:3
put them in...j — Acts 5:18
JAILER *warden*
the j to guard them — Acts 16:23
j reported these words to Paul — Acts 16:36
JAIRUS
ruler of synagogue — Mark 5:22; Luke 8:41
JAMES
1 *son of Zebedee* — Matt 4:21
brother of John — Matt 10:2
called as apostle — Matt 10:2ff
martyred — Acts 12:2
2 *son of Alphaeus* — Matt 10:3
called as apostle — Matt 10:3ff
3 *brother of Jesus* — Matt 13:55; Mark 6:3
church leader — Acts 12:17;15:13
4 *Judas' father* — Luke 6:16
JAR *container, jug*
j full of sour wine — John 19:29
golden j holding the manna — Heb 9:4
JASON
Christian of Thessalonica
Acts 17:5-9; Rom 16:21
JASPER *precious stone*
was like a j stone — Rev 4:3
of crystal-clear j — Rev 21:11
JEALOUS *envious, zealous*
Jews, becoming j — Acts 17:5
I will make you j — Rom 10:19
love is kind...not j — 1 Cor 13:4
JEHOSHAPHAT
king of Judah ancestor of Jesus — Matt 1:8
JEPHTHAH
judge of Israel — Heb 11:32
JEREMIAH
prophet — Matt 2:17;16:14
JERICHO
city in Jordan Valley N of Dead Sea
Luke 18:35; Mark 11:30
JERUSALEM
city of Roman period — Matt 2:1,3;21:1,10;
Luke 13:34; Acts 11:2,22
new Jerusalem — Rev 3:12;21:2,10
JESSE
father of David — Matt 1:6; Acts 13:22;
Rom 15:12
JESUS
1 *name of the Lord* — Matt 1:21; Luke 1:31
birth in Bethlehem
Matt 1:18-25; Luke 2:1-7
youth in Nazareth — Matt 2:19ff
baptized
Matt 3:13ff; Mark 1:9ff; Luke 3:21;
John 1:31ff
tempted
Matt 4:1-11; Mark 1:12; Luke 4:1ff
called disciples
Matt 4:18ff; Mark 1:16ff; Luke 5:1ff
transfigured
Matt 17:1ff; Mark 9:2ff; Luke 9:28ff
triumphal entry to Jerusalem
Matt 21:1ff; Mark 11:1ff; Luke 19:29ff
crucified
Matt 27:31ff; Mark 15:20ff; Luke 23:26ff;
John 19:16ff
resurrected Christ
Matt 28:1ff; Mark 16:1ff; Luke 24:13ff;
John 20:11ff
ascended to the Father
Mark 16:19; Luke 24:50ff; Acts 1:9ff
2 *Jewish Christian called Justus* — Col 4:11
JEW(S)
originally an inhabitant of Judah
the name Judean shortened to Jew during exile
later term for all Israelites in the land and in
the Diaspora — Matt 27:11;
Mark 7:3; Luke 23:51; John 4:9; Acts 22:3;
Rom 3:1; Gal 3:28; Rev 2:9
JEWISH
pertaining to Jews — John 2:6; Acts 13:6
JEZEBEL
woman at Thyatira — Rev 2:20
JOANNA
wife of Chuza — Luke 8:3
ministered to Jesus — Luke 24:10
JOB
showed great endurance — James 5:11
JOEL
prophet — Acts 2:16
JOHN
1 *father of Peter* — John 1:42
2 *the Baptist* — Matt 3:1
baptizing — Matt 3:13
beheaded — Mark 6:25
birth foretold — Luke 1:13
son of Zacharias — Luke 1:57ff
praised by Jesus — Luke 7:28
preached — John 1:15
3 *the apostle* — Matt 10:2
called by Jesus — Matt 4:21

Sons of Thunder — Mark 3:17
inner circle — Matt 17:1
request refused — Mark 10:35ff
assigned the care of Mary — John 19:26,27
with Peter — Acts 3:1,3
4 *Jewish leader* — Acts 4:6
5 *Mark, evangelist* — Acts 12:12,25
JOIN *bring together, couple*
God...j-ed together — Matt 19:6
j-ed him...believed — Acts 17:34
j...me in suffering — 2 Tim 1:8
JOINT *juncture*
together by the j-s — Col 2:19
both j-s and marrow — Heb 4:12
JONAH
prophet of Israel — Matt 12:39;16:4; Luke 11:32
JOPPA
seaport W of Jerusalem — Acts 9:36
JORAM
son of Jehoshaphat — Matt 1:8
JORDAN
river in Palestine — Matt 3:6
JOSEPH
1 *husband of Mary*
Matt 1:18;2:13; Luke 2:16; John 6:42
2 *brother of Jesus* — Matt 13:55
3 *brother of James the Less* — Matt 27:56
4 *of Arimathea* — Matt 27:57ff
in Sanhedrin (Council) — Mark 15:43
disciple of Jesus — John 19:38
provided tomb — Matt 27:57
5 *ancestor of Jesus* — Luke 3:24
6 *ancestor of Jesus* — Luke 3:30
7 *surname Barsabbas* — Acts 1:23
8 *Barnabas* — Acts 4:36
9 *son of Jacob* — Acts 7:9ff; Heb 11:22
JOSES
1 *brother of James the Less* — Mark 15:40
2 *brother of Jesus* — Mark 6:3
JOSHUA
Moses' successor — Acts 7:45; Heb 4:8
JOURNEY *traveling, trip*
a bag for *your* j — Matt 10:10
nothing for *your* j — Luke 9:3
Sabbath day's j away — Acts 1:12
on frequent j-s — 2 Cor 11:26
JOY *delight, happiness*
with great j — Matt 2:10
enter into the j — Matt 25:21
j in heaven over one — Luke 15:7
j in the Holy Spirit — Rom 14:17
love, j, peace — Gal 5:22
make my j complete — Phil 2:2
JOYFULLY *full of joy, happy*
to praise God j — Luke 19:37
accepted j the seizure — Heb 10:34
JUDAH
1 *son of Jacob* — Matt 1:2
2 *tribe* — Heb 7:14; Rev 5:5;7:5
3 *land* — Matt 2:6
JUDAISM *Jewish way of life*
manner of life in J — Gal 1:13
advancing in J — Gal 1:14
JUDAS
1 *Iscariot* — Matt 10:4
used by Satan — Luke 22:3
son of Simon — John 6:71
treasurer — John 13:29
betrayed Jesus — John 18:2
2 *Jesus' brother* — Matt 13:55; Mark 6:3
3 *apostle* — Luke 6:16; Acts 1:13
4 *Judas of Galilee* — Acts 5:37
5 *of Damascus* — Acts 9:11
6 *Barsabbas* — Acts 15:22,27
JUDE
brother of Jesus — Matt 13:55; Mark 6:3
brother of James — Jude 1
JUDEA
Roman province in Palestine based on earlier
Judah
Matt 2:1; Mark 1:5; Luke 2:4; John 11:7
JUDGE (n) *leader*
unrighteous j said — Luke 18:6
one Lawgiver and J — James 4:12
JUDGE (v) *pass judgment*
not j lest you be j-d — Matt 7:1
Son...world to j — John 3:17
Law...not j a man — John 7:51
not come to j the — John 12:47
able to j...thoughts — Heb 4:12
adulterers God will j — Heb 13:4
JUDGMENT *condemnation*
in the day of j — Matt 10:15
j, that the light — John 3:19
resurrection of j — John 5:29
My j is just — John 5:30
after this *comes* j — Heb 9:27
incur a stricter j — James 3:1
not fall under j — James 5:12
kept for the day of j — 2 Pet 3:7

JUMP
j of the great day — Jude 6
to execute j upon all — Jude 15
His j-s are true — Rev 19:2
JUMP *leap*
j-ed up, and came — Mark 10:50
JUST *fair, right*
My judgment is j — John 5:30
the j for the unjust — 1 Pet 3:18
JUSTICE *fairness, righteousness*
j and mercy and — Matt 23:23
acknowledged...j — Luke 7:29
grant to your slaves j — Col 4:1
JUSTIFICATION *vindication*
because of our j — Rom 4:25
j of life to all men — Rom 5:18
JUSTIFY *declare guiltless*
wishing to j himself — Luke 10:29
these He also j-ied — Rom 8:30
God...j-ies — Rom 8:33
seeking to be j-ied — Gal 2:17
JUSTUS
  1 *Joseph, apostolic candidate*
  also called Barsabbas — Acts 1:23
  2 *Titus, Corinthian disciple* — Acts 18:7
  3 *Jewish Christian* — Col 4:11

K

KEEP *hold, guide, preserve*
to k the Passover — Matt 26:18
if anyone k-s My — John 8:51
he will k My word — John 14:23
k-ing faith and a — 1 Tim 1:19
k yourself free from — 1 Tim 5:22
KEY *unlocking tool*
k-s of the kingdom — Matt 16:19
the k of knowledge — Luke 11:52
k-s of death and of — Rev 1:18
k of the bottomless pit — Rev 9:1
KID *young goat*
never given me a k — Luke 15:29
KIDRON
  brook and valley between Jerusalem and Mount
  of Olives — John 18:1
KILL *take life*
unable to k the — Matt 10:28
k-ed, and be raised — Luke 9:22
do you seek to k Me — John 7:19
Arise, Peter, k and — Acts 10:13
the letter k-s, but — 2 Cor 3:6
who k their father — 1 Tim 1:9
k a third of mankind — Rev 9:15
KIND (adj) *good, tender*
He Himself is k — Luke 6:35
love is k — 1 Cor 13:4
be k to one another — Eph 4:32
KIND (n) *group, variety*
all k-s of evil — Matt 5:11
k-s of tongues — 1 Cor 12:28
every k of impurity — Eph 4:19
KINDNESS *tenderness*
with deeds of k — Acts 9:36
k and...of God — Rom 11:22
joy, peace, patience, k — Gal 5:22
compassion, k — Col 3:12
tasted the k of the — 1 Pet 2:3
godliness, brotherly k — 2 Pet 1:7
KINDRED *relative*
no one...of k spirit — Phil 2:20
KINDLE *cause to burn, stimulate*
had k-d a fire — Luke 22:55
K afresh the gift — 2 Tim 1:6
KING *monarch, regent*
born K of the Jews — Matt 2:2
Are You the K of — Matt 27:11
your K is coming — John 12:15
no k but Caesar — John 19:15
K of k-s and Lord — 1 Tim 6:15
God, honor the k — 1 Pet 2:17
KINGDOM *domain, monarchy*
k of heaven is at — Matt 3:2
showed Him...k-s — Matt 4:8
Thy k come — Matt 6:10
sons of the k — Matt 13:38
keys of the k — Matt 16:19
in My Father's k — Matt 26:29
enter the k of God — Mark 10:24
to give you the k — Luke 12:32
cannot see the k of — John 3:3
preaching the k — Acts 28:31
k of His beloved Son — Col 1:13
to His heavenly k — 2 Tim 4:18
faith conquered k-s — Heb 11:33
heirs of the k — James 2:5
KINSMAN *relative*
my k-men according — Rom 9:3
Herodion, my k — Rom 16:11
KISH
  father of King Saul — Acts 13:21
KISS (n) *expression of affection*
You gave Me no k — Luke 7:45

betraying...with a k — Luke 22:48
with a holy k — Rom 16:16
with a k of love — 1 Pet 5:14
KISS (v) *expression of affection*
Whomever I...k — Mark 14:44
not...to k my feet — Luke 7:45
KNEE *part of body*
every k shall bow — Rom 14:11
every k should bow — Phil 2:10
KNEEL *bend, rest on knee*
k-ed...before Him — Matt 27:29
man ran...knelt — Mark 10:17
He knelt down — Luke 22:41
KNIT *joined together*
k together in love — Col 2:2
KNOCK *smite, strike*
k, and it shall be — Matt 7:7
stand outside and k — Luke 13:25
he k-ed at the door — Acts 12:13
at the door and k — Rev 3:20
KNOW *experience, understand*
left hand k what — Matt 6:3
k...by their fruits — Matt 7:20
I never knew you — Matt 7:23
God k-s your hearts — Luke 16:15
you shall k the truth — John 8:32
I k My own — John 10:14
k-ing that His hour — John 13:1
k that I love You — John 21:15
and k all mysteries — 1 Cor 13:2
who knew no sin — 2 Cor 5:21
k the love of Christ — Eph 3:19
value of k-ing Christ — Phil 3:8
k...I have believed — 2 Tim 1:12
k...eternal life — 1 John 5:13
I k your deeds — Rev 2:2
KNOWLEDGE *information*
in accordance with k — Rom 10:2
K makes arrogant — 1 Cor 8:1
k, it will be done — 1 Cor 13:8
have no k of God — 1 Cor 15:34
love...surpasses k — Eph 3:19
treasures of...k — Col 2:3
grow in...grace and k — 2 Pet 3:18
KORAH
  rebelled against Moses — Jude 11

L

LABOR (n) *work or childbirth*
in l and hardship — 2 Cor 11:27
fruitful for me — Phil 1:22
faith and l of love — 1 Thess 1:3
cried out, being in l — Rev 12:2
LABOR (v) *toil, work*
l-ed over you in vain — Gal 4:11
we l and strive — 1 Tim 4:10
LABORER *workman*
l-s for his vineyard — Matt 20:1
Call the l-s and pay — Matt 20:8
l-s into His harvest — Luke 10:2
l is worthy of his — Luke 10:7
LACK (n) *deficiency, need*
l of self-control — 1 Cor 7:5
little had no l — 2 Cor 8:15
LACK (v) *be deficient, need*
am I still l-ing — Matt 19:20
One thing you l — Mark 10:21
not l-ing in any gift — 1 Cor 1:7
if any...l-s wisdom — James 1:5
LAD *boy*
l here who has five — John 6:9
LADY *woman*
elder to the chosen l — 2 John 1
LAKE *pool, water*
standing by the l — Luke 5:1
wind...upon the l — Luke 8:23
into the l, and were — Luke 8:33
into the l of fire — Rev 20:10
LAMB *young sheep*
send you out as l-s — Luke 10:3
Behold, the L of God — John 1:29
Tend My l-s — John 21:15
l before its shearer — Acts 8:32
Worthy is the L — Rev 5:12
blood of the L — Rev 12:11
LAME *crippled, disabled*
the l walk — Matt 11:5
l from his mother's — Acts 14:8
LAMECH
  father of Noah — Luke 3:36
LAMENT (v) *mourn, wail*
will weep and l — John 16:20
weep and l over her — Rev 18:9
LAMENTATION *weeping*
made loud l over him — Acts 8:2
LAMP *light*
l of the body is the — Matt 6:22
l-s are going out — Matt 25:8
l-s in the upper room — Acts 20:8
l shining in a dark — 2 Pet 1:19

seven l-s of fire — Rev 4:5
LAMPSTAND *candlestick*
puts it on a l — Luke 8:16
will remove your l — Rev 2:5
LAND *country, earth*
darkness...all the l — Matt 27:45
owned a tract of l — Acts 4:37
LANDOWNER *landlord*
slaves of the l — Matt 13:27
kingdom...like a l — Matt 20:1
I who planted a — Matt 21:33
LANGUAGE *speech, word*
in figurative l — John 16:25
speak in his own l — Acts 2:6
many kinds of l-s — 1 Cor 14:10
LAODICEA
  city in Asia Minor — Col 2:1
  location of early church — Col 4:15; Rev 1:11; 3:14
LARGE *big, great, huge*
a l upper room — Mark 14:15
a l multitude — Luke 7:11
what l letters — Gal 6:11
LAST *final, utmost*
first will be l — Matt 19:30
The l Adam — 1 Cor 15:45
at the l trumpet — 1 Cor 15:52
in these l days — Heb 1:2
it is the l hour — 1 John 2:18
the first and the l — Rev 1:17
LATIN
  one of three languages written on Jesus' cross — John 19:20
LAUGH *be amused, mock*
for you shall l — Luke 6:21
began l-ing at Him — Matt 9:24
LAW *scripture, statute*
abolish the L or the — Matt 5:17
Our L...not judge — John 7:51
by that l He ought — John 19:7
by a l of faith — Rom 3:27
L brings...wrath — Rom 4:15
not under l — Rom 6:14
Is the L sin — Rom 7:7
the L is holy — Rom 7:12
L...become our tutor — Gal 3:24
thus fulfill the l — Gal 6:2
L...nothing perfect — Heb 7:19
LAWFUL *legal, right*
not l for him to eat — Matt 12:4
Is it l to heal — Matt 12:10
l...man to divorce — Mark 10:2
All things are l — 1 Cor 6:12
LAWGIVER *lawmaker*
one L and Judge — James 4:12
LAWLESS *illegal, without law*
l one will be — 2 Thess 2:8
are l and rebellious — 1 Tim 1:9
from every l deed — Titus 2:14
LAWYER *interpreter of law*
a l, asked Him a — Matt 22:35
one of the l-s said — Luke 11:45
Woe to you l-s — Luke 11:52
LAY *place, put*
l up...treasures — Matt 6:20
laid Him in a tomb — Mark 15:46
l-s down His life — John 10:11
l l down My life — John 10:15
have you laid Him — John 11:34
I l in Zion a stone — Rom 9:33
l-ing aside falsehood — Eph 4:25
l-ing hold of...hope — Heb 6:18
LAZARUS
  1 *beggar* — Luke 16:20-25
  2 *brother of Mary and Martha* — John 11:1,2,5,11,43
LAZY *idle, slothful*
You wicked, l slave — Matt 25:26
beasts, l gluttons — Titus 1:12
LEAD (v) *direct, guide*
not l us into — Matt 6:13
l the elect astray — Mark 13:22
led Him...crucify — Mark 15:20
and l-s them out — John 10:3
led by the Spirit — Rom 8:14
Led captive a host — Eph 4:8
that l-s to salvation — 2 Tim 3:15
LEADER *director, guide*
the l as the servant — Luke 22:26
Obey your l-s — Heb 13:17
LEADING (adj) *chief, noted*
number...l women — Acts 17:4
l men of the Jews — Acts 28:17
LEAF *foliage*
puts forth its l-ves — Matt 24:32
a fig tree in l — Mark 11:13
LEAP *jump, spring*
baby l-ed in her — Luke 1:41
and l for joy — Luke 6:23
l-ed up and began — Acts 14:10

LEARN *get knowledge*
I from Me	Matt 11:29
l-ed to be content	Phil 4:11
He l-ed obedience	Heb 5:8

LEARNING (n) *knowledge*
l of the Egyptians	Acts 7:22
great l is driving	Acts 26:24

LEAST *insignificant*
l in the kingdom	Matt 5:19
he who is l…is	Matt 11:11
l of the apostles	1 Cor 15:9
very l of all saints	Eph 3:8

LEATHER *animal skin*
a l belt about his	Matt 3:4
and wore a l belt	Mark 1:6

LEAVE *abandon, depart, forsake*
l the ninety-nine	Matt 18:12
Peace I l with you	John 14:27
I am l-ing…world	John 16:28

LEAVEN *yeast*
heaven is like l	Mark 1:6

LEAVE *abandon, depart, forsake*
l the ninety-nine	Matt 18:12
Peace I l with you	John 14:27
I am l-ing…world	John 16:28

LEAVEN *yeast*
heaven is like l	Matt 13:33
little l leavens the	1 Cor 5:6

LEAVENED *raised by yeast*
until it was all l	Matt 13:33; Luke 13:21

LEGAL *lawful*
Give me l protection	Luke 18:3
give her l protection	Luke 18:5

LEGION *division, group*
twelve l-s of angels	Matt 26:53
My name is L	Mark 5:9
man who had…l	Mark 5:15
L; for many demons	Luke 8:30

LEG *part of body*
not break His l-s	John 19:33

LEND *loan*
l, expecting nothing	Luke 6:35
l me three loaves	Luke 11:5

LENGTH
breadth and l and	Eph 3:18
l and width…equal	Rev 21:16

LEOPARD *animal*
beast…was like a l	Rev 13:2

LEPER *one having leprosy*
a l came to Him	Matt 8:2
cleanse the l-s	Matt 10:8
home of Simon the l	Mark 14:3

LEPROSY *infectious disease*
his l was cleansed	Matt 8:3
a man full of l	Luke 5:12

LEPROUS *having leprosy*
ten l…met Him	Luke 17:12

LET *allow, permit*
L the children alone	Matt 19:14
l this cup pass from	Matt 26:39
L not your heart be	John 14:1

LETTER *epistle or symbol*
smallest l or stroke	Matt 5:18
You are our l	2 Cor 3:2
l caused you sorrow	2 Cor 7:8
large l-s I am writing	Gal 6:11

LEVEL *flat, plain*
stood on a l place	Luke 6:17
will l you to the ground	Luke 19:44

LEVI
1 *tribe*	Rev 7:7
2 *two ancestors of Jesus*	Luke 3:24,29
3 *apostle*	Mark 2:14; Luke 5:27,29

LEVITE
descendant of Levi	Luke 10:32; John 1:19

LIAR *one telling lies*
l shall be a l like	John 8:55
hypocrisy of l-s	1 Tim 4:2
we make Him a l	1 John 1:10

LIBERTY *freedom*
spy out our l	Gal 2:4
the *law* of l	James 1:25

LIBYA
country in N Africa	Acts 2:10

LICK *lap up*
dogs were…l-ing	Luke 16:21

LIE (n) *false statement*
the father of l-s	John 8:44
truth of God for a l	Rom 1:25
no l is of the truth	1 John 2:21

LIE (v) *make false statement*
l to the Holy Spirit	Acts 5:3
not l to one another	Col 3:9
impossible…God to l	Heb 6:18

LIE (v) *recline, rest*
lying in a manger	Luke 2:12
Jesus saw him **lying** there	John 5:6
veil l-s over their heart	2 Cor 3:15

LIFE *living* or *salvation*
anxious for your l	Matt 6:25
loses his l for My	Matt 16:25
His l a ransom for	Matt 20:28
to inherit eternal l	Mark 10:17
l is more than food	Luke 12:23
but have eternal l	John 3:16
out of death into l	John 5:24
I am the bread of l	John 6:35
lays down his l	John 10:11
resurrection and…l	John 11:25
truth, and the l	John 14:6
lay down his l for	John 15:13
walk in newness of l	Rom 6:4
the Spirit gives l	2 Cor 3:6
Christ, who is our l	Col 3:4
an undisciplined l	2 Thess 3:11
receive…crown of l	James 1:12
lay down our l-ves	1 John 3:16
book of l of the lamb	Rev 13:8

LIFT *exalt, raise*
Son of Man be l-ed	John 3:14
He was l-ed up	Acts 1:9
l-ing up holy hands	1 Tim 2:8

LIGHT *brightness, lamp*
the l of the world	Matt 5:14
body will be full of l	Matt 6:22
l of revelation to	Luke 2:32
There was the true l	John 1:9
I am the l	John 8:12
while you have…l	John 12:35
l of the gospel	2 Cor 4:4
walk as children of l	Eph 5:8
Father of l-s	James 1:17
if we walk in the l	1 John 1:7

LIGHTNING *flash of light in sky*
l…from the east	Matt 24:27
appearance…like l	Matt 28:3

LIKENESS *similarity*
the l of sinful flesh	Rom 8:3
made in the l of men	Phil 2:7

LILY *flower*
l-ies of the field	Matt 6:28
"Consider the l-ies, how	Luke 12:27

LINEN *type of cloth*
left the l sheet	Mark 14:52
wrapped Him…l	Mark 15:46
saw the l wrappings	John 20:5
clothed in fine l	Rev 19:14

LION *wild animal*
like a roaring l	1 Pet 5:8
first creature…l	Rev 4:7

LIPS *part of mouth*
honors Me with…l	Matt 15:8
fruit of l that give thanks	Heb 13:15

LIQUOR *alcoholic drink*
drink no wine or l	Luke 1:15

LISTEN *hear, heed*
L…another parable	Matt 21:33
care what you l to	Mark 4:24
l-ing to the word	Luke 5:1
My Son…l to Him	Luke 9:35

LITTLE *small quantity*
O men of l faith	Matt 6:30
forgiven l, loves l	Luke 7:47
a l leaven leavens	1 Cor 5:6
l children, abide	1 John 2:28

LIVE (v) *reside* or *be alive*
not l on bread alone	Matt 4:4
l even if he dies	John 11:25
because l l	John 14:19
shall l by faith	Rom 1:17
Christ died and l-d	Rom 14:9
no longer l who l	Gal 2:20
to l is Christ	Phil 1:21
worship Him who l-s	Rev 4:10

LIVESTOCK *domestic animals*
my oxen and my fattened l	Matt 22:4

LIVING (adj) *alive*
Son of the l God	Matt 16:16
given you l water	John 4:10
I am the l bread	John 6:51
l and holy sacrifice	Rom 12:1
became a l soul	1 Cor 15:45
temple of the l God	2 Cor 6:16
word of God is l	Heb 4:12

LIVING (n) *what is alive*
God…of the l	Matt 22:32
judge the l and the	1 Pet 4:5

LOAD *burden*
My l is light	Matt 11:30
one shall bear his own l	Gal 6:5

LOAF *portion of bread*
shall ask him for a l	Matt 7:9
five l-ves and two	Matt 14:17

LOATHE *despise, detest*
you did not despise or l	Gal 4:14

LOATHSOME *detestable*
l and malignant sore	Rev 16:2

LOCK (v) *secure, shut*
l-ed quite securely	Acts 5:23
l up…the saints	Acts 26:10

LOCUST *grasshopper*
food was l-s and wild	Matt 3:4
came forth l-s upon	Rev 9:3

LOD / LYDDA
town of Benjamin SE of coastal Jaffa	Acts 9:32-38

LODGE *dwell, spend the night*
find l-ing and get	Luke 9:12
with whom we were to l	Acts 21:16

LOG *beam, wood*
l out of your own eye	Matt 7:5
l…in your own eye	Luke 6:41

LOINS *lower back*
having girded your l	Eph 6:14

LOFTY *grand, high*
every l thing raised up	2 Cor 10:5

LOIS
grandmother of Timothy	2 Tim 1:5

LONELY *alone, isolated*
l place by Himself	Matt 14:13
to a l place and rest	Mark 6:31

LONG (adj) *extended*
you make l prayers	Matt 23:14
if a man has l hair	1 Cor 11:14

LONG (v) *desire, want*
l-ing to be fed	Luke 16:21
l l to see you	Rom 1:11
angels l to look	1 Pet 1:12
l for the pure milk	1 Pet 2:2

LOOK *see, stare*
L at the birds of	Matt 6:26
l-ing up…heaven	Matt 14:19
plow and l-ing back	Luke 9:62
l on the fields	John 4:35
l on Him…pierced	John 19:37
l-ing for the blessed	Titus 2:13
l-ing for…heavens	2 Pet 3:13

LOOSE *release*
l on earth shall be	Matt 16:19
you l on earth	Matt 18:18

LORD *personal name of God*
Different Greek words are translated as Lord
Lord (*Kyrios, refers to either the Father or the Son*)	Matt 1:20; John 11:2; Acts 5:19; 2 Cor 5:6; 1 Thess 4:16
Lord (*Despotes*)	Luke 2:29; Acts 4:24; Rev 6:10
Lord God (*Kyrios Theos, refers to either the Father or the Son*)	Luke 1:32; Rev 1:8;11:17;16:7;18:8
Lord Jesus (*Kyrios Iesous*)	Mark 16:19; Luke 24:3; Acts 4:33;7:59
Lord Jesus Christ (*Kyrios Iesous Christos*)	Acts 15:26; Rom 1:7;5:1; 1 Cor 1:10; Eph 1:2,3; 1 Thess 5:9; James 2:1

LORD *human master, ruler*
his l commanded	Matt 18:25
write to my l	Acts 25:26

LOSE *mislay, suffer loss*
his life shall l it	Matt 10:39
that which was **lost**	Matt 18:11
not l his reward	Mark 9:41
whoever l-s his life	Luke 9:24

LOSS *damage, what is lost*
damage and great l	Acts 27:10
might not suffer l	2 Cor 7:9
all things to be l	Phil 3:8

LOST (adj) *missing, ruined*
l sheep…of Israel	Matt 10:6
the wine is l	Mark 2:22

LOST (n) *without God*
sent only to the l	Matt 15:24

LOT
nephew of Abraham	Luke 17:28; 2 Pet 2:7

LOT *portion or decision process*
tear it, but cast l-s	John 19:24
l fell to Matthias	Acts 1:26

LOUD *great, noisy*
Jesus cried…l voice	Matt 27:50
heard…a l voice	Rev 1:10

LOVE (n) *compassion, devotion*
l will grow cold	Matt 24:12
abide in My l	John 15:10
Greater l has no one	John 15:13
demonstrates His…l	Rom 5:8
separate us from…l	Rom 8:39
l edifies	1 Cor 8:1
l is kind	1 Cor 13:4
Pursue l	1 Cor 14:1
l of Christ controls	2 Cor 5:14
through l serve one	Gal 5:13
fruit…is l	Gal 5:22
speaking…truth in l	Eph 4:15
l of money is a root	1 Tim 6:10
for l is from God	1 John 4:7
God is l	1 John 4:16
l casts out fear	1 John 4:18

MIDIAN — MOON (Column 1)

birds which fly in m — Rev 19:17

MIDIAN
land SE of Canaan in desert — Acts 7:29

MIDST *middle, within*
I am in their m — Matt 18:20
above reproach in the m of a — Phil 2:15

MIGHT *strength*
strength of His m — Eph 1:19

MIGHTY *powerful*
m in the Scriptures — Acts 18:24
the m hand of God — 1 Pet 5:6

MILE *distance, measurement*
one m, go with him — Matt 5:41
m-s from Jerusalem — Luke 24:13

MILETUS
town in Asia Minor
— Acts 20:15,17; 2 Tim 4:20

MILK
m to drink, not — 1 Cor 3:2
pure m of the word — 1 Pet 2:2

MILL *grinding stones*
women...at the m — Matt 24:41
and the sound of a m will not be — Rev 18:22

MILLSTONE *grinding stone*
m be hung around — Matt 18:6
stone like a great m — Rev 18:21

MINA
measure of gold or silver coin — Luke 19:13ff

MIND *memory, thought*
He opened...m-s — Luke 24:45
with one m in the — Acts 2:46
to a depraved m — Rom 1:28
m set on the flesh — Rom 8:7
the m of Christ — 1 Cor 2:16
m-s were hardened — 2 Cor 3:14
with humility of m — Phil 2:3

MINDFUL *aware*
m of the...faith — 2 Tim 1:5

MINISTER (n) *one who serves*
a m and a witness — Acts 26:16
a m of Christ Jesus — Rom 15:16
is Christ then a m — Gal 2:17
I was made a m — Eph 3:7
faithful m in the — Eph 6:21
His m-s a flame of — Heb 1:7
a m in the sanctuary — Heb 8:2

MINISTER (v) *give help, serve*
angels were m-ing — Mark 1:13
follow Him and m — Mark 15:41

MINISTRY *service*
He began His m — Luke 3:23
to the m of the word — Acts 6:4
m of the Spirit — 2 Cor 3:8
m of reconciliation — 2 Cor 5:18
fulfill your m — 2 Tim 4:5
a more excellent m — Heb 8:6

MIRACLE *supernatural event*
m-s had occurred — Matt 11:21
He could do no m — Mark 6:5
perform a m in My — Mark 9:39
this m of healing — Acts 4:22
works m-s among you — Gal 3:5
wonders and...m-s — Heb 2:4

MIRE *mud*
wallowing in the m — 2 Pet 2:22

MIRROR *image reflector*
see in a m dimly — 1 Cor 13:12
natural face in a m — James 1:23

MISERABLE *bad, unhappy*
Be m and mourn — James 4:9
m and poor and blind — Rev 3:17

MISERY *sorrow, suffering*
Destruction and m — Rom 3:16

MISLEAD *lead astray*
that no one m-s you — Mark 13:5
m-ing our nation — Luke 23:2

MISSILES *what is thrown or shot*
m of the evil one — Eph 6:16

MISTREAT *treat badly, wrong*
slaves...m-ed them — Matt 22:6
pray for...who m — Luke 6:28
mocked and m-ed — Luke 18:32
m and to stone them — Acts 14:5

MOCK *ridicule, scorn*
soldiers also m-ed — Luke 23:36
God is not m-ed — Gal 6:7

MONEY *currency*
no m in their belt — Mark 6:8
m in the bank — Luke 19:23
love of m is a root — 1 Tim 6:10

MONEYCHANGERS
the tables of the m — Matt 21:12
coins of the m — John 2:15

MONSTER *enormous animal*
belly of the sea m — Matt 12:40

MOON
m will not...light — Matt 24:29

signs in...and m — Luke 21:25

MORALS *principles*
Bad...good m — 1 Cor 15:33

MORNING *dawn*
the m star arises in your hearts — 2 Pet 1:19
the bright m star — Rev 22:16

MORSEL *piece of bread*
after the m, Satan — John 13:27

MORTAL *what eventually dies*
life to your m bodies — Rom 8:11
m...immortality — 1 Cor 15:53
in our m flesh — 2 Cor 4:11

MOSES
called by God to lead the people of Israel
— Matt 17:3; Luke 16:29

MOTH *insect*
m and rust destroy — Matt 6:19
thief comes near, nor m — Luke 12:33

MOTHER
When His m Mary — Matt 1:18
take...and His m — Matt 2:13
Who is My m — Matt 12:48
Honor your...m — Matt 19:19
Behold, your m — John 19:27

MOTHER-IN-LAW
m lying sick in bed — Matt 8:14
m against daughter-in-law — Luke 12:53

MOTIVES *attitudes, intentions*
disclose the m of — 1 Cor 4:5
than from pure m — Phil 1:17
judges with evil m — James 2:4
ask with wrong m — James 4:3

MOUNT (n) *hill, mountain*
went out to the M of Olives — Mark 14:26
Lamb was standing on M Zion — Rev 14:1

MOUNT (v) *climb up*
m-ed on a donkey — Matt 21:5

MOUNT ZION
see **OLIVES, MOUNT OF**

MOUNTAIN
m-s, Fall on us — Luke 23:30
withdrew...to the m — John 6:15
faith...remove m-s — 1 Cor 13:2

MOURN *grieve, lament*
Blessed...who m — Matt 5:4
shall m and weep — Luke 6:25
Be miserable and m — James 4:9

MOUTH
out of the m of God — Matt 4:4
confess with your m — Rom 10:9

MOVE *change position, stir*
m-d with compassion — Mark 1:41
He was deeply m-d — John 11:33
in Him we live...m — Acts 17:28
m-d by the...Spirit — 2 Pet 1:21

MULTIPLY *increase*
will supply and m your seed for — 2 Cor 9:10
and peace be m-ied — 2 Pet 1:2

MULTITUDE *crowd, number*
send the m-s away — Matt 14:15
He summoned the m — Mark 8:34
Him a great m — Luke 23:27
cover a m of sins — James 5:20
love covers a m of — 1 Pet 4:8

MURDER *premeditated killing*
Whoever commits m — Matt 5:21
m-ed the prophets — Matt 23:31
full of envy, m — Rom 1:29

MURDERER *killer*
m from...beginning — John 8:44
this man is a m — Acts 28:4
no m has eternal — 1 John 3:15

MUSIC *harmony, melody*
heard m and — Luke 15:25

MUSICIAN *skilled in music*
harpists and m-s — Rev 18:22

MUSTARD *type of plant*
kingdom...like a m — Matt 13:31
faith as a m seed — Matt 17:20
It is like a m seed — Luke 13:19

MUZZLE *gag*
You shall not m the ox — 1 Cor 9:9

MYRIADS *countless*
m of angels — Heb 12:22
number...was m — Rev 5:11

MYRRH *spice*
frankincense and m — Matt 2:11
mixture of m and — John 19:39

MYSTERY *hidden truth, secret*
God's wisdom in a m — 1 Cor 2:7
know all m-ies — 1 Cor 13:2
into the m of Christ — Eph 3:4
the m of the gospel — Eph 6:19
the m of the faith — 1 Tim 3:9

MYTHS *fables*
to pay attention to m — 1 Tim 1:4
will turn aside to m — 2 Tim 4:4
attention to Jewish m — Titus 1:14

N

NAAMAN
Ben-hadad's commander — Luke 4:27

NAHOR
Abraham's grandfather — Luke 3:34

NAHUM
ancestor of Christ — Luke 3:25

NAILED (v) *attached*
you n to a cross — Acts 2:23
n it to the cross — Col 2:14

NAILS (n) *finger ends or pins*
imprint of the n — John 20:25
my finger into the place of the n, — John 20:25

NAKED *unclothed*
n...you clothed Me — Matt 25:36

NAKEDNESS *unclothed*
or persecution, or famine, or n, — Rom 8:35
shame of your n — Rev 3:18

NAME *designation, title*
Hallowed be Thy n — Matt 6:9
n-s of the twelve — Matt 10:2
such child in My n — Matt 18:5
n-s are recorded — Luke 10:20
will come in My n — Luke 21:8
baptized in the n — Acts 2:38
of faith in His n — Acts 3:16
other n under heaven — Acts 4:12
n-s are in the book — Phil 4:3

NAPHTALI
tribe / district — Matt 4:13; Rev 7:6

NARD *fragrant ointment*
perfume of pure n — Mark 14:3; John 12:3

NARROW *limited*
Enter by the n gate — Matt 7:13
the way is n — Matt 7:14

NATHAN *a son of David*
the son of N, — Luke 3:31

NATHANAEL
disciple of Jesus — John 1:49; 21:2

NATION *government, people*
n...rise against n — Matt 24:7
n should not perish — John 11:50
men, from every n — Acts 2:5
tongue...people and n — Rev 5:9

NATIVE *indigenous*
the n-s showed us — Acts 28:2
n-s saw the creature — Acts 28:4

NATURAL *normal*
n man...not accept — 1 Cor 2:14
is sown a n body — 1 Cor 15:44

NATURE *essence*
of the same n as you — Acts 14:15
n itself teach you — 1 Cor 11:14
We *are* Jews by n — Gal 2:15
of the divine n — 2 Pet 1:4

NAZARENE
1 *of Nazareth* — John 18:7
2 *follower of Jesus* — Acts 24:5

NAZARETH
town of Galilee — Matt 2:23
home of Joseph, Mary, and Jesus
— Luke 4:16; John 1:45

NECK *part of body*
millstone be hung on n — Matt 18:6
risked their own n-s — Rom 16:4

NEED *necessity, obligation*
ministered to...n-s — Acts 20:34
n-s of the saints — 2 Cor 9:12
supply all your n-s — Phil 4:19

NEEDLE
the eye of a n — Matt 19:24
n than for a rich — Mark 10:25

NEEDY *destitute, poor*
not a n person among them — Acts 4:34

NEGLECT *disregard, ignore*
n so great a salvation — Heb 2:3
n to show hospitality — Heb 13:2
do not n doing good — Heb 13:16

NEIGHBOR *one living nearby*
love your n, and — Matt 5:43
And who is my n — Luke 10:29
love your n as — Gal 5:14

NEST
birds...have n-s — Matt 8:20
n in its branches — Matt 13:32

NET *snare*
casting a n into — Matt 4:18
left the n-s and — Mark 1:18
n *full* of fish — John 21:8

NEW *fresh, recent*
n wine into old — Mark 2:22

A n commandment | John 13:34
he is a n creature | 2 Cor 5:17
a n and living way | Heb 10:20
making all things n | Rev 21:5
NEWBORN *just born*
like n babes, long | 1 Pet 2:2
NEWNESS *freshness*
walk in n of life | Rom 6:4
in n of the Spirit | Rom 7:6
NEWS *report, tidings*
the n about Jesus | Matt 14:1
n about Him went | Mark 1:28
n of a great joy | Luke 2:10
n of your faith | 1 Thess 3:6
NICODEMUS
Pharisee | John 3:1,4,9
in Sanhedrin | John 7:50; 19:39
NICOLAITANS
sect in Ephesian and Pergamum church
| Rev 2:6,15
NICOLAS
deacon, servant | Acts 6:1-6
proselyte from Antioch | Acts 6:5
NIGHT *darkness*
over their flock by n | Luke 2:8
a thief in the n | 1 Thess 5:2
tormented day and n | Rev 20:10
NINEVEH
capital of Assyria visited by Jonah
| Matt 12:41; Luke 11:32
NOAH
built an ark; saved from Flood | Matt 24:37;
Luke 3:36; 17:27; Heb 11:7; 2 Pet 2:5
NOBLEMAN *of high rank*
A certain n went to | Luke 19:12
NOISE *loud sound*
from heaven a n | Acts 2:2
NONSENSE *foolishness*
appeared...as n | Luke 24:11
NORTH *direction of compass*
and west, and from n and | Luke 13:29
three gates on the n | Rev 21:13
NOTICE *attention, seen*
not n the log | Matt 7:3
deeds to be n-d by | Matt 23:5
NOURISH *feed, sustain*
n-es and cherishes it | Eph 5:29
constantly n-ed on | 1 Tim 4:6
she might be n-ed | Rev 12:6
NULLIFY *annul, make void*
unbelief will not n | Rom 3:3
the promise is n-ied | Rom 4:14
n the grace of God | Gal 2:21
NUMBER (n) *group, total*
increasing in n daily | Acts 16:5
his n is six hundred | Rev 13:18
NUMBER (v) *count, enumerate*
hairs...all n-ed | Matt 10:30
n-ed with the eleven | Acts 1:26
NURSE (v) *suckle an infant*
who n babes in | Mark 13:17
breasts...never n | Luke 23:29

O

OAR *pole used in rowing*
straining at the o-s | Mark 6:48
OATH *declaration, vow*
make no o at all | Matt 5:34
priests without an o | Heb 7:21
OBED
ancestor of Jesus | Matt 1:5; Luke 3:32
OBEDIENCE *submission*
the o of the One | Rom 5:19
leading to o of faith | Rom 16:26
in o to the truth | 1 Pet 1:22
OBEDIENT *willing to obey*
o from the heart | Rom 6:17
o to the...death | Phil 2:8
Children, be o to | Col 3:20
OBEY *follow commands, orders*
and the sea o Him | Matt 8:27
o God rather than | Acts 5:29
o your parents | Eph 6:1
O your leaders | Heb 13:17
may o Jesus Christ | 1 Pet 1:2
OBJECT *implement or goal*
o like a great sheet | Acts 10:11
god or o of worship | 2 Thess 2:4
OBLIGATION *duty*
under o, not to the | Rom 8:12
o to keep the...Law | Gal 5:3
OBSERVE *keep or notice*
O how the lilies | Matt 6:28
o-ing the traditions | Mark 7:3
the word...o it | Luke 11:28
o days and months | Gal 4:10

OBSTACLE *hindrance*
an o or a stumbling | Rom 14:13
OBSTINATE *stubborn*
disobedient and o | Rom 10:21
OBTAIN *get possession of*
may o eternal life | Matt 19:16
o the gift of God | Acts 8:20
o-ed an inheritance | Eph 1:11
for o-ing salvation | 1 Thess 5:9
OCCUR *happen, take place*
lest a riot o | Matt 26:5
predestined to o | Acts 4:28
OFFEND *insult or violate*
Pharisees were o-ed | Matt 15:12
sake of the one o-ed | 2 Cor 7:12
OFFENSE *anger or transgression*
they took o at Him | Matt 13:57
of the o of Adam | Rom 5:14
and a rock of o | 1 Pet 2:8
OFFER (v) *give, present*
o both gifts and | Heb 5:1
o-ed Himself | Heb 9:14
prayer o-ed in faith | James 5:15
o...spiritual sacrifices | 1 Pet 2:5
OFFERING (n) *contribution*
presenting your o | Matt 5:23
any o for sin | Heb 10:18
OFFERINGS
Burnt Offering | Mark 12:33; Heb 10:6,8
Drink Offering | Phil 2:17; 2 Tim 4:6
Incense Offering | Luke 1:10
OFFICE *function or position*
sitting in the tax o | Luke 5:27
to the o of overseer | 1 Tim 3:1
OFFICIAL *one in authority*
o of the synagogue | Luke 8:41
court o of Candace | Acts 8:27
OFFSPRING *descendants*
Being...the o of God | Acts 17:29
you are Abraham's o | Gal 3:29
and the o of David | Rev 22:16
OIL
prudent took o in | Matt 25:4
not anoint...with o | Luke 7:46
OINTMENT *salve*
anointed...with o | John 11:2
OLD *aged, obsolete*
wine into o wineskins | Matt 9:17
be born when he is o | John 3:4
o self was crucified | Rom 6:6
o things passed away | 2 Cor 5:17
men of o gained | Heb 11:2
serpent of o...devil | Rev 12:9
OLIVES, MOUNT OF
mountain E of Jerusalem | Matt 24:3; Mark 11:1
place where Jesus prayed
| Matt 26:30; Luke 22:39-41
OMEGA
last letter of Gr. alphabet | Rev 1:8
title of Jesus Christ | Rev 21:6
expresses eternalness of God | Rev 22:13
ONE *single unit*
Are You the...O | Matt 11:3
joy...over o sinner | Luke 15:7
I...Father are o | John 10:30
they may all be o | John 17:21
o body in Christ | Rom 12:5
o died for all | 2 Cor 5:14
o Lord, o faith | Eph 4:5
o God...o mediator | 1 Tim 2:5
husband of o wife | 1 Tim 3:2
ONESIMUS
Christian slave of Philemon
| Col 4:9; Philem 10
ONESIPHORUS
Ephesian Christian | 2 Tim 1:16;4:19
OPEN (adj) *not shut, exposed*
the doors were o | Acts 16:26
before you an o door | Rev 3:8
OPEN (v) *expose, free, unfasten*
knock...shall be o-ed | Matt 7:7
o-ed a door of faith | Acts 14:27
and o-s the door | Rev 3:20
worthy to o the book | Rev 5:2
OPPONENT *adversary*
friends...with your o | Matt 5:25
protection from my o | Luke 18:3
OPPORTUNITY *occasion*
o to betray Him | Matt 26:16
o for your testimony | Luke 21:13
an o for the flesh | Gal 5:13
not give...devil an o | Eph 4:27
OPPOSE *contend, resist*
o-d the ordinance of | Rom 13:2
men also o the truth | 2 Tim 3:8
God is o-d to the | James 4:6
OPPOSITION *hostility*
these are in o | Gal 5:17

gospel...much o | 1 Thess 2:2
OPPRESS (v) *trouble, tyrannize*
healing all...o-ed | Acts 10:38
the rich who o you | James 2:6
OPPRESSED *afflicted*
vengeance for the o | Acts 7:24
o by the sensual conduct | 2 Pet 2:7
OPPRESSION *affliction*
for o of My people | Acts 7:34
ORACLE *revelation*
entrusted with the o-s | Rom 3:2
of the o-s of God | Heb 5:12
ORDAIN *invest, set apart*
law as o-ed by angels | Acts 7:53
been o-ed through angels | Gal 3:19
ORDEAL *difficulty, trial*
great o of affliction | 2 Cor 8:2
at the fiery o | 1 Pet 4:12
ORDER (n) *arrangement*
to give you this o | 2 Thess 3:10
the o of Melchizedek | Heb 5:6
ORDER (v) *command or request*
o-ed him to tell no | Luke 5:14
confidence...to o you | Philem 8
ORDINANCE *statute*
opposed the o of God | Rom 13:2
contained in o-s | Eph 2:15
ORIGINATE *bring into being*
not o from woman | 1 Cor 11:8
all things o...God | 1 Cor 11:12
ORPHAN *fatherless child*
not leave you as o | John 14:18
visit o-s and widows | James 1:27
OUTBURST *sudden release*
jealousy, o-s of anger | Gal 5:20
OUTCAST *rejected*
o-s from...synagogue | John 16:2
OUTCRY *strong cry or protest*
a single o arose | Acts 19:34
o of those who | James 5:4
OUTSIDER *stranger*
toward o-s | 1 Thess 4:12
OUTWARD *external*
is o in the flesh | Rom 2:28
OVERCOME *conquer, master*
I have o the world | John 16:33
but o evil with good | Rom 12:21
have o the evil one | 1 John 2:13
who o-s shall inherit | Rev 21:7
OVERFLOW *flood, inundate*
I am o-ing with joy | 2 Cor 7:4
o-ing with gratitude | Col 2:7
OVERLOOK *ignore or view*
widows were...o-ed | Acts 6:1
having o-ed the time | Acts 17:30
OVERPOWER *subdue*
Hades shall not o | Matt 16:18
attacks him and o-s | Luke 11:22
OVERSEER *director, leader*
the o-s and deacons | Phil 1:1
the office of o | 1 Tim 3:1
o...above reproach | Titus 1:7
OVERSHADOW *engulf, obscure*
Most High...o you | Luke 1:35
o-ing the mercy seat | Heb 9:5
OVERSIGHT *supervision*
exercising o not | 1 Pet 5:2
OVERWHELM *crush, overcome*
o-ed by...sorrow | 2 Cor 2:7
OWE *be indebted*
Pay...what you o | Matt 18:28
O nothing to anyone | Rom 13:8
that you o to me | Philem 19
OWN (adj) *belonging to*
calls his o sheep | John 10:3
in his o language | Acts 2:6
OWN (n) *belonging to*
He came to His o | John 1:11
provide for his o | 1 Tim 5:8
OWNER *possessor*
when the o...comes | Matt 21:40
who were o-s of land | Acts 4:34
OX *bull used as draft animal*
o or his donkey | Luke 13:15
o fall into a well | Luke 14:5
not muzzle the o | 1 Tim 5:8

P

PAIN *discomfort, hurt*
suffering and p | Matt 8:6
no longer be...p | Rev 21:4
PALACE *royal residence*
took Him...into the p | Mark 15:16
luxury...royal p-s | Luke 7:25
PALLET *bed, mat*
they let down the p | Mark 2:4
take up your p and | Mark 2:9
PALM *type of tree*
branches of the p | John 12:13

PIECE *part, portion*
thirty p-s of silver — Matt 27:3
gave Him a p...fish — Luke 24:42
woven in one p — John 19:23
PIERCE *penetrate*
sword will p...soul — Luke 2:35
p-d His side — John 19:34
p-d to the heart — Acts 2:37
PIETY *reverence*
learn to practice p , — 1 Tim 5:4
because of His p — Heb 5:7
PILATE, PONTIUS
Roman governor of Judea — Matt 27:2; Luke 3:1
presided at Jesus' trial
Matt 27:11ff; Mark 15:2ff; Luke 23:1ff;
John 18:28-38
warned by his wife — Matt 27:19
orders Jesus' crucifixion
Matt 27:24ff; Mark 15:15; Luke 23:24,25;
John 19:15,16
PILLAR *column or memorial*
p and support of the truth — 1 Tim 3:15
feet like p-s of fire — Rev 10:1
PILOT *steersman*
the p and...captain — Acts 27:11
inclination of the p — James 3:4
PINNACLE *highest point*
had Him...on the p — Matt 4:5
p of the temple — Luke 4:9
PISIDIA / PISIDIAN
district of Asia Minor — Acts 13:14;14:24
PIT *deep hole, dungeon*
to p-s of darkness — 2 Pet 2:4
the bottomless p — Rev 9:1
PITCH (v) *set up*
tabernacle...Lord p-ed — Heb 8:2
PITCHER *container*
carrying a p of — Mark 14:13; Luke 22:10
PITY (v) *have compassion*
take p on us — Mark 9:22
most to be p-ied — 1 Cor 15:19
PLACE *area, space*
love the p of honor — Matt 23:6
a p called Golgotha — Matt 27:33
I go to prepare a p — John 14:2
PLAGUE *contagious disease*
p of the hail — Rev 16:21
the seven last p-s — Rev 21:9
PLAIN *flat area*
p indication of God's — 2 Thess 1:5
broad p of the earth — Rev 20:9
PLAN *design, scheme*
p and foreknowledge — Acts 2:23
PLANT (n) *growth from soil*
p which My...Father — Matt. 15:13
PLANT (v) *put into soil*
p-ed a vineyard — Mark 12:1
I p-ed, Apollos — 1 Cor 3:6
PLATTER *shallow dish*
on a p the head of — Matt 14:8
his head on a p — Mark 6:28
PLAY *take part*
We p-ed the flute — Matt 11:17
stood up to p'' — 1 Cor 10:7
p on the flute — 1 Cor 14:7
PLEAD *appeal, beseech*
Elijah...p-s with God — Rom 11:2
PLEASE *satisfy*
how he may p his — 1 Cor 7:33
p all men in all — 1 Cor 10:33
striving to p men — Gal 1:10
to walk and p God — 1 Thess 4:1
impossible to p — Heb 11:6
PLEASING *agreeable, gratifying*
not as p men but — 1 Thess 2:4
p in His sight — 1 John 3:22
PLEASURE *gratification*
work for His good p — Phil 2:13
lovers of p rather — 2 Tim 3:4
passing p-s of sin — Heb 11:25
PLEDGE *promise*
the Spirit as a p — 2 Cor 5:5
p of our inheritance — Eph 1:14
PLENTIFUL *abundant*
harvest is p — Matt 9:37; Luke 10:2
PLOT *plan, scheme*
Jews p-ted together — Acts 9:23
p-ing against Him — Luke 11:54
PLOW *dig the soil*
his hand to the p — Luke 9:62
ought to p in hope — 1 Cor 9:10
PLUNDER (n) *booty, loot*
and distributes his p. — Luke 11:22
PLUNDER (v) *rob*
he will p his house — Matt 12:29
POINT *particular time*
grieved, to the p of — Matt 26:38
obedient to the p of — Phil 2:8

to the p of shedding — Heb 12:4
POISON *lethal substance*
p of asps is under their lips''; — Rom 3:13
full of deadly p. — James 3:8
POLL TAX *income and head tax*
collect customs or p — Matt 17:25
give a p to Caesar — Matt 22:17
POLLUTE *contaminate*
even the garment p-d by the flesh. — Jude 1:23
PONDER *think deeply*
p-ing what kind of salutation — Luke 1:29
p-ing them in her heart — Luke 2:19
PONTUS
region in N Asia Minor — Acts 2:9; 1 Pet 1:1
homland of Aquila — Acts 18:2
POOL *pond*
put me into the p — John 5:7
in the p of Siloam — John 9:7
POOR *impoverished, needy*
are the p in spirit — Matt 5:3
a p widow came — Mark 12:42
p you always have — Mark 14:7
sake He became p — 2 Cor 8:9
not God choose the p — James 2:5
PORTICO *porch*
in the p of Solomon — John 10:23
one accord in...p — Acts 5:12
PORTION *part, share*
received his p in this ministry — Acts 1:17
and bringing a p of it — Acts 5:2
have no part or p in this matter — Acts 8:21
in many p-s and in many ways, — Heb 1:1
POSSESS *control, take*
p-ed by Beelzebul — Mark 3:22
sell all you p — Mark 10:21
p-ed with demons — Luke 8:27
do not p silver and — Acts 3:6
POSSESSION *ownership*
charge of all his p-s — Matt 24:47
selling their...p-s — Acts 2:45
POSSIBLE *can be done*
all things are p — Matt 19:26
p with God — Luke 18:27
POSTERITY *descendants*
had left to us a p, — Rom 9:29
POTTER *one who molds clay*
p have a right over the clay, — Rom 9:21
vessels of the p are broken — Rev 2:27
POTTER'S FIELD
burial place bought with Judas money
Matt 27:3ff
also called **Field of Blood**
POUR *cause to flow*
p-ed it upon His — Matt 26:7
p forth of My Spirit — Acts 2:17
POVERTY *destitution, want*
through His p might — 2 Cor 8:9
your tributation and your p — Rev 2:9
POWER *authority, strength*
Thine is...the p — Matt 6:13
the right hand of p — Mark 14:62
clothed with p from — Luke 24:49
you shall receive p — Acts 1:8
gospel...p of God — Rom 1:16
the p of our Lord — 1 Cor 5:4
p of sin is the law — 1 Cor 15:56
p of Christ...dwell — 2 Cor 12:9
prince of the p of — Eph 2:2
p of His resurrection — Phil 3:10
timidity, but of p — 2 Tim 1:7
by the word of His p — Heb 1:3
quenched the p of — Heb 11:34
p-s...been subjected — 1 Pet 3:22
POWERLESS *without strength*
He might render p — Heb 2:14
PRACTICE (n) *custom, habit*
disclosing their p-s — Acts 19:18
laid aside...evil p-s — Col 3:9
PRACTICE (v) *engage in*
p-ing hospitality — Rom 12:13
learn to p piety — 1 Tim 5:4
the one who p-s sin — 1 John 3:8
PRAETORIUM / PRAETORIAN *palace*
1 *Pontius Pilate's palace in Jerusalem*
Matt 27:27; Mark 15:16; John 18:28,33
2 *Herod's palace at Caesarea* — Acts 23:35
3 *Imperial palace guards in Rome* — Phil 1:13
PRAISE (n) *acclamation, honor*
his p is not from men — Rom 2:29
anything worthy of p — Phil 4:8
a sacrifice of p — Heb 13:15
Give p to our God — Rev 19:5
PRAISE (v) *extol, glorify*
I p Thee, O Father — Matt 11:25
heavenly host p-ing — Luke 2:13
disciples began to p — Luke 19:37
leaping and p-ing God — Acts 3:8

PRAY *ask, worship*
p for...persecute — Matt 5:44
by Himself to p — Matt 14:23
p and ask, believe — Mark 11:24
until I have p-ed — Mark 14:32
Lord, teach us to p — Luke 11:1
they ought to p — Luke 18:1
I have p-ed for you — Luke 22:32
p-ed with fasting — Acts 14:23
if I p in a tongue — 1 Cor 14:14
p without ceasing — 1 Thess 5:17
p for one another — James 5:16
p-ing in the...Spirit — Jude 20
PRAYER
ask in p, believing — Matt 21:22
you make long p-s — Matt 23:14
whole night in p — Luke 6:12
My house...of p — Luke 19:46
devoting...to p — Acts 1:14
offering p with joy — Phil 1:4
but in everything by p — Phil 4:6
p-s...not be hindered — 1 Pet 3:7
p-s of the saints — Rev 5:8
PREACH *exhort, proclaim*
Jesus began to p — Matt 4:17
as you go, p — Matt 10:7
teach and p in their — Matt 11:1
p-ing...repentance — Mark 1:4
p the gospel to all — Mark 16:15
p the kingdom of — Luke 4:43
he p-ed Jesus to him — Acts 8:35
p...the good news — Acts 13:32
how shall they p — Rom 10:15
we p Christ crucified — 1 Cor 1:23
He...p-ed peace — Eph 2:17
p the word — 2 Tim 4:2
PREACHER *one who proclaims*
hear without a p — Rom 10:14
appointed a p and an — 1 Tim 2:7
Noah, a p of — 2 Pet 2:5
PRECEPTS *commandments*
as doctrines the p of — Matt 15:9; Mark 7:7
PRECIOUS *beloved or costly*
more p than gold — 1 Pet 1:7
with p blood — 1 Pet 1:19
PREDESTINED *foreordained*
purpose p to occur — Acts 4:28
foreknew, He also p — Rom 8:29
God p before the ages — 1 Cor 2:7
p us to adoption — Eph 1:5
p according to His — Eph 1:11
PREDETERMINED
p plan...of God — Acts 2:23
PREGNANT *with child*
Elizabeth...became p — Luke 1:24
PREPARATION *readiness*
distracted with...p-s — Luke 10:40
Jewish day of p — John 19:42
making p-s, he fell — Acts 10:10
p of the gospel of — Eph 6:15
PREPARE *make ready*
will p Your way — Matt 11:10
kingdom p-d for — Matt 25:34
to p Me for burial — Matt 26:12
p-d spices and — Luke 23:56
I go to p a place — John 14:2
worlds were p-d by — Heb 11:3
PRESENCE *appearance*
the p of His glory — Jude 24
the p of the Lamb — Rev 14:10
PRESENT (v) *give, offer*
p Him to the Lord — Luke 2:22
p yourselves to God — Rom 6:13
p your bodies a — Rom 12:1
p you before Him holy — Col 1:22
PRESERVE *protect*
p the unity of the — Eph 4:3
be p-d complete — 1 Thess 5:23
PRESS *compel, force*
measure, p-ed down — Luke 6:38
I p on toward...goal — Phil 3:14
PRETEND *deceive, feign*
spies who p-ed to — Luke 20:20
PREVAIL *triumph*
growing mightily and p-ing — Acts 19:20
p when thou art judged — Rom 3:4
PRICE *cost, value*
it is the p of blood — Matt 27:6
p of his wickedness — Acts 1:18
kept back some...p — Acts 5:2
bought with a p — 1 Cor 7:23
PRIDE *exaggerated self-esteem*
envy, slander, p — Mark 7:22
boastful p of life — 1 John 2:16
PRIEST *intermediary*
all the chief p-s — Matt 2:4
show yourself to the p — Matt 8:4
faithful high p — Heb 2:17
have a great high p — Heb 4:14
Thou art a p forever — Heb 5:6

PRIESTHOOD *office of priest*
His p permanently — Heb 7:24
royal p, a holy nation — 1 Pet 2:9
PRINCE *ruler*
to death the P of life — Acts 3:15
p of...the air — Eph 2:2
PRISCA / PRISCILLA
wife of Aquila — Rom 16:3
co-worker with Paul
— Acts 18:2,18,26; 1 Cor 16:19
PRISON *jail*
beheaded in the p — Matt 14:10
I was in p, and — Matt 25:36
opened...the p — Acts 5:19
spirits *now* in p — 1 Pet 3:19
PRISONER *one who is confined*
a notorious p — Matt 27:16
p of the law of sin — Rom 7:23
Paul, a p of Christ — Philem 1
PRIVATE *not public*
reprove him in p — Matt 18:15
but *I did so* in p — Gal 2:2
PRIZE *reward*
one receives the p — 1 Cor 9:24
p of the upward call — Phil 3:14
PROCEED *go forth*
p-s out of the mouth — Matt 4:4
p-s from...Father — John 15:26
PROCLAIM *announce, declare*
p justice to the — Matt 12:18
he *began* to p Jesus — Acts 9:20
first to p light — Acts 26:23
faith is being p-ed — Rom 1:8
p...eternal life — 1 John 1:2
PROCLAMATION *declaration*
p with which I was entrusted — Titus 1:3
made p to the spirits — 1 Pet 3:19
PROCONSUL *Roman governor*
the p, Sergius Paulus — Acts 13:7
p-s *are available* — Acts 19:38
PRODUCE (n) *yield of the soil*
the p of the vineyard — Luke 20:10
precious p of...soil — James 5:7
PRODUCE (v) *bring forth*
cannot p bad fruit — Matt 7:18
they p quarrels — 2 Tim 2:23
faith p-s endurance — James 1:3
PROFANE
sinners, for the unholy and p — 1 Tim 1:9
PROFESS *confess, declare*
P-ing to be wise — Rom 1:22
They p to know God — Titus 1:16
PROFIT (n) *benefit, gain*
not seeking my...p — 1 Cor 10:33
business...make a p — James 4:13
PROFIT (v) *reap an advantage*
what does it p a — Mark 8:36
the flesh p-s nothing — John 6:63
it p-s me nothing — 1 Cor 13:3
PROFITABLE *useful*
not all things are p — 1 Cor 6:12
godliness is p — 1 Tim 4:8
p for teaching — 2 Tim 3:16
PROMINENT *well-known*
a p member of the — Mark 15:43
of p Greek women — Acts 17:12
p men of the city — Acts 25:23
PROMISE (n) *agreement, pledge*
p of the Holy Spirit — Acts 2:33
the p made by God — Acts 26:6
the p is nullified — Rom 4:14
children of the p — Rom 9:8
commandment...a p — Eph 6:2
heirs of the p — Heb 6:17
precious...p-s — 2 Pet 1:4
the p of His coming — 2 Pet 3:4
PROMISED *made an agreement*
p long ages ago — Titus 1:2
He who p is faithful — Heb 10:23
PRONOUNCE *declare officially*
Pilate p-d sentence — Luke 23:24
God...p-d judgment — Rev 18:20
PROOF *evidence*
furnished p to all — Acts 17:31
p of your love — 2 Cor 8:24
p of the Christ — 2 Cor 13:3
PROPER *suitable*
fulfilled...p time — Luke 1:20
is it p for a woman — 1 Cor 11:13
as is p among saints — Eph 5:3
PROPERTY *goods or land*
who owned much p — Matt 19:22
selling their p and — Acts 2:45
things...common p — Acts 4:32
PROPHECY *proclamation*
p...fulfilled — Matt 13:14
have *the gift of* p — 1 Cor 13:2
no p...of human will — 2 Pet 1:21
the spirit of p — Rev 19:10

PROPHESY *predict, proclaim*
did we...p in Your — Matt 7:22
P to us...Christ — Matt 26:68
speaking...p-ing — Acts 19:6
who p-ies edifies — 1 Cor 14:4
PROPHET *spokesman for God*
written by the p — Matt 2:5
persecuted the p-s — Matt 5:12
Beware...false p-s — Matt 7:15
He...receives a p — Matt 10:41
the p Jesus — Matt 21:11
false p-s...arise — Mark 13:22
p of the Most High — Luke 1:76
great p has arisen — Luke 7:16
Are you the P — John 1:21
reading Isaiah the p — Acts 8:30
a Jewish false p — Acts 13:6
All are not p-s — 1 Cor 12:29
and some *as* p-s — Eph 4:11
beast and...false p — Rev 20:10
PROPHETESS *speaker for God*
there was a p, Anna — Luke 2:36
calls herself a p — Rev 2:20
PROPHETIC *predictive*
not...p utterances — 1 Thess 5:20
p word...sure — 2 Pet 1:19
PROPITIATION *atonement*
a p in His blood — Rom 3:25
p for the sins — Heb 2:17
He himself is the p — 1 John 2:2
p for our sins — 1 John 4:10
PROSELYTE *convert*
both Jews and p-s — Acts 2:10
a p from Antioch — Acts 6:5
God-fearing p-s — Acts 13:43
PROSPER *flourish, succeed*
and save, as he may p — 1 Cor 16:2
may p and be in good health — 3 John 1:2
PROSPERITY *success, wealth*
our p depends upon this — Acts 19:25
know how to live in p — Phil 4:12
PROSTRATE *fall down flat*
falling down, p-d — Matt 18:26
PROTECT *guard, shield*
He will...p you — 2 Thess 3:3
p-ed by the power of — 1 Pet 1:5
PROTECTION *safe-keeping*
legal p from my opponent — Luke 18:3
I will give her legal p — Luke 18:5
PROUD *exaggerated self-esteem*
scattered those who were p — Luke 1:51
opposed to the p — James 4:6
PROVE *establish, test*
p to be My disciples — John 15:8
p...the will of God — Rom 12:2
p yourselves doers — James 1:22
PROVERB *adage, short saying*
quote this p to Me — Luke 4:23
to the true p — 2 Pet 2:22
PROVIDE *furnish, supply*
p...way of escape — 1 Cor 10:13
not p for his own — 1 Tim 5:8
God had p-d — Heb 11:40
PROVINCE *district or territory*
asked from what p he was — Acts 23:34
arrived in the p — Acts 25:1
PROVISION *supply, requirement*
p-s of the law — Matt 23:23
no p for the flesh — Rom 13:14
PROVOKE *evoke, excite*
love...is not p-d — 1 Cor 13:4,5
not p your children — Eph 6:4
PROWL *roam in search*
devil, p-s about like — 1 Pet 5:8
PRUDENT *careful, wise*
the p took oil in — Matt 25:4
you are p in Christ — 1 Cor 4:10
PSALMS *sacred songs*
P must be fulfilled — Luke 24:44
speaking...in p — Eph 5:19
PUBLIC *open*
of his p appearance — Luke 1:80
beaten us in p — Acts 16:37
refuted...Jews in p — Acts 18:28
made a p display — Col 2:15
made a p spectacle — Heb 10:33
PUNISH *chastise, penalize*
p Him and release — Luke 23:16
I p-ed them often — Acts 26:11
p all disobedience — 2 Cor 10:6
PUNISHMENT *penalty*
fear involves p — 1 John 4:18
the p of eternal fire — Jude 7
PUPIL *student*
p is not above his — Luke 6:40
PURCHASE *buy*
p-d with His...blood — Acts 20:28

p for God with Thy — Rev 5:9
PURE *genuine, undefiled*
Blessed are the p in — Matt 5:8
whatever is p — Phil 4:8
love from a p heart — 1 Tim 1:5
p milk of the word — 1 Pet 2:2
the city was p gold — Rev 21:18
PURIFICATION *cleansing*
Jewish custom of p — John 2:6
He...made p of sins — Heb 1:3
PURIFY *make clean*
p...a people — Titus 2:14
p your hearts — James 4:8
p-ied your souls — 1 Pet 1:22
PURITY *not corrupted*
love, faith *and* p — 1 Tim 4:12
with p in doctrine — Titus 2:7
PURPLE *color*
dressed Him...p — Mark 15:17
a seller of p fabrics — Acts 16:14
clothed in p and — Rev 17:4
PURPOSE *intention, reason*
rejected God's p — Luke 7:30
for this p I have — Acts 26:16
according to His p — Rom 8:28
PURSE *bag, pouch*
Carry no p, no bag — Luke 10:4
p-s...do not wear — Luke 12:33
PURSUE *chase, follow*
p righteousness — 2 Tim 2:22
P peace with...men — Heb 12:14
PUT *place*
p on the Lord Jesus — Rom 13:14
p on the new self — Eph 4:24
P on the full armor — Eph 6:11

Q

QUALITY *character*
test the q of each — 1 Cor 3:13
imperishable q of a — 1 Pet 3:4
QUANTITY *amount*
a great q of fish — Luke 5:6
QUARREL (n) *altercation*
are q-s among you — 1 Cor 1:11
the source of q-s — James 4:1
QUART *measure*
A q of wheat for a — Rev 6:6
QUEEN *female sovereign*
The Q of the South — Matt 12:42
Candace, q of the — Acts 8:27
QUENCH *extinguish*
not q the Spirit — 1 Thess 5:19
q-ed...power of fire — Heb 11:34
QUESTION (n) *inquiry, problem*
Jesus asked...a q — Matt 22:41
in controversial q-s — 1 Tim 6:4
QUESTION (v) *ask*
He *began* to q them — Mark 9:33
to q Him closely on — Luke 11:53
Q those who have — John 18:21
QUICK (adj) *rapid*
q to hear, slow to — James 1:19
QUICK (n) *deepest feelings*
cut to the q and — Acts 5:33
were cut to the q — Acts 7:54
QUIET (adj) *calm, still*
lead a...q life — 1 Tim 2:2
gentle and q spirit — 1 Pet 3:4
QUIET (v) *become calm, still*
Be q, and come out — Mark 1:25
telling him to be q — Luke 18:39
QUIRINIUS
Roman governor at time of Judean census — Luke 2:2
QUOTE *repeat a passage*
will q this proverb — Luke 4:23

R

RABBI / RABBONI
respectful form of address
— Matt 23:7;26:25; Mark 10:51
master, teacher — John 1:49;6:25;11:8;20:16
RACA *worthless fool*
shall say...R — Matt 5:22
RACE (n) *nation, people*
advantage of our r — Acts 7:19
you are a chosen r — 1 Pet 2:9
RACE (n) *competition of speed*
in a r all run, but — 1 Cor 9:24
r...set before us — Heb 12:1
RADIANCE *brightness*
r of His glory — Heb 1:3
RADIANT *shining brightly*
His garments...r — Mark 9:3
RAGE (n) *violent anger*
with r as they heard — Luke 4:28
were filled with r — Acts 19:28
RAGE (v) *be very angry*
Why...Gentiles r — Acts 4:25

RAHAB
ancestor of Jesus
  example of faith | Matt 1:5
Heb 11:31; James 2:25

RAIN (n)
r on *the* righteous
  ground…drinks the r | Matt 5:45
Heb 6:7

RAIN (v) *fall down, pour*
it r-ed fire and | Luke 17:29
not r…for three | James 5:17

RAINBOW *colored arc in sky*
a r around the throne | Rev 4:3
r was upon his head | Rev 10:1

RAISE *elevate, lift*
Heal…r *the* dead | Matt 10:8
He will be r-d up | Matt 20:19
three days I will r | John 2:19
Jesus God r-d up | Acts 2:32
r-d a spiritual | 1 Cor 15:44
r-d us up with Him | Eph 2:6
God is able to r *men* | Heb 11:19

RANK *position*
a Man…higher r | John 1:30

RANSOM (n) *payment*
His life a r for | Matt 20:28
gave Himself as a r | 1 Tim 2:6

RAVAGE *devastate*
r-ing the church | Acts 8:3

RAVEN *type of bird*
Consider the r-s | Luke 12:24

RAVENOUS *wildly hungry*
inwardly are r wolves | Matt 7:15

RAVINE *gorge*
Every r shall be filled | Luke 3:5
r of the Kidron | John 18:1

READ
r-ing…Isaiah | Acts 8:28
prophets…are **read** | Acts 13:27
Moses is **read** | 2 Cor 3:15
Blessed is he who r-s | Rev 1:3

READY *equipped, prepared*
Make r the way | Matt 3:3
you be r too | Matt 24:44
be r in season | 2 Tim 4:2
r to make a defense | 1 Pet 3:15

REALIZE *achieve or understand*
r-d through Jesus | John 1:17
to r…assurance | Heb 6:11

REALM *area, kingdom*
kingdom is not…r | John 18:36

REAP *cut, gather*
neither do they r | Matt 6:26
neither sow nor r | Luke 12:24
sows…another r-s | John 4:37
r eternal life | Gal 6:8
your sickle and r | Rev 14:15

REAPER *harvester*
the r-s are angels | Matt 13:39

REASON (n) *explanation*
this r the Father | John 10:17
this r I found mercy | 1 Tim 1:16
For this r, rejoice | Rev 12:12

REASON (v) *analyze, argue*
Pharisees began to r | Luke 5:21
r-ing in…synagogue | Acts 17:17
as a child, r as a | 1 Cor 13:11

REBELLIOUS *defiant*
are lawless and r | 1 Tim 1:9
there are many r | Titus 1:10

REBUILD *restore*
r it in three days | Matt 26:61
r the tabernacle | Acts 15:16

REBUKE (v) *scold*
r-d the winds | Matt 8:26
Jesus r-d him | Matt 17:18
He r-d the fever | Luke 4:39
Do not sharply r | 1 Tim 5:1
reprove, r, exhort | 2 Tim 4:2

RECEIVE *encounter, take*
freely you r-d | Matt 10:8
who r-s you, r-s Me | Matt 10:40
the blind r sight | Matt 11:5
ask…you shall r | Matt 21:22
r-d up into heaven | Mark 16:19
This man r-s sinners | Luke 15:2
as many as r-d Him | John 1:12
r you to Myself | John 14:3
R the Holy Spirit | John 20:22
you shall r power | Acts 1:8
to give than to r | Acts 20:35
one r-s the prize | 1 Cor 9:24
r the crown of life | James 1:12
whatever…ask we r | 1 John 3:22
r-d the mark of | Rev 19:20

RECKONED *accounted for*
his wage is not r | Rom 4:4
r…as righteousness | James 2:23

RECLINE *lean, lie down*
r on the grass | Matt 14:19
r *at* the table in | Luke 13:29

r-ing on Jesus' | John 13:23

RECOGNIZE *be aware, know*
r that He is near | Matt 24:33
I did not r Him | John 1:31

RECOMPENSE (n) *reward*
received a just r | Heb 2:2

RECOMPENSE (v) *compensate*
be r-ed for his deeds | 2 Cor 5:10

RECONCILE *bring together*
r-d to your brother | Matt 5:24
be r-d to God | 2 Cor 5:20
r them both in one | Eph 2:16
r all…to Himself | Col 1:20

RECONCILIATION
now received the r | Rom 5:11
the r of the world | Rom 11:15
the ministry of r | 2 Cor 5:18
the word of r | 2 Cor 5:19

RECORD (v) *register, write*
are r-ed in heaven | Luke 10:20

RECOVER *reclaim, become well*
and they will r | Mark 16:18

RED *color*
the sky is r | Matt 16:2
a great r dragon | Rev 12:3

REDEEM *buy back*
Christ r-ed us | Gal 3:13
He might r those | Gal 4:5

REDEMPTION *deliverance*
r is drawing near | Luke 21:28
r…in Christ Jesus | Rom 3:24
r of our body | Rom 8:23
r through His blood | Eph 1:7
in whom we have r | Col 1:14
obtained eternal r | Heb 9:12

REED *tall marsh grass*
the r…to beat Him | Matt 27:30
and put it on a r | Matt 27:48

REFINE *purify*
gold r-d by fire | Rev 3:18

REFRAIN *abstain*
to r from working | 1 Cor 9:6
R his tongue…evil | 1 Pet 3:10
r from judging | Rev 6:10

REFRESH *renew, replenish*
times of r-ing may | Acts 3:19
r my heart in Christ | Philem 20

REFUGE *protection, shelter*
who have fled for r | Heb 6:18

REFUSE (v) *decline*
r-d to be comforted | Matt 2:18
can r the water | Acts 10:47
not r Him who is | Heb 12:25

REFUTE *prove wrong*
he…r-d the Jews | Acts 18:28
to r those who | Titus 1:9

REGAIN *recover*
r-ed their sight | Matt 20:34
want to r my sight | Mark 10:51
he might r his sight | Acts 9:12

REGARD (n) *respect*
like him in high r | Phil 2:29

REGARD (v) *esteem, respect*
highly r-ed by him | Luke 7:2
you r one another | Phil 2:3
did not r equality | Phil 2:6

REGENERATION *renewal*
r when the Son | Matt 19:28
the washing of r | Titus 3:5

REGION *area*
the r-s of Galilee | Matt 2:22
to the r of Judea | Mark 10:1
same r…shepherds | Luke 2:8

REGISTER *enroll*
to r for the census | Luke 2:3

REIGN *rule*
death r-ed…Adam | Rom 5:14
He must r until | 1 Cor 15:25
also r with Him | 2 Tim 2:12
He will r forever | Rev 11:15
will r with Him | Rev 20:6

REJECT *decline, refuse*
the builders r-ed | Matt 21:42
who r-s you r-s Me | Luke 10:16
He who r-s Me | John 12:48

REJOICE *be glad*
r-d exceedingly | Matt 2:10
r at his birth | Luke 1:14
multitude was r-ing | Luke 13:17
you would have r-d | John 14:28
r-ing in hope | Rom 12:12
yet always r-ing | 2 Cor 6:10
R in the Lord | Phil 4:4
I r in my sufferings | Col 1:24
r, O heavens | Rev 12:12

RELATIVE *kinsman*
among his *own* r-s | Mark 6:4
your r Elizabeth has | Luke 1:36

RELEASE (n) *liberation*
r for you the King | Mark 15:9
r to the captives | Luke 4:18

RELEASE (v) *set free*
he r-d Barabbas | Matt 27:26
wanting to r Jesus | Luke 23:20
efforts to r Him | John 19:12
you r-d from a wife | 1 Cor 7:27
r-d us from our sins | Rev 1:5
R the four angels | Rev 9:14

RELIEF *lessening of burden*
r of the brethren | Acts 11:29

RELIGION *system of belief*
about their own r | Acts 25:19
sect of our r | Acts 26:5
pure and undefiled r | James 1:27

RELIGIOUS *devout, pious*
r in all respects | Acts 17:22
thinks…to be r | James 1:26

RELY *depend, trust*
r upon the Law | Rom 2:17

REMAIN *abide, be left*
flee to Egypt, and r | Matt 2:13
dove…r-ed upon | John 1:32
not r in darkness | John 12:46
not r on the cross | John 19:31
let her r unmarried | 1 Cor 7:11
gospel might r | Gal 2:5
He r-s faithful | 2 Tim 2:13

REMEMBER *recall, recollect*
Peter r-ed the word | Matt 26:75
R Lot's wife | Luke 17:32
r the words of | Acts 20:35
to r the poor | Gal 2:10

REMEMBRANCE *memory*
do this in r of Me | Luke 22:19
in r of Me | 1 Cor 11:25

REMNANT *remaining part*
r that will be saved | Rom 9:27
a r according to God's | Rom 11:5

REMOVE *take away or off*
not fit to r His | Matt 3:11
r this cup from Me | Luke 22:42
R the stone | John 11:39
as to r mountains | 1 Cor 13:2

RENDER *inflict, repay*
r to Caesar the | Matt 22:21
R to all what is due | Rom 13:7

RENEW *make new, revive*
inner man…r-ed | 2 Cor 4:16

REPAY *pay back*
in secret will r | Matt 6:4
is Mine, I will r | Rom 12:19
no one r-s…evil | 1 Thess 5:15

REPENT *change mind*
R, for the kingdom | Matt 3:2
r-ed long ago in | Matt 11:21
r and believe | Mark 1:15
one sinner who r-s | Luke 15:7
R,…be baptized | Acts 2:38
all…should r | Acts 17:30
r and turn to God | Acts 26:20

REPENTANCE *penitence*
with water for r | Matt 3:11
baptism of r | Mark 1:4
r for forgiveness | Luke 24:47
appropriate to r | Acts 26:20
r without regret | 2 Cor 7:10
r from dead works | Heb 6:1
to come to r | 2 Pet 3:9

REPORT *account, statement*
r concerning Him | Luke 7:17
has believed our r | John 12:38

REPRESENTATION *likeness*
exact r of His nature | Heb 1:3

REPROACH (n) *dishonor*
without stain or r | 1 Tim 6:14
the r of Christ | Heb 11:26

REPROACH (v) *accuse, rebuke*
He…to r the cities | Matt 11:20
He r-ed them for | Mark 16:14

REPROOF *correction, rebuke*
for teaching, for r | 2 Tim 3:16

REPROVE *correct, rebuke*
r him in private | Matt 18:15
r, rebuke, exhort | 2 Tim 4:2
whom I love, I r | Rev 3:19

REPTILE *snake*
r-s and creatures | James 3:7

REPUTATION *character*
seven men of good r | Acts 6:3
a r for good works | 1 Tim 5:10

REQUEST *desire, petition*
r-s be made known to | Phil 4:6
r-s which we have asked | 1 John 5:15

REQUIRE *demand, insist*
your soul is r-d | Luke 12:20
r-d of stewards | 1 Cor 4:2

REQUIREMENT *necessity*
r-s of the Lord — Luke 1:6
r of the Law — Rom 8:4
law of physical r — Heb 7:16

RESCUE *deliver, redeem*
His angel and r-ed me — Acts 12:11
r the godly from — 2 Pet 2:9

RESERVE *retain, store up*
r-d in heaven — 1 Pet 1:4
r-d for fire — 2 Pet 3:7

RESIDE *dwell, live*
r-d in…Nazareth — Matt 2:23
those who r as aliens — 1 Pet 1:1

RESIST *oppose, withstand*
not r him who is — Matt 5:39
none…able to r — Luke 21:15
r-ing the Holy Spirit — Acts 7:51
he who r-s authority — Rom 13:2
R the devil — James 4:7

RESPECT (n) *regard*
please *Him* in all r-s — Col 1:10
to your masters…r — 1 Pet 2:18

RESPECT (v) *esteem*
They will r my son — Matt 21:37
not fear God nor r — Luke 18:4
R what is right — Rom 12:17
wife…r her husband — Eph 5:33

RESPOND *answer, reply*
how you should r — Col 4:6
Peter r-ed to her — Acts 5:8

REST (n) *remainder*
to the r…parables — Luke 8:10

REST (n) *tranquility*
I will give you r — Matt 11:28
no r for my spirit — 2 Cor 2:13
not enter My r — Heb 3:11
no r day and night — Rev 14:11

REST (v) *settled, refresh*
r-ed on the seventh — Heb 4:4
r from their labors — Rev 14:13

RESTORE *reestablish, replace*
his hand was r-d — Mark 3:5
r-ing the kingdom — Acts 1:6

RESTRAIN *hold back*
r-ed the crowds — Acts 14:18
what r-s him now — 2 Thess 2:6

RESULT (n) *consequence, effect*
not as a r of works — Eph 2:9
have *its* perfect r — James 1:4
as a r of the works — James 2:22

RESULT (v) *follow, happen*
sin r-ing in death — Rom 6:16
proved to r in death — Rom 7:10
r-ing in salvation — Rom 10:10

RESURRECTION
who say…no r — Matt 22:23
r of the righteous — Luke 14:14
being sons of the r — Luke 20:36
r of judgment — John 5:29
the r and the life — John 11:25
r of the dead — Acts 24:21
if there is no r — 1 Cor 15:13
power of His r — Phil 3:10
hope through the r — 1 Pet 1:3
This is the first r — Rev 20:5

RETRIBUTION *punishment*
stumbling block…r — Rom 11:9
dealing out r to — 2 Thess 1:8

RETURN *go back or repay*
r-ed to Galilee — Luke 4:14
Repent…and r — Acts 3:19
not r-ing evil for — 1 Pet 3:9

REVEAL *expose, make known*
r them to babes — Matt 11:25
blood did not r *this* — Matt 16:17
Son of Man is r-ed — Luke 17:30
glory…to be r-ed — Rom 8:18
r-ed with fire — 1 Cor 3:13
to r His Son in me — Gal 1:16
lawlessness is r-ed — 2 Thess 3:7
r-ed in the flesh — 1 Tim 3:16

REVELATION *divine disclosure*
r to the Gentiles — Luke 2:32
r of…judgment — Rom 2:5
the r of the mystery — Rom 16:25
awaiting…the r — 1 Cor 1:7
through a r of Jesus — Gal 1:12
by r…made known — Eph 3:3
The R of Jesus — Rev 1:1

REVENGE *vengeance*
Never take…r — Rom 12:19

REVERENCE *respect, awe*
in r prepared an ark — Heb 11:7
service with r and — Heb 12:28

REVILE *use abusive language*
Do you r God's high — Acts 23:4
are r-d, we bless — 1 Cor 4:12
r-d for the name of — 1 Pet 4:14
r angelic majesties — Jude 8

REVIVE *bring back to life*
r-d your concern — Phil 4:10

REVOLT *rebellion*
stirred up a r — Acts 21:38

REWARD *prize*
your r in heaven — Matt 5:12
not lose his r — Matt 10:42
looking to the r — Heb 11:26
receive a full r — 2 John 8

RHODA
Christian servant girl — Acts 12:13

RHODES
Mediterranean isle — Acts 21:1

RICH (adj) *wealthy*
woe to you who are r — Luke 6:24
a certain r man — Luke 16:1
being r in mercy — Eph 2:4
r in good works — 1 Tim 6:18

RICHES *wealth*
deceitfulness of r — Matt 13:22
choked with…r — Luke 8:14
abounding in r — Rom 10:12
r of His grace — Eph 1:7
r of Christ — Eph 3:8
His r in glory — Phil 4:19
uncertainty of r — 1 Tim 6:17
Your r have rotted — James 5:2

RIGHT (adj) *correct or direction*
r eye makes you — Matt 5:29
what your r hand is — Matt 6:3
Sit at My r hand — Matt 22:44
the r hand of God — Mark 16:19
at the r time Christ — Rom 5:6
r hand of fellowship — Gal 2:9
whatever is r — Phil 4:8
forsaking the r way — 2 Pet 2:15

RIGHT (n) *due, prerogative*
not have a r to — 1 Cor 9:4
my r in the gospel — 1 Cor 9:18

RIGHTEOUS (adj) *virtuous*
ninety-nine r — Luke 15:7
coming of the R One — Acts 7:52
r *man* shall live by — Rom 1:17
none r, not even one — Rom 3:10
many will be made r — Rom 5:19
prayer of a r man — James 5:16

RIGHTEOUS (n) *moral one*
sends rain on the *r* — Matt 5:45
r into eternal life — Matt 25:46

RIGHTEOUSNESS
to fulfill all r — Matt 3:15
and thirst for r — Matt 5:6
kingdom and His r — Matt 6:33
you enemy of all r — Acts 13:10
through one act of r — Rom 5:18
breastplate of r — Eph 6:14
pursue r, faith — 2 Tim 2:22
the crown of r — 2 Tim 4:8
peaceful fruit of r — Heb 12:11
not achieve the r — James 1:20
suffer for…r — 1 Pet 3:14

RIOT *tumult, uprising*
lest a r occur — Matt 26:5
r was starting — Matt 27:24
accused of a r — Acts 19:40

RIPE *fully developed*
harvest…is r — Rev 14:15

RISE *go up, issue forth*
nation will r — Matt 24:7
r-n, just as He said — Matt 28:6
children will r up — Mark 13:12
R and walk — Luke 5:23
R and pray — Luke 22:46
Lord has really r-n — Luke 24:34

RIVER
baptized…Jordan R — Mark 1:5
r-s of living water — John 7:38
r of the water of life — Rev 22:1

ROAD *path, way*
the rough r-s smooth — Luke 3:5
garments in the r — Luke 19:36
the Lord on the r — Acts 9:27

ROAR (n) *loud deep sound*
pass away with a r — 2 Pet 3:10

ROB *steal*
do you r temples — Rom 2:22
I r-bed…churches — 2 Cor 11:8

ROBBER *thief*
crucified two r-s — Mark 15:27
he fell among r-s — Luke 10:30
a thief and a r — John 10:1
r-s of temples — Acts 19:37

ROBBERY *theft*
they are full of r — Matt 23:25
you are full of r — Luke 11:39

ROBE *cloak, garment*
put a scarlet r on — Matt 27:28
walk…in long r-s — Mark 12:38
wearing a white r — Mark 16:5
bring…the best r — Luke 15:22

washed their r-s — Rev 7:14
a r dipped in blood — Rev 19:13

ROCK *stone*
his house upon the r — Matt 7:24
upon this r I will — Matt 16:18
the r-s were split — Matt 27:51
hewn out in the r — Mark 15:46
a r of offense — Rom 9:33

ROD *staff, stick*
Aaron's r which budded — Heb 9:4
rule them with a r — Rev 19:15

ROLL *move*
r-ed away the stone — Matt 28:2
Who will r away the — Mark 16:3

ROMANS
citizens of Roman Empire — John 11:48; Acts 16:21,37

ROME
Italian city — Acts 2:10
Roman Empire capital — Acts 18:2
Paul held there — Acts 28:14,16

ROOF
removed the r above — Mark 2:4
r and let him down — Luke 5:19

ROOM *chamber*
go into your inner r — Matt 6:6
a large upper r — Mark 14:15
no r for them in — Luke 2:7
r for the wrath — Rom 12:19

ROOT (n) *source*
no r, it withered — Mark 4:6
if the r be holy — Rom 11:16
of money is a r — 1 Tim 6:10
no r of bitterness — Heb 12:15
the R of David — Rev 5:5

ROOT (v) *establish or tear out*
r up the wheat — Matt 13:29
r-ed and grounded in — Eph 3:17

ROT *decay*
riches have r-ted — James 5:2

ROYAL *kingly*
a certain r official — John 4:46
fulfilling the r law — James 2:8
a r priesthood — 1 Pet 2:9

RUIN (n) *destruction*
r of that house was great — Luke 6:49
rebuild its r-s — Acts 15:16

RUIN (v) *destroy*
skins will be r-ed — Luke 5:37
he who is weak is r-ed — 1 Cor 8:11

RULE (n) *authority, government*
will walk by this r — Gal 6:16
above all r and — Eph 1:21
according to the r-s — 2 Tim 2:5

RULE (v) *govern*
r over the Gentiles — Rom 15:12
peace of Christ r — Col 3:15
r them with a rod — Rev 2:27

RULER *king, monarch*
come forth a R — Matt 2:6
r of the demons — Matt 9:34
r-s of the Gentiles — Mark 10:42
the r of this world — John 12:31
Who made you a r — Acts 7:27
be subject to r-s — Titus 3:1

RUMOR *gossip, hearsay*
wars and r-s of wars — Matt 24:6; Mark 13:7

RUN *move rapidly*
Peter arose and ran — Luke 24:12
disciple ran ahead — John 20:4
who r in a race — 1 Cor 9:24

RUSH *move quickly*
herd r-ed down the — Matt 8:32
horses r-ing to battle — Rev 9:9

RUST *corrosion*
moth and r destroy — Matt 6:19
r will be a witness — James 5:3

RUTH
in Messianic line — Matt 1:5

S

SABAOTH
Lord of Sabaoth is same as Lord of Hosts — Rom 9:29; James 5:4

SABBATH *day of rest*
is Lord of the S — Matt 12:8
S was made for man — Mark 2:27
on the S to do good — Mark 3:4
the cross on the S — John 19:31
a S day's journey — Acts 1:12
are read every S — Acts 13:27
S rest for the people — Heb 4:9

SACKCLOTH *coarse cloth*
long ago in s and ashes — Matt 11:21
sun became black as s — Rev 6:12

SACRED *consecrated, holy*
perform s services — 1 Cor 9:13
known…s writings — 2 Tim 3:15
table and the s bread — Heb 9:2

SERVANT *helper, slave*
s-s of a new covenant	2 Cor 3:6
they s-s of Christ	2 Cor 11:23
s of Christ Jesus	1 Tim 4:6

SERVE *help, work for*
s God and mammon	Matt 6:24
If anyone s-s Me	John 12:26
s-ing the Lord	Rom 12:11
through love s one	Gal 5:13

SERVICE *ministry, work*
spiritual s of worship	Rom 12:1
for the work of s	Eph 4:12
s with reverence	Heb 12:28

SETH
line of Jesus	Luke 3:38

SETTLED *arranged or inhabited*
s in the lawful	Acts 19:39

SEVEN *number*
s other spirits more	Matt 12:45
forgive...s times	Matt 18:21
John to the s churches	Rev 1:4
s golden lampstands	Rev 1:12

SEW *fasten, join*
No one s-s a patch	Mark 2:21

SEVERE *difficult, hard*
a s earthquake had	Matt 28:2

SEXUAL
not in s promiscuity	Rom 13:13
from s immorality	1 Thess 4:3

SHACKLES *fetters*
s broken in pieces	Mark 5:4
with chains and s	Luke 8:29

SHADE *protection*
nest under its s	Mark 4:32

SHADOW *image of shade*
his s might fall on	Acts 5:15
s of the heavenly	Heb 8:5

SHAKE *quiver, tremble*
s off the dust	Matt 10:14
A reed s-n by the	Matt 11:7
heavens will be s-n	Luke 21:26
he shook the creature	Acts 28:5
voice shook the earth	Heb 12:26

SHAME *disgrace, dishonor*
worthy to suffer s	Acts 5:41
glory is in their s	Phil 3:19
put Him to open s	Heb 6:6

SHARE (n) *portion*
give me the s	Luke 15:12
I do my s	Col 1:24

SHARE (v) *partake, participate*
s it...yourselves	Luke 22:17
s all good things	Gal 6:6
may s His holiness	Heb 12:10
s the sufferings of	1 Pet 4:13

SHARON
and S saw him	Acts 9:35

SHARP *cutting*
Put in your s sickle	Rev 14:18

SHAVE *cut or scrape*
they may s their heads	Acts 21:24
her whose head is s-d	1 Cor 11:5

SHEARER *wool cutter*
lamb before its s	Acts 8:32

SHECHEM *city in Ephraim hill country*
	Acts 7:16

SHED *pour out*
swift to s blood	Rom 3:15
s-ding of blood	Heb 9:22

SHEEP *animal*
lost is of...Israel	Matt 10:6
s from the goats	Matt 25:32
my s which was lost	Luke 15:6
His life for the s	John 10:11
s hear My voice	John 10:27
Tend My s	John 21:17
Shepherd of the s	Heb 13:20

SHEEPSKINS *coverings*
they went about in s	Heb 11:37

SHEET
s over *his* naked	Mark 14:51
object like a great s	Acts 10:11

SHELTER *cover, refuge*
under the s of Cypress	Acts 27:4
s of a small island	Acts 27:16

SHEPHERD (n)
sheep without a s	Matt 9:36
strike down the s	Matt 26:31
s-s...in the fields	Luke 2:8
I am the good s	John 10:11
the great S	Heb 13:20
the Chief S	1 Pet 5:4

SHEPHERD (v)
s My people	Matt 2:6
S My sheep	John 21:16
to s the church	Acts 20:28
s the flock of God	1 Pet 5:2

SHIELD *protection*
the s of faith	Eph 6:16

SHINE *be radiant, glow*
light s before men	Matt 5:16
s-s in the darkness	John 1:5
lamp s-ing in a dark	2 Pet 1:19
light is...s-ing	1 John 2:8

SHIP *boat*
escape from the s	Acts 27:30

SHORT *lacking*
days shall be cut s	Matt 24:22
s of the grace	Heb 12:15

SHOULDER *part of body*
lay them on men's s-s	Matt 23:4
lays it on his s-s	Luke 15:5

SHOUT *cry out loudly*
s-ed back, "Crucify Him!"	Mark 15:13
s for about two hours,	Acts 19:34

SHOW *manifest, reveal*
S us the Father	John 14:9
God s-s no partiality	Gal 2:6
s hospitality	Heb 13:2
if you s partiality	James 2:9

SHOWER *abundant flow*
A s is coming	Luke 12:54

SHREWD *cunning*
be s as serpents	Matt 10:16

SHRINE *object of worship*
who made silver s-s	Acts 19:24

SHUT *close*
s your door, pray	Matt 6:6
power to s up the sky	Rev 11:6

SICK *unwell*
lying s with a fever	Mark 1:30
Lazarus was s	John 11:2
anyone among you s	James 5:14

SICKLE *cutting tool*
sharp s in His hand	Rev 14:14
Put in your s	Rev 14:15

SICKNESS *illness*
every kind of s	Matt 4:23
authority over...s	Matt 10:1
s is not unto death	John 11:4

SIDON
Phoenician Port	Luke 6:17;10:13,14;
	Acts 12:20;27:3

SIGHT *perception, vision*
blind receive s	Matt 11:5
three days without s	Acts 9:9
by faith, not by s	2 Cor 5:7

SIGN *indication or wonder*
a s from You	Matt 12:38
s of Your coming	Matt 24:3
show s-s and	Mark 13:22
s-s in sun and moon	Luke 21:25
beginning of *His* s-s	John 2:11
s of circumcision	Rom 4:11
Jews ask for s-s	1 Cor 1:22
tongues are for a s	1 Cor 14:22
s-s...false wonders	2 Thess 2:9

SILAS
co-worker with Paul	
	Acts 15:22,32,40;16:19,25; 17:4,10,14
also SILVANUS	

SILENCE *quietness*
s the ignorance	1 Pet 2:15
s in heaven	Rev 8:1

SILENT *quiet*
But Jesus kept s	Matt 26:63
women keep s	1 Cor 14:34

SILOAM
1 *tower in Jerusalem*	Luke 13:4
2 *water pool in Jerusalem*	John 9:7,11

SILVANUS
see SILAS

SILVER *precious metal*
not acquire...s	Matt 10:9
thirty pieces of s	Matt 26:15

SIMEON
1 *tribe*	Rev 7:7
2 *devout Jew*	Luke 2:25
3 *ancestor of Jesus*	Luke 3:30
4 *Christian prophet*	Acts 13:1
5 *Simon Peter*	Acts 15:14

SIMON
1 *apostle*	Matt 4:18; Mark 1:16
see also PETER	
2 *the Zealot*	
	Matt 10:4; Mark 3:18; Luke 6:15
3 *brother of Jesus*	Matt 13:55; Mark 6:3
4 *leper*	Matt 26:6; Mark 14:3
5 *a Pharisee*	Luke 7:40,43
6 *of Cyrene*	Matt 27:32
carried Jesus' cross	
	Mark 15:21; Luke 23:26
7 *father of Judas*	John 6:71;13:2
8 *Magus sorcerer*	Acts 8:9,13,18
9 *the tanner*	Acts 9:43;10:6,32

SIN (n) *transgression*
an eternal s	Mark 3:29
forgive us our s-s	Luke 11:4
takes away the s	John 1:29
wash away your s-s	Acts 22:16
wages of s is death	Rom 6:23
died for our s-s	1 Cor 15:3
Him who knew no s	2 Cor 5:21
pleasures of s	Heb 11:25
confess your s-s	James 5:16
a multitude of s-s	James 5:20
confess our s-s	1 John 1:9
s is lawlessness	1 John 3:4

SIN (v) *transgress*
Father, I have s-ned	Luke 15:18
s no more	John 8:11
all have s-ned	Rom 3:23
that you may not s	1 John 2:1

SINAI
mountain where law received	
	Acts 7:30; Gal 4:24

SINCERE *without deceit*
be s and blameless	Phil 1:10
mindful of the s faith	2 Tim 1:5
s love...brethren	1 Pet 1:22

SINFUL *wicked*
s generation	Mark 8:38
I am a s man	Luke 5:8
likeness of s flesh	Rom 8:3

SING
after s-ing a hymn	Mark 14:26
s-ing...thankfulness	Col 3:16
sang a new song	Rev 5:9

SINK *fall*
they began to s	Luke 5:7
these words s into your ears	Luke 9:44

SINNER *wrongdoer*
a friend of...s-s	Matt 11:19
one s who repents	Luke 15:7
merciful to me...s	Luke 18:13
God...not hear s-s	John 9:31
while we were yet s-s	Rom 5:8
came...to save s-s	1 Tim 1:15

SISTER
a s called Mary	Luke 10:39
commend...our s	Rom 16:1
younger women...s-s	1 Tim 5:2

SIT *recline, rest*
who s in darkness	Luke 1:79
dead man sat up	Luke 7:15
where the harlot s-s	Rev 17:15

SKIN *covering*
will burst the s-s	Mark 2:22

SKULL *bony framework of head*
Place of a S	Matt 27:33

SKY *heavens*
for the s is red	Matt 16:2
will appear in the s	Matt 24:30
s was shut up	Luke 4:25
gazing...into the s	Acts 1:10
s was split apart	Rev 6:14

SLANDER (n) *defamation*
s-s, gossip	2 Cor 12:20
and s be put away	Eph 4:31

SLANDER (v) *defame*
why am I s-ed concerning	1 Cor 10:30
they s you as evildoers	1 Pet 2:12

SLANDERER *defamer*
s-s, haters of God	Rom 1:30

SLAUGHTER (n) *brutal killing*
as a sheep to s	Acts 8:32
in a day of s	James 5:5

SLAVE *bondservant*
s above his master	Matt 10:24
good and faithful s	Matt 25:21
shall be s of all	Mark 10:44
is the s of sin	John 8:34
neither s nor free	Gal 3:28
as s-s of Christ	Eph 6:6

SLAVERY *servitude*
received a spirit of s	Rom 8:15
to a yoke of s	Gal 5:1

SLAY *destroy, kill*
and were intending to s them	Acts 5:33
Lamb that was slain	Rev 5:12

SLEEP (n) *rest*
overcome by s	Acts 20:9
for you to awaken from s	Rom 13:11

SLEEP (v) *slumber*
found them s-ing	Matt 26:43
we shall not all s	1 Cor 15:51

SLOW *not quick*
to hear, s to speak	James 1:19
Lord is not s	2 Pet 3:9

SMALL *little*
For the gate is s	Matt 7:14
a few s fish	Mark 8:7
he was s in stature	Luke 19:3

tongue is a **s** part	James 3:5

SMITE *hit, strike*

s the earth	Rev 11:6
He may **s** the nations	Rev 19:15

SMOKE *mist, vapor*

and fire, and vapor of **s**	Acts 2:19
s rises up forever	Rev 19:3

SMOOTH *no roughness*

the rough roads **s**	Luke 3:5
s...flattering speech	Rom 16:18

SMYRNA

city in Asia Minor	Rev 1:11;2:8

SNAKE *serpent*

he will not give him a **s**	Matt 7:10
s instead of a fish	Luke 11:11

SNARE *trap*

table become a **s**	Rom 11:9
s of the devil	1 Tim 3:7

SNOW *ice flakes*

as white as **s**	Matt 28:3
like white wool, like **s**	Rev 1:14

SOBER *serious, temperate*

words of **s** truth	Acts 26:25
be alert and **s**	1 Thess 5:6
Be of **s** spirit	1 Pet 5:8

SODOM

city **S** of Dead Sea,	
city destroyed by God	Luke 17:29;
	Rom. 9:29; Jude 1:7

SOIL *earth, ground*

fell into the good **s**	Mark 4:8
produce of the **s**	James 5:7

SOLDIER *military man*

s-s took Him away	Mark 15:16
s-s also mocked	Luke 23:36
s-s pierced His side	John 19:34
a devout **s**	Acts 10:7
good **s** of Christ	2 Tim 2:3

SOLEMN *deeply earnest, serious*

bound...a **s** oath	Acts 23:14

SOLOMON

Son of David, king of Israel	Matt 1:6; 6:29

SON *male descendant*

she gave birth to a **S**	Matt 1:25
This is My beloved **S**	Matt 3:17
the carpenter's **s**	Matt 13:55
I am the **S** of God	Matt 27:43
S of Man...suffer	Mark 8:31
her first-born **s**	Luke 2:7
If You are the **S**	Luke 4:3
man had two **s-s**	Luke 15:11
only begotten **S**	John 3:16
S also gives life	John 5:21
become **s-s** of light	John 12:36
sending His own **S**	Rom 8:3
image of His **S**	Rom 8:29
not spare His own **S**	Rom 8:32
fellowship with His **S**	1 Cor 1:9
if a **s**, then an heir	Gal 4:7
shall be a **S** to Me	Heb 1:5
abide in the **S**	1 John 2:24
He who has the **S**	1 John 5:12

SON OF GOD

Messianic title indicating deity of Jesus Christ

Matt 4:3;8:29;16:16; Mark 1:20;3:11;14:61;
Luke 1:35; John 3:18;11:27; Acts 8:37

SON OF MAN

Messianic title of Jesus Christ

Matt 8:20;9:6; Mark 2:10; 10:33;
Luke 12:10;18:31; John 6:27;13:31

SONG *melody, music*

hymns...spiritual **s-s**	Eph 5:19
And they sang a new **s**	Rev 5:9

SORCERER *witch*

immoral persons...**s-s**	Rev 21:8
the dogs and the **s**	Rev 22:15

SORCERY *witchcraft*

idolatry, **s**, enmities	Gal 5:20
deceived by your **s**	Rev 18:23

SORDID *filthy*

fond of **s** gain	1 Tim 3:8
the sake of **s** gain	Titus 1:11
not for **s** gain	1 Pet 5:2

SORROW *grief, sadness*

s...turned to joy	John 16:20
if I cause you **s**	2 Cor 2:2

SOSTHENES

1 synagogue leader	Acts 18:17
2 Corinthian believer	1 Cor 1:27

SOUL *life, spirit*

unable to kill the **s**	Matt 10:28
exchange for his **s**	Matt 16:26
My **s** is...grieved	Matt 26:38
and forfeit his **s**	Mark 8:36
My **s** exalts the Lord	Luke 1:46
your **s** is required	Luke 12:20
one heart and **s**	Acts 4:32
an anchor of the **s**	Heb 6:19
able to save your **s-s**	James 1:21
save his **s** from	James 5:20

war against the **s**	1 Pet 2:11

SOUND (adj) *accurate, stable*

back safe and **s**	Luke 15:27
the **s** doctrine	1 Tim 4:6

SOUND (v) *express*

trumpet will **s**	1 Cor 15:52
angels who are about to **s**	Rev 8:13

SOUR *distasteful, tart*

offering...**s** wine	Luke 23:36
received the **s** wine	John 19:30

SOURCE *origin*

s of eternal salvation	Heb 5:9
s of quarrels	James 4:1

SOW *plant, spread*

birds...do not **s**	Matt 6:26
s good seed	Matt 13:27
s-ed spiritual things	1 Cor 9:11
whatever a man **s**-s	Gal 6:7

SOWER *planter*

s went out to sow	Matt 13:3
s sows the word	Mark 4:14

SPAIN

S European land	Rom 15:24,28

SPARE *save or be lenient*

not **s** His own Son	Rom 8:32
I will not **s** anyone	2 Cor 13:2
God did not **s** angels	2 Pet 2:4

SPEAK *proclaim, tell*

the dumb to **s**	Mark 7:37
s that...we know	John 3:11
Never did a man **s**	John 7:46
s with other tongues	Acts 2:4
we **s** God's wisdom	1 Cor 2:7
If I **s** with tongues	1 Cor 13:1

SPEAR *weapon*

pierced...with a **s**	John 19:34

SPECK *particle*

s out of your eye	Matt 7:4
s that is in your brother's	Luke 6:42

SPEECH *message, word*

in cleverness of **s**	1 Cor 1:17
I am unskilled in **s**	2 Cor 11:6

SPICE

prepared **s-s** and	Luke 23:56
wrappings with...**s-s**	John 19:40

SPIES *clandestine persons*

s who pretended	Luke 20:20
welcomed the **s**	Heb 11:31

SPIN *make thread*

nor do they **s**	Matt 6:28
neither toil nor **s**	Luke 12:27

SPIRIT

are the poor in **s**	Matt 5:3
authority over...**s-s**	Matt 10:1
put My **S** upon Him	Matt 12:18
blasphemy...the **S**	Matt 12:31
yielded up His **s**	Matt 27:50
S like a dove	Mark 1:10
s...not have flesh	Luke 24:39
born of...the **S**	John 3:5
worship in **s** and	John 4:24
gave up His **s**	John 19:30
pour forth of My **S**	Acts 2:17
Jesus, receive my **s**	Acts 7:59
power of the **S**	Rom 15:19
taught by the **s**	1 Cor 2:13
pray with the **s**	1 Cor 14:15
walk by the **S**	Gal 5:16
fruit of the **S** is love	Gal 5:22
one body and one **S**	Eph 4:4
be filled with the **S**	Eph 5:18
sword of the **S**	Eph 6:17
not quench the **S**	1 Thess 5:19
division of soul and **s**	Heb 4:12
the **s-s** now in prison	1 Pet 3:19
S who bears witness	1 John 5:7
see also **HOLY SPIRIT**	

SPIRIT OF GOD

S descending as a	Matt 3:16
being led by the **S**	Rom 8:14
S dwells in you	1 Cor 3:16
worship in the **S**	Phil 3:3
see also **HOLY SPIRIT**	

SPIRIT OF THE LORD

S is upon Me	Luke 4:18
see also **HOLY SPIRIT**	

SPIRITUAL *of the spirit*

the Law is **s**	Rom 7:14
s service of worship	Rom 12:1
raised a **s** body	1 Cor 15:44
with every **s** blessing	Eph 1:3
hymns and **s** songs	Eph 5:19
offer up **s** sacrifices	1 Pet 2:5

SPIT

began to **s** at Him	Mark 14:65
and **s** upon	Luke 18:32
He **s**pat on...ground	John 9:6
I will **s** you out	Rev 3:16

SPLIT *divide*

and the rocks were **s**	Matt 27:51

sky was **s** apart	Rev 6:14

SPONGE *absorbent matter*

taking a **s**, he filled	Matt 27:48
a **s** with sour wine	Mark 15:36

SPOT *speck*

no **s** or wrinkle	Eph 5:27

SPOTLESS *no defects*

unblemished and **s**	1 Pet 1:19
s and blameless	2 Pet 3:14

SPREAD *stretch out*

s the news about	Mark 1:45
death **s** to all men	Rom 5:12

SPRING (n) *water source*

s-s without water	2 Pet 2:17
s of the water of life	Rev 21:6

SPRING (v) *jump, leap*

s-ing up to eternal	John 4:14
root of bitterness **s**-ing	Heb 12:15

SPY *investigate*

s out our liberty	Gal 2:4

SQUARE *area or shape*

city is...a **s**	Rev 21:16

STAFF *rod*

or sandals, or a **s**	Matt 10:10
a mere **s**; no bread	Mark 6:8

STAIN *blemish*

without **s**...reproach	1 Tim 6:14
s-s and blemishes	2 Pet 2:13

STAND *maintain position*

love to **s** and pray	Matt 6:5
s-ing by the cross	John 19:25
why do you **s** looking	Acts 1:11
s by your faith	Rom 11:20
s before...judgment	Rom 14:10
s firm in the faith	1 Cor 16:13
foundation...**s-s**	2 Tim 2:19
I **s** at the door	Rev 3:20

STANDARD *banner or rule*

s of the Law	Acts 22:12
s of sound words	2 Tim 1:13

STAR *heavenly body*

His **s** in the east	Matt 2:2
morning **s** arises	2 Pet 1:19
wandering **s-s**	Jude 13
s fell from heaven	Rev 8:10
the bright morning **s**	Rev 22:16

STATE *position*

s of expectation	Luke 3:15
of our humble **s**	Phil 3:21
s has become worse	2 Pet 2:20

STATEMENT *assertion*

let your **s** be	Matt 5:37
trap Him in a **s**	Mark 12:13
catch Him in...**s**	Luke 20:20
This is a difficult **s**	John 6:60

STATURE *height*

in wisdom and **s**	Luke 2:52
he was small in **s**	Luke 19:3
measure of the **s**	Eph 4:13

STEADFAST *established, firm*

be **s**, immovable	1 Cor 15:58
hope both sure and **s**	Heb 6:19

STEAL *rob, take*

thieves break in...**s**	Matt 6:19
Do not **s**	Mark 10:19

STEPHANAS

Corinthian Christian	1 Cor 1:16;16:15,17

STEPHEN

deacon	Acts 6:5,8
martyred	Acts 7:59;8:2

STEPS *distance or movements*

in the **s** of the faith	Rom 4:12
follow in His **s**	1 Pet 2:21

STEWARD *supervisor*

and sensible **s**	Luke 12:42
s-s of the mysteries	1 Cor 4:1
above reproach...**s**	Titus 1:7

STEWARDSHIP *responsibility*

an account of your **s**	Luke 16:2
a **s** entrusted to me	1 Cor 9:17
s of God's grace	Eph 3:2

STILL *motionless or quiet*

sea, Hush, be **s**	Mark 4:39
they stood **s**	Luke 24:17

STIMULATE *excite*

s one another to	Heb 10:24

STING *pain*

where is your **s**	1 Cor 15:55
s of death is sin	1 Cor 15:56

STIR *agitate*

s-red up the water	John 5:4
s up all the multitude	Acts 21:27

STOCKS *confinement*

their feet in the **s**	Acts 16:24

STOMACH *part of body*

Food is for the **s**	1 Cor 6:13
s was made bitter	Rev 10:10

STONE (n) *rock*

foot against a **s**	Matt 4:6

will give him a **s** — Matt 7:9
rolled away the **s** — Matt 28:2
s-**s** will cry out — Luke 19:40
six **s** waterpots — John 2:6
first to throw a **s** — John 8:7
Remove the **s** — John 11:39
s-**s**, wood, hay — 1 Cor 3:12
as to a living **s** — 1 Pet 2:4
A **s** of stumbling — 1 Pet 2:8

STONE (v) *throw stones*
people will **s** us — Luke 20:6
seeking to **s** You — John 11:8
went on **s**-ing Stephen — Acts 7:59
they **s**-d Paul — Acts 14:19

STOP *cease*
s weeping for Me — Luke 23:28
s sinning — 1 Cor 15:34

STORE *accumulate*
place to **s** my crops — Luke 12:17
s-d up your treasure — James 5:3

STORM *tempest, whirlwind*
there arose a great **s** — Matt 8:24
mists driven by a **s** — 2 Pet 2:17

STRAIGHT *direct*
Make His paths **s** — Matt 3:3
Make **s** the way — John 1:23

STRANGE *foreign*
to teach **s** doctrines — 1 Tim 1:3
went after **s** flesh — Jude 7

STRANGER *alien, sojourner*
I was a **s** — Matt 25:35
hospitality to **s**-**s** — Heb 13:2

STRAW *stalk of grain*
wood, hay, **s** — 1 Cor 3:12

STRAY *wander*
s-**s** from the truth — James 5:19
s-ing like sheep — 1 Pet 2:25

STREET *road, way*
on the **s** corners — Matt 6:5
s of the city…gold — Rev 21:21

STRENGTH *force, power*
with all your **s** — Mark 12:30
s which God supplies — 1 Pet 4:11
sun shining in its **s** — Rev 1:16

STRENGTHEN *make strong*
s your brothers — Luke 22:32
s-ed in the faith — Acts 16:5
Him who **s**-**s** me — Phil 4:3
s-ed with all power — Col 1:11
s your hearts — 2 Thess 2:17
who has **s**-ed me — 1 Tim 1:12

STRETCH *extend*
S out your hand! — Mark 3:5
I have **s**-d out My hands — Rom 10:21

STRIFE *discord, quarrel*
of envy, murder, **s** — Rom 1:29
and **s** among you — 1 Cor 3:3
enmities, **s**, jealousy — Gal 5:20

STRIKE *hit*
s Your foot against a stone — Matt 4:6
s…the shepherd — Matt 26:31

STRIVE *contend, struggle*
s together with me — Rom 15:30
s-ing to please men — Gal 1:10
we labor and **s** — 1 Tim 4:10
s-ing against sin — Heb 12:4

STRONG *powerful, steadfast*
grew **s** in faith — Rom 4:20
act like men, be **s** — 1 Cor 16:13
be **s** in the Lord — Eph 6:10
weakness…made **s** — Heb 11:34
I saw a **s** angel — Rev 5:2

STRUGGLE (n) *conflict*
our **s** is not against — Eph 6:12
have shared my **s** — Phil 4:3

STUBBORNNESS *intractable*
s…unrepentant heart — Rom 2:5

STUMBLE *fall, trip*
eye makes you **s** — Matt 5:29
a stone of **s**-ing — Rom 9:33
all **s** in many *ways* — James 3:2

STUMBLING BLOCK *obstacle*
You are a **s** to Me — Matt 16:23
to Jews a **s** — 1 Cor 1:23
s of the cross — Gal 5:11

SUBJECT (adj) *under authority*
demons are **s** to us — Luke 10:17
church is **s** to Christ — Eph 5:24
s to…husbands — Titus 2:5
be **s** to the Father — Heb 12:9

SUBJECT (v)
creation was **s**-ed — Rom 8:20
them **s** themselves — 1 Cor 14:34
all things are **s**-ed — 1 Cor 15:28

SUBJECTION *under authority*
He continued in **s** — Luke 2:51
s to the governing — Rom 13:1
all things in **s** — 1 Cor 15:27

SUBMISSIVE *yielding*
Servants, be **s** — 1 Pet 2:18
s to…husbands — 1 Pet 3:5

SUBMIT *yield to*
s yourself to decrees — Col 2:20
S therefore to God — James 4:7

SUDDENLY *abruptly*
lest He come **s** — Mark 13:36
s…from heaven — Acts 2:2

SUFFER *experience pain*
Son of Man must **s** — Mark 8:31
s and rise again — Luke 24:46
worthy to **s** shame — Acts 5:41
we **s** with Him — Rom 8:17
creation…**s**-**s** — Rom 8:22
if one member **s**-**s** — 1 Cor 12:26
s-ing for the gospel — 2 Tim 1:8
Christ also **s**-ed — 1 Pet 2:21

SUFFERINGS *distress*
s of this present — Rom 8:18
sharers of our **s** — 2 Cor 1:7
fellowship of His **s** — Phil 3:10
rejoice in my **s** — Col 1:24
share the **s** of Christ — 1 Pet 4:13

SUFFICIENT *enough*
bread is not **s** — John 6:7
My grace is **s** — 2 Cor 12:9

SUMMER *season*
know that **s** is near — Matt 24:32
yourselves that **s** is now near — Luke 21:30

SUMMON *call, gather*
He **s**-ed the twelve — Mark 6:7
when I find time, I will **s** you — Acts 24:25

SUN *heavenly body*
shine forth as the **s** — Matt 13:43
signs in the **s** — Luke 21:25
not let the **s** go down — Eph 4:26
clothed with the **s** — Rev 12:1

SUPPER *meal*
made Him a **s** — John 12:2
eat the Lord's **S** — 1 Cor 11:20
marriage **s** of the — Rev 19:9
the great **s** of God — Rev 19:17

SUPPLICATION *petition*
by prayer and **s** — Phil 4:6
He offered up both prayers and **s**-**s** — Heb 5:7

SUPPLY *provide*
He who **s**-ies seed — 2 Cor 9:10
my God shall **s** — Phil 4:19
s moral excellence — 2 Pet 1:5

SUPPORT (n) *strength*
worthy of his **s** — Matt 10:10
pillar and **s** of the truth — 1 Tim 3:15

SUPPORT (v) *uphold*
first defense no one **s**-ed me — 2 Tim 4:16
ought to **s** such men — 3 John 8

SURE *secure, true*
But be **s** of this, that if — Matt 24:43
a hope both **s** and steadfast — Heb 6:19

SURPASS *excel*
s-ing riches of His — Eph 2:7
which **s**-es knowledge — Eph 3:19

SURROUND *encircle*
witnesses **s**-ing us — Heb 12:1

SWALLOW (v) *take in*
and **s** a camel — Matt 23:24
s-ed up in victory — 1 Cor 15:54

SWEAR *take oath, vow*
who **s**-**s** by heaven — Matt 23:22
began to…**s** — Matt 26:74
brethren do not **s** — James 5:12

SWEAT *perspiration*
s…like drops of — Luke 22:44

SWEET *fresh, pleasant*
s aroma of the knowledge — 2 Cor 2:14
it will be as **s** as honey — Rev 10:9

SWIFT *fast, rapid*
s to shed blood — Rom 3:15
bringing **s** destruction upon — 2 Pet 2:1

SWINDLER *cheater*
a drunkard, or a **s** — 1 Cor 5:11
revilers, nor **s**-**s** — 1 Cor 6:10

SWINE *pig*
your pearls before **s** — Matt 7:6
Send us into the **s** — Mark 5:12

SWORD *weapon with blade*
perish by the **s** — Matt 26:52
s of the Spirit — Eph 6:17
than any two-edged **s** — Heb 4:12
s of My mouth — Rev 2:16

SYCAMORE *tree*
climbed up into a **s** — Luke 19:4

SYCHAR
town in Samaria — John 4:5

SYMPATHY *mutual feeling*
s to the prisoners — Heb 10:34

SYNAGOGUE *assembly*
pray in the **s**-**s** — Matt 6:5

He went into their **s** — Matt 12:9
flogged in the **s** — Mark 13:9
chief seats in…**s**-**s** — Luke 20:46
outcasts from the **s** — John 16:2
taught in **s**-**s** — John 18:20
reasoning in the **s** — Acts 17:17
but are a **s** of Satan — Rev 2:9

SYRIA
NE of Israel — Matt 4:24; Acts 15:23,41;20:3

T

TABERNACLE
assembly and area for sacrificial worship
Mark 9:5; Acts 7:44; Heb 8:2; 9:11; Rev 21:3

TABITHA
see DORCAS

TABLE *furniture*
crumbs…master's **t** — Matt 15:27
t-**s**…moneychangers — Matt 21:12
dogs under the **t** — Mark 7:28
drink at My **t** — Luke 22:30
in order to serve **t**-**s** — Acts 6:2
t of the Lord — 1 Cor 10:21

TABLET *writing surface*
he asked for a **t** — Luke 1:63
t-**s** of human hearts — 2 Cor 3:3

TAIL
t-**s** like scorpions — Rev 9:10
his **t** swept away a third — Rev 12:4

TAKE *get, grasp*
T My yoke upon — Matt 11:29
T, eat; this is My — Matt 26:26
t up your pallet — Mark 2:9
t-**s** away the sin — John 1:29
day that He was **t**-n — Acts 1:22

TALENT
measure of money — Matt 18:24;25:15,25

TALK (n) *conversation, speech*
no…silly **t** — Eph 5:4
their **t** will spread — 2 Tim 2:17

TALK (v) *converse, speak*
Paul kept on **t**-ing — Acts 20:9
t-ing about things not proper — 1 Tim 5:13

TARES *weeds*
t…among the wheat — Matt 13:25
gather up the **t** — Matt 13:30
parable of the **t** — Matt 13:36

TARSUS
birthplace of Paul — Acts 21:39
capital of Cilicia — Acts 22:3

TASTE *test flavor*
shall not **t** death — Matt 16:28
t death for everyone — Heb 2:9
t-d…heavenly gift — Heb 6:4

TASTELESS *without taste*
salt has become **t** — Matt 5:13; Luke 14:34

TAX *charge, tribute*
sitting in the **t** office — Matt 9:9
pay **t**-es to Caesar — Luke 20:22
t to whom **t** is *due* — Rom 13:7

TAX-GATHERER *tax collector*
t-**s** do the same — Matt 5:46
many **t**-**s** and sinners — Matt 9:10
Matthew the **t** — Matt 10:3
a friend of **t**-**s** — Matt 11:19
he was a chief **t** — Luke 19:2

TEACH *instruct*
He *began* to **t** them — Matt 5:2
t-ing…in parables — Mark 4:2
Lord, **t** us to pray — Luke 11:1
Spirit will **t** you — Luke 12:12
He will **t** you all — John 14:26
t strange doctrines — 1 Tim 1:3
allow a woman to **t** — 1 Tim 2:12
she **t**-es and leads — Rev 2:20

TEACHER *instructor*
T, I will follow You — Matt 8:19
not above his **t** — Matt 10:24
why trouble the **T** — Mark 5:35
the **t** of Israel — John 3:10
call Me **T** and Lord — John 13:13
t of the immature — Rom 2:20
as pastors and **t**-**s** — Eph 4:11
t of the Gentiles — 1 Tim 2:7
false **t**-**s** among you — 2 Pet 2:1

TEACHING (n) *instruction*
amazed at His **t** — Matt 7:28
My **t** is not Mine — John 7:16
contrary to sound **t** — 1 Tim 1:10

TEAR *crying*
His feet with her **t**-**s** — Luke 7:38
God…wipe every **t** — Rev 7:17

TELL *relate, speak*
See that you **t** no one — Matt 8:4
t you about Me — John 18:34
t you the mystery — Rev 17:7

TEMPLE *structure for worship*
pinnacle of the **t** — Matt 4:5
will destroy this **t** — Mark 14:58

veil of the t	Luke 23:45
Destroy this t, and	John 2:19
you are a t of God	1 Cor 3:16
t of the Holy Spirit	1 Cor 6:19
his seat in the t	2 Thess 2:4
the Lamb, are its t	Rev 21:22

TEMPT *test, try*
being t-ed by Satan	Mark 1:13
lest Satan t you	1 Cor 7:5
t-ed beyond what	1 Cor 10:13
Himself does not t	James 1:13

TEMPTATION *testing, trial*
not lead us into t	Matt 6:13
not enter into t	Matt 26:41
time of t fall away	Luke 8:13
t has overtaken you	1 Cor 10:13
the godly from t	2 Pet 2:9

TEN *number*
has the t talents	Matt 25:28
seven heads and t horns	Rev 17:3

TEND *take care of*
T My lambs	John 21:15
T My sheep	John 21:17

TENDER *gentle, young*
branch has already become t	Matt 24:32
t mercy of our God	Luke 1:78

TERAH
father of Abraham	Luke 3:34

TERRIBLE *dreadful*
into t convulsions	Mark 9:26
so t was the sight	Heb 12:21

TERRIFY *frighten*
t you by my letters	2 Cor 10:9
It is a t-ing thing	Heb 10:31

TERROR *intense fear*
t-s and great signs	Luke 21:11

TERTIUS
Paul's scribe	Rom 16:22

TEST (n) *trial*
put Him to the t	Luke 10:25
you fail the t	2 Cor 13:5

TEST (v) *try*
Spirit…to the t	Acts 5:9
fire itself will t	1 Cor 3:13
t the spirits to see	1 John 4:1

TESTIFY *give witness*
they t against you?	Matt 27:13
Jesus Himself t-ied	John 4:44
they are willing to t	Acts 26:5

TESTIMONY *witness*
t against Jesus	Matt 26:59
t of two men is true	John 8:17
t concerning Christ	1 Cor 1:6
ashamed of the t	2 Tim 1:8
This t is true	Titus 1:13

TETRARCH
governor of a region	
Matt 14:1; Luke 3:1,19; Acts 13:1	

THADDAEUS
apostle	Matt 10:3; Mark 3:18

THANK (v) *express gratitude*
God, I t Thee	Luke 18:11
I t God always	1 Cor 1:4

THANKS (n) *gratitude*
giving t, He broke	Matt 15:36
a cup and given t	Matt 26:27
But t be to God	Rom 6:17
not cease giving t	Eph 1:16
always to give t	2 Thess 1:3

THANKSGIVING *gratitude*
supplication with t	Phil 4:6
t and honor and	Rev 7:12

THEFT *robbery*
t-s, murders	Mark 7:21
nor of their t-s	Rev 9:21

THEOPHILUS
addressee of Luke's gospel and Acts	
	Luke 1:3; Acts 1:1

THESSALONICA
Macedonian city	Acts 27:2; Phil 4:16
visited by Paul	Acts 17:1,11,13

THIEF *robber*
t comes…to steal	John 10:10
a t in the night	1 Thess 5:2

THIGH *part of leg*
on His t…a name	Rev 19:16

THINK *ponder, reflect*
not t…to abolish	Matt 5:17
not to t more highly	Rom 12:3
t as a child	1 Cor 13:11
t-s he is something	Gal 6:3
beyond all that we…t	Eph 3:20

THIRD *number*
raised…the t day	Matt 16:21
raised on the t day	1 Cor 15:4
to the t heaven	2 Cor 12:2

THIRST (n) *craving, dryness*
in hunger and t	2 Cor 11:27

THIRST (v) *having a craving*
t for righteousness	Matt 5:6
in Me shall never t	John 6:35
no more, neither t	Rev 7:16

THIRSTY *lacking water*
I was t, and you	Matt 25:35
If any man is t	John 7:37
one who is t come	Rev 22:17

THOMAS
apostle	Matt 10:3; Mark 3:18; Luke 6:15
doubted Jesus' resurrection	John 20:24-28

THORN *sharp point*
fell among the t-s	Matt 13:7
a crown of t-s	Matt 27:29
a burning t bush	Acts 7:30
t in the flesh	2 Cor 12:7

THOUGHT *concept, idea*
Jesus knowing…t-s	Matt 9:4
heart come evil t-s	Matt 15:19
every t captive	2 Cor 10:5

THREE *number*
or t have gathered	Matt 18:20
deny Me t times	Matt 26:34
t days I will raise	John 2:19

THRESHING FLOOR
clear His t	Matt 3:12; Luke 3:17

THROAT *part of neck*
t is an open grave	Rom 3:13

THRONE *seat of sovereign*
it is the t of God	Matt 5:34
sit upon twelve t-s	Matt 19:28
Thy t…is forever	Heb 1:8
to the t of grace	Heb 4:16
a great white t	Rev 20:11

THUNDER (n)
and peals of t	Rev 4:5
sound of loud t	Rev 14:2

THYATIRA
city in Asia minor	
home of Lydia	Acts 16:14
early church	Rev 1:11;2:18,24

TIBERIAS
city on W shore of Sea of Galilee	John 6:23
Sea of	John 6:1;21:1
see also GALILEE, SEA OF	
see also GENNESARET, LAKE OF	

TIBERIUS
Roman emperor	Luke 3:1
see also CAESAR	

TIDINGS *information, news*
bring glad t of good	Rom 10:15

TIME *day, period, season*
signs of the t-s	Matt 16:3
My t is at hand	Matt 26:18
deny Me three t-s	Luke 22:61
My t is not yet	John 7:6
not…you to know t-s	Acts 1:7
is the acceptable t	2 Cor 6:2
grace…in t of need	Heb 4:16
for the t is near	Rev 1:3

TIMOTHY
companion of Paul	Acts 17:15;18:5;
	Phil 1:1; Col 1:1; Heb 13:23

TITHE (n) *tenth*
t-s of all that I get	Luke 18:12
mortal men receive t-s	Heb 7:8

TITHE (v) *pay a tithe*
you t mint and dill	Matt 23:23
you pay t of mint	Luke 11:42

TITUS
co-worker with Paul	2 Cor 2:13;8:23; Gal 2:1

TODAY *present time*
t you…be with Me	Luke 23:43
same yesterday and t	Heb 13:8

TOIL (n) *labor, work*
t is not *in* vain	1 Cor 15:58
your t and preseverance	Rev 2:2

TOIL (v) *work hard*
they do not t nor	Matt 6:28
nor t in vain	Phil 2:16

TOMB *grave, sepulchre*
like whitewashed t-s	Matt 23:27
laid Him in a t	Mark 15:46
Lazarus out of the t	John 12:17
outside the t	John 20:11

TOMORROW *future time*
not be anxious for t	Matt 6:34
us eat and drink, for t we die	1 Cor 15:22

TONGUE *speech, talk*
impediment of his t	Mark 7:35
and his t loosed	Luke 1:64
no one…tame the t	James 3:8

TONGUE *language*
speak with new t-s	Mark 16:17
speak with other t-s	Acts 2:4
t-s of men…angels	1 Cor 13:1
if I pray in a t	1 Cor 14:14
every tribe and t	Rev 5:9

TOOTH
and a t for a t	Matt 5:38

TOPAZ *precious stone*
the ninth, t	Rev 21:20

TORMENT (n) *pain, torture*
this place of t	Luke 16:28
their t was like	Rev 9:5
the fear of her t	Rev 18:15

TORMENT (v) *annoy, harass*
t us before the time	Matt 8:29
do not t me	Luke 8:28

TOUCH *feel, handle*
t the fringe of His	Matt 14:36
not to t a woman	1 Cor 7:1

TOWER *fortress structure*
and built a t	Matt 21:33; Mark 12:1
he wants to build a t	Luke 14:28

TOWN *city, village*
except in his home t	Matt 13:57; Mark 6:4
welcome in his home t	Luke 4:24

TRADE (n) *business, occupation*
of the same t	Acts 18:3
t of ours	Acts 19:27

TRADE (v) *buy or sell*
t-d with them	Matt 25:16

TRADITION *custom*
sake of your t	Matt 15:3
hold to the t of men	Mark 7:8
hold…to the t-s	1 Cor 11:2
my ancestral t-s	Gal 1:14

TRAIN *guide, instruct*
t-ed to discern good	Heb 5:14
heart t-ed in greed	2 Pet 2:14

TRAMPLE *crush, hurt*
Jerusalem…t-d	Luke 21:24

TRANCE *daze, dream*
he fell into a t	Acts 10:10
in a t I saw a vision	Acts 11:5
fell into a t	Acts 22:17

TRANSFIGURED *changed*
He was t before them	Matt 17:2; Mark 9:2

TRANSFORM *change*
t-ed by the renewing	Rom 12:2
t-ed into the same	2 Cor 3:18
who will t the body	Phil 3:21

TRANSGRESS *break, overstep*
disciples t the	Matt 15:2
no man t and defraud	1 Thess 4:6

TRANSGRESSION *trespass, sin*
not forgive your t-s	Matt 6:15
dead in our t-s	Eph 2:5

TRANSGRESSOR *sinner*
a t of the law	Rom 2:25;2:27; James 2:11

TRANSLATED
Immanuel…t means	Matt 1:23
Golgotha, which is t	Mark 15:22
Messiah…t means	John 1:41

TRAP (n) *snare*
come…like a t	Luke 21:34
table become…a t	Rom 11:9

TRAP (v) *catch*
they might t Him	Matt 22:15
in order to t Him	Mark 12:13

TRAVAIL *intense pain*
woman is in t	John 16:21

TRAVEL *journey*
you t about on sea	Matt 23:15
Jesus…began t-ing	Luke 24:15

TREAD *walk on*
t upon serpents	Luke 10:19
t-s the wine press	Rev 19:15

TREASURE (n) *valuable thing*
opening their t-s	Matt 2:11
for where your t is	Matt 6:21
have t in heaven	Matt 19:21
t in earthen vessels	2 Cor 4:7
stored up your t	James 5:3

TREASURY *place of valuables*
into the temple t	Matt 27:6
money into the t	Mark 12:41

TREE *woody plant*
good t bears good	Matt 7:17
the fig t withered	Matt 21:19
a sycamore t	Luke 19:4
autumn t-s without	Jude 12
eat of the t of life	Rev 2:7

TREMBLING (n) *fear, reverence*
came t and fell down	Luke 8:47
with fear and t	Phil 2:12

TRESPASS *fault, sin*
caught in any t	Gal 6:1
dead in your t-es	Eph 2:1

TRIAL *testing*
if we are on t today	Acts 4:9
which was a t to you	Gal 4:14
perseveres under t	James 1:12

TRIBE *common ancestry*
judging…twelve t-s	Luke 22:30
men from every t	Rev 5:9

TRIBULATION *affliction*
will be a great t	Matt 24:21
world you have t	John 16:33
exult in our t-s	Rom 5:3
my t-s on your behalf	Eph 3:13
out of the great t	Rev 7:14

TRIBUNAL *court*
his seat on the t	Acts 25:6
before Caesar's t	Acts 25:10

TRIUMPH *victory*
His t in Christ	2 Cor 2:14
mercy t-s over	James 2:13

TROAS
city in Asia Minor	Acts 16:8,11
visited by Paul	Acts 20:5; 2 Cor 2:12

TROPHIMUS
companion of Paul	Acts 20:4; 2 Tim 4:20
Ephesian Christian	Acts 21:29

TROUBLE (n) *affliction*
day has enough t	Matt 6:34
have t in this life	1 Cor 7:28

TROUBLE (v) *bother, disturb*
Herod…was t-d	Matt 2:3
why t the Teacher	Mark 5:35
your heart be t-d	John 14:1

TROUBLED (adj) *disturbed*
soul has become t	John 12:27
Do not be t	Acts 20:10

TRUE *actual, real, reliable*
There was the t light	John 1:9
gives you…t bread	John 6:32
let God be found t	Rom 3:4
signs of a t apostle	2 Cor 12:12
This testimony is t	Titus 1:13
t grace of God	1 Pet 5:12
faithful and t Witness	Rev 3:14

TRUMPET *wind instrument*
do not sound a t	Matt 6:2
at the last t	1 Cor 15:52
voice like…at t	Rev 1:10

TRUST (n) *confidence, hope*
put My t in Him	Heb 2:13

TRUST (v) *commit to*
not t in ourselves	2 Cor 1:9
t in the Lord	Phil 2:24

TRUSTWORTHY *reliable*
It is a t statement	1 Tim 1:15;3:1;4:9; 2 Tim 2:11

TRUTH *genuineness, honesty*
full of grace and t	John 1:14
worship in…t	John 4:24
t shall make you free	John 8:32
the way, and the t	John 14:6
exchanged the t of	Rom 1:25
t of the gospel	Gal 2:5
speaking the t in love	Eph 4:15
the word of t	2 Tim 2:15
the t is not in us	1 John 1:8

TUNIC *cloak, garment*
or even two t-s	Matt 10:10
all the t-s and garments	Acts 9:39

TURN *change or move*
t from darkness to	Acts 26:18
he who t-s a sinner	James 5:20
t away from evil	1 Pet 3:11

TUTOR *teacher*
t-s in Christ	1 Cor 4:15
Law…become our t	Gal 3:24

TWELVE *number*
summoned His t	Matt 10:1
t legions of angels	Matt 26:53
when He became t	Luke 2:42
a crown of t stars	Rev 12:1

TWINKLING *flicker*
in the t of an eye	1 Cor 15:52

TWO-EDGED
than any t sword	Heb 4:12
His mouth…t sword	Rev 1:16

TYRE
Phoenician seaport	Matt 15:21; Acts 21:3

U

UNBELIEF *lack of faith*
wondered at their u	Mark 6:6
help my u	Mark 9:24
continue in their u	Rom 11:23

UNBELIEVER *non-believer*
a place with the u-s	Luke 12:46
wife who is an u	1 Cor 7:14
ungifted men or u-s	1 Cor 14:23
bound…with u-s	2 Cor 6:14
worse than an u	1 Tim 5:8

UNBELIEVING *doubting*
O u generation	Mark 9:19
u husband is	1 Cor 7:14
blinded the…u	2 Cor 4:4
evil, u heart	Heb 3:12

UNBLEMISHED *without defect*
u and spotless	1 Pet 1:19

UNCEASING *continuous*
sorrow and u grief	Rom 9:2

UNCHANGEABLENESS
the u of His purpose	Heb 6:17

UNCIRCUMCISED
who is physically u	Rom 2:27
the gospel to the u	Gal 2:7

UNCIRCUMCISION
has become u	Rom 2:25
who are called U	Eph 2:11
the u of your flesh	Col 2:13

UNCLEAN *not clean or not holy*
authority over u	Matt 10:1
u spirits entered	Mark 5:13
eaten anything…u	Acts 10:14
nothing is u in itself	Rom 14:14

UNCONTENTIOUS
gentle, u, free from	1 Tim 3:3
be u, gentle	Titus 3:2

UNCOVER *expose*
head u-ed while	1 Cor 11:5
pray to God with head u-ed	1 Cor 11:13

UNDEFILED *uncorrupted*
holy, innocent, u	Heb 7:26
marriage bed be u	Heb 13:4
pure and u religion	James 1:27
imperishable and u	1 Pet 1:4

UNDERGO *experience*
"But I have a baptism to u	Luke 12:50
Thy Holy One to u decay.	Acts 2:27
God raised did not u decay.	Acts 13:37

UNDERSTAND *comprehend*
Hear, and u	Matt 15:10
to u the Scriptures	Luke 24:45
Why do you not u	John 8:43
none who u-s	Rom 3:11
things hard to u	2 Pet 3:16

UNDISCIPLINED
in an u manner	2 Thess 3:7
leading an u life	2 Thess 3:11

UNFADING *lasting*
u crown of glory	1 Pet 5:4

UNFATHOMABLE
How…u His ways	Rom 11:33
u riches of Christ	Eph 3:8

UNFRUITFUL *not productive*
my mind is u	1 Cor 14:14
u deeds of darkness	Eph 5:11

UNGODLINESS *sinfulness*
remove u…Jacob	Rom 11:26
lead to further u	2 Tim 2:16

UNGODLY *sinful, wicked*
who justifies the u	Rom 4:5
Christ died for the u	Rom 5:6
destruction of u men	2 Pet 3:7
their own u lusts	Jude 18

UNHOLY *not holy*
no longer consider u	Acts 10:15
for the u and profane	1 Tim 1:9

UNITED *joined, union*
become u with Him	Rom 6:5
love, u in spirit	Phil 2:2
not u by faith	Heb 4:2

UNITY *united, union*
perfected in u	John 17:23
all attain to the u	Eph 4:13
perfect bond of u	Col 3:14

UNJUST *unfair*
For God is not u	Heb 6:10
the just for the u	1 Pet 3:18

UNKNOWN *not known*
To An U God	Acts 17:23
as u yet well-known	2 Cor 6:9

UNLEAVENED *non-fermented*
first day of U Bread	Matt 26:17
you are in fact u	1 Cor 5:7

UNMARRIED *single*
I say to the u	1 Cor 7:8
let her remain u	1 Cor 7:11

UNPRINCIPLED *unscrupulous*
conduct of u men	2 Pet 2:7
error of u men	2 Pet 3:17

UNPROFITABLE *without value*
u and worthless	Titus 3:3
grief…u for you	Heb 13:17

UNQUENCHABLE
burn…with u fire	Matt 3:12
into the u fire	Mark 9:43

UNRIGHTEOUS *evil, wicked*
rain on…the u	Matt 5:45
in a…little thing	Luke 16:10
God…is not u	Rom 3:5
u shall not inherit	1 Cor 6:9
u under punishment	2 Pet 2:9

UNRIGHTEOUSNESS *evil*
not rejoice in u	1 Cor 13:6
cleanse us from all u	1 John 1:9
All u is sin	1 John 5:17

UNRULY *disorderly*
admonish the u	1 Thess 5:14
who leads an u life	2 Thess 3:6

UNSEARCHABLE *inscrutable*
u are His judgments	Rom 11:33

UNSKILLED *lack of training*
u in speech, yet I	2 Cor 11:6

UNSTABLE *unreliable*
u in all his ways	James 1:8
enticing u souls	2 Pet 2:14

UNWILLING *reluctant*
they were u to come	Matt 22:3
He was u to drink	Matt 27:34
u to be obedient	Acts 7:39

UNWISE *foolish*
walk, not as u men	Eph 5:15

UNWORTHY *not deserving*
We are u slaves	Luke 17:10
u of eternal life	Acts 13:46

UPRIGHT *erect*
he stood u and began to walk	Acts 3:8
Stand u on your feet	Acts 14:10

UPROAR *loud noise*
there arose a great u	Acts 23:9

UPROOT *tear out*
u-ed and be planted	Luke 17:6

URBANUS
Roman Christian	Rom 16:9

URGE *entreat, encourage*
thought it necessary to u the	2 Cor 9:5
u the young men to be	Titus 2:6
I u you therefore	Rom 12:1

URIAH
husband of Bathsheba	Matt 1:6

USE *utilization*
for honorable u	Rom 9:21
not make full u of	1 Cor 7:31

USEFUL *beneficial*
u to me for service	2 Tim 4:11
vegetation u to those for	Heb 6:7

USELESS *worthless*
they have become u	Rom 3:12
without works is u	James 2:20

UTTER *express*
u words of…truth	Acts 26:25
unless you u by the tongue	1 Cor 14:9

UTTERANCE *expression*
was giving them u	Acts 2:4
in faith and u	2 Cor 8:7
u may be given	Eph 6:19
through prophetic u	1 Tim 4:14

V

VAIN *empty or profane*
our preaching is v	1 Cor 15:14
I have labored over you in v	Phil 2:16

VALUE *worth*
you are of more v	Matt 10:31
one pearl of great v	Matt 13:46
v of knowing Christ	Phil 3:8

VANISH *disappear*
v-ed from…sight	Luke 24:31
and then v-es away.	James 4:14

VANITY *futility, pride*
arrogant words of v	2 Pet 2:18

VAPOR *smoke*
You are just a v	James 4:14

VARIOUS *different*
v diseases and pains	Matt 4:24
led on by v impulses	2 Tim 3:6
encounter v trials	James 1:2
distressed by v trials	1 Pet 1:6

VEGETABLE *plant*
weak eats v-s only	Rom 14:2

VEIL *cover, curtain*
v of the temple	Matt 27:51
enters within the v	Heb 6:19

VENGEANCE *revenge*
defended him and took v for	Acts 7:24
V is Mine, I will	Heb 10:30

VESSEL *utensil*
v-s of wrath	Rom 9:22
treasure in…v-s	2 Cor 4:7
be a v for honor	2 Tim 2:21
as with a weaker v	1 Pet 3:7
v-s of the potter	Rev 2:27

VIAL *small container*
alabaster v of	Matt 26:7
she broke the v	Mark 14:3

VICTORIOUS *triumphant*
v from the beast — Rev 15:2
VICTORY *triumph*
He leads justice to v — Matt 12:20
swallowed up in v — 1 Cor 15:54
v that has overcome — 1 John 5:4
VILLAGE *small town*
Go into the v — Matt 21:2
entered a certain v — Luke 10:38
VINDICATE *justify*
wisdom is v-d by — Matt 11:19
Was v-d in the Spirit, — 1 Tim 3:16
VINE *stem of plant*
fruit of the v — Matt 26:29
I am the true v — John 15:1
VINEDRESSER *gardener*
My Father is the v — John 15:1
VINE-GROWERS
rented it out to v — Matt 21:33
and destroy the v — Mark 12:9
VINEYARD *grapevines*
laborers for his v — Matt 20:1
Who plants a v — 1 Cor 9:7
VIOLENT *destructive*
a v, rushing wind — Acts 2:2
a persecutor and a v aggressor — 1 Tim 1:13
VIPER *snake*
You brood of v-s — Matt 3:7; Luke 3:7
VIRGIN *unmarried maiden*
v shall be with child — Matt 1:23
kept her a v — Matt 1:25
comparable to ten v-s — Matt 25:1
v-'s name was Mary — Luke 1:27
if a v should marry — 1 Cor 7:28
VISIBLE *manifest, seen*
He should become v — Acts 10:40
becomes v is light — Eph 5:13
things which are v — Heb 11:3
VISION *dream, foresight*
Tell the v to no one — Matt 17:9
young men...see v-s — Acts 2:17
VISIT *come or go to see*
you did not v Me — Matt 25:43
For He has v-ed us — Luke 1:68
v orphans...widows — James 1:27
VOICE *sound, speech*
v...heard in Ramah — Matt 2:18
v...out of the cloud — Mark 9:7
v of one crying in — Luke 3:4
v of the Son of God — John 5:25
v has gone out — Rom 10:18
v of the archangel — 1 Thess 4:16
His v shook...earth — Heb 12:26
if anyone hears My v — Rev 3:20
with a v of thunder — Rev 6:1
VOID *empty, invalid*
faith is made v — Rom 4:14
cross...be made v — 1 Cor 1:17
VOMIT *throw up*
returns to its own v — 2 Pet 2:22
VOW *solemn promise*
not make false v-s — Matt 5:33
he was keeping a v — Acts 18:18
VOYAGE *journey*
we had finished the v from Tyre — Acts 21:7
v was now dangerous — Acts 27:9
VULTURE *bird*
the v-s will gather — Matt 24:28
the v-s be gathered — Luke 17:37

W

WAGE *salary*
w is not reckoned — Rom 4:4
the w-s of sin — Rom 6:23
worthy of his w-s — 1 Tim 5:18
WAIL *lament, mourn*
weeping and w-ing — Mark 5:38
WAIT *expect*
creation w-s eagerly — Rom 8:19
w-ing for the hope — Gal 5:5
WALK *follow, go along*
Rise, and w — Matt 9:5
w-ed on the water — Matt 14:29
w in newness of life — Rom 6:4
we w by faith — 2 Cor 5:7
w by the Spirit — Gal 5:16
w in love — Eph 5:2
w as children of light — Eph 5:8
if we w in the light — 1 John 1:7
w by its light — Rev 21:24
WALL *structure*
you whitewashed w — Acts 23:3
w-s of Jericho fell — Heb 11:30
a great and high w — Rev 21:12
WANDER *roam*
w-ed...the faith — 1 Tim 6:10
w-ing stars, for whom — Jude 13

WAR *battle, conflict*
w-s...rumors of w-s — Matt 24:6
w against the law — Rom 7:23
w in your members — James 4:1
w against the soul — 1 Pet 2:11
judges and wages w — Rev 19:11
WARN *give notice*
w-ed...in a dream — Matt 2:12
w you whom to fear — Luke 12:5
Moses was w-ed — Heb 8:5
WASH *bathe, clean*
do not w their hands — Matt 15:2
ceremonially w-ed — Luke 11:38
w in the pool of — John 9:7
w the disciples' feet — John 13:5
w away your sins — Acts 22:16
w-ed...saints' feet — 1 Tim 5:10
w-ed with pure — Heb 10:22
who w their robes — Rev 22:14
WASTE (v) *destroy, use up*
perfume been w-d — Mark 14:4
WATCH (n) *guard*
keep w with Me — Matt 26:38
w over their flock — Luke 2:8
w over your souls — Heb 13:17
WATCH (v) *observe*
W out and beware — Matt 16:6
you not keep w — Mark 14:37
WATER (n) *flood, liquid*
baptize you with w — Matt 3:11
a cup of cold w — Matt 10:42
walked on the w — Matt 14:29
no w for My feet — Luke 7:44
one is born of w — John 3:5
given you living w — John 4:10
John baptized with w — Acts 1:5
of w with the word — Eph 5:26
formed out of w — 2 Pet 3:5
by w and blood — 1 John 5:6
sound of many w-s — Rev 19:6
WATER (v) *make moist*
Apollos w-ed — 1 Cor 3:6
WAVES *billows*
w were breaking — Mark 4:37
wild w of the sea — Jude 13
WAY *manner or path*
Make ready the w — Matt 3:3
Pray...in this w — Matt 6:9
w is broad that leads — Matt 7:13
teach...w of God — Mark 12:14
into the w of peace — Luke 1:79
I am the w — John 14:6
belonging to the W — Acts 9:2
the w of salvation — Acts 16:17
unfathomable...w-s — Rom 11:33
w of escape — 1 Cor 10:13
new and living w — Heb 10:20
the w of the truth — 2 Pet 2:2
WEAK *feeble*
but the flesh is w — Matt 26:41
must help the w — Acts 20:35
who is w in faith — Rom 14:1
God...chosen the w — 1 Cor 1:27
WEAKNESS *fault*
Spirit...helps our w — Rom 8:26
bear the w-es — Rom 15:1
w of God is stronger — 1 Cor 1:25
it is sown in w — 1 Cor 15:43
perfected in w — 2 Cor 12:9
WEALTH *riches*
w of their liberality — 2 Cor 8:2
rich by her w — Rev 18:19
WEAPON *armament*
and torches and w-s — John 18:3
w-s of righteousness — 2 Cor 6:7
WEARY *tired*
all who are w — Matt 11:28
w of doing good — 2 Thess 3:13
WEAVE *interlace*
after w-ing a crown — Matt 27:29; Mark 15:17
WEDDING *marriage*
come to the w feast — Matt 22:4
a w in Cana — John 2:1
WEEK *period of time*
first day of the w — Matt 28:1
I fast twice a w — Luke 18:12
WEEP *cry, sorrow*
Rachel w-ing for her — Matt 2:18
w-ing and gnashing — Matt 13:42
he...wept bitterly — Matt 26:75
saw the city...wept — Luke 19:41
w for yourselves — Luke 23:28
Jesus wept — John 11:35
why are you w-ing — John 20:13
w with...who w — Rom 12:15
WEIGHT *heaviness*
eternal w of glory — 2 Cor 4:17
WELCOME *gladly receive*
no prophet is w-d Him — Luke 4:24
multitude w-d Him — Luke 8:40

who fears Him...w — Acts 10:35
she...w-d the spies — Heb 11:31
WELL (n) *water shaft*
Jacob's w was there — John 4:6
a w of water — John 4:14
WELL (v) *healthy, healed*
I shall get w — Matt 9:21
faith has made you w — Luke 18:42
WELL-PLEASED *satisfied*
in whom I am w — Matt 3:17
in Thee I am w — Luke 3:22
God was not w — 1 Cor 10:5
WHEAT *grain*
gather His w into — Matt 3:12
to sift you like w — Luke 22:31
unless a grain of w — John 12:24
WHITE *color*
make one hair w — Matt 5:36
clothing became w — Luke 9:29
fields...w for harvest — John 4:35
clothed in w robes — Rev 7:9
WHITEWASHED *wall covering*
like w tombs — Matt 23:27
you w wall — Acts 23:3
WHOLE *entire*
leavens the w lump — 1 Cor 5:6
keeps the w law — James 2:10
WICK *candle thread*
a smoldering w — Matt 12:20
WICKED *evil, ungodly*
taking...some w men — Acts 17:5
righteous and the w — Acts 24:15
WICKEDNESS *evil*
repent of this w — Acts 8:22
spiritual forces of w — Eph 6:12
WIDOW *husband is dead*
devour w-s' houses — Matt 23:14
w put in more — Mark 12:43
Honor w-s — 1 Tim 5:3
visit orphans...w-s — James 1:27
WIFE *married woman*
who divorces his w — Matt 5:32
Remember Lot's w — Luke 17:32
have his own w — 1 Cor 7:2
head of the w — Eph 5:23
husband of one w — 1 Tim 3:2
w-ves, be submissive — 1 Pet 3:1
w of the Lamb — Rev 21:9
WILD *untamed*
locusts and w honey — Mark 1:6
being a w olive — Rom 11:17
WILDERNESS *barren area*
preaching in the w — Matt 3:1
into the w...tempted — Matt 4:1
crying in the w — Mark 1:3
manna in the w — John 6:31
WILL *attitude, purpose*
Thy w be done — Matt 6:10
the w of My Father — Matt 7:21
not My w, but — Luke 22:42
nor of the w of man — John 1:13
who resists His w — Rom 9:19
what the w of God — Rom 12:2
knowledge of His w — Col 1:9
come to do Thy w — Heb 10:9
an act of human w — 2 Pet 1:21
WIN *succeed*
we will w him over — Matt 28:14
that I might w Jews — 1 Cor 9:20
won without a word — 1 Pet 3:1
WIND
reed shaken by...w — Matt 11:7
w and the sea obey — Mark 4:41
He rebuked the w — Luke 8:24
violent, rushing w — Acts 2:2
every w of doctrine — Eph 4:14
driven by strong w-s — James 3:4
WINDOW *opening*
sitting on the w sill — Acts 20:9
basket through a w — 2 Cor 11:33
WINE *strong drink*
new w into old — Matt 9:17
gave Him w to — Matt 27:34
made the water w — John 4:46
full of sweet w — Acts 2:13
not get drunk with w — Eph 5:18
not addicted to w — 1 Tim 3:3
WINESKINS *animal skin bag*
w into fresh w — Matt 9:17
w into old w — Luke 5:37
WINGS
chicks under her w — Matt 23:37
sound of their w-s — Rev 9:9
WINNOW *scatter*
His w-ing fork — Matt 3:12
WINTER *season*
even spend the w — 1 Cor 16:6
WIPE *pass over, rub*
w-d His feet — John 11:2

sins...**w-d** away	Acts 3:19
w away every tear	Rev 21:4

WISDOM *discernment*

w given to Him	Mark 6:2
kept increasing in **w**	Luke 2:52
made foolish the **w**	1 Cor 1:20
any of you lacks **w**	James 1:5

WISE *judicious, prudent*

you being *so* **w**	2 Cor 11:19
Who...you is **w**	James 3:13

WITHER *dry up*

with a **w-ed** hand	Mark 3:1
the fig tree **w-ed**	Mark 11:20

WITNESS (n) *testimony*

w to all the nations	Matt 24:14
He came for a **w**	John 1:7
My **w** is true	John 8:14
you shall be My **w-es**	Acts 1:8
For God is my **w**	Phil 1:8
w of God is greater	1 John 5:9
Christ, the faithful **w**	Rev 1:5

WITNESS (v) *testify*

John bore **w**	John 1:32
bear **w** of Me	John 15:26
Spirit...bears **w**	Rom 8:16
three that bear **w**	1 John 5:8

WOLF *animal*

the midst of **w-ves**	Matt 10:16
w snatches them	John 10:12

WOMAN *female, lady*

looks on a **w** to lust	Matt 5:28
w-en...grinding	Matt 24:41
Blessed among **w-en**	Luke 1:42
W, behold, your son	John 19:26
not to touch a **w**	1 Cor 7:1
w is the glory of **w**	1 Cor 11:7
w to speak in	1 Cor 14:35
His Son, born of a **w**	Gal 4:4
w clothed with...sun	Rev 12:1

WOMB

baby leaped in...**w**	Luke 1:41

WONDER *marvel, sign*

were filled with **w**	Acts 3:10
Why do you **w?**	Rev 17:7

WOOD *cut tree*

stones, **w**, hay	1 Cor 3:12

WOOL *cloth or hair*

scarlet **w** and hyssop	Heb 9:19
white like white **w**	Rev 1:14

WORD *message, speech*

every **w** that proceeds	Matt 4:4
these **w-s** of Mine	Matt 7:24
sower sows the **w**	Mark 4:14
the W was God	John 1:1
the W became flesh	John 1:14
w-s of eternal life	John 6:68
abide in My **w**	John 8:31
glorifying the **w**	Acts 13:48
too deep for **w-s**	Rom 8:26
hearing by the **w**	Rom 10:17
the **w** of the cross	1 Cor 1:18
fulfilled in one **w**	Gal 5:14
no unwholesome **w**	Eph 4:29
sanctified by...**w**	1 Tim 4:5
the **w** of truth	2 Tim 2:15
the faithful **w**	Titus 1:9
w of God is living	Heb 4:12
doers of the **w**	James 1:22
pure milk of the **w**	1 Pet 2:2
the W of Life	1 John 1:1
The W of God	Rev 19:13

WORK (n) *act, deed, labor*

see your good **w-s**	Matt 5:16
the **w-s** of Christ	Matt 11:2
the **w** of the Law	Rom 2:15
faith apart from **w-s**	Rom 3:28
not...a result of **w-s**	Eph 2:9
for the **w** of service	Eph 4:12
began a good **w**	Phil 1:6
fruit in...good **w**	Col 1:10
rich in good **w-s**	1 Tim 6:18
faith without **w-s**	James 2:20

WORK (v) *perform, produce*

not **w** for the food	John 6:27
w together for good	Rom 8:28
So death **w-s** in us	2 Cor 4:12
w out your salvation	Phil 2:12
anyone will not **w**	2 Thess 3:10

WORKER *laborer*

w is worthy of his	Matt 10:10
God's fellow **w-s**	1 Cor 3:9
beware...evil **w-s**	Phil 3:2
pure, **w-s** at home	Titus 2:5

WORKMAN *craftsman*

w-men of similar *trades*	Acts 19:25
approved...as a **w**	2 Tim 2:15

WORKMANSHIP *craftsmanship*

we are His **w**	Eph 2:10

WORLD *earth, humanity*

the light of the **w**	Matt 5:14
the field is the **w**	Matt 13:38
Go into all the **w**	Mark 16:15
gains the whole **w**	Luke 9:25
God so loved the **w**	John 3:16
Savior of the **w**	John 4:42
w cannot hate you	John 7:7
the light of the **w**	John 8:12
overcome the **w**	John 16:33
have upset the **w**	Acts 17:6
sin entered...the **w**	Rom 5:12
reconciling the **w**	2 Cor 5:19
unstained by the **w**	James 1:27
flood upon the **w**	2 Pet 2:5
Do not love the **w**	1 John 2:15

WORLDLY *earthly*

w fables fit only	1 Tim 4:7
avoid **w**...chatter	2 Tim 2:16

WORM *creeping animal*

their **w** does not die	Mark 9:48
he was eaten by **w-s**	Acts 12:23

WORMWOOD

used *figuratively*	Rev 8:11

WORSHIP *bow, revere*

in vain do they **w**	Matt 15:9
w in spirit and truth	John 4:24
w in the Spirit	Phil 3:3
w Him who lives	Rev 4:10
who **w** the beast	Rev 14:11

WORTHLESS *useless*

your faith is **w**	1 Cor 15:17
w for any good	Titus 1:16
man's religion is **w**	James 1:26

WORTHY *having merit*

w of his support	Matt 10:10
is not **w** of Me	Matt 10:37
is **w** of his wages	Luke 10:7
manner **w** of the	Rom 16:2
w of the gospel	Phil 1:27
world was not **w**	Heb 11:38
W is the Lamb	Rev 5:12

WOUND *injury*

bandaged...his **w-s**	Luke 10:34
by His **w-s** you were	1 Pet 2:24
fatal **w** was healed	Rev 13:3

WRAPPINGS *cloth coverings*

bound...with **w**	John 11:44
linen **w** lying *there*	John 20:5

WRATH *anger, indignation*

from the **w** to come	Matt 3:7
w of God abides on	John 3:36
God who inflicts **w**	Rom 3:5
children of **w**	Eph 2:3
w of God will come	Col 3:6
the **w** of the Lamb	Rev 6:16

WRETCHED *miserable*

W man that I am	Rom 7:24
that you are **w**	Rev 3:17

WRITE *enscribe*

w a certificate	Mark 10:4
with His finger **wrote**	John 8:6
w...King of the Jews	John 19:21
W in a book	Rev 1:11

WRITINGS *literary work*

not believe his **w**	John 5:47
known the sacred **w**	2 Tim 3:15

WRITTEN *enscribed*

w by the prophet	Matt 2:5
about whom it is **w**	Matt 11:10
Law **w** in...hearts	Rom 2:15
name has not been **w**	Rev 13:8
w in the Lamb's	Rev 21:27

WRONG *do evil, harm*

Love does no **w**	Rom 13:10

WROUGHT *accomplished*

been **w** in God	John 3:21

Y

YAHWEH

see **YHWH** and **LORD**

YEAR *period, time*

thirty **y-s** of age	Luke 3:23
y of the LORD	Luke 4:19
priest *enters*, once a **y**	Heb 9:7
sacrifices **y** by **y**	Heb 10:1
y-s as one day	2 Pet 3:8
reign...thousand **y-s**	Rev 20:6

YESTERDAY *past*

Y at the seventh hour	John 4:52
same **y** and today	Heb 13:8

YHWH

Hebrew tetragrammaton for name of God,
probably pronounced Yahweh
Translated usually as Lord, which is the way it
is found in the New Testament

YIELD *produce*

y-ed up His spirit	Matt 27:50
not **y** in subjection	Gal 2:5
y-s the peaceful	Heb 12:11

YOKE *wooden bar*

Take My **y** upon	Matt 11:29
to a **y** of slavery	Gal 5:1

YOUNG *early age, youth*

finding a **y** donkey	John 12:14
y men...visions	Acts 2:17
urge the **y** men	Titus 2:6

YOUTH *young*

things from my **y** up	Mark 10:20
life from my **y** up	Acts 26:4

Z

ZACCHEUS

tax collector who followed Jesus	Luke 19:2,5,8

ZACHARIAS

father of John the Baptist	Luke 1:5,12,18;3:2

ZAREPHATH

Phoenician town	Luke 4:26

ZEAL *fervor, passion*

have a **z** for God	Rom 10:2
your **z** for me	2 Cor 7:7

ZEALOT

member of radical Jewish nationalist party
Matt 10:4; Mark 3:18; Luke 6:15; Acts 1:13

ZEALOUS *fervent*

all **z** for the Law	Acts 21:20
z of...*gifts*	1 Cor 14:12
z for good deeds	Titus 2:14
be **z**...and repent	Rev 3:19

ZEBEDEE

father of James and John
Matt 4:21;27:56; Mark 1:19;10:35;
Luke 5:10; John 21:2

ZION

1 *hill/city of David which is Jerusalem*
Matt 21:5; John 12:15

2 *after Temple built, name extended to top of*
hill, Mount Zion

3 *applied to all of Jerusalem as city spreads*
John 12:15; Rom 11:26

4 *used in the corporate sense for the people*
and land 1 Pet 2:6

5 *used eschatologically for heavenly Jerusalem*
Heb 12:22; Rev 14:1

THE BIBLICAL WORLD OF THE PATRIARCHS MAP 1

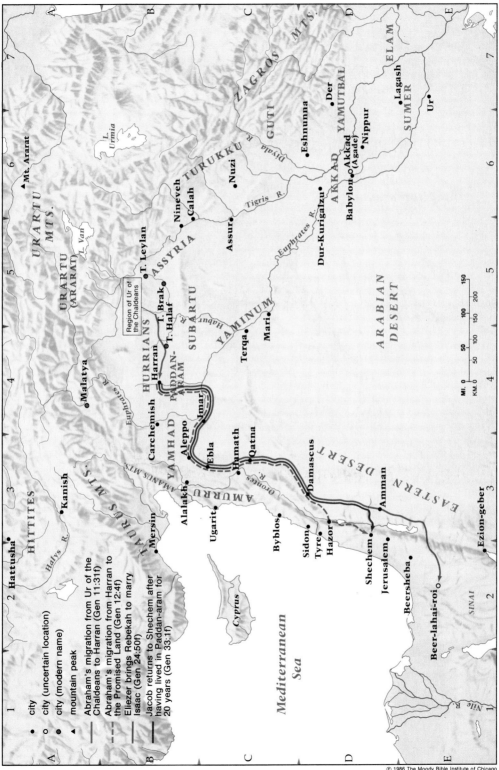

Legend:
- • city
- ○ city (uncertain location)
- ◉ city (modern name)
- ▲ mountain peak

— Abraham's migration from Ur of the Chaldeans to Harran (Gen 11:31f)

–·– Abraham's migration from Harran to the Promised Land (Gen 12:4f) Eliezer brings Rebekah to marry Isaac (Gen 24:50f)

— Jacob returns to Shechem after having lived in Paddan-aram for 20 years (Gen 33:1f)

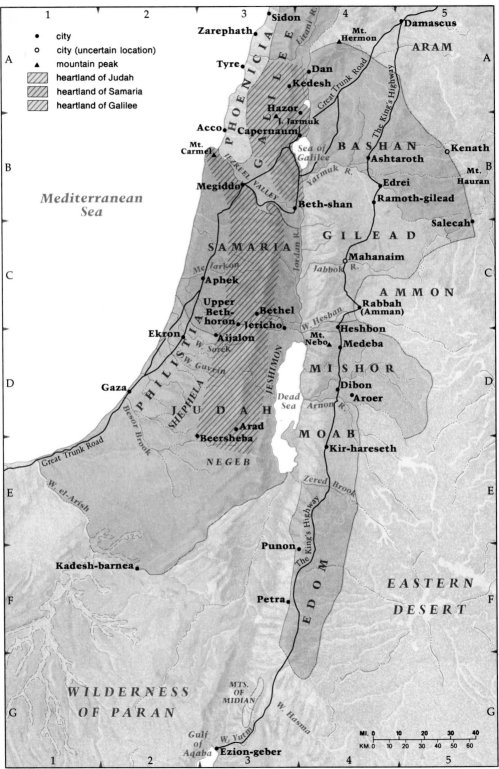

MAP 2   PALESTINE: POLITICAL REGIONS

- city
- ○ city (uncertain location)
- ▲ mountain peak
- heartland of Judah
- heartland of Samaria
- heartland of Galilee

Mediterranean Sea

Sidon
Zarephath
Tyre
Dan
Kedesh
Acco
Capernaum
Mt. Carmel
Hazor
J. Jarmuk
Megiddo
Beth-shan
Aphek
Upper Beth-horon
Bethel
Ekron
Jericho
Aijalon
Gaza
SHEPHELA
Arad
Beersheba
NEGEB

Damascus
Mt. Hermon
ARAM
BASHAN
Ashtaroth
Kenath
Mt. Hauran
Edrei
Ramoth-gilead
Salecah
GILEAD
Mahanaim
AMMON
Rabbah (Amman)
Heshbon
Mt. Nebo
Medeba
MISHOR
Dibon
Aroer
MOAB
Kir-hareseth

PHOENICIA
GALILEE
JEZREEL VALLEY
SAMARIA
PHILISTIA
JUDAH
JESHIMON

Sea of Galilee
Dead Sea

Great Trunk Road
The King's Highway
Liani R.
Yarmuk R.
Jordan R.
Jabbok R.
W. Hesban
Arnon R.
Zered Brook

Punon
Kadesh-barnea
Petra
EDOM
EASTERN DESERT

Great Trunk Road
W. el-Arish
Besor Brook
Me Jarkon
W. Sorek
W. Guvrin

WILDERNESS OF PARAN
MTS. OF MIDIAN
W. Hasma
Gulf of Aqaba
W. Yutm
Ezion-geber

MI. 0   10   20   30   40
KM. 0   10   20   30   40   50   60

© 1986 The Moody Bible Institute of Chicago

THE ROUTE OF THE EXODUS

MAP 3

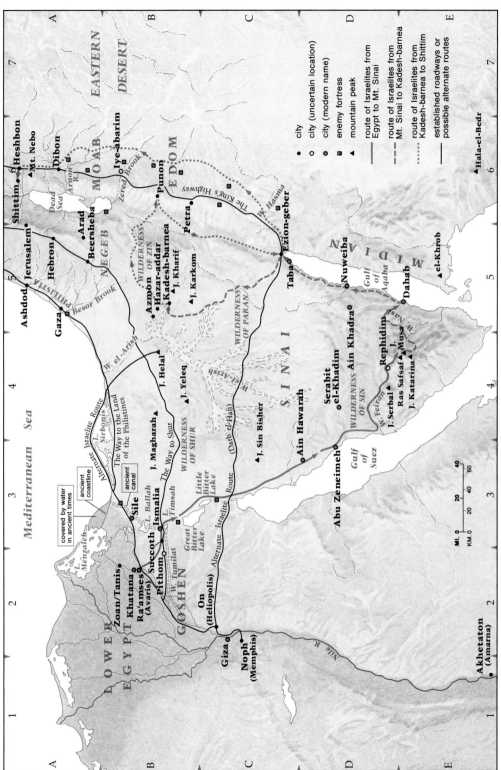

Legend:
- city
- city (uncertain location)
- city (modern name)
- enemy fortress
- mountain peak
- route of Israelites from Egypt to Mt. Sinai
- route of Israelites from Mt. Sinai to Kadesh-barnea
- route of Israelites from Kadesh-barnea to Shittim
- established roadways or possible alternate routes

MAP 4

THE TWELVE TRIBES OF ISRAEL

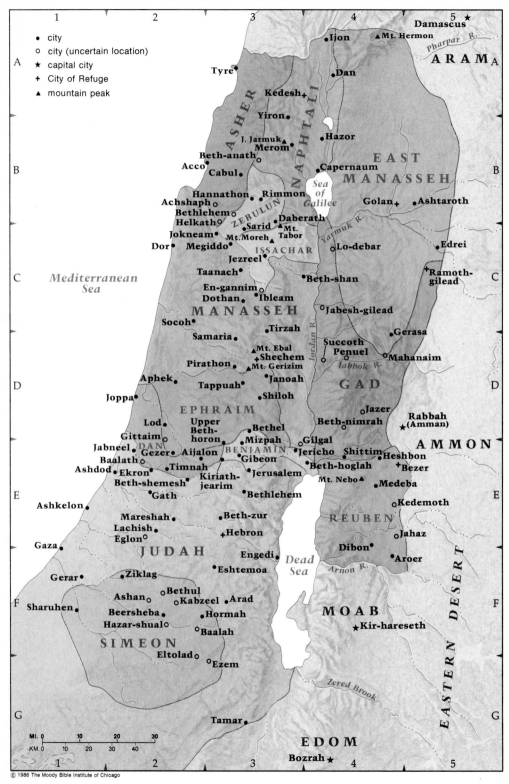

- • city
- ○ city (uncertain location)
- ★ capital city
- ✛ City of Refuge
- ▲ mountain peak

Damascus ★

Ijon
Mt. Hermon
Pharpar R.
ARAM

Tyre

Kedesh ✛
Dan

ASHER
Yiron

NAPHTALI

J. Jarmuk ▲
Merom
Hazor

Beth-anath
Acco
Cabul

EAST
MANASSEH

Capernaum
Sea of Galilee

Hannathon
Rimmon
Achshaph
Bethlehem
Helkath
ZEBULUN
Sarid
Daberath
Mt. Tabor

Golan ✛
Ashtaroth

Jokneam
Mt. Moreh
Dor
Megiddo

ISSACHAR
Jezreel

Lo-debar
Edrei

Taanach
Beth-shan
Ramoth-gilead ✛

Mediterranean Sea

En-gannim
Dothan
Ibleam
Jabesh-gilead

MANASSEH

Socoh

Samaria
Tirzah
Succoth
Penuel
Gerasa

Jordan R.

Mahanaim

Pirathon
Mt. Ebal ▲
Shechem
Mt. Gerizim

Jabbok R.

GAD

Aphek
Tappuah
Janoah

Joppa
Shiloh

EPHRAIM

Jazer
Rabbah
(Amman) ★

Lod
Upper Beth-horon
Bethel
Beth-nimrah

Gittaim
Mizpah
Gilgal
AMMON

Jabneel
Gezer
Aijalon
BENJAMIN
Jericho
Shittim
Heshbon

DAN
Baalath
Gibeon
Beth-hoglah
Bezer ✛

Ashdod
Ekron
Timnah
Jerusalem
Mt. Nebo ▲
Medeba

Beth-shemesh
Kiriath-jearim

Gath
Bethlehem
Kedemoth

Ashkelon

Beth-zur
REUBEN

Mareshah
Lachish
Hebron ✛
Jahaz

Eglon
Dibon

Gaza
JUDAH
Engedi
Aroer

Eshtemoa
Dead Sea
Arnon R.

Gerar
Ziklag

Bethul
Kabzeel
Arad

Ashan
Hormah

Sharuhen
Beersheba

Hazar-shual
Baalah

MOAB

SIMEON
Kir-hareseth ★

Eltolad
Ezem

EASTERN DESERT

Zered Brook

Tamar

EDOM

MI. 0   10   20   30
KM. 0   10   20   30   40

Bozrah ★

KINGDOMS OF SAUL, DAVID & SOLOMON   MAP 5

1 2 3 4 5

A **Aleppo**

MI. 0   50   100
KM. 0   50   100   150

**Tiphsah
(Thapsakos)**

Euphrates R.

Cyprus

HAMATH

Orontes R.

B **Arvad** **Hamath**

**Kadesh
on the
Oróntes**

Tadmor

*Mediterranean
Sea*

Byblos **Lebweh** **Sadad**

Qaryatein

Litani R.

C **Sidon** **Damascus**

Tyre **Dan**

Hazor

Acco

Megiddo **Ramoth-
gilead** **Salecah**

D **Beth-shan**

Jordan R.

Shechem

Joppa **Rabbah
(Amman)**

Gezer

PHILISTIA **Gibeah**

Ashdod **Jerusalem**

Gaza **Gath**

*Dead
Sea*

E **Raphia** **Beersheba**

Kir-hareseth

W. el-Arish **Tamar**

EASTERN DESERT

W. Sirhan

**Kadesh-
barnea** **Petra**

SINAI

• city
◉ city (modern name)
□ city fortified by Solomon
— boundary of Solomon's Kingdom
░ Saul's Kingdom
░ territory conquered by David
░ area effectively under Solomon's
economic control (1 Kgs 4:24)

Ezion-geber

*Gulf of
Aqaba*

G

1 2 3 4 5

© 1986 The Moody Bible Institute of Chicago

MAP 6 · THE DIVIDED KINGDOM: ISRAEL & JUDAH

- • city
- ○ city (uncertain location)
- ★ capital city
- + sanctuary city
- ▲ mountain peak

Byblos

Beirut

Sidon

Damascus

PHOENICIA

Mt. Hermon

Litani R.

Tyre

Dan

ARAM

Kedesh

Hazor

Acco

Mt. Carmel

Kishon R.

Sea of Galilee

Ashtaroth

Mt. Tabor

Yarmuk R.

Edrei

Mt. Hauran

Megiddo

Taanach

Beth-shan

Ramoth-gilead

Mt. Gilboa

Ibleam

Jordan R.

Jabesh-gilead

Tirzah

Succoth

Mahanaim

Samaria

Mt. Ebal

Mt. Gerizim

Shechem

Penuel

Jabbok R.

Joppa

Aphek

Shiloh

ISRAEL

Rabbah (Amman)

Bethel

Gezer

Jericho

AMMON

Ashdod

Aijalon

Jerusalem

Heshbon

Gath

Bethlehem

Mt. Nebo

Medeba

Ashkelon

Mediterranean Sea

Mareshah

Gaza

PHILISTIA

Hebron

Dibon

JUDAH

Dead Sea

Arnon R.

Besor Brook

Beersheba

MOAB

Kir-hareseth

W. el-Arish

Zered Brook

F

Bozrah

EASTERN DESERT

EDOM

Kadesh-barnea

WILDERNESS

MI. 0   10   20   30   40
KM. 0 10 20 30 40 50 60

THE ASSYRIAN EMPIRE

MAP 7

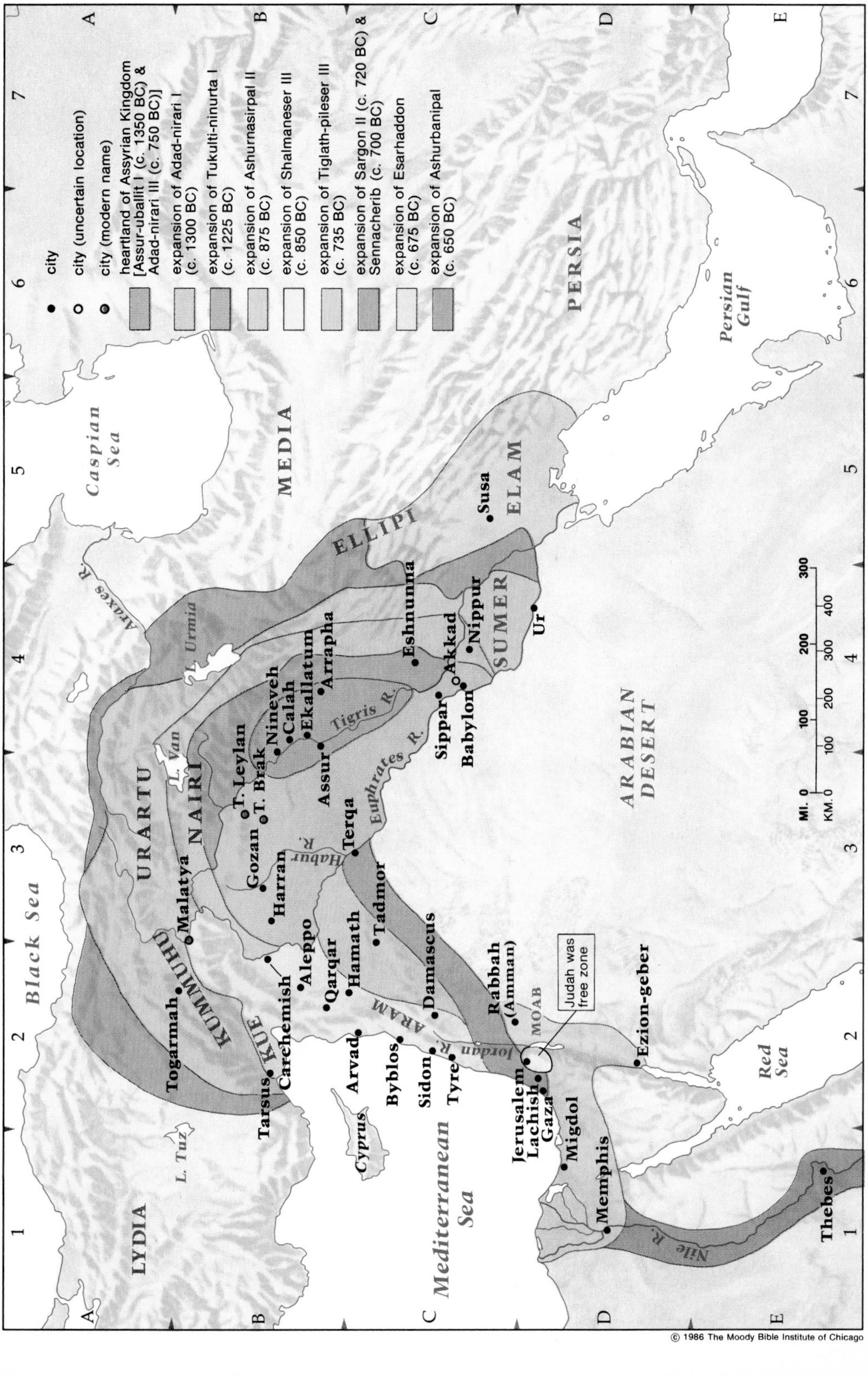
city
city (uncertain location)
city (modern name)
heartland of Assyrian Kingdom [Assur-uballit I (c. 1350 BC) & Adad-nirari III (c. 750 BC)]
expansion of Adad-nirari I (c. 1300 BC)
expansion of Tukulti-ninurta I (c. 1225 BC)
expansion of Ashurnasirpal II (c. 875 BC)
expansion of Shalmaneser III (c. 850 BC)
expansion of Tiglath-pileser III (c. 735 BC)
expansion of Sargon II (c. 720 BC) & Sennacherib (c. 700 BC)
expansion of Esarhaddon (c. 675 BC)
expansion of Ashurbanipal (c. 650 BC)
Black Sea
Caspian Sea
Mediterranean Sea
Red Sea
Persian Gulf
LYDIA
URARTU
NAIRI
KUMMUHU
KUE
MEDIA
ELLIPI
ELAM
SUMER
PERSIA
ARAM
MOAB
ARABIAN DESERT
L. Tuz
L. Van
L. Urmia
Araxes R.
Tigris R.
Euphrates R.
Habur R.
Jordan R.
Nile R.
Togarmah
Malatya
Tarsus
Carchemish
Aleppo
Qarqar
Hamath
Arvad
Byblos
Sidon
Tyre
Cyprus
Damascus
Tadmor
Gozan
Harran
T. Leylan
T. Brak
Terqa
Nineveh
Calah
Ekallatum
Assur
Arrapha
Eshnunna
Sippar
Babylon
Akkad
Nippur
Ur
Susa
Rabbah (Amman)
Judah was free zone
Jerusalem
Lachish
Gaza
Migdol
Ezion-geber
Memphis
Thebes
MI. 0 100 200 300
KM. 0 100 200 300 400
A B C D E
1 2 3 4 5 6 7

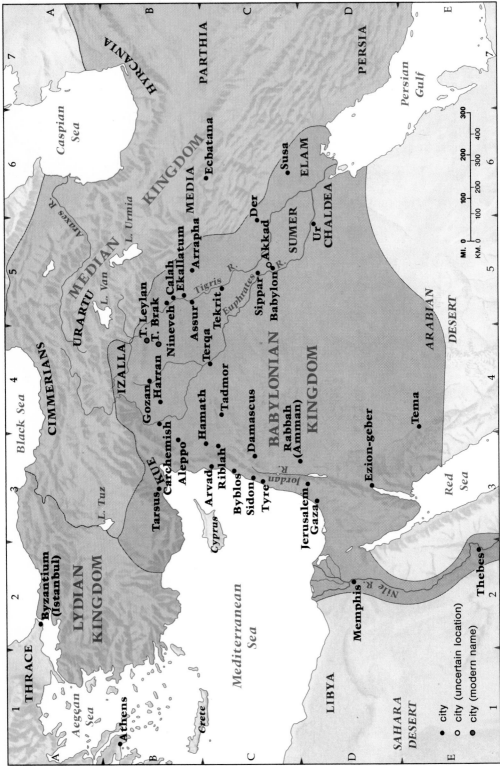

MAP 8

THE BABYLONIAN EMPIRE

© 1986 The Moody Bible Institute of Chicago

THE GREEK EMPIRE

MAP 9

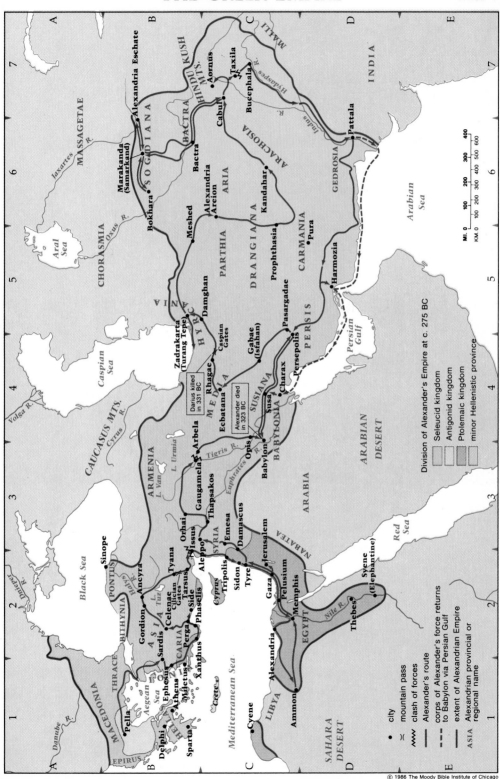

Division of Alexander's Empire at c. 275 BC

- Seleucid kingdom
- Antigonid kingdom
- Ptolemaic kingdom
- minor Hellenistic province

- • city
-)(mountain pass
- ∧∧∧ clash of forces
- —— Alexander's route
- - - corps of Alexander's force returns to Babylon via Persian Gulf
- —— extent of Alexandrian Empire
- ASIA Alexandrian provincial or regional name

Darius killed in 331 BC

Alexander died in 323 BC

MAP 10

OLD TESTAMENT JERUSALEM

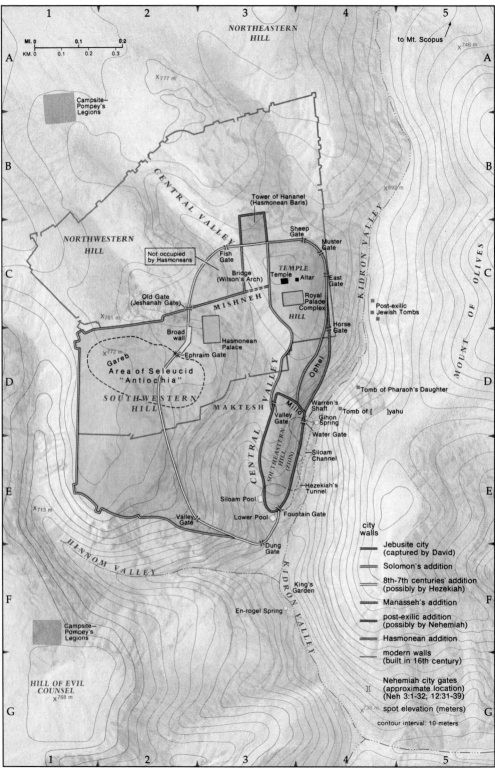

MI. 0   0.1   0.2
KM. 0 0.1 0.2 0.3

A

Campsite—
Pompey's
Legions

x777 m

NORTHEASTERN
HILL

to Mt. Scopus

x746 m

A

B

CENTRAL VALLEY

NORTHWESTERN
HILL

Tower of Hananel
(Hasmonean Baris)

Sheep
Gate

Muster
Gate

x692 m

KIDRON VALLEY

MOUNT OF OLIVES

B

Not occupied
by Hasmoneans

Fish
Gate

Bridge
(Wilson's Arch)

TEMPLE

Temple ■ Altar

East
Gate

Post-exilic
Jewish Tombs

C

Old Gate
(Jeshanah Gate)

MISHNEH

Royal
Palace
Complex

HILL

Horse
Gate

x761 m

Broad
wall

Hasmonean
Palace

Ephraim Gate

Gareb

x772 m

Area of Seleucid
"Antiochia"

SOUTHWESTERN
HILL

MAKTESH

CENTRAL VALLEY

Ophel

Tomb of Pharaoh's Daughter

Tomb of [   ]yahu

D

Millo

Warren's
Shaft

Valley
Gate

Gihon
Spring

SOUTHEASTERN HILL (ZION)

Water Gate

Siloam
Channel

Hezekiah's
Tunnel

E

x713 m

Siloam Pool

Valley
Gate

Lower Pool

Fountain
Gate

Dung
Gate

city
walls

HINNOM VALLEY

KIDRON VALLEY

King's
Garden

Campsite—
Pompey's
Legions

En-rogel Spring

Jebusite city
(captured by David)

Solomon's addition

8th-7th centuries' addition
(possibly by Hezekiah)

Manasseh's addition

post-exilic addition
(possibly by Nehemiah)

Hasmonean addition

modern walls
(built in 16th century)

F

HILL OF EVIL
COUNSEL
x768 m

Nehemiah city gates
(approximate location)
(Neh 3:1-32; 12:31-39)

x738 m spot elevation (meters)

contour interval: 10 meters

G

© 1986 The Moody Bible Institute of Chicago

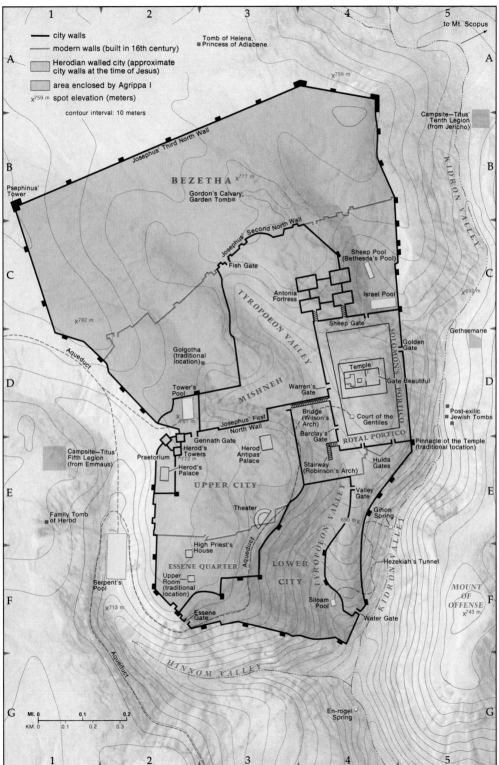

city walls
modern walls (built in 16th century)
Herodian walled city (approximate city walls at the time of Jesus)
area enclosed by Agrippa I
x759 m spot elevation (meters)

contour interval: 10 meters

Tomb of Helena, Princess of Adiabene

Campsite—Titus' Tenth Legion (from Jericho)

to Mt. Scopus

Josephus' Third North Wall

BEZETHA x777 m

Psephinus' Tower

Gordon's Calvary; Garden Tomb

Josephus' Second North Wall

Fish Gate

Sheep Pool (Bethesda's Pool)

Antonia Fortress

Israel Pool

TYROPOEON VALLEY

Sheep Gate

x692 m

Gethsemane

x792 m

Aqueduct

Golgotha (traditional location)

MISHNEH

Temple

SOLOMON'S PORTICO

Golden Gate

Gate Beautiful

Tower's Pool

Warren's Gate

x761 m

Josephus' First North Wall

Bridge (Wilson's Arch)

Barclay's Gate

Court of the Gentiles

ROYAL PORTICO

Post-exilic Jewish Tombs

Campsite—Titus' Fifth Legion (from Emmaus)

Gennath Gate

Herod's Towers x772 m

Praetorium

Herod Antipas' Palace

Herod's Palace

Stairway (Robinson's Arch)

Hulda Gates

Pinnacle of the Temple (traditional location)

UPPER CITY

Family Tomb of Herod

Theater

Valley Gate

Gihon Spring

690 m x

High Priest's House

ESSENE QUARTER

Aqueduct

LOWER CITY

TYROPOEON VALLEY

Hezekiah's Tunnel

MOUNT OF OFFENSE x743 m

Serpent's Pool

Upper Room (traditional location)

x713 m

Essene Gate

Siloam Pool

Water Gate

KIDRON VALLEY

HINNOM VALLEY

MI. 0   0.1   0.2
KM. 0   0.1   0.2   0.3

En-rogel Spring

KIDRON VALLEY

MAP 12

THE MINISTRY OF JESUS

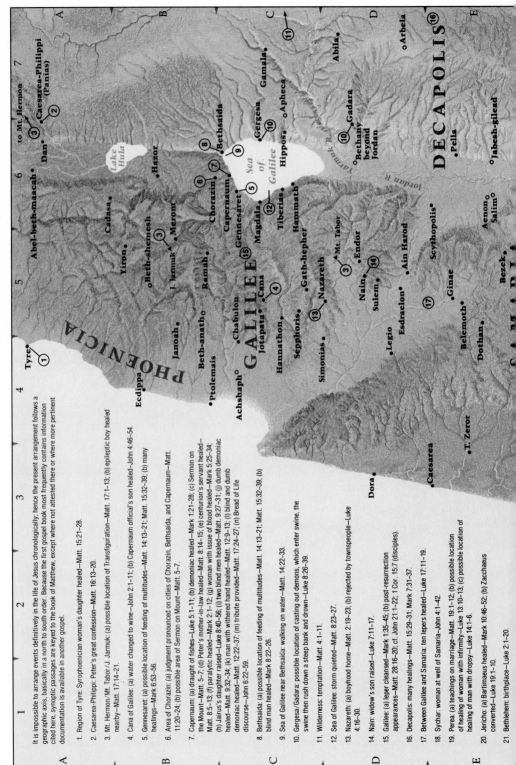

It is impossible to arrange events definitively in the life of Jesus chronologically; hence the present arrangement follows a geographic axis, basically in a north to south order. Because the first gospel book most frequently contains information cited here, synoptic passages are keyed to the book of Matthew, except where not attested there or where more pertinent documentation is available in another gospel.

1. Region of Tyre: Syrophoenician woman's daughter healed—Matt. 15:21-28.

2. Caesarea-Philippi: Peter's great confession—Matt. 16:13-20.

3. Mt. Hermon/Mt. Tabor/J. Jarmuk: (a) possible location of Transfiguration—Matt. 17:1-13; (b) epileptic boy healed nearby—Matt. 17:14-21.

4. Cana of Galilee: (a) water changed to wine—John 2:1-11; (b) Capernaum official's son healed—John 4:46-54.

5. Gennesaret: (a) possible location of feeding of multitudes—Matt. 14:13-21; Matt. 15:32-39; (b) many healings—Mark 6:53-56.

6. Area of Chorazin: (a) judgment pronounced on cities of Chorazin, Bethsaida, and Capernaum—Matt. 11:20-24; (b) possible area of Sermon on Mount—Matt. 5-7.

7. Capernaum: (a) draught of fishes—Luke 5:1-11; (b) demoniac healed—Mark 1:21-28; (c) Sermon on the Mount—Matt. 5-7; (d) Peter's mother-in-law healed—Matt. 8:14-15; (e) centurion's servant healed—Matt. 8:5-13; (f) paralytic healed—Mark 2:1-12; (g) woman with issue of blood healed—Mark 5:25-34; (h) Jairus's daughter raised—Luke 8:40-56; (i) two blind men healed—Matt. 9:27-31; (j) dumb demoniac healed—Matt. 9:32-34; (k) man with withered hand healed—Matt. 12:9-13; (l) blind and dumb demoniac healed—Matt. 12:22-37; (m) tribute provided—Matt. 17:24-27; (n) Bread of Life discourse—John 6:22-59.

8. Bethsaida: (a) possible location of feeding of multitudes—Matt. 14:13-21; Matt. 15:32-39; (b) blind man healed—Mark 8:22-26.

9. Sea of Galilee near Bethsaida: walking on water—Matt. 14:22-33.

10. Gergesa/Gadara: possible location of casting out demons, which enter swine, the swine then rush down a steep bank and drown—Luke 8:26-39.

11. Wilderness: temptation—Matt. 4:1-11.

12. Sea of Galilee: storm quieted—Matt. 8:23-27.

13. Nazareth: (a) boyhood home—Matt. 2:19-23; (b) rejected by townspeople—Luke 4:16-30.

14. Nain: widow's son raised—Luke 7:11-17.

15. Galilee: (a) leper cleansed—Mark 1:35-45; (b) post-resurrection appearances—Matt. 28:16-20; cf. John 21:1-22; 1 Cor. 15:7 (disciples).

16. Decapolis: many healings—Matt. 15:29-31; Mark 7:31-37.

17. Between Galilee and Samaria: ten lepers healed—Luke 17:11-19.

18. Sychar: woman at well of Samaria—John 4:1-42.

19. Perea: (a) teachings on marriage—Matt. 19:1-12; (b) possible location of healing of woman with infirmity—Luke 13:10-13; (c) possible location of healing of man with dropsy—Luke 14:1-6.

20. Jericho: (a) Bartimaeus healed—Mark 10:46-52; (b) Zacchaeus converted—Luke 19:1-10.

21. Bethlehem: birthplace—Luke 2:1-20.

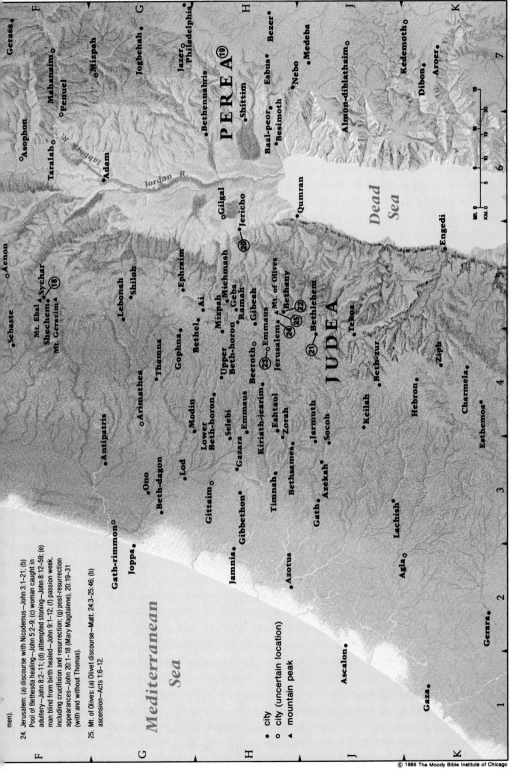

MAP 12

F

24. Jerusalem: (a) discourse with Nicodemus—John 3:1–21; (b) Pool of Bethesda healing—John 5:2–9; (c) woman caught in adultery—John 8:2–11; (d) attempted stoning—John 8:12–59; (e) man blind from birth healed—John 9:1–12; (f) passion week, including crucifixion and resurrection; (g) post-resurrection appearances—John 20:1–18 (Mary Magdalene), 20:19–31 (with and without Thomas).

25. Mt. of Olives: (a) Olivet discourse—Matt. 24:3–25:46; (b) ascension—Acts 1:6–12.

- **●** city
- **○** city (uncertain location)
- **▲** mountain peak

Mediterranean Sea

Jordan R.

Jabbok R.

PEREA ⑲

JUDEA

Dead Sea

MAP 13

THE MISSIONARY JOURNEYS OF PAUL

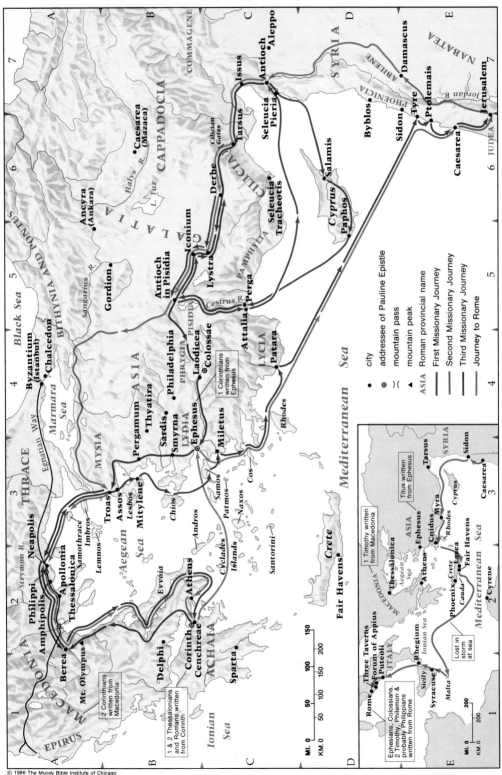

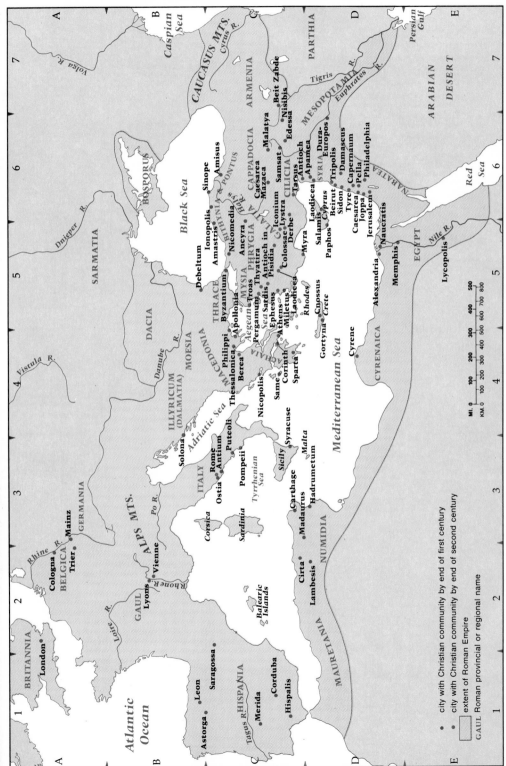

- • city with Christian community by end of first century
- • city with Christian community by end of second century
- extent of Roman Empire
- GAUL Roman provincial or regional name

MAP 15

MODERN ISRAEL

Legend:

- • city
- ◦ city (modern name)
- —— international boundary
- – – 1949 Armistice boundary
- ---- disputed boundary
- —— international zone as designated by the United Nations Partition Accords—November, 1947
- territory allocated to Israel by the United Nations Partition Accords—November, 1947
- territory gained by Israel as a result of the 1948 War and 1949 Agreements (Jerusalem is a divided city)
- territory occupied by Israel after the 6-Day War—June, 1967 (not fundamentally altered after Separation of Forces Agreement following Yom Kippur War—October, 1973)
- territory occupied by Israel after the 6-Day War—June, 1967; returned to Egypt under terms of the Camp David Accord—September, 1978 (return completed—April, 1982)
- Lebanese territory temporarily occupied by Israel—March, 1978 to June, 1978

Labels on map:

Sidon • Damascus
LEBANON • Mt. Hermon
Litani R.
Kiryat Shmona
SYRIA
Pharpar R.
Nahariya
Safed
GOLAN HEIGHTS
Acco
Haifa
Sea of Galilee
Tiberias
Nazareth
Yarmuk R.
Megiddo • Afula
Beth-shan
Hadera • Jenin
Netanya
Jabbok R.
Nablus • Shechem
Tel Aviv
WEST BANK
Amman
Ramallah
Rehovot • Jericho
Jerusalem
Mediterranean Sea
Hebron
Gaza • Engedi
GAZA STRIP
Dead Sea Arnon R.
Beersheba
JORDAN
El-Arish
Dimona
W. el-Arish
Zered Brook
Mitzpeh Ramon
EGYPT
Petra
Israeli tourist resort on narrow Egyptian coastal strip; under negotiation
Eilat
Taba • Gulf of Aqaba

MI. 0 10 20 30 40
KM. 0 10 20 30 40 50 60